WORD
BIBLICAL
COMMENTARY

WORD
BIBLICAL
COMMENTARY

VOLUME 40

2 Corinthians

RALPH P. MARTIN

WORD BOOKS, PUBLISHER • WACO, TEXAS

Word Biblical Commentary
2 CORINTHIANS
Copyright © 1986 by Word, Incorporated

Library of Congress Cataloging in Publication Data
Main entry under title:

Word biblical commentary.

   Includes bibliographies.
   I. Bible—Commentaries—Collected works.
BS491.2.W67   220.7′7   81–71768
ISBN 0–8499–0239–8 (v. 40)   AACR2

Printed in the United States of America

4 5 6 7 8 9 9   AGF   9 8 7

IN MEMORIAM

Glenn Wesley Barker
(1920–1984)

Beati mortui qui in Domino moriuntur . . .
ut requiescant a laboribus suis:
opera enim illorum sequuntur illos.
(Revelation 14:13)

Contents

Editorial Preface

The launching of the *Word Biblical Commentary* brings to fulfillment an enterprise of several years' planning. The publishers and the members of the editorial board met in 1977 to explore the possibility of a new commentary on the books of the Bible that would incorporate several distinctive features. Prospective readers of these volumes are entitled to know what such features were intended to be; whether the aims of the commentary have been fully achieved time alone will tell.

First, we have tried to cast a wide net to include as contributors a number of scholars from around the world who not only share our aims, but are in the main engaged in the ministry of teaching in university, college, and seminary. They represent a rich diversity of denominational allegiance. The broad stance of our contributors can rightly be called evangelical, and this term is to be understood in its positive, historic sense of a commitment to scripture as divine revelation, and to the truth and power of the Christian gospel.

Then, the commentaries in our series are all commissioned and written for the purpose of inclusion in the *Word Biblical Commentary.* Unlike several of our distinguished counterparts in the field of commentary writing, there are no translated works, originally written in a non-English language. Also, our commentators were asked to prepare their own rendering of the original biblical text and to use those languages as the basis of their own comments and exegesis. What may be claimed as distinctive with this series is that it is based on the biblical languages, yet it seeks to make the technical and scholarly approach to a theological understanding of scripture understandable by—and useful to—the fledgling student, the working minister as well as to colleagues in the guild of professional scholars and teachers.

Finally, a word must be said about the format of the series. The layout in clearly defined sections has been consciously devised to assist readers at different levels. Those wishing to learn about the textual witnesses on which the translation is offered are invited to consult the section headed "Notes." If the readers' concern is with the state of modern scholarship on any given portion of scripture, then they should turn to the sections on "Bibliography" and "Form/Structure/Setting." For a clear exposition of the passage's meaning and its relevance to the ongoing biblical revelation, the "Comment" and concluding "Explanation" are designed expressly to meet that need. There is therefore something for everyone who may pick up and use these volumes.

If these aims come anywhere near realization, the intention of the editors will have been met, and the labor of our team of contributors rewarded.

General Editors: *David A. Hubbard*
Glenn W. Barker†
Old Testament: *John D. W. Watts*
New Testament: *Ralph P. Martin*

Author's Preface

Paul's second letter to the Corinthians can claim at least one distinction in the Pauline corpus and in the history of interpretation: it is both the paradise and the despair of the commentator. No other New Testament book, it seems, is in need of such careful exposition; and hands and minds more skilled than the present interpreter's have confessed that this letter is one of the most difficult writings in the New Testament. It is necessary to set the scene and investigate—as far as this is possible at our distance from apostolic times—the background of Paul's tempestuous dealings with the Corinthian congregation. Much, however, has to remain speculative in our inquiries, and we can only hope that we have guessed accurately at Paul's meaning in several parts of the letter, e.g., in the identity of the opposition he encountered at Corinth.

Yet the enterprise is well worth the effort. The value of 2 Corinthians to the people of God, whether clergy or laity, is self-evident, and it has a special claim on the thoughtful pastor who is searching for his or her job description as a "minister of the new covenant" and an agent of "reconciliation"—both key terms in this epistle. C. K. Barrett offers the value-judgment that this letter contains "the fullest and most passionate account of what Paul meant by apostleship," and thus what he regarded as central to ministry. That wise remark is surely an incentive to ministers of the Gospel, whether experienced or novices, to seek out the meaning of 2 Corinthians as both a historical document and a *vade mecum* for their service.

The setting of the letter in Paul's missionary career and apostolic experience is explored in some detail, and a new proposal is offered to account for the letter's emphases. The *Explanation* sections have tried to bring out the pastoral dimension of the letter.

Nor are church people left out in Paul's writing. Indeed, they occupy a central part in his letter to the congregation at Corinth. The key element in Paul's relations with this community may well be stated as reconciliation. And that is a timely item on the church's theological and ecumenical agenda in every age, not least our own.

Ivor H. Jones has some thoughtful words on this subject. Noting that today's world has little room for the message of reconciliation, human or divine, even though there is obvious need for such, he continues:

> Perhaps it is that we have become aware of the great complexity of human relationships and grown suspicious of umbrella words that might shield us from the truth. For example, in modern family life (a situation where reconciliation is still spoken of) we have become aware of the many pressures and tensions which complicate the attempts of any couple to 'make it up.' . . . Reconciliation has reference to real relationships, and real relationships can be bafflingly complex (*The Contemporary Cross*, 125).

The last sentence may well stand as a summary of what 2 Corinthians is all about; and it will be the aim of the following commentary to elucidate what those broken relationships between apostle and congregation were, and how Paul sought *in persona Christi* (as he says, 2:10) to call back these people to the apostolic standards of belief and practice as a way of repairing the breach, so restoring amity and warm friendship. Whether he did succeed we may never know for certain, but that 2 Corinthians does hold a key to open the door to better relationships with God and our fellows cannot be doubted.

After a time of dearth, with the notable exception of such standard works as those by A. Plummer, H. Lietzmann-W. G. Kümmel, C. K. Barrett, J. Héring, and F. F. Bruce, the interest in 2 Corinthians has blossomed with the appearance or announcement of titles that promise to be invaluable to the English-speaking reader and student. I refer to the notice given of translations of D. Georgi's work on the opponents of Paul in this letter, and R. Bultmann's Meyer commentary (ed. E. Dinkler), "the subject of [his] last lectures before [his] retirement" (in 1951), as his preface indicates. Also forthcoming is a work on chapters 8, 9 by Hans Dieter Betz. Most regrettable of all from my standpoint, the recent publication of Victor Paul Furnish's *II Corinthians* as volume 32A in the Anchor Bible series came too late for much use to be made of it, and all I can do is to mention it here. Its mammoth size and comprehensive treatment will be welcomed by all serious researchers.

I am grateful to a cluster of persons who have significantly contributed to this work, stretching back to teachers and colleagues in theological education, notably T. W. Manson at Manchester for whom reconciliation was a central part of his understanding of Paul. More recently, several student assistants have given support: Richard E. Menninger, who produced an excellent draft of several of the letter's chapters and did some valuable basic research; J. David Jackson, who helped with editing and proofreading; Michael Milway, whose classroom paper on the literary structure of the epistle sketched the nature of the problem; and Janet M. Gathright, whose skill in preparing the manuscript deserves an accolade and a "thank you." George Van Alstine came to my aid with valued proofreading. Patricia Losie and Jeanie Thorndike helped with index making. I tender thanks to all these good folk, though the remaining blemishes must be laid to my account.

Finally, the volume joins its partners in this series with the hope that it may serve the needs of readers and give them some fresh insight into Paul's "weighty and forceful" letter (2 Cor 10:10).

Fuller Theological Seminary   RALPH P. MARTIN
Pasadena, California
Lent, 1985

As this volume is the first in the New Testament field to be completed since the homecall in May 1984 of Glenn W. Barker, it is fitting that his notable contribution as General Editor should be recognized, and this book is dedicated to his memory.

Abbreviations

A. General Abbreviations

A	Codex Alexandrinus	LL.	Late Latin
ad	comment on	LXX	Septuagint
Akkad.	Akkadian	M	Mishna
א	Codex Sinaiticus	masc.	masculine
Ap. Lit.	Apocalyptic Literature	mg.	margin
Apoc.	Apocrypha	MS(S)	manuscript(s)
Aq.	Aquila's Greek Translation of the Old Testament	MT	Masoretic text
		n.	note
Arab.	Arabic	n.d.	no date
Aram.	Aramaic	Nestle	Nestle (ed.) *Novum Testamentum Graece* revised by K. and B. Aland
B	Codex Vaticanus		
C	Codex Ephraemi Syri		
c.	*circa,* about	no.	number
cf.	*confer,* compare	NS	New Series
chap.,chaps.	chapter, chapters	NT	New Testament
cod., codd.	codex, codices	obs.	obsolete
contra	in contrast to	OL	Old Latin
D	Codex Bezae	OS	Old Syriac
DSS	Dead Sea Scrolls (see **F.**)	OT	Old Testament
ed.	edited, edition, editor; editions	p., pp.	page, pages
		pace	with due respect to, but differing from
e.g.	*exempli gratia,* for example	par.	paragraph
Egyp.	Egyptian	Pers.	Persian
et al.	*et alii,* and others	Pesh.	Peshitta
et passim	and elsewhere	Phoen.	Phoenician
ET	English translation	pl.	plural
EV	English Versions of the Bible	Pseudep.	Pseudepigrapha
		Q	Quelle ("Sayings" source in the Gospels)
f., ff.	following (verse or verses, pages, etc.)		
fem.	feminine	qt.	quoted by
FS.	Festschrift	q.v.	*quod vide,* which see
ft.	foot, feet	rev.	revised, reviser, revision
gen.	genitive	Rom.	Roman
Gr.	Greek	RVm	Revised Version margin
Heb.	Hebrew	Samar.	Samaritan recension
Hitt.	Hittite	*sc.*	*scilicet,* that is to say
ibid.	*ibidem,* in the same place	Sem.	Semitic
id.	*idem,* the same	sing.	singular
i.e.	*id est,* that is	Sumer.	Sumerian
impf.	imperfect	s.v.	*sub verbo,* under the word
infra.	below	Syr.	Syriac
in loc.	*in loco,* in the place cited	Symm.	Symmachus
Jos.	Josephus	Targ.	Targum
Lat.	Latin	Theod.	Theodotion

TR	Textus Receptus	vol.	volume
tr.	translation, translator, translated	v, vv	verse, verses
		vs.	versus
UBS	The United Bible Societies Greek Text	vg	Vulgate
		WH	Westcott and Hort, *The New Testament in Greek*
Ugar.	Ugaritic		
u.s.	*ut supra,* as above	x	number of times words occur
viz.	*videlicet,* namely		cur

B. Abbreviations for Translations and Paraphrases

AmT	Smith and Goodspeed, *The Complete Bible, An American Translation*	LB	The Living Bible
		Moffatt	J. Moffatt, *A New Translation of the Bible*
ASV	American Standard Version, American Revised Version (1901)	NAB	The New American Bible
		NASB	New American Standard Bible
		NEB	The New English Bible
AV	Authorized Version	NIV	The New International Version
Beck	Beck, *The New Testament in the Language of Today*	Ph	J. B. Phillips, *The New Testament in Modern English*
BV	Berkeley Version (The Modern Language Bible)	RSV	Revised Standard Version
		RV	Revised Version—1881–1885
GNB	*Good News Bible*	TEV	Today's English Version
JB	The Jerusalem Bible	Wey	R. F. Weymouth, *The New Testament in Modern Speech*
JPS	*Jewish Publication Society Version of the Old Testament*	Wms	C. B. Williams, *The New Testament: A Translation in the Language of the People*
KJV	King James Version		
Knox	R. A. Knox, *The Holy Bible: A Translation from the Latin Vulgate in the Light of the Hebrew and Greek Original*		

C. Abbreviations of Commonly Used Periodicals, Reference Works, and Serials

AAS	*Acta apostolicae sedis*	AH	F. Rosenthal, *An Aramaic Handbook*
AASOR	Annual of the American Schools of Oriental Research	AHR	*American Historical Review*
AB	Anchor Bible	AHW	W. von Soden, *Akkadisches Handwörterbuch*
ABR	*Australian Biblical Review*		
AbrN	*Abr-Nahrain*	AION	*Annali dell'istituto orientali di Napoli*
AcOr	*Acta orientalia*		
ACW	Ancient Christian Writers	AJA	*American Journal of Archaeology*
ADAJ	Annual of the Department of Antiquities of Jordan	AJAS	*American Journal of Arabic Studies*
AER	*American Ecclesiastical Review*	AJBA	*Australian Journal of Biblical Archaeology*
AfO	*Archiv für Orientforschung*		
AGJU	Arbeiten zur Geschichte des antiken Judentums und des Urchristentums	AJSL	*American Journal of Semitic Languages and Literature*
		AJT	*American Journal of Theology*

ALBO	Analecta lovaniensia biblica et orientalia	AUSS	Andrews University Seminary Studies
ALGHJ	Arbeiten zur Literatur und Geschichte des hellenistischen Judentums	BA	Biblical Archaeologist
		BAC	Biblioteca de autores cristianos
ALUOS	Annual of Leeds University Oriental Society	BAR	Biblical Archaeology Review
AnBib	Analecta biblica		
AnBoll	Analecta Bollandiana	BASOR	Bulletin of the American Schools of Oriental Research
ANEP	J. B. Pritchard (ed.), Ancient Near East in Pictures	BASP	Bulletin of the American Society of Papyrologists
ANESTP	J. B. Pritchard (ed.), Ancient Near East Supplementary Texts and Pictures	BBB	Bonner biblische Beiträge
		BCSR	Bulletin of the Council on the Study of Religion
ANET	J. B. Pritchard (ed.), Ancient Near Eastern Texts	BDB	E. Brown, S. R. Driver, and C. A. Briggs, Hebrew and English Lexicon of the Old Testament
ANF	The Ante-Nicene Fathers		
Ang	Angelicum		
AnOr	Analecta orientalia	BDF	F. Blass, A. Debrunner, and R. W. Funk, A Greek Grammar of the NT
ANQ	Andover Newton Quarterly		
Anton	Antonianum	BeO	Bibbia e oriente
AOAT	Alter Orient und Altes Testament	BETL	Bibliotheca ephemeridum theologicarum lovaniensium
AOS	American Oriental Series	BEvT	Beiträge zur evangelischen Theologie (BEvTh)
AP	J. Marouzeau (ed.), L'année philologique	BFCT	Beiträge zur Förderung christlicher Theologie (BFCTh)
APOT	R. H. Charles (ed.), Apocrypha and Pseudepigrapha of the Old Testament		
		BGBE	Beiträge zur Geschichte der biblischen Exegese
ARG	Archiv für Reformationsgeschichte	BGD	W. Bauer, F. W. Gingrich, and F. Danker, Greek-English Lexicon of the NT
ARM	Archives royales de Mari		
ArOr	Archiv orientální		
ARSHLL	Acta Reg. Societatis Humaniorum Litterarum Lundensis	BHH	B. Reicke and L. Rost (eds.), Biblisch-Historisches Handwörterbuch
ARW	Archiv für Religionswissenschaft	BHK	R. Kittel, Biblia hebraica
ASNU	Acta seminarii neotestamentici upsaliensis	BHS	Biblia hebraica stuttgartensia
		BHT	Beiträge zur historischen Theologie (BHTh)
ASS	Acta sanctae sedis	Bib	Biblica
AsSeign	Assemblées du Seigneur	BibB	Biblische Beiträge
ASSR	Archives des sciences sociales des religions	BibLeb	Bibel und Leben
		BibOr	Biblica et orientalia
ASTI	Annual of the Swedish Theological Institute	BibS(F)	Biblische Studien (Freiburg, 1895–) (BSt)
ATAbh	Alttestamentliche Abhandlungen	BibS(N)	Biblische Studien (Neukirchen, 1951–) (BibSt)
ATANT	Abhandlungen zur Theologie des Alten und Neuen Testaments (AThANT)	BIES	Bulletin of the Israel Exploration Society (= Yediot)
ATD	Das Alte Testament Deutsch	BIFAO	Bulletin de l'institut français d'archéologie orientale
ATR	Anglican Theological Review		

BJRL	*Bulletin of the John Rylands University Library of Manchester*	*ConNT*	*Coniectanea neotestamentica*
		Corp Herm.	Corpus Hermeticum
BK	*Bibel und Kirche*	*CQ*	*Church Quarterly*
BKAT	Biblischer Kommentar: Altes Testament	*CQR*	*Church Quarterly Review*
		CRAIBL	*Comptes rendus de l'Académie des inscriptions et belles-lettres*
BL	*Book List*		
BLE	*Bulletin de littérature ecclésiastique*		
		CrQ	*Crozier Quarterly*
BLit	*Bibel und Liturgie*	CSCO	Corpus scriptorum christianorum orientalium
BO	*Bibliotheca orientalis*		
BR	*Biblical Research*	CSEL	Corpus scriptorum ecclesiasticorum latinorum
BS	*Biblische Studien,* Freiburg		
BSac	*Bibliotheca Sacra*	*CTA*	A. Herdner, *Corpus des tablettes en cunéiformes alphabétiques*
BSO(A)S	*Bulletin of the School of Oriental (and African) Studies*		
		CTJ	*Calvin Theological Journal*
BT	*The Bible Translator*	*CTM*	*Concordia Theological Monthly*
BTB	*Biblical Theology Bulletin*	*CurTM*	*Currents in Theology and Mission*
BTS	*Bible et terre sainte*		
BU	Biblische Untersuchungen		
BVC	*Bible et vie chrétienne*	*DACL*	*Dictionnaire d'archéologie chrétienne et de liturgie*
BWANT	Beiträge zur Wissenschaft vom Alten und Neuen Testament		
		DBSup	*Dictionnaire de la Bible, Supplément*
BZ	*Biblische Zeitschrift*	*DISO*	C.-F. Jean and J. Hoftijzer, *Dictionnaire des inscriptions sémitiques de l'ouest*
BZAW	Beihefte zur *ZAW*		
BZET	Beihefte z. Evangelische Theologie		
		DJD	Discoveries in the Judean Desert
BZNW	Beihefte zur *ZNW*		
BZRGG	Beihefte zur *ZRGG*	*DOTT*	D. W. Thomas (ed.), *Documents from Old Testament Times*
CAD	*The Assyrian Dictionary of the Oriental Institute of the University of Chicago*		
		DS	Denzinger-Schönmetzer, *Enchiridion symbolorum*
CAH	*Cambridge Ancient History*	*DTC*	*Dictionnaire de théologie catholique (DTHC)*
CAT	Commentaire de l'Ancien Testament		
		DTT	*Dansk teologisk tidsskrift*
CB	*Cultura bíblica*	*DunRev*	Dunwoodie Review
CBQ	*Catholic Biblical Quarterly*		
CBQMS	Catholic Biblical Quarterly— Monograph Series	EBib	Etudes bibliques (EtBib)
		EBT	*Encyclopedia of Biblical Theology*
CCath	Corpus Catholicorum	*EDB*	L. F. Hartman (ed.), *Encyclopedic Dictionary of the Bible*
CChr	Corpus Christianorum		
CH	*Church History*		
CHR	*Catholic Historical Review*	EHAT	Exegetisches Handbuch zum Alten Testament
CIG	*Corpus inscriptionum graecarum*		
CH	*Corpus inscriptionum iudaicarum*	EKKNT	Evangelisch-katholischer Kommentar zum Neuen Testament
CIL	*Corpus inscriptionum latinarum*		
CIS	*Corpus inscriptionum semiticarum*		
CJT	*Canadian Journal of Theology*	*EKL*	*Evangelisches Kirchenlexikon*
ClerRev	*Clergy Review*	*EncJud*	*Encyclopaedia judaica* (1971)
CNT	Commentaire du Nouveau Testament	*EnchBib*	*Enchiridion biblicum*
		ErJb	*Eranos Jahrbuch*
ConB	Coniectanea biblica	*EstBib*	*Estudios biblicos*

ETL	*Ephemerides theologicae lovanienses* (*EThl.*)	HSM	Harvard Semitic Monographs
ETR	*Etudes théologiques et religieuses* (*EThR*)	HTKNT	Herders theologischer Kommentar zum Neuen Testament (HThKNT)
EvK	*Evangelische Kommentar*	*HTR*	*Harvard Theological Review*
EvQ	*The Evangelical Quarterly*	HTS	Harvard Theological Studies
EvT	*Evangelische Theologie* (*EvTh*)	*HUCA*	*Hebrew Union College Annual*
Exp.	*The Expositor*	*HUTh*	*Hermeneutische Untersuchungen zur Theologie*
ExpTim	*The Expository Times*		
FBBS	Facet Books, Biblical Series	*IB*	*Interpreter's Bible*
FC	Fathers of the Church	*IBD*	*Illustrated Bible Dictionary*, ed. J. D. Douglas and N. Hillyer
FRLANT	Forschungen zur Religion und Literatur des Alten und Neuen Testaments	ICC	International Critical Commentary
FTS	Frankfurter Theologischen Studien	*IDB*	G. A. Buttrick (ed.), *Interpreter's Dictionary of the Bible*
		IDBSup	Supplementary volume to *IDB*
GAG	W. von Soden, *Grundriss der akkadischen Grammatik*	*IEJ*	*Israel Exploration Journal*
GCS	Griechische christliche Schriftsteller	*Int*	*Interpretation*
GKB	Gesenius-Kautzsch-Bergsträsser, *Hebräische Grammatik*	*ITQ*	*Irish Theological Quarterly*
GKC	*Gesenius' Hebrew Grammar*, ed. E. Kautzsch, tr. A. E. Cowley	*JA*	*Journal asiatique*
		JAAR	*Journal of the American Academy of Religion*
GNT	Grundrisse zum Neuen Testament	JAC	Jahrbuch für Antike und Christentum
GOTR	*Greek Orthodox Theological Review*	*JANESCU*	*Journal of the Ancient Near Eastern Society of Columbia University*
GRBS	*Greek, Roman, and Byzantine Studies*	*JAOS*	*Journal of the American Oriental Society*
Greg	*Gregorianum*	*JAS*	*Journal of Asian Studies*
GThT	*Geformelet Theologisch Tijdschrift*	*JB*	A. Jones (ed.), *Jerusalem Bible*
GuL	*Geist und Leben*	*JBC*	R. E. Brown et al. (eds.), *The Jerome Biblical Commentary*
HALAT	W. Baumgartner et al., *Hebräisches und aramäisches Lexikon zum Alten Testament*	*JBL*	*Journal of Biblical Literature*
		JBR	*Journal of Bible and Religion*
		JCS	*Journal of Cuneiform Studies*
HAT	Handbuch zum Alten Testament	JDS	Judean Desert Studies
		JEA	*Journal of Egyptian Archaeology*
HDR	Harvard Dissertations in Religion	*JEH*	*Journal of Ecclesiastical History*
		JEOL	*Jaarbericht . . . ex oriente lux*
HeyJ	*Heythrop Journal*	*JES*	*Journal of Ecumenical Studies*
HibJ	*Hibbert Journal*	*JETS*	*Journal of the Evangelical Theological Society*
HKAT	Handkommentar zum Alten Testament		
HKNT	Handkommentar zum Neuen Testament	*JHS*	*Journal of Hellenic Studies*
		JIBS	*Journal of Indian and Buddhist Studies*
HNT	Handbuch zum Neuen Testament	*JIPh*	*Journal of Indian Philosophy*
		JJS	*Journal of Jewish Studies*
HNTC	Harper's NT Commentaries	*JMES*	*Journal of Middle Eastern Studies*
HR	*History of Religions*	*JMS*	*Journal of Mithraic Studies*

JNES	Journal of Near Eastern Studies	LSJ	Liddell-Scott-Jones, *Greek-English Lexicon*
JPOS	Journal of the Palestine Oriental Society	LTK	Lexikon für Theologie und Kirche (LThK)
JPSV	Jewish Publication Society Version		
JQR	Jewish Quarterly Review	LUÅ	Lunds universitets årsskrift
JQRMS	Jewish Quarterly Review Monograph Series	LW	Lutheran World
JR	Journal of Religion	McCQ	McCormick Quarterly
JRAS	Journal of the Royal Asiatic Society	MDOG	Mitteilungen der deutschen Orient-Gesellschaft
JRE	Journal of Religious Ethics	MeyerK	H. A. W. Meyer, Kritisch-exegetischer Kommentar über das Neue Testament
JRelS	Journal of Religious Studies		
JRH	Journal of Religious History		
JRS	Journal of Roman Studies	MGWJ	Monatsschrift für Geschichte und Wissenschaft des Judentums
JRT	Journal of Religious Thought		
JSJ	Journal for the Study of Judaism in the Persian, Hellenistic and Roman Period		
		MM	J. H. Moulton and G. Milligan, *The Vocabulary of the Greek Testament*
JSNT	Journal for the Study of the New Testament		
JSOT	Journal for the Study of the Old Testament	MNTC	Moffatt NT Commentary
		MPAIBL	Mémoires présentés à l'Académie des inscriptions et belles-lettres
JSS	Journal of Semitic Studies		
JSSR	Journal of the Scientific Study of Religion	MPG	Patrologia Graeca, ed. J. P. Migne, 1844 ff.
JTC	Journal for Theology and the Church	MScRel	Mélanges de science religieuse
JTS	Journal of Theological Studies	MTZ	Münchener theologische Zeitschrift (MThZ)
Judaica	Judaica: Beiträge zum Verständnis . . .	MUSJ	Mélanges de l'université Saint-Joseph
KAI	H. Donner and W. Röllig, *Kanaanäische und aramäische Inschriften*	MVAG	Mitteilungen der vorder-asiatisch-ägyptischen Gesellschaft
KAT	E. Sellin (ed.), Kommentar zum A. T.		
KB	L. Koehler and W. Baumgartner, *Lexicon in Veteris Testamenti libros*	NAB	New American Bible
		NAG	Nachrichten von der Akademie der Wissenschaften in Göttingen
KD	Kerygma und Dogma	NCB	New Century Bible (new edit.)
KJV	King James Version	NCCHS	R. C. Fuller et al. (eds.), *New Catholic Commentary on Holy Scripture*
KIT	Kleine Texte		
LCC	Library of Christian Classics	NCE	M. R. P. McGuire et al. (eds.), *New Catholic Encyclopedia*
LCL	Loeb Classical Library		
LD	Lectio divina	NClB	New Clarendon Bible
Leš	Lešonénu	NEB	New English Bible
LLAVT	E. Vogt, *Lexicon linguae aramaicae Veteris Testamenti*	NedTTs	Nederlands theologisch tijdschrift (NedThTs)
		Neot	Neotestamentica
LPGL	G. W. H. Lampe, *Patristic Greek Lexicon*	NFT	New Frontiers in Theology
		NHS	Nag Hammadi Studies
LQ	Lutheran Quarterly	NICNT	New International Commentary on the New Testament
LR	Lutherische Rundschau		

NIDNTT	C. Brown (ed.), *The New International Dictionary of New Testament Theology*
NKZ	*Neue kirchliche Zeitschrift*
NorTT	*Norsk Teologisk Tidsskrift (NTT)*
NovT	*Novum Testamentum*
NovTSup	Novum Testamentum, Supplement
New Docs	*New Documents Illustrating Early Christianity*, A Review of Greek Inscriptions etc. ed. G. H. R. Horsley. North Ryde, NSW, Australia
NPNF	Nicene and Post-Nicene Fathers
NRT	*La nouvelle revue théologique (NRTh)*
NTA	*New Testament Abstracts*
NTAbh	Neutestamentliche Abhandlungen
NTD	Das Neue Testament Deutsch
NTF	Neutestamentliche Forschungen
NTS	*New Testament Studies*
NTTS	New Testament Tools and Studies
Numen	*Numen: International Review for the History of Religious*
OCD	*Oxford Classical Dictionary*
OIP	Oriental Institute Publications
OLP	Orientalia lovaniensia periodica
OLZ	*Orientalische Literaturzeitung*
Or	*Orientalia* (Rome)
OrAnt	*Oriens antiquus*
OrChr	*Oriens christianus*
OrSyr	*L'orient syrien*
OTM	Oxford Theological Monographs
OTS	Oudtestamentische Studiën
PAAJR	Proceedings of the American Academy of Jewish Research
PCB	M. Black and H. H. Rowley (eds.), *Peake's Commentary on the Bible*
PEFQS	*Palestine Exploration Fund, Quarterly Statement*
PEQ	*Palestine Exploration Quarterly*
PG	*Patrologia graeca*, ed. J. P. Migne

PGM	K. Preisendanz (ed.), *Papyri graecae magicae*
PhEW	*Philosophy East and West*
PhRev	*Philosophical Review*
PJ	*Palästina-Jahrbuch*
PL	*Patrologia Latina*, ed. J. P. Migne
PO	Patrologia orientalis
PRU	*Le Palais royal d'Ugarit*
PSTJ	*Perkins (School of Theology) Journal*
PVTG	Pseudepigrapha Veteris Testamenti graece
PW	Pauly-Wissowa, *Real-Encyklopädie der klassischen Altertumswissenschaft*
PWSup	Supplement to PW
QDAP	*Quarterly of the Department of Antiquities in Palestine*
RA	*Revue d'assyriologie et d'archéologie orientale*
RAC	*Reallexikon für Antike und Christentum*
RArch	*Revue archéologique*
RB	*Revue biblique*
RBén	*Revue bénédictine*
RCB	*Revista de cultura biblica*
RE	*Realencyklopädie für protestantische Theologie und Kirche*
RechBib	Recherches bibliques
REg	*Revue d'égyptologie*
REJ	*Revue des études juives*
RelArts	Religion and the Arts
RelS	*Religious Studies*
RelSoc	Religion and Society
RelSRev	*Religious Studies Review*
RES	*Répertoire d'épigraphie sémitique*
RestQ	*Restoration Quarterly*
RevExp	*Review and Expositor*
RevistB	*Revista biblica*
RevScRel	*Revue des sciences religieuses*
RevSém	*Revue sémitique*
RevThom	*Revue thomiste*
RGG	*Religion in Geschichte und Gegenwart*
RHE	*Revue d'histoire ecclésiastique*
RHPR	*Revue d'histoire et de philosophie religieuses (RHPhR)*
RHR	Revue de l'histoire des religions

RivB	*Rivista biblica*	SD	Studies and Documents
RNT	Regensburger Neues Testament	SE	Studia Evangelica I, II, III (= TU 73[1959], 87 [1964], 88 [1964], etc.) (*StEv*)
RQ	*Revue de Qumrân*		
RR	*Review of Religion*	*SEÅ*	*Svensk exegetisk årsbok*
RSO	*Rivista degli studi orientali*	*Sef*	*Sefarad*
RSPT	*Revue des sciences philosophiques et théologiques (RSPhTh)*	*Sem*	*Semitica*
		SHAW	Sitzungsberichte heidelbergen Akademie der Wissenschaften
RSR	*Recherches de science religieuse (RechSR)*		
RscPhTh	*Revue des Sciences Philosophiques et Théologiques*	SHT	Studies in Historical Theology
RSV	Revised Standard Version	SHVL	Skrifter Utgivna Av Kungl. Humanistika Vetenskapssamfundet i Lund
RTL	*Revue théologique de Louvain (RThL)*		
RTP	*Revue de théologie et de philosophie (RThPh)*	SJLA	Studies in Judaism in Late Antiquity
RTR	*The Reformed Theological Review*	*SJT*	*Scottish Journal of Theology*
RUO	*Revue de l'université d'Ottawa*	*SMSR*	*Studi e materiali di storia delle religioni*
RV	Revised Version		
		SNT	Studien zum Neuen Testament (StNT)
SAH	*Sitzungsberichte der Heidelberger Akademie der Wissenschaften (phil.-hist. Klasse), 1910 ff.*	SNTSMS	Society for New Testament Studies Monograph Series
		SO	Symbolae osloenses
SANT	Studien zum Alten und Neuen Testament	SOTSMS	Society for Old Testament Study Monograph Series
SAQ	Sammlung ausgewählter kirchen- und dogmengeschichtlicher Quellenschriften	*SPap*	*Studia papyrologica*
		SPAW	Sitzungsberichte der preussischen Akademie der Wissenschaften
SB	Sources bibliques		
SBFLA	*Studii biblici franciscani liber annuus*	SPB	Studia postbiblica
		SR	*Studies in Religion/Sciences religieuses*
SBJ	*La sainte bible de Jérusalem*		
SBLASP	Society of Biblical Literature Abstracts and Seminar Papers	SSS	Semitic Study Series
		ST	*Studia theologica (StTh)*
SBLDS	SBL Dissertation Series	*STÅ*	*Svensk teologisk årsskrift*
SBLMasS	SBL Masoretic Studies	*StBibT*	*Studia Biblica et Theologica*
SBLMS	SBL Monograph Series	STDJ	Studies on the Texts of the Desert of Judah
SBLSBS	SBL Sources for Biblical Study		
		STK	*Svensk teologisk kvartalskrift*
SBLSCS	SBL Septuagint and Cognate Studies	Str-B	[H. Strack and] P. Billerbeck, *Kommentar zum Neuen Testament*
SBLTT	SBL Texts and Translations	StudNeot	Studia neotestamentica, Studia
SBM	Stuttgarter biblische Monographien		
		StudOr	Studia orientalia
SBS	Stuttgarter Bibelstudien	SUNT	Studien zur Umwelt des Neuen Testaments
SBT	Studies in Biblical Theology		
SC	Sources chrétiennes	SVTP	Studia in Veteris Testamenti pseudepigrapha
ScEs	*Science et esprit*		
SCR	*Studies in Comparative Religion*	*SWJT*	*Southwestern Journal of Theology*
Scr	*Scripture*	SymBU	Symbolae biblicae upsalienses (SyBU)
ScrB	*Scripture Bulletin*		

TAPA	*Transactions of the American Philological Association*	UNT	Untersuchungen zum Neuen Testament
TBl	*Theologische Blätter (ThBl)*	*US*	*Una Sancta*
TBü	Theologische Bücherei (ThBü)	*USQR*	*Union Seminary Quarterly Review*
TBT	*The Bible Today*	*UT*	C. H. Gordon, *Ugaritic Textbook*
TD	*Theology Digest*	UUÅ	Uppsala universitetsårsskrift
TDNT	G. Kittel and G. Friedrich (eds.), *Theological Dictionary of the New Testament*	*VC*	*Vigiliae christianae*
TextsS	Texts and Studies	*VCaro*	*Verbum caro*
TF	*Theologische Forschung (ThF)*	*VD*	*Verbum domini*
TGI	*Theologie und Glaube (ThGI)*	*VF*	*Verkündigung und Forschung*
Th	*Theology*	*VKGNT*	K. Aland (ed.), *Vollständige Konkordanz zum griechischen Neuen Testament*
ThA	*Theologische Arbeiten*		
ThBer	*Theologische Berichte*	VS	Verbum salutis
THKNT	Theologischer Handkommentar zum Neuen Testament (ThHKNT)	*VSpir*	*Vie spirituelle*
		VT	*Vetus Testamentum*
TLZ	*Theologische Literaturzeitung (ThLZ)*	VTSup	Vetus Testamentum, Supplements
TNTC	Tyndale New Testament Commentary	WA	M. Luther, Kritische Gesamtausgabe (= "Weimar" edition)
TP	*Theologie und Philosophie (ThPh)*		
TPQ	*Theologisch-Praktische Quartalschrift*	WBC	Word Biblical Commentary
TQ	*Theologische Quartalschrift (ThQ)*	WC	Westminster Commentary
		WDB	*Westminister Dictionary of the Bible*
TRev	*Theologische Revue*		
TRu	*Theologische Rundschau (ThR)*	*WHAB*	*Westminster Historical Atlas of the Bible*
TS	*Theological Studies*		
TSK	*Theologische Studien und Kritiken (ThStK)*	WMANT	Wissenschaftliche Monographien zum Alten und Neuen Testament
TT	*Teologisk Tidsskrift*		
TTKi	*Tidsskrift for Teologi og Kirke*	*WO*	*Die Welt des Orients*
TToday	*Theology Today*	*WTJ*	*Westminster Theological Journal*
TTS	Trierer Theologische Studien	WUNT	Wissenschaftliche Untersuchungen zum Neuen Testament
TTZ	*Trierer theologische Zeitschrift (TThZ)*		
TU	Texte und Untersuchungen	*WZKM*	*Wiener Zeitschrift für die Kunde des Morgenlandes*
TynB	*Tyndale Bulletin*		
TWAT	G. J. Botterweck and H. Ringgren (eds.), *Theologisches Wörterbuch zum Alten Testament (ThWAT)*	*WZKSO*	*Wiener Zeitschrift für die Kunde Süd- und Ostasiens*
		ZA	*Zeitschrift für Assyriologie*
TWNT	G. Kittel and G. Friedrich (eds.), *Theologisches Wörterbuch zum Neuen Testament (ThWNT)*	*ZAW*	*Zeitschrift für die alttestamentliche Wissenschaft*
TZ	*Theologische Zeitschrift (ThZ)*	*ZDMG*	*Zeitschrift der deutschen morgenländischen Gesellschaft*
UBSGNT	United Bible Societies Greek New Testament	*ZDPV*	*Zeitschrift des deutschen Palästina-Vereins*
UF	*Ugaritische Forschungen*	*ZEE*	*Zeitschrift für evangelische Ethik*

ZHT	Zeitschrift für historische Theologie (ZHTh)	ZRGG	Zeitschrift für Religions-und Geistesgeschichte
ZKG	Zeitschrift für Kirchengeschichte	ZST	Zeitschrift für systematische Theologie (ZSTh)
ZKNT	Zahn's Kommentar zum NT	ZTK	Zeitschrift für Theologie und Kirche (ZThK)
ZKT	Zeitschrift für katholische Theologie (ZKTh)	ZWT	Zeitschrift für wissenschaftliche Theologie (ZWTh)
ZMR	Zeitschrift für Missions-kunde und Religions-wissenschaft		
ZNW	Zeitschrift für die neutestamentliche Wissenschaft		

D. Abbreviations for Books of the Bible, the Apocrypha, and the Pseudepigrapha

OLD TESTAMENT

Gen	2 Chr	Dan
Exod	Ezra	Hos
Lev	Neh	Joel
Num	Esth	Amos
Deut	Job	Obad
Josh	Ps(Pss)	Jonah
Judg	Prov	Mic
Ruth	Eccl	Nah
1 Sam	Cant	Hab
2 Sam	Isa	Zeph
1 Kings	Jer	Hag
2 Kings	Lam	Zech
1 Chr	Ezek	Mal

NEW TESTAMENT

Matt	1 Tim
Mark	2 Tim
Luke	Titus
John	Philem
Acts	Heb
Rom	James
1 Cor	1 Peter
2 Cor	2 Peter
Gal	1 John
Eph	2 John
Phil	3 John
Col	Jude
1 Thess	Rev
2 Thess	

APOCRYPHA

1 Esd	1 Esdras	Ep Jer	Epistle of Jeremy
2 Esd	2 Esdras	S Th Ch	Song of the Three Children (or Young Men)
Tob	Tobit		
Jud	Judith	Sus	Susanna
Add Esth	Additions to Esther	Bel	Bel and the Dragon
Wisd Sol	Wisdom of Solomon	Pr Man	Prayer of Manasseh
Sir	Ecclesiasticus (Wisdom of Jesus the Son of Sirach)	1 Macc	1 Maccabees
		2 Macc	2 Maccabees
Bar	Baruch		

E. Abbreviations of the Names of Pseudepigraphical and Early Patristic Books

Adam and Eve	Books of Adam and Eve	1–2–3 Enoch	Ethiopic, Slavonic, Hebrew Enoch
2–3 Apoc. Bar.	Syriac, Greek Apocalypse of Baruch	Ep. Arist.	Epistle of Aristeas
Apoc. Abr.	Apocalypse of Abraham	Ep. Diognetus	Epistle to Diognetus
Apoc. Mos.	Apocalypse of Moses	Jub.	Jubilees
Asc. Isa.	Ascension of Isaiah	Mart. Isa.	Martyrdom of Isaiah
As. Mos.	Assumption of Moses	Odes Sol.	Odes of Solomon
Bib. Ant.	Ps.-Philo, Biblical Antiquities	Pss. Sol.	Psalms of Solomon
		Sib. Or.	Sibylline Oracles

T. Abr.	Testament of Abraham	Ign. *Eph.*	Ignatius, Letter to the Ephesians
T. 12 Patr.	Testaments of the Twelve Patriarchs	*Magn.*	Ignatius, Letter to the Magnesians
T. Benj.	Testament of Benjamin, etc.	*Phld.*	Ignatius, Letter to the Philadelphians
T. Levi	Testament of Levi, etc.	*Pol.*	Ignatius, Letter to Polycarp
Acts Pil.	Acts of Pilate		
Apoc. Pet.	Apocalypse of Peter	*Rom.*	Ignatius, Letter to the Romans
Gos. Eb.	Gospel of the Ebionites		
Gos. Eg.	Gospel of the Egyptians	*Smyrn.*	Ignatius, Letter to the Smyrnaeans
Gos. Heb.	Gospel of the Hebrews		
Gos. Naass.	Gospel of the Naassenes	*Trall.*	Ignatius, Letter to the Trallians
Gos. Pet.	Gospel of Peter		
Gos. Thom.	Gospel of Thomas	*Mart Pol.*	Martyrdom of Polycarp
Prot. Jas.	Protevangelium of James	Pol. *Phil.*	Polycarp to the Philippians
Barn.	Barnabas	*Adv. Haer.*	Irenaeus, Against All Heresies
1–2 Clem.	1–2 Clement		
Did.	Didache	*De Praesc.*	
Diogn.	Diognetus	*Haer.*	Tertullian, On the Proscribing of Heretics
Herm. Man.	Hermas, Mandates		
Sim.	Similitudes		
Vis.	Visions		

F. Abbreviations of Names of Dead Sea Scrolls and Related Texts

CD	Cairo (Genizah text of the) Damascus (Document)	1QSa	Appendix A (*Rule of the Congregation*) to 1QS
Hev	Naḥal Ḥever texts	1QSb	Appendix B (*Blessings*) to 1QS
Mas	Masada texts		
Mird	Khirbet Mird texts	3Q*15*	Copper Scroll from Qumran Cave 3
Mur	Wadi Murabbaʿat texts		
p	Pesher (commentary)	4QFlor	*Florilegium* (or *Eschatological Midrashim*) from Qumran Cave 4
Q	Qumran		
1Q, 2Q, 3Q, etc.	Numbered caves of Qumran, yielding written material; followed by abbreviation of biblical or apocryphal book	4QMess ar	Aramaic "Messianic" text from Qumran Cave 4
		4QPrNab	Prayer of Nabonidus from Qumran Cave 4
QL	Qumran literature		
1QapGen	*Genesis Apocryphon* of Qumran Cave 1	4QTestim	*Testimonia* text from Qumran Cave 4
1QH	*Hôdāyôt* (*Thanksgiving Hymns*) from Qumran Cave 1	4QTLevi	*Testament of Levi* from Qumran Cave 4
1QIsa^{a,b}	First or second copy of Isaiah from Qumran Cave 1	4QPhyl	Phylacteries from Qumran Cave 4
1QpHab	*Pesher on Habakkuk* from Qumran Cave 1	11QMelch	*Melchizedek* text from Qumran Cave 11
1QM	*Milḥāmāh* (*War Scroll*)	11QtgJob	*Targum of Job* from Qumran Cave 11
1QS	*Serek hayyaḥad* (*Rule of the Community, Manual of Discipline*)		

G. Abbreviations of Targumic Material

Tg. Onq.	*Targum Onqelos*	*Tg. Ps.-J.*	*Targum Pseudo-Jonathan*
Tg. Neb.	*Targum of the Prophets*	*Tg. Yer. 1*	*Targum Yerušalmi I* *
Tg. Ket.	*Targum of the Writings*	*Tg. Yer. 11*	*Targum Yerušalmi II* *
Frg. Tg.	*Fragmentary Targum*	*Yem. Tg.*	*Yemenite Targum*
Sam. Tg.	*Samaritan Targum*	*Tg. Esth I,*	
Tg. Isa	*Targum of Isaiah*	*II*	*First or Second Targum of Esther*
Pal. Tgs.	*Palestinian Targums*	* optional title	
Tg. Neof.	*Targum Neofiti I*		

H. Abbreviations of Other Rabbinic Works

ʾAbot	*ʾAbot de Rabbi Nathan*	*Pesiq. Rab Kah.*	*Pesiqta de Rab Kahana*
ʾAg. Ber.	*ʾAggadat Berešit*	*Pirqe R. El.*	*Pirqe Rabbi Eliezer*
Bab.	*Babylonian*	*Rab.*	*Rabbah* (following ab-
Bar.	*Baraita*		breviation for biblical
Der. Er. Rab.	*Derek Ereṣ Rabba*		book: *Gen. Rab.* [with
Der. Er. Zuṭ.	*Derek Ereṣ Zuṭa*		periods] = *Genesis Rab-*
Gem.	*Gemara*		*bah*)
Kalla	*Kalla*	*Sem.*	*Semaḥot*
Mek.	*Mekilta*	*Sipra*	*Sipra*
Midr.	*Midraš;* cited with usual	*Sipre*	*Sipre*
	abbreviation for biblical	*Sop.*	*Soperim*
	book; but *Midr. Qoh.* =	*S. ʿOlam Rab.*	*Seder ʿOlam Rabbah*
	Midraš Qohelet	*Talm.*	*Talmud*
Pal.	*Palestinian*	*Yal.*	*Yalquṭ*
Pesiq. R.	*Pesiqta Rabbati*		

I. Abbreviations of Orders and Tractates in Mishnaic and Related Literature

ʾAbot	*Pirqe ʾAbot*	*Kil.*	*Kilʾayim*
ʿArak.	*ʿArakin*	*Ma ʿaś.*	*Ma ʿaśerot*
ʿAbod. Zar.	*ʿAboda Zara*	*Mak.*	*Makkot*
B. Bat.	*Baba Batra*	*Makš.*	*Makširin* (= *Mašqin*)
Bek.	*Bekorot*	*Meg.*	*Megilla*
Ber.	*Berakot*	*Me ʿil.*	*Me ʿila*
Beṣa	*Beṣa* (= *Yom Tob*)	*Menaḥ.*	*Menaḥot*
Bik.	*Bikkurim*	*Mid.*	*Middot*
B. Meṣ.	*Baba Meṣiʿa*	*Miqw.*	*Miqwaʾot*
B. Qam.	*Baba Qamma*	*Moʿed*	*Moʿed*
Dem.	*Demai*	*Moʿed Qat.*	*Moʿed Qaṭan*
ʿEd.	*ʿEduyyot*	*Ma ʿas. S.*	*Ma ʿaśer Šeni*
ʿErub.	*ʿErubin*	*Našim*	*Našim*
Giṭ.	*Giṭṭin*	*Nazir*	*Nazir*
Ḥag.	*Ḥagiga*	*Ned.*	*Nedarim*
Ḥal.	*Ḥalla*	*Neg.*	*Nega ʿim*
Hor.	*Horayot*	*Nez.*	*Neziqin*
Ḥul.	*Ḥullin*	*Nid.*	*Niddah*
Kelim	*Kelim*	*Ohol.*	*Oholot*
Ker.	*Keritot*	*ʿOr.*	*ʿOrla*
Ketub.	*Ketubot*	*Para*	*Para*

Pe ʾa	Pe ʾa	Ta ʿan.	Ta ʿanit
Pesaḥ.	Pesaḥim	Tamid	Tamid
Qinnim	Qinnim	Tem.	Temura
Qidd.	Qiddušin	Ter.	Terumot
Qod.	Qodašin	Ṭohar.	Ṭoharot
Roš. Haš.	Roš Haššana	T. Yom	Tebul Yom
Sanh.	Sanhedrin	ʿUq.	ʿUqṣin
Šabb.	Šabbat	Yad.	Yadayim
Šeb.	Šebi ʿit	Yebam.	Yebamot
Šebu.	Šebu ʿot	Yoma	Yoma (= Kippurim)
Šeqal.	Šeqalim	Zabim	Zabim
Soṭa	Soṭa	Zebaḥ	Zebaḥim
Sukk.	Sukka	Zer.	Zera ʿim

J. Abbreviations of Nag Hammadi Tractates

Acts Pet. 12		Melch.	Melchizedek
Apost.	Acts of Peter and the Twelve Apostles	Norea	Thought of Norea
Allogenes	Allogenes	On Bap. A	On Baptism A
Ap. Jas.	Apocryphon of James	On Bap. B	On Baptism B
Ap. John	Apocryphon of John	On Bap. C	On Baptism C
Apoc. Adam	Apocalypse of Adam	On Euch. A	On the Eucharist A
1 Apoc. Jas.	First Apocalypse of James	On Euch. B	On the Eucharist B
2 Apoc. Jas.	Second Apocalypse of James	Orig. World	On the Origin of the World
Apoc. Paul	Apocalypse of Paul	Paraph. Shem	Paraphrase of Shem
Apoc. Pet.	Apocalypse of Peter	Pr. Paul	Prayer of the Apostle Paul
Asclepius	Asclepius 21–29	Pr. Thanks.	Prayer of Thanksgiving
Auth. Teach.	Authoritative Teaching	Prot. Jas.	Protevangelium of James
Dial. Sav.	Dialogue of the Savior	Sent. Sextus	Sentences of Sextus
Disc. 8–9	Discourse on the Eighth and Ninth	Soph. Jes. Chr.	Sophia of Jesus Christ
		Steles Seth	Three Steles of Seth
		Teach. Silv.	Teachings of Silvanus
Ep. Pet. Phil.	Letter of Peter to Philip	Testim. Truth	Testimony of Truth
Eugnostos	Eugnostos the Blessed	Thom. Cont.	Book of Thomas the Contender
Exeg. Soul	Exegesis on the Soul		
Gos. Eg.	Gospel of the Egyptians	Thund.	Thunder, Perfect Mind
Gos. Phil.	Gospel of Philip	Treat. Res.	Treatise on Resurrection
Gos. Thom.	Gospel of Thomas		
Gos. Truth	Gospel of Truth	Treat. Seth	Second Treatise of the Great Seth
Great Pow.	Concept of our Great Power		
Hyp. Arch.	Hypostasis of the Archons	Tri. Trac.	Triparite Tractate
Hypsiph.	Hypsiphrone	Trim. Prot.	Trimorphic Protennoia
Interp. Know.	Interpretation of Knowledge	Val. Exp.	A Valentinian Exposition
Marsanes	Marsanes	Zost.	Zostrianos

Note: The textual notes and numbers used to indicate individual manuscripts are those found in the apparatus criticus of *Novum Testamentum Graece*, ed. E. Nestle and K. Aland et al. (Stuttgart: Deutsche Bibelgesellschaft, 1979²⁶). The patristic citations are mainly drawn from *From the Fathers to the Churches* (London: Collins, 1983).

General Bibliography

Barker, G. W., Lane, W. L., and **Michaels, J. R.** *The New Testament Speaks.* New York: Harper and Row, 1969. **Bornkamm, G.** *The New Testament: A Guide to Its Writings.* Tr. R. H. and I. Fuller. Philadelphia: Fortress, 1973. **Cullmann, O.** *The New Testament: An Introduction.* Philadelphia: Westminster, 1968. **Dibelius, M.** *A Fresh Approach to the New Testament and Early Christian Literature.* New York: Scribner's, 1936. **Enslin, M. S.** *Christian Beginnings: The Literature of the Christian Movement.* New York: Harper, 1956. **Feine, P., Behm, J.,** and **Kümmel, W. G.** *Introduction to the New Testament.* Tr. A. J. Mattill, Jr. Nashville: Abingdon, 1966; 1st ed. in E. T. See Kümmel. **Fuller, R. H.** *A Critical Introduction to the New Testament.* London: Duckworth, 1966. **Goguel, M.** *Introduction au nouveau Testament. IV/2: les épîtres pauliniennes.* Paris: Leroux, 1926. **Grant, R. M.** *A Historical Introduction to the New Testament.* New York: Harper and Row, 1963. **Guthrie, D.** *New Testament Introduction.* Chicago: Inter-Varsity Press/London: Tyndale Press, 1963 (2d ed.), 1970 (3d ed.). **Harrison, E. F.** *Introduction to the New Testament.* Grand Rapids: Eerdmans, 1964. **Hunter, A. M.** *Introducing the New Testament.* Philadelphia: Westminster, 1957². **Koester, H.** *Introduction to the New Testament.* Vol. 2. Philadelphia: Fortress, 1982. **Kümmel, W. G.** *Introduction to the New Testament.* Rev. ed. Tr. H. C. Kee. Nashville: Abingdon, 1975. **Martin, R. P.** *New Testament Foundations.* Vol. 2. Grand Rapids: Eerdmans/Exeter: Paternoster Press, 1978. **Marxsen, W.** *Introduction to the New Testament.* Tr. G. Buswell. Philadelphia: Fortress, 1968. **McNeile, A. H.** *Introduction to the New Testament.* Rev. ed. C. S. C. Williams. Oxford: Clarendon, 1953. **Michaelis, W.** *Einleitung in das Neue Testament.* 2d ed. Bern: Berchthold Haller Verlag, 1954. **Moffatt, J.** *An Introduction to the Literature of the New Testament.* New York: Scribner's/Edinburgh: T. & T. Clark, 1911; 3d ed., 1918. **Perrin, N.** *The New Testament: An Introduction.* New York: Harcourt Brace Jovanovich, 1974; rev. D. C. Duling, 1982. **Price, J. L.** *Interpreting the New Testament.* New York: Holt, Rinehart & Winston, 1961. **Riddle, D. W.,** and **Hutson, H. H.** *New Testament Life and Literature.* Chicago: University of Chicago Press, 1946. **Robert, A.,** and **Feuillet, A.** *Introduction to the New Testament.* Tr. P. W. Skehan. New York: Desclée, 1965. **Vielhauer, Ph.** *Geschichte der urchristlichen Literatur.* Berlin: de Gruyter, 1975. **Wikenhauser, A.** *New Testament Introduction.* Tr. J. Cunningham. New York: Herder & Herder, 1958. **Zahn, T.** *Introduction to the New Testament.* Tr. J. M. Trout *et al.* Edinburgh: T. & T. Clark, 1909.

Commentary Bibliography

Alford, H. "ΠΡΟΣ ΚΟΡΙΝΘΙΟΥΣ." In *The Greek Testament* 2, 3d ed. London: Rivingtons, 1857. **Allo, E. B.** *Saint Paul: seconde épître aux Corinthiens.* EB. Paris: J. Gabalda, 2d ed., 1956. **Bachmann, P.** *Der zweite Brief des Paulus an die Korinther.* ZKNT. Leipzig: Verlagsbuchhandlung Werner Scholl, 1918. **Barclay, W.** *The Letters to the Corinthians.* Edinburgh: St. Andrews Press/Philadelphia: Westminster Press, reprint 1975. **Barrett, C. K.** *A Commentary on the Second Epistle to the Corinthians.* New York: Harper & Row/ London: A. & C. Black, 1973. **Beasley-Murray, G. R.** "2 Corinthians," *The Broadman Bible Commentary,* vol. 11. Nashville: Broadman Press, 1971. **Beet, J. A.** *II Corinthians.* London: Hodder & Stoughton, 1882. **Bernard, J. H.** "The Second Epistle to the Corinthians." In *The Expositor's Greek Testament* 3, ed. W. R. Nicoll. London: Hodder & Stoughton, 1897. **Boor, W. de.** *Der zweite Brief des Paulus an die Korinther.* Wuppertal: R. Brockhaus, 1972. **Bruce, F. F.** *1 and 2 Corinthians.* NCB. Grand Rapids: Eerdmans/ London: Marshall, Morgan & Scott, 1971. **Bultmann, R.** *Der zweite Brief an die Korinther.* Ed. E. Dinkler. MeyerK 6. Göttingen: Vandenhoeck & Ruprecht, 1976. ———. *Exegetische Probleme des zweiten Korintherbriefes.* Reprint. Darmstadt: Wissenschaftliche Buchgesellschaft, 1963. **Calvin, J.** *The Second Epistle of Paul the Apostle to the Corinthians and the Epistles to Timothy, Titus, and Philemon.* Calvin's New Testament Commentaries 10. Tr. T. A. Smail. Grand Rapids: Eerdmans, 1964. **Denney, J.** *The Second Epistle to the Corinthians.* The Expositor's Bible. London: Hodder & Stoughton, 1894/New York: Armstrong, 1903. **Evans, E.** *The Epistles of Paul the Apostle to the Corinthians.* The Clarendon Bible 13. Oxford: The Clarendon Press, 1930. **Fallon, F. T.** *2 Corinthians.* New Testament Message 11. Wilmington, Del.: M. Glazier/Dublin: Veritas, 1980. **Filson, F. V.** "The Second Epistle to the Corinthians." In IB 10. New York: Abingdon Press, 1953. **Furnish, V. P.** *II Corinthians.* AB 32A. Garden City, N.Y.: Doubleday, 1984. **Goudge, H. L.** *The Second Epistle to the Corinthians.* WC. London: Methuen & Co., 1927. **Hanson, R. P. C.** *2 Corinthians.* Torch Bible Commentaries. London: SCM, 1967. **Harris, M. J.** "2 Corinthians." In *The Expositor's Bible Commentary,* ed. F. E. Gaebelein. Grand Rapids: Zondervan, 1976. **Héring, J.** *The Second Epistle of Saint Paul to the Corinthians.* Originally CNT. Tr. A. W. Heathcote and P. J. Allcock. London: Epworth Publishing Company, 1967. **Hodge, C.** *An Exposition of the Second Epistle to the Corinthians.* New York: A. C. Armstrong & Son, 1891. Reprint. Edinburgh: Banner of Truth, 1959. **Hughes, P. E.** *Paul's Second Epistle to the Corinthians.* NICNT 47. Grand Rapids: Eerdmans/London: Marshall, Morgan & Scott, 1962. **Kennedy, J. H.** *The Second and Third Epistles of St. Paul to the Corinthians.* London: Methuen & Co., 1900. **Lietzmann, H.** *An die Korinther 1/2.* With supplement by W. G. Kümmel. HNT 9. Tübingen: J. C. B. Mohr (Paul Siebeck), 1969. **Menzies, A.** *The Second Epistle of the Apostle Paul to the Corinthians.* London: Macmillan & Co., 1912. **Meyer, H. A. W.** *Kritisch-exegetischer Handbuch über den zweiten Brief an die Korinther.* MeyerK 6. Göttingen: Vandenhoeck & Ruprecht, 1840. **Plummer, A.** *A Critical and Exegetical Commentary on the Second Epistle of St. Paul to the Corinthians.* ICC 47. Edinburgh: T. & T. Clark, 1915. **Strachan, R. H.** *The Second Epistle of Paul to the Corinthians.* MNTC 7/2. London: Hodder & Stoughton/New York: Harper & Brothers, 1935. **Tasker, R. V. G.** *The Second Epistle to the Corinthians.* TNTC 8. Grand Rapids: Eerdmans, 1958. **Thrall, M. E.** *The First and Second Letter of Paul to the Corinthians.* The Cambridge Bible Commentary. Cambridge: University Press, 1965. **Wendland, H. D.** *Die Briefe an die Korinther.* NTD 7. Göttingen: Vandenhoeck & Ruprecht, 1964. **Wilson, G. B.** *2 Corinthians.* A Digest of Reformed Comment. Edinburgh: Banner of Truth, 1979. **Windisch, H.** *Der zweite Korintherbrief.* MeyerK 6. Göttingen: Vandenhoeck & Ruprecht, 1924.

Introduction

1. CORINTH: CITY AND CHURCH

Bibliography

Barrett, C. K. "Titus," *Neotestamentica et Semitica*. FS M. Black. Ed. E. E. Ellis and M. Wilcox. Edinburgh: T. & T. Clark, 1969. 1–14. ———. *The New Testament Background: Selected Documents*. London: SPCK/New York: Macmillan, 1956. **Conzelmann, H.** "Korinth und die Mädchen der Aphrodite. Zur Religionsgeschichte der Stadt Korinth." *NAG* 8 (1967) 247–61. Reprinted in his *Theologie als Schriftauslegung: Aufsätze zum Neuen Testament*. Munich: Kaiser, 1974. 152–66. ———. *1 Corinthians*. Hermeneia. Tr. J. W. Leitch. Philadelphia: Fortress, 1975. **de Waele, F. J.** "Korinthos." In Pauly, A. and Wissowa, G. *Real-Encyklopädie der klassischen Altertumswissenschaft*, supp. VI, 182–200. 1935. **Doughty, D. J.** "The Presence and Future of Salvation in Corinth," *ZNW* 66 (1975) 61–90. **Fascher, E.** "Die Korintherbriefe und die Gnosis." In Tröger, K. W., ed. *Gnosis und Neues Testament*, 281–91. Gütersloh: Mohn, 1973. **Finegan, J.** *Light from the Ancient Past*. Princeton: University Press, 1946–1965. ———. *Handbook of Biblical Chronology*. Princeton: University Press, 1964. **Grant, R. M.** *A Historical Introduction to the New Testament*. London: Collins/New York: Harper & Row, 1963. **Gunther, J. J.** *Paul: Messenger and Exile*. Valley Forge, PA: Judson, 1972. **Hock, R. F.** "Paul's Tentmaking and the Problem of His Social Class." *JBL* 97 (1978) 555–64. ———. "The Workshop as a Social Setting for Paul's Missionary Preaching." *CBQ* 41 (1979) 438–50. ———. *The Social Context of Paul's Ministry: Tentmaking and Apostleship*. Philadelphia: Fortress, 1980. **Holmberg, B.** *Paul and Power. The Structure of Authority in the Primitive Church as Reflected in the Pauline Epistles*. ConB 11. Lund: Gleerup, 1983. **Jervell, J.** "Der schwache Charismatiker." In *Rechtfertigung*. FS E. Käsemann, ed. J. Friedrich, W. Pöhlmann, & P. Stuhlmacher, 185–98. Tübingen: J. C. B. Mohr, 1976. **Jewett, R.** *A Chronology of Paul's Life*. Philadelphia: Fortress, 1979. **Koester, H.** and **Robinson, J. M.** *Trajectories through Early Christianity*. Philadelphia: Fortress, 1971. **Kümmel, W. G.** *Introduction to the New Testament*.[2] Tr. H. C. Kee. London: SCM Press/Nashville: Abingdon, 1975. **Lenschau, T.** "Korinthos." In Pauly, A. and Wissowa, G. *Real-Encyklopädie der klassischen Altertumswissenschaft*, suppl. IV, 991–1036. 1924. **Luedmann, G.** *Paul, Apostle to the Gentiles. Studies in Chronology*. ET. Philadelphia: Fortress, 1984. **Martin, R. P.** *The Spirit and the Congregation: Studies in 1 Corinthians 12–15*. Grand Rapids: Eerdmans/Exeter: Paternoster Press, 1984. **Marxsen, W.** *Introduction to the New Testament*. Tr. G. Buswell. Philadelphia: Fortress, 1968. **McNeile, A. H.** and **Williams, C. S. C.** *An Introduction to the Study of the New Testament*.[2] Oxford: Clarendon Press, 1953. **Murphy-O'Connor, J.** *St. Paul's Corinth. Texts and Archaeology*. Wilmington, Del.: M. Glazier, Inc., 1983. ———. "The Corinth St. Paul Saw," *BA* 47.3 (1984) 147–59. ———. *1 Corinthians*. NT Message. Dublin: Veritas/Wilmington, Del.: Glazier, 1979. **Papahatzis, N.** *Ancient Corinth: The Museums of Corinth, Isthmia and Sicyon*. Athens: Ekdotike Athenon, 1977. **Robinson, J. A. T.** *Redating the New Testament*. London: SCM/Philadelphia: Westminster Press, 1976. **Schmithals, W.** *Gnosticism in Corinth*. Tr. John E. Steely. Nashville: Abingdon, 1971. **Smallwood, E. M.** *The Jews under Roman Rule*. Leiden: Brill, 1976. **Theissen, G.** *The Social Setting of Pauline Christianity. Essays on Corinth*. Tr. J. H. Schütz. Philadelphia: Fortress Press, 1982. **Thiselton, A. C.** "Realized Eschatology at Corinth." *NTS* 24 (1977–78) 510–26. **Wilson, R. McL.** "Gnosis at Corinth." In *Paul and Paulinism: Essays in Honour of C. K. Barrett*, ed. M. D. Hooker & S. G. Wilson, 102–14. London: SPCK, 1982.

Yamauchi, E. "Pre-Christian Gnosticism, The New Testament and Nag Hammadi in Recent Debate." *Themelios* 10 (1984) 22–27.

First-century Corinth was the leading commercial center of southern Greece. (For an account of recent archaeological work on the site and its environs, see Papahatzis, *Ancient Corinth.*) Its favorable geographical situation contributed to this, for it was located on the isthmus connecting northern Greece with the Peloponnesus, and it boasted two harbors, Lechaeum to the west, and Cenchreae to the east. (See Pausanias, *Description of Greece* 2.3, for the harbors of Corinth; cf. 1.5 for early attempts to dig a canal across the isthmus; Strabo, *Geography* 8.6.20*a*, calls Corinth "wealthy" because of its being "situated on the isthmus and [it] is master of two harbors"; Horace, *Odes* 1.7.2, has the phrase "double-sea Corinth.") It thus became an emporium for seaborne merchandise passing in either direction, and a considerable number of roads converged on it. See the map in J. Murphy-O'Connor, *St. Paul's Corinth,* 20, and the account in Pausanias, *Description* 2.4, 5.4. Sailors were able to avoid the dangerous route around the Peloponnesus, and a more northerly trip across the Aegean Sea, away from storms, was made possible. Tribute to Corinth's topographical position, which made unnecessary the voyage around Cape Malea, is given in Strabo, *Geography* 8.6.20*a:* "To land their cargoes here was a welcome alternative to the voyage to Malea for merchants from both Italy and Asia." For evidence of delays caused by rough seas around Malea, see Pliny, *Ep.* 10.15.

Like most seaports throughout history, Corinth took on an international reputation. Of this fact Cicero's treatise *On the Republic* 2.7–9 is cognizant: "Maritime cities also suggest a certain corruption and degeneration of morals; for they receive a mixture of strange languages and customs, and import foreign ways as well as foreign merchandise, so that none of their ancestral institutions can possibly remain unchanged." There must have been considerable intermixing of races in its population, and this resulted in a variety of religious cults. Corinth's chief shrine was the temple of Aphrodite, the Greek goddess of love and life (Pausanias, *Description* 5.1). In Corinth her cult appeared in a debased form, due to the admixture of certain Oriental influences. This meant a low moral tone and sexual perversion in a possibly attested cult of sacred prostitution. According to Strabo, *Geography* 8.6.20, "the Temple of Aphrodite was so rich that it owned more than a thousand temple-slaves, courtesans, whom men and women had dedicated to the goddess." But Conzelmann (12) doubts the relevance of this description to the city of Paul's day on the ground that Strabo's reference to "prostitutes in the temple service" (of Aphrodite)—ἱεροδούλους ἑταίρας—is anachronistic because he is referring to the city in the pre-146 B.C. period, not the city he visited in 29 B.C.; and Pausanias is silent on the issue. J. Murphy-O'Connor (*St. Paul's Corinth,* 56) notes that sacred prostitution was never a Greek custom, and—if Corinth was an exception—it becomes impossible to account for the silence of other ancient Greek authors. Because of the luxury and vice of Corinth the word "corinthianize"—κορινθιάζεσθαι—(i.e., to fornicate) was coined as an infamous sign of the wealth and immorality for which the city was renowned in the ancient world. But Aristophanes (*ca.* 450–385 B.C.) may have invented the verb as part of Athenian disdain for the region in southern Greece during the Peloponnesian War, or else the term reflects the rivalry of Athens whose trade was jeopardized by Corinth. Yet the term was widely popular. Plays such as *Korinthiastēs* (Κορινθιαστής, i.e., "The Harlot") were written by Philetaerus (4th cent. B.C.) and Poliochus, according to Athenaeus, *Deipnosophistae* 7:313c, 13:559a. On the cited passage of Athenaeus, *Deipnosophistae* 13:573c–574c, which refers to "the Corinthian prostitutes [who] entered the temple of Aphrodite and prayed for the salvation of the Greeks," see Conzelmann, "Korinth," 256 = *Theologie,* 160 f., and Murphy-O'Connor, *St. Paul's Corinth,* 126, 127. Plato, *Republic* 404D, uses *korinthia korē,* "a Corinthian girl," to mean a prostitute (ψέγεις ἄρα καὶ Κορινθίαν κόρην; "you would frown then on a Corinthian girl?").

In such a place, by the grace of God and the ministry of his servant Paul, a church was formed. A large proportion of its members must have been drawn from the pagan world, with its heterogeneous standards of life and conduct. Yet they would be familiar with Jewish teaching as converts to the faith of the synagogue (Acts 18:4; see Murphy-O'Connor, *1 Corinthians* ix, x). Not surprisingly, issues of Christian morality and behavior dominate the first epistle; and in 2 Corinthians 6:14–18 a strong warning is issued against association with unbelievers. "Also, the tendencies to factiousness and instability have a real psychological basis in both the blend and the clash of racial character to be found in such a cosmopolitan city" (Strachan, *Commentary,* xiv).

A section of the church belonged to the Jewish colony, the so-called Dispersion, which was naturally represented in such a commercial center. See Philo, *Leg. ad Gaium,* 281, 282, for the presence of Corinth in the list of cities of the Jewish *diaspora.* Jewish exiles from Sicyon (to the northwest of Corinth) may have fled when their city was destroyed in 146 B.C. There were common trade links to draw them (Strabo, *Geography* 8.6.23c). Murphy-O'Connor (*St. Paul's Corinth,* 79) suggestively remarks that after A.D. 67 when Vespasian sent six thousand young men to work on the Corinth canal (Josephus, *JW* 3:540) the nucleus of Jewish communities in Corinth would have been augmented. Jewish legal rights in such situations include the right to assembly, permission to send the temple tax to Jerusalem, and to be exempted from any civic activity which would violate their sabbath observance (Smallwood, *Jews,* 120–43). E. M. Smallwood (225) suggests that by Paul's time the Jewish presence at Corinth would be considered a *politeuma,* i.e., a corporation of resident aliens with permanent rights of domicile and empowered to manage its own affairs through self-appointed officials. Hence we read of a synagogue ruler (Acts 18:8, 17), and a debated inscription [SYN]AGŌGĒ HEBR[AIŌN], "Synagogue of the Hebrews," may testify to the site of their meeting place (Smallwood, 138; Barrett, *New Testament Background,* 51; J. Finegan, *Light from the Ancient Past* II [1969] 360–63).

Acts 18:1–11 tells us that the church was formed as a result of Paul's preaching in the local synagogue. Nonetheless, it is probably correct to assume that the preponderance of the church members were Gentile, converted to Christ from a pagan milieu. These were called to be God's people in the "Vanity Fair" of the Roman Empire. Murphy-O'Connor (*BA,* 147) writes of Corinth in Paul's day as "a wide-open boomtown," comparing it with San Francisco of the gold rush days.

Corinth had attained eminence as a city much earlier than Paul's arrival there, owing to its commercial advantages, but it had been destroyed by the Roman conqueror L. Mummius about two hundred years before the apostle's visit. (There are several accounts of this destruction of Corinth by the Romans: Pausanias, *Description* 7.16.7–10, who dates it in 146 B.C.; Strabo, *Geography*, 8.6.23*b*, who uses an eyewitness, the Greek historian of Rome, Polybius [*ca.* 203–120 B.C.]; and Dio Cassius, *Roman History* 21, who adds the detail that Mummius was concerned to enslave all Corinthians as a punitive measure.) After lying in ruins for about a century, it was reconstructed by Julius Caesar in 46–44 B.C. and peopled as a Roman colony. Our authority here is Appian, *Roman History* 8.136. He supplies the datum that Julius Caesar sent in a band of colonists. The sentence that those were sent "to Carthage and some to Corinth" links the repopulating of the two cities, and provides a fixed point of chronology. "Thus the Romans won the Carthaginian part in Africa, destroyed Carthage, and repeopled it again 102 years after its destruction." The two cities of Carthage and Corinth fell in 146 B.C.; so their rebuilding is dated 44 B.C. Possibly this occurred sooner since Julius was assassinated on the Ides of March in 44 B.C. and Augustus (Octavian) was in no position to execute the plan to reestablish the colonies before the end of 43 B.C. at the earliest (Murphy-O'Connor, *St. Paul's Corinth*, 114). It may be preferable to keep the date flexible, and allow the time of Corinth's rebirth by the Romans to fall between 46 B.C. when Julius Caesar was engaged in his Africa campaign and his death two years later. He may well have grasped the strategic importance of Corinth as a commercial center; cf. Cicero, *On the Agrarian Law* = *Against Rullus* 2.87, who pays tribute to Corinth's economic importance. This historical background may account for Roman names that appear in the Corinthian letters (1 Cor 1:14: Crispus, Gaius; 16:17: Stephanas, Fortunatus, Achaicus).

In the first century the city was heavily populated, and its place as a political and commercial center can be gauged from the Romans' having made it in 27 B.C. the capital city of the senatorial province of Achaia in southern Greece. Strabo, *Geography* 17.3.25, gives the account of Caesar Augustus' determination to create two kinds of Roman province in 27 B.C.: "provinces of Caesar," or imperial provinces, and "provinces of the people," senatorial provinces, governed by a proconsul. Achaia fell into the latter category until A.D. 15 when "it was decided to relieve them [Achaia, Macedonia] of their proconsular government for the time being and transfer them to the emperor" (Tacitus, *Ann.* 1.76). And while its reputation for moral corruption made the "Corinthian life" synonymous with luxury and licentiousness, its pretensions to philosophy and literary culture made the phrase "Corinthian words" a token of polished and cultivated speech (see Aelius Aristides, *Orations* 46:20–31); but this tribute is much later than Paul's day.

In this great and busy center Paul spent a year and a half or more in the course of his second missionary journey (Acts 18:11, 18), having arrived in the city probably in the winter of A.D. 50/51. (Gallio's accession on July 1, 51, as proconsul of Achaia in southern Greece is one of the fixed points of apostolic chronology. The evidence, set forth in J. Finegan, *Handbook of Biblical Chronology* [1964], 316–18, may also be construed to fix the date twelve months later [A.D. 52]; see J. J. Gunther, *Paul: Messenger and Exile* [1972] 57, 171f., and, for the earlier dating, F. F. Bruce, *New Testament History* [1969] 282, 298; J. A. T. Robinson, *Redating the New Testament* [1976] 31, 35; E. M. Smallwood, *Jews under Roman Rule* [1976] 213, n. 35. Conclusively for the earlier date see R. Jewett, *A Chronology of Paul's Life* [1976] 36–40, and J. Murphy-O'Connor, *St. Paul's Corinth* [1983] 141–52.) Paul found hospitality in the home of Aquila and Priscilla, a Jewish couple, eminent for their devotion, who had come from Rome following the decree of Claudius in 49 (this is the traditional date; Murphy O'Connor, 130–139, wishes to date this edict in A.D. 41, with further arguments adduced by G. Luedmann, *Paul,* 162–71). With them Paul carried on his trade of tentmaking (see R. F. Hock, *JBL* 97 [1978] 555–64; *CBQ* 41 [1979] 438–50; and *The Social Context* [1980]).

Beginning his ministry in the synagogue, he was soon compelled by the opposition of the Jews to seek another place of meeting, which he found in the house of Justus, a converted proselyte. There he preached the Gospel, encouraged by a vision from God. Divine blessing was manifest in the conversion of his hearers and in the establishment of a Christian community despite the Jews' attempt to invoke the civil power against him (Acts 18:4–18). The converts seem to have been drawn from the lower classes (1 Cor 1:26–29), but not exclusively so (cf. 1 Cor 4:10; 10:27; 11:17–34; 12:24, 25; see Theissen, *Social Setting,* 70–99). They were not free from the prevailing tendency to intellectual pride (cf. 1:18–20; 3:18, 19; 8:1). Added to this was a proneness to sensual sin, equally characteristic of their native city (5:1–11; 6:15–18; 11:21), though there is probably a theological reason for these symptoms (as outlined by R. P. Martin, *The Spirit and the Congregation: Studies in 1 Corinthians 12–15* [1984]).

Internal evidence from the first canonical letter suggests that several features marred the life of this church. There was a factious spirit that divided the church into rival groups and showed itself in bickering which drew them to civil courts to settle their disputes (chap. 6). This party rivalry destroyed the unity of Christ's body (chap. 12) and was seen even at the Lord's table meal (11:17 ff.). Also, the Corinthians boasted of their "knowledge" (8:1) and "freedom" (6:12; 8:9; 10:23). These two terms have suggested to some scholars that a species of Judaeo-gnostic thought and practice had penetrated the church and influenced the thinking and conduct of some of the members. See W. Schmithals, *Gnosticism in Corinth* (ET 1971) 117–285; W. Marxsen, *Introduction to the New Testament* (ET 1968) 75. But arguing against this is R. McL. Wilson, "Gnosis at Corinth" (1982) 102–14. Much turns on the precise definition of "gnosticism," a slippery term. See the latest report in E. Yamauchi, "Pre-Christian Gnosticism" (1984), 22–27.

Numerous signs of this "heretical theology in Corinth" (Schmithals's term) have been identified: the value placed on esoteric "knowledge" (γνῶσις, *gnōsis,* 1 Cor 1:5; 8:1, 7, 10, 11; 12:8; 13:2; 14:6; this feature reappears in the second letter: see 2:14; 4:6; 8:7; 10:5; 11:6); and "freedom" claimed and used in many ways. To these Corinthian catchwords must be added "spiritual" (πνευματικός, *pneumatikos*), which is found fourteen times in 1 Corinthians as against four times in the other undisputed Pauline letters. Individual Corinthians evidently set themselves above the constraints of community order and control; and each church member became a law to himself or herself (1 Cor 8:9; 10:23; 14:32–40). Other signs were a denial of a future resurrection (chap. 15; cf. 2 Tim 2:18); a high value placed on sacramental efficacy as conferring "protection" (chap. 10) with a devaluating of ethical seriousness; an importance attached to demonstrations of the Spirit—τὰ πνευματικά—(14:1 ff.); the setting up of a clique of Spirit-endowed persons (14:37); strange marriage practices (chap. 7; cf. 1 Tim 4:3); and possibly a disavowal of interest in the earthly Jesus with a resulting concentration on the heavenly "eon" Christ (12:3) and a consequent passing over of the kerygma centered in the cross (1:18 f., 23; cf. J. M. Robinson, "Kerygma and History in the New Testament," in *Trajectories through Early Christianity* [with H. Koester, 1971], 34: "It would seem to be this heretical interpretation of the kerygma in terms of an already consummated eschaton for the initiated that is behind the various Corinthian excesses to which Paul addresses himself in 1 Corinthians"). At 2:8 the christological title "Lord of glory" is probably borrowed from Paul's Corinthian opponents and turned against them as it is anchored in the cross, namely, by insisting that Jesus became Lord only by first submitting to humiliation and death.

The attractiveness of this interpretation is that it makes all the facets of the Corinthians' erroneous teaching and practice spring from a single source. However, it begs the question of whether second-century gnostic ideas appeared so early in the apostolic age (a theme we shall take up later). Some have explained the contents of the Corinthian correspondence without any recourse to gnosticizing ideas (e.g., J. C. Hurd, Jr., *The Origin of 1 Corinthians* [1965; 2d ed., 1983]), but it is more likely that at Corinth we see the beginning of that accommodation of the Christian Gospel to hellenistic mysticism which was later to blossom in the various gnostic schools. F. F. Bruce's term "incipient gnosticism" may well be flexible enough to account for the Corinthian phenomena (F. F. Bruce, *1 and 2 Corinthians*, 21, cf. R. McL. Wilson, "How Gnostic were the Corinthians?" *NTS* 19 [1972–73] 65–74). R. M. Grant, *A Historical Introduction to the New Testament* [1963] 204–206, bases his conviction that "there were Gnostics at Corinth, and that Gnosticism was essentially a way of viewing the Christian gospel" on the Corinthians' claim to adopt a fully realized eschatology, drawn in part from Jewish apocalypticism. But this is challenged by D. J. Doughty, "The Presence and Future of Salvation in Corinth," *ZNW* 66 [1975] 61–90, who argues that the controversy at Corinth turns not on the futurity of salvation, but rather on the understanding of salvation as such. The two ideas are linked, however (see R. P. Martin, *The Spirit and the Congregation;* A. C. Thiselton, "Realized Eschatology").

When we turn to 2 Corinthians we find that the data available to us to attempt a description of the Corinthians' "theology" are not the same. Whereas in 1 Corinthians the church leaders and members have written to consult Paul, and whereas he had received rumored reports (1 Cor 1:11; 11:18) of the problems there, in the second letter the sources of information are more indirect. We have to infer from the texts the nature of the debate between Paul and his congregation, some of whom at least seemed to be under the influence of intruding teachers, especially emissaries referred to in chaps. 10–13. Already in 2:17; 3:1–18; 4:2–6, in the canonical sequence of the letter, Paul is confronting those whose teaching is at odds with his version of the kerygma, and we shall have to discuss the most likely reason for the way these texts set the ground of the debate. Part of the reason is personal: Paul is accused of vacillation and insincerity. But there is a theological difference between his message and the "gospel" brought to Corinth (11:4). Its "alien" character is in part christological (5:16), in part eschatological (5:1–10), in part related to the presence and power of "spirit" (πνεῦμα, *pneuma;* 11:4) that conferred presumed authority on these teachers. At its heart was evidently an exegesis of the Old Testament and in particular an understanding of the role of Moses. The latter gave them an assurance that they were superior to Paul, who looked distinctly "inferior" by comparison (see 11:5, 6; 12:11). The point at issue has to do with rhetorical prowess and a commanding presence, two features that Paul's ministry lacked. On the negative side, as Jervell ("Der schwache Charismatiker") and Holmberg (*Paul and Power,* 78, 79) have suggested, was the undeniable fact that, although Paul was known as a remarkable leader in the churches (12:12), he was a weak person physically (10:10) and could not heal himself (12:7; cf. Gal 4:13 f.). The Corinthian adversaries may well have reasoned that he was no demonstration of God's power since his claim to be an apostle and his experience of weakness contradicted each other (cf. E. Käsemann, *Die Legitimität des Apostels,* 38–43). For them "a sick charismatic and wonderworker [would be] astonishing" as being a *contradictio in adjecto* (Jervell, loc. cit., 192, 194). They insinuated, therefore, that he was no true apostle, since they took as their criterion the picture of the itinerant "holy man" preacher, whose credentials were the possession of the spirit (πνεῦμα) and the right to claim the Corinthian province as their jurisdiction (10:13–18), evidently in the name of the *Überapostel,* the "super-apostles," in Jerusalem (11:5; 12:11). The question is posed to the interpreter at this point: can we identify, however tentatively, the type of "charismatic" ministry brought by these teachers which stands at odds with Paul's self-conscious defense of his apostleship? In a later section we will try to set this question in a broader framework. Here we may pause to reflect on J. M. Robinson's conclusion: "Paul was primarily confronted with a distorting transmission of traditions about Jesus as a glorious miracle worker, and he replied, with an ironic presentation of himself within that succession, to document the invalidity of such a scope for the traditions; and by repudiating such knowledge of Jesus" (*Trajectories,* 59 ff.). For a similar conclusion, see R. H. Fuller, *A Critical Introduction to the New Testament* (London: Duckworth, 1966), 49 f.

2. PAUL'S VISITS TO CORINTH

Paul's motives and movements in connection with his visits to this city form a difficult complex, but the suggested list of events is likely, and we shall base our discussion of his Corinthian correspondence with special reference to 2 Corinthians on this reconstruction. The following is a tentative outline, to be reviewed after some issues of literary composition have been discussed. We return to the proposed itinerary later (p. xlvi).

(1) Paul plants the church (Acts 18:1 ff.). (2) Paul leaves Corinth and goes to Ephesus (Acts 18:18 f.). (3) He sends the Corinthians a letter, now lost, to which he refers in 1 Corinthians 5:9, though some scholars believe that 2 Corinthians 6:14–7:1 may be a fragment of it. (4) He learns from "members of Chloe's household" (1 Cor 1:11) that the church in Corinth is split into factions. (5) About the same time, Paul receives a letter from the Corinthians asking for his advice and guidance on certain issues affecting the ordering of worship and Christians' relations with the outside world (1 Cor 7:1). (6) He responds to their factiousness and answers their request for advice by writing the letter we know as 1 Corinthians. This letter possibly is taken by Titus (cf. 2 Cor 12:18, though this verse more probably refers to the "severe letter" visit of item 10 below), who subsequently returns to Ephesus where Paul is. (7) Timothy is sent to Corinth on a special mission (1 Cor 4:17; 16:10). (8) In the meantime a serious crisis breaks out in Corinth, fomented by a ringleader who launches a personal attack on Paul (2 Cor 2:5–11; 7:8–13). Timothy is evidently at a loss to deal with it and returns with the news to Ephesus. (9) On receiving Timothy's report, Paul pays a brief visit to Corinth to deal with the issue in person. This he later refers to as the occasion of a "painful visit" (2 Cor 2:1). He is humiliated before the church and has to return to Ephesus in great distress. (10) He now writes a powerful letter of remonstrance, at great cost to himself, in order to deal with the crisis (2 Cor 2:4; 7:8). This is known as the "tearful" or the "severe letter," which is either lost or only partially preserved in 2 Corinthians 10–13. Titus is instructed to meet Paul at Troas. (11) According to the plan outlined in 1 Corinthians 16:5 ff., but after some delay caused by the "intermediate visit" to Corinth (mentioned as item 9 above), Paul leaves Ephesus for Macedonia. He comes to Troas and cannot find Titus; so he goes on to Macedonia to intercept him (2 Cor 2:12 f.). (12) Paul meets Titus, who relates that the worst is over, and the rebellion is quelled (2 Cor 7:6–16). (13) He writes the letter we have as 2 Corinthians, either in its entirety (in which case the last four chapters are aimed at clearing up the remaining pockets of resistance and opposition in the church) or, more probably, in part (that is, what we know as chaps. 1–9). This letter he sends from Macedonia through Titus, accompanied by two other brethren. (14) Subsequent to the sending of 2 Corinthians 1–9, Paul learns that renewed troubles have broken out at Corinth and that a group in the church is in danger of being won over by emissaries who have challenged Paul's authority and introduced a rival teaching (2 Cor 10:10; 11:27; 12:6 f.). This groundswell of opposition confirms Paul's latent fears that all is not well in the church. He writes chaps. 10–13 to confront this problem. (15) Paul himself reaches Corinth (Acts 20:2) where, less than a year later, he writes the epistle to the Romans.

3. CORRESPONDENCE WITH THE CHURCH AT CORINTH

Although we can almost certainly place the writing of 1 Corinthians at one point in Paul's missionary career, it is difficult to fix a more precise time of composition. 1 Cor 16:8 shows that he wrote shortly before the feast of Pentecost, which we may place early in May of A.D. 54 or, less probably, 55. We infer, too, from 16:1 f. that the collection at Corinth for the poor believers in Jerusalem had not yet been started. In 2 Cor 8:10 and 9:2 he writes that the Corinthians began the collection "last year." As McNeile and Williams say, "The relation between the dates of the two epistles depends upon this phrase" (*An Introduction to the Study of the New Testament* [1953] 133; but see Kümmel, *Introduction to the New Testament*, 282; Gunther, *Paul*, 77). It is clear that 2 Corinthians was written from Macedonia after Paul had left Ephesus. Eager to learn the results of the visit by Titus to Corinth to enforce the apostle's views and gauge the response to his "tearful letter," Paul had no heart to embrace the opportunity to preach at Troas when his emissary did not appear there. Finally they met in Macedonia. Titus brought the good news that Paul's letter had done its work well, producing in the Corinthians a repentant sorrow. His joy at learning that the crisis was over is the immediate occasion of what we know as 2 Corinthians (at least chaps. 1–9), written in the autumn of A.D. 55 or, less likely, 56, and the last four chapters a short while later. This is the traditional view at its simplest.

> He had been racked with fear that they might defy his authority by refusing to listen to the pleadings and to follow the directions in his sorrowful letter. His relief was unbounded when he heard from Titus that they had accepted his letter in the right spirit, and had shown their penitence by dealing strongly—almost too strongly—with the offender. And he at once wrote this letter. It was not a moment for dealing with Christian doctrine or Church practice; the letter is simply a pouring out of the man himself (A. H. McNeile-C. S. C. Williams, *Introduction*, 138; see also C. K. Barrett, "Titus," in *Neotestamentica et Semitica* [M. Black *Festschrift*, ed. E. E. Ellis & M. Wilcox, 1969] 1–14).

Whereas the contents of 1 Corinthians fall into well-defined sections, corresponding largely to the matters on which the church had written to Paul for advice, in 2 Corinthians the flow of Paul's writing is erratic and less well-ordered, especially in the first seven chapters. Before we come to grips with some critical problems of the letter, it will be necessary to set down an analysis of the contents and then in a final section to say something about its contribution to our understanding of Paul's missionary history.

4. AN ANALYSIS OF 2 CORINTHIANS

Introduction (1:1–11): notes of salutation (vv. 1, 2) and thanksgiving (vv. 3–11).
  I. *Paul justifies his conduct toward the Corinthians* (1:12–7:16)
    A. *The question of Paul's journeys to Corinth* (1:12–2:13): Paul has changed his voyage plans and has consequently been accused of vacillation. He defends himself by explaining that he wants to spare both them and him fresh pain like that of the "painful visit" (see below). He explains his movements from Troas to Macedonia, where Titus had brought him news.

B. *First defense of the apostolic ministry* (2:14–7:4)
  1. *The faithfulness of the apostle* (2:14–3:6): The Christian apostle is the "aroma of Christ to God among those who are being saved." He has confidence in the message he proclaims and needs no "letters of recommendation." Believers who respond to the Gospel are living letters, proving the validity of the new covenant applied by the Holy Spirit to their hearts.
  2. *The superiority of the apostle in the new covenant* (3:7–4:6): This excellence of the new covenant is contrasted with the Mosaic order.
  3. *The weaknesses and sufferings of the apostle* (4:7–5:10)
     a. *His past and present experiences* (4:7–12) as he bears about in his body the dying of Jesus.
     b. *His hope* (4:13–5:10) in God's eternal glory certified by the resurrection of Christ, to show that his apostolic life is oriented to the future.
  4. *The apostle as ambassador and servant of God* (5:11–6:10): A blend of doctrine (5:11–6:1) and practice (6:2–10) in an exposition of the Gospel of God's reconciliation.
  5. *Double conclusion* (6:11–7:4): "Our heart is open to you: open to us your heart completely." In the middle of this passage is inserted an exhortation not to refuse the offer of reconciliation which would be akin to associating with unbelievers (6:14–7:1).
C. *Again, Paul's journeys* (7:5–16): The long exposition of his apostolic ministry is followed by a return to personal issues, taking up the thread of 2:13. Titus had brought him good news, gladdening his heart.
II. *The collection for the Jerusalem church* (8:1–9:15)
  A. *Recommendations for the collection and delegates* (chap. 8): The Macedonian churches have been generous. In the collection that Titus has begun to organize at Corinth, let the Corinthians imitate this Macedonian generosity and, above all, the sacrifice seen in the incarnate Lord. Their extra resources should meet the needs of the poor. Three brothers sent by Paul are commended warmly to the Corinthians.
  B. *A second recommendation* (chap. 9): The collections would have to be organized promptly to prove to the Macedonians that Paul's estimate of the Corinthians' zeal was correct. One who gives generously receives generously from God. Present service is turned to the glory of the Gospel and cements the love between Gentile and Jewish elements in the church.
III. *Polemical argument and defense* (10:1–13:10), in the light of a fresh crisis at Corinth
  A. *Paul defends himself and his work against personal accusations* (chap. 10): Paul clears himself of the charge of "living as a worldly person" (10:2, 3) and points out to those who deny his legitimate apostolic ministry that the Lord himself has authorized.
  B. *Paul's self-eulogy* (11:1–12:18): Paul regrets the need to speak thus of himself, but it is for the sake of the Corinthians and of the Gospel. He will take the part of a "fool" and recount his story. He is in no

way inferior to those who claim connection with the "super-apostles"; indeed, he is more disinterested than they. There follows (11:21–12:18) his "kerygmatic autobiography," his *apologia pro vita sua*, which is also *pro evangelio suo*. He enumerates his claims, works, sufferings, extraordinary gifts from God, and, at the same time, his weaknesses, especially his "thorn in the flesh." In a final touch of irony he clears himself and his colleagues of any suspicion of covetousness: they had never cost the Corinthians any money!

C. *Final notices* (12:19–13:10): The apostle fears that the third visit will be a time for stern measures. He issues a last call for the church to reform its life and expresses his confidence in them.

Conclusion (13:11–13): Final appeal and greetings, ending with the trinitarian formula of apostolic prayer.

5. AN OUTLINE OF 2 CORINTHIANS

   I. Address (1:1, 2)
  II. The past experience of Paul reviewed (1:3–11)
      A. Praise and encouragements (1:3–7)
      B. Paul's trial in Asia (1:8–11)
 III. Transition to the letter's first theme (1:12–14)
  IV. Paul's self-defense of his travel plans (1:15–2:13)
      A. Travel plans reviewed (1:15–22)
      B. Paul's travel plans explained and his earlier letter justified (1:23–2:11)
      C. Paul's concern for Corinth (2:12, 13)
   V. The main theme: Paul's apostolic ministry (2:14–7:16)
      A. The Apostle's adequacy for ministry (2:14–3:6)
      B. Life under the two covenants (3:7–18)
      C. Apostolate, kerygma, ministry (4:1–6)
      D. Paul's ministry: its glory and frailty (4:7–18)
      E. The heavenly dwelling (5:1–10)
      F. The motives for Paul's preaching and living (5:11–15)
      G. Living in the New Age (5:16–21)
      H. Paul's appeal for an open heart (6:1–13)
      I. The temple of the living God (6:14–7:1)
      J. The final appeal and Titus's good report (7:2–16)
  VI. The collection (8:1–9:15)
      A. The commendation of the Macedonians (8:1–6)
      B. The appeal to the Corinthians (8:7–15)
      C. The mission of Titus (8:16–24)
      D. Commendation of the brothers to Achaia (9:1–5)
      E. The collection and the unity of the church (9:6–15)
 VII. Fresh troubles in Corinth (10:1–13:10)
      A. Paul's self-vindication (10:1–11)
      B. The issue of Paul's ministry (10:12–18)
      C. The emissaries identified and opposed (11:1–15)
      D. Paul's "Fool's Story" (11:16–12:10)

E. Paul's apostolate justified (12:11–18)
F. Warnings and a third visit promised (12:19–13:10)
VIII. Conclusion (13:11–13)

6. LITERARY PROBLEMS IN 2 CORINTHIANS

Bearing in mind that the bulk of 2 Corinthians is related to Paul's relief at the Corinthians' change of attitude, we may now address ourselves to some more complex literary details.

The Issues

As a frontispiece to our study of the literary theories and submissions that have been proposed to explain the contents of 2 Corinthians, we begin with a short account of what data constitute the difficulties.

Reading through the letter, we notice a break in the flow of Paul's thought as we move from 2:13 to 2:14. The same phenomenon of a caesura is seen at the transition from 7:4 to 7:5. Up to the point in his argument recorded at 2:13, Paul has been recounting the travel arrangements that brought him to Troas and Macedonia where he was to meet Titus. Then at 2:14 a lengthy section is opened, extending to 7:4. The themes here are somewhat independent of his contacts with Corinth—at least at face value, though we shall argue that the term "digression" is inappropriate (*pace* Harris, 317, 331)—and fall into the category of a defense of his apostolic ministry. Yet at 7:5 Paul picks up the thread of his previous narration and relates how he found Titus, who brought news of the Corinthians' acceptance of the letter of rebuke (7:6–13).

At 6:13 we again reach a hiatus in Paul's thought. He is speaking of his "children," i.e., his Corinthian converts, calling on them to give him a welcome, "Open wide your hearts" to me as my heart is open to you at Corinth (6:11). Strangely, then, that appeal is broken off by a discourse of warning, apparently aimed at admonishing the readers not to get entangled with unbelievers. That section extends to 7:1, 2, at which point, in an equally remarkable way, Paul's thought pattern picks up the appeal left at 6:13. He continues: "Make room for us in your hearts" (7:2), with a renewed appeal to them to believe the sincerity of his motives (7:3). Is this a simple digression as his thought is led off on a tangent? Or have we evidence of a separate composition that is stitched into the fabric of the extant letter, yet with the seams obviously showing at both ends? Or is this hortatory appeal for reconciliation illustrated by this section which may or may not have had an earlier form?

Chaps. 8 and 9 pose similar, if not identical, problems. They are both devoted to a consideration of the collection for the Jerusalem church, referred to at 8:4 and repeated at 9:1. The question is why the two discussions should stand back-to-back in this way. One argument for treating these two chapters as separate compositions is not simply the presence of duplicate discussions; rather, where at 7:5 Paul is addressing his readers at a time of crisis in his own life and while he shares these trials with the Macedonians, when he gets to 8:1, 2 the Macedonians are evidently looking back on afflictions that are past. We question this line of reasoning (see pp. 249, 250). Moreover, chap. 9 is targeted at the Achaeans (9:2; i.e., residents in southern Greece), whereas chap. 8 is concerned with the Corinthians themselves. This is a double-edged datum. It may prove that these two chapters were originally addressed independently to different groups; it may equally show that Paul shifts his audience, writing first to the church at Corinth, and then in a subsequent chapter, turning to speak to a wider clientele in Achaia.

The final literary conundrum demands a fuller treatment. Its occasion is posed by the break, self-evident to all readers of our letter in its canonical shape, at the point of transition between 9:15 and 10:1. The new chapter is different from its preceding section in both style and substance. Up to the end of chap. 9, Paul's tone has been conciliatory and confident, based on the cementing of restored relations with the Corinthians now that the ugly crisis has been resolved—at least in the main. At 10:1 Paul's tone is suddenly aggressive as he launches into a violent and sarcastic attack with his apostolic standing again a subject of heated debate. Paul is clearly on the defensive.

Several explanations of this abrupt and unheralded change of writing have been forthcoming, and we shall comment on these now that we have stated the issues.

For a number of researchers the above data compel the conclusion that our present 2 Corinthian letter is made up of separate "notes." G. Bornkamm, "The History" (see later), has offered a reconstruction that sees no fewer than five or six compositions, including a "Letter of Defense" (2:14–6:13; 7:2–4) sent with Titus to deal with the influence of itinerant Christian missionaries who were disturbing the Corinthians and challenging Paul's authority. In it Paul defends himself and explains the change in his travel plans, announcing a promised visit to the city. He had visited Corinth where he suffered a rebuff (2:5–6) and witnessed a defection from his Gospel. On his return to Ephesus he wrote and sent a "Letter of Tears" (chaps. 10–13) in defense of his apostolic work. After an imprisonment at Ephesus (referred to in 1:8–10) he went to meet Titus whom he eventually found in Macedonia. With news of the Corinthians' return to allegiance, Paul then penned a "Letter of Reconciliation" (1:1–2:13; 7:5–16), followed later by one or two "Letters" devoted to commending Titus and the brothers (chap. 8) and commending the leaders who were to arrange the collection (chap. 9). Paul next traveled to Corinth where he wintered prior to his last journey to Jerusalem. As a final touch to his reconstruction of apostolic movements and compositions, Bornkamm submits that our present configuration in 2 Corinthians is the work of an editor who presented the fragments as a "connected whole," designed as Paul's last will and testament to the churches. At this point the redactor added 6:14–7:1 as an exhortation to loyalty centered in Paul's teaching. Testamentary literature as a biblical genre includes a feature in which the patriarch or prophet heralds the future and warns of apostates to come. This fact explains why chaps. 10–13 come at the close of the letter, to be rounded off by an apostolic admonition and final prayer (13:11–13).

Other variations on this partition or fragment hypothesis have been offered, and these will be noted below. A second option is that the letter as we have it is a unity comprised substantially in the order of our chapters and describing events which flow in a connected, sequential pattern. Thus the breaks are accounted for on the supposition of Paul's habits of digression or else the interruptions in his dictation occasioned by natural diversions such as a night's sleep that supposedly intervened between his composing of chaps. 9 and 10. Finally, the remaining possibility—which this commentary adopts—is that the chapters are in order (with the exception of the section 6:14–7:1, which is in sequence but had a previous setting), but that chaps. 10–13 represent a later work of Paul called forth by fresh outbreaks of trouble at Corinth. We shall consider these possible solutions after a brief excursus to survey the variations that have been canvassed.

EXCURSUS: NOTE ON THE HISTORY OF THE COMPOSITION OF 2 CORINTHIANS

Bibliography (excluding commentaries used later)

Bates, W. H. "The Integrity of 2 Corinthians." *NTS* 12 (1965–66) 50–69. **Batey, R.** "Paul's Interaction with the Corinthians." *JBL* 84 (1965) 139–46. **Betz, H.-D.** "2 Cor. 6:14–7:1: An Anti-Pauline Fragment?" *JBL* 92 (1973) 88–108. **Bornkamm, G.** *Die Vorgeschichte des sogenannten zweiten Korintherbriefes.* SAH Phil.-hist. Klasse. Heidelberg: Winter, 1961: partial ET. "The History of the Origin of the So-Called Second Letter to the Corinthians." In *The Authority and Integrity of the New Testament.* London: SPCK (1965) 73–81 (from *NTS* 8 [1962] 258–64). **Buck, C. H.** "The Collection for the Saints." *HTR* 43 (1950) 1–29. **Drescher, R.** "Der zweite Korintherbrief und die Vorgänge in Korinth seit Abfassung des ersten Korintherbriefs." *TSK* 70 (1897) 43–111. **Fee, G. D.** "2 Corinthians 6:14–7:1 and Food Offered to Idols." *NTS* 23 (1977) 140–61. **Fitzmyer, J. A.** "Qumrân and the Interpolated Paragraph in 2 Cor 6:14–7:1." *CBQ* 23 (1961) 271–80. **Georgi, D.** *Die Gegner des Paulus im 2 Korintherbrief.* WMANT 11. Neukirchen-Vluyn: Neukirchener Verlag, 1964. **Gnilka, J.** "2 Cor 6:14–7:1 in the Light of the Qumran Texts and the Testaments of the Twelve Patriarchs." In J. Murphy-O'Connor, *Paul and Qumran: Studies in New Testament Exegesis.* London: Chapman, 1968. **Goguel, M.** *Introduction au nouveau Testament. IV/2: les épîtres pauliniennes.* Paris: Leroux, 1926. **Halmel, Anton.** *Der zweite Korintherbrief des Apostels Paulus.* Geschichte und literarkritische Untersuchungen. Halle: Niemeyer, 1904. **Hausrath, Adolf.** *Der Vier-Capitelbrief des Paulus an die Korinther.* Heidelberg: Bassermann, 1870. **Hyldahl, N.** "Die Frage nach der literarischen Einheit des zweiten Korintherbriefes." *ZNW* 64 3/4 (1973) 289–306. **Kennedy, J. H.** *The Second and Third Epistles of St Paul to the Corinthians.* London: Methuen, 1900. **Koester, H.** *Introduction to the New Testament.* Vol. 2: History and Literature of Early Christianity. Philadelphia: Fortress, 1982. **Krenkel, M.** *Beiträge zur Aufhellung der Geschichte und der Brief des Apostels Paulus.* 2d ed. Braunschweig: Schwetschke, 1895. **Kuhn, K. G.** "Die Schriftrollen vom Toten Meer." *EvT* 11 (1951) 72–5. **Kümmel, W. G.** *Introduction to the New Testament.* Rev. ET by Howard Clark Kee. London: SCM/Nashville: Abingdon, 1975. **Lake, K.** *The Earlier Epistles of St. Paul.* London: Rivington's, 1927. **Lambrecht, J.** "The Fragment 2 Corinthians 6:14–7:1: A Plea for its Authenticity." In *Miscellanea Neotestamentica II,* ed. T. Baarda et al. NovTSup 47, 143–61. Leiden: Brill, 1978. **Marxsen, W.** *Introduction to the New Testament.* Tr. G. Buswell. Philadelphia: Fortress, 1968. **Munck, J.** *Paulus und die Heilsgeschichte.* København: Munksgaard, 1954. Tr. Frank Clarke, *Paul and the Salvation of Mankind.* London: SCM, 1959. **Nickle, K. F.** *The Collection: A Study in Paul's Strategy.* SBT 48. London: SCM Press, 1966. **Perrin, N.** *The New Testament: An Introduction.* New York: Harcourt Brace Jovanovich, 1974; rev. ed. D. C. Duling,

1982. **Pherigo, L. P.** "Paul and the Corinthian Church," *JBL* 68 (1949) 341–50. **Plummer, A.** *The Second Epistle of St. Paul to the Corinthians.* ICC. Edinburgh: T. & T. Clark/New York: Scribner's, 1915. **Price, J. L.** "Aspects of Paul's Theology and Their Bearing on Literary Problems of Second Corinthians." In *Studies in the History and Text of the New Testament*, FS K. W. Clark. Ed. B. D. Daniels and M. J. Suggs, 95–106. Grand Rapids: Eerdmans, 1967. **Schenke, Hans-Martin** and **Fischer, Karl Martin.** *Einleitung in die Schriften des Neuen Testaments.* I. Die Briefe des Paulus und Schriften des Paulinismus. Berlin: Evangelische Verlagsanstalt, 1978. **Schmithals, W.** "Die Korintherbriefe als Briefsammlung." *ZNW* 64 3/4 (1973) 263–88. ———. *Die Gnosis in Korinth.* FRLANT 66. Göttingen: Vandenhoeck & Ruprecht, 1965. Tr. John E. Steely, *Gnosticism in Corinth.* Nashville: Abingdon, 1971. **Semler, J. S.** *Paraphrasis II. Epistolae ad Corinthos.* Halle: 1776. **Stephenson, A. M. G.** "A Defence of the Integrity of 2 Corinthians." In *The Authorship and Integrity of the New Testament.* SPCK Theological Collections 4, 82–97. London: SPCK, 1965. ———. "Partition Theories on 2 Corinthians." *Studia Evangelica II.* 1. TU 87. Berlin: Akademie, 1964. **Thrall, M. E.** "A Second Thanksgiving Period in 2 Corinthians." *JSNT* 16 (1982) 101–24. **Vielhauer, Ph.** *Geschichte der urchristlichen Literatur.* Berlin: de Gruyter, 1975. **Watson, Francis.** "2 Cor. x–xiii and Paul's Painful Visit to the Corinthians." *JTS* 35 (1984) 324–46. **Weiss, J.** *Das Urchristentum.* 1917. Tr. F. C. Grant, *Earliest Christianity: A History of the Period AD 30–150.* Vols. 1, 2. New York: Harper & Row, 1959. **Wendland, H. D.** *Die Briefe an die Korinther.* NTD 7. Göttingen: Vandenhoeck & Ruprecht, 1968–1972.

The extremes of approach to this topic are seen in Philip E. Hughes, on the one side, who maintains that "modern denials of its [2 Corinthians] unity are unsupported by any evidence of an objective nature or even circumstantial nature" (*Commentary*, xxi). On the other hand, there are Anton Halmel, who divided the epistle into nine elements which he rearranged in order to find three distinct letters (*Der zweite Korintherbrief*), and Walter Schmithals, who subscribed to a theory that 1 and 2 Corinthians together comprise a collection of letters (*Briefsammlung*) involving nine individual dispatches from Paul to the Corinthians. Schmithals's arrangement ("Die Korintherbriefe," 288) produced the following:

Brief (Letter) A: I 11:2–34.
Brief B: I 6:1–11 + II 6:14–7:1 + I 6:12–20 + 9:24–10:22 + 15:1–58 + 16:13–24 (*Vorbrief*).
Brief C: I 5:1–13 + 7:1–8:13 + 9:10–22 + 10:23–11:1 + 12:1–31*a* + 14:1*c*–40 + 12:31*b*–13:13 + 16:1–12 (*Antwortbrief*).
Brief D: I 1:1–4:21.
Brief E: II 2:14–6:2 (*Zwischenbrief*).
Brief F: I 9:1–18 + II 6:3–13 + 7:2–4.
Brief G: II 10:1–13:13 (*Tränenbrief*).
Brief H: II 9:1–15 (*Kollektenbrief*).
Brief I: II 1:1–2:13 + 7:5–8:24 (*Freudenbrief*).

See further H.-M. Schenke-K. M. Fischer, *Einleitung*, 106.

Apparently, J. S. Semler in 1776 in *Paraphrasis II. Epistolae ad Corinthos* was the first to challenge the unity of the epistle. He separated out 12:14–13:13 as a later codicil and entertained the possibility that chap. 9 was a note sent elsewhere than to Corinth (perhaps to Achaia). The first theory, however, to enjoy the endorsement of a representative section of New Testament scholars was introduced in 1870 in a book by Adolf Hausrath, *Die Vier-Capitelbrief des Paulus an die Korinther.* Not surprisingly, the theory became known as "the four-chapter hypothesis." Accordingly, chaps. 10–13 were identified as the "tearful letter" (*Tränenbrief*) of 2:3–4:9; 7:8, 12, which was written prior to chaps. 1–9. The proponents of this view include Kennedy (1900), Plummer (1915), Lake (1927), Goguel (1926), Strachan (1935), Filson (1953), Hanson (1967), and Watson (1984).

A variation of the four-chapter hypothesis, although it is newer than Hausrath's theory in its popularity, is in fact an older model for reconstructing the Corinthian correspondence. The antecedents for this view are rooted in Semler's argument (1776). Accordingly, chaps. 10–13, rather than being identified as the "tearful" letter, are instead held to have been written after chaps. 1–9. This is the thesis adopted in our commentary. We should include among those who follow the present interpretation: Krenkel (1895), Drescher (1897), Windisch (1924), Pherigo (1949), Buck (1950), Munck (1954), Batey (1965), Bruce (1971), Barrett (1973), and Furnish (1984).

All this is not to say that defenders of the unity of 2 Corinthians are espousing a lost cause. In fact, the integrity of the epistle has been (and is being) championed by several scholars, including Bernard (1903), Lietzmann (1909), Menzies (1912), Goudge (1927), Allo (1936), Tasker (1958), Guthrie (1961–1970), Hughes (1962), Kümmel (1963), Stephenson (1965), Bates (1965), Price (1967), Hyldahl (1973), and Harris (1976).

The question of the proper placing of chaps. 10–13 has caused the most discussion respecting the literary analysis of 2 Corinthians. Other difficulties, however, have been debated and have caused increased disagreement among the commentators. Some critics have isolated the substance of 2:14–7:4 as a distinct letter. Evidently Halmel (1904) was the first (with minor variations) to reach this conclusion. He was followed by Schmithals (1956), Georgi (1958), and recently by Bornkamm (1961), whose argument was endorsed with small adaptations by Marxsen (1968), Perrin (1974), and Koester (1982). Moreover, a few scholars have identified 2:14–7:4, not as a separate letter, but as of a piece with chaps. 10–13 as part of the "tearful" letter; these include, Weiss (1917), Bultmann (1947), and Vielhauer (1975).

Located within this larger passage (2:14–7:4) is a small pericope, 6:14–7:1, which even on its own is rather enigmatic. It is seemingly out of place and to a degree also out of character for Paul. Karl Georg Kuhn (1951) was one of the first to discover the literary relationship between this paragraph and various Qumran writings. Since then it has been regarded by Bultmann (1947), Fitzmyer (1961), Bornkamm (1965), and Gnilka (1968) as a non-Pauline interpolation. Betz (1973) has even argued, on the basis of its similarity to the theology of Paul's opponents in Galatians, that it represents an anti-Pauline tract.

The remaining problems are confined to understanding the relationship between chaps. 8 and 9, and further, how and where the two chapters fit into the scheme for the Corinthian correspondence. A few scholars have followed the early lead by Semler (1776) who separated the two chapters. Weiss (1917), and recently, Bornkamm (1965), Nickle (1966), Héring (1967), Wendland (1968), and Barrett (1973) have advocated this division. By and large, the view has been greeted with relatively little acclaim, but Betz's forthcoming study (1985?) will reopen the issue in support of Semler's hypothesis.

As we have seen from the data setting out the problems, the integrity of 2 Corinthians has also been challenged historically on four fronts: (1) chaps. 8 and 9; (2) 2:14–7:4; (3) 6:14–7:1; and (4) chaps. 10–13. In turn we shall consider the components of the debate, centering on each of these four problematic areas.

(1) The transition between chap. 7 and chap. 8 is noticeably abrupt, but understandably so. The subject changes from the apostle's self-confession to the collec-

tion for the poor Christians in Jerusalem. What comes as a surprise, but is left without an obvious explanation, is 9:1 where Paul seemingly introduces the collection as if previously nothing had been said concerning it. We might expect, however, that if Paul were indeed introducing a new subject, he would likely have employed his customary περὶ δέ rather than the resumptive περὶ μὲν γάρ. Furthermore, when Paul mentions "the brothers" in 9:3, 5, he assumes that his readers know of whom he speaks. Yet only in 8:6, 16 ff. is there any indication of the identity of these men.

For Bultmann, the only way to make sense of Paul boasting to the Macedonians about the gracious response to the collection in Achaia (9:2), when he also uses the generous giving of the Macedonians to inspire generosity in Achaia (8:1–5), is to regard chapter 9 as a separate and earlier letter. But Bultmann's reconstruction does not solve the apparent dilemma which takes the form of a circular argument (you should give as they gave; they should give as you gave). The circularity remains despite the attempt to remove it by rearranging the time-line (i.e., by having chap. 9 precede chap. 8).

Windisch makes a case of the alleged different reasons for the coming of the brothers in 8:20 as opposed to the reason offered in 9:3–5. In the former, the men become witnesses to Paul's responsibility and trustworthiness with the monies collected. In the latter, the men are sent ahead to prepare the collection before Paul's arrival. However, in order for this to militate against the unity of chaps. 8 and 9, one would have to overlook first the fact that in 8:20 only one man is in mind, but in chap. 9 both brothers (perhaps including Titus) are in view, and second, the possibility that the brothers' role had a dual function.

Nevertheless, it remains a problem, if we hold to the unity and sequence of the two chapters, to explain the awkward transition from 8:24 to 9:1. With F. F. Bruce (225), it seems reasonable to maintain that there was a short break in dictation precisely here. The train of thought was broken by a brief intermission.

(2) A second problem arises in the discontinuity between 2:13 and 2:14. In the preceding paragraphs Paul had been discussing his travel plans respecting Corinth; but beginning in 2:14 he launches into a discourse concerning his apostleship, only to return in 7:5 to his travel plans. In fact, if 2:14–7:4 were extracted from the text, Paul's mentioning of Titus and Macedonia in 2:12, 13 would flow perfectly into the mention of Paul's rendezvous with Titus in Macedonia as explained in 7:5–16. We are left to decide whether 2:14–7:4 represents (a) an interpolation, and if so, what explains its awkward placement here, or (b) a "noble digression" (as Bengel called it), and if this, what might be the occasion for the digression.

The most convincing evidence that 2:14–7:4 is not an interpolation is the verbal link between 7:4 and 7:5–7 and running on to 7:16 (see the *Commentary*, pp. 214–16). The connection would be extremely uncanny had it not been purposed by the author. Several terms in 7:4 reappear in comparable form in 7:5–7. This is the argument offered by H. Lietzmann (131, with Thrall, 109, in agreement):

> The strict linkage between verses 5 ff. and verse 4 is clear (παρακλήσει [4] = παρακαλῶν [6], παρεκάλεσεν [6], and παρακλήσει [7]; χαρᾷ [4] = χαρῆναι [7]; θλίψει [4] = θλιβόμενοι [5]), so that the theories of interpolation which bind 7:5 closely to 2:13 run into particular difficulties.

With Allo, we can find an explanation for the apparent discontinuity between 2:12–13 and 2:14–17 by suggesting that the thought of Macedonia in 2:13 evoked in the apostle a spirit of thanksgiving for what had transpired there, viz., the arrival of good news from Corinth via the hand of Titus (see Thrall, 107). After all, the verses preceding the awkward transition are not altogether different from the chapters following (so Thrall, 112–116).

(3) Several peculiarities have made suspect the authenticity of the small pericope in 6:14–7:1. (a) The verses form a self-contained unit which exhibits no apparent relation to, or dependence upon, the Corinthian situation. (b) It interrupts the flow of thought: Paul began in 6:11, 12 with an exhortation about having "open hearts," but finishes the thought later in 7:2–4, "make room for us in your hearts." (c) It contains eight New Testament *hapax legomena:* ἑτεροζυγοῦντες, μετοχή, συμφώνησις, βελιάρ, συγκατάθεσις, μολυσμός; so also ἐμπεριπατήσω and εἰσδέξομαι (Old Testament citations found in LXX); and παντοκράτωρ (which is found only in Revelation). (d) It betrays a similarity to certain writings found at Qumran: the triple dualism of uprightness/iniquity, light/darkness, Christ/Beliar; the rejection of idolatry; the temple-of-God theology; the resistance to carnality; the concatenation of Old Testament texts (see Betz, Fitzmyer, Harris).

However, to conclude on the basis of these peculiarities that 6:14–7:1 is therefore an interpolation is not to solve all the problems. It is equally as difficult to understand why the compiler placed the text amidst an apparently irrelevant exhortation as it is to explain why Paul digressed on an ethical homily. Some scholars have tried to belittle the unnatural connection between 6:13 and 6:14, attempting to find similarities between 6:14–7:1 and the preceding contexts (e.g., Harris). But we believe that a more attractive hypothesis is that the digression is in keeping with the letter's having been composed in stages (so also Stephenson, Bates, Bruce, Guthrie, Tasker, Hughes, and Kümmel), or more plausibly still, that Paul has taken over a preformed piece and used it with a design to enforce his hortatory appeal for reconciliation (see *Commentary,* pp. 190–95).

There are Pauline features in the paragraph. Fee discovers at least three: the church as God's temple; the emphasis on righteousness; and the contrast between light and dark. Lambrecht adds to the list the concept of the tension between "the already" and "the not yet." Schmithals (*Gnosticism,* 94, 95) defends the Pauline authorship—but not its place in 2 Corinthians—on the basis that the passage seems to assume the very kind of situation Paul had discovered in Corinth. And we might add that a similar attitude to that which is expressed in the present pericope is found in 1 Cor 10:14 ff.: "Therefore, my beloved, flee from idolatry. . . ."

It seems possible that the paragraph not only marks a seeming intermission in dictation but that during the break in writing Paul had encountered a tract from, or one resembling something from, the Qumran community's library. Paul did not quote what he read verbatim (for certain it would not have mentioned "Christ"), but reworked it into his epistle as something which might profit the Corinthians too. Its purpose, we shall submit, is seen in the use Paul makes of its emphasis to enforce his paraenetic call for reconciliation by showing that, failing their acceptance of his offer, the Corinthians will be ranging themselves with unbelievers. In 7:2 the apostle resumed where he had left off before the inserted appeal.

(4) Doubtless, the literary problem that has received the most attention is the relationship between chaps. 1–9 and chaps. 10–13. The last four chapters introduce a pronounced and unexpected change of tone. The previous chapters were mainly— but not exclusively—filled with unbridled joy, but all that changes to scathing remonstrance in chaps. 10–13. The apostle is rather straightforward in the beginning regarding any appeal made to the Corinthians, but that tone also is forsaken for irony after 10:1. Furthermore, twice in chaps. 10–13 Paul promises (or rather threatens) an imminent third visit to Corinth (12:14; 13:1), but nothing is said of such a visit in chaps. 1–9, especially where one might expect it (in 1:15–2:13) had it indeed been planned when that portion was penned (so Harris).

If therefore we suspect that chaps. 10–13 represent a separate letter, we have still to determine whether it was written and sent prior to, or after, chaps. 1–9. Moreover, we are enjoined to explain why alternative explanations for the abrupt change, other than that 10–13 was a different letter from 1–9, fail to suffice as adequate reasons.

The arguments offered in support of the view that chaps. 10–13 belonged to an earlier letter are basically four (originally articulated by Kennedy and later elaborated by Lake). Here we give an overview of the four arguments shortly to be scrutinized in detail. The first two contributions argue that the sections must have been isolated letters; the second two would suggest that chaps. 10–13 preceded 1–9: (a) chaps. 1–9 are mainly full of praise, but 10–13 are generally characterized by condemnation (as above). (b) The vocabulary is used differently, which intimates that 2 Corinthians was not intended to be an integrated unit. For example, καυχᾶσθαι, "to boast," with its cognates, is a favorable word in the apostle's mind during the early chapters. Paul "boasts" to the Corinthians about the generous gifts made by Macedonians. Yet the word is used with an unfavorable nuance in chaps. 10–13. He requires of the Corinthians that they bear with him in his "boasting"; it is as though he were out of his mind, being moved by a desire to express a "fool's speech" (Koester, *Introduction,* 129; cf. J. Zmijewski, *Der Stil der paulinischen "Narrenrede"* [Köln-Bonn: Hanstein, 1978]). (c) Passages in chaps. 10–13 demonstrate a perspective that looks forward to certain events, whereas chaps. 1–9 seem to be looking back on these same events. For example, "it was to spare you that I did not come again to Corinth" (1:23), which quite naturally could have been preceded by a statement such as, "If I come again I shall not spare . . . " (13:2). (d) When Paul said that he wanted to preach "beyond" Corinth, the apostle must have been located east of Corinth (presumably in Ephesus) and thinking of proceeding toward Rome (even Spain? see Rom 15:24, 28). If instead he was in Macedonia (north of Corinth), then "beyond" Corinth would have meant south, and it is doubtful that he wanted to go in that direction. Since, therefore, he was in Ephesus when he wrote chaps. 10–13, and presumably in Macedonia when he wrote chaps 1–9 (7:5 ff.), and because, historically, we can assume that he was in Ephesus before Macedonia, then 10–13 was written (in Ephesus) prior to 1–9 (in Macedonia).

The third argument (c) above is not necessarily conclusive, because as Buck ("The Collection") has argued, the passages in chaps. 1–9 which supposedly refer back to events found in 10–13 may instead be found to allude to events detailed in 1 Corinthians. Furnish in fact argues the exact opposite: it is inconceivable that the kind of confidence shown by the apostle about the collection (chaps. 8, 9) postdates chaps. 10–13 where Paul defends himself against the charge of "deceit" and "fraud" (Furnish, 38).

The fourth argument (d) overlooks the fact that Rome (and Spain) might naturally have been referred to as the land "beyond." The Gospel and the Great Commission were born in Jerusalem; from there and from Antioch the mission went forth. Naturally, Rome was "beyond" Corinth from this perspective, as in Rom 15:24–29.

Conclusion

The unity of 2 Corinthians can be defended against the charges that chaps. 8 and 9 are not compatible in their present configuration, that 2:14–7:4 is an interpolated paragraph, and likewise that 6:14–7:1 is a non-Pauline or anti-Pauline interpolation which is a "foreign body" (*Fremdkörper*) in its present canonical setting. The reasons given in the survey above, which discussed internal evidence, are buttressed

by the external evidence that no manuscript or patristic authority ever divides
the epistle. We have no textual evidence which supports any partitioning; but the
probative force of this contention is weakened if the earliest textual evidence postdates the work of a redactor (so Bornkamm: see earlier p. xxxix).

The supposition, however, that chaps. 10–13 represent a later letter than chaps.
1–9, can be deduced if we accept (as argued above) that they were different letters
and that chaps. 10–13 could not have been written first. A positive argument for
the same conclusion might observe that the mission of Titus as described in 12:18
can cogently be identified with the mission of Titus (and two brothers) as viewed
in 8:16–24; 9:3–5. This is not to say that it is impossible that 2 Corinthians was
indeed one letter; but if it was, we should be ready to explain a substantial intermission between chap. 9 and chap. 10, a gap best explained by Paul's receiving word
from or about Corinth which altered his attitude toward them. If this were true,
however, we might have expected Paul to have destroyed chaps. 1–9 and rewritten
them since they were out of character with the present situation at Corinth. But
the composition in chaps. 1–9 may well have left Paul's hands en route to Corinth
by the time he was apprised of an outbreak of further troubles in that city. Therefore,
the more attractive hypothesis is that chaps. 10–13 were a separate letter written
after chaps. 1–9.

According to the present theory we have espoused, the historical situation surrounding the Corinthian correspondence can be constructed as follows:

A.D. 50–51   Paul establishes the church at Corinth.
51–54   Paul writes to Corinth (letter A; now lost, see 1 Cor 5:9).
54   Paul writes to Corinth after having heard oral reports of the church's problems (letter B; our 1 Corinthians).
(Spring) 55   Paul's emergency visit to Corinth. He is confronted and is required to
leave in a hurry (2 Cor 1:15 ff.).
(Summer) 55   Paul writes again to the Corinthians (the "tearful" letter C of 2 Cor 2:4;
7:8, now lost).
(Fall) 55   Paul is met by Titus in Macedonia. He receives word that the Corinthians
had experienced a change of heart; therefore he dispatches another letter
to say that he is pleased and confident (letter D; 2 Cor 1–9).
56   Paul receives word that the Corinthians' attitudes have taken a turn for
the worse; therefore he writes to correct them and to defend his apostolic
authority (letter E; 2 Cor 10–13). He later visits the city where (presumably
but not certainly) he is well received. If this was the case, then he was
able to winter there and compose the epistle to the Romans.

We may turn to address the literary phenomena of our epistle in some detail
and review the strengths and weaknesses of the solutions proposed to solve the
problems created by the data.

Résumé

A. The "Painful Visit."

In 2 Corinthians (if we think of the letter as a unity as it stands in our Bible),
Paul made up his mind to visit Corinth twice—once immediately, crossing directly
by sea from Ephesus, and then again after going from there to Macedonia (1:15 f.).
The first of these visits was made; but the second was not made at that time because
the first was so painful that Paul could not bring himself to go a second time
(1:23; 2:1). But that a second visit, unrecorded in Acts, which knows only the
visits of chaps. 18 (initial visit for church planting) and 20 (a return visit from

Macedonia), is required is confirmed in 12:14 and 13:1 f., which speak of "the third time" he proposes to come to Corinth.

Paul's visits to the city, therefore, may be tabulated thus:

> 1. A first visit (Acts 18:1–11) was made in the course of Paul's second missionary journey.
>
> 2. A second visit (the so-called interim visit) followed when Paul heard adverse reports subsequent to the sending of 1 Corinthians. He decided to pay this visit, which was a painful and humiliating experience for him. Following this he quickly returned to Ephesus and sent to Corinth a letter, written "out of much affliction and anguish of heart" (2 Cor 2:4) in an attempt to rectify the matter. This is often referred to as the "tearful" or "severe letter." From Titus, the bearer of the severe letter, whom he met in Macedonia, he heard improved news and, as we have seen, his relief occasioned the writing of 2 Corinthians, or at least chaps. 1–9 or the greater part thereof.
>
> 3. He spent the next winter at Corinth, fulfilling the promise of 2 Cor 12:14 and 13:1 f., which explicitly allude to a third visit (Acts 20:2).

Can we trace the "severe letter" which follows the second, sorrowful visit to Corinth? Along with that question comes, for many modern scholars, a doubt: can the *whole* of 2 Corinthians be regarded as expressing satisfaction that the church has acted favorably to the apostle, for which response the apostle expresses his relief? In Kümmel's words, "the crucial problem is the question whether 1–9 and 10–13 could have been parts of the same letter" (*Introduction* [2], 290). These two matters are really quite separate, but they are matched in the modern assumption that part of the "severe letter" may survive in 2 Cor 10–13, which (it is held) do not really belong in a letter of thanksgiving and congratulation.

B. *The "Severe Letter."*

1. Some have proposed that this may be canonical 1 Corinthians. It is suggested that the matters in Paul's first letter which caused grief to the Corinthians were his reproaches of their lax discipline and disorderly conduct (esp. chaps. 5, 6, 11). But this identification is rejected by most contemporary scholars because Paul's language describing his state of mind while writing it (2 Cor 2:4) is thought to be extravagant if 1 Corinthians is in mind. However, it is at least possible—but not probable—that his words give a flashback to his subjective reactions while he was writing the first letter, though he had managed to conceal his feelings.

J. Moffatt (*Introduction to the Literature of the New Testament* [3], 119, 122n) objects that 1 Corinthians is permeated by a spirit of calm, practical discussion. Its occasional outbursts of emotional tension (e.g., in chaps. 5, 6) could not have caused Paul even a momentary twinge of compunction. The language in 2 Cor 2:4 and 7:8 is too definite to be explained as the mere recollection of one or two isolated sentences in an epistle of the size and general character of 1 Corinthians. Moffatt also criticizes the view (held by J. Denney, 2 f., among others, including Hughes and Stephenson) that the offender referred to in 2 Cor 2:5–8 and 7:12 is the same as the incestuous person of 1 Cor 5:1–5. Moffatt argues against the identity of the person in 2 Cor 7:12 with the sinner of 1 Cor 5 on the ground that Paul would not have dealt so lightly with the offense of the incestuous person.

2. A second conjecture as to the identity of the "severe letter" is that the letter in question—minus its beginning—is preserved in 2 Cor 10–13. This is a widely held modern theory, first proposed in 1870 by A. Hausrath, who maintained, as we observed, a double thesis—first, that 2 Cor 10–13 form a separate letter, mutilated at the beginning; and second, that this letter is identical with that letter

written with tears (*Tränenbrief*), spoken of in 2 Cor 2:4. On what does this view rest?

a. *The change of tone between chaps. 1–9 and 10–13.* In the former part Paul writes with considerable relief at what he has heard of the change of attitude on the part of the Corinthians. Hostility is absent; friendly relations seem to have been restored. But (so it is held) the latter chapters are "written in remonstrance, anger, satire, and self-defence" (McNeile-Williams, *Introduction*², 139). The claim that these two sections are incongruous was made as early as 1776 by Semler, who detached 12:14–13:14 as a later epistle and thought of chap. 9 as a separate "note," written independently of the Corinthian letters.

Would the apostle, having expressed his happiness over the success of an earlier and more severe letter and having given some hint of his regret after writing the severe letter, close his epistle with such unparalleled invective in self-defense as is found in 2 Cor 10–13? The contrast between the two hypothetical sections of 2 Corinthians must not be overstated, however. There are evidences in chaps. 1–7 of the opposition to Paul which still persisted (see Stephenson, "A Defence," 87 ff.; also idem, "Partition Theories on 2 Corinthians," *SE* II. 1. [1964] 639 ff.; Bates, "The Integrity," 56–69; J. L. Price, "Aspects," 100). In 1:17 f. he argues strongly in self-defense, while in 2:6 he speaks of the offender as being punished by the majority, implying that there was a minority who did not agree with Paul's authoritative pronouncement on the case. Also, 2:17 and 4:2–5 advert to those who vexed the apostle's soul by their lack of fidelity to the true Gospel, and in 5:12 f. we read of their attitude to Paul himself. These evidences suffice to show that chaps. 1–7 do not give the impression that the Corinthians are now *wholly* on the side of Paul. His relief is occasioned by the responses of the majority, which was a big step forward, but he must still deal with the more dangerous minority; and it is possible that Paul commends the majority in the first part of the letter before turning his severe words of rebuke to the still recalcitrant minority in the closing chapters. But these positions are tenuously held, and we will have to argue in the *Commentary* that Paul's allusions to "the majority" (οἱ πλείονες) do not necessarily have a smaller group of "still unsubdued rebels" in contrast. Further, the severe references to "all" in chaps. 2 and 7 are noteworthy, whether it is true that these verses relate to the fact that the Corinthians were basically on Paul's side and had (momentarily) entertained an intruder (so Barrett), or that Paul and Titus were too optimistic in believing that the disaffection was finally put down and disposed of, or that a new situation was created by the appearing of emissaries subsequent to the sending of chaps. 1–9.

b. *Differing references to the apostle's visits.* There are, according to Kennedy and K. Lake (Kennedy, *The Second and Third Epistles,* 81 ff.; Lake, *The Earlier Epistles,* 159 f.; see too Bruce, 166–70; D. Guthrie, *Introduction*³, 433 ff.; the case is revisited by F. Watson, "2 Cor x–xiii," 326 f.), three pairs of passages to support the contention that chaps. 10–13 precede chaps. 1–7. These are:

I	paired with	II
10:6		2:9
13:2		1:23
13:10		2:3

It is evident that the references in the latter part of the epistle (our column I) are all forward-looking, whereas those in the earlier section (column II) are all in the past. If the sequential order of these parts is reversed, i.e., if column I precedes column II in time, both groups of references could relate to the same visit.

Lake's argument is ingenious but not conclusive. In comparing 13:2 with 1:23

we should note that in the latter verse Paul is concluding his explanation of his altered plans following his painful visit, while the former refers to his intended severity toward those who are still recalcitrant and might, with good reason, look ahead to the visit he anticipates paying from Macedonia. It is the apostle's hope in 13:10 that on this next visit he will not have to use sharpness, but this is the same hope expressed in 2:3; the difference is that in the earlier reference he thinks back to the expression of sentiment in a prior letter, while in 13:10 he contemplates the effect of the present letter on the Corinthians. There is no obvious reason for placing 10:6 before 2:9, since the context of the latter does not suggest that their obedience is now complete. If, however, in 2:9 the apostle is saying that in his former letter he was seeking proof of their obedience, it is reasonable to assume that the answer he received was not one hundred per cent convincing, and he still looks forward to its completion in 10:6, even if we do not postulate the emergence of a new situation after chaps. 1–9 were written.

c. *Differing attitudes towards self-commendation.* It is alleged that two irreconcilable— "almost schizophrenic" (the description is that used by R. P. C. Hanson, *Commentary*, 20)—attitudes toward self-commendation are found in 2 Corinthians: in 3:1 the apostle deprecates it; in chaps. 10–13 he is at great pains to engage in it. In 5:12 he asserts, "We are not commending ourselves to you again." Since both 3:1 and 5:12 use the word "again," it is an attractive suggestion that Paul is thinking of the wording of chaps. 10–13 sent at an earlier date.

But 3:1 clearly alludes to the practice of some of Paul's Corinthian opponents to arm themselves with letters of commendation, to which Paul himself strongly objects. Indeed, he sees no need for such letters: the Corinthians themselves are his commendation. The same thought is present in 5:12. In chaps. 10–13, however, Paul is addressing those who still oppose him and dispute his credentials, presumably because they have been encouraged to do so by the coming of emissaries (11:4) who make Paul's apostolate the center of their attack (10:7, 8; 11:12; 13:13). For them a different approach was clearly necessary.

On these three grounds, if their plausibility is granted, the epistle is regarded as a hypothetical fusion of two separate pieces of correspondence. In addition to our remarks above, however, there are other considerations which make this view doubtful or argue that it is at least not proved.

In the first place, if the hypothesis is true, an explanation is needed for Paul's mention (in 12:18) of Titus's previous visit (as Kümmel observes, *Introduction*[2], 290). Obviously, if chaps. 10–13 constitute the "severe letter," this visit could not have been the occasion on which Titus conveyed the severe letter; yet the language is more naturally read as referring to the time when he took the severe letter and, having reported the changed conditions to the apostle, was sent back with 2 Corinthians (cf. 8:16 f.).

Second, it seems likely from 2:1 ff. and 7:12 that the reason for the severe letter was the wrongdoing of some individual (see later, pp. 237, 238, and C. K. Barrett, in his *Essays on Paul*, chap. 6). Yet there is no mention of this in chaps. 10–13. The explanation that this omission can be accounted for by supposing that such a reference was contained in that part of the severe letter which is no longer extant—either accidentally lost or purposely suppressed while the offender was still living—is very feeble.

Finally, we may note that there is no manuscript authority for dividing the epistle into two parts. It is asked, "Can we suppose that interpolations so serious as to amount . . . to the formation of an entire Epistle out of heterogeneous fragments— or even the interpolation of any one of the passages in question [6:14–7:1; 8–9; 10–13]—can have taken place without leaving so much as a ripple upon the stream of textual tradition?" (A. Robertson, *Hastings' Dictionary of the Bible*, vol. 1 [1898], 497; Tasker, 25. But this argument is not unanswerable, as noted by Barrett, *Commentary*, 14 f., and J. J. Gunther, *Paul: Messenger and Exile*, 74 f.). Moreover, the partition theory requires an extraordinary weaving together of two separate epistles, each only partially preserved. One is missing its close, the other its beginning; the two truncated fragments happen to join together to make a single epistle with the appearance of a whole.

3. There is a third answer to the question of the identity of the severe letter: that it is no longer extant. Since the *entire* letter mentioned in 1 Cor 5:9 has certainly not survived (see earlier, p. xxxiv), there is strong presumption in favor of the view that the other correspondence between Paul and the Corinthians has also been lost. According to its proponents (e.g., Hughes, Tasker, Kümmel, and especially Allo, excursus xiv), this view is believed to face fewer difficulties than the other views, though it leaves us without any data for reconstructing the subject matter of the letter. One can assume that the letter contained nothing of sufficient general interest to warrant its preservation or that it was suppressed or destroyed because it dealt with some personal opponent of the apostle (2 Cor 2:5 ff.); or conceivably just because it was effective in calling the congregation to Paul's side, it was allowed to disappear, thus drawing a veil over an unhappy episode. But that kindly explanation needs to account for the fact that, *ex hypothesi*, chaps. 10–13 *have* survived.

We must nevertheless account for the obvious change of tone at the end of 2 Cor 9, which J. Héring (11) has likened to the sudden onset of a storm after a clear sky and calm weather. H. Lietzmann proposed a solution found in the psychology of the apostle. He imagined that a bout of insomnia depressed Paul's mood and caused him to adopt a different tone on the day when he came to write chap. 10 (138; but see Moffatt's just dismissal of this suggestion, *Introduction*[3], 123). Though it may be difficult to take this idea seriously, it does lead some writers to a second possibility—that the writing of 2 Corinthians took many days, and a distinct time interval lapsed between the writing of chaps. 9 and 10. Possibly more disquieting news reached Paul as he was in the course of his letter, and this inflamed his wrath against the "false apostles" who were none other, in his eyes, than "ministers of Satan" (11:13–15). In any case, it is said—on the basis of evidence in Phil 3:1—that Paul's literary manner includes the phenomenon of abrupt digressions. Finally, if those researchers are correct in supposing that, after addressing the majority in chaps. 1–9, Paul directs his attack to a still unsubdued vociferous minority in the church, this change of theme would quite naturally call forth a different emotional reaction. Lietzmann-Kümmel find the explanation in the apostle's change of intention:

> In 2 Corinthians 1–9 Paul has spoken only to the church: now [in chapter 10] he is dealing with his opponents against whom his anger is flaring up, and with it all kinds of things about the church that he had kept back in chapters 1–9 are coming out again (*Kommentar*, 139; cf. A. Wikenhauser, *New Testament Introduction* [New York: Herder & Herder, tr. J. Cunningham, 1958] 397 f.; J. Munck, *Paul and the Salvation of Mankind*, 171).

All these explanations have been offered. In our view, none is conclusive, and several suggestions look to be question-begging and thus improbable. We are left then to offer a third option, since it is not adequate simply to say negatively that a given theory is open to question. A rival proposal must be offered for testing, and preferably one that both accounts for the complex phenomena of 2 Corinthians and throws light on its setting in the life of Paul at the time of its composition.

4. There remains one further distinct possibility to account for the literary phenomena of 2 Corinthians as it stands in our canonical text. This proposal is built on the assumption that the sequence of the chaps. 1–9 and 10–13 is correct but that there is a compositional hiatus set between the writing of the two parts of the present letter. This view rests on Semler's initial insight, viz., that chaps. 10–13 are separate from the earlier parts of the letter as it stands; but it declines to accept Hausrath's logical conclusion that the four chapters are out of order. Stated by Windisch in 1924, this view was championed by a few writers, but it has gained fresh credibility in the past generation, thanks to Barrett, Bruce, Furnish, and (in part) Harris, each of whom has espoused it. The last correctly sees the utility of such a position: first, it reckons with the elements of increased seriousness in Paul's defense in 10–13 over the milder tone of 1–9. This fact suggests that a new outbreak of opposition to Paul's apostolic authority gave increased virulence to Paul's counterattack, as seen in chaps. 10–13. Second, the sequence of events relative to Titus's visits in 8:17, 18, 22 can be kept intact, since it is the same occasion that is (naturally) referred to as a past occurrence at 12:18 (see Barrett, *Essays on Paul*, chap. 7).

This fourth proposition is the one accepted in the subsequent commentary, and it remains to be shown—at the exegetical level—that this view has probability. The most that can be gained in this field of inquiry is probability. Yet, as Batey ("Paul's Interaction") remarks, the view leaves certain loose ends and puts a question mark over the outcome of Paul's Corinthian mission. Did chaps. 10–13 actually help recover Paul's apostolic standing and salvage his integrity from attack by intruders? We may never know. But that very uncertainty may well explain the setting of our letter in the wider frame of Paul's *theologia crucis*, as our closing section will argue (see pp. lii–lxi). And inferentially, Paul's later visit to Corinth, according to Acts 20, may suggest a happy ending to the Corinthian crisis. But, to be sure, we have no direct word from Paul to that effect.

C. *The Problem of 2 Cor 6:14–7:1.*

There is one outstanding problem remaining. It has been strongly claimed by many scholars, some of whom have otherwise defended the unity of the epistle, that the second half of 2 Cor 6 breaks the connection of thought and may therefore be regarded as an interpolated fragment from another genuine epistle (see T. W. Manson, "The Corinthian Correspondence," *Studies in the Gospels and Epistles*, ed. M. Black [Manchester: Manchester University Press, 1962] 222). Since it deals with the problem of the believers' relationships with unbelievers, and since the apostle says in 1 Cor 5:9, "I wrote to you in my letter not to associate with immoral people," it is an attractive hypothesis that the 2 Corinthians passage is in mind. Moreover, 1 Cor 5:10 f. shows clearly that Paul's advice had been misunderstood, and it is at least conceivable, as some have concluded from 2 Cor 6:14–7:1, that he wrote advising believers to have nothing to do with unbelievers (J. C. Hurd, Jr., *The Origin of 1 Corinthians*, rev. ed. [Macon, Ga: Mercer Press, 1983]). Furthermore, 6:13 gives an excellent introduction to 7:2, and removing 6:14–7:1 improves the flow of the argument.

Yet before concluding that the section must be an interpolation, the investigator must be satisfied that this is not another example of the apostle's tendency to digress (see the classic essay, E. Stange, "Diktierpausen in den Paulusbriefen," *ZNW* 18 [1917–18] 115 f.). The change from 6:13 to 6:14 is abrupt, and the tone differs from the preceding sections. Such a digression would be unpardonable in a treatise, but the same rigid literary rules cannot be applied to letter-writing. If Paul composed the letter in stages over a length of time, one of his breaks may have come here, and he may have taken up a new theme on resuming the letter. Such an explanation would seem more satisfactory than trying to find an unnatural connection with the preceding context, unless we can trace a continuing theme.

On the other hand, if the section really does go back to the letter referred to in 1 Cor 5:9, how do we explain its present position in 2 Corinthians? It is difficult to believe that anyone would intentionally place it here, and the only recourse is therefore to suppose that it got there accidentally (but see G. D. Fee's attempt to relate the section to the problem of idol meats in 1 Cor ["I Corinthians vi.14–vii.1 and Food Offered to Idols," *NTS* 23 (1976–77) 140–61]. The drawback to this suggestion is, as Fee grants, that idol meats are not specifically mentioned either in this passage or its immediate context). But this idea is difficult to sustain in the absence of any supporting manuscript evidence, particularly as it involves the insertion of a fragment in the middle of an existing manuscript, and there is no break in the textual tradition to encourage this view. Even if we grant the work of a later redactor who assembled Pauline fragments into our present document (so Bornkamm), we have still to offer a rationale for placing 6:14–7:1 at this point in the final work. The scantiness of our present knowledge of the preservation of the Pauline epistles, however, allows for such a hypothesis, and recent studies of the origin of this passage in the light of the Qumran scrolls have added further testimony to the idea that this is an independent Pauline—or non-Pauline—fragment which has become attached loosely to this part of 2 Corinthians. We return to the issue after the exegetical discussion, pp. 211, 212, and try to suggest a reason for the inserting of this independent pericope at this point in the letter and at this stage of Paul's argument.

7. THE SETTING OF 2 CORINTHIANS IN PAUL'S LIFE

Bibliography

Barrett, C. K. "Paul and the 'Pillar' Apostles." In *Studia Paulina in honorem Johannis de Zwaan,* 1–19. Haarlem: Bohn, 1953. **Black, David Alan.** *Paul, Apostle of Weakness. Astheneia and Its Cognates in the Pauline Literature.* New York: Lang, 1984. **Brown, R. E.** and **Meier, J. P.** *Antioch and Rome. New Testament Cradles of Catholic Christianity.* New York: Paulist Press, 1983. **Bruce, F. F.** *New Testament History.* London: Nelson/New York: Doubleday, 1969. ———. *Paul, Apostle of the Heart Set Free.* Grand Rapids: Eerdmans. UK title *Paul, Apostle of the Free Spirit.* Exeter: Paternoster, 1977. **Catchpole, D. R.** "Paul, James and the Apostolic Decree." *NTS* 23 (1977) 428–44. **Dunn, J. D. G.** "The Incident at Antioch." *JSNT* 18 (1983) 3–57. ———. *Jesus and the Spirit.* London: SCM/Philadelphia: Westminster, 1975. ———. *The Unity and Diversity of the New Testament.* Philadelphia: Westminster/London: SCM, 1977. **Fee, G. D.** "Eidolothyta Once Again: An Interpretation of 1 Corinthians 8–10." *Bib* 61 (1980) 172–97. **Fuchs, E.** "La faiblesse, glorie de l'apostolat selon Paul (Etude sur 2 Co 10–13)." *ETR* 2 (1980) 231–53. **Gnilka, J.** *Der Philipperbrief.* HTKNT 10. Freiburg, Basel, Wien: Herder, 1968. **Güttgemanns, E.** *Der leidende Apostel und sein Herr.* FRLANT 90. Göttingen: Vanderhoeck & Ruprecht, 1966. **Hengel, M.** *Acts and the History of Earliest Christianity.* Tr. J. Bowden. London: SCM Press, 1979. ———. *Between Jesus and Paul.* Tr. J. Bowden. London: SCM Press, 1983. **Hickling, C. J. A.** "Is the Second Epistle to the Corinthians a Source for Early Church History?" *ZNW* 66 (1975) 284–87. **Holmberg, B.** *Paul and Power. The Structure of Authority in the Primitive Church as Reflected in the Pauline Epistles.* ConB 11. Lund: Gleerup, 1978. **Jewett, R.** "The Agitators and the Galatian Congregation." *NTS* 17 (1970–71) 198–212. **Käsemann, E.** *Die Legitimität des Apostels. Eine Untersuchung zu II Korinther 10–13.* Darmstadt: Wissenschaftliche Buchgesellschaft, 1956. (Originally in *ZNW* 41 [1942] 33–71). **Martin, R. P.** *Carmen Christi. Philippians 2:5–11 in Recent Interpretation and in the Setting of Early Christian Worship.* SNTSMS 4.

Cambridge: Cambridge University Press, 1967: 2d ed. Grand Rapids: Eerdmans/Exeter: Paternoster Press, 1983. ————. *Philippians.* NCB. Grand Rapids: Eerdmans, 1980. ————. *Reconciliation: A Study of Paul's Theology.* London: Marshall, Morgan & Scott/ Atlanta: John Knox, 1981. **Moore, G. F.** *Judaism in the First Three Centuries of the Christian Era.* Cambridge, Mass: Harvard University Press, 1927–30. **Reicke, B.** *The New Testament Era.* Tr. D. E. Green. London: A. & C. Black, 1968. **Robinson, W. C., Jr.** "Word and Power (1 Corinthians 1:17–2:5)." In *Soli Deo Gratia: New Testament Studies in Honor of William Childs Robinson,* ed. J. M. Richards, 68–82. Richmond: John Knox, 1968. **Schütz, J. H.** *Paul and the Anatomy of Apostolic Authority.* SNTSMS 26. Cambridge: University Press, 1975. **Tannehill, R. C.** *Dying and Rising with Christ.* BZNW 32. Berlin: Töpelmann, 1967. **Theissen, G.** *The Social Setting of Pauline Christianity. Essays on Corinth.* Tr. J. H. Schütz. Philadelphia: Fortress, 1982.

This section will seek to place the letter in Paul's life as a missionary and church leader whose apostolic standing was a subject of heated debate at Corinth. To achieve our aim we shall need to sketch the course of apostolic history in outline, and indicate, according to one theory, the way Paul's vocation was shaped by the flow of events that led to the composing of our letter called 2 Corinthians. This task is best done by a series of statements which mark the train of events relating to Paul's role as apostle in the early church, as seen through his letters and the data of Acts, however problematic these data in Acts may appear to be. In this way our endeavor will be to show that the contents and chief emphases of 2 Corinthians are best appreciated by setting the letter in a historical and theological *Sitz im Leben* in Paul's missionary career. And we will be indirectly challenging C. J. A. Hickling's position ("Is the Second Epistle to the Corinthians a Source of Early Church History?"; he responds negatively to his question by seeing the letter as not consisting of a "locally directed polemic" occasioned by Paul's opponents at Corinth [286]). Hickling, to be sure, rightly emphasizes "the personal factors that emerge strongly in the confrontation" between Paul and the Corinthians. But when he denies the force of "doctrinal" issues separating Paul and his readers, with the opponents forming a third member of the triangle of relationships, he cuts himself off from a valuable source of information, and he thus does not allow the setting of the letter to come to the aid of exegesis.

1. A suitable *terminus a quo* is the so-called "famine" visit of Acts 11:27–30. Paul and Barnabas came to Jerusalem from Antioch on the Orontes where they had united to lead a mission church that was Gentile in ethnic composition (Acts 11:19–21) and that cherished its freedom from Jewish restrictions (see J. P. Meier, *Antioch and Rome,* 32–35). Yet the visit of Acts 11:29, 30 was intended to forge a link of practical support and concern between the mother church in Jerusalem and the mission areas of Paul's ministry. If this visit may be equated with the events of Gal 2:1–10, it will follow that a concordat (of Gal 2:7) was reached by which the "pillar" apostles (οἱ στῦλοι) and Paul agreed on spheres of service (cf. 2 Cor 10:12–18) and tacitly refused to accept the insinuations of the "false brothers" who sought to infiltrate the ranks of Gentile congregations in Galatia as *agents provocateurs* (Gal 2:4, 5). Paul and Barnabas are seen as genuine representatives of the Gentile mission, with credibility in the eyes of the Jerusalem leaders. Yet Antioch, in sending its delegates both in Acts 11 and to the council of Acts 15, was expressing

a concern to retain the link with the mother church (Holmberg, *Paul and Power*, 18–20).

2. This agreement led to the outbreak of Judaizing opposition to the Pauline mission, with the center of the controversy the question of circumcision. This issue provoked much discussion on a broader front at that time. The place of circumcision and whether it was required to be practiced on Gentile inquirers as a *sine qua non* of entry into the Jewish community were spotlighted in the case of Izates of Adiabene, who initially wished to identify himself with the Jews but not to the point of accepting the rite of circumcision. (See Josephus, *Ant.* 20.34–48.) The concession was evidently made that he could "worship God without being circumcised, if indeed he had fully decided to be a devoted adherent of Judaism; for it was this that counted more than circumcision." In this event, Eleazar of Galilee persuaded him otherwise, and he was circumcised privately (F. F. Bruce, *New Testament History*, 266). In turn, there were political pressures exerted on Jewish Christians at a time when the Zealot movement in Judea aimed to force Jews to close ranks against paganizing influences (see Reicke, *The New Testament Era*, 202–3; R. Jewett, *NTS* 17 [1970–71] 198–212; for the evidence of Josephus, *Ant.* 20.102, 186 f.). The Jewish believers in Jesus would be caught in a double bind: on the one hand, they were anxious to honor their patriotism by declaring themselves to be loyal to the ancestral faith and its tradition; on the other side, they could see how Paul's reported actions (later to be garbled according to the witness of Acts 21:18–25) would—if left unchecked—offer a frontal assault on the Jewish religion and in turn lead to the church's becoming exclusively Gentile and so cut off from its Jewish roots. The author of Acts hardly gives this case a full hearing and views it only as a threat to the Pauline message and mission praxis that rests on the free, untrammeled grace of God apart from ritual or cultic observance. So the protestation of the Jewish Christians is given in stark terms in Acts 15:1, 2: "Some men came down from Judea [to Antioch?] and were teaching the brothers: 'Unless you are circumcised according to the custom taught by Moses, you cannot be saved.' " This sentiment, in all its frankness, needs to be read in the light of Acts 15:11 where Peter's response is couched in language replete with Paul's theological idiom and missionary topicality: "We believe it is through the grace of our Lord Jesus Christ that we [Jewish Christians] are saved, just as they [i.e., Gentile believers] are."

Paul and Barnabas were, therefore, delegated by the Antiochenes to go to Jerusalem to confer with the Jewish Christian leaders. This, in our view, is the background to the so-called council of Jerusalem, *ca.* A.D. 50.

3. At the conference reported in Acts 15:1–19, a three-cornered discussion got underway, though we have only minimal information and several questions are unresolved. The central issue that provoked the meeting in the first instance (Acts 15:5) was that of the rite of circumcision which, it was insisted from the Jewish Christian side, must be imposed on Gentile converts to the messianic faith. Peter led off as the first contributor to the debate. He stood in the role of "bridge-man" (to use J. D. G. Dunn's phrase, *Unity and Diversity*, 385, following Hengel, *Acts*, 92–98), ostensibly spanning the gap between the different factions, and providing a link to unite Jewish and Gentile suscepti-

bilities both on the basis of his own experience after the Cornelius episode (Acts 10, 11) and in concurrence with the arrangement already made in Galatians 2:4, 7.

Paul is the second voice to be heard (Acts 15:12) as he summarily reported the success that had followed the initial evangelism he conducted in Syria, Cilicia, and Antioch (cf. Gal 1:21). Then it was James, the Lord's brother, who proposed a *modus vivendi* from the Jewish Christian side and evidently aimed at quieting the apprehensions of that group. The "decree" (v 20), however, neatly circumvents the question of circumcision, and instead concentrates on a less heated topic, namely, table fellowship between Jewish and non-Jewish parties and the requirements to be met if such cordiality was to be continued. The Gentiles are left in no doubt that they are under obligation (derived from the Noachian laws of Judaism that were believed to be God's original intention to unite all people in accepting a basic moralistic and dietary code, derived from Gen 9:4; see G. F. Moore, *Judaism*, 1:274 f., 339) to abstain from the items as listed. Paul—and maybe Peter—may not have been present at this phase of the conference, since in Acts 21:18–25 James announces the decree as something evidently new to Paul (v 25, "*we* have written," seems to exclude Paul; so Hengel, *Acts*, 117: "there James presents it [the decree] as something new and apparently unknown to him").

4. The situation, following the council, developed in a way that caused alarm among the more zealous Jewish Christians. We may postulate the reasons for their consternation: Paul's mission preaching in Acts 13, 14 opened the door to the evangelization of pagans en masse. In that preaching no mention of circumcision was made, as indeed the matter had been glossed over at the Jerusalem meeting. According to Acts 14:23, Paul quickly followed up his initial evangelism by proposing a rudimentary church organization involving a Jewish structure, the appointing of "elders" to oversee the nascent communities. The Jewish believers responded to what occasioned their fear by nominating Judas and Silas to enforce the decree at Antioch. Paul's presence at Antioch is clearly certified in the text (Acts 15:35), but it is a moot point whether he and Barnabas should be associated with the decree in this chapter or at Acts 16:4. It seems clear that Luke's purpose is to highlight the harmony between various factions and their leaders. It is noteworthy that at Corinth where matters germane to the items of the decree were warmly debated, especially εἰδωλόθυτα, "food offered to idols" (1 Cor 8:1–10; see G. D. Fee, *Bib* 61 [1980] 172–92), he never once appeals to *that* authority. Instead, in 1 Corinthians Paul's court of appeal is much more personal than to any document, even if it may have emanated from an august source, the Jerusalem hierarchy. He appeals to what Büchsel calls "the obligation of love" (*Liebespflicht: TWNT* 2: 379: see R. P. Martin on "Idols, Meat offered to," *IBD* part 2 [1980] 680, 681).

Peter's behavior at Antioch, according to Gal 2:12, was the cause of further Jewish Christian concern. The emissaries from James attacked his practice of consorting with Gentiles: the issue was apparently not that of table fellowship per se, as in Gal 2:12, but the easygoing attitude that led Peter to sit down with *uncircumcised* people. Hence Paul writes in that verse: "he was afraid of those who belonged to *the circumcision group*" (NIV, italics added).

5. The record of the confrontation between Paul and Peter at Antioch (Gal 2:11–14) poses its own set of problems to the modern interpreter. (See Holmberg, *Paul and Power*, 32–34; Dunn, "The Incident," *JSNT*, with responses. The modern consensus [see Holmberg, 34, n. 117] is that Paul "lost" his case at Antioch, and thus his alienation from Antioch began at this point: Hengel, *Acts*, 123.) The issue under dispute was the question of whether new Christians should "live as Jews" (2:14) by following "Jewish customs" (ἰουδαΐζειν), a phrase Paul interprets to mean both the accepting of the kosher laws in regard to food and the practice of circumcision. Peter vacillated at these points where the Jewish Christians were insistent (reinterpreting the decree—it may be, in their own interests—to include circumcision), and on his side, Paul was emphatic, since he interpreted the council's meeting in his own way (see Holmberg, *Paul and Power*, 21, 22). He regarded Peter's tame acceptance of Jewish Christian pressure as intolerable; it was nothing short of a move away from "the truth of the Gospel" (Gal 2:5), agreed upon in the working arrangement of the earlier concordat. At this point, as D. R. Catchpole ("Paul, James and the Apostolic Decree," *NTS* 23 [1977] 428–44) suggests, Paul hardened his attitude to the decree. It was seen not as a gesture of conciliation leading to unity, but as a step backward and a capitulation to the *Urgemeinde*, the primitive Jerusalem church, with its limitation on mission. Up to this juncture and turn of events, Paul may well have tolerated the value of the decree, possibly because it was concerned in its first drafting with matters such as a detestation of idolatry and immorality and the adoption of food rules which Paul took to be axiomatic for his converts, or at least as a matter of indifference (1 Cor 6:18–20; 8:4–8: "Food does not bring us near to God"). It may be that he did not treat these issues as central to the kerygma (Rom. 14:14–18) or that his attitude is explained by his flexibility. As F. F. Bruce (*Paul*, 186) put it: "Where the principles of the gospel were not at stake, he was the most conciliatory of men." More likely still, we may see in Paul's later resistance to and passing over of the decree the final development of his repugnance *from the beginning.* Again Catchpole is surely correct in detecting three aspects of the decree that would have made the formula distasteful to him: its Mosaic character, its implicit separation of Jew and Gentile on ethnic grounds, and its observance of a levitical code based on ceremonial cleanness. The Paul who wrote 2 Cor 3:1–18; Gal 3:28, 29; and Rom 3:27–31 is hardly likely to have been enthusiastic at a formulation of Christianity that served only to accentuate both the Jewishness and exclusiveness of that faith on ritualistic grounds. So Paul was driven to conclude that the decree was an attempt to put the clock back and to turn the course of the Christian mission into antiquated channels.

Such a momentous conclusion, however, had far-ranging repercussions for Paul in his missionary vocation based on theological convictions, not pragmatic grounds, namely:

a. It sharpened the focus of his Gospel to a point where justification apart from the works of the law became a pivotal issue, and the results of this narrowed focus are seen in the polemical statements in Galatians and Philippians with a more measured exposition in the letter to the Romans—at least up to chap. 4. "Justification by faith" became, under the exigencies of this turn of events, a clarion call of the Pauline mission since it served to show the distinctiveness of Paul's missionary theology vis-à-vis the Jewish Christians' counterclaim. Whether "justification" had a larger purpose as providing a groundwork for Paul's theology in toto may be doubted; and we have sought to argue that a more comprehensive term such as "reconciliation" takes over as representing the quintessence of Paul's message to the Gentiles adumbrated in 2 Cor 5:18–21 and fully fashioned in Romans, once the debate with the Jewish Christians receded from view (see R. P. Martin, *Reconciliation: A Study of Paul's Theology*, especially 149–54).

b. Paul's stance set him in inevitable opposition to the "pillar" apostles, whose authority he now proceeded to challenge, partly in pursuance of his loyalty to "the truth of the Gospel" which he felt they had betrayed and partly in response to the insinuation that began to appear from this quarter of Jewish Christianity that he was in fact no true apostle—indeed, that he was no apostle at all (note the correct translation of 2 Cor 12:12, obscured in the RSV), or if E. Käsemann, *Die Legitimität* (11, 12), is correct on the basis of 2 Cor 10:7, not even a Christian person. This innuendo is clearly in his sights at the time of the Corinthian crisis, and sets the agenda of his writing of 2 Cor 3–7; 10–13, chapters which in different ways resist the insinuation that he has no apostolic status. Moreover, they demonstrate what he regarded as his valid credentials over against the opponents who attempt to found their apostolate in the figure of Moses, and appeal to the self-styled "super-apostles" (2 Cor 11:5; 12:11, NIV) as authorities to justify their status as "servants of Christ" (2 Cor 11:23) and "apostles of Christ" (2 Cor 11:13).

c. Paul's isolation from Jerusalem was a somewhat ambivalent entity. He still professed a concern for national Israel κατὰ σάρκα, i.e., on its ethnic base (Rom 9:1–5; 10:1–2), and still was willing to reach out in compassion and in practical ways to aid the "poor saints" in the holy city (2 Cor 8, 9; Rom 15:25–31; cf. Gal 2:10). Nonetheless, the evidence of a break with his former colleagues is only too apparent: he separated from his original sponsor (Acts 9:26–28), Barnabas (Acts 15:36–41), and he found a congenial partner in Silas, shifting his power base from Antioch to Asia. Indeed, we may see how Antioch as a church center increasingly moved in the direction of a rapprochement with Jewish Christianity with its acceptance of the primacy of Peter in Matthew's Gospel (Matt 14:28 f.; 16:16 ff.; 17:24; 18:21; cf. R. E. Brown and J. P. Meier, *Antioch and Rome*, 45–72; M. Hengel, *Acts*, 98), its desire to keep open some lines of communication with the ancestral faith in spite of persecution, and its openness to Christian nomism and particularism as safeguards against too radical a version of the Pauline Gospel (e.g., Matt 5:17–20; 7:21; 10:5, 6; 15:24; 19:28; 23:2, 3, 23).

Paul's chief centers of ministry are now located in the Roman world: at Philippi, where his mission church building is hailed as "the beginning of the gospel" (Phil 4:15; see Gnilka, *Der Philippenbrief*, 177; Martin, *Philippians*, NCB, 165), at Corinth and at Ephesus. In these church communities Paul works out the logic of his chosen position. He proclaims and applies a universal, law-free, circumcisionless Gospel, detached from ceremonial restrictions and cultic taboos which, once they were reintroduced either from the Jewish (as in Philippians) or hellenistic side (as in Colossians), had to be resisted in the name of Paul's teaching of *sola gratia, sola fide*.

In 2 Cor 10:12–18 Paul handles a theme of some complexity. We may leave the details to be considered later. But the main topic is obvious. Paul wants to justify his mission to Corinth on the ground that he is working within the "proper limits" (the μέτρον τοῦ κανόνος of the true apostle: so Käsemann, *Legitimität*, 43–51, who sees the term as embracing Paul's entire apostolic calling and the validity of his mission everywhere) God has assigned him. He has no intention of going "beyond our limits" (10:15) to trespass on the turf which rightly belongs to "others," presumably Jewish Christian leaders whose derogatory attitude to Paul's mission at Corinth lies in the background. He has been accused of having no right to be at Corinth where Peter and Barnabas were evidently well known and received (1 Cor 9:5, 6; see C. K. Barrett, "Cephas and Corinth," *Essays on Paul,* chap. 2). This paragraph is one of the clearest statements, along with Rom 15:17–22, of Paul's self-defensive response to those who alleged that he was an interloper. With fervency and boldness he retorted that his apostolic writ did run to these Gentile areas which God had given him—and which the "pillar" men had earlier accepted (Gal 2:7–9)—as his bailiwick (see C. K. Barrett, "Paul and the 'Pillar' Apostles").

The point of this discussion is that, with Paul's disaffection in regard to Antioch as a base of missionary operations, he was temporarily without a spiritual *Heimat* and vulnerable, since he could be regarded as an itinerant preacher doing very much solo work without a legitimating "home" base. The "letters of recommendation" carried to Corinth by Paul's competitors have to be seen in this light. "Thus they always represented some specific Christian community. Paul did not" (Theissen, *Social Setting,* 50). Hence he articulates his insistence that at Corinth he is working the Lord's work among people to whom he has been sent (1 Cor 1:1; 15:58; see B. Holmberg, *Paul and Power,* 30, 31 *et passim*) and has his credentials in human lives (3:1–3; cf. 1 Cor 9:1, 2).

d. So we reach, by this circuitous route, the occasion of 2 Corinthians and its *Sitz im Leben* in Paul's missionary career. Not the least consequence of the train of events which led to his stand against Jewish Christians, and especially in the person of the emissaries he confronts in 2 Cor 10–13, was a new expression of his confidence in his own apostleship.

The emphasis on Paul's "rightful apostolate" has been regarded by Holmberg (*Paul and Power,* 7) as occasioned by the presence of rival apostles at Corinth and their initial success in ousting him from his position of authority in that community. So it is concluded that it was this new factor (seen in 11:4, where ὁ ἐρχόμενος, "he who comes," implies a visit of emissaries hitherto unknown, armed with a rival gospel) which led to Paul's stance. "What Paul threatens to do in 2 Cor 10:1–6 and 13:10 is thus something he has never before attempted at Corinth," namely, to engage in fierce polemic and exert his God-given right (ἐξουσία) as a "divine apostle." The issue in this discussion turns on Paul's consciousness of being such an apostle, possessing a powerful apostolate.

But what is noteworthy is that *it was reformulated in a surprisingly novel manner.* The pressure of these events which set him apart from Jewish Christian leaders and their emissaries to Corinth and brought him under a cloud of suspicion made it inevitable that he would define his role as a suffering apostle whose power is seen in his frailty and inherent weakness (2 Cor 4:7–12;

12:9, 10; 13:3, 4, 9). Paul's credentials are not found in written documents but in the lives of his people (2 Cor 3:1–3). More particularly he appeals to the inner reality rather than the tangible and evidential (4:16–18; 5:12; 13:3). See D. A. Black, *Paul, Apostle of Weakness* (1984), who coins the expression "the weakness of the cross" (239). This self-evaluation is a natural corollary of Paul's new insights into soteriology, or the way God saves believers. The cross, for Paul, took on a new dimension as the place of divine humiliation and self-giving, expressed in Christ's surrender of all he had or could be (2 Cor 8:9; Phil 2:6–11).

With some justification we may trace to this time in his life a clear articulation of a *theologia crucis* in contradistinction to both a *theologia gloriae* ("theology of glory") which was prevalent at Corinth among a hellenistic group there and a nomistic bid to bracket the cross with an insistence on circumcision as equally necessary to salvation. "If righteousness could be gained through the law, Christ died for nothing!" (Gal 2:21, NIV) is one of his most forthright denials of the latter proposal.

The genesis of Paul's teaching on Christ's cross as the locus of divine power-in-weakness (1 Cor 1:18–2:5) and of his own ministry as "weak in him" may go far to explain the statistical phenomena addressed by Black's recent study (*Paul* [1984], 18–21). He shows—but does not ask why the evidence leads to a conclusion—that Paul's term for "weakness" (ἀσθένεια) is most frequent in the Corinthian letters (29x out of a total of 44 uses; in 2 Cor the ratio is 14x out of 44; these 14x are all in 2 Cor 10–13). "In these two letters (and to a lesser degree in Romans) he develops weakness into a *theological* formulation" (Black, 85, his italics). This is true. The question now is posed: what led Paul to make this formulation? It can hardly have been only "the loneliness and discouragement of his disappointing visit to Athens (Acts 17)," as Black surmises (101). A deeper cause is suggested, and we propose that it lay in the coherence of his own experience of isolation from earlier missionary support, the nature of the Corinthian crisis which struck a blow at his apostolic authority, and his need to redefine the Gospel in terms of a clear distinction from Judaism and Jewish Christian ideology. In consequence, he came to define the message as "the word of the cross" (1 Cor 1:18), and God's power was traced to the hidden wisdom of Christ's weakness by which the mighty were overcome (1 Cor 1:27–29). "Crucified in weakness" (2 Cor 13:4), Christ achieved salvation by surrendering his glory, by self-giving in taking the slave's condition, and by obedience to death. Paul's language coheres precisely with this new insight born out of the experiences that came to him at this crucial time in his life and career (see J. H. Schütz, *Paul and the Anatomy of Apostolic Authority*, 235–48; W. C. Robinson, Jr., "Word and Power," for his important conclusion: *Theologia crucis* is a theology not just for conversion; the word of the cross is the power of God for all of Christian life [82]).

Robinson's allusion to "the use of pre-formed material in a concrete situation" (loc. cit., 79) may be illustrated by an appeal to Phil 2:6–11, the Christ-hymn that celebrates the odyssey of the redeemer from eternity to his final glory as ruler of all. This *carmen Christi* has been intensively studied, and we may pick out from the complexities of recent discussion several items that bear upon the mind of Paul at the time of his writing 2 Corinthians. We may take as a working hypothesis the dating of Philippians in Paul's

Ephesian ministry, i.e., at the same time that the Corinthian crisis was filling his mind. Granted, in the Philippian letter Paul uses a traditional piece of hymnic material; but its setting is clearly paraenetic, leading to the hortatory appeal of 2:12, which in turn has the pastoral situation of 2:1–4 in its sights.

One way that Paul has utilized the preformed hymn is to pick up the theme of "obedience" in his *applicatio* at 2:12. By common consent Phil 2:6–8 is centered on the obedience of the one who entered our human lifestream at great cost and consented to accept a life of humiliation and self-denial of his rights, as δοῦλος, "a slave." Clearly δοῦλος has its counterpart in κύριος, "Lord," which is the title now bestowed on the exalted Christ (v 11). But the inclusion of the earthly name "Jesus" in the ascription of praise at v 11 is meant to look back to the first part of the hymn and to cast its shadow across his earthly existence, traced in a course of several actions that are denoted by stark reflexive verbs but with no explicit subject in vv 6–8. All we know from the original draft of the hymn is that a heavenly being (v 6) who existed as the divine image consented to embark on a life of self-abnegation. The inclusion of Ἰησοῦς in the acclamation formula of v 11 is designed to point back to that earthly life, which is no charade or mock example as though the heavenly one was simply going through the motions as a piece of histrionics. He was really involved—since his name, now revealed at the enthronement, is "Jesus," which is attached to the title of exaltation, "Lord."

This is precisely Paul's point at 1 Cor 12:1–3 where the cry ἀνάθεμα Ἰησοῦς, "Jesus [be] damned"—as offensive to Paul surely as to the present-day Christian believer—was heard at Corinth as some members were disclaiming the earthly Jesus in favor of concentrating their religious aspirations on the heavenly eon, Christ. Their enthusiastic reaching out to Christ as world ruler and Lord of the congregation is coolly received by Paul, whose Gospel has to hold together the earthly Jesus with the exalted Lord if it is not to evaporate into a "docetic" philosophy or a species of gnostic religiosity akin to prevalent hellenistic cult devotion. Paul's antidote is to be seen in 2 Cor 4:9–12 where the frequent allusion to the name "Jesus" is not an accident, but serves to enforce Paul's major thrust against his opponents.

Also, it seems fairly certain that Paul in taking over this "hymn to Christ" has redacted it—by the insertion of v 8c: θανάτου δὲ σταυροῦ, "the death of the cross"—to enforce its appeal, and to anchor the incarnational motifs of vv 6–8 in the saving event which involved the redeemer's death on a cross. The function of that coda (in v 8c) along with the elements of his earthly humiliation and obedience is to reveal to the Philippians that it is the *crucified Jesus* whom they acknowledge as Lord (v 11). Their life "in Christ Jesus" (v 5) is to be governed by that control, and the reminder—based on a *theologia crucis*—is Paul's way of summoning his reader to face the outworking of what the Christian life is all about (cf. R. P. Martin, *Carmen Christi*[2] [1983] xii–xxxix).

This setting of the cross at the heart of the hymn, as it is molded under Paul's design, shows where the paraenetic appeal lies: it assists in giving a kerygmatic dimension to the readers' lives in Christ by anchoring what they understand as life under Christ's lordly control (a conviction shared by Paul and his readers) in a "theology of the cross." The cross, in the understanding Paul has learned at this phase of his mission, is not a station on the road to glory or a temporary diversion quickly to be passed over in a retelling of the story of Christ (as the church to which 1 Cor 15 was written was imagining; see R. P. Martin, *The Spirit and the Congregation,* chap. 6). Rather the cross is of the *esse* of Christian existence and the decisive criterion of what Paul calls in 2 Cor 10:7 Χριστοῦ εἶναι, "being Christ's person" (Käsemann, *Legitimität,* 11). Jesus' death is not rightly seen as a mere fact of past history or an episode that was soon to be swallowed up in the glory of the risen one. It is the hallmark of all that characterized Jesus' historical person and saving significance, and to proclaim him is to proclaim the cross (1 Cor 1:18). To treat the cross in any other way—as in the case of those to whom Paul writes 2 Cor 5:11–21—is to subvert its meaning. Worse, it is to range oneself with those (as in 2 Cor 6:14–7:1; 11:13–15) who are elsewhere called "the enemies of Christ's cross" (Phil 3:18). (See further for connections between Paul's opponents in 2 Cor 10–13 and Philippians, R. P. Martin, *Philippians,* NCB, 22–36, 143, 144.)

The obverse side of this teaching is the practical application of the kerygma of the cross to the apostolic ministry. Now it is seen—for the first time by any Christian leader in the *Urchristentum* of whom we have record—that the *esse* of the church is its role as a suffering people, and that the title to service is written in Paul's own self-designation as "dying with Christ" (2 Cor 4:10, 11; 2 Cor 13:4). Rightly, therefore, does R. C. Tannehill (*Dying and Rising,* 177) remark: "The past dying with Christ and the present dying with Christ in suffering are not two unrelated things, but the same thing taking place on two different levels." Yet that place of weakness is also paradoxically the seat of apostolic authority (ἐξουσία: 2 Cor 10:8; 13:10)—but it is power harnessed to the service of love in seeking to build up, not pull down, and enlisted to encourage people to grow in the maturity of faith (2 Cor 1:24).

Here we may see the sequence of historical happenings that brought Paul to a lonely place. When viewed in a theological frame of reference and seen *sub specie aeternitatis,* the events that led him to face the Corinthian crisis produced, in the alchemy of divine overruling, a magnificent exposition of what the Christian life is all about, how the church of Christ should see its existence and mission in the world, and the ways that Christian service in a true apostolic succession should be spelled out in this and all generations.

8. Features of 2 Corinthians

From the attempt we made above to set the letter in its niche within Paul's life and experience as the apostle to the Gentiles and to observe how its chief emphases were called out by the confluence of events that precipitated the critical Corinthian situation, we may go on to draw out its main insights into Paul's conception of his life, his ministry, and his message. The first part of the letter reflects what must have been one of the most distressing experiences of Paul's life. He had been personally opposed and insulted by an individual or a group in the church at Corinth, which taunted him with insincerity and duplicity (1:17), charged him with making promises he did not fulfill, and accused him of arrogantly asserting authority he did not possess. The first section of the letter (chaps. 1–7) is concerned to explain and to justify his actions in the light of his apostolic ministry. The final chapters (10–13) suggest the presence of a new threat, occasioned by the arrival of Judeo-Christian emissaries, and a fresh outbreak of hostility to Paul by attacking his apostleship and person, but this time at a deeper level, more serious than the personal insults leveled at him in the situation referred to in chaps. 2 and 7. Now in chaps. 10–13 the gravamen is that he is no true apostle, but a religious fraud. Overall, the areas of his writing suggest the following items of teaching in the letter.

1. He relates his experience in the humiliating circumstances of opposition he has known and also in the course of his recent apostolic trials in Asia Minor (1:8–11). He had almost despaired of his life and seemed completely dejected; yet he had come to a new awareness of God's presence and power and was led to trust him more fully (4:7–12 is a poignant expression of this).

2. He claims over against his detractors that he has those very credentials they challenged and denied to him. Yet the credentials are not his property, rather they are proof of God at work through him (see on 12:12; Holmberg, *Paul and Power*, 78, 79). The call of God in his own soul, the living proof of his ministry in the changed lives of those converted under that ministry, the "signs of an apostle" in what God had wrought through him, and especially his persistence and resolution (ὑπομονή: cf. 6:4)—all these accredit him as truly a servant of God. His detractors made a threefold assault on him: they attacked his person, his teaching, and his character, see 10:1, 10; 11:6; and Paul's reply in 10:7; 13:4; for the second assault, see 2:17; 10:12–18; 11:7–12; 12:13; 11:4; which he answers in 2:17; 4:2, 5; 10:12–18; 11:1–4, 22–30; 12:1–12; and for the third insinuation against his character, see 1:15–17; 10:9, 11; 11:16–19; 12:16–19; and Paul's defense in 1:15–24; 3:1–6; 5:13; 7:2–4; 10:18; 11:16–19; 12:14–18.

We may notice the grounds on which Paul was attacked: he was accused of vacillation (1:17 f., 23), pride and boasting (3:1, 12; 5:12), lack of success in preaching (4:3), physical weakness (10:10), "rudeness" of speech, deficient in rhetorical skill (11:6), being an ungifted person (4:7–10; 10:10; 12:7–10; 13:9), dishonesty (12:16–19), posing as a "fool" (5:13; 11:16–19; 12:6), and lack of apostolic standing (11:5; 12:12). Above all, he is held to be a deceiver (4:8) and a charlatan (10:1), a blatant denial of the power of the Christian message (13:2–9).

3. Finally, the emphasis falls on an appeal for generosity on the part of the Corinthians. Chaps. 8 and 9 relate to this theme. Those at strife among themselves at Corinth had to look further afield to the needs of the church outside, especially the poor "saints" at Jerusalem. The supreme model is that of the incarnate Lord (8:9).

Above all, 2 Corinthians is a very human document, opening a window into the inner life of the apostle. R. H. Strachan's words (xxix) are a tribute to this feature:

> The letter is an artless and unconsciously autobiographical description of the ways in which Paul was accustomed to meet slander and calumny, physical danger and bodily suffering, disloyalty and ingratitude, from those for whom he had given of his best, the disillusionment and disappointment that invaded his spirit from time to time.

The personal element obviously comes to the fore often in this epistle, and this accounts for one of its outstanding values. M. Hengel, *Between Jesus and Paul,* tr. J. Bowden (Philadelphia: Fortress, 1983), 69, has called 2 Corinthians Paul's most personal letter. Yet we should not overlook the way that apostle and Gospel are so closely bound together in these chapters. What was at stake at Corinth was nothing less than the essence of the kerygma as expressed in the way of the cross (*theologia crucis*) for proclamation and daily living.

The epistle has many lessons to teach Christians and indeed all who take Paul as a religious leader and spiritual guide in a serious fashion. We should be ready to forgive (2:10), grateful for uplifting news (2:13, 14; 7:6), courageous and hopeful in trying circumstances (4:8–10), recognizing that affliction is the church's true glory (4:8–10, 16–18; 6:3–10). There should be true ambition in pleasing God (5:9). We should see that life contains paradoxes (6:10). There should be a concern to aid poor church members (chaps. 8, 9). We should not be eager to defend ourselves against the attacks of others, but there are times when it is right and necessary to do so, especially when the integrity of the Gospel is at risk (chaps. 10, 11). We should be glad to suffer as God wills (12:8–10). We should be strictly honest (8:16–22; 12:17, 18).

The call of the Gospel is "come . . . and die" with Christ (4:10–12) in expectation of God's future which, at present veiled from our eyes, is grasped by faith (5:7) and awaited with confidence. This two-beat rhythm (death/ life; distress/consolation; affliction/glory; weakness/strength) runs through the epistle and finds its heart in the incarnate (8:9), atoning (5:18–21), and enthroned Lord (4:5) whose "grace" and strength meet every human need (12:10; 13:13), for he "died and was raised" (5:15) and lives by God's power (13:4). Yet his present power is seen in the paradox of the suffering apostle (4:7; 13:4) who "acts out" in his ministry the Gospel he proclaims and embodies (5:20). As James Dunn puts it, Paul "experiences Christ as the Crucified as well as the Exalted; indeed, it is only when he experiences Christ as crucified that it is possible for him to experience Christ as exalted, only when he experiences death as the dying of Christ that it is possible to experience the risen life of Christ" (*Jesus and the Spirit,* 334).

Perhaps the central element in this letter is the close link uniting Paul's person and ministry with the kerygma he is charged to make known. Apostle and Gospel go together in indissoluble unity, just as Christ Jesus and his apostle Paul are closely associated as "Lord" and "servant" (4:5). They remain two distinct persons, however inextricably joined (4:10; 13:3: Güttgemanns, *Der leidende Apostel,* 134, has a novel way of expressing this relationship. He appeals to the "real presence" of the crucified Jesus as Lord in Paul's apostolic existence, so that the "body" of Paul becomes the place where there is an appearing and a presence of the earthly Jesus); yet given the contingent situation at Corinth and the reality of conflict and isolation in Paul's missionary career, he writes in such a way that at times the two merge by their intimate association with the Gospel, which is both Christ's and Paul's. So a decision for Paul is at the same time a decision for the Gospel (so Bultmann, 149); and that decision is equally one registered for Christ.

I. Address   (1:1, 2)

Bibliography

Barrett, C. K. *The Signs of an Apostle.* London: Epworth Press, 1970. **Carrez, M.** "Le 'nous' en 2 Corinthiens." *NTS* 26 (1979–80) 474–86. **Delling, G.** "Merkmale der Kirche nach dem Neuen Testament." *NTS* 13 (1966–67) 297–316. **Dobschütz, E. von.** "Wir und Ich bei Paulus." *ZSTh* 10 (1933) 251–77. **Doty, W. G.** *Letters in Primitive Christianity.* Philadelphia: Fortress Press, 1973. **Evans, O. E.** *Saints in Christ Jesus: A Study of the Christian Life in the New Testament.* Swansea: John Penry Press, 1975. **Fridrichsen, A.** *The Apostle and His Message.* Uppsala: Lundequistska Bokhandeln, 1947. **Hainz, J.** *Ekklesia.* Strukturen paulinischer Gemeinde-Theologie und Gemeinde-Ordnung. Regensburg: Verlag Friedrich Pustet, 1972. 127–29. **Kirk, J. A.** "Apostleship since Rengstorf: Towards a Synthesis." *NTS* 21 (1975) 249–64. **Kramer, W.** *Christ, Lord, Son of God.* SBT 50. Tr. B. Hardy. London: SCM Press, 1966. § 13e, 42b. **Lofthouse, W. F.** " 'I' and 'We' in the Pauline Epistles." *BT* 6 (1955) 72–80. **Ollrog, W.-H.** *Paulus und seine Mitarbeiter.* WMANT 50. Neukirchen-Vluyn: Neukirchener Verlag, 1979. **Rissi, M.** *Studien zum zweiten Korintherbrief.* ATANT 56. Zurich: Zwingli Verlag, 1969. 43. **Snaith, N. H.** *The Distinctive Ideas of the Old Testament.* London: Epworth Press, 1944. 21–50.

Translation[a]

[1]*Paul, apostle of Christ Jesus by the will of God, and brother Timothy, to the church of God that is at Corinth and to all the saints who are in the whole of Achaia.* [2]*Grace to you and peace from God our Father and the Lord Jesus Christ.*

Notes

[a]The translation throughout is based on *Novum Testamentum Graece*, ed. E. Nestle and K. Aland *et al.* (Stuttgart: Deutsche Bibelgesellschaft, 1979[26]). References to Bratcher signify *A Translator's Guide to Second Corinthians* by R. G. Bratcher (New York: United Bible Societies, 1983), and to Diglot, *A Greek-English Diglot,* ed. R. G. Bratcher (London: British and Foreign Bible Society, 1964).

Form/Structure/Setting

Epistolary salutation in the Pauline letters follows the pattern of contemporary letter-writing practices, with obvious Christian features added (see Doty, *Letters,* 21–47). The names of sender and addressees are given at this point in the letter; and there is an expression of greeting. In the case of this epistle Paul adds a self-description as "apostle of Christ Jesus," and the colorless Greek greeting χαίρειν becomes the rich Pauline χάρις, "grace."

The placing of Timothy's name alongside that of Paul is not apparently intended to connote a shared responsibility for authorship. To be sure, the following letter oscillates between the use of the singular ("I") and the plural ("we"); and this feature has been discussed at some length (see Windisch, 33, 34; von Dobschütz, "Wir und Ich"; Lofthouse, " 'I' and 'We' "; Carrez "Le 'nous' "). But there is no suggestion that Paul consciously looked to

Timothy to lend support to his apostolic convictions or that Timothy was a coauthor.

On the contrary, it is more probable that Timothy is mentioned in the letter's prescript because he needed Paul's endorsement of all he had sought to do as he undertook an intermediate mission between the visits of Acts 18:3 and 20:4. In that interim we may postulate (on the basis of Acts 19:22) a visit made by Timothy subsequent to the sending of 1 Corinthians. Paul may well have dispatched him to report on the Corinthian crisis, inferred from 1 Cor 4:17–21, where v 17 is an example of an epistolary aorist, "I am sending to you Timothy." See too 1 Cor 16:10 for Timothy's errand.

The fact that 2 Corinthians does not allude to this mission may suggest that Paul is kindly drawing a veil of secrecy over an event that turned out disastrously for his own authority at Corinth. If so, Timothy's name in the address will be Paul's attempt to rehabilitate his colleague, who had been insulted and rejected as his emissary. This is an uncertain inference, though Windisch's statement of there being no conflict between Timothy and the Corinthians at the time of Paul's writing is difficult to prove. Allo cautions that we know so little about Timothy's movements that we cannot say if he did actually get to Corinth; it is hazardous to postulate a hypothesis of Timothy's having been the victim of an attack, Allo concludes (1, 2). Yet there is no denying the reasonableness of the suggestion—for which there are some indications in the text—that part of Paul's purpose in including Timothy's name was to reestablish his standing in the eyes of the church at Corinth (so Strachan, 40).

Comment

1. Paul introduces himself as ἀπόστολος Χριστοῦ Ἰησοῦ, "apostle of Christ Jesus"—a title authorized to him by the phrase διὰ θελήματος θεοῦ, "by the will of God." The note of apostolic authority is sounded again at 1:21; 2:17; 4:5; 5:20; 10:8; 13:10. These verses pay eloquent tribute to Paul's self-consciousness as God's servant uniquely set apart and commissioned for the task of ministry in the framework of the "new covenant" (cf. 3:6). In these self-designations it was Paul's awareness of the divine "will" both for his own life and for the mission of Christ to the Gentiles that impelled his service at every point. See Fridrichsen, *The Apostle;* and for "apostle" as the "keyword" in Paul's relations with the churches, see Hainz, *Ekklesia,* 128, 129.

"Apostle" is a pivotal term in this letter, to be understood both negatively and affirmatively. In the former sense, what Paul writes about his vocation and ministry has to be seen in direct opposition to the claims made by other teachers on the Corinthian scene. Paul does not hesitate to label such men "false apostles" (ψευδαπόστολοι: 11:13; see Kramer, sec. 13e). He tacitly concedes that they laid claim to the title "apostle," and it was important for him to define *his* understanding of the term over against *their* perception of it. Paul's criteria are the proclamation of the Gospel (11:4) and the marks of its true preacher (Rissi, *Studien,* 43). On the positive side, "this epistle contains . . . the fullest and most passionate account of what Paul meant by apostleship" (Barrett, 53; see his *Signs,* 35–46). On the meaning of the term "apostle," see especially J. A. Kirk, "Apostleship since Rengstorf: Towards a Synthesis," and J. Roloff, *Apostolat-Verkündigung-Kirche,* (Gütersloh: Verlag Mohn, 1965) 9–37, for a table of possible meanings of the term in Paul's understanding.

Timothy is designated "the brother," a term that recurs in 1 Thess 3:2; Col 1:1. More endearing descriptions such as "my beloved and faithful child/son" (1 Cor 4:17) and Paul's "son" (Phil 2:22) are found, as well as tributes in the Pastoral epistles. The word "brother" suggests a quasi-official function (as in 8:22) and would support the idea of Timothy as Paul's envoy to Corinth, whether or not his mission had suffered defeat there. On Timothy's role in the Pauline mission churches, see W.-H. Ollrog, *Paulus und seine Mitarbeiter*, 20–23.

"Church" (ἐκκλησία) is found nine times in the letter, usually in the sense of the local congregation of God's people of the new covenant. The exception is 11:28 where "all the churches" has an ecumenical ring about it, at least as far as the Pauline communities were concerned. See below.

ἐν Κορίνθῳ, "at Corinth." On Corinth as a Greek city in Paul's day and earlier see pp. xxviii–xxx; the verbal form in the phrase τῇ ἐκκλησίᾳ τοῦ θεοῦ τῇ οὔσῃ should be observed in the light of K. L. Schmidt's contention (*TDNT* 3:506) that what is in view is the "one great church" with its local manifestation or outcropping at Corinth. He argues that it is a mistake to render "the Corinthian church"; rather it is the one church of God that appears on the scene at Corinth.

Σὺν τοῖς ἁγίοις πᾶσιν τοῖς οὖσιν, κτλ. Two matters invite comment in this phrase: (1) the description of Christians as "the holy ones" (οἱ ἅγιοι) and (2) the addressees of the letter in a region wider than just the church(es) in the city of Corinth. Paul's phrase takes into his purview the congregations located in the entire region of Achaia. "Achaia" became, after 27 B.C., the name of the whole of Greece (Pauly-Wissowa, *RE* 1:193 f.), whereas in pre-Roman times it denoted a smaller territory on the northern coast of the Peloponnese. Paul's usage here (and in 1 Cor 16:15; cf. Rom 15:26; 1 Thess 1:7, 8) probably reflects the earlier designation. In Acts 17:34 converts made in Athens are evidently not counted in Paul's remark (in 1 Cor 16:15) that some Corinthians were the first believers in Achaia. See Goudge, 1, for uncertainty as to Paul's exact delimitation of Achaia, though it is clear that he regarded Corinth as the chief city of the province in general (Lietzmann-Kümmel, 99; Bultmann, 24). Lietzmann's theory that the designation of Corinth in the province of Achaia as the "root of the later constitution of a metropolitan" church is, however, justly criticized by Hainz, *Ekklesia*, 130.

The adjectival noun ἅγιος as a title for Christians has its roots in the Old Testament. It derives from a Hebrew word meaning "to separate" (קדשׁ, *qdš*), and the LXX renders such a root by ἅγιος in its adjectival form. The saints are the separated ones in a double sense; negatively, there is separation from evil, and on the positive side, dedication to God and his service (see Snaith, *Distinctive Ideas*, 29, 30).

In the Old Testament, Israel is God's holy people in precisely these two ways. It is a nation set apart by God's election (see A. Asting, *Die Heiligkeit im Urchristentum* [FRLANT 46; Göttingen: Vandenhoeck & Ruprecht, 1930] 133–51) from the rest of the ancient world (Num 23:9; Ps 147:20); and its national life is distinctive as a witness to God because it is called to be "a holy nation" (Ex 19:5, 6; Lev 11:44, 45; 19:1, 2; Deut 7:6; 14:2). The church is successor to the sacred community of Israel (see 1 Pet 2:9, 10) as the term "saints" denotes. We may observe the added reminder that *hagioi* is found only in the plural in the New Testament, except at Phil 4:21 where, however, the singular form of the word refers to a group. It is applied to all New Testament believers, not to a select body of spiritual elite. See Evans, *Saints,* 29–34, and G. F. Hawthorne, *Philippians* (WBC 43 [Waco: Word Books, 1983] 6) for the moral imperatives associated with the calling of the church as a "holy" company (see 1:12; Evans, 71). The Corinthians, no less than the Philippian believers, are summoned to be God's "saints" as his own people marked by a distinctive way of life and demonstrating the reality of their election by allegiance to God in ethical behavior of the highest order. On the equivalence of ἅγιοι and ἐκλεκτοί (elect) and κλητοί (called), see Delling, "Merkmale," 305.

2. Paul's salutation merges into a benediction-like prayer: χάρις ὑμῖν καὶ εἰρήνη, "grace and peace to you," represents a christianized adaptation of the customary wish expressed in letters of the Greco-Roman culture, namely χαίρειν, "greeting," or πλεῖστα/πολλὰ χαίρειν, "abundant greetings." See E. Lohmeyer, "Briefliche Grussüberschriften," *ZNW* 26 (1927) 158–73, and its critique by G. Friedrich, "Lohmeyers These," *ZNW* 46 (1955) 273, 274, who maintains that the prescript language is Paul's own creation. In Paul's hands the term χαίρειν becomes charged with the force of a powerful, performative wish-prayer which conveys the idea of God's favor (χάρις) to those who do not deserve it ("the primary fact of the Gospel," Menzies, 4) and his strength to match human weakness (see 12:9 for this meaning of χάρις, "grace"). See J. Moffatt, *Grace in the New Testament* (London: Hodder & Stoughton, 1931) 19, and G. D. Fee, "ΧΑΡΙΣ in II Corinthians I. 15," *NTS* 24 (1977–78) 533–38.

Paul adds to "grace" the prayer for God's "peace" (εἰρήνη) in what became for him a standard collocation (Rom 1:7; 1 Cor 1:3; Gal 1:3; Phil 1:2; Col 1:2; 1 Thess 1:1; 2 Thess 1:2; Philem 3: cf. Eph 1:2). "Peace" is a stylized greeting drawn from the semitic world (see J. A. Fitzmyer, "Some Notes on Aramaic Epistolography," *JBL* 93 [1974] 214–16) but its Christian overtones are clearly to be heard in the following phrases, "from God our Father and the Lord Jesus Christ." The nomenclature is here significant, with God's essential title given as "Father" (see on 1:3) and Jesus Christ receiving his usual Pauline appellation, "Lord" (κύριος). On this title see Kramer, sec. 47b, emphasizing how Jesus' lordship spells out "the authority to whom all are answerable for their every action." The coordination of God the Father and Jesus the exalted Lord is no less remarkable and endorses J. G. Machen's observation that "everywhere in the Epistles . . . the attitude of Paul toward Christ is not merely the attitude of man to man, or scholar to master; it is the attitude of man toward God" (*The Origin of Paul's Religion* [New York: Macmillan, 1921] 198).

Explanation

Paul's opening section focuses attention on an issue that will preoccupy him in the remainder of the letter, if in various ways. It is the question of his apostolic authority in the congregation. Clearly this authority was under fire at Corinth and was a matter of warm debate. So it is fitting that at the outset Paul should clearly indicate that such authority as he has is derived from "the Lord himself" (as 13:10 remarks) and is exercised for the "upbuilding" of the church (10:8; 12:9).

The church too is prominently in his sights as God's "holy people," called to reflect the divine character and serve him in the world. Moral problems were a plague-spot at Corinth, and in the last four chapters Paul will have to deal severely with various offending groups. It is again appropriate that at the beginning the nature of the church as God's "sanctified" people should be displayed and held up before this congregation as its calling.

II. The Past Experience of Paul Reviewed (1:3-11)

A. Praise and Encouragements (1:3-7)

Bibliography

Cuming, G. J. *Hippolytus: A Text for Students.* Bramcote: Grove Books, 1976. **Deichgrä-ber, R.** *Der Gotteshymnus und Christushymnus in der frühen Christenheit.* SUNT 5. Göttingen: Vandenhoeck & Ruprecht, 1967. 64–87. **Jeremias, J.** *The Prayers of Jesus I. "Abba."* SBT 2d ser. 6. London: SCM, 1967. 11–65. **Kleinknecht, K. T.** *Der leidende Gerechtfertigte.* WUNT 2d ser. 13. Tübingen: Mohr, 1984. **O'Brien, P. T.** *Introductory Thanksgivings in the Letters of Paul.* NovTSup 49. Leiden: Brill, 1977. 233–58. ———. "Thanksgiving within the Structure of Pauline Theology." In *Pauline Studies: Essays Presented to F. F. Bruce,* ed. D. A. Hagner and M. J. Harris, pp. 50–56. Exeter/Grand Rapids: Paternoster Press/Eerdmans, 1980. **Rissi, M.** *Studien zum zweiten Korintherbrief.* **Robinson, J. M.** "Die Hodajot-Formel in Gebet und Hymnus des Frühchristentums." In *Apophoreta,* FS E. Haenchen, 194–235. BZNW 30. Berlin: Töpelmann, 1964. **Sanders, J. T.** "Hymnic Elements in Eph 1–3." *ZNW* 56 (1965) 214–32. **Schubert, P.** *Form and Function of the Pauline Thanksgivings.* BZNW 20. Berlin: Töpelmann, 1939. **Tannehill, R. C.** *Dying and Rising with Christ. A Study in Pauline Theology.* BZNW 32. Berlin: Töpelmann, 1966. 90–98. **Turner, N.** *Christian Words.* Edinburgh; T. & T. Clark, 1981. **Warfield, B. B.** "Some Difficult Passages in the First Chapter of 2 Corinthians." *JBL* 6 (Dec. 1886) 27–39. **White, J. L.** "Introductory Formulae in the Body of the Pauline Letters." *JBL* 90 (1971) 91–97. **Wiles, G. P.** *Paul's Intercessory Prayers: The Significance of the Intercessory Prayer Passages in the Letters of St. Paul.* SNTSMS 24. Cambridge: University Press, 1974. 226–29.

Translation

[3] *Blessed (be) the God and Father of our Lord Jesus Christ, the Father of mercies and the God of all encouragement.* [4] *He encourages us in all our trial, so that we can encourage those who are in any trial by the (same) encouragement with which we ourselves are encouraged by God.* [5] *For just as Christ's sufferings overflow to us, so also does the encouragement that we receive through Christ overflow.* [6] *If we are facing trials, it is for your encouragement* [a] *and salvation. If we are encouraged, it is for your* [b] *encouragement which (God) produces as you remain steadfast under the same sufferings that we suffer.* [7] *And our hope for you is firmly grounded, because we know that, as you share the sufferings, so too (you share) in the encouragement.*

Notes

[a,b] In vv 6, 7 the manuscript evidence shows a great deal of confusion as to the order of the words (see Bultmann, 29, 30). We have translated the text of א A C supported by bo sa vg syr[p], p[46], which Bultmann rightly regards as original. The meaning, however, is not affected,

with the exception of a decision (followed by B. B. Warfield) to omit "and salvation" with B 33. But this decision is poorly based and omission of the words καὶ σωτηρίας is explained on the principle of scribal puzzlement over difficult words.

Form/Structure/Setting

Paul's use of the formula "Blessed be God" is taken from the synagogue liturgy in which "blessing" (ברכה, *berākāh*), i.e., a tribute of acclamation, was said as an ascription of praise to Israel's God. See S. Singer, *The Authorised Daily Prayer Book*, for examples, and Deichgräber's section (*Gotteshymnus*, 64–87) on "Introductory Eulogy" in the New Testament letters, as well as at Qumran (e.g. 1 QH 3:19 ff.), and in later Christian prayers (e.g., *1 Clem* 59:2, 3; *2 Clem* 1:4–8; Hippolytus, *Apost. Tradition*, sec. 4; Cuming's text, 1–10).

It is a common feature in the later New Testament epistles for writers to break out into an expression of praise at the opening of their letters (Eph 1:3–14; 1 Pet 1:3–9). But where these examples are rich in gratitude to God for the blessings of redemption, the praise of God in our text is specifically focused on Paul's recent past experience of being delivered from some trial in Asia (1:8). Deichgräber, *Gotteshymnus* (87), calls this an example of "a special intervention in a definite case of need."

The form "Blessed is/be God" has been studied in the light of the Qumran hymns, especially the *Hodayoth* scroll, and some far-reaching conclusions drawn as to the nature of early Christian worship (see J. M. Robinson, J. T. Sanders; the topic is briefly discussed by R. P. Martin, in *New Testament Interpretation*, ed. I. H. Marshall [Exeter: Paternoster/Grand Rapids: Eerdmans, 1977] 233, 234). One positive gain of this study has been to set the public reading of the New Testament epistles in congregational worship services where the liturgical language of invocation and praise has its natural place. Paul evidently felt himself at one with his congregations as they assembled for worship (1 Cor 5:3–5; cf. Col 2:5), and it is only to be expected that he would have them in his sights as a worshiping company when he addressed them through his letters. This may well explain the heavy concentration on the prayer- and praise-idiom in the opening parts of his letters (B. Rigaux, *The Letters of St. Paul*, tr. S. Yonick [Chicago: Franciscan Herald Press, 1968] 120–22, and L. G. Champion, *Benedictions and Doxologies in the Epistles of Paul*, [Oxford: publ. privately, 1934]).

The section (1:3–7) is rich in all the telltale marks of *liturgica*, namely, (1) the fulsome description of God as "the Father of mercies," drawn from synagogue prayers; (2) the descriptive participial clause, "He who encourages" (v 4)—for examples in the Greek Old Testament Psalter see Pss 102:1 ff.; 135:3 f., 143:1; 146:7 ff., which employ the participle and the definite article in hymnic patterns: see E. Norden, *Agnostos Theos*, Untersuchungen zur Formengeschichte religiöse Rede (Stuttgart: Teubner, 1956 ed.) 166 ff.—which introduces the key-term "encouragement" (παράκλησις), which in turn runs like a thread through this paragraph and indeed the rest of the letter (see later); and (3) at least one specimen of a chiastic structure in v 5:

A   overflow (περισσεύει)   B'   our encouragement through Christ

B   Christ's sufferings   A'   overflows (περισσεύει)

A more elaborate structural analysis is attempted by Kleinknecht, (*Der leidende Gerechtfertigte*, 243 f.), which brings out the centrality of παράκλησις and θλῖψις.

Comment

The opening section breaks out into jubilant thanksgiving to God (vv 3, 4). O'Brien, *Introductory Thanksgivings*, 254–58, gives a full comment on Paul's habit of opening his letters with thanksgiving related to the epistolary situation of his readers, whatever formal characteristics mark his vocabulary usage; he argues that the form εὐλογητός, "blessed," is used of God's blessing which Paul shared, while εὐχαριστεῖν, "to thank," is restricted in Pauline usage to gratitude expressed to God for his work in the lives of Paul's addressees. The second verb is found at v 11. He further suggests that εὐχαριστεῖν is a word suitable to Gentile readers, whereas εὐλογεῖν is primarily a Jewish formulation. But see W. L. Knox, *Some Hellenistic Elements in Primitive Christianity* (London: Oxford University Press, 1944) 3–7, for a different account on the interrelation of the two verbs, pointing to the OT-Jewish background of εὐχαριστεῖν. The chief themes of Paul's rejoicing are contained in the reasons for the apostle's outburst. One reason is given in this section; the next is picked up in vv 8–11.

Paul is glad that, in spite of the many troubles that have weighed upon him, he has known the special strength given by God (v 4). Suffering for Christ's sake was ever his destiny as the apostle to the Gentiles (1 Thess 2:2: cf. Col 1:24; Eph 3:13). In Luke's narrative this vocation was made known to him at the commencement of his Christian life (cf. Acts 9:15, 16). Out of that continuing experience came Paul's sense of kinship with his churches which often had to endure trial in a pagan world. And he joins together his vocation with that of his people who in passing through troubled times learn with him to receive divine encouragement and to minister that encouragement to others. This is the theme before us.

3. ὁ πατὴρ τῶν οἰκτιρμῶν, "the Father of mercies," is obviously a semitic expression, patterned on the prayer of the synagogue. "O our Father, merciful Father" (אָב הָרַחֲמִים, *'āb hāraḥᵃmîm*) introduces the Jewish confession of Israel's faith, the *shemaʿ* (A. Marmorstein, *The Old Rabbinic Doctrine of God* [New York: KTAV Publ., reprint, 1968] 56). Other examples, including the prayers at Qumran (e.g., 1QH 10:14; 11:29, which have "God of mercies"; "Father of mercies" as a precise ascription has not appeared in DSS: O'Brien, 241) are given in R. Deichgräber, *Gotteshymnus*, 93, 94. See too J. Jeremias, "Abba," 27, who concludes that the phrase is more than just "merciful Father"; it characterizes what God is in himself, the fountain of mercy (similarly Windisch, 38, who speaks of the phrase as implying not simply "merciful Father" [gen. of quality] but God as "the creator and original source of mercy" [objective gen.]). He is the Father "from whom mercy comes" (Lietzmann-Kümmel),

citing Exod 34:6; Ps 25:6; 68:17, (LXX 69:16) and he shows his favor in his "comfort" (Rom 15:5).

παράκλησις, "encouragement," is a key-word controlling the following discussion (Windisch: on the verb see O. Schmitz-G. Stählin, *TDNT* 5:773–99; Tannehill, *Dying and Rising*, 90–98; O'Brien, *Introductory Thanksgivings*, 242–47). The root in verb and noun forms is found ten times in five verses. The same Greek root is frequently found throughout the epistle (in 8:4, 17 as a noun; in 2:8; 5:20; 6:1; 8:6; 9:5; 10:1; 12:8, 18 as a verb; other references in 2 Cor are 2:7; 7:4, 6, 7, 13; 13:11). The various contexts dictate that no one meaning is sufficient, and "no single translation will suffice" (Barrett, 60). Clearly, with a background in this paragraph of Paul's trials and his deliverance we need the emphasis on "comfort" (Heb. נחם, *niham*) which has a special nuance implying Paul's share in the messianic deliverance promised in the Old Testament (Isa 40:1; 51:3, 12, 19) and described in the role of messiah as Israel's "comforter." "Comfort," however, though preferred by Barrett, is an ambiguous modern rendering; and we opt for "encourage"/"encouragement" rather than "comfort" (RSV, NIV) or "consolation" (NEB, Héring). TEV/GNB paraphrases as "the God from whom all help comes!" See F. V. Filson, "The God of all Comfort—2 Cor. 1:3–7," *TT* 8 (1951–52) 495–501.

4. Ἐπὶ πάσῃ τῇ θλίψει ἡμῶν, "in all our trial"; this term "trial" often has an eschatological flavor, denoting the stress to come on the church as a prelude to the end-time (see R. P. Martin, *Philippians* [NCB, 1976 = 1980] 164). In this context it is more closely linked with "the sentence of death" in v 9. See later for the probable reason why Paul feared a premature death. But the second allusion to θλῖψις, "trial," in v 4 widens the scope of the term to include the lot of Christians in the world where hostility for the Gospel's sake may well be expected. NIV, which renders "trouble/troubles," is decidedly weak and fails to catch the sense of Paul's trial and the Corinthians' affliction as their lot destined by their allegiance to the Gospel; it also minimizes the "divine purpose" (Rissi, *Studien*, 34) that runs through all these experiences. Rissi notices too how Paul's strengthening by God in time of trial leads him to be able to help others.

εἰς τό + infinitive (δύνασθαι), "so that we can," may indicate either purpose or result (BDF § 402.2), probably the latter here. Windisch (39) gives illustrations from Epictetus (*Diss* III. 23.8) and Seneca (*Cons. ad Polyb.* 15.5) of the principle that in human experience sufferers can aid those in like circumstances to their own.

5, 6. τὰ παθήματα τοῦ Χριστοῦ, "Christ's sufferings," is a notable crux. Barrett, 61, indicates how two ideas are combined: (1) the sufferings experienced by Christ, which are "extended so as to reach and be shared by others"; and (2) messianic sufferings, based on a Jewish doctrine of חבלי המשיח (*heblê hammašîah*), lit., "the afflictions of messiah," implying not the sufferings endured by the messiah but rather sufferings associated with him in the messianic age and as a prelude to the coming age of bliss. In the context that includes the phrase that such messianic sufferings "overflow to us" (i.e., "which fall to our lot," Lietzmann-Kümmel) it is preferable to adopt the second alternative. Paul has in view Christ's ongoing sufferings that are endured in the church under the trial and specifically the apostolic ministry in his (Paul's) own person (Phil 3:10; cf. Col 1:24; Eph 3:13) and his labor for Christ's cause. There is thus a divine purpose in Paul's suffering which is borne for the Gospel's sake. See E. Best, *One Body in Christ*, (London: SPCK, 1955) 131, 132, and E. Güttgemanns, *Der leidende Apostel und sein Herr: Studien zur paulinischen Christologie*. FRLANT 90 (Göttingen: Vandenhoeck & Ruprecht, 1966) 323–28.

Paul also knew divine succor and strength, called here "encouragement we receive through Christ." That too reaches out to include his congregations, especially the Corinthians who caused him so much pain (cf. 4:12, 11:28). This is how presumably we should understand the enigmatic phrase that follows: if we are facing trials (εἴτε δὲ θλιβόμεθα, whence the term θλῖψις in v 4), it is for your encouragement (BDF § 231.2 for ὑπέρ, "on your behalf") *and salvation*. The final words, καὶ σωτηρίας, are difficult. They are best understood, not as personal salvation which might imply that Paul was a savior figure, though he does play something of a mediating role between Christ and the Corinthians (Windisch, 39). But the term means either the church's protection from evil or its preservation in its wholeness or health, its chief good ("zu eurem Besten," Bultmann, 29; the word σωτηρία can mean that, as in Acts 27:34; Phil 2:12 on which see J. H. Michael, "Work out your own salvation," *Expositor* 9th ser. 12 [1924], 439–50, and R. P. Martin, *Philippians* [NCB 1976 = 1980], 103, citing Phil 1:19, 28). The close connection between Christ's passion (Phil 3:10) and Paul's experience is brought out in J. D. G. Dunn, *Jesus and the Spirit* (London: SCM Press, 1975) 332, 449, 450.

6. Εἴτε παρακαλούμεθα, ὑπὲρ τῆς ὑμῶν παρακλήσεως τῆς ἐνεργουμένης ἐν ὑπομονῇ τῶν αὐτῶν παθημάτων ὧν καὶ ἡμεῖς πάσχομεν, "If we are encouraged, it is for your encouragement which (God) produces as you remain steadfast under the same sufferings that we suffer."

The main translation issue is to know how to take the participle ἐνεργουμένης, whether or not it is a true passive, "which is effected," i.e., "made effectual by your steadfastness," or is to be seen as a "divine passive." In the latter case God's working is in view (so K. W. Clark, "The meaning of ἐνεργέω and καταργέω in the New Testament," *JBL* 54 [1935] 93–101) as he effects in their steadfastness the encouragement the Corinthians need. We have followed this second line. Barrett, 62, gives an active sense to the participle, which is less acceptable.

Either way, the meaning is tolerably clear, however. When Paul undergoes apostolic sufferings, it is to benefit the churches (4:12). When God encourages him in his trials, the effect is seen in the strength also given—but not magically nor mystically (Bultmann, 31; Strachan, 47, 48)—to afflicted believers. Just how the Corinthians were suffering, we cannot say, apart from the obvious way in which suffering is the lot of the people of God in a hostile world (cf. 2 Tim 3:12). But it is important to observe here a practical outworking of Paul's teaching in 1 Cor 12:26; Rom 12:15, and just as important, it is necessary to stress, with Bachmann (35), that in this opening section we meet the situation that was at the heart of the debate between Paul and his Corinthian converts. Suffering and divine encouragement given to Paul in his weakness are the very issues that spoke to the Corinthian scene (especially in the confrontation in chaps. 10–13); so this introduction "fixes" the exact particularity of our letter as Paul's response of "strength-in-weakness" directed to the Corinthians' questioning of his apostleship because he was a suffering figure and carried no exemption from trial, as his enemies in the last four chapters evidently pointed out to the Corinthians. This conclusion may stand even if Paul's idioms of "affliction-comfort" are—in part—based on the figure of the righteous sufferer in Jewish thought (so Kleinknecht, *Der leidende Gerechtfertigte*, 245–49).

7. Καὶ ἡ ἐλπὶς ἡμῶν βεβαία ὑπὲρ ὑμῶν, εἰδότες ὅτι ὡς κοινωνοί ἐστε τῶν παθημάτων, οὕτως καὶ τῆς παρακλήσεως, "And our hope for you is firmly grounded, because we know that, as you share the sufferings, so too (you share) in the encouragement."

What unites the apostle's present trials and the carryover of his encouragement into the lives of his people is a "confidence" (lit., "hope," ἐλπίς, which in the New Testament has the normal meaning of "strong assurance"; and for Paul, is "never tinged with nervousness or alarm, as in secular contexts" [Turner, *Christian Words*, 214]), the confidence he cherished that all is well with his readers. His hope is "firm" (βεβαία), a commercial term meaning what is secure and gilt-edged as a reliable security. It has some reference to the divine promises (Rom 4:16), and Paul will use it later as a verb (in 1:21) for the divine character. Paul knows that God can be counted on both to sustain the church in trouble and to bring it through as in 1 Cor 15:58. This is the chief reason for his exultant praise (v 3) which leads into the language of prayer (v 7: see Wiles, *Paul's Intercessory Prayers*, 228). The key-term is κοινωνοί, "sharers," implying a joint participation in a reality outside the believers' experience (H. Seesemann, *Der Begriff KOINONIA im Neuen Testament*, BZNW 14 [Giessen: Töpelmann, 1933] 73–83 on Phil 1:5). In this case it is a common sharing in divine παράκλησις, "encouragement," which, Paul remarks, sustains the church in ὑπομονή, i.e., endurance of their trials (Bultmann, 31). We should, however, observe with O'Brien, *Introductory Thanksgivings*, 247, 248, that while the Corinthians share in the messianic woes, they do not endure precisely the same trial (θλῖψις) that the apostle met (v 6). In fact, we do not know the precise nature of the church's sufferings, yet they are linked with "Christ's afflictions."

Explanation

Paul is glad that, in spite of the many troubles that have weighed upon him—and in the light of 11:28 we should not exclude his "anxiety for all the congregations" committed to his pastoral charge, especially at Corinth—he has known the special strength afforded him by God (v 4).

There is a divine purpose in human suffering that is borne for the Gospel's sake. Thereby the cause of Christ is advanced (see Acts 14:22; Col 1:24 ff.). But one special reason is given in our passage. Those who receive encouragement from God are qualified to enter sympathetically into the experience of others whose pathway leads them through a vale of tears (vv 4, 6, 7). "Sympathy is love perfected by experience" adds Goudge, so Paul the apostle is not a man who lives a detached existence, untroubled by hard knocks in life; and by the same token he is no aloof pastor, remote from the people to whom he ministers. And the conclusion from this moving section seems clear: *"Qui in uno genere afflictionum fuit, in eo potissimum potest alios consolari; qui in omni in omni"* (Bengel), that is, "he who has experienced one kind of affliction is particularly qualified to console others in the same and all circumstances."

B. Paul's Trial in Asia   (1:8–11)

Bibliography

Baumert, N. *Täglich Sterben und Auferstehen. Der Literalsinn von 2 Kor 4, 12–5, 10.* SANT 34. Munich: Kösel-Verlag, 1973. **Deissmann, A.** *Light from the Ancient East.* Tr. R. M. Strachan. London: Hodder & Stoughton, 1927. ———. *Bible Studies.* Tr. A. Grieve. Edinburgh: T. & T. Clark, 1903. **Dunn, J. D. G.** *Jesus and the Spirit.* London: SCM Press, 1975. 206, 259. **Hemer, C. J.** "A Note on 2 Corinthians 1:9." *TynB* 23 (1972) 103–7. **Hoffmann, P.** *Die Toten in Christus.* Münster: Aschendorff, 1966. 234, 247, 328 f., 344. **Nägeli, Th.** *Der Wortschatz des Apostels Paulus.* Göttingen: Vandenhoeck & Ruprecht, 1905. 30. **Singer, S.** *Authorised Daily Prayer Book.* London: Eyre and Spottiswoode, 1925. **Stanley, D. M.** *Christ's Resurrection in Pauline Soteriology.* AnBib 13. Rome: Pontificio Istituto Biblico, 1960. 129–131. **Steinmetz, F. J.** " 'So dass wir keinen Ausweg mehr sahen' (2 Kor 1, 8). "Apostolische Mühsal bei Paulus—und heute." *GuL* 41 (5, 1968) 321–26. **White, J. L.** *The Form and Function of the Body of the Greek Letter.* Missoula, MT: Scholars Press, 1972. **Young, N. M.** ". . . 'To make us rely not on ourselves but on God who raises the dead'—2 Cor 1, 9b as the Heart of Paul's Theology," *Die Mitte des Neuen Testament.* FS Eduard Schweizer, ed. U. Luz and H. Weder, 384–98. Göttingen: Vandenhoeck & Ruprecht, 1983.

Translation

⁸ *We want you to know, then, brothers, about the affliction that came to us [in the province of] Asia. We were under extreme pressure beyond our power [to cope], so that we despaired even of life itself.* ⁹ *Indeed, it seemed to us that we had received the death sentence, that we should trust no longer in ourselves, but in the God who raises the dead.* ¹⁰ *It is God who rescued us from so menacing a death,* ᵃ *and he will rescue* ᵇ *us. We have set our hope on him that* ᶜ *he will rescue us yet again,* ¹¹ *if you also work with us by your prayer. Then from many people* ᵈ *thanks may be rendered to God on* ᵉ *our behalf for the gracious gift granted us through the help of many people.*

Notes

ᵃ ἐκ τηλικούτου θανάτου. The plural forms τηλικούτων θανάτων are read by P⁴⁶, 630 1739ᵛ·¹· vg: *de tantis periculis* syrᵖ Orig. Ambst. and evidently translated by TEV: "such terrible dangers of death." See Bratcher, *Translator's Guide,* 11. Kümmel, 197, regards the later reference to the plural (in 11:23) as influencing the scribe. Allo's translation "such a prolonged death" implies that it was the danger of death that was continual (11:23; 1 Cor 15:31) and this rendering would be permissible if the plurals were authentic. On the other hand, G. Zuntz, *The Text of the Epistles* (London: Oxford University Press, 1953) 104, regards the plural ("out of such tremendous, mortal dangers") as bearing "the stamp of genuine Pauline diction. . . . The singular clearly arose from the pedantic idea that no one could risk more than one death." But we may query whether the text speaks only of "mortal dangers" and the "risk" of death. Does it not rather reflect Paul's encounter with death itself? If so, the singular form has to be correct.

[b] καὶ ῥύσεται is read by P[46] ℵ B etc., whereas a present tense of the verb (καὶ ῥύεται) is presumably an attempt (in the later uncials D[3] E F G K L M syr[h] vg) to "improve" the meaning. See G. Zuntz, *Text*, 197.

[c] Retaining ὅτι with ℵ A and TR, whereas P[46] B D* 1739 omit. The latter omission is preferred by Zuntz, *Text*, 196, and Barrett, 57 n. 2, who judges the older text to be "awkward and repetitive." Bultmann, 34, sees here an instance of a periphrastic doublet resulting from the dictation to the scribe.

[d] Lit., "from many faces (= persons)." P[46] G M have a singular ἐν πολλῷ προσώπῳ which Héring wants to take as "in the presence of many people" giving to πρόσωπον the OT meaning of "face" (cf. Allo, 13 f.; Plummer, 21 f.; Tasker, 44; Bachmann ["von vielen Angesichtern," 44]), but this is difficult, as Hughes, 23 f., notes. The best attested text has plural forms: ἐκ πολλῶν προσώπων, but this looks tautologous in view of the parallel phrase διὰ πολλῶν later in the verse. See *Comment*.

[e] Reading ὑπὲρ ἡμῶν rather than ὑπὲρ ὑμῶν (P[46] B D[2] and uncials).

Form/Structure/Setting

Bachmann (35) wishes to see a new section of Paul's thought opening at v 8. He calls attention to the address "brothers" (ἀδελφοί) and the introductory formulation (οὐ γὰρ θέλομεν ὑμᾶς ἀγνοεῖν, "for we do want you to know," cf. Phil 1:12) as well as the stylistic difference between vv 8 ff. and vv 3–7. After the liturgical style and rhetorical idiom in the earlier verses, v 8 introduces a section which lacks these features. So, Bachmann infers, we should see 1:8 as beginning the major division of the letter (from 1:8 to 7:16).

Bultmann (32) objects that 1:8–7:16 is no unified section, and maintains that the opening part (the *proem*) extends to v 11. He notes the connective γάρ, "for," "then," as indicating a connection with vv 3–7 and 8–11, and comments convincingly that the "sufferings" and "encouragement" (in vv 3–7) point forward to some specific occasion, referred to in vv 8–11. Similar conclusions are reached by P. T. O'Brien, *Introductory Thanksgivings*, 235, 236. As further evidence that Paul has some specific occasion in mind (which Hoffmann, *Die Toten*, 328, denies on insufficient grounds) and that Paul's bitter experience of θλῖψις in Asia affected his writing of this letter (especially 4:16–5:10), we may appeal to the lexical note in BGD, xxvii, on the verb ῥύομαι with ἐκ τοῦ θανάτου: this does not mean "preserve from death" in general, but "rescue from a(n actual) situation in which death was threatened."

This pericope is linked by a series of catch-phrases, notably at v 10 (ἐρρύσατο . . . ῥύσεται . . . ῥύσεται: "he delivered . . . he will deliver . . . he will deliver"). Allo (13) and Menzies (9) prefer to retain the textual variant ῥύεται (in v 10), found in a large number of manuscripts, on the ground that this reading (present tense) will then produce the chronological series: past, present, future. But the omission of ῥύεται makes better sense.

The positioning of the words in v 11 is also artistic; hence the slightly ambiguous result, making literal translation difficult. The sentence appears to be overloaded (so Héring); there is a "a fussy mode of expression" (Windisch). Plummer writes understandably of "a perplexing sentence." Perhaps the reason is the chiastic form in 11*b:*

A   ἐκ πολλῶν προσώπων ⎯⎯⎯⎯⎯⎯⎯⎯ B'   εὐχαριστηθῇ

B   χάρισμα   ⎯⎯⎯⎯⎯⎯⎯⎯ A'   διὰ πολλῶν

Much depends on how εὐχαριστηθῇ ("thanks may be rendered" or "God may be thanked") is taken. Héring wants to adopt an alternative meaning of εὐχαριστεῖν as "to request" or "to bestow favor." He then renders the entire part-sentence: "In order that the favour which you do me (τὸ εἰς ἡμᾶς χάρισμα) may be bestowed through the prayers of many people (διὰ πολλῶν εὐχαριστηθῇ)." At all events Paul is expressing his indebtedness to the Corinthians for their intercessions which have resulted in many persons opening their mouths in praise to God for his delivering mercies shown to him. The "grace" (χάρισμα) is the work of God freely given (a divine passive construction, making God the hidden agent), even if human caring is not neglected. On the passive voice of the verb εὐχαριστηθῇ see P. Schubert, *Form and Function of the Pauline Thanksgivings*, 46 ff., and O'Brien, *Introductory Thanksgivings*, 250–54; cf. BDF § 312.2.

Comment

8. οὐ γὰρ θέλομεν ὑμᾶς ἀγνοεῖν, lit., "for we do not wish you not to know" (with parallels in 8:1; Rom 1:13; 11:25; 1 Cor 10:1; 12:1; 1 Thess 4:13; see White, *Form and Function* for this disclosure formula). Paul uses this idiomatic expression as a way of calling attention to the second reason for his thanks to God. He sets the deliverance he has known against the background of "the affliction that came to" him in the Roman province of Asia. Evidently some particular event, or set of events, is in his mind, but it is not easy to pinpoint the precise detail (Allo, 15–19, has an extended note on the kinds of peril Paul faced). The text (in vv 8, 9) suggests an experience that drove Paul to the edge of despair (the verb ἐξαπορεῖν in the passive, "to be in great difficulty" [BGD], recurs in 4:8 as well as Ps 87:16, LXX: "It is a kind of paroxysm of anguish which banishes all hope," remarks Héring) and led him even to the gate of death. He was "burdened" (ἐβαρήθημεν, like an overladen ship) by a grievous trial. Paul even adds one of his favorite expressions καθ' ὑπερβολήν, "extreme," lit., "excessively," as in Rom 7:13; 1 Cor 12:31; 2 Cor 4:17; Gal 1:13. And the added emphasis "beyond our power" (ὑπὲρ δύναμιν) is found in 8:3; cf. 1 Cor 10:13. Such pleonasms point to the intensity of the experience Paul endured and has in his vivid recall.

9, 10. "We had received" (ἐσχήκαμεν: the tense of the verb is perfect, which is how Menzies understands it: "we received in our own mind the answer 'Death' and feel it to this day"). But this is to overtranslate, and we should regard the tense as the same as the aorist (as in 2:13); see BDF § 343; Hughes, 9; Windisch, 46; Bultmann, 32. The sense, then, is that Paul, on reflection, accepted the sentence of death and "ceased rebelling against the idea of his premature death" (Héring, 5). But there is no denying that his language is weighed down with thoughts of death's inevitability—as he viewed his circumstances at a time of great affliction in Asia. For how much credibility we should give to the inference that Paul was a prisoner in Ephesus and whether any or all of the so-called "prison letters" (especially Phil, Col, Philem) originated at this time and from Ephesus, see the survey of the data (mainly inferential) in Martin, *Philippians* (NCB) 48–57.

The description of God as one "who raises the dead" (see Deut 32:39; 1 Sam 2:6, LXX) is drawn from a well-attested understanding of God's power in the Jewish liturgy. The second prayer in the Eighteen Benedictions runs: "Thou, O Lord, art mighty forever, thou makest the dead to live" (Str-B 3:242; Singer, *Authorised Daily Prayer Book*, 44). On Rom 4:17 which repeats the thought of God's power over death, see E. Käsemann, *Perspectives on Paul*, tr. M. Kohl (Philadelphia: Fortress Press, 1971) 90. But we should be careful to include with the appeal to Rom 4:17 the reminder that for Paul the God who "raises the dead" derives not from his acquaintance with Jewish prayers but from "the radical faith" (Bultmann, 33) in the God who raised the once-crucified Jesus to life. And Paul relates this demonstration of divine grace to his own circumstances of need (Windisch, 48).

God's deliverance lifted Paul from the threat of "so great a death" as τηλικοῦτος θάνατος literally means. Yet as Barrett notes, "so great" is colorless and unimaginative: hence we render "so menacing a death" (NIV is hardly strong enough with "such a deadly peril"). Past deliverance gives the apostle an assurance that God will rescue him in the future; but in 2 Cor 5:1–10 Paul will go on to explain what that confidence entails, in both life and death. The theological basis for his hope (ἐλπίς) is provided in Rom 4:17, 18: Abraham in hope believed that God gives life to the dead and calls things that are not as though they were. For the tense, see Moulton, *Grammar* 1:145; BDF § 343.2, possibly suggesting with Héring that Paul could not resist the pressure of events that bore down on him as "the death sentence."

The last turn of phrase (τὸ ἀπόκριμα τοῦ θανάτου) is much disputed. The options are that Paul was referring (1) to the riot in the Ephesian theater (Acts 19:23–41, which may or may not be connected with a time of social anarchy which followed the assassination of the proconsul, M. Junius Silanus: see G. S. Duncan, *St. Paul's Ephesian Ministry* [London: Hodder & Stoughton, 1929] 100–107); (2) to a much more perilous risk to his life, arising from the same breakdown of law and order, suggested by his being exposed to the beasts in the arena (1 Cor 15:32: see B. B. Warfield, *JBL* 6 [1886] 34; A. J. Malherbe, "The Beasts at Ephesus," *JBL* 87 [1968] 71–80); (3) to a sentence of death passed on Paul in the civil courts (so Deissmann, *Bible Studies*, 257, who calls attention to the technical language in this phrase, like our modern expression, "death-warrant," and D. M. Stanley, *Christ's Resurrection*, 129). But (4) this last suggestion is denied by C. J. Hemer, "A Note," who insists that the term is not juridical but has a neutral flavor. While it may be rendered "verdict," it has, Hemer contends, no forensic connotation. The answer God gave was "death," i.e., Paul would not escape death before the Parousia (5:1–10) nor was he exempt from bodily sufferings (12:8, 9). But this reconstruction lifts the verse out of its immediate context since Paul did not die in Asia but lived to tell the tale and write 2 Corinthians! (5) Others (e.g., Allo, 18, who interprets the language of vv 8–10 to refer to bodily sickness which was longstanding and recurrent; M. J. Harris, "2 Corinthians 5:1–10: Watershed in Paul's Eschatology?" [*TynB* 22 1971] 57, who also interprets the allusion to severe sickness; cf. H. Clavier, "La santé de l'apôtre Paul," in *Studia Paulina in honorem Johannis de Zwaan* [Haarlem: 1953] 66–82) relate Paul's trial to the onset of serious health problems, noting that the danger seems to have arisen from within Paul's life rather than from outside (Barrett, Allo: see on his "stake in the flesh," 12:7; but this connection is by no means obvious).

A lot depends, in reaching a tentative decision in the matter, on the meaning of the "thorn" and how much weight we should give to the Jewish link between a sickness leading a person near to death and God's healing described as "resurrection" (Ps 85:6; 119:25; Hos 6:2; see E. Jacob, *Theology of the Old Testament,* tr. A. W. Heathcote and P. J. Allcock [London: Hodder & Stoughton, 1958] 308). On the other side, the clause "that we should trust no longer in ourselves" suggests a set of circumstances where Paul might have extricated himself by personal effort but chose not to do so. That hardly fits in with a bout of sickness, and we should probably think of some hardship ("serious physical violence," so Strachan, 52, leading to exposure to death itself, from which only God could save him, v 10: see O'Brien, *Introductory Thanksgivings,* 249) suffered out of loyalty to the Gospel, which he refused to compromise. N. M. Young, ". . . To make us rely," submits that this verse holds the key to unlock the secret of Paul's entire theology—a bold claim! Héring (3) makes the perceptive remark that Paul feared the prospect of death not for his own sake, but because death would prematurely cut short the eschatological mission of evangelizing Gentiles and so delay the end-time.

11. Paul "remembers that God acts through the prayers of his people" (Barrett, 67) in a sequence of thought similar to Phil 1:19. The picturesque verb (συνυπουργούντων; lit, "working together to support [me]"), a participle which RSV translates as an implied imperative ("you also must help us by prayer," but TEV renders the verb form as a clause of attendant circumstances, "as you help us by means of your prayers"; our translation offers a third option), recalls the part played by the intercessions of Paul's friends who stood with him in his apostolic mission (2 Thess 3:1–3). The value Paul set upon these prayers of supplication is seen in the consequence: many people will have occasion to give thanks to God for the "favor" (χάρισμα; i.e., his deliverance [Dunn, *Jesus and the Spirit,* 206]) freely granted (εὐχαριστηθῇ) by God in answer to "the many," i.e., the loyal Corinthians who have prayed for Paul. Normally we associate Paul's prayers for his congregations with what he has to say regarding prayer; here it is their prayers for him that are praised. "The many" (οἱ πολλοί) suggests the majority of the Corinthian church who had recently declared their allegiance to the apostolic ministry in a time of testing and had dissociated themselves from the recalcitrant person(s) who had fomented a rebellion against Paul (2:6; 7:12). This exegesis, we submit, is preferable to that which sees two classes of persons in Paul's word "many" (ἐκ πολλῶν . . . διὰ πολλῶν). If the text is not corrupt—a suggestion made because it looks overloaded and convoluted—Paul's wording is deliberately emphatic in praising "the many" who were on his side. Otherwise, with Bratcher's suggestion (*Translator's Guide,* 12), we might think that Paul's commendation of the first group of "many" is meant to influence a second group. So he translates: "Many people will pray [to God] for us, and God

will answer their prayers and bless us. And so many [others] will thank God for blessing us." But this seems a needless expedient. Cf. Baumert, *Täglich Sterben*, 106.

Explanation

In retelling this account—even if with some tantalizing obscurities—of his ordeal in Asia, Paul makes it plain that he was saved from the jaws of death by God's signal mercy and favor in answer to his prayer. Yet God worked through the prayers of his people (v 11), and Paul does not forget this side of the story as well. Those who prayed for him (and Paul's verb in v 11 is remarkably expressive to remind us that prayer is both a work, as in Col 4:12, 13, and a privilege to be in partnership with those in need) are invited to share his gladness. There is no finer stimulus to our prayers than when we hear from some friend at home or abroad that he or she is rejoicing in an answer to our praying on his or her behalf.

III. Transition to the Letter's First Theme (1:12–14)

Bibliography

Bultmann, R. *Theology of the New Testament 1.* Tr. K. Grobel, London: SCM Press, 1952. 211–20. **Hahn, F.** "Das Ja des Paulus und das Ja Gottes. Bermerkungen zu 2 Kor 1:12–2:11." FS Herbert Braun, ed. H.-D. Betz & L. Schottroff, *Neues Testament und christliche Existenz,* 229–38. Tübingen: J. C. B. Mohr, 1973. **Jewett, R.** *Paul's Anthropological Terms: A Study of Their Use in Conflict Settings.* AGJU 10. Leiden: Brill, 1971. 402–46, 458–60. **Pierce, C. A.** *Conscience in the New Testament.* SBT 15. London: SCM Press, 1955. **Rissi, M.** *Studien zum zweiten Korintherbrief,* 43. **Schnackenburg, R.** *The Moral Teaching of the New Testament.* Tr. J. Holland-Smith and W. J. O'Hara, New York: Herder and Herder, 1968. 287–96. **Spicq, C.** "Conscience." *EBT* 1. 131-134. **Thrall, M. E.** "The Pauline Use of ΣΥΝΕΙΔΗΣΙΣ." *NTS* 14 (1967–68) 118–25.
———. "2 Corinthians 1:12: ΑΓΙΟΤΗΤΙ or ΑΠΛΟΤΗΤΙ?" In *Studies in New Testament Language and Text,* ed. J. K. Elliott, 366–72. NovTSup 44. Leiden: Brill, 1976.

Translation

[12] *Our confidence* [a] *is this: the testimony of our conscience that we behaved in the world, and more particularly in our dealings with you, with honesty* [b] *and sincerity like that of God,* [c] *not with worldly* [d] *wisdom but [in reliance on] the grace of God.* [13] *Now we are not writing to you anything different from what you read or from what you recognize.* [e] *And I hope that you will recognize it fully,* [f] [14] *just as you have recognized us partially, that we are your confidence, as you too are our confidence, in the light of the Day of the Lord Jesus.*

Notes

[a] καύχησις, "reason for boasting" (BGD), in this context seems to refer more specifically to Paul's "confidence" in his life and ministry as commissioned by God than a claim to "our boast" (NIV). The root καυχ- is found 29 times in 2 Cor, a total exceeding Paul's usage in all his other epistles. The idea of "boasting" is especially important in 2 Cor 10:13: see later. On the importance of the word for Paul see R. Bultmann, *TDNT* 3:646–54.

[b] Reading ἁπλότητι (ℵ² D F G lat syr), meaning "simplicity." The rival reading is ἁγιότητι (holiness) attested by P⁴⁶ ℵ* A B. The consonants are obviously similar, leading to scribal confusion. Paul, however, does not elsewhere use precisely the word ἁγιότης; the contrast with "worldly wisdom" and what Paul writes in v 13 endorse the choice for ἁπλότητι (Lietzmann, 101), and the context requires a term to denote Paul's self-defensive posture against insinuations of duplicity (Barrett). Ἁπλότης is found in this epistle at 8:2; 9:11, 13; 11:3; Rom 12:8. See M. E. Thrall, "2 Cor 1:12," for a balanced defense of the reading ἁγιότης, granting that the evidence is plentiful on both sides. Her strongest point in favor of "holiness" is that Paul may well have been accused of corrupt practice (4:2; 12:16 [and 2:17, which she does not cite]) in the matter of the collection (371, 372). But, as she admits, even then, ἁπλότης would be the more natural opposing partner to πανουργία.

[c] τοῦ θεοῦ, "of God," clearly belongs to the two preceding nouns in a hendiadys (Bultmann, 37).

ᵈ σαρκικῇ, lit., "fleshly." Σάρξ, "flesh," often carries for Paul a negative connotation of a person's proud self-assertiveness and independence of God. 1 Cor 1:21–2:16 describes the folly of human wisdom when it sets itself in opposition to God. A uniform translation is not possible; we have opted for "worldly" in the sense of pertaining to this "world" (αἰών, the term in 1 Cor 2:8; or κόσμος, as in 1 Cor 1:20; 7:31, 33).

ᵉ There is a play on the words ἀναγινώσκω and ἐπιγινώσκω (though P⁴⁶ B omit this second verb, evidently by mistake: Barrett, 63 n.2). The pun "apprehend and comprehend" has been suggested. Paul's claim is that there are no hidden, esoteric meanings in his letters, so "you don't have to read between the lines" (Moffatt's transl.) to get the sense. But see under next section.

ᶠ ἕως τέλους, lit., "to the end"; 1 Cor 13:12b suggests the translation "completely, fully" in contrast to "in part" (so here ἀπὸ μέρους in v 14). See Windisch, 57, 58, who cites P. Oxy. XIV. 1681 for this meaning of ἀπὸ μέρους; and this contrast makes ἕως τέλους an adverbial expression equivalent to εἰς τέλος in classical Greek.

Form/Structure/Setting

The form of this pericope is one of *apologia*. Paul is clearly on the defensive, and needs to state unambiguously that his motives in past dealings with the Corinthians have been always well-intentioned and sincere, i.e., without duplicity. The charge of "fickleness" leveled at him will come to the surface at v 17. Here he meets the objection in advance. This explains the heavy "theological" appeal in vv 12, 14, especially the appeal to the eschatological "Day of the Lord Jesus" when all human motives will be exposed and judged (1 Cor 4:4, 5).

Two sets of contrast play off the insinuation and Paul's spirited rebuttal: (1) "earthly (σαρκική) wisdom" vs. "the grace of God." The same contrast recurs in 10:4: "we do not wage war according to the flesh (κατὰ σάρκα), for the weapons of our warfare are not fleshly (σαρκικά) but are powerful from God." "Grace" (χάρις) and "power" (δύναμις) are virtual synonyms: see 12:9. (2) As was already noted, there is a play on the root γνω- (v 13): What we are writing to you is in no way different from what you read (ἀναγινώσκετε) or can understand (ἐπιγινώσκετε). This suggests that Paul is accused of deliberate obscurity in his letter-writing style in order to conceal his mixed motives (Strachan). Or else Paul is being reproached for saying the opposite of what he had in mind. The dialectic of v 17 suggests that this second interpretation is preferable.

The pericope is framed by an *inclusio*, that is, the framing of a writer's thought by identical or similar ideas at the beginning and the end of the section. καύχησις ἡμῶν ("our confidence," v 12) is picked up at v 14 ("we are your confidence," καύχημα ὑμῶν). This puts the emphasis where the apostle wants it to rest, namely, on establishing mutual relations of integrity and probity between the two groups (himself, the Corinthian believers) at a time when the relationships were sorely strained.

Comment

12–14. The chief thrust of the paragraph (which is best taken as a unit) is to convey Paul's asseveration of his own reliability as an apostle, which was the target of his enemies' attack at Corinth. He warmly responds in several ways: (1) his conscience (see C. A. Pierce, *Conscience;* M. E. Thrall, "The Pauline Use"; H. C. Hahn–C. Brown, *NIDNTT* 1: 348–53) is clear that his conduct has been exemplary as he has relied on God's help. "Conscience" (συνείδησις) may be picking up a term much in vogue at Corinth (Pierce, 60–65). The Corinthians, on this theory, were appealing to their "conscience" to justify certain types of moral behavior (as in 1 Cor 8, 10: so Jewett, *Paul's Anthropological Terms,* 436: "it was . . . the Corinthians who introduced συνείδησις into Christian theology"). Paul entered the debate on the side of an insistence that conscience alone is not an infallible guide and must be subordinated to a wider network of issues that bear on a person's relationship to God and his or her neighbor's well-being. Pierce's negative judgment, however, that "conscience" in Paul leads only to a person's experience of guilt and remorse has been criticized by Thrall with reference to 2 Cor 4:2; 5:11. She argues that "Paul's conscience can bear witness to the holiness and sincerity of his conduct in 2 Cor 1:12" (125). Pierce (86) has to regard 1:12 as an "exception to make trial of [the] rule."

In the case of Paul's claim that *his* conscience is clear, he is willing to have his moral actions ("how we behaved in the world"—a possible allusion to his role as apostle to the nations, as in Rom 15:19, as Bultmann, 37, thinks; but more likely the term κόσμος coupled with ἀναστραφῆναι [BDF § 219.4] refers to the whole apostolic demeanor [as in 4:2; 5:7; 10:2 f.; 12:18] over against the lifestyle of his enemies) examined by divine norms, "to be determined by his belief" (R. Schnackenburg, *Moral Teaching,* 294). Already at 1:12 Paul is meeting the objection of those who impugned his apostolic character (Rissi, *Studien,* 43) and he will return to the assertion of his "sincerity" in 2:16, 17.

Those standards were his "probity" and "sincerity" set against his relationship *coram Deo,* and marked his life as a person who, renouncing all confidence in the σάρξ ("flesh," Phil 3:3), relied on God's grace which enabled and empowered his ministry (1 Cor 15:10; see the contrast in 1 Cor 2:5: μὴ . . . ἐν σοφίᾳ ἀνθρώπων ἀλλ᾽ ἐν δυνάμει). "Sincerity" (εἰλικρίνεια) connotes the idea of testing to prove the genuineness of an article or a person. Paul claims to have consented to such evaluation—by God.

Then (2) his letters were not intended to deceive; rather he has striven to say exactly what was in his mind, against the charge of double-dealing that he will shortly take up (v 17) as he reviews his travel plans and travel promises. His letters were so transparent, he avers, that "we are not writing to you anything different from" (οὐκ ἄλλα . . . ἀλλ᾽ ἤ, "nothing other than," a classical expression, BDF § 448.8) that which the Corinthians may readily understand. "What he wrote is what he meant" (Bultmann, 39), and tribute will later be paid to the effective letter-writing practice of the apostle (10:10).

(3) Paul's recognition of the seriousness of the pastoral problem is seen in the rather tortuous wording of v 14. This feature is explained by Paul's running together of two ideas in the same sentence, a temporal (now . . . then) and descriptive (in part . . . completely) contrast (Windisch, 57). At present the Corinthians know only part of Paul's story; he hopes they will bear with him as he tells it in detail. Then they will see why he acted as he did. The upshot will be a restored relationship of mutual trust, based on a

reciprocal confidence. He already has firm faith in *their* integrity as Christian believers; he trusts that such a confidence will now come from them to him as they express their acceptance of his honesty. The Parousia of the Lord Jesus is the day when all motives will be disclosed (1 Cor 4:2–5); at that time it will be the Corinthians who will be shown for what they are, not Paul who will be on trial (Bultmann, 40). Rather, then his work will be vindicated (1 Thess 2:19; Phil 2:16). That such a confident expectation is not the end of the story is clear from 12:21.

Explanation

This paragraph can only be understood in the light of what follows in vv 15–22. Paul is leading up to a frank statement of his change of mind by declaring the motives that inspired all his dealings, his words, and his letter-writing habits. The pericope has its value in pinpointing the importance of motive in Christian behavior, and incidentally we learn that there is sometimes a need to make our motives transparently clear and intelligible to others. Occasionally—to paraphrase a dictum—a Christian's actions in dealing with his or her fellow-believers must not only be done in the right way but must also be seen to be done in the right way.

IV. Paul's Self-Defense of His Travel Plans (1:15–2:13)

A. Travel Plans Reviewed (1:15–22)

Bibliography

Delling, G. *Die Taufe im Neuen Testament.* Berlin: Evangelische Verlagsanstalt, 1963. 105–107. **Dinkler, E.** "Die Taufterminologie in 2 Kor. 1, 21 f," in *Neotestamentica et Patristica.* Freundesgabe Oscar Cullmann. NovTSup 6, Leiden: Brill, 1962. 173–91. Reprinted in *Signum Crucis.* Aufsätze zum Neuen Testament und zur christlichen Archäologie. Tübingen: J. C. B. Mohr, 1967. 99–117. **Dunn, J. D. G.** *Baptism in the Holy Spirit.* SBT 15, 2d ser. London: SCM Press, 1970. 131–34. **Fee, G. D.** "ΧΑΡΙΣ in II Corinthians 1:15: Apostolic Parousia and Paul-Corinth Chronology." *NTS* 24 (1977–78) 533–38. **Hahn, F.** "Das Ja des Paulus und das Ja Gottes. Bermerkungen zu 2 Kor 1, 12—2, 1." In *Neues Testament und christliche Existenz,* FS H. Braun, ed. H.-D. Betz and L. Schottroff, 229–39. Tübingen: Mohr, 1973. **Hill, E.** "The Construction of Three Passages from St. Paul, Romans 8:20–21, 2 Corinthians 1:20, 2 Corinthians 3:10." *CBQ* 23 (1961) 296–301. **Kramer, W.** *Christ, Lord, Son of God,* 1963, sec. 53, 54a. **Panikulam, G.** *Koinonia in the New Testament. A Dynamic Expression of Christian Life.* AnBib 85. Rome: Biblical Institute Press, 1979. 59–63. **Potterie, I. de la.** "L'onction du chrétien par la foi," *Bib* 40 (1959) 12–69. **Rieger, J.** "Siegel und Angeld." *BibLeb* 7 (1966) 158–61. **Thrall, M. E.** "Christ Crucified or Second Adam?" In *Christ and Spirit in the New Testament.* FS C. F. D. Moule, ed. B. Lindars and S. S. Smalley, 143–50. Cambridge: University Press, 1973. **Trimaille, M.** and **Coune, M.** "Les Apôtres, envoyés authentiques du Dieu fidèle (2 Cor 1:18–22)." *AsSeign* 38 (1970) 42–50. **Unnik, W. C. van.** "Reisepläne und Amen-Sagen. Zusammenhang und Gedankenfolge in 2 Korinther 1:15–24." In *Studia Paulina,* 1953, 215–34; reprinted in *Sparsa Collecta. The Collected Essays of W. C. van Unnik.* NovTSup, Part One, 29. Leiden: Brill, 1973. 144–59.

Translation

[15] *On the ground of this confidence I was intending to come to you first so that you might have a second opportunity to do a favor,* [a] *and* [16] *then, having been with you, to go my way to Macedonia. From Macedonia [I planned] to come to you once more and to be helped on my way to Judea with your support.* [17] *With this as my intention, surely I was not fickle? Or do I make my [travel] plans on a human level, that there should be on my part a vacillating attitude, saying "Yes" and "No"* [b] *in the same breath?*

[18] *But as certain as God is trustworthy, our message to you was not a "Yes"-and-"No".*

[19] *For the Son of God, Jesus Christ, who was proclaimed among you by us—that*

is, by myself, Silvanus and Timothy, was not "Yes"-and-"No". Rather, the "Yes" has always been a reality in him.

²⁰ *To all the divine promises, however many they are, the "Yes" is in him; and that is why it is through him that we say* ᶜ *our Amen to God for his glory.* ²¹ *Now it is God who confirms both us and you in our relationship to Christ. He has anointed us,* ²² *set his seal upon us, and imparted the Spirit to us as a pledge.*

Notes

ᵃ χάριν, "favor," is read by ℵ* A C D G K and lesser witnesses in vg syrᵖ·ʰ copˢᵃ arm. The rival reading χαράν, "joy" (attested by ℵᶜ B L P copᵇᵒᵖᶜ Theodoret), is evidently a scribal effort to account for the apostle's thought in context, "softening the idea from 'grace received' to 'joy experienced'." So B. B. Warfield, "Some Difficult Passages," *JBL* 6 (1886) 36, who interprets Paul's mind (on the basis of χαράν as original): "he was confident, at that time, that his coming would bring joy." But χαράν is clearly secondary, and unless χάρις and χαρά are taken as equivalent in meaning (so Chrysostom, *Hom. 3 in 2 Cor*, Migne *PG* 81 col. 408: χάριν δὲ ἐνταῦθα τὴν χαρὰν λέγει and endorsed by Bleek, *TSK* [1830] 622), χάριν must be accepted on the principle of *lectio difficilior potior*, the harder reading is to be preferred. See *Comment* on p. 25 in this context.

ᵇ This translation does not overlook the view that the best-attested reading has τὸ ναὶ ναὶ καὶ τὸ οὒ οὒ; in the same breath Paul is alleged to be saying "Yes, yes" and "No, no." The shorter reading τὸ ναὶ καὶ τὸ οὒ (ᴾ⁴⁶ 424ᶜ vg Pelagius) is poorly endorsed and is probably due to assimilation to the wording of v 18. But in English translation such duplication is hardly needed to enforce the point, though Héring (10) champions the shorter reading and thinks that the doubling of the "Yes" and "No" is a late attempt to harmonize Paul with Matt 5:37 (cf. Jas 5:12). He notes the conjecture that the text may have read: "so that my Yes means No and my No a Yes." There is no support for this, however. See F. Hahn, "Das Ja," 234–37, for the emphasis that belongs to Paul's "Yes" in this context. But his restoration of the original text as ἵνα ᾖ παρ᾽ ἐμοὶ τὸ ναὶ ναὶ καὶ οὒ, while understandable as a way the text evolved, is hardly convincing.

ᶜ δι᾽ ἡμῶν is given a different nuance by Hill, "2 Cor 1, 20," 298, who wishes to observe the placing of the phrase at the close of the sentence. The sense then is: "therefore it is also through *him* that the Amen goes to God at the *doxa* (or doxology) (which is offered) through us." Perhaps δι᾽ ἡμῶν here is related to our approving of what happens when Christ offers our worship to the Father. For this meaning of τῷ θεῷ see John 9:24. The repetition of ἐν αὐτῷ with δι᾽αὐτοῦ ("through him," Christ) and δι᾽ἡμῶν ("through us") is remarkable, as Thüsing, *Per Christum in Deum* (Münster: Aschendorff, 1965), 178, notes. Christ cannot be equated with the Amen (as Hill, 299, suggests) since it is illogical to make him equivalent to the "Yes" and the "No" at the same time (Thüsing, 179). Rather Christ speaks the Amen in our response, and our response is Christ's speaking the praise of God (Thüsing, 180).

Form/Structure/Setting

Paul reverts to an expression of his "confidence" (πεποίθησις) in the Corinthians' readiness to believe him, a hope expressed in v 14. He, however, finds it necessary to rehearse the circumstances which led to a change of his travel plans and which raised against him the charge of being "fickle." V 17 contains a key phrase which is somewhat obscured in rsv ("was I vacillating when I wanted to do this?"). The literal translation is: "When I therefore was thus intending (to change my plans), did I act with *the* fickleness" (τῇ ἐλαφρίᾳ; note the definite article) of which I am now accused? The definite article here and before the "Yes" and "No" in the same verse "probably indicates that Paul is quoting what is being said about him at Corinth" (Tasker,

47). The allegation of vacillation—blowing hot and cold at the same time— arose directly out of a reneging of Paul's travel promises (vv 15, 16).

In 1 Cor 16:5–7 he expressed the hope of visiting Corinth for an extended stay after first traveling to Macedonia, presumably to collect the money raised for the Jerusalem church in its need. Now he explains that that original plan had to be modified, and he decided—for reasons that are unclear to us—to pass quickly through Corinth en route to Macedonia. Thence he would return to Corinth, and he wanted to experience their goodwill in sending him on his way to Judea with the collection, augmented doubtless with what the Corinthian church had raised for this cause (1 Cor 16:1–6). The point at issue, and the source of contention—or at least misunderstanding—between the apostle and the Corinthians was the shift from a lengthy visit (1 Cor 16:7: cf. 15) to what turned out to be a fleeting stopover in Corinth; and we are curious to know why (a) his original plan would have brought δευτέραν χάριν to them, and (b) if the "second" χάρις, "favor" never materialized, did Paul later hold out a hope that the situation could be salvaged in such a way that he could write (in 8:7), "see that you excel in this χάρις also"?

Much depends on the precise sense given to χάρις in 1:15. G. D. Fee, "ΧΑΡΙΣ in II Corinthians I.15," has offered an attractive proposal that the word means, not what the Corinthians were to receive from Paul's renewed presence with them, but "a double opportunity" for them to show kindness to him in support of his apostolic mission and to give evidence of God's grace (χάρις) working in them and through them in the matter of the collection (χάρις in 8:7). They wanted him to stay in their midst; he implies that it was his original intention to visit them first (πρότερον, v 15) on the way to Macedonia and to have them expedite that northerly journey, much in the spirit of Rom 15:23, 24, which has the same *mise en scène*, namely, the collection for the saints.

The church at Corinth would be revisited when Paul returned from Macedonia and yet again they would have the chance to speed him en route to Jerusalem. But that arrangement broke down because Paul crossed over to Ephesus from Macedonia and refused to visit Corinth again since on that earlier visit he had been met by strong opposition and public insult (2:5; 7:12; 12:21). This visit was painful to him (it is elaborated in 1:23–2:4), and Paul had no alternative—from his point of pastoral sensitivity—but to forgo the plan of 1:15 and indeed to renege on his promise given in 1 Cor 16: 5–7. Now, at a later time, in composing 2 Cor 1–9 he is at pains to explain why he never kept his promise of a return visit (1:23; 2:1). So his revised itinerary, which he details in order to rebut the criticism of indecision and a failure to keep his first promise, centers on what is most at stake at Corinth: his credibility as a true apostle of Jesus Christ. This feature explains a remarkable stylistic feature of this section, which is Paul's heavily weighted theological language in vv 18–22 (Wendland, 170, 171, who, however, associates "grace" more with the apostle's role as bearer of divine power and one whose presence will convey God's grace to the community).

The setting we have sketched, however tentatively, helps us to make sense of the earlier section (vv 12–14), for Paul is leading up to a frank statement of his change of mind by declaring the motives that inspired all his dealings, his words, and his letter-writing habits.

Comment

15. With most commentators (e.g., Bultmann, 41) but not all translators, (e.g., TEV which translates "I made plans at first to visit you"), προτέρον, "first," goes with πρὸς ὑμᾶς ἐλθεῖν, not with ἐβουλόμην: "I wanted to come to you first of all," ἵνα δευτέραν χάριν σχῆτε: "that you might have a double opportunity for showing kindness." Fee, 536, notes that the verb is "to have" rather than λάβητε (Rom 1:5; 5:17; "take") or δέξησθε (2 Cor 6:1; "receive"). In this context, on Fee's understanding, the "grace" is both experienced and proved by service to others (Windisch's rendering is "Gnadenerweisung," 63) specifically in the collection for the saints in Jerusalem. Most commentators, however, think in terms of what the Corinthians were anticipating by Paul's presence among them, and δευτέραν χάριν is variously rendered "benefit" (KJV/AV, RV, NEB, NIV, Menzies, Goudge, Denney, Hughes), a second "kindness" (Barrett), "a second opportunity for rejoicing" (Héring), "double delight" (Moffatt), "second sign of his esteem" (Allo), "a second proof of my goodwill" (BGD, 877, but the entry also notes how χάρις and χαρά run closely together). Our translation follows Fee ("a double opportunity for kindness"), with a variation.

If Paul is referring to his visit to Corinth when he was affronted (2:1), Bultmann asks, why did he not say ἦλθον, "I came," in place of ἐβουλόμην . . . ἐλθεῖν, "I was intending to come"? But this query overlooks the fact that Paul is relating what his original plan was, namely, an arrangement that included a second visit after he had been to Macedonia (v 16). It is the second member of the pair of visits that was the occasion of dispute between Paul and his readers. As it turned out, that *third* visit is spoken of in 2 Corinthians only in prospect (12:14; 13:1 f.).

16. "To be helped on my way to Judea" (lit., "to have you send me [ὑφ᾽ ὑμῶν προπεμφθῆναι] on my way to Judea"). Something more than "escort me to the ship" is in view (the verb has this sense in Acts 21:5). It looks clearly as if Paul had planned to have some Corinthian delegates join him in bringing the collection to Jerusalem, once the money had been raised in Achaia (1 Cor 16:3, 4; Rom 15:26). Windisch (63) speaks of a plan to have "an escort from Corinth"; but the party that sets out from Greece did not include Corinthian Christians according to Acts 20:2–4. The probable reason for this was that the disaffection at Corinth was by no means settled.

17. τοῦτο οὖν βουλόμενος μήτι ἄρα τῇ ἐλαφρίᾳ ἐχρησάμην; "With this as my intention, surely I was not fickle?" Paul now addresses the nub of the debate over his travelogue. He is defending himself against a specific charge: τῇ ἐλαφρίᾳ; ἐλαφρία "vacillation," "levity" (BGD), but, as we observed, the definite article denotes "the fickleness with which you charge me" (Windisch; Barrett, who, however, sees that the issue is one where Paul had canceled a promised visit, i.e., according to our reconstruction, he had not returned to Corinth from Macedonia but had sailed on to Ephesus). This seemed to his

opponents to be the mark of a "worldly man" (RSV: a person whose decisions are made κατὰ σάρκα, "inspired by merely human motives," Héring, 9). σάρξ, "flesh," stands in antithesis to the (Holy) Spirit who, Paul claimed, guided and possessed him (v 22). The same allegation against Paul recurs in 10:2: "some reckon that we are living on a merely human level" (ὡς κατὰ σάρκα περιπατοῦντας). ἵνα ᾖ παρ᾽ ἐμοὶ τὸ ναὶ ναὶ καὶ τὸ οὔ οὔ, literally, "that there should be on my part, Yes, yes and No, no." Clearly there is an implied accusation of duplicity. The ἵνα is used to express a result clause (BDF § 391.5: Moulton, *Grammar* 1:210). To allege that Paul was a person whose actions were motivated by σάρξ, his self-interest, means "that I am found saying 'Yes' and 'No' in the same breath" (Héring). The "Yes" has specifically to do with his promise to revisit Corinth. We cannot, then, agree with Strachan's judgment (55) that "the utterance (of v 18) has only a slight connection with his apology for a change of plan."

18. The theological reasoning, commencing with πιστὸς δὲ ὁ θεός ("But as certain as God is trustworthy") invites us to think that Paul has more to defend than his reputation. It was bad enough that his detractors attacked him as vulnerable and shifty (after all, he had changed his plans more than once, though there were good reasons to do so, and they were closely connected with his concern for his readers' well-being, 1:23). It was worse when they went on to insinuate that his message was just as unreliable and unsure. The purpose of vv 18–22 is to defend the apostolic ministry which, for Paul, was intimately bound up with the message God had entrusted to him and his co-workers. Paul's appeal that his message has self-consistency has led M. E. Thrall, "Christ Crucified," 143, 144, to see a reply to this charge in vv 18, 19; the question will recur in chap. 3 and at 4:4. He does this in several ways, as follows:

(1) There is an appeal to God's character as πιστός, "faithful" or "covenant-keeping," and so he is the "guarantor" of his promises (Lietzmann-Kümmel, 103). See Deut 7:9 LXX: θεὸς πιστός, ὁ φυλάσσων διαθήκην καὶ ἔλεος τοῖς ἀγαπῶσιν αὐτόν, corresponding to the title of God as הָאֵל הַנֶּאֱמָן, ha-ʾel hanneʾeman, "the faithful God." This text, along with Isa 49:7; Ps 89:38; Prov 14:5, 25, is cited by van Unnik, "Reisepläne und Amen-Sagen," 221, 222, as grounds for his thesis that the key to an understanding of these vv (18–24) is Paul's word-play on the semitic root אמן (ʾmn, as in "Amen," v 20).

(2) The γάρ, "for," in v 19 has to be given due weight (van Unnik, 218) since Paul moves on to ground his proclamation as sincere and free from all charge of making "airy promises" (Héring) on the person of his Lord who is the great affirmation of God's truth and promises (v 20). There is, Paul avers, no duplicity in the "Son of God" (on this christological title see W. Kramer, *Christ, Lord, Son of God,* 54a, d; M. Hengel, *The Son of God,* tr. J. Bowden [London: SCM Press, 1976] 7–15) with special references to the divine OT promises. Jesus Christ was a minister of the circumcision "in the interest of the truth of God, with a view to the confirmation of the promises" (Denney, 39: he gives this translation in italics). The affirmative ring of Paul's Christology (ἀλλὰ ναὶ ἐν αὐτῷ γέγονεν: "rather the 'Yes' has always been a reality in him") stands in contrast to the preachers of 2:17 and looks on further to 11:4.

20. (3) So the next step in the chain of argument follows on logically. In Christ the OT finds its fulfillment—and Paul is claiming a wide scope for this fulfillment as is clear from ὅσαι γὰρ ἐπαγγελίαι θεοῦ, ἐν αὐτῷ τὸ ναί (a nominative construction where the more natural reading would be πάσαις ταῖς ἐπαγγελίαις τοῦ θεοῦ, ὅσαι γὰρ εἰσίν γέγονεν ἐν αὐτῷ τὸ ναί: BDF § 466.2): "for all the promises of God [find] their affirmation in him."

τὸ ναί, the "Yes," leads on to the believer's endorsement in the liturgical language of the "Amen" (1 Cor 14:16, which also has the article: the root in Heb., אמן, ʾmn, suggests solidity, firmness, expressing agreement with the prayer or creedal confession uttered). The context of the church at worship is clear from 1 Cor 14 (see R. P. Martin, *The Spirit and the Congregation* [Grand Rapids: Eerdmans, 1984] 71), and it may well be traced here: see C. F. D. Moule, *The Phenomenon of the New Testament*, SBT 1, 2d ser. (London: SCM Press, 1967) 54, 68.

Such a liturgical response is issued "to the glory of God," an acclamation where the apostle's thought loves to come to rest (as in Phil 2:11, as Lohmeyer remarks, *Kyrios Jesus. Eine Untersuchung zu Phil 2, 5–11* [Heidelberg: C. Winter, 2d ed. 1961] 60–62).

Δι᾽ ἡμῶν, "through us" is hardly "through the faith of us" (Plummer, 30); it is rather "through our spoken utterance" of the Amen that believers ascribe praise to God, however true it may be generally that "our faith" answers to the divine faithfulness.

21, 22. (4) ὁ δὲ βεβαιῶν ἡμᾶς σὺν ὑμῖν εἰς Χριστὸν . . . θεός, "Now it is God who confirms both us and you in our relationship to Christ." Yet one further corollary from Paul's theological exposition of God's covenant faithfulness is to be drawn. This is the appeal to human experience, specifically his own self-consciousness as the "divine apostle" whose message, attacked at Corinth, he is determined to see vindicated. At the same time Paul is concerned to defend his own character as being as unambiguous as the word he is commissioned to deliver. Denney (38) wisely recalls that ὁ λόγος ἡμῶν ("our word" in v 18) carries a double weight; it covers what Paul said regarding his travel plans and also the substance of his mission preaching at Corinth. So Paul will launch out into a cryptically written *apologia* respecting the apostolic ministry. It is endorsed by God (ὁ βεβαιῶν, "the one who guarantees" is from the Hebrew verb to "confirm," to "fulfill a promise," according to van Unnik, 227: see Rom 15:8 and H. Schlier, *TDNT* 1: 600–3: but Barrett, 78, 79 doubts the linguistic link with אמן, ʾmn that van Unnik wishes to establish). 1 Cor 1:6 is a good parallel, with its statement that the apostle's testimony about Christ is confirmed (ἐβεβαιώθη) in his people who are then (1 Cor 1:8) said to be "confirmed" to the end-time (βεβαιώσει ὑμᾶς ἕως τέλους). So the verb denotes the initiation of believers in the Christian life and experience, brought about by the preacher's witness and including the believer's becoming incorporated into the divine possession (περιποίησις; cf. Eph 1:14). βεβαίωσις is also a legal and commercial term to designate properly guaranteed security: see BGD (138) and Deissmann, *Bible Studies* (104 ff.). Such an act of God's grace confers privilege which makes the Christian a partaker of Christ himself (εἰς Χριστόν). The latter idea is also taken from the phrase καὶ χρίσας ἡμᾶς θεός: "and God has anointed us," with an obvious wordplay χρίσας . . . Χριστός:

in the Anointed one (= Χριστός, Christ) God has "anointed us" (L. Cerfaux, *Christ in the Theology of St. Paul*, tr. G. Webb and A. Walker [London, 1959] 498). The verb (χρίειν) conjures up OT associations of God's servants (judges, kings, prophets) who were set apart and commissioned for their office by the pouring out of oil over their heads. If that is the background here, the anointing will refer to the bestowal of charismatic gifts intended to equip men and women for God's work by the coming of the Spirit (cf. Isa 61:1–3, cited in Luke 4:18, 19; Acts 4:27; 10:38), though Denney's point (51) is worth consideration that the primary reference in our text is the anointing to the apostolic office. The result is that whereas God is said to confirm (present tense) "us" as faithful disciples of Christ—and Paul adds "with you" to include the Corinthian readers—the latter part of the text restricts both anointing and sealing by the Spirit (καὶ σφραγισάμενος ἡμᾶς καὶ δοὺς τὸν ἀρραβῶνα τοῦ πνεύματος ἐν ταῖς καρδίαις ἡμῶν: lit., "having sealed us and set the Spirit in our hearts as a pledge") to the Christian apostles. Of the four participles (βεβαιῶν, χρίσας, σφραγισάμενος, δούς), Windisch observes that the first "strengthening"/"confirming" indicates a lasting and continuing effect, while the other verbs speak of an event already accomplished (so too, Panikulam, *Koinonia*, 60–62, who approves also of Windisch's idea that βεβαιῶν ἡμᾶς εἰς Χριστόν looks like an abbreviated form of βεβαιῶν τὴν κοινωνίαν ἡμῶν τὴν σὺν Χριστῷ: confirmed in the fellowship with Christ, as in Col 2:7).

This conclusion would be less debatable if there was only one setting of the three activities: guaranteeing, anointing, the sealing of the Spirit as a pledge of final salvation (there are surely not four clear images here, as Barrett, 80, thinks since τοῦ πνεύματος, "of the Spirit," is not a partitive but explanatory genitive as in 5:5: see Delling, *Die Taufe*, 106). The "giving of the Spirit" in particular has been linked with baptism (so E. Dinkler, "Die Taufterminologie," 177–90, who wishes to relate all four verbs to the act of baptism in company with Windisch (73), Lietzmann-Kümmel, Allo, Denney and Bultmann: see too G. W. H. Lampe, *The Seal of the Spirit* [London: Longmans, 1951] 3–7, 61, 62 and contrast J. D. G. Dunn, *Baptism in the Holy Spirit* [London: SCM Press, 1970] 131–34, who denies any direct—or even indirect—reference to baptism in water). "Seal" (σφραγίζω) is not here used in an eschatological sense (Rev 7:2 ff.; 14:1 ff.), but rather it denotes the claiming of property as belonging to a rightful owner: Deissmann, *Bible Studies*, 238 f. It is elsewhere used of circumcision (Rom 4:11; *Barn* 9:6); and it is undeniable that "sealing" (σφραγίς) became a dramatic description of the Spirit's action in baptism (Eph 1:13; 4:30; Hermas, *Sim.* 8:6; 2 *Clem* 7:6, 8:6; Abercius' Inscription, and the later patristic evidence of baptism as *signaculum fidei*: J. Ysebaert, *Greek Baptismal Terminology: Its Origin and Early Development* [Nijmegen: Dekker & Van de Vegt, 1962] 204 f., 226, 265–71, 379–87), as did the receiving of the Spirit as a "down-payment" (ἀρραβών, OT עֵרָבוֹן, *ʿērābôn*, another commercial term used in the papyri for a payment which obligates the contracting party to make further payments; cf. Gen. 38:18; see BGD 109), as in Eph 1:14. Barrett makes out a better case for seeing here a comprehensive statement of the entire rite of initiation into the new life in Christ, involving conversion, faith, baptism and the reception of the Spirit.

Finally, we come back to the purpose of this stately description of all that

God and Christ and the Spirit (an implicit and inchoate trinitarian "division of labor" is probably to be seen in the vv). Either Paul is moved along by his initial thoughts based on his wordplay with the root]מא, *'mn*, "amen," from which he then extracts the maximum value, into a tangential discussion of all that the apostolic ministry has effected under God, or his focus is more narrow. In the latter case, he is entering a defensive plea on behalf of his own trustworthiness and authority as both an honest person (see 1:12) and a commissioned apostle whose message is to be trusted as God-given. If this latter purpose is in view, all his remarks are polemically and defensively slanted, and this piling up of images (with a notable use of participles in vv 21, 22; E. Norden, *Agnostos Theos,* 384, traces here a strong semitic influence)— God as faithful, Christ as the affirmation of divine promises, your amen in a service of worship which points to God's confirming work, and our commissioning and being set apart by the Spirit—is intended to rebut the innuendo that Paul's apostolic ministry is not to be believed. On the contrary, he concludes, the apostle and his coadjutors (v 19: see J. Hainz, *Ekklesia* [1972], 299; E. E. Ellis, "Paul and his Co-Workers," *NTS* 17 [1970–71] 437–52; Windisch, 67, remarks that the three men are "proclaimers as commissioned and believing heralds of the exalted Lord") are men of probity, since they have all the marks to validate their ministry, whatever appearances to the contrary (namely, that Paul changed his itinerary plans) there may be.

Explanation

This short paragraph illustrates some typical Pauline traits and opens a window of access to his sense of pastoral responsibility and concern. He is obviously writing as a person whose reliability had been questioned, and not without reason. He had indeed deemed it wise to alter his plans to visit Corinth as originally promised. But for Paul more was at stake than his personal reputation. If the messenger was double-tongued, what were the Corinthians to make of the message he came to Corinth to deliver as God's word? That probing question haunts the writer as he joins his own ministry and its validity with a self-defense of his past dealings with the Achaean readers. Paul has yet to give a reason for his altered travelogue; in fact, when he does (in 1:23–2:13; 7:5–16), much is left in obscurity and our questions posed to the text are often left unanswered. But what is not in doubt is Paul's appeal to his message as divinely authenticated by God's own character, Christ's person, and Christian experience as life-in-the-Spirit.

Of these realities Paul was in no doubt, and for him and his partners, Silas and Timothy—and for those who seek to follow their example in ministry—they constituted the substance of what he called "the Gospel," which centers in Christ. "The proclaimed Christ is their legitimation" (Hainz, *Ekklesia,* 131). The thrust of this passage is essentially positive, and therein lies its timeless quality, for "nobody has any right to preach who has not mighty affirmations to make concerning God's Son, Jesus Christ—affirmations in which there is no ambiguity, and which no questioning can reach" (Denney, 41).

B. Paul's Travel Plans Explained and His Earlier Letter Justified (1:23–2:11)

Bibliography

Barrett, C. K. *The Signs of an Apostle.* 41–44. ———. " Ὁ ΑΔΙΚΗΣΑΣ (2 Cor 7.12)." In *Verborum Veritas.* FS G. Stählin. Wuppertal: Verlag Rolf Brockhaus, 1970; reprinted in *Essays on Paul,* London: SPCK, 1982, 108–17. **Batey, R.** "Paul's Interactions with the Corinthians." *JBL* 84 (1965) 139–46. **Binder, H.** *Der Glaube bei Paulus.* Berlin: Evangelische Verlagsanstalt, 1968. 57. **Cox, S.** "That Wicked Person," *Exp.* 1st ser. 3 (1875) 355–68. **Daniel, C.** "Un mention paulinienne des esséniens de Qumran." *RQ* 5 (1966) 553–59. **Friedrich, G.** "Glaube und Verkündigung bei Paulus." In *Glaube im Neuen Testament,* FS H. Binder, ed. F. Hahn and H. Klein, 93–113. Biblisch-Theologische Studien 7. Neukirchener-Vluyn: Neukirchener Verlag, 1982. **Hahn, F.** "Das Ja des Paulus und das Ja Gottes." In *Neues Testament und christliche Existenz,* 229–39. **Hainz, J.** *Ekklesia. Strukturen paulinischer Gemeinde-Theologie und Gemeinde-Ordnung,* 132–41. **Jones, Ivor H.** *The Contemporary Cross: A Study for Passiontide—A Theme and Four Biblical Variations.* London: Epworth Press, 1977. **Lampe, G. W. H.** "Church Discipline and the Interpretation of the Epistles to the Corinthians." In *Christian History and Interpretation,* Studies presented to John Knox, ed. W. R. Farmer et al., 353–54. Cambridge: University Press, 1967. **Ljungman, H.** *PISTIS. A Study of Its Presuppositions and Its Meaning in Pauline Use.* ARSHLL 64. Lund: C. W. K. Gleerup, 1964. **Schweizer, E.** *Church Order in the New Testament.* Tr. F. Clarke. SBT 32. London: SCM Press, 1961.

Translation

²³ *I call upon God as a witness against me [if I am not telling the truth]: it was to spare you that I did not come again to Corinth.*
²⁴ *This does not mean that we are ruling over your faith, but we are working with you for your joy, because it is by faith that you stand firm.*
²·¹ *So* ᵃ *I decided not to pay you another painful visit.* ² *For if I cause you sorrow, then who is to cheer me? Certainly not* ᵇ *the person who is made sorrowful on my account.* ³ *I wrote moreover as I did so that, when I came, I might not be saddened* ᶜ *by those who ought to make me rejoice, for I was confident that my joy is the joy of you all.* ⁴ *For I wrote to you out of great distress and anguish of heart, with many tears, not to make you sorrowful but to make you know the love which I have in great measure* ᵈ *for you.* ⁵ *But if anyone has caused sorrow, he has caused sorrow not to me but in some measure—I mustn't put it too strongly—to all of you.* ⁶ *The censure in question, which was inflicted on that person by the majority [of church members] is enough for him,* ⁷ *so that on the other hand, you should rather forgive and console him to prevent his being swallowed up by excessive sorrow.* ⁸ *So I urge you, therefore, to affirm your love for this person.* ⁹ *The reason I wrote to you was to see if* ᵉ *you would pass the test and be obedient in everything.* ¹⁰ *If you forgive anyone, I also do the same. For what I have forgiven—if indeed there was anything to forgive—it was done on your account in the presence of Christ,* ¹¹ *to prevent Satan from taking advantage of us; for we know well his designs.*

Notes

[a]The reading δέ ("but"; D* has τέ, "and") is found in ℵ A G lat syr^p and the Byzantine witnesses. P⁴⁶ B 69 and syr^h have γάρ ("for"). As Barrett remarks, if γάρ links on to 1:23 it gives a reason for Paul's decision not to revisit Corinth and 1:24 is parenthetic: "I act so as not to spare you . . . for I had made up my mind." This makes good sense, provided we could be sure that 1:24 has been slipped in as an aside and "that 2:1 . . . supplies the reason for Paul's delay in visiting the Corinthians (1:23 f.)": so B. M. Metzger, *Textual Commentary*, 576. But see *Comment*.

[b]The revised punctuation suggested by Héring makes admirable sense. It involves placing the question mark after με ("me") and taking εἰ μή as a strong denial, "certainly not."

[c]D G 1739 lat syr^h expand the phrase to λύπην ἐπὶ λύπην (based on Phil 2:27), i.e., "sorrow upon sorrow."

[d]While περισσοτέρως (lit., "even more," "to a much greater degree") is undisputed, it is unclear whether it goes with the verb "to have love" and so qualifies the extent of Paul's love (as in the translation above) or with εἰς ὑμᾶς, "especially for you" (so Barrett).

[e]εἰ ("if," "whether") is read by A B as ᾗ, a Greek letter which could either be a variant of εἰ (which has the strong attestation of ℵ C D it vg syr cop^{bo}) or the dative feminine singular of the relative pronoun, "in which [matter]." But the final phrase "in everything" (εἰς πάντα) is difficult then to understand. See Moulton, *Grammar* 2:72. The omission of εἰ by P⁴⁶ is accidental, caused by the scribe's eye wandering to the next word εἰς.

Form/Structure/Setting

This section forms a lengthy *apologia* for Paul's nonappearance at Corinth; Bultmann (47) writes, "Now at last Paul gives the actual reason for the change of his travel plans." But we should also include, with I. H. Jones, *The Contemporary Cross* (36), the answer to a second criticism, namely, the tone of his harsh letter (2:4). On the first reason, much depends on the specific understanding of the adverbs in 1:23; 2:1. "Again" (πάλιν) may be attached to the verbs in two quite different ways: (1) Paul is saying, "I decided not to come to you again"—pointing back to his initial visit to Corinth, Acts 18:1–18—"in such circumstances that my coming would be this time one which causes me sorrow" (see R. Batey, "Paul's Interaction," *JBL* 84 [1965] 139–46); (2) Paul's statement runs: "I had already visited you in circumstances that I found painful, and I decided not to have the same experience twice." Since the phrase "in sorrow" (ἐν λύπῃ) immediately follows the adverb (πάλιν) the second view is preferable, but not indubitably so. If it is preferred, we can postulate an intermediate visit between the first visit of Acts 18:1–18 and the visit promised in 1:15, and presumably in 12:14; 13:1. It was on the first one of the projected two visits that Paul encountered this trouble at Corinth; therefore he abandoned the second one. This explains the need for such an "apology," i.e., a reasoned statement to account for his course of action. In this case, he has to explain why he did not make good his promise to revisit the church. If option (1) above is championed, we are left in the dark as to the flow of events leading to Paul's writing 2 Corinthians, since it is clear from all the evidence that his initial visit at the time of Acts 18 was not attended by "sorrow," of which he now writes in retrospect.

The explanatory style of writing means that Paul's previous actions have been misunderstood, either innocently or maliciously. The issue of how culpable the Corinthians were in their discernment of the apostle's motives turns on (a) the identity of the person referred to in 2:5 ("if anyone [τις] has caused sorrow," he has caused sorrow not to me [only] but in some measure . . . to all of you); and (b) the degree of confidence Paul expresses in phrases such as "all of you" (ἐπὶ πάντας ὑμᾶς . . . πάντων ὑμῶν . . . πάντας ὑμᾶς in vv 3, 5), which reveals that the church as a whole was on his side. Indeed, at 7:11 he can write: "in every way you showed that you were innocent (ἀγνούς) in the matter" of dealing with the "one who committed the wrong" against Paul (7:12), who disguises himself in the following phrase, "it was not on account of the one who was wronged." The church's dealing with the situation led to Paul's encouragement, part of which was occasioned by Titus's report that "his spirit has been refreshed by you all" (v 13, ἀπὸ πάντων ὑμῶν), and once more Paul is led to express confidence in the church (7:16).

As a general background to those two matters which are vital to an understanding of both 1:23–2:11 and 7:5–13, we may begin with some items that form a consensus, as listed and considered by Allo (54–63) and by C. K. Barrett (" Ὁ ᾿ΑΔΙΚΗΣΑΣ," 109–11). The injury done at Corinth was not a doctrinal aberration which led to a theological dispute, and 1:24, τῇ γὰρ πίστει ἑστήκατε, however we translate it, hardly says categorically, as Allo assumes, that Paul is recalling his readers to the apostolic truth they have abandoned. Second, the double reference in 7:12 with the verb ἀδικεῖν, "to wrong," "to treat unjustly," "to injure" (see BGD), shows that the issue was a disaffection between fellow Christians. Third, it was committed by a single individual as the primary reason for the disagreement (2:5, 6, 7, 8, 10; 7:12: all these vv speak of a specific person, most clearly in the last v). The altercation was a serious one, leading to Paul's change of travel plans and impelling him to write a letter to deal with the situation created by this person's attitude (1:23; 2:1, 3, 4; 7:8). The ramification of this one individual's opposition to Paul touched the life of the entire church (2:5), yet Paul himself was the object of the attack, as is clear from 2:5; 7:12. It is open to question whether the attack was directed against Paul's person or his ministry and/or his teaching. At the time when the incident took place, the Corinthians either failed to see its gravity or else they sided with the man. Whether it was a landslide of opposition to Paul, or only part of the church that formed a faction against him as they ranged themselves with the individual, is not exactly clear. 2:5, 6 can mean either "not all of you, but only some" of you were drawn in to the opposition, or "all of you" were affected, since to injure one Christian was to involve the entire fellowship: the former seems to point to a "dissident minority" (Barrett's term), whose existence compelled Paul to test the obedience of the whole church (2:9). Some Corinthian church members then formed a pocket of resistance and Paul (evidently) was fearful that their influence, fomented by the ringleader, would spread to lead the entire church into "disobedience."

At a later time, presumably following the arrival of the "severe letter" and perhaps because Titus was on hand at Corinth, the guilty person had repented, though a shadow was cast over the church's relationship to Paul (since 7:9 speaks of the church's being called to penitence "to clear themselves," 7:11) and some residual problems had to be dealt with. Most notably (2:10; 7:6–13), the disciplinary action taken by the church against the offender—or by a majority (οἱ πλείονες, 2:6) against both the man and his supporters—was harsh. The individual was in danger of being swallowed up in despair; so Paul emphasizes his own forgiveness, and calls on the church to assure the offender of Christian love in restoring him. Paul's final fear is that too severe a "reproof" (ἐπιτιμία, 2:6) will lead only to the church's further division and factious state (2:10, 11).

The two questions we posed earlier may be now addressed. (a) On the identity of the individual who offended Paul, we think that Barrett's case for regarding him as an intruder on the scene, a visitor to Corinth and not a Corinthian church member, is cogently presented. At a time during or subsequent to the first of the two-member visits, promised in 1:15, 16, Paul encountered this man whose presence at Corinth he speaks of in a way that dissociates him from the church as a whole; and at 7:12 he treats the man as the third person in a triangle of relations between himself and the Corinthians. Just how the man insulted Paul is not clear, but we may guess that it was he who raised the charge of Paul's failure to keep promises made (according to 1 Cor 16:1–8) of a lengthy visit to Corinth. Then if Paul, taxed with this failure, left the scene hurriedly and did not return to Corinth but instead wrote the letter of 2:4 from Ephesus, the man would have had more grounds for accusing Paul of "insincerity" and "double-dealing" (to which he replies in 1:12).

This sketch of the situation that led to Paul's letter and the church's handling of the problem virtually excludes the view that the "man who offended" is to be identified with the incestuous person of 1 Cor 5:1 (as Cox, Denney, Hughes, and more recently, Lampe have maintained): such a view would mean that ὁ ἀδικήσας was the man who had cohabited with his (step-) father's wife, and the person in ὁ ἀδικηθείς was the (step-) father. Lampe's stronger argument is that the restoration of the sinner in 2:7 ff. seems to be an act of the whole church in its discipline, and the verb in 2:9 and 7:12 refers to a previous correspondence, taking ἔγραψα, "I wrote," as a true aorist going back to Paul's advice in 1 Cor 5:5. But neither argument is compelling, as we shall observe.

Another kind of moral offense is suggested (see Strachan, 70; Windisch, 238) if what is in Paul's mind is the scene of 1 Cor 6, where, it is submitted, ἀδικεῖν carries its strict legal sense and refers to Christians' going to the civil courts to settle their differences. Paul's strong language, however, is not accounted for in this view, nor is his personal involvement, which seems clear, explained on either of the interpretations just given. Bultmann (51, 52) puts the point clearly: "In no circumstance can ἀδικήσας ("one who wronged") be the 'incestuous person' of 1 Cor 5, because such conduct was not a personal insult against Paul, but a direct outrage against the community; and it is quite overlooked that Paul cannot be satisfied with the excommunication required in 1 Cor 5:5 but wants the matter settled by a personal pardon (on his part, 2:10)." Moreover, the point at issue in 2 Cor 2 is not a moral question (1 Cor 5) nor a legal dispute, but Paul's having to endure "rude and disagreeable conduct" (Menzies).

We are left with the most obvious reading of the text, that Paul had been affronted by an individual at Corinth in one of several ways. Either Paul was directly involved in a confrontation with a church member during his second visit (the most popular view, see W. G. Kümmel, *Introduction to the New Testament,* 1st ed. [Nashville: Abingdon Press, 1966] 208; but see 2d ed. [1975] 283, for a different emphasis), or after he had left Corinth on his second visit, there was "an act of flagrant disobedience and revolt" (Barrett)—but for this conclusion there is little direct evidence; or Paul was insulted in the person of one of his fellow workers, such as Timothy (Barrett's own position, but opposed by Allo, 62, who also rejects the suggestion that Titus was the object of attack, 74–76). Of these options the most likely—because it requires fewest inferences from the text—is the first one, with the caveat that the man in question seems to have been an intruder on the Corinthian scene.

If this working hypothesis is sound, we can quickly notice the most probable reply to question (b), namely, how far were the Corinthians involved in the insult directed at Paul's person? Paul's tone (in 2:2, 4 [referring to a "tearful letter," written more in sorrow than in anger] and 7:8) is to be weighed; the conclusion seems rightly drawn that this man had influenced at least a substantial section of the church who subsequently needed to repent of their disaffection and alienation from the apostle and who had shown undue rigor in imposing a disciplinary reprimand upon the anti-Paul ringleader. Paul's concern for the well-being of the whole church stands out clearly in both chapters, and 7:11, 12 can best make sense—as indeed will the rest of the epistle, as Barrett observes—if Paul's chief regard was the state of his relations with the local church, relations that were put under a cloud by all that had transpired prior to Titus's report that the "tearful letter" had worked and the church as a whole had been won back to Paul's side.

Comment

23. ἐγὼ δὲ μάρτυρα τὸν θεὸν ἐπικαλοῦμαι, κτλ, "I call upon God as a witness" (as in Rom 1:9; Phil 1:8; 1 Thess 2:5, 10), is a mild example of oath-taking for which Deissmann, *Light from the Ancient East* [4] (London: Hodder & Stoughton, 1927), 304, provides a loose parallel in a hellenistic curse-formula. But there are OT precedents for this sentiment (Ruth 1:17; 1 Sam 14:44; 2 Sam 3:35; 1 Kgs 2:23). Ἐπὶ τὴν ἐμὴν ψυχήν, lit., "against my soul" (Moffatt), implies that "if he is lying, God will punish the perjury." More likely, the words reflect the Hebrew עַל־נַפְשִׁי, ʿal-napšî, and are a way of saying "myself." Thus they are part of Paul's habit of confessing that all lives are open to divine scrutiny. The point is that he is most anxious to clear the air by stating the reason behind his change in travel plans: it was "to spare you," the Corinthians, that Paul chose not to revisit Corinth as he had promised. The adverb οὐκέτι (in this context meaning "not again") is linked with the verb ἦλθον ("I came"), and together these words "I did not come again" indicate the grounds on which Paul was accused of ἐλαφρία ("fickleness," 1:17).

24. οὐχ ὅτι κυριεύομεν ὑμῶν τῆς πίστεως, ἀλλὰ συνεργοί ἐσμεν τῆς χαρᾶς ὑμῶν, "This does not mean that we are ruling over your faith, but we are working with you for your joy." In acting thus Paul will declare his motive. The decision to spare the church more pain (in addition to that "grief" mentioned in 7:8, 11) was made in no high-handed manner, as though Paul were a dictator

(κύριος) who wanted to domineer (κυριεύειν) over their faith (so Héring), but Héring is surely wrong in regarding v 24 as a digression: rather it provides the basis for v 23, as Bultmann says: οὐχ ὅτι offers the rationale underlying the previous v (cf. Phil 4:17). The apostle is a fellow worker (συνεργός as in 1 Cor 3:5–9) whose hallmark is service to the community of faith and whose desire is to sustain its "joy" in the Lord, rather than his own satisfaction (so Lietzmann-Kümmel). Yet Paul here is still the apostle in relation to the church—otherwise there would be no need to explain his course of action—and it is their Christian standing (τῇ . . . πίστει ἑστήκατε: πίστις, "faith," may mean here their loyalty to Paul's apostolic Gospel as in 1 Thess 3:8; 1 Cor 16:13; see F. Hahn, "Das Ja des Paulus," 231) that Paul is concerned to promote. See Rom 11:20: σὺ δὲ τῇ πίστει ἕστηκας, "by faith then you stand." Bultmann, *TDNT* 6:218, wants to see here an emphasis on Christian standing attained by faith, an interpretation criticized by H. Binder, *Der Glaube*, 57. E. Schweizer, *Church Order*, § 23e, notes how Paul "is obviously striving to establish the Church as the real bearer of responsibility" in the exercise of its discipline, as in Gal 6:1; 2 Thess 3:14.

2:1. ἔκρινα δὲ ἐμαυτῷ τοῦτο, τὸ μὴ πάλιν ἐν λύπῃ πρὸς ὑμᾶς ἐλθεῖν, "So I decided not to pay you another painful visit." At length the contrast is explicitly made: Paul wished only for the Corinthians χαρά ("joy") and, if he had paid them "another painful visit" (the phrase, ἐλθεῖν ἐν corresponds to the Aramaic verb ב אתא, ’aṯā’ bᵉ, "to come with," "to cause," "to bring"), the result would have been the direct opposite: λύπη, "grief" (2:3). Moreover, his own "joy" would have been sacrificed, when he wished only to share in their joy as faithful believers. So he decided not to visit Corinth until the altercation was settled.

2. εἰ γὰρ ἐγὼ λυπῶ ὑμᾶς, "If I cause you sorrow" refers to the letter of 2:4 and its immediate impact (7:8), together with the situation that caused Paul to write as he did. The person responsible for the pain now stands revealed as ὁ λυπούμενος, "the person who made me sorrowful." Héring (14) makes clear the drift of Paul's thought by his repunctuation, which we have adopted (cf. BDF § 442.8). Paul did not expect to find any consolation until the matter—ἐξ ἐμοῦ, "on my account": "the sorrow occasioned by my presence" at a time when this man opposed Paul—had been settled. Then he would be gladdened, not unnaturally so, even if Windisch thinks Paul is egotistical here! But it is the language of love that speaks (Bultmann, 50).

3. καὶ ἔγραψα τοῦτο αὐτὸ ἵνα μὴ ἐλθὼν λύπην σχῶ ἀφ᾽ ὧν ἔδει με χαίρειν, "I wrote moreover as I did so that, when I came, I might not be saddened by those who ought to make me rejoice." Paul looks ahead to a future visit (12:14; 13:1) which he expects will be an occasion of rejoicing. He gives one reason for the letter, prefaced by a difficult phrase: καὶ ἔγραψα [ὑμῖν] τοῦτο αὐτὸ. The KJV/AV retains the words "unto you" based on ὑμῖν of the inferior reading in the TR. Three possibilities are open: (1) "I wrote precisely for this reason": so BDF § 160, 290.4, Bultmann and Héring, and the intent is to give an added force to the following clause. (2) "I wrote like this," assuming that τοῦτο αὐτὸ is the direct object of the verb (taken as a true, not epistolary aorist) and points back to an excerpt from the letter, perhaps in 1:23 or 2:1, or looks forward prospectively to "that I may not come and

be made sorrowful" (see Héring, 15, who thinks τὴν ἐπιστολήν, "the letter," may be the assumed object). (3) Barrett supports a view similar to (2) but with the words τοῦτο αὐτὸ summarizing the main drift of the letter: "I wrote to just this effect." No certain decision is possible, and our translation is intentionally as vague as Paul's Greek.

The sentence ends on the note of confident joy. Paul could well have said, "my sorrow is the sorrow of you all" (Bachmann, 94) based on v 5, but instead he accentuates the positive, knowing well that the issue is disposed of, as chap. 7 will reveal. His joy derives from the joy shared by all the church; and neither one is possible without the other (against Windisch, 81, who wants to see a causal relation making the Corinthians' joy dependent on Paul's).

4. ἐκ γὰρ πολλῆς θλίψεως καὶ συνοχῆς καρδίας ἔγραψα ὑμῖν διὰ πολλῶν δακρύων, "For I wrote to you out of great distress and anguish of heart, with many tears." This verse opens a window into the writer's inner life at the time the letter was composed and sent; it needs to be read in the light of 7:8, which raises the issue of whether Paul felt he had written too strongly. Here, however, all is tenderness and anguish on his part; θλῖψις ("distress") is not the experience of 1:8, even if the word is the same. συνοχή ("anguish") is a natural partner (as in similar wording in Rom 2:9; 1 Thess 3:7; cf. Ps. 106:39; 24:17, LXX). The third part of the description is διὰ πολλῶν δακρύων: "with" (for διά in this sense see BDF § 223.3 and in our letter 3:11; 5:7; Rom 14:20) "many tears." The letter in question cannot therefore be our 1 Cor (so Denney, Hughes and earlier commentators generally); it must be the letter sent directly following Paul's visit ἐν λύπῃ "in sorrow" (cf. 7:8) and committed to Titus's hands as its bearer (7:6 ff.).

At first glance the reason for the letter—οὐχ ἵνα λυπηθῆτε ἀλλὰ τὴν ἀγάπην ἵνα γνῶτε ἣν ἔχω περισσοτέρως εἰς ὑμᾶς, "not to make you sorrowful but to make you know the love which I have in great measure for you," with its introductory οὐχ ἵνα—seems to be at odds with 7:8 ("I made you sorry with the letter"). But we should distinguish Paul's immediate and direct purpose in writing a letter at great cost to himself and the way such a letter was perceived when it was read at Corinth, its "direct result," as Bultmann calls it (51). While the contents of this letter may not have survived (for the view that 2 Cor 10–13 is the letter, see the *Introduction*), we may conjecture that it was filled with Paul's assurance that any "change of heart" (μετάνοια, 7:9 ff.) the Corinthians may be led to adopt would be met with his love; indeed he is confident that they will see the gravity of the situation and return to his side. So "love" (ἀγάπη) stands in a prominent place in this sentence since it is his deeply felt concern for the church's good and for the individual offender (vv 8–10) that really motivated the letter.

5. εἰ δέ τις λελύπηκεν οὐκ ἐμὲ λελύπηκεν, ἀλλὰ ἀπὸ μέρους, ἵνα μὴ ἐπιβαρῶ, πάντας ὑμᾶς, "But if anyone has caused sorrow, he has caused sorrow not to me but in some measure—I mustn't put it too strongly—to all of you." This verse opens a new subsection of the present letter. At last we have "some indication of the root cause of the unhappy situation" (Héring, 15) that prevailed in the background of Paul's dealings with the church. At the center of the picture was an individual (τις, v 5; τοιοῦτος, vv 6, 7) who caused

the pain that Paul has so frequently alluded to. The fact that Paul speaks in such personal terms rules out the identity of the man as someone who has aspersed the character of one of his associates (e.g., Timothy, Titus). The personal pronoun in v 10 clinches the point that Paul himself was the object of this man's outburst.

Yet Paul has to grant that the offender's stand has brought grief to the entire church. This is seen in the enigmatic words ἀλλὰ ἀπὸ μέρους, ἵνα μὴ ἐπιβαρῶ, πάντας ὑμᾶς: the sorrow has been caused not to me (only) "but in some measure [qualifying the verb, and not delimiting the number of persons involved]—so as not to exaggerate, to you all," though it is possible, with Moffatt's translation and following Lietzmann-Kümmel, to take Paul's phrase ἀπὸ μέρους to imply that he does not wish to overstate the case, yet he acknowledges that the pain has been caused "not so much to me as to all of you—at any rate, to a section of you."

6. ἱκανὸν τῷ τοιούτῳ ἡ ἐπιτιμία αὕτη ἡ ὑπὸ τῶν πλειόνων, "The censure in question, which was inflicted on that person by the majority [of church members], is enough for him." This last-mentioned rendering would lead on to the thought that the vote of "censure" (ἐπιτιμία) had been cast by the majority (ὑπὸ τῶν πλειόνων) and had resulted in the individual's being distressed, perhaps by the severity of the reprimand, or perhaps by its duration if, for instance, it involved a permanent exclusion from the church's fellowship or its *agapē* meal (1 Cor 11:17–22; Acts 2:44–46; 2 Pet 2:12, *v.1.*, and the references given in R. J. Bauckham, *Jude, 2 Peter*, WBC 50 [Waco: Word Books, 1983] 84, 85, to which may be added *Did* 10:6: "If anyone is holy, let him come. If not, let him repent" for a possible exclusion formula used at an *agapē* meal; cf. 1 Cor 16:22). In this case Paul's words are directed partly to the "main body" (Barrett's rendering) who decreed the offender's reproof and are calling for a moderation in their treatment, and partly to the minority who had sided with the man and are appealing to them to know how Paul's chief interest is the unity of the church, which, he is confident, has been restored. The term οἱ πλείονες, "the many," however, may be an inclusive title corresponding to the Hebrew הרבים, *hā-rabbîm*, used in Dan 9:27; 11:33, 39; 12:3 (citing Isa 53:11) and at Qumran for the community as a whole and in plenary session (see C. Daniel, "Une mention paulinienne," though M. Black, *The Scrolls and the Christian Faith* [London: Thomas Nelson & Sons, 1961] 177, and M. Delcor, "The Courts of the Church of Corinth and the Courts of Qumran," *Paul and Qumran*, ed. J. Murphy-O'Connor [London: Chapman, 1968] 79, 80, point out that Paul's use of the term need not be directly drawn from the Scrolls but comes from OT precedent, and a pastoral procedure rather than a juridical one, familiar to the Essenes, is in Paul's text).

7. ὥστε τοὐναντίον μᾶλλον ὑμᾶς χαρίσασθαι καὶ παρακαλέσαι, μή πως τῇ περισσοτέρᾳ λύπῃ καταποθῇ ὁ τοιοῦτος, "so that on the other hand, you should rather forgive and console him to prevent his being swallowed up by excessive grief." Whatever the penalty meted out, Paul is now ready to suggest a different attitude, presumably since the "short, sharp shock" has done its remedial work: μᾶλλον, "on the contrary," is the hinge on which his counsel turns. The ἐπιτιμία ("censure," "reproof," "reprimand": Bultmann connects "this"

[αὕτη] action with 7:11 as Titus reported what the letter led to, rather than "punishment," so Barrett's conclusive study, 90) has proved "sufficient" (ἱκα-νόν) to turn him around from his misdemeanor and opposition, and it is time to make amends: Let the church—we are required to add in a phrase such as "you should" or "you must" before the verb (Windisch, 87)—now act rather "to forgive" (χαρίζεσθαι: to be gracious or generous corresponding to ἀφιέναι) him and console (or "encourage," παρεκαλέσαι) him, so that he "may not be swallowed up by excessive sorrow," which would perhaps lead him to abandon the faith altogether. The apostle's deep interest in this man's welfare is only too obvious, and the temper of this verse hardly compares with the stern measures required in 1 Cor 5:5 in the community's dealing with the immoral man there. So we have one further sign that the two cases are not the same (Bruce, 185).

Once more we have to ask whether the church is dealing with one of its own members or is being asked to address the problem of an outsider who, although a believer, has moved onto the scene as Paul's rival and adversary. The tenor of v 7 is indecisive in settling the question. But the next verses do illumine the matter.

8, 9. Διὸ παρακαλῶ ὑμᾶς κυρῶσαι εἰς αὐτὸν ἀγάπην, "So I urge you" (a different nuance of this verb from that in the preceding verse, yet required by the context; perhaps there is an undertone of Paul's apostolic authority here, yet with a novel twist; see C. J. Bjerkelund, Parakalô. Form, Funktion und Sinn der Parakalô-Sätze in der paulinischen Briefen [Oslo: Universitetsforlaget, 1967] 154). The readers may have been expecting him to endorse their action and "confirm" (κυρῶσαι) whatever discipline they had imposed. Instead Paul uses the verb to issue the call: now "affirm" your love for him. The mixing of a legal term (κυρίόω: BGD) and a non-legal one (ἀγάπη) is striking, as noted by Bachmann and Barrett.

Paul's pastoral attitude of restoration and forgiveness may seem to be different from that first perceived in the terms of his letter (in 7:8). So he goes on to make clear that his original intention was to put the church to the test (δοκιμάζειν) and see whether they were in fact on his side ("obedient," ὑπήκοοι). It is not explicitly said to whom this obedience is due; but 7:9 specifies their repentance, and we know that Paul has their coming to a new disposition vis-à-vis his apostolic ministry in view in that chapter. Yet such an acceptance of his ministerial status has to be viewed in the light of 1:24, which makes Paul *both* a servant-figure *and* an appointed leader who expects obedience in his congregations (the latter role is stressed by Bultmann, 53, citing 7:15; 10:6; Phil 2:2; Philem 21; 2 Thess 3:14). What is clear is that Paul is more interested in the church and its well-being than in establishing his victory over the offending individual who, once more, looks to be an intruder on the scene (Barrett).

10. ᾧ δέ τι χαρίζεσθε, κἀγώ· καὶ γὰρ ἐγὼ ὃ κεχάρισμαι, εἴ τι κεχάρισμαι, δι' ὑμᾶς ἐν προσώπῳ Χριστοῦ, "If you forgive anyone, I also do the same. For what I have forgiven—if indeed there was anything to forgive—it was done on your account in the presence of Christ." The close involvement of the church—Paul's major interest, as we have seen—comes to the fore here. Reversing the expected order of events, he says: ᾧ δέ τι χαρίζεσθε, κἀγώ, as

you forgive this person, I join you in my forgiveness of the offense. And my act of pardon and acceptance has been given δι᾽ ὑμᾶς: for your sakes, and in the presence of our common Lord (ἐν προσώπῳ Χριστοῦ, perhaps "as though Christ were present" [cf. 1 Cor 5:4], as he summons Christ as a witness and guarantor; so Bratcher, *Translator's Guide*, 24; Windisch, 91).

11. To do otherwise would have disastrous consequences: ἵνα μὴ πλεονεκτηθῶμεν ὑπὸ τοῦ Σατανᾶ, "that Satan may be prevented from taking advantage of us" (the verb πλεονεκτεῖν means "to outwit, cheat, defraud," but in the passive "to be outwitted by Satan" [BGD] means to allow Satan to rob the church of one of its group). Two measures would bring about this result of the enemy's success in the matter. If, on the one hand, the offender were to be lost to the church by lapsing into "excessive despair" and remorse, then Satan's work would be achieved; if, on the other side, Paul and the church were to withhold their love and acceptance, the church's enemy would be just as pleased. As it is, neither extreme will come about, and "Satan" (a Hebrew word for the archenemy of God and man, especially in his role of prosecutor and accuser; cf. Job chs. 1–2; M. Dibelius, *Die Geisterwelt im Glauben des Paulus* [Göttingen: Vandenhoeck & Ruprecht, 1909] 53 f., for Satan's role as an accuser of Christians, and for his opposition to the church, see J. Weiss, *Earliest Christianity*, vol. 2, tr. F. C. Grant [Gloucester, MA: Peter Smith, 1970 reprint] 602 f.) will not win the day, "for we know well" (Rev 2:24) his νοήματα, his evil "thoughts" as he lays plans to ensnare the feet of unwary Christians (1 Pet 5:8; *Barn* 2:8–10; *Test. Dan* 6:3). νοήματα, RSV "designs," has "some adverse implications" in Paul's letter (3:14; 4:4; 10:5; 11:3 [Bruce]).

Explanation

Paul's pastoral attitudes are much on display in this pericope. He finds it needful to explain why he acted as he did, presumably because this apparent going back on his promise was the bone of contention at Corinth. He was under fire and his apostolic character was assailed because he did not visit Corinth as he had originally planned. Doubtless this course of action was held against him by someone at Corinth who used it as grounds for an attack on him personally. Paul saw this affront not so much as a personal insult to be borne, but as a denigration of his apostolic work and an obstacle to be removed (4:3).

His counter-reply was to unfold the reasons for his nonappearance and to paint in the background of the sending of a "sorrowful letter" (2:4). Grief and joy mingle in this paragraph, as he rehearses the pain that was caused and deeply felt and the relief that came once the offender had relented in his opposition. The group in the church that had sided with him were also won back.

It is now a time for making amends. Paul's skillful *pastoralia* points the way forward. The severe reprimand has worked; it is time to forgive and reinstate the errant brother. The loyal Corinthians must affirm their love for him and set about restoring the church's unity of spirit—a concern always present in Paul's pastoral handling of all congregational disputes. Wisely

Paul steers a course between the Scylla of indifference and dissension on the one hand, and the Charybdis of rigorism and an unforgiving spirit on the other. The strains of Paul's "care of the churches" (11:28) did not blind him to what must be done at Corinth: a firm stand and a severe letter with its reproof were needful, but now such a sternness may, indeed must, be replaced by a warm, generous, appealing gesture of pardon and restitution to the church's fellowship. To fail here is to play exactly into Satan's hands. The enemy "knows" what can and does divide Christians; but we take refuge in that "we know" (2:11) what he knows and can circumvent his ploys.

C. Paul's Concern for Corinth   (2:12, 13)

Bibliography

Barrett, C. K. "Titus." In *Essays on Paul*, 118–31. London: SPCK; Philadelphia: Westminster Press, 1982. **Hemer, C. J.** "Alexandria Troas." *TynB* 26 (1975) 79–112. **Rissi, M.** *Studien zum zweiten Korintherbrief*. 15–17. **Robinson, J. A. T.** *Redating the New Testament*. London: SCM Press, 1976. 47–52, 54, 55.

Translation

[12] *When I came to Troas [to proclaim [a]] the Gospel of Christ, in spite of there being an opportunity [b] opened by the Lord for me,* [13] *I had [c] no relief for my spirit [d] because I could not find [e] my brother Titus. For that reason I bade them farewell [f] and went off to Macedonia.*

Notes

[a]The verb is added to fill out Paul's text which runs literally: "I came to Troas for (εἰς) the Gospel" (εὐαγγέλιον, which functions as a *nomen actionis*, as though the verse ran: εἰς τὸ εὐαγγελίζεσθαι Χριστόν).

[b]The Greek has a metaphor, literally, "a door having been opened for me by/in the Lord." See 1 Cor 16:9; Col 4:3 for Paul's usage elsewhere of this Rabbinic idiom for "an opportunity set before a person" (Str-B 3:484 f.).

[c]The perfect tense ἔσχηκα, "I had," in place of the aorist for historical narration: Moule, *Idiom Book*, 145; BDF § 343.2; cf. 1:9.

[d]Paul's πνεῦμα ("spirit") is Paul himself (Bultmann, 55, citing Rom 1:9; 2 Cor 7:13; 1 Cor 16:18). The parallel is 7:5 where (unusually) σάρξ ("flesh") is used as synonymous with πνεῦμα.

[e]The dative of an infinitive (τῷ εὑρεῖν) is found only here in the NT (BDF § 401). But see Héring, 17.

[f]The verb is ἀποταξάμενος, aorist middle, meaning "having said farewell (to), taken leave (of)" (BGD).

Form/Structure/Setting

This short section rounds off Paul's recital of his travel plans. The paragraph provides a link with 7:5 where the arrangement to meet Titus at Troas on his return from Corinth is picked up in the narrative form. As it happened, on not finding Titus, Paul moved across to Macedonia where the storytelling is resumed at 7:5 ff.

Bultmann (55) makes the suggestion that this pericope stresses Paul's intense longing to know how things were at Corinth, and so is still part of his apologetic writing, though cast in narrative style. It is clear the narrative breaks off at 2:14 to be completed in chap. 7, leaving 2:14–7:4 as a lengthy excursus devoted to an exposition of the apostolic ministry. But the link between 2:13 and 7:5 is not axiomatic for Rissi (*Studien*, 15 f.), who notes that (a) 7:5–7, which exemplifies Paul's experience of God's comfort through guidance, is connected to 7:2–4, whose theme is divine consolation in his distress, and (b) the reference in 2:12 to Paul's "proclamation of the Gospel" spills over into 2:14–17 where he has to deal polemically with false preachers. These observations are worth pondering in our attempt to see the structure of 2 Corinthians. But there is still no denying the verbal links, linguistic agreement, and stylistic congruity between 2:12, 13 and 7:5:

ἐλθὼν	paired with	ἐλθόντων ἡμῶν
εἰς τὴν Τρῳάδα		εἰς Μακεδονίαν
οὐκ ἔσχηκα ἄνεσιν		οὐδεμίαν ἔσχηκεν ἄνεσιν
τῷ πνεύματί μου		ἡ σὰρξ ἡμῶν

Barrett ("Titus," 130, n. 25) concludes that the change from first person to third person in effect militates against regarding 2:13 and 7:5 as originally a continuous piece of writing, interpolated by 2:14–7:4 as a separate document.

Comment

12. ἐλθὼν δὲ εἰς τὴν Τρῳάδα, "When I came to [the] Troas" or possibly "the Troad." The definite article may point back to 1:23, which, however, does not mention Troas (Barrett, BDF § 261.1).

"Troas" is, however, here clearly not the province but Alexandria Troas, the port of embarkation for sea travelers from Asia to Macedonia (Acts 16:8, 11; 20:5 f.; cf. 2 Tim 4:13). This journey of Paul's is not recorded in Acts, and took place after his "trial" in Asia (1:8). For a study of what we know of ancient Alexandria Troas, see Hemer, *TynB* 26 (1975) 79–112, with the observation "Troas is unexpectedly prominent in the New Testament texts" (95).

θύρας μοι (dative of advantage) ἀνεῳγμένης ἐν κυρίῳ: lit., "a door stood wide open"—giving force to the perfect tense—"for me by the Lord," presumably the risen Christ whose Gospel Paul was charged to proclaim (Gal 1:15 f.; 1 Cor 1:17: ἀπέστειλέν με Χριστὸς . . . εὐαγγελίζεσθαι; cf. 1 Cor 9:16).

As to what historical circumstances led Paul to see "a door standing open" for evangelism at Troas we can only guess. Windisch (94) thinks that it implies at least the provision of a house for his lodging and then for a "base of operation" to launch his mission (cf. Lydia's home in Acts 16:15, and house settings in general for both discussion and Christian hospitality: see H. J.

Klauck, *Hausgemeinde und Hauskirche im frühen Christentums* [Stuttgart: Verlag katholisches Bibelwerk, 1981]). There must have been more to the phrase, and we should see here a measure of success in preaching and church formation at Troas. When Paul came to leave Troas (prematurely?) he did so with reluctance: ἀποταξάμενος αὐτοῖς, lit., "having said farewell to them" (v 13). Héring notes the "solemn character" of this farewell. And Rissi (*Studien*, 16) sees in this decision to leave a successful mission enterprise in its early days an "ultimate sign of his love" for the Corinthian church, about whose welfare Paul was deeply concerned. He was eager to rendezvous with Titus in order to learn from him how matters fared at Corinth.

13. Paul found no rest (ἄνεσιν) in spirit, in spite of burgeoning opportunities at Troas. The reason was the absence of Titus whom he had arranged to meet there. This is the first reference to Titus in this letter; see chap. 7 and *Comment* there for this important person in Paul's dealings with Corinth, and also C. K. Barrett ("Titus").

So Paul took his leave of "the people at Troas" (implied in αὐτοῖς, Lietzmann-Kümmel, 107), and went on to Macedonia on the other side of the Thracian sea, presumably by boat (as Ignatius did, *Polyc.* 8) as he was eager to meet Titus as soon as possible. But perhaps Paul had to go by the land route in the winter season when the sea lanes were closed. He would know therefore that Titus also would be on that road. A crossing of the Hellespont was still involved, and Barrett ("Titus," 124) conjectures that the two men missed each other. This may explain Paul's distress when he did reach Macedonia (7:5: "for even [καὶ] when we came into Macedonia, we found no relief" until Titus arrived, 7:6). But Titus's nonappearance to greet Paul in Macedonia may equally be explained by his tardiness in reaching Macedonia from Corinth.

This trip of Paul's is usually identified with the one in Acts 20:1 and may be dated near the end of A.D. 55 (see *Introduction,* pp. xxxiv, xlvi; cf. Barrett, "Titus," 123 f.; Robinson, *Redating,* 50, 55).

Explanation

The agitation that troubled Paul's spirit and made his ministry at Troas less than it might have been is clear from this text. When pastoral concerns weighed heavily upon him he could not put his heart in evangelistic opportunity. In the event, it was better for him to quit Troas and press on to meet his colleague on his return from Corinth. No good purpose is served, we learn, in any Christian's attempting a piece of service when his or her real interests lie elsewhere; and pastoral responsibility stood high on Paul's agenda at this time.

V. The Main Theme: Paul's Apostolic Ministry (2:14–7:16)

A. The Apostle's Adequacy for Ministry (2:14–3:6)

Bibliography

Baird, W. "Letters of Recommendation. A Study of 2 Cor. 3:1–3." *JBL* 80 (1961) 166–72. **Bartelink, G. J. M.** "Θεοκάπηλος et ses synonymes chez Isidore de Péluse." *VC* 12 (1958) 227–31. **Barth, G.** "Die Eignung des Verkündigers in 2 Kor 2, 14–3, 6." In *Kirche*, FS G. Bornkamm, ed. D. Lührmann and G. Strecker, 257–70. Tübingen: J. C. B. Mohr, 1980. **Betz, H.-D.** *Der Apostel Paulus und die sokratische Tradition*. BHT 45. Tübingen: J. C. B. Mohr, 1972. **Collange, J.-F.** *Enigmes de la deuxième épître de Paul aux Corinthiens*. SNTSMS 18. Cambridge: University Press, 1972. **Collins, J. N.** "Georgi's 'Envoys' in 2 Cor 11:23." *JBL* 93 (1974) 88–96. **Daniel, C.** "Un mention paulinienne des esséniens de Qumran." *RQ* 5 (1966) 553–59. **Denis, A. M.** "La fonction apostolique et la liturgie nouvelle en Esprit. Etude thématique des métaphores pauliniennes du culte nouveau." *RScPhTh* 42 (1958) 401–36, 617–56. **Egan, R. B.** "Lexical Evidence on Two Passages." *NovT* 19 (1977) 36–42. **Friesen, I. I.** *The Glory of the Ministry of Jesus Christ. Illustrated by a Study of 2 Cor 2:14–3:18*. Theologischen Dissertationen 7. Basel: Fr. Reinhardt, 1971. **Georgi, D.** *Die Gegner des Paulus im 2 Korintherbrief*. WMANT 11. Neukirchen-Vluyn: Neukirchener Verlag, 1964. **Hickling, C. J. A.** "The Sequence of Thought in II Corinthians Chapter Three." *NTS* 21 (1974) 380–95. **Jaubert, A.** *La notion d'alliance dans le judaïsme aux abords de l'ère chrétienne*. Paris: Editions du Seuil, 1963. **Käsemann, E.** *Die Legitimität des Apostels. Eine Untersuchung zu II Korinther 10–13*. Darmstadt: Wissenschaftliche Buchgesellschaft, 1956. (Also in *ZNW* 41 [1942] 33–71.) **Kinsey, A. B.** "The Triumph-Joy." *ExpT* 21 (1910) 282 f. **Knox, W. L.** *St. Paul and the Church of the Gentiles*. Cambridge: University Press, 1939. 129–31. **Lane, W. L.** "Covenant: The Key to Paul's Conflict with Corinth." *TynB* 33 (1982) 3–29. **Lohmeyer, E.** *Vom göttlichen Wohlgeruch*. Heidelberg: Carl Winter, 1919. **Lührmann, D.** *Die Offenbarungsverständnis bei Paulus und in paulinischen Gemeinde*. WMANT 16. Neukirchen: Neukirchener Verlag, 1965. **Manson, T. W.** "2 Cor 2:14–17: Suggestions Towards an Exegesis." In *Studia Paulina* (de Zwaan FS), ed. J. Sevenster and W. C. van Unnik, 155–62. Haarlem: Erven F. Bohn, 1953. **Marshall, P.** "A Metaphor of Social Shame: ΘΡΙΑΜΒΕΥΕΙΝ in 2 Cor 2:14." *NovT* 25 (1983) 302–17. **Moore, G. F.** "Conjectanea Talmudica: 2 Cor 2:14–16: The Savour of Life or of Death." *Journal of the American Oriental Society* 26/2 (1905) 329, 30. **Pope, R. M.** "Studies in Pauline Vocabulary 1: of the Triumph-Joy." *ExpTim* 21 (1910) 19–21. **Prat, F.** "Le triomphe du Christ sur les Principautés et les Puissances (Col 2:15)." *RSR* 3 (1912) 201–29. **Provence, T. E.** " 'Who Is Sufficient for These Things?' An Exegesis of 2 Corinthians 2:15–3:18." *NovT* 24 (1982) 54–81. **Prümm, K.** "Phänomenologie der Offenbarung laut 2 Kor." *Bib* 43 (1962) 396–416. ———. *Diakonia Pneumatos. Der 2 Korintherbrief als Zugang zur apostolischen Botschaft*. Vols. 1, 2. Rome/Freiburg/Wien: Herder, 1960–67. **Rissi, M.** *Studien zum zweiten Korintherbrief*. **Wilckens, U.** *Weisheit und Torheit. Eine exegetisch-religionsgeschichtliche Untersuchung zu 1 Kor. 1 und 2*. BHT 26. Tübingen: J. C. B. Mohr, 1959. **Williamson, L., Jr.** "Led in Triumph: Paul's Use of *Thriambeuō*." *Int* 22 (1968) 317–32.

Translation

[14]*But thanks be to God, who is ever leading us in his triumph in the cause of Christ and through us is making known the fragrance of the knowledge of God in all places.* [15]*For we are an aroma of Christ to God among those on the road to salvation—and among those on the road to ruin.* [16]*Among those in the latter case [we are] a deadly fume* a *that leads to death, but for those in the former a life-giving fragrance that leads to life. And who is adequate for this [kind of ministry]?* [17]*For we do not go about adulterating God's message as our many* b *[opponents] do. No, we speak as those who do so with sincerity, whose word is from God and given in the sight of God and as servants of Christ.*

[3:1]*Are we starting over again recommending ourselves to you? Or do we require, as some do, letters of recommendation to you or from you?* [2]*You yourselves are our letter, written in your* c *hearts, read and recognized by all people;* [3]*and you clearly show yourselves [to be] a letter of Christ, composed by our ministry [to you], written not in ink but by the Spirit of the living God, not on stone tablets but on tablets of the human heart.* d [4]*This is the confidence we have through Christ in the presence of God.* [5]*It is not that we are adequate in ourselves to reckon anything to our credit, but our adequacy comes from God,* [6]*who indeed gave us our adequacy to be servants of a new covenant, based not on the letter but on the Spirit; for the letter kills, but the Spirit imparts life.*

Notes

a ὀσμὴ ἐκ θανάτου εἰς θάνατον is a difficult expression in Greek, recognized by the omission of ἐκ by D G and the Byzantine uncials generally. Evidently later copyists were perplexed and the text does read more smoothly without the preposition; the fume of death that leads to death (see Godet, 90, who thinks ἐκ was added later in imitation of Rom 1:17). So the omission is adopted in our translation which makes θανάτου adjectival. If with Barrett, the ἐκ is retained as *lectio difficilior* (the "harder reading" principle), then it is a matter of exegesis to interpret ἐκ θανάτου, either with Barrett, "an odour issuing from death and leading to death" (but what does this really mean? see Barrett, 101), or Collange (35, 36), who, rejecting the interpretations of Hughes (ἐκ . . . εἰς is a superlative) and of Plummer and Lietzmann (who explain the rhetorical phrase as a progression), relates the expression to how Paul's life is perceived; in the eyes of unbelievers he seems as a man given over to death and so his ministry seals their fate in a sentence of death (citing 4:10 ff.).

b οἱ πολλοί is read by ℵ A B C K P Ψ 88 1739 Byz vg cop^bo,sa eth, with λοιποί ("in the way others do," Héring's translation, read by P46 D G syr^ph and Marcion; and note that λοιποί is rejected by Metzger's UBSGNT Committee as "too offensive an expression for Paul to have used" here, but accepted by Godet, 91, 92. See *Comment*, p. 50.

c ἐν ταῖς καρδίαις ὑμῶν is, however, weakly attested (ℵ, 33, 88, 436, 1881, eth), yet seems required by the context (Barrett, Héring, Bultmann, Provence). καρδίαις ἡμῶν ("our hearts") is the reading of P46 A B C D etc. but may be due to assimilation to 7:3. See Bultmann, *Theology*, 1:222.

d καρδίαις is clearly the "more difficult reading," smoothed over by F K vg syr^p cop^bo,sa to read καρδίας (genitive), accepted by Moulton-Turner, *Grammar*, 3:214. But the LXX text used here probably explains καρδίαις, which is to be preferred.

Form/Structure/Setting

τῷ δὲ θεῷ χάρις (v 14) is an elliptical construction (BDF § 128.6) drawn from the model of classical Greek and often used by Paul (Rom 6:17; 7:25;

1 Cor 15:57; 2 Cor 8:16; 9:15), "Thanks (be) to God." The order of words here is the same as 1 Cor 15:57, and the accent falls on "God—to whom be praise!" (so Plummer, Hughes, Bachmann).

With Collange, *Enigmes* (22, 23), and Bornkamm, "The History of the Origin," in *The Authorship and Integrity of the New Testament* ([London: SPCK, 1965] 75–77, but see *Introduction*, pp. xxxix–xl), this sentence may mark the opening of a letter originally independent and added in here when the fragments of 2 Corinthians were assembled, and so the v may be redactional, setting the stage for the following exposition of the apostolic ministry. The phrase ἐν παντὶ τόπῳ, lit., "in every place," coupled with πάντοτε, "always," in v 14 suggests an apologetic plea for the universal character of Paul's mission and ministry, to be entered against his opponents who are clearly in view in this longer section (2:17; 3:1; 4:2, 10).

The liturgical flavor of v 14 (seen also in the participial forms that follow the verbless acclamation) is further enhanced by cultic or sacrificial terms that follow ("fragrance," ὀσμή; "aroma," εὐωδία). Such terms are designed to enforce the claim of Paul's work as "pleasing to God," as the OT sacrifices were so regarded (Lev, Ezek).

Yet "smell" is an ambivalent term: it may be a poisonous fume or a pleasant fragrance. So Paul develops a set of parallelisms (v 15), climaxing in a rhetorical question which holds a tacit claim that may (Georgi, *Die Gegner*, 224) or may not (most commentators and especially Hickling, "The Sequence") be taken directly from what Paul's rivals were saying: "we are competent" to exercise our ministry. Paul will answer the question in 3:5: ἡ ἱκανότης ἡμῶν ἐκ τοῦ θεοῦ, "our capability comes (only) from God," and does not depend on the sources that his opponents evidently appealed to (2:17; 3:1).

Yet Paul, who disdained any method that could lead to a cheapening of the message, did appeal to his ministry at Corinth as evidential (3:2: again a paronomasia—γινωσκομένη καὶ ἀναγινωσκομένη): the Corinthians are as letters "read and recognized" by everyone who cares to examine his work, which is likened to a letter written on the Corinthians' hearts, v 2: see 1 Cor 9: 1, 2.

A final appeal is made to OT prophecy, specifically Ezekiel's hope (11:19; 36:26) that one day God's word would be engraven, not on stone tablets (Ezek 31:18) but on the "fleshly tablets of the heart" ("fleshly," σαρκίναις, here is a contrasting term to "stone," λιθίναις, drawn from LXX; and σάρξ/σαρκινός has an unusual meaning for Paul). But he is evidently led to it by the analogy of a letter, a thought in turn derived from "the letters of recommendation" which were being flourished before the Corinthians by his adversaries who carried such to accredit their mission (Collange, *Enigmes*, 44).

The imagery of the "letter," however, shades off into a contrast between two covenants. The transition is from v 3—the letter is "ministered" (διακονηθεῖσα) by us—to v 6: ministers (διακόνους) of a new covenant. Paul's role is that of "servant" (διάκονος, v 6) of the new covenant given in Jeremiah's oracle (Jer 31:31–4; but also in 32:37–40; 50:5; and Ezek 36:26 f.). This concept of what ministry Paul claimed for himself lies at the heart of his discussion of ἱκανότης ("competence"), which in turn goes back to the question posed in 2:16*b*. Vv 1–3 prepare for the statement of "specific self-awareness of the apostle" (Bultmann, *TDNT* 6:8) in v 4: "such confidence" we have, based not on ourselves but on God who has equipped us by his Spirit to dispense the new covenant which leads to life (v 6) in the same Spirit.

The carefully arranged structure of the passage may now be seen, following Provence, "Who Is Sufficient?" 57, 58. The stage is set by 2:15, 16 with its parallelism: Paul's ministry and preaching have a "double effect" (Bultmann, 70) and he is called on—by the exigencies of the situation at Corinth—to clarify why this is so. The chiastic schema looks like this:

The issue (2:16b)

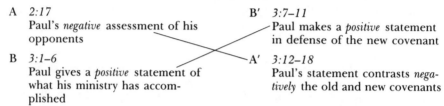

A *2:17*
Paul's *negative* assessment of his opponents

B *3:1–6*
Paul gives a *positive* statement of what his ministry has accomplished

B' *3:7–11*
Paul makes a *positive* statement in defense of the new covenant

A' *3:12–18*
Paul's statement contrasts *negatively* the old and new covenants

Granted that this neat arrangement gives the impression of being too tidy, it still remains the case that a central motif runs through the section 2:7–3:18 and is continued into 4:1–6, which summarize and recapitulate the earlier passage. That passage offers a rationale for Paul's two-sided ministry, for which God has equipped him. It has four parts: (1) he is not afraid to preach undistorted truth (A); (2) the Holy Spirit has changed lives through his work (B); (3) like the new covenant, his ministry shares God's glory (B'); (4) unlike Moses' ministry, his ministry takes away the veil of hard-heartedness (A').

Comment

2:14. God is praised for one special reason: θριαμβεύοντι ἡμᾶς ἐν τῷ Χριστῷ. The meaning of the verb is much debated (see Bultmann, 66, who gives four senses, ranging from "to celebrate a triumph," whether military [Appian, *Rom. Hist. Pun.* 20, of Scipio Africanus] or religious [θρίαμβος as a hymn to Dionysus], to "cause to triumph" [KJV/AV and older commentators, but now out of fashion: see earlier discussions by Pope, Kinsey, and Héring who take the verb in a causative sense as a kind of *hiphil:* but against this, L. Williamson, "Led in Triumph," *Int* 330, n. 45]. Bengel's rendering *qui facit ut semper triumphemus in Christo* is also open to objection as lacking lexical support and also is inappropriate in Paul's context).

"To lead in a triumphal procession" (Delling, *TDNT* 3:160; this rendering is accepted by Rissi, *Studien,* 17, and Friesen, *Glory,* 25) has more secure support (see BGD, 363); and Williamson and Collange concur in giving a paradoxical nuance: Paul is the conquered slave exposed to public ridicule (1 Cor 4:9, 10, 13) . . . and, at the same time, "he is the joyful participant in Christ's victory celebration. It is, in fact, just the kind of paradox Paul loved!" (Williamson, 325 f.). See Collange, *Enigmes,* 24, 25, who appeals to 4:10 and 12:9, and sees in the paradox of "strength-in-weakness" Paul's theme developed in the succeeding chapters of the letter (see Marshall, 312, in response to Egan, 37). Collange makes a telling point that Paul needs to justify his kind of ministry in the eyes of the readers who were being influenced by the "triumphalistic" tenor of Paul's opponents, a motif reinforced by Marshall's argument that the verb carries the nuance of social disgrace, linked with "the thorn" of 12:7. This background to Paul's writing in 2 Corinthians is opposed by Hickling, "The Sequence," who brings the charge of circularity against this reconstruction of false teaching which *ex hypothesi* Paul is answering in those chapters and indeed throughout the letter. Hickling's position (381) is that "it was not their beliefs that he is here in chap. 3 controverting in addition to their slanders on his person and claims, but only the latter." He therefore dismisses the influence of "opponents" as "quite limited" when we ask what motivated the direction of Paul's thought. All he will concede is that Paul is "vindicating his entitlement to a greater respect than he was being accorded."

But Paul's defense of his apostolic ministry and the distance he sets between himself and the "many" (2:17) who have a diametrically opposite idea of ministry is a *theological* issue, with practical ramifications. It cannot be dismissed simply as a "personal rather than a doctrinal" matter, since for Paul "ministry" and "gospel" are two sides of the same coin. For this reason we regard Collange's point (made above and in his *Enigmes*, 56, 57) as well taken, and providing a reason for Paul's wording, otherwise difficult to explain in context. Besides, Hickling himself (394, n. 3) is compelled to bring in the admission that the passage contains "diversified theological motifs" at the close of his interesting study.

The next participle, φανεροῦντι, "is making known" (RSV "spreads," linked with "fragrance of the knowledge of him"), is also a polemical term in this setting, with an eye on those who claimed to manifest the divine power in their lifestyle and ministry (cf. 13:3–10: the issue is one of "evidence" of apostolic credentials; so Georgi, 224; Käsemann, *Die Legitimität*, 51–66; Betz, *Der Apostel Paulus*, 133).

Paul's verb has to be understood in the light of 4:2: "it is by the making known (φανέρωσις) of the truth" that the true commendation (συνιστάνοντες) is shown. The verb at 2:14 is preparing for the debate over apostolic qualifications, a subject hotly discussed at Corinth, just as vv 15, 16 will be expanded on in 4:3–6, leading to Paul's self-description as a "pottery vessel" (4:7) to mark his own frailty and humanity. Yet he is charged with delivering the "treasure" of God's message, here likened to the "fragrance of God's revelation" (γνῶσις, "knowledge," another highly charged and volatile term at Corinth, closely associated with φανέρωσις as key terms in the debate at Corinth centered on the issue, How is the divine known and revealed? See Lührmann, *Das Offenbarungsverständnis*, 45–66, 159 ff., for the polemical setting: against Prümm, *Bib* 43 [1962] 399, who minimizes the contextual relevance of the Corinthian crisis for Paul).

Paul's metaphor (ὀσμή, "fragrance," but perhaps a more neutral term such as "odor" should also be entertained, as Paul will [v 15] distinguish two sorts of smell) may be drawn from the use of incense scattered along the victor's route in a Roman imperator's return from a campaign (Windisch, Plummer, Hughes). The point of this illustration is that it explains how ὀσμή can be understood as εἰς θάνατον, leading to death for prisoners, and εἰς ζωήν, leading to life for the victorious army. But the evidence for this practice is weak (Collange, 29; but see Knox, *St. Paul*, 129 n. 5; Lietzmann, Friesen,

The Glory, 26), and the same criticism stands against Lohmeyer's suggestion (*Vom göttlichen Wohlgeruch*, 33 ff.) that "perfume" is a general term for the divine presence in many religions (e.g., Euripides, *Hippolytus*, 1392: the goddess Artemis appears as ὦ θεῖον ὀσμῆς πνεῦμα: "O divine spirit of fragrance").

A more specific application to OT wisdom literature (Sir 24:15; 39:14; 50:15; Bultmann, 68, 69) makes Paul link "the knowledge of God" with wisdom under the common figure of a sweet odor (Prümm, *art. cit.*). But with this view as with the appeal to OT sacrifices, described as εὐωδία (v 15: Gen 8:21; cf. Exod 29:18; Lev 1:9, 13, 17; Ezek 20:41, so Strachan, Denis, Stumpff, *TDNT* 2:808–10), the difficulty remains that v 15 makes a distinctive contrast based on two reactions.

T. W. Manson, "2 Cor 2:14–17," is therefore able to meet this objection with his appeal to rabbinic literature (citing Str-B 3:498 f., but we have noted that G. F. Moore, "Conjectanea Talmudica," laid the groundwork for this suggested background as long ago as 1905). The Torah is often called a medicine or drug (סם, *sam;* סַמָּא, *sammā'* in Aramaic) which may bring benefit or harm according to the circumstances of its use. In fact, the medicine is unchanged—it is the Torah; but those who come into contact with it find it to be either an elixir of life (סם חיים, *sam ḥayyim*) or a deadly poison (סם המות, *sam ha-māwet*), i.e., to Israel it is life, to the Gentiles it is death. Paul is taking this twofold effect of Torah and is applying it to his Gospel, or more concretely, the γνῶσις τοῦ θεοῦ which Paul was charged to make known in his ministry. Provided we can make the short transition from "perfume" (ὀσμή) to "medicine" (as in *Yoma* 72*b*, to which Manson appeals, 158; but Kümmel, 198, objects; a reply to Kümmel is noted below), we can see the linkage. Paul's apostolic work is to offer Christ as the repository of divine knowledge (cf. Col 2:3), which may either be accepted as life-conferring or rejected (in which case it is death-dealing). In Christ is the remedy for sin; if it is taken, it is a life-giving medicine; if it is refused, the apostle's ministry acts like deadly poison. Hence the claim in v 17 that Paul does not offer an adulterated word from God, as his rivals are said to do. On Manson's theory, the issue is christological; and this may well tie in with recent discussion of οἱ πολλοί, "the many," in the light of 11:4.

15. ἐν τοῖς σῳζομένοις καὶ ἐν τοῖς ἀπολλυμένοις. The present participles denote "those on the way" to either "salvation" or "perdition" (4:3; cf. 1 Cor. 1:18; Phil 2:18; 1 Pet 2:7). We observe the progression from v 14 which (if redactional) simply makes the statement: the preaching is an odor. Perhaps Paul's pointed application follows: Yes, and *we* are the sweet smell of Christ (the anointed one, Χριστός, from χρίειν, to pour oil: here would be a link with medicine, in reply to Kümmel above). Paul's Gospel proclamation was intended to lead to the hearer's "salvation" (σωτηρία: see W. Förster-G. Fohrer, *TDNT* 7:966–1004, esp. 992: it is an eschatological term, announcing that the day of God's promised deliverance for Israel [cf. 6:2] has arrived, to be greeted by faith and with gratitude: see Rom 10:1, 11; 11:14; 1 Cor 9:22; 10:33; 1 Thess 2:16. But it is given a wider application by Paul as "apostle to the nations" [Rom 1:5] to include the Gentiles [Rom 10:12–17]). The converse is ἀπώλεια, "destruction, ruin, loss," also an eschatological codeword for existence apart from God: see U. Wilckens, *Weisheit und Torheit*, 21–23, on the two participles σῳζόμενοι . . . ἀπολλύμενοι).

16. Obviously ὀσμή ("odor") here must carry two opposite meanings corresponding to the way it is appreciated. To the "lost" it is a fume, ἐκ θανάτου εἰς θάνατον, either "deadly" in itself, or carried by Paul who "embodied" a sentence of death (4:10–12), or suggesting only a dead Jesus to the unreceptive (Barrett, 101). To those who respond, the proclamation of Paul is a fragrance ἐκ ζωῆς εἰς ζωήν, that is, one that issues from life—Jesus' risen life (Barrett)—or that speaks of Paul's own life-in-Christ, hidden yet no less real (Phil 1:23; cf. Col 3:3) and that leads the hearer to "eternal life" (Rom 6:23). The same apostle and Gospel (the two terms are correlative, and neither is understood apart from the other [Bultmann, *Theology* 1:59 f.]) thus produced two quite diverse results.

Such weight is attached to this ministry that Paul can ask rhetorically: καὶ πρὸς ταῦτα τίς ἱκανός; who, then, is competent—or possibly "equipped"—for these things? Not only the office or the teaching is at stake, but rather it is the person who bears this responsibility that prompts a sudden outburst (Windisch, 99; Georgi, *Die Gegner*, 221 f.). Bultmann (72) rightly sees that the implied question is, How can I be such a messenger?

The issue is that of ἱκανότης ("competence, capability, adequacy," but much more a matter of true authority and evidence for it), a term obviously ventilated at Corinth. Paul will return to the matter in 3:5, 6, and the next v suggests that there were those in Paul's mind who did lay claim to both ἱκανότης and to some success in discharging a ministry as δοῦλοι Χριστοῦ, "servants of Christ" (11:23; cf. 11:13: "they masquerade as apostles of Christ"). See Georgi, *Die Gegner*, 224: "the opponents had very probably spoken of their competence and connected this in quite direct relation with God," even answering Paul's question "we are competent," since they showed all the marks of a divine-man (θεῖος ἀνήρ) type of hellenistic religion, mixed with a Jewish tradition; and their claim was to be "inspired . . . filled by God and ἔνθεοι" (Georgi, 147). Barrett (103) agrees in part, though he doubts whether the designation "divine-man" is justified; that doubt is considerably reinforced by C. H. Holladay's monograph *Theios Aner in Hellenistic Judaism,* whose subtitle, "A Critique of the Use of This Category in New Testament Christology," shows the book's intent (SBL Dissertation Series 40 [Missoula: Scholars Press, 1977] esp. 34–40).

At all events, we may be confident that there is a polemical tone to the question in v 16; otherwise it becomes difficult to connect it to the next v.

17. οὐ γάρ ἐσμεν κτλ., *"for* we are not," etc. The connective γάρ is to be given full weight. Paul's earlier question "who is equipped?" presumes a negative answer (Barrett, Collange: against Plummer, Bachmann, Lietzmann, Héring, who boldly adds in [We are]). Or, at least, when the answer is given in 3:5 f. it is a considerably modified affirmative. Instead, here Paul puts a distance between his concept of ministry and that cherished and propagated by his opponents. It is clear how he viewed their pretentious claims. They are no better than "hucksters (who) adulterate . . . they act for profit" (so Bengel, who anticipated recent discussion on Paul's verb καπηλεύοντες, a verb that combines two meanings: (1) to dilute as wine may be "watered down" (Barrett) and (2) to make a profit by selling shoddy goods (Windisch, *TDNT* 3:606–9; Bartelink quotes the witness of the later Isidore of Pelusium who writes [using this verb] of certain church leaders who dishonor their office

by listening to pretty women, and then begin teaching false doctrine). The verb is a *hapax* in the NT and found only twice in LXX (cf. Isa 1:22 for an interesting allusion to mixing water with wine). Plato (*Protagoras* 313) uses it of pseudo-sophists and mock philosophers in his day: "the sophist is a merchant or retailer in knowledge" (κάπηλος), and Philostratus, *Life of Apollonius* 1.13, has the verb σοφίαν καπηλεύειν, "to hawk wisdom around."

The term is obviously one of disparagement, directed against "the many" (οἱ πολλοί) who seemed to Paul to be on the scene at Corinth (for their interest in the profit-motive, see 11:7–10, 20; 12:13; cf. Georgi, *Die Gegner*, 234 ff.). But their conduct was worse than avarice in Paul's eyes (4:2; 11:4: they distort the truth and introduce an alien gospel). "Many" says nothing of their number, but testifies to their influence in introducing a rival message which surely has no connection with Qumran teachings (so Daniel, "Une mention"). Rather it is a pseudo-Christian preaching which Paul reprobates.

On the other side, Paul's message is "from God" (ἐκ θεοῦ) and proclaimed "in God's presence" (κατέναντι θεοῦ) and ἐν Χριστῷ, "in Christ," i.e., as Christ's servant ought to do, pointing on to 4:5. It is fanciful to see in these three phrases a groundplan of chapters 3–7: ἐκ θεοῦ = 3:1–4:12; κατέναντι θεοῦ = 4:13–5:10; ἐν Χριστῷ = 5:14–7:1, as Prümm, *Diakonia Pneumatos* 1.93 ff. does. But, as Collange indicates, the suggestion is worth following up that vv 14–17 do prepare for the later sections of the epistle, as we have seen (p. 46).

Above all, Paul and his associates are "persons of" (the meaning of ὡς, Bultmann, 73) εἰλικρίνεια, "sincerity," "probity," whose word can be trusted (cf. 1:12, for the polemical setting), and the twofold ἀλλά ("but") marks off Paul from the intruders who have caused disturbance at Corinth, not by their presence only but by their utterance. Hence the rejoiner λαλοῦμεν, "we speak." The need for such a forthright apology will be clear in 3:1–3, which is hardly a "digression" (Bultmann, 73) but necessary to justify 2:16–17.

3:1. Paul's spirited defense may have seemed too brash: so ἀρχόμεθα πάλιν ἑαυτοὺς συνιστάνειν; "are we starting over again" (πάλιν; but it may go with the verb συνιστάνειν, yielding the same general sense) "to recommend ourselves?" The adverb πάλιν encourages us to ask when it was that Paul did recommend himself (cf. 4:2; 5:12 for the same idea). Was it at the time of 1 Corinthians (e.g., 1 Cor 9:1, 2, Bruce, Héring, Hughes) or does this v presuppose chaps. 10–13 of 2 Corinthians (especially 12:19) as an earlier letter? Or is the allusion to the "tearful letter" of 2:4, which may well be lost to us? It is difficult to say. See *Introduction*, pp. xl–li.

"Letters of commendation" are seen in Acts 9:2; 22:5; 18:27; Rom 16:1 (the last two references are to Christian documents used to established credibility; συνίστημι, a verb found 16 times in NT, with 13 references in Paul, who uses the verb 8 times in our letter; cf. Georgi, *Die Gegner*, 241 ff., who remarks on the identity and credentials of the bearer, as in Rom 16:2 of Phoebe. So Georgi concludes that this verb is the ruling idea in the polemical issue between Paul and the "many" alien teachers in the Corinthian church).

Paul has no use for such external witnesses, well known in the ancient world (cf. C. W. Keyes, "The Greek Letter of Introduction," *American Journal of Philology* 56 [1935] 28–44), even if their pedigree was to be respected. "To you" (πρὸς ὑμᾶς) suggests to Käsemann, *Die Legitimität*, 25, that the letters emanated from the mother-church in Jerusalem (but this idea is challenged by Georgi, *Die Gegner*, 245, who thinks that the adversaries of Paul, with their free-wheeling, charismatic approach to the Christian faith, would scarcely have been amenable to the hierarchical, institutional control of the Jerusalem church: "for them it was not authority [*Recht*] that authenticated the Spirit, but the Spirit who authenticated authority"). At all events, these men came to Corinth armed with these credentials; possibly such were lists of their "spiritual" exploits (cf. 11:21–33).

Paul will have occasion (in 10:12, 18) to repel this kind of status-conferring activity, and his appeal will be to his sufferings as the "signs of an apostle" (11:21–33; 12:12). At this point he is more interested in "letters" (ἐξ ὑμῶν) "from you," and that inquiry leads him to consider his pastoral work at Corinth.

2. The Corinthians' Christian standing is the test of what he regarded as valid ministry: "you yourselves are our letter, written on your hearts," as the readers' own experience gave evidence of the worth of all that Paul had done as church-planter (1 Cor 3:6–10). Only the reading ἐν ταῖς καρδίαις ὑμῶν, "*your* hearts," can make sense of the participles that follow, for the drift of Paul's thought is that the letter, written on the Corinthians' changed lives (καρδία, "heart," is the seat of religious activity, where the Spirit works, and the center of human personhood: J. Behm, *TDNT* 3:609–16), is also a witness to the world. It is "read and recognized" (we earlier noted the pun, which cannot really be reproduced in English) by "all the world." Perhaps this last phrase implies a veiled innuendo that Paul's opponents were shady in their dealings with the Corinthians and not anxious to have their interest in the church too well scrutinized (so 11:20; 12:16, 17). On the other hand, Paul's work is known "in all places" (2:14) and open to public view.

3. The verb φανεροῦν/φανεροῦσθαι, "to show," "to be manifest," has already formed part of Paul's self-confession (2:14), and he will return to it, in its noun form, in 4:2. In v 3 the context is different, but probably still with an eye on the overall issue: Where is the true source of authority? What are genuine credentials for ministry? The Corinthians themselves gave evidence that they are "a letter of Christ" (ἐπιστολὴ Χριστοῦ, where the genitive is subjective: they are a letter whose author is Christ). Yet they would not have become this had Paul not "ministered" (διακονηθεῖσα ὑφ'ἡμῶν) to them. His faithful service (διακονία) is the token Paul appeals to in support of the claim and rebuttal that underlie these verses. It is "obviously" (taking φανερούμενοι as middle with Héring, and polemical with Lührmann) the case that their lives are a communication from Christ, but only because of "our efforts" in service.

Διακονία, "ministry," is a favorite term for the apostle (51 times, counting the verb and noun, of which 20 references occur in 2 Cor but 6 are found in chaps. 8, 9 in reference to the collection, so the meaning is not uniform). Christ's message, to be delivered to the Achaeans, is yet acknowledged to be an action of the divine Spirit who thereby authorized Paul's ministry (see W. Baird, *JBL* 80 [1961] 166–72, citing Josephus, *Ant.* 6. 298, for the verb διακονεῖν to mean "to deliver a message").

Paul's agile mind moves abruptly from "letter" to "covenant" (Provence, 60), as the phrase διακονία τοῦ πνεύματος, "the ministry of the Spirit" becomes the ruling idea henceforth in this chapter (Prümm). Collange, *Enigmes*, 51, puts it illustratively: two rivers (letter/covenant) flow into a wider expanse; and, we may add, what these two ideas have in common is "the Spirit," (πνεῦμα) who brings new life by writing Christ's letter on the human heart and marking the onset of a new covenant age, of which Paul's ministry is the sign.

"Not with ink" (v 3*b*)—οὐ μέλανι—would suggest a link with papyrus, but the contrast is heart/Spirit and stone/Moses' law (at least by inference). Paul goes back to Exod 31:18, LXX: πλάκας λιθίνας γεγραμμένας τῷ δακτύλῳ τοῦ θεοῦ, "stone tablets, written with the finger of God," cf. Exod 32:19; Deut 9:17. The most striking change is that "with the finger of God" becomes "by the Spirit of the living God," in turn an exceptional title—found only here in the Bible—for the Holy Spirit. The texts in Exodus refer to the Mosaic covenant; but it is Jer 31 (38):33 which alone, in OT, mentions a "new covenant," with the law placed "in their minds" (διάνοιαν) and written "on their hearts" (ἐπὶ καρδίας αὐτῶν); but, as Collange, *Enigmes* (51), observes, there is no contrast with the *law* of Moses (as distinct from the old covenant) and no reference to the Spirit. On this topic see R. P. Martin, "Writing and Writing Materials," "Papyrus," in *Dictionary of the Bible and Religion,* ed. W. Gentz (Nashville: Abingdon, 1986).

It is to Ezekiel (11:19; 32:26) that we must turn for these two allusions; and clearly those vv are in Paul's mind, when he writes of a "new spirit" and "tablets of stone" set over against "tablets of flesh." Yet Paul has innovated in a remarkable way: he has assimilated "heart of stone" to "tablets of stone," with the latter phrase used to connect with Moses' law. That it is this connection which he proceeds to explore in the balance of the third chapter of our letter will become clear.

4. πεποίθησιν δὲ τοιαύτην ἔχομεν, "this is the confidence we have." The conclusion drawn here harks back to 3:1–3 (Plummer, Hughes)—or better, to 2:17 (Strachan, Godet, Windisch, Provence, 62). The term is chosen to buttress Paul's self-conscious awareness that he is acting as a "minister of the new covenant," with a freedom that he enjoyed (3:12, 17, 18; Bultmann, *TDNT* 6:1–12). But the word also expresses Paul's relations with the Corinthian community (four of the six occurrences of πεποίθησις, "confidence," are in 2 Cor). So ἔχομεν, "we have," ought to be regarded as a declaration: "*we have* this assurance with good reason; it is no illusion" (Godet's paraphrase), and the verb ἔχειν, "to have" runs through the letter of 2:14–7:4, expressing Paul's sense of being taken up into God's purposes (3:12; 4:1, 7, 13; 5:1, 12, [14]; 6:10; 7:1: so Prümm, *Diakonia Pneumatos* 1, 111; 2, 36, 39).

Such confidence, Paul would hold to, only if suitably qualified, as in the phrase διὰ τοῦ Χριστοῦ, "through Christ," perhaps a formula to show Paul's role as one through whom Christ has worked among the Corinthians (M. Bouttier, *En Christ,* Etude d'exégèse et de théologie paulinienne [Paris: Universitaires de France, 1962] 33 f.). The second phrase is πρὸς τὸν θεόν, "in the presence of God," and goes back to 2:17*b* to denote the sphere in which Paul's ministry is exercised. He claims no virtue for himself, but proceeds to express in a heavily loaded sentence that his "sufficiency" is a gift of God in grace (1 Thess 2:4; 1 Cor 15:10: cf. Eph 3:7, 8; 1 Tim 1:12, 14).

5. οὐχ ὅτι ἀφ᾽ ἑαυτῶν ἱκανοί ἐσμεν λογίσασθαί τι ὡς ἐξ ἑαυτῶν, ἀλλ᾽ ἡ ἱκανότης ἡμῶν ἐκ τοῦ θεοῦ, "it is not that we are adequate in ourselves to reckon anything to our credit, but our adequacy comes from God."

At length we have reached the terminus of Paul's journey which started at 2:16 with the rhetorical question: Who is competent for these responsibilities? The key term is ἱκανός, which is picked up at this verse. "Not that we are adequate (ἱκανοί) in ourselves (ἀφ᾽ ἑαυτῶν) . . . but our adequacy (ἱκανότης) comes from God." Perhaps there is an allusion to Joel 2:11, καὶ τίς ἔσται ἱκανὸς αὐτῇ; "and who can endure it (the great and terrible day of the Lord's judgment)?" So in the divine presence (πρὸς τὸν θεόν, v 4) man as a human being is acutely aware of his frailty and finitude, and the appropriate attitude is humility, since man is only a mere mortal, while God is the "self-sufficient one" (Heb. ᾽el shaddai = שַׁדַּי, šadday, LXX ὁ ἱκανός in Ruth 1:20; Job 21:15; 31:2; 40:2; and Ezek 1:24[A]; it is a common title for God in Aquila, Symmachus as in Philo; see Knox, *St. Paul*, 131, n. 1). But Georgi, *Die Gegner*, 223, 224, is not convinced.

The object of Paul's disavowal of adequacy in himself is then stated: "to reckon anything (λογίσασθαί τι) to our credit," lit., "as from ourselves," (ὡς ἐξ ἑαυτῶν) a clumsily worded phrase (Collange, *Enigmes*, 60) but powerfully evocative (Allo, Héring, Collange who brings out a semicommercial nuance; Georgi, *Gegner*, 223, sees it as a Corinthian catchword as in 10:2, 7, 11; 11:15; 12:6). Rather (ἀλλά), "our adequacy comes from God" (ἐκ τοῦ θεοῦ; ἐκ matching ἐξ ἑαυτῶν). We cannot avoid concluding that this remark is polemically slanted and addressed to Paul's adversaries who made it their boast that they were the "well-endowed ones," with pneumatic gifts and imposing credentials to support their claim. On this v, see C. H. Dodd, *BT* 28 (1977) 101–16.

6. ὃς καὶ ἱκάνωσεν ἡμᾶς διακόνους καινῆς διαθήκης, "who indeed gave us our adequacy to be servants of a new covenant." Paul writes with precision even if, as is likely, he seems to be indebted to a catechetical tradition known to his readers. Certainly there are unusual turns of phrase in this v. Specifically (1) "God has qualified" (ἱκάνωσεν) us, and the aorist tense suggests to some (Hughes, Plummer, Windisch) that Paul is looking back to his conversion-call to ministerial office as Christ's servant (see S. Kim, *The Origin of Paul's Gospel* [Grand Rapids: Eerdmans, 1982] 11); then (2), "servants of the new covenant" (καινῆς διαθήκης corresponding to an expression in the *Damascus Document* [CD] 6:19; 8:21; 19:34; 20:12; and possibly in 1QpHab 11:3; but, most important, to be traced to Jer 31:31–4 and evident in Lk 22:20[D]: 1 Cor 11:25; cf. Heb 8:8; 9:15; 12:24); and finally (3) the enigmatic οὐ γράμματος ἀλλὰ πνεύματος, the covenant is based "not on the letter but on the Spirit." On the other hand, this verse stands in tandem with 2:16b as the following parallelism will show:

3:6		2:16b
ἱκάνωσεν	paired with	ἱκανός
ἡμᾶς		τίς
διακόνους		πρὸς ταῦτα;
καινῆς διαθήκης		

The key terms listed take us to the heart of Paul's counterarguments raised against those who devalued his work at Corinth, and led the Achaean Christians into what he regarded as false paths. He lays claim to God's seal of approbation in the root ἱκαν-, "sufficient, capable," with special reference to service. Eschewing all claim to being self-appointed or relying on native endowments, he sees his life *coram Deo*, as God sees it in its weakness, and he knows that only God can equip him (as in 1 Cor 15:9: ὃς οὐκ εἰμὶ ἱκανὸς καλεῖσθαι ἀπόστολος).

The transition to "service" (διακονία) is smooth, and since Jeremiah 31 has already been in his mind (3:3), it is only to be expected that Paul's thoughts will move on to consider the "new covenant" that stands in some tension with Moses' law. But Paul may well have been responding to his opponents if we are right to see their claim as ἀπόστολοι/διάκονοι Χριστοῦ (11:15, 23) mirrored also here. For Paul selects exactly the term that is under discussion at Corinth (Georgi's evidence is impressive, *Die Gegner*, 31–49; see too Collins, *JBL* 93 [1974] 88–106) and re-mints it, in this context, by the descriptive phrase which he never troubles to explain: καινῆς διαθήκης, "of the new covenant." Possibly he can simply quote it because his readers were well aware of its significance (so W. C. van Unnik, "La Conception," 111), or it may be that his enemies had appropriated the term διαθήκη, a rich OT word, as E. Jacob, *Theology of the Old Testament* (tr. A. W. Heathcote and P. J. Allcock [London: Hodder & Stoughton, 1958]) 209–17 on בְּרִית, *bᵉrît*, "covenant," shows, to make claims on their own behalf (so A. Jaubert, *La notion d'alliance*, 447). Or, it may be, as W. L. Lane, "Covenant," *TynB* 33 (1982), suggestively proposes, that the Corinthians were failing to see in the apostle the "messenger of the covenant lawsuit [Heb. רִיב, *rîb*] God has brought against his rebellious vassals at Corinth" (18). More probably the accent falls on καινή, "new," since Paul is going to appeal to the elements of "newness" in the Gospel he was commissioned to proclaim, though it does seem clear that he has to overcome some misunderstanding of what the *"new* covenant" entailed, specifically, that it was not a sign of a renovated Judaism but of a new chapter in God's dealing with humankind, "the eschatological new redemptive order" (E. Käsemann, "The Spirit and the Letter," *Perspectives on Paul*, tr. M. Kohl [Philadelphia: Fortress Press, 1971] 150). In support of this addition (καινῆς) to διαθήκης we may note how Paul loves to set "old" and "new" in antithesis as marking the transition from the old order of sin and death to the new, eschatological age of fulfillment in Christ (1 Cor 5:7: παλαιὰ ζύμη . . . νέον φύραμα; Rom 7:6: παλαιότης γράμματος . . . καινότης πνεύματος; Gal 4:24: δύο διαθῆκαι; cf. Col 3:9, 10: παλαιὸς ἄνθρωπος. . . . καινὸς ἄνθρωπος; Eph 4:22, 24 idem).

The stark contrast of γράμμα/πνεῦμα, "letter/Spirit," is hardly resolved by the way Paul's sentence concludes: "for the γράμμα kills, but the πνεῦμα imparts life." A lot of involved debate has centered on this remark, which has to be viewed in the light of similar statements in Rom 2:29; 7:6. The axiom looks like a piece of traditional teaching, introduced to round off the discussion on Paul's efficacious ministry: the latter imparts life to the responsive hearers (going back to 2:15, and so forming a kind of *inclusio* or an envelope framework in which the ending matches the opening). The unbelieving reaction, which leads to death, is what is meant by the γράμμα killing those who stay with it—and so refuse to move on into the era of the new age. The death is the "eschatological sentence" that awaits those who remain in the old eon (4:4).

The term γράμμα naturally refers to OT as Scripture, and of all the various possibilities open to the interpreter (see Provence, 62–68, for a convenient resumé), the most satisfactory is that which sees in γράμμα a certain interpretation of the Torah which prevailed at Corinth. This view would correspond with Cranfield's explanation (*The Epistle to the Romans* 1 [ICC; Edinburgh: T. & T. Clark, 1975] 339 f.) of γράμμα as a misuse of Moses' law seen as an end in itself and which fails to appreciate its true purpose (Rom 10:4: τέλος) as leading to Christ, its fulfillment (Gal 3:24). But a more severe attitude to Moses will occupy Paul as he moves into the section of 3:7–18, and we may surmise that, if v 6 belonged to catechetical instruction on which he is relying (Collange, *Enigmes*, 63, 64, 66), then it was the virulent opposition at Corinth that drove him to bring a sharper focus to the "old covenant" with its Torah basis as a "dispensation" (διακονία) of both "death" and "damnation" (3:7, 9).

On a broader canvas, we have suggested that the crisis of authority vis-à-vis Jewish Christianity, accentuated by troubles at Corinth, may have led Paul to give a more nuanced meaning to the law at this point in his ministry. See *Introduction*, pp. lvii–lxi.

Explanation

In a lengthy section such as 2:14–3:6 with its many subthemes, it is helpful if we can isolate the central, master subject. Clearly Paul is on the defensive, and concerned to demonstrate (as far as that is possible) the validity of his apostolic ministry in a context where it is under suspicion. His detractors are aiming their shafts at his person and challenging his "competence"; but (*pace* Hickling, "The Sequence") the issue is deeper than personal. Underlying the debate over ministry is the theological tension of what kind of ministry is it that carries the divine approval. The pragmatic question, What is the ministry that succeeds? can only be answered in the light of the more searching issue, Where is the seat of authority in ministry?

Paul concedes as a premise (2:14) that God in Christ has launched a victory campaign, of which the end is not in doubt. The good news of messianic triumph has to be proclaimed, and men and women have to be called to share in the new age of the Spirit. The point in disputation at Corinth has to do *with the credentials of those charged to carry this message.*

For Paul's opponents (2:17) evidently regarded themselves as accredited "servants of Christ" (11:23 has this term of later troublemakers at Corinth) and came to the city armed with "letters of authority" that gave evidence of their prowess and exploits in Christian service. By contrast, Paul's ministry looked feeble and ineffectual. So he must make a robust "defense," while at the same time attacking the basis of accreditation that his rivals trusted.

He disdained the use of "written letters." Yet his appeal is multifaceted. Out of his own character as sincere (2:17) he draws the further conclusion that the Corinthian converts are his testimonial; and by contrast with external tokens he appeals to the inner working of God's Spirit in their lives to show itself in their "newness of life."

No one can claim to be adequate, left to one's own resources and strength. So the final court of appeal is to God's enabling (3:5, 6); and the only endorsement of the ministry worth having is that which passes muster in God's sight and is true to Christ (the names *God/Christ* recur frequently, e.g., 2:17; 3:4). The herald will not be a popular figure since the message as God's word promotes either salvation or ruin, depending on how it is regarded (2:15, 16). At all cost, it must not be watered down, and so falsified. The hearers must be confronted with an "either . . . or" decision. And, in the end, says C. S. Lewis, there are only two classes of people; those who say to God, Thy will be done; and those to whom God says, thy will be done.

B. Life under the Two Covenants   (3:7–18)

Bibliography

Balch, D. L. "Backgrounds in 1 Cor 3: The Sayings of the Lord in Q: Moses as an Ascetic in 2 Cor 3." *NTS* 18 (1971/72) 351–64. **Barth, G.** "Die Eignung des Verkündigers in 2 Kor 2, 14–3, 6." 257–70. **Chevallier, M.-A.** *Esprit de Dieu, Parole d'Hommes.* Neuchâtel: Delachaux & Niestlé, 1966. 91–99. **Collange, J.-F.** *Enigmes de la deuxième épître de Paul aux Corinthiens.* **Doeve, J. W.** *Jewish Hermeneutics in the Synoptic Gospels and Acts.* Assen: Gorcum, 1954. **Dunn, J. D. G.** "2 Corinthians III. 17—'The Lord is the Spirit,'" *JTS* 21 n.s. (1970) 309–20. **Dupont, J.** "Le chrétien, miroir de la gloire divine après II Cor III. 18." *RB* 56 (1949) 392–411. **Ellis, E. E.** "How the New Testament Uses the Old" in *New Testament Interpretation.* Ed. I. H. Marshall. Exeter: Paternoster Press/Grand Rapids: Eerdmans, 1977. 199–219. **Feuillet, A.** *Le Christ sagesse de Dieu, d'après les épîtres pauliniennes.* Paris: Gabalda, 1966. 113–61. **Fitzmyer, J. A.** "Glory Reflected on the Face of Christ (2 Cor 3:7–4:6) and a Palestinian Jewish Motif." *TS* 42 (1981) 630–44. ———. " 'To Know Him and the Power of His Resurrection' Phil 3, 10." In *Mélanges bibliques en hommage au R. P. Béda Rigaux,* ed. A. Descamps and A. de Halleux, 422–24. Gembloux: Duculot, 1970. **Friedrich, G.** "Die Gegner des Paulus im 2. Korintherbrief." In FS O. Michel *Abraham unser Vater,* ed. O. Betz, M. Hengel, P. Schmidt, 181–215. AGJU 5. Leiden: Brill, 1963. **Friesen, I. I.** *The Glory of the Ministry of Jesus Christ.* **Göttsberger, J.** "Die Hülle des Moses nach Ex 34 und 2 Kor 3." *BZ* 16 (1924) 1–17. **Grech, P.** "2 Corinthians 3, 17 and the Pauline Doctrine of Conversion to the Holy Spirit." *CBQ* 17 (1955) 420–37. **Greenwood, D.** "The Lord is the Spirit: Some Considerations of 2 Cor 3:17." *CBQ* 34 (1972) 467–72. **Griffiths, D. R.** " 'The Lord is the Spirit' (2 Corinthians 3:17, 18)." *ExpT* 55 (1943–44) 81–83. **Hanson, A. T.** "The Midrash in II Corinthians 3: A Reconsideration." *JSNT* 9 (1980) 2–28. **Hermann, I.** *Kyrios und Pneuma. Studien zur Christologie der paulinischen Hauptbriefe.* SANT 2. München: Kösel-Verlag, 1961. 17–19, 38–56. **Hickling, C. J. A.** "The Sequence of Thought in II Corinthians, Chapter Three." *NTS* 21 (1974) 380–95. **Hill, E.** "The Construction of Three Passages from St. Paul . . . 1 Corinthians 3:11." *CBQ* 23 (1961) 296–301. **Hugedé, N.** *La métaphore du miroir dans les épîtres de s. Paul aux Corinthiens.* Neuchâtel: Delachaux & Niestlé, 1957. 17–24, 32. **Jervell, J.** *Imago Dei. Gen. 1, 26 f. im Spätjudentum, in der Gnosis und in den paulinischen Briefen.* FRLANT 76. Göttingen: Vandenhoeck & Ruprecht, 1960. **Kim, S.** *The Origin of Paul's Gospel.* WUNT 4. Tübingen: J. C. B. Mohr, 1981; Grand Rapids: Wm. B.

Eerdmans, 1982. **Le Déaut, R.** "Traditions targumiques dans le corpus paulinien?" *Bib* 42 (1961) 28–48. **McNamara, M.** *The New Testament and the Palestinian Targum to the Pentateuch.* AnBib 27. Rome: Pontifical Biblical Institute, 1966. ———. *Targum and Testament. Aramaic Paraphrases of the Hebrew Bible: A Light on the New Testament.* Grand Rapids: Wm. B. Eerdmans, 1972. **Meeks, W. A.** *The Prophet-King. Moses Traditions and the Johannine Christology.* NovTSup 14. Leiden: Brill, 1967. **Moberly, R. W. L.** *At the Mountain of God. Story and Theology in Exodus 32–34.* Sheffield: JSOT Press, 1983. 106–9. **Moule, C. F. D.** "2 Cor 3:18b, καθάπερ ἀπὸ κυρίου πνεύματος." In *Neues Testament und Geschichte,* ed. H. Baltensweiler and B. Reicke. FS. O. Cullmann. Zurich: Theologischer Verlag, 1972. 231–37. **Patte, D.** *Early Jewish Hermeneutic in Palestine.* SBL Dissertation 22. Missoula: Scholars Press, 1975. **Provence, T. E.** "Who is Sufficient for These Things? An Exegesis of 2 Corinthians ii:15–iii:18." *NovT* 24 (1982) 54–81. **Schmithals, W.** *Gnosticism in Corinth.* Tr. John E. Steely. Nashville: Abingdon, 1971. **Schulz, S.** "Die Decke des Moses. Untersuchungen zu einer vorpaulinischen Überlieferung in II Cor 3:7–18." *ZNW* 49 (1958) 1–30. **Smith, William H., Jr.** "The Function of 2 Corinthians 3:7–4:6 in Its Epistolary Context." Ph.D. diss., Southern Baptist Theological Seminary, 1983. **Ulonska, H.** "Die Doxa des Moses," *EvT* 26 (1966) 378–88. **Unnik, W. C. van.** "'With Unveiled Face,' An Exegesis of 2 Corinthians iii. 12–18." *NovT* 6 (1963) 153–69 (in *Sparsa Collecta,* Part I: NovTSup 29. Leiden: Brill [1973] 194–210). **Wainwright, A. W.** *The Trinity in the New Testament.* London: SPCK, 1962. 217, 225–27.

Translation

⁷ *Now if the ministry that leads to death, engraved in letters of stone, appeared with [such] glory that the Israelites were not able to fix their eyes on Moses' face because of his glory, although it was transient,* ⁸ *how much more glorious will be the ministry of the Spirit!* ⁹ *For if the ministry* ᵃ *that leads to condemnation was glorious, how much more will the ministry that leads to righteousness abound in glory!* ¹⁰ *Indeed, that which had partial glory has really lost whatever glory it had, compared with the surpassing glory [of the new covenant].* ¹¹ *For if the transient [ministry] had its moments of glory, how much is the enduring ministry filled with glory!*

¹² *Since, then, we really do have such a hope, we speak with great freedom born of confidence.* ¹³ *We are not like Moses who was in the habit of putting a veil over his face to prevent the Israelites from fixing their eyes [to see] the significance of what was about to be done away.* ¹⁴ *But [this happened because] their minds were obtuse; for until the present day, the same veil remains at the reading of the old covenant, and since the veil is not lifted, it is not evident that [only] in Christ is the glory done away.* ¹⁵ *But until today, as often as Moses is read, a veil lies over their mind;* ¹⁶ *yet "whenever there is a turning to the Lord, the veil is removed."* ¹⁷ *"The Lord" represents the Spirit; and wherever the Spirit of the Lord is, there is freedom.* ¹⁸ *And we, all of us, with faces uncovered, beholding as in a mirror the glory of the Lord are being transformed into the same image [of God] from one degree of glory to another; this is the work of the Lord, who is the Spirit.*

Notes

ᵃ Reading the nominative διακονία with B D² and Byzantine witnesses. The dative τῇ διακονίᾳ has strong support (P⁴⁶ ℵ A C D* G) and would yield: "if there was glory in the ministry that leads to condemnation, how much more. . . ." Hardly a different meaning, and it appears that διακονία is the *lectio difficilior*, changed to make for easier reading. But see UBSGNT and Nestle[26]. Barrett (109) and Collange, *Enigmes* (79), prefer the nominative reading, but "le sens reste tout à fait le même," as the latter justly remarks.

Form/Structure/Setting

A question that has exercised recent interpreters is presented by Windisch (112) in a short paragraph. Taking a cue from Göttsberger, "Die Hülle," he proposed that 3:7–18 is a Christian midrash on Exod 34:29–35 added to show the superior glory of the new administration (*Amt*)' in Christ to the old. He offered several reasons for this novel idea: (1) on stylistic grounds the section is unlike the surrounding vv, with which it is not connected; (2) it lacks the apologetic motif that we observed in 2:16*b*–3:6, and which will be resumed at 4:1 ff.; (3) the theme is "Christianity and Judaism," not Paul's position vis-à-vis Jewish Christianity; and (4) it has all the marks of being a literary unit, independent of the epistolary situation in which it is now found.

Windisch's hypothesis has been taken up and expanded by Schulz, "Die Decke," and Georgi, *Die Gegner,* the former noting the *hapax legomena* in the vv (e.g., "old covenant," 3:14, the classical expression ἡνίκα ἄν, "whenever," in 3:15, 16; and "to turn to the Lord" in 3:16, among the more obvious examples listed by Schulz, 11), the latter subjecting the section to a literary-critical analysis (274–82). Both conclude that Paul has taken over a preformed Jewish Christian midrash and "glossed" it by adding his own comments. The result (Georgi, *Die Gegner,* 282) is seen in the way that an original document extolling Moses' glory has been edited and utilized by Paul as a further contribution to his debate at Corinth.

Attractive as this theory appears—and the different style and the presence of some unusual lexical terms in 3:7–18 are to be noted—we are left with the following questions: (1) How did Paul have recourse to such a composition, and why did he insert it here, albeit in a redacted form? (2) How can we account for the sets of antithesis, "death/spirit," "condemnation/righteousness" that are already found in Romans and Galatians (Prümm, "Röm. 1–11 und 2 Kor. 3," *Bib* 31 [1950] 164–203; idem, "Gal. und 2 Kor. Ein lehrge-haltlicher Vergleich," *Bib* 31 [1950] 27–72).

Collange, *Enigmes* (68), adds some other criticisms: (3) The hypothesis is very complicated, requiring us to know how much is part of the "original treatise" and how much is Paul's own work (e.g., in the contrasts of vv 9, 11 which Schulz [5] regards as "typically Pauline"). (4) It raises the issue of Paul's tact; would he wish to cite a document evidently highly regarded by his readers, then to denigrate its contents by his emendations in what would seem to them to be a cavalier way? For example, Schulz, 2, postulates an original text of v 18, noting its rhythmic-hymnlike form (Plummer, 103), and suggests that it is part of an anti-Pauline Jewish Christian midrash, on which Paul has added corrective, christological comments to identify the εἰκών ("image") as Jesus Christ in his exaltation (Rom 8:29; Schulz, 25, 26). (5) The complex proposal overlooks Paul's flexible thought, and thus alters the meaning of the text.

Less ambitious is Moule's hint (*The Birth of the New Testament,* 3d ed. [New York: Harper & Row, 1982] 70, n. 1) that we have here the development of a synagogue sermon preached by Paul on some previous occasion. This suggestion would go far toward explaining two puzzling features in our section: (1) the unusual style in the context of a pastoral letter, and (2) the phenomenon of Paul's exegetical method whereby he *seems* to be commenting on a Scripture lection (Exod 34) and applying lessons to a specific problem. Also we note the fact that v 12 refers to παρρησία, "boldness in speaking," leading to the central theme, which is the Christian's freedom in Christ (v 17), and the διακονία πνεύματος, "the ministry of the Spirit," in the new order of eschatological fulfillment. There is also the small point that the issue, centrally placed in this letter, of Paul's "authority" is aptly explored by a sermon on δόξα, usually rendered "glory" but which also can be construed as a possession conferring authority on God's representatives whether Moses or Paul, who are the two antithetical figures in those vv (so J. Jervell, *Imago Dei,* 176–80). That equation may explain why Paul chose to introduce the "sermon," in the form of a *midrash pesher,* i.e., an interpretative exposition of OT text(s) and its/their contemporary application, at this juncture of his letter to Corinth.

As to the structure of the section, we can appreciate that it is artistically composed. The most noteworthy literary device is the presence of three statements (in vv 7–11) which utilize the rabbinical exegetical *middah* of "the light and the heavy" (*qal-wāḥômer,* קל־וחומר, Str-B 3:223–26), which translates into English as "if then . . . how much more" (as in the Latin *a minori ad maius*):

vv 7 f.: εἰ δὲ . . . . . πῶς οὐχὶ μᾶλλον
v 9: εἰ γὰρ . . . . . πολλῷ μᾶλλον
v 11: εἰ γὰρ . . . . . πολλῷ μᾶλλον

Also to be noted are sets of contrast in antithetic parallelism:

θάνατος (v 7)	πνεῦμα (v 8)
death	Spirit
κατάκρισις (v 9)	δικαιοσύνη (v 9)
condemnation	righteousness
τὸ καταργούμενον (v 11)	τὸ μένον (v 11)
what is disappearing	what is remaining

Plummer (91 f.) has observed another striking literary feature. This is the recurring use of γὰρ ("for") in 3:9, 10, 11. The particle introduces an explicative statement which follows, in each case, the three statements of contrast. So the pattern is remarkable, as W. H. Smith has detected: there is a paraphrase of an OT reference, followed by a contrast (in vv 7–11 it is the *qal-wāḥômer* device that is used (A. T. Hanson, "The Midrash in II Corinthians 3: A Reconsideration," *JSNT* 9 [1980] 2–28; D. Patte, *Early Jewish Hermeneutic in Palestine* [SBL Dissertation Series 22, Missoula: Scholars Press, 1975] 109–15), in turn succeeded by an explicative statement.

Vv 12–15 carry the same hallmark of this pattern:

v 12: opening paraphrastic statement;
vv 13, 14: the structure is one of contrast, but instead of
πῶς οὐχὶ μᾶλλον, "how much more" we have οὐ . . . ἀλλά: *not* as Moses
. . . *but* their minds were dulled. For (γὰρ) to this very day . . .
v 15: But (ἀλλὰ) to this day

If this midrashic pattern aids our exegesis, it shows how the points of
antithesis are not (a) the Christian's παρρησία ("boldness") over against Moses'
veiled face (v 13), but (b) the Israelite's disability to gain direct access to
God—because Moses wore a veil that concealed the divine glory—and the
Christian's direct access through Christ (v 14), a thought that becomes central
in vv 16–18 (so Smith, challenging van Unnik, " 'With Unveiled Face,' " 159–
68, who supports (a) above). So the sets of antithesis are:

1. Israelites	*vs*	Christians, based on the earlier contrasts, i.e.	
2. Moses	*vs*	Paul	(vv 12, 13)
3. Law	*vs*	Spirit	(vv 7, 8)
4. Letter	*vs*	Covenant	(v 6)

Under 1. we may conclude that what prevented the Israelites from seeing
the divine glory was their πώρωσις (ἐπωρώθη, "their minds were obtuse,"
in v 14) as in Rom 11:7, 8, 25, "Israel has experienced *a hardening* in part"
(NIV, italics added).

Another midrashic pattern is found in vv 16–18 where the key term is
κύριος ("Lord"). This rabbinic exegetical method is based on the equation
(the principle of analogy: *gezerah šawa*) of two disparate texts in the OT,
with the formula "This is that" (J. W. Doeve, *Jewish Hermeneutics*, 98). By
this method Paul is able to seize on the reference to κύριος in Exod 34 and
apply it to the Spirit by a conviction that E. E. Ellis has dubbed "eschatological
exegesis," i.e., the writer views the OT promises and prophecies as having
fulfillment in his own time and experience; or alternatively, as "charismatic
exegesis," i.e., the new age of the Spirit gives fresh meaning to an ancient
text and makes it relevant to the (Christian) writer's needs (E. E. Ellis, "How
the New Testament Uses the Old," 207, 214).

Comment

7. The preceding v has stated a stark antithesis: τὸ γράμμα ἀποκτέννει, τὸ
δὲ πνεῦμα ζῳοποιεῖ, "The letter kills, but the Spirit imparts life." Now Paul
proceeds to unpack that statement in an elaborately drawn set of contrasts.
Under the dual terms γράμμα/πνεῦμα he will consider the relative association
of the two covenants, linked with Moses and Christ/the Spirit. The entrée
to Paul's thought may well be as simple as Jervell (*Imago Dei*, 178 f.) surmises:
the γράμμα refers primarily to the "letters of recommendation" (3:1–3), and
points to the controversy with the "false brethren" who carried them. By
contrast, Paul's ministry is authenticated by the "power" (*Vollmacht*) of the
Spirit who has produced a different kind of letter—one that is "spiritual"

(*geistig*). But if that is the starting point of the following discussion, it is considerably extended in the way Paul's exegetical excursus proceeds. For he moves on to what is at the heart of his theology: his office as a "minister of the new covenant," which is a variant of all that he understood by "his Gospel" (Gal 1:1, 12; 3:1–4). Any "other" gospel (Gal 1:8, 9) leads to death, whereas it is his evangelical work at Corinth that has brought new life in the Spirit (cf. Rom 8:9–11, 14–17; Gal 5:25); and with the end result that the *imago Dei* is restored to its full splendor in the freedom of God's children (Rom 8:21, 29; 1 Cor 15:43, 49; Phil 3:21). So vv 17, 18. Thus it is legitimate to see Paul's thought soaring to embrace this far-reaching disquisition before returning to the local scene at Corinth where again the εἰκών ("image") motif will be used to good effect (4:4–6). The primary antithesis is Moses/Paul, which shades into the contrast Moses/Christ or Moses/the Spirit, since Paul boldly associates himself with "the Lord" as Moses did—in Exodus 34—in identifying himself with Yahweh's gift, the Torah.

It is clear that Paul found no fault with Torah, the law itself (Rom 7:12, 14), but he knew from his own experience that the law set a high standard which it beckoned a person to attain, yet it provided no power to achieve the goal. The trouble lay with "man" as σάρξ ("flesh"); so human frailty and proneness to evil allowed the σάρξ to turn the law of God (which God intended as good) into a death-dealing instrument (Rom 7:13). The reason why the law became our enemy is given in Rom 8:3*a*, and Paul can glide into a set of equations when he comes to assess humankind's alienation from God: sin, flesh, Satan, law all lead to the ultimate end of death (see R. P. Martin, *Reconciliation: A Study of Paul's Theology* [London: Marshall, Morgan and Scott; Atlanta: John Knox Press, 1981] 48–67, for an overview of the relevant texts).

Thus Paul can write phenomenologically, that is, based on what he knows of human experience, that the law produces "a διακονία (an administration) that leads to death," i.e., the "death" of Rom 6:23; 8:6; cf. Eph 2:2; 4:18, "cut off from the life of God . . . due to their hardness (πώρωσις) of heart."

ἐν γράμμασιν ἐντετυπωμένη λίθοις, lit., "engraved in letters on stone," seems to look back to 3:1–3, where "the letters of commendation" are set in contrast to what is written (ἐγγεγραμμένη) by the divine Spirit on the human hearts, not on "tablets of stone" (ἐν πλαξὶν λιθίναις). The reference now is to Moses' receiving the law in Exod 34:29 f., 35. "In these verses the biblical text merely says that the skin of Moses' face shone because he had been talking with God. In Jewish tradition (the Septuagint included) this passage is interpreted to mean that (the skin of) Moses' face was rendered glorious" (McNamara, *Targum and Testament*, 111; cf. idem, *The New Testament and the Palestinian Targum*, 168–88).

This train of thought seems evident in the way the text proceeds: the Mosaic order was "inaugurated with glory" (ἐγενήθη ἐν δόξῃ: so rendered by Godet and Plummer with reference to the Sinai theophany; but Allo [86] points out that the allusion is rather specifically to the receiving of the Law and the way Moses' face was changed into a luminous splendor, *un éclat lumineux;* cf. Bachmann).

Δόξα, "glory, radiance" is a key word in this section. It occurs 19 times in 2 Cor chap. 1–8, of which 15 references are in chaps. 3, 4. It is more a theological code-word than a graphic description (see A. M. Ramsey, *The Glory of God and the Transfiguration of Christ* [London: Longmans, 1949]; and for the OT setting and the development of the word, L. H. Brockington, "The Septuagintal Background to the New Testament Use of δόξα," in *Studies in the Gospels: Essays in Memory of R. H. Lightfoot*, ed. D. E. Nineham [Oxford: Blackwell, 1955] 1–8; and for the semantic link with εἰκών, "image," v 18, see R. P. Martin, *Carmen Christi: Philippians 2:5-11* [SNTSMS 4, Cambridge: University Press, 1967; 2d ed., Grand Rapids: Wm. B. Eerdmans, 1983] 102–20).

The brilliance of this light on Moses' face had one dire effect: the Israelites could not "fix their eyes" (ἀτενίσαι: not in the Hebrew Bible and LXX but in Exod 34:30, Aaron and the people were afraid to come near Moses: ἐφοβήθησαν ἐγγίσαι αὐτόν) on him. Paul does not comment on this "fear," but regards the luminosity as too dazzling to "behold," a verb that denotes intensity and fixedness set on a heavenly form (Windisch; cf. Acts 1:10; 6:15; 10:4; *1 Clem* 7:4; 9:2; 17:2; 19:2; 36:2). Philo, *Life of Moses* 2.70, however, says, "their eyes could not endure the dazzling brightness that flashed from him like the rays of the sun." The second alteration that Paul makes to the MT/LXX is to add τὴν καταργουμένην to τὴν δόξαν τοῦ προσώπου. Here he qualifies the privilege Moses had in possessing a radiant "face" (πρόσωπον, twice in Exod 34:29; over one half of the 22 occurrences of this word in Paul are in 2 Corinthians: E. Lohse, *TDNT* 6:67–69; C. F. D. Moule, "Peculiarities in the Language of II Corinthians," in his *Essays in NT Interpretation*, 159–61), which in this passage stands in antithetic relation to "heart" (καρδία; cf. 5:12, where it is polemical as in the OT tradition [1 Sam 16:7], and we may suspect that Paul's interest in the LXX of Exodus 34 is similarly governed). So he exploits the inference (drawn in v 13) that the glory was "fading" or merely transient, in defiance of some Jewish and Samaritan traditions that Moses retained a radiant face until the day of his death (Str-B 3:516, citing *Tg. Onq.* on Deut 34:7: "Moses was one hundred and twenty years old when he died . . . the splendor of his face's glory had not changed": van Unnik, " 'With Unveiled Face,' " 198 n. 4). The derogatory addition of τὴν καταργού-μενην, "although it was transient" (a verb Paul normally uses of the cessation of human enemies whose power to hurt is canceled by the victorious Christ: Rom 6:6; 7:2, 6; 1 Cor 15:24, 26; cf. 2 Thess 2:8; 2 Tim 1:10), has alerted writers such as Schulz, "Die Decke," (3 f.) and Georgi (*Die Gegner*, 274)—following Windisch (114)—to see a Pauline coda to an original text that praised Moses as a "divine man" figure, whose δόξα marked him out as special. It is certainly notable that Moses' glory is so limited and said to be "transient," and this feature will be again the subject of comment in v 11 where the new age in Paul's mind is superior because it lasts (μένον). The complementary v 8 pursues a different tack, however.

8. The contrast is now drawn, introduced with πῶς οὐχὶ μᾶλλον: "how much more" will (ἔσται) "the ministry that leads to righteousness be glorious." The point to be made is that the temporary nature of the δόξα on Moses' face is not the only feature of its weakness: the degree of δόξα in the new covenant is superior. That new eon of the Spirit is described by a verb, ἔσται, "will be" (future), that seems to point to what is to be. The sense may be

either logical (Bultmann, 84; Barrett, 116, "logical, not chronological," as though it awaited the Parousia when God's glory will be fully revealed, as in Rom 8:18), or eschatological if we may regard πνεῦμα ("Spirit") as a bridge joining the present and the future (so Hermann, *Kyrios und Pneuma,* 31–34). More likely, with Collange, *Enigmes* (78) and Bouttier, *En Christ* (45–48), the two meanings are not to be divorced, yet with the eschatological dimension predominant, since for Paul the future has already begun in the age of the Spirit, of which believers have a foretaste (1:22; 5:5; Rom 8:23; cf. Eph 1:14). See on v 12, ἔχομεν, "we have," implies a present possession, fully assured now even if the fullness awaits a future consummation (cf. 5:1).

9. One further point of distinction: the old order led to κατάκρισις, "condemnation," because it did nothing to alleviate the human condition as sinful (Rom 8:3) or because the law provoked sin in arousing sinful tendencies (Rom 7:7–20; Gal 3:19: τῶν παραβάσεων χάριν προσετέθη, the law "was added because of transgressions"), see Strachan, 81. Paul is not explicit in our v. All he says is that the end result of nomistic religion is divine judgment, whereas the ministry of the Spirit confers the blessing of "righteousness" (δικαιοσύνη). This comes about (1) by supplying divine power to overcome the old eon of sin and death, so E. Käsemann, " 'The Righteousness of God' in Paul," *New Testament Questions of Today,* tr. W. J. Montague (London: SCM Press, 1969) 173–74; (2) by introducing believers to a new world, a καινὴ κτίσις (5:17), so P. Stuhlmacher, *Gerechtigkeit Gottes bei Paulus* (FRLANT 87; Göttingen: Vandenhoeck & Ruprecht, 1965) 76, and Barrett, 117; (3) by offering all that God has done to justify guilty people, so Bruce, 191; or (4) by producing righteousness in human lives, so E. Hill, *CBQ* 23 (1961) 299–301; see too J. Reumann (and J. A. Fitzmyer & J. D. Quinn), *Righteousness in the New Testament* (Philadelphia: Fortress Press, 1982) 50, 51. The new order, then, "excels" (περισσεύει), a verb often used by Paul to set apart the new age of salvation in contrast to the old order (Collange, 79); and this endorses the element of "already begun" which is to be seen in ἔσται, "will be," a future that is brought into the present, though not without remainder.

10. The γάρ, "for," "indeed," establishes the foundation on which the previous deductions have been grounded and formulated. We may translate "thus it is quite true that," with Collange and Godet, while Georgi (*Die Gegner* 275, 278) sees one more instance of Paul's redaction of an existing text as he slipped in the negative ἐν τούτῳ τῷ μέρει, lit., "in this part" (of the whole; see later for another sense) to negate what was said positively about the law which was extolled by the double description of Moses. In Exod 34:29–35 it is Moses' face that is "lit up" (δεδόξασται) in vv 29, 35, and "the skin of his face shone": καὶ ἦν δεδοξασμένη ἡ ὄψις τοῦ χρώματος τοῦ προσώπου αὐτοῦ (v 30).

There is a conscious debt to Jewish tradition, by no means uncomplex, to do with the glory that shone on Moses' face or illumined his appearance (ὄψις in LXX and Philo). The main sources are Philo, *Life of Moses* 2.69, 70; *Exod Rabbah* 47.5, 6 with its interesting comment: "Moses knew not that the skin of his face sent forth beams" (on Exod 34:29). Such beams derive from Moses' intimacy with God (Exod 33:22), or from the *Shekinah,* or from the ink left on the pen with which he wrote the Ten Words and that passed through his hair, producing "beams of splendor." In *Pesiq. Rab Kah.* 32 Moses is a godlike figure whose "face emitted beams of light" (on Exod 34:20); *Midr Tanḥuma* 51 (on Num 10:1–2, which interrogates the text on the question, How is Moses a god [Exod 7:1]? Answer: he had a rod [=scepter], Exod 4:16, which is a mark of royalty, and he has "horns" [Heb. קֶרֶן, *qeren*, which is equated with "the trumpet" of Ps 47:5, "God has gone up with a shout, the Lord with the sound of the horn": see W. A. Meeks, *The Prophet-King*, 193]: *Pesiq. R.*, *Piska* 10.6, Moses takes the beams from God's angel, citing Hab 3:4; so his face was one of "radiance, surpassing and brilliant," and *Piska* 15.3, which softens the entire episode of Exod 34:30).

W. H. Smith, who surveys this material, points out that it is not uniform, and Paul does not agree with any one source. Indeed much of the data is later than the apostle's time. The question of the veil, found positively only in *Pesiq. R.*, will be considered at our v 12. Here we are interested in a single item: the body of this material is in agreement that Moses' face emitted "beams" (from קֶרֶן *qeren*, "horn"), however they are explained; and his face (or the skin) shone. Most texts link this aura of radiance with his ascent at Sinai, and two sources concur that Moses was not aware of it. Philo and *Pesiq. R.* are in agreement with MT/LXX in attributing fear to those who saw the leader's face, but they diverge from the OT in saying that the people could not see Moses' countenance.

The two issues on which Paul and his sources are in agreement are: Moses' face was illuminated, and it was glorious. But v 10, while ostensibly drawing on Exod 34:29–35, modifies that Old Testament tradition considerably, as if Paul were responding to some Jewish (or Jewish Christian) apologetic on Moses' behalf. Paul's sentence adds up to this paradoxical conclusion: that which had glory did not have glory! The paradoxical feature is caused by some difficult words: ἐν τούτῳ τῷ μέρει, lit., "in this respect" or "in this case" (Barrett, Allo), namely, as far as concerns the glory of the Gospel. So the meaning of 9:3 is a clue, for in that v the sense has to be "in this case" (BGD, 1 b θ). But an appeal, with Bachmann and Héring, to 1:14; 2:5, gives a restrictive nuance to μέρος, and we find this view preferable (cf. Georgi, *Die Gegner*, 275). Hence, "that which has been glorified within limits or partially" (i.e., because it has only a transient quality about it, a meaning of καταργουμένην in v 7 which Bultmann supports with his translation *die vergänglich war*, the participle being a substitute for a verbal adjective, BDF § 65.3) has not really been glorified at all with respect to/on account of (εἵνεκεν; BDF § 216.1) the new, *surpassing* glory." ὑπερβαλλούσης, "surpassing": the verbal adjective is one of the key expressions in this epistle in a variety of contexts (4:17; 11:23; 12:7). So Paul paradoxically gives a certain measure of approval to the OT idea of the Sinai covenant as expressing God's glory. But the good is now replaced by the better; indeed by the best, which elsewhere Paul puts in more personal language: "the surpassing (τὸ ὑπερέχον) worth of knowing Christ Jesus my Lord" (Phil 3:8).

11. εἰ γὰρ τὸ καταργούμενον διὰ δόξης, πολλῷ μᾶλλον τὸ μένον ἐν δόξῃ. A summary conclusion in verbless form completes the thought: "for (γὰρ) if the transient was with glory, how much rather has the permanent its glory." Διὰ δόξης, "with glory," and "in glory" (ἐν δόξῃ) are hard to distinguish (so

Windisch, Lietzmann-Kümmel), though some do. If there is a fine line of distinction, it is that the old order was accompanied, at its inception, with God's glory displayed, whereas the enduring new order is glorious (ἐν + dative having adjectival force, as in Phil 4:19, "glorious riches." See too Moule, *Idiom Book*, 58, and the "exegetical overkill" in Collange, 83, who extracts a great deal from the prepositional phrase, all of which is true [e.g., the cross of Jesus has overthrown all previous ideas of "glory"], but such considerations are hardly relevant here).

12. This v marks a new section. So far Paul has laid down three propositions, each using the *a minori ad maius* contrast:

1. The glory which lit up Moses' face was transient, whereas the age of the Spirit is invested with a glory that gives life (v 6). This is the "polemical term" (*Kampfbegriff:* so G. Barth, "Die Eignung," 267) around which the subsequent discussion gathers. And the point under debate is what constitutes the "criterion and norm for understanding the churchly office" of apostolic preachers (idem, 270).
2. The glory of the old era was there but had its limitations (i.e., it led to condemnation), where the new age has a superior aim, to bring in divine "righteousness," God's saving power.
3. The Mosaic order possessed only a restricted life, seen in that the glory faded; the glory of the new world is permanent.

In one sense, Paul's argument can rest here, for to his own satisfaction and given his premises he has proved his point. This is that the ministry of the new covenant is God's way of offering life to men and women, and it has no rivals with such credentials (cf. Gal 2:21). If the issue is whether Paul's own claim to be "a minister of the new covenant" (3:6) is central, then his case rests on the indisputable logic he has drawn—partly using exegetical details from Exod 34, and partly making an appeal to his apostolic service which centers on a "writing of the Spirit" that places its mark on the human lives at Corinth.

The new paragraph that opens at v 12 has, at first glance, a different theme. The subject matter is Moses' head covering (κάλυμμα), and it is not easy to see the transition from v 12, which *is* intelligible, to vv 13 ff., which appears to introduce some extraneous matters, e.g., Moses' veil, the hardness of the Jewish heart as Moses' veil becomes a veil set over their minds, and Christians' experience, shared by a wider audience than Paul and his apostolic band, of encountering the divine splendor, "with unveiled faces." Some commentators despair of the task of relating vv 13–18 to the foregoing (Strachan, 87, 88, who speaks of a "sudden tangent of thought which would neither convince nor conciliate" his opponents); others less temperately are wholly dismissive of the vv, referring to them as "a passage like a cock-and-bull story" (*"du coq à l'âne,"* Collange, *Enigmes*, 89), with little meaning and less relevance. These are hasty judgments. Yet we can sympathize with Schulz ("Die Decke," 7–9) and Georgi (*Die Gegner*, 275, 279), who see in 3:12–18 a Pauline gloss on a preformed Judeo-Christian document. Their view is that it was Paul's opponents who made the link between Moses' veil and the hardness of Israel; and so Paul's responsibility is restricted only to what are deemed his insertions into the pre-existing text. But this is speculative, for the reasons we have given, even if some recent writers (e.g., G. Friedrich, "Die Gegner," 181–215, esp. 184) have accepted the provenance of 3:7–18 as a theological tractate from a Judaizing source; or have modified it (e.g., G. Barth, "Die Eignung," 260, 269, who sees the opponents as hellenistic-Jewish Christian "charismatics" who moved around the Pauline churches). Yet this latter position virtually overthrows the observation that Paul's exegetical method has an appeal to those trained in rabbinical methods.

The most ingenious way of joining v 12 to what follows is that of van Unnik, " 'With Unveiled Face,' " based on certain semantic equivalents. The two terms brought together are (1) παρρησία, "boldness of speech," arising from confidence and freedom and (2) the Aramaic idiom גלה ראש, galleh rēʾš, —"to uncover the head"—as a sign of freedom. With a parallel expression גלה אפין, galleh ʾappîn, "to uncover the face," it is possible to render "to have freedom to speak," and this is an idiomatic rabbinic phrase. Van Unnik assumes that, for Paul as bilingual, this argument would be persuasive and would be his reply to those who made much of Moses as an OT mediator. Paul points to the veil, which covered Moses' face (and mouth?), and draws out the symbolic meaning: Moses did not have the παρρησία, "boldness," which we as Christians have (3:18). And Paul's line of defense is to indicate how Moses suffered under liabilities that do not apply to the apostolic communities of the new covenant. But this background is so involved that we may wonder if the first readers would have been able to appreciate it—or even follow it. The same verdict has to be recorded against an implied contrast—what R. W. L. Moberly calls a "daring parallelism"—between Moses (with bull horns) and the calf that became the object of veneration. He appeals to the Hebrew "horn" (qeren) and the antithesis of "veil" (masweh in connection with the root ʾwr "to shine," At the Mountain, 106–9). But this requires reading into the OT text far more than could be expected.

Granted that Paul did draw out certain items from the "Moses-midrash" that are not explicit in the OT, we should still seek a solution to the exegetical difficulties by a suggestion that reads as little into the text as possible, and that focuses on what, on other grounds, is the central issue in the entire chapter, namely, Paul's defense of the apostolic service.

Two preliminary matters need to be borne in mind: (1) the claim of v 12 involves just this estimate of Paul's ministry which is the spoken communication authorized by God (3:5) and expressive of the terms of the "new covenant" (3:6); and (2) the verbal links of 3:12–18 connect it with the preceding (διαθήκη, κάλυμμα, καρδία, πνεῦμα) and with what is to come at 4:1–6 ([διακονία] κεκαλυμμένον [2x], νοήματα, δόξα, εἰκών, κύριος, καρδία, πρόσωπον). These links are impressive in number and significance, and give rise to the idea that 3:12–18 is no independent section, loosely appended to chap. 3, but integral to it; and also that the shift of interest still keeps the focus of Paul's thought on his preaching ministry, its authority and effectiveness. The difference, however, is that at 3:12 he turns to address another challenge: How can he account for the lack of response among his own Jewish compatriots? The undertone is polemical, since the charge no doubt is still intended to undermine his office, but the ground of attack is new. He must answer the allegation that he has had little success (in contrast to the "many" [2:17] opponents who styled themselves "servants of Christ" and saw in Moses a powerful, triumphalist figure), and that he, unlike Israel's leader who was given a nimbus of radiance, has only a feeble presence (4:7–12, 17; 5:12, 13; 6:4–10; 10:1, 10; 11:6; 12:5–10; 13:4—all vv that reveal Paul's innate frailty, with the only "glory" being that which rejoices in his sufferings).

But Paul does have παρρησία, a word with a long, variegated history (see Bultmann, 87, 88). In hellenistic Judaism it means the right to have access to God, with a good conscience (cf. 1:12; 4:2). In Christian circles it is connected to both "freedom" (ἐλευθερία) and "authority" (ἐξουσία). In the context it is part of what Paul has already said in regard to his πεποίθησις (v 4), rendered "confidence"; but here it is polemically slanted, and prepares for 4:1, as we can see:

3:12 ἔχοντες οὖν τοιαύτην ἐλπίδα πολλῇ παρρησίᾳ χρώμεθα, "since then we really do have such a hope, we speak with great freedom"
4:1: ἔχοντες τὴν διακονίαν ταύτην . . . οὐκ ἐγκακοῦμεν, "since we have this ministry . . . we are not discouraged."

Some conclusions stand out from this parallelism: (1) παρρησία has its counterpoint in ἐγκακεῖν, "to lose heart." Because Paul knows what such "boldness" means, he has the antidote to faintheartedness. (2) The "boldness" is directed to his fellow men and women, not primarily to God, and springs out of his "sincerity" (2:17) which is opposed to all "deceit" (δόλος, 4:2). (3) Paul's sense of assurance is one that rests on hope (ἐλπίς), where we might have expected him to extol his διακονία. Instead, he appeals to "hope," in turn based on what is permanent, not transitory (3:11; he will return to this contrast in 4:16–18), that is, a new covenant of which he is called to be a διάκονος and so possessed of δόξα-ἐξουσία, valid authority (see earlier, p. 53). It is natural, then, that he will set this calling side by side with Israel's great leader, both positively and negatively. His daring innovation is to assert that he has παρρησία to challenge Moses as the last word in God's salvation-history (see Georgi, *Die Gegner;* C. K. Barrett, *From First Adam to Last* [London: A. & C. Black, 1962] chap. 3) and to affirm a new final age of that salvation-history. As Bultmann (88) aptly puts it, " 'we speak with great freedom' corresponds to 'I am not ashamed of the Gospel' (Rom 1:16)."

13. So Paul's boldness is immediately offset by Moses who too shared his moments of glory. The link with v 12 is broken syntactically, and we are required to add a verb: "but [it is with us] not as [it was] with Moses" (BDF § 482). Nor is it with Christians as it was with Moses in v 7, where the accent falls on a natural sequence: Moses' face was lighted up with a radiance, and it was such an aura that repelled the Israelites. The same radiant brilliance required the placing of a veil over his face πρὸς τὸ μὴ ἀτενίσαι τοὺς υἱοὺς Ἰσραὴλ εἰς τέλος τοῦ καταργουμένου ("to prevent the Israelites from fixing their eyes [to see] the significance of what was about to be done away").

The center of this clause is the word τέλος, which may mean either of two things: termination or goal. The English word "end" is also capable of being taken in either sense, e.g., the end of the day or "the chief end of man" (Westminster Catechism). One v where both meanings seem intricately joined is Phil 3:19 (H. Köster, *NTS* 8 [1961–62] 325 f.); and Rom 10:4 *could* include both nuances: Christ brings the law to its appointed fulfillment, and in so doing he ends its regime as a way to righteousness. Most commentators see in Paul's wording at 3:13 a statement that Moses' veil was put in place in order that (πρὸς τὸ μὴ + infinitive expressing purpose: Plummer, Bachmann, Georgi; BDF § 402.5) the Israelite people should not fix their gaze (ἀτενίσαι: see on v 7) on the glory that was coming to an end. Moses' interview with Yahweh was terminated and the source of the radiation was withdrawn; so the skin of his face was losing its glow, as suntan fades when we are no longer exposed to the sun's rays. The purpose was to avoid the people's disappointment.

But it is uncertain if this is the true sense, and it can be argued, on the other hand, that τέλος should be taken as "goal" or "purpose" (Ziel, according to Rissi, 31, 32; Provence, 75) or indeed "ultimate significance" (Héring, 24, implying that the people misunderstood what the glowing face of Moses and his intimate communion with God was all about; this reading of τέλος answers Provence's critical point, art. cit., 76 n. 62). The chief support for this latter view is the way the text goes on: ἀλλὰ ἐπωρώθη τὰ νοήματα αὐτῶν, the ἀλλὰ ("but") starting a fresh line of application as Paul proceeds to move from Israel in Moses' time to Israel κατὰ σάρκα, "in natural descent," in his own day (v 14). The subject of τοῦ καταργουμένου, "of what was disappearing" or "fading," or (as we prefer) "being done away," is not δόξα (a feminine noun), but either κάλυμμα ("veil") or νόμος ("law") in agreement with the neuter or masculine participial ending. Even so, there is a hiatus, because ἀλλὰ, on this view, has to open a fresh section of thought, and cannot provide a reason for it by contrast with v 13.

So we consider Collange's interpretation (Enigmes, 96, 97) preferable, which sees the key word, not in κάλυμμα but in the verb ἀτενίζω, which has a strong meaning, "to gaze at intensely." The fault of Israel—though not of Moses, who in this v is seen in a good or neutral light (Hickling, "The Sequence," 391)—is that they persisted in looking at a face that symbolized a "ministration" (διακονία) which in turn was on the way out. The fading glow on Moses' face betokened the temporary nature of nomistic religion. But the Jews, both in Moses' day and ἄχρι(γὰρ)τῆς σήμερον ("until the present day"), have shown their obtuseness by looking to Moses as the final embodiment of God's salvation. This neat exegesis virtually adds up to the idea given in translation as Héring's rendering, which we have adopted.

14. Paul finds the condemnation of Israel, both ancient and modern, in the place accorded to the veil. Moses' act in putting it on was for reverential reasons, as well as prudential. But he also took it off (Exod 34:34; the verb יסר, ysr, is middle: "he took it off himself"; so too LXX περιῃρεῖτο); and Israel in the nation's unbelief maintained the place of the veil as a sign of Moses' authority. But, says Paul in his rejoinder, this is exactly the mistake they have made and still make.

Ἐπὶ τῇ ἀναγνώσει τῆς παλαιᾶς διαθήκης, "at the reading of the old covenant" (ἐπί is given a local sense by Bachmann; or "when the old covenant is read," a temporal sense: so Plummer), refers to the public reading of Torah (Acts 13:15 where ἀνάγνωσις, "reading," translates the Hebrew מקרא, miqrāʾ: B. Gerhardsson, Memory and Manuscript: Oral Tradition and Written Transmission

in Rabbinic Judaism and Early Christianity, ASNU 22 [Lund: Gleerup, 1961]
67–70). What is exceptional is the phrase "the old covenant" for Torah,
the books of Moses. Paul evidently coined the expression (perhaps based
on Jer 31:31; so H. Seesemann, *TDNT* 5:720 n. 13), and its next occurrence
is as late as Melito of Sardis, *On the Passion* (before A.D. 190). The phrase,
moreover, is pejorative, with the emphasis on "old" (as in Heb 8:13). The
point is clearly made when the next clause is introduced, obscure as it is:
μὴ ἀνακαλυπτόμενον ὅτι ἐν Χριστῷ καταργεῖται. "The same veil remains" (μένει;
cf. v 11 for the verb) over human hearts, Paul concludes as a sad comment
on Jewish synagogue worship. The reason for this blindness is expressed in
"as long as the veil is unlifted" (a kind of accusative absolute, but this would
need the participle μὴ ἀποκαλυπτόμενον, yet it is the rendering supported by
Allo, Moffatt, Bachmann), or "since the veil is unlifted" as predicative to
μένει (so Luther, Héring), or the sense is "the unlifted veil is explained by
the knowledge that [only] in Christ is the law done away" (so Cramer, *Catenae,*
370.9, cited by Bultmann). Much depends on how the ὅτι is understood.
Bultmann opts for a causal sense; it could equally be explicative, with the
subject παλαιὰ διαθήκη or that which is tantamount to the "old covenant,"
namely, its δόξα ("glory"). The subject cannot be "veil," since the verb καταργεῖται, "is done away," hardly goes with it (Bachmann), and in other neighbor-
ing vv (7, 11, 13) it is the glory of the "old covenant" that is on the road
to passing away. Moreover, καλύπτειν, "to veil," must be accorded the same
meaning as in v 18 where the participle recurs. Alternatively, we could agree,
with Collange (99), that the subject of καταργεῖται is indeterminate, and refers to the interpretation given by Paul's opponents to Moses and his covenant.

Of the various possibilities, we have stressed in our rendering the ὅτι as
explicative and have taken "the fact that the glory fades in Christ" as the
result of Jewish resistance. The veil is still in place for them as they read
Moses' law, and "veiled from them is the fact that only in Christ is the glory
of the Old Testament done away" (so Moffatt; cf. Bachmann, Godet). The obverse side of this negative assessment of the OT is seen in Luke 24:45, 46
where the disciples' "minds" are opened (and no longer obtuse) and they
can then see the OT as full of messianic prefigurations (cf. Luke 24:27, 32).

15. Unlike the Emmaus disciples, these people in Paul's sights, who are
his compatriots, though in this context, his adversaries who claimed to be
"true Israelites" (11:22), suffer under the liability of a "veil over their minds"
(ἐπὶ τὴν καρδίαν αὐτῶν: καρδία, "heart," is the equivalent of νόημα in v 14)
so that "whenever (ἡνίκα ἄν: a NT *hapax,* but it is taken directly from Exod
34:34 LXX: ἡνίκα δ᾽ ἄν εἰσεπορεύετο Μωυσῆς ἔναντι κυρίου λαλεῖν αὐτῷ, περιηρεῖτο
τὸ κάλυμμα: "whenever Moses went before the Lord to speak with him, he
removed the veil") Moses (= the Torah, as in Acts 15:21) is read, a veil
lies over their heart." The last word holds the clue: we are again faced with
Paul's rebuttal of those "who gloried in appearance (πρόσωπον), not in heart
(καρδία)." See 5:12 for the explicit antithesis. Taking their stand on Moses
and all he stood for as an authority figure (their Moses typology is well depicted
by J. H. Schütz, *Paul and the Anatomy of Apostolic Authority,* SNTSMS 26 [Cam-
bridge: University Press, 1975] 173, 174, 185: Paul's enemies appealed to

the principle of tradition in the OT Scriptures; the *persona* of Moses as θεῖος ἀνήρ, "divine man," was their model; the Christian pneumatic was, like Moses, a spirit-filled person, and in their hands the "veil" was a sign of Moses' dignity par excellence, to which they aspired, and like Moses, they "turned to the Lord" for their glorification), Paul's opponents are seen to be under a self-delusion, with the same veil on which they prided themselves acting as a curtain to separate them from the truth as Paul saw it.

16. Moses, on whom they patterned their lifestyle, did wear a veil, to be sure. But he "took it off himself" in Yahweh's presence (Exod 34:34, LXX) in order to hold communion. Is Paul here reproving his opponents' practice of seeing in the veil a token of Moses' authority, in which they claimed a share? The wording of v 16 parallels, if not exactly, the LXX, but is Paul's re-reading of the LXX intended to draw out the lessons he wished to make positively?

If the subject of ἐπιστρέψῃ, "he/it turns," is primarily Moses, this is obviously a kind of "historicizing" that Paul undertakes: "whenever Moses turned to Yahweh, he removed the veil" (so Schulz, "Die Decke," 15, 16). But why would Paul rewrite the OT text if his interests were solely and exclusively historical? Nor can the implied subject be "the people of Israel," since it is harsh to infer a change of subject in such a short sentence as v 16 is.

The text may refer to the Jewish people, either in Paul's day ("whenever a Jew is 'converted'," ἐπιστρέφειν being the semantic term for שׁוּב, šûb, "to repent": Gal 4:9; 1 Thess 1:9, etc.; see Le Déaut, "Traditions targumiques," 46, 47) or in the future hope of Rom 11:25, 32, where, however, the verb ἐπιστρέφειν or the noun ἐπιστροφή, "conversion," "turning," is not found. Then the aorist subjunctive of ἐπιστρέψῃ followed by the present tense (περιαιρεῖται) implies the suddenness of conversion. As soon as a person turns to the Lord, in a trice the veil drops off (so Godet), while Hughes interprets the present as an assurance of what will happen in the future in God's design for the Jewish people, or a spiritual Israel, Israel κατὰ πνεῦμα (Héring). Barrett (122) opts for the subject as καρδία of v 15, but this overlooks the Exodus background. All these interpretations seem forced; but they may yield an added dimension to Paul's exegesis (see *Explanation*).

Instead, we propose a generalized subject of the verb ἐπιστρέψῃ with ἡνίκα δὲ . . . πρὸς κύριον as complement, "whenever there is a turning to the Lord," granting the text is modeled on Exod 34:34. Paul's insistence lies not in the "turning" but in the removing of the veil, and it is this act that he wished to get home to his readers. Moses was in the habit of going in (imperfect, εἰσεπορεύετο) to Yahweh's presence; then he would drop the veil ἕως τοῦ ἐκπορεύεσθαι, "until he came out." "Going in" . . . "coming out" are incidental; the action that counts for Paul is what Moses did "before the Lord"— he took off the veil. The conclusion is in response to those who attached a mystical significance to the veil. That Paul vehemently denied, and his thought moves on to v 18: "we all, with veils removed," see the Lord's glory by the Spirit's action over against the γράμμα-quality of the old order (3:6).

17. This v is a parenthesis, with a consensus emerging that it stands as Paul's *pesher* or interpretative comment on v 16. The text there spoke of Moses' turning to the Lord (= Yahweh). The updating procedure in Paul's exegetical method is to refer ὁ κύριος, "the Lord," in quotation marks (with

an anaphoric article, N. Turner, *Grammatical Insights into the New Testament* [Edinburgh: T. & T. Clark, 1965] 126 f.), to the Spirit (τὸ πνεῦμα), with the copulative ἐστιν being treated as the exegetical *significat*, "it represents." "The Lord" in the passage just cited means [for us] the Spirit (see Dunn, "2 Corinthians III. 17," against Hermann, *Kyrios und Pneuma*, 39 ff., with a modification in Moule, "2 Cor 3:18*b*," 231, 232). A final blow at Paul's opponents with their Moses typology would be registered if we could accept Hickling's novel interpretation (394, n. 3). He sees the Exodus text as reinterpreted to mean that when Moses ascended the mountain, he met the Spirit, the source of freedom. But Moses' mind was archetypally "hardened," and he descended with the Ten Words of legalistic religion. So Moses was the first to suffer πώρωσις, "hardening," and Israel thereafter simply followed his (bad) example. But this has the sound of a strained exegesis.

"The Spirit" is usually taken as the Holy Spirit, but it is a case of his dynamic action rather than the person of the Spirit that is in view (1 Cor 15:45; so Barrett, 123; Collange, 109; Hermann, 17–58). Yet the role of the Spirit as revealer of the knowledge of God has been powerfully championed by Chevallier, *Esprit de Dieu*, 93–97, and his way of linking v 17 to v 18 is suggestive. The Jewish interpreters of the Exodus story read that Moses went in to find communion with God; but as they still are veiled, that access is denied them, unlike their leader. When we seek "the Lord" by the Spirit, it is the Spirit of the Lord that grants us access to God, Paul concluded.

Paul's term for access, on this reading, is "freedom" (ἐλευθερία), a term found only here in 2 Corinthians. It is linked with παρρησία, "boldness," in v 12, and is the conclusion of Paul's argument for the value and validity of the apostolic ministry, that is, to proclaim a message of "freedom in Christ" (Gal 5:1; Rom 8:2), which spells our heritage as God's children (Rom 8:14–17) and as part of his creation (Rom 8:19–25).

18. This is a noble conclusion, to which Paul's disquisition has been leading. ἡμεῖς δὲ πάντες, "but we all," reaches out to widen the scope of what the Spirit of God does. Paul's thinking is christological to the extent that for him Christ is the living embodiment (εἰκών, image) of God's revelation. The new covenant, of which Paul is a διάκονος, carries the title it does because in Christ the καινὴ κτίσις, "new creation" (5:17), has dawned, the new eon of salvation and righteousness.

Moses' veil acted as a barrier to Israel, but the veil is removed in Christ (v 14), and to that extent "every Christian has become a Moses" (Héring 27 n. 21). Christians are said to be τὴν δόξαν κυρίου κατοπτριζόμενοι, either "beholding" or "reflecting" the glory of the Lord. Both meanings are feasible, but Kümmel's point tips the scale. The translation "we reflect" removes the contrast of the Christians with the Jews, who because of their veil cannot see; so the rendering "we behold" is to be preferred, and is forcefully maintained by Hugedé, *La métaphore du miroir*, 17–24, 32.

The object of the participle is God's glory revealed in his "image" (εἰκών: 4:4–6; cf. Col 1:15; Heb 1:1–4; John 1:18; and Phil 2:6 if μορφή there has its semantic equivalent in δόξα/εἰκών; see R. P. Martin, *Carmen Christi: Philippians 2:5–11*, 99–133).

The verb μεταμορφούμεθα, "are being transformed," strongly suggests a link with Christ as God's "image" who is the prototype (*Abbild*: Jervell's term,

Imago Dei) for all who belong to him and in whom he is taking shape (Gal 4:19). See 1 Cor 15:44–49 on which we may refer to M. J. Harris, *Raised Immortal* (London: Marshall, Morgan & Scott, 1983) 114–33; R. P. Martin, *The Spirit and the Congregation: Studies in 1 Corinthians 12–15* (Grand Rapids: Eerdmans/Exeter: Paternoster Press, 1984) 129–42, for a consideration of recent discussion.

This process of "transformation" (μεταμορφοῦσθαι: cf. Rom 12:2) is gradual and progressive, ἀπὸ δόξης εἰς δόξαν, from one stage of glory to yet a higher stage (*2 Bar* 51:3, 7, 10), climaxing in the goal reached in Rom 8:17, 29, 30 (cf. A. R. C. Leaney, "Conformed to the Image of His Son," *NTS* 10 [1963–64] 470–79).

The agent in this process is described cryptically as καθάπερ ἀπὸ κυρίου πνεύματος, most simply, "as from the Lord, who is the Spirit" (Barrett), or the Lord whom we know as the Spirit (cf. Moule), or "as from the sovereign Spirit" (W. L. Knox, *St. Paul,* 131 f.), or as from the Spirit who is "the functional means by which Jesus continued after his death to promote Christianity" (Greenwood, "The Lord is the Spirit," 471). The exegetical knot can only be untied as we can relate the two genitive nouns, κυρίου and πνεύματος, and several options are possible. Probably the simpler rendering is the best, as we have chosen, with Schmithals's view of the text as glossed being the last resort (*Gnosticism,* 315–25).

At all events, the discussion reaches its peak with Paul's asseveration that believers in Christ live in a new age where "glory" is seen in the Father's Son and shared among those who participate in that eon. It is the Spirit's work to effect this change, transforming believers into the likeness of him who is the groundplan of the new humanity, the new Adam, until they attain their promised destiny as "made like to his Son" (Rom 8:29) and enjoy the full freedom that is their birthright under the terms of the new covenant.

Explanation

Since these vv (7–18) have been scrutinized in some detail, it remains now to pull together the results of the exegesis into something like a coherent statement. We may be pardoned for a neglect of Paul's central themes which we are in danger of losing amid a welter of exegetical suggestion and countersuggestion. So we propose a fairly straightforward résumé of the apostolic argument in the interests of clarity and as a way to get at the heart of a tortuous passage.

At this point in the Pauline statement of the apostolic ministry, we are now prepared for a series of contrasts in which the old and the new covenants are discussed together. There are three lines of approach which the apostle takes. Vv 7–11 express two of them.

First, the law set the standard, but offered no power to reach it. For that reason Paul does not mince his words: the law "kills" (v 6); it is "the ministry that leads to death" (v 7) which, in turn, produces "condemnation" (v 9). These strong terms can only mean that the law set the target of a perfect standard; but men and women, who are sinfully weak, are unable to attain it.

Paul finds no fault with the law in itself (Rom 7:12, 14), but he discovers that the law mocked and taunted by calling him to an impossibly high level, yet offering him no assistance or dynamic for attainment. In this way, what God intended as good is turned into a death-dealing instrument (Rom 7:13)— and the reason? We may refer to Rom 8:3*a*: the law is weakened by human inadequacy, "the flesh."

Second, Paul goes on to teach that the law had an honorable purpose, but it was only temporary. The illustration of the law's "parenthetic character" (as Gal 3:16 ff. describes it) is seen in the way in which the glory of both the law (vv 7, 11) and the lawgiver, Moses (v 7), was only a passing one. The background reference is clearly Exod 34:29–35, which describes the splendor that shone from Moses' face when he returned from communion with God. That radiance, however, faded in time and at length disappeared. From the lawgiver, Paul argues to that which he represents, viz., ancient Judaism whose glory, once historically a reality, is now fading away; indeed, its day is over, and its impermanence has given way to that which has come to stay, viz., the Gospel (vv 10, 11).

All of this contrast adds up to one firm conclusion: the Christian ministry is meant, by divine intention, to supersede the old Judaic ceremonial order. The glory of God is to be sought now, not in the law or the Temple or the priesthood, but in the face of Jesus Christ (2 Cor 4:6; Titus 2:13). John's prologue says the same thing exactly (John 1:17), as does the main argument of the letter to the Hebrews (chap. 8 in particular).

Having taken his readers thus far, Paul is now ready for a third element in the distinction between the two covenants. The law betokened a barrier between God and the people of Israel, both in Moses' day and in Paul's. Why did the lawgiver place a veil over his radiant face (v 13; Exod 34:33)? Part of the reason was to prevent the people's disappointment when they saw the glory fading; but Exod 34:30 reports that "they were afraid to come near him," partly because of the "radiation" of his face (Exod 34:29 reads literally that "the skin of his face sent forth beams").

Paul finds in this circumstance a profound explanation, for the veil which Moses wore is no mere historical detail. It speaks of a barrier which still hides the truth from the Jewish reader of the OT.

When the Jews of Antioch, Ephesus, or Corinth hear the law read in the Sabbath worship of the synagogue (vv 14, 15), they fail to perceive its true significance. They imagine that it is the final revelation of God, not (as Paul has shown) a preparatory agency making them ready to receive the Christ (Gal 3:24). Therefore they remain hardened and blinded (4:3, 4; Rom 11:25), in spite of their inestimable privileges as God's ancient people to whom the law was first entrusted (Rom 3:1, 2; 9:4, 5).

But whenever a Jew turns to the Lord, how different is the result as the veil is lifted and "Christ in all the Scriptures" is made known! Paul's own experience was a living proof of the validity and force of this "eschatological exegesis" of the OT which, through Christian eyes, takes on an added dimension.

Vv 17, 18 require a comment. The crux is the sentence "the Lord is the Spirit." If we recall that the preceding verse is taken originally from Exod

34:34, though Paul is novel in the way he applies it, we are on the right track. Then v 17 is a comment on the reference to Moses' turning in toward God's presence: "Now in the verse mentioned, the Lord whom Moses approached means *for us* the Spirit who leads a person to turn to Christ and confess his lordship" (cf. 1 Cor 12:3). This is Paul's apparent meaning.

The office of the Holy Spirit is further described in vv 17*b*, 18; he brings the Jewish believer out of bondage to liberty, and transforms all believers, Gentiles as well as Jews, into God's pattern, viz., the archetype of perfect humanity, Christ Jesus, as a progressive experience and by communion with the living God (Rom 8:29; Gal 4:19; Phil 3:21; 1 John 3:2). So "every Christian has become a Moses" (Héring), beholding the divine glory in this life in anticipation of perfect conformity to Christ in the next.

C. Apostolate, Kerygma, Ministry (4:1–6)

Bibliography

Bain, John A. "2 Cor iv.3–4." *ExpT* 18 (1906–07) 380. **Baumert, N.** *Täglich Sterben und Auferstehen.* 115–17, 318–46. **Benoit, P.** "Qumrân et le Nouveau Testament." *NTS* 7 (1960–61) 289, 290. **Bouttier, M.** "Le tesson. 2 Cor 4, 6–11." *AsSeign* 40 (1972) 37–42. **Cranfield, C. E. B.** "Minister and Congregation in the Light of II Cor 4:5–7." *Int* 19 (1965) 163–67. **Davies, S.** "Remarks on the Second Epistle to the Corinthians 4:3, 4." *BSac* 25 (1968) 23–30. **Doeve, J. W.** "Some Notes with Reference to τὰ λόγια τοῦ θεοῦ." *Studia Paulina.* FS de Zwaan. 111–23. **Fitzmyer, J. A.** "Glory Reflected on the Face of Christ (2 Cor 3:7–4:6) and a Palestinian Jewish Motif." *TS* 42 (1981) 639–44. **Hopfl, H.** "2 Cor iv.3,4." *ExpTim* 18 (1906–07) 428. **Iverach, J.** "The Ministry of Light." *Exp* 4th series 3 (1891) 92–103. **Kim, S.** *The Origin of Paul's Gospel.* Grand Rapids: Wm. B. Eerdmans, 1982. **Larsson, E.** *Christus als Vorbild.* ASNU 23. Lund/Uppsala: Gleerup, 1962. 279–89. **MacRae, G. W.** "Anti-Dualism Polemic in 2 Cor 4.6?" *SE* IV/1 (1968) 420–31. **Martini, C.** "Alcuni temi letterari di 2 Cor 4,6 e i racconti della conversione di San Paulo negli Atti." *Studiorum Paulinorum Congressus.* AnBib 17–18 (1961) I, 461–74. **Muellensiefen, W.** "Satan der θεὸς τοῦ αἰῶνος τούτου. 2 Kor. 4.4?" *TSK* 95 (1923–24) 295–98. **Rissi, M.** *Studien.* 58–60. **Schmithals, W.** *Gnosticism in Corinth.* Tr. J. E. Steely. Nashville: Abingdon, 1971. **Smith, William H., Jr.** "The Function of 2 Corinthians 3:7–4:6 in Its Epistolary Context." Ph.D. diss., Southern Baptist Theological Seminary, 1983. **Zorell, F.** " 'Deus huius saeculi' (2 Cor 4.4)." *VD* 8 (1928) 54–57.

Translation

¹ *Therefore, since we have this ministry, as we have had mercy shown* [*to us*], *we are not discouraged.* ᵃ ² *We have repudiated shameful practices devised in secret; we do not employ cunning methods nor do we tamper with God's word, but by an open declaration that reveals the truth, we recommend ourselves to everyone's conscience as living in God's sight.* ³ *Yet if even our gospel preaching is veiled, it is veiled only to those on the way to perdition,* ⁴ *that is, to those nonbelievers whose minds the god*

of this age has blinded to stop them from seeing the revealed splendor of the Gospel, that is the glory of Christ who is the image of God. ⁵*For it is not ourselves we are proclaiming but Jesus Christ as Lord; we ourselves are simply your slaves—for Jesus' sake.* ⁶*For it is the God who said, "Light shall shine out of darkness," who has shone in our hearts to illumine them with the knowledge of God's glory seen in the face of Christ.* ᵇ

Notes

ᵃReading ἐγκακοῦμεν, where a few, inferior texts (C Ψ 0243 TR) have ἐκκακοῦμεν, "we grow weary." The confusion is understandable in view of the phonetic similarity between the verbs and also the link in thought: "since weariness could well be the cause of neglect of duty" (Barrett, who so renders ἐγκακοῦμεν).

ᵇThe shorter reading has Χριστοῦ, "of Christ" (offered by A B 33 1739* copˢᵃ arm Marcion Tert. and later Fathers), and is accepted on the principle of *lectio brevior potior*, "the shorter reading is stronger" (so Metzger, *Textual Commentary*, 579). But the addition of Ἰησοῦ to the *nomen sacer* has impressive attestation (incl. P⁴⁶ ℵ and uncials, with D F G reversing the order to Χριστοῦ Ἰησοῦ).

Form/Structure/Setting

The links between 2:14–17 and 4:1–6 suggest that Paul is employing a literary device known as "ring-composition," i.e., his closing thoughts revert to his earlier statements and complete the circle of ideas. The section 2:14–17 described the opponents of his Gospel and characterized their sad condition as οἱ ἀπολλύμενοι, "those on the road to perdition" (cf. 4:3, ἐν τοῖς ἀπολλυμένοις). Such teachers are labeled "pedlars of God's word" (cf. 4:2), whereas Paul claimed to be acting out of motives of "sincerity" (ἐξ εἰλικρινείας, 2:17; cf. 4:2) and always under the eye of God (2:17, κατέναντι θεοῦ; cf. 4:2 ἐνώπιον τοῦ θεοῦ, as "living in God's sight"). Moreover, the substance of Paul's kerygma is given as "the knowledge of God" (2:14, τῆς γνώσεως αὐτοῦ, with which is linked τῆς γνώσεως τῆς δόξης τοῦ θεοῦ, "the knowledge of God's glory," in 4:6). It seems clear that Paul's thought is consciously picking up the terms of his earlier indictment of the false teachers in 2:14–17 and is continuing his polemic against them.

Bultmann (101) sees also points of contact between 4:1–6 and the argument in 3:7–18. The common theme is the apostolic office whose hallmark is a "confidence" (πεποίθησις, 3:4) which leads in turn to Paul's forthrightness in speaking out the message of God (παρρησία, 3:12). He is marked off from the corrupt teachers of 2:17 and also from those referred to in 4:2. What divides the two ministries goes back to chap. 3 in the following ways:

(a) Paul's ministry (διακονία, 4:1) is the same as that mentioned at 3:8, 9, with a contrast drawn at 3:7 (there its opposite is "a ministry that leads to death"). (b) Because of this possession (ἔχοντες, "having," 4:1), Paul's ministry can be "bold" (3:12, ἔχοντες . . . πολλῇ παρρησίᾳ χρώμεθα), and he does not become despondent (οὐκ ἐγκακοῦμεν). Also he has set his face against "secret dealings" (τὰ κρυπτὰ τῆς αἰσχύνης, 4:2) and is able to speak out boldly, 3:12. (c) The recognition of God's mercy shown to him (4:1) points back to 3:4 (διὰ Χριστοῦ, "through Christ," he was summoned to his missionary service).

(d) As a telling point, the "veiled gospel" of 4:3 f. continues the debate over Moses' veil (3:13–18), with a common term not only in κάλυμμα ("veil"), but also in νοήματα ("minds") in 4:4 and 3:14 f. and the verbs αὐγάσαι (4:4), "to see," and ἀτενίσαι (3:13), "to behold," "to fix one's eyes."

The conclusion seems clear. Paul is building on his earlier debate with his adversaries in chap. 3, and responding to another line of criticism brought against his Gospel and his ministry. We may infer that the line of this critique ran: Paul has every reason to be discouraged since his person is marked by weakness and his message is ineffectual (see on 10:10). It is as though his hearers were groping in darkness, and his preaching cannot help them because it lacks the demonstrable signs of power to convince them of its authenticity. Paul tackles these issues head-on in 4:1–6; and so he closes his elaborate discussion opened at 2:14.

Comment

1. The διὰ τοῦτο (rendered "therefore," "for this reason") may well look forward to what is to come in the next clause, since it is not easy to connect 4:1 with the *immediately* antecedent section. The ground for Paul's assertion lies in the awareness he has of the mercy of God (καθὼς ἠλεήθημεν, "as we have had mercy shown [to us]"; cf. Matt 5:7 for this sense of "finding mercy" or favor from God. For Paul it has to do with his call to service; cf. 1 Tim 1:13). Another way of expressing this thought is seen in 3:4 (Bultmann).

"This ministry" (τὴν διακονίαν ταύτην) is that of the new covenant outlined in chap. 3, notably at 3:6, 8 where διακονία τοῦ πνεύματος, "ministry of the Spirit," looks on to 3:18. So it is just possible that there is a latent contact between 3:18 and 4:1; but it is latent.

Paul's commission to apostolic service is part of his "conversion," and several commentators find in this allusion to divine mercy or grace (1 Cor 15:10; cf. 1 Tim 1:13–16) an echo of his conversion (so Prümm, *Diakonia;* Lietzmann; Windisch; Plummer; Barrett; cf. Bultmann's objection which may be overruled by Kim's full discussion, *The Origin,* 5–11, 26, citing 1 Cor 7:25 as grounds for clarifying the aorist tense of the verb, "we have had mercy shown," in 4:1).

The upshot of Paul's confidence (stated in 3:4, 12) in his ministry as given him by God is that "we are not discouraged," a verb that can have several shades of meaning extending from "we do not get tired" (Luther), or "we do not neglect our tasks" (Windisch, 132; Barrett) to "we do not despair" (Lietzmann, 114) or "act in a cowardly way" which is "ashamed of the gospel" (Rom 1:16). Bultmann opts for the last meaning on the strength of what Paul avers in 3:12, "we are very bold." The advantage with this choice is that it focuses on Paul's affirmation of faith in his message (v 2), and the verb is not simply a subjective feeling (so in 4:16). Paul would fall victim to despair if he doubted the authenticity of the message entrusted to him. ἐγκακέω, "to lose heart," or better, "to behave weakly," is always in the NT prefaced by the negative οὐ or μὴ, and so indicates perseverance (Collange, *Enigmes,* 128). Parallel expressions are in 5:6–8; 7:16; 10:1–2, and ὑπομονή ("perseverance") recurs at 1:6; 6:4; 12:12. In this v "the mercy of God has found him, and made him simple, strong, sincere" (Iverach, "The Ministry," 94, citing Bengel: *"misericordia Dei, per quam ministerium accipitur facit strenuos et sinceros,"* i.e., "the divine mercy by which ministry is received, makes us active and sincere"). Baumert, *Täglich Sterben,* 318–46, has a full lexical note on ἐγκακεῖν in which he shows that the verb does not connote primarily physical or psychical exhaustion or distress (*Angst*) but distaste and aversion. Paul is thus confessing that he does not find his mission service a source of disagreeable revulsion; rather he glories in it, because he finds his hope in the one who called him and in the message of the cross (Gal 6:14). The relevance of this sentiment to Paul's life at the time of his writing 2 Corinthians is to be seen. See *Introduction,* pp. lii–lxi.

2. There is a bridge to his negative language in this v expressed by the strong adversative "but" (ἀλλά). It is the idiom of renunciation that he has turned away deliberately from one course of action to follow another (cf. Phil 3:7–14, a classic statement of this *renuntiatio* motif, which confirms that v 2 may well be a side glance at what happened at a decisive moment in Paul's life, at his conversion: so Plummer, Hughes, Collange). Or else, the following verb may point to the crisis of his Ephesian ministry (see *Introduction,* pp. lx, lxi).

However, Paul had his immediate sights trained on what his Corinthian accusers have leveled at him (Strachan; Schmithals, *Gnosticism,* 183, 184) and is launching out into an offensive assault on what his opponents are guilty of: shameful "intrigues that are hatched in secret" (the *Bible du Centenaire* has this vivid translation: "les intrigues qui se trament en cachette"). The phrases τὰ κρυπτά, "hidden acts," and αἰσχύνη, "shame," are used in Phil 3:19 also in this negative way.

Paul elaborates: "we do not practice cunning methods," lit., "we do not walk (περιπατέω, an OT verb for human conduct: H. Seesemann, *TDNT* 5: 940–46) with cunning" (ἐν πανουργίᾳ: a noun found six times in the New Testament, of which three occurrences are in our letter, 4:2; 11:3; 12:16; the word means, literally, "ready or able to do anything"; and since this is a pretentious claim based on an impossible feat, it comes to be linked with craftiness, trickery, pretense: see BGD, 608). From 12:16 we learn that Paul has been accused of making this false claim, but the reference may be ironical. The same accusation underlies 1:12.

Both his lifestyle and his preaching were attacked. "The word of God" is explained by vv 4, 5 as Paul's missionary message, his kerygma (cf. 2:17). He is accused of tampering (δολοῦν) with the Gospel perhaps by not requiring circumcision of his Gentile converts (Barrett)—but circumcision is hardly a burning issue in 2 Corinthians. More likely, what was questioned was Paul's handling of the Old Testament (for λόγος τοῦ θεοῦ in this sense, see Rom 9:6; cf. 3:2 on which see Doeve, "Some Notes") and his claim that "the veil" of 3:14–16 was removed only in Christ. If so, this train of thought naturally leads to the next phrase, connected by the contrasting ἀλλά, "but."

τῇ φανερώσει τῆς ἀληθείας συνιστάντες ἑαυτούς, "by an open declaration of the truth we recommend ourselves." The key part of this disavowal is that Paul will not "recommend himself" (cf. 3:1; 5:12). His court of appeal is not in any of the self-advertised claims such as his rivals at Corinth brought onto the scene; rather he places his confidence in openly stating—as opposed to a veiled message (v 3)—the truth of the Gospel for all to see. φανέρωσις, "open declaration," is a favorite Pauline expression in this letter (10 times; it is scarcely borrowed from the Corinthians, as Schmithals, *Gnosticism*, 190, supposes with his idea that Paul sets the *phanerōsis* of the truth against their rejoicing in the *phanerōsis* of the spirit in 1 Cor 12:7). The expression has parallels with the Qumran community's teaching (CD 2.12 f. "And He made known His Holy Spirit to them by the hand of His anointed ones, and He proclaimed the truth [to them]. But those whom He hated He led astray." But J. Murphy-O'Connor in *Paul and Qumran* [London: Chapman, 1968] 198–99, has noted the uncertainty of the textual reading). For that reason, Paul can direct his appeal to the human "conscience" (συνείδησις, see R. P. Martin, *Dictionary of the Bible and Religion* [Abingdon, 1986] under this word). Barrett, *Signs*, 85–86, makes the important point that Paul's ministry is validated by the Gospel he proclaims, not vice versa. Above all—unlike his opponents—Paul labors ἐνώπιον τοῦ θεοῦ, "as living in God's sight."

3. The underlying charge is that Paul's Gospel is obscure (Lietzmann; Schmithals, *Gnosticism*, 184), or better, that Paul had offered an interpretation of the Mosaic veil that his enemies found fault with. The latter view explains the εἰ δὲ καὶ, "yet even if," and the emphatic place of ἔστιν, "is," in the sentence. It is freely conceded that the Gospel *is* veiled—but only to those who insist on having it so by clinging to an understanding of the veil that keeps it in place, and failing to appreciate that the covering is done away with in Christ. They are, alas, "those on the way to perdition" (for the same term used of Paul's enemies, see 2:15; 1 Cor 1:18; Phil 1:28; 3:19; cf. 2 Thess 2:10). Since it is problematic how τοῖς ἀπολλυμένοις, "to those who are perishing," is to be related to the next clause beginning ἐν οἷς, "to those," which is strictly incorrect and should be αὐτῶν, i.e., "whose minds the god of this age has blinded." Bain, "2 Cor iv.3–4," *ExpTim* 18 (1906–07) 380, makes an attractive proposal to the effect that ἐν τοῖς ἀπολλυμένοις is neuter, not masculine. So he renders: "it is veiled in (or by) the things that are perishing, in (or by) which the God of this world." The advantage is seen when we consider whether τῶν ἀπίστων, "of unbelievers," is tautological, and if not, to whom it refers. But Paul's syntax is not always precise, and ἐν οἷς may be explicative or resumptive, as in our translation (cf. rsv, "in their case"). Windisch (135) explains the solecism as a result of Paul's dictation style (*Diktierstil*).

4. The god of this αἰών, "age," is Satan, in Paul's demonology (cf. 11:13–15; see R. P. Martin, *Reconciliation: A Study of Paul's Theology* [1981] 51–54, for some general background to Paul's thought in this area). The Jewish doctrine of two ages is important for the apostle; so Satan controls this age under God's decree. For Paul this malevolent power is seen in the blinding of human minds to prevent the light of the Gospel from penetrating. Those who are blinded are οἱ ἄπιστοι (whose minds, νοήματα: a term used in this letter of "the reasonings of Paul's adversaries who tried to show how his ministry lacked apostolicity," Collange, *Enigmes*, 134), a designation ordinarily used for unbelievers outside the church (see 1 Cor 14:23), but here slanted to those who were false brothers intent on doing Satan's work by undermining Paul's (11:13–15). This is an important datum for interpreting 6:14 (see *Com-*

ment there). So "those on the way to perdition" can apply to the same foes of Paul's message, though the term means (strictly) outsiders who reject the public preaching of the cross (1 Cor 1:18; cf. 2 Thess 2:10). The two phrases οἱ ἀπολλύμενοι and οἱ ἄπιστοι are identical here (Bultmann, 108).

εἰς τὸ μὴ αὐγάσαι, "to stop them from seeing," is a difficult clause, because the verb αὐγάζω, found only here in the NT and rare in the LXX, can have three nuances: "to shine" (so Bachmann, Prümm); "to illuminate"—but this would require a direct personal object, which is lacking in the best textual authorities; and "to see clearly," which is preferred by most commentators (Lietzmann, Windisch, Barrett, Bultmann) as fitting in with the contrast of Satan as blinding human minds. This fits in with the "veiling" of 3:13 (Moses' example), and by contrast 3:18.

The object of the verb is indeed τὸν φωτισμόν, lit., "illumination," which goes with a string of following genitives (τοῦ εὐαγγελίου τῆς δόξης τοῦ Χριστοῦ) and is best treated as adjectival. It describes the δόξα, "glory," as "revealed." Moreover, the chief object is the Gospel, which is the issue under consideration in this paragraph. Paul goes on to describe the content of his kerygma in the following way: its "glory" (a looking back to chap. 3 where Moses' δόξα and the Christian counterpart are set in opposition) is none other than Christ himself, "who is the image of God." The piling up of genitives suggests to Jervell (*Imago Dei*, 214, 215) that this reference to the exalted Christ as εἰκὼν τοῦ θεοῦ is a traditional formulation inserted from a hymnic or confessional source utilized also in Phil 2:6; Col 1:15; 1 Cor 15:45 f., 49. Εἰκών here, in these christological texts, means that Christ is not only the full representation of God, but the coming-to-expression of the nature of God, the making visible (here are links with φανερόω–φανέρωσις, "revelation" words in this context) of who God is in himself: see R. P. Martin, *Carmen Christi: Philippians 2:5–11²*, 110–13, for references to endorse V. Taylor's judgment that "in His face we see the *shekinah* present in visible form" (*The Names of Jesus* [London: Macmillan, 1954] 127).

5. οὐ γὰρ ἑαυτοὺς κηρύσσομεν ἀλλὰ Ἰησοῦν Χριστὸν κύριον, "for it is not ourselves we are proclaiming but Jesus Christ as Lord." For Paul to preach the Gospel was to preach Christ (Gal 1:16; 1 Cor 1:23; Phil 1:15–18, to give only a few representative texts). Here Paul makes two additional points: he proclaims Jesus Christ as Lord (κύριος: a snatch of early Christian catechism, according to Rom 10:9; 1 Cor 12:3; Phil 2:11; Col 2:6, all implying that those who respond to Paul's call in the Gospel attest that they are accountable to the sovereign Christ for the moral direction of their lives: see W. Kramer, *Christ, Lord, Son of God*, tr. B. Hardy [London: SCM Press, 1966] 169–73, sec. 47). The second element is by way of disavowal: "it is not ourselves that we are proclaiming." Once again Paul appears to be reacting to criticism, and facing the allegation that he *was* preaching himself by way of commendation (3:1; 5:12). He categorically denies this by asserting that his role is rather one of δοῦλος, a slave, not its antithesis, a κύριος, "lord, owner" (see 1:24 for the cognate verb κυριεύειν: "we do not rule over your faith"). Paul rejoices in the self-designation "slave of Jesus Christ" (Rom 1:1; Phil 1:1; Gal 1:10), and G. Sass, "Zur Bedeutung von δοῦλος bei Paulus," *ZNW* 40 (1941) 24–32, has built on the foundation of E. Lohmeyer's insight, *Philipper* (MeyerK;

Göttingen: Vandenhoeck & Ruprecht, 1930), *ad* Phil 2:7, to the effect that "to be a servant, in the religious language of Judaism, meant to be one chosen by God." The stress in the title "δοῦλος of Christ" falls, therefore, not on servitude but privilege, just as the *ʿebed Yahweh* of Isaiah's servant poems is a character chosen by God to fulfill a mission and counts it a joyous task, even if such a mission involves suffering. Paul's addition of διὰ Ἰησοῦν, "for Jesus' sake," contributes a note that will be enlarged in a later paragraph (4:10–12, which reiterates the human name of Jesus). The vocation to a suffering apostolate is freely acknowledged, and Paul finds no reason to hide it, even if his detractors scorned his frailty and ragged demeanor (10:10). See on v 7.

6. ὅτι ὁ θεὸς ὁ εἰπών, ἐκ σκότους φῶς λάμψει, κτλ., "for it is the God who said, 'Light shall shine out of darkness.'" The train of thought reverts to the contrast of darkness/light in v 4. Obviously Paul has OT Scripture in mind; but what text specifically is in view when the words ἐκ σκότους φῶς λάμψει, "light shall shine out of darkness," are cited, with the introductory formula ὁ θεὸς ὁ εἰπών: it is "the God who said"? The common view is to quote Gen 1:3, but that reads γενηθήτω φῶς, "let there be light!" Another possibility is to appeal to Isa 9:1, "the people who walk in darkness (ἐν σκότει) . . . on you light will shine (φῶς λάμψει ἐφ᾽ ὑμᾶς)." This prophetic promise does have Paul's verb and is in the same future tense. But it is not a direct oracle of Yahweh who speaks the promise. Perhaps, with Collange, *Enigmes*, 139, we should include the role of the servant in Isa 49:6; cf. 42:6, 16; 60:1–2 who is said to be a "light to the nations," a *testimonium* Paul (and Luke in Acts 13:47; 26:18, 23) saw fulfilled in the apostolic ministry (Rom. 1:5; 15:8–13, 15, 16; so Martini, "Alcuni temi letterari," AnBib 17–18, 1, 461–74). In the latter case, Paul may well have his own conversion-call in mind, with its traditional associations of light, the heavenly voice, and a commission to service (so Kim, *Origin*, 6–8; the aorist of the verb ἔλαμψεν, "has shone," is appealed to as reaching back to the Damascus road Christophany, which made known to Paul the revelation of Christ as "the image of God," idem, 229–32).

The God who brought light to birth in creation and in the new creation has made his light (ἔλαμψεν, "he shone," but in the Hebrew causative sense of "to make to shine") to shine in human hearts. The purpose of such illumination is to impart knowledge (γνῶσις; this term is sometimes taken to suggest an anti-gnostic [Jervell, *Imago Dei*, 218 n. 172] or anti-dualistic counterblast [MacRae, "Anti-Dualist Polemic"]; but this remains unproved). The knowledge of God's glory is what the Pauline Gospel is all about. And for him it is focused "in the face" (ἐν προσώπῳ) or "person" of Christ. The risen Lord is the subject who both illumines his servants and summons them to his service (again, Paul's own experience is in view; cf. Gal 1:15, 16; 1 Cor 9:16; 15:8–10) and the object whom Paul and his associates are charged to make known and so to bring saving truth to light (see Eph 3:7–11 for a meditative reflection on Paul's ministry as bringing light to cosmic and human intelligences).

The reference to "glory . . . in the face of Christ" reverts to the preceding discussion in chap. 3, especially at 3:7 (Moses' face and the fading glory) and 3:18 (the unveiled face of believers who behold the glory of the Lord), as Fitzmyer shows ("Glory," 639–44) and William H. Smith's dissertation has developed. The Qumran parallels (1QH 4.5–6, 27–29; 1QSb 4.24–28; 1QS 2.2–4) are important. All these texts emphasize the shining of God's face on his people. Paul borrows the imagery to enforce his central thrust: in the new age of eschatological fulfillment God's glory is found, not in the Old Testament or the Mosaic covenant, but in Christ who is the εἰκών, "image," of God.

Explanation

"Of the various temptations which beset the Christian minister, one of the chief and deadliest is the temptation to preach himself" (Cranfield, "Minister," 163): "It would be hard to describe the Christian ministry more comprehensively in so few words" as in 4:5 (Barrett, 134). These two quotations aptly and tellingly fix the purpose of the entire pericope.

Admittedly Paul's writing is polemically angled throughout as he continues his running debate with his detractors at Corinth. They charged him with all manner of unworthy motives and the discrediting liabilities of physical weakness and theological perversity. In reply, Paul builds his case on several firm bases: the presence of tradition in the church, as he cites the formulary of the lordship of Christ (4:5); his own conversion-call with its overtone that the one who summoned him revealed himself as "God's presence all-divine" (4:4), the glory of God in human form (4:6); Paul's charge to enlighten the nations as the new "servant of God" (4:5), sent on a mission to all peoples; and his own probity as a person who renounced devious ways and recourse to questionable methods to gain a popular appeal (Gal 1:10; 4:16).

In these ways this short section holds out much encouragement to Christian leaders in every age, and these few verses offer a directory of ministry that can apply to situations in all cultures and circumstances. Other aspects of these vv can only be appreciated after we have seen the details of 4:7–18. See *Explanation* on pp. 93–95.

D. Paul's Ministry: Its Glory and Frailty (4:7–18)

Bibliography

Baumert, N. *Täglich Sterben und Auferstehen.* 72–82, 82–88. **Bishop, E. F. F.** "Pots of Earthenware." *EvQ* 43 (1971) 3–5. **Bultmann, R.** *Der Stil der paulinischen Predigt und die kynisch-stoische Diatribe.* FRLANT 13. Göttingen: Vandenhoeck & Ruprecht, 1910. **Chavasse, C.** "Studies in Texts—2 Cor. 4:7." *Th* 54 (1951) 99–100. **Cobb, W. H.** "Aἰώνιος II. Cor. iv.17 and v. 1." *JBL* 3 (June & December, 1883) 61. **Dahood, M. J.** "Two Pauline Quotations from the Old Testament." *CBQ* 17 (1955) 19–24. **Güttgemanns, E.** *Der leidende Apostel und sein Herr.* FRLANT 90. Göttingen: Vandenhoeck & Ruprecht, 1966. **Harman, A. M.** "Aspects of Paul's Use of the Psalms." *WTJ* 32

(1969) 1–23. **Joüon, P.** "Reconnaissance et action de grâce dans le NT." *RScR* 29 (1939) 112–14. **Kleinknecht, K. T.** *Der leidende Gerechtfertigte.* WUNT 2d.ser.13. Tübingen: Mohr, 1984. **Leivestad, R.** " 'The Meekness and Gentleness of Christ' (II Cor. x.1)." *NTS* 12 (1965/66) 156–64 (162). **Noack, B.** "A Note on II Cor. iv.15." *ST* 17 (1963) 129–32. **Perrin, N.** "The Use of (παρα)διδόναι, in connection with the Passion of Jesus in the New Testament." In *Der Ruf und die Antwort der Gemeinde.* FS J. Jeremias, ed. C. Burchard. Göttingen: Vandenhoeck & Ruprecht, 1970. 204–12. **Popkes, W.** *Christus Traditus.* Eine Untersuchung zum Begriff der Dahingabe. ATANT 49. Zurich: Zwingli Verlag, 1967. 150–51. **Proudfoot, C. M.** "Imitation or Realistic Participation? A Study of Paul's Concept of 'Suffering with Christ.' " *Int* 17 (1963) 140–60. **Rey, B.** "L'homme nouveau d'après St. Paul." *RScPhTh* (1965) 161–95. **Rissi, M.** *Studien zum zweiten Korintherbrief.* 47–53. **Robinson, J. A. T.** *The Body. A Study in Pauline Theology.* SBT 5. London: SCM Press, 1952. 75–78. **Robinson, W. C., Jr.** "Word and Power (1 Corinthians 1:17–25)." In *Soli Deo Gloria,* FS W. C. Robinson, ed. J. M. Richards. Richmond: John Knox, 1968. 68–82. **Schweizer, E.** "Dying and Rising with Christ." *NTS* 14 (1967–68) 1–11. ———. "Die 'Mystik' des Sterbens und Auferstehens mit Christus bei Paulus." *EvT* 26 (1966) 239–57. **Siber, P.** *Mit Christus Leben.* Eine Studie zur paulinischen Auferstehungshoffnung. Zurich: Zwingli Verlag, 1971. 67–76. **Spicq, C.** "L'image sportive de 2 Corinthiens 4, 7–9." *ETL* 14 (1937) 209–29. **Tannehill, R.** *Dying and Rising with Christ. A Study in Pauline Theology.* BZNW 32. Berlin: Töpelmann, 1967. 84–90.

Translation

⁷ *But we have this treasure in clay pots, to show the preeminent power as God's, not our own.* ⁸ *We are hard pressed in every way, but not crushed by it; thrown into perplexity, but not left to despair;* ⁹ *harassed, but not abandoned; knocked down, but not knocked out.* ¹⁰ *We always bear in our bodily existence the dying of Jesus, so that the life too of Jesus may be displayed in our mortal existence.* ¹¹ *For we as living persons are always* ᵃ *being handed over to death for the sake of Jesus, so that the life of Jesus may also be displayed in our mortal nature.* ¹² *Thus death is at work in our case, but it is life for you.*

¹³ *But since we possess the same spirit of faith as that shown by the Scripture writer,* ᵇ *"I believed, and so I spoke," we too believe, and thus we speak* ¹⁴ *in the knowledge that he who raised up Jesus* ᶜ *[from death] will raise up us also with Jesus and lead us with you into his presence.* ¹⁵ *For all this will happen on your account, so that as grace extends to yet more people, it may cause gratitude to abound to God's glory.*

¹⁶ *So we are not discouraged. But even if our outward person is wasting away, our inward person is being renewed day by day.* ¹⁷ *For our affliction, light and momentary, is producing for us out of all proportion an eternal weight of glory* ¹⁸ *as we set our gaze not on what is seen but what is not seen; for what is seen is transient, but what is not seen is eternal.*

Notes

ᵃThe bulk of textual authorities read ἀεί, "always," but P⁴⁶ F G syrᵖ Iren Tert Ambrosiaster have εἰ, "if." If the latter is preferred, the reading will produce the following: "for if we as living persons are being handed over . . . it is that the life of Jesus may be displayed," etc.

ᵇLit., κατὰ τὸ γεγραμμένον runs "according to what has been written." This is an unusual formula of citation to introduce OT Scripture; it is unique in the NT. Bultmann's suggestion (123) is that it is a legal form, referring to A. Deissmann, *Bible Studies,* 250. But there are rabbinic parallels; cf. J. Bonsirven, *Exégèse rabbinique et exégèse paulinienne* (Paris: Beauchesne et ses fils, 1939) 32; G. Schrenk, *TDNT* 1:749.

In translation a certain amount of paraphrase may be permitted here (so rsv; Barrett, "as that referred to in the Scripture passage"; Héring, "which inspired the Scripture passage"; "of which Scripture speaks" is Collange's rendering.)

ᶜThe reading is "he who raised up the Lord Jesus" (τὸν κύριον Ἰησοῦν, by א C D G K L P Ψ TR and the main versions), but the shorter reading, attested by P⁴⁶ B 33 has strong—if Alexandrian—support. Yet Origen and 1739 are witness for Caesarea, while there are Latin supports for the omission of κύριον, and cop and arm agree. The distribution of the data suggests that the original form of the text was τὸν Ἰησοῦν later expanded to include κύριον on grounds of piety and reverence. So Metzger, *Textual Commentary,* ad loc. See W. Kramer, *Christ, Lord, Son of God,* sec. 3h, and n. 738.

Form/Structure/Setting

This section is interesting because it combines several features of Paul's literary style: the use of images (v 7), and the rhetorical device, beloved by hellenistic moralists, of "lists of trials," Gr. περιστάσεις (*Peristasenkataloge,* as Bultmann, *Der Stil,* 19, called this feature), using antithesis and paronomasia in the manner of the Stoic diatribe. See *Der Stil,* 25 ff., 79 ff. with reference to Epictetus, *Diss.* II.19, 24; and Seneca, *Ep.* 41.4.

See further on these "lists" Prümm, *Diakonia,* 232 f.; Georgi, *Die Gegner,* 194 f. But, as Collange, *Enigmes* (149), notes, the OT-Jewish tradition is not to be passed over, e.g., the "afflictions of the righteous" in the Psalms (Pss. 3:2, LXX; 12:5; 22:5; 34:19). See H. Schlier, *TDNT* 3:139–48; and under *Comment* later.

Above all, there is paradox, as in vv 11, 12 where "life" and "death" are combined in an epigrammatic way. And the "seen" and the "unseen" are set in paradoxical juxtaposition (v 18), while the present and the future are held together in uneasy tension by Paul's obvious hyperbolic reference to "light affliction" he now experiences, offset by his future expectation of a "weight of glory" (a Hebraic pun, since כָּבוֹד, *kābôd,* in the OT, usually rendered "glory," has as its basic meaning "heaviness") which is part of the age to come (αἰώνιος, "eternal," v 17).

Then, there is recourse to OT Scripture in order to buttress the Pauline appeal to παρρησία, "confidence" (v 13). This citation is unusual in that it is introduced by the phrase κατὰ τὸ γεγραμμένον, "as that shown by the Scripture writer" (see under *Notes*). Normally Paul prefers the introductory formula καθὼς or καθάπερ γέγραπται, "as it is written," or (once) κατὰ τὰς γραφάς (1 Cor 15:3, 4 where he is borrowing from a *paradosis*). See E. E. Ellis, *Paul's Use of the Old Testament* (Edinburgh: Oliver and Boyd, 1957). Moreover, the substance of the quotation—Ps 115:1 (LXX; the MT 116:10 is slightly different) is without parallel in the use the rabbis make of the OT (Str-B 3:517). Paul ignores the context of Ps 115 (yet Kleinknecht, *Der leidende Gerechtfertigte,* 260 f., sees a point of comparison between Paul and the righteous sufferer, the psalmist), but fastens on the two verbs, "believe," "speak," in order to justify his apostolic ministry as proclamation. There may be a piece of Pauline apologetic here, as he defends his Gospel at Corinth. An even more closely connected way of relating the psalmist and the apostle is suggested by Dahood, "Two Pauline Quotations" (23), but as this proposal involves some textual emendation it is less than convincing. He proposes that the MT *he²ᵉmantî kî ²adabbēr ²anî ᶜanîtî mᵉôd*, "I believe when I speak: I was greatly afflicted," should be revocalized with *²adabbēr* becoming *²adubbar* (puᶜal of *dibbēr*, to drive, pursue, persecute) and *ᶜanîtî* being read as *ᶜunnētî* (cf. Ps 119:71). The reconstructed sentence now runs: "I trusted even though I was persecuted; I have suffered much."

A final literary device—if we may so dub it—is the evident stress placed on the human name of Jesus by itself; it occurs some six times in the space of five vv (10–14), which on any showing is a high ratio of use. Granted that v 14 has a variant reading with the addition of κύριον (Lord) to "Jesus," it is still a remarkable feature that calls out for explanation. Bengel attributes the recurring name to Paul's meditative spirit (*singulariter sensit [Paulus] dulcedinem eius*, "[Paul] seems peculiarly to have felt its sweetness," cited by Güttgemanns, *Der leidende Apostel*, 112, n. 101). Denney quotes P. W. Schmiedel as putting the repetition down to accident and, in part, to the fact that Christ's death is here regarded as a purely human occurrence, not the redemptive deed of the messiah. But this idea is open to objection; there is nothing in the context to warrant such a conclusion. Denney himself wants to see Paul's conscious paralleling of his own missionary career accompanied by its hazards and exposure to death (vv 11, 12) with Jesus' earthly ministry and crucifixion. An alternative proposal is that Paul is appealing to Jesus' "example" (see Proudfoot, "Imitation or Realistic Participation?") as setting a model for Christian living, i.e., for all believers to follow; or more likely as indicating the way the true apostle of Christ will take, namely, the path to suffering and obedience, as Jesus did (so Güttgemanns, *Der leidende Apostel*, 112–19; Collange, 153, 154; cf. E. J. Tinsley, *The Imitation of God in Christ*, London: SCM Press, 1960). For this latter interpretation the strong point of support is that Paul is seen to be continuing his running debate with the Corinthians who, because he was known to be a weak and afflicted person, were casting aspersion on his claim to be a genuine "apostle of Christ." It seems that only on this understanding of the raison d'être of these few vv can we make sense of some further idiosyncratic features of the text: (1) the unusual phrase "the dying of Jesus" (τὴν νέκρωσιν τοῦ Ἰησοῦ, v 10); (2) the rare expression, "in our mortal nature" (ἐν τῇ θνητῇ σαρκὶ ἡμῶν, v 11; σάρξ, "flesh," is not customarily used with this nuance by Paul); (3) the conclusion (v 15), which brings in the Corinthians as the direct beneficiaries of Paul's "conformity" to Jesus (preferring *Nachfolge* to *imitatio*, with many interpreters: see H.-D. Betz, *Nachfolge und Nachahmung Jesu Christi im Neuen Testament* [Tübingen: J. C. B. Mohr, 1967]).

Comment

7. "But" (δέ) sets up a contrast with the foregoing. Paul has extolled the glory of the Gospel, which focuses its beams that shine from God's act to spotlight the supreme revelation in the person/face (πρόσωπον) of [Jesus] Christ (v 6). In him we see the knowledge of God displayed in its glorious form and light. But Paul's thought quickly turns to the realities of the situation

of his missionary labors—there is no nimbus of glory surrounding the messengers of such a glorious Gospel. Rather they are as a "claypot" (ὀστράκινον σκεῦος), a thought of human frailty and bodily weakness (Ps 30:13; Jer 22:28, translating the Hebrew כְּלִי, *keli* in the LXX version as σκεῦος). Several suggestions as to the background of Paul's imagery have been made. We may dismiss summarily the rather fanciful notion of Chavasse, "Studies," that Paul's word is dependent on the narrative in Jud 7:16–20 (Gideon's use of "empty jars," into which torches were fitted as lamps) in spite of some superficial resemblances in the language forms used. The following are to be more seriously entertained as suggestions: (1) Allo remarks on the element of fragility which is true of clay vessels, and he goes on to relate this inherent weakness and frangible character to Paul's human frame (vv 8–10). (2) But Barrett argues that the contrast is more one of the treasure of the contents and the "cheapness" of those who carry it. A good illustration is in *Sifre* Deut 48 (84a on Deut 11:12): as it is not possible for wine to be stored in golden or silver vessels, but only in one which is least among the vessels, an earthenware one, so also the words of Torah can be kept only with one who is humble in his own eyes; cf. *b. Ta'an.* 7a where it is remarked that "glorious wisdom in a repulsive earthen vessel" describes R. Jehoshua ben Hanaiah, whose outward appearance was unattractive (cf. 2 Cor 10:10, and 10:1; 11:6, cited by W. L. Lane, *NIDNTT* 3 [1978] 914). (3) The fact that pottery vessels were used as receptacles for wick lamps has suggested to T. W. Manson, "2 Cor. 2:14–17," *Studia Paulina,* 156, that the contrast is between "the small pottery lamps, cheap and fragile, that could be bought in the shops of Corinth" (see *BAR* 11 [1985] 42–56 for oil lamps in the Herodian period) and Christ's followers who have only "frail mortal bodies" which nevertheless bear about a light derived from the central source of light in the face of Jesus Christ," citing Phil 2:15 as well as 4:6, 10—two contrasting vv. There is much to favor this idea, not least that it capitalizes on the common theme of light that shines in a dark place. But C. Spicq, "L'image sportive," 210, enters an objection that vases in antiquity were not the commonplace, rough-hewn items of domestic furniture of little value but were "decorated with athletic figures" and highly prized. (4) This leads to Collange's view (*Enigmes,* 146) that σκεῦος is a title of honor and dignity (see Acts 9:15, σκεῦος ἐκλογῆς, "a vessel of election," as Paul is called by the risen Lord). It carries this distinction of esteem because it speaks of human beings as instruments in the divine hands (Isa 10:15; 54:16 f.), the master potter (Jer 18:1–11). Paul is, according to this interpretation, celebrating his honored place in the succession of Israel's prophets (especially the ʿebed Yahweh of Isa chapters 40–55) whom God chose to be his servants. Conceivably the title looks back to Paul's conversion and call (Gal 1:15, 16; see S. Kim, *The Origin of Paul's Gospel* [1982] 93–99).

What follows, then, is either a sign that weak and disposable clay vessels demonstrate only too clearly that they have no inherent worth, or a tribute to God's action in human, specifically apostolic, lives where the divine power is displayed, since Paul did not rush to volunteer as a candidate for the apostolic office. Either way, the clause with ἵνα signifies purpose: "to show"—the verb must be added *ad sensum*—"that the preeminence (ὑπερβολή) of power may be God's, and not derived from (ἐξ) us" (Barrett's translation).

8. But the mention of "power" (δύναμις) must be strictly qualified (see

C. H. Powell, *The Biblical Concept of Power* [London: Epworth Press, 1963]; B. Holmberg, *Paul and Power: The Structure of Authority in the Primitive Church as Reflected in the Pauline Epistles* [Philadelphia: Fortress Press, 1978]). Paul is not a source of power in his ministry. On the contrary, he has received whatever authority he is called to exercise (see 10:8; 12:9; 13:10); and to outward appearance (10:7, 10) he is just the opposite of an impressive, commanding, self-sufficient persona. In a telling series of antitheses he offers an insight of his self-evaluation, calling into play the rhetorical figures of speech that enforce his main point, stated clearly in 13:4: ἡμεῖς ἀσθενοῦμεν ἐν αὐτῷ, ἀλλὰ ζήσομεν σὺν αὐτῷ ἐκ δυνάμεως θεοῦ εἰς ὑμᾶς, "we are weak in him, but with him we shall live through the power of God (displayed) toward you."

θλιβόμενοι, "hard-pressed," "afflicted"; the verb recalls the bitter experiences of the Psalmists (3:2, LXX; 12:5; 22:5; 34:19) who endured hardship out of loyalty to Yahweh and his cause. Interestingly, there is a distinct link between θλῖψις ("affliction") and στενοχωρία (lit., "narrow place," so suggesting "difficulty," "hardship," "anguish"; see BGD) in both hellenistic (Epictetus, *Diss.* I. 25, 26) and biblical writers (e.g., Job 18:11; Deut 28:53 ff.; Isa 8:22; 30:6; Esth 1:1g, LXX). This suggests a stereotyped formulation. But Paul's use of this association (also in Rom 2:9; 8:35) needs to be seen in the light of what he will later write in 6:4; 12:10, where there is no such antithesis present. The root θλίβω/θλῖψις also looks back to 1:3–11 and ahead to 7:5 where the "affliction" is clearly precipitated by the crisis at Corinth. The verb στενοχωρέω, "to crush," as in a narrow defile, and so "to be confined" or "hard-pressed" (in the passive voice), recurs in 6:12 also in direct reference to the Corinthian situation. It seems then that Paul's antithesis, while owing some indebtedness to literary convention and conceivably a personal recall of the narrow pass, only sixty feet in places, in the Taurus mountains (the "Cilician Gate," near Tarsus), is also prompted by his recent experiences at Corinth. He was subjected to fierce testing as Christ's apostle as his authority was challenged; yet he now confesses to not being left in a "tight spot" and so "cornered," in the modern idiom. God graciously made a way out for him to take (7:6) and his attitude to the errant church at Corinth that caused him so much grief was not such to "restrict" his affection for them (6:11–13), οὐ στενοχωρεῖσθε ἐν ἡμῖν. The limiting factor was on the Corinthians' side (στενοχωρεῖσθε δὲ ἐν τοῖς σπλάγχνοις ὑμῶν). See later.

"Thrown into perplexity, but not left to despair" hardly does justice to Paul's paronomasia and lyricism: ἀπορούμενοι ἀλλ᾽ οὐκ ἐξαπορούμενοι, the ἐξ is added to supply perfective force (Moulton, *Grammar* 1:237; 2:310; Robertson, *Grammar*, 596). The latter verb is rare, occurring in the Greek Bible only in Ps 87:16 (LXX). But its use at 1:8 fixes its sense here. Paul in his conflict "despaired" that he would escape with his life, so great was the peril he met in Asia. This v qualifies the earlier statement to the extent that Paul did not feel himself abandoned by God even when he faced great perplexity.

Διωκόμενοι, "harassed," is the participle from διώκειν, "to pursue, chase, hunt"—a term used of seeking a quarry. The noun διωγμός, "persecution," is linked with θλῖψις in Mark 4:17; Rom 8:35; 2 Thess 1:4, to describe the ordeal of Christian witness under attack. Paul's autobiography in 12:10 includes this term as well as στενοχωρία (the impasse which creates difficulty). Here again Paul acknowledges the depth of the trial, yet he confesses that God did not abandon him in it (ἐγκαταλείπειν, "to abandon," used of a person's sense of being forsaken by others, 2 Tim 4:10, 16, and by God, Mark 15:34 = Matt 27:46, citing Ps 22:2; cf. Heb 13:5; the latter sense is drawn from LXX as in Gen 28:15; Jos 1:5. Acts 2:27 may be added to complete the NT usage of the word, certifying that God did not desert his servants in the hour of need).

9. καταβαλλόμενοι ἀλλ᾿ οὐκ ἀπολλύμενοι, "knocked down, but not knocked out." This is a colloquial attempt, following J. B. Phillips, to express the most obvious example of paronomasia in Paul's list. The first verb is unique, being found only here in the NT; it carries the idea of being thrown down to the ground. The companion verb ἀπόλλυμι has already been used of those on the road to final perdition (2:15; 4:3), namely, unbelievers as well as the adversaries of the apostle. Paul seems to be claiming here that while his opponents are powerful—they can knock him down—they are not able to subvert his apostleship or destroy his work.

10. The life of the apostle offers a strange paradox, signified by his close union with the suffering Jesus (13:3, 4). His apostolic career "in the body" is the place where the "dying" (νέκρωσις) is seen; Paul's term is rare, found only here and in Rom 4:19. His preferred designation is "death" (θάνατος, 45 times elsewhere) to denote the demise of the earthly Jesus on the cross. Paul's intimate association of his apostleship with Jesus' death is a major theme of his ministerial life, as A. Schlatter (*Paulus, der Bote Jesu* [4] [Stuttgart: Calwer Verlag, 1969] 553) puts it: "As Jesus' herald, he told the story of the passion; he not only told it, but he experienced it too; cf. Phil 3:10." See too R. Tannehill, *Dying and Rising,* especially 84–90; E. Schweizer, "Die 'Mystik' des Sterbens und Auferstehens mit Christus bei Paulus," *EvT* 26 (1966) 239–57, and E. Güttgemanns, *Der leidende Apostel,* 97–119, who questions the propriety of the term "mysticism" in regard to Paul's sufferings. The νέκρωσις strictly refers to a process or a state of dying rather than the act when death supervenes. Windisch, Strachan, Plummer, Bultmann (*TDNT* 4:899) all regard Paul as speaking of the extended process of his life regarded as a continual dying (as in 6:9; 1 Cor 15:31: cf. R. P. Martin, *The Spirit and the Congregation* [Grand Rapids: Wm B. Eerdmans, 1984] 121–23). But Tannehill (*Dying,* 85 ff.) and Güttgemanns (*Der leidende Apostel,* 114–17), from the parallel with Rom 4:19, argue for a rough equivalence of the terms "dying," νέκρωσις, and "death," θάνατος, inasmuch as Paul does not say "the sufferings of death," but talks of his carrying in his mortal existence "an objective event" (Collange), i.e., Jesus' once-for-all death (Rom 6:7–10) as the theme of his mission preaching. The "carrying" motif may go back to v 7, as a "vessel" carries the treasure of the Gospel, committed to the apostles.

Yet death for Jesus was not the end; his (risen) life was taken up after death, and he lives in power (13:4; see Rom 1:3, 4; 4:24 f.). That life is now seen displayed in the "bodies" (rsv, but the Greek is singular, ἐν τῷ σώματι) of his apostles. The "body" (see J. A. T. Robinson, *The Body,* 75–78) is thus both the locus of Paul's commitment to the Gospel of a crucified Jesus (Gal 6:14) and the medium of the display—φανερωθῇ, "may be displayed," is emphatic by its position at the end of the sentence—of divine power. We know that a major debating point at Corinth was precisely the issue: Where is the real φανέρωσις, the true manifestation, of divine strength (see on 4:2; 5:10, 11)? Paul's opponents appealed to their charismatic presence and signs (12:12). Paul himself saw the power of God in his weakness (12:1–10: see W. C. Robinson, "Word and Power") because there he identified with him who was "crucified in weakness" (13:3). And in particular Paul saw his office as "minister of the new covenant" (3:6), which is modeled on the righteous sufferer in Israel, yet christianized by Paul's awareness of living in the new age with its christological center (so Kleinknecht, *Der leidende Gerechtfertigte*, 268–78, esp. 277).

11. The preferred reading ἀεί, "always," refers to Paul's life as a constant struggle: "all our days" (Collange) we as living persons are "being delivered up to death." The technical verb παραδιδόναι, "to hand over"—used regularly of Jesus' destiny as a suffering figure who is fulfilling his life in God's plan as one required (δεῖ) to suffer (see Popkes, *Christus Traditus*, 150, 151, and N. Perrin, "The Use of (παρα) διδόναι") suggests that this is Paul's fate decreed by God. Popkes speaks of Paul's destiny to suffer as a "core" element in his thought. He did not choose to live a risky life, as if he were a foolhardy person (an innuendo possibly to be seen in the background of 12:1–10 and in Phil 1:26–30: R. P. Martin, *Philippians* [NCB 1976 = 1980] ad loc.), or one who emulated the stoic ideal of a person challenged to bravery by life's vicissitudes (see H. Braun, "Das 'stirb und werde' in der Antike und im NT," *Gesammelte Studien zum Neuen Testament* [Tübingen, J. C. B. Mohr, 1962] 136–58, and esp. 186–91). Rather, he suffered in line with his apostolic vocation, and that is the proof that such a calling is God's purpose for his life and that he is a "true" apostle (12:12, RSV). "For Jesus' sake," lit., "because of Jesus" (διὰ ['Ιησοῦν] = *propter*, Plummer, 131; Popkes, 150), i.e., on account of loyalty to the Gospel of his death and resurrection, gives the rationale for Paul's sufferings and exposure to death. See A. Schweitzer, *Mysticism*, 125–27, who insists on seeing the language as meaning "a physical union between Christ and the Elect" (people)—a most improbable idea (for a critique see A. C. Thiselton, "Schweitzer's Interpretation of Paul," *ExpTim* 90 [1978–79] 20–25 and D. M. Stanley, "The Theme of the Servant of Yahweh," *CBQ* 16 [1954] 385–425, especially 412 ff., who argues for a background in the "servant" role [Isa 40–55]).

The outcome (or purpose, so taking ἵνα with J. D. G. Dunn, *Jesus and the Spirit*, 327, 328) is that "the (risen) life of Jesus may be displayed." Again, observe the key word φανερωθῇ ("displayed"), indicating the locus of Paul's authority, not in ecstatic signs or external credentials but in "our mortal existence" (ἐν τῇ θνητῇ σαρκὶ ἡμῶν). There is hardly a distinction to be drawn between σάρξ, "flesh," here and σῶμα, "body," in the previous v (so in 7:5 and 2:13 where σάρξ and πνεῦμα, "spirit," are virtual synonyms). The "flesh" is weak for several reasons: it is attacked by sin (Rom 6:12) and it is liable to corruption (1 Cor 15:53, 54; Martin, *The Spirit and the Congregation*, 134, 135).

12. ὥστε ὁ θάνατος ἐν ἡμῖν ἐνεργεῖται, ἡ δὲ ζωὴ ἐν ὑμῖν, "thus death is at work in our case, but it is life for you." A surprising conclusion, says Collange, *Enigmes*, 159, since we are not prepared for it. And Calvin and Godet dismiss

it cavalierly as ironical, while Plummer thinks it was added on prudential grounds, as a tactful aside. Güttgemanns (*Der leidende Apostel,* 99) remarks that it is polemically slanted against Paul's adversaries. But this cannot be, since ἐν ὑμῖν, "for you," a clear dative of advantage, does not have them in view. It is the Corinthians who are the beneficiaries: "life is *for you."* Proudfoot, "Imitation," especially 155, finds a reason in the mystical life that was mediated as though sacramentally through the church as the body of Christ. Collange (following Bachmann, Lietzmann, Barrett, Thrall) argues that the contrast death/life follows the pattern of the preceding vv and refers to Paul's apostolic labor. Outwardly, Paul's missionary service seems a failing enterprise: death is relentlessly active in his person, robbing him of his power; but Paul counts this disability worth it since his converts at Corinth are receiving the message of "life that leads to life" (2:16). Maybe there is a side-glance at the blessings of the new covenant (3:6) in contradistinction to the old order that spells death (3:6–11).

13, 14. ἔχοντες δὲ τὸ αὐτὸ πνεῦμα τῆς πίστεως κατὰ τὸ γεγραμμένον . . . εἰδότες ὅτι ὁ ἐγείρας τὸν κύριον Ἰησοῦν καὶ ἡμᾶς σὺν Ἰησοῦ ἐγερεῖ καὶ παραστήσει σὺν ὑμῖν, "But since we possess the same spirit of faith as that shown by the Scripture writer . . . in the knowledge that he who raised up Jesus [from death] will raise up us also with Jesus and lead us with you into his presence." Here is the opening of a new section, discussing the apostolic service and Paul's faith. The centerpiece is the assertion, πιστεύομεν, "we believe" (v 13). Paul's confidence is traced back to a like assurance he found in the psalmist whose words are given verbatim: ἐπίστευσα, διὸ ἐλάλησα, "I believed, and so I spoke." What has led Paul to join his witness to that of the psalmist? If his somber verdict in v 12 is taken at face value, would it not counsel his silence? (Plummer). Is he returning to share with his readers, who have been distanced from him, as the community is different from the apostle (v 12), what they now have in common? (Strachan, 96, who with Schlatter thinks that "the *same* spirit of faith" unites Paul and the Corinthians). We should rather start from Paul's conscious desire to identify with the psalmist (Ps 116) for whom the issue was one of life and death. So he regards his spoken ministry as a testimony to his faith—and the psalmist's—in the triumph of life over death. As a Christian, moreover, he grounds his faith in the God "who raised Jesus" from death to new life, drawing on a confessional dictum (so W. Kramer, *Christ, Lord, Son of God,* sec. 3a-i, 20–26) and enlarging it to include God's care for his people and servants as well as his Son Jesus, whose presence beyond death is a sure article of Paul's faith (Phil 1:20–23; 1 Thess 4:16–18; 5:10). Notice the frequent mention of the human name Jesus (six times in vv 10–14), as though to emphasize the commonality of trust shared by the earthly Lord and his people who not only live "in Christ" but share a life with him (M. Bouttier, *En Christ,* 53), both now and at the Parousia which A. Deissmann takes to be the point of σύν, "with," with Ἰησοῦ (*Light from the Ancient East* [London: Hodder & Stoughton, ET 1927] 303, n. 1; similarly Kümmel). But it is more likely to have a broader reference to "personal fellowship between Christ and the apostle" (W. Grundmann, *TDNT* 7:784), whether in life or beyond death. See the references to recent discussion on σὺν Χριστῷ, "with Christ," in R. P. Martin, *Philippians* (NCB, 1976 = 1980, 78, 79), and for the broader implications of this appeal to the human Jesus seen in the frequent mention of his earthly name, see the *Introduction*, pp. lx, lxi.

The closing part of the sentence, which is heavy with stereotyped phrases betraying the presence of traditional material, is typically in the Pauline manner. He will elsewhere employ paraenetic matter from tradition and then add a comment to apply it to his readers' situation. So he writes: "and lead us with you (σὺν ὑμῖν) into his presence." This is an elliptical remark, lacking a complement to the verb παραστήσει—it would be ἑαυτῷ, "to himself"— (Reicke-Bertram, *TDNT* 5:835–40) which is associated with the Parousia of Christ (Rom 14:10) or the final day of God's purposes (Eph 5:27). But it can be a more immediate reference to entry into the Lord's presence here and now (1 Cor 8:8; Col 1:22, 28). The future tense, however, points to a final consummation with the note of judgment struck, a thought Paul will return to in 5:10.

15. τὰ γὰρ πάντα δι᾽ ὑμᾶς, "For all this will happen (supplying a verb in the future tense) on your account." Paul's pastoral regard shines out in this cryptic, verbless remark, as he is reminded that his sufferings and their vindication at the future resurrection find their raison d'être in the benefit that accrues to his Corinthian friends, both in life and death (so 7:3: see G. Stählin, " 'Um mitzusterben und mitzuleben.' Bemerkungen zu 2 Kor 7, 3," in *Neues Testament und christliche Existenz*. FS Herbert Braun, ed. H.-D. Betz and L. Schottroff [Tübingen: J. C. B. Mohr, 1973] 503–21). So much is clear from the general drift of v 15, which may be read as Paul's tribute of praise to God as his people rejoice in his grace and turn their joy into thanksgiving. But the sentence is loaded with exegetical difficulties. These center on one main issue: is the verb περισσεύσῃ, "overflow," "abound," transitive, requiring an object, or intransitive with no object? In the latter case, it may have a causative sense, as in Barrett's rendering, "the grace . . . may cause gratitude to abound to the glory of God," which we have followed. This is preferable to seeing περισσεύειν as finding its direct object in εὐχαριστίαν, so RSV, "it may increase thanksgiving," since as B. Noack, "A Note on II Cor iv. 15," says, for Paul grace abounds through God's will, not through human action. His solution, however, is to emend χάρις, "grace," as the subject to εὐχαριστία, "thanks," and so render "that the abounding grace might be to the greater glory of God because there are more Christians to thank Him for His grace." But to duplicate εὐχαριστία seems harsh and tautologous.

Noack and Moule (*Idiom Book*, 108) take the phrase διὰ τῶν πλειόνων as "through your increasing number" (so Bratcher, *Translator's Guide*, 47, 48), and this implies, from Paul's standpoint, an evangelistic desire to see the good news of God's grace reaching ever-increasing circles of men and women in his world. This may well be a Pauline sentiment (cf. 1 Cor 9:19–23; Rom 15:14–29), but has been questioned as to whether it is relevant in this context. If the v is not a tangential observation but is closely related to the Corinthian scene, we may propose that οἱ πλείονες, "the many," refers to the main body of the church or the majority, of whom he has already written (2:6, in reference to the entire congregation exercising public discipline, or at least the considerable number who were on Paul's side). It is possible, then, that Paul has this section of the Corinthian church in his sights, and is expressing thankfulness that "a majority of the church at Corinth had grasped their dependence on the grace of God" (Barrett). The upshot is that they, since they are thought of as having come over to Paul's position regarding the recent disaffection, would have a more sober opinion of themselves as they reflect on the way these restored relations are due to divine grace, and should express their thankful hearts of praise to God. This line of interpretation is eminently reasonable. But we have opted for the former view—that Paul is calling the readers to celebrate the grace that extends to more and more unbelieving persons—on the ground that he is still in a combative mood. He is disavowing an interest in increasing his own apostolic stature by seeing more people becoming believers; this is a counterblast to his opponents who made such a claim. He is anxious to see the grace of God in wider display—but only so that gratitude may *abound to God's glory*, not his own. Our view of περισσεύειν as a Corinthian watchword supports this interpretation (see Martin, *The Spirit and the Congregation*, 154, n. 13).

16. "So (διὸ) we are not discouraged." The verb οὐκ ἐγκακοῦμεν picks up the earlier reference in v 1. The connecting διὸ gives the reason for Paul's indomitable spirit. Earlier he reflected on God's mercy shown to him; here it is the recall of God's power in raising Jesus from the dead. These articles of faith bolster him in a testing time. Yet he cannot deny the obvious facts of his mortal existence. ἀλλ᾽ εἰ καὶ, "but even if" (see M. Thrall, *Greek Particles*, 36–39, on ἀλλά followed by γέ) is a disclaimer, granting the realities of the situation. Paul now faces the inevitable result of wear and tear on his human frame. ὁ ἔξω ἡμῶν ἄνθρωπος, "our outward person," relates to his life as a mere man, "subject to a thousand troubles and under sentence of death" (Barrett) because of his mortality (1 Cor 15:42–50, 53). The contrast is then drawn with ὁ ἔσω [ἄνθρωπος] ἡμῶν, "our inward [man]" which is being renewed (ἀνακαινοῦται) "day by day." The last-named adverbial phrase ἡμέρᾳ καὶ ἡμέρᾳ, an obvious Hebraism (Esth 3:4; Ps 68:20; BDF § 200; but see Barrett who doubts the OT setting of the precise phrase), gives us a clue when we read it in the light of 1 Cor 15:31: "I die every day" (καθ᾽ ἡμέραν ἀποθνῄσκω). Paul's physical existence was wasting away and the death sentence was already in process. Yet his "inmost self" (Rom 7:22, RSV) is undergoing renewal—not by absorption, as in hellenistic and gnostic thought, but by the hope of resurrection which entails a future for the outward person in his bodily existence (σῶμα). So B. Rey, "L'homme nouveau," as cited by Collange. This is an important observation, marking off Pauline anthropology from Plato, *Rep.* IX 589A, Epictetus, *Diss.* II 7.3, 8.14, and even Philo, *Quod Det. Pot.* 22 f., all of whom make the human person a composite of a material shell and a precious kernel, the soul, which aspires to be immortal. No such dichotomy is really to be found in Paul who, in this passage, comes closest to making the human being a hybrid of body and soul (see later our comment on 5:7). But it is more likely that Paul's idiom is shaped by the exigencies of his polemic, since in other places he draws no such radical distinction between body and soul, as though the outer frame were like an envelope or container to house the immaterial, immortal soul. "For him the person is one, indivisible whole" (Fallon, 47), and in using the language of his opponents he seems to be taking over their dualism. They made much of the "inner person"

(the soul), regarding it as detachable from bodily existence (Güttgemanns, *Der leidende Apostel*, 115). But 5:7 and 12:2, 3 speak differently, and all that Paul is attempting is to set side by side the totality of the human person seen from opposing angles in order to draw the conclusion that this life is running down, and the eternal destiny set for the person is already in the making. That hope is not a shedding of the existing "body," but its being taken up into God's purpose in the eschatological body that awaits the resurrection. Of this hope we already have a foretaste in the "new person" given at baptism (Col 3:10: the new Adam) and indwelt by Christ (Eph 3:16; 4:22, 24) through the Spirit (1:22; 5:5). It is what Paul calls in his own idiom "the heart" (καρδία: 2 Cor 5:12; Rom 2:29; 10:9, 10, etc.); and 1 Peter 3:4, "the hidden person of the heart" (ὁ κρυπτὸς τῆς καρδίας ἄνθρωπος) epitomizes Pauline thought. If this is so, we have a valuable key to unlock the mystery of the text of 4:17–5:10.

17. Paul's apostolic "affliction" (θλῖψις; cf. 1:8) refers to his trial as that which life demands of him as suffering apostle. Euphemistically it is dubbed "light" (ἐλαφρόν, a neuter adjective standing for an abstract noun) and "momentary" (παραυτίκα, a NT *hapax:* see Bachmann for illustrations of the contrast "momentary" versus "lasting" [τὸ μέλλον or τὸ ἔπειτα]). Here the contrast is made with the twin notions of light versus heavy. The "eternal weight of glory" (αἰώνιον βάρος δόξης) is a phrase with a built-in paronomasia since δόξα, on its semitic groundplan (כָּבוֹד, *kābôd*), speaks of "heaviness," "weight." Similarly, the "transitory" θλῖψις is matched by an "eternal" vindication by God. Paul enforces the point with his adverbial expression καθ᾽ ὑπερβολὴν εἰς ὑπερβολήν, lit., "far beyond all measure," to register the fact that his present suffering will reap a reward from God far out of proportion to its bitter experience. Cf. Wis. Sol. 3:5: "having been disciplined a little, they (the righteous) receive a great good," cf. Rom 8:18.

18. μὴ σκοπούντων ἡμῶν τὰ βλεπόμενα ἀλλὰ τὰ μὴ βλεπόμενα, "as we set our gaze not on what is seen but what is not seen." The use of μὴ (and not οὐ) with σκοπούντων ἡμῶν is a salutary reminder that the verb carries a conditional force (Héring, against Denney): "*provided* we do not fix our attention on what is visible," for then we should most certainly have cause to be discouraged and feel depressed by life's conditions and trials. Per contra, as Paul deliberately averts his gaze from what is to be seen by eyesight (τὰ βλεπόμενα) to the invisible world of God's providence and rule, so he is not disheartened in his service to the point of neglecting his ministerial office (Barrett). The verb is σκοπέω, to "set one's sight" (see E. Fuchs, *TDNT* 7:415–19), usually in the sense of "regard as your aim" (so J. B. Lightfoot *ad* Phil 2:4) in distinction from the colorless βλέπω, which means simply "to look," "to regard." Σκοπέω, found only (in NT) in the writings of Paul (with the sole exception of Luke 11:35), carries with it the nuance of estimating the worth of an object, a gaze which is more like acuity than merely "seeing" something, and a realization of the purpose of what we see. The paradox will be evident in the juxtaposing of σκοπεῖν and βλέπειν in this verse, μὴ σκοπούντων . . . τὰ βλεπόμενα, i.e., not allowing our aim in life to be determined by what passes before our vision, for such "phenomena" are only surface impressions of reality, which is open only to the eye of faith (as in Heb 11). This recall

lifts the level of the future prospect of v 17 and makes it relevant for the present, not only in regard to Paul's service but also his assurance of God's reward. For the present his eyes are trained "on the mark"; it is the goal of the glory of Christ (Denney), or at least the glorious world where Christ reigns in splendor (4:4–6), and where his service exerts its renewing power in human lives.

The reason is now supplied. The visible reality is πρόσκαιρα, "transient," whereas for Paul those aspects of reality which are hidden from the naked eye share the life of God; they are αἰώνια, "eternal," as God is eternal. The former are destined to pass away as Paul's mortal life is "being wasted away" (διαφθείρεται, in v 16). The invisible realities on which Paul encourages his readers to set their gaze are part of the new world where fellowship with God is the most real of all life's experiences (Collange, *Enigmes*, 179). Again, a polemical note underlies this seemingly Platonic dictum: what Paul is concerned to assert is that eternal reality lies in the world of nonsensory perception. His opponents were fond of claiming exactly the opposite on the basis of their adherence to the outer "form" (εἶδος, 5:7) of life. Paul's orientation to life is grounded on "faith" (again 5:7; περιπατοῦμεν . . . διὰ πίστεως), which in turn is directed to the unseen world of God and has its hope cast in the future. To the continued debate on the locus of reality—whether it is present or future, and whether it is gained by a rapture as the bodily existence is transcended or is bound inextricably to a "new creation" (see 5:17) of bodily dimension as a gift of God—he will turn in the argument of 5:1–10.

Explanation

"This ministry" looks back to the contrast with the Mosaic order which, Paul declares, is superseded in Christ. But equally the phrase looks around at the Corinthian scene where Paul's apostolic mission is under fire. So he must be defensive and explain how it is that such ministry can be justified.

Obviously Paul faced, at this period in his career, the temptation of "losing heart" (twice repeated in 4:1, 16). We might press Paul for a reason for this denial: "we do not yield to discouragement." If he relied solely on human resources or was foolhardy enough to practice "disgraceful, underhand ways" in order to gain some cheap victories (v 2), then he might well concede a mood of despair. For the human heart remains hard and obdurate, strangely resistant to love's appeal. Possibly we should hear in these verses the innuendo that Paul's ministry was ineffectual and weak; it produced no great response in terms of "results." So he must account for this lack of "success," as his opponents evaluated his absence of credentials. Yet he *is* confident, with a persuasion that rests on several grounds: (1) His own sincerity, he claims, is self-evident (v 2). (2) The Gospel he brought to Corinth is thereby reinforced by the character of its messengers who convey it (v 2*b*), and it needs no external corroboration, for it shines by its own light. (3) The failure of many to respond is not due to any lack of adequacy or relevance of the message. Rather, the reason lies in the satanic grip on the human heart and mind (v 4). (4) Yet Paul is glad to report *some* visible proof of his work in the lives of the Corinthians whose increasing number are a tribute of praise to God.

They do not serve to build up his own ego or promote his personal interests (v 15). He does not proclaim himself (v 5). He preaches "Jesus Christ as Lord," whose authority he seeks to bring to bear on the situation at Corinth. And God's radiance in Jesus' person is one compelling sign of the finality of the new order that has taken over from the Judaic dispensation (3:7–18), as Paul himself had known that glory in his conversion-commission encounter which may be in the background of his writing here (vv 4–6).

Such a message as vv 5, 6 describe may well, without exaggeration, be called a "treasure" whose value is in no way diminished by the cheap and disposable pots that carry it. This is how Paul saw himself—having no inherent worth save as a messenger and transmitter; or to use his metaphor, as an earthenware jar in which some commodity was carried. His favorite self-designation is "servant" (v 5) or "honored vessel," useful for allowing the Lord of glory to shine forth through his feeble and often threatened life (v 7).

The purpose of the arrangement by which the truth of God is deposited in frail vessels is then made plain (v 7b). So far from being protected and preserved unharmed from "the slings and arrows of outrageous fortune"— as possibly Paul's opponents like the "super-apostles" and their emissaries of 11:5, 13–15 believed themselves to be specially favored—Christ's messengers are consigned to a life of humiliation and risk. And this is in order to leave the unmistakable impression that the power of the message does not derive from the ingenuity and skill of the pleaders but comes solely from the inherent truth of the message as God's word (a looking back to 2:17). So Paul's assertion (v 7) is one of his most revealing summaries of the nature of the debate at Corinth, with ramifications that touch the meaning of Christian service in every age.

> Man's wisdom is to seek his strength in God alone;
> And even an angel would be weak who trusted in his own.
> *William Cowper*

"Dying, and look, we are alive" (6:9); "I die every day" (1 Cor 15:31) may be dismissed, at first glance, as a piece of Pauline rhetoric. But the passage that follows (vv 8–10), in a series of eloquent contrasts and memorable phrases, leads to this conclusion (vv 11, 12). Put in simple language, his apostolic work required that he should share in his Lord's humiliation in the confidence that he will also share in his triumphant life (v 14). And the poignancy of this remark is not lost if we are near the truth in our reconstruction of the setting of the entire letter of 2 Corinthians 1–9, with chaps. 10–13 following in succession. In regard to this letter we suggest that it came out of a distressful period in the writer's life when he knew himself to be bereft of human support and saw the prospect of his life's mission evaporating before his eyes as his congregations at Ephesus and Corinth were in danger of sliding away from him as their apostolic "father in God." See *Introduction*, pp. lviii–lxi.

But the hope of final vindication, when death will lead through resurrection to the last home-gathering of the church, is not the apostle's exclusively. When Paul is introduced to his Lord's presence (v 14), those who are with him in Christ will share the victory too. That was his eager longing (Phil 1:21–23; 3:10, 11), although it was no escapist death wish which had taken possession of his outlook (conceivably the Philippian letter came out of the same period of his life, written while he was a *détenu* at Ephesus and reflecting his present circumstance and its aftermath). If God willed the continuance of his apostolic trials and labors, as he tells the Philippians (Phil 1:24), his congregations will benefit, and the result must be that "as the abounding grace of God is shared by more and more, the greater may be the chorus of thanksgiving that ascends to the glory of God" (v 15, NEB).

Meanwhile, no other proof of the finitude and frailty of the apostle's physical frame is needed than the reminder in v 16. His body, in its weakness and exposure to hazard, is constantly in the process of decay both in the normal course of "growing old" and—more so—in pursuit of his apostolic mission. "This slight momentary affliction" (v 17) must be one of his greatest understatements! But it serves to highlight where his hope is set: the real life of the spirit is being renewed and revitalized by the power of God (v 16).

And the outcome for him is not in doubt. His horizon is bounded by an eternal prospect (v 18), as with the eyes of faith he is enabled to see beyond the visible and tangible—the external credentials and demonstrable signs by which his adversaries at Corinth set so much store—to the eternal realities of that world where God's glory shines in the person of Christ (4:6). Moving to the fulfillment of that hope will entail both death and Parousia. So to that theme he moves on in chap. 5.

E. The Heavenly Dwelling (5:1–10)

Bibliography

Baumert, N. *Täglich Sterben und Auferstehen: Der Literalsinn von 2 Kor 4, 12–5, 10.* SANT 34. Munich: Kosel-Verlag, 1973. **Berry, R.** "Death and Life in Christ." *SJT* 14 (1961) 60–76. **Bornkamm, G.** "Der Lohngedanke im Neuen Testament." In *Studien zu Antike und Urchristentum.* BzET 28. Munich: Kaiser Verlag, 1959. **Bruce, F. F.** "Paul on Immortality." *SJT* 24 (1971) 457–74. **Cassidy, R.** "Paul's Attitude to Death in II Corinthians 5:1–10." *EvQ* 43 (1971) 210–17. **Collange, J.-F.** *Enigmes de la deuxième épître de Paul aux Corinthiens.* Cambridge, 1972. **Conzelmann, H.** *An Outline of the Theology of the New Testament.* Tr. J. Bowden. London: SCM Press, 1969. **Cox, S.** "The Earnest of the Spirit." *Exp* 2d ser. 7 (1884) 416–26. **Danker, F. W.** "Consolation in 2 Corinthians 5:1–10." *CTM* 39 (1968) 552–56. **Davies, W. D.** *Paul and Rabbinic Judaism* [2]. London: SPCK, 1955. **Dodd, C. H.** "The Mind of Paul: Change and Development." In *New Testament Studies.* Manchester: University Press, 1953. **Ellis, E. E.** "II Corinthians v. 1–10 in Pauline Eschatology." *NTS* 6 (1959–60) 211–24. **Feuillet, A.** "La demeure céleste et la destinée des chrétiens: Exégèse de II Cor 5:1–10 et contribution à l'étude des fondements de l'eschatologie paulinienne." *RScR* 44 (1956) 161–92, 360–402. **Hanhart, K.** "Paul's Hope in the Face of Death." *JBL* 88 (1969) 445–57. **Harris, M. J.** "2 Cor 5:1–10: A Watershed in Paul's Eschatology?" *TynB* 22 (1971) 32–57. ———. "Paul's View of Death in 2 Corinthians 5:1–10." In *New Dimensions in New Testament Study,* ed. R. N. Longenecker and M. C. Tenney. Grand Rapids: Eerdmans,

1974. 317–28. ———. *Raised Immortal: Resurrection and Immortality in the NT.* London: Marshall, Morgan & Scott, 1983. **Hettlinger, R. F.** "2 Corinthians 5:1–10." *SJT* 10 (1957) 174–94. **Hodge, C.** *An Exposition of the Second Epistle to the Corinthians.* Reprint. Grand Rapids: Eerdmans, 1959. **Jeremias, J.** "Flesh and Blood Cannot Inherit the Kingdom of God." *NTS* 2 (1956) 151–59. **Jewett, R.** *Paul's Anthropological Terms: A Study of Their Use in Conflict Settings.* AGJV 10. Leiden: Brill, 1971. **Kennedy, H. A. A.** *St. Paul's Conception of the Last Things.* London: Hodder and Stoughton, 1904. **Knox, W. L.** *St. Paul and the Church of the Gentiles.* Cambridge: University Press, 1939. **Lang, F. G.** *2 Korinther 5, 1–10 in der neueren Forschung.* BGBE 16. Tübingen: Mohr, 1973. **Lincoln, A. T.** *Paradise Now and Not Yet: Studies in the Role of the Heavenly Dimension in Paul's Thought with Special Reference to his Eschatology.* SNTMS 43. Cambridge: University Press, 1981. **Manson, T. W.** "ΙΛΑΣΤΗΡΙΟΝ." *JTS* old ser. 46 (1945) 1–10. **Mattern, L.** *Das Verständnis des Gerichtes bei Paulus.* ATANT 47. Zurich: Zwingli Verlag, 1966. **Mitton, C. L.** "Paul's Certainties. The Gift of the Spirit and Life beyond Death: 2 Corinthians 5:1–5." *ExpT* 69 (1958) 260–63. **Moule, C. F. D.** "St Paul and Dualism: the Pauline Conception of Resurrection." *NTS* 12 (1965–66) 106–23. Reprinted in *Essays in New Testament Interpretation,* chap. 14. Cambridge: University Press, 1982. **Robinson, J. A. T.** *The Body.* SBT 5. London: SCM Press, 1952. **Roetzel, C. J.** *Judgement in the Community: A Study of the Relationship between Eschatology and Ecclesiology in Paul.* NovTSup. Leiden: Brill, 1972. **Schlatter, A.** *Paulus, der Bote Jesu.* **Schmithals, W.** *Gnosticism in Corinth.* Tr. J. E. Steely. Nashville: Abingdon, 1971. **Schweitzer, A.** *The Mysticism of Paul the Apostle.* Tr. W. Montgomery. New York: H. Holt and Co./London: A & C Black, 1931. **Sevenster, J. N.** "Einige Bemerkungen über den 'Zwischenzustand' bei Paulus." *NTS* 1 (1954–55) 291–96. ———. "Some Remarks on the ΓΥΜΝΟΣ in II Cor. v. 3." In *Studia Paulina,* FS. de Zwaan. Haarlem: Bohn, 1953. **Stevens, G. B.** *The Pauline Theology.* New York: Scribner's, 1892. **Thrall, M. E.** *Greek Particles in the New Testament.* Grand Rapids: Eerdmans, 1962. **Thornton, L. S.** *The Common Life in the Body of Christ.* London: Dacre Press, 1942. **Vos, G.** *The Pauline Eschatology.* 1930 ed. Reprint. Grand Rapids: Baker, 1979. **Wagner, G.** "Le tabernacle et la vie 'en Christ.' Exégèse de 2 Cor. 5:1–10." *RHPR* 41 (1961) 379–93. **Watson, N. M.** "2 Cor. 5:1–10 in Recent Research." *ABR* 23 (1975) 33–6. **Whiteley, D. E. H.** *The Theology of St. Paul.* Philadelphia: Fortress, 1966.

Translation

[1] *For we know that if the earthly tent we live in is dismantled, we have a house from God, one not built by human hands, eternal, in the heavens.* [2] *And indeed in this [tent] we groan, longing to put on our heavenly house,* [3] *since indeed [a] we shall put it on, [b] and we shall not be found naked.* [4] *For while we remain in this tent, we groan and are burdened, because we do not desire to be unclothed, but clothed, in order that what is mortal may be swallowed up by life.* [5] *The one who prepared [c] us for this very purpose [is] God, who also gave us the Spirit as a pledge.* [6] *Accordingly, we are always confident and know that while we are at home in the body, we are away from the Lord,* [7] *for we live by faith, not by sight.* [8] *We are confident [I repeat] and would rather be away from the body and be at home with the Lord.* [9] *And so our ambition, whether we are at home or away, is to please him.* [10] *For we must all appear before the judgment seat of Christ, in order that each one may receive recompense for what he has done in the body, [d] whether good or bad.*

Notes

[a] εἴπερ, found in P[46] B D G, suggests more strongly that the "supposition agrees with the fact" (Liddell and Scott, 1:489). The text (εἰ γε) is supported by C and most of the MSS. But

see M. J. Harris's remark cited by Lincoln, *Paradise*, 212, n. 50. The context alone, however, can decide, as Thrall, *Greek Particles*, 86–91, allows.

ᵇ *ἐνδυσάμενοι* is found in P⁴⁶ ℵ B D² (cf. RSV) and appears to be an older reading. *ἐκδυσάμενοι* is contained in a later MS such as D*. Plummer, 148, views the latter reading as an "early alteration to avoid apparent tautology." On the basis of external evidence, he probably is correct (Barrett, 149, n. 2; Schmithals, *Gnosticism*, 263 f.). But to include the former one makes the apostle's statement appear trite (Metzger, *A Textual Commentary on the Greek New Testament* [New York: United Bible Societies, 1975] 579, 580—though Metzger himself disagrees with the decision of the committee); thus Bultmann (137, 138) argues that only the second reading is really clear. At this point, however, we opt for the first reading and depart from Aland's 26th edition.

ᶜ The Western text (D F G lat) supports *κατεργαζόμενος*.

ᵈ P⁴⁶ lat have *τὰ ἴδια τοῦ σώματος*.

Form/Structure/Setting

In the first section (5:1–5) Paul continues (*γάρ*, "for") the exposition begun in 4:7. He extends his argument concerning the contrast between the temporary and the permanent, the seen and unseen (4:18; cf. 1 Cor 15:51–58). To keep the contrast before his readers, Paul describes in 5:1 the antithesis of the Christian's present body, namely, the future "spiritual" body.

Present	*Spiritual*
τοῦ σκήνους	οἰκοδομὴν (cf. Heb 11:9,10)
ἐπίγειος	οἰκίαν ἀχειροποίητον
καταλυθῇ	αἰώνιον ἐν τοῖς οὐρανοῖς

These opposites reflect Paul's earlier teaching to the Corinthians concerning the same idea.

σῶμα ψυχικόν (1 Cor 15:44)	σῶμα πνευματικόν
σώματα ἐπίγεια (1 Cor 15:40)	σώματα ἐπουράνια
σπείρεται ἐν φθορᾷ (1 Cor 15:42)	ἐγείρεται ἐν ἀφθαρσίᾳ

Paul sees this earthly body as subject to wear and tear. Yet, there is something that will replace it, namely, a body that is free from the frailties that hinder the earthly vessel.

In 5:2–4 Paul continues his discussion of the spiritual body, but why he does so is unclear. He speaks of putting on (*ἐπενδύσασθαι*) the heavenly body over the earthly tent (5:2). But into this discussion Paul brings the idea of being unclothed, naked (*γυμνός*, 5:3). We do not know for sure what was Paul's reason for including 5:2–4 in the epistle. Is Paul speaking of the Christian taking on the spiritual body at death or at the Parousia? Or does the Christian "already" have this body? Furthermore, does the idea behind "being naked" suggest an intermediate state (the period between the death of a Christian and the putting on of the spiritual body at Parousia) or does this suggest the concept of judgment as depicted in the Old Testament? There is no consensus as to the purpose for Paul's writing of 5:2–4, though, at least, we can highlight three suggested reasons.

(1) One possible reason is that Paul has shifted his eschatology, for if Paul in 2 Corinthians sees the Christian receiving a spiritual body at death,

then this marks a change from his position in 1 Corinthians which viewed the resurrection body as available to the Christian only at the Parousia (1 Cor 15:51–58; cf. 1 Thess 4:13–18; Phil 3:20, 21). One who sees such a shift is Knox, *St. Paul*, 121–45, who argues that Paul did indeed change his view of the time at which the Christian receives a spiritual body. (There is also debate on whether or not Paul is consciously counteracting gnostic ideas [see Baur, Windisch, Käsemann, Kümmel, Friedrich, Bornkamm, Rissi, Schmithals; cf. Barrett 28–30]. What can safely be said is that regardless of the identity of Paul's opponents there is some gnostic element in the background of his thinking.) Since Paul's Jewish eschatology was probably not satisfactory for Greek minds (Knox, *St. Paul*, 26, 69–71; cf. 136 n. 8, where Knox cites hellenistic literature as a means of supporting his point [cf. σκῆνος in Wisd. Sol. 9:15]; for the opposite view see Manson "ΙΛΑCΤΗΡΙΟΝ," 1–10), Knox (128) understands that 2 Corinthians is "largely devoted to a complete revision of Pauline eschatology." In 2 Corinthians Paul, under the influence of hellenistic thinking, teaches the equivalent of the gnostic promise that at death the soul takes on a "robe" of divine fire (*Corp. Herm.* 10.18; Windisch; Bultmann, *Theology*, 1:201, 2).

Davies, *Paul and Rabbinic Judaism*, 310–18, who also believes that Paul now teaches that a spiritual body is to be received at death, attacks Knox's view on the ground that the ideas of Paul, though similar in terminology, are not necessarily strictly hellenistic (cf. Grundmann, *TDNT* 2:63–64, and Schweitzer, *Mysticism*, 134). The desire to be free from this body, as well as the idea of a possession of the spirit (Davies, 144), can be seen also as Jewish (cf. Sevenster, "Some Remarks," 208–10). Furthermore, Knox's argument is weak in the fact that he does not convince us with regard to Paul's sudden change to incorporate the Greek understanding of death in his thinking (Sevenster, "Einige Bermerkungen," 295). Knox's theory, *St. Paul* (1–26), that Paul's visit to Athens was the basis for the apostle's change undercuts his position (Davies, 314) because the impression given in Acts 17 is that Paul left Athens a disappointed person on more pragmatic grounds.

While Davies has argued against the hellenistic influence as the reason behind Paul's change in eschatology, nevertheless he does see a change. He sees that change occurring because Paul came to view the Age to Come in a different manner. In 1 Corinthians 15, where Paul was quite certain of being alive at the Parousia, the apostle concentrates on the general resurrection. But in 2 Corinthians 5, Paul shows an "unconscious ambiguity of thought," for he now is concerned with his own death and the intermediate state. Since his conversion, Paul has come to realize that the Age to Come has been actualized in the next world and at death the Christian will receive his spiritual body (Davies, 317–18; Whiteley, *Theology*, 206–7; Bruce, "Paul," 470, 71).

But not all are convinced that Paul has shifted his thinking about eschatology. Berry disagrees with the notion that Paul has changed his mind about the time at which the Christian receives the spiritual body. For Berry, Paul has not changed his position, but rather expresses his fear of entering the "interim" state in a bodiless, or naked, state (64). Berry is not alone in this thinking (Stevens, *Pauline Theology*, 343, n. 1; Kennedy, *St. Paul's Conception*, 264–81; Plummer 160–64; Thornton, *Common Life*, 284–86; Goudge, 45–55).

For Berry, Paul does not present anything new in 5:2–4 (62; cf. 5:1). But because of an increased awareness on Paul's part that death was close at hand, his hope centers now on the idea that he wishes to avoid death. Paul does not fear death *per se* but the fear centers on being a soul apart from the body. Harris, "2 Cor 5:1–10: A Watershed . . . ?" concludes (56): "The eschatology of this passage cannot be deemed a temporary aberration in his thought. Nor, on the other hand, do the modifications of outlook and clarification of doctrine in 2 Cor 5 constitute a radical revision of Pauline eschatology, since the cardinal concepts of his eschatology—Parousia, resurrection, judgment—were not abandoned, but (in the case of the Parousia-resurrection motif) merely redefined in the light of new insights." See too his "Paul's View."

One notes that Paul was probably not offering a doctrine different from his earlier teaching (5:1; see 1 Cor 15; Ellis, "II Cor. v. 1–10," 217; Vos, *Pauline Eschatology*, 172–205). To have done so would have left Paul open to the charge of fickleness, something which he has already encountered and answered (1:15–23; see 2:17). Cassidy argues ("Paul's Attitude" [210–17] that there is a completely different time-frame for believers who have died. Thus, they are not subject to the same aspects of time as those remaining on earth. As a result, they do not experience the "intermediate state," even though theoretically this period exists. But Cullmann's position that those who died are still anticipating a better age (Rev 6:10, "How long, O Lord?") holds a strong counterposition to Cassidy (see O. Cullmann, *Christ and Time* [2], tr. F. V. Filson [Philadelphia: Westminster Press/London: SCM Press, 1950] 239–42).

In short, Christians are groaning (στενάζομεν, 5:2, 4) and are burdened (βαρούμενοι, 5:4) as they wait for the new building of God. Paul seeks to be clothed over his earthly body (ἐπενδύσασθαι, 5:2) and does not wish to be found naked (γυμνός; cf. *m. Ber.* 3:5: the *shema*ʿ must be recited by a person who is clothed). Possibly repelling the gnostic idea that happiness results in being unclothed (Bultmann, 137–38; cf. Plato and Philo), as well as showing the Jewish fear of nakedness (Barrett, 154, 155), Paul longs to escape death and to be clothed with his resurrection body. Thus 5:2–4 appear to reflect a change in Paul's understanding of his life's expectancy rather than a change in eschatology. As our *Comment* (see below) will show, Paul is quite cognizant of the subject of the intermediate state. To be sure he does not elaborate on it, but he does point out that he is not looking forward to it (Barrett, Hughes).

(2) A second proposed reason why Paul wrote 5:2–4 is offered by Ellis, "II Cor. v. 1–10." He views the discussion of 5:2–4 as emphasizing the corporate body rather than individual bodies (so Lang, *2 Korinther 5:1–10*, 179–82; Watson, "2 Cor 5:1–10"): "Paul's primary thought is not of individual bodies at all, but of corporate solidarities which inhere in Adam and in Christ, the old aeon and the new aeon" (Ellis, 217). In fact, Ellis does not view the present passage as dealing with the intermediate state in any way (224). Following the reasoning of Robinson, *The Body* (76), Ellis understands Paul to mean that to think of the resurrection hope is not to think of the individual, but of the church (see Robinson, 81, 82).

The position of Ellis highlights the Christian's existence ἐν Χριστῷ, "in

Christ." In this view it is held that the resurrection of the body commences at the believer's baptism (Robinson, 79, 80; cf. Eph 5:26–27). At that time the Christian becomes one spirit with the Lord (1 Cor 6:17) and puts on Christ (Gal 3:27). This action is seen as the beginning of the replacement of one body (ἐν Ἀδάμ, "in Adam") by the other body (ἐν Χριστῷ "in Christ"; Robinson, ibid.). The goal of the Christian is eventually to be "absent from the body." Ellis interprets (222) this phrase to mean that one is no longer a partaker in the "solidarities of the mortal body" (i.e., the σῶμα ψυχικόν, "a natural body"; cf. 1 Cor 15:44). The key moments become "baptism" and the "Parousia" (Robinson, 79): at the former the Christian begins the process of the resurrection; at the latter the completion of this transformation is achieved (ibid., 80, 81; Ellis, 218). For a critique of Ellis's position see Hughes (184, 185); Harris, *Commentary* (349); and idem, "2 Cor 5:1–10," in *TynB* 22 (1971) 39, 40.

The position of Ellis does not see a shift in Pauline theology. For Paul, the Parousia is still the time when the Christian receives the final reward from God. The death of a Christian is more of a dissolving of the old solidarity than a completion of the new. Rather, Ellis offers the idea that the apostle was speaking of the corporate body. The Christian does not enter the "naked" state, for the Christian already has a "body." For Ellis the naked state refers to the concepts of guilt and shame (219–22).

There is a Greek "tinge" to Paul's teaching in 5:2–4, but it seems unlikely that his main target is gnosticism (against Bultmann, 141). Possibly he is simply relating his fear of the "interim" period, a fear common to Jewish people. Moreover, he may be engaged in addressing an eschatological debate at Corinth, a debate that is reflected in his new concern with the interim state. To be sure, Paul is much concerned with death, but his death never dominated his writing. Rather, the possible debate, in conjunction with the increasing likelihood of his death, has prompted Paul to write 5:2–4.

(3) The foregoing provides us with a third possible reason behind 5:2–4. It is to be sought in the Corinthians' situation; and it is polemic (cf. Lang, *2 Kor.*, 183; the opposite view to 5:1 is that the earthly house was being identified with the heavenly at Corinth). The insistence that Paul's thinking here regarding the afterlife has been mainly influenced by his opponents has led to this new proposal. This suggestion refuses to see a sharp break between 4:16 and 5:1 ff. Still less does it envisage Paul as a confused or erratic thinker—or to use Windisch's homely metaphor, a gardener plucking flowers at random and arranging them into a bouquet of mixed varieties. Bultmann (132) writes of 5:1–5 as a digression which does not have the apostolic ministry in view. Rather, in opposition, this third interpretation views the apostle's thought as coherent and as continuing on into chap. 5 with the same objective in view: that is, to rebut the teaching of his opponents (clearly shown in Lincoln, *Paradise*, 59–71, and to an extreme in Lang, *2 Korinther 5, 1–10*, who makes a polemical setting the *leitmotif* of 5:1–10). The issue lies in determining the two "forms" of Christian existence ascribed to being "in Christ" (Collange, 198). His opponents claimed that their Christian status was achieved now; Paul responds by pointing to the future, with its promise of a somatic resurrection (Harris, *Raised Immortal*, 223, 224).

A sharper focus is put on the debate once we pose the question, How did the two understandings of being a Christian differ? The issue is not death and resurrection, but the distinction between soul and body (see Fallon, 47). From his opponents' viewpoint, the soul could attain to God only by a mystical ascent. At present the soul was held in a prisonlike existence in the body where it was weighed down and where it cried out for deliverance. Such release could come as the body wasted away, or was destroyed, or put off as clothing, or was left as an exile might leave a foreign land for home. The soul would thus be liberated and attain its glory by revitalizing the "inner person" by becoming a house of God, by putting on new garments of immortality, or being returned from exile.

Paul's disquisition in 5:1–10 aims to repel all these assertions. It is less concerned with the right way of conceiving a future existence, and more with relating the kerygma to present existence (Lang, *2 Kor.*, 194, who puts his thought epigrammatically: Paul is not saying that one cannot stay in two places at one time; what he is saying is that one cannot serve two masters, as two attitudes to life are seen in 5:7, the contrast between πίστις, "faith," and εἶδος "sight," "form"). He uses the language of his disputants in the hellenistic Jewish tradition but modifies it to suit his purpose. (Lincoln, *Paradise*, 59, traces this emphasis to Paul's desire to oppose "the claims of the 'super-apostles' [in 11:5; 12:11] to present glory and to the Spirit's manifestation in their ecstasies, their rhetorical gifts and impressive appearance.") Specifically, glory, for Paul, will come only at the Parousia, not in any ecstatic experience. The present life is shot through with suffering rather than the glory of ecstasy. "Ecstasy" is an ambivalent term (5:13). When it comes (12:2, 3) it is a gift of God, but more important is the call to serve the Lord in daily life (5:9, 10).

V 5 closes the first part of our passage. It would not be appropriate for Paul to end on a note of despair, and he does not disappoint his readers. The confidence of Paul is based on the pledge (ἀρραβών) of God. This idea of pledge seems to make 5:5 a verse of transition to summarize the confidence of 5:1–4, and, at the same time, provide the basis for the hope of 5:6.

The second section (5:6–10) continues on the upbeat note of optimism introduced in 5:5. 5:6–8 is an awkward construction grammatically (see Héring, 38, n. 8; Hughes, 178, n. 53). Characteristic of Paul, he spontaneously interjects an explanatory parenthesis (v 7) and thus his thought is not sequentially clear. But it seems that v 7 holds the key to the discussion (see later), and the third option considered above (pp. 100, 101) commends itself. Nevertheless, 5:6–8 reflects a "victory" over any problem associated with the interim state. (Possibly this is a reference to the eschatological-anthropological debate at Corinth.) While Paul prefers to be alive at the Parousia, he acknowledges in 5:8 that to be absent from the body is still better than to be absent from the Lord (cf. Phil 1:23; Martin, *Philippians* [NCB, 1976 = 1980] 79). Hettlinger (176–79) picks up on this "sudden change" in attitude and argues that Paul's contentment with the afterlife shows that 5:4 could not have included the concept of disembodiment. But this again overlooks the evidence of 5:2–4, as well as ignores the possibility that Paul could have two minds about death (Berry, 66–68).

But Paul is not satisfied to emphasize the future only. Indeed, he is concerned with present issues at Corinth. In 5:9, 10 he warns the Corinthians that the goal, while time remains, regardless of one's state at the Parousia (Conzelmann, *Theology*, 165), is to please the Lord (5:9). The time is coming for judgment to be passed on how the Christians behave (5:10). Thus Paul ends this passage, 5:1–10, as he opened it. This earthly tent, or body, will pass away only at death and there is something better for those who are faithful to the call: to see the present experience of believers as incomplete since they await the resurrection as a future event.

Comment

1. οἴδαμεν γάρ, "For we know." That Paul continues his theme of 4:16–18 is seen in his use of γάρ, as well as the structure of 5:1 (see p. 97). By including οἴδαμεν Paul probably wants to convey assurance to the believers (Bruce, 201) and remind them of previous teaching (Berry, 61, 62; see 1 Cor 15:42–45). Collange, *Enigmes*, 183, thinks Paul is recalling the teaching of Jesus in a synoptic logion (Mark 14:58: so Lincoln, *Paradise*, 62). Thus contra Knox (see p. 98), Paul is not preparing his readers for something new, but something already known. That this "something known" is revealed and not learned through human knowledge is suggested by Paul's use of οἶδα instead of γινώσκειν, also "to know" (Seesemann, *TDNT* 5:120–22). But this is not a distinction that is always true (see p. 151). The use of a *Wissenformel* (as in 1:7; 4:14; 5:6, 11 [16]) has suggested to a number of commentators (Windisch, Héring, Ellis [213], Bultmann [132]) that Paul is responding to his critics by citing agreed Christian tradition (see Prümm, *Diakonia*, 1:40, 174).

Expanding his idea that what is seen is temporary (4:18), Paul describes the human body as ἡ ἐπίγειος ἡμῶν οἰκία τοῦ σκήνους, "the earthly tent we live in" (cf. RSV). The metaphor of a tent, possibly reflecting the close proximity of the Feast of Tabernacles, or Booths (Lev 23:42), to the time of the writing of 2 Corinthians (Manson, "ΙΛΑCΤΗΡΙΟΝ," 8, 9; Wagner, "Le tabernacle"), suggests that the body is a temporary structure. But it is doubtful if Paul sees the tent as an outer covering of the real self (Schmithals, *Gnosticism*, 262; cf. Hipp. VI, 9:4–5; VII, 29:22). Indeed, he may be consciously opposing this notion. We possibly press Paul too much to account for his view of man in dualistic terms, namely, σῶμα—ψυχή (or σῶμα—πνεῦμα). Sevenster ("Remarks," 210–12) is probably correct when he writes that Paul left the question of what the tent covers unanswered, for the apostle was not primarily interested in the death of an individual; rather the concern of Paul was the eschatological sequence of *Heilsgeschichte*.

This tent soon will be καταλυθῇ—"dismantled." Kümmel, *Theology*, 239, 240, and Hughes, 162, n. 18, suggest that Paul has death in mind when he speaks of dismantling. If καταλύειν and ἀναλύειν are synonyms (ἀναλύειν is also used for the idea of dismantling a tent in 2 Macc. 9:1; cf. BGD 57), then from Phil 1:23 we see that death is in Paul's view in 5:1. Also, we could rightly expect the notion of ἀλλαγῆναι ("change," cf. 1 Cor 15:51, 52; see Hodge [354 n.] for concerns of textual problems in 15:51) if Paul was speaking of the change at the Parousia. Barrett (151) sees that both possibilities—

death and the Parousia—are in Paul's mind when he talks of the tent being dismantled. This position is possible in light of Paul's use of the subjunctive (see below). But in view of Paul's concentration on "taking off" (5:3*b*) and the point that the Parousia, in Paul's thought, suggests a change (1 Cor 15:51), it appears that the intention of this passage was concerned primarily with death, and in particular the necessary corollary that death must precede resurrection—a point made in 1 Cor 15:12–28 (see R. P. Martin, *The Spirit and the Congregation*, 109–18). Regardless of which possibility influenced him, Paul is suggesting, as he has in 4:18, that something better awaits those who share the apostolic faith. Thus Paul is attempting to give meaning to the present situation by referring to the future (Bornkamm, *Paul*, 230).

We note that ἐάν commands the subjunctive καταλυθῇ and reflects a conditional situation. The doubt expressed by Paul, however, is not directed toward the veracity of the apodosis (for we know Paul to be certain about a new body, 1 Cor 15:51–58); rather, the sentence construction of 5:1 expresses uncertainty in the apostle's mind concerning whether or not he will experience this dismantling before the change at the Parousia. Another possibility is that Paul is driven by the exigencies of debate to assert that the future house must await death, i.e., against "realized" eschatologists at Corinth who telescoped the future hope at or beyond death into a present experience, begun in a baptismal resurrection (1 Cor 4:8; 15:12).

If death should occur, there is a replacement for the earthly tent, namely, οἰκοδομὴν ἐκ θεοῦ, "a house from God," one that is permanent, not temporary, αἰώνιον ἐν τοῖς οὐρανοῖς, "eternal in the heavens" (cf. Job 16:19; Heb 11:16; Phil 2:10; 1 Cor 15:49; John 3:12). This permanent dwelling, this spiritual body, is one that is ἀχειροποίητον, "made without hands" (see Collange, *Enigmes*, 186; Mark 14:58; Col 2:11). To say that this new house was made without hands is not to negate that God created man (Gen 2:7). It is to say that the tent is of the earth and that there is both a need (1 Cor 15:22) and a desire (5:8) for something else, wholly from God.

Schmithals's assertion (*Gnosticism*, 263) that Paul emphasizes the features of the new habitation instead of the habitation itself is correct to a point. But it is not conclusive that Paul did this to overturn the gnostic argument that rejected the celestial corporeality (ibid., 160 f.; 176; so Sevenster, "Some Remarks" [210], who correctly asserts that parallel meaning of words does not necessarily imply agreement in ideas). It is also possible that Paul highlighted these "differences" between the earthly and the heavenly to support his contention that there is something unseen even though "the seen" is wasting away. Most scholars believe that Paul is more concerned with hope in the light of trouble, the temporary in view of eternity, than with a running battle with the gnostics. But the local situation at Corinth may well explain these expressions found only here in Paul.

Because Paul uses ἔχομεν, from ἔχειν, "to have" (present tense), some writers (Schlatter, *Paulus*, 544; Robinson, *The Body*, 80, 81; Hettlinger, "2 Corinthians 5:1–10," 185) have concluded that Paul sees the Christian as having a new body before death (Lincoln, *Paradise*, 211, n. 38, lists several other interpreters but raises serious objection). Ellis identifies the body put on at baptism (1 Cor 12:13; Gal 3:27). Thus, by being initiated into the corporate Body of Christ (Ellis calls [218] the house in 5:1 the Messianic Community; cf. Mark

14:58), the Christian is never "bodiless." But to press Paul at this point as holding that the Christian already has the house of God misunderstands Paul's use of Body of Christ, and also ignores 5:2 which speaks of the longing for this house. How can one have in possession something for which he still longs? Furthermore, if the Temple is the body, why associate the Temple with a tent? (Barrett, 152). Most likely the object of ἔχομεν is the hope that there is a house prepared (cf. John 14:2) for the believer (Barrett, 151) akin to the Jerusalem which is above (Gal 4:26). But see Lincoln, *Paradise*, 63. This interpretation is consistent with the tone of 4:16-18; there is hope, but it is for something yet to be grasped. See Rom 8:24, 25 (cf. Phil 3:20 f.) for this dimension of hope in Pauline thought, which in this field of inquiry is precisely his line of argument in 1 Cor 15 and 1 Thess 4 (Lincoln, 64, 65).

2. That our interpretation of ἔχομεν, "we have," is probably correct is also seen in the first part of 5:2: καὶ γὰρ ἐν τούτῳ στενάζομεν, τὸ οἰκητήριον ἡμῶν τὸ ἐξ οὐρανοῦ ἐπενδύσασθαι ἐπιποθοῦντες, "and indeed in this [tent] we groan, longing to put on our heavenly house." Paul's phrase ἐν τούτῳ, "in this," refers to "in the tent." While ἐν τούτῳ could also equal "for this reason" (John 16:30; 1 Cor 4:4; cf. Bruce, 202), the evidence suggests otherwise. Since the antecedent of the demonstrative must be σκῆνος, "tent," there was probably little doubt in the mind of Paul or his readers. Furthermore, Paul uses ἐν τούτῳ again (5:4), but this time he includes the word "tent" (see ἐν τῷ σκήνει). Hughes's suggestion (167, n. 27) that ἐν τούτῳ be rendered "meanwhile" (as in NIV) leaves us with a colorless introduction to 5:2. But see Bultmann, 136.

Since Christians dwell in an earthly tent, they are subject to groaning (στενάζειν). But against Bruce, 202, the reason for groaning is not a negative but a positive one. That Paul would groan and despair at unkind circumstances seems highly unlikely (Phil 4:11-13), even if he was under a "death sentence" (1:9; cf. Bruce *Paul,* 468; cf. 4:8-12; 11:23-7). Paul's use of στενάζειν (the verb meaning "to groan" occurs here, 5:4, and Rom 8:23) suggests that it is in anticipation of something to come that one groans, not in distress at what is. Rom 8:23 shows this to be the case. The groaning is in conjunction with the help of the Spirit, itself a gift of God, for we groan eagerly (Rom 8:25; cf. 5:5; see Black, *Romans* [NCB; Grand Rapids: Eerdmans, 1973 = 1981] 122). Why groan eagerly with the Holy Spirit's indwelling unless there was something good to follow? The groaning in Rom 8:23 is a sign of hope (Murray, *Romans* [NICNT; Grand Rapids: Eerdmans, 1959] 1:306). This line of reasoning appears similar to what is in our passage.

The reason for Paul's groaning is that it is part of the believers' desire: ἐπιποθοῦντες ("longing," present participle) ἐπενδύσασθαι ("to put on") the οἰκητήριον . . . τὸ ἐξ οὐρανοῦ ("heavenly house"; cf. 2 Peter 1:13 ff.). The groaning is seen in a positive vein, for Paul is expecting something good to happen (Barrett, 152). We should note that Paul's desire is to put on over what already is on. This is seen in ἐπενδύσασθαι (BGD, 284; like an "overcoat," Barrett, 153). Hodge's claim (115; cf. Feuillet, "La demeure," and Bultmann, 136, who think also that the verbs as noted are hardly distinguishable) that ἐπενδύσασθαι and ἐνδύεσθαι are synonyms ignores 5:3, where Paul longs not to give up his earthly body (ἐκδυσάμενοι), but rather put the heavenly garment over it (ἐπενδύσασθαι, 5:4). He wishes for no interval to transpire as would be the case in the event of his demise before the Lord's return. The change in metaphor—house to garment—makes even clearer what Paul is thinking. As was discussed earlier (see pp. 97–99), it appears that Paul did not change his outlook concerning the point at which Christians receive their resurrection body. This is seen in Paul's choice of ἐπενδύσασθαι. Why seek to "put on over" unless one fears being unclothed? The point is that Paul groans, longs for, the outer garment to be placed over his earthly garment, namely, his physical body. If this were to happen, and it would happen for certain (he held) at the Parousia (1 Cor 15:51 ff.), then Paul would avoid the interim period, in which he would be naked (γυμνός).

3. The textual problems related to this verse have been discussed (see notes a and b, pp. 96, 97: εἴ γε καί, "since indeed"). Paul is confident that the hope of a Christian will come to pass (Thrall, *Greek Particles*, 85–91). If the tent is dismantled, there awaits the Christian a house from God. But is this house obtained at death or at the Parousia? It is now time to present the evidence for our conclusion offered above.

As was discussed on 5:2, Paul is anticipating the putting of the heavenly garment over the earthly one, without the loss of the latter. He desires to avoid the experience of death, but if death comes, this will not result in a permanent state of being unclothed. Paul has already assured the Corinthians that the dead in Christ will put on a new body (1 Cor 15:52, 54). This, in addition to what 5:2 teaches, leads us to see that Paul still keeps both ideas about the resurrection before the people, both the dead in Christ and those remaining alive will be clothed at the Parousia, which is the topic of 5:2. But the evidence for our position is more than simply circumstantial.

5:4 yields the sense, as will be shown, that Paul seeks to avoid the period between death and the Parousia, the so-called *Zwischenzeit*, or *Zwischenzustand*, for he wishes, as he did in 5:2, to put the new body on over his corporeal frame. But whether in death or life, the Christian will put on the new body at the Parousia.

Paul's desire is to put on the new corporeality so as not to be found naked (γυμνός). As a Jew Paul would abhor nakedness (Barrett, 153; Knox, 137; see *m. Ber.* 3:5, quoted above), for this would suggest that a man "ceases to be truly and properly man" (Hughes, 171). However, we must not press Paul to argue for a dualistic appraisal of man. (The minority view here—shared by Ellis, "II Cor," Hanhart, "Paul's Hope," and Lang, *2 Kor 5*, 188—is that εὑρίσκεσθαι, "to be found," is to be taken in a judicial sense, and so the fear is that Paul will enter the next life exposed by God as one denuded [γυμνός] of good works. This is hardly cogent.) To say death has occurred—i.e., bringing inevitably the sense of nakedness—is to say that man becomes incomplete. We remember that the Greeks looked forward to dying, for it represented a flight of the soul from the body and as such it promised a desirable goal (*Corp. Herm.* 1:26; 10:8; Philo *Leg. Alleg.* II 57, 59; Plato *Rep.* IX 577B, *Phaedo* 67DE). What does Paul's inclusion of γυμνοί in 5:3 mean? To evaluate Paul's mention of γυμνότης as either an "afterthought" (Plummer, 147) or a "spasm of unbelief" (Moule, "Dualism," 121) is unsatisfactory. Ellis's (220, 21) argument that Paul's idea of nakedness refers to the shame and guilt of judgment is weak because judgment does not come in this passage until 5:10 and then only for Christians (cf. Oepke *TDNT* 1:774; 2:318; cf. Sevenster, "Some Remarks," 204 f.). Also to see Paul fighting the Greek understanding of nakedness is inadequate (cf. Davies, *Paul,* 191–200: contra Schmithals, *Gnosticism,* 204). To be sure, Paul was not unaware of the gnostic idea of disembodiment (Bultmann, *Theology* 1:201, 202), but he does not view it as a state to be desired. Rather, death is now a real possibility to Paul; and it is one that he does not cherish.

For Paul the interim period is a bodiless one (1 Cor 15:35–38). It is, to be sure, a period that is temporary (1 Cor 15:42–44). But there *is* an interval (1 Cor 15:37). Although Paul actually gives little detail about the interim state for it does not appear to be in his sights, yet he does express the desire to bypass this period. But why does he seek to avoid the interim period unless this time of nakedness offered something less than the ultimate realization of hope (5:4)? If death results in the Christian's receiving the resurrection body, why look forward to the Parousia? (See G. E. Ladd, *A Theology of the New Testament* [Grand Rapids: Eerdmans, 1974] 554.) What need was there for God to redeem creation (Rom 8:23–27) if the salvation of the Christian was consummated at death? If death were the answer to all hope, we would think that Paul would desire death, but this is not what we find. Rather, he considers it still an enemy (1 Cor 15:26). He is thankful that he has escaped death (1:10) and he desires to finish his ministry in this life (Phil 1:20–24; 1 Cor 9:23–27).

But while Paul in 5:3 and 5:4 expresses the desire to be clothed, to be alive at the Parousia, he is unwilling to paint the intermediate state as a condition of horror. For one thing, Paul does not hold that the Christian is separated from Christ at death (Rom 8:30 ff.). Rather, to leave this life is to be with Christ (5:8; Phil 1:23). Paul's goal (against Schmithals) is to finish this age alive and enter the next age without having to pass through a stage of being "naked." And, as 5:4 reveals, this "skipping" the interim stage remains in Paul's mind. But he is not overwhelmed to the point of despair by the prospect of leaving this world. Rather, though his goal is the Parousia, the outcome of death is still a plus for the Christian.

4. οἱ ὄντες ἐν τῷ σκήνει στενάζομεν, "while we remain in this tent we groan," resumes the thought introduced in 5:2. Paul groans for the spiritual body. He groans so as to express his desire to put on the new body. To this idea of groaning is added βαρούμενοι, "being burdened." This idea of burdening suggests being weighed down either by affliction or with anxiety (RSV, "we sigh with anxiety"). In the light of Paul's desire to answer his critics, the former understanding of βαρούμενοι (present participle, βαρέω) appears to be better (see 1:8 and the play on words in 4:17). Alternatively, circumstances do not "get" to Paul to threaten him (Phil 4:11–13; cf. 2 Cor 4:7–12). Furthermore, if the interpretation of 5:2 is correct, then Paul is simply expressing concern to receive the new body. But he seems to be answering some point here, namely, that he was a suffering apostle, and must fend off the charge of a fruitless ministry (so Hanhart, "Paul's Hope," but with an unusual view of γυμνός).

Paul proceeds to explain that he is distressed and burdened ἐφ' ᾧ οὐ θέλομεν ἐκδύσασθαι ἀλλ' ἐπενδύσασθαι, "because we do not desire to be unclothed" (see Moulton, *Grammar* 1:107; Turner, *Grammatical Insights,* 131) "but clothed." Hettlinger's translation, "not because we wish," is untenable. Paul wishes to "put on over" (ἐπενδύσασθαι) and escape the "taking off" of the earthly garment (ἐκδύσασθαι). We have argued already (p. 103) that Paul believes that the spiritual body is not available to the Christian until the Parousia. The idea that those who die do not consciously experience an interval between death and the Parousia (Bruce, 204) also apparently misses the point. Paul has spoken twice of the desire to "put on over," to have his resurrection body without losing his earthly body. This would not be necessary unless Paul wanted to avoid the result of death. He does not entertain the prospect of death enthusiastically. Probably Cullmann, *Christ and Time* [2], 231–41, is correct in saying that those who enter the bodiless state, though better off (5:8; cf. Phil 1:23), still experience the tension of "already, but not yet" ("How long, O Lord?" is the cry according to Rev 6:9; cf. Heb 11:39 f.). The point is that Paul's fear of the result of death can be best understood and with less problems if we see the interim state as a state which Paul fears, namely, a period of nakedness.

This last idea is further demonstrated in the use of the ἵνα, "in order that," clause that completes 5:4. Paul longs for the Parousia, the "putting on over," so that he may experience this ultimate result: καταποθῇ τὸ θνητὸν ὑπὸ τῆς ζωῆς, "what is mortal may be swallowed up by life." We see a parallel in 1 Cor 15:54 which says that death is "swallowed up" in victory. The Christian who is alive at the Parousia will avoid death because what is mortal— that which is not yet dismantled in death (Jeremias, "Flesh and Blood," *NTS* 2 [1956] 154)—is swallowed up by the living. Life is a gift from God. It (ζωή = "immortal life": see Harris, *Raised Immortal,* 220–26) remains to be given, for life is not a possession of human beings as yet (Schmithals, *Gnosticism,* 268).

Paul concludes his short digression on the fate of the dead in Christ. From his viewpoint it is much better to await the Lord's coming than to experience death (cf. Isa 25:8). This is simply an expansion of teaching put forward earlier in 1 Corinthians. Now that Paul realizes that it is very possible he will experience death himself, he reveals his preference. A spiritual body is to be desired instead of having to enter the interim period of waiting. This has been the theme of 5:2–4, but the hope of the resurrection is not lost as far as the dead are concerned (5:3). The hope of Christians, whether alive or dead, remains unchanged (Héring, 38).

We might pause to ask why Paul said so little concerning the interim state. By now the reason should be apparent. The hope of Paul is the resurrection of Christ, the pivot on which *Heilsgeschichte* turns since it looks forward to the hope that is yet to be consummated. From 4:13 to our present verses, Paul has stressed that which lies beyond what is seen. His short digression on the interim state simply reveals Paul's desire to avoid this nakedness. But Paul is not concerned to give us a detailed theology of a mystery that had not been revealed to him. More likely, his point is to write about the events of eschatology, not the death of individuals (Sevenster, "Some Remarks," 212), especially as these matters formed the nub of his debate with Corinthian teachers. They (as referred to in 1 Cor 15:12) "considered themselves to be enjoying heavenly existence to the full already [and] did not envisage a further stage of embodiment" (Lincoln, *Paradise,* 67). The issue, then, is his apostolic authority derived from the kerygma which, in turn, is based on an eschatology not yet realized; the debate at Corinth was centered on future events in themselves.

So, it appears that the Corinthians have already been exposed to the idea of the interim state. Possibly in a general manner, Paul had discussed the topic (as well as written to the Corinthians [1 Cor 15:12–19]) concerning those who have already died. He had already addressed this concern of the Corinthians. Thus, it appears that the matter of the interim state has been dealt with before and Paul simply reiterates what was said earlier. But there is a sharper point put on the later teaching because of the opponents' claim that they have no need of a future resurrection.

5. ὁ δὲ κατεργασάμενος ἡμᾶς εἰς αὐτὸ τοῦτο θεός, ὁ δοὺς ἡμῖν τὸν ἀρραβῶνα τοῦ πνεύματος, "the one who prepared us for this very purpose [is] God, who also gave us the Spirit as a pledge." While 5:4 displayed the dislike of Paul for the interim state, it would be inconsistent for him to be paralyzed with fear concerning this prospect. Paul's theme for several verses has been one of hope, which by its nature emphasizes what is not seen and not yet attained. "The one who prepared us for this very purpose is God," repeats the thought of the last clause of 5:4. The whole of creation awaits God's final action (Rom 8:23–27), at which time perfect fellowship will be restored and eternal life completed. The hope of the people should be in θεός, God, (placed at the end of the clause for emphasis). He has created (κατεργασάμενος; aorist participle) his people for this very thing (αὐτὸ τοῦτο). Probably Paul has in mind the endowment of Christians with heavenly bodies (Phil 3:21). This would revive Paul's theme of the unseen, and of the permanent taking over from the temporary and terrestrial. But now Paul introduces the reason for this hope. It is more than simply a "shot in the dark." Rather, Paul is convinced that what God will do in the future is ensured by what he has done in the past and what he is doing in the present (the use of the aorist implies an act already completed yet with present effect).

Paul's basis for his assurance of the permanent triumphing over the temporary is the ἀρραβών (pledge) given to believers. This pledge is the πνεῦμα (Spirit). God has already imparted the Holy Spirit, referred to in δοὺς, "given," (aorist participle) as his pledge or deposit. The use of ἀρραβών (see on 1:22; cf. Gen 38:17, 18, 20) refers to a down payment, something to assure that the "final installment will come" (1:22). What the Christian has now is a present possession, which promises more to come (Cox, 424; Vos, *Eschatology,* 165; Hughes, 41 f.). To be sure, Paul describes the Holy Spirit as the instrument of God for the renewal of the "inner man" (ἔσω ἄνθρωπος). But also Paul is sure that the saving power that raised Jesus from the dead is also available to people in the present (Rom 8:11). God gave part of himself to be enjoyed now, as well as offering us the assurance that eternal life awaits the Christian (Cox, 425; Mitton, "Paul's Certainties").

Moule believes ("St. Paul and Dualism," 118–20) that Paul groans because the apostle understands that God has only prepared us for the exchange; there is to be no addition of a new garment. Moule views God as planning the "naked" state and so requiring that everyone must recognize this "process of mortality" (ibid., 119). There is no possibility of avoiding the exchange;

what is worked out is life's hardship. The process of exchange occurs not only at death but throughout life. The crisis Paul fears is the using up of and the parting with our strength and health in obedience to God (ibid., 121). The Holy Spirit is simply a pledge that there will indeed be an exchange. Thus Moule translates 5:5a *"but* it is God who has made [?] us for this very thing; viz. to strip off clothing (and receive new clothing in exchange)" (ibid., 118 n. 1). But this interpretation implies that God's creation was brought into being for the purpose of dying. Also, Moule eliminates the significance of Paul's compound verb, ἐπενδύσασθαι, for this scholar argues that Paul is denying the idea of putting on over or that he is offering nothing more than wishful thinking. Such conclusions we find inadequate, and thus hold to the position that the naked state can be avoided. God has prepared us for the new life, not for the interim stage (Lincoln, *Paradise,* 212, n. 46).

6. Grammatically speaking, 5:6 is an anacoluthon. θαρροῦντες οὖν πάντοτε καὶ εἰδότες ὅτι ἐνδημοῦντες ἐν τῷ σώματι ἐκδημοῦμεν ἀπὸ τοῦ κυρίου, "accordingly, we are always confident and know that while we are at home in the body we are away from the Lord." It appears that Paul abandons his original thought after 5:6 and interjects a spontaneous interpretation in the form of an explanatory parenthesis (5:7; Bultmann, 141), a feature characteristic of Paul (see Hughes 178, n. 53). That Paul inserts a change of thought from his original intention is seen in his redundant use of θαρροῦμεν, "we are confident," in 5:8. Paul probably meant to say, "Being therefore always of good courage, and knowing that to be at home in the body is to be away from the Lord, we are willing rather," etc. It appears that, as Paul was writing or dictating this letter, he came to the end of 5:6 and realized that some may understand that this life means separation from Christ. Of course, from 5:5 we see that this is not what he meant. To correct any possible misunderstanding, therefore, Paul inserts 5:7.

The contents of this earthen vessel (4:7–11) are priceless. And though the vessel, the tent, is fragile and temporary, there is no room for despondency (Barrett, 157). οὖν, "therefore, accordingly," relates back to the hope discussed in 5:5. There is no reason for Paul to despair since the Spirit is with him. "Despair is an experience to which he [Paul] does not submit; for to despair is to disown the Spirit and to disown the Spirit is not to be a Christian at all" (Tasker, 82). Thus, θαρροῦντες πάντοτε ("always confident") describes those who treasure the pledge of God.

Paul's use of καὶ, "and," could be taken to mean "because" (NEB). If this is true, then it would suggest that the reason Paul has confidence is that he is away from the Lord and at home in the body. But this force of καὶ is unlikely, both on contextual grounds and on the basis of what we know of Paul. With respect to the former, the οὖν, as already pointed out, points back to Paul's hope and assurance in 5:5. Thus Paul expresses confidence in God's work, not in his environment. The latter argument is even more obvious, for Paul has the ability, with help from God, not to allow circumstances to dull his peace of mind (Phil 4:10–13). Furthermore, his firm hope is to put on the heavenly garment, something that Paul surely feels will bring him home to the Lord (Phil 3:21). Thus καὶ does not carry the force of "because," but simply connects this thought.

ἐνδημῆσαι ἐν τῷ σώματι, "to be at home in the body," expresses Paul's awareness that some Christians do remain in the body. As suggested above, Paul does not want his readers to think that dying in Christ is a terrible thing. On the contrary (5:8), he sees it as a great improvement in relation to this life. To be "in the body" (notice Paul has dropped all metaphors for body) has its disadvantages, among which is "being away from the Lord." Goudge describes the wording "being at home in the body" as a deplorable interpretation. His point is that the present body is not worthy to be called our home. But Paul is not suggesting that communion with the Lord is nonexistent during the Christian's earthly pilgrimage (Knox, St. Paul, 140, 141). Rather, Paul is saying that the Christian is away from the Lord only in comparison with the prospect of seeing him face to face (1 Cor 13:12; cf. Bruce, 205; Martin, The Spirit and the Congregation, 53–56). If Paul had wanted to maintain the idea of total separation between creation and Creator, he could have used ἀποδημεῖν, as did Philo. Paul holds that through the Spirit the believer can always have communion with the Lord. Thus, to be at home in the body is the confession that those who are alive "reside" (Strachan, 99) in the body. But to reside in the body is to postpone the fulfillment of greater fellowship between the Christian and the Lord. While we remain in this body, ἐκδημοῦμεν ἀπὸ τοῦ κυρίου, "we are away from the Lord." The idea behind ἐκδημῆσαι is that the Christians are in a strange land (BGD, 238; Liddell and Scott, 1:504; cf. 1 Peter 2:11; Heb 11:13–16; Ep. Diognetus 5). While Christians are in communion with God they are nevertheless in a foreign land, continuing their pilgrimage. As long as one is on the earth, that perfect fellowship desired between the believer and the Lord remains elusive.

7. διὰ πίστεως γὰρ περιπατοῦμεν, οὐ διὰ εἴδους, "for we live by faith, not by sight." But it may appear that Paul does not feel that his argument concerning the present communion between the believer in the body and Christ was sufficiently clear. As though Paul wanted to stress that being at home in the body does not imply an "absolute" sense of being away from the Lord, the apostle inserts, and somewhat awkwardly, a parenthesis which reads διὰ πίστεως γὰρ, κτλ., "for we live (lit., "walk") by faith, not by sight." Paul wants to be sure that the Corinthians retain hope even though what they hope for is unseen (cf. Rom 8:24). Thus Paul presents in 5:7 the thought of the invisibility of Christ, not his absence per se (Barrett, 158), as the idea behind 5:6 expresses it. Faith can be real, for Christ is real. Faith believes in things unseen (cf. 4:18) and is the basis for the Christian's walk while "at home in the body."

We note that περιπατοῦμεν is rendered in the present tense, thus suggesting the idea of "walking" as our experience in this lifetime. The "walk" (i.e., conduct, BGD, 649) of a follower of Christ is made possible through πίστις, "faith." The use of διά with the genitive (πίστεως) denotes the idea of "by means of" (Moule, Idiom Book, 56, 57). The hope of God, given in the Holy Spirit as a pledge, is unseen by the human eye. But the demand of God is that those who want to please him must believe in him (Heb 11:6). The Christian has hope, even though he is away from the Lord, because as a believer he walks in the confidence that Christ is real, but unseen (see 1 Pet 1:8, 9).

But to get a complete idea of what Paul means by 5:7 is difficult because his use of εἶδος is debated. The question centers upon whether εἶδος, "sight," is to be given an active or passive meaning. Kittel argues (*TDNT* 2:374, 375), that εἶδος is not to be understood in the active sense (cf. Liddell and Scott, 1:482); thus διὰ εἴδους means "on the basis of what is seen" (see Hughes, 176, n. 2; Plummer, 151 f.). Kittel would take 5:7 as suggesting that the believer is controlled not by the things he cannot see, but by the faith that they do exist (we walk by faith, not by the appearance of things). However, Kümmel points out (121, 203) that εἶδος can have an active sense (Num 12:8, LXX), and thus 5:7 would emphasize that faith in Christ is the determining factor in the Christian's life even though he remains invisible (Tasker, 82; we walk by faith in Christ even though we cannot see him). In terms of context, Paul probably meant the latter, for to evaluate εἶδος in a passive sense as understood by Kittel loses Paul's use of it as an antithesis to faith. This parenthesis (5:7) has been inserted to correct any misunderstanding presented in 5:6. The faith of the Christian overcomes the problem set by the invisibility of the Lord. To be away from the Lord is not to be out of communion with him. Rather our walk with him in fellowship, though not yet perfected, is possible because of faith (Bruce, 205). Barrett argues (159) that the passive sense of εἶδος could also mean "we live by believing in the absent and invisible Christ, not by looking at visible forms." If this is true, then regardless of our choice as to the meaning of εἶδος, the emphasis of 5:7 centers on faith in Christ as possible even if 5:6*b* be true.

The polemical side to this statement cannot be ignored, confirming Bultmann's estimate (141) of vv 1–5 as "a polemical excursus." He treats the phrase διὰ πίστεως γὰρ περιπατοῦμεν κτλ. as "a fundamental antignostic Christian remark," citing H. Jonas, *Gnosis und die spätantiker Geist* (Göttingen: Vandenhoeck & Ruprecht, 1954) II.1.48. The polemical nature of v 7 is recognized by an array of interpreters, listed by Lincoln, *Paradise* 68, 213, n. 60. Paul's opponents built their hope on "what they saw" in ecstatic vision and thus gloried in the "outward" (5:12), not recognizing that the eschaton is future (1 Cor 13:12). Their pretensions to present power (12:12) were based on what they "saw" (contrast 4:18). This, for them, was the "form" (εἶδος, *Gestalt*; see Jervell, *Imago Dei*, 270) of reality. Paul contradicts this, since faith is not yet realized in vision. He thus relativizes the value of their ecstatic experiences (Fallon), and unifies the human person (as in 12:2, 3), refusing to separate the "pure" soul from the "imperfect" body. He denies the dichotomy that would view the person as composed of two separable parts, a body of lesser value, and a soul which alone is capable of an intimacy with the divine. For Paul the human person is one and indivisible. Dualistic separation into body and soul is no part of his anthropology (see Jewett, *Paul's Anthropological Terms*, 275–77, who argues that the use of σῶμα in v 6 is modified by vv 8, 10; this proposal suggests that Paul is indebted to his opponents for the language of the earlier vv).

8. That 5:7 is a parenthesis, a break in Paul's train of thought, is seen in the way he opens 5:8. θαρροῦμεν ("we are confident"), though redundant, picks up the thought dropped in 5:6, namely, that whether in or out of the body, the Christian can be of good courage (see Héring, 39; Bultmann, 141). The Christian can always be confident whether in the body, for God has given a pledge; or out of the body, for ἐκδημῆσαι ἐκ τοῦ σώματος . . . ἐνδημῆσαι πρὸς τὸν κύριον ("to be out of the body [is to be] at home with the Lord")

is the greater hope of the Christian (Martin, *Philippians*, 79, *ad* Phil 1:21–23; see too Lincoln, *Paradise*, 69).

In comparison with 5:6, Paul in this v makes several changes. He reverses the order of being at home and being away from home. The meanings of these two words were discussed above. In 5:6 to be in the body was a present reality, marked by a present participle; so to be away from the Lord was described in the finite present tense. But in 5:8 Paul uses the aorist infinitive (ἐκδημῆσαι and ἐνδημῆσαι, probably inceptive in nature) to signify a once-for-all turn of events. Death will usher the believer into the presence of the Lord. The phrase πρὸς τὸν κύριον suggests both motion toward (linear) and place of rest (punctiliar; Moule, *Idiom Book*, 52, 53; but both grammatical points are challenged by Harris, *TynB* 22 [1971] 46). This could also be Paul's way of suggesting the intimate fellowship that awaits the Christian (Hughes, 178, n. 52; cf. Moulton, *Grammar* 2:467), thereby overcoming the lack of fellowship hinted at in 5:6. The point of 5:8 is clearly that there is an alternative to being away from the Lord. εὐδοκοῦμεν μᾶλλον, "we would rather," suggests a distinct preference (so most commentators, but not Berry, "Death," 65. Collange, *Enigmes* [233, 234] shows the weakness of this view; but doubts remain).

What comes as somewhat of a surprise is that Paul writes εὐδοκοῦμεν μᾶλλον, "we would rather" be away from the body. The surprise comes because it appears from 5:2–4 that Paul was fearing just this event. The event of his death suggested to him a bodiless state, a condition that he groaned to avoid. But in 5:8 he expresses the desire to enter that state. In short, Paul prefers nakedness to present life (Héring, 39). Hettlinger, "2 Cor 5:1–10" (176–79), is quick to point out that this "fondness" for the interim period negates the position that Paul considers nakedness a bodiless state. Why long for something that is feared? The point is that Paul sees nakedness as a state not to be feared ultimately because it looks forward to a prospect of embodiment.

To adopt this position, that 5:8 is a reversal of 5:3, or even more, a denial of our findings for 5:3, is to assume that Paul (or anyone) can hold only one view about a certain idea. This, as Berry suggests (66–68), is not necessarily so. Paul could easily have two minds about death. On the one hand, he could shrink from death, for it held possibilities that he would like to avoid. On the other hand, to be free from this body would lead to a greater level of fellowship with Christ since the Parousia would intervene, bringing to an end all the service "in the body." In other words, to die was not the consummation of salvation for the Christian, but it was, in terms of fellowship with Christ, better than staying in the body. This is exactly his train of thought in Phil 1:20–26.

That Paul expressed his wish to depart from the body and to be with Christ is not to say he developed a death wish. His ministry was important to him as a sacred trust from God (4:1; 1 Thess 2:1–8; 1 Cor 9:23 ff.; cf. 2 Tim 4:7). This is seen especially in Phil 1:21–26 where Paul, for the sake of the Philippians, views staying alive as a benefit, even though he desires to be with Christ.

From this there appears little development in terms of Paul's eschatology from 1 Thessalonians to 1 Corinthians 15 to 2 Corinthians 5:1–10 (Vos, *Pauline Eschatology*, 172–205). But Harris (*TynB* 22 [1971]) sees a movement in Paul's thinking *away from* the apocalyptic idiom and hope of an imminent Parousia, intensely desired, based on a realization that death may well supervene for him before the end-time. So the movement is *toward* a more nuanced type of eschatological thought, where the future discloses more of what the present reality of Christ's rule conceals. These "altered eschatological perspectives" (56) are due to Paul's experience in 2 Corinthians 1:8–11 and his own expectancy of receiving a σῶμα πνευματικόν at his death. Paul also abandoned the hope of "sleeping" in the grave or Sheol until the Parousia. What is missing, however, in Harris's reconstruction is a concern to relate Paul's teaching in 2 Cor 5 to the contingency of the situation at Corinth at this particular juncture of his apostolic ministry, and a recognition of the polemical character of his writing in these vv. Paul, increasingly aware of his feeble hold on life (4:7–12; 6:9) and the looming prospect of an imminent death, reflects on the seriousness of it and on the fact that the dead in Christ are with the Lord (Héring, 39; Barrett, 159; Lincoln, *Paradise*, 69–71). The same setting in Paul's life is found in Phil 1:20–26; 2:17, and Rom 15:31. These writings, along with 2 Cor, conceivably come out of the same period of Paul's experience of fear and isolation.

9. διὸ καὶ φιλοτιμούμεθα, "and so, our ambition is." The use of διὸ alerts Paul's reader that the apostle is ready to present a logical conclusion (Moule, *Idiom Book*, 164). Paul writes that it is the Christian's ambition (φιλοτιμούμεθα) to please the Lord. The idea behind φιλοτιμεῖσθαι is "to aspire" (BGD, 861) or "to devote oneself zealously to a cause" (Hughes, 178, n. 54). The cause is to please (or be acceptable to BGD, 318) the Lord (εὐάρεστος τῷ κυρίῳ εἶναι). See Rom 12:1 f.; 14:18; Phil 4:18; Col 3:20; Eph 5:10; Heb 13:21; *1 Clem* 35:5 [62:2].

Paul also makes it clear, in light of 5:6–8, that it makes no difference what state the Christian may be in when the Parousia happens (εἴτε ἐνδημοῦντες, εἴτε ἐκδημοῦντες, "whether at home or away"; Kümmel notes [121] that these participles are the reverse of 5:6; but it appears to make little difference whether we supply "the body" or "the Lord"; see Barrett, 159). The condition of the believer at the Parousia is immaterial for the saving event (Conzelmann, *Theology*, 165; cf. 1 Thess 5:9, 10). Whether asleep or alive, the Christian will receive the resurrection body at the Parousia. The point is that (as will be expanded in 5:10) at all times the person should seek to please the Lord (cf. John 8:29; 1 John 3:22; *Did* 4:12; *Barn* 19:2).

We may ask, Was Paul suggesting that the dead in Christ, the persons in a state of nearer presence to Christ (Héring, 39), could possibly not please Christ? In other words, are the "naked" persons still involved in a struggle between doing right and wrong? It does not appear so. For one thing, if Paul did hold this, it would lessen the attraction of being at home with the Lord. Furthermore, as 5:10 will show, the judgment of Christians is restricted to "things done in the body." This strongly suggests that there is no chance of doing wrong in the intermediate state, which logically leads us to conclude that there is no way to displease Christ once we are at home with him. Filson argues (230, 231) that Paul nowhere suggests a "moral striving" for those who are asleep in Christ. What he adds is the exhortation to make efficient use of the time left to one. At the point of receiving the letter, the Corinthians who read it were "alive." Thus, Paul is saying in 5:9 that regardless of how the "end" comes about—through death or the Parousia—the Christian is not relieved of his or her responsibility to please the Lord. Until the end happens, Christians are responsible to account for their conduct, if it should fall below the standard of good behavior (5:10). The polemical point of this v is seen in Paul's use of the verb φανερωθῆναι, "to appear," in the next v, a term much in vogue at Corinth to denote the "God-manifest" character of Paul's opponents (see on 4:2, 3). Paul's word (δεῖ: "it is necessary") shows how he gave a special twist to the claim to reveal the divine presence in human life (see on 4:2). It is only by a life of goodness in the concrete situations of bodily existence (τὰ διὰ τοῦ σώματος, and we note the P[46] and Latin readings "in his own body") that a person's claim to be representing God is shown to be authentic. Paul has clearly put his adversaries in his sights here.

10. Paul concludes at 5:10, and reaches the end of the "digression" (if that is the right term) of 4:7–5:10 by setting before the Corinthians the stimulus for behavior that is pleasing to the Lord. Though the Christian's future is secure no matter what his state at the Parousia, Paul writes against false security. (The first readers would be aware of 1 Cor 9:27, which suggests that the Christian could be "rejected" on the basis of conduct; Rissi, *Studien*, 98, suggests that faith must be renewed to the close of life.)

τοὺς γὰρ πάντας, "for all of us," denotes the sum total of Christians (Moulton, *Grammar* 3:203). That Paul considered all Christians liable to judgment is also evident from δεῖ, "it is necessary." The requirement is φανερωθῆναι, "to appear" (aorist infinitive), not in the sense of a simple "showing up" but in the sense of being laid bare, for all the world to see the true nature of one's character (Hughes, 180; cf. 1 Sam 16:7; Heb 4:13; cf. 1 Cor 4:5). The place we stand is ἔμπροσθεν τοῦ βήματος τοῦ Χριστοῦ, "before the judgment seat of Christ." While God judges the world (Rom 3:6), Christ is named also as judge (Rom 2:16; cf. Matt 25:31; John 5:22; Rom 14:10). This does not appear to be a contradiction; it is rather a statement that God judges the world, but that he chooses to do so through Christ (Barrett, 160).

A question arises as to whether this judgment in 5:10 is universal or is restricted to Christians. From earlier Pauline writings, it appears that there is a judgment intended for Christians (Héring, 39; cf. 1 Cor 3:10–15). The possibility of not pleasing God while here in the body is put before the Corinthians as something to be avoided. The inference is that Paul's desire is to please God, even if it means displeasing men (Collange, *Enigmes*, 243). We know from 1 Cor 3:10–15 that salvation is not lost simply because one believer's life is not as pleasing as another one's. But the solemnity of this judgment should not be overlooked either (Tasker, 82). The tribunal of Christ for the Christian is needed to complete God's justice, both in terms of holiness and impartiality (see below). The life of faith does not free the Christian from the life of obedience (Hughes, 180 f.; cf. Tasker, 83; Denney, 185; and Bultmann, 146, denying any inconsistency between justification by faith alone and 5:10).

That God's judgment is universal is seen in that no one escapes, not even Christians. ἕκαστος, "each one," must stand before the judgment seat of Christ (see C. J. Roetzel, *Judgement in the Community,* 175, who brings out the polemical setting of v 10: at the judgment "Paul's Gospel will receive its vindication and those who oppose him and his Gospel can expect eschatological ruin [φαῦλον]," a point of view ignored by L. Mattern, *Das Verständnis des Gerichtes bei Paulus,* 151–58). And though this idea of everyone receiving judgment takes in Christians, Plummer (157) correctly points out that judgment is not rendered en masse, but in each case, one by one (cf. "we all must appear"). The reason that all Christians (Bruce, 206) stand before Christ and are addressed individually ("ein jeder," see Bornkamm, "Der Lohngedanke," 74) is ἵνα κομίσηται, "in order to receive recompense." The purpose of the "appointment" before Christ is heralded by the ἵνα clause. The Christian will receive (note how the use of the middle voice for κομίσηται stresses the action of the agent; this fits in well with the remainder of this verse) or "receive back" or "receive what is one's own" ("reap" or "get back for one's self," Liddell and Scott 1:975, 76) "in proportion to his deeds" (Moule, *Idiom Book,* 53). The basis of this recompense for the Christian is τὰ διὰ τοῦ σώματος πρὸς ἃ ἔπραξεν, "what he has done in the body." The last phrase can refer to both deeds and words, since both are under the auspices of the Christian (Plummer, 58). (Note a textual consideration: ἴδια, added in some witnesses, intensifies the retributive form of κομίζεσθαι, but Hughes, 181, n. 57, submits that the optional reading does not affect the meaning; see Note *d,* p. 97). The διά could be instrumental ("by means of the body," Barrett, 160) or temporal ("while in the body"). Both ideas amount to the same thing (Bultmann, 145). Though Paul would definitely not overlook the latter idea, the former seems more likely in light of the phrase πρὸς ἃ ἔπραξεν. The important point to note is the aorist tense of the verb rendered "receive." Paul's use of it strongly suggests a constative force. If so, the Christian's behavior is viewed by Christ as a unity, and not as a concatenation of individual acts (Hughes, 181, n. 58). This is further seen in Paul's statement εἴτε ἀγαθὸν εἴτε φαῦλον, "whether good or bad," which he uses to describe ἃ ἔπραξεν. Plummer notes (158 f.) that "whether good or bad" is constructed with a change to the singular neuter. Thus, though each individual is judged on the basis of his or her behavior, the person's habitual action, and not his individual acts, are the basis for judgment. Specifically, what is at issue is the reader's attitude to Paul's teaching at Corinth. Thus God's judgment is also impartial, for what is due to a person is what is given that person.

But we should not characterize this recompense as solely a penal operation (Hughes, 181). Paul is suggesting that those who do well will receive good. This is consistent with his picture in 1 Cor 3:10–15. The Christians whose work turns out to be gold, silver, and costly stones, will receive their reward (1 Cor 3:14; cf. Matt 16:27). If, however, they build their Christian life with only wood, hay, or straw, though they escape with their life, they suffer loss (1 Cor 3:15). Since Paul urged his readers to please the Lord, there must be a "positive reinforcement" for just such action. The Christian is not excused from doing good, and is liable for his or her actions (Eph 6:8; Col 3:25).

In this verse Paul does not clearly indicate exactly when this manifestation will take place, whether at death or at the Parousia. But it is hard not to assume that the recompense follows closely on the heels of the appearance before Christ (Plummer, 159). Likewise, Paul does not explain the idea of reward (cf. 1 Cor 3:14) though whatever lies behind this concept surely includes God's approval (Barrett, *1 Corinthians*, 88, 89).

Explanation

These verses (5:1–10) bring to a close Paul's disquisition (4:7–5:10) on the question concerning why his ministry (and that of those with him) proceeds in spite of overwhelming odds and why it has its credentials in spite of his suffering. While the ministry of death (3:7) has a sign, the Torah, the Christian looks to the unseen world, for this is permanent (5:1). Paul has shown that the earthly body, though wasting away, is the home of the Spirit (cf. the idea in 1 Cor 6:19). The Spirit, the pledge from God, is the basis for believing that God has something better in store for his people. There will come the day when the Christian will receive his or her permanent dwelling, the spiritual body, from God. It is a future prospect, not a present possession as his opponents were laying claim to. And though Paul desires to put on the heavenly body over the earthly body and not see death (his constant exposure to risk, among many reasons, is the one reason that this would impugn even more his ministry in the eyes of his opponents), the Spirit is the proof that God will meet both the dead in Christ and those who are alive at the Parousia.

Though Paul digressed in these verses concerning his fear of the naked state, the theme, especially in the second half (5:6–10), was the hope of God and its impetus to constrain the Christian to practical obedience. Until death, or the Parousia, occurs, the Christian must seek to please the Lord, for the Christian stands accountable for his or her actions as a Christian.

F. The Motives for Paul's Preaching and Living   (5:11–15)

Bibliography

Black, D. A. *Paul, Apostle of Weakness: Astheneia and Its Cognates in the Pauline Literature.* New York: Peter Lang, 1984. **Carrez, M.** "Le 'nous' en 2 Corinthiens: contribution à l'étude de l'apostolicité dans 2 Corinthiens." *NTS* 26 (1980) 474–86. **Cerfaux, L.** *Christ in the Theology of St. Paul.* Tr. G. Webb and A. Walker. New York: Herder & Herder, 1959. **Collange, J.-F.** *Enigmes de la deuxième épître de Paul aux Corinthiens.* SNTSMS 18. Cambridge: University Press, 1972. **Denney, J.** *The Death of Christ.* London: Tyndale, 1951. **Dunn, J. D. G.** "Paul's Understanding of the Death of Jesus." In *Reconciliation and Hope,* FS L. Morris, ed. R. Banks. Grand Rapids: Eerdmans, 1974. ———. "The

Incident at Antioch." *JSNT* 18 (1983) 3–57. ———. *Jesus and the Spirit*, 1975. **Ellingworth, P.** " 'We' and 'I' in 2 Corinthians: a Question." *BT* 34 (2, 246 [1983]). **Enslin, M. S.** "The Constraint of Christ." *CrQ* 11 (1934) 315–22. **Fahy, T.** "St. Paul's 'Boasting' and 'Weakness.' " *ITQ* 31 (1964) 214–27. **Furnish, V. P.** *Theology and Ethics of Paul.* Abingdon: New York, 1968. **Glombitza, O.** "Mit Furcht und Zittern. Zum Verständnis von Phil. 2:12." *NovT* 3 (1959) 100–06. **Gollwitzer, H.** " 'Hinfort nicht mehr,' Predigt über 2 Kor 5, 15. . . ." *EvTh* 14 (1954) 1–6. **Hahn, F.** " 'Siebe, jetzt ist der Tag des Heils.' Neuschopfung und Versöhnung nach 2 Korinther 5, 14–6, 2." *EvTh* 33 (1973) 244–53. **Hanson, B.** "School of Suffering." *Dialog* 20 (1981) 39–45. **Hendry, G. S.** "ἡ γὰρ ἀγάπη τοῦ Χριστοῦ συνέχει: 2 Cor 5:14." *ExpTim* 59 (1947–48) 82. **Lofthouse, W. F.** "Singular and Plural in St. Paul's Letters." *EvT* 57–58 (1946–47) 179–82. **Manson, T. W.** "2 Cor 2:14–17: Suggestions towards a Exegesis." In *Studia Paulina.* FS de Zwaan. Haarlem: Bohn, 1963. **Martin, R. P.** *Reconciliation: A Study of Paul's Theology.* London: Marshall, Morgan & Scott/Atlanta: John Knox, 1981. ———. *Worship in the Early Church.* London: Marshall, Morgan & Scott, 1964; Grand Rapids: Eerdmans, 1974 ed. **Meyer, H. A. W.** *Kritisch-exegetischer Kommentar über den zweiten Brief an die Korinther.* Göttingen: Vandenhoeck & Ruprecht, 1856. **Otis, W. S. C.** "Exposition of 2 Cor 5:14." *BSac* 27 (1870) 545–64. **Reumann, J.** *Righteousness in the New Testament,* 1982. **Romaniuk, K.** "L'origine des formules pauliniennes 'le Christ s'est livré pour nous.' " *NovT* 5 (1962) 55–76. **Schlatter, A.** *Paulus, der Bote Jesu.* Stuttgart: Calwer, 1956. **Spencer, A. B.** "The Wise Fool (and the Foolish Wise): A Study of Irony in Paul." *NovT* 23 (1981) 349–60. **Spicq, C.** "L'étreinte de la charité." *ST* 8 (1956) 123–32. **Stuhlmacher, P.** "Das paulinische Evangelium." In *Das Evangelium und die Evangelien.* WUNT 28. Tübingen: Mohr, 1983. 157–82. **Wood, J. E.** "Death at Work in Paul." *EvQ* 54 (1982) 151–55.

Translation

[11] *Therefore, since we know the fear of the Lord, we attempt to persuade [a] men; we stand open to God and, I hope, also open in your consciences.* [12] *For we are not again commending ourselves to you, but giving you an occasion to boast on our behalf [b] so that you may have something to set against those who boast of what is seen and not [c] of what is in the heart. [d]* [13] *For if we are out of our minds, it is for God; if we are of sound mind, it is for you.* [14] *For the love of Christ compels us, since we have concluded that [e] one has died for all. Therefore, all died.* [15] *And he died for all that those who are living might no longer live for themselves, but for the one who died for them and was raised.*

Notes

[a] p[46] contains the reading πείθωμεν (subjunctive) instead of πείθομεν.

[b] p[46] b ℵ have ὑπὲρ ὑμῶν ("to boast in yourselves") instead of ὑπὲρ ἡμῶν. Barrett (162, n. 1) suggests that one would have expected ὑπὲρ ὑμῶν αὐτῶν or ὑπὲρ ἑαυτῶν. It is possible ὑπὲρ ὑμῶν could be interpreted to show that because of what Paul has done for the Corinthians they had reason to boast on their own account. As will be seen in the *Comment*, the context leads us toward an appreciation of the reading ὑπὲρ ἡμῶν. But Barrett raises a good question when he asks, if p[46] B ℵ are in error, why only these early MSS? Collange, *Enigmes*, 248, prefers the "harder reading" (ὑπὲρ ὑμῶν) on the ground that this sense means that Paul is appealing to the Corinthians' conscience as the tribunal where his apostolic work is confirmed. They are his "children" (6:12). But this seems forced, and Lietzmann's verdict that the *lectio difficilior* turns out to be "meaningless" is upheld.

[c] The text is attested by ℵ B. οὐκ is attested by D C G. This change could have been an attempt to balance with the beginning οὐ, "not," but the use of ἵνα probably rules out this option.

ᵈOur text is found in P⁴⁶ ℵ B (μὴ ἐν καρδίᾳ). In C D², we read οὐ καρδίᾳ and D* F G we find οὐκ ἐν καρδίᾳ.

ᵉThere is weak evidence (ℵ³ C* vg) of an endeavor to construct a conditional sentence. But the MSS (ℵ* B C² D) supporting the text appear to rule out this endeavor (see, however, BDF § 451.2, suggesting that εἰ may have been elided before εἰς, the next word).

Form/Structure/Setting

Barrett (163) calls the passage (5:11–21) "one of the most pregnant, difficult, and important in the whole of the Pauline literature." Of this passage, 5:11–15 forms a foundational part. One aspect of Paul's thought, found in earlier parts of this epistle, continues in these verses. The apostle's penchant for presenting the Gospel in terms of paradox is evident in 5:11–15. The preceding verses (especially 4:1–18) have pictured the treasure of the Gospel and its container, the earthen vessel. Though the figures of speech change, the contrast remains. In 5:11–13 Paul asserts his dignity and authority as God's messenger, yet this assertion is based on his portrait of himself as a slave (see Barrett). This paradox is continued in the representation of the Son of God as the servant of God (5:14, 15). The paradox is used as a teaching aid by Paul.

Paul is concerned to argue that his ministry is worthy of apostolic credibility. Spurred on by the fear of the Lord, Paul's goal is to persuade his hearers. But the understanding of this goal is somewhat blurred by Paul's desire not to have his defense (of apostolic integrity) made a ground for personal boasting (5:12). (5:11b may be a parenthetical remark to overcome just such a charge; Schmithals, *Gnosticism*, 188.) Thus, the themes of boasting in the Gospel and not boasting in oneself are played off against each other throughout the passage as a continuation of the paradox motif.

Paul attempts to hold both sides of the motif in tension. The Corinthians should have a reason to boast, namely, that he is an example of God's handiwork. But their doubt of Paul's sincerity forces him to place before them the facts, which consist of an asseveration that he has worked hard and openly for the Corinthians. Paul faces a dilemma in that there is nothing else for him to do but to remind them of his upright ministry.

This passage (5:11–15) opens in a way that suggests that it is a conclusion to 5:1–10 as well as a transition to what follows (see *Comment*). Paul presents his ministry as controlled by the fear of the Lord; he also justifies it in light of its mission. Paul's ministry is an avenue through which God reconciles the world. Though 5:18–20 brings out the rationale of reconciliation, 5:14, 15 provides the basis of reconciliation in the lives of the messengers and their audience, that is to say, Jesus' death and the love it creates in his people. Paul has risen to a new life through God's calling. Furthermore, he stands before God in openness; thus it is inevitable that his ministry to the Corinthians is likewise open to the scrutiny of others, in particular his converts at Corinth. All of Paul's action, whether in or out of the mind (5:13), is for others.

Our verses show Paul's desire to be accepted by the Corinthians. The paradox of being a slave satisfies God's demand, but our study will show that Paul was having trouble satisfying the Corinthians, whose suspicions

had been aroused by Paul's detractors on the scene. Though Paul will conclude
5:11–21 by concentrating on reconciliation, we should not let this concept
of the hesitancy on the part of the Corinthians slip from our attention. Once
again in 6:1–13; 7:2–13*b*, Paul will rehearse what has been done on behalf
of the Corinthian church. Though this reflects Paul's work, it should point
to God as an indication of the veracity of Paul's ministry.

Comment

11. Εἰδότες οὖν, "Therefore, since we know." In the opening verses of
this passage, Paul relates just how seriously he takes the admonition of 5:10.
While it is sometimes difficult to ascertain the degree of difference between
οἶδα and γινώσκω, nevertheless it is safe to assume Paul's choice of the former
is meant to underline the deep consciousness of his awe for God (see comment
on 5:1; also Héring, 40). Just how much this awe influences Paul's life is
seen in what follows.

In a sense, then, Paul is concluding his argument of the previous verses.
He has described, in the form of a digression (4:7—5:10), the manner of
his ministry. (Unlike the lives of the "super-apostles" and their emissaries
[11:5, 13–15], Paul's life is characterized by weaknesses and shortcomings,
at least from the opponents' standpoint.) This argument culminates in 5:9,
which speaks of the goal of every Christian, which is to please the Lord. As
if this is not enough, Paul adds the motivation of the necessity of appearing
before the Lord to receive a reward, good or bad, depending on the Christian's
faithfulness to God's call. With this standard before his readers, Paul is ready
to conclude with the idea of how it affects his ministry. The use of οὖν ("therefore") suggests that he is ready to offer an inference from his thinking.

However, οὖν may play a double role. Though it is the commonest inferential conjunction found in the New Testament (occurring almost 400 times),
it can also be used in a transitional manner (so Robertson, *Grammar*, 1191). After having described the style of his ministry (4:7—5:10), Paul changes his
emphasis in 5:11. He will be concerned in 5:11–21 to show that the aim of
his ministry is to aid in the reconciliation of the world to God (5:18–21). His
ministry is an avenue through which God calls the sinful world back to himself (and of course we cannot overlook Paul's desire for the Jews, his own
compatriots, in the ministry, Rom 9–11). With this verse (5:11) Paul points
to the goal of his service. Hence, οὖν marks the conclusion of his digression (Hughes, 186) as well as the opening of his rhapsody on reconciliation.

τὸν φόβον τοῦ κυρίου, "the fear of the Lord." That Paul is greatly influenced
by the meaning of 5:10 is seen in this phrase. He has set down this genitive,
leaving open before his readers the question of whether it is subjective or
objective. It is doubtful that the apostle is suggesting the Lord's fear (in a
subjective sense), for it would make little sense for Paul to be motivated by
the Lord's personal fear (of him? besides, what would the Lord fear?). More
likely Paul sees κυρίου as the object (Tasker, 83). That is, Paul fears the Lord.

But what is the nature of this fear? Most likely Paul is not speaking of a
"terror" of the Lord (so KJV/AV, Ambrose, Beza). The terror or the horror,

of standing before the throne of God is reserved for the ungodly (Rom 2:1–11; cf. Rev 6:15–17). That "terror" is not in Paul's mind is also seen in the importance "fear" plays in the Christian life (see below). It hardly makes sense that Paul would highlight fear, if it meant terror, for he has just pointed out the desire to be with the Lord (5:8).

In a positive vein, Paul is probably speaking in terms that go beyond the fear that leads to wisdom (Job 28:28; Eccl 12:13; Prov 9:10; Sir. 1:18). Paul is using fear in a deeper sense, that is, one that includes the dimension of hope (Bruce, 206). This is not to say that φόβος does not lead to wisdom, nor is it to say that this φόβος does not see the Lord as judge. But here Paul uses φόβος to convey the "reverential awe which the Christian should feel towards the Master whom he loves and serves and at whose hand he will receive the things done in the body" (Hughes, 186).

As will be seen, this fear is both a lodestar and a dynamic for Paul's life and service. This fear has led him to live a life marked by wisdom, in the biblical sense of the term. Paul's ministry has been in accordance with God's will (Acts 9:15, 16). He has been trustworthy, and his service to the Lord has been done so as to please him, whether in life or in death (5:9). Paul's "fear" of the Lord leads him to highlight φόβος in the Christian's life as a means to ensure a right standing before Christ (Barrett, 163). Christians should not fail to supply a right motive for their endeavors; and if they do fail, they will suffer a loss to their shame (1 Cor 3:10–15). But the fear of the Lord not only leads to the correct way in which to live, but also to the source which enables a life to be so lived.

For Paul, φοβος is important as a healthy attitude which promotes reliance on the Spirit in power (1 Cor 2:4). This is seen in Paul's use of the phrase "in fear and trembling" (Phil 2:12) which are no doubt human attitudes (see Martin, *Philippians* [NCB, 1976 = 1980] 103; cf. 1 Cor 2:3; 2 Cor 7:15; Eph 6:5). Balz, *TDNT* 9:213–14, n. 132, sees this phrase as christologically oriented, since for Paul fear is an essential aspect of faith. There is need of filial fear for it brings "out the radical and total dependence of the believer on the saving work of God" (Balz, *TDNT* 9:214). This does not mean that fear determines the life of a believer, but rather that one must continually respect God as judge, even after conversion (Rom 11:20). Yet, God's role as judge does not lead to the uncertainty of terror, but to hope, based on God's trustworthy character (see 1:18). To be sure, faith is predicated on the fear of God, the fear that respects God as judge, and simultaneously appeals to this judge, through the Spirit, for the strength to live a worthy life. If one lives a pleasing life, then, in hope and anticipation, one can look forward to standing before Christ (so Plummer, 168; see Glombitza, "Mit Furcht und Zittern," 105, 106, who sums up that fear is so essential to faith that it cannot be simply explained in terms of terror).

The result of this examination of the term for fear is important to keep in mind, for to miss the significance of this appeal is to miss the essence of Paul's defense of his integrity in 5:11–13. Having shared his sense of fear in the context of his desire to please God (5:6–10), Paul has laid the foundation of the argument based on his motives for serving the Corinthians. His life is marked by dependence on God, as well as faith in him. To the Corinthians Paul presents himself as one who has been honest and aboveboard as he has sought to love them. He has done nothing out of motives of selfish ambition, but has served them with their best interests always in mind. As Paul will suggest, his credentials consist not of external "honors," but of a life marked by dedication to God and to the people to whom he sent Paul. Here is, then, "the new standard for evaluation" of Paul's ministry (Bultmann, 147).

ἀνθρώπους πείθομεν, "we attempt to persuade men." The knowledge of the fear of the Lord leads Paul to attempt to persuade men and women. But the question before us is what lies behind Paul's understanding of persuasion (πείθειν).

One idea that Paul probably meant to convey with his use of πείθομεν, "we persuade," is that he seeks to convince the Jews and Greeks alike to accept God's salvation (but contra Bachmann, Godet, Plummer, Hughes, 186). The missionary idea in the verb is also remarked on by other writers (Windisch, Prümm). From 5:9–10, it would be hard not to see Paul as motivated to take the Gospel to the world (see Acts 18:4; 19:8, 26; 26:28; 28:23). This makes even more sense in light of Paul's thesis of reconciliation (5:18–20) in that he believes himself to be an instrument of reconciliation. In light of judgment day, Paul presses on to evangelize (Schlatter, *Paulus*, 556, 557; cf. Tasker, 83).

But also in view of Paul's defense of his motives (5:11*b*–13), it appears that he has in mind to persuade the Corinthians of the genuineness of his ministry and motives. Paul's authority as an apostle is under attack (3:1–3; 10:1–18). He has had to persuade certain members of the church of his personal integrity (1:12–14; 4:1, 2; 6:3–10; 7:2–4). In fact, much of 2 Corinthians is a defense of his personal character, so much so that Hughes writes, "This whole epistle may be described as a vindication of his genuineness" (186, 187).

Thus Paul's use of πείθομεν has a double flavor; he tries to persuade men and women that Christ is the means of salvation, and he attempts to persuade them of his purity of motive. As Denney says, "The first [nuance] is suggested by the general tenor of the passage, and the second seems to be demanded by what follows" (187).

The present tense of πείθομεν informs us that Paul's attempt at persuading is an ongoing endeavor. And if Bultmann's cue (*Probleme*, 13) is correct that πείθειν is an opponent's word, then the picture unfolds even more meaningfully. As it was in the case of the Galatians, so it may be here with the Corinthians. We read that some had accused Paul of seeking human approval through unscrupulous means (Gal 1:10, πείθω; see Burton, *Galatians* [ICC; New York: Scribner's, reprint 1970] 30). If Paul was not deflecting an opponent's barb, then it is highly possible that he would have employed παρακαλεῖν in lieu of πείθειν in 5:11 (so Bultmann). The use of the former would have hinted at a more positive meaning in Paul's statement, as an appeal to loyalty rather than an attempt to overcome opposition. (When we come to the comment on 5:12, 13, we shall see the basis for the attack against Paul. Apparently the apostle did not exhibit the outward signs of "super-apostleship" as did some on the Corinthian scene.)

Schmithals, (*Gnosticism*, 189–92), sees Paul's attack directed not at this "super-apostolic" front, but at the gnostic criticism that found fault with Paul's

nonecstatic method of communicating the Gospel. Schmithals connects 5:11*a*
with 5:13 because of the γάρ in the latter verse. By matching ἀνθρώπους πείθομεν
to εἴτε σωφρονοῦμεν and θεῷ πεφανερώμεθα to εἴτε ἐξέστημεν, he then draws a
parallelism. He further concludes that the use of φανέρωσις (1 Cor 12:7) is
congruent with πεφανερώμεθα and πεφανερῶσθαι in 5:11*b*, in terms of a "making
manifest of the Pneuma in ecstasy." This, however, does not take into account
Paul's use of φανερωθῆναι in 5:10. Moreover, Schmithals confesses that he
finds no parallel in gnostic writings to support the theory he espouses (see
Barrett, 164).

θεῷ δὲ πεφανερώμεθα, "we stand open to God." In contrast to trying to
persuade men, Paul has no question in his mind that he has "persuaded"
God. He stands open (πεφανερώμεθα) before God. The perfect tense suggests
that this is an accomplished state, thus leading him to believe in his heart
that he could come before God (5:10) and be acquitted (1 Cor 4:4). The
opportunity to receive a "good" reward is well in Paul's reach. What this
thought does is to introduce the reader into the main concern of 5:11–13,
namely, the integrity of Paul's ministry (and apostleship) before both God
and man. He well knows that a person can deceive himself, but that God
cannot be so treated, for nothing is hidden from his eyes. Paul is secure in
his position, for it is God's judgment that matters (Barrett, 164).

Paul's reasoning is this: If this ministry has received the "seal of approval"
from God (1 Cor 9:1, 2), then consequently his ministry is in God's will.
This in turn should lead the Corinthians to view his ministry as sincere,
not false, and as from God and not self-authenticated. In other words, if
Paul could stand before God in clear conscience, then what does he have
to hide or cover up (or overcome) in the eyes of the Corinthians? Furthermore,
if the fear of the Lord is well entrenched in Paul's mind and heart, why
would he do anything to jeopardize his standing before God by preaching
a false gospel before men? That God was fully aware of Paul's service (of
which God had approved) is a "brake" upon any desire to please himself
(Tasker, 83). As Paul is (and will be) transparent before God, so he is likewise
before men and women (Bruce, 206).

ἐλπίζω δὲ καὶ ἐν ταῖς συνειδήσεσιν ὑμῶν πεφανερῶσθαι, "and, I hope, also
open in your consciences." Paul continues his proposal that he is nothing
less than genuine in the eyes of the Corinthians. One might note Paul's switch
to the singular pronoun "I" in ἐλπίζω, "I hope," from the plural "we/us"
in the earlier part of 5:11. This does not have to be a source of consternation
for those exegeting this passage, but it raises some questions.

The oscillating singular and plural "I/we" may conceal a mention of the
group(s) with which Paul regularly commences (1 Cor 1:1; Phil 1:1; Col 1:1;
2 Thess 1:1; in the case of 2 Cor, Paul mentions Timothy) and concludes
(Rom 16:1; 1 Cor 16:19, 20; Eph 6:21; Phil 4:21, 22; Col 4:7–18; Titus 3:15;
for 2 Cor see "the saints" in 13:13) his letters. Possibly the plural pronouns
could include the Christian community (see 1:1*b*; 13:13), whether Paul speaks
of the local congregation or the Church as worldwide. Also, Paul may be
thinking of ministers as a whole (Plummer, 169; see Cerfaux, *Christ*, 176, n.
25, and Carrez, "Le 'nous,' " who summarizes the "we" passages as follows:
[1] the action of the entire community, as it participated in Paul's ministry;

[2] apostolic solidarity experienced by himself and team members; [3] his claim to hold a place among the apostles; [4] his personal solidarity with the Corinthian church, 486).

That we cannot identify with certainty the antecedent of the "we/us" should not disturb us in our interpretation of this (and similar) passages (for any conjecture is probably close to the truth). Rather, we should concentrate on Paul's use of "I." The singular personal pronoun may be Paul's way of emphatically pointing to his own example. This stands to reason in light of the general tenor of 5:11. By switching from "we" to "I," Paul is taking his stand in the pleading of his case. His appeal takes on a personal nature as he relates his convictions to the congregation. In short, the switch to "I" spells out the pathos of Paul's request.

That this request is one that has already been made and is continued is clear from the perfect tense of πεφανερώμεθα. Paul's target is the consciences of the Corinthians. (See *Comment* on 4:2, for Paul's commending himself to each person's conscience.) In light of his own integrity, he has not slighted the Corinthians (1:12). He has come preaching nothing other than the cross (1 Cor 2:1–5; note also in the same passage that Paul openly disregarded any claim to superiority over others on the basis of eloquence or wisdom). He has brought the Gospel to them. If, indeed, this is the case, then his opponents have no ground whatever to attack Paul or accuse him. The Corinthians should know this. (Note that 5:11 is Paul's rare use of the plural συνειδήσεσιν, "consciences," thus suggesting he is seeking the commitment of each and everyone; Plummer, 169.) If each individual would search down deep, he or she would know of Paul's truthfulness.

It appears that Paul is hoping for such an outcome. The use of ἐλπίζω, "hope," followed by a perfect infinitive (πεφανερῶσθαι; cf. 1 Cor 16:7; Phil 2:19, 23; 1 Tim 3:14) suggests the idea of "believe" (Hughes, 188) or "think" (Barrett, 164; cf. BFD § 350). Thus, it seems feasible that Paul holds some confidence that the Corinthians will reflect and then follow the correct path. They will not see Paul's actions as selfish (i.e., an attempt to overcome an unofficial, or inferior, apostleship); rather they will appear as honoring the Gospel.

One cannot say, however, that Paul presents an unbiased portrait of himself. He has placed his plea in juxtaposition to God's approval of his ministry. Hence, Paul hints, and somewhat strongly, that those who reject him and his ministry are liable to condemnation in light of 5:10. Those who profess to follow Christ are not to reject one approved of God. There is no prejudice or jealousy in Paul's conscience. What we see is a "clear" conscience, communicating the demands of God ("As a man is in his conscience, so he is before God," Hughes, 187). Since Paul must stand before God and since he has been sincere before men and women, there is no need to offer any further "credentials" as to the soundness of his call. This observation has moved Schmithals (*Gnosticism*, 188) to see 5:11*b* as a parenthetical remark aimed at overcoming the charge that Paul is attempting to commend himself again.

12. οὐ πάλιν ἑαυτοὺς συνιστάνομεν ὑμῖν, "For we are not again commending ourselves to you." Try as Paul may to avert it, this latest presentation of his activity would probably be taken as a self-commendation (see Bultmann,

Probleme 13, 14). He had sought to avoid this in 3:1 (see *Comment*), for after discussing his sincerity (1:1—2:17) Paul again has to ask, "what else is necessary from me to validate my ministry?" (3:1–3). Once more in this verse Paul shows that he is not seeking glory for himself (note use of οὐ in an emphatic role, and also he reverts to the plural personal pronoun). As in 4:2 and as will be the apostle's *apologia pro vita sua et evangelio* in 7:4, his "being on the front line" of mission service is sincere, open to each one's conscience. But we can surely have empathy with Paul's frustration at those close to his heart who were not accepting that service as well-meaning and selfless. Paul found himself in a dilemma. One horn was the realization that any self-commendation that did not point to God was wrong (1 Cor 1:31). Yet, the other horn required that Paul must do something else to convince the Corinthians of his faithfulness, that he was presenting the Gospel, as it was intended. Upon closer examination (which will follow) it does appear that Paul escaped the dilemma.

ἀλλὰ ἀφορμὴν διδόντες ὑμῖν καυχήματος ὑπὲρ ἡμῶν, "but giving you an occasion to boast on our behalf." It should come as no surprise that Paul is not concerned with his own conscience (5:11); rather he seeks to provide some justification for those who are sympathetic to his cause. Moreover, by convincing at least some of the Corinthians of the truthfulness of his Gospel, he desires that they may have strength and reason to become instruments of reconciliation.

Paul probably has in mind a "filial" relationship with his readers (6:13). Paul's relations with his people are often described in the language of "parents-children" (see B. Holmberg, *Paul and Power*, 80, who notes the variety of images that cluster around the notion of fatherhood, not least—for Paul— the right of the parent to expect obedience [1 Cor 4:21; 2 Cor 1:9; 7:15; 10:6; Phil 2:12; Philem 21] and the call to imitation [1 Cor 4:16; 10:33–11:1; 1 Thess 1:6; Phil 3:17; 4:9; Gal 4:12; see W. P. de Boer, *The Imitation of Paul* [Kampen: Kok, 1962]). Paul is giving (διδόντες; for the absolute use of the participle instead of the indicative, see Moule, *Idiom Book*, 179; Moulton, *Grammar* 3:343; also Hughes, 140, 141, n. 10, and 188, n. 5; cf. 7:5, 7; 8:19, 20, 24; 9:11; see Rom 5:11) something to the Corinthians, and this object is an ἀφορμή ("occasion," "incentive," Hughes, 188; it occurs in 11:12 and is a term set in a polemical context, Collange, *Enigmes*, 247, n. 2) qualified by καύχημα ("boasting"). Action was needed to help preserve some form of unity in the Corinthian church. Possibly Paul hoped that both his proponents (through his life) and his opponents (through the power of the Gospel) would have common ground for meeting and that he would cease to be a forum of debate and disagreement.

That Paul was putting himself forward as an example is unavoidable, but, as will be seen in 5:12c, what he appealed to was not himself but the Gospel. His role was to be a faithful and true worker for the Gospel (Barrett, 165). If all could see the power of God at work in his life and ministry, then the Gospel, not Paul, would be the thing actually commended.

ἵνα ἔχητε πρός, "so that you may have something to set against." In this purpose (or result) clause (note ἵνα, "so that": for ἔχειν, see Acts 4:14; 25:26; Titus 2:8), Paul explains why he is giving the Corinthians an occasion to boast. The purpose of this gift is that the "pro-Pauline" Corinthians will have a defense against Paul's opponents. Building on the assumption that he views the Corinthians as knowing that he is faithful, Paul marches onward.

Much has been made about the grammatical object of ἔχητε ("may have [something]," note ἔχητε is subjunctive, following ἵνα). Some supply τι or λέγειν τι or καύχημα ("something to boast against those," so Hodge; cf. Bultmann, 150) or even ἀφορμήν ("a resource at hand," so Plummer, 170; cf. καύχημα/ἔχειν in Rom 4:2; Gal 6:4, and ἀφορμήν/λάβειν in Rom 7:8, 11). Better yet is Hughes's suggestion (188, 189) that Paul is not so much giving the Corinthians something new as he is reminding them of what they already know. Through their personal acquaintance with Paul and the testimony of their own consciences, the Corinthians do have reasons to set before those who attack him and, in so doing, attack the Gospel. What Paul stands for is a source of truth (13:8), which is "both a starting point for an operation and the resources with which an operation can be launched" (Tasker, 84; cf. Rom 4:2; 7:11; 1 Tim 5:14). The basis of this operation—the demonstration of the Gospel through the successful defense of Paul's ministry—is described in the remainder of 5:12.

τοὺς ἐν προσώπῳ καυχωμένους καὶ μὴ ἐν καρδίᾳ, "those who boast of what is seen and not of what is in the heart." Apparently Paul is not the only one "boasting." His opponents—those mentioned in the stern letter (Filson, 333)—also boast. But Paul is quick to point out the different sources of the two acts of boasting. (The verb καυχᾶσθαι, "to boast," is more often used of Paul's own attitude, with an interesting result when we take note of its occurrence. The verb is found 59 times in the NT, with Paul's usage totaling 55. Of these, 29 references are in our epistle, especially in chaps. 10–13 [Collange, *Enigmes*, 247, n. 2].) Those set against Paul have "super" credentials which they use to lord it over the Corinthians on the ground of Paul's inferiority. Among the possibilities for ridicule are (a) Paul's lack of personal knowledge of Jesus (Strachan, 106; cf. 5:16), (b) his poor relationship with the Jerusalem church (the confrontation reported in Gal 2:11–16 shows how Paul may have been defeated at the hands of the Jewish Christians at Antioch: see Dunn, "The Incident"; Stuhlmacher, "Das paulinische Evangelium," esp. 175–78; and *Introduction*, pp. lvi, lvii), (c) his lack of a forceful personality (10:10), (d) his dependence on others (10:16), (e) his inferior oratory skills (11:6), and (f) the fact that his grounds for boasting are "negative" accomplishments (11:21–31; see Hodge, 131). For those who did not have these "flaws," their place of pride was in the πρόσωπον, similar in meaning to εἶδος (5:7), hence the idea of things seen, "external things" (BGD, 721). This is perhaps the only place in our letter where the circumcision controversy conceivably peeps through (cf. Rom 2:25–29); but this is dubious (Phil 3:3–5), though Bultmann suggestively makes ἐν προσώπῳ equivalent to κατὰ σάρκα (cf. 10:2, 3).

What Paul wishes to convey is that his concern is not with himself but with God and his people, in this case, the Corinthians. Those who glory in the outward speak of their inward inclinations (Matt 12:34b). Paul is saying that he has done nothing save what was in his heart (ἐν καρδίᾳ, the center and source of the entire inner life, BGD, 403, 404; cf. Gal 2:6). An apostle does not pride himself on external qualifications (Calvin). A true minister, if he must glory in appearance, will do so in weakness and not in strength

(Denney, 189–90). Here is a nodal point in Paul's running debate with the Corinthians, centered on the *Evidenzproblem,* as Betz calls it (*Der Apostel Paulus,* 133; see later pp. 409, 473, 477), the issue of what credentials for apostolic ministry are valid.

The one who follows the prescription of Paul's opponents is vulnerable to the temptations of self-aggrandizement, at the expense of those who receive his ministry. But Paul has come in a clear conscience, motivated by the fear of the Lord (5:11) to offer a "pure" ministry to the Corinthians. As he allows the Gospel to operate in and through his life, Paul, by using himself as an example, commends the Gospel to all. The Corinthians have taken the offensive (Denney, 188) against those who would thwart the Gospel (by attacking Paul). They can boast on Paul's behalf, for the power of God has shone through in weakness (12:9). Paul was not out to impress or to be served, but to be true to his calling, which was grounded in the Gospel (cf. 1 Thess 2:4–8; also Acts 20:24; 26:19). Hence, if the Corinthians would simply remember Paul's example, then he could escape the dilemma mentioned earlier, for he had to do nothing else to prove his integrity. This is seen in greater detail in 5:13.

13. εἴτε γὰρ ἐξέστημεν, θεῷ. εἴτε σωφρονοῦμεν, ὑμῖν, "For if we are out of our minds, it is for God; if we are of sound mind, it is for you." Paul continues his rejoinder against those who question his sincerity of motive. (Paul did not seek to be a "hero" or superman; Fahy, "St. Paul's 'Boasting,' " 216.) On the surface, it comes into view that no matter the state of Paul's mind or disposition, he does nothing for himself; all is done for God and the Corinthians. But under the surface is the mystery of what he means by ἐξίστασθαι, "to be out of one's mind." The total understanding of this passage may be beyond our grasp.

The meaning of ἐξιστάναι, found here in contradistinction (Hughes, 190) to σωφρονεῖν (of sound mind; "mental health," BGD, 802), may denote a type of mental derangement (at least in the eyes of Paul's opponents, Plummer, 172). 5:13 is the only time the verb is used in the epistle, and indeed in the Pauline corpus. Usually in the rest of the NT this verb is translated "to be amazed" (Matt 12:23; Mark 2:12; Luke 8:56; Acts 2:7, 12; 8:13; 9:21; 10:45; 12:16; see LXX of Exod 19:18; Ruth 3:8 where the verb from חָרַד, hārad ["to tremble"], is rendered ἐξέστη; see Luck, *TDNT* 7:1102). Also, the related noun ἔκστασις ("ecstasy") either means "amazement" (Mark 5:42; 16:8; Luke 5:26; Acts 3:10) or is used to describe an event in which someone is "not in his right mind" because of a vision or trance (Acts 10:10; 11:5; 22:17). Moreover, one could ask why Paul does not use μανία ("insanity") or μαίνομαι ("to be insane"; see Plato, *Phaedrus* 244), terms used when he was before Festus (Acts 26:24, 25), to describe his "madness." Hence, this line of reasoning leads us to doubt seriously that Paul was speaking of "mental illness," though his opponents possibly saw his fanaticism (11:1, 16–32) as "religious mania" (Hughes, 191, 192; Strachan, 106; Lietzmann; and Wendland think Paul's opponents viewed him as stricken with megalomania exhibited in trances, since he felt his work marked an epoch in *Heilsgeschichte*).

More likely, Paul describes here ecstatic experiences when he speaks of "being out" of his mind toward God (Dunn, *Jesus and the Spirit*, 215, 216). If θεῷ ("to God") is a dative of reference, then probably ἐξιστάναι *could* refer to insanity. But surely ὑμῖν ("to you") is a dative of advantage, and it is highly unlikely that Paul would not use both datives in the same way (Tasker, 85, Bultmann, 151). If θεῷ is then also a dative of advantage, this rules out insanity as a meaning for ἐξίστασθαι, for how would Paul's "mental illness" benefit God? Rather, this verb emphasizes "stress of great spiritual emotion" (Tasker, 84), or better, elation.

The ecstatic experience(s) that Paul here refers to might be speaking in tongues (1 Cor 14:18; Denney, 192) or experiences that accompanied the vision described in 2 Cor 12:7 (Barrett, 166). At first glance the aorist suggests a one-time event in Paul's life (Allo), such as the Damascus event or his "angry" (sorrowful) visit (Bachmann) or the vision of 12:7. But this aorist also could be a timeless one, betraying his custom (Plummer, 172; Moulton, *Grammar* 1:134). Having presented himself continually to the Corinthians in reasoned speech and relying on clear preaching (note perfect tenses in 5:11) Paul could be suggesting an ongoing experience with his use of ἐξιστάναι. (In the Greek the aorist "extended its province at the expense of the perfect," so Robertson, *Grammar*, 843). This falls in line with the continuous tense (present) of σωφρονοῦμεν, so the second verb of 5:13 may carry along the first. Also Barrett's suggestion (167) that σωφρονεῖν has been associated too closely with speech and instruction, and not enough with the wider context of rationality (encompassing more than speech and instruction) provides a basis on which to affirm the contradistinction between ἐξιστάναι and σωφρονεῖν. That is, these two verbs remain opposites, not because they speak of insanity and sanity respectively, but refer to ecstatic and rational behavior (so Bultmann, followed by Kümmel; Güttgemanns, *Der leidende Apostel*, 301; Georgi, *Die Gegner*, 196). Thus, Paul is dividing into categories his behavior toward God, namely, ecstatic; and toward the Corinthians, namely, rational and controlled. (The people could then boast of having an apostle who does both well, so Schlatter, *Paulus*, 557, 558; cf. Lietzmann, 124.)

This, then, is the closest we can come to getting underneath the surface to the meaning of this verse. At most, we can say that, whether Paul speaks of his exceptional behavior or his ordinary, all of his actions are directed toward someone else (Plummer, 173). If he had visionary experiences—on which his opponents prided themselves—they were moments of intimacy between God and himself, and not to be paraded as flamboyant claims. If he speaks in a rational manner, it is no less then that his apostolic ministry carries the hallmark of genuine value, since this "sober" address serves to promote the good of the Corinthians who "may receive more fully [than by what occurs in an ecstasy] the benefits of his apostolate" (Fallon, 50). This tightens up and summarizes his plea of 5:11, 12. He has done nothing to push himself forward except to be a minister of the Gospel; rather he is intent on seeking to please God and to serve his fellows (see Hodge, 132).

14. ἡ γὰρ ἀγάπη τοῦ Χριστοῦ συνέχει ἡμᾶς, "For the love of Christ compels us." This verse marks an end to Paul's explicit proof that he is not commending himself, and the beginning of his manifesto on reconciliation (though one can see that the force behind his selflessness is founded on Christ's love).

Before us are two questions that relate to the understanding of this clause: (1) what type of genitive is τοῦ Χριστοῦ ("the love *of Christ*"), and (2) what is the meaning of συνέχει?

With regard to the first question, ἡ ἀγάπη τοῦ Χριστοῦ could be a subjective genitive (Christ's love for us) or an objective genitive (our love for Christ). The consensus is that it is the former. (See Bultmann, *Theology* 1:304–5; Denney, 193; Godet, 179; Hodge, 133; Plummer, 173; see too Robertson, *Grammar*, 499, though he admits that the genitive in 5:14 lends itself to either point of view [cf. Gal 2:20; Rom 8:35–39]. Also Spicq, "L'éntreinte," 124, is correct to point out that Christ's love for Paul is reason for Paul's love for Christ. Spicq [132] also suggests that the idea of a subjective/objective genitive is the wrong emphasis, rather it should be ἀγάπη–συνέχει–κρίναντας. These three terms demonstrate the zeal of Paul for the Gentiles, as well as the heroism of the early church, especially the mystery of the cross. That is, the believer appreciates the love in Christ, learned in suffering. Also see Héring, 41, 42. For ἀγάπη used with an objective genitive, see 2 Thess 2:10; Luke 11:42; Lietzmann, 124, sees a mystical double meaning.) This reasoning falls in line with what follows, in that Paul portrays what Christ has done for the sinner (cf. Barrett, 167; see Rom 5:8).

Our second question centers on the meaning of συνέχει (from συνέχειν, "hold in one's grip"). In only one other passage do we find Paul using συνέχειν (Phil 1:23; G. F. Hawthorne, *Philippians*, WBC [1983] 43, 47, takes it to mean that Paul's action is constrained, in this case by two conflicting desires; see Köster, *TDNT* 7:882–85). This idea of "to compel," or "to control," is supported by many (RSV, Barrett, 168; BGD, 789, "urge"; Hodge, 133; also see Lietzmann, 124, "exert domination"; NEB, "leaves us no choice"). The weakened sense of "restraining from self-seeking" (Plummer, 173; Strachan, 107), as though to provide a reason for not boasting (so Bultmann, 152), does not do justice to Paul's position (see below). Schlatter is closer to the true idea when he sees Paul as explaining why he has so much love in his heart for the Corinthians (*Paulus*, 558, 559). Furnish's understanding (*Theology*, 167) of συνέχειν as signifying "sustaining" is partially correct, but once again the context demands a more nuanced reading. If ἡ ἀγάπη τοῦ Χριστοῦ is a subjective genitive, then Paul is shut in as between two walls by Christ's love for him. Because of this love, Paul has one purpose—selfless devotion to God and his fellow human beings (as summed up in 5:13). "God has the first word. He establishes the relationship. This is laid down once and for all in Rom. 8. His resolve, election and calling are decisive [Rom 11:29]. From Him proceeds everything that may be called ἀγάπη" (so Stauffer, *TDNT* 1:50).

The idea behind συνέχειν is deeper than a "moral influence" of the love of Christ, acting so as to restrain one's behavior in terms of boasting. In 5:14, Paul is not looking back to 5:11–13 (though he builds on 5:13) as much as he is looking forward to his theme of reconciliation. The love of Christ compels ("allows," Hendry, "ἡ ἀγάπη," 82) us to be included in Christ and his mission. The point is that "compels" signifies a positive force. Paul cannot but follow his plan of ministry because it is God's plan. What Christ has done for Paul is the basis of the apostle's life. (This compelling power of Christ's love is clearly seen in Phil 1:21; 3:7–11. "It is the logic which demands his [Paul's] willingness to suffer the loss of all things for Christ's sake; and it is the reason for his overmastering ambition to win Christ, to be found in Christ, and to know Christ," Hughes, 193.)

κρίναντας τοῦτο, "since we have concluded." Remembering that Paul is moving on in his argument and focusing on Christ's love, we may remark that this small clause is an important springboard into the rest of 5:14, 15. The aorist participle κρίναντας conveys the idea that Paul has decided upon something (τοῦτο) (See BGD, 451). This "something," which is spelled out in 5:14–15, is probably based on a judgment formed in the past, at or soon after his Damascus road experience (Hughes, 193, n. 22). We should not let the aorist tense rule out any period of time for contemplation. Possibly Paul is including in his writing a period of reflection between conversion and missionary activity (Gal 1:17, 18; so Plummer, 174), a time of deliberation and thought (Otis, "Exposition," 558). This last point helps to paint a picture of a Paul who was sure, even after the test of time, that Christ's love, exhibited so tenderly in his passion, was the dominating force in his life. (For Hughes, 193, Paul's conclusion is his "rational ground of his security in Christ.")

ὅτι εἷς ὑπὲρ πάντων ἀπέθανεν, "that one died for all." With the remainder of 5:14, 15, Paul lays the foundation for his doctrine of reconciliation. The bedrock of this conviction is Paul's evaluation of Jesus' death, its hope for the Christian, as well as its call to service. A solid understanding of 5:14, 15 will shore up Paul's argument about his motive for preaching. In addition this understanding will set the stage for 5:16–20.

In short, 5:14, 15 are vv that speak of representation and renewal (Martin, *Reconciliation*, 97–101). Two areas of concern in our present clause have to do with the words ὑπέρ and πάντων. The clause begins by defining the content of what Paul concluded in the preceding clause; that a summary is to follow is signaled by the recitative conjunction ὅτι, "that." What he concluded is that one (εἷς), namely, Christ, died for all. The aorist ἀπέθανεν (cf. Rom 6:10, 14:9) points back to and treats the crucifixion as a historical event. (This is further seen in the pre-Pauline tradition found in 1 Cor 15:3.) But what does Paul mean by ὑπέρ (for)? Does he mean "for" in the sense of "instead of" (substitution) or in the sense of "for the benefit of"? Or do the two meanings overlap?

These last questions center on whether or not ὑπέρ carries with it the same force as ἀντί (see Moulton, *Grammar* 3:258), with respect to substitution (see Mark 10:45; Matt 20:28; 1 Tim 2:6). Some writers do not see ὑπέρ as on a par lexically with ἀντί; for example, Meyer, 129, 130, and Filson, 334, hold ὑπέρ to carry a weak force and maintain that the preposition means "on their behalf and for their good." While "instead of" includes the concept of "for the benefit of," the converse is not necessarily true. (Thus, Filson's position that Christ's death, though mainly confirming the idea of "for the benefit of," also contains an element of substitution, is highly suspect.) The context of our verse demands that ὑπέρ carry the force of "instead of" (so Collange, *Enigmes*, 254, citing Delling, "Der Tod Jesu in der Verkündigung des Paulus," *Apophoreta* [FS E. Haenchen; Berlin: Töpelmann, 1964] 85–96)." "Therefore, all have died," the extension of ὅτι εἷς ὑπὲρ πάντων ἀπέθανεν, implies that ὑπέρ is used with substitutionary force, otherwise this extension cannot be valid (so Hughes, 193 and Bultmann, 152, 153, rendering *"an Stelle von"* rather than *zugunsten von*). That is, this extension cannot be a true conclusion unless Christ died as a proxy for all (how could all have died except that Jesus' death was a substitution for all?). Moreover, ὑπέρ is used with substitutionary force in other texts, such as 5:20; Philem 13; Eph 6:20; also see 8:23, cf. Moulton, *Grammar* 1:105. In 1 Tim 2:6 ἀντί and ὑπέρ are used in association with each other and this association suggests substitutionary force. (See Hughes 193, 194, n. 24; also cf. Euripides, *Alcestis*, 682, 690, 700, 701, for repeated use of ὑπέρ with substitutionary meaning. The prefix and preposition occur in Pheres' speech in response to Admetus' plea that the old man should have been willing to die for him [ὑπερθνῄσκειν] and so spare young Alcestis, i.e., to take his place and die in his stead, which Alcestis has done.) That much is clear. But it remains to be discussed whether the grammatical point can prove a theological argument. For some older writers it may and can. Others are not so sure that "substitute" is the best term in the theological vocabulary to denote Christ's saving action for sinners. Let us review the options.

To take ὑπέρ as meaning anything less than "instead of" is "to destroy the mainspring of the Apostle's argument" (Hughes, 193). Hence, it appears that ὑπέρ carries the force of substitution (so Robertson, *Grammar* 631, 632; Hodge, 135; Denney, *Death,* 83–85; Strachan, 107; see Moule, *Idiom Book,* 64, 65). As Tasker, 86, writes, "Christ's death was the death of all, in the sense that He died the death they should have died; the penalty of their sins was borne by Him [1 Cor 15:3; 2 Cor 5:20]; He died in their place." (See Athanasius, *De Incarn.* 8.)

Barrett assumes (168, 169) a moderate stance toward the meaning of ὑπέρ πάντων, for he insists that neither substitution nor representation is "exactly" what Paul had in mind. Rather, he seems to infer that the death of Christ opened the way to renewal (5:15). While we agree this is the result of Christ's death, it appears that Barrett has unwittingly omitted an important function of Jesus' death. Dunn, "Paul's Understanding," especially 140, 141, also wishes to question whether substitution is the most appropriate word to use in this context, and he argues strongly for "representation" as conveying more the idea of Christ's acting on his people's behalf. The latter term avoids, in his view, the one-sidedness and the narrowness that attaches to "substitution."

A break through the impasse may be possible if we give full weight to the argument of K. Romaniuk, "L'origine des formules pauliniennes, 'le Christ s'est livré pour nous.'" He speaks of the formulation "Christ was delivered up 'for us'" as having a setting in baptism; and with Collange, *Enigmes,* 255, we should look to Rom 6:1–14 as the best parallel text to illumine our v. Paul is consciously recalling the baptismal occasion, with his participle κρίναντας, coupled with a recitative ὅτι, and harking back to his proclamation that "Christ died" for those who are baptized in his name. The death he died on the cross—his atoning act—now becomes the place where they too find release from their guilty past and the entrance to a new life (Gollwitzer, "Hinfort," 5). They are "baptized into his death," meaning that they avail themselves of the benefits of his passion since he did for them what they could never do for themselves (hence, substitution), and they share in the blessings his death on their behalf has brought (hence, representation). So Christ is their corporate representative who acted both in their name and in their place. "Proxy" is perhaps the preferred term since it speaks of one authorized to act for others, yet one who has intimate connections with both parties. It thus avoids the chief objection to the term "substitute," namely, that Christ *could* be introduced as an extraneous third party mediating between God and man, and having only a loose attachment to both sides. "Representative" may be too weak, since what Christ did in our name is equally done in a unique fashion. Because we were powerless to save ourselves, he took our sin and made it his own.

Related to the meaning of ὑπέρ is the adjective πάντες, "all." For whom did Christ die, all of mankind or the ones who accept Christ? In one sense the answer is both. That the death of Christ was a benefit for all humankind is an *a priori* of theology (Barrett, 168). But as will be seen below, πάντων (in 5:14d and 5:15) can speak only of those who have accepted the message of reconciliation (Otis, 559). Filson is correct when he writes, "The word 'all' expresses the fact that the benefit becomes effective only through faith" (334, 335).

ἄρα οἱ πάντες ἀπέθανον, "Therefore, all died." In the preceding discussion it was seen that Paul viewed Jesus' death in traditional terms of both "substitution" and "representation"; in this sentence the emphasis falls more on the latter aspect. But the background of a death ὑπέρ πάντων by the יהוה עבד, ᶜebed Yahweh (the servant of God), in Isaiah 53 means that we should not make the distinction too artificial. If the v reflects missionary preaching (Popkes, *Christus Traditus*, 255 ff.) and has in view Christ's role as fulfilling the ᶜebed Yahweh destiny as his people's mediator and deliverer, who "bore their guilt" (Isa 53:5, 10, 11) as their proxy, then the "all" who benefit are clearly the people of God, and the servant Christ both acted *for* them and *in their place*. See O. Cullmann, *Christology*, 51–82; H.-R. Weber, *The Cross: Tradition and Interpretation*, tr. E. Jessett (Grand Rapids: Eerdmans/London: SPCK, 1978) 50–63, on the place of Isaiah 53 in early soteriology.

"All died" (ἀπέθανον, aorist) signifies those who accept Jesus. But is this a physical death? Although Paul surely knew the threat of death for the Christian (1:9), it makes little sense to speak of it here because those still alive, reading Paul's words, would not as yet have experienced death. Rather, Paul is speaking of the "symbolic" death that Christians die to self based on Christ's death to sin (Barrett, 169). As we see in Rom 5:12–19, the actions of both Adam and Christ had unusual consequences (Hughes, 195; see Col 2:20, 3:3 for ἀπεθάνετε, and Rom 6:1–11; cf. Kümmel, *Theology*, 214, 215). Adam represents wayward man, living for himself; Jesus is the progenitor of a new race, the representative of the new humanity. Those coming to Christ die to the old life and rise to the new (Rom 6:1–11; see Martin, *Worship*, 104, 105, for the issue of what is meant by the symbolism of "baptism into Christ," based on Old Testament prophetic action). Jesus' dying for all (i.e., his people) meets the demands of God's plan (Rom. 5:6, 8); our dying for him is our only possibility for new life in sanctification (Rom 6:8; see Hughes, 195, 196; cf. Gal 2:20).

Thus, Paul has built his case logically. He does nothing out of selfishness. As an example of how this is possible, Paul cites what Jesus has done. Volun-

tarily Christ laid down his life, both in terms of physical life and of his willingness to serve God's purpose. Because of this Paul is compelled to do likewise.
Paul's "selfless" attitude toward the Corinthians is a result of Christ's love
for him. Christ's death is both a necessary and sufficient impetus for him
not to boast in himself and yet, at the same time, to seek to be approved
of God.

15. καὶ ὑπὲρ πάντων ἀπέθανεν, "And he died for all." This sentence is simply
a rehearsal of his opening premise of 5:14. Paul, however, here brings out
a third part of a triad, namely, moral renewal.

ἵνα οἱ ζῶντες μηκέτι ἑαυτοῖς ζῶσιν, "that those who are living might no longer
live for themselves." Those who have died (5:14d) have "become free for a
new life" (Windisch, 182). There is the power of renewal in Jesus' death.
(Probably Paul wanted his readers to see his own life as an example of this
renewal; hence, his ministry is one of purity.) Note the use of ἵνα, "that,"
but to express purpose rather than result.

The living (οἱ ζῶντες, present participle) no longer (μηκέτι) live (ζῶσιν,
subjunctive) to themselves (as did Paul's opponents). Plummer, 175, on the
basis of 4:17, sees the οἱ ζῶντες as referring only to those who are physically
alive. But this appears untenable, for it is not consistent with our understanding of death, as given in 5:14d. Rather, the οἱ ζῶντες appears as those who
are spiritually alive as people, freed from the bondage of sin. He who accepts
the atonement of Christ puts to death his "unregenerate life [Gen 2:7; Rom
6:23], in which the old sinful self was regarded as the proper centre of reference, and begets a new life which is centred upon Another" (Tasker, 86).
(See again Paul's teaching on baptism and death in Rom 6:1–11 referred to
above; R. Tannehill's point, *Dying and Rising*, 70, 71, expounding the cross
as the eschatological event which gives meaning to baptism is well taken.)

ἀλλὰ τῷ ὑπὲρ αὐτῶν ἀποθανόντι καὶ ἐγερθέντι, "but for the one who died
for them and was raised." The antithesis of living for self is living for the
one who died for all. We note that ἀποθανόντι is an aorist participle and
active, suggesting not only a historical fact, but that Jesus voluntarily laid
down his life; the aorist participle ἐγερθέντι (from ἐγείρειν) suggests also the
historical fact of the resurrection ("a dead saviour is a contradiction in terms,"
Hughes, 196). But we also note that ἐγερθέντι is passive, thus highlighting
God's action in the resurrection (cf. Rom 1:4 which interprets the Easter
event as a divine vindication of who Jesus is).

The death and resurrection of Jesus make it possible to communicate the
new life to those who have died (5:14d) and are now living (5:15a) (see
Rom 4:25 which brings together, in a cited soteriological tag, the results of
Christ's death and rising: see Martin, *Reconciliation*, 140). There is some question as to whether the construction of 5:15b suggests both participles are
to be connected with τῷ ὑπὲρ αὐτῶν. If the second participle is not related
to τῷ ὑπὲρ αὐτῶν, then the flow of the sentence is broken, leaving us with a
translation "he died for them and rose" (for his own benefit). This breaks
up the logic of Paul's argument. If Jesus has not risen for the benefit of
"them," then it seems unlikely that the concept of a "renewed" life would
be on Paul's mind. More natural is the suggestion to associate both participles
with τῷ ὑπὲρ αὐτῶν and thus preserve the apostle's argument (see Plummer,
175).

Thus Paul has completed his triad—substitution, representation, and renewal. This argument adroitly summarizes Paul's indication that the "constraining love" of Christ compels him to live a life of renewal as one honoring God through an honest portrayal of the Gospel, and a sincere ministry. This has been made possible by the work of Christ, something that propels Paul onward. Moreover, Paul's conclusion focuses on the meaning of Christian and apostolic existence, and offers a "measuring rod" for a true evaluation of his ministry (Bultmann, 154).

Explanation

In the verses of this section, Paul has described the desired outcome for one who fears the Lord. From this fear, he is summoned to perform his ministry in light of God's requirement that all Christians stand before his Son in judgment. What Paul has in view is the paradigm that pervades the NT. This paradigm is that God's love, demonstrated in Christ's death and resurrection, compels a Christian to live a life dedicated wholly to God. In turn, this motive power touches other Christians, for it calls us to reflect God's love by exhibiting total dedication to fellow Christians.

But unfortunately, Paul has not been accepted as such an apostle. Instead, because he exemplified God's power through weakness, his credentials as a minister of the Gospel are in doubt. Desiring a "powerful" leader and preacher, some of the church at Corinth have attacked Paul as being inferior. The underlying premise is that a strong preacher would not have his life characterized by weakness and tribulation. This, however, is the secret of Paul's stand.

Reminding the Corinthians that Jesus died for all his people, Paul points out that this leads the same people to die also. Not a physical death, but a spiritual one, in the sense of crucifying self is in Paul's sights. By accepting such a call to "Come and die" (Bonhoeffer), the Christian is vulnerable to persecution. But it is in just such a demeanor that the Christian allows God's power to be seen. Moreover, the one who dies to himself should—by that token—not to be accused by others of a self-seeking ministry. Needless to say, this was not to be so in the case of Paul (as it has not been in the case of many saints down through church history).

Regardless of the opinion of others, Paul holds to his position of "boasting in the Gospel." Paul wishes his critics, as well as his supporters, to see his life-in-weakness as a result of God's work. "Fear of the Lord" and "living for Jesus" go hand in hand. The power of God is within the grasp of those who accept this station; the warning against misusing his investment is our motivation to use this "power" wisely, a paradox Paul elaborates in 12:9, 10; 13:1–4, on which see David A. Black, *Paul, Apostle of Weakness:* "Only when Paul is 'weak'—persecuted, insulted, humiliated, poor, sick, despised, unloved by his own converts [and we may add, isolated from his erstwhile confrères; see *Introduction,* p. lviii]—(is it) that God's might comes into view and Paul can claim 'I am strong' " (151). "Death to self and life for God" is the motto of Paul in this passage. T. W. Manson's words ring true:

The death of Christ is something in which all his followers have a share; and equally they share in his risen life, which means that they can no longer live their old selfish life but must live for him who inaugurated the new life for them by dying and rising again ("2 Cor 2:14–17," 156).

G. Living in the New Age (5:16–21)

Bibliography

Bouttier, M. *En Christ.* Etude d'exégèse et de théologie pauliniennes. 1962. **Brauch, M. T.** "Perspectives in 'God's Righteousness' in Recent German Discussion." In **Sanders, E. P.** *Paul and Palestinian Judaism,* 523–35. London: SCM/Philadelphia: Fortress Press, 1977. **Bultmann, R.** *Theology of the New Testament.* Tr. K. Grobel. Vol. 1. London: SCM, 1952. 270–84. **Cambier, J.** "Connaissance charnelle et spirituelle du Christ dans 2 Cor. 5:16," in *Littérature et théologie pauliniennes.* Recherches bibliques v, 72–92. Bruges: Desclée de Brouwer 1960. **Collange, J.-F.** *Enigmes de . . . Corinthiens.* 258–80. **Conzelmann, H.** *An Outline of the Theology of the New Testament.* Tr. J. Bowden. London: SCM, 1969. **Dunn, J. D. G.** "Paul's Understanding of the Death of Jesus." In *Reconciliation and Hope,* ed. R. Banks, 125–44. Grand Rapids: Eerdmans/Exeter: Paternoster, 1974. **Dupont, J.** *La réconciliation dans la théologie de saint Paul.* Paris/Bruges: Descleé de Brouwer, Publications Universitaires de Louvain, 1953. ———. *Gnosis: La connaissance religieuse dans les épîtres de St. Paul.* Louvain/Paris: Gabalda, 1949. **Fitzmyer, J. A.** "Reconciliation in Pauline Theology." Chap. 7 in *To Advance the Gospel.* New York: Crossroad, 1981. **Fraser, J. W.** "Paul's Knowledge of Jesus: II Corinthians V. 16 Once More." *NTS* 17 (1970–71) 293–313. **Goppelt, L.** *Christologie und Ethik.* Göttingen: Vandenhoeck & Ruprecht, 1968. 147–64. **Hainz, J.** *Ekklesia.* 272–80. **Hanson, A. T.** *Studies in Paul's Technique and Theology.* Grand Rapids: Wm. B. Eerdmans, 1974. 72, 73. **Hofius, O.** "Erwägungen zur Gestalt und Herkunft des paulinischen Versöhnsgedankens." *ZNW* 77 (1980) 18–99. **Johnson, H.** *The Humanity of the Saviour.* London: Epworth, 1962. 101–104. **Käsemann, E.** *Perspectives on Paul.* Tr. M. Kohl. ET. London: SCM/Philadelphia: Fortress Press, 1971. 32–59. ———. "Some Thoughts on the Theme 'The Doctrine of Reconciliation in the New Testament.'" In *The Future of our Religious Past,* ed. J. M. Robinson. London: SCM/New York: Harper and Row, 1971. ———. "The Righteousness of God in Paul." In *New Testament Questions of Today,* tr. W. J. Montague. London: SCM/Philadelphia: Fortress Press, 1969. **Kertelge, K.** *'Rechtfertigung' bei Paulus. Studien zur Struktur and zum Bedeutungsgehalt des paulinischen Rechtfertigungsbegriff.* Neutestamentlichen Abhandl. 3 Münster; Aschendorff, 1966. 99–107. **Lohse, E.** "Das Amt, das die Versöhnung predigt." In *Rechtfertigung,* FS E. Käsemann, ed. J. Friedrich, W. Poehlmann, P. Stuhlmacher, 339–49. Tübingen: J. C. B. Mohr, 1976. **Lyonnet, S. and Sabourin, L.** *Sin, Redemption and Sacrifice. A Biblical and Patristic Study.* Rome: Pontifical Biblical Institute, 1970. **Marshall, I. H.** "The Meaning of Reconciliation." In *Unity and Diversity in New Testament Theology: Essays in Honor of George E. Ladd,* ed. R. A. Guelich, 117–32. Grand Rapids: Wm. B. Eerdmans, 1978. **Martin, R. P.** *Reconciliation. A Study of Paul's Theology.* London: Marshall, Morgan & Scott/Atlanta: John Knox, 1981. 90–110. **Martyn, J. L.** "Epistemology at the Turn of the Ages: 2 Corinthians 5:16." In *Christian History and Interpretation. Studies Presented to John Knox,* ed. W. R. Farmer et al., 269–87. Cambridge: University Press, 1967. **McDonald, J. I. H.** "Paul and the Preaching Ministry." *JSNT* 17 (1983) 35–50. **Michel, O.** " 'Erkannen dem Fleisch nach' (II Kor 5, 16)." *EvT* 14 (1954) 22–29. **Reumann, J.** (with Fitzmyer, J. A., and Quinn, J.). *Righteousness in the New Testament.* Philadelphia:

Fortress Press, 1982. **Rey, B.** "L'homme nouveau d'après St. Paul." *RScPhTh* (1965) 161–95. **Sabourin, L.** "Note sur 2 Cor. 5, 21: Le Christ fait péché." *Sciences ecclésiastiques* 11 (1959) 419–24. **Schlier, H.** "La notion paulinienne de la Parole de Dieu." In *Littérature et théologie pauliniennes* (1960) 127–41. **Stanton, G. N.** *Jesus of Nazareth in New Testament Preaching.* SNTSMS 27. Cambridge: University Press, 1974. 88–93. **Stuhlmacher, P.** "Erwägungen zum ontologischen Charakter der καινὴ κτίσις bei Paulus." *EvT* 27 (1967) 1–35. ———. *Gerichtigkeit Gottes bei Paulus.* FRLANT 87. Göttingen: Vandenhoeck & Ruprecht, 1965. ———. "Jesus als Versöhner." In *Jesus Christus in Historie und Theologie,* FS H. Conzelmann. ed. G. Strecker. Tübingen: Mohr, 1975. **Tannehill, R. C.** *Dying and Rising with Christ: A Study in Pauline Theology.* BZNW 32. Berlin: Töpelmann, 1967. **Thrall, M. E.** "Salvation Proclaimed: V. 2 Corinthians 5:18–21." *ExpTim* 93 (1982) 227–32. **Thüsing, W.** "Rechtfertigungsgedanke und Christologie in den Korintherbriefen." In *Neues Testament und Kirche,* FS R. Schnackenburg, ed. J. Gnilka, 301–24. Freiburg/Basel/Wien: Herder, 1974. **Williams, A. T.** "Reconciliation with God." *ExpTim* 32 (1919–20) 280–82. **Ziesler, J. A.** *The Meaning of Righteousness in Paul.* SNTSMS 20. Cambridge: University Press, 1972. 158–65.

Translation

[16] *Therefore from now we judge no one from an outward point of view. Though [a] we may have judged Christ from such a viewpoint, now we do so no longer.* [17] *So, if anyone comes to be in Christ, there is a new creation; the old order has gone, to be replaced by the new [in every way [b]].* [18] *And this new order in all respects is God's doing, who reconciled us to himself through Christ and has given us the ministry of reconciliation.* [19] *Its terms are that in Christ God was reconciling the world to himself, not charging humankind's offenses against them. And he has entrusted us with the message [c] of reconciliation.* [20] *We are then ambassadors for Christ, with God making his plea through us. We implore you, in Christ's behalf, Be reconciled to God!* [21] *God appointed him (who was without any acquaintance with sin) to be a sin-offering on our behalf, that in him we might become the righteousness of God.*

Notes

[a] εἰ καί, "though" is read by P[46] B ℵ* D*. The added δέ interposed between εἰ and καί in the majority of MSS changes the meaning little, but the reverse order to καὶ εἰ, "even if," in G and vg and the reading εἰ δέ, "but if," in K do change the emphasis (Barrett; but Bultmann pronounces K's reading "impossible"). Collange (262) takes the καί in a comparative sense, with a comma between εἰ and καί. He renders, "In the same way, if we knew Christ according to the flesh, we now know him so no longer," appealing to BDF § 453.1.

[b] Taking τὰ πάντα as adverbial rather than the indeterminate subject of γέγονεν. Cf. 1 Cor 13:7. But τὰ πάντα, though read by many MSS and Marcion (on theological grounds, so claiming the superiority of the new covenant), may be a later addition, omitted by P[46] ℵ B C D* vg etc. τὰ πάντα may well have been added by dittography with the scribe's eye wandering to the next v (τὰ δὲ πάντα).

[c] τὸν λόγον, "the message" is the best attested and simplest reading, while P[46] elaborates to τὸ εὐαγγέλιον, "the Gospel of reconciliation" and D F G join the two nouns, "the Gospel of the message of reconciliation."

Form/Structure/Setting

The link with the foregoing is plain (ὥστε, "so then, therefore," v 16; ὥστε repeated in v 17), suggesting the way Paul had entered upon a new world-view as a person who has died to himself and is alive in Christ (vv 14, 15). Throughout this extended section he is offering reasons for his apostolic conduct and its motivations. In particular, he now states the two constraints that are placed on his ministry—and both have to be seen in the light of his ongoing debate with the Corinthian church. They are:

1. He, along with all who share his "status" as "in Christ," inhabits a new world. A new eon has been inaugurated by the cross and resurrection of Jesus, and Paul sees the whole of life through fresh eyes because of the new order of creation that has arrived at the "turning point of the ages" (*Aeonenwende*). See J. L. Martyn, "Epistemology," who makes a lot of the eschatological "shift" implied in living in the new order over against the old eon.

2. The other reality is the knowledge of God's reconciliation which is expressed by his recital of a piece of traditional teaching in vv 18–21 on which he has supplied interpretative comment.

Both these hermeneutical keys have been the subject of much recent scholarly study, so it will be well to treat them at length, under the headings of (a.) the horizon of the passage (5:16–21); (b.) the structure of the verses (18–21); (c.) the distinctive elements, especially in vv 18–21 seen as Paul's redaction of an existing tradition; and (d.) the application of this tradition-historical exercise to Paul's situation at Corinth. From the vantage point of such conclusions as may be drawn it may be possible to approach the exegesis with a fresh alertness to what the Pauline text means in context.

a. *The horizon,* that is, the purpose of an author's writing insofar as that purpose may be ascertained and understood from its setting in the larger whole of the writing, *may first be described.* This will inevitably involve a certain amount of recapitulation of his previous chapters, but it is required in order to set 5:16–21 in perspective.

At 2:14 Paul has just concluded a narrative recital of events that, he explains, led him to move from a promising situation near Troas on the Asian coast and sail over to Macedonia. The narrative sequence is picked up again at 7:5 where he returns to his theme. In the interval he seems to digress and offer a resounding defense of his ministry and the Gospel he preached. What led him to this extended "diversion" (if that is the right word) in his letter?

A quick answer may be seen in his understanding of his mission. At Titus's return and meeting with Paul in Macedonia, the news of the situation was uplifting to Paul's spirits (7:6), and it was time to celebrate the return of the Corinthian church (or at least the majority of its members) to the loyalty they once displayed to Paul. The disaffection in the main was over and it was an occasion for jubilant thankfulness to God that Paul's Gospel and its advocacy in the apostolic ministry had overcome its detractors. The extravagant language of 2:14 is explained: God leads us in triumph, "[carrying] us along in the victorious progress of the Messianic triumph, which is sweeping through the world," as T. W. Manson paraphrases the verb (see earlier, p. 46). Moreover, the progress of that triumph involves the success attending the life-giving message entrusted to Paul who, with his party, is like a fragrance of life to those who accept the Gospel and yet a smell of doom and death to those who reject it. The latter are they who have fallen prey to an adulterated version of the apostolic preaching (2:17) and remain in a state of blindness like the unbelievers over whom Satan still has power (4:3, 4).

The inference is that the message and the messenger are in some way interconnected; to reject the message is to despise the ones who bring it and embody it in their lives (4:7). Conversely, the Corinthians who have turned away from Paul, perhaps some of whom are still holding out and refusing to come over to his side, are rejecting not only his person but the very thing the apostle stood for and represented in his person, "the word of God" with life-imparting power. The kerygma is a divine fragrance containing the "knowledge of God" (2:14), but Paul can boldly claim "we are the aroma of Christ" (2:15), since it is in our persons and ministry that "God is making his appeal" to you (5:20).

The entire section (2:14–7:4) should be read as Paul's appeal. It is not so much a digression from what he had said about the "tearful letter" pledging reconciliation if the Corinthian malcontents will deal radically with the offender (2:1–11), nor simply a rehearsal of past events up to the time of his leaving Troas and reaching Macedonia. It is an extension of the same spirit he had shown in calling them to repentance (2:2; 7:8–11) and obedience (2:9), and it is a fervent yet reasoned appeal to any who were still unyielding to the pressure of his earlier appeal and whose friendly attitude to himself he has reason to doubt. The plea is a renewed call to them to leave their hostile dispositions and suspicions of both his message and his ministry and accept his proffered reconciliation, already given to the ringleader (2:5–11; 7:12).

The section in chapters 2–7, then, is arranged methodically in a set of contrasts (cf. McDonald, "Paul and the Preaching Ministry").

(1) *Paul's teaching* is opposed to a different understanding of the Christian message which featured a promoting of Moses as a "divine man" (θεῖος ἀνήρ) lawgiver (3:1–18); a reliance on worldly success and lordly power to validate its preachers (4:1–15); and a type of eschatological thinking that saw the future already contained in the present and denied a future hope of resurrection (4:16–5:10; its slogan is "we walk by sight," which Paul counters). Above all, this type of teaching raised hostility to Paul, who was dismissed scornfully as "out of his mind" (5:13). The only answer he could give in retort was to appeal to Christ's love for him (5:14, 15) which has not only provided him with a motive power and a driving force for his ministry; it has most recently enabled him to forgive his enemies at Corinth (2:10), and now he extends to them and others who are still recalcitrant the same reconciliation. The appeal then embodied a piece of traditional "church teaching" on God's reconciliation of the world through Christ (5:18–21), offered to enforce Paul's contention that this christological emphasis (5:16) meant the arrival of a new age in human history where "the new has come" (5:17), but also to state that his attitudes to these Corinthian persons and problems were fashioned according to the new life that the new age had brought with it.

(2) *Paul's person* belongs to that new eon. He and his followers share a glory more illustrious than Moses (3:18), and what occurred in his conversion (4:6) and his commission (4:5) have set the pattern for his ensuing life and

ministry (4:7–12). It is essentially a career of human weakness and full reliance on God who will raise the dead at the end-time. The Spirit is our "first installment" (5:5) of the powers of the new age, but the end is not yet. Meanwhile Paul walks "by faith" (5:7) and anticipates the resurrection in the future. The same tension between present possession and future hope is found in his mention of reconciliation.

God has reconciled the world in Christ; but the task of proclaiming the reconciliation goes on, and, adds Paul, it must be applied to concrete human situations such as the one staring the Corinthians in the face. So he slips in the aside, "Be reconciled to God" (5:20), as his earnest yet tender plea. So sure is he of the rightness of what he is doing in this move to secure full restoration that he can call upon God as his ally (6:1) and build on the fact that God is "working together" (συνεργοῦντες) with him, as he is with God in this endeavor. There are no hard feelings on his side (6:11); there should be no continuing resistance on theirs (6:12) as he works toward a complete reconciliation. His final appeal, "Mend your ways . . . live in peace" (RSV) is renewed—perhaps with a worsened situation in view—in the closing verse (13:11), preparatory to the liturgical ending (13:13).

With this short attempt to "set the stage" we can look more closely at the passage in question.

b. *The structure of the verses (18–21)*. Our discussion will be helped if we set down Paul's writing in lines, adopting a more prosaic translation.

[18] All this is God's doing,

1a who reconciled us to himself through Christ
1b and gave us the ministry of reconciliation,[19] namely,
2a God was reconciling the world to himself in Christ
    [not reckoning their trespasses against them]
2b and committing to us the message of reconciliation
3b [20] We act then as ambassadors for Christ, as God
    entreats through us [we beg on Christ's behalf, Be
    reconciled to God]

3a	[21] The one who did not know sin	(a)
	on behalf of us	(b)
	sin	(c)
	he made	(d)
	that we	(a')
	should become	(d')
	the righteousness of God	(c')
	in him.	(b')

On three grounds this short exposition of Paul's teaching on reconciliation seems to have incorporated and adapted traditional material already in existence. First, in a context where the appeal is to pastoral problems at Corinth and is (presumably) addressed to believers in the church there, it is remarkable that Paul has used kerygmatic idioms more suited to a preaching of the Gospel to unbelievers outside the church. The call "Be reconciled to God" is the "language of evangelism" (as I. H. Marshall calls it in "The Meaning of Reconciliation," 129), and is evidently explained by the secondary use Paul is making of the traditional preaching forms to enforce his concern for the Corinthians to be restored to good relations with himself as an apostolic leader (see 2 Cor 6:11–13).

Second, the literary structure of the section suggests a carefully prepared piece of soteriological credo, that is, a specimen of confessional statement expressing in summary form what the first Christians believed about God's redemptive work in Christ. The two vv (18, 19) stand together as dependent upon each other, the latter verse enlarging and explaining what is contained in the former. Thus, line 1a (God reconciled *us*) is taken up and repeated with modification in line 2a (God or God-in-Christ reconciled *the world*). Similarly line 1b is parallel with line 2b and the terms "ministry" and "message" go together.

The structure in vv 20, 21 is a little more complicated. Matching thoughts are repeated but in inverse sequence. The verbs in v 20 ("act as ambassadors," "entreat," "beg") seem to be unnecessarily repetitious; this suggests a special reason for their use. At v 21 it is fairly easy to see, even in the English translation, how the different lines are matched to form a series of contrasts. The first part refers to the redeemer's work; the second half applies the benefits to the redeemed people.

Attempts have been made to trace a word-order chiasmus, suggesting a criss-cross arrangement, in the last verse, but its symmetry is less than perfect, as C. K. Barrett concedes. The most he is willing to grant is that "Paul is moved by the subject with which he is dealing to write in an exalted style that suggests the language of hymn or liturgy" (163). All we know of Paul's literary habits indicates that when he uses hymnic or poetic speech he borrows compositions already formed and does not compose "on the run." Also his epistolary method is to add interpretative or explanatory or corrective comments to existing hymnic periods in such a way that leads to a break in strict symmetrical forms. Examples of this practice are seen in Rom 3:24–26; Phil 2:6–11; and Col 1:15–20.

This reminder brings us to the third reason for suspecting a pre-Pauline statement embedded in our text. Two lines look out of place, and we suggest that they were added by Paul's hand as he incorporated the formulation into his letter.

v 19*b:* not reckoning against them their trespasses
v 20*c:* we beg (you) on Christ's behalf, Be reconciled to God.

The interesting thing is that both these suggested additions are full of Pauline language. The verb "to reckon" is used elsewhere in a similar context (Rom 4:3f., 5f., 9, 11). The second verb "to beg" is in 2 Cor 8:4; 10:2; Gal 4:12. We suggest that these two lines are Paul's interpretative "glosses" on a preformed tradition, and added to accomplish a double objective. On the one side (v 19), Paul wanted to make it clear that the "reconciliation of the world" was achieved by what God did in not holding trespasses against humankind—it is noteworthy that the line says "against *them,*" whereas elsewhere in the paragraph the language is first person plural (we, us)—and so he cleared them of guilt. It is the idiom of justification that Paul inserts, perhaps to safeguard the teaching against false understanding. Maybe "reconciliation" was thought of as an automatic process or divine fiat, and Paul wished to anchor its rationale firmly in an act of God's power that dealt with human sin (exactly his teaching in Rom 4:25; 5:15–18, 20). On the other side, v 20 opens with a somewhat harsh apostolic appeal as Paul appears in the role of "ambassador" (πρεσβεύομεν: see Lohse, "Das Amt," 340). He does not use this title (πρεσβευτής) of himself elsewhere, except at Philem 9 (where the reading is disputed), and the term reflects an authority only later accorded to Paul (as in Eph 6:20). So we conclude that the appeal, "acting as Christ's ambassador," is softened by the more moderate and tender call, "we beg (δεόμεθα) on Christ's behalf, Be reconciled to God," with an eye on the Corinthian malcontents who were still resisting Paul's apostleship. This is evidently the sense of the appeal in 2 Cor 6:1.

As an extension of this third argument based on linguistic features we may go on to inquire if there are characteristically non-Pauline expressions in these verses. "Righteousness of God" in v 21 may be suspected since, while it is undeniable that Paul's salvation-teaching centered precisely on this phrase, it is normally (as in Rom) used of the power of God that introduced a new age of grace and forgiveness for the world. But in v 21 in our text the thought of Christians "becoming the righteousness of God in him [Christ]" is not paralleled elsewhere in Paul—the nearest he comes to it is 1 Cor 1:30, but with a significant difference: "our righteousness" stands in some uneasy tension with the divine righteousness. In other words, the anthropological application in 2 Cor 5:21 of the term sits awkwardly with the apostle's attested usage in other places.

The same doubt about another phrase in v 21 may be registered. "He made him to be sin for us" is a difficult sentence to explain precisely, because we do not know the background of the expression. Three possibilities are surveyed by L. Sabourin and S. Lyonnet (*Sin, Redemption, and Sacrifice*, 250–56; cf. L. Sabourin, "Note," 419–24): (*a*) Christ was treated as a sinner in his own person; (*b*) Christ identified himself with sin in his incarnation (as in Rom 8:3); (*c*) Christ became a sacrifice for sin. Their conclusion is that (*c*) is preferable, and cogent reasons are given for tracing this part-verse to the suffering servant motif in Isaiah 53, especially the teaching of Isa 53:10: "When thou makest his soul an offering for sin" (Heb., RSV marg.). If this is so, it points in the direction of yet another instance of Paul's borrowing of traditional teaching, for this verse falls under the rubric of an established modern consensus, namely: "Paul never makes use of any of the Servant language, except where he is quoting tradition which he has received from pre-Pauline Christianity" (R. H. Fuller, *The Mission and Achievement of Jesus*, SBT 12 [London: SCM Press, 1954] 57).

Our conclusion may be stated. In the course of a discussion with the Corinthian church Paul introduces a piece of accepted teaching on the theme of reconciliation. Arranged suggestively in lines, it has the appearance of a creedal statement, with an introductory phrase ("All this comes from God"). At key points in the quoted material Paul has inserted lines (vv 19*b*, 20*c*) partly to elaborate the meaning, partly to correct the sense of the preformed tradition. In so doing he has underscored those elements of the teaching on reconciliation that were in need of special emphasis.

So Paul, in quoting a current formulation, intended to make it his own. "The pre-existing tradition is used to give a sharper profile to the apostle's own theology" (E. Käsemann, "The Saving Significance of the Death of Jesus in Paul," *Perspectives*, 44). Yet, Käsemann continues, "it is impossible to miss the fact that this tradition thereby takes on a new intention." What that "new intention" may have been fails to be considered.

c. *Distinctive elements in the apostle's teaching (vv 18–21)*. For Paul the "reconciliation of the world" is interpreted in terms of justification, as God does not impute trespasses to man's account and in this way shows himself as the one who "justifies the ungodly" (Rom 4:5). The call to live in God's justifying grace is one of perennial application. Christians are spoken of as "already justified" by the past act of God's setting the world right with himself (Rom 4:25; 5:1; 8:30, 33). To that extent the gift can be gratefully received and God's completed action in Christ celebrated as already fully and finally accomplished. There is, however, another side to Paul's thought. The present reality of living in God's favor of grace brings with it a sure confidence that at the future judgment the verdict of acceptance will be confirmed (Gal 5:5; Phil 1:11; 3:9). There is an open-ended aspect of justification that keeps the final day of acquittal in view (1 Cor 4:5) (see K. P. Donfried, "Justification and Last Judgment in Paul," *ZNW* 67 [1976] 90–110; but cf. J. Reumann's critique, *Righteousness*, 82). The continual tension "already justified . . . not yet finally saved" runs through Paul's correspondence and provides a basis for his paraenetic (i.e., hortatory) counsel to the churches.

The same tension is seen with "reconciliation," which Paul reinterprets by inserting into a traditional formula both the negative element of God's not reckoning trespasses and the positive aspect of the need for Christians to be reconciled to God and so "not to receive the grace of God in vain" (6:1). These two matters deserve extended comment, along with a third feature that sets the teaching in this context on a firm Pauline base. This third item will be treated first.

(1) Paul's earlier discussion had centered on a reminder that is singularly lacking in 5:18–21. The explicit mention of the cross and resurrection of Jesus is made in vv 14, 15: "one has died for all . . . he died for all that those who are living might no longer live for themselves, but for him who died for them and was raised." These words pick up and state clearly what were central assertions in Paul's public proclamation which in turn was based on teaching he had received (1 Cor 15:3 ff.). In his hands the statements, "Christ died . . . he was raised," became a summary of his message (e.g., Rom 8:34; 2 Cor 13:4). But it was not only the past event that interested Paul. He was concerned to underline the continued relevance of Jesus' death and resurrection to the Christian life. He died . . . and we died in him; he was raised . . . and God will raise us up (4:14; 1 Cor 6:14; cf. Rom 6:1–11; 1 Thess 5:10).

The effect of the cross and resurrection is to lead responsive believers to break with their old "self"-life (Gal 2:20) and to live henceforward under the dominion of Christ the Lord (Rom 14:7–9). Paul has therefore safeguarded his use of the "reconciliation" paragraph in 5:18–21 by prefacing it with a clear reminder that God's deed avails little unless it is "applied" to those who are its beneficiaries. To maintain—as the credo evidently did in its stark simplicity and monumental grandeur—that "God reconciled the world in Christ" is only part of the kerygma, albeit an indispensable foundation. There must be a corresponding personal dimension, otherwise the profound teaching remains *in abstracto* and detached from human experience. The objective kerygma requires a complementary call to faith; and Paul's "faith" is a close identification with Christ in his death and rising that becomes part of the fabric of the Christian's life as he or she thereby "dies" to self and rises to "walk," to "serve," to "live" in newness under Christ's lordship (Rom 6:6; 7:6; cf. Col. 2:6). The verbs refer to life in the new eon (5:17: see Tannehill, *Dying and Rising*, 39–43).

(2) If our position is correct that the line "not reckoning their trespasses against them" (5:19*b*) is from Paul's own hand, its value may now be assessed. As we have remarked, the "non-reckoning" of human guilt is basic to his discussion in Rom 4–5. The novel feature added here is a carefully worked-out explanation of the "mechanics" of God's action in v 21.

It involves several steps that we can tabulate even at the risk of appearing to give to Paul's words more logical coherence than they may originally have had. Obviously we do not have access to any early Christian "doctrine of the Atonement" constructed as a piece of dogmatic theology. The best we can do is to summarize some ideas or convictions (see v 14: "we conclude," "we have reached this conviction," or possibly there is an implicit appeal to a soteriological credo, see earlier p. 130): so Héring, 41. With this caveat, the following scheme may be set down:

(a) *Identification.* "God was in Christ reconciling the world to himself" (RSV) is capable of being taken in several ways. See *Comment.* The phrase "in Christ" may go with "God" to form a composite expression, thus "God-in-Christ" and the participle of the verb follows. Or else "in Christ" is the means through which God reconciled the world (so Barrett). The latter translation seems better to continue the thought of v 18 which attributes the initiative to God. Nonetheless it still remains true that Paul's Greek is less than precise; yet it is also true that the flow of his argument is to show how God himself is personally involved both in his acting through the agency of Christ (v 18, διὰ Χριστοῦ) and by coming himself in Christ (ἐν Χριστῷ, v 19) to our world. We may take Paul's text to convey this: in Christ God became one of our human race and identified himself with it.

(b) *Representation.* J. D. G. Dunn ("Paul's Understanding," 130) has rightly focused on 5:14, 15 as "one of the most explicit expressions of Paul's understanding of Jesus as representative man": "One has died for all, therefore all humankind (οἱ πάντες) died." At face value this is taken to mean that Christ assumed the role of the last Adam and, as a human being, died because there was no other way for mortals because they are all mortal. "His death is an acknowledgment that there is no way out for fallen men except through death." Only through death, therefore and as a consequence, does the New Man emerge in risen life. That hope of new life, however, is restricted to believers in a way not parallel with the earlier statement that "Christ died, therefore all died." The death is common to all humanity, Christ included; the resurrection (in v 15) embraces only those who "acknowledge the Risen One as Lord."

The insistence on Christ as the representative man is correct, but we may hesitate to follow Dunn in taking the death of "all" (in v 14) to refer to "all humankind." The representation of Jesus is that of his people; it is they who are described as having died in the person of their representative; and as F. F. Bruce (207) comments, "The 'all' of this passage is synonymous with the second 'many' of Rom. 5.15, 19." Moreover, as we noted earlier, it cannot be a physical death as a terminus of life that is in view, since the "all" continue to live (v 15), albeit no longer to themselves but under a new head. The death is to the old order of self-interest: "He died for us that we might die to ourselves," observes Calvin, echoing Mark 8:34. The death of "all" not only seals the grave on the old way of life, but liberates the persons who share Christ's death that they may share his resurrection newness, "to become free for a new life with new goals and purposes" (Windisch, 182).

In the statements "one died *for* all," "he died *for* all," the meaning of the preposition is obviously important. Tasker (86) argues (rightly, in our judgment) against the view that when Paul wrote "Jesus *died for all,* the inference must be that all were liable to death which was the penalty of sin." He concludes, "it is not this truth that Paul is now stressing." He, however, takes the first part of the verse in precisely the way which he has rejected for its second half. "The apostle means that Christ's death was the death of all, in the sense that He died the death they should have died; the penalty of their sins was borne by Him; He died in their place." Whether this notion of substitution that is traditionally attributed to this verse is demanded in v 21 has already been noted and will be considered again later. It is doubtful, however, if it can be exclusively sustained as an interpretation of vv 14, 15, where the phrase "for all" (ὑπὲρ πάντων) speaks more of the representative task of Christ who, acting on his people's behalf, died, i.e., so identified himself with their humanity and plight that his death to sin can be regarded as an act of obedience and surrender in which they have a share. The preposition in v 20 (twice repeated, ὑπὲρ Χριστοῦ . . . ὑπὲρ Χριστοῦ) describes the apostolic ministry in a similar way: it is representative of Christ, not only in that Paul acts for Christ as his servant but that God is personally present in Paul's ministry, "as though God were entreating through us." Paul's preaching is given a word-of-God character by this close identification (cf. 1 Thess 2:13), and proclamation is nothing less than the voice of God through Paul, as J. Murphy-O'Connor makes clear (*Paul on Preaching* [London: Sheed & Ward, 1964] 72–76). If this parallelism may be used, it would lead us to conclude that Christ's oneness with the race means his acting in their name and offering to God on their behalf as their proxy an oblation of filial obedience and allegiance that God accepted and because of which he acted forgivingly to restore the race of sinners. At this point in the chapter Paul, it seems, says no more than "he died for others" by acting representatively in their name, with the consequence that his act has the profound effect of changing personal attitudes and dispositions. They for whom he died no longer live for themselves but for him. But that he did for them what they could never do for themselves is brought out in vv 18–21.

(c) *Imputation.* The puzzling question, How is the sinful race restored to divine favor? is posed later, at v 21. The answer is given in terms of a transference or, to use Paul's word, "imputation" (Rom 4:4–8). The elements are presented in their bare simplicity. The sinless Christ took our condemnation, that for us there might be condemnation no more. On its positive side, the happy result of this "transaction" is that as Christ in his sinlessness took responsibility for our wrongdoing, we are gifted with that entity ("the righteousness of God") that permits our acceptance with God. If this way of expressing the exchange is most suitable, then the appropriate term is "substitution" used to denote an interchange of guilt and righteousness, while "imputation" stresses how the two sides of the matter are related: (a) becomes (b), so that (b) may become (a).

The moment the process of transference is stated in these bald terms, we are struck by the fact that Paul elsewhere never so speaks and in other places he gives a more positive content to the matter. His attested teaching on the uniqueness of the redeemer in both his filial relation to God as "Son" and his pre-existence as being "sent"—to which M. Hengel has drawn attention (*Son of God* [London: SCM, ET 1976] 12–15)—does not include a statement of his sinlessness. Indeed it has been argued that Rom 8:3—Christ "came in the likeness of sinful flesh"—points in the other direction, namely that his complete humanity involved a taking of man's fallen nature. This is debatable, of course; and the debate, chronicled by Harry Johnson in his monograph *The Humanity of the Saviour*, continues. (See too D. M. Baillie, *God was in Christ* [London: Faber, 1948] 16–18, for a comment on the history of this discussion in Barth and Edward Irving.) It is more significant to observe another part of Paul's discussion in Romans where the notion of "interchange" (M. D. Hooker's phrase, "Interchange in Christ," *JTS* 22 [1971] 349–61) seems clear and so would offer a parallel. "For as by one man's disobedience many were made/constituted sinners, so by one man's obedience many will be made/constituted righteous" (Rom 5:19). The essence of that summarizing statement is well stated by Cranfield: "The many will be constituted righteous through Christ's obedience"—to God—"in the sense that, since God has in Christ identified Himself with sinners and taken upon Himself the burden of their sin, they will receive as a free gift from Him that status of righteousness which Christ's perfect obedience alone has deserved" (*The Epistle to the Romans,* ICC [Edinburgh: T. & T. Clark, 1975] 1:291).

With that explanation in mind we may observe the distinctive elements in 2 Cor 5:21: (i) Nothing is said there of Christ's freely willed obedience (classically stated in Phil 2:6–8). Instead God "made" him to be sin, perhaps in the sense of "appointed" or "designated." See *Comment.* (ii) Adam's "trespass" (παράπτωμα, Rom 5:18) is not used as a foil to display more brightly the illustrious obedience of the last Man. Interestingly, it is precisely this term for human sin—"trespasses" (παραπτώματα)—that Paul has inserted in 5:19 using the language of imputation. (iii) "Becoming the righteousness of God in him" poses its own problems, not least being the unexampled way this phrase "righteousness of God" is used. Paul's normal usage (Rom 1:17; 3:21; 10:3 may be taken as characteristic, since they appear at pivotal points in that epistle) carries the sense of a disclosure of divine power leading to salvation and new life for the world (see J. Reumann, *Righteousness*). The thought of believers "becoming" (see γενώμεθα, v 21) part of that enterprise is strange for Paul, and is in no way parallel with Rom 5:19, where believers are "constituted righteous," i.e., justified by Christ's vicarious obedience. In other words, the idioms of 2 Cor 5:21 are not justification terms and state simply a substitutionary exchange. The issue of how God has dealt with human sin is left open and no rationale, such as the Pauline justification teaching offers, is given to throw light on the pressing moral conundrum: how did Christ's identification with sin open the way for Christians to receive his righteousness? The v then needs to be understood in the light of Paul's teaching elsewhere, and to that extent to be amplified and corrected by what we have in Romans. In specific terms, Christ's sharing our sin, whether as a sin-offering or a sacrifice or a savior figure modeled on Isaiah 53's יהוה עבד, *ʿebed Yahweh*, is viewed by Paul as *his obedience* or *faithfulness to his mission as filial redeemer of the new humanity*. Those who stand as beneficiaries of his saving work are given acceptance with God because they are "justified" or "constituted righteous" in their status before God, *coram Deo*. This has come about by God's gracious decision not to reckon trespasses against them exactly as in Rom 5:18 f., and to accept the filial obedience of the righteous one, the last Adam, on their behalf. To that extent "they become God's righteousness in him," i.e., they are not divinized by God *but given the salvific status as men and women rightly related to God*. That conclusion, we submit, emerges from Paul's insertion of his distinctive comment in v 19: "not counting their trespasses against them."

(d) *Reconciliation.* And so we come to the quintessence of this stately creedal paragraph. Paul is led to this theme by reflecting on the new order that came into being with Christ. The epitome of what he had discovered about the new age is summed up in "the love of Christ" that impelled him to his service (5:14). That love expressed itself supremely in the cross, a theme to which Paul returns in Romans 5:1–11 where he offers a concise statement of his understanding of reconciliation.

The "cross of the messiah" raised for Paul, as for Jewish hearers, an intractable problem. If he was simply an earthly messiah, seen from a "human point of view" (v 16: κατὰ σάρκα, a phrase with a negative connotation in Paul, suggesting horizons bounded by man's forlorn and arrogant wisdom), there is a fundamental contradiction in the statement that he was crucified. Whoever died in this manner fell under the deuteronomic rubric of a divine curse (Deut 21:23); he was "under a ban" (חרם, *ḥērem*) and an outcast from Israel's community (see M. Hengel, *Crucifixion*, tr. J. Bowden [Philadelphia: Fortress Press, 1977] 85). In another place Paul lets us see how the puzzle was solved. "Christ became a curse *for us*," he remarks (Gal 3:13) to account for the strange fulfillment of the deuteronomic text. Here he denies the basis of the alleged objection. "We do not now regard him from an earthly viewpoint," since no nationalist or politicized categories will suffice, and "Christ" (= messiah) is a term Paul came to use less as a title of office meaningful only to Jews, and more as a personal appellation (see N. A. Dahl, "The Problem of Messiahship in Paul," in *The Crucified Messiah* [Minneapolis: Augsburg, 1974] 37–47; M. Hengel, " 'Christos' in Paul," in *Between Jesus and Paul*, tr. J. Bowden [Philadelphia: Fortress Press, 1983] chap. 4).

As a universal person, set free from all limiting restrictions, Christ ushered in the new era, at the "turn of the ages" (v 17). It was like a new order of creation, remarks Paul as he reflects on the Genesis creation story not for the first time in his letter (4:6). The old world, with its enslavements and fears and ruled by its god (4:4), is on the way out; already it is replaced by the new age, promised in the glowing words of the exilic prophet (Isa 51:9 ff. and 54:9 f.; cf. Isa 42:9 and 43:18 f. for the contrast between the old/new worlds) and already entering human experience as forgiveness and accompanied by baptismal joy. But we must be careful not to reduce the phrase to "new creature," in a way similar to that which the rabbis promised to pious converts to Judaism (see *Comment*). Paul is not describing *in this context* the personal dimension of a new birth; rather he is announcing as a kerygmatic statement *the advent of the new creation "in Christ,"* the dramatic recovery of the world, formerly alienated and dislocated, by God who has acted eschatologically in Christ, i.e., the world is placed now under his rule.

It is strange that C. K. Barrett should write in reference to v 18: "Up to this point Paul has been describing the work of God *in nobis,* that is, the new creation that takes effect in and for a man who by faith comes to be in Christ." The flow of Paul's argument suggests the opposite. It is God's work "outside of us" (*extra nos*), objectively viewed and independent of human application that Paul has recited, at least until he reaches the quoted formula of v 18. Then, in our view, follows a piece of cosmic soteriology stated as a Christian "confession of faith"—the language is both personal ("reconciled *us*") and universal ("the world"), except for v 19*b*—and expressing in non-Pauline terminology the achievement and the demands of reconciliation. The note of authority runs through the statement, since those who are charged to undertake "the ministry of reconciliation" are no less than "ambassadors for Christ." As was earlier observed, this singular title prompts the inquiry whether the next line, "we beg you on Christ's behalf, be reconciled to God," may be a Pauline aside, slipped in to temper the appeal. We proceed to test this assumption by remarking that in the quoted sentence the verb καταλλάγητε, "be reconciled," takes on an altered nuance since it is applied to pastoral problems at Corinth and so is lifted out of its earlier cosmic setting.

The semantic field of the verb "to reconcile" ([κατ] αλλάσσειν) has been investigated by several scholars (see F. Büchsel, *TDNT* 1: 251–59; J. Dupont, *La réconciliation;* and now J. A. Fitzmyer, "Reconciliation"). At its simplest the verb denotes "the action by which peace is made between personal enemies," as Moses brought together his estranged compatriots (Acts 7:26: the verb here is συνήλλασεν). It is the work of a mediator whose office is "to make hostility cease," "to lead to peace." Applied to divine-human relations, the verb "to reconcile" does not describe a change of feelings or disposition whether of man to God or of God to man but rather "an objective change of the situation" in which God and man face each other, as Collange, *Enigmes,* remarks (268). Reconciliation "denotes a change in the relations between God and man and more particularly a change in man himself" (T. W. Manson, *On Paul and John,* SBT 38 [London: SCM, 1963] 52). The verses of Paul's text say two important things: it is God who has acted to reconcile men and women to himself, and this reconciliation is effected through the mediation of Christ, with the thought left implicit that the phrase "through Christ" (διὰ Χριστοῦ, v 18) includes his cross and resurrection. If, as is likely, v 19 should read "in Christ God was reconciling the world to himself," then the "in Christ" (ἐν Χριστῷ) formula is to be explained either as a stylistic variant of the more normal "through Christ" (so F. Neugebauer, *In Christus* [Göttingen: Vandenhoeck & Ruprecht, 1961] 85 f.; Lietzmann, 125, or the sign of a more obvious non-Pauline usage [Collange, 272; the usage would be even stranger if we adopted Collange's translation following Allo, 170, to the effect, "God was in Christ, reconciling . . .")]).

The periphrastic tense of the verb in v 19, "God was (ἦν, imperfect of the verb "to be") reconciling (καταλλάσσων, participle)," has caused an exegetical problem. Does it imply that reconciliation is a process (Plummer), or an incomplete action (Windisch), or "open-ended" in that while from God's side the reconciliation is total, there is the possibility that "some men may not accept their being reconciled to God" (von Allmen, "Réconciliation du monde et christologie cosmique," *RHPR* 1 [1968] 32–45, esp. 37, n. 20])? Collange believes that the shift in verb tenses is slight and is made on grounds of rhythm and style, with the imperfect tense disguising an aorist of past action. The last-named explanation may be too simple, and we are bound to observe that the ambiguity in 5:18, 19 is not present in Rom 5:1–11 where reconciliation is an event in past time, once and for all.

The difficulty for the interpreter comes when it is noted that the verb is used passively (as in v 20), referring to the action of a person in giving up his hostility to another individual. Then, the offended person is appealed to that he may set aside his enmity or anger. Josephus (*Ant.* 7:184) uses the verb of David who was asked to be reconciled to his erring son Absalom and let his anger cease. In 2 Maccabees, as Dupont (*La réconciliation,* 13) says, there are several examples of situations where Israel has justly deserved God's wrath because of apostasy and is suffering in consequence. Judgment has a salutary effect as the people pray for Yahweh to be reconciled to them and cease from his anger (2 Macc 1:5). Martyrs whose suffering is both for their own sins (2 Macc 7:18) and on behalf of the nation as a whole offer especially powerful prayers since their sufferings have a vicarious value. They bear the divine wrath, so (the prayer proceeds) in effect "let the people be spared." God is implored to be reconciled to the nation (2 Macc 7: 32 ff.).

A sharp point may be put on the Pauline text if we ask whether this usage in Jewish literature offers a genuine parallel. There is an obvious difference. The Maccabean martyrs urge God to be reconciled to them, and they offer both their lives and their sins to him as acts of vicarious piety and merit. This picture stands in direct contrast to Paul's teaching, whether that teaching was inherited or is his own formulation. Consistently the stress falls, in the apostolic preaching, on God as the originator of the act of reconciliation; he is always the subject and never the direct object of the verb. He is never said to be reconciled to us; on the contrary the passive "be reconciled" is directed to men and women (or "the church," since verse 20*c* is the solitary place where this imperative form of the verb is found, and we shall argue that it has specific and specialized reference to Paul's Corinthian scene). To be sure, it may well be insisted that God's wrath (ὀργὴ θεοῦ, Rom 1:18; 3:5) and judgment (δικαιοκρισία τοῦ θεοῦ, Rom 2:5) are terms that presuppose God's being "offended by the sins of men," and he has "dealt with the sins which aroused his wrath," so removing the barrier on his side to the establishment of peace and friendly relations. This line of exposition goes on to conclude that "in dying Christ exhausted the effects of divine wrath against sin" (Marshall, "Reconciliation," 123). But it has to be said in all fairness that our passage hardly demonstrates this construction (though it *could* be inferred, as by Denney), since it says no more than that God in Christ has acted in such a way as to restore friendly relations between the world and himself. "He has reconciled us to himself" means simply "he has put us in right relations with himself." As Dupont expresses it, "God does not reconcile himself to the world, he reconciles the world to himself" (*La réconciliation*, 15).

The participial phrase in v 20*b*, "God making his appeal through us," needs discussion from an exegetical standpoint. The basis of that appeal is, as we have seen, God's decisive act in the person of Christ by which the world is returned to God from its estrangement. "Reconciliation" is a word that rests on prior disagreement and animosity; but, in this case, on whose side? Undoubtedly the cause is double-sided. On God's side there is that manifestation of his holy love called his "righteousness" in the light of which the world stands both condemned and "lost"; it is alienated and under the foreign domination of evil powers. On the human side, there is all that is summed up in terms such as "enmity," "hostility," "bondage," "fear," "despair"—language of the human condition, which is part of Paul's anthropology (Rom 5:1–11; 8:1, 2, 12–17; Gal 4:3–9: cf. Eph 2:1–3; 4:18). This barrier too must obviously crumble and fall if a genuine rapprochement is to take place.

The "appeal" rests on the prior move God has made. Paul's ministry comes to his contemporaries with the news that God has taken the initiative and now offers peace. His hearers are bidden to receive it with a trustful welcome, not so much to lay aside their suspicion and enmity (though it is hard to deny that element: see Denney, cited under *Comment*) as to greet the good news with joyful acceptance. Or, as Paul would more carefully express it, with the obedience of faith (Rom 1:5; 6:16; 16:26). The office of ambassador is one that "stands upon [its] dignity" (Denney, 216; Collange, *Enigmes*, 274), since Paul's text sounds the note of authority in its call for such obedience.

But we must notice two matters that demand caution in the above comment. We have had to introduce Paul's teaching on "enmity" and "peace" from other places to flesh out these sentences of our passage. And the "appeal" is a general one, not directed to the Corinthians, *who do not come into the picture until v 20c.* The result is that, while the call "Be reconciled to God" may be a legitimate extension of the apostolic kerygma, there is no proof of this. The call is issued with the Corinthian congregation and its pastoral problems in view, and should primarily be interpreted in that context. The awkward point of connection in v 20 may be explained once we postulate a non-Pauline origin of the clause, "We are then [acting as] ambassadors for Christ, with the conviction (ὡς [see Collange, 274 f.]; this is not translated in rsv) that God is *making his plea* through us." The verb is παρακαλοῦντος

—a frequent term in Paul, especially in 2 Corinthians—but with the normal sense of Paul or God "comforting" or "exhorting" or "strengthening" his people (see *Comment* on 1:3–7) and not in the sense of directing an appeal to sinners. Paul's customary usage of the verb in this context is seen in 6:1: "We exhort (παρακαλοῦμεν) you not to receive God's grace in vain."

d. *Application of this teaching to the Corinthian scene.* "Reconciliation" is a noble term in a pericope (5:18–21) on which Calvin rightly remarks, "Here is a remarkable place, if there is such in the entire writing of Paul" (*est hic insignis locus, si quis alius est in toto Paulo*). And regarding v 21 Hughes writes, "There is no sentence more profound in the whole of Scripture." Certain features of the apostolic message of Christ's work stand out. But much is tantalizingly obscure. We may affirm the divine initiative in reconciliation, both in its origin and total execution. Humankind plays only a passive role as those who are "acted upon" by being "reconciled" and then "appealed to" (Bultmann; Denney as cited later, p. 155). The cosmos is affected, presumably in the sense of being brought back to harmony with the creator and reinstated in right relations with him, "becoming the righteousness of God" in Christ. The pre-Pauline teaching and provenance here are demonstrable (*pace* Stuhlmacher, *Gerichtigkeit Gottes*, 74–77; J. Reumann, *Righteousness*, 51, 52 does not advert to a discussion of the provenance of v 21). E. Käsemann ("Some Thoughts," 53) offers three pointers to this conclusion: (*i*) Paul does not normally use "sin" (ἁμαρτίαν[ἐποίησεν, v 21]) in the sense of "punishment for sin"; (*ii*) the close of v 21 is less christological than 1 Cor 1:30; (*iii*) "righteousness" is here used in a way different from Paul's attested usage. The Pauline clause in v 19, however, we may submit, has recast the setting of what follows. It has introduced the framework of justification and so ensured, from Paul's perspective, that the "double imputation"—our sin is borne by Christ/Christ's holy status is transferred to us—is understood in categories that Paul's teaching regarded as central, namely: (*a*) God has reconciled the cosmos which is made up of sinful men and women; (*b*) he has taken action to deal with their sins in Christ; (*c*) reconciliation is intimately related to personal and moral concerns having to do with his apostolic responsibility at Corinth; and (*d*) "righteousness" is God both setting men and women right with himself and justifying himself; by God's doing so Paul's own Gospel is "justified," i.e., vindicated. Not least in importance is the Pauline announcement in v 17, not of a refurbished Judaism with the old order of Moses revamped but of a new age with a new covenant (ch. 3) and a new start made to world history (see E. Käsemann, "Paul and Israel," in his *New Testament Questions of Today*, tr. W. J. Montague [London: SCM, 1969] 183–87).

The focal point of this enterprise is "Christ became sin," again presumably on the cross, though that fact is not mentioned explicitly. It could be that the "original version" of this soteriological credo simply announced the new age by divine fiat—E. Güttgemanns (*Der leidende Apostel und sein Herr*, 312–17) goes so far as to postulate a gnostic doctrine of creation's "self-redemption," which Paul opposes in v 18: "all is God's doing"—and connected the divine condemnation of the sinless Christ with a new status accorded to those who belong to him. But once vv 18–21 are introduced by vv 14–15, there can be no mistaking the dimension set by the self-giving of the historical Jesus, his death on the cross, and his resurrection.

In taking over this preformed credo, Paul has clarified its meaning in ways we have already drawn attention to. In one other regard he has done something editorially that has put a fine point on the teaching *in the light of his customary method attested elsewhere.*

Paul has added, "We implore you [Corinthians] on Christ's behalf [who did so much for us, ὑπὲρ ἡμῶν], be reconciled to God!" The apostle, in tempering the strident apostolic voice to suit a more affectionate tone, repeated in 6:11–13, has recast the kerygmatic announcement to give it a personal dimension. He has taken language more germane to a call to unbelievers and has applied it to the strained relationships with the church by calling on them to accept his God-given authority implicit in his apostolic office (10:8; 13:10, 11) and to return to his side as children to a grieved father (6:11–13). How far this winsome appeal reflects the kerygma addressed to sinners is an open question. Given the scantiness of the evidence in Paul, we may never know whether he or others called on the hearers in synagogue or marketplace to be reconciled to God. The inference is that they did not, any more than that their message was a pleading with or commanding men and women, "Be justified before God." The language is more declaratory than hortatory, as the data in Acts (13:39) and the capital epistles indicate.

But the link between kerygma and exhortation to Christians is important. In both cases, for Paul if not so clearly for his predecessors, the announcement of reconciliation is *expressible only in personal terms,* whether we recall Christ's obedience to God or the believer's response to all that reconciliation involves as a vital, loving relationship set up with persons always in view. In a helpful summary Wiard Popkes (in a private communication) writes in regard to our present passage's exegesis:

> Paul wants to describe the new kind of life which he lives and which determines his outlook and behaviour. He approaches the matter from three angles: (i) new creation, (ii) reconciliation, and (iii) the righteousness of God. All of these concepts reflect God's character. He is the creator, the father and the judge. All of them reflect our situation. Without Christ we belong to the old, perishing creation; we are alienated from God; and we stand under the judgment of sin. All of the terms reflect the great change brought about by God in Christ. We stand in the new world; our personal relation to God has been restored; and we are free from judgment.

To this final statement perhaps one more item needs to be added. Paul interjects the pastoral call "Be reconciled to God" to professing Christians as if to emphasize (a) the continual claim of the new life embarked on by the act of justification and grace (see 6:1); and (b) the need for Paul's apostolic authority expressed in the proclamation he has quoted as commonly accepted material to be reestablished at Corinth where it was under attack. Against those who prided themselves on "the outward" and despised "the inward" (5:12) Paul's kerygma centered in the weakness of the crucified Christ (13:4*a*) and the frailty of his messengers (4:7–12; 13:4*b*). But Paul appeals now to the greatness of his Gospel that in some way embodies his own office as herald. So to be open to *his* apostolic person is part of the human response to the message. To alienated "children" (6:13; cf. 1 Cor 4:15–21) at Corinth, the call is renewed, "Be reconciled to God."

Comment

16. ἀπὸ τοῦ νῦν, "from now on," "henceforward," marks the transition from the old order κατὰ σάρκα, "according to the flesh," i.e., human life organized without reference to God and his purposes, to the new (κατὰ πνεῦμα; the Spirit initiates the new age according to 3:6). It is not an exclusive allusion to Paul's conversion (Lietzmann ["νῦν is the moment of conversion," 126], Windisch, 185) nor to an eschatological moment of crisis resolved and actualized by faith (Bultmann, 156). Rather it refers to "the decisive event through which the believer has entered the new life, i.e., to the fact that "one died for all; therefore, all died." . . . [It is] the time of God's decisive act which changed the situation of men in the world" (R. C. Tannehill, *Dying and Rising*, 67). The adverb νῦν carries the same nuance in 6:2: "*now* is the acceptable time [of salvation]; *now* is the day of salvation."

In specific terms Paul is appealing to the "new time," the eschatological hour of the world's destiny and deliverance when in Christ "all (τὰ πάντα, *si vera lectio*) has become new" (v 17). One aspect of that new age is that believers have a true insight into the author of that salvation. He is seen—Paul's verb is γινώσκειν, "to know," akin to the Hebrew יָדַע, *yada῾*, but in v 16a εἰδέναι has no appreciable difference of meaning. Both are used of knowing God or Christ with an intimacy and personal quality that leads to fellowship (see H. Seesemann, *TDNT* 5:121; J. Dupont, *Gnosis*, 186).

There is a subtle play, however, on the two parts of the v, obvious not from the change in verb but in the adverbial modifier κατὰ σάρκα, which attaches to ἐγνώκαμεν . . . γινώσκομεν rather than to Χριστόν (but see Bultmann, 156: the Χριστὸς κατὰ σάρκα is for him Christ in his worldly accessibility, before his death and resurrection [citing Phil 2:7]). Much turns on whether the particle εἰ καὶ introduces a real or an unreal condition. The latter would be Paul's way of constructing a hypothetical case for argument's sake (as in Gal 5:11). But that seems unlikely here. Rather he is conceding a knowledge of the earthly Jesus as real—to himself as to his opponents who made a lot of such privilege (Héring; compare 10:7). Paul grants that such knowledge would be limited to an appreciation of Him as Jewish messiah and yet he qualifies such a concession by inferring that it would place a roadblock in the way of faith in Him as Lord of all creation. It would be a human achievement (σάρξ, "flesh"; cf. Phil 3:3), and Paul cannot accept such knowledge since it is narrowly circumscribed, i.e., he denies that this way of knowing Christ has any scope in a person's relationship to God (see Barrett, 172). What is needed is to appreciate him as "the whole Christ" by the Spirit and by faith (J. W. Fraser ["Paul's Knowledge," *NTS* 17, 293–313]). More pertinent, in the new creation this is how he views all other people according to their standing in him, in the new eschatological situation (so Fraser)—and, we must go on to add, this is how he expects the Corinthians to view him and his ministry. The model is the crucified and risen Lord, and Paul wishes his work to be judged by that criterion (vv 14, 15).

17. The same idea, that in Christ there is a new way of "seeing" since he has made all things new, is repeated. ἐν Χριστῷ governs the expression καινὴ κτίσις, "new creation," not τις, "anyone." So it is less than correct to interpret the v as describing a person's conversion after the analogy of new birth (John 3: 3, 5, 7). But see J. Reumann, *Righteousness*, 51 and n. 65, for the translation "new creature." The accent falls on a person (τις) entering the new order in Christ, thus making the καινὴ κτίσις an eschatological term for God's age of salvation (Bultmann, *Theology* 1, 306–8) based on Isa 51:9 f.; 54:9 f.: cf. 42:9; 43:18 f. rather than the rabbinic teaching of "new creature" (see W. D. Davies, *Paul and Rabbinic Judaism*, 2d ed. [London: SPCK, 1955] 121 ff.). Paul is talking of a "new act of creation," not an individual's renovation as a proselyte or a forgiven sinner in the Day of Atonement service. There is even an ontological dimension to Paul's thought (so P. Stuhlmacher, "Er- wägungen"), suggesting that with Christ's coming a new chapter in cosmic relations to God opened and reversed the catastrophic effect of Adam's fall which began the old creation (Kümmel, 205). To conclude: ἐν Χριστῷ, καινὴ κτίσις in this context relates to the new eschatological situation which has emerged from Christ's advent (unlike the sense of Gal. 6:14, 15).

Tannehill (*Dying and Rising*, 68, 69) has correctly noted that this eschatologi- cal change must not be transformed into a subjective one, as if it were merely the individual's viewpoint which had changed. "If Paul were only able to assert that 'for me' or 'in my view' the old world has passed away, he would not be able to argue as he does that others may no longer judge him according to the flesh, for they would be as entitled to their viewpoint as he is to his. Paul's own argument in these verses depends upon the reality of the presence of the new aeon."

τὰ ἀρχαῖα, "the old order" means the old world of sin and death, but also the realm of the σάρξ, "flesh." It has "gone" in the sense that its regime is broken, though its power remains (Gal 5:16–21, 24) to be neutralized in Christ. γέγονεν καινά, lit., "it has become new," picks up the original Pauline description of καινὴ διαθήκη, "new covenant" in chap. 3, and fastens the arrival of the newness in Christ to the apostle's ministry as a servant of that new dispensation (Collange, *Enigmes*, 264, 265).

18. It is important to see this linkage to chap. 3, since the common feature of Paul's διακονία, "ministry," is now elaborated in some detail. As we have noted (see *Form/Structure/Setting*), Paul offers now an interpretative commen- tary on some creedal παράδοσις of well-accepted soteriological teaching. His use of this device is well known, namely, he will claim the agreement of his readers by citing what he and they have in common possession. The reason is clear to see: the quarrel between Paul and his readers is not simply personal; it is above all about the kerygma. Hence Paul's recourse is made to tradition (παράδοσις), with a parallel instance in 1 Cor 15:1–11 (see R. P. Martin, *The Spirit and the Congregation*, chap. 6).

The introductory formula is τὰ δὲ πάντα ἐκ τοῦ θεοῦ: lit., "all things then come from God." The antecedent to τὰ πάντα is left open. Presumably it goes back to what is given in vv 14, 16, 17 (so Bengel, with agreement from Windisch, Bultmann, Barrett, Collange). Héring and Reicke (*TDNT* [5:885– 95]), however, render τὰ πάντα as "the universe" since this is a technical term, and Héring (and Güttgemanns, *Der leidende Apostel:* see above, p. 149) justifies the entrance of the cosmic idiom on the ground that Paul is setting off his teaching against a gnostic idea that the demiurge took the initiative in reconciliation. This may be possible but it is unproven. Nonetheless, the immediate referent is better regarded as v 17 with its statement of the new eon in Christ and the making of "all things new" (if τὰ πάντα, "all things," is read; if it is not to be included in the text, the plural forms are seen in ἀρχαῖα, "old" and καινά, "new"). "All things" are God's work in the new creation. Now Paul must define exactly what is implied in that new age. He proceeds to spell it out in terms of reconciliation which (on our understanding of the text) had a *Vorlage* which *did* speak of cosmic restoration. In his hands the teaching is given a new twist: he has located reconciliation in forgiveness and as a matter of personal relations, with his eye on the Corinthian scene (v 19b); and he has interjected a pastoral plea (in v 20c) for his readers no longer to range themselves with the "unbelievers" (οἱ ἄπιστοι, 4:4; 6:14). In the readers' case it is not their need to respond to the public kerygma that is in view, but rather to accept his proffered friendship on the principle that to accept his Gospel is to accept his apostolic office.

The aorist participial verb form τοῦ καταλλάξαντος (ἡμᾶς ἑαυτῷ), "who reconciled" (us to himself) is descriptive of God's past action, located in the mediation of Christ (διὰ Χριστοῦ). The initiative of God who is always spoken of as the one originating reconciliation (see Dupont, *La réconciliation,* 15) and the part played by his Son are the allied themes, both historical and eschatological (for διὰ Χριστοῦ, see M. Bouttier, *En Christ,* 31–35; and for the general teaching of reconciliation through Christ's cross, Bachmann and Collange). The next v continues the theme but with a different emphasis marked by a periphrastic verb.

Part and parcel of God's activity is his design to commit this message to his servants, notably Paul (δόντος ἡμῖν τὴν διακονίαν τῆς καταλλαγῆς, "has given us the ministry of reconciliation"). Διακονία, "ministry," is a keyword, denoting Paul's office as herald of the cross and resurrection. The content of such a proclamation follows.

19. ὡς ὅτι—"that is," RSV; "that," NIV—is puzzling, often taken as a simple ὅτι after verbs of speaking or feeling (so Plummer, Hughes, Windisch), but there is no such verb here except by inference. Godet (191) gives a comparative sense to ὡς and connects it with the previous v: God has reconciled us because—as it must be—God was in Christ, etc. More convincingly, Lietzmann prefers the view of BDF § 396 that ὡς ὅτι should be regarded as a simple ὡς (so T. Muraoka, "The Use of ΩΣ in the Greek Bible," *NovT* 7 [1964] 51–72, esp. 65). It should be treated here as opening a quotation, i.e., in the recitative sense.

God is spoken of as taking action with several possibilities of construction, listed by Collange: (1) "God was reconciling the world (which was in Christ)"— a most implausible view; (2) "God was, reconciling the world to himself," equally difficult; (3) "God was reconciling the world in (= through) Christ," i.e., by his agency (Plummer; Hughes; Godet; Bruce; Tasker; Barrett; Bultmann; Thrall, "Salvation Proclaimed," 228); and (4) "God was in Christ, reconciling the world" (Allo; Bachmann; Collange, who makes the chief point that there is a verbal symmetry between καταλλάσσων ["reconciling"] and the other participles, λογιζόμενος and θέμενος, in the v; the upshot is that "reconciling" stands apart from the sentence "God was in Christ"; but this is a dubious expedient. M. J. Harris, "Prepositions and Theology in the Greek New Testament," *NIDNTT* 3:1193, offers a better rationale for the reading, "God was in Christ, reconciling the world," namely, that "it was only because God in all his fullness had chosen to dwell in Christ [Col 1:19] . . . that reconciliation was accomplished." But again this view turns the statement into a revelatory one [Christ as the locus of divine revelation] rather than a soteriological one, which is preferable). Our option is for (3), with most commentators and giving weight to the thought as chiefly soteriological, not incarnational as is sometimes maintained when "God was in Christ" is kept separate (see Bruce). The periphrastic tense (participle + verb ἦν, "was") denotes an element of contingency that, although the reconciliation is complete from God's side, there is the possibility that some people may not accept it (von Allmen, "Réconciliation," 37) or that, with an eye on his readers, they may not have entered into the full experience of reconciliation (Thrall, "Salvation Proclaimed," 231).

The two parallel participles μὴ λογιζόμενος αὐτοῖς, "not charging [their trespasses] against them," and θέμενος ἐν ἡμῖν τὸν λόγον, "having entrusted to us the message (of reconciliation)," belong together as explaining what the reconcilement entailed. If we are correct in tracing Paul's own coda to the general statement in the first line, it is his way of insisting that reconciliation includes—and is expressed in—the non-imputation of sins (as Rom 4:3 ff. clarifies, with an appeal to Ps 32 [31]:2: "Happy is the man to whom Yahweh does not reckon sin"). λογίζεσθαι [τινί τι], "to reckon," is a characteristic of Paul's soteriology and its idioms. παράπτωμα, "trespass," too is frequent in Paul (sixteen times, but only here in our epistle).

Paul's own ministry is then described as a setting forth of the "word of reconciliation." What God has done needs to be proclaimed and his offer extended to the hearers. The nature of that response must now be considered, and is debated. But there can be little doubt that Denney's five pages (211–15) are a strong summing-up of what it is all about to preach the Gospel of reconciliation, for Paul and for those who seek empathy with him as a Christian teacher. They deserve to be cited *in extenso*, at least in significant extracts.

To Paul the estrangement which the Christian reconciliation has to overcome is indubitably two-sided; there is something in God as well as something in man which has to be dealt with before there can be peace. Nay, the something on God's side is so incomparably more serious that in comparison with it the something on man's side simply passes out of view. It is God's earnest dealing with the obstacle on His own side to peace with man which prevails on man to believe in the seriousness of His love, and to lay aside distrust. It is God's earnest dealing with the obstacle on His own side which constitutes the reconciliation; the story of it is "the word of reconciliation"; when men receive it, they *receive* (Rom. v. 10) the reconciliation. "Reconciliation" in the New Testament sense is not something which *we accomplish* when we lay aside our enmity to God; it is something which *God accomplished* when in the death of Christ He put away everything that on His side meant estrangement, so that He might come and preach peace. To deny this is to take St. Paul's Gospel away root and branch. He always conceives the Gospel as the revelation of God's wisdom and love in view of a certain state of affairs as subsisting between God and man. Now, what is the really serious element in this situation? What is it that makes a Gospel necessary? What is it that the wisdom and love of God undertake to deal with, and do deal with, in that marvellous way which constitutes the Gospel? Is it man's distrust of God? is it man's dislike, fear, antipathy, spiritual alienation? Not if we accept the Apostle's teaching. The serious thing which makes the Gospel necessary, and the putting away of which constitutes the Gospel, is God's condemnation of the world and its sin; it is God's wrath, "revealed from heaven against all ungodliness and unrighteousness of men" (Rom. i. 16–18). The putting away of this is "reconciliation": the preaching of *this* reconciliation is the preaching of the Gospel.

When St. Paul says that God has given him the ministry of reconciliation, he means that he is a preacher of this peace. He ministers reconciliation to the world. His work has no doubt a hortatory side, as we shall see, but that side is secondary. It is not the main part of his vocation to tell men to make their peace with God, but to tell them that God has made peace with the world. At bottom, the Gospel is not good advice, but good news. All the good advice it gives is summed up in this—Receive the good news. But if the good news be taken away; if we cannot say, God has made peace, God has dealt seriously with His condemnation of sin, so that it no longer stands in the way of your return to Him; if we cannot say, Here *is* the reconciliation, receive it,—then for man's actual state we have no Gospel at all.

When Christ's work was done, the reconciliation of the world was accomplished. When men were called to receive it, they were called to a relation to God, not in which they would no more be against Him—though that is included—but in which they would no more have Him against them. There would be no condemnation thenceforth to those who were in Christ Jesus.

The very universality of the expression—reconciling a world to Himself—is consistent only with an objective reconciliation. It cannot mean that God was overcoming the world's enmity (though that is the ulterior object) it means that God was putting away His own condemnation and wrath. When this was done, He could send, and did send, men to declare that it was done; and among these men, none had a profounder appreciation of what God had wrought, and what he himself had to declare as God's glad tidings, than the Apostle Paul.

20. ὑπὲρ Χριστοῦ οὖν πρεσβεύομεν ὡς τοῦ θεοῦ παρακαλοῦντος δι᾽ ἡμῶν. δεόμεθα ὑπὲρ Χριστοῦ, καταλλάγητε τῷ θεῷ, "We are then ambassadors for Christ, with God making his plea through us. We implore you on Christ's behalf, Be reconciled to God!" "This verse holds the key to the argument of v 18–21" (Collange, *Enigmes*, 273). Paul is appealing to the Corinthians both to embrace the fruits of divine reconciliation—inasmuch as they have moved away from his Gospel—and to heed and accept his proffered gesture of friendship (to be elaborated in 6:1–2, 11–13; 7:2–4).

He opens his case with a cited passage *ex hypothesi*, "We are then ambassadors (οὖν πρεσβεύομεν) for Christ, with God making his plea (ὡς τοῦ θεοῦ παρακαλοῦντος) through us," only to slip in an aside in order to enforce the *paradosis* and to temper it with a verb of tenderness and affection as well as to address the readers directly, in the imperative mood. δεόμεθα, "we implore," in our view turns the traditional teaching in a new direction. It is Paul's *applicatio*, as he holds out the offer of what reconciliation should mean in the situation of the Corinthian malcontents. "Be reconciled to God" is both the language of the kerygma (so I. H. Marshall; see earlier, p. 138) and Paul's adaptation of that kerygmatic appeal and *paraklēsis* to the pastoral requirements at Corinth. As we observed above, the linguistic data with the unusual terms (πρεσβεύομεν: Bornkamm, *TDNT* 6:651–83; the verb καταλλάσσειν in the passive imperative mood: see F. Büchsel, *TDNT* 1:256; the use of ὡς to denote "with the conviction that," BDF § 425.3; T. Muraoka, *NovT* 7 [1964] 58 ff.) all speak in favor of tracing here a piece of preformed material, redacted by the writer to ensure that its relevance will not be lost. The phrase "God making his plea through us" is also an unusual form, but highly suggestive in its indication that, while the human preacher is charged to deliver the word of reconciliation, it is not his or her voice that is to be heard but the very call and invitation of God which resonates in that proclamation. The value of this observation for a doctrine of Christian communication is clear. "Not simply is it [the case] that Paul heard God's call and answered it (Gal 1:15, 16): nor that he discovered the secret of his life's work in preaching (1 Cor 9:16). Rather, he came to see that in the proclamation of this message God was himself present . . . The daring claim to be acting and speaking for God would be audacious enough. Paul's wording goes beyond that as he reverses the roles and insists that when he speaks the kerygma God himself is the chief actor and it is his voice that men and women hear and his authority that is brought to bear upon people's lives" (cited from the present writer's *The Worship of God: Some Theological, Pastoral and Practical Reflections* [Grand Rapids: Eerdmans/Exeter: Paternoster Press, 1982] 104, 105).

The setting of this remark, "God making his plea through us," has been well characterized by J. Hainz, *Ekklesia*, 273: "To this event of reconciliation the apostle belongs. The ministry of reconciliation (διακονία τῆς καταλλαγῆς) which God gave him has the same origin as the reconciliation itself. In both Paul sees the activity of God. The same God who reconciles us to himself through Christ is also the author of the apostolate as a ministry of reconciliation, which is to be proclaimed through the apostle." The rationale behind this assertion is the fact that for Paul "his proclamation is the explication of the event of reconciliation," not as a continuation of it but as a making present (*Vergegenwärtigung*) of the action of God in Christ. So the apostle is representative of Christ and God at one and the same time. (This idea will be elaborated at 6:1, 3–10 as at 1:18 f.; 12:19; 13:3. So Hainz, 277– 80.)

The situational dimension of this teaching is brought out by Fallon, 52: "Reconciliation to God through the gospel and thus implicitly in this context to Paul as the apostle of the true gospel are part of God's ongoing work . . . to accept the true gospel means also to accept Paul as an authentic apostle of it."

21. The evidence for this verse as a piece of creedal material handed on to the Corinthians, akin to 1 Cor 11:23 ff.; 15:3 ff., is noteworthy; so Käsemann, "Some Thoughts," 53, who (as we observed) builds his case on two arguments: the fact that ἁμαρτία is here used of punishment for sin rather than sin as a power, which is the normal Pauline use; and the notion of "imparted" righteousness at the close of the v. (See too J. Reumann, *Righteousness;* P. Stuhlmacher, *Gerechtigkeit*, 74–77, esp. 77, n. 2, has objected to Käsemann's deduc-

tions, but not convincingly. Collange, 275, adds in the features of the tenuous link between vv 20 and 21 and the rhythmic and striking character [on stylistic grounds] of v 21 to support the thesis that here we have a traditional formula, cited to put a seal on Paul's appeal.)

We have already (p. 140) discussed the central issue in this soteriology: what is meant by "God appointed (ἐποίησεν) him [to be] sin"? Our conclusion is that the text is leaning on an Old Testament testimony, namely, Isa 53:10 where "offering for sin" (חַטָּאת, אָשָׁם, *ḥaṭṭāʾt ʾāšām*) is what is implied in ἁμαρτία (so Bruce, 210; Hofius, "Erwägungen," 196f., but only a cautious assessment is given by Thrall, 230, 231). The drawing on language derived from the ʿebed *Yahweh,* the servant of God, motif in the Old Testament would help to explain the unusual idiom here (the closest parallel is Gal 3:13) and be accounted for by recourse to an early Christian exegetical tradition which made much of Isaiah 53, an OT *testimonium* to which Paul does not apparently appeal in his rationale of the cross and the resurrection, except by invoking tradition. See O. Cullmann, *The Christology of the New Testament,* tr. S. C. Guthrie and C. A. M. Hall (London: SCM, 1959) 76. Against this view, see Bachmann who argues that the verb "made" is out of character, where we should expect "gave," "offered," "presented," but our rendering is explained by the non-Pauline character of the v as a whole, so there is no need to be embarrassed by the absence of Pauline parallels; see too Collange who regards Gal 3:13 as similar, and Barrett who follows Windisch in appealing to Rom 8:3 and finds here a forensic, rather than a cultic, flavor to ἁμαρτία when connected with δικαιοσύνη, "righteousness." But if the pre-Pauline or non-Pauline character of v 21 is proven on other grounds, here would be an extra confirmation, albeit in a negative way. The argument runs that where Paul does have recourse to cultic imagery, whether levitical (Rom 3:24–26: the proposal to equate Jesus in 2 Cor 5:21 with the goat for Azazel in Lev 16 is bizarre, though Héring, 45, favors it) or sacrificial in general (Rom 4:24, 25; 8:32; Phil 2:6–11), he is beholden to tradition. So both halves of v 21 are full of extra-Pauline (i.e., traditional) echoes: the preexistent (so Windisch; but this is unlikely in spite of a conceivable parallel with the *harpagmos,* "act of snatching," of Phil 2:6: he did not choose amiss in "deciding" to enter upon human existence) or the historical Jesus did not consent to sin, and at the cross by his death he was appointed a "sacrifice for sin," and as our representative "suffered all the consequences of human sin, including its penalty" (Thrall, 230).

The purpose of God's appointment of the innocent Christ ("the one who did not know sin" is Hebraic, utilizing the verb γινώσκειν = OT יָדַע, *yadaʿ,* "to have acquaintance with": Windisch [198] cites Rom 7:7 [cf. Rev 2:24] for this sense of γνῶναι ἁμαρτίαν; there is another idea of "knowing" which implies acceptance or approval, cf. Matt 7:23; both meanings would be accurate) is declared. It is twofold: on the one side, God identified his Son with the human condition in its alienation and lostness; on the other side, God declared that believers might become righteous with a righteousness that is his own (cf. NEB: "that in him we might be made one with the goodness of God himself"). The middle link of connection in this equation is that God in Christ has acted sovereignly to establish this new order, thus making "righteousness of God" (δικαιοσύνη τοῦ θεοῦ) not so much an individual quality available to faith as a gift (so Bultmann, 167; cf. his *Theology* 1:270–87, and his article "ΔΙΚΑΙΟΣΥΝΗ ΘΕΟΥ," *JBL* 83 [1964] 12–16; Conzelmann, *Outline*, 214–20) as a technical term for the eschatological act of God in power by which the world is set right with the divine purpose (so P. Stuhlmacher, *Gottesgerechtigkeit*, following E. Käsemann, in *New Testament Questions of Today*, 168–82). See the summaries in M. T. Brauch, "Perspectives," 523–35, and J. Reumann, *Righteousness*, 50–52. Collange, *Enigmes*, 278–80, strives to combine these two ideas, the personal and the cosmic, in company with K. Kertelge, '*Rechtfertigung*,' who, apropos of our v speaks of the way God has acted, in his righteousness, on man's behalf, thereby instituting a new era of divine-human relations (304). The strong point in seeking to combine the two elements is the place accorded to γενώμεθα . . . ἐν αὐτῷ, "that we might become . . . in him," which is equivalent to being "in Christ" (ἐν Χριστῷ, v 17). It is through their faith-nexus with Christ who was "appointed" (giving to ἐποίησεν this sense, as in Mark 3:14; Acts 2:36) to act for humankind that believers come to share in the benefits of his reconciling deed and enter the new world of acceptance *coram Deo*, as God is well pleased with his Son's ever-pleasing relationship. So "righteousness" relates to "God's whole intervention in Jesus" (Ziesler, *The Meaning of Righteousness*, 159).

Explanation

The lengthy, weighty passage in vv 16–21 has many facets but one master theme. In it Paul is setting down the Christian conviction that in the Christ event a new world has been born and a new age has supervened on world history. Phrases like "a new creation," "reconciliation," and "righteousness of God" are all virtual synonyms for this new eon which has radically affected *both* divine-human *and* all earthly relationships.

God has inaugurated the new age at his sovereign instigation (v 18) and by a set of events so unparalleled that, even if the idiom is OT and a bewildering kaleidoscope of forensic (v 19) and cultic (v 21) images is conceivably pressed into service, Paul or his source has left the modern reader at a loss to handle all these statements adequately. We may sympathize with Bengel's bewilderment: *quis auderet sic loqui, nisi Paulus praeirit?* (Who would have dared to speak thus, unless Paul had first led the way?) One or two things stand out, however.

First, the thrust of the text, especially in the Pauline redaction, is inalienably personal. The cosmic transformation, implied in v 19, is recast in Paul's hands, in such a way that we cannot fail to see that at its heart is the forgiveness of sins and a new relationship with God through Christ that unites us with our creator as reconciled persons.

Then, Paul's purpose is eminently practical and pastoral. He calls on a piece of soteriological credo to enforce the call "Be reconciled to God," issued here to errant Christians who were doubting both Paul's kerygma and his own attitude to them. So he turns the kerygma of the world's salvation into a version of his own Gospel; and armed with that version, he implores his readers to apply the message and to live as "reconciled children" of God and as his own true converts (6:13).

H. Paul's Appeal for an Open Heart   (6:1-13)

Bibliography

Betz, H.-D. *Lukian von Samosata und das Neue Testament.* TU 76. Berlin: Akademie, 1961. **Brillet, G.** "Voici les jours de salut (2 Cor. 6:10)." *AsSeign* 26 (1962) 21–36. **Congar, Y.** "In the World and not of the World." *Scr* 9 (1957) 53–59. **Ellis, E. E.** *Prophecy and Hermeneutic in Early Christianity.* Grand Rapids: Wm. B. Eerdmans, 1978. **Fascher, E.** "Theologische Beobachtungen zu *dei.*" In *Neutestamentliche Studien für Rudolf Bultmann,* ed. W. Eltester, 248–54. Berlin, Töpelmann, 1954. **Fridrichsen, A.** "Paulus und die Stoa." *ConNT* IV (1944) 27–34. **Friedrich, G.** *Amt und Lebensführung: Eine Auslegung von 2 Kor. 6:1–10.* Neukirchen-Vluyn: Neukirchener Verlag, 1963. **Furnish, V. P.** "The Ministry of Reconciliation." *CurTM* 4 (1977) 204–18. **Harnack, A. Von.** "'κόπος (κοπιᾶν, οἱ κοπιῶντες) im frühchristlichen Sprachgebrauch." *ZNW* 27 (1928) 1–10. **Höistad, R.** "Eine hellenistische Parallele zu 2 Kor 6, 3ff." *ConNT* IX (1944) 22–27. **Kamlah, E.** *Die Form der katalogischen Paränese im NT.* WUNT 7. Tübingen: J. C. B. Mohr, 1964. **Kleinknecht, K. T.** *Der leidende Gerechtfertigte.* WUNT 2nd series, 13. Tübingen: Mohr, 1984. **Martin, R. P.** *Reconciliation. A Study of Paul's Theology.* **Mealand, D. L.** "As having nothing and yet possessing everything: 2 Cor. 6:10c." *ZNW* 67 (1976) 277–79. **Müller-Bardorff, J.** "Nachtlicher Gottesdienst im apostolischen Zeitalter." *TZ* 81 (1956) 347–52. **Neumann, M.** "Ministry, Weakness, and Spirit in II Corinthians." *ClerRev* 59 (1974) 647–60. **Rood, L. A.** "Le Christ comme δύναμις θεοῦ." *RechBib* 5 (1960) 93–108. **Schoeps, H. J.** *Theologie und Geschichte des Judenchristentums.* Tübingen: J. C. B. Mohr, 1949. ———. *Paul.* Tr. G. A. F. Knight. London: Lutterworth Press, 1961. **Schrage, W.** "Leid, Kreuz und Eschaton: Die Peristasenkataloge als Merkmale paulinischer theologia crucis und Eschatologie." *EvT* 34 (1974) 141–75. **Stählin, G.** "'Um mitzusterben und mitzuleben' Bemerkungen zu 2 Kor 7, 3," In *Neue Testament und christliche Existenz.* FS. H. Braun. ed. H.-D. Betz and L. Schottroff, 503–21. Tübingen: J. C. B. Mohr, 1973. **Stoger, A.** "Die paulinische Versöhnungstheologie." *TPQ* 122 (1974) 118–31. **Von Hodgson, R.** "Paul the Apostle and First Century Tribulation Lists." *ZNW* 74 (1983) 59–80. **Werff, B.** "Teurgeefs ontvangen Genade, 2 Cor 6:1–2." *GThT* 7 (1906) 114–16. **Wibbing, S.** *Die Tugend- und Lasterkataloge im NT.* BZNW 25. Berlin: Töpelmann, 1959.

Translation

[1] *Thus, as co-workers [with him],*[a] *we exhort* [b] *you not to receive God's grace in vain.* [2] *For he says,*

> *In an acceptable time I heard you*
> *and in a day of salvation I helped you.*

Look, now is the acceptable time [of salvation]; look, now is the day of salvation. [3] *We do not put a stumbling-block in anyone's path so that the ministry* [c] *may not be faulted.* [4] *Rather, in every way, as God's servants,* [d] *we commend* [e] *ourselves; in great endurance, in moments of affliction, anguish, and distress,* [5] *in beatings, in*

imprisonments, in social disorders, in labors, in times of sleeplessness, and hunger,
⁶in purity, in knowledge, in patience, in kindness, in the Holy Spirit,ᶠ in genuine
love, ⁷in the message of truth, in the power of God; through the weapons of righteousness,
both on the right hand and on the left, ⁸through glory and dishonor, through bad
reputation and good; as deceivers, yet true men; ⁹as unknown, yet well-known; as
dying, and yet we live; as being chastened,ᵍ yet not killed; ¹⁰as sorrowing, yet always
rejoicing; as poor, yet making many rich; as having nothing, yet possessing everything.
¹¹We have spoken freely to you, Corinthians and opened ourʰ hearts wide. ¹²We
do not withhold our affection from you, but you withhold affection from us. ¹³In
returnⁱ—as I speak to [my]ʲ children—you do the same to us.

Notes

ᵃAlthough "with him" is not represented in the original, the English calls for a complement.
See *Comment.*

ᵇ𝔭⁴⁶ D F G have παρακαλοῦντες instead of παρακαλοῦμεν.

ᶜThe Western Text (D F G it vg syr) favored by NIV, RSV adds ἡμῶν, thus "our ministry."
Though "our ministry" is a natural emphasis, the suggestion of Barrett (182, n. 1), that ἡ διακονία
should be not restricted to Paul's activity, deserves examination.

ᵈδιάκονοι, being in the nominative, cannot be used as accusative (see Robertson, *Grammar,*
454). Hence "as God's workers we commend," not "we commend ourselves as God's workers"
(see *Comment*).

ᵉThe text is supported by 𝔭⁴⁶ ℵ* C D*. Other variants are συνιστάνοντες found in B 1175,
and συνιστῶντες located in ℵ² D² TR.

ᶠThough no definite article is found in the text, most commentators see this as a reference
to the third person of the Trinity (*contra* Barrett).

ᵍThe more common πειραζόμενοι ("undergoing testing") is found in the Western text (D* F
G it Ambst), but our textual reading παιδευόμενοι appears better supported: it is certainly *lectio
difficilior.*

ʰWe find ὑμῶν, "your," in 𝔭⁴⁶ ℵ B. This is probably the result of the error of itacism (see
Metzger, *The Text of the New Testament,* 191, 192). If the older reading is taken, this verse makes
little sense. Bruce reminds us that antiquity of attestation is not always an indication of a true
reading (213).

ⁱLit., "in recompense." See Moule, *Idiom Book,* 160 f., for use of the accusative. See also
Comment.

ʲThough "my" is not represented in the Greek text, Pauline penchant demands the English
"my." See *Comment.*

Form/Structure/Setting

Our passage under study provides a fitting climax to Paul's exposition of
the theme of his ministry (5:20). To enforce his appeal, he urges the Corinthians to receive God's grace in a wholehearted way (6:1). He highlights this
exhortation by quoting Scripture (Isa 49:8, LXX) and adding his *pesher* comment, namely that the time of prophetic fulfillment is now. The present is
both the right time to act for God and the right time for God to act. But
6:2 appears as a parenthesis breaking Paul's train of thought. (Here is another
example of how Paul's dictation did not produce a flowing discussion.)

This break alerts us to the fact that Paul is presently to diverge from his
theme of reconciliation to a new theme of commending himself to the Corinthians as one worthy of God's ministry and worthy of their love. In 6:3, he
begins his apology, which is his defense of his ministry, by showing there is
no reason for the Corinthians, at least with respect to his work, to have

received the grace of God in vain. His ministry is faultless to the degree that Paul commends himself again to them. He does this commending in a series of examples of contrasts, as found in 6:4–10. It will be well to examine this commendation in detail.

We enlist the aid of Collange (*Enigmes*, 281–301) in analyzing this section. This scholar believes that Paul used a preexisting text when he came to include 6:4–10 in our epistle (290). This idea may have grounds for support when we notice the interesting design of the passage. It appears that the verses before us are composed of four stanzas (4*b*–5; 6–7*a;* 7*b*–8*a;* 8*b*–10), in which a rich and unusual vocabulary is found. The closest parallel is in 2 Enoch 66:6 (Windisch, 206, who speaks of "an amazing set of parallels"). Sprinkled throughout these verses are terms that reflect stereotype expressions used by contemporary moralists. It may be possible that Paul has reworked a pre-formed passage, for we also notice that some of the terms are polemical, possibly with a direct view to his opponents. Also, we can locate some terms that appear autobiographical for Paul. In short, Paul has probably taken a text of stoic nature (so Höistad, "Hellenistische Parallele," 22–27; and Fridrichsen, "Paulus und die Stoa," 27; but this is challenged by Kleinknecht, *Der leidende Gerechtfertigte*, 264, 265, 268, who appeals to the Jewish righteous sufferer model) and edited it to fit his purpose (see the section of 6:14–7:1 for another example where Paul has taken an already existing text—in that case possibly Essene in background—and reworked it to his advantage).

(1) In the first stanza (4*b*–5), Paul gives us nine forms of suffering that he has endured. ὑπομονή ("endurance") is set at the head as a "text" (see Kleinknecht, ibid., 256). These nine forms are broken down into three groups of three. The first group (θλῖψις, ἀνάγκη, στενοχωρία) describes the suffering of Paul in general terms ("generic tribulations," so von Hodgson, 63). In fact, these terms reflect the eschatological nature of his ministry (Collange, 293). We note that the preposition ἐν, "in," begins a run (eighteen times repeated to be exact) that carries into 6:7. We also note the tie between θλῖψις and ἀνάγκη (1 Thess 3:7) and between θλῖψις and στενοχωρία (2 Cor 4:8; Rom 8:35). For Paul, this is a designation of his existence as an apostle (Collange, 293, 94).

The second group of three in this first stanza focuses on concrete examples of Paul's suffering, namely, πληγή, φυλακή, and ἀκαταστασία. The third group concentrates on aspects of Paul's suffering that appear to be voluntary (κόπος, ἀγρυπνία, and νηστεία). When these last six terms are considered together, there are two important points to notice. The first observation is the similarity of 6:5 and 11:23, 27. Except for ἀκαταστασία (which is found only again in 12:20 [Collange, 294, n. 2]) the terms of 6:5 are all repeated in 11:23, 27. The latter passage appears as an expansion and refinement of the former, but the precise meanings are not necessarily the same. Taken together, both passages describe the *peristaseis*, "lists of trials," of the apostolic ministry, however.

Furthermore, a second point is to be noted. Four of the terms (πληγή, φυλακή, ἀγρυπνία, and νηστεία) are used by Paul nowhere except in 6:5 and 11:23, 27. The fifth one (κόπος) is one of Paul's favorite idioms in outlining his missionary work (1 Thess 2:9; 3:5; 2 Thess 3:8; 2 Cor 10:15). From this it should be apparent that Paul has characterized his ministry in 6:4*b*–5. Yet, this first stanza was not written in isolation from other parts of our epistle. Paul will again (11:23, 27) bring to the attention of his readers his credentials for being considered a true apostle.

(2) In our second stanza (6–7*a*) Paul turns from the external circumstances (Barrett, 186) of his life to the inward marks that delineate his moral character. To help his readers catch the flavor of this description, Paul employs such literary tools as alliteration and chiasmus. He commences this stanza with four couples of virtues. The first two couples (ἀγνότητι–γνώσει; μακροθυμίᾳ–χρηστότητι) are preceded by ἐν and marked by Paul's use of alliteration (Collange, 295), or at least assonance. Moreover, it can be argued that Paul exudes polemical tendencies toward Corinthian libertinism (Collange, 295). This is noted in connection with ἀγνότης, "purity," which stands at the head of the second stanza (cf. 12:20, 21; but more probably it is purity of motive, as in 4:2, that is in mind).

The closing part of our present stanza lists the remaining two sets of virtues. This time however, Paul uses double terms to describe these virtues. And in doing so, Paul utilizes the rhetorical device of chiasmus, a criss-cross arrangement:

$$
\text{ἐν} + \begin{array}{l} \text{A} \quad πνεύματι\ ἁγίῳ \\ \text{B} \quad λόγῳ\ ἀληθείας \end{array} \quad\times\quad \begin{array}{l} \text{B}' \quad ἀγάπῃ\ ἀνυποκρίτῳ \\ \text{A}' \quad δυνάμει\ θεοῦ \end{array}
$$

Looking closer, we see that Paul has employed idioms that reflect in his language usage both stereotype and polemics. With respect to λόγος ἀληθείας, "message of truth," we see an expression that is consonant with the view found elsewhere in the NT that the Gospel is true (Collange, 296; see Eph 1:13; Col 1:5; 2 Tim 2:15; Jas 1:18). In addition, the use of ἀλήθεια in this context exhibits polemical tendencies. This can be seen many times in our epistle (1:18; 2:17; 4:2; 7:14; 11:10; 12:6; 13:8). The reader will be prepared for a treatment of the opponents that are described as being false, i.e., bogus, making claims that cannot be sustained as true. Hence the titles ψευδαπόστολοι, "false apostles," and "deceitful workers" (ἐργάται δόλιοι; 11:13). The position that Paul is concerned to be polemical is also shown in that the parallel component of λόγος ἀληθείας in our chiastic structure is most likely polemical as well (Collange, 296). We note in 12:15–17 that Paul expounds his love for the Corinthians and that in a sarcastic tone ("Yet, crafty fellow that I am, I caught you by trickery") he confesses that his love is genuine (i.e., with no δόλος [cunning], and so ἀνυπόκριτος [with no insincerity]).

(3) Our third stanza (7*b*–8) is set off mainly because of the change of forms that are used and that break the pattern in the passage. Paul has concluded his (seemingly endless) use of ἐν, "in," and introduces the preposition διά. This preposition, rendered "through," helps to develop a different slant to Paul's argument. In the first stanza, Paul elucidates the outward circumstances surrounding his ministry; the second stanza echoes his moral rectitude. In short, the writer is describing his apostleship. However, in our third stanza, Paul prepares to describe both the means by which he performs his ministry

(7*b*) and the paradoxical consequences that result from this work (8*a;* see Collange, 297). Once again we note a chiastic construction; this time in 8*a:*

Paul has introduced the idea of a ministry that produces varying evaluations. This thought will continue throughout the remainder of vv 8*b*–10. The idea of antithetical components could be Paul's way of demonstrating that even the true minister of God may encounter a negative reaction to his well-intentioned work. This is seen in that Paul has to overcome the accusations of his opponents. His ministry is not above attack, but we note that, for every complaint hurled against his apostleship, Paul produces a positive rebuttal. Since v 8*a* has this antithetical or paradoxical nature, it goes better with 8*b*–10 than with what precedes it (Collange). We also detect the presence of assonance and homoioteleuton (words with similar endings) in 8*a*, produced by terms (δυσ-φημίας/εὐ-φημίας) that belong together.

(4) In the fourth and final stanza (8*b*–10) of our present passage (6:4–10), Paul launches into a catalogue of the "vicissitudes of the apostolic life" (Bruce, 212; Héring, 48) by composing a mosaic that contrasts the worldly and divine. In this strophe we find seven specimens of paradox: impostors/true; unknown/well-known; dying/living; punished/preserved from death; sorrowful/always rejoicing; poor/making many rich; having nothing/having everything.

The literary form of 6:8*b*–10 differs somewhat from the rest of the passage. The first term of each antithesis is introduced by ὡς, "as," which replaces the διά of the preceding stanza. The second term is preceded by either καὶ (the first, second, third, fourth, and seventh antitheses) or δέ (the fifth and sixth antitheses). It should be noted that καὶ fulfills the adversative function. So the alternation of καὶ and δέ is more stylistic than substantive.

Though the fourth stanza is made up of paradoxes, a close examination reveals that each term is not necessarily contradictory of its partner. More likely, the last term complements the first (see *Comment*). That this was Paul's intention can be seen in his use of paronomasia. This is especially evident in 9*a* where we find ἀγνοούμενοι and ἐπιγινωσκόμενοι. Paul wishes to show that, in spite of the negative accusations brought against his ministry, God has brought him safely through. Moreover, he again uses polemical thoughts to undergird the argument that both terms of the paradox can actually be true. That is, it is true Paul has been slandered and misjudged. But what he shows in 8*b* (see 3:12; 4:2), in 9*a*, and in 10*b, c* is that, while the descriptions of his ministry are real, the substance or veracity of each negative evaluation is lacking. The proof is in the fact that the apostle has remained under God's care. This in itself should prove the truthfulness of his apostleship. He does not need the aid of "letters of recommendation" (3:1–3). Rather, in light of his opponents' attacks, Paul has survived as the true apostle of God.

It should be easy to see the emotion that accompanied this passage. The gravity of Paul's appeal is mirrored in the structure of 6:4–10. This section, especially vv 6–10, may be one of the most lyrically attractive readings of Paul, comparable with 1 Corinthians 13. Our section has been called one of the high peaks of the Pauline epistles (Hughés, 238). The evidence for such a verdict appears in the mounting effect of the structure of this passage, though the "effect he [Paul] desires upon his readers is that of truth, not of verbal bravura" (Hughes, 226, n. 67).

6:1–13 closes with a heartfelt appeal to the Corinthians (6:11–13). Paul has opened his heart to them, possibly by saying more than he intended ("I have let my tongue run away with me," Barrett, 191). But he looks for a reciprocal response on behalf of the Corinthians. They, not Paul, have withheld affection, something a "father" (Paul's own term, 1 Cor 4:14, 15) finds disconcerting and perplexing.

Collange (*Enigmes*, 281–84, 300, 301) has hypothesized that 6:3–13 represents the ending to one of two editions of a letter prepared by Paul. In general, 2:14—6:2 constitutes the basic letter of Paul. Faced by two sets of readership, he constructed two separate endings so as to be able to send two different letters. Specifically the Corinthians (Christians living in Corinth) were to receive a letter composed of 2:14—6:2 plus 6:3–13 with chap. 8 added. Another letter (2:14—6:2 plus 6:14—7:4) was to go to the people of "Achaia," i.e., those living in southern Greece, who are also addressed in chap. 9. In the eyes of Collange, the ending (6:13) of our passage is the conclusion of a letter.

This proposal has received little support, especially in that no MS evidence can be found to support two separate editions. The MS evidence suggests that 2 Corinthians never circulated in any form other than as it is found in the canon. We cannot, of course, tell whether it was redacted at a precanonical stage or stages to produce a literary unit. Yet, it appears that Collange has used this proposal to overcome (all too easily, it may be) the difficulties surrounding 6:14—7:1 by suggesting that 6:1 is directly linked to 6:14. Following Windisch, he submits that, after Paul's παρακαλοῦμεν, "we exhort," it is natural to expect a piece of paraenesis such as appears in 6:14–7:1. Thus he neatly explains the hiatus between 6:13 and 14.

Comment

1. Συνεργοῦντες δὲ καί, "Thus, as co-workers [with him]." In the preceding verses Paul has just described the nature of his ministry. This ministry may be characterized in the entreaty Paul gives in 5:20. From 6:1, 2 we can learn of the content of this entreaty (see *Form/Structure/Setting*). Before examining this content, we need, however, to examine the participle συνεργοῦντες, "as co-workers."

The phrase "thus, as co-workers" comes across as incomplete in the English (any translation requires a complement; Barrett, 183). The question is posed "with whom" is Paul working? (Note Paul's use of first person plural; see *Comment* on 5:11.) There have been several suggestions offered as possible answers to this question. One is that συνεργοῦντες (present participle of συνεργέω) has its complement in "other teachers" (see Plummer, 189). But for this suggestion to be supported, one would have to overcome a dilemma.

Either the first person plural speaks only of Paul or the translation of συνεργοῦντες comes out as "co-working with ourselves." The first solution is highly suspect in that if Paul wanted to single out himself, he would have used the first person singular (see *Comment* on 5:10). The second view is to be dismissed because it is meaningless.

Others have suggested that the complement of the participle is the Corinthians (so Chrysostom, Bachmann, Allo). But this position is also called into question because Paul has just finished urging the Corinthians to accept him as a worthy minister of the Gospel (5:11–13). Moreover, he will again resume this theme (6:3–12; 7:2–7). Why speak to somebody as though they were fellow-workers, if indeed, they have been accused of being just the opposite?

The best option for the complement of συνεργοῦντες is God (so Calvin; Hodge, 152; Denney, 225; Tasker, 91; Plummer, 189; Héring, 46; Barrett, 183; Hughes, 216, 217; Collange, 285, who cites 1 Thess 3:2 where Timothy is συνεργὸς τοῦ θεοῦ ἐν τῷ εὐαγγελίῳ τοῦ Χριστοῦ, according to D* 33 lat: see F. F. Bruce, *1 & 2 Thessalonians* WBC [1982] 82). This is seen in an earlier statement, in which the apostle speaks of being "God's fellow-worker" (1 Cor 3:9; the idea of working with God is not foreign to Paul's mind; so Hughes, 216). Better yet, the context of 6:1 supports our choice, "with God" as the complement. In 5:20, as was seen, Paul is being used by God as an avenue through which the message of reconciliation flows. Taken with what follows ("we exhort you not to receive God's grace in vain") there is an unbroken logic. Paul cooperates with God in bringing the message of reconciliation to the Corinthians; Paul cooperates with God in exhorting the Corinthians not to receive this message in vain. Hence, though the original has no explicit complement (Bruce, 211) we insert the words "with him" in our translation. (We note that while the antecedent for "him" is usually taken to be God [KJV/AV, RSV, NIV, GNB, NEB, Phillips], it could be taken to be Christ [so Plummer, 189].)

παρακαλοῦμεν, "we exhort you" (παρακαλεῖν, "to exhort," was used in 5:20). The appeal was made through Paul (and his fellow-workers?) as an appeal for reconciliation. God has made peace with humankind. But apparently this exhortation needs rehearsing for, as will be seen, Paul again has to exhort the Corinthians (Barrett, 183, takes the object of παρακαλοῦμεν to be all Christians). This time, though, Paul is not bringing the message of reconciliation to the Corinthians for the first time; rather he urges the Corinthians that they do not receive the grace of God in vain, i.e., by failing to act upon what he has told them and so opposing his ministry. But the phrase has been given a wider connotation. Let us review the options, in a mini-*Auslegungsgeschichte*.

μὴ εἰς κενὸν τὴν χάριν τοῦ θεοῦ δέξασθαι ὑμᾶς, "not to receive God's grace in vain." Immediately upon reading this clause, we are faced with two imposing questions: (1) What does Paul mean to say when he speaks of "receiving God's grace in vain"? and, (2) What may have led the Corinthians to receive grace in this manner? We shall answer these questions in the order just presented.

One explanation of what Paul means to "have received the grace" (χάρις;

seen in Christ's redemptive act, discussed in 5:21; cf. 1 Cor 15:10) of God "in vain" ([εἰς]κενόν; "empty"; "to no purpose"; "without result"; see LXX Lev 26:20; Job 39:16; Isa 29:8; Jer 6:29; 28:58; 1 Thess 3:5; Gal 2:2; Phil 2:16) is to view Paul as thinking that some receive God's grace only by external means. This may reflect the idea found in the Parable of the Four Seeds (Mark 4:1–9, 13–20; Matt 13:1–9, 18–23; Luke 8:4–8; 11–15) where some, after receiving the message (seed) of the kingdom with joy, fall away during times of difficulty and persecution (Matt 13:5, 20, 21). But we concur with Hughes (217) that it is doubtful in 6:1 that Paul is considering either a counterfeit faith or the concept of perseverance. Also, δέξασθαι, "to receive," is an aorist infinitive, suggesting an event of the past (conversion, so Plummer, 190), though an aorist infinitive does not always imply an event prior to the action of the main verb (see Héring, 46).

Another possibility is that Paul envisages a person who, after first receiving the grace of God, then proceeds to lose this grace. But this is not what Paul teaches elsewhere. In Phil (1:6) we find that Paul was confident that God, who had begun a good work in them, would carry it through to completion.

A third possibility of what Paul means by receiving God's grace in vain is proposed by Hodge (154). He sees that the statement under consideration speaks to humankind in general and that this is a declaration of Paul's preaching method. But Hodge gives a strange twist to the verse when he writes that "not to receive the grace of God in vain" is tantamount to exhorting all men not to reject salvation. This statement as quoted is strange because it implies that something has been received. Furthermore, as Héring asks (46), how can anyone be exhorted not to have done something? (The point is that the aorist δέξασθαι suggests that something has already taken place. Thus, one cannot exhort somebody to avoid doing something that has already transpired.) Also, Hodge ignores Paul's focus of attention on the Corinthians, instead of humankind, as exhibited by ὑμᾶς ("you").

In the light of Paul's thinking in 5:10 ("the judgment seat of Christ") it appears that the best answer to the question is that the grace of God has been given in vain because it has not produced the desired results. Barrett pertinently writes (183) that "it is no forgone conclusion that all will cease to live to themselves and live henceforth for Christ" (5:14, 15). Paul had brought to the Corinthians the Gospel of reconciliation. In essence, their failure to "practice" their profession constituted a "denial of the logical implications of the Gospel" (Hughes, 218). Having learned that Jesus died for them, they had not yet died to themselves. And this failure to die was partially exhibited in their failure to have stood by Paul. This "frustration of grace" (so Barclay, Commentary ad loc.) is an example of nongratitude for God's love (Filson, 345).

Yet Paul had not left them with a theoretical statement only. He had provided an example for them ("a paradigm of reconciliation") when he forgave the offender whom he encountered on his painful visit. (See 2:8–11, especially v 10; cf. 7:12a.) That is, Paul enacted a "parable of reconciliation" when he showed how the forgiveness of God works and how it is to affect one's life. In turn, the Corinthians should also receive the offender and not be unduly rigorous in punishing this one (2:7). But something deeper is at stake, since Paul's role as a Christian leader and teacher has been seriously questioned at Corinth. So, reconciliation should take place between Paul and the church. That this has been effected before the writing of 2 Cor 1–9 can be seen in chap. 7. But the point is clear. God has reconciled the world to himself and if his people believe this, then there should be reconciliation among them. If Paul's Gospel is true, then the Corinthians should receive him as well as his message ("So to be open to *his* apostolic person is part of the human response to the message," Martin, *Reconciliation,* 110; cf. Furnish, "The Ministry," 216–18). Therefore, it appears that the meaning behind Paul's understanding of receiving the grace of God in vain is to accept the apostolic kerygma only to abandon it, or to have a counterfeit faith based on an easygoing adherence to what his rivals would promote at Corinth (11:4: "if you accept a different gospel" brought by bogus teachers, 11:13–15). It is to fail to grow and mature in the Christian life, as evidenced by a life under the control of the one who died for believers (unlike the results in the Corinthians seen later in 12:21). And what better way for Paul to show this than to forgive and accept the one who was at an earlier time an enemy. Likewise the Corinthians are exhorted to share Paul's spirit and come over to his side.

With our first question now answered, we turn to the second. If Paul sees the Corinthians failing to respond properly to his Gospel, what may have been the reason for this failure? Whereas we answered the first question with some degree of certainty, the answer to the second one remains in the realm of conjecture, with several options to be noted in the history of interpretation. Possibly the Corinthians, in pursuit of selfish concerns, had not exhibited any growth. This becomes a possibility in light of Paul's scathing remarks in 1 Cor 3:1–3, or the Corinthians could have been influenced by the false apostles (2:17; later in 11:1–15 this influence becomes a real threat) who proclaimed a gospel different from Paul's (11:4; note that in 11:4 Paul uses ἐδέξασθε, from the same verb as in 6:1). If the latter is true, we see a reflection of the situation Paul encountered in Gal 3:1–3, where it appears that members of the church support the position that they themselves can contribute something to obtaining salvation. This is what Paul, especially in the Corinthian letter, calls καύχησις, "boasting," a term applicable to any effort to usurp the sovereignty of God and to subvert his grace (Collange, *Enigmes,* 285). If this is attempted, grace (Augustine recalls that grace is freely [*gratis*] given) loses its distinctive character (P. S. Watson, *The Concept of Grace* [London: Epworth Press, 1959] chap. 6). One is no longer appreciative of the deed done on his behalf and thus does not feel compelled to live a life for the one who died for him (see Denney for this idea). Maybe the reason for the Corinthians' lack of growth is a combination of the two possibilities offered. Regardless, the grace of God bestowed on the Corinthians has not led them to live for the one who died and rose again for them (5:15; the Corinthians evidently still resist Paul's appeal in 6:13; 7:2). Bruce, 211, quotes Acts 20:24.

2. λέγει γάρ, "For he says." This verse appears as a parenthesis (Tasker, 92), interrupting Paul's theme of exhortation. Yet, the inclusion of Isa 49:8 (quoted almost exactly from the LXX) extends Paul's argument in 6:1 by stressing the urgency of the moment. The use of λέγει without a stated subject

is not uncommon in the epistles (Rom 9:25; 10:8; 15:10; Gal 3:16; Eph 4:8; 5:14; also cf. Heb 8:8, 13; Jas 4:6; sometimes we find φησίν, "it says," used likewise, 1 Cor 6:16; Heb 8:5). The translation of λέγει can be either "he (God) says" or "it (Scripture) says" without affecting the meaning (see Hughes, 219, n. 58). Either of these suggestions for translation should include quotation marks (so Plummer, 190; contra Goudge who thinks the subject of λέγει is the servant of Deutero-Isaiah; this, however, contradicts the context of Isa 49:8, in which God, not the servant, is the one speaking ["Thus saith the Lord"]).

καιρῷ δεκτῷ ἐπήκουσά σου καὶ ἐν ἡμέρᾳ σωτηρίας ἐβοήθησά σοι, "In an acceptable time, I heard you and in a day of salvation I helped you." We may ask, why does Paul insert this verse? Part of the answer may lie in the idea that he is emphasizing the urgency of the time, as well as its expediency.

For Paul the coming of Christ marked the inauguration of the messianic age, the better time when God in his mercy accepts man in grace (Barrett, 183). Paul is claiming that prophecy has been fulfilled. The time (καιρός) was acceptable. Plummer views the use of δεκτός (acceptable) as showing that the emphasis is on what is acceptable for men (190, 191). He cites Luke 4:19, which uses Isa 61:1, 2 (also, see H. Conzelmann, *Theology of St. Luke*, tr. G. Buswell [London: Faber, 1960] 36, who sees a contrast between Paul and Luke; for only the latter, not the former, sees Jesus' ministry as the acceptable year of the Lord; cf. I. H. Marshall, *Luke: Historian and Theologian*, [Grand Rapids: Zondervan/Exeter: Paternoster Press, 1970] 120, 121). But Plummer's position overlooks that both Isa 61:2 (שְׁבַת־רָצוֹן יהוה, *šᵉbat-rāṣôn Yhwh*, "Yahweh's year of grace") and Isa 49:8 (בְּעֵת רָצוֹן, *bᵉʿat rāṣôn*, "a season of grace") speak of the acceptance of men by God (Hughes, 220). See too Bultmann, 169.

In this acceptable time God has "heard," ἐπήκουσα ("listened," from ἐπακούειν, which may be a technical term for hearing prayer, Betz, *Lucian*, 61), and helped (ἐβοήθησα) his people. This may be seen in the way Paul combines the themes of help from God and servanthood (Hughes 219, 220). For one thing, the Corinthians could testify that God's grace had come to them (and in essence he had heard their prayer). Next, Paul the ambassador of God with the message of reconciliation was also an example of God's grace (expressed, so Paul thought, in his ministry as well as in his action toward the offender). Also, the concept of Jesus as the servant, the one responsible for the implementation of the age of reconciliation, the "acceptable time," could be suggested by Isa 49:8. Therefore Isa 49:8 reminds the Corinthians of their acceptance of grace, made possible by Paul, in the transforming power of their Savior. "In the faithful discharge of his apostolic office Paul, the servant of the Servant, had made himself their servant; they had been brought into the participation of the eschatological messianic kingdom and all its blessings" (Hughes, 219, 220).

Ἰδοὺ νῦν καιρὸς εὐπρόσδεκτος, ἰδοὺ νῦν ἡμέρα σωτηρίας, "Look, now is the acceptable time of salvation; Look, now is the day of salvation." Paul drives home his argument in the preceding part: the anticipation of the servant has become a reality among you, Corinthians. What we have here may be Paul's use of the interpretative method called *pesher*, as he analyzes the Old

Testament quotation and makes its contemporary fulfillment the point to be grasped (so Ellis, *Paul's Use of the Old Testament* [Edinburgh: Oliver & Boyd, 1957] 143; Bruce, 211, "avail themselves now of the grace of God"; cf. Heb 3:12–15).

Paul has changed the δεκτός of the Isaianic citation to a strengthened form, namely εὐπρόσδεκτος (so Barrett, 183, who translates "Behold, now is the 'welcome' time"). That the attention of the Corinthians is sought is evident from the double use of ἰδού, "look," and νῦν, "now."

It is easy to see that the use of "now" suggests the urgency of accepting God's grace (O. Cullmann, *Salvation in History*, tr. S. G. Sowers *et al.* [New York: Harper & Row/London: SCM, 1967] 248). There is no time to lose. Plummer is probably correct in stating that this is more an exhortation to act than a fear expressed of the shortness of time (191). But this urgency is also predicated by Paul's view that his preaching is part of the eschatological event itself (see Bultmann, *Exegetica* [Tübingen: J. C. B. Mohr, 1967] 164). His coming to the Corinthians with the Gospel, the message of reconciliation, provides the word of the cross that creates a crisis in the sense that one must respond to the demands of the age that was initiated with the resurrection of Christ (as in 5:16, with its double νῦν, "now").

Cullmann takes the νῦν to mean not only the moment, but the interim period as well (254, 255). There is a time-frame, with its before and after, for each individual, as well as for humankind (and creation) as a whole. For Paul God has acted; men and women must accept. There was the beginning point before Christ came, and for each individual (set by death, Heb 9:27) as well as for creation (Matt 13:24–50) there is a termination point. Act now, Paul urges, for this is the acceptable (and only) time to do so.

But we cannot leave 6:2 without pointing out that salvation is probably not the only issue in Paul's mind. In view of his emphasis on the need to live a life worthy of God (5:9, 10, 14, 15) and in view of our understanding of 6:1 (not to receive God's grace in vain), Paul is probably urging the Corinthians to rededicate their lives to the Christian ideal. Paul's preaching does not end with the call to be reconciled to God; his preaching is also directed to the goal of guiding people on their path in Christian living, which he will later elaborate (6:14—7:1). Since the "now" signifies the acceptable time for God's grace, the opportunity to receive his favor, the "now" also declares an age of responsibility. The one reconciled to God is also called upon not to receive God's grace in vain by despising both the message and the messenger (Hughes, 220). God, through Paul, has opened the way to "eschatological existence" (Barrett, 184), a divine moment (καιρός) when he has chosen (δεκτός, "acceptable" may look to the Hebrew רָצוֹן, *rāṣôn*, God's good pleasure) to act in saving power (see O. Cullmann, *Christ and Time*, tr. F. V. Filson [London: SCM, 1951] 37–59, for a fine exposition of καιρός as a term denoting the realization of the salvation-historical event, with its offer and demand). The interconnectedness of God's call and his requirement is seen in Mark 1:15 where the καιρός, the time appointed for the kingdom to appear (cf. *Pss. Sol.* 17:24) is matched by the summons to repentance and trustful obedience to God. Paul's text declares that "now" (νῦν) that "day of Yahweh" is here, with its twofold insistence. As G. Friedrich (*Amt und Lebensführung,*

29 f.) puts it well, νῦν marks at the same time the triumphal joy and the dutiful exhortation that belong together.

3. μηδεμίαν ἐν μηδενὶ διδόντες προσκοπήν, "We do not put a stumbling-block in anyone's path." Grammatically, this verse resumes the construction of 6:1, with v 2 a parenthesis. The participle of 6:3 is the "first of an extraordinary series extending to verse 10" (Barrett, 184; [also Moulton, *Grammar*, 3:343, who calls these participles durative in nature]; because of Barrett's observation, he includes "In thus exhorting you" in his translation). διδόντες, lit., "giving," appears to carry with it the connotative sense of the present (Barrett, 184). From this we see the connection of συνεργοῦντες, "working together" and διδόντες "giving," and soon will be added a third participle to this line, συνιστάντες, "commending," (Plummer, 191). Paul is working together with God to provide the Corinthians with the best possible opportunity both to accept and to live out God's grace.

Paul has just written that "now" is time to accept God's offer of reconciliation (5:20, 21) and to live a life that reflects this happy relationship (6:1, 2; cf. 5:14, 15; Bultmann, 169). In continuity with these ideas, Paul suggests (and he is leading up to 6:4, which again refers to his example of ministry) that he puts nothing before the Corinthians that would bring dishonor to God by leading them astray. He seeks to avoid any kind of προσκοπή ("stumbling-block"; this word in the Greek New Testament is a *hapax legomenon* [Stählin, *TDNT* 6: 745–59], but note a cognate verb in 11:12 and cf. its cognate noun πρόσκομμα [Rom 9:32–33; 14:13, 20; 1 Cor 8:9; also see 1 Pet 2:8]). We shall discuss the possibilities that are included in the meaning of προσκοπή.

What we can say now is that any stumbling-block would not come from Paul. This is seen in the phrase μηδεμίαν ἐν μηδενί; μηδεμία literally means "nothing." The idea behind ἐν μηδενί can be taken to mean either "before anybody" (taking μηδενί to be masculine; so vg., Chrysostom, NIV, RSV, Phillips) or "in anything" (viewed as neuter, so KJV/AV, NEB, Plummer, Filson, Barrett, Hughes). We have opted for the latter translation of ἐν μηδενί in light of Paul's counterpart in 6:4, ἐν παντί, "in everything." Thus, there is consistency here on Paul's part that may not be seen if we took the former translation. Regardless of the translation for ἐν μηδενί, one thing is sure: Paul again presents his ministry to the Corinthians as honest and God-approved.

ἵνα μὴ μωμηθῇ ἡ διακονία, "so that the ministry may not be faulted" (μωμᾶσθαι: the verb is found only twice in the NT, here and at 8:20: both refer to Paul's ministry as under a cloud of suspicion). In this clause Paul answers the implied question of why he seeks not to put a stumbling-block ("offence," Barrett) before the Corinthians. The ἵνα, "so that" implies purpose and commands the subjunctive mood (note use of μή to state a purpose negatively; cf. Matt 7:1). What is in Paul's mind at this juncture is his ministry (though ἡ διακονία—literally—states simply "the ministry"; see *Notes* on inclusion of "our" ministry; so NIV, RSV, NEB, Hughes). He is not out to vindicate his own person (cf. 5:12). The term διακονία is picked up in what follows, namely, the elliptical ὡς θεοῦ διάκονοι, "as ministers of God" (4).

That his ministry is in his mind is seen in the use of μωμηθῇ (subjunctive of μωμάομαι). The idea behind the verb (found used in Greek since Homer, but rare in LXX; cf. Wisd Sol 10:14) is the idea of blame. μῶμος; Momus, from the same root, is the name of the Greek god of mockery and ridicule (Hughes, 221). Probably Paul was concerned with more than simply finger-pointing, for his message *was* inalienably offensive (1 Cor 1:23; contrast Gal 5:11). More likely, Paul feared his ministry would be considered a "laughing-stock," that is, in light of his desire to present his ministry as pure, his weakness would be taken as trivial. He wanted to convince the Corinthians so that no one could accuse his ministry of leading people (unbelievers and converts alike) away from God. If this were proved against Paul, then he would indeed be a source of ridicule (Plummer, 192).

Paul realizes the serious responsibility placed upon a minister to be a good example to the congregation (Hughes, 221). This is seen in 6:3, as well as in 6:4–10. The Corinthians' conduct, especially in regard to the way they have doubted Paul's integrity and been diverted to other teachers, has been inconsistent; Paul has been accused of bringing disrepute on himself, possibly by his supposed vacillation regarding his travel plans (1:17) and certainly by his frailty and proneness to suffering (4:7–12, to be developed in chap. 6). But with 6:3 Paul begins an "apology" for his past life and actions. He has put no obstacle in the paths of the Corinthians, no stumbling-block such as self-commendation, boasting, avarice (12:14–18), selfish motives, or anything that denies the transforming power God can have in lives (4:7). All of these suggestions are reasons (or excuses, so Denney) not to accept Paul's Gospel. On a broader front, it is sadly true that an immoral or improper life on the part of a minister will quickly cause God to be mocked and blasphemed, thus leading the observant person to reject the Gospel (Filson, 346).

We reiterate, however, that Paul was not concerned to "apologize" for his own person. ("His ministry, not his person, is what matters," says Barrett, 184; Bruce, 212, is discerning when he points out the sad situation of Paul's converts listening to the insinuations of his opponents; see 1 Cor. 10:32–11:1). He was a messenger of reconciliation and while the message may—indeed must—offend (1 Cor 1:23; Gal 5:11), the messenger must not do anything to direct the people away from the real cause of the σκάνδαλον, which is the cross. Paul's argument, beginning in 5:11, has been one of demonstrating that nothing he has done has been for self-promotion, but for the advancement of the Gospel (he has maintained an unblemished ministry, Héring, 47). Hence, it follows that Paul focuses on his ministry in this verse. His conduct has been open and wholesome (1:12–14), not dependent on spurious letters of recommendation, as his adversaries claimed (3:1; Hughes, 202), nor built on his own reputation which was under fire at Corinth. Hence the wording of 4:7 is the key to Paul's *apologia pro vita sua* here, and the train of reasoning will be elaborated at 10:1–6 in response to a more virulent outbreak of opposition.

4. ἀλλ' ἐν παντὶ συνιστάντες ἑαυτοὺς ὡς θεοῦ διάκονοι, "Rather, in every way, as God's servants, we commend ourselves." The theme of commendation, which is one Paul has addressed earlier (3:1; 4:2), comes up again as a way in which to prove that the ministry is honorable before God. The phrase ἐν παντί, "in every way" plays off the earlier one, ἐν μηδενί, "in no way," and

shows that Paul perceives his ministry as something of which he can be candidly "proud" if in a paradox (as in 1 Cor 15:9, 10: "I, yet not I": see R. P. Martin, *The Spirit and the Congregation* [1984] 99, 100).

We note that διάκονοι, "servants," is in the nominative and not the accusative, as might be expected. Hence, the thrust of the clause is "we, as ministers of God, commend ourselves" or "we commend ourselves as ministers do" (so Windisch, Bachmann: the nominative may be termed generic), and not "we commend ourselves as ministers of God (see Robertson, *Grammar*, 454). This difference in nuance suggests that Paul already considered himself a servant (or minister) of God. He was not out to prove he was a servant; rather, because he is a servant, he can put forth what he does as an example of the power of God (12:9). Through purity and sincerity of motive (5:11–13), and in spite of suffering and persecution (6:4b–11), Paul brings the wealth of the Gospel to the Corinthians. He defends his ministry by putting together—or, if Collange (*Enigmes*, 290) is correct, drawing on a preformed text, a suggestion that would account for the anacoluthon at v 4 [*ab initio*]—a series of statements in the form of "a kind of breviary of God's servant" (Collange 291, 300), a *vade mecum*, that set down the Identi-kit picture of how Paul saw apostolic ministry.

Though wanting not to be accused of promoting his own person, Paul cannot resist setting himself up as an example (συνιστάνειν, "to prove or show," see Kasch *TDNT* 7:896–98; BGD, 790; cf. Phoebe who is called a διάκονος whom Paul "commend(s)" [συνίστημι] in Rom 16:1), though it may be a reversal of 5:12. Apparently, the apostle, so moved by his love for the Corinthians, and so alarmed at the situation, speaks again, in great detail, of his credentials. He is unable to keep his word as given in 5:12. Thus, his heart (in 6:4a) overrules his logic (3:1; 5:12), and he commends himself one more time. The issue of how this deprecating of self-commendation fits in to the matter of the order of the chapters is mentioned in Introduction, pp. xlix, 1.

We can see even more why Paul has reversed himself from his position given in 5:12. In fact, 6:4b–10 is somewhat of a climax to the section commencing with 5:11. Paul now, as the argument closes, pummels his reader with datum after datum on why he is who he says he is. And if we pay close attention to his list, we will be rewarded by insight into Paul's inner mind as revealed in this apology.

This frank, if laconic, resumé of his life has been called Paul's "blizzard of troubles" (Chrysostom). We can almost picture the pace at which Paul writes (or dictates or, maybe, draws on) this list, as he assails his readers with information (see 4:8–12; 11:23–29; 1 Cor. 4:9–13). Moule (*Idiom Book*, 196) considers our present passage the beginning of a section of emotive writing, logical to a point, though the uneven use of prepositions makes precision of interpretation somewhat difficult (see *Form/Structure/Setting*).

Though following a break in the Greek text, since as we saw there is an anacoluthon with the nominative phrase ὡς θεοῦ διάκονοι left in suspension, ἐν ὑπομονῇ πολλῇ, "in great endurance," may go with what precedes it (Hughes, 222) but it rather introduces what follows (Kleinknecht, *Der leidende Gerechtfertigte*, 256). With the listings of trials and hardships that follow, it is easy to see that much patience, or endurance (ὑπομονή: "an attitude of patient and persevering waiting in the midst of trials," so C. Spicq, " 'ΥΠΟΜΟΝΗ, *patientia*,' " *RSPhTh* [1930], 83–106, esp. 103 f.) is called for if one is to remain faithful to God, and thus, witness for him. Barrett (185) sees a stoic model in what follows, as Paul has expressed the utility of suffering (1:6; cf. Rom 2:7; 5:3; also see Jas 1:3; Dio Chrysostom 8:15–17: so Höistad, "Hellenistischen Parallele," 22–27). Whatever was in Paul's mind, some in the early church appreciated his example (see *1 Clem* 5 for a tribute to the Roman martyrs, including Paul).

ἐν θλίψεσιν, "in afflictions." The plural may be taken as "moments of trial." Paul's attitude of great endurance (Héring, 47) is followed by a list of trials of a general nature but with an eschatological overtone (see 4:8–17) and an "existential" nuance (Collange, 294). "Affliction" is prominent in this epistle (1:4, 8; 2:4; 4:8, 17; 7:4; 8:2, 13) though not in other letters. "Affliction" ("hardships," NEB; "troubles" in NIV slights Paul's intensity) is a way of life for the Christian apostle. The Acts of the Apostles records that Paul was well acquainted with affliction. This is seen in Paul's preaching to those in Antioch (14:22) and those of Ephesus (20:23). The Johannine Jesus had indeed told his disciples that affliction was part and parcel of being in the world (John 16:33), yet the power of God is seen in that affliction cannot separate Paul (or anybody in Christ) from the love of Christ (Rom 8:35; this thought alerts us to the appeal of Paul's logic: his ministry was beset by suffering, yet he stood as a true minister of God, for he lived as one loved and affirmed by that office).

ἐν ἀνάγκαις, "in anguish" (again a plural form) denoting "times of stress." Given the plural, ἀνάγκη carries with it the idea of necessity (Filson; Tasker, 93, there are some "hardships of which no mitigation was possible"; cf. Rom 13:5). Yet it is not "blind chance" like εἱμαρμένη (destiny) or τύχη (luck) which are synonymous terms in Greek fatalism (see R. P. Martin, *Carmen Christi*, 307–9). Rather if it is "necessity," it is a destiny to which Paul the servant of God is committed as part of his inner compulsion (the δεῖ is integral to God's eschatological plan, embracing both the message and the messenger: see E. Fascher, "Theologische Beobachtungen zu δεῖ," 248–54). So it is a "seeing" necessity, open-eyed to the sense of privilege in serving God and his Gospel. Most likely too the idea of suffering is involved with Paul's use of ἀνάγκη (see 12:10; Barrett considers torture as included in these sufferings; cf. Diodorus Siculus 4.43.5). But also the idea of the necessity of preaching the Gospel (1 Cor. 9:16) may be in Paul's mind, and that conviction is his "great and overruling necessity" (Hughes, 224). Hence, Paul sees his burden for sharing the message of reconciliation as well as the sufferings that accompany this sharing as a proof of his apostleship.

ἐν στενοχωρίαις, lit., "in distresses." In addition to situations which Paul cannot, or does not, seek to escape, there are also situations that appear totally overwhelming (4:8; 12:10; Rom. 8:35). Lit., στενοχωρία means "straits" and speaks of a narrow place from which no escape is possible (Filson, 347). Yet, surprisingly, Paul writes (in 4:8) as if a "way through" the impasse could be found, but he is not writing with exactitude here, and if pressed, he would probably confess that "distresses" have to come to him *qua* apostle, even if they have no power to deter him from his mission. The defile is narrow—

and there is no alternative route, but there *is* a way of exit, at the end. Though we probably would receive little return for trying to isolate what events fit into which categories (most likely these categories overlap such as afflictions, hardships, deprivations) we do well to see the patience required in enduring these calamities ("burning paradoxes," Héring, 47) and remaining yet faithful to the cause.

5. ἐν πληγαῖς, "in beatings." With this Paul shifts to a more specific description of the perils of his ministry, both involuntary and voluntary in nature. That Paul was a victim of beatings is a foregone conclusion of his understanding of apostolic ministry. In 11:23, 24, the apostle will speak of how much more severe his beatings have been when compared with the ease of life enjoyed by those he dubs the "false apostles" (see 11:13). Five times he received from Jews thirty-nine lashes, as well as being beaten three times with Roman rods. Probably included in this latter is the occasion at Philippi (Acts 16:23), where the *lictores* (ῥαβδοῦχοι) carried these rods (ῥάβδοι, *fasces*) as a badge of office (Acts 16:35, 38).

ἐν φυλακαῖς, "in imprisonments." Again we look to 11:23 and Acts 16:23–40 to learn of some of the imprisonments, though these surely are not the only times (Hughes, 225: *1 Clem* 5:6 says he was in chains on seven occasions).

ἐν ἀκαταστασίαις, "in disorders." Of these social upheavals ("calamities," NEB; "tumults," RSV) we have numerous accounts in the Acts of the Apostles: Pisidian Antioch (13:50), Iconium (14:5), Lystra (14:19), Philippi (16:22), Thessalonica (17:5), Corinth (18:12), Ephesus (19:23–41), Jerusalem (21:27–36, cf. 1 Cor 14:33; 2 Cor 12:20 for the word, in a different setting).

ἐν κόποις, "in labors." Into this list (6:4–10) of dangers, Paul inserts some more hardships, but with a different twist, namely that the next are of the voluntary nature. Probably Paul is thinking of those labors ("fatigues,"; see Trench, *Synonyms*, [Grand Rapids: Eerdmans, 1976 ed.], 378) exerted for Christ and the apostolic mission (Trench goes on to say that the labor spoken of is not so much the exertion of effort, as the "weariness which follows on this straining of all his powers to the utmost"). While the labor of Christ's servants (6:4a) is not in vain (1 Cor 15:58), it is unlikely Paul has in mind the "physical" labor of an occupation or trade (see 1 Thess. 2:9; 2 Thess 3:8; contra Barrett, 186, with respect to Paul's desire to impose no financial burden on the church at Corinth [9:7, 9, 10; 1 Cor 9:12, 15]). Rather, as Harnack, "κόπος(κοπιᾶν)" has shown, the terms for labor in this word group refer to Paul's missionary activity. A good illustration is in Phil 2:16 (Martin, *Philippians*, NCB, 106).

ἐν ἀγρυπνίαις, "in sleeplessness," also translated "watchings" (Hughes, 225). The usage is plural to denote seasons of insomnia. Paul has in mind voluntary periods where he went without sleep, as in vigils, in order to devote more time to ministry. Apparently this was a frequent event occasioned by Paul's exposure to risk, or more likely, by his desire to "watch and pray" (cf. Eph 6:18; Heb 13:17). See too 11:27. Héring, 47, prefers the former option against Müller-Bardorff, "Nachtlicher Gottesdienst," cols. 347 n. 1, 348, 349).

ἐν νηστείαις, "in hunger." We may suppose that Paul had several occasions where he was forced by his work, which included much travel, to miss nourishment ("fastings," Filson, 348). This is seen from 11:27, in which there is the connection between λιμός (hunger) and νηστεία. It is more logical here, however, that Paul was speaking of the formal religious practice of fasting (cf. Matt. 6:16, 17) that exhibited spiritual discipline (Barrett, 186), since he is talking of voluntary renunciations. But Hughes (226) may be correct in suggesting that Paul's periodic abstinence from eating was due to his desire not to be a burden on anyone (11:7, 9; 1 Cor. 9:12–14).

6. ἐν ἁγνότητι, "in purity." After listing the many traumas that have overtaken him, Paul again picks up the idea of personal reaction ("great endurance" 6:4) as inward proof of his ministry (Tasker, 93). This shift of thought is seen to be "a breathing place in the outburst of the apostle's feeling" (Denney). The appeal to purity ("innocence," see Barrett, 186; cf. 7:11) carries with it the idea of complete integrity of life (Filson, 348), as well as moral purity (Tasker, 93, 94; note ἁγνότης occurs only here and in 11:3, though the latter reading is not certain. See *Notes* on 11:3; also cf. 1 Thess. 2:10; Phil 4:8). Friedrich, *Amt*, 42, finds an allusion to sexual purity in contrast to the state of the church, which leads Paul to mourn over examples of Corinthian libertinism (see 12:20, 21). But it is purity of intention (3:13; 4:2) that is more probable in this context.

ἐν γνώσει, "in knowledge." To get behind the meaning Paul intended, with the use of γνῶσις, is difficult. Most likely it is not a statement reflecting a "secret" knowledge. (For Windisch it is the work of an inspired charismatic giving knowledge as in 1 Cor 12:8; yet the ideas of patience and kindness that are partners speak of qualities different from an intellectual elitism. Hughes is correct when he points out that this knowledge, or "understanding" [NIV] is available to all believers in Christ, regardless of ability or status.) The consensus is that Paul uses γνῶσις here to connote that he is aware of the saving knowledge offered in Christ (5:20; so Hughes, 187; Tasker, 94; Filson, 348). Γνῶσις plays an important role in the Corinthian debate (see *Introduction,* p. xxxi) and one central meaning is the soteriological sense of the content of the divine "plan of redemption" (*Heilsplan*), set against a Jewish-hellenistic background (see C. K. Barrett, *Essays on Paul*, 6–14; E. E. Ellis, " 'Wisdom' and 'Knowledge' in 1 Corinthians," in *Prophecy and Hermeneutic in Early Christianity;* and espec. J. Dupont, *Gnosis*, 379–416). There is evidence to support this point from our letter (2:14; 4:6; 11:6; see Col. 2:3). But Barrett's suggestion (186) is that in this context the term for "knowledge" carries a specialized sense of an intelligent apprehension and application of Christian truth (Barrett, *1 Corinthians*, 37). He supports his conclusion by the use of γνῶσις in 1 Pet 3:7 where husbands are urged to live considerately with their wives, according to knowledge (κατὰ γνῶσιν). This idea includes the element of "Christian insight and tact, a conscience sensitive to God's will" (J. N. D. Kelly, *1 Peter*, HNTC [New York: Harper & Row, 1969] 132, 133). Seen in the light of what follows, this interpretation makes sense. The concepts of patience, kindness, and genuine love (as well as in 6:8–10) are part of the portrait of a Christian leader who is truly interested in the welfare of his or her charge. To be sure, the use of γνῶσις here includes the awareness of Jesus' person as the one who brings in a new age, based on his death and its atoning value (5:16, 18–20). But Paul is well aware that this is not

enough. Others have misused this knowledge (10:4, 5; 11:13–15). There must
be the ability to apply the knowledge to human situations. Paul has the "wisdom such as is given from God" (Chrysostom), and he uses what he knows
in the correct way; he uses it in accordance with God's will not only to share
the good news of the Gospel, but also to live it before his readers, even if
they disdain his lowly demeanor and lack of rhetorical, sophistic expertise
(10:10; 11:6).

ἐν μακροθυμίᾳ, "in patience." The idea of longsuffering, or patience, reflects
the disposition with which Paul has faced these bitter experiences (cf. 6:4).
Plummer views this "patience" as suggesting the endurance of these deeds
(6:4b–5) without anger (Jas 1:19) or revenge (Rom 12:19; cf. Filson, 348).
Hughes (227) extends this idea to differentiate between ὑπομονή (6:4) and
μακροθυμία. The latter refers to Paul's attitude to the injustices imposed by
those of the church, whereas the former reflects how he handled the calumnies
of the enemies outside the church (see the terms used in ethical lists of
Eph 4:2; Col 3:12, 13). This suggests one reason for the use of two different
words, though it may simply be a stylistic alternation.

ἐν χρηστότητι, "in kindness." χρηστότης, coupled with μακροθυμία, speaks
of the outgrowth of love for others as a result of God's love for man (Gal
5:22; 1 Cor 13:4: see also Eph 2:7; Titus 3:4). We know that Paul considers
love as patient and kind (1 Cor 13:4; he includes love at the end of 6:6).
What Paul is suggesting is "goodness in action" (Tasker, 94). In all these
trials, Paul has exhibited the "life-changing proof" that comes only from
the power of God, namely, as a result of the giving of the Holy Spirit. While
these hardships attest weakness on Paul's part, they reflect strength on God's,
which is the paradox of 12:9; 13:3, 4. The true minister of God evinces kindness and longsuffering as well as many other qualities (Col 3:12, 13). To
do otherwise would not promote God's working. Paul loves his people, unlike
the example of the false apostles who seek to promote their own interests
and not the interests of the Corinthians (11:13–15, 20; 12:14–17, on which
Héring comments: "He has not sought after their goods, but themselves,
that is their good" [96]).

ἐν πνεύματι ἁγίῳ, "in the Holy Spirit." The inclusion of this phrase has
raised questions as to its meaning. Is it to be translated (and understood)
as the third person of the Trinity, the Holy Spirit, or is it meant to convey
the idea of a "spirit of holiness" or even "holy zeal" (le zèle la sainte énergie:
so Godet, who traces this virtue to the action of the Holy Spirit)? Moreover,
if it is an allusion to the Holy Spirit as the Spirit of God, why include it in
a list of human virtues?

The problem presented by our second question has led Plummer (196,
197), to view ἐν πνεύματι ἁγίῳ as being equal to "a spirit that is holy." The
point is that it seems unlikely that into a list of the qualities of a dedicated
Christian life, the apostle inserted the mention of the Holy Spirit. Furthermore, if Paul meant this phrase to signify the Holy Spirit, then he would
have put the title either at the head of the list, or its conclusion, for emphasis.
Plummer is following this line of thinking because of Paul's desire to distinguish between a false and true minister.

While we agree with Plummer's last point, it appears that he has overlooked the use of the expression in an identical manner elsewhere (Rom 5:5; 9:1; 14:17; 15:13, 16; 1 Cor 6:19; 12:3; 2 Cor 13:13; 1 Thess 1:5, 6; 4:8). That is, in several other places Paul uses πνεῦμα ἅγιον for the Holy Spirit. Furthermore, if Paul was concerned to denote a spirit of holiness, he could have penned πνεῦμα ἁγιωσύνης (cf. Rom. 1:4; Hughes, 228, n. 69). H. B. Swete writes (*The Holy Spirit* [London: Macmillan, 1910], 196–97) that it is not the person, but the gift of the Spirit that is intended by Paul. Swete concludes that Paul is concerned to show "the Spirit which is common to all true ministers of God, distinguishing them from false apostles." Hence, we find Plummer's position, though interesting, still unconvincing. (In light of Swete's work, Hughes, 229, comments that "Plummer is right in effect, though not in principle.")

Barrett holds (186, 187) a view similar to that of Plummer's, noting that it is surprising that Paul should include the Holy Spirit in this list. Barrett thus concludes that Paul uses "spirit" in terms of the human spirit, and "holy" in terms of its ethical quality. He bases his findings on Paul's use of πνεῦμα as an element of the human make-up (Rom 1:9; 8:16; 11:8; 1 Cor 2:11; 4:21; 5:4, 5; 7:34; 14:14, 32; 16:18; 2 Cor 2:13; 7:1, 13; 12:18; Gal 6:1, 18; Phil 4:23; 1 Thess 5:23; Philem 25). However, he omits an important piece of evidence. In each of these references, the term ἅγιος (holy) is missing. Thus, while Paul includes the πνεῦμα in a descriptive summary of the human spirit, he separates this part of the human make-up from the third person of the Trinity by use of the adjective "holy." Therefore, we conclude that when Paul writes πνεῦμα ἅγιον he means or implies a reference to "the Holy Spirit" (so the consensus, Hughes, Tasker, Filson, NIV, KJV/AV, RSV, NEB), but with emphasis on the "power" that derives from him (see D. P. Francis, "The Holy Spirit. A Statistical Inquiry," *ExpTim* 96 [1985] 136 f. concluding from tables of occurrences that, in the NT as a whole, " 'power' references to the Holy Spirit do not contain the definite article, but references to the Holy Spirit as a person do").

But we are still faced with the question of why Paul inserts this reference to the Holy Spirit in the list. There seem to be several good answers which, though only partial in themselves, when taken *in toto*, present convincing logic. For one thing, Paul is writing in free style and is not concerned with logical niceties (Swete). Next, Paul, who has an excellent ear for words and phrases, starts a series of double terms (Hughes; see *Form/Structure/Setting*) and needs this phrase to pair with δύναμις θεοῦ, and both have a polemical slant (Wibbing, *Die Tugend*, 100). Also, Paul is not apt to divorce the gifts of the Spirit from the Spirit himself (Allo). In addition, Paul is listing some of his favorite phrases that demonstrate the work of the Spirit (love, longsuffering, kindness—Gal 5:22, 23). Therefore, whether planned or spontaneously, the person of the Holy Spirit fits in (at least in Paul's mind) with the list of these positive attributes, and in fact gives a rationale to that list by showing that divine power-in-the-Spirit matches the apostle's too human weakness, the point under discussion at Corinth.

ἐν ἀγάπῃ ἀνυποκρίτῳ, "in genuine love." The conclusion of these Christian qualities is highlighted by the climactic reference to love. This quality, or fruit, is the primary description of the Spirit's work (Bengel); so it makes even more sense to view ἐν πνεύματι ἁγίῳ as the Holy Spirit. Note that Paul has not dropped his concern to show that his actions toward the Corinthians are sincere. His use of ἀνυπόκριτος ("unfeigned," KJV/AV; "genuine," RSV) is meant to show that he is totally and purely committed to the Corinthians (Rom 12:9). His love is "unhypocritical" (Hughes, 229) and refers to life in the new age (6:2) that has broken into the present (Stauffer, *TDNT* 1: 51).

7. ἐν λόγῳ ἀληθείας, "in the message of truth." With the beginning of this verse Paul shifts attention from inward qualities to his preaching ministry. He begins this shift with "the message (or word) of truth." The RSV has interpreted this genitive in terms of description ("truthful speech"). This usage is found in several places (1:12, 13; 2:17; 4:2; 10:11; see Plummer, 197; Héring, 47, who calls it the "imperturbable courage with which the apostle continues" his preaching mission). But in light of the message of reconciliation (5:20) and his urging of 6:2, it appears Paul probably meant the idea of "message" or "proclamation" (Hughes 229, 230, "the proclamation of the revealed truth of the Gospel"; Tasker, 94). This can be seen from Eph 1:13 ("you heard the word of truth, the gospel of your salvation") and Col 1:5 ("the word of truth, the gospel"). Tasker, 94, is correct to see this phrase as more than a merely human activity: it is parallel with the charism of 1 Cor 12:8 (see R. P. Martin, *The Spirit and the Congregation*, 11–14).

ἐν δυνάμει θεοῦ, "in the power of God." That what Paul is preaching is more than human speech is seen in this phrase. For δύναμις, see C. H. Powell, *The Power of God* (London: Epworth Press, 1963). The genuineness of Paul's message and person is made apparent by the power manifested in his preaching and experienced by his Corinthian listeners (Hughes, 230; cf. Rom 1:16; 15:19; 1 Cor 1:18; 2:4–5; 2 Cor 4:7; 1 Thess 1:5). Paul's convincing manner was due not to his own eloquence but to God's power (1 Cor. 2:3–5; 1 Thess 2:13). And this was displayed best in his ability to serve with patience and strength in spite of trying circumstances ("power experienced becomes power communicated," Hughes, 230). The context here needs to be borne in mind when we come to 12:12 and ask what the "signs of an apostle" really consist in, given Paul's self-confessed frailty and finitude.

διὰ τῶν ὅπλων τῆς δικαιοσύνης τῶν δεξιῶν καὶ ἀριστερῶν, "through the weapons of righteousness, both on the right hand and on the left." Paul, being fond of military metaphors (10:3, 4; Rom 13:12; cf. Eph 6:13–18; and see Rom 6:13; Philem 2; 1 Tim 6:12; 2 Tim 2:4 in the Pauline corpus; they are studied as NT paraenesis by E. Kamlah, *Die Form der katalogischen Paränese*, 85–92, 189–96), portrays the power of God and the truth of the Gospel as being energized by weapons from above. The Christian is equipped with his or her armor (weapons, NIV, RSV, NEB) as a means to survive and overcome the evils of this world (1 QS 1:4–5; *T. Dan.* 6:10, see Murphy-O'Connor *Paul and Qumran* [London: G. Chapman, 1968] 57, but there is no precise equivalent at Qumran to Paul's phrase: Kleinknecht, *Der leidende Gerechtfertigte*, 265, n. 73). If this genitive (τῆς δικαιοσύνης, "of righteousness") is one of definition, then we may be reading a report of the moral rectitude of Paul, or more properly of his tacit claim to be a "minister of righteousness" in the new order of grace that dispenses "righteousness" (3:9) over against his adversaries. They are characterized as mock "servants of righteousness" (11:15) whose deeds belie this title which they may have claimed for themselves (Georgi, *Die Gegner*, 245–49; Lincoln, *Paradise Now and Not Yet* [1981] 56 f.). So Bultmann's idea that the genitive δικαιοσύνης should be classified as objective, "weapons for the (defense) of righteousness" (174), may not be wide of the mark (see W. Schrage, "Leid," 157, for two kinds of weapons, offensive and defensive). Barrett (188) sees an allusion to the Gospel here, in similar vein. But, if this genitive is one of origin (so Tasker), then we are pointed to the source of the weapons. Paul, being justified by God, is now supplied with the qualities that reflect evidence of the indwelling Holy Spirit (Bruce, 212; see J. Reumann, *Righteousness in the New Testament*, 52, 53).

After using the preposition ἐν no less than eighteen times (6:4*b*–7), Paul changes to διά, "through." This appears to be both a natural change and a stylistic one. ἐν, "in," would not have been a suitable preposition to use here. Likewise, though Paul is not concerned primarily with style, nevertheless, he may have wanted to break the monotonous string of prepositions (see Hughes, 231, n. 73; Plummer, 199).

Just how much significance to attribute to Paul's use of weapons "on the right and left" is debatable. Many interesting suggestions have been given. One is that Paul seeks to show that, whether in good fortune (right side) or bad (left, Lat. *sinister*), one must wield the weapons of righteousness (Chrysostom, Allo). Another is that the right hand is a symbol of offense (sword or javelin) and the left the symbol of defense (shield; cf. Eph 6:16, 17; Lietzmann, 128; Oepke, *TDNT* 5:293). The third, and probably correct one, is that Paul simply meant to show that one equipped with the weapons of righteousness is thoroughly equipped (Barrett). And the phrase may be introductory to what follows in vv 7*b*–10, as shown in Kleinknecht's form-analysis (*Der leidende Gerechtfertigte*, 256) and conclusion that Paul is explaining what the ministry of the new covenant is all about (269).

8. διὰ δόξης καὶ ἀτιμίας, "through glory and dishonor." Paul continues his use of διά, "through" in the first half of this verse, but now he shifts the focus of his attention. After characterizing his preaching ministry, Paul turns to the response which that ministry has received. He provides us with this picture by giving a series of double terms. These terms are connected by καί (that is, until v 10) and are the opposite of each other (Héring, 48). In a masterful and graphic manner, Paul elucidates the "vicissitudes of the apostolic life" (Bruce, 212; cf. 4:8, 9; 1 Cor 4:10–13). Whether these "antitheses" are the products of Paul's proponents and opponents respectively, or the reflections of the fickleness that can be found in one person, he is quite open to the reality that positive and negative opinion can come with the apostolic calling (see John 15:18–20; cf. Hughes, 231, 232).

Paul's use of δόξα, "glory," here conveys the classical Greek meaning of good opinion or reputation (cf. John 5:44; 12:43; Hughes 231, n. 74). In the eyes of some, Paul is held in high esteem (Gal 4:14), he is "honored" by some (KJV/AV, RSV, NEB). In contrast, others have little or no regard for him (10:10; 11:23–33; 1 Cor 4:10; Phil 1:15–18; 2 Thess 2:2).

Likewise, διὰ δυσφημίας καὶ εὐφημίας, "through bad reputation and good," an assonance in the original. This phrase, in essence, repeats the preceding one (contra Plummer), though we might note that any report, whether δύσφημος ("slanderous," Filson, 349; see 1 Macc 7:38; 3 Macc 2:26; Josephus, *Ant.* 16: 90) or εὔφημος ("auspicious"; Philo; Josephus, *c. Apion* 2, 248), can come both from within and outside the church (1 Cor 4:13; Rom 3:8; see Phil 4:8 for the adjective εὔφημος. with two possibilities of meaning [R. P. Martin, *Philippians*, NCB, 159] in an ethical word list).

While the minister of God is to be faithful and loving in the face of "whispers behind the back," there is the other side of the temptation, namely, to be well spoken of. One must resist this temptation, which can lead to pride and complacency. Thus Hughes is adroit (232) when he summarizes Paul's idea that he was demonstrating his steadfastness to his ministry for "no evil report, however false, can harm him and no good report, however true, can distract him."

ὡς πλάνοι καὶ ἀληθεῖς, "as deceivers, yet true [men]." Paul continues the contrasts, but in a different literary way. The διά drops out and is replaced by ὡς, "as." Also, the context requires the ὡς ("yet" Plummer, 199) to be taken as adversative (see Moule, *Idiom Book,* 178). Another item to notice is that with this phrase (as well as all the phrases in 6:8–10), both contrasting terms, in a loose sense of the word, are true. It was not that Paul actually deceived anyone, but that indeed he was considered a "deceiver" or "imposter" (Plummer). It seems he has been accused of doing just that (12:16–18; for a different reason, see 1 Cor 15:15). Note that πλάνοι is related to the verb πλανάω, "lead astray, cause someone to wander" (BGD 665; see the evidence cited from Philo, Josephus, Test. of the Twelve Patriarchs, *Sib. Or.* 3:721). Apparently there were several occasions on which Paul had to defend his words (Rom 9:1–2; 2 Cor 11:31; Gal 1:20). In fact, the accusation that Paul was a deceiver did not cease at his death (see Pseudo-Clementine lit., where Paul is compared to Simon Magus; on this see Schoeps, *Theologie,* 128, 431, and on a wider front, A. Lindemann, *Paulus im ältesten Christentum* (BHT 58. Tübingen: J. C. B. Mohr, 1979); as Hughes, 233, relates, Paul's "genuineness" is sometimes suspect even today, though old stereotypes of Paul as "the enemy of his people" are disappearing: see D. A. Hagner, "Paul in Modern Jewish Thought," in *Pauline Studies: Essays Presented to F. F. Bruce* [Exeter: Paternoster Press, 1980] 143–65).

Regardless of others' evaluation of him, Paul knows his standing before God is secure. It is true standing, held with good conscience (4:2; 5:11). He had been faithful to God's call; he was open and sincere to the Corinthians. At this point, unlike in chapter 11, Paul rebuts this accusation in a mild manner. He offers no criticisms or sarcasm, but simply reports that he is also known as true. For Paul the truth will vindicate his ministry (see 13:8).

9. ὡς ἀγνοούμενοι καὶ ἐπιγινωσκόμενοι, "as unknown, yet well-known." Immediately we notice that both participles are perfect passive, thus suggesting that Paul was concerned to show that the action was on the part of others. Hughes attempts (233, 234) to convince us that ἀγνοούμενοι refers to Paul's relinquishing of his fame as Saul of Tarsus, and his embracing the role as the despised "Paul the apostle." But it is hardly the case that Paul in his days as a Pharisee went unnoticed, as one who was "obscure" (Lietzmann,

128). Rather, in light of ἐπιγινώσκειν, "to know exactly" (BGD, 291; cf. Josephus, *Ant.* 20, 18; Rom 1:32; Col 1:6), it appears that the first participle of this phrase supports the view that some considered Paul as lacking the credentials for apostleship (see *Comment* on 5:12, 12:12). In short, he was unknown as a "true" or "super" apostle. This assessment comes out in detail in chaps. 10–13. Many of Paul's contemporaries, with a flick of the hand, could dismiss him as a "nobody" (Filson, 350), one whom they need not fear (10:2, 10). In their eyes, he could be overlooked; and in essence to be unknown, for Paul, is to be ignored (Tasker, 95; Plummer, 199; see 3:1).

Yet, Paul was recognized by some—and in particular by God—as a "full-fledged" apostle. In short, he was understood for who he truly was. But by whom? His use of ἐπιγινώσκειν in 1:13, 14 expresses the hope of being understood by the Corinthians. Moreover, 1 Cor 13:12 speaks of being fully understood by God (ἐπεγνώσθην). Hence, both God and the Corinthians appear to be in his mind. (Schoeps offers the view that Paul also had in mind the honest recognition as an apostle by the pillars of Jerusalem. See his treatment in *Paul*, 68; Barrett, 189; and we may be reading an indirect *cri de coeur* at a time when he felt isolated and bereft of human support. See *Introduction*, pp. lvii–lix.) Paul has already displayed his confidence that God sees him in openness and approval (5:8–11). Also, he presents this opportunity for scrutiny to the Corinthians, though with less certainty (5:13). Thus, in 6:9a though Paul is more confident of being well known to God, his energy may be diverted in greater intensity toward the Corinthians. See too Héring, who is right to point out the contrast between the visible appearance and the essential reality of Paul's life, though this scholar and Schoeps, *Theologie*, 128, 431, probably go too far in suggesting that Paul saw himself as Isaiah's suffering servant (Isa 52:2, 3) in spite of the datum in Acts 13:47.

ὡς ἀποθνῄσκοντες καὶ ἰδοὺ ζῶμεν, "as dying, and yet we live." Paul continues "his paradoxical rhetoric" (Barrett, 189), in terms both practical and theological. It is quite easy to see how the term "dying" (ἀποθνῄσκων, present participle of ἀποθνῄσκειν) related to his daily activities. Time and time again, Paul had been exposed to the perils of death (Acts 14:19; 1 Cor 15:30; 2 Cor 1:8, 9; 11:23–26). At some undefined time Paul was literally under the sentence of death (1 Cor 4:9) unless the language is figurative (as it may be in 1 Cor 15:32). Yet, miraculously, he escaped. The term ἰδού ("behold," "see") describes the joy and victory in Paul's mind (so Filson, 350) as well as sounding the note of surprise, i.e., it is contrary to all expectation (so Bengel). He is alive and continues to live in spite of his often-threatened apostolic existence (11:23; ἐν θανάτοις πολλάκις).

At the same time, Paul probably is concerned with more than the "practical" aspects of his "dying" and "living." There are theological implications also. Paul had indeed "died" in order to live for Christ (5:14, 15; Rom 6:1–14; Gal 2:20). He had this life now even though he required the "old nature" to be put to death (see Col 3:5). The power of God was exhibited in Paul's life, for even if he had died (4:10–12; 5:1–10), he would not be separated from Christ (Rom 8:35–39, which cites and redefines the Psalmist's lament [Ps 43:23: ἕνεκα σοῦ θανατούμεθα ὅλην τὴν ἡμέραν, "for your sake we die all the day long"]).

In summary, Paul was constantly aware of death (noted by present participle) but God's power for triumph over death was also known to the apostle. Whether in practical terms, as he faced the "cheating of death" (Hughes, 234), or in theological terms the eschatological travail of the man of faith (4:10–12; Barrett, 190), Paul was constantly both dying and living (Héring, 48 nn. 9, 11). He hoped to convince his readers that only one so dedicated as he was to the Gospel would be an instrument for God's power (Ps 118:17, 18, which is referred to the second part of the v). To be sure, Paul had little to commend himself in terms of external credentials. But, inwardly and christologically (based on 4:10, 13:4) he was the epitome of humble service and yet effectual ministry. His ministry called him to die both "physically" and "spiritually," yet the power of God enabled Paul to "live" in triumph, both now and in what the future might bring him. The wider context of Paul's experience of "suffering with Christ" and "living with him"—a phrase which occurs at 7:3—is richly treated in G. Stählin, "Um mitzusterben," especially 511–21, and Kleinknecht, *Der leidende Gerechtfertigte*, 274, 275, 281, 282, who argues from 6:1 that the antithesis of vv 9, 10 demonstrates how the grace of God was not ineffectual in Paul's case. On the contrary, the ministry of the new covenant he exercised showed that he belonged to the "new age" (5:17) where the signs of the new creation are "always rejoicing," "making many rich," and "having nothing." These characteristics of ministry are based on the christological plan of 8:9, 13:1–3, and are informed by the teaching of the "righteous afflicted" in apocalyptic thought. This *Denkfigur* (model) provides the pattern for Paul's self-understanding, but is radicalized by Paul's view of the cross and the new age, since the present experience of this man is "shot through" (*"perforiert"*) with intimations of the new eon of Jesus' resurrection life.

ὡς παιδευόμενοι καὶ μὴ θανατούμενοι, "as chastened, yet not killed." Collange, *Enigmes*, 299, points to the close affinity between the thought of Paul in 6:9 and Ps 118 (117):17, 18. In this latter text we read:

> I did not die, but survived
>   to recount Yahweh's acts.
> Yahweh severely chastised me,
>   but he did not give me over to death.
> (L. C. Allen, *Psalms 101–150* WBC [1983] 119)

Possibly, if Psalm 118 is a thanksgiving liturgy (Allen, ibid., 122–24), and if Paul is considering his perils as chastisement, then it could be that the preceding "dying and living" of 6:9 triggered the recall of this Psalm in Paul's mind and he uses its idiom (LXX reads παιδεύων ἐπαίδευσέν με ὁ κύριος). And we note his allusion to Ps 116 in the Hallel collection in 4:8 f. (see *Comment* there).

The meaning behind παιδεύειν is a divine discipline or punishment (BGD, 604; "chastened," KJV/AV, Hughes). In the OT and Jewish works we see that the discipline of Yahweh is likened to the action of a father for the correction and training of his children, and is meant to be received as evidence of God's loving concern (Prov 3:11–12; Job 5:17; Pss 94:12; 119:67, 75; Jer 31:18, 19; *Pss Sol* 18:4 [παιδεία σου]; for the New Testament, see Heb 12:5–13; Rev 3:19). No doubt Paul viewed his strife and sufferings in this way (cf. for his actions 1 Cor 5:5; 11:32). No doubt also, the opponents of Paul who considered him as "unknown" pointed to the apostle's past as a Pharisee and persecutor of the church as grounds for God's anger in consigning him to a life of pain and hardship. But Paul strives to show that rather than his suffering being a mark of divine wrath, it is a sign of divine love (Hughes, 235). The textual correction to πειραζόμενοι, "being tested," weakens the sense, and the reading is secondary.

Paul learned, though it was a painful lesson, that God chastises in order to bless (1:9; 4:11; cf. Heb. 12:5, 12). All this happening (6:4*b*, 5; cf. 11:23–33) had led Paul to a deeper realization of Christ's presence and drawn him closer to God as 12:11 will explain. And yet, in spite of the pain, Paul could shout with the Psalmist (118:15, 16) that he had victory. Paul had been spared death (see 1:8–11: in our v this is an example of the practical side of the preceding clause in 6:9, Barrett, 190). This was proof that God was working for the best in Paul's life. He was "subjected to God's disciplinary correction, yet rescued from death by God's grace and power" (Filson, 350).

10. ὡς λυπούμενοι ἀεὶ δὲ χαίροντες, "as sorrowing, yet always rejoicing." With all the disappointments, frustrations, and dangers of his apostolic life, it was inevitable that Paul, being human, would feel sorrow. Λύπη, "sorrow," also includes the idea of grief, BGD, 481. It is a key noun and verb in our letter with eighteen references out of a total Pauline usage of twenty-three times: it resembles—by contrast—the χαρά-χαίρειν (joy-rejoice) collocation in Philippians (Collange, *Enigmes*, 299). There were many events in Paul's life that inevitably brought him grief. The lost state of his own people, the Jews, caused him no little pain (Rom 9:2). Other churches for which he cared were a source of concern (2 Cor 11:28). But no doubt the Corinthians were a major cause of his sorrow. To say the least, they were divided (1 Cor 1:10–13; 3:1–9), immature (1 Cor 3:1–3), morally lax (1 Cor 5:1–8; 2 Cor 12:20, 21), selfish (1 Cor 11:17–34), as well as easily diverted with respect to entertaining wrongheaded motives about the resurrection (1 Cor 4:8; 15:1–58) and reluctant to remain loyal to Paul (2 Cor 10–13); all these items come to a head to the point that Paul wrote to them in tears and anguish of heart (2:4). See *Introduction*, pp. xlvii–li.

All this notwithstanding, Paul rejoiced (2:3; 7:4, 7, 9, 13; 13:9; see too Rom 12:12, 15; 14:17; 15:13, 32; 16:19; 1 Cor 16:17; Gal 5:22 [where χαρά, "joy," is mentioned as a fruit of the Spirit]; Phil 1:4; 2:17; 3:1; 1 Thess 2:19f., 3:9, 5:16). This was an "inalienable feature of his life" (Barrett, 190). No matter the situation or context, Paul was not overcome with a defeatist mood. Rather he exhibited a "perennial spring of joy" (Tasker, 96). This is seen in his insertion of ἀεί, "always." Paul was constantly rejoicing in the Lord (see esp. Phil. 4:4: see above for χαρά-χαίρειν found sixteen times in that letter: R. P. Martin, *Philippians* [NCB] *passim*).

Paul would be the last to complain about his sorrow in the sense of plunging him into bitterness. For him, life's disappointments meant an opportunity to build up the people of God (13:9). Thus, Paul takes the idea of weakness and strength one step farther. His weakness, confirmed to him by the Corinthians' slowness in accepting him and illustrated in the emotion of sorrow, is an occasion for God to work (Barrett, 190).

ὡς πτωχοὶ πολλοὺς δὲ πλουτίζοντες, "as poor, yet making many rich." To

those with standards of reference it was quite obvious that Paul possessed
little of the world's goods. Yet he is not alluding to the economic condition
of poverty here, however true it may be that in some cases, especially for
the benefit of the Corinthians, he had chosen to forsake any remuneration
for his service rendered to the churches (11:7–10; 12:13; 1 Cor. 9:12, 15,
18: the reason for this attitude is discussed in Holmberg, *Paul and Power*,
92–95). The poverty is more likely a spiritual one (Collange, 299). Yet, how
did he make the πολλοί, "many," rich?

Paul considers himself rich because of the surpassing value of knowing
Jesus Christ (Phil 3:8). The Corinthians, even if they shared liberally their
money with him and his collection (and it appears they did have it to share:
see 9:11), could not supply the riches which Paul has in God. There are
riches for Paul in the "glory of Christ Jesus," (4:6: so Bultmann, 176) for
God supplies all his needs (Phil 4:19; cf. Eph 1:7; 2:7, 8). Paul possessed
and shared the riches of the Gospel (cf. Eph 3:8). At 8:9 he will point to
the supreme illustration of what is at the heart of his Gospel, namely, the
incarnation when the eternal Son became "poor" in accepting our human
lot so that we might become "rich," i.e., enriched by divine grace. Material
poverty and wealth are clearly not in view here (*pace* J. D. G. Dunn, *Christology
in the Making* [Philadelphia: Westminster, 1980] 122). So we are led to conclude that it is doubtful if Paul planned to make many rich, in this instance,
with the collection described in chaps. 8 and 9, as Chrysostom thought.

ὡς μηδὲν ἔχοντες καὶ πάντα κατέχοντες, "as having nothing, yet possessing
everything." In this clause Paul expands the thought of the preceding one.
In doing so he uses the Greek word play of ἔχοντες . . . κατέχοντες (see 1
Cor 7:30). The latter, being an intensive compound, leads to the translation
"having all things to the full" (Hughes, 238, n. 78). Echoing what he has
just said, Paul contrasts earthly riches with heavenly riches. The latter are
eternal; the former temporal.

The truly rich, who are those who actually possess something worthwhile,
are those who also possess "eternal security" (1 Cor 3:21, 22). In the world's
eyes Paul—being homeless, penniless, hated, ridiculed, despised—looked
poor. But it appears unlikely that this same world could fail to notice the
"other-worldly gleam in his eye" (Hughes, 237). Not only that, but also his
ability to rise above his "poverty" with love and joy (as we know from Phil
4:10–20) convinced people that at least he believed he was possessor of all
things. The ἔχειν ("to have") formula has been seen in 3:4, 12; 5:1. Paul
has confidence, hope, and certainty. He does not have the hallmarks of success
and protection from harm and disaster that appear to have characterized
his opponents and because of which they chided that he was no real apostle.
He has no wealth, no power as a charismatic force, no wonder-working ability
to create an impression, no ecstasy to attest his being a "special" person
(Collange, 300). But he does have what really matters: Christ, as a "man in
Christ" (12:1; cf. 10:7). Lietzmann sees the model of a stoic in these denials
and there is parallel sentiment expressed in Phil 4:10–13. (Yet it is clear
that Phil 4:13 puts a novel slant on his "self-sufficiency.") Citing Epictetus
(*Diss.* 2.14,24), Lietzmann sees the contrasts of sick and happy, dying and
happy, exiled and happy, and disgraced and happy as reflected somewhat

in Paul (also compare Philo, *Quod Det. Pot.* 34). But Mealand, "As having nothing," argues that such concepts are common, not necessarily borrowed, ones. Paul can use an occasional idea, or sentence, and infuse theological meaning into it, thereby creating an ethical paraenetic framework. So 6:10 is something in which "the reader hears a familiar tone" (ibid. 277–79). Kleinknecht, *Der leidende Gerechtfertigte,* 267, 268, finds in this phrase some evidence of Paul's role as "pious sufferer."

Hence, Paul concludes his section which has its aim in setting out his life story with the trials and triumphs that he has known. He has provided his readers with nothing new in the sense that they probably knew as much from Paul's reputation among the congregations. But once again Paul has presented the readers with the picture of the servant of Christ. To belong to Christ (1 Cor 3:23) is to possess nothing in this world (Barrett, 191). But this leads one to see that the Lord Jesus, as apprehended by the faith of Paul, has given to his servant all things. The apostle is truly a sincere and *bona fide* minister for God, for he bears the marks of God's loving discipline and enjoys the riches that only Christ could give.

11. τὸ στόμα ἡμῶν ἀνέῳγεν πρὸς ὑμᾶς, Κορίνθιοι, "we have spoken freely to you, Corinthians." This sentence which our translation puts idiomatically reveals several things about Paul. First, he apparently has become aware that he has drifted from his original theme of God's grace (6:1, 2). Second, the emotional feeling of Paul is strongly expressed for the Corinthians. Of Paul's letters that we have, in addition to this v, only in Gal 3:1 and Phil 4:15 do we find Paul addressing his readers by name. Chrysostom views that address as a "mask of great love and warmth and affection"; but Collange, *Enigmes,* 283, 300, noting that Κορίνθιοι is a *hapax* in Paul, uses this singular allusion to argue that the v belongs to one edition of his writings; whereas in 7:2 ff. the Corinthians are not mentioned by name, since Paul has turned to a wider constituency in the province of southern Greece and in a separate letter (see earlier p. 164). Third, Paul has drawn closer to the Corinthians, even in the few moments that he has dictated (note use of στόμα "mouth"; with ἀνοίγειν used intransitively the sense is "to speak freely") this portion of the epistle (6:3–10).

This drawing closer is seen in that his mouth has been opened and remains opened toward the Corinthians (ἀνέῳγεν is perfect tense of ἀνοίγειν; "I have let my tongue run away with me," Barrett, 191; Héring, 49; Bruce, 213). Paul has spoken in complete freedom (see Aeschylus, *Prometheus Vinctus* 609–11; cf. Jud 11:35 f.; Job 3:1; Sir 51:25 along with Ezek 16:63; 29:21; Eph 6:19). He considers the Corinthians his friends in spite of the heartaches he has endured on their behalf. That Paul is closer to the Corinthians is seen in the second part of 6:11.

ἡ καρδία ἡμῶν πεπλάτυνται, "and opened our hearts wide." In one sense, Paul's "explosion" has been cathartic. He has, after all, commended his example to the Corinthians (in spite of his earlier intention to do otherwise, 5:12). In the process of this opening up of his emotion, Paul has revealed the attitude of his inner heart. πεπλάτυνται is the perfect of πλατύνειν, "to open wide" (while the verb form here could be passive, a middle voice would emphasize Paul's participation in the process; see Héring, 49). It has come to Paul's mind that there is room for the Corinthians in his heart (see Chrysostom, cited in *Explanation;* cf. 3:2; 7:3; Phil 1:7). Especially in letter writing Paul betrays his love for the Corinthians (a concession his readers unwittingly grant from the evidence of 10:10). This is just one more reason for the Corinthians to have something about which to boast (5:12). We note that 6:11 reminds us of Ps 119:32*b* but the recall is more in language than in meaning, as the text (Ps 118:32, LXX) shows: ὅταν ἐπλάτυνας τὴν καρδίαν μου, "since you have enlarged my heart."

12. οὐ στενοχωρεῖσθε ἐν ἡμῖν, "We do not withhold affection from you." Naturally, if Paul is enlarging his heart, he expects this pastoral outgoing to be reciprocated. However, this has not been the case, at least up to the present, in his dealings with the Corinthians.

This verse is a difficult one to put into English idiom and, at the same time, to keep near to the original (a perusal of versions and commentaries reveals this). "We are not restricted" (cramped, squeezed) for space (BGD, 766; Lucian, *Nigr* 13, *Tox* 29; LXX) lies behind στενοχωρέω. This verb, as found in 4:8, carries with it the idea of "being crushed" because of being forced into a narrow space ("straitened," KJV/AV). In 6:12 the tone is different. Paul has not allowed the Corinthians to be squeezed out of his affections. The ill feelings toward Paul could have pushed the Corinthians to a neglected corner of Paul's heart. Rather, with a reversal of thought, this is the charge made by Paul against them that *they* have turned *from* him to embrace an alien gospel, a defection which took on a more ominous cast later at 11: 4–6.

στενοχωρεῖσθε δὲ ἐν τοῖς σπλάγχνοις ὑμῶν, "but you withhold your affections from us." Literally, "we are restricted in your bowels." The idea of σπλάγχνα; Heb. רחמים, *raḥᵃmîm* ("bowels" [cf. 1:3; 7:15]) is more elegantly rendered "affection" in the English. To the Greeks the vital organs—heart, liver, lungs— were the center of the affections; Filson, 351; the meaning is "the self as moved by love," so Bultmann, *Theology* 1:221, 222.) If anyone was withholding affection in this case, it was the Corinthians. Paul, in spite of his poor reception, demonstrated his affection toward the Corinthians. Unfortunately, gossip and slander (exactly as in 12:20) had filled their hearts to the point there was no room for Paul (note that καρδία, "heart," and σπλάγχνα can be interchangeable as synonyms, so Hughes, 240 n. 2; Bultmann, 177; Collange, 301, n. 1; see H. Köster *TDNT* 7:548–59). Surprisingly, a heart full of love and affection expands, while one filled with selfishness and suspicion has a strong tendency to shrink. For this antithesis in popular Greek moral philosophy, see Bultmann, 178, citing Epictetus, *Diss.* 1. 25, 26–29.

13. τὴν δὲ αὐτὴν ἀντιμισθίαν, "In return." Paul continues the double theme of love and the request for love. Implicitly, he demonstrates his love in that he avoids giving a censure or rebuke which could have appropriately followed his appraisal of their disaffection for him. Explicitly, he asks now for a return of his love.

Ἀντιμισθία (lit., a "recompense" only here and in Rom 1:27) is a *quid pro quo*, something given in fair exchange (NEB; see Hughes, 240, n. 3). The use of τὴν αὐτὴν ἀντιμισθίαν underlines the idea of "sameness." Paul is appealing to the Corinthians, requesting that they return what he has given them, namely, love. Grammatically there is a question of what to do with the accusative cases τὴν αὐτὴν ἀντιμισθίαν. Some see this phrase as adverbial (Alford; Moule, *Idiom Book*, 34), thus "opening your hearts with the recompense." More likely (Moule, *Idiom Book*, 160, 161; see too 35, 36) this is taken in apposition with the main clause (see below; Barrett, 192; BDF, § 154; Robertson, *Grammar*, 486; Moulton, *Grammar*, 3:245). Still others (Plummer, Allo) conclude that the verb governing ἀντιμισθίαν has dropped out (see Hughes, 240, n. 3).

Compounding the sentence is Paul's parenthesis, ὡς τέκνοις λέγω, "as I speak to [my] children" (see BDF, § 465.2; after the affectionate parenthesis ὡς τέκνοις λέγω, Paul forgets the opening construction; so too Plummer. This last point may help to explain why Paul, who was dictating this letter, gave us a writing that is in many places awkwardly constructed). Also, related to the presence of this parenthesis is the question whether or not we should supply the English "my" to qualify children (the original does not contain μου). In light of Paul's penchant for considering his "charges" as his children (in his corpus see 1 Cor 4:14, 17; Gal 4:19; 1 Tim 1:2, 18; 2 Tim 1:2; 2:1; Titus 1:4; Philem 10; a paternal quality in John, see 1 John 2:1, 28; 3:7, 18; 4:4; 5:21), in addition to his desire to have their love in return, it appears only natural that he as their spiritual father should seek love from his spiritual children (Hughes, Tasker, Filson). Paul is not speaking in "school-room language" (R. A. Knox), but as one who loves the Corinthians. "It is not a large demand, if a father claims affection from his children" (Plummer, 204), though Paul appeals, more than demands, since his undoubted apostolic authority cannot compel it (1:24: cf. 13:7–10) (Barrett).

πλατύνθητε καὶ ὑμεῖς, lit., "you too open," so "you do the same to us." The main clause of this verse sums up Paul's appeal. He is asking only for "fair play" (Bruce, 213). He has opened up his heart in love. Now may his "children" do likewise in return. (One wonders whether, in this idea of wanting the Corinthians to "open up," Paul was also expecting the Corinthians to come out boldly and declare their interest. See above, 6:11.)

Paul continues his appeal that the Corinthians open their hearts in 7:2, but in the present arrangement of the text 6:14—7:1 interrupts that thought. On this see the next section.

Explanation

The language of Paul used in 6:1–13 illustrates a high point of this epistle. In it, Paul has again brought to the attention of his readers that his is the message of God and the message he brings is that of reconciliation. Reconciliation implies being brought into a relationship of peace with God. Yet this relationship includes responsibility which can only be discharged by living a life that reflects this peace. To this Paul directs their attention, and from his example he seeks to show his love for them.

The series of examples and opposites in 6:4b–10 conveys the weakness through which he acted in power (12:9, 10). Paul's ministry is a paradox, but it is the kind of ministry that God accepts. Now, Paul hopes, the Corinthians will do likewise and come over to his side. For Paul these events mark an open heart, enlarged to accept the Corinthians. Hence, as their spiritual father he asks for their love.

With these verses Paul seeks "reconciliation" with the Corinthians. In this section we may see at length the raison d'être of including the passage which expounds God's *Heilsplan,* his saving work, in (5:18–21) and why Paul has permitted the call "Be reconciled to God" (5:20) to stand as the centerpiece of that soteriological statement. The language of the kerygma is pressed into the service of Paul's hortatory appeal to the Corinthians. They are no longer to remain with an unbelieving world which judges his ministry a failure and a shame (v 8) but instead to come over to God's evaluation of his person and work as a true minister of God (v 4). In this apostolic *vade mecum,* a directory of the apostle's trials and triumphs, we see the kind of service that God's chosen messengers are called to, what they may expect to experience and, above all, how they may gain comfort from seeing how Paul acted and reacted in regard to his destiny, his ἀνάγκη (v 4).

The nub of the appeal is still the validity of Paul's apostolate and its credentials. From one viewpoint those credentials are dubious because they consist in a litany of his troubles. Yet as Paul seeks a full reconciliation with himself— and, by extension, with his Gospel—he can invoke the aid of God (v 1) to secure what he desires: a vindication of his life's service, at a time when it seemed all his efforts were in vain (Phil 2:16). He looks to the Corinthians to prove him wrong (6:1: "do not receive God's grace in vain").

As a final comment on a topic of interest, namely, Paul's role as a pastor and based on 6:13, we may turn to an early commentator, John Chrysostom (*Hom.* 13.1, 2). Here is his reflection on Paul's relationship as "father" to his spiritual children.

> Just as what brings heat makes things expand, so it is the gift of love to stretch hearts wide open; it is a warm and glowing virtue. Love caused Paul to open his mouth and expand his heart. "I do not love only by words," he says, "my heart itself joins in the song of love and so I speak with confidence with my whole mouth and my whole heart." Nothing was wider than the heart of Paul which embraced all the saints, just like the individual lover, in close bonds of love. And yet his love did not stretch to breaking point, nor become weak, but remained whole in every case. What wonder that he had such feeling for the saints when even in the case of unbelievers his heart embraced the whole world?
>
> And so he did not say, "I love you," but—and this is more emphatic—"We have spoken frankly to you, we have opened wide our hearts." We have all men in our heart; and not merely that alone, but with ample room. For he who is loved wanders in the inmost heart of the lover without any fear: accordingly Paul says: "On our part there is no constraint; any constraint there may be is in yourselves." Notice that the reproach is uttered with restraint, which is the mark of lovers. He did not say, "You people do not love me," but, "Not in an equal measure," nor does he wish them to be too bitterly reproached.
>
> It is evident in all his writings how he burns with love for the faithful. Choose quotations out of every epistle. Writing to the Romans, the apostle says: "I long to see you," and, "I have often made it my object to come to you," and "If in any way at all I may have a prosperous journey to you." To the Galatians he speaks as follows: "My little children, with whom I am again in travail"; to the Ephesians again: "For this reason I kneel in prayer on your behalf"; to the Thessalo-

nians: "What is our hope or joy or crown of boasting? Is it not you?" For he said that he carried them round both in his heart and in his chains.

Furthermore, he writes to the Colossians: "I wish you to see how great a conflict I have on your behalf and on behalf of those who have not seen my face in the flesh so that your hearts can have comfort," and to the Thessalonians: "Like a nurse who cherishes her charges, thus we yearn for you, and we wanted to give you not only the gospel but even our lives." "On our part there is no constraint," he says. He does not say only that he loves them, but that he is loved by them, that in this way too he may draw them to him. And about them he bears this witness: "Titus has come bringing us your longing, your tears, and your eagerness."

I. The Temple of the Living God (6:14–7:1)

Bibliography

Betz, H.-D. "2 Cor. 6:14–7:1: An Anti-Pauline Fragment?" *JBL* 92 (1973) 88–108. **Collange, J.-F.** *Enigmes de la deuxième épître de Paul aux Corinthiens.* Cambridge: University Press, 1972. 305–13. **Dahl, N. A.** "A Fragment and its Context: 2 Corinthians 6:14–7:1." In *Studies in Paul.* Minneapolis: Augsburg, 1972. 62–69. **de Jonge, M.** *The Testaments of the Twelve Patriarchs.* Leiden: Brill, 1953. **Derrett, J. D. M.** "2 Cor 6:14ff. a Midrash on Dt. 22, 10." *Bib* 59 no. 2 (1978) 231–50. **DeVries, S. J.** "Note Concerning the Fear of God in the Qumran Scrolls." *RQ* 5 (1964–66) 233–37. **Driver, G. R.** *The Judean Scrolls.* Oxford: Basil Blackwell, 1965. **Ellis, E. E.** "A Note on Pauline Hermeneutics." *NTS* 2 (1955–56) 127–33. **Fee, G. D.** "II Corinthians VI.14–VII.1 and Food Offered to Idols." *NTS* 23 (1977) 140–61. **Fitzmyer, J. A.** "Qumran and the Interpolated Paragraph in 2 Cor 6:14–7:1." in *Essays on the Semitic Background of the New Testament,* 205–17. London: Chapman, 1971. **Gnilka, J.** "2 Cor 6:14–7:1 in Light of the Qumran Texts and the Testaments of the Twelve Patriarchs." In *Paul and Qumran,* ed. J. Murphy-O'Connor, 48–68. London: Chapman, 1968. **Gunther, J. J.** *St. Paul's Opponents and Their Background.* NovTSup 35. Leiden: Brill, 1973. 308–13. **Huppenbauer, H. W.** "Belial in den Qumrantexten." *TZ* 15 (1959) 81–89. **Jewett, R.** *Paul's Anthropological Terms: A Study of their Use in Conflict Settings,* 1971. **Jones, Ivor H.** *The Contemporary Cross.* London: Epworth, 1973. **Ker, R. E.** "Fear or Love? A Textual Note." *ExpTim* 71–72 (1959–61) 195–96. **Kuhn, K. G.** "Les rouleaux de guerre de Qumrân." *RB* 61 (1954) 193–205. **Moffatt, J.** "2 Corinthians VI.14–VII.1." *ExpTim* 20 (1908–9) 429–30. **Pagels, E. H.** *The Gnostic Paul.* Philadelphia: Fortress, 1975. **Rensberger, D.** "2 Corinthians 6:14–7:1—A Fresh Examination." *StBibT* 8 (1978) 25–49. **Schenk W.** *Gemeinde in Lernprozess die Korintherbriefe.* Bibelauslegung für die Praxis 22. Stuttgart: Katholisches Bibelwerk, 1979. **Schick, E.** *Die Wahrheit siegt durch die Liebe: Priesterliche Existenz nach dem zweiten Korinthbrief.* Stuttgart: Katholisches Bibelwerk, 1975. **Schütz, J. H.** *Paul and the Anatomy of Apostolic Authority.* SNTMS 26. Cambridge: University Press, 1975. 165–86. **Skeat, T. C.** "Early Christian Book Production: Papyri and Manuscripts." In *Cambridge History of the Bible,* vol 2, ed. G. W. H. Lampe, 54–79. Cambridge: University Press, 1969. **Thrall, M. E.** "The Problem of II Cor. VI.14–VII.1 in some Recent Discussion." *NTS* 24 (1977) 132–48.

Translation

¹⁴ *Do not be mismated with unbelievers. For what partnership do righteousness and lawlessness have? Or what fellowship has light with darkness?* ¹⁵ *What harmony is there between Christ and Belial?* ᵃ *Or what portion does a believer have with an unbeliever?* ¹⁶ *And what agreement can God's temple have with idols? For we are* ᵇ *the temple of the living God. As God said: I will dwell in their midst, and walk with them, and I will be their God and they shall be my people.*

> ¹⁷ *Therefore, come out from their midst*
> *and be separate,*
>   *says the Lord.*
> *Touch nothing unclean;*
>   *and I will receive you.*
> ¹⁸ *And I will be a father to you,*
>   *and you shall be my sons and daughters,*
>   *says the Lord Almighty.*

¹ *Since then, beloved, we have these promises, let us cleanse ourselves from every defilement of flesh and spirit, perfecting holiness in the fear of God.* ᶜ

Notes

ᵃ See Hughes (248, n. 12) for a helpful explanation concerning the variant spellings of βελίαρ, such as βελίαν (D K ψ), βελίαβ (F G) and βελίαλ (*pc* lat; vg). βελίαλ represents בְּלִיַּעַל, *b*ᵉ*liyya‘al* (*BGD*, 139) which strongly suggests that the better attested βελίαρ resulted from the interchange (dissimilation, Bruce, 214) of λ and ρ. This happened, for example, with the alteration of κλίβανος to κρίβανος and φαῦλος to φαῦρος. The number of variants indicates great uncertainty regarding the final consonant. Note Barrett and NIV translate "Beliar"; the NASB, NEB, and RSV translate "Belial." Hughes remarks (250) that if Beliar were changed to Belial it is far more likely that the first "l," not the second, would be changed. However, the change of γλωσσαλγος to γλωσσαρος shows that this is not a hard and fast rule (Plummer, 208).

ᵇ The majority of MSS support ὑμεῖς γὰρ ναὸς θεοῦ ἐστε (P⁴⁶[א²]C D² F G itᵍ vg), but the strong witness of both Alexandrian and Western strains (א* B D* 33 81* itᵈ copˢᵃ,ᵇᵒ) leads us to prefer the Nestle-Aland²⁶ text. Metzger concludes (*Textual Commentary*, 580) that the reading with ὑμεῖς was probably suggested to a scribe in view of 1 Cor 3:16 "that God's spirit lives in you" (οἰκεῖ ἐν ὑμῖν). This makes sense also, because we see the use of the second person in 6:14, 17. Similar problems of deciding between ἡμεῖς and ὑμεῖς can be found in 7:12; 8:8; 19; 1 Cor 7:15. On the other hand, there appears no reason to change the "you" to "we."

ᶜ Only P⁴⁶ contains ἀγάπη instead of φόβῳ. Ker, "Fear or Love?" 195–96, argues that the phrase ἐν·ἀγάπῃ θεοῦ is a more familiar NT saying than ἐν φόβῳ θεοῦ. The latter, for Ker, betrays a Septuagintal influence. Though he is arguing *contra mundum*, Ker does have the support of the earliest MS. See Jude 21, for the phrase ἐν ἀγάπῃ. But more likely the reading of P⁴⁶ is mistaken (Barrett, 193, n. 2).

Form/Structure/Setting

Anyone familiar with this passage in modern discussion of 2 Corinthians is sure to be aware of the critical questions that it provokes. Such questions will momentarily be delayed as a subject of consideration, for the structure of this passage needs first to be examined.

The passage itself is a self-contained entity composed of a statement (6:14*a*) followed by five antithetical questions (6:14*b*, *c*, 15*a*, *b*, 16*a*). Each of these questions is designed to enforce the thrust of the admonition of 6:14*a* not to "become yoke-mates with unbelievers." The questions illustrate the need to be separate, i.e., to avoid association with evil.

An impetus for this call to holiness is provided in the author's intention to explore the imagery of believers as the temple of God (viewed collectively 6:16*b*). To show that the "Christian temple" is to be free of "idols" (as was the case with the Jewish Temple) the writer of our passage presents a catena of Old Testament texts. These texts are sometimes a quotation (16*d*), but many times a paraphrase (16*c*) or a redaction of Old Testament vv (6:18, *a*, *b*). Intermingled with these exhortations are promises that reflect the author's desire to portray a lifestyle, not simply to achieve holiness as an end in itself (see Betz, "2 Cor 6:14–7:1"). There are three promises (6:16*c–d;* 17*c;* 18) that become the basis for the concluding exhortation to (1) refrain from all defiling of flesh and spirit; and (2) live as "perfecting" holiness (7:1), i.e., bringing it to completion. The passage thus concludes as it commenced, with a charge to live a holy and separated life unto God. The theme of detachment from the pagan world is consistently held throughout the passage.

With this structure in mind, scholars have struggled with questions regarding the placement and composition of this passage. For one thing, it becomes difficult to see any transition between 6:13 and 14. 6:13 concludes with Paul's appeal for the Corinthians to "open wide their hearts." Suddenly, we find the admonition to avoid being yoked together with nonbelievers (6:14). In like manner, the conclusion of our passage (7:1), which speaks of avoiding contamination of the flesh and spirit does not lead smoothly into 7:2, a v describing once again the desire for the writer to enter the hearts of the Corinthians. Thus, one crucial question facing interpreters is the integrity of 2 Cor 6:14–7:1. Does it belong here or is it an interpolation?

But a second question focuses on the authorship of this passage. Is it authentic in terms of Pauline writing, or is it the creation of someone else? Arguments against Pauline authorship can be summarized under four headings: (1) the large number of *hapax legomena* (nine terms in all as a maximum count: see later) in such a short passage; (2) the extreme spirit of exclusiveness (based on a levitical or cultic code) shown by its author, an attitude that is seemingly out of character when related to the former Pharisee who had been "liberated" from the law; (3) an affinity with Qumran (see Schweizer, *TDNT* 7:126, n. 225) such as the presence of dualistic contrasts (i.e., the antithetical questions), the idea of the community as a temple, and the catena of Old Testament scriptural texts loosely strung together, and (4) the "un-Pauline" use of "flesh" and "spirit" in 7:1. (Two helpful summaries of the questions surrounding this passage are found in the works of Hughes, 241–44, and Rensberger, "2 Corinthians 6:14–7:1.")

The reasons mentioned above have led several scholars to conclude that 6:14–7:1 is not from Paul. Fitzmyer, "Qumran," sees the passage as a "Christian reworking of an Essene paragraph and is to be read as a non-Pauline interpolation" (217). Dahl, "A Fragment," (64, 65), in like manner, concludes that 6:14–7:1 is a "slightly Christianized piece of Qumran theology . . . of non-Pauline origin." Gnilka, "2 Cor 6:14–7:1," follows suit and views the author as an unknown Christian other than Paul. Betz, "2 Cor 6:14–7:1," goes to the extreme by arguing that this is an anti-Pauline argument, portraying the position of Paul's enemies at Galatia. (For the use made of this theory in exegeting Paul's opponents in Galatians, see Betz, "Spirit, Freedom, and Law, Paul's Message to the Galatian Church," *SEÅ* 39 [1974] 145–60.)

These arguments are worth attention, but they are not necessarily convincing. There are several *hapax legomena* in these verses (ἑτεροζυγοῦντες, μετοχή, συμφώνησις, βελιάρ, συγκατάθεσις and μολυσμός: [ἐμπεριπατήσω, εἰσδέξομαι and παντοκράτωρ appear also as Pauline *hapax legomena*, but these are contained in OT renderings and hardly seem sufficient to count as original on the part of the author]), but this is not so unusual. For one thing, Pauline outbursts containing a high percentage of *hapax legomena* are not uncommon (1 Cor 4:7–13 has six *hapaxes* and 2 Cor 6:3–10 [the verses preceding this passage] has four; also cf. 11:22–29; as Hughes [242] writes, there are some fifty *hapaxes* in 2 Cor alone). Furthermore, as Fee points out, "II Cor vi.14–vii.1" (144, 145), the argument based on *hapax legomena* needs to be utilized with greater precision, for since verbs and nouns, such as ἐλπίζω–ἐλπίς, γινώσκω–γνῶσις and πιστεύω–πίστις are related, why not μετέχω–μετοχή and μολύνω–μολυσμός? Also is ἑτεροζυγέω that much different from similar compounds with ζυγός and σύζυγος? We can also see that συμφώνησις and συγκατάθεσις simply follow the pattern of other Pauline compound words formed with the prefix συγ(μ). The only *hapax* to give any substantial evidence against Pauline authorship is βελιάρ (Thrall, "The Problem," 138), and it is hardly reasonable to think that a term, so entrenched in Jewish thinking (see below) should necessarily be excluded from Paul's thinking (Allo, 190). Thus, Fee (147) appears to be correct in concluding that "the authenticity of this passage is not called into question by the *hapax legomena*." With Paul's academic training and linguistic abilities (Hughes, 242) the use of different words should not surprise us. Yet on balance the high proportion of unusual and rare terms is remarkable, and requires explanation.

The argument that these vv (6:14–7:1) exhibit too much exclusiveness is more weighty. A proponent of this argument is Betz, "2 Cor 6:14–7:1," who, in the process of arguing that 6:14–7:1 is anti-Pauline, speaks of the advocacy of Torah observance, but that is something absent from this passage (Rensberger, "2 Corinthians 6:14–7:1," 26). Taken to its logical conclusion, the inference is that Paul—if he was so out of sympathy with the teaching of these vv here—would be considered a libertine. If 6:14–7:1 were anti-Pauline, then it would follow that a "Pauline" passage would exhibit tendencies that commended a life free from all moral restrictions. But this seems unwise in light of his insistence on living a holy life (Rom 8:9; 1 Cor 6:12–20). Paul has argued that believers are free from the law (Rom 7:4–6; Gal 2:19; cf. Rom 10:4), but he does not conclude that "law-free" living means permission to please oneself (Rom 6:12–19; Gal 5:13–25). And his converts who took this line are uniformly reprobated (Rom 3:8; 6:1, 15; Gal 5:13). Also, one must remember that the tone of exclusiveness comes from the OT quotations, possibly reflecting the reason he was misunderstood, as was the case in 1 Cor 5:10. But it is the appeal to OT cultic religion, seen in the vv appealed to, that constitutes a major roadblock in the way of believing that Paul would use this set of OT images.

We have to observe the Qumran affinities noted in this passage (Gunther, "St. Paul's Opponents," 312). But, as Bruce remarks (214), these features are not peculiar to Qumran (see *Comment*). Most likely, to see the influence of Qumran as the main reason for many points in 6:14–7:1 is to fall into the trap of "parallelomania" (see S. Sandmel's article by this title in *JBL* 81 [1962] 1–13; cf. Fitzmyer, 205, n. 1). To evaluate this question requires a verse-by-verse examination (see later), but it can be said that, if we are seeking certain proof, there is hardly a clear demonstration that this section had an Essene or Jewish-Christian author (Thrall, "The Problem," 138). ("It cannot be proved that the section [6:14–7:1] is Pauline. But even less can it be proved that it could not come from Paul or that it must come from Qumran," so concludes W. G. Kümmel, *Introduction to New Testament*[2], 1975, 288.) Yet on reflection it is striking that there are these close parallels with the mentality that prevailed at Qumran.

There is also the question of whether or not the appeal to the Pauline use of flesh and spirit (7:1), admittedly unusual, is strong enough to rule out apostolic authorship. This consideration will be discussed in detail later, but for now it appears reasonable to remark that this is not an overwhelming reason to reject authenticity (Hughes, 242).

All in all, there will never be a consensus on the authenticity of this passage. Both sides (divided over whether Pauline or non-Pauline authorship is more feasible) can make a case. In light of the discussion above, we are led to believe that in all probability Paul had some control over this passage. This, we hope, will become clear in the *Comment*. But we stop short of accepting the following unequivocal position: "There is, in short, no *prima facie* evidence that this passage could not have been written by the Apostle Paul" (Hughes, 242).

Such a denial by Hughes leaves unanswered the question of why Paul made such a decided "jerk" (Barrett) in his thinking. Also, though some of Paul's terminology here does not have to be confined to Qumran, can we find another passage in the NT exhibiting such a close relationship with the Essene thinking? Furthermore, though Fee cautions against putting too much stock in the many *hapaxes* found in our passage, we must ask ourselves why there are so many in such a short piece of literature. In short, it is difficult to attribute this passage solely to Paul's dictation and originality. That is, while it appears more or less certain that Paul had some control over the writing of 6:14–7:1 and it is not a case of direct borrowing, it is quite doubtful this paragraph came unaided from Paul's mind. Rather than to say that it is non-Pauline or simply to say that it is genuinely Pauline, we adopt Rensberger's view (with some modifications) as a viable option.

His argument is that the mixture of Pauline and non-Pauline features probably resulted from Paul's use of a piece of tradition put together previously by a Christian of Essene background (41). This submission gains credibility when we consider that possibly 6:14–7:1 is the writing mentioned in 1 Cor 5:9. As will be argued, Paul had a point to make when he incorporated 6:14–7:1. We may identify this section as a preformed passage that was in his mind as an independent unit when he came to this part of 2 Corinthians. But though he is the final "redactor" of this Essene work and has "Paulinized" it, we cannot judge it to be uniquely Pauline. Rather, we see 6:14–7:1 as

authentic in the sense that Paul was the one to place it in the letter at this
curious juncture. Our modification of Rensburger will be seen in the *Comment*.
It is sufficient to say here that we disagree with seeing the immediate target
of 6:14–7:1 to be the opponents of chaps. 10–13. Rather, it appears to us
that the section's chief targets are Christians in danger of merging with unbelievers. The aim of the *Vorlage* (original draft) was to ensure a holy community
by warning Jewish Christian believers to avoid all contact with Gentiles who
were (traditionally) stained by the twin sins of idolatry and immorality (see
Acts 15:19, 20; G. F. Moore, *Judaism in the First Centuries of the Christian Era*,
vol. 1 [1946] 274, 275, 339). Whether Paul reproduced this teaching to deal
with problems in 1 Cor 5, only to have his instruction misunderstood, we
cannot exactly say. What does seem plausible to account for the presence
of this rigorous pericope in 2 Cor and at this point in the letter is the reinforcing provided by the passage of Paul's teaching on reconciliation (5:14–21)
and the defense of his apostolic ministry (6:1–13), which ended on a tender
note (6:13). Now, as a final thrust, he adopts a different tack and tone. He
inserts a warning lest the Corinthians should range themselves with the world
of unbelievers that is still hostile and unreconciled; and by continuing to
disbelieve his integrity and his Gospel the Corinthians would fail to heed
the call, Be reconciled to God (5:20). Hence the opening line compares them
to unbelievers (ἄπιστοι; cf. 4:3, 4) to stab them awake to their condition and
peril if they refuse to join him.

   With a possible solution to the question of the authorship and setting,
we now return to a previous question, namely the integrity of our passage.
There are three possible answers to this question: The passage was (1) put
in its present place by accident, or (2) inserted by an interpolator, or else
(3) it is located in its present context by Paul's design. Let us review these
suggestions.

   1. The first solution appears the least likely. It is doubtful that Christians
of the first century used codices that would allow for an accidental placement
of this passage in 2 Corinthians (Allo). Most likely a papyrus scroll was used
(see T. C. Skeat, "Early Christian Book Production"). Furthermore, there
is no textual evidence to suggest that "any copy of the Epistle ever lacked
this passage" (Plummer, 205). Thus, it appears that the earliest editions of
2 Corinthians contained our passage. (See Plummer, xxv; cf. Betz, 108; Rensberger, 26.)

   2. With regard to the second option—that an interpolator inserted this
pericope into a copy of the letter—we are faced with the perplexing question
of why it is put in here at this precise place. That is, if a final redactor put
the finishing touches on 2 Corinthians, why did he insert 6:14–7:1 in such
an awkward place, so alien to its context (see Barrett, 23, 24)? J. Moffatt,
(*First Epistle to the Corinthians* [MNTC; London: Hodder & Stoughton, 1938]
xxiv) suggests that it is part of the "Previous Letter" (referred to in 1 Cor
5:9; Strachan, 3), but again this suggestion is faced with the question of the
reason for its present placement. Denney (238) suggests that Paul himself
is the interpolator who, upon reading over the letter, inserted this paragraph.
But, again, we are confronted with the task of explaining why the insertion
was made at this point. Several reasons have been offered, in addition to
the one we have just made. See *Comment*.

3. An array of scholars (Filson, 352; Tasker, 30; Bruce, 214; Barrett, 194; Plummer, 208; Héring, 49; Hughes, 243, 44; Thrall) considers this passage as part of the original letter (that is, it is here by the author's set purpose). It was not unnatural for Paul to "dart" (Plummer) to a parenthetical thought. We must not forget that Paul was dictating a letter (Hughes, 243), not writing a dispassionate treatise. Furthermore, as will be seen, 6:14–7:1 is not that much out of touch with its context (Thrall). In 6:1, 2 there is a call to holiness. Then Paul abruptly changes direction and begins a digression that includes some *hapaxes*. He has paraded the qualities of his apostolic life in paradoxical fashion before the Corinthians (6:3–10); then, having assured them that he loves them (6:11–12), he asks for a reciprocal acceptance (6:13). But upon establishing his concern for them, he embarks on a final appeal, which many interpreters believe to be a digression, by supplying the reason why he feels they are liable to close him out of their hearts. Though the congregation has reacted strongly to Paul's teaching (1 Cor 5:9, 10), the Corinthians apparently have yet to break completely their ties with idolatry (1 Cor 10:14–22). Possibly Paul senses an uneasy awareness on the part of the Corinthians concerning this failure (Bruce, 214), thus leading to his confidence that they will follow the logic of his call in 1 Cor 10:14: "So, my dear friends, avoid idolatry." Furthermore, it remains possible (but unlikely, we think) that he would sometimes break into overenthusiastic preaching, forgetting that the converts were his audience (Tasker, 30). Upon relieving his mind or remembering his main thought of 6:13, Paul returns to his appeal to come into the heart of the Corinthians (Plummer). (With a more complex proposal, Collange, *Enigmes*, 282–84; 302–17, suggests that Paul had two editions of the letter which begin at 2:14. These were the same letters except for separate endings, one included 2:14–6:13 [addressed to the Corinthians] and the other was 2:14–6:2 and 6:14–7:4 [addressed to other Christians in Achaia]. This thesis has met with little acceptance [see Thrall, 141–44; Rensberger, 27].)

Though this third option has been championed by many (and is well stated by Hughes), it appears too ill-defined with regard to the areas of concern mentioned earlier, namely, the passage's strong affinity with Qumran, and its apparent, sudden introduction into the sequence of chapter 6. Yet we also cannot agree with those who see the vv as non-Pauline, and as put there in 2 Corinthians by accident or an interpolator other than Paul. It seems more probable that Paul borrowed a writing of Essene origin, placed the finishing touches on it, and added it to this letter because of a specific intention. That intention, we repeat, has to be seen as Paul's continued appeal to his alienated children to believe his Gospel of reconciliation and thereby to break with the unbelieving world with which—however unwittingly—they have identified themselves. In our view, and against most interpreters, we see 6:14–7:1 as integral to Paul's closing argument begun in chap. 5 and completed in 7:3 ff. It is not a digression but a logical development.

Comment

14. Μὴ γίνεσθε ἑτεροζυγοῦντες ἀπίστοις, "Do not be mismated with unbelievers." The use of the present imperative with μή (μὴ γίνεσθε, i.e., "do not

get into," BDF § 354) suggests that the Corinthians were, in Paul's mind, already engaged in the process of joining themselves to the ἄπιστοι, "unbelievers": see especially 4:2, 3 for this term. This situation could be reflected in 1 Cor 5:9–11, but more likely it looks to the issue of their opposition to the apostolic kerygma as brought by Paul and embodied in his person. See *Comment* on "righteousness" in 6:7 and its opposite in 11:15. For Paul is exhorting the Corinthians not to continue becoming unequally yoked, i.e., "incongruously joined," (*Greek-English Diglot*) with unbelievers (6:14; Hughes, 245, n. 6). That Paul is concerned to show this is seen in what follows (see discussion of Structure in *Form/Structure/Setting*).

ἑτεροζυγοῦντες, "mismated" ("double harness," so Barrett, 195). This is the first of the *hapax legomena* (see *Form/Structure/Setting*) in this passage. The prohibition of being doubly yoked is found in the Old Testament (see Str-B 3:521: possibly anticipating the OT references that follow). Lev 19:19 (רבע, *rbᶜ*) speaks against mismating animals, and Deut 22:10 prohibits the union of ox and donkey (cf. tractate *Kil.* 8:2. Derrett argues that of the two OT passages, the Deuteronomic one is clearly the better choice. He bases his position on the idea that 6:14–7:1 is a midrash on Deut 22:10. His reasoning is convincing to a point, but his insistence that the charge against the ἄπιστοι represents one of unreliable financial integrity weakens his argument). This metaphor of "mixtures" (כלאים, *kilʾayim*) is taken up by Paul and adroitly applied to his audience. There is to be a distinction between the Christian and the non-Christian (unbeliever). But does Paul use non-believer (ἄπιστος) in the technical sense?

To take ἄπιστοι in the technical sense is not without its problems. Rensberger (29–31, 41–44) views the ἄπιστοι as the "opponents" of Paul, or at least people who were doing the work of adversaries. He is right to point out that the main topic of 2 Cor is not that of relations with non-Christians, a theme found in 1 Corinthians (e.g., 10:14–20). He also bases his position on the use of ἄπιστοι in 4:3, 4. For Rensberger, the word has a double meaning. It is used for non-Christians, but also Paul has in mind the false apostles who oppose him. Collange (*Enigmes,* 305) also believes that Paul is thinking of his opponents. We have partly supported this view (and it may be also sustained by reference to 1 Cor 14:22, if there ἄπιστοι are the Corinthians: see J. Murphy-O'Connor, *1 Cor,* 130), but it has its challengers, and it needs sharper focus.

For one thing, it is queried, to say that ἄπιστοι in 6:14 denotes Paul's opponents overlooks the technical use of the term in 1 Cor 6:6; 7:12–15; 10:27; 14:22–24 (cf. Rom 11:20, 30; 1 Tim 1:13; 5:8; Titus 1:15; see also Luke 12:46; Rev 21:8; BGD 85). Furthermore, Thrall's contention ("The Problem," 143) that if ἄπιστοι was meant by Paul to refer to his opponents it would have been included in 2 Cor 10–13 (which it is not) has not been answered. But, in reply, the theme of righteousness/unrighteousness *is* applied in those chapters. In light of the context, Paul has urged the Corinthians to open wide their hearts (6:13). Possibly the purpose of the passage is to remind the Corinthians not to open so wide their hearts as to permit illicit unions to enter in their lives. The sudden change of direction at this point is to show that opening wide to Paul does not allow for deviation from the narrow way of allegiance to his Gospel. And this deviation would be in the form of close and consequential union with unbelievers. So the union has a specific reference, as we suggested, and Paul is classing the Corinthians with unbelievers for precise reasons. Betz, 90, also sees a meaning for ἄπιστοι other than relating to pagan nonbelievers. He views the term as referring to those who do not keep the Torah; see Bultmann, *TDNT* 6:208–15. But Betz builds (108) his conclusion on the thesis that 6:14–7:1 is an anti-Pauline fragment, reflecting the *Sitz im Leben* of the letter to Galatia, a thesis that is founded on an unprovable supposition: "For reasons unknown to us (a redactor) has transmitted a document among Paul's letters which in fact goes back to the movement to which Paul's opponents in Galatia belong," so Betz, 108. But he fails to elaborate on these "unknown reasons." Also, the idea of keeping the Torah, so important to Betz's thesis, does not appear in 6:14–7:1 (cf. Rensberger, 26), nor indeed in 2 Corinthians as a whole, where νόμος (law) is singularly absent.

If, however, a broader scope is given to ἄπιστοι here, we may ask what kind of union and to what extent Christians are to refrain from becoming yokefellows with non-Christians. On the one hand, it appears unlikely that Paul was asking the Corinthians to cease all contact with the Gentile world. He recognized that this was an impossibility (1 Cor 5:10), though his counsel was evidently misunderstood. In terms of business and ordinary social kindness, Paul would exhort the believers to be good witnesses (Filson, 352). Paul did not ask his converts to come out of the world (or even "to abstain from non-Christian dinner parties," Barrett, 196). Also, we note how Paul became "all things to all men" (1 Cor 9:20–23).

Rather, Paul warns against compromising the integrity of faith (Hughes, 246). Any action that would cause believers to link up with the world in thought or act (through indifference or connivance) must be avoided. Specifically, marriage (1 Cor 7:12–15) was one source of possible mismating. (This is the commonest understanding of 6:14a, though probably it is too narrow; Denney, 240; Plummer, 206.) Also, the question of eating idol meat appears—at least obliquely—to fall under Paul's consideration (1 Cor 10:27, 28; see Fee). Possibly the apostle also had in mind the taking of grievances to pagan courts (1 Cor 6:1–8). But whatever Paul had in view in terms of particular relationships, in general the extent of such contact and commerce should not be such that the Christians forget that they are members of the holy people of God (a topic dominating the rest of the passage; see Barrett, 196; Strachan, 4). Hughes is correct (246) when he writes: "The metaphor of the yoke which he (Paul) uses here shows that he is thinking of close relationships in which, unless both parties are true believers, Christian harmony cannot be expected to flourish and Christian consistency cannot fail to be compromised." And that sentiment is exactly true when applied to the specific situation of Paul's relations as apostle to a recalcitrant group at Corinth, as we proposed (pp. 194, 195).

τίς γὰρ μετοχὴ δικαιοσύνῃ καὶ ἀνομίᾳ; "For what partnership do righteousness and lawlessness have?" With this clause, Paul begins a series of five rhetorical questions, all of them consisting of antitheses. Each question commences with the interrogative pronoun τίς ("what"), and the answer to each question is taken to be obvious, since the questions are rhetorical.

Paul begins with γὰρ ("for"), thereby showing the logical conclusion to the preceding clause. In what follows, he gives a clear demand for a distinction between believer and nonbeliever. ("Paul is not thinking in terms of an abstract theology, but of actual personal relationships in the life of a pagan city," Strachan, 5.) Under the influence of a loving God, Paul sees a New Testament, or Christian, "Puritanism" (Denney, 237–47) as the natural and needed response to God's grace (6:1, 2). Though he does not exhort Christians to "leave" the world, nevertheless, it has been asked if Paul's former Pharisaic training with its concern for purity and distinctiveness, to the point of "separation"—hence the name Pharisee—is not in evidence in the following words he uses (Strachan, 4). But the issue is two-edged, since Paul's missionary faith does not agree with such a separatist tendency.

μετοχή, "partnership" ("sharing," so Filson, 352), is another *hapax legomenon*. (See Philo *Spec. Leg.* 4:203–18; cf. *Pss. Sol.* 14:6.) Most interpreters see δικαιοσύνη, "righteousness" as a term used here by Paul in an ethical sense (Gnilka, 57; Reumann, *Righteousness*, 52). This can be confirmed in Paul's practical use of δικαιοσύνη found in Rom 6:13–19; 14:17; 2 Cor 6:7; 11:15; Phil 1:11. By practical is meant right human living, not "God's gracious gift of acquittal" (cf. Rensberger, 31, who sees the δικαιοσύνη/ἀνομία antithesis as at the "heart of the question of 'Paulinicity' " with respect to 6:14–7:1). The idea of practical living is found in Rom 6:13–19 (Collange, *Enigmes*, 306, noting the contrast in 1QH 14) where Paul repeatedly contrasts the idea of being a slave to righteousness with being a slave to ἀνομία, "lawlessness" ("wickedness" NIV; "iniquity," Barrett; "atheism," Héring). Not only that, this passage in Romans also speaks of the contrast between holiness and uncleanness, a link found likewise in our present passage (cf. Heb. 1:9). Such a Pauline thought concerning righteousness, though not the most characteristic of his usage, is not out of keeping (Barrett, 197). The use is found in Qumran, but this simply shows that both Paul and the Qumran writers had been influenced by the OT (ibid.). Thus, Betz's contention (91, n. 12) that what we have is un-Pauline, should be dismissed (see Rensberger, 31). And this argument is more defensible if Paul does have a polemical purpose in view, namely, to oppose his Gospel of righteousness to the claims of his rivals in 11:15, who professed to be "servants of righteousness." See above, pp. 194, 195.

ἤ τίς κοινωνία φωτὶ πρὸς σκότος; "Or what fellowship has light with darkness?" This antithesis is "fundamental" to understanding the daily victory of the Christian, for in this "parable" we see the incompatibility of belief and unbelief (Hughes, 247). The metaphor of darkness and light as moral qualities are common in the NT, both in the Pauline corpus (Rom 13:12; 1 Thess 5:5; Eph 5:11–14) and outside it (John 1:4–9; 12:36; and Luke 16:8). The Christian has been called out of darkness into the light (1 Pet 2:9), for Christ is the light of the world (John 8:12; 9:5) and the unbeliever is destined for outer darkness (Matt 8:12; 22:13; 25:30). Yet the most important reference is to 2 Cor 4:4–6; 11:14, where "darkness" is the lot of unbelievers, a fate the Corinthians are risking by yielding to satanic overtures, masquerading as "light."

Paul writes of κοινωνία, "fellowship," which is one of the key words of his vocabulary. But the idiom here is exceptional. (See R. P. Martin, *IBD* 1:

307–8, for some general analysis of the term: cf. idem, *The Family and the Fellowship* [Grand Rapids: Eerdmans/Exeter: Paternoster, 1979] chap. 3, to be supplemented by G. Panikulam, *Koinonia in the New Testament,* AnBib 85 [Rome: Pontifical Biblical Institute, 1979], and J. Hainz, *Koinonia: "Kirche" als Gemeinschaft bei Paulus,* BibU. 16 [Regensburg: Verlag F. Pustet, 1982], esp. Excursus zu 2 Kor 6, 14, 204–5: he remarks on the unusual construction κοινωνία + dative and πρòς σκότος, as illustrative of the non-Pauline character of the section.)

The metaphors of light and darkness are also found in the Qumran literature. This is seen in the War Scroll where the sons of light are pitted against the sons of darkness (see 1QS 1:9–11; also cf. 1QS 2:16, 17; 3:3, 13, 19, 20, 24, 25; 1QM 1:1, 3, 9, 11, 13; 13:5–6, 9, 15–16; 1QH 12:6; 4QFlor 1:9). It might be noted that the expression "sons of darkness" does not appear in the NT, though 1 Thess 5:5 comes near to it (see Fitzmyer, 208, n. 7). This supports the position of Barrett (197) that the idea of light and darkness is not dependent directly on the Qumran influence but simply reflects the difference between those who are saved and those who are condemned (2:15). Yet one cannot easily dismiss the possibility that such a contrast reflects Qumran teaching, and thus the case for affinity between 6:14–7:1 and an Essene "author" of the first draft of 6:14–7:1 cannot be ruled out.

15. τίς δὲ συμφώνησις Χριστοῦ πρòς βελιάρ, "What harmony is there between Christ and Belial?" Yet again, we have two more *hapaxes.* The concept of "harmony" (Barrett, 197 f.; "agreement," BGD 780, 781; "Syncretism of Christian and pagan cults," Héring, 50) continues the logical chain of antitheses. There is nothing unique about the contrast between Christ and the devil (or Antichrist figure, Bruce, 214 f.; see *Notes* for discussion of variants of the spelling *Belial*). The significance lies in the use of the term *Belial* itself, especially if one attributes this passage to Paul (see Thrall, "The Problem," 138, who views Belial as the "only piece of real evidence" [of the *hapaxes*] militating against Pauline authorship of this passage). One would expect, if Paul authored or even reworked a pre-Pauline tradition, that he would have used or substituted the more common term for the devil, namely, Σατανᾶς, Satan (διάβολος, devil, is found only in Eph 6:11 in the Pauline corpus).

The meaning behind Belial (see Foerster, *TDNT* 1: 607) is not found in the OT as referring to a person (Gnilka, 54; but compare 1 Sam 2:12). Rather it is not uncommon to find Belial (בְלִיַּעַל, *beliyyaʿal*) in the OT suggesting the idea of "worthlessness" (Hughes, 248–50, n. 12), in the sense of evil, or lawlessness (see Deut 13:13; 15:9; 2 Sam 22:5; Ps 18:4; Nah 1:11, 15). Thus, it appears that the author of 6:14–7:1 probably did not draw the term *Belial* (meaning a person) from the OT.

There is, however, considerable evidence that Belial in later Jewish literature came to represent a personalized force opposed to God (*Jub.* 1:20; *T. Reub.* 4:11; *T. Sim.* 5:3; *T. Levi* 19:1; *T. Dan.* 4:7; 5:1; *T. Naph.* 2:6; 3:1; *Asc. Isa* 3:11), especially at Qumran: "Blessed be the God of Israel . . . , but cursed be Belial with his hostile purpose . . ." (1QM 13:1–4; cf. 1QS 1:18, 24; 2:19, 5; 1QM 1:1, 5, 13; 4:2; 11:8; 13:4, 11; 14:9; 15:3; 18:1, 3; 1QH 6:21; 4QFlor 1:8, 9; 2:2; see Huppenbauer, "Belial," 81–89). Yet, one notes that Belial is always the adversary of God, never of the messiah (Murphy-

O'Connor, 55). Thus there is the likelihood that a Christian writer, possibly Paul, changed "God" to "Christ." We might also note that there is the possibility that the demonological teachings of the DSS are reflections on such works as *Jub, T. Levi* and *T. Naph.* (see Milik, *Ten Years of Discovery in the Wilderness of Judaea*, SBT 26 [London: SCM, 1959] 34, 35). Moreover, the idea that Belial opposed the messiah is found in *T. Lev* 8:12. If de Jonge's ("The Testaments," 90, 91) argument is correct—that *T. Levi* (chap. 18) is a hymn to Jesus Christ—then the concept of Christ versus Belial may not be uniquely a Qumranian idea (contra Fitzmyer, 213: "Considering the . . . contrast of . . . Christ and Beliar, it is difficult to deny the reworking of Qumran expressions and ideas" [see also ibid., n. 19]). But a Christian interpolation into *T. Levi* 18 has been suspected (see Gnilka, "2 Cor 6:14–7:1," 55; H. C. Kee, in *The Old Testament Pseudepigrapha, Apocalyptic Literature and Testaments*, ed. J. H. Charlesworth, vol. 1 [New York: Doubleday, 1983] 776–80, 794 f.; and M. Philonenko, *Les interpolations chrétiennes des Testaments des douze Patriarches et les manuscrits de Qoumrân* [Paris: Presses Universitaires de France, 1960]).

Admittedly, since Belial is found in the New Testament only at 6:15, we are forced at least to consider the possibility that 6:14–7:1 is of Qumran provenance. Otherwise, why does the text speak of Belial? Yet, the fact that Belial is a *hapax legomenon* is not sufficient to conclude that 6:15 emanated from a Qumran source. There is evidence, as suggested in the preceding paragraph, that the contrast between Christ and Belial was not unheard of in Christian circles. Also, Driver, *The Judean Scrolls*, 488, regards it likely that Belial and Satan were used interchangeably (cf. *Asc. Isa*). If so, then a Christian writer, specifically Paul, could have possibly used the term Belial. This still leaves unanswered the question why he chose the term here when he has used the term *Satan* to oppose Christ in other instances. To say simply that Paul just used "literary prerogative" as a stylistic variant is not enough (though it cannot be ruled out). But if Barrett is correct (198) when he suggests that Paul's rabbinic training may have influenced the choice of words, then we may be closer to a solution. In *Sifre Deut* 117 (on 15:7–9); *Sanh.* 111*b*, is found the idea of "having no yoke" (בלי עול, *beli ʿôl*), that is "having thrown off the yoke of God." This idea may be in the background of the teaching of 6:14. The point is that the believers in Corinth were not to be "unequally" yoked with those who were "unbelievers," those in the dark, those of iniquity, namely, those who were not ruled by God. If this line of reasoning is followed, then, the idea of Belial as a figure opposing God developed simultaneously, though independently, in the NT and Qumran literature (see Driver, *The Judean Scrolls* 490, 491). In 6:15 Paul simply allowed his mind to associate Belial with his thesis of 6:14 since he was ruminating on the nature of satanic opposition to his cause at Corinth (see 11:14 where Satan is mentioned explicitly, though in reliance on a Jewish story about Satan's transformation in Eden: see *Comment* there and on 11:3: Collange, *Enigmes*, 308). What remains unanswered by those who look to Qumran to illumine our passage is to explain how Belial is included in a letter if the term was not known, at least to some degree, by the Corinthians. Yet what remains unanswered by those who favor a genuine Pauline text is the question why Paul did not redact "Belial" to read "Satan," since he most likely "Paulinized" the passage to read specifically "Christ" as the one opposing the force of evil.

ἢ τίς μερὶς πιστῷ μετὰ ἀπίστου; "Or what portion does a believer have with an unbeliever?" Paul once again explicitly reiterates the contrast between believer and unbeliever. He insists that there is no μερίς, "portion" (Bruce, 214: the word is found in Col 1:12; Fitzmyer, "Qumran," 210, 11, traces a contrasting parallel with *gôral ʾel*, "lot of God," at Qumran) between these two. (Note Paul's use of the preposition μετά, "with," probably a stylistic variation, Hughes, 246, n. 9.)

There is the question as to whether or not πιστός is used here in the technical sense of "believer in Christ" (see Bultmann, *TDNT* 6:215). Barrett (199) takes the use of the word as "semi-technical." That is, the original meaning of πιστός was one of "worthy of belief, reliable, faithful" (Gnilka, "2 Cor 6:14–7:1," 57). This adjective was used both of God (1 Cor 1:9; 10:13; 2 Cor 1:18; 1 Thess 5:24; 2 Thess 3:3) and humans (1 Cor 4:2, 17; 7:25; Gal 3:9; Col 1:2, 7; 4:7, 9). In later Pauline (or deutero-Pauline) writing (1 Tim 4:10, 12; 5:16; also see Eph 1:1), it is clearer that πιστός speaks of one who places faith in Jesus Christ. Before us is the issue whether or not 6:15 reflects at least a semitechnical use of the description. In light of both 6:14 and Paul's use of ἄπιστοι as referring to unbelievers (2 Cor 4:4; 1 Cor 6:6; 7:12–15; 10:27; 14:22–24) we can safely say that 6:15 reflects πιστός as a designation of the follower of Jesus and in particular the Pauline adherent, given the contextual setting of this pericope, in our view. To be sure, a believer in Christ was necessarily faithful and dependable, and thus the term became a technical one without losing its original intention. See above on v 14 for ἄπιστοι.

16. τίς δὲ συγκατάθεσις ναῷ θεοῦ μετὰ εἰδώλων, "And what agreement can God's temple have with idols?" Paul concludes his list of five antithetical questions with a reference to the temple of God (an allusion reminiscent of 1 Cor 6:19). The *hapax* συγκατάθεσις, "agreement" ("union": Philo *De Post. Caini* 175; Epictetus; Dionys. Hal. 8, 79; Polybius 2, 58, 11;21, 26, 16) contrasts the ναὸς [θεοῦ], "temple," "sanctuary" (of God [cf. 1 Cor 3:16–17; 6:19], a synonym for the church; for a discussion of "temple" as used of individuals and of a corporate body, see below) and εἴδωλα, "idols." Since, for Paul, the Temple of God in Jerusalem had been replaced in *Heilsgeschichte* by the Temple of God (the believing community), it is doubtful if he saw only opposition between the "Temple of God" and an actual temple of idols (Plummer, 208). Moreover, the apostle is relating to the Corinthians his "horror of idolatry" and all that this sin entails (see Barrett, 199; cf. 1 Cor 5:10, 11; 6:9; 8; 10:7, 14, 19; 12:2; Gal 5:20; Col 3:5; 1 Thess 1:9). For Paul idolatry suggests the element of the licentious and immoral behavior that accompanied the sin of worshiping false deities. This connection is clearly made in Wisd Sol 14:12: "for the idea of making idols was the beginning of fornication, and the invention of them was the corruption of life." That is, more than simple abstinence from idol worship is in Paul's mind. As this passage has shown, Christians must separate themselves from those who are idolaters (cf. 1 Cor 10:7, 14; see too 1 Cor 5:10, 11; 6:9, 10). This is especially evident in the OT catena that follows. What was true about the physical Temple in

Jerusalem is applied to the spiritual temple of believers; the introduction of an "idol" causes the temple to be defiled and so rendered unworthy of God.

Of note is the fact that the image of temple was strong in Qumran (Kuhn, "Les rouleaux," 203, n. 1; B. Gärtner, *The Temple and the Community in Qumran and the New Testament* [SNTSMS 1; Cambridge: University Press, 1965]; R. J. McKelvey, *The New Temple—The Church in the New Testament* [Oxford: University Press, 1968]); see 1QS 2:11, 17; 4:5; 1QH 4:19; CD 20:9; cf. *T. Reub.* 4:6). The Qumran community viewed itself in opposition to the Temple at Jerusalem (see Cullmann, *Christology*, 157–73) and thus regarded itself as a "spiritual community." And even though Qumran was also adamantly opposed to idols, there is no explicit contrast of idols with the Temple of God in Qumran literature (Fitzmyer, "Qumran," 213). Thus, it appears that Paul probably borrowed this imagery from the OT and not from the DSS (Barrett, 199). This makes sense especially in light of his dependence on the OT in the remainder of chapter 6.

ἡμεῖς γὰρ ναὸς θεοῦ ἐσμεν ζῶντος, "for we are the temple of the living God." Paul is emphatic to get his point across. This is seen in the illative use of γάρ, "for." He gives the reason to explain why the Christian has no room for idolatry. There is only one place appropriate for God to dwell and that is in the soul of living beings (Plummer, 209).

Paul makes a plea that he considers himself part of the community of God. His use of ἡμεῖς, "we," a plural form also found in 7:1, suggests one or possibly two ideas. For one thing, it appears that the ναὸς θεοῦ, "the temple of God," is meant in a corporate (1 Cor 3:16), not individualistic sense (1 Cor 6:19; Fitzmyer, "Qumran," 214; Filson, 354). This can be seen in the OT vv that follow. The context suggests that the individual as the temple was not the primary thought on Paul's mind in our present v (Fitzmyer, 214, n. 20; contra Lietzmann, 129). For Paul, the ναός (the sanctuary, the most sacred part of the temple structure as opposed to τὸ ἱερόν, the Temple area [so Goudge, 71]) was now equated with the church as a spiritual reality (see Bruce, 215). Those who had been claimed by God had not been called in isolation, for they were "the temple of the living God."

This discussion of the "corporate" concept of the Temple of God is not to contradict or rule out the idea that the Holy Spirit dwells in each believer ("God can only dwell in the midst by dwelling in each one" [Calvin]). That Paul was thinking of the individual as the temple of God cannot be dismissed, for it easily could have been in his mind (but in 1 Cor 3:16, 17 [cf. 2 Cor 5:10] it is the church in view, as Godet, 214, allows; see Kuhn, "Les rouleaux," 203, n. 2). Yet the tone of this passage (6:14–7:1) is set by an address to the body as a whole as it existed in Corinth. It was a natural development for people who considered themselves to be the legitimate heirs "of Old Testament promises" to see themselves as the temple of God (Barrett, 199).

A second idea that the inclusion of "we" suggests is that the audience of the Corinthians as a whole has not been ignored by the writer of the section. That is, though there is nothing unique about the use of "we," it does suggest that the insertion of 6:14–7:1 was not made at random, thus confirming our view that Paul is in fact extending and enforcing his plea begun at 5:20.

Paul has addressed the Corinthians in general, especially at 6:13. The point is that the use of "we" in 6:16 is not incongruent with 6:13. Rather it enhances the application. Paul has not changed the focus of his instructions. Those who have sought to keep their hearts closed to Paul must refrain from allowing this to continue by joining with idolaters. (Note that the temple of God, in terms of Johannine understanding, is the body of Christ, understood as his physical being; cf. John 2:14–22; see Héring, 50, n. 19.)

One more note on this clause is Paul's description of God as the ὁ θεὸς ὁ ζῶν ("living God"). The concept of a new beginning to Christian existence (Héring, 50), not as evident in the Corinthian church as Paul would have liked (1 Cor 5:6–8), is set before the church again. The corporate figure is a composition of individuals taking their place in the new creation (2 Cor 5:17) and in the new age of the Spirit (see 2 Cor 3:3). The God of the universe makes his home (his "true dwelling-place") in the "hearts" of believers, not in a temple made with hands (a thought of both Paul, according to Acts 17:24, and Stephen, as in Acts 7:48, from whom the apostle may have heard this idea: see M. Hengel, *Between Jesus and Paul* [London: SCM, 1983] 22, n. 138). But the task of witnessing to the new life is to be a shared task of the community of believers. The living God, the one who provides the only way to life—through rebirth—is in Paul's mind and is conveyed by a favorite element of his apostolic teaching, namely the temple-concept (Hughes, 252, 253).

καθὼς εἶπεν ὁ θεὸς, "As God said." To keep the point of separation and distinctiveness before the Corinthians—demanded by the analogy of the temple of God—Paul betrays his *pesher* style (see Derrett; E. E. Ellis, *Paul's Use of the Old Testament*, 139–49). He proceeds to emphasize his understanding of the antithetical nature of Christ and Belial with a catena of OT quotations. For such a "chain" of OT citations, we may compare chaps. 9–11 of Romans.

He introduces this chain with a not-so-usual citation formula, "As God said." More often, he employs the formula "he says" or the like (cf. Rom 9:15, 25; 2 Cor 4:6; 6:2; see Gal 3:16). Gnilka shows ("2 Cor 6:14–7:1," 58) that the unusual formula of 6:16b is paralleled in the DSS (CD 6:12–13; 8:9; cf. 19:22). When the Qumran Essenes sought to "validate" the ordinances of the community, an appeal to "God has said" would preface this proof. Gnilka's suggestion cannot be taken as conclusive proof that Qumran influence is behind the formula (Barrett, 200). Paul could have chosen to use this phrase, and there are partial examples in Rom 9:15, 25; 2 Cor 4:6; cf. Gal 3:16. It is difficult, however, to ignore the Qumranian influence that is present in this phrase. Whatever the reason, there is no room for misunderstanding on the part of the Corinthians as to the force of Paul's use of the OT.

As will be observed, Paul does not slavishly follow nor cite verbatim his OT text in Greek (LXX). While he does not corrupt the true meaning of the texts, he appears to alter (Filson, 354) the wording so as to continue his theme of the separation of God's people from defiling associations. This again possibly reflects Paul's use of the *pesher* method. (Each adaptation is seen as a deliberate attempt to conform the text to the current context and to point to the polemical issues at stake. Specifically, as we saw in chap. 3, Paul and his opponents have rival methods of scriptural exegesis, especially in relation to the fulfillment-theme: see D. Georgi, *Die Gegner*, 265–82. The deviations found in 2 Cor 6:16*b*–18 are "evidently designed for a messianic age interpretation of the prophecies" [so Ellis, "A Note," 130]; see also discussion above on 6:2 concerning Paul's appeal to fulfilled prophecy as a means of showing that the messianic age has dawned.)

Ἐνοικήσω ἐν αὐτοῖς καὶ ἐμπεριπατήσω, "I will dwell in their midst and walk with them." To impress on his readers even more the joyful reality, yet the solemn gravity of being God's temple, Paul introduces this *testimonium*. Verse 6:16*b* appears as the combination of both an OT paraphrase and an almost direct quotation of Lev 26:11, 12. The paraphrase could well be from Ezek 37:27, which speaks of a dwelling place (κατασκήνωσις—"taking up lodging," BGD, 418, a term found in Polybius 11, 26, 5; Diodorus Siculus 17, 95; LXX). Paul uses ἐνοικεῖν, "to dwell," which appears as a verb which was not used of God in the LXX (Barrett, 200; Plummer, 209; Windisch, 216, n. 3; see BGD, 267). This use of a word denoting an idea stronger than "to tabernacle among them" (Plummer) suggests that, as God sought to be present among the Israel of the OT (see Lev 26:9), he has now established his everlasting rule over his people. This rule is characterized by dwelling among them (see the application in John 1:14; 14:23; Rev 21:3). Paul wants his readers to understand that the divine dwelling place is in his temple, namely, the followers of God (Héring, 50). As the Holy of Holies (the ναός) was the dwelling place of the divine presence in the Tabernacle, God has a dwelling place in the new age, namely, the chosen people (cf. Exod 25:8; 29:43–46; 2 Sam 7:14, 27; Isa 52:4, 11; Ezek 20:34; Philo, *De Somn.* 1:148, 2:248; cf. Knox, *St. Paul and the Church of the Gentiles*, 164).

That God will "walk" (ἐμπεριπατεῖν) among his people begins an almost word-for-word quotation of Lev 26:12, which continues through to the end of 6:16. The idea of "walking" (i.e., to move about) is usually found in the form περιπατεῖν; the compound form is only in Lev 26:12 and 2 Cor 6:16 (see too Exod 25:8; 29:45). There is a change in pronouns from the second to third person, which accounts for the variation between Lev 26:12 (LXX) and 6:16*b* and which may be the effect of the paraphrase of Ezek 37:27, a verse constructed with the pronoun "you." It is doubtful that this slight change affects the meaning of 6:16*b* (Hughes, 253). Rather the tension between separation and nonseparation is held constant. The people of God are the temple of God, for he dwells in their midst and walks among them.

καὶ ἔσομαι αὐτῶν θεός, καὶ αὐτοὶ ἔσονται μου λαός, "And I will be their God and they will be my people." Except for the pronoun, this is a direct quotation from Lev 26:12. It is the ancient language of the covenant (Bruce, 215; see Ezek 11:20; 36:28; cf. Rev 21:3; also see Ezek 37:26, 27; Jer 31:31–34). God has chosen to dwell among those who believe in him. By virtue of the fact that he has acted to inaugurate a new age (6:1, 2), this is a new dwelling with the added dimensions of depth and effect. No one can break the new covenant; those under that covenant have the opportunity to be sharers in the new creation (5:17). Note the LXX's reading of διαθήκη ("covenant") for מִשְׁכָּן, *miškān*, in Lev 26:11, "I will put my dwelling place among you."

Yet, Paul has stated before (5:10; 6:1) and repeats here that this privilege carries with it a demand (Plummer, 209). The essence of such a demand is the call to holiness of living (cf. Lev 11:44; Matt 5:48), which is expanded in the verse to follow.

17. διὸ ἐξέλθατε ἐκ μέσου αὐτῶν καὶ ἀφορίσθητε, λέγει κύριος, καὶ ἀκαθάρτου μὴ ἅπτεσθε, "therefore, come out from them and be separate, says the Lord. Touch nothing unclean." Paul concludes his contrasts between Christ and Belial with both an exhortation and a promise. The negative exhortation is a reminder to the Corinthians that they are to live as befits the temple of God. If this vocation is taken seriously by them, there remains a promise, namely, that God will be among his people. With this promise in mind Paul reiterates the way of living that will ensure that the promise will come to pass.

Paul begins 6:17 (the "practical conclusion" of vv 14–16, so Plummer, 209) with the strong inferential conjunction διό, "therefore." Therefore, since believers and unbelievers have distinctive ways of life (at least on the spiritual plane), and since the church is the temple of God, and since he has promised to live among his people, God commands his people to "come out of the midst of them."

ἐξέλθατε ἐκ μέσου αὐτῶν, "come out from their midst." The verb ἐξελθεῖν ("to go out," "to come away from," "to escape"; cf. John 10:39) is in the aorist imperative, thus showing Paul's desire for immediate and decisive withdrawal on the part of the Corinthians (Plummer, 209: "For Paul the necessity of sanctification follows from the premise," so Wendland, 141; cf. Rev 18:4). That God has promised his presence to his people is underscored by the command to be holy like God.

It appears that the first three lines of 6:17 are drawn from Isa 52:11 ("Depart, depart, go out, go out from there, touch nothing unclean, go out from the midst of her"). In the OT setting, the people of Israel, seen as a priestly community, are ordered to leave Babylon, and so to separate themselves from this pagan city. As Isa 52:11 goes on to say, those who are leaving are to carry the vessels of Yahweh. This leaves open the possibility that the writer of Isa 40–55 had cultic cleanness in mind. Betz argues ("2 Cor 6:14–7:1," 95, 96) that 6:14–7:1 is urging a "cultic-ritual separation from the unclean." (For Betz, since Paul already considers the church holy [1 Cor 6:11; also see Bultmann, *Theology* 1:133–152, 276–78], the apostle could not have penned 6:17 because the thrust of 6:14–7:1 is a call to be holy. But it seems that Betz has overlooked that Paul's desire in 2 Cor [see 6:1, 2] is for the people to achieve what as yet they do not exhibit, namely, holiness. The tension is a common one in the Corinthian correspondence; it is that of "already a holy people, but not yet dedicated to God," as in 1 Cor 5:7, 8; see J. Jeremias, *The Eucharistic Words of Jesus*, tr. N. Perrin [London: SCM, 1966] 59, 60.) But the Christians are called to leave the ranks of the unbelieving ("Babylon") and subscribe to a new kind of purity. There is a transitional process from a cultic understanding (in Isa 52:11) to an ethical one in 2 Cor 6:17 (Bruce, 215). As Barrett writes (201), "If the people of God cease to be separate in moral holiness from the rest of mankind, they cease to be the people of God." On the tension between indicative and imperative, see P. Tachau, *'Einst' und 'Jetzt' im Neuen Testament* (FRLANT 105 [Göttingen: Vandenhoeck & Ruprecht, 1972] 116–29).

Another part of this command is seen in ἀφορίσθητε, "be separate," (from ἀφορίζειν; aorist imperative). The third part is again in the imperative, ἀκαθάρτου μὴ ἅπτεσθε, "touch nothing unclean" (from ἅπτεσθαι). These last two verbs simply reinforce the thrust of 6:17a. The Corinthians are to become holy. In between the second and third parts is found the phrase λέγει κύριος ("says the Lord": See Ellis, *Paul's Use*, 107–13) which is possibly Paul's attempt at emphasizing the divine and authoritative origin of these commands, namely, the Lord. We may note two other items. First, ἀκαθάρτου ("unclean") could be a neuter ("unclean thing") or a masculine ("unclean person") word. Regardless of which is preferred, Paul probably has idolatry in general in his mind (Betz, 96; cf. Plummer, 210). Second, Bruce is right (215) to point out that the demand to "come out," found here in 6:17, echoes the similar command in 1 Cor 5:10. But there is no identity (on our understanding), and the text in 6:17 may well be a nuanced application if Paul is directing his call to the Corinthians to forsake the false teachers.

κἀγὼ εἰσδέξομαι ὑμᾶς, "And I will receive you." V 17 concludes with a promise. This promise, the second of three promises found in 6:14–7:1, appears to be based on Ezek 11:17, LXX; 20:34, 41, LXX; (Héring, 50; cf. Zeph 3:20, which also has the phrase εἰσδέξομαι ὑμᾶς, as does Ezek 20:34). Of note is the fact that εἰσδεχέσθαι ("welcome," BGD, 232; cf. Josephus, *Ant.* 14, 285; *1 Clem* 12:3) is found only here in the NT. Betz ("2 Cor 6:14–7:1," 96–98) holds that this is not a quotation from Ezek 20:34 but rather an interpretation of 2 Sam 7:14, an allusion to which follows in 6:18. Once again this view is based on his desire to show that 6:14–7:1 is entirely anti-Pauline. For Betz, the second promise can only be fulfilled if the people observe cultic purity (96: "Thus, the cultic purity of the community becomes the precondition for the second promise"). But the thrust of 6:14–7:1 is not a call to earn holiness, but for the Corinthians to live as though they were holy, as indeed they are in one sense—by divine calling ("saints," 1:1). For Paul urges them (in light of accepting him as a true apostle) to keep their hearts open to him by keeping their hearts open to God. This could come only by living separately, though not apart, from the pagans and in particular by ceasing to cast doubt on his Gospel. Paul was concerned with ethical, not physical separation from the nonbelieving world. It is hardly possible that cultic separation was in his mind, in spite of the cultic idioms that are pressed into service.

18. καὶ ἔσομαι ὑμῖν εἰς πατέρα καὶ ὑμεῖς ἔσεσθέ μοι εἰς υἱοὺς καὶ θυγατέρας, "And I will be a father to you and you will be my sons and daughters," This third promise (though some, such as Betz, consider 17b–18 as one promise) is probably a repetition of Nathan's prophecy of David (so Collange, *Enigmes*, 312; cf. Schlatter, *Paulus*, 579) as found in 2 Sam 7:14 ("I will be a father to him and he will be my son"; cf. 4QFlor 1:2). We can see that Paul has changed the singular third person pronoun to a second person plural. This appears to be necessary in order to keep consistency with respect to the subject of the community of believers as a whole and to enforce the paraenetic call to his readers.

In line with this last thought, Paul "expands" the scope of the community addressed to include women. He does this by adding θυγατέρας, "daughters" to the v from 2 Sam. Many (Plummer, Barrett, Hughes, Héring) see this as an attempt by the apostle to raise women up to a place of equality with men. Possibly the OT text Isa 43:6 recalled this in Paul's mind (Schlatter, *Paulus*, 579) but the point is well taken. The king of 2 Samuel (Solomon) has been equated with the Christian Lord in 6:18. In him, all men and women participate in the community of God, namely, the temple of God (see Barrett, 201). While there are many unresolved issues concerning Paul's attitude to the social position appointed for women in the church and society (Col. 3:18; 1 Cor 11:11–16; 14:33*b*–36; cf. Eph. 5:22–33; 1 Tim 2:11–15), there appears little doubt of his conviction regarding them in terms of spiritual equality (Gal 3:28, even if this v is a pre-Pauline baptismal formulation). The inclusion of the feminine noun may well point forward to the discussion in 11:2, 3 and denote Paul's self-conscious role as "groomsman" (as in John 3:29*b*; Heb *šôš^ebîn;* cf. 1 Macc 9:39) who mediated between Christ the bridegroom and the church as the new Eve (Str-B 2:429; cf. 1:500–04).

λέγει κύριος παντοκράτωρ, "says the Lord Almighty." The term "almighty" ("all-sovereign," Barrett, 201) is found only here in the Pauline corpus, and in Rev, where it occurs nine times. As for the OT usage, it is probably pointless to cite a single passage as the prime source of Paul's quotation (e.g. 2 Sam 7:8; Jer 51:7; Collange, *Enigmes* 310), for this phrase is used with great frequency as the LXX equivalent of "Lord of hosts" (*yhwh ṣ^ebā'ôt*) (Héring). In all probability, this was Paul's way of concluding his argument. But it is a remarkable way to end a list of OT citations, and points to a quoted source which has been pressed into service by Paul. The will of the Lord is that his sons and his daughters should recognize the holiness of their Father. He has called them out and promised them a filial relationship. The word of the Almighty has gone forth in a way reminiscent of the Old Testament oracular utterances, attributed to the prophets. Perhaps Paul is here taking the prophets' mantle in his appeal: cf. 1 Cor 14:37.

With this formula Paul concludes his mosaic of OT quotations and interpretations. As on other occasions he has used a catena of OT verses (Rom 3:10–18; 9:25–33; 15:9–12) brought together into a self-contained unit. Fitzmyer ("Qumran," 215, 216) raises the question whether Paul constructed this catena himself or utilized an already existing *florilegium*. It used to be said that Paul could not have employed a pre-existing work of OT quotations since no list was thought to exist prior to the evidence in the early Christian fathers. This view, however, was changed with the discovery of 4QFlor in which various texts of the OT are found in groups (see Fitzmyer, 59–89). This suggests that Paul used an existing set of *testimonia*, possibly also found in the texts cited above from Romans. But the manner in which Paul used and wove these verses together makes one wonder if this was a creation of Paul himself (see Bruce, 216, who raises a doubt), or more probably from an unknown Essene source on which he has drawn for his own reasons.

7:1. ταύτας οὖν ἔχοντες τὰς ἐπαγγελίας, ἀγαπητοί, "Since then, beloved, we have these promises." οὖν, "since then" (or "therefore"; cf. W. Nauck, "Das οὖν paräneticum," *ZNW* 49 [1958] 134, 135), provides a conclusion to Paul's elaboration on τὰς ἐπαγγελίας, "promises"; cf. the intent of 6:16*b*, 17*b*, 18. In Rom 15:8 the promises are messianic, as elsewhere in Paul; but here they have an ecclesiological slant. The use of ταύτας, "these," standing first as emphatic clarifies any uncertainty regarding which promises Paul has in mind. Those assurances just mentioned are within the reach of the Corinthians. What God has done is apparent to Paul and, it is hoped, will be so to the Corinthians. The promises are the "indicative" on which the following paraenesis is built (see Betz, "2 Cor 6:14–7:1," 98; note present participle of ἔχειν, "to have"). "The thought here follows the movement of indicative [leading to] imperative" (Collange, *Enigmes*, 312). God has fulfilled his promises and will continue to do so if the "imperatives" are carried out. He will walk among his people, but if the Corinthians are to have God dwell among them, then this dwelling must be purified (Plummer, 211). Hence, Paul exhorts the Corinthians to strive for holy living by basing his call on divine promises (see Schniewind-Friedrich, *TDNT* 2:573–83).

That Paul is ultimately concerned for the Corinthians' welfare is seen in his calling them ἀγαπητοί ("beloved"). This is not an idle usage by Paul. Although the apostle is using a familiar form of address (BGD, 6), he is not liberal in its use in his letter-writing habits (only once more in this letter, in 12:19; twice in 1 Cor 10:14; 15:58, twice in Phil 2:12; 4:1, and finally, once in Rom 12:19). Paul was not ashamed to be counted in association with the Corinthians, as will be seen also in our discussion of καθαρίσωμεν (see below). Despite his ill-treatment the apostle once again "opens" his heart to them by identifying with them. Whether 6:14–7:1 is from the "previous letter" or, more probably, is in its rightful place in 2 Cor, the use of a term of endearment is a pointer to Paul as the author (or redactor) of this piece. Would an interpolator or redactor be so careful as to include the note of "tenderest affection" (Hughes, 257)? It is doubtful that someone quite removed from the original setting would have taken such care and initiative to include ἀγαπητοί, unless he was striving (artificially) for verisimilitude. But, according to our theory of the function of 6:14–7:1, the personal appeal is exactly in order. It picks up the call to reconciliation in 5:20.

καθαρίσωμεν ἑαυτοὺς ἀπὸ παντὸς μολυσμοῦ σαρκὸς καὶ πνεύματος, "let us cleanse ourselves from every defilement of flesh and spirit." Paul continues in his desire to be counted on the side of the Corinthians so that he can call them over to his side. After addressing them as "beloved," he strengthens this bond by using the hortatory subjunctive, καθαρίσωμεν, "let us cleanse." If Paul had not wanted to draw close to the Corinthians he could have couched the following demand in terms of "you must do." Rather, he exhorts both the church and himself. In short, "he reaffirms his loving oneness with them" (Hughes, 257).

The use of καθαρίζειν (cf. Jos. *Ant.* 11, 153) reminds us of cultic language (Barrett, 202; but not to the extent claimed by Betz). Anything that stands in the way of becoming like God the Father is to be removed. This has been the thrust of 6:14–18. The promise of God's approval and fellowship is based on the Christian's desire and effort to be cleansed. It is doubtful if holiness is the goal of this purification process as Betz ("2 Cor 6:14–7:1," 98, 99) interprets it. In one sense the Corinthians are holy for they have received the grace of God. However, Paul desires that they revert to the standard which they were first called to follow (6:1, 2). As we observed, Betz appears to overlook the tension in Paul's joining together of the "indicative" and the "imperative." (See Tachau, *'Einst' und 'Jetzt,'* cited above.) By doing so he fails to see that Paul could hold the position he does. The goal of purification is not to strive for holiness (contra Betz, 98) but to demonstrate that holiness is the result of salvation. The reflexive verb simply implies a personal stake in the process.

The object of cleansing is to remove every "defilement" ($\mu o\lambda \upsilon \sigma \mu \acute{o}\varsigma$). This is the last *hapax* of the passage (though we find its cognate verb in 1 Cor 8:7). (Once again it becomes difficult to accept Betz's contention [98, n. 73], that purification is not in Paul's mind.) The idea of defilement is connected with idolatry (1 Esdr 8:80; 2 Macc 5:27; cf. Jer 23:15, LXX), a point drawn from the previous verses. Paul, in logical fashion, exhorts his readers to purify or cleanse themselves. To accomplish this the objects or reasons for defilement must be removed.

Paul includes the whole spectrum of possibilities of defilement, when he writes "let us cleanse ourselves from all defilement of flesh and spirit" ($\sigma \alpha \rho \kappa \grave{o}\varsigma$ $\kappa \alpha \grave{\iota}\ \pi \nu \epsilon \acute{\upsilon}\mu \alpha \tau o\varsigma$). This inclusion of "flesh and spirit" has sparked no small disagreement over the integrity of these words. Gnilka ("2 Cor 6:14–7:1," 58) calls this reference "the absolutely untheological use of 'flesh' and 'spirit.'" The point of contention is that this usage does not appear to be "normal" Pauline anthropology, which employs the terms as two powers, not two parts of the human person as here (Collange, *Enigmes*, 313; cf. E. Schweizer, *TDNT* 7:125). For one thing, Paul usually has in mind the "intrinsically evil" side of humanity when he uses $\sigma \acute{\alpha}\rho \xi$, "flesh." Characteristically, Paul would say that "flesh" is incapable of being cleansed of sin. Likewise, Paul would normally consider $\pi \nu \epsilon \hat{\upsilon}\mu \alpha$, "spirit," as "intrinsically good," not in need of cleansing (see Tertullian, *Adv. Marcionem* 5:12. Marcion read $\alpha \H{\iota}\mu \alpha \tau o\varsigma$ [of blood] in place of $\pi \nu \epsilon \acute{\upsilon}\mu \alpha \tau o\varsigma$ [of spirit], because his anthropological dualism had room only for bodily sins; but he may have been influenced by 1 Cor 15:50). Thus, some would maintain that Paul could not have possibly written in this way.

The purification of flesh and spirit also smacks of a Qumranian theology. We read in 1QS 3:8, "By subjecting his soul to all the commandments of God he purifies his flesh." Gnilka (59) interprets this purification and sanctification as a result of the effort of the individual. This dissection of man into flesh and spirit is well attested at Qumran (1QH 13:13, 14; 15:21, 22; 17:25). Once again we have the evidence that the sons of light who wish to take part in the holy war must be "perfect in spirit and flesh" (1QM 7:5). Thus Fitzmyer ("Qumran," 215) concludes that 2 Cor 7:1 strongly resembles Essene thought.

But it may be asked if this is necessarily cogent enough to eliminate the possibility that Paul could have penned these words ("defilement of flesh and spirit"). Barrett (202), for one, does not rule out the possibility that Paul could have used the collocation in a nontheological manner. He could have been using popular language to designate the makeup of a person, both material and immaterial (Plummer, 211). In Col 2:5 the text speaks of the writer being "absent in the flesh" ($\tau \hat{\eta}\ \sigma \alpha \rho \kappa \grave{\iota}\ \check{\alpha}\pi \epsilon \iota \mu \iota$) but "present in the spirit" ($\tau \hat{\wp}\ \pi \nu \epsilon \acute{\upsilon}\mu \alpha \tau \iota\ \ldots\ \epsilon \H{\iota}\mu \iota$). Also, in 7:5 we read that "the flesh" of Paul had no rest, as we compare that with 2:13, that his "spirit" had no peace.

Thus, it is possible that Paul could use σάρξ and πνεῦμα in a nontechnical sense. But R. Jewett, *Paul's Anthropological Terms*, 184, 185, has maintained that at 7:1 the text stands in the Jewish apocalyptic tradition, so that "spirit" is none other than God's spirit given to man (cf. *T. Naph.* 10.9, "Blessed is the man who does not defile the holy spirit of God which has been placed and breathed into him"). This meaning would be close to Paul in 1 Cor 3:6, 6:17–19. Moreover, as we saw, "flesh" and "spirit" follow each other in 2:13 and 7:5 but in reverse order (Jewett, 133; Lietzmann, 131; Bultmann, 56).

Further light is shed by 1 Cor 7:34 where Paul comments, "Her aim is to be devoted to the Lord in both body (σῶμα) and spirit (πνεῦμα)" (cf. 1 Cor 5:3, 5; Jewett, 120). This appears to be a concern for the outward and inward man (Barrett, 202), without being a reproduction of gnostic thought ("Gnostics maintained that it was impossible to cleanse flesh as to cleanse filth," so Plummer, 211).

These examples are sufficient to show that the expression "defilement of flesh and spirit" does not have to be non-Pauline, however unusual it may be. Paul could have used the combination of flesh and spirit to depict the total picture of human nature of which the "intercommunion of the parts is so close, that when either is soiled the whole is soiled" (Plummer, 211; see Rensberger, "2 Cor 6:14–7:1," 39). He could have taken this from other sources than Qumran. We find such a combination in *T. Jud.* (13:4) and Isa 31:3 (בשׂר, *bāśār* and רוח, *rûaḥ*). Thus, even though this was not Paul's normal mode of expression in v 1, the evidence suggests a loose usage.

ἐπιτελοῦντες ἁγιωσύνην ἐν φόβῳ θεοῦ, "perfecting holiness in the fear of God." The result of the act of catharsis will be an ἐπιτελεῖσθαι in ἁγιωσύνη ("perfecting in holiness"). The present participle ἐπιτελοῦντες (from ἐπιτελεῖν, "bring about sanctification," BGD, 302; cf. *Ep. Arist.*, 133) suggests an advancement in holiness (Hughes, 258, n. 22). Paul appears to some readers to be promoting the idea that the Corinthians are to obtain holiness by way of the observance of cultic ordinances (as described in 6:17; Betz, "2 Cor 6:14–7:1," 98, n. 76; cf. Delling, *TDNT* 8:61, 62). But to take this position suggests that what is being advocated is instant holiness in this life. This is quite inconsistent with Paul in other places (see Phil 3:12–15 against such perfectionist teaching; Martin, *Philippians* 137, 138: the Pauline believer is always *in statu viatoris*, on the road between the starting point and the goal). Rather, the idea of advancing in holiness depicts a repeated act of self-consecration (Plummer, 212), a constant drive to live as God's people. There is a goal to be reached when believers are said to bring holiness to completion (Bruce, 216; cf. 8:6, 11; Phil 1:6; 1 Thess 3:3; Rom 1:4). To rest content and self-satisfied with an unholy life is to receive the grace of God in vain (6:1, 2). Paul struggled (Phil 3:12–16) with the paradox of two kinds of perfection, and, in this context, in his view the Corinthians were set aside (considered holy) for God had called them (1:1); yet they needed to act out their status-in-Christ. This is precisely the paradox of reconciliation, of which we spoke earlier (see pp. 164, 165).

The living of the holy life is done ἐν φόβῳ θεοῦ, "in fear of God." We saw earlier that Paul's ministry, especially with the Corinthians in mind, was motivated by this reverence (5:11) and both there and here we trace a polemical thrust in his appeal to God to vindicate the teaching. The way a person acts, even after conversion, affects the person's standing before God (5:10, a testing not—for Paul—in terms of salvation, but in terms of reward). The motive of "right" living remains a part of the apostle's teaching, and not least when his credibility as an apostle is at stake.

The "fear of God" is a principle of life found in the Jewish wisdom literature (Pss 2:11; 5:7; Prov 1:7, 29, 8:13; Eccles 12:13; Sir. 1:11–30). It is not clear whether the ἐν, "in," suggests the sphere in which the perfecting of holiness takes place or the means by which it is accomplished (Plummer, 212). Probably it is the former in light of our discussion in 5:11. But the ethical demand is not lost. Christians must fulfill both the negative (cleanse their flesh and spirit) and the positive (complete their holiness) duty (so Tasker, 100). Above all, Pauline believers are summoned to make good their profession by heeding Paul's apostolic entreaty and "becoming what they are."

Explanation

If we lay all the critical problems aside, the meaning of this passage is reasonably clear. Those who profess to have accepted God's grace must not deceive themselves. Rather, through living in a way that is holy (set aside for God's service) they must seek to be separate (in the twofold sense of "holy," both negative and positive: see *Comment* on 1:1). Yet to be an effective witness, believers must be seen and accessible. That is, they discharge their calling to the world only if they are in the world.

Paul's exhortation to be separate stops short of exhorting them to become recluses. What Paul apparently had in mind was the breaking of "spiritual ties" with the Gentile world. Until that was accomplished, God's promises remained stifled. In that event, the Corinthians could not enjoy the full measure of the "sanctified" life, nor practice the quality of life that will receive reward (1 Cor 3:10–15; 2 Cor 5:10). The tie with the world had to be broken so that the temple of God would be pure. An important result of this failure to cleanse themselves was that the true ambassador for God was likewise shut out of the Corinthians' lives, and they had ranged themselves on the side of the unbelieving world which needs to be "reconciled"—as they did insofar that they were opposing Paul's Gospel.

While this short section has obvious elements of Christian counsel for the believers' attitudes to the world and society and its direct application is to contrast Christian and pagan morality, thereby setting out "the ideal of the Christian life" (Denney), its primary point should not be lost. Coming between two impassioned appeals (6:11–13; 7:2, 3) to the Corinthian congregation to be reconciled to Paul, the pericope warns the readers of their danger and cautions them not to remain alienated from the Pauline Gospel. Using idioms that betray a preformed piece of teaching on the sacral nature of Christian living—temple, idols, separation, cleansing, holiness—and within a quasi-dualistic frame (God vs. idols; Christ vs. Satan; unbelievers vs. God's people) Paul enforces a single point: the call to reconciliation involves a whole-hearted commitment and pledge of loyalty to him and to his proclamation as the "divine apostle." The tone is strident and severe, but evidently such was needed. Paul now moves deftly into a short resumption (7:2, 3) to moderate what he may have regarded as too impersonal and rigorous.

At the heart of these verses which run from 5:11 to 7:3 stands indeed one central theme with three variations. The overarching consideration is to lay a basis for reconciliation with the Corinthian church, and the three elements are (1) the suffering apostolate, (2) the partnership of apostle and people, and (3) a celebration of God's work of grace in human lives (so Ivor Jones, *The Contemporary Cross*, 120–25).

J. The Good Report of Titus   (7:2–16)

Bibliography

Barrett, C. K. "Ο ΑΔΙΚΗΣΑΣ (2 Cor. 7.12)." In *Essays on Paul*, 108–17. ———. "Titus." In *Essays on Paul*, 118–31. **Carrez. M.** "Le 'nous' en 2 Corinthians." *NTS* 26 (1979–80) 474–86. **Jones, I. H.** *The Contemporary Cross*. London: Epworth Press, 1973. **Lampe, G. W. H.** "Church Discipline and the Interpretation of the Epistles to the Corinthians." In *Christian History and Interpretation*, Studies presented to John Knox, ed. W. R. Farmer *et al.*, 337–61. Cambridge: University Press, 1967. **Moncure, J.** "Second Corinthians 7:8–10." *RevExp* 16 (1919) 476–77. **Olivier, F.** "Συναποθνῄσκω. D'un article de lexique à Saint Paul, II Corinthiens, vii, 3." *RThPh* 17 (1929) 103–33. **Schütz, J. H.** *Paul and the Anatomy of Apostolic Authority*. SNTMS 26. Cambridge: University Press, 1975. 233–34. **Stählin, G.** "Um mitzusterben und mitzuleben. Bermerkungen zur 2 Kor. 7,3." *Neues Testament und christliche Existenz*. FS H. Braun. ed. H.-D. Betz and L. Schottroff, 1973. 503–21.

Translation

²*Make room for us* [*in your hearts*]; *we have wronged no one, we have ruined no one, we have taken advantage of no one.* ³*I do not say this to condemn you,*[a] *for I have said previously that you*[b] *are in our hearts; thus we die or live*[c] *with you.* ⁴*I have much confidence in you; I take great pride in you. My encouragement is complete; I am overflowing with joy in all our distress.*

⁵*For when we came into Macedonia our body found*[d] *no rest but on all sides we were distressed; strife from without; fears*[e] *from within.* ⁶*But God, the one who encourages the downcast, encouraged us with the coming of Titus.* ⁷*And not only with his coming, but also in the encouragement you gave to him. He told us of your desire* [*for me*], *of your mourning, of your zeal for me, so that my joy was even more than before.* ⁸*Even if my letter hurt you, I do not regret it. Though I did regret it—for I see*[f] *that letter hurt you for a while—*⁹*now I rejoice, not that you sorrowed but that your sorrow led to repentance. For you experienced godly sorrow so that you suffered no loss through us.* ¹⁰*For godly sorrow produces*[g] *repentance that leads to salvation and leaves no regret, but worldly sorrow leads to death.* ¹¹*See what earnestness this godly sorrow has produced*[h] *in you,*[i] *but also what eagerness to clear yourselves, what indignation, what fear, what longing, what zeal, what punishment. In every instance you have demonstrated your innocence in*[j] *this matter.*

[12] *So then,*[k] *when I wrote to you it was not on account of the offender, or of the offended, but on your account, so that before God you could see your*[l] *earnestness toward us.* [13] *Because of this we are encouraged.*[m] *In addition*[n] *to our encouragement, we rejoiced more than ever at the joy of Titus because his spirit has been refreshed by all of you.* [14] *For I boasted to him about you and you did not embarrass me. And as we have spoken the truth in all things*[o] *to you, likewise our*[p] *boasting to*[q] *Titus about you has proved true.* [15] *His affection abounds toward you when he recalls everyone's obedience, for he was received with fear and trembling.* [16] *I rejoice in that I have complete confidence in you.*

Notes

[a]The text is supported by ℵ B C P. We have the reading *οὐ πρὸς κατάκρισιν λέγω* in D E F G K L. Most likely this second reading is a later correction (so Plummer). On the literary form (epidiorthosis—a subsequent correction of a previous impression) see BDF § 495.3.

[b]Note that B omits *ἐστε*.

[c]*συζῆν* has weaker attestation (B[3] K L P) than does *συνζῆν* (ℵ B* C D E F G).

[d]Nestle-Aland[26] has the perfect *ἔσχηκεν* (ℵ C D Ψ 0243), while some MSS (P[46] B F G K) have the aorist *ἔσχεν*, as an attempt to "correct" the tense (see BDF § 343.2).

[e]P[46] has *φόβος* (singular).

[f]This verse is extremely difficult with respect to its text and punctuation. Some question surrounds the correct reading. The possibilities are *βλέπων* (P[46*] vg), or *βλέπω* (P[46c] B D* it sa Ambst), or *βλέπω γὰρ* (ℵ C D[1] F G ψ 0243 vg[mss] syr[bo]). Scholars such as Lachmann and Hort supported *βλέπων*, "seeing." They took the Vulgate rendering *videns* as correct, especially in light of the scribal practice of contracting the ending *-ων* to *-ω*. It is noted that Hughes (269, n. 6) likewise supports the reading of *βλέπων*. This reading, however, has weaker textual support, but Barrett and Windisch suggest the final *ν* has been lost in transmission.

Better attestation is found for the reading of *βλέπω*. Barrett considers this reading the most difficult of the three and thus he supports it (210). He receives some support for his position from the minority of the UBSGNT committee (*A Textual Commentary on the Greek New Testament,* in which see 581) which takes *βλέπω* to be an attempt by a copyist to overcome the difficult syntax of 7:8. But when we look to the reading that has the greatest support, we are left with *βλέπω γὰρ*. The majority of the committee noted this support and was led to include it in the text. But even this majority reflected the uncertainty that surrounds our text for we note that *γὰρ* is inserted in brackets in Nestle-Aland[26].

In the question of the correct reading of the text we are also confronted with the correct punctuation of the verse. One view is that *βλέπω [γὰρ] ὅτι ἡ ἐπιστολὴ ἐκείνη εἰ καὶ πρὸς ὥραν ἐλύπησεν ὑμᾶς* should be considered a parenthetical statement (NIV; Hughes, 269, n. 6). It appears that some scribes saw *εἰ καὶ μετεμελόμην* as a new portion of the letter, for B inserts *δὲ* between *εἰ* and *καὶ*. This supports placing a full stop before *εἰ καὶ μετεμελόμην*. The thought beginning with "Though I did regret it" is interrupted by the statement, "for I see that letter hurt you for a while." This sequence should be continued at the beginning of v 9. The KJV/AV has presented us with an awkward punctuation of 7:8 and, when examined, has the clause beginning with *βλέπω* as stating the reason why Paul made the Corinthians sorry rather than the reason why he regretted having hurt them (see Tasker, 104, 105; Hodge; also see *Comment*).

[g]*ἐργάζεται* is found in ℵ* B C D P 81 1175, while ℵ[2] F G Ψ 0243 have *κατεργάζεται*. Plummer (222) contends that the latter reading is due to assimilation to the next clause, which indeed includes *κατεργάζεται*.

[h]Some MSS (ℵ[2] D Ψ vg) include *ὑμᾶς* after *λυπηθῆναι*, but the text is supported by P[46] ℵ* B C F G 0243 33 81 630 1739 1881 Ambst.

[i]*ἐν* is found before *ὑμῖν* in ℵ[2] C F G P 104 326 365 629 2464 2495 Ambst. This preposition is omitted in (P[46]) ℵ* B D K L Ψ 0243 6 33 81 630 *Clem.*

[j]A few MSS (D[1]) include *ἐν* before *τῷ πράγματι*, but there is overwhelming evidence to omit this. Possibly *ἐν* was introduced by later scribes to ease the construction (so Plummer).

[k]*ἄρα* carries with it the force of *ὥστε*, "so then."

[l]This verse is another example of how easily *ἡμεῖς* and *ὑμεῖς* can become a source of confusion.

Variant readings are ἡμῶν τὴν ὑπὲρ ἡμῶν (G d vg^ms), ὑμῶν τὴν ὑπὲρ ὑμῶν (א D* F 0243 629) and ἡμῶν τὴν ὑπὲρ ὑμῶν (323 945 lat Ambst). As will be seen in the *Comment*, the context demands what is found in the text of Nestle-Aland[26], i.e., ὑμῶν τὴν ὑπὲρ ἡμῶν. The second variant results from a desire to harmonize with 7:4; so Bultmann, 62, while the other readings hardly give a tolerable sense.

   ^m There are some scholars who take v 12 to include the words διὰ τοῦτο παρεκεκλήμεθα (RSV; see Héring 56 and note).

   ^n δὲ is omitted in P^46 81 104 365 629 630 1175.

   ^o πάντοτε (C F G 81 sy^h co) and πάντων (326) are alternate readings.

   ^p ὑμῶν is found is B F.

   ^q The text is supported by P^46 א^2 C 0243. ἡ πρὸς Τίτου is found in D F G P Ψ 365 614 1175.

Form/Structure/Setting

The present passage resumes the plea of Paul found in 6:11–13. He has opened his mouth to them—a biblical idiom (Jud 11:35 f.; Job 3:1; Sir 51:25; Matt 5:1, which all use some form of ἀνοίγειν τὸ στόμα, "to open the mouth" in readiness for speaking). Paul beckons the Corinthians to open their hearts to him and, following the insertion of 6:14–7:1 and continuing the appeal launched in 5:20 ff., he again takes up his exhortation (7:2). In order to convince the Corinthians that such action on their part has been beneficial, Paul has written in polemical fashion. He now reminds them that he has wronged no one (ἀδικεῖν; cf 1 Cor 6:8, but it has a veiled allusion here to what will follow in 7:12), though he has been wronged, both by the offender and by the false apostles. Also, Paul writes that he has corrupted (φθείρειν) no one and that his actions have not hurt the church. In addition, the apostle has not taken advantage of (πλεονεκτεῖν) anyone. This is an accusation that he, at least indirectly, brings in defense against his opponents (see 12:17, 18). Contrary to the "super-apostles" (11:4–7), Paul has preached the true Gospel and asked nothing in return (11:9), except to be loved. The Corinthians should open their hearts to Paul, for he has done nothing to injure them. When compared with his opponents the apostle is the only one who truly deserves to be in the Corinthians' hearts. This is the final element in the task of mutual reconciliation, for "Paul was not one to plead for reconciliation without making a healing gesture himself" (Jones, *The Contemporary Cross*, 61).

With the uprightness of his actions rehearsed, Paul launches into the first of two related themes that permeate the remainder of this passage.

(1) Paul has confidence (παρρησία) in the Corinthian church (7:4). As a result of the news that Titus brings, Paul knows that he can now rely on the Corinthians to be obedient to him (7:4; cf. 7:11). And in relating this truth to the Corinthians, Paul returns (after a long exposition, 2:14–7:4) to the subject of Titus. In 2:13, Paul had been describing his "ordeal" of waiting for Titus to return from Corinth with the news of the church's response to the "severe letter." This letter had troubled Paul (7:8) and he found little rest while waiting for the return of Titus. But upon the return of Titus, Paul learns the good news that Titus has to share. Paul, who has been enheartened many times (1:3–7), is gladdened by the report of Titus that all is well in the Corinthian church with respect to Paul and the faithful church members. For now all is well, but we are forced to keep the door open for

the onset of further trouble. If we assume chaps. 10–13 were written after chaps. 1–9, then obviously Paul's troubles were not behind him. If the last point is true, then we are led to ask why Paul can be so happy in chap. 7 in light of the problems announced in 10–13? Did Titus misread the situation? Did the confidence that Paul here shows miscarry? Or was only a majority of the church won over to his cause? Did the opponents of 10–13 intrude on the Corinthian scene *after* Titus' return to Paul in Macedonia? These questions need to be considered in our study of 2 Cor. Our preference is for the last-named option. See *Introduction.*

(2) Upon hearing the news, Paul shares with his readers the second of the themes in our present passage, namely, joy (χαρά). In the passage we not only see the joy of Paul but also that of Titus. Titus feels loved by the Corinthians, which is part of the story Paul does not overlook. Thus, the welcome news of Titus brings Paul both confidence and joy (7:16).

But 7:8–13 convey that much has happened prior to the accession of this confidence and joy. Paul wrote the "tearful" (or severe) letter. (See *Introduction,* pp. xlvii–li, for a discussion of the theories concerning the identity of this letter. There is nothing to suggest otherwise than that the letter mentioned in 7:8 and the one in 2:4 are one and the same. Most likely, then, this letter has been lost or been destroyed—a not unthinkable supposition, since it served its immediate purpose, as indicated in this chap.) This letter caused him great concern, for he feared that the reaction of the Corinthians would be entirely negative. Yet, he sees that this letter was necessary, for it was used by God (7:9) to promote "godly sorrow" which led to repentance (7:10). This sorrow is not the kind that fails to change a person's relationship to God (and his ambassador), but it is the kind that produces the desire for reconciliation and the means by which to restore a broken fellowship. In Paul's eyes this godly sorrow brought about several changes in the Corinthians (7:11). Surprisingly, Paul had been sure that these changes were well within the reach of the Corinthians. The apostle was so confident of the Corinthians (even more so than Titus) that he wrote the tearful letter, not to condemn anyone, but to allow the Corinthians the opportunity to prove before God their devotion to himself (v 12: there is another way to take this v; see *Comment*). By showing the Corinthians their misbehavior, Paul helped to guide them back to the path on which they were to walk. Because of this return to his side, Paul rejoiced in the Corinthians (v 16).

Paul closes the passage with an explanation of the impact that the Corinthians' attitude had on Titus (7:13b–15). Titus has been renewed by the change in the Corinthians, a prospect Paul had been sure in his brighter moments would be realized (7:14). (Of course, we are not amazed at Paul's confidence after the fact. In 7:8, he states that he was unsure of the outcome of the letter. But from 7:14, it appears that *before* Paul wrote this letter he was confident the Corinthians could [if so inclined] return to his side. It appears that the apostle saw potential in the Corinthians, though at the same time he was not completely sure that they would realize it. We cannot overlook the polemical manner in which Paul speaks. He claims to be standing for the truth, a posture that was—according to him—not true of his adversaries.) Titus's report had been more than ample proof to Paul of the sincerity of the Corinthians, for they had obeyed Titus as an emissary of Paul (we remember that another emissary of Paul, namely Timothy, had not fared so well; see Barrett, "Titus"; Kümmel, *Introduction to the New Testament* [2] [1975] 286, 287). Because of this, Paul had confidence in the Corinthians, which was a basis for joy. The good report of Titus was evidently a personal blessing for Paul in every way (ἐν παντί: v 16).

On the form of this section, while it appears at first glance to be a straightforward piece of narrative prose, some pattern has been detected (by Lietzmann, 131). It seems that the initial remark of v 4 with its three terms παράκλησις, χαρά, and θλῖψις has set the model for what follows. Thus

v 4: παρακλήσει	paired with	v 6: παρακαλῶν
		παρεκάλεσεν
		v 7: παρακλήσει ᾗ
		παρεκλήθη
		v 13: παρακεκλήμεθα
v 4: χαρᾷ	paired with	v 7: χαρῆναι
		v 9: χαίρω
		v 13: ἐχάρημεν, χαρᾷ
v 4: θλίψει	paired with	v 5: θλιβόμενοι

We may also observe how a fourth term (καύχησις, "pride" in v 4) is picked up in v 14, where the word is better rendered "boasting." But the repetition is noteworthy. These verbal links are also more than interesting; they contribute significantly to the question of the origin of 2 Corinthians by showing that the connection between 7:2–4 and 7:5–16 is intimate, as Lietzmann (cited in our *Introduction*, p. xliii) has remarked.

The section overall exhibits the feature of a "ring-composition" (*inclusio*) with the παρακαλεῖν verb at both the beginning (v 6) and conclusion (v 13): see Bultmann, 63.

Comment

2. Χωρήσατε ἡμᾶς, "Make room for us [in your hearts]." Paul resumes the appeal of 6:12, 13. The interruption is ended as Paul returns to his argument that they, the Corinthians—not he—are responsible for a less than desirable relationship at this point. χωρήσατε, "make room" (aorist imperative of χωρεῖν, see Philo, *De Ebrietate* 32; Jos. *BJ*, 6.131; *Sib. Or.* 3, 8; see BGD, 889, 890), carries with it the idea of expansion. While χωρεῖν certainly includes the cognitive element (Matt 19:11, "not everyone can receive [understand; χωροῦσιν] this saying"; this usage has led Allo and Héring to view Paul's use of χωρεῖν in 7:2 to be restricted to the intellectual plane [Héring, 53, n. 4]), there is more depth to the term, especially in light of Paul's emotional appeal of 6:11–13. Paul is speaking personally, not in an official way (Bultmann, 179: *nicht amtlich, sondern persönlich;* but see later). He had exhorted the Corinthians to take him into their hearts (Strachan, "make a place for me," 124). He now asks for a reciprocal move to his taking of them into

his heart (Barrett, 203). The text does not include "in your heart" but the context demands it. The KJV/AV ("Receive us") is insufficient, without an additional phrase *ad sensum.*

οὐδένα ἠδικήσαμεν, "we have wronged no one." Once again Paul puts before his readers the thought that his motives are pure (4:2; 5:12, 13; 6:3) and that the slanderous attacks against his person are wrong. He does this here with three aorist verbs used in asyndeton (this alerts us to the staccato "rapidity" with which Paul is evidently dictating this letter as well as his emotional involvement). Paul quickly negates reasons which may continue to cause the Corinthians to refuse him a place in their hearts (Plummer, 213).

The fact that ἠδικήσαμεν, ἐφθείραμεν, and ἐπλεονεκτήσαμεν are all in the aorist tense (i.e., denoting point action in past time) and all are preceded by a negative substantive (οὐδένα) may signify that in Paul's mind there was not a single instance in which he harmed anyone. Hughes views this construction as pointing to a definite time when Paul was in Corinth (260, n. 26). No doubt Paul is reacting to charges against him, the specifics of which are contained in 7:2*b*. This threefold denial of Paul, highlighted by the placing of οὐδένα, "no one," before each of the aorists, is an attempt to convince the Corinthians that there is no reason for them to be estranged from him (Tasker, 101).

ἠδικήσαμεν (from ἀδικεῖν) conveys the idea of treating another person unjustly (Filson, 356; see 7:12; Gal 4:12; Philem 18; Col 3:25). ἐφθείραμεν ("ruined," from φθείρειν) presents the possibilities of either financial or moral ruin. Paul may have been accused of urging people to abandon practices that were lucrative but unchristian (Strachan, 124, 125). Or, he might have been cited for causing ruin by "taking" people's money in order to help others in distant lands. (This can be seen in light of Paul's mission concerning the offering, specifically in the Gentile mission. It has been suggested in connection with 12:16–18 that Paul had been accused of taking the offering [see chaps. 8, 9] and using it for himself.) In terms of morals, possibly some barbs were aimed at his conduct or example (Filson, 356; BGD, 857), thereby suggesting that he was accused of corrupting (RSV) others (cf. ἀπολλύναι in 1 Cor 8:11; Rom 14:15 is parallel; so Bultmann, 179, and we may recall 2:17 in our letter). Such an attack could have come from the Jewish Christians who considered Paul's doctrine as "thoroughly immoral" (Plummer, 213). Since some of Paul's disciples misinterpreted their freedom in Christ, the Jewish Christians could easily point a finger at those who used their liberty as a license to sin (Rom 3:8; 6:1; Gal 5:13); we may anticipate that a similar charge would be brought in 12:21 and 13:2, for the lack of mutual restraint by the Corinthians could have been an argument used by the Jewish Christians that the Gentiles "lacked" something, namely, obedience to the law in circumcision. The point against this, however, is that circumcision is not otherwise an issue in 2 Corinthians, and it is significant that νόμος, "law," does not occur in the entire letter (Kleinknecht, *Der leidende Gerechtfertigte,* 270, n. 91).

οὐδένα ἐπλεονεκτήσαμεν, "we have taken advantage of no one." The KJV/AV has "defraud," but this is possibly too definite (Plummer, 213), for it may limit the meaning simply to the question of financial dealings (Filson,

356). Though financial deception may be one meaning, the use of πλεονεκτεῖν (Dionys. Hal. 9, 7; Diod. Siculus 12, 106; Plut., *Marc.* 29, 7; Ps.-Lucian, *Amor.* 27) in 12:14–18 suggests a deeper meaning. The idea of "overreaching" (Lietzmann, *übervorteilen*) or "exploiting" (NIV) someone else carries with it the larger meaning of using that person to one's own advantage, financially or otherwise (BGD, 667; except for 1 Thess 4:6, πλεονεκτεῖν is found only in 2 Cor in the NT [7:12; 12:17–18; 2:11]).

Because of the Gospel's demand—made through God's ambassador, namely Paul—any sacrifice by the Corinthians could have been misconstrued by Paul's opponents as an attempt on the apostle's behalf to ruin or destroy the church members. Also, any attempt by Paul to correct a situation that called for the exercise of "authority" could likewise be viewed as an attempt to inflict "injury." One example is the man guilty of incest. Paul's solution was to have this offender "handed over to Satan" (1 Cor 5:5). This action possibly included excommunication (5:2, 7, 12), since the realm outside the church was seen as Satan's domain (4:4: see Eph 2:2; Col 1:13; cf. 1 John 5:19). Such a measure would seem drastic to someone who held the generally accepted opinion in NT times that to be outside the circle of the eschatological people of God (namely, the visible church) was to be liable to God's judgment (1 Cor 11:32). See G. W. H. Lampe, "Church Discipline," esp. 353 f. And though Paul's command to hand the man over to Satan was given in the hope of reforming and disciplining him (as well as purifying the church), it is not difficult to see how Paul's opponents could use such an expulsion to discredit Paul as an authority figure who was out to exercise undue pressure on the church even at the expense of a third party (Hughes 260, 261). More likely, however, the reference is to the case of the (different) man who insulted Paul during the interim visit (2:5–11), since it seems most probable that Paul's verb in v 2 is looking ahead to vv 12, 13 of our chapter and has in mind the occasion of the wrong given and suffered. From the earlier discussion in chap. 2 we learn that the church had reacted—and overreacted—to Paul's injury and had disciplined the person with extreme harshness. This treatment is regarded as Satan's ruse (2:11: see *Comment*), and Paul now returns to face the charge that he had initially promoted a severely strong disciplinary measure in this case. This allegation was unfounded, as he explains in 2:6, 7, but doubtless his enemies were making capital of it as a *cause célèbre*.

Probably in the report of Titus (7:6–16) Paul received news of the accusations hurled at him. (This may suggest that all was not well in the church even at the time of the writing of our passage.) The three aorist verbs of 7:2*b* are presumably synonymous terms in Paul's mind. If he had wanted to mark a gradation in the sense of making each accusation seem worse than the preceding one, he would have reversed ἐφθείραμεν and ἐπλεονεκτήσαμεν (Héring, 53). But Paul, dictating more under emotion than in logical terms, simply wished to remind the Corinthians that he has hurt no one, not even in the final analysis the chief offender of v 12.

3. πρὸς κατάκρισιν οὐ λέγω, "I do not say this to condemn you." See *Notes* for this literary figure. It seems safe to assume that Paul realized that his previous work in Corinth had not been wasted on all. He was hoping that a relationship still existed between a father and his children, going back to

6:13. Paul's defense of his ministry has been in response to the attack of his opponents. But the response had been made as much to the Corinthians as to anyone, so as to keep the relationship with them in full view. This is what Paul cherished most of all. While the apostle has presented an apology in order to win back the hearts of the Corinthians, this statement was necessitated by an attempt on the part of his adversaries to discredit Paul. Since Paul has learned from Titus (7:7–16) of the Corinthians' concern for him, he does not want to jeopardize this happy turn of events, and the *bonheur* thereby created. Though he has been hurt by the Corinthians, nevertheless he does not consider *them* his enemies. Rather, Paul wants to remind his audience that he is not condemning them (κατάκρισις, a forensic term; cf. 1 Cor 6:4). Since 7:2 probably alludes to the insinuations of the false apostles (Héring, 53) who were trading on Paul's severity, he goes out of his way to explain that the target of his wrath is not the Corinthians. Paul is seeking to clear himself, not to accuse the Corinthians (Barrett, 203). This chapter may well be groundplan for the more vigorous attack on his traducers in chaps. 10–13, as a more threatening situation emerged (11:4).

προείρηκα γὰρ ὅτι ἐν ταῖς καρδίαις ἡμῶν ἐστε εἰς τὸ συναποθανεῖν καὶ συζῆν, "for I have said previously that you are in our hearts; thus we die or live with you." Paul earlier remarked how wide his heart is opened toward the Corinthians (6:11) and how much affection flows from his person to them (6:12). He now extends and deepens this commitment to them by relating to what extent he will go to preserve the relationship intact. συναποθανεῖν, "to die together" (see Philo, *Spec. Leg.* 1, 108), and συ[ν]ζῆν, "to live together," are two verbs that both tell how much the Corinthians mean to Paul. At first glance, this is not necessarily a thought that originated in Christian circles. Horace wrote of Lydia (*Odes* 3.9.24: *Tecum vivere amem, tecum obeam libens*) that, "with you I would love to live, with you I would gladly die." And Electra professes a similar sentiment to Orestes: σὺν σοὶ καὶ θανεῖν αἱρήσομαι καὶ ζῆν, "with you I shall choose to die and live" (Euripides, *Orest.* 307 f., cited by Bultmann, 179). But a closer parallel is Ittai's protestation to David, "wherever my lord the king shall be, whether for death or for life (ἐὰν εἰς θάνατον καὶ ἐὰν εἰς ζωήν), there also will your servant be" (2 Sam 15:21). See Olivier, "Συναποθνῄσκω," 103–33, and Stählin, "Mitzustirben" esp. 508–11, who gives more examples ranging from Homer (*Il.* 18.32 ff.) and Plutarch (*Antonius* 71: of Antony's love for Cleopatra) to the devotion of Tristan and Isolde and of Romeo and Juliet. In a different context (Bruce, 217) Paul sees this thought as grounded in Christ and raised to a higher plane (Héring, 53). It is doubtful that Paul is speaking in necessarily theological terms here. Though he may be thinking of the concept of death and resurrection (Filson, 356), more likely he is simply explaining the degree of his love (Barrett, 204; "As a pastor he gives himself to his people, grateful or ungrateful, without reserve").

His choice of the words "death" and "life" brings to mind similar ideas of Paul's in a new context: Rom 8:38, 39, "For I am convinced that neither death or life . . . will be able to separate us from the love of God that is in Christ." In either verse, Rom 8:38 or 2 Cor 7:3, we could have expected "life" to precede "death." But possibly owing to Paul's excitement in dictating such thoughts (Plummer, 214), or to the fact that his life was such a series of deadly perils (Denney, 250, 251), or to both factors, the apostle prefers the order found in the text (see Bruce, 217), which is the sequence in the expressions, both OT and classical, quoted above. His affection for the Corinthians is no secret. In his experience of living (probably Paul's intent behind his use of συζῆν, so Plummer), Paul would never exclude the Corinthians from his love, even if he did see death as a possibility because of them (Strachan: "you are in my very heart, and you will be there in death and life alike," 124).

We may again wonder if Paul is attempting to discriminate between "I" and "we," for he uses λέγω, "I say," and ἐν ταῖς καρδίαις ἡμῶν, "in our hearts." Plummer observes (and correctly so) that if Paul was concerned to direct attention solely to himself (as possibly he did in 5:12) he should have used ἐν τῇ καρδίᾳ. Most likely, he intentionally includes his associates in his thoughts (7:11, 12). The interchange between "I" and "we" is "quite intelligible" (Plummer, 214). This alternation of "I"/"we" in 7:2–13 illustrates the thesis stated by M. Carrez, "Le 'nous' en 2 Corinthiens," to the effect that "this we/you expresses the possible participation of the community in Paul's ministry. Paul is the bearer of this ministry, the community is his field of activity" (478). But the question is raised: since the community has its own ministry, how much of the "you" is included in the "we"? Part of the answer is seen in the passage before us where "I" alternates with "we," and on this fact Carrez tells us (482, 483) that the practice of alternating the pronouns shows Paul's way of doing things. He uses the "we"-form when he wants to stress his good attitudes in his relations with the community, thereby showing the link between the Corinthians and himself that results from the exercise of his ministry (so 7:2, 3). A little farther on, Paul mentions the apostolic struggle in which he has a stake and of which he is the center (7:5). In his view, "a close relationship exists between what happens to him (expressed by 'we') and the consequences of his actions for and his intervention in the community's behavior. Paul never despairs even in the worst of situations (cf. 4:7–10), because whatever the cause of the despair it may be transformed into a motive for encouragement. When he suffers the apostle brings encouragement in a true communion which goes out from him to the community's members. This solidarity, which belongs to the apostolic office, will become the apostolic characteristic of all ministries exercised for the community's welfare."

Carrez's conclusion is borne out by this section, therefore: "The 'we' is not only a literary device, or stylistic trait. It is theologically important because there are contrasts within the term (whether Paul means 'I' or 'we the apostles') . . . within the relationships: Christ/Paul/Apostles/Ministers/Community, the 'we' . . . is to be deciphered in the tension between 'I' and 'you,' a relationship which involves Christ and which is both rich and complex as between the author and the addressees of the letter" (486).

Some importance has been made of Paul's use of προείρηκα, "I have said previously" (perfect of προλέγειν), which probably reflects 6:11 (cf. 1:6; 3:12; 4:12; cf. 13:2; Gal 1:9; 3 Macc 6:35). This has led Tasker to note that Paul was aware of a break, or a digression, in thought from 6:11–13. It is doubtful

Paul would be referring back to something written only a few verses before unless there was a consciousness of his going off in another direction. The point is that Paul would not make an apparent attempt to bring his readers' attention back to his thought of affection for them unless he had drifted from it. "If this deduction is legitimate, it is an argument against the view that 6:14–7:1 is an interpolation from another letter" (Tasker, 102).

4. Πολλή μοι παρρησία πρὸς ὑμᾶς, πολλή μοι καύχησις ὑπὲρ ὑμῶν, "I have much confidence in you; I take great pride in you." Having told the Corinthians how much he loves them, Paul returns to a subject he had discussed earlier in this epistle. In 2:12, 13, Paul had related how he had entered Troas hoping to find Titus and learn of the reaction of the Corinthian church to the "severe letter." Paul is ready now to build on what Titus has told him. Much had been overcome and Paul is proud to tell others that he considers the Corinthians as his own people. 7:4 appears as a transition from his "apology for ministry" beginning at 2:14 to the resumption of the account of Paul's meeting with Titus.

Paul uses alliteration in this verse, and he is especially fond of the letter π (Plummer, 215; 8:22; 9:5, 8; 13:2). He has much, or great, confidence in the Corinthians as a result of the good report of Titus (7:7). πολλή μοι, "I have much," is repeated twice. παρρησία, "confidence," has been translated as "boldness of speech" (KJV/AV; Barrett ["great freedom," 193]; Denney, 248; see 3:12: Bultmann denies this [180], remarking that Paul is writing personally, not as an apostle; but this is not so even if the tone is tender). This appears as the original meaning of the word (Filson, 356; Tasker 102). In light of 6:11 and Paul's declaration of his openness to the Corinthians, it could be that παρρησία carries with it this narrow meaning. There, however, is evidence that suggests that Paul meant more than this.

The general use of παρρησία in the NT reflects the understanding of the word as meaning boldness or confidence (BGD, 630, 631; Eph 3:12; 1 Tim 3:13; Heb 3:6; 6:16; 10:19, 35; 1 John 2:28; 3:21; 4:17; 5:14). Most commentators have opted for this meaning (Plummer, 215; Héring, 53 ["assurance"]; Tasker, 102; Bruce, 217; Strachan, 125 ["absolute confidence"]; Filson, 356; RSV, NIV). In view of the good report of Titus, Paul has confidence in his readers. Though we think that Paul used παρρησία in the general sense of confidence rather than forthright speech, this does not affect the meaning of the passage, for boldness of speech can reflect confidence of the heart (Hughes, 262). See too W. C. van Unnik, "The Christian's Freedom of Speech," *BJRL* 44 (1961–62) 466–88, who argues for the sense of "frankness" (NEB) in this v (473, 474).

A result of this confidence is that Paul has great pride in the Corinthians (Schütz, *Paul*, 234). He has a reason for his boasting (καύχησις) just as he sought to be a reason for their boasting (5:12). We note that apparently Paul boasted to Titus of the Corinthians before the former went to them (7:14). Paul was not making a "fair-weather" stand, as though he would support them only if he was heeded. Rather, as a matter of optimism based on his conviction that the truth will prevail (13:8), the apostle had pride in these people. For the fundamental issue at stake, see 11:10 with *Comment*. Now, however, after the good report of Titus, he is even more confident of the potential for loyalty of the Corinthian church. This unwavering confidence in the Corinthians is also seen in 9:2. (For use of ὑπέρ here, see Moule, *Idiom Book*, 64.)

πεπλήρωμαι τῇ παρακλήσει, ὑπερπερισσεύομαι τῇ χαρᾷ ἐπὶ πάσῃ τῇ θλίψει ἡμῶν, "My encouragement is complete; I am overflowing with joy in all our distress," a sentence which holds together three key terms to be elaborated in vv 5–13 (Lietzmann). For Paul, confidence and joy are means to encourage (παρακαλεῖν). We know that "encouragement" was an important component in Paul's relationship to the Corinthians (see on 1:3–7). The problems and difficulties associated with keeping true to the Gospel melt away in view of the uplift he has received from the Corinthians, though its source is traced ultimately as coming from Christ (1:5b). This would lead Paul to refrain from self-congratulation and instead to dwell on his role as an instrument for the proclamation of the grace of God (5:20; cf. 5:10, 11; 6:1). The encouragement of the Corinthians, a factor so real to Paul, is a sure sign of blessing from God. The use of the perfect πεπλήρωμαι, lit., "I am completed," may be Paul's way of showing that the Corinthians have for some time been a source of happiness and now the fruit of his patience has appeared. (Often πληροῦν is found with a genitive [Acts 2:28; 13:52] but the dative is not totally unfamiliar; see Rom 1:29; 3 Macc 4:16; 2 Macc 6:5; 7:21.)

Paul closes the v with a "double climax" (Plummer, 215). While Paul is filled with comfort, he is overflowing (ὑπερπερισσεύομαι, only here and in Rom 5:20: see G. Delling, "Zum steigernden Gebrauch vom Komposita mit ὑπέρ bei Paulus," *NovT* 11 [1965] 127–53) with joy (χαρά; Plummer translates the article τῇ [with the joy], but this is awkward in the English; see BDF § 195 [2], concerning the use of "to fill" with the dative). This joy is in the midst of affliction or distress (ἐπὶ . . . τῇ θλίψει). The ἐπί, "in," does not suggest that Paul builds his joy upon distress (Plummer); rather in the midst of all that Paul endures, he finds comfort and much joy.

The idea of receiving joy in the midst of affliction strongly suggests that Paul wrote this part of the epistle while enduring suffering. He has not reached the point that he could say that his troubles were over. (We must not forget that Paul had other church responsibilities to consider: see 11:28). If suffering was to remain a part of Paul's life, then it is possible that chaps. 10–13 were written after chaps. 1–9. Though our present passage marks a high note in Paul's life, nevertheless it does not rule out that hardship could still plague him (Barrett, 204). Some interpreters (e.g., Fallon, 5, 61) go on to deduce that there is a change in Paul's circumstances between the time of 7:4 ff. and 8:1, 2, where evidently (it is said) the afflictions of the Macedonian churches are past (see later p. 249).

According to some influential views about the literary structure of 2 Corinthians, at 7:4 we are reading the close of a separate "Letter of Defense," which opened at 2:14, ran on to 6:13, and included 7:2–4. In this view the separate letter was entrusted to Titus who was commissioned to use it to counteract the false teachers' mission at Corinth, to reassert Paul's authority, to restart the collection (if all went well), and to announce and explain Paul's changed itinerary, namely, his intention to visit Corinth before his going to Macedonia and then to come again to Corinth on his return trip. But, as we saw in our review of the proposal (*Introduction*, pp. xxxix, xl) of this reconstruction, news came back to Paul that the situation at Corinth was still tense and necessitated his presence, in the so-called "interim visit," followed by the "Letter of Tears" (chaps. 10–13). After that letter had done its work, we learn in 7:5–16 that Paul met Titus in Macedonia from which place he sent a final "Letter of Reconciliation" (1:1–2:13; 7:5–16), as a prelude to making arrangements for the collection (chaps. 8, 9). But this is only one reading of apostolic movements, as we have seen.

5. καὶ γὰρ ἐλθόντων ἡμῶν εἰς Μακεδονίαν οὐδεμίαν ἔσχηκεν ἄνεσιν ἡ σάρξ ἡμῶν, "For when we came into Macedonia our body found no rest." γάρ, "for," shows a link to what is immediately preceding (Bruce, 217), though some want to attribute this to a redactor who forged an editorial link between two discrete compositions (2:14–7:4 and 7:5–16: see above). ἐλθόντων ἡμῶν, "when we came," a genitive absolute construction, returns the course of the letter as we have it to Paul's thought of 2:13. Paul had been diverted—but only apparently (2:14–7:4)—from the account of his meeting with Titus in order to vindicate his apostolate and to thank God for his place in that ministry. The exposition had continued for some length. Though 7:3, 4, do not refer directly to his Macedonian account, they do pave the way for Paul to return to the topic of 2:13. In 7:5 Paul is going to review his reason for joy despite discomfort. This review partially tells of Paul's adventure in Macedonia.

οὐδεμίαν ἔσχηκεν ἄνεσιν ἡ σάρξ ἡμῶν, "our body found no rest." Paul's use of σάρξ, here "body," lit., "flesh," has caused much controversy (see also *Comment* on 7:1). In the light of the connection of 2:13 and 7:5 it does appear that Paul is not using σάρξ in the sense of its technical, or theological, meaning of man's unredeemed nature, the perverse "self." (See Martin, *Reconciliation*, 59–61; Jewett, *Paul's Anthropological Terms*, 114–16.) Rather, the v is using it in the popular sense, to denote "Paul's weak physical body" (Jewett, 134).

In 2:13 Paul confessed, οὐκ ἔσχηκα ἄνεσιν τῷ πνεύματί μου, "I found no rest in my spirit." It does appear that Paul, whether speaking of flesh (7:5) or spirit (2:13), is alluding to his human person as frail (as in 12:7). In our present context it appears that he uses πνεῦμα, "spirit," and σάρξ, "flesh," as synonymous terms (Hughes, 265; Bultmann, 56), both reflecting his sense of agitation because of the absence of Titus. It is unfair to insist that Paul should use the same terms in always the same manner ("Language was made for man, not man for language," Plummer, 217). Other translations for σάρξ are "bodies" (rsv using a plural), "flesh" (kjv/av), and the simple pronoun "I" or "we" (*Translator's Guide*). In any case, the idea is of subjection to weariness and pain as endured by the physical body (Filson, 357; cf. Héring, 54), but here occasioned by the nonarrival of Titus (2:13) as well as the trials spoken of in the v.

The idea of rest (ἄνεσις) carries with it the notion of "relaxation" (Bruce 217; cf. 2:13; 8:13) or "relief" (BDG, 65). Until Paul learns that he as apostle is valued in the eyes of the Corinthians he finds no relief from strain. A sensitive person such as Paul here mirrors the frailty of the human person under the stresses and pressures of daily living (Tasker, 102, 103). That this was a constant phenomenon can be seen in his use of ἔσχηκεν (perfect of ἔχειν, "to have"; see *Notes* for textual support of the aorist tense, ἔσχεν:

BDF § 343.2). This would suggest that Paul could possibly still feel the strain (if there was continued trouble in Corinth) in spite of the good news of Titus (Denney, 252). If this is so, then the Corinthian situation, though possibly under control, still weighed on Paul's mind.

ἀλλ᾽ ἐν παντὶ θλιβόμενοι, "but on all sides we were distressed." Strictly speaking, the participle θλιβόμενοι (from θλίβεσθαι [cf. 4:8] "to be afflicted" or "to be distressed," BGD, 362) is an anacoluthon (BDF § 468[1]), for we see that the construction begins with a finite verb and continues with a participle (a construction of which Paul is quite fond). The use of ἐν παντί, "on all sides" or "in every way" (6:4; 9:8; 11:6, 9) is a way of saying that much of Paul's activity has encountered great opposition. This is illustrated in what follows in 7:5. Yet, the limpid remark in v 5 does not specify, in any detail, exactly what these afflictions were.

ἔξωθεν μάχαι, ἔσωθεν φόβοι, "strife from without; fears from within." The idea of μάχαι, lit., "strifes," carries with it the idea of "battling" or "quarreling" (BGD, 496). This could be a reference to adversaries in Macedonia (Bruce, 217; Plummer, 217, 218; see 1 Cor 15:30–32, 16:9 for Paul's trials in the Aegean region), whether Christian or non-Christian in origin (Barrett, 207; Tasker, 103; Filson, 357; see Acts 16:23; 17:5; Phil 1:30; 1 Thess 2:2) or adverse circumstances (Bultmann, 56). The "fears within" most likely include the fear of failure at Corinth, a "troublesome anxiety on account of the Corinthian church" (Bultmann, 56). Paul had sent Titus to deliver the letter so that the Corinthian situation might be remedied. The report of the reaction of this letter weighed on Paul's spirit. Furthermore, if Titus was overdue in keeping the rendezvous, this too would be a cause for extra fear within Paul. (Héring also considers states of depression and illness as reason for fear within [54]. Possibly with the weakness of the flesh, Paul is referring also to his "thorn"; see 12:7; Bruce, 217.)

6. ἀλλ᾽ ὁ παρακαλῶν τοὺς ταπεινοὺς παρεκάλεσεν ἡμᾶς ὁ θεὸς ἐν τῇ παρουσίᾳ Τίτου, "But God, the one who encourages the downcast, encouraged us with the coming of Titus." It is at this point that Paul finally reports to the Corinthians the arrival of Titus. Paul's phrase "the one who encourages" is a tribute to God and a reminder of the encouragement God gives. In 1:3, 4 we read about the God of all encouragement, the one who encourages his people (παρακαλεῖν; see Comment there for translation options, i.e., "comfort," "console," as well as "encourage"). This is reminiscent of Isa 49:13, καὶ τοὺς ταπεινοὺς τοῦ λαοῦ αὐτοῦ παρεκάλεσεν, "he encouraged the outcasts of his people." See too Ps 112 (113):6, (ὁ θεὸς ἡμῶν ὁ . . .) καὶ τὰ ταπεινὰ ἐφορῶν), "(our God) . . . raises the poor" (RSV, 113:7). "He sets on high those who are lowly," according to Job 5:11, τὸν ποιοῦντα ταπεινοὺς εἰς ὕψος (ταπεινός = עָנִי, ʿanî), i.e., lowly, not despised: so Bultmann, 57; and Kleinknecht, Der leidende Gerechtfertigte, 249, 250). The allusion is all the more remarkable since its OT v in Isaiah occurs in the same chapter from which Paul drew a testimony in 6:2 (Isa 49:8). Kleinknecht (ibid., 249, n. 19) notes how the LXX couples Yahweh's comfort and "the outcasts," thereby demonstrating divine vindication (δικαιοσύνη) as opposed to the Hebrew text which separates God's people and the "afflicted ones," though in parallelism. To ensure that the Corinthians know who the comforter is, Paul inserts in apposition (possibly as an after-

thought, Barrett, 207) the term ὁ θεός, God. Paul sees that the encouragement he received at the news from Corinth is actually from God. His invoking God's name may be a traditional formulation, but it is nonetheless a real religious experience.

God comforts τοὺς ταπεινούς, "the downcast." Though ταπεινός can be seen as meaning humble (so Bruce, 218), most likely here it means the downcast, or depressed (RSV, NIV; Tasker, 103; Barrett, 207; Filson, 357; Plummer, 218; Strachan, 124). In the light of 7:5, it appears that Paul is not concerned with the ethical force of "humility" (Hughes, 266, n. 3). In 7:5 he has shown how the pressures of life have weighed heavily on him and the idea of humility is not in his mind, except indirectly—unless Kleinknecht's argument (*Der leidende Gerechtfertigte,* 250) is cogent that Paul is consciously identifying himself with the righteous sufferer in Jewish ideology. Paul, in sharing the lot of the downcast, is lifted up at the arrival of Titus, for both the message and the messenger were a source of comfort and joy for Paul.

ἐν τῇ παρουσίᾳ Τίτου, "with the coming of Titus." The preposition ἐν ("with," "by," or "at") suggests more the instrumental case than the locative (Plummer, 218, 219). Titus was a heaven-sent "means" for the renewal of Paul's spirit. παρουσία ("coming"; "arrival"; "staying," Plummer 218, 219; see Deissmann, *Light from the Ancient East,* 372, 382) is another example of a term of popular use utilized in a technical sense. It came to be associated with the glorious advent of Jesus Christ. Here it is used simply to refer to the arrival of Titus (another example of Paul's alternation between popular and technical use of certain terms; cf. "flesh" and "spirit"). All in all, 7:5, 6 show that Paul's love for the Corinthians is a multifaceted dynamic (Strachan, 125). Yet it was not Titus's arrival that cheered but the uplifting news that came with that arrival (so Bultmann, 57), and the fact that Titus had come from Corinth where he had succeeded in his mission (see v 7). Paul writes of "us" because he has the apostolic work at Corinth in view (Carrez, "Le 'nous'," 483).

7. οὐ μόνον δὲ ἐν τῇ παρουσίᾳ αὐτοῦ ἀλλὰ καὶ ἐν τῇ παρακλήσει ᾗ παρεκλήθη ἐφ' ὑμῖν, "And not only with his coming, but also in the encouragement you gave to him." Paul is quick to point out that seeing Titus again, though a source of joy for him, was not the only basis for his comfort. "Encouragement" (KJV/AV has "consolation") is a recurring theme in 2 Corinthians (see on 1:3–7; 7:6, 13). The trials Paul had endured on behalf of the Corinthians had not caused him to give up hope. God was always giving Paul fresh heart, and one way in which this encouragement had been felt by him was the joy he experienced at hearing the good news from Corinth. We know that Paul had suffered in order that the Corinthians might be comforted. In turn, for him to be comforted is yet another means by which the Corinthians are comforted (1:6b). In short, Paul's goal was to enhearten the Corinthians. But, as can be seen, if the Corinthians are open to Paul, this responsiveness is also a source of joy to him. Moreover, Titus has been encouraged. His trip to Corinth has been successful (at least in its immediate result). He has returned to him. Seeing Titus again would be a reason for Paul to rejoice. Another reason for him to have joy was that he saw the joy of Titus ("A joy shared is by that fact so much greater," Filson, 357, 58).

The basis for the joy present in Titus's case is that he had received encouragement. He had received this encouragement (παρεκλήθη, aorist passive of παρακαλεῖν) from the Corinthians, who had perhaps unexpectedly but quite obviously reacted to Paul's letter in a positive manner. (One wonders whether or not the severe letter went with Titus or was sent ahead of him [Héring, 54, n. 8]. In support of the latter idea, it appears that the letter took quick effect, so that we would have thought it reached Corinth before Titus, thus allowing time for such a drastic change to take place. On the other hand, we might have expected Paul to mention the name of the courier who preceded Titus, if indeed Paul did send the letter in advance.) That the Corinthians were the basis for Titus's encouragement (and subsequently the joy of Paul) is possibly seen in the phrase ἐφ᾽ ὑμῖν, "in you." Plummer (219) takes the view that this phrase is to be translated "over you" (see 1 Thess 3:7: see too Bultmann, 57), but this suggestion ignores the depth of feeling that seems to be evident from 7:7b. Titus is convinced of their new direction and thus a translation "in you" (Tasker, 103) appears to capture better the flavor of Paul's thought. Titus is comforted, and with the news he brings to Paul in detail, the apostle can take comfort in the Corinthians' change of heart (μετάνοια, vv 9, 10).

ἀναγγέλλων ἡμῖν τὴν ὑμῶν ἐπιπόθησιν, "He told us of your desire [for me]." Paul relates to the Corinthians the essentials of the report of Titus. One might have expected—in strict grammar—a finite verb rather than the participle ἀναγγέλλων ("to report, announce," from ἀναγγέλλειν, but Paul is evidently moved as he writes, and is concerned to present the positive message, not to observe the niceties of grammar: see examples of participial forms in 5:12; 9:11).

No doubt what Paul heard from Titus brought joy to him for he learned of the ἐπιπόθησις (v.l. ἐπιποθία, Rom 15:23), "longing," "desire" of the Corinthians for him. This is a rare noun in biblical Greek (it recurs in 7:11; and is found in Ezek 23:11 [Aq.]; cf. Clement of Alexandria, Strom. 4, 21, 131; Damascius, De Princ. 38; Etym Mag. 678, 39), though the verb ἐπιποθεῖν is common in both Paul (Rom 1:11; 1 Thess 3:6; Phil 2:26) and the LXX. For ἐπιποθεῖν as a desire to see fellow Christians, see especially Phil 1:8 (Martin, Philippians, NBC, ad loc., citing C. Spicq, "Epipothein, Désirer ou chérir?" RB 64.2 [1957] 184–95). What is to be brought out in the English translation is the supplying of an object of this desire. Having known that Paul once refrained from visiting them (2:11), the Corinthians long to see him again. But instead of Paul's coming to them it was Titus who came as his emissary. Now, with the reconciliation having taken place, the door appears open for a warm and loving reception of the apostle himself. Both the KJV/AV and RSV omit any reference to Paul as the object of the Corinthians' longing, but we agree with Barrett (208) that such an object is needed ad sensum. Most likely the Corinthians understood Paul to be writing that he indeed is the one for whom they long (Strachan, 124). Thus to include "for us" (Barrett, 208) or "for me" (NIV; Filson, 358) in the translation does nothing to destroy the meaning behind 7:7. In the light of the latter part of 7:7 which includes the words "for me," ζῆλον ὑπέρ ἐμοῦ, we have felt justified in including the words "for me" in our translation.

Another point of interest is Paul's triple use of ὑμῶν, "for you," in 7:7;

each time it is placed between the article and the noun for special emphasis (Hughes, 267, n. 5). A gesture that seems on the surface to be only action on Paul's behalf becomes action on the Corinthians' part as well. Denney (252, 253) remarks on the counterpart to Paul's love for the Corinthians, namely, that the Corinthians long to restore to its original level their relationship with Paul (Filson, 358). For Denney, Paul's use of ὑμῶν suggests a change of heart in the Corinthians, which would be a definite source of comfort for both Paul and Titus (see Tasker, 103; 1:6 [2x]; and 12:19 for similar use of the pronoun ὑμῶν).

τὸν ὑμῶν ὀδυρμόν, "of your mourning." The idea behind ὀδυρμός is that of mourning or lamentation (see Josephus, *BJ* 5.31; *Ant.* 2.238; 2 Macc 11:6). Paul is not specific in identifying that for which the Corinthians mourn. Possibly it is for the grief they have caused for Paul (Tasker 103), as well as the sorrow experienced when they learned that Paul felt he could not visit them (Barrett, 208; but see his essay on 7:12 for the sense of "lamentation" other than a confession of guilt). Paul had wanted to come (1:23), but because of the painful visit had thought it better to send Titus. The sorrow implied in the Corinthians' reaction paves the way for the mention of μετάνοια, "repentance" (v 10).

τὸν ὑμῶν ζῆλον ὑπὲρ ἐμοῦ, "of your zeal for me." The proof of the new outlook toward Paul, anticipated in the desire of the Corinthians, as well as in the grief over any wrongdoing, is made firm in that they have zeal, or ardor, for him. Note the gradation of terms here, with "zeal" as the climax (Bultmann, 58). Most likely this zeal was exhibited in their desire to put things right, i.e., in reconciliation in the light of his correction. Also, this zeal may be seen in that the Corinthians now defend Paul (possibly) against his attackers, a loyalty that was missing before he sent the letter (Barrett, 208). Also, the confidence (7:16) Paul had in the Corinthians was a further source of comfort for him because he could proceed without fear of a return by the Corinthians to their earlier ways (Hughes, 267). But in this he may have been too optimistic in his conclusion. The use of ὑπὲρ ἐμοῦ ("for me") again shows the personal note of comfort that the apostle experienced. The absence of the definite article with this possessive pronoun construction is to be observed (BDF § 272).

ὥστε με μᾶλλον χαρῆναι, "so that my joy was even more than before." χαρῆναι ("to rejoice"; aorist infinitive deponent of χαίρειν) coupled with μᾶλλον ("more, greater": BDF § 244.2, 246: cf. 60.3: a feature of this paragraph) has led to three possible interpretations. (1) One is that Paul is saying that he rejoiced instead of only being comforted. (2) A second interpretation is that Paul saw that his joy outweighed his previous distress (Windisch, "*im Gegensatz dazu,*" i.e., rather than mourning or sorrow: Bultmann, 58). (3) A third possible interpretation of this clause is that his joy increased when he heard Titus's report. The last option appears to be the most likely. For one thing, 7:13 tells us that the happiness of Titus was a bonus for Paul, as an additional reason to rejoice. The return of Titus was indeed a reason for rejoicing, but the report he brought with him was even a greater reason (for essentially Titus reported that the wayward community [i.e., the Corinthian church] has returned). As was pointed out above, the use of ὑμῶν, "your," demonstrates that Paul (and Titus) based his comfort on the new traits (concern, grief, zeal) exhibited by the Corinthians. This too would support the third choice for understanding this clause. This is not to say that suggestions numbered (1) and (2) for interpreting the closing of 7:7 are to be excluded from Paul's thinking: rather it is to admit that these two possibilities are included in the third. Paul truly rejoiced, in addition to being encouraged, and no doubt his distress seemed small compared with the joy he now experienced on behalf of the Corinthians. But Paul's thought throughout 7:5–16 speaks of his meeting with Titus and the pleasant surprise of the good news from Corinth (Plummer, 219). As always with Paul, his joy was enhanced at the joy of another (e.g., Phil 2:27, 28), especially with regard to the mission that Titus undertook (Hughes, 268).

8. ὅτι εἰ καὶ ἐλύπησα ὑμᾶς ἐν τῇ ἐπιστολῇ, οὐ μεταμέλομαι, "even if my letter hurt you, I do not regret it." Here begins a subsection to remark on the effectiveness of the "tearful letter." Paul does not attempt to skirt the issue that the Corinthians suffered pain under his rebuke. In v 7 Paul spoke of their "mourning" (ὀδυρμός). In the present verse, Paul speaks of causing them sorrow (ἐλύπησα, aorist of λυπεῖν, "to irritate, offend, insult," and so "to cause pain"). He writes to say that he is aware of the hurt that came to them. Yet this verse is not an apology in the sense that the apostle is sorry to have hurt them. εἰ καὶ ("even if"; for the use of εἰ καὶ instead of καὶ εἰ; see Plummer, 113) he caused the Corinthians to sorrow, he does not now regret it (μεταμέλεσθαι, "to regret," including the idea of changing one's mind, BGD, 511; the rendering, "repent" [KJV/AV] is a source for some confusion, see Moncure, "Second Corinthians 7:8–10," 467, 468; there appears to be a semantic difference between μεταμέλεσθαι [Matt 21:30, 32; Heb 7:2] and μετανοεῖν [12:21; Acts 2:38; 3:39], though Plummer cautions against drawing too hard and fast a line). As will be seen below, Paul considers that their salutary hurt was an important component of their repentance. And for this he has no regret.

Yet, it seems that there was a past time when Paul regretted having sent the "severe letter." εἰ καὶ μετεμελόμην, βλέπω [γὰρ] ὅτι ἡ ἐπιστολὴ ἐκείνη εἰ καὶ πρὸς ὥραν ἐλύπησεν ὑμᾶς, "Though I did regret it—I see that letter hurt you for a while . . ."). The concessive use of εἰ καὶ (Moule, *Idiom Book*, 167; Thrall, *Greek Particles in the NT*, 79, 80) suggests that at one time Paul may have weighed the risk of the possible outcome of the letter. After all, he was writing ostensibly out of love, not hate (2:4). There could have been further alienation between him and the Corinthians, as well as further embarrassment for Paul, if this appeal had been rejected. But this regret is now a thing of the past, for when Paul wrote 2 Corinthians he had already heard the good report from Titus of the Corinthians' change of heart. The pain of the Corinthians was not the end of Paul's relationship with them, but rather a needful step to deepening and enriching it.

The remainder of v 8 is a "tortuous" (Héring, 54) construction (for the textual questions see *Notes*). Most likely Paul realized that to say he did not regret sending the letter (either chaps. 10–13 or more probably one now lost; Barrett, 209) might come across to the Corinthians as a cruel sentiment. Probably at the time Paul regretted sending a letter, but after hearing from

Titus, he saw that his anxiety was needless. Irrespective of whether we take βλέπω or βλέπων as the correct reading, it appears that we have εἰ καὶ μετεμελόμην as a protasis, and νῦν χαίρω, "now I rejoice," as an apodosis. "If I did [once] regret it . . . I now rejoice" is Paul's thought in v 8. What lies between can be considered a parenthesis (Plummer, 220). Though this parenthesis is rather awkward when seen as a written statement, it would be possible to account for it in dictation, when the speaker was evidently emotionally moved.

Tasker has rightly pointed out that the KJV/AV has punctuated this verse incorrectly (104, 105). Rather than treating βλέπω [γὰρ] ὅτι ἡ ἐπιστολὴ ἐκείνη εἰ καὶ πρὸς ὥραν ἐλύπησεν ὑμᾶς as a parenthesis, the KJV/AV places a full stop (period) at the end of v 8. This is incorrect because it suggests that Paul was giving the reason he made them sorry rather than saying why he regret-ted—for a while—the sending of the letter. In other words, Paul is not saying, in a tautology, I made you sorry, for I see I made you sorry (Hodge, 181). He is giving the reason why he had some regret. See Bultmann, 58, 59, for the argument on the basis of this temporal parenthesis (as above), citing Gal 2:5 and Philem 15 (and, we may add, 1 Thess 2:17 too).

The use of ἐκεῖνος, "that," suggests that the letter (lit., "that letter") is now something remote from Paul's mind at the time of writing now (Plummer, 220). It refers to part of the past he now wishes to forget. This letter is no longer needed because the Corinthians have repented. Their pain, though sharp, lasted but "for an hour" (πρὸς ὥραν). The use of the preposition πρός to denote an allusion to time has its main idea as expressing duration (Moule, *Idiom Book*, 53). Plummer argues that in this usage the duration could be of a short or long period (220; Philem 15; Gal 2:5). But the meaning is clear regardless of the length of time that the Corinthians were hurting. The pain of the Corinthians has now passed. Paul did not sorrow anymore because he had written the "severe letter." If its effects had been disastrous, then possibly Paul would have continued to regret that he had written the letter. But, as will be seen, he rejoices inasmuch as the Corinthians have returned to his side.

9. νῦν χαίρω, "now I rejoice." This is the continuation of the conditional sentence of v 8, if an asyndeton. If Paul did regret, he now rejoices, and this latter fact is already known to the Corinthians (7:4, 7).

His rejoicing is not at the pain of the Corinthians. Paul would never think of rejoicing over the suffering of his converts (cf. 1:24: ἀλλὰ συνεργοί ἐσμεν τῆς χαρᾶς ὑμῶν); see too 1 Thess 2:19, 20.

οὐχ ὅτι ἐλυπήθητε, "not that you sorrowed," is Paul's implicit declaration that the Corinthians' pain was not a direct source of satisfaction to him. Instead, Paul is happy that the sorrow and pain of the Corinthians has led to their repenting of past opposition.

ἀλλ᾽ ὅτι ἐλυπήθητε εἰς μετάνοιαν, "but that your sorrow led to repentance." Paul rejoices in the effect of the "severe letter." By design it caused the Corinthians pain and hurt ("It vexed him to vex them," Denney, 254). But the Corinthians were not embittered toward Paul (a fear latently expressed in 7:8) or God. Rather they were led to repent.

An interesting note is that Paul rarely uses μετάνοια, lit., "change of mind"

(BGD, 511, 512). It is found only in the Pauline corpus in 2 Cor 7 twice (here and v 10; "feel pain that leads to repentance," ibid.) and in Rom 2:4 and 2 Tim 2:25. (Furthermore for Paul, the verb μετανοιεῖν occurs only in 2 Cor 12:21.) This rare use does not belittle Paul's message of forgiveness, so often made part of the theme of reconciliation (Plummer, 221). But Paul's avoidance of the term may be accounted for on the score that μετάνοια "did not stress sufficiently God's action in salvation" (Fallon, 64). That is, with its Jewish equivalent, חשׁוּבה, t*šûbāh, "a turning," it denotes a human experience (see on 3:16: could there be a "veiled" allusion to Moses' action in 7:9? The Corinthians have followed Moses' example, and "turned to the Lord"). In the other instances, Paul's use of "repentance" is related to God and is addressed to Christians. Thus, prominent in the apostle's mind is the thought that the Corinthians have realized their wrong toward God and have sought to make amends. Yet, the Corinthians must have equally felt sorrow at their actions toward Paul. This is suggested by the previous vv and also by our discussion of chap. 5. In that place it was submitted that Paul considered their improper behavior toward him and his apostolate as an affront to God. To mistreat God's representative placed the Corinthians in a precarious position because it involved a wrong attitude to the Gospel. To be sure, Paul would point his people to God in repentance. But most likely Paul also sees in their "change of mind" a reflection on their attitude toward him personally (see Filson, 358, 359). But there is no great distinction in meaning, as Bultmann (149 on 5:12) has forcefully brought out. He writes: "The decision for the Gospel and for Paul is one and the same. When the Corinthians do not understand him, they do not understand the Gospel as well, since this misunderstood claim . . . is not in regard to the person (of Paul), but in regard to the claim of the apostle and also of the Gospel."

Strachan takes a different approach to v 9 when he seeks to base a psychological understanding of Paul on it (127, 128). There is a return of confidence between Paul and the church for this "great religious psychologist"—as he calls him—feels free to open up old wounds and talk about mistakes and regrets again. He can do this because he is not intending to promote himself, but rather he sees this as an example of true repentance. The Corinthians have accepted Paul's rebuke and it has led them to repentance. The work of the "severe letter" has been used by God to repair the relationship between Paul and the Corinthians, as well as direct them back toward God (see use of εἰς in the phrase εἰς μετάνοιαν, "to repentance"). But this exegesis does not center on the chief issue of Paul's concern for the Gospel.

ἐλυπήθητε γὰρ κατὰ θεόν, "for you experienced godly sorrow." This clause makes it clear that the sorrow of the Corinthians was more than superficial. The sorrow of the Corinthians is called κατὰ θεόν, lit., "according to God," "godly." This phrase is also found in Rom 8:27 (see Gal 1:4; 4 Macc 15:2). Paul is here paving the way for a discussion of the two types of grief (see 7:10). Godly grief, or sorrow, is a grief that leads individuals to view their conduct as God does. The phrase κατὰ θεόν does not mean sorrow through which God works, but sorrow in accordance with his will (cf. *Test. Gad* 5.7: ἡ γὰρ κατὰ θεὸν ἀληθὴς μετάνοια φυγαδεύει τὸ σκότος καὶ φωτίζει τοὺς ὀφθαλμοὺς καὶ γνῶσιν παρέχει τῇ ψυχῇ καὶ ὁδηγεῖ τὸ διαβούλιον πρὸς σωτηρίαν, "for according to God's truth, repentance destroys disobedience, puts darkness to flight,

illumines the vision, furnishes knowledge of the soul, and guides the delibera-
tive power to salvation" [H. C. Kee's tr. in *The OT Pseudepigrapha* vol. 1,
ed. J. H. Charlesworth]). Such a grief allows submission to God's scrutiny
and does more than simply impart sorrow over pain or affliction (Héring
calls it "contrition," 55). This may be further understood in the clause that
follows.

ἵνα ἐν μηδενὶ ζημιωθῆτε ἐξ ἡμῶν, "that you might suffer no loss through
us." Lietzmann (132) considers this clause as consecutive, so that the suffering
endured is a result of the godly sorrow. But it is better to see this clause
with ἵνα as expressing purpose. The reason for the godly sorrow is that no
loss has come about. This latter conclusion appears the more logical (Windisch, 231; Bultmann, 59).

The γάρ, "for," of 7:9 opens a summary remark. Paul is rejoicing because
the sorrow of the Corinthians has led to repentance, which is a desirable
grace only possible if the sorrow is of the godly type. To take Lietzmann's
line in interpreting the clause is to miss the intent of Paul's "severe letter."
That intent was not to produce godly sorrow so that the Corinthians would
suffer. Rather, the purpose of this sorrow was to ensure reconciliation, in
hope that the Corinthians would be none the worse for the experience. Indeed,
it would be profitable. The use of "godly sorrow" therefore probably suggests
that the ἵνα clause is final (Barrett 210).

We may inquire about "the loss" that the Corinthians avoided. The use
of ζημιωθῆναι ("to suffer loss," "forfeit," see BGD, 338, for Philo, Josephus)
is related to the phrase ἐξ ἡμῶν, "through us." What would the Corinthians
have lost, and how was it related to Paul? Héring (55) suggests that one
element of the loss would have been that Paul would not have returned to
Corinth. The possibility that Paul would not have visited the Corinthians
again, had they remained recalcitrant, seems logical. If his painful visit had
prevented his promised return trip (1:23), it could have been that a further
rebuke would have made a third visit impossible. In this we agree with Héring.
But it is doubtful that this was the thought uppermost in Paul's mind. Though
he could be bold (10:1, 2), to say that the main loss to have been inflicted
upon the Corinthians would have been his absence may be too presumptuous,
even for Paul. Besides, as has been discussed, he wanted to avoid all actions
that suggested pretense. For Paul to have acted as Héring surmised would
have played into the hands of his opponents who may have taken ζημιωθῆναι
as *their* watchword (see Bultmann, 59, n. 41, who thinks more of the church's
reproach).

More likely is Hughes' idea (269, 270), that the "loss" is related to the
"reward" in the next life and it is this thought that guides Paul's writing
(as in 1 Cor 3:10–15). There Paul earnestly desired that the building materials
for the Corinthians should be gold, silver, and precious stones (valuable
items), not hay, straw, and stubble, i.e., worthless. Since he was their spiritual
father (6:13), he had chosen not to spare them pain if this could possibly
correct the situation. To have eschewed this responsibility would have made
them vulnerable to great loss and placed a great blame on him (5:9, 11:
Plummer, 221). As a minister of the Gospel (5:18–20), he could not do this
and stand confidently before the Lord. Filson is right in saying that Paul
felt the authority to impose sanctions and penalty on the Corinthians (359),

but one wonders how Paul could have exercised any control if they continued to reject his authority. The next v sets the warning in perspective by relating their change of attitude to "salvation" in place of "death," its opposite. But if "salvation" there means "health, integrity," the loss (ζημιοῦσθαι) may indeed turn out to be a deficiency in the church's desire for wholeness, which becomes Paul's prayer-wish for them in 13:11.

10. ἡ γὰρ κατὰ θεὸν λύπη μετάνοιαν εἰς σωτηρίαν ἀμεταμέλητον ἐργάζεται, "For godly sorrow produces repentance that leads to salvation and leaves no regret." Paul continues to focus on the idea of "godly sorrow." κατὰ θεόν conveys, we suggest, the idea of "a manner agreeable to the mind and will of God" (Hodge, 182). We saw in 7:9 that godly sorrow is the road to true repentance. "Godly sorrow in its outworking leads to repentance unto salvation" (Hughes, 271). There is a question as to whether ἀμεταμέλητος with the sense of "not to be regretted" (BGD, 45; see Polybius 21, 11, 11; 23, 16, 11; cf. Philo, *Leg. All.* 3.211 f.) goes with μετάνοια ("repentance") or σωτηρία ("salvation"; note that εἰς expresses the idea of leading to; see Moule, *Idiom Book,* 68). Some take the feminine accusative ἀμεταμέλητον to agree with its nearest noun σωτηρίαν (Hodge, 183), and grammatically speaking, this is correct. But this is questionable because it prompts the question of why would one regret salvation. The majority of commentators take ἀμεταμέλητον to go with μετάνοια (so Strachan, 128; Bruce, 218; Plummer, 221; Lietzmann, 132; Tasker, 105, 106; Héring, 55). Going one step further, some see the adjective as attached to both nouns (Hughes 271, n. 11), or at least as producing the compound thought of repentance-unto-salvation (Barrett, 211).

Also of interest is the question of who is the subject of the sorrowing. Is it a general statement, as a truism regarding all Christians, or specifically the Corinthians? Or is it narrower in the sense that Paul is the one having no regret? Moncure views ἀμεταμέλητον as an echo of οὐ μεταμέλομαι in 7:8. V 10 can then be paraphrased as follows: "For your feelings were hurt in accord with God's will, producing repentance unto salvation—that's why I don't regret it" (Moncure, "Second Corinthians," 467, 468). This suggestion (see Hughes, 272) is an interesting one. It does cohere with Paul's discussion of regret in 7:8. In that verse, Paul reviews how he had at one time regretted having sent the letter. But the report of Titus provides the reason for Paul not to continue to be regretful. The Corinthians have repented. Because of this "turning around" (again 3:16 should be recalled as an act of conversion that leads to life in the new age of 5:17), Paul sees renewed hope in the Corinthians.

Such godly sorrow reminds him of the message he brings, which is one of reconciliation (5:18–21). Possibly then Paul sees in 7:10 the same idea as is found in 5:18–21. With the flame rekindled, there is an even greater proof that the Corinthians will have not received the grace of God in vain (6:1). This may have been in his mind in 7:4 when Paul speaks of the great encouragement he has received from the Corinthians. Godly sorrow is the only sorrow that leads to life, just as the Pauline Gospel does (2:16: ἐκ ζωῆς εἰς ζωήν).

ἡ δὲ τοῦ κόσμου λύπη θάνατον κατεργάζεται, "but worldly sorrow leads to death." In contrast to godly sorrow is the sorrow that is of the world (τοῦ κόσμου, a phrase equal to κατὰ σάρκα in 10:3). This sorrow is a type that includes pain and regret, similar to godly sorrow. However, the result in this case is not repentance, but death (see 2:16 for Paul's Gospel with this sad result). Worldly sorrow comes about because of the unwelcome consequence of sin. The person who exhibits this response of worldly sorrow may indeed seek to avoid similar future actions and their consequences. But in no instance is the person driven to God, for that individual feels no deep-seated remorse over actions taken against God. Rather it is more a regret that one has acted foolishly or been discovered in a lapse, like king Saul's admission, "I have played the fool, and erred exceedingly" (1 Sam 26:21). Repentance involves the whole person—knowing, feeling, willing (Strachan, 128)—and is more than an emotional reaction (Denney, 257). "Recognition of sin by itself is not repentance; it may be defiance. Nor is sorrow for sin repentance, if it be alone in the mind; it may be remorse or despair. Abandonment of sin, by itself, may be no more than prudence" (cited in Strachan, 128).

The criterion in evaluating the worth of an individual's "sorrow" lies in its effect. Worldly sorrow results in death. Paul speaks in similar fashion in Rom 7:13. In that v Paul writes ἡ ἁμαρτία, ἵνα φανῇ ἁμαρτία, διὰ τοῦ ἀγαθοῦ μοι κατεργαζομένη θάνατον, "sin, in order that it might be recognized as sin, produced death in me through what is good." In Romans it is the law, here it is Paul's Gospel, that is "good." Of note is Paul's use of κατεργάζεται, "works out," both in Rom 7:13 and in 2 Cor 7:10. In the latter, this verb is used in contrast to ἐργάζεται in v 10a, "works." While the difference may be attributed to the stylistic manner of Paul, possibly a distinction should be preserved. The former verb might have been used to "emphasize the inevitability of the outworking in death of the sorrow of the world" (Hughes, 272, n. 12). The result is "death" (Rom 6:15, 21, 23; 7:5), which means alienation from God (Martin, *Reconciliation*, 63–67, surveying the different meanings of θάνατος in Paul).

The contrast in 2 Cor 7:10 between the two types of sorrow is reminiscent of Esau and of David (so Windisch, 231; Hughes, 273). Though the former was of a sorrowful heart (Gen 27:38), nevertheless no change was brought about (Heb 12:16, 17). In contrast, David acknowledged his sin (Ps 51:1–11) and was restored to God's favor (Ps 51:12–19). The contrast between Peter's failure and recovery and Judas' fall (cf. Matt 27:3: μεταμεληθείς, repented = felt regret; Matt 21:30, 32. Contrast Luke 22:31–34) is even more obvious. Had the Corinthians expressed only remorse at being chastened, then Paul would have had great reason to be pained, for he could have seen through their hypocrisy. However, they reacted with godly sorrow that leads to repentance in turning *back* to his message and turning *from* the false prophet (2:16, 17) by turning *to* the Lord of the new eon. They had responded to Paul's gestures of love (in the "severe letter"). In the end they avoided the path that allows sin to produce "spiritual death." As Denney (256) writes, "If death is to be defined at all, it must be by contrast with salvation: the grief which has not God as its rule can only exhaust the soul, wither up its faculties, blight its hopes, extinguish and deaden all."

11. ἰδοὺ γὰρ αὐτὸ τοῦτο τὸ κατὰ θεὸν λυπηθῆναι πόσην κατειργάσατο ὑμῖν σπουδήν, "See what earnestness this godly sorrow has produced in you."

Paul is quick to point out that the effect of the sorrow of the Corinthians is not death, but life. This will be seen in his list of seven (is the number significant? asks Bultmann, 61, but skeptically) nouns found in 7:11, all pointing to an "excellent change" (Plummer, 222).

Also, Paul is alert to bring the effect of their repentance to the forefront. ἰδού, "see," "behold": Paul is looking back both to 7:7 (Plummer 222) and to 7:10 (Barrett 211; cf. 5:17; 6:2, 9; 12:14). The godly sorrow produced (note aorist passive, κατειργάσατο) in the Corinthians verifiable results. For Paul this must have been a heartwarming event. The news of Titus has raised him "from the trough of his former apprehensiveness to the crest of a great wave of consolation" (Hughes, 274).

Grammatically speaking, the noun used to introduce this upsurge of spirit is σπουδή "earnestness" (repeated in v 12). This carries with it the idea of eagerness as well (BGD, 763, 764), thus suggesting that not only were the Corinthians serious about salvaging their relationship with Paul ("earnest care," Hughes, 274) and achieving reconciliation (Bultmann, 61), they were also bent on doing this with dispatch (the noun recurs frequently in chap. 8, esp. 8:8, 16).

ἀλλὰ ἀπολογία, "but also what eagerness to clear yourselves" (RSV). The adversative use of ἀλλά, "not only this, but also," introduces a new element in an emphatic manner to denote an idea reaching a climax (BDF § 448.6). Beginning with ἀπολογία (lit., "defense," "desire to clear oneself," Denney, 256), the apostle places an anaphoric ἀλλά before each of the following six nouns. Noting that πόσος, "how much, what," is linked with σπουδή (see Hughes, 274, n. 14) we maintain that there is a continuity in the linking of eagerness, or earnestness, with each noun. Since this idea is in mind, it would be redundant to render it in our English translation throughout the verse.

Paul's use of ἀπολογία with respect to the actions of the Corinthians means more than an "apology" in the modern sense of the word (contra Hodge, 185). Also, it is equally unlikely that the idea of "excuse" is behind the word (see Héring). In addition, Plummer's idea that the Corinthians were trying to demonstrate that they had no part in the actions of the offenders is rather weak (222). It is difficult to convince Paul that they were not complacent when they failed to act on Paul's behalf. Rather Strachan is closer to the mark when he suggests that the Corinthians were "keen to clear themselves" of any further desire to condone the action of the offender or to make any more excuses for their past actions (128). Or more probably they wanted to defend themselves against Paul's accusation that they had accepted false prophets (Fallon, 65). Hughes (274) is right to note that since the Corinthians were aroused to give an account of their actions—even if their account entailed admission of guilt (Barrett sees ἀπολογία as a forensic term, 211: idem, "Ο ΑΔΙΚΗΣΑΣ," 113)—this was an improvement over an earlier lethargy. This rebirth of the Corinthians, as noted by Paul, continues his motif of 7:10, namely, that godly sorrow motivates people to seek correction in the sight of God.

ἀλλὰ ἀγανάκτησιν, "what indignation." The Corinthians were indignant, but at whom? It could be at the perpetrator(s) who caused many of the problems, either the offender (Barrett, 211; Héring, 55; Bultmann, 61), or the false apostles (Filson, 360; Fallon, 65), or the indignation could be addressed at themselves, for they brought much shame upon the reputation of the church at Corinth (Denney, 256; Plummer, 223; Tasker, 106; Strachan, 129; Hughes, 274). In light of our understanding of ἀπολογία, it appears that Paul understood the indignation of the Corinthians to be directed primarily at themselves, though surely some of their present hostility was directed at the adversaries of Paul. This point can be seen in view of Paul's urging of the Corinthians to receive the offender and to let go of any ill-feelings toward him (2:5–11; note that ἀγανακτεῖν, "to be indignant, angry," is used several times in the synoptics, but the use of the noun is found in the NT only in our verse).

ἀλλὰ φόβον, "what fear." This fear, or alarm (Strachan, 129), could have been the healthy fear that the Corinthians had for Paul as apostle (Barrett, 211; Filson, 360; Denney, 257; Hughes, 274; Fallon, 65). This can be seen in the light of 1 Cor 4:21 ("shall I come with a whip?") and 7:15 (which speaks of receiving Titus with respect). However, Paul could be speaking of the fear of God (5:11; cf. Héring). The Corinthians had been in danger of inviting divine wrath, for they had mistreated God's representative. To be sure, Paul does use φόβος with respect to both man and God, but Plummer is too minimizing when he cites the unlikelihood of Paul's putting "fear of himself in the foreground" (223). The use of fear suggests "reverential awe" in the face of Paul's claim to be acting for God (5:20) as a "divine apostle."

ἀλλὰ ἐπιπόθησιν, "what longing." As in verse 7:7, the Corinthians longed "to be reunited with him who had brought the Gospel to them, to welcome him as their own genuine apostle, and to see the restoration of their former relationship of trust and affection" (Hughes, 274).

ἀλλὰ ζῆλον, "what zeal." The idea of zeal can be taken in either a good sense (Rom 10:2; 2 Cor 9:2; 11:2) or a bad one (as "jealousy, envy," Rom 13:13; 1 Cor 13:4; 2 Cor 12:20; James 3:14, 16). Sometimes the sense is obscure (Gal 4:18). Most likely the former sense is meant by Paul here, especially since this list is one of positive attributes of the Corinthians. Nevertheless, the positive force can be aimed at several targets. On the one hand, Paul could now envision the Corinthians having zeal for him. The Corinthians now honor his apostolic authority and imitate his example (Hughes, 275). They are zealous for Paul and show it by their return to his Gospel. On the other hand, the Corinthians exhibited zeal in that they were against the evil of the day, especially toward those who oppose Paul ("they were full of moral earnestness, which made lax dealing with him [the offender] impossible," Denney, 257). Included in this zeal, of course, is zeal for God (Plummer, 223). The use of "concern" for ζῆλος in the NIV is weak, missing almost entirely the depth of Paul's emotion.

ἀλλὰ ἐκδίκησιν, "what punishment." ἐκδίκησις can mean both "revenge" and "punishment." While a consensus is that this idea of requital (Hughes, 275) is centered on the one who opposed Paul (note, though, that Hughes is referring to the immoral member of 1 Cor 5), there is some question as to whether the term denotes vengeance or punishment. The KJV/AV has "revenge," while the RSV has "punishment." In the light of Paul's spirit expressed in 2:5–11, the cold emotion of spite was probably missing and both ἐκδίκησις and ἀδικήσας (along with ἐπιτιμία in 2:6) are terms borrowed from criminal law (Bultmann, 61), as are the three words (ἁγνός, πρᾶγμα, and possibly συνιστάναι) in the next v. It is more in keeping that the apostle would commend the Corinthians for heeding his advice and punishing anyone who assailed him or his Gospel (for it is the ruling idea that to attack Paul is to attack God). But Paul was more concerned that a wrong had been righted than that he has been avenged on his enemy.

ἐν παντὶ συνεστήσατε ἑαυτοὺς ἁγνοὺς εἶναι τῷ πράγματι, "In every instance you have demonstrated your innocence in this matter." At the end of 7:11, Paul expressed his satisfaction with the Corinthians. They have stood the test (2:9; see Bruce, 218: cf. 13:5–7) though it has been a painful process for everyone concerned. "In every instance" (note ἐν παντί, with a dative of respect, is singular, not plural as translated in KJV/AV, "in all things") the church has shown itself pure (ἁγνός), i.e., legally blameless, in this context. Paul's use of συνεστήσατε (aorist of συνιστάνειν) can express the idea of commending (a frequent verb in our letter: 3:1; 4:2; 5:12; 6:4; 10:12, 18; 12:11) or proving (Rom 3:5; 5:8; Gal 2:18). Noting Paul's use of the verb in 2 Cor, we may conclude that the uppermost thought in his mind was probably the element of commendation or confirmation as valid (Bultmann 61, n. 45), though at least we can also say that Titus was convinced of the Corinthians' change (Barrett, 212).

What the Corinthians did by their actions was to demonstrate their "innocence." The meaning of ἁγνός can include the concept of purity (11:2). For Paul, the verb εἶναι, "to be" (instead of γινέσθαι; see Plummer, 223) suggests probably that he is seeing the Corinthians as now having attained the verdict of acquittal. Plummer argues that Paul does not want even to hint that he considered them formerly guilty. But this position ignores the fact that Paul has argued that there has been repentance in the Corinthian church, for we may question why repentance is mentioned if Paul did not think something was amiss. Clearly Plummer is wrong, and Bachmann, 304, who argues that εἶναι is not an imperfect but a "real" present (see too Allo) is right. The Corinthians had been guilty of complacency but now, after having taken the action described in 7:11a, they were "established" as being on Paul's side. Where Paul seeks to avoid bringing up and so exacerbating an unpleasant subject is in the vague reference to "this matter" (τῷ πράγματι). Paul's usual idea behind πρᾶγμα is that of a task or an undertaking (Rom 16:2; 1 Thess 4:6). If the term is considered a legal one (so Héring; Bultmann renders Rechtsfall in the light of 1 Cor 6:1–11; cf. 6:1: τις . . . πρᾶγμα ἔχων, "one . . . has a grievance"), then in essence Paul has declared the Corinthians not guilty, presumably because they are to be dissociated from the offender who, on this showing, was not one of them (so Barrett, "Ο ΑΔΙΚΗΣΑΣ [2 Cor 7:12]," 113, 114).

12. ἄρα εἰ καὶ ἔγραψα ὑμῖν, "So then, when I wrote to you." This verse is similar to 2:9. For the use of ἄρα as inferential and not interrogative (ἆρα) see Moule, Idiom Book, 164. It is taken as a connective by M. E. Thrall, Greek Particles in the New Testament, 10, 11, as well as inferential (ibid., 36). We may note that placing ἄρα, "so then," at the beginning of the Pauline sentence is well-attested (cf. 2 Cor 5:14; 1 Cor 15:18; Rom 10:17; Gal 5:11; 6:10).

Plummer (224) views ἄρα as equivalent to ὥστε when connected to a finite verb (cf. 1 Cor 7:14; Rom 7:21; Gal 3:17). With this opening Paul once again alludes to the "severe letter" (see *Form/Structure/Setting*), whose central theme is not personal injury, but the fractured relationship between the apostle and the community, which needs to be put right (Bultmann, 62).

οὐχ ἕνεκεν τοῦ ἀδικήσαντος, "it was not on account of the offender." With this clause we get an insight into the Semitic thinking of Paul. He presents clear alternatives. He could have written the "severe letter" primarily on the account of someone other than the Corinthians (namely, the offender or himself), or he could have constructed the letter mainly for the Corinthians themselves. But in negating the first purpose, this is not to negate it absolutely (Plummer, 224). Rather it is to highlight the importance of the second. Plummer cites the example of Hos 6:6 ("I desire mercy and not sacrifice"), and rightly points out that the verse "does not prohibit sacrifice; it affirms that mercy is much the better of the two" (ibid., cf. Mark 9:37; Luke 10:20; 14:12; 23:28). Paul is not without remembrance of the one who offended him, or of himself (see next clause); rather he is more concerned with the outcome of his letter-writing, namely, that the Corinthians manifested their earnestness before God.

Héring (56) does not interpret the writing of the letter by Paul in terms of a purpose (so he interprets Paul as saying, "I wrote in order to provoke the zeal of the Corinthians"). Rather, he translates ἕνεκεν as causal ("I am comforted on account of your zeal"). But he appears to be in the minority (see Moule, [*Idiom Book*, 83] who says that what follows ἕνεκεν is "practically a final clause"; see BDF § 216.[1], where ἕνεκεν is shown to be quite similar to διά plus the accusative and thus ἕνεκεν is usually not causal; also cf. BGD, 264).

Unresolved problems of the identity of the offender (ὁ ἀδικήσας from ἀδικεῖν, "to wrong") remain. At best we can only offer what seems the most logical conjecture in our review of options. (1) At first glance it appears that the offender is that one mentioned in 1 Cor 5:1–5, i.e., the man accused by Paul of sexual immorality and some form of incest. But closer scrutiny reveals that this link fails to be sustained in our present v. If Paul is the "offended," as seems clear, then it is doubtful that he would take the sin described in 1 Cor 5:1–5 in such a personal way (but see Lampe, "Church Discipline," 353–55). Moreover, if we allow that the offender (ὁ ἀδικήσας) is the man mentioned in 1 Cor 5:1–5, then the offended one (ὁ ἀδικηθείς) becomes (strictly) the father of the offender. If this were true, then we would have expected a stronger reaction from the Corinthians at the act of cohabiting with a person's mother or stepmother while the father was still living. Also, the approach of Paul to the offender, as recorded in 7:12, does not match his apodictic pronouncement in 1 Cor 5:5, 7, 13 (Kümmel, *Introduction*[2], 283, 284).

(2) Another possibility for the identity of the offender is that he is the person mentioned in 1 Cor 6:1–11, namely, the one taking a fellow church member to court to bring suit against him (Windisch, 237–39). This view has received little support (Bultmann, 62, notes the personal elements in 2 Cor 2:7, which are lacking in 1 Cor 6). (3) Most likely the offender (note the singular ἀδικήσαντος here and the singular "such a one" in 2:7) was one

who confronted Paul face to face, probably during the painful visit ("a turbu-
lent Corinthian," Plummer, 225; see too Bruce, 218; Barrett, 212, 213). These
several allusions to "anyone" (2:5), "such a one" (2:6, 7, 8), "to him" (2:10),
"the one who does wrong" (7:12) point to a specific individual in the light
of 2:7, 8, and should not be glossed over in favor of the view that Paul is
referring to "those members of the Corinthian community who decided for
the opposing apostles," as though the singular was a generalizing one (as
Fallon, 65, 66, thinks). To the details of the "wrong" committed against
Paul we are not privy. Whatever it was, Paul lost face and had to regain his
standing by writing the "severe letter." Though the "crime" of the Corinthians
was probably indifference to the actions of the offender, a new relationship
needed to be restored between Paul and the church. Thus Paul is an example
("paradigm") of reconciliation, for he is restored to the offender, and the
Corinthian church has again taken to Paul with zeal (Martin, *Reconciliation*,
91, 92).

(4) That the offender was probably a single individual we can be more
or less certain, but we are less likely to ascertain, however, whether or not
he was a member of the church. Barrett calls him an "anti-Pauline intruder"
(213). See too his essay "O AΔIKHΣAΣ (2 Cor 7.12)," summarizing Allo and
developing a stronger theory of the offender's relation to the Corinthians.
But one may question whether the church would have been so quick to follow
an outsider, or at least to tolerate an outsider's opinion. If we follow Barrett's
line of reasoning, it is required that we assume that the person was a strong
character with power to sway the congregation—or at least a sizable proportion
of it—to his side, and against the apostle. Hence Paul can now write that
the church as a whole was "guiltless" in this affair, and once they had been
"written to" (in the "tearful letter") they were quick to show a conversion
to Paul's cause.

(5) Or, pursing a different tack, we may opine that, possibly unaware of
the seriousness of the situation, the church sided with no one. But the apostle
took this as meaning that the Corinthians had sided with the offender. While
the extent of the opposition is unknown to us, a reasonable assumption is
that an influential minority affected the majority. The value of this reconstruction is that it leaves chaps. 10–13 to stand on their own as a witness to a
much more serious threat to Paul's apostolic mission and ministry. It requires
a positing of these four chapters as written to a later and developed situation,
which arose after the scenarios of chaps. 1–9. The intruders of 11:4, 20,
are, then, not to be equated with the offender in 2:7 (as Fallon imagines,
and others). This distinction seems clear, and it is accepted here in agreement
with Barrett's sagacious dictum: "it helps to make good sense of the whole
epistle" (loc. cit. 115).

οὐδὲ ἕνεκεν τοῦ ἀδικηθέντος, "or of the offended." We have assumed that
the offended person was Paul. Some (e.g., Filson, 361) believe that Timothy
or some other Pauline friend is the one offended, but the personal nature
of these verses rules out anyone but the writer himself as the party injured.

ἀλλ' ἕνεκεν τοῦ φανερωθῆναι τὴν σπουδὴν ὑμῶν τὴν ὑπὲρ ἡμῶν πρὸς ὑμᾶς ἐνώπιον
τοῦ θεοῦ, "but on your account, so that before God you could see your earnestness toward us." Paul had not written the "severe letter" because of the

offender, nor because of himself. Rather, his purpose (note ἕνεκεν followed by genitive of the articular infinitive φανερωθῆναι) in composing the letter was to have the Corinthians see their "indebtedness to and fundamental loyalty toward the apostle" (Barrett, 214; note Goudge: "This verse of course describes, not S. Paul's purpose in writing his severe letter, but the purpose which the letter had actually served, and which God had intended it to serve," 77). A drastic action was needed to shock (Bruce, 219) the Corinthians into seeing just how much the situation had deteriorated. ("The main object was to get the Corinthians to realize their true state of mind respecting the Apostle," Plummer, 225). In short, the letter, though causing a trauma, was for the benefit of the Corinthians (see Denney, 258). πρὸς ὑμᾶς probably carries with it the idea of "to you," though it could include the thought of "with you" or "among you" (see Héring, 56). On the textual issues in this v see *Notes*.

But we miss the force of Paul's thinking if we fail to note that the Corinthians came to realize their concern (σπουδή) to be reconciled to Paul "before God" (ἐνώπιον τοῦ θεοῦ). This phrase is placed at the end of the sentence for reasons of emphasis (Plummer, 225). If God judged the renewed spirit of the Corinthians as true, then true it indeed was. Reflecting on Paul's earlier self-vindication as being transparent before God and man (5:10, 11), we see that he has helped the Corinthians do likewise. And how has he done this? This was accomplished by his being the example of reconciliation. He preached reconciliation in 5:18–20; in 2:10 he has forgiven the offender; in 7:12 he has shown that the Corinthians have been restored to their rightful place vis-à-vis Paul. *Coram Deo*, the Corinthians actually have within them the essence of what it takes to continue a right relationship with God and his messenger, namely, Paul. Plummer points out that Paul's responsibility before God is also in the apostle's thinking. This is consistent with 5:10, 11 ("God would judge of his reason for writing and of the words which he said," ibid., 226).

13. διὰ τοῦτο παρακεκλήμεθα, "because of this we are encouraged." A case can be made for placing a full stop (period) after these words and including them in v 12 (Tasker, 107; see also *Notes*). The τοῦτο, "this," is probably referring to the earnestness of the Corinthians, as seen in 7:12 (cf. 7:7, 11). The hope of the Corinthians' again expressing zeal towards Paul has been realized (we must remember that to receive Paul as God's envoy, was, in the apostle's mind, to accept the demands of the Gospel). For Paul this action of the Corinthians is a source of encouragement (παράκλησις: see *Comment* on 1:3–7). Such an attitude has been and continues to be a benediction for Paul (note the perfect tense of this verb παρακεκλήμεθα, "we are encouraged"). The idea of encouragement resumes the thought of 7:6 as an *inclusio*, i.e. an "envelope" device, bringing two identical ideas together, as well as echoing Paul's opening comments of the epistle (1:3–7).

Ἐπὶ δὲ τῇ παρακλήσει ἡμῶν, "In addition to our encouragement." This sentence marks a new paragraph, as it reviews the past vv (6, 7), and explains the course of events at greater depth. Paul has made it plain that he has been gladdened by the Corinthians in their "repentance" (7:7, 9–12). And in this encouragement Paul was not thinking only of himself. As was explained in 7:6, Paul was also uplifted both by the person and message of Titus. Once again the apostle returns to this thought. The placement of δέ (Plummer, 226) overrules the attempt (in KJV/AV) to connect the following words in the Greek (note KJV/AV translates "in your comfort") with the preceding. If the KJV/AV is followed, then the v reads "we were comforted in your comfort." This reading does not fit the context (see *Notes*).

Though the common meaning of ἐπί with the dative is "upon" or "at," there is a different understanding of the preposition in 7:13. It is better translated "in addition to" (Tasker, 107) or "over and above" (Plummer, 226; Bultmann, 63, *ausser*). This is borne out in what follows (cf. H. E. Dana and J. R. Mantey, *A Manual of Grammar of the Greek New Testament* [Toronto: Macmillan, 1955] 107). Paul is rehearsing the pleasure he received from the reaction of Titus to the Corinthians' repentance. For Paul, the joy of Titus was a reason to rejoice ("Friendship redoubleth joys," Bacon). "Just as the consolation Titus received was the basis of Paul's consolation, so Titus's joy is the ground of his joy" (Bultmann, 63).

περισσοτέρως μᾶλλον ἐχάρημεν ἐπὶ τῇ χαρᾷ Τίτου, "we rejoiced more than ever at the joy of Titus." The joyful demeanor of Titus was an additional reason for Paul's joy. Paul is so concerned to show how Titus's joy increased his that he gives us a pleonastic construction. He strengthens the comparative περισσοτέρως (from περισσῶς, which means "beyond measure") by adding the redundant μᾶλλον. The combination of the two terms gives us the idea of "even much more" (BGD, 651; BDF § 60.3, § 246). This is not a unique construction, since we find similar examples in Mark (7:36) and Paul (Phil 1:23). Also, this is a construction found in classical Greek (see Plummer, 226; Hughes, 278, n. 21). The procedure of accumulating several comparatives was intended to heighten the comparison.

As will be discussed below, there may be more to Titus's joy than appears on the surface. To be sure, Titus's being joyful meant that he had received a good report from the Corinthian church. Also, his joy was in and of itself another component for Paul's rejoicing. But we wonder (along with Filson 361, 62) if Titus had at the first been prone to doubt whether the Corinthians would reform in any manner at all. (After all, the earlier treatment of Timothy at the hands of the Corinthians would do nothing to raise the spirits of Titus— or of Paul.) Any doubt on Titus's part would make his being convinced that much harder. But if indeed Titus was convinced, then Paul had a double reason for welcoming his colleague's happy experience. Not only was Paul relieved that Titus was refreshed (see below) but he could also verify that indeed the change that took place with the Corinthians was deep and solid; it was nothing that would vanish overnight. However, if chaps. 10–13 come later in sequence, we may query whether Titus's joy at the Corinthians' return was all that secure and permanent. The reason for Titus's joy was a twofold foundation on which Paul could build. Note the more common use of ἐπί, "at," in the clause under study. Its use here is as a dative of reference.

ὅτι ἀναπέπαυται τὸ πνεῦμα αὐτοῦ ἀπὸ πάντων ὑμῶν, "because his spirit has been refreshed by all of you." Paul explains why Titus was and is joyful. We see this explanation in the causal use of ὅτι, "because"; or possibly the ὅτι clause is the object of the ἐχάρημεν, "we rejoiced." Titus is rejoicing because of the positive action of the Corinthians. His response to their change of heart is seen by Paul as a refreshing of the human spirit. Again we have the "untheological" (Barrett, 214) use of πνεῦμα (cf. 2:13; 7:1). The idea behind ἀναπέπαυται is that of "rest" or "refreshment" (BGD, 58, 59). (Note that we meet the same idea with respect to Paul's spirit in 1 Cor 16:18; also cf. Philem 7, 20, where τὰ σπλάγχνα is a substitute for τὸ πνεῦμα. On the Jewish background see Str-B 3:486.) Perhaps what Titus had was a respite from the critical situation, rather than a lasting cessation from a burden of pastoral interest ("a truce as distinct from a peace," Plummer, 226). This can possibly be seen in the difference between ἀναπαύειν and παύειν ("stop," "relieve," BGD, 638; cf. Matt 11:28, 29; 1 Pet 3:10). The least that can be said is that probably Paul's use of the perfect does imply that Titus was still in a state of refreshment (Hughes, 279, n. 22). But we must note that if the conclusion of Plummer is right, then possibly the Corinthian situation could still be improved.

One might have expected ὑπό, "by" instead of ἀπό (cf. Matt 16:21; Luke 7:35; 17:25; Jas 1:13). But just this substitution of terms continues the sense of causality, carrying with it a concept of "because of" (BDF §§ 113, 210.2). Titus is joyful because of what the Corinthians have decided about Paul.

From this decision, we can see that the majority of the church was behind Paul. We might wish to stop short of saying "everyone" in the church, in the light of the idea of only οἱ πλείονες, "a considerable number" (so Windisch, 86), not the entire group, who sanctioned punishment for the offender (see 2:6). Yet the point is clear: where disunity, or at least lethargy, existed previously, unity now prevails. In 7:13, Paul uses ἀπὸ πάντων ὑμῶν, "for all of you." Again we see "all" in v 15 (πάντων ὑμῶν; cf. 2:5, πάντας ὑμᾶς). Likewise the phrase "everything" (πάντα) is found in 7:14. This gives us a good reason to underline a motif of unity in this v (see Filson, 362, who takes this element of unity in the church as a reason to question the literary unity of chaps. 1–9 and 10–13, but Barrett has a better argument, as we noted earlier). The church has responded to Titus, and this expression of unity is a sure sign of loyalty to Paul. This was important, for soon Paul would be looking to the Corinthians to provide further grounds of his boasting by moving ahead with the offering for the saints (8:24; 9:3).

14. ὅτι εἴ τι αὐτῷ ὑπὲρ ὑμῶν κεκαύχημαι, οὐ κατῃσχύνθην, "For I boasted to him about you and you did not embarrass me." Paul elucidates further the reason why Titus's joy meant so much to him. No doubt since the report was positive, Paul had good feelings. And, since his companion rejoiced, Paul has a double reason to rejoice. But while this victory was important, it was more than just a triumph because of restored relationships. Paul, so to speak, had declared himself concerning the Corinthians. In essence, in spite of possible inner misgivings, Paul had boasted to Titus that all would be well, a bold endeavor at that time, to say the least.

The use of εἰ (sometimes "if") is here relative rather than conditional (Tasker, 108; see Barrett, 214, "If I had made any boasts to him about you," for a literal translation; this has been called a good Greek construction; see also K. Beyer, *Semitische Syntax im Neuen Testament I,* 1 [Göttingen: Vandenhoeck & Ruprecht, 1962] 81, 228). Apparently Paul had boasted (κεκαύχημαι; the idea of boasting [καύχησις] occurs almost thirty times in 2 Cor, i.e. more than in all of the other genuine Pauline letters combined: see earlier, p. 125) to Titus concerning the Corinthians. The use of the perfect may be an attempt by Paul to emphasize that the action in the past remains a force in the present. Despite the bleakness of the situation at Corinth and before the sending of the "severe letter," Paul had risked embarrassment by predicting that all would be well. The use of τι, "anything," could be a "tactful" reminder to the Corinthians that at that moment when Titus left bearing the "severe letter" there was not a lot of which Paul could be proud (Filson, 362). In many instances, however, those who care will provide more hope than possibly a situation warrants. Paul did this for himself and for Titus. That the latter was apprehensive might have been expected, for he probably did not want the rude reception that had been accorded some of his co-workers, namely Paul and Timothy. We are left on the outside looking in with respect to the degree of suspicion that Titus raised, but we can be quite sure from our text that Paul held more assurance with regard to the Corinthians than Titus did.

Paul's confidence was rewarded. He did not suffer shame, or embarrassment (κατησχύνθην, aorist passive of κατασχύνειν) but even more, as Bultmann (63) notes, his work at Corinth was not overthrown, an idea parallel with Phil 1:20 (ἐν οὐδενὶ αἰσχυνθήσομαι, "I will in no way be ashamed"). The word carried with it the idea of humiliation or being despised (1 Cor 11:22). The notion of dishonor (or disfigurement) is seen in 1 Cor 11:4, 5. Paul risked much and was rewarded with much more. He had boasted "about" the Corinthians. The preposition (ὑπέρ) is closer to the idea of "on behalf of" than "concerning" (i.e., ὑπέρ instead of the more common περί, see BFD, § 231). In essence, Paul had related the truth to Titus with a frankness that had always marked his relationship with the Corinthians (Héring). See the allegation rebutted in 1:12–14, using καύχησις from καυχᾶσθαι, in this v. ἀλλ' ὡς πάντα ἐν ἀληθείᾳ ἐλαλήσαμεν ὑμῖν, "And as we have spoken the truth in all things to you." Paul reiterates what is to him the obvious. His speech is true (Hughes, 279). The use of ἀλλά conveys the idea of "on the contrary" (Plummer, 227). Rather than leading to Paul's shame, what he had boasted to Titus has turned out to be true. The Corinthians would be reconciled to Paul. He had spoken to them, ἐν ἀληθείᾳ, "in truth." No doubt Paul takes a polemical stab at his opponents, who questioned his credibility and reliability (1:13 f., 15–23). For as Paul will say in 13:8, he is constrained by the truth, i.e., the apostolic message (4:2). So the issue, after all, is Paul's apostolic standing at Corinth, and his version of the kerygma.

οὕτως καὶ ἡ καύχησις ἡμῶν ἡ ἐπὶ Τίτου ἀλήθεια ἐγενήθη, "likewise our boasting to Titus about you has proved true." This clause continues the theme of truth's claim. Paul boasted to Titus about the Corinthians' integrity. It had proved to be the case, for Titus was well pleased and stands ready to return and assist with the collection (8:16, 17).

The employment of ἐπὶ Τίτου, "to Titus," underlines that this optimism of Paul was presented "before" Titus (BDF § 234). Note a similar use in Mark 13:9 (". . . you will stand before governors and kings . . ."); the idea of the Latin term *coram* is seen here, as in *coram Deo*: see on v 12: cf. also Acts 25:9; 1 Cor 6:1). Titus had to "judge" (M. Zerwick and M. Grosvenor,

A Grammatical Analysis of the Greek New Testament, II [Rome: Biblical Institute Press, 1979] 549) the soundness of Paul's boasting. And what better way to judge than to go to see the situation at first hand? Paul risked much on behalf of the Corinthians. Apparently Titus was finally convinced concerning the Corinthians, for when he was at Corinth he started work on the collection (8:6). Thus, it seems unlikely that a renewed outbreak of revolt was taking place in Corinth during Titus's stay, for one cannot so readily promote a positive work especially where money is involved, if there is much negative feeling to overcome (Barrett, 215).

15. Καὶ τὰ σπλάγχνα αὐτοῦ περισσοτέρως εἰς ὑμᾶς, "his affection abounds toward you." It would come as little surprise if the Corinthians were now happy at this point in the reading of 2 Corinthians. Still, further, Paul encourages the Corinthians in the light of the timeliness of their action by relating in fuller detail the emotions of Titus (which Paul interprets as also including himself). The σπλάγχνα ("affection," "heart," lit., "bowels"; see H.-H Esser, *NIDNTT* 2:600: "the noun refers to the whole man, viz., in his capacity to love or as one who loves," as in 6:12) of Titus has gone out to the Corinthians because of the reception granted him (see below). A question surrounds Paul's intent behind the use of περισσοτέρως, lit., "even more," "especially"; or "even much more," as in 7:13, which adds μᾶλλον. The question is whether this adverb is used comparatively or in an elative way, to signify "the most." By NT times, the superlative was being replaced with the comparative (BDF § 60). Nevertheless, we must ask whether Paul was hinting that Titus had made a previous visit to Corinth before the one that resulted in the good report. Hughes conjectures (293, 294) that Titus had made such a visit to Corinth, possibly as a bearer of the lost epistle (1 Cor 5:9) but, more likely, as one of the brethren mentioned in 1 Cor 16:11. This reconstruction suggests that Titus's love for the Corinthians increased "more" after his second visit (KJV/AV). Some interpreters (e.g., Hughes, 280) supply a superlative force to περισσοτέρως ("he feels the most abundant affection for you"). Plummer suggests that the term could simply describe the manner in which Titus showed affection without regard to a comparison (227). Thus, Titus demonstrated affection "very abundantly." Regardless of what is decided on the syntactical point, Titus had a warm place in his heart for the Corinthians, thereby showing the sincerity of their ready acceptance of him as Paul's delegate.

ἀναμιμνῃσκομένου τὴν πάντων ὑμῶν ὑπακοήν, "when he recalls everyone's obedience." A true test of commitment to Paul is "obedience," his favorite expression for human response to the Gospel message, and to his apostolic work. In these words of Paul, we see for the first time a specific description of Titus's treatment. In 7:6, 13, Paul has related how Titus had been refreshed and convinced of the change that had come over the Corinthians. In 7:15 Paul went on to report that indeed things went well for Titus with respect to his own standing as well as Paul's. In short, Titus enhanced the favorable attitude of the Corinthians toward Paul by recalling (ἀναμιμνῃσκομένου) the warm-hearted reception afforded him. This is seen especially in the final words of v 15, but we must not overlook the impression made on Titus by the obedience of the Corinthians (τὴν πάντων ὑμῶν ὑπακοήν). Plummer believes that Titus had made specific demands upon the Corinthians and that these demands had been complied with universally (228). Whether such "demands" were in the form of a Pauline imperative or simply initiated by Titus on his own is unclear. What is clear is that Titus was recognized as an emissary of Paul and of God and thus respected and obeyed as Paul expected to be obeyed (2:9). This is important, for Titus was to do future business with the Corinthians (8:6, 16, 17; Bruce, 219). Possibly this was part of the obedience, that the Corinthians responded in a positive manner to his instruction regarding the collection. Titus was so impressed by the action of the Corinthians that he himself initiated a subsequent visit (8:17). But, as will be seen presently, there was another dimension to the reception of Titus (see Denney, 258–61).

ὡς μετὰ φόβου καὶ τρόμου ἐδέξασθε αὐτόν, "for he was received with fear and trembling." The use of ὡς here may have its commonest meaning of "as," but Héring sees it as possessing causal force ("because," 57). This is not out of the question (cf. Matt 6:12; see BDF § 453; also see Windisch, 241). Even better is the epexegetical sense, called "explanatory extension" by T. Muraoka, "The use of ΩΣ in the Greek Bible," *NovT* 7 (1964) 61.

The phrase μετὰ φόβου καὶ τρόμου, "with fear and trembling," is Pauline: but cf. Isa 19:16 from which it may be taken. We find it in no other NT writer (1 Cor 2:3; Phil 2:12; cf. Eph 6:5). This phrase appears to reflect the anxiety over the duty required of a person. But it is not in the sense of "nervous panic"; rather, it betokens "a solicitous anxiety lest we should fail in doing all that is required of us" (Hodge, 190). Filson suggests that even before Titus's arrival, guilt was beginning to work in the conscience of the Corinthians (303). So they may have opened their hearts up to Paul before Titus arrived. Or, if the "severe letter" arrived ahead of Titus, the rebuff of Paul could have weighed upon their minds. In either case, with "reverence and respect" (Phillips), the audience awaited the arrival of someone (maybe Paul), so that the church could demonstrate a changed heart to their human founder. Perhaps this v reflects the alarm expressed in 7:11 (Bruce, 219).

Strachan gives a curious twist to the sense when he interprets the phrase here to mean that the "reverence and trembling" were not directed at Titus (129). But it seems strange to say this in the light of the opening words of v 15. True, Titus would sense that much of the Corinthians' love should be directed toward Paul. But to imply that their affection excluded Titus is to overlook the fact that he interpreted such affection as also meant to include himself. Also, the warm reception for Titus almost totally rules out any notion of a disaffection in Corinth against Paul at that time. It hardly makes sense for Titus to have been welcomed (δέξασθαι: cf. 6:1 for the verb) if "there was no recalcitrant minority" (Barrett, 215), at least in the days after the letter had done its work.

16. χαίρω ὅτι ἐν παντὶ θαρρῶ ἐν ὑμῖν, "I rejoice in that I have complete confidence in you." This verse repeats the thought of 7:4 closing the "ring" as a literary formulation. All in all, Paul is satisfied that the Corinthians have understood the message and the mission as he does (Barrett, 215). The use of ὅτι could mean "because" (RSV, Filson 363) or "that" (KJV/AV). There

appears little difference in the options (Plummer, 228). The use of θαρρῶ (from θαρρεῖν; "to have confidence, courage"; "perfect confidence," Bruce, 219, RSV; "complete confidence," NIV, NEB) is also seen in 5:6, 8; 10:1, 2. This latter v presents an antithesis, and Paul is evidently citing what the opponents said of him, that he was "arrogant," where the verb has negative connotations; also see *Comment* on 10:1, 2. Though one may opt for understanding θαρρῶ as meaning "I have courage" (based on παρρησία, 5:6, 8), the context of v 16 suggests the idea of being able to depend on someone (BGD, 352), or have confidence (Tasker, 108) that the letter had worked to transform the community's behavior (Bultmann, 64).

In the light of Titus's testimony, Paul is now confident in the Corinthians. They have reformed as needed. Paul is confident not only in their present sincerity, but also in their action predicated for the future. Paul is about to write concerning the subject of the collection. Because of the turn of events, he can have "confidence" in them. It may be that this term for confidence was misunderstood at Corinth, and was later to form the butt of his enemies' attack in 10:1, where they evidently quote it against him. The phrase ἐν ὑμῖν, "in you," can be compared to Paul's use of ἐν found elsewhere (Gal 1:24; 4:20; Phil 1:30; cf. Phil 2:5 where E. Lohmeyer, *Kyrios Jesus: Eine Untersuchung zur Phil 2, 5–11*, SHAW 4 [Heidelberg: Winter, 1928, ²1961] 13 sees a kind of paradigmatic meaning, corresponding to the Hebrew ב, *bᵉ*; *'Aḇoṯ* 3:7). But Bultmann, 64, makes ἐν ὑμῖν equal to εἰς ὑμᾶς in 10:1. His confidence lies in them ("in respect of you," Hughes, 282, n. 25). As Plummer (288) writes, "Their past good works and present loyalty give him courage in pressing this matter [the collection] upon them." The "paradigm" would then be their readiness to resume the collection as in 9:2.

Thus 7:16 can be understood in terms of a transition. The preceding verses have described Paul's return of confidence in the Corinthians (7:4–16). What follows in chaps. 8, 9, is an opportunity for the Corinthians to demonstrate the confidence in practical terms. While Hughes may be correct in describing 7:16 as the "perfect transition," it is too ambitious and simplistic when he says, "It [7:16] is the delicate pin around which the whole of the epistle pivots" (282).

Explanation

Though Paul already knows the outcome of Titus's visit to the Corinthians, nevertheless he spells out for them the circumstances in which he learned the news. In our passage, Paul concludes his appeal to gain full access to the hearts of the Corinthians. He reminds them that he had done nothing to hurt any of them. And in reminding them he is quick to describe his confidence in them. The confidence is a result of their acceptance of his rebuke, and their consequent return to his side.

The essence of this reconciliation should not be overlooked. Paul initiated this restoration by risking the delicate relationship altogether. This is seen in his writing the "tearful letter" and sending a close friend to report on its effect on the congregation. In short, Paul is so relieved and refreshed by the results that he reviews the past in order to show how much had taken

place. The word Paul uses to describe the results of his efforts is "joy."
For Barclay there are three great joys found in our passage (*The Letters to
the Corinthians*, 226). They are: (1) the joy of reconciliation, (2) the joy of
seeing one's faith and confidence in someone else justified, and (3) the joy
of seeing someone who is loved accepted and treated well. Essentially, the
fifteen vv under study comprise some of the most joyful ever written by Paul.

The power of God is seen at its best when a relationship between two
parties is restored, first, between an individual and God, and second, between
two sets of human beings. We may illustrate this facet in a stanza which
Hester Hawkins composed for her parents' golden wedding anniversary:

> Yet Thy love hath never left us,
> In our griefs alone to be;
> And the help each gave the other
> Was the strength that came from Thee.

For Paul, the restored relationship was a new beginning. Though an individual had opposed him, the situation in Corinth had now brightened considerably. With this in mind, Paul continues to expand his horizon in Macedonia.
He can count on the church's loyalty, which is due to be tested when more
troubles appear later (chaps. 10–13), and he can proceed toward the completion of the offering started the year before (8:10–12). This was to be carried
out by Titus.

Though Paul had taken some time to get to the good report of Titus
(2:14–7:4), this delay (in the form of an extended defense of apostolic ministry)
does not mute the uplifting note of our present passage. Paul is confident
that he holds a place in the hearts of the Corinthians, which was not always
the case. He is now confident that God's work will continue. The Corinthians
have been restored to God's messenger, which is a sure sign to Paul that
the Corinthians are obeying God in his apostolic person. Needless to say,
the good report of Titus was as music in the ears of Paul.

This pericope is a concrete illustration of Paul's "joy in the midst of trouble," where trouble came to him from those in the church who were most
highly regarded and loved. In the *Introduction* (pp. lviii–lxi) we have tried to
show the historical context of Paul's sense of isolation from his former colleagues and his fear (see 7:5) that his apostolic labors in the Aegean region
were in danger of being lost. This setting gives an added poignancy to these
verses.

Pastorally, no one has captured the Pauline sentiments in 7:2–4 better
than John Chrysostom (*Hom. in 2 Cor*, 14.1, 2) from whom we may quote:

> Again Paul begins his discourse with love, restraining the bitterness of reproof.
> He had reproached them and reproved them on the score that when he loved
> them they did not return his love, but had broken away from his love and allied
> themselves to men of evil life. But again he thinks it necessary to soften his reproof
> and says, "Make room for us in your hearts," that is, "Love us." The favor which
> he asks is not at all burdensome but one which is actually more advantageous to
> those who give than to those who receive. Nor does he say, "You must love,"
> but—a word full of compassion—"Make room for us in your hearts." "Who now,"

he asks, "has driven us out of your hearts? Who has cast us out? Why do we find your hearts closed to us?" Now the apostle has said above, "It is you who have closed your hearts to us," and in this passage he expresses himself more clearly. He declares, "Make room for us in your hearts," and again in this way he draws them to himself. For there is nothing which so draws a man to return love, as when he understands that he who loves him is urgently longing for his affection.

"As I have said before," he remarks, "you are so dear to us that we are always together, whether we live or die." Now the greatest power of love is this, that even when spurned the one who loves is willing to live and die with the beloved. You are not merely in our hearts, but in them in the way I have said. It is possible that a man could love and try to avoid danger; but it is not so with us.

"I am filled with consolation." What consolation? Obviously that which flows from you: because you have changed your ways, you have consoled me by your deeds. It is characteristic of a lover to complain that he is not loved, and then to fear that by going too far in his accusations he may cause sorrow. And so Paul says: "I am filled with consolation, I am running over with joy."

What he means is this: "You have caused me great sorrow, but you have made it up to me in full and brought me comfort: not only have you dispelled my sorrow, you have made me full of joy."

Then he shows how great his joy really is. Not only does he say: "I am running over with joy," but he adds, "in all our troubles." So great, he says, was the pleasure which you brought me that it could not be diminished by all that we are suffering. It has overwhelmed all our troubles so that we cannot feel them for joy.

VI. The Collection (8:1-9:15)

A. Commendation of the Macedonians (8:1-6)

Bibliography

Bornkamm, G. *Paul.* Tr. D. M. G. Stalker. New York: Harper & Row, 1971. Original *Paulus.* Stuttgart: Kohlhammer, 1969. **Bruce, F. F.** "Paul and Jerusalem." *TynB* 19 (1968) 3–25. **Buck, C. H.** "The Collection for the Saints." *HTR* 43 (1950) 1–29. **Dahl, N. A.** "Paul and Possessions." In *Studies in Paul.* Minneapolis: Augsburg Publishing House, 1977. **Davies, W. D.** *The Gospel and the Land.* Berkeley, Los Angeles, and London: University of California Press, 1974. **Dockx, S.** "Chronologie paulinienne de l'année de la grande collecte." *RB* 81 (1974) 183–95. **George, A. R.** *Communion with God in the New Testament.* London: Epworth Press, 1953. **Georgi, D.** *Die Geschichte der Kollekte des Paulus für Jerusalem.* TF 38. Hamburg-Bergstedt: H. Reich. Evangelischer Verlag, 1965. **Hainz, J.** *Koinonia.* "Kirche" als Gemeinschaft bei Paulus. BU 16. Regensburg: Verlag Friedrich Pustet, 1982. 104, 151–61. ———. *Ekklesia.* 101 f., 241–44. **Hengel, M.** *Acts and the History of Earliest Christianity.* Tr. J. Bowden. London: SCM Press, 1979. **Holmberg, B.** *Paul and Power: The Structure of Authority in the Primitive Church as Reflected in the Pauline Epistles.* ConB NT Series 11. Lund: Gleerup/Philadelphia: Fortress Press, 1978. 35–57. **Keck, L. E.** "The Poor among the Saints in the New Testament." *ZNW* 56 (1965) 100–29. ———. "The Poor among the Saints in Jewish Christianity and Qumran." *ZNW* 57 (1966) 54–78. **Luedemann, G.** *Paul, Apostle to the Gentiles: Studies in Chronology.* Tr. F. Stanley Jones. Philadelphia: Fortress Press, 1984. **McDermott, J. M.** "The Biblical Doctrine of KOINONIA." *BZ* 19 (1975) 64–77, 219–33. **Munck, J.** *Paul and the Salvation of Mankind.* Tr. Frank Clarke. London: SCM Press/Atlanta: John Knox, 1959. 288–92, 295–97. **Nickle, K. F.** *The Collection: A Study in Paul's Strategy.* SBT 48. London: SCM Press, 1966.

Translation

¹ *We draw to your notice, brothers, the grace of God given to the churches of Macedonia how that* ² *in much testing by reason of adversity, the welling up of their joy and their deepdown*[a] *poverty have flowed out in the wealth of their generosity.* ³ *For—as I can testify—they gave up to the limit of their means and even beyond it; and did so spontaneously,* ⁴ *begging us with great insistence that they might have the privilege of joining in the act of service to the [Jerusalem] saints.*[b] ⁵ *And they did this, not just as we had hoped, but most importantly by giving themselves to the Lord*[c] *and to us, by the will of God,* ⁶ *so that we requested Titus that, as he had previously begun this gracious service [for them], so he would also bring the same service to completion for you.*

Notes

[a] κατὰ βάθους. βάθος is read by P⁴⁶ D* *pc.*

[b] For the addition of δέξασθαι ἡμᾶς added from the MS marg. and the scribal gloss (ἐν πολλοῖς τῶν ἀντιγράφων. οὕτως εὕρηται: "it is found thus in many of the copies") which exists as a curiosity,

see B. M. Metzger, *The Text of the New Testament*, 2d ed. (New York: Oxford University Press, 1968) 194.

ᶜκυρίῳ. θεῷ read by P⁴⁶, some cursives and Latin texts with "Ambrosiaster" is less well attested. See *Comment*.

Form/Structure/Setting

As to the life-setting of Paul's writing in chaps. 8, 9, there are two matters to consider. First, the two chapters would seem to be written out of different situations and addressed to different audiences: chap. 8 uses the example of the Macedonian churches to influence the Corinthian readers, whereas chap. 9 is a letter of recommendation of certain unnamed brothers to the churches in Achaia, i.e., southern Greece. This is the original hypothesis of J. S. Semler in 1776 (see *Introduction*, pp. xlii–xliii and B. Rigaux, *The Letters of St. Paul*, tr. S. Yonick [Chicago: Franciscan Herald Press, 1968] 110). It also offers an incentive to the Corinthians to be generous, and to that extent there is a measure of overlap in the two chapters. But it is not easy to see why Paul should send out two discussions about the collection in what appear as two successive chapters.

It is possible that chap. 8 was sent out separately to the Corinthian church, whereas chap. 9 is intended for a wider clientele in the whole of southern Greece (Achaia); or, it may be, as Windisch suggests (268), that chap. 9 as a second composition is an expansion of Paul's treatment of the matter of the collection (*zweite Erörterung der Kollektensache*). Denney (279, 280) sees the solution in 9:1 which, he insists, is in the typical Pauline manner of handling a delicate matter (cf. Phil 3:1). Paul's use of the definite article in περὶ . . . τῆς διακονίας, "concerning *this* service" (9:1) and the sense of τὸ γράφειν (9:1) taken to mean "it is superfluous for me to be writing you *as I do*" combine to move the discussion—by a smooth transition—from one approach by Paul to the collection to another. But Héring speaks for most commentators when he remarks that Paul "seems to introduce a fresh topic not yet dealt with" (65) at 9:1.

The second observation to do with life-setting would clearly tip the scales in favor of regarding both chapters as independent compositions. Chap. 8 follows hard on the heels of 7:5–16 in our canonical letter. It was clearly written at a time when Titus had just arrived from Corinth to rendezvous with Paul in Macedonia and while the Macedonians were in the throes of a critical situation which Paul shared. Yet beginning at 8:1, 2 the tone of the letter is different, more tranquil and optimistic. Titus was evidently about to leave for Corinth as the bearer of the letter now contained in 1:1–2:13; 7:5–16, and the Macedonian crisis of financial straits is apparently resolved (8:2; note the past tense of the perfect participle δεδομένην, "given," in 8:1). We may suppose that if chap. 8 was a separate document it was sent to Corinth with the brethren who were to accompany Titus (8:17, 18) and may be dated in the summer, or better, the fall of A.D. 55 (or 56) (see Dockx, "Chronologie"). Chap. 9, if it is indeed a separate composition as many researchers think, will have been written later than chap. 8 since the sending of delegates of 9:3 looks to these scholars to be in addition to the mission of the brethren in 8:18, 22. The audience in chap. 9 seems to be wider than the narrower focus of chap. 8. In the earlier chapter Paul is still confronting the Corinthian church now that it has reacted favorably to the appeal of the "tearful letter"; in chap. 9 it is Achaia as a province (9:2) that is in his sights, and the more local scene at Corinth has faded from view. Chap. 9 will have gone to southern Greece prior to Paul's visit early in A.D. 56 (or 57) (Fallon 7, 76).

The matter, however, can be resolved another way, and much depends on whether the brothers of 8:18, 22 are the same as those referred to in 9:3. This equation turns on the link which connects 8:19, 24 and 9:2, 3: Paul's προθυμία and καύχημα–καύχησις—his readiness and pride—are treated in both places, and it is singular that Paul should repeat *in identical terms* the pastoral regard he has for his readers if they in fact are two diverse groups. (But the first term [προθυμία] does in fact refer to two different sets of people.) A stronger point is that the phrase "a year ago" (8:10; 9:2) is common to both chapters. But this repeated time-phrase hardly *proves* that the two chapters are not so different. One remaining issue has to be faced. If, as we shall maintain, the brothers of 8:18, 22 are Macedonian Christians, does this fact militate against seeing them in 9:3 (where perhaps the tense is *not* epistolary aorist: so "I have sent the brothers," ἔπεμψα, referring to a previous event, i.e., in chapter 8), since the "Macedonians" are said to join Paul in his subsequent visit to Corinth? So Nickle, *The Collection,* 19. But it is scarcely a compelling argument for identifying the two men in chap. 8 as Judean Christians, as we shall note. And we know so little of Paul's movements at this time that we cannot deny that the two Macedonian leaders may well have been followed by a larger contingent from the same province at a later time; this is especially so if the witness of Acts 20:4 is accepted as reliable (Munck, *Paul,* 288–92; Nickle, *The Collection,* 63 f.; Holmberg, *Paul,* 38, 61; cf. J. A. T. Robinson, *Redating the NT,* 50–53).

So we regard chap. 9 as a separate composition but written in swift succession to chap. 8, and addressed to the same readers but, bearing in mind the language of 1:1—"to the church of God which is at Corinth, with all the holy people who are in the whole of Achaia"—we shall regard the addressees as comprising a total audience of Christians in the city and beyond in the province.

The specific request of this section is held back until v 7. Paul will preface what turns out to be a new section (Bultmann, 255) of the letter by citing the example of the Macedonian churches whose response and continuing fidelity to his Gospel remained an important paradigm. The Macedonians are mentioned no fewer than thirteen times in the Pauline letters (J. Gnilka, *Der Philipperbrief,* HTKNT 10 [1968] 177), and it is often their characteristics of poverty and generosity that are evoked in the apostle's allusions to them. Paul's calling them to the attention of the Corinthian readers (γνωρίζομεν δὲ ὑμῖν: H. Conzelmann, *1 Corinthians* [Hermeneia; tr. J. W. Leitch; Philadelphia: Fortress, 1965] 250, speaks of a note of "ceremonious introduction" attaching to the use of this verb [γνωρίζειν, "to make known, reveal," BGD, 163] in 1 Cor 12:3; 15:1; Gal 1:11 and here) is a calculated design to pave the way for his later appeal to the church to follow the Macedonians' good example, with v 6 acting as a bridge to connect Titus's action in raising the collection at Macedonia with his endeavor to take up the same work at Corinth.

In this part of the letter which some (see above and also in the *Introduction*, pp. xlii, xliii) have argued is an independent composition, Paul turns to consider the great collection which he was gathering in the Gentile churches for the impoverished Jewish Christians (called "the saints" in v 4) at the mother church in Jerusalem. It formed "one of the great enterprises of his career" (Allo, 204), at least during the mid-fifties A.D., and may rightly be called an "illustrative model of his theology" (Georgi, *Die Geschichte der Kollekte*, 79). In this way he was accomplishing several goals (listed in Nickle, *The Collection*, and Holmberg, *Paul and Power*, 35–43, drawing on the fundamental work of Georgi, *Die Geschichte der Kollekte*, and summarized in Martin, *The Worship of God: Some Theological, Pastoral and Practical Reflections* [Grand Rapids: Eerdmans, 1982] 69–73. See the "Note on the Pauline Collection," pp. 256–58): (1) he was making good his promise, given to the "pillar"-apostles, to remember the poor at Jerusalem (see Gal 2:10, a pledge he may not have been able to make good, on account of Galatian intractability: see Luedemann, *Paul*, 87, 88); (2) he was conveying the concern and generous compassion of the gentile congregations on the basis of equality and "sharing" (2 Cor 8:11–15; Rom 15:25–27); (3) he was seeking to bind together the two ethnic "wings" of the church, and to indicate his continuing sense of indebtedness to Israel as the "mother church" (9:13, 14) with an undertone, much ventilated in recent discussion, following Munck, of (4) preparing to make possible and so to greet the eschatological fulfillment of Israel's conversion when the gentile believers would make their pilgrimage to Jerusalem bearing gifts (see Munck, *Paul*, citing Isa 2:2–5; 60:5–22; Mic 4:1–5). The fact that the collection was designated for the "saints" (8:4) *at Jerusalem* is all-important (see K. L. Schmidt, *TDNT* 3:510), and anchors Paul's resolve to come to the aid of the mother church in his understanding of salvation-history which had at its heart the unity of the church made up of Jews and Gentiles who had entered the community of the new Israel by faith in messiah Jesus (Gal 3:23–4:7: see Eph 2:11–22 for the final statement of this article of Pauline *heilsgeschichtlich* theology).

The above survey of the role of the collection in Paul's salvation-historical approach may help to account for the heavy use of religious language in his diction. Terms such as "grace" (8:1; 4, 6), "fellowship" (8:4; 9:13), "ministry" or "service" (8:4; 9:1, 13), "sign of love" (8:7) and later "blessing" (εὐλογία, 9:5, 6), "liturgy" (λειτουργία in 9:12) are all derived from the vocabulary of human relationships with God and sacred acts of worship (see the complete list in Dahl, "Paul and Possessions" 37, 38). The raising of a collection—and it is striking that neither here nor in Phil 4:10–20 does Paul even once mention money (ἀργύριον, χρυσίον) (Plummer, 230; Denney, 263)—is invested with a sacral-liturgical aura, and never treated as a mundane secular enterprise. On the idioms which are both cultic and judicial, see J.-L. Leuba, *New Testament Pattern*, tr. Harold Knight (London: Lutterworth Press, 1953) 118f., and note how χάρις, "grace," in vv 1, 6 forms an *inclusio*, as the same word marks the opening and the close of this disquisition.

Also to be observed in these and succeeding vv is the way Paul grounds his paraenetic call in a theological justification. The central statement is made in 8:5 that the Macedonians gave themselves to the Lord in "the will of God" (διὰ θελήματος θεοῦ). It is not accidental that Paul uses the same term [ἀπόστολος] . . . διὰ θελήματος θεοῦ, 1:1, of his own apostolic commission (Windisch, 248). So closely did Paul see his own apostolic work as bound up with God's service that he can link the phrase "and to us" (καὶ ἡμῖν; see Carrez, "Le 'nous'," NTS 26 [1979–80] 479) with the Macedonians' dedication to God. This pericope is an indirect recall to the Corinthians that at least in the Macedonian province (where cordial relations with the churches prevailed, Phil 4:1; 1 Thess 2:19, 20) Paul's authority was not in doubt. Contrast the fortunes of the collection in Galatia and at Corinth with the exemplary giving of the congregations in northern Greece.

The churches in Macedonia, of which Philippi is the best known, were renowned for their "wealth of generosity" as we learn also from Phil 1:3–5 (on which see P. T. O'Brien, Introductory Thanksgivings in the Letters of Paul, NovTSup 49 [Leiden: Brill 1977] 23, and Dahl, "Paul and Possessions," 34: both interpret the "remembrance" of the Philippians as their aid to Paul; cf. R. P. Martin, Philippians, NCB, ad loc.) and Phil 4:10–19. Their "joy" coupled with "deep-down poverty" is an item of their history that can only be known from what Paul's letter here says, though Héring (58) speculates that the testing of the Macedonian churches may have been caused by severe earthquakes which, in Claudius' reign, shook several provinces. But there is no independent evidence of this for northern Greece. We may trace their economic hardship to persecution (e.g., Phil 1:29, 30: 1 Thess 1:6; 2:14; 3:3 f.; cf. 2 Thess 1:4–10) rather than to a general depression, since Barrett (219) draws attention to their flourishing trade. Yet Plummer, 233, quotes Livy (45.30) to the effect that "the Romans . . . had taken possession of the gold and silver mines . . . and had taxed the right of smelting copper and iron. . . . The Macedonians said that their nation was like a lacerated and disjointed animal," though this evidence is much earlier than Paul's time. Later on Strabo, Geog. 9.5.2, describes Macedonia's topography as bearing on its economy: the plain of Thessaly is "a most fortunate land, except that much of it is subject to flooding" (πλὴν ὅση ποταμόκλυστός ἐστιν).

Comment

1. Γνωρίζομεν δὲ ὑμῖν, ἀδελφοί, τὴν χάριν τοῦ θεοῦ τὴν δεδομένην ἐν ταῖς ἐκκλησίαις τῆς Μακεδονίας, "we draw to your notice, brothers, the grace of God given to the churches of Macedonia." ἡ χάρις τοῦ θεοῦ, "the grace of God," is a key term which sets the stage for Paul's appeal to the example of the Macedonian communities and their generosity in supporting the collection for the Jerusalem saints (v 4). For this support see Rom 15:26. The opening ascription is to God's generosity (χάρις) in his gifts-in-grace (χαρίσματα: see E. Käsemann, "Ministry and Community in the New Testament," in Essays on New Testament Themes, tr. W. J. Montague [London: SCM, 1964], 64 f., who states that "other charismata only exist because of the existence of this one charisma," God's gift in Jesus Christ [Rom 6:23]). This χάρις given to his people looks ahead to 8:9 where Christ's self-offering is

in view and is seen as the act of supreme "grace." The link-term is in 8:5 where the Macedonians "gave themselves" (ἑαυτοὺς ἔδωκαν) both to the Lord and to the apostolic mission (καὶ ἡμῖν, "to us"). They did so, because of divine grace at work in (ἐν: for this preposition meaning "for," "on behalf of," see BDF § 220.1) their lives and because, as the theological basis of such self-giving makes clear, of Christ's decisive act (cf. Gal 1:4, τοῦ δόντος ἑαυτὸν ὑπὲρ τῶν ἁμαρτιῶν ἡμῶν, "who gave himself for our sins": see Hainz, *Koinonia*, 139, for some penetrating observations here. See too J. D. G. Dunn, *Jesus and the Spirit* [London: SCM Press/Philadelphia: Westminster, 1975] 202–4).

"Macedonia" here refers to the Roman province in northern Greece, extending from Apollonia in the west to Philippi in the east. Its place in Paul's mission is important, as Phil 4:15 testifies (see R. P. Martin, *Philippians*, NCB [1976 = 1980] 165, for details). The relation between "grace" and the Macedonian generosity is none too clear, so Paul proceeds to explain.

2. ὅτι ἐν πολλῇ δοκιμῇ θλίψεως ἡ περισσεία τῆς χαρᾶς αὐτῶν καὶ ἡ κατὰ βάθους πτωχεία αὐτῶν ἐπερίσσευσεν εἰς τὸ πλοῦτος τῆς ἁπλότητος αὐτῶν, "how that in much testing by reason of adversity, the welling up of their joy and their deepdown poverty have flowed out in the wealth of their generosity." "How that" is not spelled out except by ὅτι. Paul's thought is moving on to consider the example he has invoked. The Macedonians had undergone "much testing" (δοκιμή, as in 2:9; 13:3, but the reference is quite different). "Adversity" is θλῖψις as in 1:8, but again the setting is obviously not the same. Their affliction is related to their extreme poverty (ἡ κατὰ βάθους πτωχεία αὐτῶν, lit., "down to the depth," which Barrett happily renders "rock-bottom"). By contrast Paul writes of their "overflow of joy" (περισσεία τῆς χαρᾶς) which "overflows" (ἐπερίσσευσεν: note the tautology) in an expression of rich generosity (note the paradox of poverty spilling over into wealth, πλοῦτος, which is obviously not material but relates to a richness that pertains to a generous spirit that loves to give and whose giving is not measured by the amount but by the sacrifice entailed). "Joy in trial" was a feature of both the Philippian and Thessalonian churches (Phil 4:4; 1 Thess 1:6).

ἁπλότης, "generosity," could be translated more strictly "singleness, simplicity, sincerity" (as in 1:12, *v.l.;* 11:3; cf. 9:11: Nickle, *The Collection*, 104, 105), but there is a body of Jewish material, given in BGD, 86, that shows how piety is expressed in generosity (as in 9:11, 13 and Rom 12:8, though BGD prefer "sincere concern" as the most suitable rendering for these vv). Yet the word "tends . . . in the direction of liberality" (Barrett, 220).

3. ὅτι κατὰ δύναμιν, μαρτυρῶ, καὶ παρὰ δύναμιν, αὐθαίρετοι, "For—as I can testify—they gave up to the limit of their means and even beyond it; and did so spontaneously." The generosity in question, which is the point of the apostle's appeal, is seen further in the extent of personal cost involved. No connective joins v 2 to v 3, so the verb has to be added *ad sensum.* (They gave) κατὰ δύναμιν, "to the limit" and beyond it (παρὰ δύναμιν, cf. 1:8), as Paul knew well from his continuing association with the Philippian church. They gave not from their surplus, but out of their limited resources. See BDF § 465.2 for the parenthesis. Moreover they gave αὐθαίρετοι, "of their own accord," a rare term used also in 8:17, and so their giving was made

"freely, spontaneously" (2 Macc 6:19; 3 Macc 6:6). Héring disputes the latter word (59), remarking that Paul had to request them to raise the collection in vv 3, 4. But where is this idea? we may ask.

4. μετὰ πολλῆς παρακλήσεως δεόμενοι ἡμῶν τὴν χάριν καὶ τὴν κοινωνίαν τῆς διακονίας τῆς εἰς τοὺς ἁγίους, "begging us with great insistence that they might have the privilege of joining in the act of service to the [Jerusalem] saints." Rather it is the Macedonians who "begged" (δεόμενοι; on the participle, functioning as an indicative, see C. F. D. Moule, "Peculiarities in the Language of II Corinthians," in his *Essays in New Testament Interpretation* [Cambridge: University Press, 1982] 158–61) Paul for the privilege (χάριν) of sharing (κοινωνίαν) in this service (διακονίας) on behalf of the fund to aid the Jerusalem church in its poverty. These latter persons are called the "saints" in their need (for this title, see Rom 15:25, 26; 1 Cor 16:1, 2; 2 Cor 9:12; and Keck, "The Poor"). For the reasons proposed for their poverty, see Martin, *Worship of God*, 69, 70, with reference to K. Holl's influential essay in which he argues that "poor" and "saints" are self-conscious designations linking poverty and piety and establishing the claim to maintenance as a sacral duty laid on Paul's mission churches. But Leuba, *NT Pattern*, 117–20, has seriously questioned this; and these criticisms have been reinforced by W. D. Davies, *The Gospel*, 199. See too the following *Note*, pp. 256–58.

χάρις, κοινωνία, διακονία are three key words in this discussion, detailed at length by Nickle, *The Collection*, 105–11; Hainz, *Koinonia*, 132–41. We should refuse to treat them as simple synonyms for the collection, though they do overlap in the range of their possible nuances. We have taken χάρις here as a human privilege, a gracious act, while recognizing that it has a theological underpinning, i.e., the Macedonians have acted in response to divine grace which prompts and disposes all human endeavor. The thought goes back to 8:1.

κοινωνία is not only a sharing or gaining of fellowship with others, but it conveys rather the idea of participation in the objective reality, the religious good (so E. Lohmeyer on Phil 1:5, cited by Hainz, 94, 95, and discussed in R. P. Martin, *Philippians* [TNTC, rev. ed. 1986] Introduction), which gives the basis and the norm by which the sharing is made possible and effective. In this case the proof of the Macedonians' desire for sharing-in-fellowship was their active support of "the service," i.e., the collection (so Bachmann, 313; and especially Prümm, *Diakonia Pneumatos* 1:507 f.; κοινωνία, he says, signifies the notion of having a share in fellowship in a work, which in this text is precisely "the service" of the collection). So διακονία, all commentators are agreed, stands for the offering that Paul was minded to collect from his people at Corinth to support the Jerusalem community. But, as we saw, since his apostolic standing was in question there and since too the collection from gentile believers to aid Jerusalem would be regarded as a seal of his apostleship, he attached great significance to this act, giving it an "ecclesiological interpretation," as Hainz remarks (139). On κοινωνία see further R. P. Martin in *IBD*, pt. 1, under "Communion," 307, 308, with special reference to A. R. George, *Communion with God*, and J. M. McDermott, "Koinonia."

5. καὶ οὐ καθὼς ἠλπίσαμεν ἀλλὰ ἑαυτοὺς ἔδωκαν πρῶτον τῷ κυρίῳ καὶ ἡμῖν διὰ θελήματος θεοῦ, "and they did this, not just as we had hoped, but most

importantly by giving themselves to the Lord and to us, by the will of God." Some connecting verb is needed to fill a caesura in Paul's prose: "and they did so" is linked with "they gave" (v 3) and anticipates the verb "giving themselves" later in v 5. If the Macedonians had made a contribution to the collection, that would have met Paul's expectation. In the event, he goes on, that hope was surpassed. They "gave themselves to the Lord" and they "gave themselves . . . to us," two part-sentences that run in tandem, and stand under the rubric of διὰ θελήματος θεοῦ, "by the will of God," which must be read in the light of 1:1. Paul is an apostle by divine calling. The Macedonians have recognized this fact, and have yielded a submission to the Lord's authority in him (the P⁴⁶ reading "God" for "Lord" is inferior, since in this argument Paul's apostleship is defined by his relationship to Jesus Christ, 1:1: see too 1 Cor 9:1, 2; Gal 1:1, 16). Yet it is equally valid to have this statement understood in the light of 1:24 where Paul disavows any right to domineer over his people. The authority is exercised in a way that serves their good (10:8; 13:10). If this line of exegesis is sound, the giving of the Macedonians is not primarily in their initial response to the Gospel nor in their approach to God in prayer (so Héring, 59); rather what Paul is alluding to is the most important (taking πρῶτον, lit., "first," as elative, as in 1 Cor 15:3, not temporal) step of their recognizing the power of the Lord at work in Paul's ministry as a justification for the collection itself.

6. εἰς τὸ παρακαλέσαι ἡμᾶς Τίτον, ἵνα καθὼς προενήρξατο οὕτως καὶ ἐπιτελέσῃ εἰς ὑμᾶς καὶ τὴν χάριν ταύτην, "so that we requested Titus that, as he had previously begun this gracious service [for them], so he would also bring the same service to completion for you." As the Macedonians had begged a place in Paul's design to raise a contribution for Jerusalem, so on the strength of this fine example Paul will ask Titus to do at Corinth (εἰς ὑμᾶς, "for you") what he had already begun to do there, namely, to gather in the collection. The final word is ἐπιτελέσῃ . . . καὶ τὴν χάριν ταύτην: it spells out the instruction that Titus should also "complete this same service of grace" (χάρις), pointing back to vv 1, 4 and looking forward to v 7 where "grace" is the activity inspired by God's grace that leads to giving. The καί "seems unnecessary" (Barrett, 221) in the remark that Titus may *also* bring this work to completion. But there may be a link to suggest that, as Titus has acted successfully as bearer of the "Letter of Tears" (2:4) in resolving the disaffection at Corinth, so he may be encouraged to add this ministry of fund-raising to his trophies (so Fallon, 70).

Explanation

The paradox of Paul's expression, "the abundance . . . of their extreme poverty" (v 2) lies at the heart of this section; and it invites the present-day reader to see how Paul regarded the meaning of Christian commitment in the most practical area of stewardship.

The Macedonians are held up as a model of the type of giving Paul commends. Out of a firm conviction that Paul's apostolic service needed support and with an equally solid desire to enter into partnership with the Jewish mother church in its straitened condition they rallied to the call. They even overcame Paul's seeming reluctance to take money for the Jerusalem poor from them in *their* poverty-stricken state. Normally we think of the fund-raiser as "begging" the would-be donors. Here it is the donors, who could least afford it, who entreated Paul for the favor of having a part in this enterprise.

Yet Christian giving, we learn, is much more than a display of compassion and a readiness to help those in distress, however commendable those virtues are. There is the underlying theological strain that comes out in Paul's idioms—all heavily weighted on the side of divine grace and service which both sets a pattern for our giving and offers a spur to challenge us to do something tangible and costly. All giving is mirrored in God's gifts to his creatures and his children, and his gifts-in-grace (*charismata*) are such that we can use them for no higher purpose than to serve the needy people who have claim on our giving.

EXCURSUS: NOTE ON THE PAULINE COLLECTION

The best starting point in any consideration of the collection for the Jewish Christians is in Paul's own words. As part of the agreement made at Jerusalem, according to Galatians 2:10, Paul accepted responsibility for "the poor." That he took the task seriously is clear from the repeated references in later letters to a ministry involving the raising of a fund for the "poor in Jerusalem" (1 Cor 16:1-4; 2 Cor 8, 9; Rom 15:27-29) as well as his intention, declared in the story of Acts, to visit the Holy City for the purpose of handing over the money so subscribed (Acts 20:16, 22; 24:17; strangely, this aspect of his visit is not prominent in Luke's detail).

The reason for the Jerusalem church's poverty can only be guessed. It may be that the church had grown in size and, with increasing numbers of widows to care for, the relief fund was overburdened (cf. Acts 6:1-7). We know that elderly Jewish families migrated to the Holy City to spend their last days and eventually to be buried there in expectation of the resurrection of the dead. Some scholars suggest that Galilean Christians undertook a similar pilgrimage to Jerusalem to await the advent of the messiah whose appearing there was anticipated. A popular view is that the experiment of a "communism of love" (to use Troeltsch's term *"religiöse Liebeskommunismus;"* see Holmberg, *Paul and Power,* 35; but this expression and what it implies is criticized by E. Haenchen, *The Acts of the Apostles,* tr. B. Noble and G. Shinn *et al.,* completed by R. McL. Wilson [Oxford: Blackwell, 1971] 233) involving the pooling of resources and the liquidation of assets (as in Acts 4:32-37; 5:1-11) had brought impoverishment. C. H. Dodd offers this reason for the failure of the Jewish Christian experiment: "They carried it out in the economically disastrous way of realizing capital and distributing it as income" (*The Epistle of Paul to the Romans,* MNTC [London: Hodder & Stoughton, 1932] 230). On the external front, we may appeal to bad harvests reported in Judea in the mid-forties of the first century (see Acts 11:27-30); and the persecuting of the church by Jewish authorities, which may well have added to its economic and social woes.

For whatever reason—and it may well have been a combination of circumstances—the Jerusalem congregations were in real economic distress. So Paul's offer of "remembering" (that is, actively aiding) them looks at first sight to be a simple, if noble, act of charity and compassion. Paul expected his Gentile churches in Macedonia and southern Greece to rally to the support of fellow Christians in their extreme need and to help them in a most practical manner. This seems clear enough from Romans 15:26 and Paul's line of reasoning in 2 Corinthians 8:13 f. and 9:12.

Karl Holl's essay in 1928 put a fresh face on this discussion ("Der Kirchenbegriff des Paulus in seinem Verhältnis zu dem der Urgemeinde," *Gesammelte Aufsätze zur Kirchengeschichte* [Tübingen: J. C. B. Mohr, 1928] 2:44–67). He maintained that "the poor" and "the saints" were both designations not of people who were in need but of the church in Jerusalem as such. They claimed to be a "holy" people whose "poverty" was akin to the condition of the "poor in spirit" of Matthew 5:3. Their self-designated status gave them a "right" to expect financial help from the Gentile churches since they were the mother church of Christendom (Holl, loc. cit., 62, speaks of "an undoubted right of taxation" [*ein gewisses Besteuerungsrecht*]). There was precedent for the "right of taxation" in the way Jewish synagogues of the Dispersion were under legal obligation to send a Temple tax to the Holy City (Matt 17:24–27). Though he did not explicitly point to the analogy of the Jewish custom, Holl went on to argue that Paul accepted this claim, a concession betrayed in the language he chose to use in words such as "abundance" (2 Cor 8:20), "service" (2 Cor 9:12), and "collection" (1 Cor 16:1 f.). Hengel, *Acts*, 188, describes how the collection may have seemed to Jewish Christians—assuming that they knew of Paul's activity on their behalf, as 2 Cor 9:13, 14 implies. But see *Comment* there.

The case presented by Holl and others seems exaggerated (so D. Georgi, *Die Geschichte der Kollekte*, 10, 11, 17; G. Bornkamm, *Paul*, 40, 41, who writes that the levy on Jerusalem "was never a regular import [*Abgabe:* impost?] . . . [and Paul] avoided terms taken from law" [*juridische Termini*], so in original *Paulus*, 62; B. Holmberg, *Paul and Power*, 77; W. D. Davies, *The Gospel*, 199; Keck, "The Poor" [1965, 1966]; along with the older work of R. N. Flew, *Jesus and His Church* [London: Epworth, 1938] 156, 157) but it is generally admitted that the collection for the saints was more than a simple expression of charity. As we look at the texts in 2 Corinthians and Romans it appears that Paul viewed this exercise as a powerful way of demonstrating the unity of the two wings of the church, both Jewish and Gentile. His appeal as "apostle to the non-Jews" was calculated to awaken in his converts a sense of gratitude for all the benefits they had received through Israel's hope in the messianic faith. Conversely, Paul fervently believed that such a sign of Gentile generosity (which was freely expressed and so gave evidence of both Gentile independence from and fellowship with Israel, according to K. Berger; "Almosen für Israel," *NTS* 23 [1976–77] 180–204 [198]) would be interpreted as a way to cement relations—often strained—between the two cultural groups and win over the Jewish Christians to the full acceptance of the validity of his own mission (see Gal 2:7–10 and Introduction, pp. lv–lviii). There is an undertone of missionary strategy here as Paul adds in the thought that the way Gentile Christians act as proof of their new life in Israel's messiah will goad the Jews into envy and encourage them to seek salvation (Rom 11:14).

There is a special dimension of this hope. It begins with the attested fact that Paul was willing to visit Jerusalem with the collection in hand, being careful to surround himself with a large number of Gentile Christians (cf. Acts 20:4). This was partly to protect the money (we assume); but more especially, it was to safeguard his reputation lest it be damaged by innuendo that he was not to be trusted with sums of money. It is clear, too, that Paul was ready for this journey even though he feared that he would not be welcomed by the Jewish Christian leadership and would be exposed to danger at Jerusalem (Rom 15:31). One side of the matter is that Paul was acting in a representative manner in offering "alms for Israel" as part of the notion that God-fearing Gentiles were encouraged to help the poor in Israel in order to express a desire to share in their faith in one God. There is evidence that some believed that such charitable gestures might make up for a lack of being circumcised, and serve to admit uncircumcised yet pious Gentiles into the covenant of Israel. If this is so, Paul's action was a powerful plea to have his Gentile churches accepted as a true part of the Israel of God. The use of idioms that Holl called attention to may thus be explained, even if there are other terms such as "brotherly love," "fellowship," "fair shares for all" (but see Georgi's interpretation in our *Comment* on 8:13, 14) that speak more of a human concern to stretch out a helping hand. The slightly flavored sacred-legal language may well be accounted for as Paul's way of overcoming resistance to the collection—especially at Corinth, where there seemed to have been a reluctance to accept responsibility, as we shall see.

One remaining item falls under consideration in this connection. Johannes Munck (*Paul and the Salvation of Mankind*, 176, 193) and others have acutely noted how the presenting of the collection fits in with the winding up of the apostle's labors in the east (Rom 15:23), and have suggested that Paul regarded his mission service among these Gentile churches as successfully completed. The Jerusalem hierarchy gathered around James the Just may well have viewed this conclusion with dismay, suspicion, and fear; hence Paul's sensitivity that the gesture of the collection might be misinterpreted as though he were acting autonomously and independently of Jerusalem's claim to be God's elect people (see the hints of an animus to Paul in Acts 21:21, 28). In any event, this is how it worked out, and Paul's intention to unify the two factions of apostolic Christianity was broken on the hard rocks of increased suspicion and a reluctance of Jewish Christians to come to his defense when he was accused of fomenting trouble in the Temple area. So as an attempt to "prod the unbelieving Jews to profess faith in Christ, Paul's project was a crashing failure," as Keith F. Nickle sums up (*The Collection: A Study in Paul's Strategy*, 155). In a similar way Paul's valiant enterprise in seeking to draw Jewish Christians and their Gentile brethren together collapsed under the weight of mounting hostility, which may have resulted from pressure from Jewish nationalists, the Zealots, who aimed to close ranks against the pagans and who could well have accused the Jewish Christians of national disloyalty in consorting with so-called "converted Gentiles."

Paul's laudable aim suffered yet one more blow. His pilgrimage to Jerusalem, bearing gifts from the nations, reflects the prophetic picture of the last days (Isa 2:2-5; 60:5-22; Mic 4), as the rabbis believed. Then, it was hoped, the obedience of the Gentiles would lead to the renewal of Israel and the onset of the new age of eschatological joy and blessedness. Paul's own work as an apostle would be validated by this climactic result, as he headed the large retinue of Gentile delegates to the Holy City (Acts 20:4). His thinking seems to oscillate between the expectation of Israel's conversion (Rom 11:26) and his continuing desire to evangelize in Rome and Spain (Rom 15:24), but clearly the two are interrelated. Thus Paul views the offering of the collection as both a "salvation-historical" validation of his own ministry against his detractors and a means of "eschatological provocation" leading to national Israel's jealousy and turning to God. Alas, here again Paul's best hopes were doomed and crushed on the anvil of Israel's continued "hardness" and "blindness" and his own increasing disfavor among his compatriots.

B. The Appeal to the Corinthians (8:7–15)

Bibliography

Barrett, C. K. "Titus." *Essays on Paul*, chap. 7. 118–31. **Betz, H.-D.** *Nachfolge und Nachahmung Jesu Christi im Neuen Testament*. BHT 37. Tübingen: J. C. B. Mohr, 1967. **Bischoff, A.** "Exegetische Randbermerkungen," *ZNW* 9 (1908) 168. **Craddock, F.** "The Poverty of Christ. An Investigation of II Corinthians 8:9." *Int* 22 (1968) 158–70. **Dahl, N. A.** "Anamnesis: Memory and Commemoration in Early Christianity." In *Jesus in the Memory of the Early Church*, 11–29. Minneapolis: Augsburg Publishing House, 1976. ———. "Form-critical Observations on Early Christian Preaching." In *Jesus in the Memory of the Early Church*, 30–36. Minneapolis: Augsburg Publishing House, 1976. **de Boer, W. P.** *The Imitation of Paul*. Kampen: Kok, 1962, 61 f. **Dunn, J. D. G.** *Christology in the Making*. London: SCM Press/Philadelphia: Westminster Press, 1980. ———. *Jesus and the Spirit*. London: SCM Press/Philadelphia: Westminster Press, 1975. **Dupont, J.** "Pour vous le Christ s'est fait pauvre (2 Cor. 8:7, 9, 13–15)" *AsSeign* 44 (1969) 32–37. **Feuillet, A.** "L'homme—Dieu considéré dans sa condition terrestre." *RB* 51 (1942) 70–73. ———. *Christologie paulinienne et tradition biblique*. Paris: Editions du Cerf, 1972. **Hanson, A. T.** *The Image of the Invisible God*. London: SCM Press, 1982. **Hamerton-Kelly, R. G.** *Pre-existence, Wisdom, and the Son of Man*. SNTSMS 21. Cambridge: University Press, 1973. **Kramer, W.** *Christ, Lord, Son of God*. Tr. Brian Hardy. SBT 50. London: SCM Press, 1966. **Larsson, E.** *Christus als Vorbild*. Tr. B. Steiner, ASNU 23. Uppsala: Gleerup, 1962. **Meeks, W. A.** *The First Urban Christians*. New Haven and London: Yale University Press, 1983. **Moffatt, J.** *Grace in the New Testament*. London: Hodder and Stoughton, 1932. **Nickle, K. F.** *The Collection*. 18, 109 f., 126 ff. **Ross, A.** "The Grace of our Lord Jesus Christ." *EvQ* 13 (1941) 219–25. **Schrage, W.** *Die konkreten Einzelgebote in der paulinischen Paränese*. Gütersloh: G. Mohn, 1961. **Theissen, G.** *The Social Setting of Pauline Christianity*. Tr. J. H. Schütz. Philadelphia: Fortress, 1982. **Veilhauer, Ph.** *Geschichte der urchristlichen Literatur*. Einleitung in das neue Testament, usw. New York & Berlin: de Gruyter, 1975.

Translation

⁷*And now, just as you overflow in every [grace-gift]—in faith, in speech, in knowledge, in all eagerness and in the love that we have aroused in you—,* ᵃ *make sure that you overflow in this gracious service as well.* ⁸*I am saying this not as an order, but I am seeking to try out the reality of your love also by using the eagerness of others [as a standard].* ⁹*For you know the generosity of our Lord Jesus Christ who—for your sakes and though he was wealthy—became poor, so that you by that poverty might become wealthy.* ¹⁰*So it is then only an opinion I am giving you in this matter; for this advice befits you, you who last year were those who were the first* ᵇ *not only to undertake this action but also to decide on it.* ¹¹*Now complete the undertaking, so that the performance matches the readiness of your decision, as your means allow.* ¹²*For if the readiness is there, this is acceptable in accordance with what a person has [to offer], not in accordance with what a person does not.* ¹³*Indeed, it is not a question of relieving others at the expense of your own affliction, but it is a matter of fair shares.* ᶜ ¹⁴*At the present time and in the circumstances, your surplus will meet their deficiency, so that then their surplus may meet your deficiency; in this*

way there will be fair shares all round. [15] *This is in line with Scripture: "He who collected much did not have too much, and he who collected little lacked nothing."*

Notes

[a] Most MSS have ἐξ ὑμῶν ἐν ἡμῖν, "your love to us" (so ℵ C D F G ψ TR lat syr), but this is the simpler reading, whereas ἐξ ἡμῶν ἐν ὑμῖν is the more difficult reading and so it is preferred. It is read by P[46] B and cop[sa,bo] as well as some church fathers. Yet the more expected reading has an attestation that is widespread. We have followed Bratcher in translation, though his *Translator's Guide* gives the RSV, GNB/TEV, NIV rendering. The latter is "your [love] for us." See Harris, 369.

[b] προενήρξασθε (ℵ B C K L P) should be read in place of the smoother ἐνήρξασθε (D F G). See 8:6.

[c] There is an alternative way to add punctuation here. The UBS text places a full stop (period) after θλῖψις, thus making the next phrase ἀλλ᾽ ἐξ ἰσότητος to be joined to v 14. The reading is thus produced: "it is not a question of relieving others at the expense of your own affliction, but as a matter of fair shares (ἐξ ἰσότητος), at the present time . . . etc." This construction is less preferable.

Form/Structure/Setting

The same group of literary features that we observed in 8:1–6 is in evidence in this section: certain anacolutha (in vv 13, 17, where the verb "to be" has to be added), a cryptic style of writing seen in v 11, and in particular an ambiguous use of ἵνα to denote either final clauses or statements of command (v 13). All these items make for a very confused passage whose sense, while tolerably clear, is far from certain. There is a note of dialectic which has been traced in this Pauline argumentation (Georgi, *Die Geschichte der Kollekte,* 66, 67).

Let us set the scene of these vv. Paul is caught in the middle of two extremes. He wishes, on the one hand, to urge the Corinthians to complete the task of the collection for the saints which they had earlier begun, at the time of Titus's previous visit (vv 6, 10: these vv refer to a visit during the previous winter while Paul was in Ephesus: so Luedemann, *Paul,* 93, n. 175, against Vielhauer, *Geschichte,* 145, who thinks of *two* previous visits of Titus, the first to deal with the collection [8:6; 12:17 ff.], the second to win back the Corinthians with the "tearful letter"). In this act they will prove the genuineness of their love (v 8) as they bring the "work of grace" (χάρις) to its completion (v 11). Paul is not averse to employing an imperative verb form to drive home his appeal (v 7: "see that you *overflow* in this gracious work as well" as in the cultivating of the well known Corinthian charismata; see 1 Cor 12–14). On the other side, he writes delicately, not wishing to issue an order (v 8) and not allowing his appeal to the Macedonians who gave "beyond their power" (8:3) to "embarrass" his readers. So he writes (v 12) on the acceptability (by God) of a gift which is based on what a person has and not (as was evidently the case with the heroic sacrifice of the Macedonians) determined by what such a person does not have. The latter phrase οὐ καθὸ οὐκ ἔχει, "not in accordance with what a person does not have" (v 12) matches what he wrote (in v 11) in calling for a fulfillment of their pledge ἐκ τοῦ ἔχειν, literally, "out of what you have." This is seemingly a tactful aside suggesting he is not calling for a superhuman effort like the Macedonian example (Windisch, 256).

Instead of issuing a mandate, Paul firmly sets his appeal on the principle of reciprocity (vv 13–15), based on an Old Testament text (using LXX). The Gentiles are in debt to Israel (Rom 15:27). Let them honor that obligation by sharing their surplus to match Jewish penury in time of need. The obverse point is then made: what is true now ἐν τῷ νῦν καιρῷ, "in this age"—if the phrase has the quasi-technical sense of Rom 3:24; 8:13; 11:5—will (so Georgi, *Die Geschichte*, 65) give place to a new situation when the riches of Israel will be available to the Gentiles. This is a thought which, if it is not purely hypothetical (so Héring, 61) and required by the principle of *quid pro quo*, has to be understood in the light of Paul's expectation in Romans 11:12, 15, concerning the restoration of Israel and the promise of life from the dead by which Gentiles will benefit (see R. P. Martin, *Reconciliation: A Study of Paul's Theology*, 132–35). But, it has to be conceded that the turning of the Corinthians' money gift designed to help famine-racked Jerusalem into the eschatological hope of spiritual bounties at the climax of the ages seems a vast shift of thought—at least to us. Incidentally, Paul is content elsewhere (Rom 15:26, 27) simply to let one thought stand, without a complementary idea that "God's people in Jerusalem" could ever enrich the gentile believers. Yet two points should not be overlooked: (1) Paul may well have expected the dénouement of history when he brought the collection to Jerusalem, and the Gentile delegates presented their offerings in fulfillment of Old Testament-rabbinic anticipation; and (2) at 8:9 he does glide from the "grace" of God (8:1) to the Corinthians' making good their promise of a generous gift (v 7) by means of an appeal to the unrivaled act of Incarnation in which the Lord Jesus Christ gave up his wealth to assume our poverty. This is "a daring but characteristic argument" (Bruce, 222). Here surely "wealth" and "poverty" are ciphers not for material prosperity and penury but for a spiritual "exchange," as the incarnate Christ became what we are in order to make us what he is, to use Irenaeus's formulation. Our becoming rich by his lowly Incarnation cannot be understood otherwise, and this illustration shows how Paul's mind can oscillate between material goods (in helping the Jerusalem saints) and spiritual enrichments that come into human experience both in fellowship with Christ now and, by a restored Israel, in God's good and future time.

Comment

7. Ἀλλ' ὥσπερ ἐν παντὶ περισσεύετε, πίστει καὶ λόγῳ καὶ γνώσει καὶ πάσῃ σπουδῇ καὶ τῇ ἐξ ἡμῶν ἐν ὑμῖν ἀγάπῃ, ἵνα καὶ ἐν ταύτῃ τῇ χάριτι περισσεύητε, "And now, just as you overflow in every [grace-gift]—in faith, in speech, in knowledge, in all eagerness and in the love that we have aroused in you—, make sure that you overflow in this gracious service as well." Paul grants that he is writing to a congregation rich in *charismata* (cf. 1 Cor 1:7, Dunn, *Jesus and the Spirit*, 266, 267). Their claim—which he does not dispute—was to have "excelled" (on περισσεύειν as a Corinthian term, see R. P. Martin, *The Spirit and the Congregation*, 154, n. 13). The catalogue of these attainments

runs as follows: they were enriched in "faith" (πίστις: 1 Cor 12:9; 13:12, 13: see *The Spirit and the Congregation*, 11, 12, 44, which draws on the distinction between "saving faith" [*Kerygmaglaube*] and "wonderworking faith" [*Wunderglaube*]); "speech" (or eloquence, λόγος); "knowledge," γνῶσις, a prime Corinthian asset, as they claimed. (The word γνῶσις is found sixteen times in 1, 2 Cor: with "speech" a couplet associated in 1 Cor 1:5). Then follow two qualities which had been questioned at the time of the Corinthians' disaffection from Paul: their "zeal" (σπουδή: see 7:7, 12) and "love" (ἀγάπη: for the curious expression τῇ ἐξ ἡμῶν ἐν ὑμῖν ἀγάπῃ, "the love I have inspired in you," Héring, 59, see *Notes*). Both terms (zeal, love) refer here to the readers' attitude to the apostle. Both responses to Paul and his apostleship had been in doubt; but now Paul is confident enough of the restored relationship—otherwise called reconciliation (5:18–21; 6:1 f.)—to build on these virtues as a basis for his paraenetic call. "Make sure" renders the imperatival ἵνα (see H. G. Meecham, "The Imperative Use of ἵνα in the NT," *JTS* o.s. [43, 1942] 179, 180; Plummer, 238, citing 2 Macc 1:9): "that you overflow (περισσεύητε, matching the earlier mention of the same verb) in this gracious service (χάρις) *as well*" (καὶ). The καὶ is significant and ταύτῃ ("*this* gracious work") is emphatic by its position in the sentence. Paul "is anxious not to seem to be finding fault" (Plummer, 238), yet he is clear that he wants to call the Corinthians to action.

8. Οὐ κατ᾽ ἐπιταγὴν λέγω ἀλλὰ διὰ τῆς ἑτέρων σπουδῆς καὶ τὸ τῆς ὑμετέρας ἀγάπης γνήσιον δοκιμάζων, "I am saying this not as an order, but I am seeking to try out the reality of your love also by using the eagerness of others [as a standard]." Paul's thought turns to the Corinthian readers, for whose sake he has introduced the example of the Macedonians. The delicateness of Paul's language (οὐ κατ᾽ ἐπιταγὴν λέγω: "I am saying this not as an order": see 1 Cor 7:6, 25 for the same permissive style of writing) shows how he sensed the need to handle tactfully those who had just come back to his side. V 10 will reiterate this kind of oblique writing. Nonetheless what is at stake is the reality (lit., "testing [for δοκιμάζειν, see 13:5] the genuine love of yours") of their commitment to his apostolic mission, to see whether it is of the same caliber as the Macedonians': hence καὶ, "also," joins the two groups. Our translation tries to make the connection even clearer by an extra verb ("using"). Paul has no doubt about the genuine love (ἀγάπης γνήσιον) of the Macedonian churches shown in their zeal (σπουδή) for the collection. Now he wishes to be certain that the Corinthians share the same quality, both of love and zeal (reverting to 7:7, 12: it is zeal for Paul's cause that is in mind). "The example of the Macedonians provides a criterion for testing the reality of their love for him and their fellow Christians" (Fallon, 71).

9. γινώσκετε γὰρ τὴν χάριν τοῦ κυρίου ἡμῶν Ἰησοῦ Χριστοῦ, ὅτι δι᾽ ὑμᾶς ἐπτώχευσεν πλούσιος ὤν, ἵνα ὑμεῖς τῇ ἐκείνου πτωχείᾳ πλουτήσητε, "For you know the generosity of our Lord Jesus Christ who—for your sakes and though he was wealthy—became poor, so that you by that poverty might become wealthy." Possibly the mention of ἀγάπη, "love," prompts Paul to appeal to the highest illustration of love-in-action (1 Cor 13, "the hymn to love," which must also be read in a christological light: see Oda Wischmeyer, *Der höchste Weg: Das 13. Kapitel des 1. Korintherbriefes* [Gütersloh: Gütesloher Verlagshaus,

1981], summarized in Martin, *The Spirit and the Congregation*, chap. 3). The reminder offered in the introducing verb γινώσκετε, "you know," is typical of the biblical usage where recourse is made to a paradigm of divine action in order to enforce an ethical call (see N. A. Dahl, "Anamnesis"). This is to be preferred to M. E. Thrall's interpretation which argues that the γὰρ in v 9 looks back to the ἵνα καὶ ἐν ταύτῃ τῇ χάριτι περισσεύητε in v 7 (*Greek Particles*, 93).

At the heart of Paul's invocation is the "grace of our Lord Jesus Christ" (a full liturgical title, suggesting the use of a creedal sentence: Kramer, *Christ, Lord, Son of God*, 66*b*, comments: "the full christological titles are well suited . . . to the solemnity of liturgical language, and that is why they are used in places where Paul is writing in an elevated style"). "Grace" (χάρις) is normally associated with Pauline introductory formulas and benedictions; here it carries the theological weight of a divine attribute, namely, love in action, expressed on sinners' behalf and reaching out to help the undeserving (see J. Moffatt, *Grace*, passim; R. P. Martin, *s.v.* "Grace" in *Dictionary of the Bible and Religion* [Nashville: Abingdon, 1986]). Christ's pretemporal life (cf. Dunn, *Christology*, 121–23, for an attempt to dispute this; but it is no more successful here than in Phil 2:6 for identical reasons, namely, only one who shared the divine existence in eternity may be said to exercise a choice to abandon it in a lowly Incarnation) is here expressed as "being rich" (πλούσιος ὤν; cf. ὑπάρχων in Phil 2:6: see my *Carmen Christi*[2], xx, xxi, 65, n. 2, for the evidence that ὑπάρχειν and εἶναι are virtual equivalents in *koine* Greek). The riches of Christ, then, are "His pre-existent status" (Héring, 60; cf. Plummer, 241: "the pre-existence of Christ is plainly taught here, as in Gal iv.5": see too M. Hengel, *The Son of God*, tr. John Bowden; and against Dunn, ibid., see A. T. Hanson, *The Image of the Invisible God*, 64–66) tantamount to his "being in the form of God" (ἐν μορφῇ θεοῦ ὑπάρχων). See further R. G. Hamerton-Kelly, *Pre-existence*, 150 f.; F. Craddock, "The Poverty of Christ," and idem, *The Pre-existence of Christ in the New Testament* (Nashville: Abingdon, 1968) 99–106.

The incarnational event is next depicted: "he became poor" (ἐπτώχευσεν: we may ask, Is the choice of this verb linked with οἱ πτωχοί, "the poor," of the Jerusalem church? Our hesitation to say yes is based on the fact that Paul's favorite expression is "collection for the *saints*," rather than "the poor": 1 Cor 16:1; 2 Cor 8:4, 5; Rom 15:25, 31). The aorist is ingressive, i.e., he took poverty as his lot (Moffatt, *Grace*, 191), but the meaning has still to be unpacked. Did he identify with us in our human condition of need (cf. Rom 8:3; Gal 4:4), or with the life of the (economically) "poor" whom he—as the Jesus in the Gospels—came to bless (Luke 4:18; 6:20; 7:22), or with the "poor in spirit," the trustful souls whose only hope lay in God, the so-called *anawim*? The last option seems the most likely—if Paul has the historical Jesus in view, as Dunn (*Christology*) maintains, appealing to Mark 10:28–30; Matt 8:20; Luke 9:58. But that assumption is by no means certain, and it could be the text is simply emphasizing the contrast "rich/poor" to accent the stupendous condescension involved in Christ's becoming human. If this interpretation is correct, it is not social status or economic deprivation or membership of one religious group that is in view. Paul wants to drive home

the single point that the Lord of glory took the form of a human being
"for your sake" (δι᾿ ὑμᾶς, in the emphatic position; Plummer, 240). And thereby
he has created the possibility—Paul's argument proceeds according to a "tel-
eological pattern" (Dahl, "Form-critical Observations," 35, 36)—that the Corinthian readers who see Christ's weakness (13:4) in his self-chosen "poverty,"
which he embraced by forsaking his heavenly glory, will be stirred to "act
out" their faith—here called "being rich" (as in 6:10; 9:11)—by contributing
to the needy saints in Jerusalem. See Meeks, *First Urban Christians*, 65, 66.
The citation in this passage is motivated by Paul's desire in v 8, which is to
test the sincerity of their love. Here is the criterion and norm by which they
may do that, he remarks. As they realize what their calling is in Christ—
and how they came to be in him—so they will see the imperative call: "This
is what you ought to do." (V 10 is a verse that functions exactly as Phil
2:12 does, i.e., to enforce the kerygmatic statement in Phil 2:5–11 by a call
to obedience. So in v 11, "now complete your action.") See Betz, *Nachfolge*,
177, 178, on the paraenetic appeal to God's saving act, not Jesus' earthly
life. Larsson, *Christus als Vorbild*, 234, argues to the contrary: "The unex-
pressed but unavoidable conclusion is that the Corinthians should part
with their earthly goods for the benefit of others. They should take the
behavior of Christ (*Handlungsweise Christi*) as their example (*zum Vorbild*)."
But this interpretation reads a lot into Paul's formulaic and evidently traditional words.

10. καὶ γνώμην ἐν τούτῳ δίδωμι. τοῦτο γὰρ ὑμῖν συμφέρει, οἵτινες οὐ μόνον τὸ
ποιῆσαι ἀλλὰ καὶ τὸ θέλειν προενήρξασθε ἀπὸ πέρυσι, "So it is then only an opinion
I am giving you in this matter; for this advice befits you, you who last year
were those who were the first not only to undertake this action but also to
decide on it." Paul's hesitancy in appearing too forceful is mirrored once
more: καὶ γνώμην ἐν τούτῳ δίδωμι, "so it is then only an opinion I am giving
[you]." The next few words, "for this is expedient for you," may be taken
in one of two ways of rendering τοῦτο γὰρ ὑμῖν συμφέρει. Is it the advice expressed as an opinion of Paul, or is τοῦτο the collection itself because, as
they at Corinth act to gather it in and send it, so thereby their genuine
love and earnestness will become apparent? Probably the former is the simpler
choice (Lietzmann, 134, 135; against Windisch, 254, and Barrett, 224). The
next problem is more thorny. Why is the decision or intention (τὸ θέλειν)
to make the collection apparently considered to be more important than is
the execution (τὸ ποιῆσαι: the issue was noted by Bischoff in 1908)? Obviously
Paul is harking back to what took place "a year ago" (see *Form/Structure/
Setting*). Now he is seeking to enforce an appeal as altogether in their best
interests (συμφέρει: see on 12:1, BGD 780). See 9:2: "I boasted concerning
you to the Macedonians, saying that Achaia was ready a year ago"—ἀπὸ πέρυσι,
as here. For the possibilities of meaning of this expression, see Allo, lvii–lx,
218, 219, who maximizes the interval between 1 and 2 Cor to nearly two
years, whereas Bachmann, Windisch, and Harris, 306, 307, opt for eighteen
or nineteen months' interval. But these attempts to be precise are largely
unconvincing since Paul is obscure here. What is required is sufficient length
of time to fit in Paul's interim visit to Corinth, the sending of the "tearful
letter" on his return to Ephesus, the danger of 2 Cor 1:8 f., the trip to

Troas and on to Macedonia where he met Titus. Luedemann, *Paul*, 97, 98, postulates sixteen months between the Corinthians' letter to Paul in Ephesus and the writing of 2 Corinthians, i.e., the spring of one year followed by the summer of the next year. See also Luedemann, 263. If this setting holds the key to understanding, then the inference is: you ought not to let me down. I know you had the determination to act then (according to 1 Cor 16:1–4); now turn that good idea which you were the first (προ–in the verb προενήρξασθε: alternatively, προ–implies that the Corinthians had begun to gather the collection *before* Titus came on the scene [Barrett, 225]; this is less likely) to think up into practical effect. So Paul in a tortuous piece of Greek (see Robertson, *Grammar*, 425) is giving a veiled compliment to his readers who needed no pressure to give a year ago. He calls on them to implement their eagerness without any further admonition on his part. He is appealing to their already avowed determination—and knows he has a personal stake in their willingness to carry through, "to convert their readiness in principle for the collection into action" (Luedemann, *Paul*, 97). This "compliment" is shown further by Paul's use of οἵτινες, which is more than a simple relative pronoun (οἵ). It carries the sense, "You were the kind of people" (Moule, *Idiom Book*, 124; Plummer 242: "the force of οἵτινες must . . . be preserved"). See too Barrett, "Titus," 125, 126.

11. νυνὶ δὲ καὶ τὸ ποιῆσαι ἐπιτελέσατε, ὅπως καθάπερ ἡ προθυμία τοῦ θέλειν, οὕτως καὶ τὸ ἐπιτελέσαι ἐκ τοῦ ἔχειν, "Now complete the undertaking, so that the performance matches the readiness of your decision, as your means allow." So ἐπιτελέσατε, "complete," must be a mild injunction, with τὸ ποιῆσαι, the direct object: "now complete the undertaking," and with the verb picking up the summons to Titus "to complete" the service (χάρις). The v goes on to mark the virtues of the Corinthians which Paul wished to see conjoined: the readiness (προθυμία, repeated in vv 12, 19; 9:2) to desire (τὸ θέλειν) and the readiness to bring such intentions to fruition (τὸ ἐπιτελεῖσθαι). The disclaimer is, "as your means allow" (ἐκ τοῦ ἔχειν, lit. "out of what you have"), but this sounds banal, so Héring, 61; yet the phrase must carry a meaning like this (BDF § 403) and be Paul's concession that he is not requiring his readers to emulate the Macedonians to the point of heroic sacrifice (Windisch, 257). Again, Paul's sensitivity to the delicate pastoral situation at Corinth is in evidence. He does not wish to appear to be taking advantage of the new situation in which the Corinthians have repented of their opposition and moved back to his side (7:9, 11).

12. εἰ γὰρ ἡ προθυμία πρόκειται, καθὸ ἐὰν ἔχῃ εὐπρόσδεκτος, οὐ καθὸ οὐκ ἔχει, "For if the readiness is there, this is acceptable in accordance with what a person has [to offer], not in accordance with what a person does not." His thought of not asking for a superhuman effort is continued. What counts is "eagerness" (προθυμία), i.e., willingness to do something, as Paul had earlier acknowledged (later reported in 9:2). Such a spirit, he continues, is "acceptable" (εὐπρόσδεκτος) (to God, as "pleasing"—εὐάρεστοι—to him in 5:9; or as a sacrifice under the new covenant as in Phil 4:18: δεκτήν . . . τῷ θεῷ; 1 Pet 2:5; *1 Clem* 35:5; 40:3, rather than to fellow Christians, as in Rom 15:31 which uses εὐπρόσδεκτος of the relief fund as pleasing to the recipients: but see earlier on "*Note on the Pauline Collection*"). Above all, the Corinthians'

willingness betrays conduct true to one's life in the new eschatological age (6:2).

Yet, in a realistic way, the Pauline call to give is moderated: the giving is in accordance (καθὸ) with what a person may have (ἔχῃ), not what he does not possess (οὐκ ἔχει: indicative mood, against a previous subjunctive; Robertson, *Grammar*, 967). "No one will be criticised if his modest means do not allow exceptional sacrifices" (Héring, 61). As to procedure here for assembling the collection, see 1 Cor 16:1, 2.

13. οὐ γὰρ ἵνα ἄλλοις ἄνεσις, ὑμῖν θλῖψις, ἀλλ᾽ ἐξ ἰσότητος, "Indeed, it is not a question of relieving others at the expense of your own affliction, but it is a matter of fair shares." The reason for such a common sense remark follows. "Indeed (γὰρ), it is not a question (ἵνα seems to mean this: Moule, *Idiom Book*, 145, takes its meaning as imperatival: "let there not be") of *relieving others at the expense of your own affliction.*" The two nouns (ἄνεσις, θλῖψις) have already been before the reader in a different context (2:13; 7:5; see too 1:8; 4:17; 8:2), and suggest that these two notions are dominating Paul's outlook. He is reflecting on past experience, in Ephesus where he encountered θλῖψις (1:8), and in Troas where he endured no ἄνεσις, "release from pressure." Now with these experiences behind him, he has no wish to lay burdens on others. (Possibly we hear here a rumble of some objection to his apostolic ministry, voiced at Corinth [Bruce, 233]. Cf. 12:16. But, to the contrary, see H.-D. Betz, *Apostel Paulus*, 116, n. 538, who finds no allusion to the collection in chaps. 10–13.) Hence his call is for "fair shares" (ἰσότης, to be added to Dahl's inventory of words referring to the collection, "Paul and Possessions," 37, 38). The term ἰσότης here and v 14 means "equality, fair dealing" and is linked with justice or righteousness (δικαιοσύνη) in Philo, *Spec. Leg.* 4.231. But in Philo, *Quis Rer. Div. Her.* 141–206 (cited in Windisch, 258; Stählin, *TDNT* 3:343–56; Georgi, *Geschichte der Kollekte*, 62–66; cf. Barrett, 226, 227) the term suggests divine power. Georgi, then, wants to see here an appeal to God's power as providing the basis for Paul's ideal, as if the text read "from God" (ἐκ θεοῦ). This is possible on the ground that it makes sense of the following v where Paul will declare that in the future (to contrast with ἐν τῷ νῦν καιρῷ, "in the present age") Gentiles will be enriched by Jerusalem's overflow—and this hope is what Paul's *heilsgeschichtlich* theology (Rom 9–11) promised as part of his understanding of how divine righteousness works, and it is not simply a human sense of "fair shares" all round, conceived as an altruistic feature. But this may be to overinterpret the text. Yet v 14 shows that Paul's thought is eschatologically controlled.

At all events, Paul is calling for a share of mutual regard and helpfulness on the part of the Corinthians to benefit Jerusalem with a future reversal of roles in prospect. But it is hardly the case that "it was not inconceivable for the Jerusalem Christians some day to become the donors of financial aid and the Corinthian Christians the recipients" (Harris, 370, who virtually dismisses this possibility, preferring with Allo, 220 and Nickle, *The Collection*, 120, 121, to think in terms of Jerusalem's spiritual fullness in the future in whose blessings the Corinthians would come to share. The emphasis, however, on material blessings from the mother church is championed by Plummer, 245; Héring, 61; Windisch, 260; and Lietzmann, 135; but with varying degrees of conviction). What follows is difficult; yet it will help us to set v 13 in perspective.

14. ἐν τῷ νῦν καιρῷ τὸ ὑμῶν περίσσευμα εἰς τὸ ἐκείνων ὑστέρημα, ἵνα καὶ τὸ ἐκείνων περίσσευμα γένηται εἰς τὸ ὑμῶν ὑστέρημα, ὅπως γένηται ἰσότης, "At the present time and in the circumstances, your surplus will meet their deficiency, so that then their surplus may meet your deficiency; in this way there will be fair shares all around." Most likely ἐν τῷ νῦν καιρῷ, "at the present time" (cf. Rom 3:26: ἐν τῷ νῦν καιρῷ: see references in R. P. Martin, *Reconciliation* 81–89) is the existing period of eschatological reality when God is righteous (δίκαιος) and justifies the ungodly who have faith in Jesus. That is, it is the era of gentile freedom-in-grace, offered to those who trust Paul's law-free Gospel. But grace imposes obligation. So the Corinthians, out of their surplus (περίσσευμα: hardly economic prosperity; rather it is their enrichments-by-grace as in 1 Cor 1:7: see above on the verb [περισσεύειν, p. 261]. It is really beside the point to allude here to the presence of some wealthy church members at Corinth: 1 Cor 1:26; 11:17–22; Rom 16:23; Theissen, *Social Setting*, 99–110) have a chance to demonstrate concern for ethnic Israel in her want, both in physical distress but also in her parlous condition *extra Christum*.

The connecting ἵνα looks on to what Paul expected in the coming age when (according to Rom 11:11, 12) Israel's reconciliation will be a vindication (δικαίωσις) of God's purpose to bless the world, and that event will presage the final homecoming of the nations (Rom 11:25, 26, 30–32). This is obviously a tremendous theological affirmation which, although expressed succinctly in v 14, merits wider treatment, which Paul will give in Rom 9–11, written only a short while later in his life. See *"Note on Israel's Salvation and the Gentiles' Reconciliation,"* pp. 268–70.

15. καθὼς γέγραπται· ὁ τὸ πολὺ οὐκ ἐπλεόνασεν, καὶ ὁ τὸ ὀλίγον οὐκ ἠλαττόνησεν, "This is in line with Scripture: 'He who collected much did not have too much, and he who collected little lacked nothing.' " Justification for this arrangement uniting the "now" and the "then" in respect of the Gentiles' share in Israel's blessings is sought in Old Testament Scripture (Exod 16:18, LXX, cited verbatim but with a different word order and some slight variation in LXX A^{a, b}: see Windisch, 259). The gathering of the manna in Israel's desert wanderings (Exod 16:13–36) is the story pressed into service, with the detail recorded that the Israelite "who collected much did not have too much, and he who collected little lacked nothing." The OT story in the v is used illustratively (Barrett, 227) but not christologically or eschatologically as in 1 Cor 10:1–5. There is no inference drawn out concerning the Church as the new Israel sustained by manna on her journey *in via*. Instead, a novel twist is given to the OT meaning with a changed emphasis from the equal amounts gathered to an equality in the supply. But the two ideas add up to the same conclusion: provision and need ought to be matched.

Explanation

By following the Macedonian believers' splendid example, Paul's readers would prove the authentic nature of their love (v 8). But an even higher, more compelling encouragement is invoked in the next v, tacked on almost as an aside, yet arresting in the picture it gives. It tells of the pre-existing Lord of glory, who became poor by choosing to accept our earthly life (Phil 2:6–11; cf. Heb 10:5–7) and at length to give his all (Mark 10:45) for his people's eternal good. "For your sake" and "you" (in v 9) are emphatic by design. It was *for you* he laid his glory aside and gave himself to the awesome consequences of humiliation.

Bach's lines in his *Christmas Oratorio,* taken from Luther, express the thought memorably, as Lietzmann notes (134):

> Er ist auf Erden kommen arm,
> dass er unser sich erbarm,
> uns in dem Himmel mache reich
> und seinen lieben Engeln gleich.

> He has come on earth as poor
> that he might have compassion for us
> to make us rich in heaven
> and like to his beloved angels.

Some principles of Christian stewardship follow (vv 10–15). Three aspects stand out: (a) there is the primary *desideratum* of a willingness to give (see 8:3; 9:5, 7) coupled with a making good of such a promise in action. Titus's responsibility (v 6) lay precisely at this point: he is bidden to ensure that what the Corinthians pledged a year ago will be forthcoming. (b) Opportunity, expressed in the phrase "according to what a person has" (v 12), is a determining factor in the matter of the amount of giving, which is not measured by the quantity of the gift alone but by the extent of the sacrifice involved (see Mark 12:43, 44). (c) The quotation from Exod 16:18 exposes the "law" of reciprocity (v 15). Paul does not intend that the Jerusalem saints should be relieved by causing the Corinthians to be burdened (v 13). But equally, God's purpose decrees that giving to Israel will enhance that plan and move history to its appointed goal (*telos*). Paul sees the climax in Israel-of-the-future (as distinct from Israel-according-to-the-flesh, Rom 2:28, 29; 9:6–8) becoming a fountainhead of blessing to the nations (*ethnē,* "Gentiles," Rom 11:12). So the reciprocal principle works in the two ways the need requires. Aside from this specific instance, the teaching still applies: let those who have share with those who have not, so that both groups may be provided for. Paul's time-bound insight has far-reaching ramifications for our world so tragically divided into privileged—at economic, social, cultural, and educational levels— and disadvantaged.

EXCURSUS: NOTE ON ISRAEL'S SALVATION AND THE GENTILES' RECONCILIATION

Bibliography

Barth, M. *Israel and the Church.* Richmond, VA: John Knox, 1969. **Davies, W. D.** "Paul and the People of Israel." *NTS* 24 (1977–8) 4–39. ———. "Romans 11:13–

24: A Suggestion." In *Paganisme, Judaïsme, Christianisme: Mélanges offerts à Marcel Simon*, 131–44. Paris: E. de Boccard, 1978. **Ellison, H. L.** *The Mystery of Israel*. Exeter: Paternoster Press, 1968. **Käsemann, E.** "Paul and Israel." In *New Testament Questions of Today*, tr. W. J. Montague, 183–87. London: SCM Press, 1969. **Munck, J.** *Christ and Israel: An Interpretation of Romans 9–11*. Tr. Ingeborg Nixon. Philadelphia: Fortress Press, 1967. **Richardson, P.** *Israel in the Apostolic Age*. SNTSMS 10. Cambridge: University Press, 1969.

A larger question is provoked by our exegesis of 8:13, 14 since, on face value, v 14 looks ahead to the future of "Jerusalem" when believing Israelites will attain their περίσσευμα ("surplus," "abundance"). What is intended, we may ask, by this phrase in the wider context of Israel's role according to Paul's eschatology, i.e., his vision of the future? But the issue also involves Paul's understanding of the Church.

How does Israel-in-the-future fit into God's plan of salvation? Paul's starting point is that Israel's messiah (Rom 9:5) came to bless all nations (Gal 3:6–9, referring to Gen 12:1–3). Israel has always had an outer shell and an inner core of the faithful, called the "remnant" who lived by grace (Rom 11:5). God, for Paul, was seen always to be working through this responsive remnant. The apostolic kerygma as Paul proclaimed it was directed to all who would believe; they were drawn from Israel's true members (Rom 2:28, 29) and equally included, under Paul's ministry, responding Gentiles. Paul himself belonged to the first group, but accepted responsibility for the second.

God's saving plan in the future will be to graft the "Jews-as-Israel" likened to cultivated olive branches (Rom 11:24), broken off because of unbelief, into the parent stem—if they do not persist in their unbelief (11:23). Already the wild olive shoots have been inserted into the stem as a tribute to Paul's ministry (11:17— a course of action, Paul recognizes, that is "contrary to nature," v 24, since he is expressing something miraculous, not what was then horticulturally practicable; cf. Matt 3:9 and J. Munck, *Christ and Israel*, 128).

By the same miracle that grafted in wild shoots, God, it is said, can return the natural branches to the parent tree, but with the clear proviso that "they do not persist in unbelief." Paul is thus asserting two principles of ecclesiology simultaneously: (a) God's people is one and the same throughout the ages (Rom 4:12; Gal 3:6ff.)—a conclusion shared by most commentators; and the new Israel or the Church is a continuation of the original Israel, where the common element is faith in God *either* in anticipation of *or* in realization of his promise in Christ. And so Jewish Christians ought to be grateful now that they have gentile partners in the same olive tree; and Gentile Christians ought to recognize their debt to Israel and not assume a false independence because "true Israel" supports them (11:18); moreover Israel's future will enrich them in due time by accelerating the close of the age (11:5; this idea is expressed possibly in 2 Cor 8:14: "their abundance may supply your want," RSV). (b) Paul's second statement holds out the hope of a "homecoming of all the people of God" based on his illustration of the olive tree. When the natural branches (Israel *qua* people of God) and the wild olive shoots (Gentiles *qua* believers) are united, they will form one tree. Two events are needed to bring about this happy result. On the one side, "the full number of the Gentiles" will be added—there is an obvious change of metaphor in Rom 11:25, which implies that the totality of the gentile world, perhaps representatively as in Rom 11:30–32, has responded to bring about "an eschatological universalism" (Bruce, *The Epistle to the Romans*, TNTC [London: Tyndale Press, 1963] 233). On the other hand, there is the anticipation that God's acceptance of his people will be like a resurrection to life in the coming age. The promise of "life from the dead" that follows on God's admittance of Israel to the community of faith has been interpreted in two quite opposite ways (C. E. B. Cranfield, *Romans*. ICC [Edinburgh: T. & T. Clark, 1979] 2:562–72). For one group of commentators, it is a figurative expression implying that Israel's final conversion to God will lead to a spiritual renewal throughout the world. But as Cranfield is quick to point out, this view hardly agrees with Rom 11:25, 26, according to which the total number of Gentiles will have already been added *before* the turning of Israel to God, and so further enrichment of the Gentiles numerically is ruled out. The alternative is to take "life from the dead" literally and see in the phrase the resurrection that will usher in the consummation. Paul is then setting in tandem association the two eschatological "events" that will be harbingers of the end-time and the final wind-up of the ages:

> (i) Israel's fall into unbelief (11:12a), however temporary, has resulted in the "riches for the Gentiles" and "the reconciliation of the world" (11:15a);
> (ii) Israel's recovery of faith (11:12b) will lead to its "fullness" in the final resurrection of the dead and the eschaton (11:15b).

The advantages of this latter interpretation may now be assessed: (a) it sets the twin nouns "rejection"/"acceptance" in obvious parallelism, with God as the implied author in both cases; (b) it allows "reconciliation" to be taken in the sense already established in Romans 5:1–11, i.e., the breaking down of barriers of estrangement between God and sinful persons, which is the leading theme of Paul's ministry to the Gentiles (2 Cor 5:18–21). Indeed, as has been claimed (Martin, *Reconciliation: A Study of Paul's Theology*, chap. 8), "reconciliation" is *the* term par excellence for the salvation of the Gentiles in Paul's formulation; (c) it permits a second parallelism between the "full number" (πλήρωμα) of the Gentiles (Rom 11:25) and the "full inclusion" (πλήρωμα) of Israel (Rom 11:12) to be drawn, and this paves the way for (d) Paul's triumphant conclusions in Rom 11:26 and 32, which have the consummation of all things (ἀποκατάστασις πάντων) in view.

"And so (οὕτως) all Israel will be saved." There is a consensus that the text does not mean every individual Israelite, but at least "Israel as a whole" (Sanday and Headlam, *Romans*, ICC [Edinburgh: T. & T. Clark, 1902] 335). Munck relates it to "the remnant" (Rom 11:5) plus "the rest" (Rom 11:7), at present hardened in unbelief but in God's good time to be aroused from unbelief and "grafted in" (Rom 11:23) (*Christ and Israel*, 134–37). The word "all" suggests completeness embracing Jews of all ages. Further, the believing Gentiles should certainly find a place in this category since (i) they have been mentioned in Rom 11:25, and (ii) they will surely feature in Paul's universalistic thought of Rom 11:32. The phrase "all Israel" looks to be an omnibus expression covering all types of believers: elect Israelites from the beginning; responsive Gentiles who hear the message from Paul's lips; and (when the Gentiles' full tally is complete) the "Israel-of-the-future" who in faith will embrace the messianic salvation. Paul concludes, with an Old Testament citation to buttress his eschatological hope, "So in this way all Israel will be saved . . . God has consigned all men (Jews and Gentiles alike in Adam, Rom 1:18–3:20; 5:12–14) to disobedience, that he may have mercy upon all" (Jews and Gentiles alike in the new Man, Jesus Christ).

C. The Mission of Titus (8:16–24)

Bibliography

Barrett, C. K. "Titus." In *Essays on Paul.* London: SPCK, 1982. Chap. 7, 118–31.
————. "Shaliah and Apostle." *Donum Gentilicium. New Testament Essays in Honour of David Daube.* Ed. E. Bammel, C. K. Barrett, and W. D. Davies. Oxford: Clarendon Press, 1978. 88–102. **Ellis, E. E.** "Paul and his Co-workers." *NTS* 17 [1971] 437–52. Also in *Prophecy and Hermeneutic in Early Christianity.* Grand Rapids: Wm. B. Eerdmans, 1978. 3–22. **Hainz, J.** *Ekklesia.* 147–57, 244, 307–10. **Moule, C. F. D.** "Peculiarities in the Language of II Corinthians." In *Essays in New Testament Interpretation,* 158–61. Cambridge: University Press, 1982. **Nickle, K. F.** *The Collection.* SBT 48. London: SCM, 1966. 18–22. **Ollrog, W.-H.** *Paulus und seine Mitarbeiter.* WMANT 50. Neukirchen-Vluyn: Neukirchener Verlag, 1979. Chap. 3. **Roloff, J.** *Apostolat-Verkündigung-Kirche.* Gütersloh: G. Mohn, 1965. **Schweizer, E.** *Church Order in the New Testament.* Tr. Frank Clarke. SBT 32. London: SCM. 7m, 23c. **Souter, A.** "A Suggested Relationship between Titus and Luke." *ExpTim* 18 (1906–07) 280. ————. "The Relationship between Titus and Luke." *ExpTim* 18 (1906–07) 335, 336.

Translation

[16] *Now thanks be to God who puts* [a] *the same eagerness on your behalf into Titus's heart.* [17] *For he not only acceded to our request, but he is himself on his way to you with all eagerness and on his own initiative.* [18] *We are sending with him the brother who is praised throughout all the congregations for his work in the Gospel.* [19] *In addition to this he has also been appointed by the congregations to be our traveling companion* [b]*—as we fulfil this service which we are rendering for the honor of the Lord himself*[c] *—and to prove our own readiness* [to help]. [20] *We are taking this precaution to avoid being blamed by anyone for the way we administer this generous gift.* [21] *For we are concerned, then, to do the right thing, not only in the Lord's eyes but also in human eyes too.*

[22] *We are sending also with them our brother whom we have often tested and proved to be eager in many matters, and now he is all the more eager because of the great confidence he has in you.* [23] *If there is any question about Titus* [d]*—he is my partner and fellow worker among you; if there is a question of our brothers—they are the delegates of the congregations, and an honor to Christ.* [24] *For this reason, show* [e] *them the proof of your love and the reason for our pride in you, so that all the congregations can see it.*

Notes

[a]$\delta\iota\delta\acute{o}\nu\tau\iota$ is read by $\aleph$ B C Byz, but Nestle-Aland[26] prints $\delta\acute{o}\nu\tau\iota$, the aorist, with P[46] $\aleph$[3] D F G L lat bo Ambr. But the latter reading, though well supported, could reflect Titus's favorable impression on the Corinthians mentioned in 7:7 (Barrett, 217). The present is therefore preferred (so RSV; Plummer, 247).

[b]The preposition $\sigma\acute{v}\nu$ is left untranslated since it goes strangely with $\tau\hat{\eta}$ $\chi\acute{a}\rho\iota\tau\iota$; it is read by P[46] $\aleph$ D G K Byz, whereas $\acute{e}\nu$ is found in B C P lat syr[p] cop arm eth, but the latter is obviously a secondary reading, changing $\sigma\acute{v}\nu$ to the more usual preposition with a nonpersonal object. See Metzger, *Textual Commentary,* 581, 582.

[c]Nestle-Aland[26] reads $\pi\rho\grave{o}\varsigma$ $\tau\grave{\eta}\nu$ [$a\grave{v}\tauo\hat{v}$] $\tauo\hat{v}$ $\kappa\nu\rho\acute{\iota}o\nu$ $\delta\acute{o}\xi a\nu$. The bracketed $a\grave{v}\tauo\hat{v}$ is omitted by B

C D* F G L but included in א D¹ Byz which have the harder reading. Barrett (217) submits that Paul wrote αὐτοῦ and added τοῦ κυρίου but as an explanatory aside: "His—I mean, the Lord's."

ᵈ εἴτε ὑπέρ Τίτου . . . εἴτε ἀδελφοὶ ἡμῶν: for this use of the preposition, BDF § 231; and for the correlative conjunctions εἴτε . . . εἴτε, see BDF § 454.3.

ᵉ ἐνδεικνύμενοι: a participle used as an imperative (BDF § 468; Moule, *Idiom Book*, 179 f.; idem, "Peculiarities," 158 f.), though this reading (B D* E F G) is challenged by א C Dᵇ·ᶜ K L P lat and many versions which have ἐνδείξασθε. The latter is due to copyists who, overlooking the semitic idiom of the use of the participle, used a finite verb. See further Moulton, *Grammar* 3:343; Lietzmann, 137, against Windisch, 267, 268. Plummer, 252, is undecided.

Form/Structure/Setting

Lietzmann is not the only reader of these vv to remark on "the complicated presentation" (*die umständliche Vorstellung*) as Paul recommends three Christian leaders en route to Corinth. The language he uses and the stylistic traits which are evident combine to produce a piece of writing which is overweighted with heavy content. Hainz, *Ekklesia,* 148, offers a key to the style of writing in his observation that the purpose is undoubtedly polemical, with Paul having to meet opposition and suspicion on two fronts. (1) He must clear the air at Corinth of any remaining doubts regarding the integrity of his motives and actions, especially where money matters are concerned (vv 20, 21: cf. 7:2; 11:20; 12:15–18), and (2) he must pave the way for the smooth transference of the collection from his gentile congregations to Jerusalem where again a favorable reception cannot be assumed (Rom 15:30, 31). Hence the pericope of 8:16–24 is full of terms and ideas that not only indicate how trustworthy and duly accredited are the "messengers" (ἀπόστολοι) of those gentile churches but—more important—how Paul is ready to distance himself from the collection itself lest it should be thought that he had a personal stake in the matter. Yet he cannot completely dissociate himself, as v 19 makes clear, though he expresses his involvement in a cumbrous, roundabout style. See *Comment.* He therefore goes out of his way to praise Titus's eagerness (vv 16, 17), to approve the mission of an unnamed yet well-reputed "brother" whom the congregations have elected to carry the money (vv 18–20), and to ensure that a third member of the party is a person who has great confidence in the Corinthians and who is also highly recommended as the churches' authorized representative (vv 22, 23). A final thrust in this piece of writing is an exhortation to welcome these men, with a none-too-subtle undertone that in so doing Paul's readers will be proving the sincerity of their professed allegiance to the apostle himself and acting out their declared repentance and allegiance to him (7:7–16).

The apostle's appeal, however, is not directed simply to his own appraisal of the integrity of the men nor to the congregation's confidence in their probity. What makes this commendation significant is the invoking of a christological approval. Two phrases are noteworthy: Paul's task—which he shares with the colleagues—of carrying the offering to Jerusalem will be πρὸς τὴν [αὐτοῦ] τοῦ κυρίου δόξαν, "for his glory, I mean, of the Lord" (v 19, see earlier in *Notes*); and the delegates of the churches are praised as δόξα Χριστοῦ, "the glory of Christ," which may be an ascription of praise or, more likely, a second "title of honor" (*Ehrentitel . . . zweite Ehrenprädikat;* so Windisch, 267) alongside ἀπόστολοι, "messengers." Both terms are therefore "relational concepts" (Hainz, *Ekklesia,* 152) not only binding the men to the churches as their representatives but signifying that they are acting with the authority of the head of the Church (i.e., the universal society of believers), the Lord of glory (so Bachmann, 326; Windisch, 267). Indeed, with Hainz, ibid., we may go further and see in all these descriptive words used of Paul's associates (additionally we will include κοινωνός [partner], συνεργός [fellow worker]) tributes of high esteem to the three individuals who are being sent to Corinth. Such reputation is given them not in their own persons but in relation to the Gospel (v 18) and the apostolic mission (observe the repetition of the verb "to send") whose work they share with Paul. So Paul's praise of them, along with the commendation of "all the churches"—a hyperbolic expression not to be unduly pressed since it cannot be true of the Corinthians as it was of the Macedonians; otherwise there would be no point in referring to it—is an oblique vindication of his own ministry as well as a safeguard of his own concern "not to put a stumblingblock in anyone's way, so that our ministry will not be discredited" (6:3) through a failure to take necessary precautions, v 21.

A final reason for these fulsome commendations has to be traced to the situation of Corinth where much mischief had been caused by bearers of "letters of recommendation" (3:1–3) who had entered on the scene with a flourish. The antidote to whatever trace of resistance still remained at Corinth is in Paul's insistence that *he* can commend by this letter his representatives as men of sterling worth and proven integrity (v 22).

Comment

16. χάρις δὲ τῷ θεῷ τῷ διδόντι τὴν αὐτὴν σπουδὴν ὑπὲρ ὑμῶν ἐν τῇ καρδίᾳ Τίτου, "Now thanks be to God who puts the same eagerness on your behalf into Titus's heart." χάρις δὲ τῷ θεῷ, "now thanks [be] to God," is a verbless ejaculation, recalling the thanksgiving period of 2:14. But the setting is different. Here Paul is elaborating the procedure for bringing in the collection, already referred to in 8:6 and to be mentioned later at 9:5. These vv speak of Paul's concern; now he is glad to see that Titus's "eagerness" (σπουδή) is the same (τὴν αὐτὴν) as his own. In typically Pauline fashion he ascribes this impulse to God's working in Titus's heart. Barrett, "Titus," 126, associates this eagerness not so much with the concern to gather in the money as with Titus's desire to retrace his steps and return to Corinth. This return, Barrett (ibid., n. 30) suggests, may have seemed irksome since it would involve traveling a long distance for a duty "very quickly discharged." But if large sums of money were involved (v 20), it may not have appeared so simple; so Paul is relieved to have Titus's warm-hearted concurrence. More likely, I think, the formal χάρις . . . τῷ θεῷ suggests that more than a simple travel arrangement was at stake, namely, Paul is glad that Titus is ready to go back to consolidate the gains already made and to put the Corinthians to a searching test: Will they contribute to the fund as a token of their good faith? (This is exactly the appeal in v 24.)

17. ὅτι τὴν μὲν παράκλησιν ἐδέξατο, σπουδαιότερος δὲ ὑπάρχων αὐθαίρετος

ἐξῆλθεν πρὸς ὑμᾶς, "For he not only acceded to our request, but he is himself on his way to you with all eagerness and on his own initiative." Titus was not only willing to go along with Paul's idea for his return trip to Corinth, but he embraced the plan with "more eagerness" than Paul had hoped, if σπουδαιότερος, a comparative adjective connected with σπουδή, is given its full flavor. Alternatively, it may simply be an elative: "most eager" (BDF § 244.2), without any sense of setting up a contrast between Titus and Paul. Plummer, 247, renders "in his characteristic earnestness," treating the adjective as speaking of a well-known quality or trait. The important thing is that he was ready to go "of his own accord" (αὐθαίρετος, the same word as in v 3, where the Macedonians gave without any pressure put on them). On the paradox here— Titus complied with a request, yet is said to be ready to go of his own accord— see Barrett, 228, who finds the solution in the manner of Paul's παράκλησις, "request," which is not so much a directive to be obeyed as a call to help which Titus was already anxious to respond to. Héring (62) detects in Paul's personal delay in coming to Corinth—hence this request of Titus—a strategic action on the apostle's part. Perhaps he wished to be involved as little as possible directly with the collection. This matter was of some consequence to him (v 20). Paul's sensitivity to the Corinthian believers shines through here, since, as we observed, his standing at Corinth as an apostle has to be still delicately managed.

18. συνεπέμψαμεν δὲ μετ᾽ αὐτοῦ τὸν ἀδελφὸν οὗ ὁ ἔπαινος ἐν τῷ εὐαγγελίῳ διὰ πασῶν τῶν ἐκκλησιῶν, "We are sending with him the brother who is praised throughout all the congregations for his work in the Gospel." συνεπέμψαμεν, "we are sending," is an epistolary aorist, i.e., a verb whose action will be past when the readers receive the letter; hence the rendering of the past tense with the present sense.

The companion of Titus (μετ᾽ αὐτοῦ, "along with him") is the brother whose description is tantalizingly vague yet fulsome: [τὸν ἀδελφὸν] οὗ ὁ ἔπαινος ἐν τῷ εὐαγγελίῳ διὰ πασῶν τῶν ἐκκλησιῶν, literally, "whose praise in the Gospel is throughout all the churches." Several possible translations make the meaning less than fully clear. (1) Is his praise current in all the (Pauline) churches or throughout "christendom"? (2) Is it his work as an evangelist (taking "in the Gospel" to mean this: cf. Eph 4:11) that is well-known? (3) Is he praised for his commitment to the work of the Gospel (i.e., active Christian service; cf. Phil 1:5; 4:3 for this meaning of εὐαγγέλιον) through all the congregations? (4) Is it a reference to a Gospel-writer (e.g., Mark, Luke)? The last-named is ruled out by the fact that there is no clear evidence before A.D. 150 of τὸ εὐαγγέλιον ("the Gospel") being used of a written composition; it is ministry by personal deed and word that is in view (see R. P. Martin, "Gospel," International Standard Bible Encyclopedia, [ed. G. W. Bromiley et al. Grand Rapids: Eerdmans, 1982] 2:529).

The choice of (3) would be wise if we are to give weight to the reason why Paul is sending this person. He has a proven reputation for faithful Christian work, as "all the congregations" testify (Windisch, 262 who notes too the pleonasm as in 1 Thess 1:8; Rom 1:8; Bachmann, 322, 323 thinks the phrase refers only to all the Macedonian churches). Probably Paul means no more than to say that this is a person who is both known and recognized in church life (Hainz, Ekklesia, 149). Yet see Comment on 10:14.

So it would appear, except that we are kept guessing as to who was the individual in question. Barrett (228), following Souter ("A Suggested Relationship"), wants to take the definite article in ὁ ἀδελφός seriously and regard the man as Titus's own natural brother, but he dismisses the inference of Souter since "brother" is too well-known a name for believers (yet E. E. Ellis, "Co-workers," 445–58, limits it mainly to those who have "Christian mission or ministry as their primary occupation," but this restriction is criticized by Ollrog, *Paulus*, 78 n. 92), and Héring (62) asks why he is not named if he was Titus's relative. Other suggestions are no more convincing. The following have been proposed: (1) Luke (so Bachmann, a nomination going back to Origen and Jerome, but often on wrong grounds, namely, that "in the Gospel" (v 18a) means a Gospel-writer: see earlier); (2) Barnabas (Chrysostom, Theodoret: refs. in Héring, 62); (3) Aristarchus (so Windisch [263] and Zahn before him), who was indeed a Macedonian and a companion of Paul according to Acts 19:29; cf. Acts 20:4; 27:2. But if a more prominent figure is to be sought, we may offer (4) Apollos' name as candidate (cf. Acts 18:24–28). For whatever reason Paul has chosen not to reveal his name, but Lietzmann (136, 137) and Windisch have a point in maintaining that Paul's letter must originally have had a name in its text, for one does not introduce unnamed persons. Yet Paul's letters do have one parallel instance of not naming an individual for his own reasons, e.g., Phil 4:2, if "true yoke fellow," γνήσιε σύζυγε, does not conceal a proper name. Nor can we share Héring's somewhat uncharitable view that there was a name in the original text which the later church expunged because "the evangelist, whoever he was, forfeited his credit later on" (62).

19. οὐ μόνον δέ, ἀλλὰ καὶ χειροτονηθεὶς ὑπὸ τῶν ἐκκλησιῶν συνέκδημος ἡμῶν σὺν τῇ χάριτι ταύτῃ τῇ διακονουμένῃ ὑφ᾽ ἡμῶν πρὸς τὴν [αὐτοῦ] τοῦ κυρίου δόξαν καὶ προθυμίαν ἡμῶν, "In addition to this he has also been appointed by the congregations to be our traveling companion—as we fulfill this service we are rendering, for the honor of the Lord himself—and to prove our own readiness [to help]." This unnamed person has several more credentials. He has been appointed (χειροτονηθείς: an election by a hand vote is suggested by the verb: see BGD, 881: "choose . . . by raising hands" [see too Windisch, 263]. The verb is a Pauline *hapax*) by the (Pauline) churches to be the apostle's συνέκδημος, "traveling associate" (cf. Acts 19:29; see Ellis, "Co-Workers," 451, n. 4, for this description applied to Paul's companions who did not have directly "religious" functions; but this deduction is not provable, and v 18 is against it). See Schweizer, *Church Order in the New Testament*, 103 (7m).

Such a man is mentioned in order to associate Paul with a wider company as he administers the service (χάρις) of "the collection," lit., "this grace which is being administered by us." The enterprise is πρὸς τὴν [αὐτοῦ] τοῦ κυρίου, "for the honor of the Lord himself"; but also [πρὸς] . . . καὶ προθυμίαν ἡμῶν, "[for] to prove our readiness." The complement of this phrase is left open, but it must be something like "to help you." Barrett (229) paraphrases with the addition of "and at our suggestion"; Héring (62) has "for our own satisfaction," which is less apt. And Kümmel (207) gives another view: the appointment of this brother served to augment Paul's overall readiness, reverting to v 16. On the textual issue with [αὐτοῦ] see *Notes*.

The puzzling phrase καὶ προθυμίαν ἡμῶν, which we rendered "and to prove our readiness [to help]," has already been noted. As Denney (277 n) observes, the expression has a doubtful sense, especially if his own suggested translation "and that we may be made of good heart" is correct. His recourse to conjecture, proposing κατά in place of καί and connecting the phrase with χειροτονηθείς: "elected as we earnestly desired," seems strained. Yet it is a strange phrase, and Paul may have added it to explicate 8:11, 12, 16 and to match his own readiness to send this delegate with what he knows of the Corinthian προθυμία a year ago.

On χειροτονεῖν, "to appoint," see Acts 14:23; *Did.* 15:1; and often in Ignatius (*Phld.* 10:1, *Smyrn.* 11:2 f., *Pol.* 7:2) for election to church office.

20. στελλόμενοι τοῦτο, μή τις ἡμᾶς μωμήσηται ἐν τῇ ἁδρότητι ταύτῃ τῇ διακονουμένῃ ὑφ' ἡμῶν, "We are taking this precaution to avoid being blamed by anyone for the way we administer this generous gift." The introductory verb στελλόμενοι is an anacoluthon (BDF § 468.1) since there is no antecedent in agreement with it. The verb στέλλεσθαι, "to stand aloof, to avoid" (so K. Rengstorf, *TDNT* 7:588–99) has a plausible synonym in φοβεῖσθαι, "to fear" (BGD, *s.v.*, 766, but see Héring [63] who regards the sense of "fear" as a "pure invention of modern scholars"), and the tense is conative: "we are seeking to avoid this lest (μή) anyone should blame us concerning this generosity which was ministered by us" is a woodenly literal rendering, which we can only improve if some kind of English paraphrase is offered. We follow Héring's proposal to understand στέλλεσθαι as "to set out on a task, to undertake" (Liddell-Scott, *s.v.*); thus the sentence flows well. Paul had organized this matter (the collection) by taking all needful precautions so as not to have his honesty come under suspicion. The merit of this proposal is that the sentence connects with the following v.

ἁδρότης, "abundance, generosity," is yet one more synonym for the collection raised for the Jerusalem saints (BGD [18, 19]: "in this lavish gift"). If taken literally, the term says that the Corinthian gift was expected to be munificent out of their "surplus" (v 14); hence the need for the safeguard of appointing delegates to ensure that such a sizable donation was not mishandled or lost through inadvertence or robbery.

21. προνοοῦμεν γὰρ καλὰ οὐ μόνον ἐνώπιον κυρίου ἀλλὰ καὶ ἐνώπιον ἀνθρώπων, RSV rendering is: "For we aim at what is honorable, not only in the Lord's eyes but also in the sight of men." An alternative translation is: "For we are concerned for" (προνοοῦμεν: προνοεῖν, "to think of beforehand, take care of, take into consideration"; see Rom 12:17 and 1 Tim 5:8 and here in Paul, which are the only NT uses: see Wisd Sol 6:8). The verb with καλά, "the right thing," are words drawn from Prov 3:4 (LXX), not as a quotation but more of an allusion. "What is honorable" in the sight of the Lord obviously counted for much in Paul's estimation; but here what is honorable "in the eyes of" people, friend and foe, is his chief interest. 1 Cor 10:32 shows his pastoral sensitivity in this area, a gesture which marked his dealings with Corinth on a wide front. In this v he has his critics and their suspicions in his sights (Bruce, 224).

22. συνεπέμψαμεν δὲ αὐτοῖς τὸν ἀδελφὸν ἡμῶν ὃν ἐδοκιμάσαμεν ἐν πολλοῖς πολλάκις σπουδαῖον ὄντα, νυνὶ δὲ πολὺ σπουδαιότερον πεποιθήσει πολλῇ τῇ εἰς ὑμᾶς, "We are sending also with them our brother whom we have often tested

and proved to be eager in many matters, and now he is all the more eager because of the great confidence he has in you." The third member of the apostolic trio who will join Titus and his "brother" has also an identity shrouded in mystery. He too is a man known for his σπουδή, "eagerness" to assist, with two added qualifications: (1) he has been often tested and tried (ἐδοκίμασεν: Rom 12:2; 1 Cor 16:3; this verb and cognates [δοκιμάζειν] will play a pivotal role in Paul's later self-defense, in chap. 13) in these many matters presumably to do with handling funds, and (2) he has great confidence which serves only to increase his eagerness (σπουδαιότερον, lit., "the more eager"). Paul writes that this man has been "often tested" in many ways by himself ("we tested"). This statement will go against Ollrog's stark conclusion (*Paulus*, 183, n. 101) that "Paul especially emphasizes that the worker [in his mission] derived his legitimacy and authority not from Paul but through the Gospel," citing as evidence 2 Cor 8:17–24. Both Paul and his colleagues, of course, gained their accreditation from the Gospel, but Paul nevertheless was careful to apply some tests to his would-be associates.

The Greek πεποιθήσει πολλῇ τῇ εἰς ὑμᾶς could be taken to imply either the unnamed person's "confidence in you" or Paul's own "confidence in you." But the latter rendering is hardly likely to be reason for an increase of this man's enthusiasm to go to Corinth, though it seems to fit the context. On the other hand, we cannot say who this brother may have been if he now, like Paul, has had his confidence in the Corinthians restored—unless he was someone close to Paul, such as Timothy. Again, we are left to puzzle over this person's precise identity and to speculate why his name is missing from our text. Windisch (266) opts for Luke, or since Paul writes of "*our* brother" (τὸν ἀδελφὸν ἡμῶν) it has been said (here Windisch cites Bleek) that Paul's natural brother or cousin is in view (cf. Acts 23:16, 17, for Paul's family connections in Jerusalem). But as to his exact identity we are quite in the dark.

23. εἴτε ὑπὲρ Τίτου, κοινωνὸς ἐμὸς καὶ εἰς ὑμᾶς συνεργός· εἴτε ἀδελφοὶ ἡμῶν, ἀπόστολοι ἐκκλησιῶν, δόξα Χριστοῦ, "If there is any question about Titus—he is my partner and fellow worker among you; if there is a question of our brothers—they are the delegates of the congregations, and an honor to Christ." The coordinate conjunctions in the phrase εἴτε . . . εἴτε set the two delegates in some sort of contrast, with the preposition ὑπέρ the equivalent of περί, "about," "concerning," BDF § 231.1. So we translate and interpret: if there is a question of Titus, [know that] he is my partner in mission (κοινωνὸς ἐμὸς, in the nominative!) and on your behalf he is a fellow worker (καὶ εἰς ὑμᾶς συνεργός: a possible chiastic structure). If there is a question of our brothers (referred to in vv 18, 22), they are messengers appointed by the congregations (ἀπόστολοι ἐκκλησιῶν) and an honor to Christ (δόξα Χριστοῦ). See Hainz, *Ekklesia*, 152.

Titus is given a warmer commendation because of his closer relationship to the writer. Paul looks on him as an intimate associate (κοινωνός; the word describes personal relationship, with a nuance of confidence and joy-in-service [*Arbeitsfreude*, according to Ollrog, *Paulus*, 77: cf. Philem 17; perhaps this is a technical term for a sharer in Christian enterprises: so Hauck, *TDNT* 3:804]) and a συνεργός. In the latter word it is hard to decide whether the prefix συν-, "with," implies "a worker with me" (Windisch, 267), or "a worker with the Corinthians," like Paul himself (1:24: συνεργοί ἐσμεν, "we are working with you"), or "a worker with God," as in 6:1 (so Bachmann, 326). The term συνεργός, "fellow worker," has a wide range of meanings in Paul. Ollrog, *Paulus*, 67, offers a formal definition: it is a person commissioned by God to work in the united "task" of mission preaching, where the chief component parts are: (1) being commissioned (1 Cor 3:9; 1 Thess 3:2); (2) assignment to a united "task" (ἔργον, 1 Cor 15:48; 16:10; Phil 2:30: its equivalent is εὐαγγέλιον, "Gospel"); (3) the work of preaching in the mission churches (1 Thess 3:2; 1 Cor 3:9; 16:16: cf. Col 4:11). Paul regarded these co-workers less as helpers than as sharers in a common enterprise (cf. Phil 1:7, 2:22).

The "brothers" (but observe how Paul has dropped the ὑπέρ ["on behalf of"] construction, and speaks of them as ἀδελφοὶ ἡμῶν, "our brothers," again in the nominative) are commended as ἀπόστολοι ἐκκλησιῶν (no article is attached to either noun), so we may render "delegates of the churches." Ἀπόστολος also has a full range of meanings; see the handy summary in Barrett, *Signs*, 70–73, idem, "Shaliah." He regards the noun in this v with Phil 2:25 as falling into the separate category of "messenger," based on the Jewish-rabbinic model of שָׁלִיחַ, šālîaḥ, "one sent," or more specifically שְׁלִיחַ צִבּוּר, šᵉlîaḥ ṣibbûr, "messenger of the [synagogue] congregation": cf. Rengstorf, *TDNT* 1:413 ff.; T. W. Manson, *The Church's Ministry* (London: Hodder & Stoughton, 1948) 31–52 (40–45). Ollrog, *Paulus*, 79–92, updates this discussion and confirms the origin of the expression in the Jewish šālîaḥ pattern with one qualification: he insists that it says nothing about the content of a person's duty but only that the enterprise of the ἀπόστολος has been commissioned. That is, the genitive ἐκκλησιῶν is as significant *in this* v as the noun ἀπόστολος (cf. 1:1 for similar reasoning on the genitive Χριστοῦ Ἰησοῦ: but ἀπόστολος has two different senses in 1:1 and 8:23, dubbed respectively "specific" and "non-specific" by Roloff, *Apostolat*, 39).

A second tribute is that these two men (or maybe three if we include Titus) are δόξα Χριστοῦ, lit., "the glory of Christ," which is on face value a title of high honor. If we wish to be more precise, we may inquire: Does it mean an inherent dignity belonging to their appointment? Is it used to bolster *these* ἀπόστολοι, whom the (Pauline) churches recognized over against the claims of the ὑπερλίαν ἀπόστολοι ("super-apostles," 11:5; 12:11), or the spurious pretensions of the ψευδαπόστολοι ("false apostles," 11:13–15) who professed to be emissaries of the Jerusalem church and who in turn are set apart from Paul's office within the class of "servants of Christ" (διάκονοι Χριστοῦ, 11:23)? Or, is it an ascription of less moment, as in the translation "they reflect Christ" (NEB mg.)? Or, if that idea is too minimal, is Georgi's interpretation better when he regards these men as "representatives of Christ's heavenly splendor" (*Repräsentanten des himmlischen Glanzes des Christus: Die Geschichte der Kollekte*, 55)? It is difficult to decide.

The contrast that seems implicit between "apostles" who have universal recognition (cf. v 18: "all the churches") and "apostles" both the "pillar" leaders (called οἱ στῦλοι in Gal 2:9) in Jerusalem (11:5; 12:11) and their emissaries—whether real or pretended (11:13)—leads on to a final question: Are Paul's delegates referred to here Macedonians (as we have assumed)? Or perhaps, after all, they are agents of the Judean churches (i.e., ἀπόστολοι ἐκκλησιῶν [sc. τῆς] Ἰουδαίας, as Holmberg [*Paul,* 47] expands the v—note that he has added the definite article!) commissioned to function as controllers of the collection and intended to witness to the unity of the Gentile and Jewish Christian congregations. So also Hainz, *Ekklesia,* 155–57; Nickle, *The Collection,* 18–22.

But these latter suggestions are most improbable, given the delicate balance of Paul's authority so recently challenged at Corinth, and the uncertainty he shows concerning whether the collection would even be acceptable at Jerusalem (Nickle, *The Collection,* 70–72, thinks it was well received; but more likely—on the basis of Acts 21:21, 28—the experiment was "a crashing failure" [Nickle's term, ibid., 155] in every sense). And the further guess that the men in question are to be identified as Judas (in v 18) and Silas (in v 23) is unfounded. There is even less reason why such proposed names should have been elided from the text (cf. Nickle, ibid., 21).

24. τὴν οὖν ἔνδειξιν τῆς ἀγάπης ὑμῶν καὶ ἡμῶν καυχήσεως ὑπὲρ ὑμῶν εἰς αὐτοὺς ἐνδεικνύμενοι εἰς πρόσωπον τῶν ἐκκλησιῶν, "For this reason, show them the proof of your love and the reason for our pride in you, so that all the congregations can see it." The key word in this sentence is ἐνδεικνύμενοι, "show": for the participle used as a command, see *Notes.* It is preferable to accept this semitic usage rather than read ἐνδείξασθε, "prove" (with א C and the Latin, Coptic, Syriac versions and Byzantine MSS). Paul is calling for a demonstration of love to these delegates on the part of the readers. He adds as a final thrust that the warm reception accorded these men confirms the sense of pride he has expressed to them about the Corinthians (for καύχησις, see especially 7:14; 9:3). But a wider audience is envisaged if εἰς πρόσωπον τῶν ἐκκλησιῶν, "before all the congregations," takes on an ecumenical sense and denotes "the universal Church" (*ecclesia catholica:* Ignatius, *Smyrn.* 8:2; *Mart. Pol.* inscr. 8:1; 19:2 [16:2?]) of the day (as Denney—see the quotation in *Explanation*—understands the phrase).

Explanation

Cicero's words (*De officiis* 2.21.75) are appropriate: "but the main thing in all public administration and public service is to avoid even the slightest suspicion of avarice" (*ut avaritiae pellatur etiam minima suspicio*). They set the stage for this section which forms the introduction of the three individuals who are being sent to Corinth to attend to the matter of the collection. The reason that Paul is careful to arrange these visits and to have these men superintend the taking of the gift lies in v 20: "we are taking this precaution to avoid being blamed by anyone for the way we administer this generous gift." A matter of Paul's mission policy follows: "for we are concerned to do the right thing, not only in the Lord's eyes, but also in the sight of all" (v 21). Hence the apostolic messengers are men of proven worth; one is of universally recognized stature (vv 19, 23) and two are valued by Paul as tested and trusted colleagues (vv 17, 22, 23). More importantly, they are attached to the Corinthians and have confidence in Paul's mission there. Now

Paul calls (v 24) for a reciprocal attitude to greet them with love and coopera-
tion.

The sequel to these missions may be read in 12:16–18, which has close
parallels with this pericope even if only two men are nominated: the one
"brother" of 12:18 would then, in this view, be identified as the person of
8:22. The third man, here spoken of as "appointed by the congregations"
(v 19) is not alluded to since in chap. 12 he needs no defense (Barrett, "Titus,"
127). Or else, as we shall propose (see pp. 447, 448) the later vv refer to
the mission of 8:6.

Of special note in this section is the high esteem in which Paul held these
associates. Denney (278, 279) has captured the sense of v 23 where Paul
praises them as "envoys of the churches, the glory of Christ":

> What an idealist Paul was! What an appreciation of Christian character he had
> when he described these nameless believers as reflections of the splendour of
> Christ! To common eyes they might be commonplace men; but when Paul looked
> at them he saw the dawning of that brightness in which the Lord appeared to
> him by the way [Acts 9, 22, 26]. Contact with the grimy side of human nature
> did not blind him to this radiance; rather did this glory of Christ in men's souls
> strengthen him to believe all things, to hope all things, to endure all things. In
> showing before these honoured messengers the proof of their love, and of his
> boasting on their behalf, the Corinthians will show it, he says, before the face of
> the Churches. It will be officially reported throughout Christendom.

D. Commendation of the Brothers to Achaia (9:1–5)

Bibliography

Bornkamm, G. "The History and Origin of the So-Called Second Letter to the Corinthians." In *The Authorship and Integrity of the New Testament*, 73–81. London: SPCK,
1965. Fuller version as *Die Vorgeschichte des sogenannten zweiten Korintherbriefes.* SAH phil.-
hist. Klasse. Heidelberg: Winter, 1961. **Dahl, N. A.** "Paul and Possessions." In *Studies
in Paul*, 22–39. **Funk, R. W.** "The Apostolic Parousia: Form and Significance." In
Christian History and Interpretation. FS John Knox, ed. W. R. Farmer *et al.*, 249–68.
Cambridge: University Press, 1967. **Georgi, D.** *Die Geschichte der Kollekte des Paulus für
Jerusalem.* 67–79. **Hainz, J.** *Ekklesia.* 242–44. **Jones, I. H.** *The Contemporary Cross.* London: Epworth Press, 1973. **Wiles, G. P.** *Paul's Intercessory Prayers.* SNTSMS 24. Cambridge: University Press, 1974.

Translation

> [1] *Now concerning the service to the saints [at Jerusalem], there is no necessity
> for me to be writing to you [as I have done]:* [2] *for I know your readiness; I boast
> about it in your case to the Macedonians, remarking that Achaia has been prepared
> since last year; and your zeal has spurred most of them.* [3] *But I have sent the brothers
> in order that our pride in you might not be proved in vain in this matter, and that
> you might be prepared just as I said you would be.* [4] *For if any of the Macedonians*

come with me and find you unprepared, we—not to mention you [a]*—may be put to shame because of this eventuality.* [b] [5] *So I deemed it needful to ask the brothers to go to you in advance and prepare in advance the gift you were making which had been already provided. I want it to be ready as really a gift, not as money wrung out of you.*

Notes

[a] Reading and paraphrasing ἵνα μὴ λέγω ὑμεῖς, since λέγω is found in p⁴⁶ C* D G cop^sa goth. The rival reading λέγωμεν (א B C² ψ Byz lat syr bo) is usually explained as a scribe's assimilation to the first person of the preceding verb καταισχυνθῶμεν. Plummer, 255, opts for the reading λέγωμεν as more widely attested. The oscillation between "I" and "we" is explained by Carrez, "Le 'nous,'" *NTS* 26 (1979–80) 480: "In 2 Cor 9:4 again referring to the collection, Paul announces his coming and so used the pronoun 'I,' but he expresses the assurance of the ministerial group by using the pronoun 'we': '*I* am afraid that, if *I* bring with me other men from Macedonia and they find you unprepared, what a disgrace it will be to *us*, not to say to *you*.' "

[b] The added reading τῆς καυχήσεως (א² Byz^pl syr) appears in KJV, but it is misleading exegetically (see Köster, *TDNT* 8:584, n. 117, who traces its influence to a borrowing from 2 Cor 11:17).

Form/Structure/Setting

For some information and discussion regarding the difficult transition from 8:24 to 9:1 see earlier, pp. 249, 250. There it was submitted that the two chapters belong to the same general letter and were written in close proximity to each other, yet they are addressed to a narrower (chap. 8) and wider (chap. 9) constituency. Thus we seek to explain the repetition and reinforcement of Paul's appeal to the churches in southern Greece in the matter of the offering for Jerusalem. See too Plummer, 252, 253, who notes how the full designation "service *to the saints*" reiterates what Paul has earlier mentioned (8:4). See Hainz, *Ekklesia,* 242.

At the center of this paragraph is the issue of Paul's "pride and boasting" (καυχῶμαι . . . καύχημα, vv 2, 3) in the Corinthians in one particular matter: their readiness to complete what was begun a year ago (8:10, 11). This pledge and the way Paul had expressed confidence in his readers to honor their promise lies at the heart of the discussion (9:2–5). Indeed, on a wider front, just this attitude of Paul's confidence in the Achaeans and their partnership with him in the apostolic mission in the Aegean sector have been regarded as "vital to the whole of 2 Corinthians chs 1–9 and provide[s] a key to its argument" (Jones, *The Contemporary Cross,* 33–37), with the note of thanksgiving, identified as another *leitmotif* running through the entire letter of chaps. 1–9, taken up in 9:11–15. The clarifying of the theme of "thankfulness to God" serves also to link together chaps. 8 and 9, but with a different emphasis to be noted.

In chap. 8 the collection is recommended on the theological ground of ἰσότης, i.e., "equality," binding together Jewish and Gentile believers in a common enterprise (8:13). In chap. 9 the same collection is seen as an opportunity for "cheerful giving" (9:7). The point is that both aspects of the same enterprise are expressions of the same spirit: Paul calls it προθυμία, "readiness" (v 2). This is evidently a key term with several applications. (1) It characterizes

Paul's appeal to the Macedonians (by inference in 9:4: there the lack of preparation on the part of the Achaeans would cause shame to Paul); (2) it was part of Paul's determination to see the job completed (8:19); and (3) it was a trait of the Corinthians a year before (8:11) which the Achaeans already shared (9:2) and which Paul wishes to see developed and expressed in their present offerings. The "boasting" of Paul to the Macedonians of the Corinthian/Achaean goodwill (9:2) is another common term, of which the two sides are that the Macedonians have set an example (8:1-5), and now the Corinthians can be shown to have profited from this incentive (9:1, 2). Thus, there is no need, with Georgi, *Geschichte der Kollekte*, 56, to argue for an incompatibility between the two chapters, especially as Georgi himself presents a strong argument for Paul's emphasis in chap. 9 on a *large* offering, requiring (so Georgi claims) the hiring of a special ship to take the delegates to Jerusalem.

The wording of 9:1 (περὶ μὲν γάρ) need not express an emphatic contrast (as in Rom 5:16; 14:5; 1 Cor 5:3; 11:7; 12:8); it may—and more probably does—introduce a subheading within the major theme (as in Rom 3:2; 1 Cor 11:18; 2 Cor 11:4; so Jones, ibid., 146, n. 68). The subplot stays within the general orbit of Paul's reasons for sending the deputation (8:18-23) and builds on his confidence expressed in his readers (8:24, a v which is picked up in 9:4). What is still untouched in the earlier chapter is now addressed: will the collection be a sign of voluntary generosity and the gift be commensurate with the Achaeans' ability to raise a "bountiful gift" (εὐλογία, 9:5)? In an epigram (whether consciously designed or not, we cannot tell; see Deissmann, *Bible Studies*, tr. A. Grieve [Edinburgh: T. & T. Clark, 1903] 144), Paul had earlier confidently anticipated the "offering" (λογεία, 1 Cor 16:1) to be forthcoming; now he is taking steps to ensure that it is εὐ-λογία, "a generous offering." This appeal for a worthy gift will be illustrated and enforced in 9:6, 7.

Comment

1. Περὶ μὲν γὰρ τῆς διακονίας τῆς εἰς τοὺς ἁγίους περισσόν μοί ἐστιν τὸ γράφειν ὑμῖν, "Now concerning the service to the saints [at Jerusalem], there is no necessity for me to be writing to you [as I have done]." The phrase περισσόν μοί ἐστιν τὸ γράφειν ὑμῖν, "there is no need for me to be writing to you," has already been commented on, and the exegetical options set down (p. 249). What is clear is that a reminder to the present readers—the Achaeans as inhabitants of a wider region than the city of Corinth which was its senatorial provincial capital (see *Introduction*, p. xxx)—is, in Paul's estimation, justified only because he knows their state. The introductory γάρ ("for, how") either (1) links with 8:24 which speaks of Paul's confidence in the Corinthians (Plummer, 252; Barrett, 232) or (2) is Paul's way of turning from the commissioners (in chap. 8) back to the collection itself (Goudge, 86), or (3) is an editorial insertion to make the link between the two chapters plain, in the final redaction of the letter (as most writers suggest who see the chapters as separate pieces: Georgi, ibid. 56-58, Bornkamm, *Vorgeschichte*, 31 f. (= *History*, 77), Fallon, 76-78). We have followed Denney, 279, 280 in adding to τὸ γράφειν ὑμῖν,

"to be writing to you," the phrase "as I have done" to mark the connection with the preceding discussion, while we are cognizant of a widening of the scope of Paul's writing. The particle μέν looks forward to v 3 (δέ): There is no need to remind you . . . but all the same I am sending the brothers. That is the sense of Paul's introductory remark in v 1, connecting with v 3. And we note well Denney's judgment (ibid.): "the statements in vv 3–5 would be unintelligible if we had not chap. viii.16–24 to explain them; and instead of saying there is no connexion between ix.1 and what precedes, we should rather say that the connexion is somewhat involved and circuitous—as will happen when one is handling a topic of unusual difficulty," and, we may add, unusual delicacy. See too J. Moffatt, *Introduction to the Literature of the New Testament* [3] (Edinburgh: T. & T. Clark, 1918): "instead of being inconsistent with what precedes, 9:1 clinches it" (128).

The continuation of Paul's discussion into chap. 9 may also be accounted for by his "embarrassment which he constantly showed about gifts" (Wiles, *Paul's Intercessory Prayers*, 237, agreeing with Moffatt, ibid., cited above).

2. οἶδα γὰρ τὴν προθυμίαν ὑμῶν ἣν ὑπὲρ ὑμῶν καυχῶμαι Μακεδόσιν, ὅτι Ἀχαΐα παρεσκεύασται ἀπὸ πέρυσι, καὶ τὸ ὑμῶν ζῆλος ἠρέθισεν τοὺς πλείονας, "For I know your readiness; I boast about it in your case to the Macedonians, remarking that Achaia has been prepared since last year; and your zeal has spurred most of them." The Achaean Christians are held up as a model. Perhaps the disaffection at Corinth was local and confined to house congregations in the city, and other churches in Achaia (of which Cenchreae is an example, Rom 16:1) may not have been so troubled. They had exhibited a keenness from the beginning (ἀπὸ πέρυσι, "a year ago," as in 8:10), and it was this spirit of "eager readiness" to support the collection that had stimulated the majority but not all of the Macedonians (τοὺς πλείονας: so Moule, *Idiom Book*, 108). Some commentators (Barrett, 233; Fallon, 77) find Paul's earlier confidence in the Achaeans a little too optimistic because it was premature and so now it is embarrassing. They put the expression of Paul's boasting (καυχᾶσθαι) down to his willingness to see his communities in the best possible light and to give them the benefit of any doubt he might have, especially when it comes to commending them to other people. But the statement *can* be the sober truth, if we are prepared to distinguish between Achaeans and Corinthians, and see the zeal (ζῆλος) of the former group as acting as a spur, with a remarkable domino effect. ἐρεθίζειν, which normally in classical Greek has a bad sense, "to irritate, to embitter" (BGD, 308), as in Col 3:21, in this v means rather "to promote healthy rivalry" (Héring, 65) and evidently carries here no pejorative sense. Windisch's fear (270, 271) that this v contradicts 8:1–5, because there Paul's analysis seems to suggest that the Corinthians were dilatory and sluggish, is unfounded. He does not consider that it was the rebellion against Paul at Corinth which put the collection into abeyance; and in any case 9:1, 2 may have a different group from the Corinthians in its view, as we noted.

3. ἔπεμψα δὲ τοὺς ἀδελφούς, ἵνα μὴ τὸ καύχημα ἡμῶν τὸ ὑπὲρ ὑμῶν κενωθῇ ἐν τῷ μέρει τούτῳ, ἵνα καθὼς ἔλεγον παρεσκευασμένοι ἦτε, "But I have sent the brothers in order that our pride in you might not be proved in vain in this matter, and that you might be prepared just as I said you would

be." "But I have sent (ἔπεμψα: probably not epistolary aorist here, parting company with RSV; Héring, 65; Fallon, 77; Barrett, 234; etc.) the brothers in order that our pride (τὸ καύχημα ἡμῶν) in you might not be proved in vain (lit., "be empty," κενωθῇ: cf. 1 Cor 9:15; Phil 2:7 [on the verb, see Martin, *Carmen Christi*, 165–69]) in this respect or matter" (ἐν τῷ μέρει τούτῳ, see *Comment* on 3:10), unlike the other matter about which Paul had occasion to congratulate the Corinthians, in 7:14. A second ἵνα clause follows to express purpose: "and that you might be prepared" to promote the collection, with Paul's none-too-subtle aside added: "just as I said" (καθὼς ἔλεγον) you would be. Barrett's rendering which places "as I was saying" in parenthesis gives a different sense, since it makes Paul's reference to apply to the Corinthians' readiness, not their pledge to give. But this is less preferable to the above translation which harks back to Paul's earlier allusion in 8:11. Here again the two biblical chapters are bound together by word association.

The "brothers" are the men mentioned in 8:6, 17–24, in our view. But if the two chapters are quite separate and were written independently of each other, a fresh delegation of more unnamed leaders is introduced (so Héring, 65; Windisch, 272, 286–88; and Georgi, ibid., 58, suggesting a three weeks interval between the composition of the two chapters and hence the two delegations). The purpose of this mission is given ἵνα μὴ τὸ καύχημα ἡμῶν τὸ ὑπὲρ ὑμῶν κενωθῇ: that our pride which we have expressed (v 2) on your behalf may not be shown to be a hollow boast, especially in regard to the collection and the Achaeans' readiness. Rather, Paul hopes they will be shown to be prepared as he had impressed on the Macedonians (v 2).

4. μή πως ἐὰν ἔλθωσιν σὺν ἐμοὶ Μακεδόνες καὶ εὕρωσιν ὑμᾶς ἀπαρασκευάστους καταισχυνθῶμεν ἡμεῖς, ἵνα μὴ λέγω ὑμεῖς, ἐν τῇ ὑποστάσει ταύτῃ, "For if any of the Macedonians come with me and find you unprepared we—not to mention you—may be put to shame because of this eventuality." The reverse of Paul's expectation is that if the readers are ill-prepared, then both he and they will lose face. The issue again relates to the collection, an occasion which may be concealed in the phrase ἐν τῇ ὑποστάσει ταύτῃ, "in this eventuality" (so Héring, 66; ὑπόστασις is lit., "reality, actual being, situation," see BGD, 847. H. Köster, *TDNT* 8:571–88, opts for the sense of "plan, project," rejecting "confidence" [RSV; NIV; Barrett, 234], "assurance," as without parallel, but see R. E. Witt, "Hypostasis," in *Amiticiae Corolla*, FS J. R. Harris, ed. H. G. Wood [London: University Press, 1933], 319–43, esp. 330). A different set of meanings is offered by Windisch (273): either "in this matter" (see Dahl, "Paul and Possessions," 38) or "in this connection." But both "in this matter" of the collection on which Paul has expressed confidence, and "in this connection" seem to be weak renderings of ὑπόστασις, as Héring notes: he therefore goes back to the etymological meaning "supposition." Paul is envisaging the fear that if the eventuality of the Achaeans not being ready is realized, then his scheme for the enterprise will collapse. And not only his project is affected; the credibility of the readers will be lost: ἵνα μὴ λέγω ὑμεῖς, "not to mention you," which is a delicately phrased aside (BDF § 495) to drive home Paul's appeal. This v speaks of a visit by certain "Macedonians" to Corinth who will be accompanied by Paul himself. This trip, we propose,

is planned as subsequent to the mission with the brothers in 9:3 and refers to the follow-up visit to Corinth of Paul and his party (Acts 20:2). The "Macedonians" in question are the persons referred to in Acts 20:4 (where for "Derbe" the Western reading gives "Doberus," a Macedonian town near Philippi [cf. Thuc. 2.98–100: Bruce, *Acts of the Apostles* (London: Tyndale Press, 1951) 370, 371]; and maybe "Derbe" goes with Timothy, thus permitting this Gaius to be equated with the man in Acts 19:29, "Gaius of Macedonia." See NEB of Acts 20:4, and, on the other side, the note in *Textual Commentary*, 475, 476; E. Haenchen, *Acts*, tr. B. Noble and G. Shinn *et al.* [Oxford: Blackwell, 1971] 52, 53).

Paul's presence with these Macedonians follows on the sending of the brothers (v 3). The linkage between the apostolic emissary here (and in 8:16–24) and Paul's own "parousia" presence is not accidental; it conforms to his regular association of persons involved in visits and his letter-writing habits (see Funk, "The Apostolic *Parousia*," 249, 254). For the nuance of the verb καταισχυνθῶμεν, "we may be put to shame," see *Comment* on 7:14; 10:8 (cf. Phil 1:20).

5. ἀναγκαῖον οὖν ἡγησάμην παρακαλέσαι τοὺς ἀδελφούς, ἵνα προέλθωσιν εἰς ὑμᾶς καὶ προκαταρτίσωσιν τὴν προεπηγγελμένην εὐλογίαν ὑμῶν, ταύτην ἑτοίμην εἶναι οὕτως ὡς εὐλογίαν καὶ μὴ ὡς πλεονεξίαν, "So I deemed it needful to ask the brothers to go to you in advance and prepare in advance the gift you were making which had been already provided. I want it to be ready as really a gift, not as money wrung out of you." "To go in advance" (προ-ἐλθεῖν) is the key word to Paul's plans. On one reading of this v it is assumed (with most commentators) that Paul will accompany these brethren; so v 4. Chap. 8 has no hint of Paul's visit; so, it is said, chap. 9 must be earlier, and we must postulate a change of plan between the earlier chap. 9 and the later arrangement in chap. 8. But this is by no means certain. If there were two deputations, and Paul intended to join the second, then all is clear.

At all events, there is an element of necessity (ἀναγκαῖον . . . ἡγησάμην; cf. 2 Macc 9:21 for an identical phrase: Phil 2:25, for identical wording) in Paul's urging (παρακαλέσαι, as in 8:6 but no reluctance on their part is envisaged, Goudge, 87) these men to undertake a journey to Corinth ahead of himself and the Macedonians. The purpose is that they might arrange in advance (note the προ- in the verb προέλθωσιν; indeed the frequency of the prefix προ- in the verbs of this v is remarkable) the gift the Achaeans had previously promised. Paul is evidently wanting to stress the need for the matter already decided to be put in hand immediately. One other reason is supplied: the gift is to be seen as a "blessing" (εὐλογία in reference to both a thank-offering and a salutation: see Bruce, 226), not as a species of "avarice" (πλεονεξία, "niggardliness," Héring, 66). Obviously we must try to read beneath the surface since these basic meanings cannot be accidental. The ready gift at Corinth will be a sign that the response was planned as a generous one (εὐλογία, a rather solemn term for the offering; so Georgi, *Die Geschichte der Kollekte*, 67, 68, referring to Jos 15:19 [LXX] of Caleb's daughter [δός μοι εὐλογίαν] and Héring, 66, citing 2 Kings 5:15 [LXX] of Naaman's present to Elisha [καὶ νῦν λαβὲ τὴν εὐλογίαν παρὰ τοῦ δούλου σου] for a gift both bountiful and set in a religious context). The opposing partner is πλεονεξία, normally rendered "covetousness" (Rom 1:29; cf. Col 3:5) or avarice, rapacity, greed, love of money, which is tantamount to idolatry (Col 3:5; cf. *T. Judah* 19:1: Delling, *TDNT* 6:266–74). The sense here is fixed by the reference to πλεονεξία in 12:17, 18, where Paul is later to face this charge, namely, that he has used the collection to line his own pocket. So in advance—if we assume that suspicions were already being raised—he turns the word around by denying that he ever expected the Corinthians to be blackmailed into giving (so Barrett, 235). But this exegesis requires a shift in meaning of πλεονεξία (*pace* BGD, 667, who say "The context calls for the pregnant meaning," i.e., "extortion"; but Plummer, 256, to the contrary, against BGD). It is better to keep its plain sense of "love of money" which in turn leads to a niggardly gift, especially as this is precisely the point of vv 6, 7. The text does not speak, in our view, of two ways of securing the gift (as voluntary act/as extortion or exaction, so RSV). Rather it is two attitudes of giving (generously/grudgingly, so Héring) that are brought together in antithesis.

Explanation

This section sets the two congregations—in Macedonia and in southern Greece—in some sort of contrast. We have already seen Paul praise the former (8:1–5); now it is the turn of the Achaeans to be gently prodded to act but also to be reminded of Paul's confidence (v 3) in them. Paul's honor is at stake because he has already set forth the Achaeans as a model of readiness to contribute. But their tardiness in completing the matter—for reasons at which we can only guess—seems to belie this honor Paul has set upon them. So now he calls upon them to fulfill this task and, in so doing, to confirm the expectation he has of them. Above all, he wants the money gift to be both freely forthcoming and generous in its amount. He picks out a number of expressive ways of getting the truth home (vv 2, 5), especially in the latter verse: "I want it to be forthcoming as a generous gift, not as money wrung out of you" (Moffatt). In terms of pastoral theology, we do well to observe the style and substance of Paul's handling of a delicate issue (money-raising is no sinecure!): there is an appeal to emulation, with the Macedonian example the benchmark; there is recourse to shame, lest Achaean slackness should in any way reflect adversely on Paul's confidence in them or on their own self-respect; and there is a recall of faithfulness in keeping one's pledge.

E. The Collection and the Unity of the Church   (9:6–15)

Bibliography

Dahl, N. A. "Paul and Possessions," in *Studies in Paul*, Appendix I, 37, 38. **Davies, W. D.** *The Gospel and the Land.* 200–203. ———. *Paul and Rabbinic Judaism.* 2d ed. London: SPCK, 1953. **Georgi, D.** *Die Geschichte der Kollekte des Paulus für Jerusalem.*

Hainz, J. *Ekklesia*, 242–45. ———. *Koinonia.* "Kirche" als Gemeinschaft bei Paulus, 141–44. **Harnack, A. von** *Mission and Expansion of Christianity in the First Three Centuries.* Tr. J. Moffatt. Vol. 1, chap. 4. London: Williams & Norgate/New York: Putnam's Sons, 1908. **Nickle, K. F.** *The Collection.* 104–6, 108–10, 134–36. **Reumann, J.** *Righteousness in the New Testament.* Philadelphia: Fortress Press, 1982. **Sevenster, J. N.** *Paul and Seneca.* NovTSup 4. Leiden: Brill, 1961. **Turner, N.** *Grammatical Insights into the New Testament.* Edinburgh: T. & T. Clark, 1965. **Wiles, G. P.** *Paul's Intercessory Prayers.* **Ziesler, J. A.** *The Meaning of Righteousness in Paul: A Linguistic and Theological Enquiry.* SNTSMS 20. Cambridge: University Press, 1972.

Translation

⁶ *To enforce the point: he who sows sparingly will also reap sparingly, he who sows generously will also reap generously.* ⁷ *Let each one give as he has decided* [a] *in his mind, not regretfully nor under constraint: for it is the cheerful giver that God loves.* ⁸ *God is able to make all grace to overflow to you, so that, in all things and at all times, you may have all you need and may overflow in every kind of good work.* ⁹ *As it is written:*

He has scattered widely, he has given to the poor;
His righteousness endures forever.

¹⁰ *He who provides seed for the sower and bread for food will provide* [b] *and increase* [b] *your seed and will augment* [b] *your harvest of righteousness.* ¹¹ *You will be made rich in every way so that you can be always generous, and through us such generosity will yield thanksgiving to God.* ¹² *This service which you render is not only providing for the needs of the saints [at Jerusalem], but overflows through many thanksgivings* [c] *to God.* ¹³ *By their approving of this service they give praise to God in that they see both the obedience that accompanies your faith which acknowledges the Gospel of Christ and the generosity of your partnership with them and everyone.* ¹⁴ *And in their prayers for you* [d] *they yearn for you because of the surpassing grace God has given you.* ¹⁵ *Thanks be to God for his gift beyond measure!*

Notes

[a] Reading προῄρηται with ℵ B C F G and most witnesses; προαιρεῖται, yielding a present tense, is found in D ψ Byz and preferred in the Bible Societies' Translator's text.

[b] These three verbs χορηγήσει, πληθυνεῖ and αὐξήσει are read as future indicative with ℵ* B C D* and minuscules. But the optative mood (χορηγήσαι, πληθῦναι, αὐξήσαι) is given by the majority of MSS, while P⁴⁶ is divided, giving two optatives, "may he provide and increase," and a future indicative for "and he will augment." Paul's train of thought evidently requires a confident assertion (Barrett, 232), not a pious hope.

[c] εὐχαριστιῶν (plural), "thanksgivings," is the reading of the overwhelming evidence (ℵ B C D G K P Byz and versions). Rival readings (εὐχαριστίαν, P⁴⁶part Cyp. Aug.) or εὐχαριστίας (arm, Ambr) are due to assimilation with v 11 which has εὐχαριστίαν τῷ θεῷ.

[d] ὑμῶν, "for you"; ℵ* B and most minor authorities have ἡμῶν, "for us," to be rejected on the principle *lectio facilior.*

Form/Structure/Setting

Paul has been recommending the brothers and their advance visit to the Achaeans. It is now time to advert to the collection itself, and especially to enforce a single plea. The collection in southern Greece should express the generosity Paul knows these churches are capable of. So generosity is a hallmark of this appeal. Then, as a second motif, the collection is shown to fit in to Paul's exposition of the Christian life which falls into the pattern of "grace/gratitude," a nexus that characterizes biblical religion. God's gift (*Gabe*) is received by our giving back to God (*Aufgabe*) in the delightful duty of thanksgiving. Finally, in a wider context, Paul uses the offering to the "saints," i.e., the Jerusalem church (v 12), as a vehicle to demonstrate how, once it is gratefully received, the collection will act as a sign of unity, binding the two wings of the church (Jewish Christian, Gentile Christian) together (or, so he hopes: whether it turned out so may be doubted, from other pieces of data: see earlier, pp. 257, 258). The climax comes in a wondrous ejaculation of praise to God (v 15), as Paul seemingly reverts to the christological motif of 8:9, but with its *immediate* occasion evidently the unity manifested between the two ethnic and religious parts of the "one Church." In a remarkable way the instruction on the Jerusalem collection coheres with his teaching on reconciliation (in 5:18–21; 6:1–13) as the Gospel of divine grace is shown to lead to union, not only with God but between churchly groups isolated by mutual suspicion and fear. Thus, this pericope anticipates Eph 2:11–22 where Paul's teaching on reconciliation in a new context is developed, enforced and applied (Martin, *Reconciliation*, chap. 9).

On formal and stylistic matters this section is replete with several interesting features: one is the illustrative material from an OT agrarian background (vv 6–10), with the citation of a proverb (v 6) full of assonance and demonstrably a chiasmus in structure; it is probably quoted from some source, although there is no extant parallel. However, the OT is certainly pressed into service in surrounding verses (vv 7, 9). Another feature is Paul's play on the word for "all," "every" (πᾶς, four times; πάντοτε, once) which is used in a marked tautological way in these vv (8, 11). Yet the overall impression is striking, and enforces Paul's statements. It is the same with his use of the verb περισσεύειν, "to overflow" (vv 8, 12: also we observe that v 8 is set in chiastic structure. The combination of the roots πασ- and περι- amounts to a conscious alliteration using the Greek letter π [so Windisch, 277]), and this accentuation of a special vocabulary is a tribute to God's generous blessing and also states the ground of the readers' ability to rise to unmeasured *giving* (v 8)—and thanks-*giving* (vv 11, 12). The pun in English exactly corresponds to the Greek play on χάρις–εὐχαριστία ("grace" producing "gratitude"). The powerful coda of v 15 picks up this association of terms, with thanks (χάρις) expressed to God for his gift (δωρεά, a new word in these two chapters to alert the reader to God's giving-in-grace [Rom 5:15, 17] as a mark of the new eschatological age of salvation). Romans 3:24, "justified freely-as-a-gift (δωρεάν) by his grace (τῇ αὐτοῦ χάριτι)," sums up the salvation-historical background of Paul's instructions on how Christians should prove their new standing before God by positive action and self-giving dedication to the needs of others, especially Israel (Gal 6:10, 16).

Comment

6. Τοῦτο δέ, ὁ σπείρων φειδομένως φειδομένως καὶ θερίσει, καὶ ὁ σπείρων ἐπ᾽ εὐλογίαις ἐπ᾽ εὐλογίαις καὶ θερίσει, "To enforce the point: he who sows sparingly

will also reap sparingly, he who sows generously will also reap generously."
The verbless interjection, τοῦτο δέ (BDF § 481 for the ellipsis), calls attention
to what is to follow: "now mark this," as though the verb were λογίζεσθε.
The previous vv have been easing the readers' minds into a consideration
of the amount of their gift. Now Paul will illustrate his point from the world
of the farmer. It is the imagery of the sower scattering seed in his field. He
begins with a rhythmical proverb: ὁ σπείρων φειδομένως/φειδομένως καὶ θερίσει
shows the chiastic structure, with the criss-cross pattern: "he who sows spar-
ingly/sparingly will he also reap."
The pattern is repeated in the lines:

$$ὁ\ σπείρων\ ἐπ'\ εὐλογίαις$$
$$\times$$
$$ἐπ'\ εὐλογίαις\ καὶ\ θερίσει$$

He who sows generously (ἐπ' εὐλογίαις lit. "with blessings") generously will he
also reap.

The term εὐλογία, "gift," "blessing," reverts to v 5. There is no precise
parallel to this sententious saying, but Aristotle, *Rhetoric* III.3.4, is often cited:
You sowed these things shamefully (αἰσχρῶς . . . ἔσπειρας), but you reaped
them in evil (κακῶς . . . ἐθέρισας); cf. Cicero, *De Oratore* ii.65.261, Rusca's
reply: *Ut sementem feceris, ita metes,* "you shall reap what you sowed." But the
Jewish literature has the same image: Prov 22:8, "he who sows injustice will
reap calamity" (LXX: ὁ σπείρων φαῦλα θερίσει κακά), which combines, as Paul
does, the agricultural motif and moral axiom. For the positive side, see Prov
11:25, LXX (ψυχὴ εὐλογουμένη πᾶσα ἁπλῆ: "every generous soul receives a
blessing").
The point of Paul's imagery is: those who contribute generously to the
Jerusalem collection will give as a farmer gives away his seed in expectation
of a rich harvest of produce. What that bountiful harvest of "blessings" (ἐπ'
εὐλογίαις: the preposition denoting manner may be colloquial, and the plural
noun indicates abundance: Plummer, 258) entails has already been described
in 8:14 (see *Comment* and *"Note on Israel's Salvation"*). The appeal is to a
motive which is not one of reward so much as a disinterested concern to
reach out to the Jerusalem saints in their need, and the issue is not the
amount of the gift so much as the involvement it reflects (8:12).
7. ἕκαστος καθὼς προήρηται τῇ καρδίᾳ, μὴ ἐκ λύπης ἢ ἐξ ἀνάγκης· ἱλαρὸν γὰρ
δότην ἀγαπᾷ ὁ θεός, "Let each one give as he has decided in his mind, not
regretfully nor under constraint: for it is the cheerful giver that God loves."
The appeal is continued and directed to thoughtfulness and joy in giving.
Clearly some words have to be added *ad sensum*, since the v lacks an introductory verb: let each one (ἕκαστος) [give] . . . καθὼς προήρηται: "as he is determined," reflecting conviction which is personal (so τῇ καρδίᾳ: "in his heart":
the phrase hardly implies "prompting of the heart" with Héring, 67; it is
more a moral resolution that is in view). μὴ ἐκ λύπης: literally "not with sorrow." Paul's use of λύπη, "sorrow, regret" recalls 7:8 ff. but the sense here
is different. In this v it is regret that betokens a grudging spirit, unwilling
to let the money go (and so a trait of πλεονεξία from v 5; but Deut 15:10

may be in mind). Nor is the gift to be ἐξ ἀνάγκης, literally, "out of necessity," through pressure being applied. λύπη and ἀνάγκη are virtual synonyms in this couplet (Plummer, 259). For ἀνάγκη, see 2 Cor 6:4; 12:10, but this setting hardly fits; rather we should look to 1 Cor 9:16: "I am *under compulsion* to proclaim the Gospel." See too Philem 14 where ἀνάγκη ("compulsion") is opposed to ἑκούσιον ("of free will"); see Thuc. 8:27; Plut. *Mor* 446E. An aphorism drawn from Prov 22:8 (LXX) sounds the positive note, where the order of words ought to be kept: "it is the cheerful giver (ἱλαρὸν . . . δότην) whom God loves (ἀγαπᾷ: the LXX has this verb as a variant to εὐλογεῖ, "God blesses," gnomic present tense: Moule, *Idiom Book*, 8). The thought of God's approving the generous and joyful giver is "thoroughly Old Testament and Jewish" (Barrett, 236, and Windisch, 277, referring to *Lev. Rab.* 34.8 [131*b*]: "when a man gives alms, let him do so with a joyful heart"; Sir 4.10, 14; 13.26; 26.4; 35:9 [LXX 35:8]: ἐν πάσῃ δόσει ἱλάρωσον τὸ πρόσωπόν σου, "with every gift put on a cheerful face"; see too Wisd Sol 7:28; yet he observes that the idea of God's love brings a new thought into the discussion). See too 'Abot̲ 5:13 on four types of almsgiving: (1) "he that is minded to give but not that others should give—he begrudges what belongs to others; (2) he that is minded that others should give but not that he should give—he begrudges what belongs to himself; (3) he that is minded to give and also that others should give—he is a saintly man; and (4) he that is minded not to give himself and that others should not give—he is a wicked man"; and by contrast the simple directive of Rom 12:8: ὁ ἐλεῶν ἐν ἱλαρότητι, "the one who shows mercy should do so with cheerfulness."

8. δυνατεῖ δὲ ὁ θεὸς πᾶσαν χάριν περισσεῦσαι εἰς ὑμᾶς, ἵνα ἐν παντὶ πάντοτε πᾶσαν αὐτάρκειαν ἔχοντες περισσεύητε εἰς πᾶν ἔργον ἀγαθόν, "God is able to make all grace to overflow to you, so that, in all things and at all times, you may have all you need and may overflow in every kind of good work." Both verbs are classed as a generic present tense. The application of the principle "generous sowing leads to bountiful harvest" is made to the moral life, and also to the readers' condition. There is a statement of God's gracious favor ("he is able to make all grace *to overflow* to you": περισσεύειν is a favorite word in Paul's Corinthian vocabulary; it is used here and quite likely in 4:15 in a transitive way for what God does: so Plummer, 260; see pp. 90, 91), coupled with God's design that, since the Corinthians have all their needs provided for (αὐτάρκεια means "self-sufficiency," a stoic term for a person's independence of things, making those individuals who adopt this philosophy complete in themselves: see Kittel, *TDNT* 1:466; J. N. Sevenster, *Paul and Seneca*, 113; but here and in Phil 4:11–13 the term clearly depicts the Christian's dependence on God and rests on finding sufficiency in Christ), they will be able to "excel" (περισσεύητε, going back to 8:7) in all good works, notably the collection. The ruling thought is that, as the Achaeans rise to their responsibility in making their offering, they may count on God to sustain this endeavor by granting them both the desire to share and the necessary ability to do so (cf. Bengel: *datur nobis, et habemus, non ut habeamus, sed ut bene faciamus*). Thus the apostle's teaching moves on from 8:12 which limits the amount to what a person has to this level where it is God who inspires and provides the ability to give as a basis for genuine "sharing" (going back to 8:14).

The form of the sentence is chiastic, with its parallel terms coming at the crucial parts of the writing. God's (χάρις) "grace" thus matches εἰς πᾶν ἔργον ἀγαθόν, "every good work," and both terms are set in the framework of the collection.

9. καθὼς γέγραπται·
  ἐσκόρπισεν, ἔδωκεν τοῖς πένησιν,
  ἡ δικαιοσύνη αὐτοῦ μένει εἰς τὸν αἰῶνα.

As it is written:
  He has scattered widely, he has given to the poor;
  His righteousness endures forever.

An Old Testament quotation is called in to make the allusion to ἔργον ἀγαθόν ("good work") clear: it is the charitable deed of helping the poor saints of Jerusalem (referred to explicitly in v 12). The key word is "poor," as in Ps 112:9 (LXX 111:9, which is here cited as a later title for one branch of Jewish Christians known as "ebionites" [a Greek form of *hā ʾebyônîm*, "the poor"], see F. F. Bruce, *New Testament History* [London: Nelson, 1969] 255, 256). The righteous man in Israel is known for his almsgiving (Dan 4:27); and "righteousness" (צְדָקָה, *ṣᵉdāqāh*) tended to be equated with giving charity in early Judaism (Str-B 3:525), which may be paralleled in Matt 6:1–4 (Reumann, *Righteousness*, 52 f., 234; Ziesler, *Meaning of Righteousness*, 134: δικαιοσύνη, "righteousness" denotes in this context "religious, moral, and compassionate activity in general"). But the word "righteousness" may also be treated as a forensic term in the sense that care for the poor is an evident token of a person's right relationship to God (Barrett, 238; Georgi, *Geschichte der Kollekte*, 71–74, who notes how "his righteousness" is associated with "the fruits of righteousness" in v 10, though the quotation is taken from Hos 10:12, LXX). So Georgi resists both Lietzmann, 138, and Windisch, 278, 279, who tend to view righteousness (as equivalent to φιλανθρωπία, "philanthropy") in moral terms. The providing of seed in v 10 goes back to God the provider in the preceding v, and the anthropological interpretation in v 9 which sees righteousness solely as an act of benevolence and charity is ruled out thereby; if it is not completely discounted, then it needs to be supplemented, just as Barrett's reading of Paul's motives in 1 Cor 16:1–4 and this v, which he sees as a simple device to help the needy Jerusalemites in their poverty and to bind together the two wings of the Church (*1 Corinthians*, 385 ff.) need to be enriched by what Paul's eschatological hope might contribute to our understanding of 9:10–15 (see Davies, *The Gospel and the Land*, 200–203).

Instead, Paul is building on God's justifying action of which the gentile Christian collection for Jerusalem is a potent sign (*ein Symptom*, Georgi, ibid., 73). Georgi, ibid., 78, makes much of the use of 1 Chron 29:16–22 in Jewish expectation. The people, in this text, are seen as offering freely and joyfully to Yahweh and his Temple in Jerusalem. In Jewish hopes based on Isa 60:5, 11, this giving would be completed as the Gentiles brought gifts ("the wealth of the nations") to Zion, and this occurrence would mark the new age. Paul may have seen the collection in this light. Yet it still remains to be shown that the Temple motif was so important for the apostle (cf. M. Hengel, *Acts and the History of Earliest Christianity*, 118). Note, however, 6:14–7:1, and we observe how Paul may be using an appeal to the Temple as exploiting his opponents' idiom, even if he wished to dissociate himself from the Temple theology of the Chronicler in 1 Chron 29 (so Georgi, ibid., 79 ff.) in spite of the witness of Acts 21:26; 24:17. Yet, as Davies, *Paul*, 74–85, and Jones, *The Contemporary Cross*, 148 f., submit, there may be a measure of sublimated nationalism still residual in the Paul of the epistles. This second view which sees Paul's interpretation of the collection in eschatological terms has much to recommend it, as the next v apparently shows.

10. ὁ δὲ ἐπιχορηγῶν σπόρον τῷ σπείροντι καὶ ἄρτον εἰς βρῶσιν χορηγήσει καὶ πληθυνεῖ τὸν σπόρον ὑμῶν καὶ αὐξήσει τὰ γενήματα τῆς δικαιοσύνης ὑμῶν, "He who provides seed for the sower and bread for food will provide and increase your seed and will augment your harvest of righteousness." It is God who provides the farmer's needs: seed for sowing and bread for eating. Once more, Paul's thought moves from the horticultural sphere of activity to the moral, or better, the eschatological. The Old Testament allusion is taken from Isa 55:10; Hos 10:12, from which vv Paul has extracted words and phrases rather than making a direct citation. Yahweh makes the earth "grow and sprout" and gives "seed to the sower and bread for eating," a reference followed by the prophet Hosea's hortatory words (LXX): "Sow for yourselves in righteousness (εἰς δικαιοσύνην) . . . seek Yahweh until the fruits of righteousness (γενήματα δικαιοσύνης) come to you." Such "fruits" would be seen in the Gentiles' willing support of the "saints" as part of God's plan for the restoration or fullness of Israel and the reconciliation of the world (Rom 11:12, 15: see earlier, pp. 268–70). These vv (8–10) have distinct bearing on our understanding of 8:14 with similar wording.

11. ἐν παντὶ πλουτιζόμενοι εἰς πᾶσαν ἁπλότητα, ἥτις κατεργάζεται δι᾿ ἡμῶν εὐχαριστίαν τῷ θεῷ, "You will be made rich in every way so that you can always be generous, and through us such generosity will yield thanksgiving to God." "You will be made rich" (πλουτιζόμενοι, a participial form, perhaps a transitive aspect of the middle voice, "enriching [others]": see N. Turner, *Insights*, 166) recalls 6:10 and 8:9. Indeed, it fixes the meaning of these references as Paul's talking of God's enrichments of grace, not material prosperity per se. Yet there is a practical side to the Gentiles' liberality. They are summoned to come to the rescue of "the poor" in Zion, and for that reason—since the offering moves God's age-old plan of universal salvation to its appointed goal (Rom 11:30–32)—what is done by the Achaean believers leads to thanksgiving arising to God. At the heart of the v is ἁπλότης, "generosity," the word as in 8:2 and v 13 of this chapter; but Barrett prefers "integrity," "goodness," which is less desirable since clearly what is the trigger of thanksgiving to God is the readers' ready and unstinted response to the claims of need (cf. Rom 12:8, which is a generalized application).

12. ὅτι ἡ διακονία τῆς λειτουργίας ταύτης οὐ μόνον ἐστὶν προσαναπληροῦσα τὰ ὑστερήματα τῶν ἁγίων, ἀλλὰ καὶ περισσεύουσα διὰ πολλῶν εὐχαριστιῶν τῷ θεῷ, "This service which you render is not only providing for the needs of the saints [at Jerusalem], but overflows through many thanksgivings to God." Here Paul's thought which has been somewhat vague and erratic in the previous v (BDF § 468.2) sums up. The first objective of the collection was to meet the needs of the saints (προσαναπληροῦσα τὰ ὑστερήματα τῶν ἁγίων [as

at 8:4]). The fact that it was not simply an exercise in charity but was directed to the specific end of helping the Jerusalem church in its destitution accounts for the language of ἡ διακονία τῆς λειτουργίας ταύτης, the service (8:4; 9:13) or administration (Georgi, *Geschichte der Kollekte,* 74) of this act of public service (λειτουργία, which may reflect a special use of the word referring to a religious enterprise, or it may be neutral, meaning the Philippians' money gift to Paul, at least in the second following reference, in Phil 2:17, 30). The terms are virtual synonyms for the collection itself (refs. in Dahl, "Paul and Possessions," 37), but there is no mistaking the solemn tones of the language Paul uses to describe a donation of money.

The offering "overflows" (περισσεύουσα: again a harking back to 8:7 is mandatory, since there Paul calls on the Corinthians to "excel" [περισσεύειν] in the grace of giving) through many thanksgivings (εὐχαριστιῶν: see *Notes;* a plural is used for emphasis, or else meaning "acts of thanksgiving"; a suggested reference to the eucharist seems misplaced, though we should not deny that "thanksgiving" often carries a liturgical overtone in Paul; cf. 1 Cor 10:16; 11:24; 14:16) to God. The final goal of all giving is God's honor, as Barrett acutely notes. It is just possible to construe the sense of διὰ πολλῶν εὐχαριστιῶν to be "through the thanksgivings of many (people)," which might then widen the embrace of the audience to include Paul's own Gentile congregations. Yet this is denied by Georgi, ibid., 74, n. 289, though for no good reason.

13. διὰ τῆς δοκιμῆς τῆς διακονίας ταύτης δοξάζοντες τὸν θεὸν ἐπὶ τῇ ὑποταγῇ τῆς ὁμολογίας ὑμῶν εἰς τὸ εὐαγγέλιον τοῦ Χριστοῦ καὶ ἁπλότητι τῆς κοινωνίας εἰς αὐτοὺς καὶ εἰς πάντας, "By their approving of this service they give praise to God in that they see both the obedience that accompanies your faith which acknowledges the Gospel of Christ and the generosity of your partnership with them and everyone." The Jerusalem believers are thought to be welcoming of the Gentiles' gift. Their δοκιμή ("approval" rather than "testing" is obviously the sense; but see *Comment* on 10:8) will lead to their joining in a chorus of praise (δοξάζοντες: "giving honor"—δόξα—"to God") offered for one reason in particular (denoted by ἐπί: "on the ground of," or "in that they see," as we have paraphrased). This occasion is twofold: the submission (ὑποταγή) that goes with the Gentiles' response (lit. "acknowledgement" or "confession," rendering ὁμολογία) to the Gospel of Christ; and the generosity (ἁπλότης) of the Gentiles' partnership (κοινωνία) with believing Israel and with everyone (εἰς πάντας). Clearly there are complex idioms here, which need inspection. And we cannot escape the conclusion that "in the fulness of his feeling the Apostle gives a compressed fulness of expression, the general meaning of which is certain, but the exact construction of which cannot in all particulars be disentangled with certainty" (Plummer, 266). Perhaps even that guarded statement is too sanguine, since a lot depends on the implied subject of the participle δοξάζοντες, which is a further anacoluthon, the nominative participle having no direct agreement. Presumably it does not agree with πλουτιζόμενοι (v 11), for then the persons in view would be the Corinthians themselves as well as others (so RSV, and RSV mg., Bruce, 228). Most commentators see the subject as the Christians at Jerusalem, "the poor saints who receive the benefits" (Barrett, 240; Héring, 68; Plummer, 266) of the collec-

tion. But there is a third possibility, namely, that the antecedent is in the adjective διὰ πολλῶν εὐχαριστιῶν (v 12), "in the thanksgivings *of the many,*" referring to the Corinthians who remained loyal to Paul's cause, and who now welcome the action of the entire church as expressed in the raising of the offering (see 1:11; 2:6 for the notion of a division within the Corinthian ranks). The allusion to "obedience" (lit., "submission," ὑποταγή) in confessing the (Pauline) Gospel seems to indicate some reaffirmed allegiance to Paul as the Gospel's proponent. In this view, the Jerusalem church does not enter the picture until the second half of the v ("your partnership with them," εἰς αὐτούς).

The collection, which may have seemed at face value simply a charitable deed, has deeper levels of meaning. It is a vindication of Paul's authority and then—as a consequence—a demonstration to the Jerusalem church of the Corinthian (*pars pro toto,* so representing the Pauline churches of the Gentile communities) confession that there is one Gospel, including both Jews and non-Jews (Rom 1:16, 17)—at least from Paul's angle of vision. This setting is highly significant in offering a reason for Paul's convoluted syntax, which (in our reconstruction) makes a strong pitch to the Jerusalem congregation to join the malcontents at Corinth in recognizing Paul's apostolic ministry. Then, the generous giving is a visible token of κοινωνία—a common sharing in divine grace (see Hainz, *Koinonia,* 141–44, for several nuances here)— that unites the two factions of Christendom in Paul's day. Raising this money gift was fraught with deeply felt theological and ecclesiological (so Windisch, 284, who speaks of "church politics" in this aspect; but the better term is von Harnack's *Liebespflicht,* "duty of love," in *Mission and Expansion,* 183 [in the original, 158]; this gesture led to "one visible expression of brotherly unity" [ibid., 183]) desires on Paul's part, namely, there is one Gospel intended for all people, and there is one Church embracing believing Jews and believing Hellenes (Rom 3:29, 30; 10:9–13; Gal 3:28, 29; 1 Cor 10:32). Strangely, Paul rounds off the phrase after κοινωνίας εἰς αὐτούς with the supplementary phrase καὶ εἰς πάντας, "and with everyone." This should strictly mean that the Gentile congregations raised money gifts for other churches and worthy causes other than the needs of the people at Jerusalem. But we have no knowledge of these actions. So we must take the phrase to be a general one in praise of the generous spirit that moves the readers, and would move them wherever there may be need (so Tasker, 129; Héring, 68, n. 10; Hainz, *Koinonia,* 144, who sees in the additional phrase a bias on Paul's part to "relativize" the claims of Jerusalem without denying the continuing "relationship of debt" between the mission churches and the mother church).

14. καὶ αὐτῶν δεήσει ὑπὲρ ὑμῶν ἐπιποθούντων ὑμᾶς διὰ τὴν ὑπερβάλλουσαν χάριν τοῦ θεοῦ ἐφ᾽ ὑμῖν, "And in their prayers for you they yearn for you because of the surpassing grace God has given you." The "saints" at Jerusalem are also bound to Paul's mission churches—at least, so he writes with expectation—by ties of prayer and common grace. The tender verb ἐπιποθεῖν, "to yearn for, show affection to," is ordinarily used of Paul's own desire to see his converts' faces (e.g., Phil 1:8 on which see R. P. Martin, *Philippians,* NCB, 67, referring to C. Spicq, "*Epipothein,* Désirer ou chérir?" *RB* 64 [1957] 184–95; Phil 2:26; Rom 1:11; 1 Thess 3:6; cf. 2 Tim 1:4). The link that unites

the Jewish and Gentile believers is the "surpassing (ὑπερβάλλουσαν, a hyper-bolic word, yet futuristic in its tendency, as Plummer notes, 267, with the caution that Paul's hopes may have been set too high; we may add that Rom 15:30, 31 gives a more dismal prospect of the collection's future on the Jewish-Christian side, and the fact that, according to Acts 20:2–5, no Corinthian is found among the delegates to Jerusalem, may show Paul's great desires to have the collection cement relations were not to be realized; see too Lietz-mann, 139, and Barrett, 242, similarly; cf. Eph 1:19; 2:7; 3:19 and earlier in our letter at 3:10) grace of God" shown to the Corinthians. There is a conscious play on the word χάρις, which up to this verse in the discussion has chiefly carried the meaning of "the collection" (Hainz, *Koinonia*, 139, 140); now it reverts to the sense found in 8:1 of God's action in human lives leading to those impulses which cause people to be generous. Thus at 9:14 we complete the circle started at 8:1 in an elaborate *inclusio*, and the two "ends" of Paul's disquisition are joined. Incidentally, there is here yet more *indicium* of the unity pervading these two chapters. χάρις will take on a different nuance again in the concluding coda of v 15, which is a doxology; hence χάρις means "thanks" to God (τῷ θεῷ) in a verbless ejaculation.

15. χάρις τῷ θεῷ ἐπὶ τῇ ἀνεκδιηγήτῳ αὐτοῦ δωρεᾷ, "Thanks be to God for his gift beyond measure!" Appropriately, then, a doxological outburst is a fitting climax: χάρις, literally, "grace," but here the one instance in chaps. 8, 9 of the meaning "thanks," is ascribed to God for his gift beyond all imagining. In a chapter full of emphasis on the Gentiles' giving, it is fitting for the writer to recall that God is the great giver; and that his gift—presumably that of his Son (8:9) or, more likely in this context, his universal Gospel announced in Paul's message and ministry—should evoke Christian praise, since it is a gift whose depth cannot be expressed (ἀνεκδιήγητος, a rare word for "indescribable"; cf. its use in *1 Clem* 49:4, 61:1 and in *1 Clem* 20:5 it stands in tandem with ἀνεξιχνίαστοι . . . ὁδοί of Rom 11:33 in Paul).

Explanation

"To give," says one ancient commentator (referred to by Strachan, 142) "is not to lose but to sow seed." The point of connection is that the fruits of generous giving are as productive and sure as the fruits of the earth in the season of good harvest. The key phrase lies in v 7: God loves the cheerful giver, since—we learn from v 15—he himself is the giver par excellence (Rom 8:32). This central idea is well brought out by Barrett (240):

> At no stage does Paul allow the caritative action of his churches to escape from the theological context which supplies its meaning, any more than he allows his theology to be without practical expression.

The section thus alternates between the horticultural imagery (seed, sower, crop, harvest) and the down-to-earth practicalities of the "collection for the saints" (v 12). In the latter case the emphasis is laid on munificence in giving and the relief of human wants. But such help is clearly set in the framework of thanksgiving to God (vv 11, 12, 15), and a demonstration of concern that promotes the oneness of believers in Judea and Paul's missionary sphere, his "field" of evangelistic and pastoral opportunities (10:13–16, esp. v 15, RSV). There is a deeply wrought-out purpose in Paul's enterprise, as we have seen. But let us not overlook at least the thread of compassion (Harnack's term, "obligation of love," cited earlier) and concern for the poor that runs through these two chapters.

Leo the Great has a sermon on the virtue of charity with words that are apposite in every age and circumstance:

> We must show more liberal bounty toward the poor and those who suffer from all kinds of affliction in order that many voices may give thanks to God . . . no other devotion of the faithful is more pleasing to the Lord than that which is directed toward the poor. Where he finds merciful concern he recognizes the reflection of his own kindness. Let the almsgiver feel happy and secure, for he will have the greatest gain if he has saved the smallest amount for himself; as the blessed apostle Paul says: "He who supplies seed to the sower both will supply bread for food and will multiply your seed and increase the harvest of your righteousness" in Christ Jesus our Lord.
>
> Sermon 10 on *Lent,* 3–5

VII. Fresh Troubles in Corinth (10:1–13:10)

A. Paul's Self-Vindication (10:1–11)

Bibliography

Bahr, G. J. "The Subscriptions in the Pauline Letters." *JBL* 87 (1968) 27–41. **Barrett, C. K.** *Essays on Paul:* "Christianity at Corinth." 1–27. **Baur, F. C.** *Paul the Apostle of Jesus Christ.* Tr. E. Zeller. London: Williams & Norgate, 1876. **Betz, H.-D.** *Der Apostel Paulus und die sokratische Tradition.* BHT 45. Tübingen: J. C. B. Mohr (P. Siebeck), 1972. **Güttgemanns, E.** *Der leidende Apostel und sein Herr.* FRLANT 90. Göttingen: Vandenhoeck & Ruprecht, 1966. **Jervell, J.** "Der schwache Charismatiker." In *Rechtfertigung,* FS E. Käsemann, ed. J. Friedrich, W. Pöhlmann and P. Stuhlmacher, 185–98. Tübingen/Göttingen: Mohr/Vandenhoeck & Ruprecht, 1976. **Käsemann, E.** *Die Legitimität des Apostels.* **Kleinknecht, K. T.** *Der leidende Gerechtfertigte.* WUNT 2nd ser. 13. Tübingen: Mohr, 1984. **Knox, W. L.** *St. Paul.* New York: Appleton, 1932. **Leivestad, R.** " 'The Meekness and Gentleness of Christ,' 2 Cor 10.1." *NTS* 12 (1966) 156–164. **Mackintosh, R.** "The Four Perplexing Chapters (2 Cor 10–13)." *Exp* 7th ser. 6 (1908) 336–44. **Marshall, P.** "Invective: Paul and his Enemies in Corinth." In *Perspectives on Language and Text,* FS F. I. Andersen, ed. E. Condrad: Winona Lake, IN: Eisenbraun (forthcoming). **Oostendorp, D. W.** *Another Jesus. A Gospel of Jewish Christian Superiority in II Corinthians.* Kampen: Kok, 1967. **Schütz, J. H.** *Paul and the Anatomy of Apostolic Authority.* SNTSMS 26. Cambridge: University Press, 1975. **Weher, U.** "Erklärung von 2 Kor 10:1–6." *BZ* 1 (1903) 64–78. **Ward, R. B.** "The Opponents of Paul." *RestQ* 10.4. (1967) 185–95. **Zmijewski, J.** *Der Stil der paulinischen "Narrenrede." Analyse der Sprachgestaltung in 2 Kor 11, 1–12, 10 als Beitrag zur Methodik von Stiluntersuchungen neutestamentlicher Text.* BBB 52. Köln-Bonn: Hanstein, 1978.

Translation

[1] *I, then, Paul myself, appeal to you by the meekness and gentleness of Christ, I who am "timid" when face to face with you, but when I am away, I am "haughty" over you.* [2] *I beg [you] that when I am present I may not have to be "haughty," with a confidence of boldness I expect [to show] to those who think that we are living according to worldly standards.* [3] *For though we are living in this world, we do not carry on a war as the world does.* [4] *Rather, the weapons we fight with are not worldly weapons, but as God empowers [us], we pull down fortresses. We demolish arguments,* [5] *and all lofty notions that oppose the knowledge of God; and we make every thought captive as it obeys Christ.* [6] *And we stand ready to avenge every act of disobedience, once your obedience becomes complete.*

[7] *Look at what is in front of you! If there is anyone who is sure that he is Christ's person,* [a] *he should consider this fact: just as he belongs to Christ, so we too belong to Christ.* [8] *Even if* [b] *I can boast [about being Christ's] and, more than that, about*

*my [our] authority, which the Lord gave us to build you up and not pull you down,
I will not be discredited by it.* **9** *[Do not think] that I am trying to frighten you
with my letters.* **10** *For some are saying, "His letters are weighty and forceful, but
his physical presence is weak and his rhetoric moves us to contempt."* **11** *Let this
person [who thinks like this] consider that what we are through our letters when
we are absent, we will be in our actions when we come to you.*

Notes

a δοῦλος is added by D* F G vg^{mss} Ambst before Χριστοῦ, "Christ's servant," P^{46} has ὁ Χριστός.
b Nestle-Aland^{26} brackets τε after ἐάν, the reading of ℵ C D ψ etc. τε is omitted by P^{46} B F
and minuscules. See Moulton, *Grammar* 3:339; BDF § 443.3; Thrall, *Greek Particles,* 96, 97.

Form/Structure/Setting

The opening of chap. 10 marks a new section of the letter. Attempts to
explain the transition from chap. 9 to the last four chapters present the reader
with a bewildering variety of choices. Beyond all doubt, we have to reckon
with several changes in the flow of the letter: changes of atmosphere, the
mood of Paul's response, and in what he expects from the Corinthians (Barrett,
244; Héring, 69, writes: "Paul is no longer the father reconciled with his
children . . . but an irritated chief who is defending himself by attacking
his opponents": a bit of an exaggeration! But it does highlight an undeniable
feature. Other scholars [cited in Plummer, 269] have tried to maintain that
chaps. 8 and 9 prepare for the polemic against opponents in 10–13. But
Plummer's question is emphatic: "Is asking for money a good preparation
for an incisive attack?" And, in any case, "when the curtain rises in 10, we
are immediately aware of a complete change of scene. Titus and the Macedonians have disappeared, along with the collection-plates" [Héring, 69]. True,
but both Titus and the Macedonian brothers are waiting in the wings for
their cue to reappear in 12:14–18, and the collection may be seen in a veiled
form in that pericope). It is not adequate to treat chaps. 10–13 as a "recapitulation" of previous sections in 1–9 (so W. H. Bates, "The Integrity of II Corinthians," *NTS* 12 [1965] 56–59). Psychological explanations, e.g., that Paul had
a sleepless night between composing the two chapters (Lietzmann, 139) and
that the new moods are due to a pause in dictation (Denney, 290, but he
acknowledges later [389] that the "break" in the flow of the dictation led
Paul to compose "in a very different strain") are not enough to account for
the new reaction which changes "a hopeful to a despairing attitude" (Barrett,
244). We may turn the argument from psychology in a new direction. It is
just conceivable that a person's mood would improve from despair to hope.
But it is unthinkable that the mood alternation would go in the reverse direction—unless fresh circumstances were called into play. If we refuse to see
chaps. 10–13 as part of the "tearful letter" (2:4–7:8), then the remaining
option is to postulate a new and worsening development in Paul's relations
with the Corinthians, which required another letter of a different tone and
temper, consonant with a more serious attack on his apostolic work at Corinth.
We may trace this development to the arrival and influence of the anti-Pauline
teachers of 11:4–18.

With this theoretical setting, we have now to inquire how Paul goes about his task. The answer involves some decision about the form and style of these four chapters. Modern discussion has agreed that these parts of the letter form an "apology" in the technical sense of the term: a statement of a person's integrity in the face of detractors (Allo, 230, who distinguishes several nuances of the word "apology" in 2 Cor. The fresh emphasis in chaps. 10–13 is that "all [the apostle's writing] becomes apologetic—or polemical, to put it more correctly. Thus we reach now his personal apology") and especially the defense of Socrates against the sophists and hostile poets and playwrights such as Aristophanes (Betz, *Der Apostel Paulus*, 17–19, 34, 35), whose play *Clouds* in particular ridicules Socrates as a bogus thinker and a charlatan. But even more is at stake. It is Paul's status as an apostolic figure and teacher that is under fire, as emissaries have appeared at Corinth to insinuate that Paul is in fact no true apostle (so F. C. Baur, *Paulus*, 289, cited by Käsemann, *Legitimität*, 33) or even not a Christian at all (so Käsemann, ibid.). It could be maintained, therefore, as Barrett (245) does, that it is not Paul's person but his Gospel that is at the front of the debate. But rather we should not set these elements in contrast, since Paul's life and work go inseparably together (Bultmann, 149). And to reject him—on grounds given at v 10, namely, that his personal presence is weak, and his utterances (= teaching) are to be despised—is in his view to turn away decisively from his understanding of the kerygma given by God. We can see this nexus illustrated in v 6 where "obedience" elicited from the reader is directed both to Christ and to Paul acting *in persona Christi*. The "autobiographical" dimension should not be overlooked, as we may observe with Kleinknecht, *Der leidende Gerechtfertigte*, 295, 296, 301. Paul's address to the church is indeed an *apologia pro vita sua* because he is inextricably bound up with the message entrusted to him as a divine ambassador (5:20). His defense is equally *apologia pro evangelio suo*. Αὐτὸς δὲ ἐγὼ Παῦλος, "I . . . Paul," is therefore a good *exemplum* of his style and purpose, for in Carrez's table ("Le 'nous' en 2 Corinthiens," 475), out of 239 uses of "I" in 2 Cor, 147 references are in chaps. 10–13: "it is in these chapters where Paul is defending his apostolate and the legitimacy of his mission with vehemence and vigor" that these personal statements are emphatic (Carrez, 482).

This evidence would seem to endorse G. J. Bahr's proposal (in "The Subscriptions") to account for αὐτὸς δὲ ἐγὼ Παῦλος, "I, then, Paul myself" and what follows in chap. 10–13 as opening and constituting the autograph subscription (ὑπογραφή) which Paul appends to chaps. 1–9 (the letter's σῶμα, "body") which had been prepared by an amanuensis. Bahr, therefore, appeals to this literary analysis to bind together chaps. 1–9 and 10–13. But the emotional content of some parts of 1–9, e.g., chaps. 6, 7, with their fractured syntax as well as the personal appeals that punctuate chaps. 1–5 (1:23, 24; 2:4; 4:15; 5:12, 13; 6:11–13; 7:2–4; 8:8; 9:1, 11) tend to militate against this theory as also against Mackintosh's idea that 10:1 shows how Paul is rebutting the charge that he "could not have written an epistle *all his own*" ("Four Chapters," 343, his italics). Besides, as Plummer, 270, says, the feeling expressed in these four chapters is of a "very different kind . . . he now exhibits fierce indignation and asserts his authority to the uttermost."

The formal expression αὐτὸς . . . ἐγὼ Παῦλος is best explained as an assertion of authority, paralleling Gal 5:2 (Plummer, 272, citing Lightfoot, *Galatians*,
ad loc.). The αὐτός makes the refutation (implied in ἐγὼ Παῦλος) more emphatic and perhaps scornful; and it serves as an introduction to these chapters
which are marked (as Plummer notes, 272) by three features: (1) strong,
personal feeling; (2) indignation at the calumnies of Paul's opponents; and
(3) the intention that, if the opposition continues, he will not spare his readers.

This section (10:1–11) is notable for the structure of the defense he makes.
Vv 1, 2 are only really intelligible if they cite the actual estimate of Paul in
the eyes of his opponents; and we may appeal to v 10 for confirmation of
the view that Paul is quoting their words as "catch-phrases" or "slogans"
(Bultmann, 184, 185). They refer to Paul's ταπεινότης, lit., "humility," but
here it must mean something like "servility" or "timidity." An even stronger
term like "obsequiousness" or even "sycophancy" may be correct. He—they
alleged—took on a mock humility when he came to Corinth (a possible allusion
to the "interim" visit of 2:1). When he left Corinth and at a safe distance
wrote letters which, they grant, were effective (v 10), he took on the character
of an arrogant, insolent man (his πεποίθησις, unbridled confidence, with the
hallmark of θαρρεῖν). This demeanor—if Bultmann's suggestion (185) is approved—is reckoned by them to be an act of "daring boldness" (τολμῆσαι,
v 2; cf. 10:12; 11:21).

They charge Paul with living as a worldly person (v 2: κατὰ σάρκα, "according to the flesh," which for them is the antithesis of πνεῦμα, "spirit"—divine
power of which they professed to be fully conscious, and which they sought
to import to Corinth, 11:4). They deny to Paul authority (ἐξουσία, v 8) as
an "official" leader in the congregation and pour scorn on his bodily weakness
(ἀσθένεια) as a sick man, and unable to heal himself (a charge which he will
address in 12:1–10). Above all, he claims to be "Christ's person" (Χριστοῦ
εἶναι, v 7). But that designation is one they claim for themselves (v 7b), and
so deny to Paul, since their estimate of Christian living and service would
exclude him.

This body of evidence seems adequate to justify the conclusion that in
Paul's *apologia* he is calling on the idioms and expressions currently being
used at Corinth. Derogatory names and descriptions of his person and claims
are quoted, only to be re-minted by Paul and given a novel twist, either by
being applied in a fresh context or else modified by a play on words (e.g.,
λογίζομαι in v 2b looks on to v 2c; λογισμούς [v 4], and v 7, λογιζέσθω; κατὰ
σάρκα in v 2 is transformed into ἐν σαρκί in v 3, with an obvious change of
meaning).

Also, Paul uses here a style of writing parallel with the devices used by
the philosophers in their debate with the sophists (Betz, ibid., 55). In this
"letter of apology" we have several exchanges of arguments used by which
the true philosopher was distinguished from the false one or by which genuine
leaders in Attic Greece were marked off from the boastful charlatan (γόης,
ἀλαζών). The popular way in which such distinctions were drawn included
the employment of sarcasm, irony, and parody. (1) Examples of sarcasm and
the stronger feature of invective (Marshall, "Invective") will be seen throughout these chapters, especially in the section 11:1–12:10 where Paul's boasting

(καύχησις) is designed to show him as self-consciously taking the role of the "fool" in a highly contrived way (see Zmijewski, *Der Stil der paulinischen "Narrenrede"*). Paul's ridicule of his opponents is seen in 10:1–11 in his exaggerated descriptions of their positions as "fortified vantage points" (v 4), a military metaphor for "lofty ideas" (v 4) which need to be "pulled down" (v 4, as Paul has the right to do, v 8). (2) His irony comes through as he does not directly negate what the opponents say about him; rather he accepts it in an *ad hominem* way, and turns their negative and prejudicial assessment of him into an affirmation of positive and personal credit (e.g., his "timidity" is a commitment to his preaching of a humiliated, now exalted, Lord: so Güttgemanns, *Der leidende Apostel*, 135–41, a section strikingly headed with the caption "Apostolic existence as christological proclamation," and appealing to the creedal Phil 2:6–11 to show how the present power of the Lord is displayed and "proclaimed" in the weakness of Paul, whose life of wretchedness [2 Cor 4:10] patterns that of the earthly Jesus). (3) The style of parody is illustrated (more clearly in 11:16–33) in the way Paul uses imitatively the literary expressions of his opponents but turns their evaluation of him on its head—a favorite trick of the true philosopher who, like Socrates, appeared innocently to disclaim knowledge of the truth in order to mock his rivals. By these literary and stylistic procedures "Paul presents this moving defense of his apostolate and Gospel" (Fallon, 83).

Metaphors abound in these few vv. There are appeals to the language of military installations (v 4) and soldiers' campaigns (v 5: αἰχμαλωτίζοντες)—these terms seem drawn from the "wars of the Maccabees" literature (see *Comment*); the rhetorical schools with their cultivation of arguments (v 5) and reasonings (v 5) are alluded to; and the twin ideas of erecting a building and demolishing it (v 8), the latter verb linked with the idea of v 4, are familiar idioms. And possibly a use is made of forensic terminology (v 6: "to punish every disobedience": cf. Rom 13:4). This section is carefully crafted as we see from the assonance of καθαιροῦντες (v 4) and ἐπαιρόμενον (v 6); and ὑπακοή (vv 5, 6) and παρακοή (v 6); the quick succession of metaphors, sometimes mixed (v 5); the thoughtful positioning of the words, e.g., in the chiasmus of v 11:

$$
\begin{array}{ccc}
\tau\hat{\omega}\ \lambda\acute{o}\gamma\omega & & \pi\alpha\rho\acute{o}\nu\tau\epsilon\varsigma \\
& \times & \\
\dot{\alpha}\pi\acute{o}\nu\tau\epsilon\varsigma & & \tau\hat{\omega}\ \check{\epsilon}\rho\gamma\omega
\end{array}
$$

and, it may be, a chiastic structure in v 10. The contrasted adjectives ἀσθενής // ἰσχυραί and ἐξουθενημένος // βαρεῖαι are set in a criss-cross fashion; "each pair helps to determine the meaning of the other" (Plummer, 282). Note too the alliterative use of words beginning with π especially πᾶν . . . πᾶν . . . πᾶσαν παρακοήν (vv 5, 6).

Comment

1. Αὐτὸς δὲ ἐγὼ Παῦλος παρακαλῶ ὑμᾶς διὰ τῆς πραΰτητος καὶ ἐπιεικείας τοῦ Χριστοῦ, ὃς κατὰ πρόσωπον μὲν ταπεινὸς ἐν ὑμῖν, ἀπὼν δὲ θαρρῶ εἰς ὑμᾶς, "I, then, Paul myself appeal to you by the meekness and gentleness of Christ,

I who am 'timid' when face to face with you, but when I am away, I am 'haughty' over you." Αὐτὸς δὲ ἐγὼ Παῦλος, "I, then, Paul myself." The formal introduction of the apostle is not accidental (assuming it is not the work of a redactor preparing to insert chaps. 10–13 into the final edition of the text: cf. Bornkamm, "History" [see *Introduction*, pp. xl–xlvi]) nor added for the sake of effect. It gives an air of authority to what follows, as in 12:13 (αὐτὸς ἐγώ, "I for my part"); Rom 9:3; 15:4; or in Gal 5:2 (ἴδε ἐγὼ Παῦλος, "now, I Paul." It is not likely that Paul is consciously detaching himself from Timothy as coauthor (1:1) as D. A. Black, *Paul, Apostle of Weakness,* 133, thinks (cf. Plummer, 271). Rather, Paul is preparing to assume the mantle of apostolic authority, which is the central theme of concern in these four chapters.

Yet his stand is moderated in two ways. First, we note his choice of the verb παρακαλῶ ὑμᾶς, "I appeal to you." There is less a note of authoritarian command and more of entreaty (as in Rom 12:1; 15:30; 1 Cor 1:10). Bjerkelund (*PARAKALÔ,* 188) has concluded in regard to Paul's use of clauses with παρακαλέω that there the verb "has neither a sense of commanding (ἐπιτάσσω) nor a sense of entreaty (δέομαι). παρακαλέω is used by Paul when the question of authority is unproblematic, and the apostle can speak to the members of the congregation as his brothers, knowing that they will acknowledge him as apostle." What is in view is a type of admonition that takes into account the moral judgment and spiritual independence of the churches (Holmberg, *Paul and Power,* 86; cf. Bjerkelund, ibid., 190). The issue of authority was *not* unproblematical at Corinth, to be sure; but Paul's coupling of παρακαλῶ and δέομαι (v 2) suggests an oblique appeal—perhaps beginning with a strong verb and moderating his stance by adopting a lower tone, δέομαι, "I beseech" (so Plummer, 273)—to a delicate matter, which he handles with tact and firmness (cf. 12:12; 13:10).

The second court of appeal is διὰ τῆς πραΰτητος καὶ ἐπιεικείας τοῦ Χριστοῦ, "by the meekness and gentleness of Christ," two character traits that refer to *either* of two situations. They may refer (1) to his earthly life (Matt 11:29: so Kümmel, 208; Windisch, 292; see G. N. Stanton, "Matthew 11:28–30," *ExpTim* 94 [1982] 3–9; see too Matt 5:5: ἐπιεικής "gentle" is not found in the Gospels; but it is a Christian trait in Phil 4:5, τὸ ἐπιεικές, "graciousness" is a suggested rendering [R. P. Martin, *Philippians,* NCB ad loc.], with the idea that Christians will have a willingness to forgo retaliation when threatened, a thought of some relevance here; 1 Tim 3:3; Titus 3:2 and especially 1 Pet 2:18). The Lord's attitude (as in Col 3:13) may well have prompted this appeal. If we inquire why Paul did not use the earthly name Ἰησοῦς, but instead spoke Χριστός, the answer could be that "Χριστοῦ may have a point, because some of [the Corinthians] professed to be in a special sense Χριστοῦ" (Plummer, 173: see *Comment* on 10:7). *Or* the two traits may refer (2) to his condescension in becoming incarnate (as in 8:9; cf. Phil 2:6–11, where his "obedience" is the center of gravity, see Güttgemanns, *Der leidende Apostel,* 140; R. P. Martin, *Carmen Christi* [2], xxiii–xxv). But both are intimately related (Barrett, 246). Both Christ's incarnation and his character were foundational as setting up a paradigm for Christian behavior. See Leivestad, "The Meekness," 156–64, whose view that 10:1 relates to the preexistent Christ is challenged by G. N. Stanton, *Jesus of Nazareth in New Testament Preaching*

SNTSMS 27 (Cambridge: University Press, 1974), 108. But see Bultmann, *Theology* 1:294. Here Paul is repeating his pastoral attitude, given in 1:23, 24, and perhaps using terms that recalled his treatment of the offender in 2:6–10 (Strachan, 9).

The relative ὅς, "who," refers to Paul, but it could have a christological dimension explored by Güttgemanns, ibid., 137, citing Rom 4:25; Phil 2:6; Col 1:13 [15]; 1 Tim 3:16 as part of a hymnic style with an introductory relative pronoun. The "deep meaning" is that Paul's character of ταπεινός, "humble" (in the good sense), is fashioned according to the model of what he knows was Christ's way of life. (As a Christian virtue, humility is praised in 1 Cor 4:21; Gal 5:23; Col 3:12; Eph 4:2; 1 Tim 6:11; 2 Tim 2:25; Titus 3:2 in the Pauline corpus, with varying nuances.) His service shared in the features set by the criterion of the humbled and crucified Christ (as in 4:7–10; 6:4–10). In context, however, as was observed above, ταπεινός carries a pejorative sense, implying that Paul was regarded by his enemies as pusillanimous (Plummer has "grovelling" in the sense of a mock humility and recalling the caricature of Uriah Heep who was "very humble" and self-abasing—but in an artful, devious way) in contrast to their strong and effective presence at Corinth (10:10; 11:20). He cites their estimate, while retaining in a double entendre his own self-estimate based on the model of the incarnate Lord. The opposite of ταπεινός is θαρρῆσαι from a verb (θαρρεῖν) rendered "to be confident, courageous" (BGD 352), as in 5:6, 8; 7:16, but in the context of 10:1 with a parallel sense *in malam partem* of "arrogant," "insolent" or (as we prefer) "haughty" (linking with Paul's later protestation in v 5: "all lofty notions," πᾶν ὕψωμα). Paul's opponents are to be heard in this innuendo, charging that when he is away from Corinth he is insisting on his rights and lording it over the congregation (εἰς ὑμᾶς: something like "over you" would express the idea of Paul's superior attitude, his "impudence," Bultmann's word, *Frechheit*).

Two contrasting attitudes are here revealed: servility and superiority. Paul takes them from his opponents, and redirects their intention to his own ends. "I am a humble follower and servant of the lowly Christ, yet have a God-given authority to represent him," notably by strong letters in my absence (v 10; cf. Polycarp, *Phil.* 3:2, for the same contrast of "present . . . absent" in regard to Paul's relations with the congregation). He returns to this contrast in 10:11.

2. δέομαι δὲ τὸ μὴ παρὼν θαρρῆσαι τῇ πεποιθήσει ᾗ λογίζομαι τολμῆσαι ἐπί τινας τοὺς λογιζομένους ἡμᾶς ὡς κατὰ σάρκα περιπατοῦντας, "I beg [you] that when I am present I may not have to be 'haughty,' with a confidence of boldness I expect [to show] to those who think that we are living according to worldly standards." Δέομαι, "I beg you," is even more conciliatory in tone, but it should be treated as a request, not a prayer (so Bachmann, and possibly Barrett, 248; but cf. Bultmann, 185, who renders *ich bitte,* not *ich bete,* but adds *euch,* "you"), for it complements the verb in v 1 rather than further tempering its appeal to excess. Hence to add "you" is legitimate. The object of the request is expressed by the suggested clause ἵνα μή . . . (BDF § 399.3), and picks up the prospect of Paul's future visit to Corinth (13:1–13). Then if these detractors are not refuted by Paul's letter and the Corinthians remain

hostile to him—there will be no choice but for him to be "haughty" (θαρρῶ) in a special way. So he writes of a confidence born of boldness (τῇ πεποιθήσει ᾗ λογίζομαι τολμῆσαι) as he reckons it, that is, directed at those who think (λογιζομένους) that we are acting in a worldly manner (κατὰ σάρκα). The sentence is convoluted and hard to unravel, but the meaning is tolerably plain. Its key lies in the twice repeated middle verb λογίζεσθαι (a key verb in these chaps.: 10:7, 11; 11:5; 12:6; cf. 3:5; and possibly a Corinthian watchword, or maybe a slogan of Paul's enemies, Bultmann, 185). It implies an evaluation and consequent action. They "imagined" (λογιζομένους: Plummer notes the subtle change in the verb's texture here, 274) that Paul was a "man of the world" in his attitudes, with motives and actions dictated by σάρξ, "flesh," i.e., self-interest. Paul takes their word and "disinfects" it by claiming it for his expectation (λογίζομαι) of his own estimate of what it would take to win back the Corinthians (i.e., a "courage" implied in θαρρεῖν in bonam partem, leading to the confidence of a person who is daring enough to risk his reputation at Corinth). The verb τολμῆσαι, "to be bold," may be another slogan in the mouths of the opponents, since they accused Paul of just the opposite, namely, ταπεινότης, = pusillanimity in v 1, reckoning him to be "capricious and shuffling, verbose and vain-glorious, at once a coward and a bully" (Plummer, 275).

The persons in this dramatic opposition to Paul are referred to indirectly: ἐπί τινας, "to those who think," a phrase in which Barrett (249) rightly suggests Paul does not have the Corinthian readers in his sights. Goudge (93, 94) is one of the few commentators to raise the question of the identity behind the veiled allusion to τινας here. He maintains (1) that the indefinite "some" (better "certain people") suggests that Paul is not referring to the Corinthians, and (2) on the other hand, that the appeal of the v presupposes that it depends upon the action of the Corinthians whether Paul has to act sternly or not. The solution to this combination of ideas is not to equate the τινας with the Corinthians themselves but with the emissaries (shortly to be revealed: see 11:4) who have presumed to interfere with Paul's apostolic mission.

These men are outsiders who "have come" (11:4) onto the scene since chaps. 1–9 were sent to Corinth. Not for the first time (cf. 1:12, 17) Paul's motives have been unfavorably weighed and found wanting. Here the σάρξ ("flesh") may well imply that Paul was no pneumatic person, singularly lacking in demonstrable, charismatic gifts of leadership (ἐξουσία; cf. v 8; 13:2 ff.: Käsemann, Legitimität, 10, relating this section to the watchword ἱκανότης, "competence," in chap. 3).

3. ἐν σαρκὶ γὰρ περιπατοῦντες οὐ κατὰ σάρκα στρατευόμεθα, "For though we are living in this world, we do not carry on a war as the world does." ἐν σαρκί, lit., "in the flesh," uses σάρξ in its neutral sense, with a change of preposition from κατά in the preceding v. (See R. Jewett, Paul's Anthropological Terms, 153, 154, for Paul's reply to the [supposed] "gnostic" attempt to equate ἐν σαρκί and κατὰ σάρκα.) Paul denies that he has lived in a way that conforms (κατά) to the world's standards, but he is quick to assert that his is a mundane existence, fraught with experience of life's vicissitudes (cf. 4:7–10; 6:4–10, and to be elaborated at 11:23–33). "In the flesh" is the literal translation,

but this has to mean that his life is set in this present world and not withdrawn from it as a recluse (1 Cor 5:10 is a good example of a similar misunderstanding already made at Corinth). His apostolic career is illustrated by the use of military language: στρατευόμεθα, "we carry on a warfare" (cf. 6:7; 1 Cor 9:7; Rom 13:12, 13; 1 Thess 5:8; Eph 6:10–17; 1 Tim 1:18; 2 Tim 2:3 f. in the Pauline corpus; and Wisd Sol 5:17–20).

4a,b. τὰ γὰρ ὅπλα τῆς στρατείας ἡμῶν οὐ σαρκικὰ ἀλλὰ δυνατὰ τῷ θεῷ πρὸς καθαίρεσιν ὀχυρωμάτων, "Rather, the weapons we fight with are not worldly weapons, but as God empowers [us], we pull down fortresses." The weapons of this war are clearly not "fleshly" (σαρκικά), Paul explains, thereby amplifying his earlier remark that he did not wage war "according to the flesh" (κατὰ σάρκα), as people in the world do it, or with a reliance on external power and influences. Perhaps there is an allusion to 4:2 where πανουργία, "cunning," and δολοῦν, "tamper" with God's message, are also linked to the verb περιπατέω, "to walk," i.e., to live as God's professed servants (cf. 12:16). Instead, the ὅπλα τῆς στρατείας ἡμῶν, "the weapons we fight with," are described as δυνατὰ τῷ θεῷ, meaning either (1) in God's sight, they are powerful (cf. BDF § 192 for the Hebraism; Moule, *Idiom Book*, 184) or (2) on God's behalf (BDF § 188.2, taking the τῷ θεῷ as *dat. commodi*, i.e., God can work powerfully through these weapons [Plummer, 276; Barrett, 251], since they are πνευματικά, directed by the Spirit, as in 1 Cor 2:4). The MSS are ambivalent between reading στρατείας (B) and στρατίας (‫א‬ C D G). The two terms must be viewed as synonymous, though strictly the former means "campaign" (the preferred sense) and the latter, "army." (For the confused orthography, see Deissmann, *Bible Studies*, 132.) V. C. Pfitzner, *Paul and the Agon Motif*, 160, writes that "the image of στρατεία pictures the life and work of the Apostle in its totality."

The effectiveness of these assets for the apostolic ministry is seen in the result clause which follows: πρὸς καθαίρεσιν ὀχυρωμάτων, "to pulling down of fortresses," an allusion to Prov 21:22, LXX: πόλεις ὀχυρὰς ἐπέβη σοφὸς καὶ καθεῖλεν τὸ ὀχύρωμα ἐφ᾽ ᾧ ἐπεποίθεισαν οἱ ἀσεβεῖς, "A wise man scales the strong cities and brings down the stronghold (ὀχύρωμα) in which the ungodly trust." The attack of sophists with a similar figure of speech is mentioned in Philo, *De Conf. Ling.* 129–31 (Windisch, 297, 298; Bruce, 230; Betz, *Der Apostel Paulus*, 68, who notes too the use of the verb τολμᾶν, "to be bold," in this setting). The wording of Philo is striking since it combines two of Paul's otherwise rare expressions and a noun which recurs in the significant passage of 13:10: "the demolishing (καθαίρεσιν) of . . . the stronghold (ὀχυρώματος) built through persuasiveness of speech (διὰ τῆς τῶν λόγων πιθανότητος) . . . to divert and deflect the mind from honoring God." Yet ὀχύρωμα is frequent in 1 Maccabees (e.g., 5:65), and it seems that Paul is indebted to several ideas from this source, e.g., αἰχμαλωτίζοντες in v 5 (1 Macc 8:10, which also has ὀχυρώματα: Plummer, 276, 277). See *Comment* on 11:32, 33.

4c, 5. λογισμοὺς καθαιροῦντες, καὶ πᾶν ὕψωμα ἐπαιρόμενον κατὰ τῆς γνώσεως τοῦ θεοῦ, καὶ αἰχμαλωτίζοντες πᾶν νόημα εἰς τὴν ὑπακοὴν τοῦ Χριστοῦ, "We demolish arguments, and all lofty notions that oppose the knowledge of God; and we make every thought captive as it obeys Christ." The metaphor of "demolishing" (καθαίρειν) continues but with a variation: now the participles—

καθαιροῦντες, "destroying" arguments, αἰχμαλωτίζοντες (v 6), "making captive" every thought, and ἐν ἑτοίμῳ ἔχοντες (in v 6), "standing ready"—continue the idea of the purpose for which Paul is equipped by the divine resources for his apostolic tasks. The term λογισμοί, "arguments," is calculated to challenge the opponents' use of reason, exactly as the defensive stance of Attic philosophy sought to ridicule the pretensions of the sophists (cf. the verdict on διαλογισμός in Rom 1:21; 1 Cor 3:20; Phil 2:14 but without this setting), and there is a play on λογίζεσθαι (v 2) commented on negatively again at 11:5.

πᾶν ὕψωμα ἐπαιρόμενον κατὰ τῆς γνώσεως τοῦ θεοῦ, "all lofty notions that oppose (lit., are raised up against) the knowledge of God." Raising a rampart against a person in the sense of opposing him is found in Job 19:6, LXX (γνῶτε οὖν ὅτι ὁ κύριός ἐστιν ὁ ταράξας, ὀχύρωμα δὲ αὐτοῦ ἐπ᾽ ἐμὲ ὕψωσεν, "Know then that Yahweh has troubled [me] by raising up his stronghold against me": suggested by Bultmann, 187), but it may be that a change of metaphor is implied, as Paul considers how his opponents have set up a wall of rivalry between himself and his Corinthian converts. His job is to tear it down, since for him this alienation is a sign that the Corinthians are blocking their access to the divine truth of the Gospel (as in 4:2–4; 6:7; 13:8, all of which identify his Gospel with God's truth that mediates the knowledge of God; cf. Wisd Sol 14:22: πλανᾶσθαι περὶ τὴν τοῦ θεοῦ γνῶσιν, men "err in their knowledge of God," in a chapter fulminating against idols and idolatry. For gnosis at Corinth, see Barrett, Essays on Paul, 6–14). The task of Paul has a single aim: to make every thought (νόημα, another polemical term for human "design" [Barrett's rendering] which is at odds with the divine will; in 2 Cor νόημα is invariably used in a negative way: 2:11; 3:14; 4:4; 11:3) captive to obey Christ. The verb αἰχμαλωτίζειν is properly "to take as prisoner of war," as Paul's mission colleagues are so designated in a good sense of the verb: see W.-H. Ollrog, Paulus und seine Mitarbeiter (1979) 76, for lists. In the bad connotation it implies that sinful aspirations to human independence (Rom 1:18–23; 7:23; cf. 2 Tim 3:6) are to be curbed and brought into submission to Christ (εἰς τὴν ὑπακοὴν τοῦ Χριστοῦ), so Plummer, 277. In practical terms such obedience to Christ involves a submission to Paul's kerygma which is in danger of losing its credibility at Corinth (11:4) as a result of the rival mission there.

6. καὶ ἐν ἑτοίμῳ ἔχοντες ἐκδικῆσαι πᾶσαν παρακοήν, ὅταν πληρωθῇ ὑμῶν ἡ ὑπακοή, "And we stand ready to avenge every act of disobedience, once your obedience becomes complete." "Obedience" as one of Paul's favorite terms for human response to Christ and his word (see Bultmann, Theology 1:314–24) now elicits his attitude to the opposition. "We stand ready" is an attempt to render ἐν ἑτοίμῳ ἔχοντες (a possible Latinism, in promptu habere = ἐν ἑτοίμῳ ἔχειν), and marks a distinction between the baneful influence of the emissaries at Corinth whose "every act of disobedience" (πᾶσαν παρακοήν) Paul is about to avenge (ἐκδικῆσαι, a forensic term), when the stranglehold these men have on the Corinthian believers is broken, and the church's return to his side (implied, as a profession of his confidence in "your obedience," ὑπακοή) becomes (ingressive use of the verb: see Héring, 71; BDF § 331) "complete." In other words, Paul distinguishes the alien intruders at Corinth whose satanic

work (11:13–15) he wants to overthrow and neutralize from the body of Pauline believers for whom he entertains optimistic hope of their recovery from the snare of deviation and seduction (11:1–4). A sharper point is put on the recurrence of the obedience/disobedience motif if Barrett (cf. *1 Corinthians*, 238 ff.) is correct in tracing this "disobedience" on the part of the intruders to their breaking the agreement entered into at Antioch (Gal 2:7–9, see *Introduction*, pp. liv–lvi). The same matter lies behind the following paragraph of 10:12–18, and accounts for its insertion in the flow of Paul's defense. This reading of the scene is to be preferred to other views: that once the Corinthians have returned from their latest defection, Paul will punish them for all past lapses by raking over their former criticisms (e.g., 1:17), or that he will then widen his campaign against all opposition in the world (Windisch, 299), or that once the community returns to the true Gospel and rejects the opponents' gospel Paul will be ready to act against the members of the community who maintain their allegiance to a false gospel (Fallon, 86).

7. τὰ κατὰ πρόσωπον βλέπετε. εἴ τις πέποιθεν ἑαυτῷ Χριστοῦ εἶναι, τοῦτο λογιζέσθω πάλιν ἐφ᾽ ἑαυτοῦ, ὅτι καθὼς αὐτὸς Χριστοῦ, οὕτως καὶ ἡμεῖς, "Look at what is in front of you! If there is anyone who is sure that he is Christ's person, he should consider this fact: just as he belongs to Christ, so we too belong to Christ." τὰ κατὰ πρόσωπον βλέπετε may be construed in a number of possible ways: (1) as an indicative mood and ironic; thus by J. A. T. Robinson, *The Body*, 26, who renders, "You see only the end of your nose," or NIV, "you are looking only on the surface of things"; (2) as a question: "Do you look on things after the outward appearance?" (J. H. Kennedy, *The Second and Third Epistle*, 184): so KJV/AV, Bultmann, 198; (3) as an imperative, "Look at what is in front of you"; so NIV mg., RSV, NEB, and in the various translations of Allo, Windisch, Héring, and Hughes who renders, "Face the obvious facts" (355). Kleinknecht, *Der leidende Gerechtfertigte*, 285–89, insists on the sense of the imperative on the grounds that this is Paul's confrontational tactic, as he bids the opponents look at his "weak" existence. It is not easy to decide which option is best, but what is important is the recall of κατὰ πρόσωπον, "face to face," "in appearance," from v 1. There Paul referred to his presence among the Corinthians; now he invites them to consider what that presence meant at a time when his initial evangelism at Corinth is under suspicion. Or possibly there is a caustic allusion to those who trusted in "appearance" and relied on external signs to accredit their ministry (5:12: so Bultmann, 189). The polemical tone to be read into this remark, where βλέπετε may have the added sense of "look out for" (as in Phil 3:2), is confirmed by what follows immediately: lit., "if there is anyone who trusts himself."

εἴ τις πέποιθεν ἑαυτῷ clearly has a specific object in Paul's sights: it is his opposition in Corinth, the men—here personalized as a single number (τις) as in Gal 5:10; Col 2:8—who made pretentious claims which Paul is seeking to resist. Barrett rightly points to v 11 as confirming that the τοιοῦτος there looks back to the τις in v 7, referring to "a particular person who claims to be in a special way Χριστοῦ" ("Cephas and Corinth," *Essays*, 35). The issue turns on what is meant by Χριστοῦ εἶναι, lit., "to be of Christ" (Käsemann, *Legitimität*, 11, 12), which was evidently a catch phrase being bandied about at Corinth. These opponents laid claims to this title, but the way in which

Paul writes of this claim (πεποιθέναι ἑαυτῷ, "to have confidence in oneself" as a species of pride; cf. Luke 18:9; see too a similar phrase in Phil 3:3 where ἐν σαρκὶ πεποιθέναι means "self-reliance" [Beare, Philippians, HNTC (New York: Harper & Row, 1959) ad loc.]) makes it is clear that he refused to believe it. But he does not deny it to them; instead he invites them to consider (λογίζεσθαι, again probably their term, and reverting in thought to v 2 and especially the critique of λογισμοί in v 4) that he too (καί) can lay claim to being Christ's person, just as they do. The καθώς . . . οὕτως link emphasizes the point of this counterassertion made to ward off the accusation that Paul had no right to be regarded at Corinth as a Christian leader or maybe as having any Christian standing.

The meaning of Χριστοῦ εἶναι is much disputed: see Baur, Paul (270–86); Hughes (356–58); Barrett (256–58); Schmithals, Gnosticism, 197–99 (cf. ibid. 200–206); Georgi, Die Gegner, 227–29; and Oostendorp, Another Jesus, 17–20, for representative opinions. Windisch (301) covers the leading options: (1) Χριστοῦ εἶναι means being a Christian simpliciter, with parallels in 1 Cor 3:23; 15:23; so too Oostendorp, 18, 19. Somewhat differently, Käsemann, Legitimität, 11, 12, follows this on the score that what is at issue is Paul's "Christian existence"; see Baur, Paul, 286, but see also Kümmel's rejoinder (208); (2) it relates to the claim that individuals at Corinth—or members of the Judeo-Christian mission who arrived there—made out to be personal disciples of the earthly Jesus (Baur, Paul, 276), and so that they were the first to plant the church there. G. Theissen (Social Setting, 46) has recently championed this view, appealing to Mark 9:41, ὅτι Χριστοῦ ἐστε, "on the ground that you belong to Christ," and he matches this description with the debate over apostolic remuneration and hospitality at Corinth, in 1 Cor 9; cf. Matt 10:10 // Luke 10:7.

(3) The term refers to the special rank of the apostle as commissioned by the Lord to serve in the congregations. The title which the opponents claimed is then virtually identical with 11:13–15, εἰς ἀποστόλους Χριστοῦ . . . οἱ διάκονοι αὐτοῦ (sc. of Satan!) . . . διάκονοι δικαιοσύνης (see Comment there for the various ways of taking these titles), and the issue turns on the question, Who has the genuine ἐξουσία, "authority," to exercise this ministry? (so Bachmann; Georgi, 227, and Betz, Der Apostel Paulus, 133, 134, who links the matter with δοκιμή in 13:1–3: who will pass the test and be approved as Χριστοῦ εἶναι? Hence the call to "look at facts," ibid., 56, i.e., produce evidence; see too F. C. Baur, Paul, 274, who links the claim to be Christ's (Χριστοῦ εἶναι) with ἐξουσία . . . εἰς οἰκοδομήν—"the strength and energy with which a man labours in the furtherance of the cause of Christianity," and he relates this group with "all who boasted of their closer outward connection with Jesus or . . . with Peter, the first of the Apostles, and found in this the true criterion of Χριστοῦ εἶναι").

(4) A gnostic-mythical relationship with the heavenly Christ is said to be at the heart of this simple phrase, Χριστοῦ εἶναι, according to Schmithals (loc. cit.) who goes on to interpret that relationship as one claimed by the πνευματικοί, the spirit-filled persons who, full of πνεῦμα, did extraordinary feats as a sign of their endowment. The sense may then be slightly ironical, as in 1 Cor 14:37 (Martin, The Spirit and the Congregation, chap. 5).

Windisch and Barrett, we believe, are correct in their preference for (3) with incorporation of elements drawn from (2) and (1). The center of debate is Paul's right to ministry, set against that of his rivals who have appeared on the Corinthian scene. They claim to be true apostles, and act accordingly. Paul, following his literary convention of irony and *apologia*, takes their claims at face value but then challenges them to offer proof. Hence the call βλέπετε [τὰ κατὰ πρόσωπον]. Moreover, he enters a counterclaim, that he too is Christ's representative with rightful authority, ἐξουσία (v 8), so when they deny that to him they are virtually casting doubt on his Christian standing. "Pressed to the limit, the question raised here is whether Paul is or is not a Christian" (Barrett, 257, who goes on to remark that Paul defends himself by appealing to his apostleship. But the two identities overlap, with a third factor entering the picture, that he claimed to be human founder of the church at Corinth, and that only a true apostle and a genuine Christian could have done this work: 1 Cor 3:10, 9:1; hence the Corinthians are rightly called "of Christ" [Χριστοῦ, 1 Cor 3:23] and so Paul shares that relationship par excellence).

8. ἐὰν [τε] γὰρ περισσότερόν τι καυχήσωμαι περὶ τῆς ἐξουσίας ἡμῶν ἧς ἔδωκεν ὁ κύριος εἰς οἰκοδομὴν καὶ οὐκ εἰς καθαίρεσιν ὑμῶν, οὐκ αἰσχυνθήσομαι, "Even if I can boast [about being Christ's] and, more than that, about my [our] authority, which the Lord gave us to build you up and not pull you down, I will not be discredited by it." Paul now clinches his counterclaim and focuses on the main point: that of ἐξουσία, "right," to be an accredited leader. The danger looms in the final verb, οὐκ αἰσχυνθήσομαι, lit., "I shall not be ashamed." But the shame is not personal and emotionally charged, even if there is a rhetorical background where the aim of the debater is to humiliate the opponent (Marshall, "Invective"). It is Paul's fear that his work at Corinth will have gone for nothing (cf. Phil 1:20 for this sense of the verb), if the competitors have their way and turn the people away from him. At risk is not only Paul's apostolic credibility, but his entire Gentile mission in the Aegean region, with its headquarters at Corinth. If this church is lost to him, his entire work is in jeopardy—as is his prospect for a future mission in the west (Rome, Spain), to say nothing of his task to get the collection to Jerusalem. See *Introduction,* pp. lvii, lviii, for these extra reasons why Paul's great apprehension at this time in his life weighed upon him. Hence we render the verb "I will not be discredited." He would lose credibility by having his claim to apostolic service fail to meet the test (ἀδόκιμος, in 13:7).

Rather, Paul anticipates that his authority (ἐξουσία) will be validated, and he is prepared to engage in some "boasting" (καυχᾶσθαι) to that end. The motif of καυχᾶσθαι is here introduced, and will be elaborated in 10:15–18 as well as chaps. 11, 12 (see *Comment* on later vv). For the moment Paul is content to enforce the ἐξουσία which he traces back to the Lord's commission (13:10). His first claim is, however, that he is "Χριστοῦ εἶναι," since the cryptic περισσότερον seems to require an insertion to make the comparison: Even if I may boast [about being Christ's] and more than that (the τε—if part of the text—is not copulative, but functions to reinforce the condition or statement as in Rom 7:7*b*) about the authority, etc. (against NIV, which is vague, and RSV, which is misleading). Paul is not talking about boasting "too much"; he is making a comparative statement (cf. Barrett for examples, and differently

Hughes, 359, n. 14). Moffatt too is equally questionable: "even supposing I were to boast somewhat freely of my authority." There is little to concede a hypothetical attitude on Paul's part. He is going definitely to play the fool.

The commission in which Paul rejoices is described as εἰς οἰκοδομὴν καὶ οὐκ εἰς καθαίρεσιν ὑμῶν, "to build you up and not pull you down." The οἰκοδομή metaphor used for the building up of the church is a well-attested one in Paul (Ph. Vielhauer, *Oikodome* [Munich: Kaiser Verlag, 1979 ed.] 77 f., 108; for the theological dimension to the word: "the logical subject is always God; the logical object is always the church [1 Cor 14:4 is a pejorative exception; cf. 1 Cor 8:1]. . . . The goal of divine purpose is not pious individuals but one holy catholic church in the profoundly and radically eschatological meaning of the NT"), especially in 1 Corinthians 14 where it occurs several times (14:19, 23, 26, 28, 35: see R. P. Martin, *The Spirit and the Congregation*, chap. 4). Its opposite is καθαίρεσις, "a tearing down," which recalls v 4, where Paul's God-given weapons have effective power to demolish strongholds. Paul asserts here his authority (ἐξουσία) to use these weapons (as in 13:10). See Bultmann, 191, who shows how this "right" is woven into Paul's καυχᾶσθαι, "boasting." Héring (72, n. 10) is one of the few to ask the question, How could Paul have "destroyed" the Corinthians? The answer is either by opposing all false notions which, in his mind and convictions, serve only to destroy, so his response is a variant of the "sentences of sacred law" (*Sätze der heiligen Rechts*), namely, "destruction to the destroyer" (1 Cor 3:16, 17), or by defaulting in the exercise of his own pastoral authority, referred to in 11:28; 13:10. Thirdly, it may be a specific reference to his right to excommunicate offenders from the community (cf. 2:5–11; 1 Cor 5:1–13 [Lampe, "Church Discipline," in *Christian History and its Interpretation*, 352–55] as J. Munck, *Paul and the Salvation of Mankind* [1959] 190, thinks. Cf. Fallon, 89).

9. ἵνα μὴ δόξω ὡς ἂν ἐκφοβεῖν ὑμᾶς διὰ τῶν ἐπιστολῶν, "[Do not think] that I am trying to frighten you with my letters." The transition from v 8 is unclear, and the sequence in the apostle's thought has been variously interpreted. The question centers on the force of ἵνα μὴ δόξω, lit., "that I might not seem" or "lest I should seem," but what is the antecedent? Of the various options (Barrett, 285 f.) the most intelligible—but it may not be the best (given Paul's intricate thought pattern)—is to connect it with "the Lord gave us authority"; then, the following clause is added to explain how that authority should be most profitably exercised, i.e., that Paul does not want to appear as frightening his readers. That assumes that the ἵνα-clause is intimately connected with the foregoing (Plummer, 281). Another possibility is that the ἵνα-clause introduces a new sentence, unattached except loosely to what precedes. Moule (*Idiom Book*, 145) views the use of ἵνα as imperative: "let me not seem to be frightening you!" would be the sense. This makes for good sequential flow. A third possibility is to take v 10 as parenthetic, and so to join v 9, where ἵνα μὴ δόξω opens a new thought, to be completed later with v 11. The flow of the sense then runs directly from v 9 to v 11: "Lest I should seem to be frightening anyone with my letters I say: let that man consider that what we are through our letters," etc. This is probably the best explanation; it goes back to the Vulgate translation (*ut autem non existimer tamquam terrere vos per epistolas*. But Plummer, 281, objects that the word *autem*, "but," has been

gratuitously introduced; so too Héring, 72, granting the need to supply δέ, which *is* in fact added by Lietzmann) and shows the continuing topic to be about Paul's letters, with a satisfactory explanation of why v 10 got stuck in here as an illustration. Other options are that we should add "only" to the verb ἐκφοβεῖν to modify it, and so make vv 8, 9 run together. The reason for Paul's shame (on this view, which is supported by Bachmann, Héring) is that he does not appear simply to wish to intimidate his readers by his letters, as "one who strikes the empty air, simply to inspire fear" (Héring, 72). But this sounds too involved, and fails to explain why v 10 stands in contradiction when it affirms that the Corinthians thought his letters *were* powerful and effectual. Windisch, 305, confesses that in his view some words have been elided, while Hughes, 361, takes the sentiment as ironical; neither proposal is likely.

10. ὅτι αἱ ἐπιστολαὶ μέν, φησίν, βαρεῖαι καὶ ἰσχυραί, ἡ δὲ παρουσία τοῦ σώματος ἀσθενὴς καὶ ὁ λόγος ἐξουθενημένος, "For some are saying, 'His letters are weighty and forceful, but his physical presence is weak and his rhetoric moves us to contempt.' " On our reading of this v it is an explanatory parenthesis, added to account for the way some at Corinth felt that Paul was trying to "frighten the wits" (ἐκφοβεῖν, with a reinforcing prefix, a NT *hapax:* Windisch, 305, but in Job 7:14; 4 Macc 9:5) out of the readers. These persons whom Paul has in his sights have to admit that he has a reputation (φησίν, "some are saying," though it is third person singular). This usage is explained either as a diatribe style (BDF § 130.3; Betz, 8, 44, 45) to introduce the formal charge brought by Paul's calumniators (cf. Bultmann, *Der Stil,* 10, 66, 67), or an indefinite verb, "people are saying," like the French *on dit* or German *man sagt,* or else a specific person is in mind, reverting to v 7, τις. The last idea is probably best, since Paul does seem to have the ringleader of opposition in view in this paragraph (so Denney, 307; Goudge, 96; Hughes, 362 n. 19; Barrett, 260).

Paul's letters to Corinth were voluminous, but in accordance with our understanding of the literary compositions sent to that city and its environs, it is the so-called "severe letter" (2:4; 7:8) that is primarily spoken of here. Its readers acknowledged that it was like the rest of Paul's correspondence βαρεῖαι καὶ ἰσχυραί, "weighty (i.e., impressive) and forceful," that is, effectual, not only because the letters revealed the writer but because of their tones of warning and instruction (Bultmann, 192). Whether Paul would have shared this estimate of his letters is problematical (cf. 1:24; see J. D. G. Dunn, *Jesus and the Spirit,* 277–80, on Paul's avoidance of the strong word ἐπιταγή, "command"; cf. 2 Cor 8:8), but he did expect the letters to be read, heeded and acted upon (1 Cor 14:37, 38; cf. Col 4:16; 1 Thess 5:27), though not to be blindly obeyed as an imperious *diktat* (Phil 3:15, 16). The compliment paid in v 10, however, is a backhanded one, since (a) it implies that Paul knows how to write effective and strongly worded letters—at a safe distance. αἱ ἐπιστολαὶ κτλ. corresponds with ἀπὼν δὲ θαρρῶ (v 1): Bultmann, 192. This point would be enforced if T. Holtz's idea is supportable, "Die Bedeutung des Apostelkonzils für Paulus," *NTS* 16 (1974) 110–48 (147, n. 5). He argues that it is only after the Council of A.D. 49/50 and the Incident at Antioch (Gal 2:11–16) that Paul developed the use of letters as a way of communicating with his churches. For it was as Paul was kept away from his converts and knew them to be vulnerable to various countermissionary activity that he relied on letters as his *alter ego* (cf. Polycarp, *Phil* 3:2, cited on p. 303). His enemies, however, put a negative construction on this policy, insinuating that Paul chose the safety of distance rather than a personal encounter (κατὰ πρόσωπον, vv 1, 7) with them in the setting of Paul's congregations. And when he did come, he was ταπεινός (v 1), i.e., obsequious and groveling in marked contrast to his attitude as expressed in his stern letters, which they interpreted as boastful, imperious, indeed uncompromisingly bold (θαρρῆσαι: Plummer, 274) and wildly reckless (τολμῆσαι, v 12).

(b) The other prejudicial side to this tribute is that the report offsets the power of his letters by an adverse comment on his physical presence (παρουσία) and his abilities of public speech (λόγος). The former is branded as ἀσθενής, "weak," probably including the sense of being sickly and infirm, retiring in the face of vigorous opposition (Windisch, 293; cf. 12:7: see H. Clavier, "La santé" in *Studia Paulina* [1953] 66–82, esp. 77; J. Jervell, "Der schwache Charismatiker," 109–14). For Paul's physique, see *Acts of Paul and Thekla,* chap. 3; for the tradition of Thekla's attraction to Paul which lured her away from her fiancé, see E. M. Howe, "Interpretations of Paul in the Acts of Paul and Thecla," *Pauline Studies,* FS F. F. Bruce (ed. D. A. Hagner and M. J. Harris [Grand Rapids: Eerdmans/Exeter: Paternoster, 1980] 33–49 [37]; but this view of ἀσθενής is not exclusively or primarily so, as Betz, *Der Apostel Paulus,* 46 f., shows with an appeal to Schmithals, *Gnosticism,* 176–79. The latter argues that what is in mind is Paul's ταπεινότης as deficient in those essential traits of the gnostic πνευματικός, namely, δύναμις, "power"; ἐξουσία, "rights to be exercised"; replete with ἀπόδειξις, "demonstration"; and λόγος, "rhetorical skill." Above all, Paul lacked ἀρετή, "divine power" (see Georgi, *Die Gegner,* 145 ff., 220 ff.) and πνεῦμα, thought of as a dynamic and impressive force to convey powerfully the triumph and effectiveness of his message. They charged that Paul was, by contrast, ἰδιώτης, "incapable of pneumatic speech," i.e., glossolalia (11:6: so Käsemann, *Legitimität,* 9, but cf. 1 Cor 14:18) or rhetorical finesse; and perhaps, if we return to the witness of 12:1–10, was unable to heal himself of the malady that rendered him so weak (cf. Jervell, loc. cit.: a person who is both "a sick/weak charismatic and a wonderworker"—they alleged—"is a contradiction in terms," 194; further discussion on this point in Georgi, *Die Gegner,* 229, n. 7; Güttgemanns, *Der leidende Apostel,* 154–56; Schmithals, *Gnosticism,* 164–66; U. Wilckens, *Weisheit und Torheit* [Tübingen: Mohr, 1959], 218; Kleinknecht, *Der leidende Gerechtfertigte,* 295–303; and now J. Jervell, "The Signs of an Apostle," tr. R. A. Harrisville, *The Unknown Paul* [Minneapolis: Augsburg, 1984] 94).

The allegation brought against his λόγος is summed up in one expressive term, ἐξουθενημένος, which is difficult to capture in translation. See 1 Cor 1:28; 6:4; 16:11; Gal 4:14. On the verb, BGD, 277, offer "to disdain, despise someone," and on 10:10 they comment, "Of the speaking ability of the apostle when he appears in person: *it amounts to nothing*" (italics in quotation: so NIV, but this rendering is decidedly weak). Rather the verdict is damningly positive: it declares that, in their ears, Paul's rhetorical ability was nonexistent and his public presentation of the message moved them to contempt and scorn. Thus they reasoned that he could be regarded as no true apostle;

rather he was bogus (γόης, a trickster). In the contest of "evidence," he made a poor showing on the twin counts where they scored—personal presence and rhetorical flair—at least in their own esteem. And on both counts he had no valid claim to "authority" (ἐξουσία).

11. τοῦτο λογιζέσθω ὁ τοιοῦτος, ὅτι οἷοί ἐσμεν τῷ λόγῳ δι᾽ ἐπιστολῶν ἀπόντες, τοιοῦτοι καὶ παρόντες τῷ ἔργῳ, "Let this person [who thinks like this] consider that what we are through our letters when we are absent, we will be in our actions when we come to you." Now it is Paul's turn to enter the lists. He offers a firm rebuttal, using a negative approach that is unusual in such a context. He comes out with a forthright denial of what "they say" (v 10). Not so much "They say, let them say" as a categorical disclaimer, "let this person (ὁ τοιοῦτος) consider (λογιζέσθω, correcting the pretentious λογισμοί of v 7; cf. v 2) that what we are . . . when absent . . . we will be (supplying with Menzies, 93, ἐσόμεθα, which is better than "we are," ἐσμεν, with Barrett) . . . when present." The person who speaks thus contemptuously is now addressed. It is not the person of 2:6, 7 but the immediate audience which will reappear in v 12 as τινες, "those who recommend themselves," and in 11:13 as οἱ . . . τοιοῦτοι ψευδαπόστολοι, "such men are false apostles." Less likely is the identification which sees Paul's immediate opponents as the "superior apostles" (ὑπερλίαν ἀπόστολοι) referred to in 11:5; 12:11, though Barrett favors this view ("Cephas and Corinth," 35–38). The contrast ἀπών/παρών picks up vv 1, 2 and so rounds off the self-contained section with a chiasmus (τῷ λόγῳ ἀπόντες/παρόντες τῷ ἔργῳ) in a ring-composition or *inclusio*. The further contrast is between ἐπιστολαί (letters) and ἔργα (actions). Cf. 1 Cor 4:20: the kingdom of God is not ἐν λόγῳ . . . ἀλλ᾽ ἐν δυνάμει, not "in word . . . but in power." The threat is resumed at 13:2, 10, when Paul will make manifest his powerful ἐξουσία, but it will be ἐξουσία at the service of love and truth (13:8) since it is designed to promote οἰκοδομή, "upbuilding," not καθαίρεσις, "pulling down" (v 8). That is the "power of Christ" (13:3, 4) acting "through him." In a word, Paul is, and means to be, consistent (Barrett, 261), matching promise and threat with a further performance. Then, he will translate word into deed (τῷ ἔργῳ). Presumably this is a remonstrance as he plans to deal with refractory church members (v 8: see *Comment*), but more particularly he is confronting the alien teachers who have seduced them (11:2, 3). The deed (ἔργον) may have a specific application, namely excommunication to the "dark domain" of Satan outside the church, as W. L. Knox (*St. Paul*, 101, 102) and J. Munck (*Paul and the Salvation of Mankind*, 190) suggest.

Explanation

"Look facts in the face" (v 7, NEB) is Paul's head-on appeal and answer to his critics' charge implied in v 1: "My critics have said that I am feeble when I'm with you in person."

The counterargument is directed against his opponents who claimed a special position as Christ's servants (v 7) and did not hesitate to criticize the apostle on the ground that he was inferior to them (v 10). *They* made out that they enjoyed a special place in the church as authoritative teachers and possessed a commanding presence. Moreover, they had one great advantage in their favor: they were at Corinth and able to influence the church there at firsthand.

It seems too that they turned their presence at Corinth to their own designs, for implicit in Paul's paragraph is the thought that he was under fire because of his absence. The point on which they had fastened was that he preferred to stay at a safe distance and to conduct his defense by correspondence (vv 9, 10). This policy, they were suggesting, was a coward's refuge, for it seemed to imply that Paul was a strong personality when he wrote his letters, but when he appeared on the scene, his personal presence was nowhere near as impressive. Perhaps too his opponents were harking back to his supposed indecisiveness of action (1:17) and failure to come to Corinth as he had promised (2:1). Now (they would explain to the Corinthians and so capitalize on Paul's nonappearance) we know the real reason; he was afraid to come, and can only terrify people by letters written from a comfortable distance (v 9).

On reading this short section the present-day Christian may well appreciate—in a way that was not possible for Paul's first readers—the timeless significance of Paul as a letter-writer. In the sixteenth-century Reformation with its recovery of the historical Paul, this aspect was not the least among the discoveries made: "The words of St. Paul are not dead words, but are living creatures that have hands and feet to carry away a man" (Luther).

B. The Issue of Paul's Ministry (10:12–18)

Bibliography (see also under 10:1–11)

Barrett, C. K. "Christianity at Corinth." In *Essays on Paul*, 1–27. ———. "Cephas and Corinth." In *Essays on Paul*, 28–39. **Betz, H.-D.** *Der Apostel Paulus und die sokratische Tradition.* **Georgi, D.** *Die Gegner des Paulus im 2. Korintherbrief.* **Gunther, J. J.** *St. Paul's Opponents and Their Background.* **Holmberg, B.** *Paul and Power.* **Horsley, G. H. R.** (ed.) *New Documents Illustrating Early Christianity (1976, 1977).* North Ryde, NSW: Macquarie University, 1981, 1982. **Käsemann, E.** *Die Legitimität des Apostels.* **Luedemann, G.** *Paul, Apostle to the Gentiles. Studies in Chronology.* Tr. F. Stanley Jones. Philadelphia: Fortress, 1984. **Munck, J.** *Paul and the Salvation of Mankind.* **Schlatter, A.** *Paulus, der Bote Jesu.* **Schütz, J. H.** *Paul and the Anatomy of Apostolic Authority.* **Schweizer, E.** *Church Order in the New Testament.* SBT 32. Tr. Frank Clarke. London: SCM. 1961. **Stuhlmacher, P.** "Erwägungen zum ontologischen Charakter der καινὴ κτίσις bei Paulus." *EvT* 27 (1967) 1–35. **Theissen, G.** *The Social Setting of Pauline Christianity.*

Translation

[12] *We do not have the effrontery to class or compare ourselves with some of those who recommend themselves. Rather, when they measure themselves by themselves and compare themselves with themselves, they appear as without understanding.* [a] [13] *We, however, will* [a] *not boast beyond proper limits, but only within the sphere of service*

which God has assigned to us as our sphere, a sphere that reaches as far as to you. ¹⁴ *For we are not overreaching our limit, as we should be doing if we had not* [*already*] *reached you, for we did come as far as to you with our preaching of Christ.* ¹⁵ *We did not go beyond the proper limits by boasting of the work done by others, but we have the hope that as your faith continues to grow, so our work may, within the sphere we have, be greatly expanded among you.* ¹⁶ *The result is that we may preach the Gospel in places beyond you. We do not wish to boast about what has already been done in another person's sphere* [*of service*]. ¹⁷ *But rather, "let the one who boasts boast only about the Lord."* ¹⁸ *For it is not the person who recommends himself who is approved, but the person whom the Lord recommends.*

Notes

ªThe text of 10:12 (end) and at the beginning of v 13 is uncertain. What is translated above is Nestle²⁶, attested by the majority witness. A shorter Western text, read by D* G it^{d. g. 61} Ambrosiaster and others, omits οὐ συνιᾶσιν. ἡμεῖς δέ, "are without understanding. We, however." The shortened version reads: "But we, measuring ourselves by ourselves and comparing ourselves with ourselves [i.e., changing the participles to refer to first person] will not boast beyond our proper limits." The allusion in the longer text to Paul's opponents now drops out, and the reference to measuring by one's own standards in v 12 takes on a good connotation (Barrett). For this sense, cf. 1 Cor 2:15, 16 cited by Käsemann, *Die Legitimität*, 45, who champions the shorter reading, on the ground that Paul is speaking of himself as a *Pneumatiker* who needed no earthly validation, only a heavenly authorization by the Spirit (cf. Schlatter, *Paulus*, 623; Georgi, *Die Gegner*, 230). But Kümmel, 208, 209, sees how difficult it then becomes to make sense of ἐν ἑαυτοῖς ἑαυτοὺς μετροῦντες, which must refer to persons other than Paul (αὐτοί marks a new subject, Plummer, 285), in spite of the classical usage of the reflexive ἑαυτούς (which was largely displaced in hellenistic Greek). And it is equally problematical how to connect v 12 with v 13 except on the assumption that there is a contrast: Paul's enemies measure themselves by themselves in place of (*statt*) a divine measuring rod, and so prove themselves to be "without understanding." Paul himself does not measure himself by himself but rather by the measuring rod (κανών) given to him by God.

Barrett (164) notes ingeniously how the witnesses to the shorter text are either Latin or Greco-Latin in provenance, and suggests that a latinized translator would make the slip in the belief that a first-person form of the verb was required. More simply, a copyist's eye could have traveled from οὐ to οὐκ causing an omission by haplography, and thus the intervening words are missing.

The shorter text, however, is supported by BDF § 416.2; Windisch, 309; Bultmann, 194, 5; Strachan, 15, 16; Héring, 73, and is usually regarded as an example of Westcott-Hort's category of "Western non-interpolations." Plummer, 285, refers to the omission as an attempt to make the original text clearer by eliminating offending words. The reading οὐ συνιᾶσιν ἡμεῖς in ℵ* 88 is an orthographical slip (Metzger, *Textual Commentary*, 583): it would yield the sense, "they compare themselves with themselves without being aware that they are doing so"—a Pauline concession he is not likely to have made.

Form/Structure/Setting

At 10:12 begins a lengthy section of the letter which is devoted to an assertion of Paul's "boldness" (τόλμα) in the face of his enemies (Bultmann, 193). Clearly "boldness" has a double meaning, similar to the words used in 10:1 (see *Comment*). For Paul, nothing was more certain than his own apostolic calling and standing (1:1), which inspired him with confidence (πεποίθησις, 1:15; 3:4, 8, 22; 10:2) and expressed itself as an acknowledgement of his ἱκανότης, "competence," under and in dependence on God (3:5) which he regarded (λογίζεσθαι) as his endowment by grace. Such confidence gave him boldness of speech (παρρησία, 3:12), especially in speaking frankly to the errant Corinthians (7:4). Above all, he laid claim to "authority" (10:8; 13:10) to be both a church planter and an apostle clothed with the right to "build up" the community of God in faith.

Now it is clear that these were impressive credentials and yet open to misunderstanding, especially in the hands of those who bore no affection for Paul. Later (at 11:4) we shall seek to identify who these opponents may have been. Here it is enough to observe how they could influence the Corinthians into thinking that Paul was no better than a religious imposter and false leader. They could allege that his "boldness" was none other than self-advertisement and proud display, which is called "boasting" (καύχησις) and "recommending oneself" (10:17, 18). Other factors enter into the opponents' charge-list against Paul's apostolate, and these items appear in due course, e.g., his cunning craftiness (12:16), and his weakness as a sick man unable to heal himself (12:7–10). One particular topic of warm debate at Corinth is handled in 10:12–18. It related to Paul's "right" to be a missionary to Corinth in the first place. Logically this is the first consideration in any attack made on Paul—and so his defense of his Gospel and the apostleship which expresses it is made here. The allegation centers on "the measure of the province God dealt out to us as our measure" (Barrett's translation, 10:13, τὸ μέτρον τοῦ κανόνος οὗ ἐμέρισεν ἡμῖν ὁ θεὸς μέτρου). All these words are difficult to render, since both μέτρον and κανών are evidently being used in a semitechnical way. The notion of measurement, however, lies at the heart of the issue and, in particular, the geographical area assigned to apostolic leaders in the early church (cf. Gal 2:7–9; cf. E. A. Judge in *New Docs* [1976] #9, [1977] #55). The point in question is the challenge which was apparently raised against Paul that he had no jurisdiction at Corinth, which may have been claimed— whether with consent or not—as Peter's bailiwick (see Barrett, "Cephas and Corinth"). See v 15 and Romans 15:19, 20 for this idea of "another's territory." So the conclusion is drawn by his rivals that Paul's mission to Corinth was illegitimate from the start, and his converts were therefore being placed under duress with the insinuation that they are followers of a pseudo-apostle and a charlatan. What was at stake was the issue of what F. C. Baur (*Paulus*, 289; E. T. *Paul*, 281) called "the genuine Christian idea of apostolic authority," or as Käsemann more recently expressed it, *Legitimitätsprinzip*, the criterion of legitimacy, to test the claim of apostolic credibility (*Die Legitimität*, 34). With a sharper focus it centers on what has been termed "the principle of nonintervention" (Holmberg, *Paul and Power*, 502, who ascribes this notion to the Cephas party whose influence he traces in the emissaries of 11:4, 13–15; cf. more moderately Barrett, "Cephas and Corinth," 35–38).

Paul's response is to offer a rationale for his initial evangelism and church building at Corinth as a pioneer missionary (cf. 1 Cor 3:6–10). He does so by maintaining the following propositions (note that, in fact, his reasoning is less clear than these statements would appear, and his style of writing is tortuous and obscure in several places, as we shall see): (1) He has power to deal effectively with the situation; it is a power not confined to his letters (10:10). He can act strongly (10:11) as well as write powerful letters. (2) He refuses to accept any "standard" for ministry other than the "measure" apportioned him by God. His opponents are branded as "foolish" (v 12, as though ἄφρονες) for making an appeal to their own authority; presumably this related to their awareness of "spirit" (πνεῦμα) and the enjoyment of charismatic powers as "signs" (12:12). (3) He makes an appeal to the church's past history in v 14. We got to Corinth first, he claims, preceding the missionary enterprise referred to in 11:4 ("he who comes . . ."); and so he staked a claim at Corinth as Gentile territory which had been ceded to him as part of the concordat of Gal 2:6–10; see Rom 15:17–20. But, as Barrett observes (167), this allocation and agreement of ministry is not a personal matter; it was an *entente* involving the Gospel as Paul knew and proclaimed it, i.e., good news intended for the Gentile world (Rom 1:13, 16; 3:29, 30; 15:16; all these texts say virtually the same thing, that Paul's mission to the non-Jews carries divine sanction and is to be recognized as valid, since it is grounded in God's all-embracing regard for all peoples who have come to share in the promise to Abraham, the father of many nations; so Rom 4:9–25; Gal 3:28, 29) and centered in reconciliation (R. P. Martin, *Reconciliation*, 153, 154). It was this message that came first to Corinth in advance of the Judeo-Christian mission with its contrary teaching (11:4). See Betz, *Der Apostel Paulus*, 130, 131, for a recognition of the contrast between Paul's κανών and ἀλλότριος κανών in vv 13, 15, with parallels.

(4) Finally, Paul hints that he has already established Corinth as a "home base" (11:12 gives the word ἀφορμή) from which he proposes to launch out to further regions of evangelistic exploration (v 16). This plan matches exactly the idea of Rom 1:1–15; 15:23, 24, 28, where he purposes an extension of his mission (to proclaim the Gospel, Rom 1:15) to Rome with the same idea of moving on westward in the ongoing endeavor to evangelize the gentile world in Spain as his divinely appointed destiny (*1 Clem* 5:6, 7: [Paul] "became a herald [of the Gospel] in East and West, and won the noble renown which his faith merited. To the whole world he taught righteousness, and reaching the limits of the West [ἐπὶ τὸ τέρμα τῆς δύσεως] he bore his witness before rulers"). So, as a concluding coda, he asserts that his mission work has the sign and stamp of God's approbation. It is this conviction that proves the basis of his "boasting" (v 17). He appeals confidently, in the spirit of an OT *testimonium*, to that which the Lord approves as "he boasts in (or about) the Lord" (Jer 9:24), for it is the Lord whose approval he seeks (v 18).

These are the leading themes in this "apology" for Paul's mission at Corinth and a justification of his apostleship on behalf of the Gentiles, "the administration of God's grace that was given to me for you Gentiles," as Eph 3:1, 2 expresses it, moving on to outline his chief emphasis in Eph 3:6. But where the language of Ephesians is stately, measured, and rhapsodic, the argument in 2 Cor 10:12–18 is "notably clumsy," containing "oddly confused expressions," "intolerable constructions" (so Windisch, 313), and replete with "chopped up pieces of sentences, violently thrown together" (Lietzmann, 143, *gehackten, grimmig hingeworfenen Satzbrocken*, with some exaggeration, surely). There is no denying the convoluted sentence structure in which Paul "ties himself in grammatical knots" (Barrett, 261). We may put this type of composition down to Paul's emotional involvement in the situation he is describing, and the way (it seems) his dictation runs ahead of his mind. And with his opponents' terms no doubt in his sights, he does not bother to explain all that his words imply. We should see in this paragraph both Paul's drawing on technical terms for mission service (Betz, *Der Apostel Paulus*, 130) and also his quoting his opponents' estimate of what they regarded as their claims, which Paul refutes by opposing his own estimate (Käsemann's insight, *Die Legitimität*, 43–51). We shall see this feature in vv 12–15. And, if Käsemann's particular argument (*Die Legitimität*, 49, 50) is convincing, what is at stake that moves Paul so passionately is nothing less than a rebuttal of the charge that he is not only a false apostle but a bogus Christian, with the inference drawn that his converts at Corinth are similarly "misbegotten," to use the metaphor of 1 Cor 4:15 (ἐν . . . Χριστῷ Ἰησοῦ διὰ τοῦ εὐαγγελίου ἐγὼ ὑμᾶς ἐγέννησα, "in Christ I begot you through the Gospel").

In spite of the angular style of this section there are some traces of rhetorical forms: (1) A pun is to be seen in v 12, with a play on ἐγκρῖναι/συγκρῖναι. The former verb means "to judge among," "to class," the latter is a weaker form meaning "to bring together," "to combine," and so "to compare." The assonance suggests a link such as "pair" and "compare" (Plummer, 286, based on Bengel's *aequiparare aut comparare*). And (2) alliteration is heard with ἐμέρισεν . . . μέτρου in v 13, as Paul reiterates the idea of "measure," "sphere" (cf. v 15, ἄμετρα).

Comment

12. οὐ γὰρ τολμῶμεν ἐγκρῖναι ἢ συγκρῖναι ἑαυτούς τισιν τῶν ἑαυτοὺς συνιστανόντων, ἀλλὰ αὐτοὶ ἐν ἑαυτοῖς ἑαυτοὺς μετροῦντες καὶ συγκρίνοντες ἑαυτοὺς ἑαυτοῖς οὐ συνιᾶσιν, "We do not have the effrontery to class or compare ourselves with some of those who recommend themselves. Rather, when they measure themselves by themselves and compare themselves with themselves, they appear as without understanding." This v opens a new section which considers the ground of the allegation brought against Paul. The issue turns on "self-recommendation" (implied in the reflexive verb form ἑαυτοὺς συνιστανόντων), and the charge against the apostle is that he is too cowardly and weak (v 10, ἀσθενής) to make any bold assertion regarding himself as an apostle and leader. He had earlier (v 11) remarked on his plan to deal strongly with the opponents at Corinth; to that extent v 12 is closely linked with the preceding. Now he seeks to ward off the accusation that he cannot make good on that threat because he is basically a flawed character. He refuses to boast (v 13, καυχᾶσθαι) and to push himself forward—unlike his competitors whose claims he must now confront and answer.

His tactic is to adopt a stance of mock humility: I really cannot rise to the level of these people so that I can rightly join myself to them (ἐγκρῖναι) or compare myself with them (συγκρῖναι). With an obvious play on words which may owe something to an antirhetorical and antisophistic posture—opposing *synkrisis* (σύγκρισις) with a denial of ὑπεροχή (cf. 1 Cor 2:1) adopted by popular philosophy (see Betz, *Der Apostel Paulus*, 119, 120), Paul answers those who said that he was boastful (3:1; 10:1). In the game of self-praise, he retorts, I haven't the skill to play (see 11:6, ἰδιώτης τῷ λόγῳ).

The two verbs, linked by assonance (as we saw), are evidently chosen to silence this kind of folly—though Paul will be forced to shift his ground later in his debate (see 12:11, "you have compelled me to play the fool [in my boasting]," a theme begun in 11:10 and continued to 12:10. The occasion, we may suspect, was the presence of the teachers at Corinth spoken of in 11:4). For the present, Paul will have none of this type of self-advertisement. The verb οὐ τολμῶμεν, "we do not have the effrontery," will be resumed in 11:21: τολμῶ κἀγώ, "I do have the audacity to boast"—when I speak as a fool. The verb τολμᾶν, "to be brave enough," so "to dare," "presume," has a wide range of meanings. The thought of a person pushing himself forward so that he does not hesitate to speak or act on his own behalf is well-attested (Epict.; 3 Macc 3:21; Philo *de Somn.* 1.54; see Betz, ibid., 67–69, for the data to show how τόλμα, "audacity," "effrontery," was part of the terminology of the philosopher-sophist debate). Paul's use of the term is ironical in 11:21, while here the charge of "effrontery" is plainly denied, with a link going back to 10:1 where Paul's "boldness" (θαρρῆσαι) is held as a charge against him.

The precise point of the debate centers on συνιστάναι ἑαυτόν, "self-commendation," which is a practice Paul will not indulge in (a denial already registered in 5:12). Again, we must add, this is his stance until he is driven from it by the exigencies of his "apology" in subsequent chapters (cf. 11:21 ff.). Then, he will be compelled to boast, though paradoxically the object of his self-approbation will be his weakness (ἀσθένεια).

In this present section the topic is self-evaluation in terms of the scope of mission service. Paul has stated his aversion from self-advertised claims. The ἀλλά, "rather," sets off his position from that of his rivals (αὐτοί), which hardly opens a new subject (as Kümmel, 208, suggests; but Bultmann, 194, rightly disputes this). The αὐτοί, "they," refers to the opponents who use as the measuring rod (μέτρον) of their service, their own self-judgment, and set up their own standards of conduct as the criterion (ἑαυτοῖς ἑαυτοὺς μετρεῖν). The result is a foregone conclusion: they find themselves well-qualified and praiseworthy. Paul's verdict on them is exactly to the contrary: "they are without understanding" (οὐ συνιᾶσιν: a negative verb used by Paul of human error in Rom 3:11; or as a noun of the human wisdom God rejects, 1 Cor 1:19).

The reason for this negative assessment will be seen in some contrasts Paul draws later; on his part he has not "overreached" himself (v 14) but has submitted to the limits of service God appointed him, and his boasting (καυχᾶσθαι) is not in himself but in the Lord who commends (συνίστησιν, repeating the verb of v 12) him (v 18).

13. ἡμεῖς δὲ οὐκ εἰς τὰ ἄμετρα καυχησόμεθα ἀλλὰ κατὰ τὸ μέτρον τοῦ κανόνος οὗ ἐμέρισεν ἡμῖν ὁ θεὸς μέτρου, ἐφικέσθαι ἄχρι καὶ ὑμῶν, "We, however, will not boast beyond proper limits, but only within the sphere of service which God has assigned to us as our sphere, a sphere that reaches as far as to you." The pronoun (ἡμεῖς) with δὲ sets out Paul's own estimate of his ministry *ex professo*. But it seems (with Barrett, 263) that we are intended to infer that "Paul's rivals have boasted of their apostolic status"; and Paul is anxious to distance himself from any such self-originated claim. So he disavows any attempt to put himself forward "beyond the limit." τὰ ἄμετρα could mean simply: we will not boast in any unmeasured way, but we will temper our

apostolic claims, having regard to the sphere God has assigned us, and not in any exaggerated way. Then the comparison with v 12 would be clearcut: they made exorbitant claims as apostolic figures, we moderate our "boast" so that it stays within the limits of our mission (Gal 2:7) given us by divine appointment. A similar view is taken in Moule, *Idiom Book*, 71.

On the other hand, the way the sentence unfolds points to a more complicated train of thought and flow of ideas. A clue is found in the following verb, ἐμέρισεν . . . ὁ θεὸς with its complement μέτρου, which in turn stands in agreement with τοῦ κανόνος. One might have expected "God gave us (ἔδωκεν) our service," but μερίζειν, "to allot, apportion," is evidently chosen to denote the assignment or a sphere of ministry (*Missionsgebiet;* Bultmann, 196) according to God's purpose (cf. 1 Cor 7:17; Rom 12:3); hence the tautological and seemingly unnecessary piling up of ἄμετρα . . . μέτρον . . . ἐμέρισεν . . . μέτρου to emphasize strongly the single point that Paul has not transgressed his allocated area of service which has been apportioned to him by God. Hence he can "boast," since the object of his καυχᾶσθαι—his "missionary field"—is not what he has chosen for himself, but rather it is what God has assigned to him (hence v 17).

The link-idea is the verb μετρεῖν in v 12: his competitors have a measuring rod (μέτρον), which they have used wrongly, since it has served only to inflate their pride and bolster their self-praise. They have failed to use the proper μέτρον; for Paul the function of such a measure is to define and delimit one's κανών, "specific sphere," definitely marked out (Plummer, 287) and open-ended (Schweizer, *Church Order*, 203, 24k, n. 779). Note that Paul is slightly unfair in this use of terms, since he denies to his opponents' μέτρον τοῦ κανόνος the very aspect he wishes to insist on for himself, namely, that he has legitimacy to move out to new territorial regions (v 16). But he could have justified this view on the ground that any "mission to the Hellenes" (Gal 2:7, 8) must include an ever-expanding domain. κανών—as in the sense of "canon"— betokens a measured length and denotes distance in a linear way (e.g., length of the radius from a circle's center, or a race track; Hughes, 366, who also finds an athletic metaphor in v 12, with ἐγκρίνειν = "compete"). But it also tends to include what is the area thus measured: hence it means territory as well as boundary limit (see, however, Judge, art. cit. [316] for meaning of κανών as "assessment"). The English "line" has the same overlap of meanings (cf. Gal 6:16): a straight line, and a person's "line," e.g., line of business, interest, etc.

This interpretation of κανών as a boundary or what is enclosed in a boundary perimeter stands opposed to the view of Käsemann, *Die Legitimität*, 43–51, Georgi, *Die Gegner*, 229, 230, and Kümmel, 209, for whom κανών means here a "standard of judgment" (*Beurteilungsmassstab:* H. W. Beyer's designation, *TDNT* 3:598–600) and concerns the legitimacy (Käsemann's term, ibid., 49) of Paul's evangelism which needed to be proved by tokens of success (held to be implied in v 15b: τῆς πίστεως ὑμῶν ἐν ὑμῖν μεγαλυνθῆναι, "as your faith continues to grow," and 1 Cor 9:2).

Barrett, "Christianity at Corinth," 18, rightly criticizes this understanding on several grounds: (1) it cannot explain the (alleged) unnecessary repetition of words for measuring rod (μέτρον, κανών); (2) ἐφικέσθαι ἄχρι καὶ ὑμῶν, "to reach even to you," relates to Paul's geographical outreach (cf. *1 Clem* 41:1 for this meaning), not his success at Corinth, while he grants that Paul's mission did include the foundation and growth of the church there.

Other meanings of κανών are (1) as a synonym for "the Gospel" of Paul, for which there is some evidence in the use of εὐαγγέλιον in v 14 (so T. Lønning, *"Kanon im Kanon": Zum dogmatischen Grundlagenproblem des neutestamentlichen Kanon*, Oslo-Munich, 1972 [as cited by Holmberg, *Paul and Power*, 46]); and (2) with a setting in Jewish apocalyptic thought, corresponding to *qan* (קן), the eschatological and juridical "right" of the creator God, which is in the background of Paul's missionary calling to be the prophet of the end-time (Stuhlmacher, "Erwägungen," 6, 7, appealing to various Jewish texts to do with measurement/measuring line: Job 38:5; *T. Naph.* 2:3; *1 Enoch* 61; 1QH 1:28; 3:27; 10:26).

Paul's allocation included Corinth: ἐφικέσθαι ἄχρι καὶ ὑμῶν, "to reach as far as to you." The infinitive expresses consequence (see BDF § 391.4) and the καὶ is emphatic: "even to you" our mission, under God, extends. So Paul concludes: you at Corinth belong to our area of competency (ἱκανότης: cf. 2:16; 3:4–6) and God's κανών was drawn to include you. The significance of this remark will be apparent (in v 14). But the main assertion is already established in the face of some rival claims: Paul was the first to preach the Gospel in Corinth, and his commission emanated directly from God (1 Cor 9:1–3, 15–18; 15:8–11).

14. οὐ γὰρ ὡς μὴ ἐφικνούμενοι εἰς ὑμᾶς ὑπερεκτείνομεν ἑαυτούς, ἄχρι γὰρ καὶ ὑμῶν ἐφθάσαμεν ἐν τῷ εὐαγγελίῳ τοῦ Χριστοῦ, "For we are not overreaching our limit, as we should be doing if we had not [already] reached you, for we did come as far as to you with our preaching of Christ." The translation we have proposed attempts to see a defense of apostolic ministry based on the verb ἐφικνεῖσθαι, "to come to, reach" (a NT *hapax*, but common in classical Gr.). The connection with v 13 is not as though v 14 explained the foregoing; rather v 14 looks on to v 15 (Plummer, 288); there is more to v 14 than the expedient to treat it as parenthetic. The verb ὑπερεκτείνειν, lit., "to stretch out beyond," is unusual and quite rare (see BGD, 840; Bultmann, 197), and this fact suggests that it may derive from the opponents' armory. They allege that Paul had "overextended himself" and gone beyond the limit in his Corinthian mission, which he further took as a theme of boastful pride (εἰς τὰ ἄμετρα καυχᾶσθαι: Betz, ibid., 130, 131). There may well be a trace of the charge that he had indicted himself as guilty of overweening pride (ὕβρις) by exalting his own mission service at the expense of a more sober estimate (σωφροσύνη, "restraint," "moderation," μηδὲν ἀγὰν, acting κατὰ μέτρον), and in the Greek tradition of the post-Homeric poets and playwrights, such an attitude invited the inevitable onset of ἄτη, "delusion, folly," leading to punishment and divine retribution. See P. Marshall, "Hybrists not Gnostics in Corinth" (forthcoming, SBL Seminar Papers), who argues suggestively that the ὑπερ- prefix and the -λίαν component as in ὑπερλίαν (11:5; 12:11) are examples of pejorative uses denoting excess which "in various constructions, [produce] *hybris* [evidence in Euripides, Aristotle, Lysias]. So the apostles who have gone beyond the bounds and who have invidiously compared [cf. v 12] their rhetoric, knowledge, achievements, and other cultural qualities

with his own, are shameful hybrists or 'boasters.' " He offers for οἱ ὑπερλίαν ἀπόστολοι (11:5; 12:11) the rendering "the hybristic apostles."

The Pauline defense is to deny that such a mission was an overreaching of his apostolic calling. The participial form of ἐφικνούμενοι implies this (RSV, "as though we did not reach" you; our translation tries to be more emphatic). Indeed, he puts in the counterclaim that he was the pioneer missionary on the scene at Corinth. His evangelistic ministry (ἐν τῷ εὐαγγελίῳ Χριστοῦ: cf. v 16: εὐαγγελίζεσθαι is the corresponding verb, "to proclaim the Gospel") was an undisputed fact, and he could appeal confidently to the readers to endorse that "we did come" (ἐφθάσαμεν; φθάνειν, "to come first, "anticipate," as in 1 Thess 4:15 and in classical usage, rather than as in later use where it means simply "to come" [1 Thess 2:16; Rom 11:31; Phil 3:16], which Bultmann, 197, prefers). But the context requires the sense: we got to you first, that is, before any rivals: so Barrett, 266; Héring, 74, since it is this thought which is carried on to the next v and forms the basis of Paul's argumentation.

The situation, moreover, requires such a response from Paul. It is undeniable that emissaries have made their presence felt at Corinth (see on 11:4). He must retort effectively that he arrived on the scene earlier, and so he claims to have staked out Corinth as his territory (κανών), since this strategy was his by design (Rom 15:17–20) and indeed by the concurrence of the "pillar" apostles in Jerusalem (Gal 2:6, 7). In line with Barrett, 267, we regard this declaration as of fundamental significance in exegeting this v and what follows. Paul is saying no more than what is well-known: he came to the city as to virgin soil. "His ideal is to be the first to plant the flag" (Héring, 75), and Corinth rightly belonged to his "sphere of service" *qua* apostle to the Gentiles (1 Cor 2:1–5; 9:1–3) which fell to his lot as an integral part of his mission activity, "in the Gospel," i.e., in his preaching ministry as in 2:12; 8:18. And he is laying claim to no less: Corinth rightfully belongs to his jurisdiction in which the rival preachers are properly to be seen as interlopers and usurpers of apostolic prerogative.

To this we may add one extra thought: it was evidently of vital concern for Paul to defend Corinth as his "home church" if he wished to have it as a base from which, in due course, to launch out on his westerly mission to Rome and beyond. More was at risk than just the disaffection of a local congregation; his present and future work "in the Gospel" were in jeopardy by a situation which could develop into a renewed slide away from Paul and his mission on the part of the Corinthian believers.

15, 16. οὐκ εἰς τὰ ἄμετρα καυχώμενοι ἐν ἀλλοτρίοις κόποις, ἐλπίδα δὲ ἔχοντες αὐξανομένης τῆς πίστεως ὑμῶν ἐν ὑμῖν μεγαλυνθῆναι κατὰ τὸν κανόνα ἡμῶν εἰς περισσείαν ¹⁶εἰς τὰ ὑπερέκεινα ὑμῶν εὐαγγελίσασθαι, οὐκ ἐν ἀλλοτρίῳ κανόνι εἰς τὰ ἕτοιμα καυχήσασθαι, "We did not go beyond the proper limits by boasting of the work done by others, but we have the hope that as your faith continues to grow, so our work may, within the sphere we have, be greatly expanded among you. ¹⁶The result is that we may preach the Gospel in places beyond you. We do not wish to boast about what has already been done in another person's sphere [of service]." The link-verb is again, as in v 14, a participle (καυχώμενοι), which does not make for smooth transition or easy comprehension, especially as the sequence of the argument takes the reader into v 16.

The first part of v 15 is tolerably clear. Paul cannot be accused of poaching on the mission territory held by others, and certainly his alleged καυχᾶσθαι, "boast," which (it is said) he evinces, based on the limits he has transgressed (τὰ ἄμετρα), is categorically refused. Alternatively, as we observed with interpreting v 13 (see *Comment*), the τὰ ἄμετρα phrase may be construed adverbially, i.e., we will not boast unfairly or in an exaggerated way or to an unwarranted degree. The former view is preferable, because the term is an opponents' watchword used as a weapon to attack the apostle. And he is simply retorting by denying it. The reason given, however, is what counts. It would be true that this allegation of *superbia* or inordinate pride (implied in καυχᾶσθαι and also in the ὑπερέκειν- root in vv 14, 16) could stand if Paul has not respected the work of "others" and has taken some of the credit that belonged to another's κανών, "sphere of mission" (v 16). Who such persons may have been is uncertain. We have the same conundrum in Rom 15:20, "lest I build on another person's foundation" (ἵνα μὴ ἐπ᾽ ἀλλότριον θεμέλιον οἰκοδομῶ). The most we can say is that this phrase may well have been part of the emissaries' charge against Paul's work; and if so, then the reference will be to the claim made for the Jewish Christian leadership that they—especially Cephas (1 Cor 1:12; 3:22; 9:5; 15:5)—were the rightful founders of the Corinthian congregation. See Barrett, "Cephas and Corinth," 35, 36, who suggests that Peter himself may have headed the mission, but Paul politely and tactfully passes over him in an oblique reference to "such a person" (10:11) and to the singular ἐν ἀλλοτρίῳ κανόνι in v 16. This veiled identity explains why Paul throughout 2 Cor 10–13 refrained from mentioning names. (See later, p. 353, for another reason.) A suggestive link with Peter is that, in the "division of apostolic labor" in Gal 2, the leadership of Peter on the Jewish Christian side is patent, and it was on the terms of this arrangement that Paul based his "apology" in 10:12–18 (Barrett, ibid., 37; but was it Peter who preached a "different Jesus" [11:4]? Hardly). So Barrett concludes (ibid., 38): "yet Peter, in the hands of those who made use of him, was on the way to ruining Paul's work at Corinth." See for similar conclusion, Holmberg, *Paul*, 50; Gunther, *St. Paul's Opponents*, 301–3.

So far—with the exception of the precise identity of the "other" person—the sentence is clear. It is the statement of Paul's expectation (ἐλπίδα . . . ἔχοντες) that, once the situation at Corinth had clarified and the church there had reaffirmed its confidence in Paul, the way would be open for him to use Corinth as a launching-pad for a mission westward ("we may preach the Gospel in places beyond you"). Clearly Paul is doing several things by means of this involved, complex sentence: (1) He is expressing his optimism (ἐλπίς is invariably in the NT "good hope" which anticipates and articulates the Christian's confidence in God's good purpose: see Moule, *The Meaning of Hope*, Facet Book 5 [Philadelphia: Fortress, 1963] passim) that all will turn out well. (2) He gives as the immediate object of the hope that the Corinthians' faith will be enlarged. (αὐξανομένης τῆς πίστεως ὑμῶν is a genitive absolute; πίστις, however, may mean either their faith in Paul's Gospel or their faithfulness to his mission, which will act as a support to his future service, as in Rom 1:11, 12: the Romans' faith will strengthen Paul's and encourage him to press on westward. Then, the increase may be related to an outreach of mission.) (3) The latter view in (2) is confirmed by the difficult phrase ἐν ὑμῖν . . . κατὰ τὸν κανόνα ἡμῶν: lit., "among you—or in your eyes (see Barrett, 267) . . . according to our sphere of mission service." What Paul sees as the result of the Corinthian loyalty is that they will recognize that he has worked at Corinth as part of his authentic bailiwick. (4) This is the basis on which he wishes to launch out to a work with a further enlargement (εἰς περισσείαν, a phrase to be attached to v 16: Héring, 75), namely, to proclaim the Gospel, i.e., the same Gospel he brought originally to Corinth (v 14), "in places beyond you" (τὰ ὑπερέκεινα ὑμῶν εὐαγγελίσασθαι). He does not pause to elaborate where such places may be. But from Romans 1:15; 15:23–39 we may, with some confidence, postulate a mission to Rome and Spain.

(5) The one negative assessment in this "grand strategy" is that thereby he will not have to answer the evident charge that is running through this entire section (vv 13, 14, 15). If Paul moves out to these regions outside the territorial limits in the eastern Mediterranean where his tasks are now at an end (Rom 15:19: πεπληρωκέναι τὸ εὐαγγέλιον τοῦ Χριστοῦ), he will have no need to justify any boasting (καυχᾶσθαι), since "work already done in another's sphere [of service]" will certainly not include what he has projected as his next step in missionary endeavor. The allusion to εἰς τὰ ἕτοιμα matches εἰς τὰ ὑπερέκεινα ὑμῶν (BDF § 184 on the genitive used with the adverb). Paul is opposing "preaching" (εὐαγγελίζεσθαι) directed to the lands (sc. μέρη) "beyond you" and a mission work already "prepared"—ἕτοιμος—by other person(s) before we came on the scene and claimed credit for it (Plummer, 290), or done by other leader(s) who did stay within their assigned limits of service, e.g., Peter at Antioch (or less probably Palestine, as Theissen, *Social Setting,* 50, n. 53, surmises). Paul increasingly felt his isolation from Antioch (*Introduction,* pp. lvi–lix; M. Hengel, *Acts and the History of Earliest Christianity,* 123–26), but here he generously allows that his rivals do have a permitted and legitimate sphere; and this meaning would be helped, if we take εἰς τὰ ἕτοιμα and attach it to ἐν ἀλλοτρίῳ κανόνι: there is for each (missionary group) a sphere, in view of what has been prepared for it, i.e., which corresponds to what God has allocated to each. Yet the construction with εἰς following the infinitive εὐαγγελίσασθαι is rough: so Windisch, 313, who pronounces it "intolerable." See Héring, 75, for some discussion which goes into the syntactical tangle of vv 15, 16.

17, 18. ὁ δὲ καυχώμενος ἐν κυρίῳ καυχάσθω· 18 οὐ γὰρ ὁ ἑαυτὸν συνιστάνων, ἐκεῖνός ἐστιν δόκιμος, ἀλλὰ ὃν ὁ κύριος συνίστησιν, "But rather, 'let the one who boasts boast only about the Lord.' 18 For it is not the person who recommends himself who is approved, but the person whom the Lord recommends." In a typically Pauline mannerism, the writer clinches his point with an OT citation, followed (in v 18) with an explanatory comment, which in turn binds together the initial part of his discussion in v 12 with its conclusion in v 18 in a "ring composition": the hook-word is συνιστάνειν, "to commend/recommend." The issue at stake is κανών and its demarcation, whether it is (1) the product of human endeavor and so it deserves the praise or blame that a person seeks either to gain or avoid for the work done in mission service, or (2) an assignment from "the Lord" who gives it validity and so is the only one who can rightly commend it as "approved" (δόκιμος; the prefiguring of 13:3–5 is apparent: Bultmann, 199).

The biblical appeal is to Jer 9:22, 23 (LXX) at the heart of which is the line:

ἀλλ᾽ ἢ ἐν τούτῳ καυχάσθω ὁ καυχώμενος:
"But in this let the boaster make his boast."

Cf. 1 Cor 1:31 for a similar use of the oracle of Jeremiah.

Paul's adaptation is to enforce the point by including the divine name (ἐν κυρίῳ) which is then taken up in the succeeding v: "not the one who commends (συνιστάνων) himself is approved (δόκιμος), but the person whom the Lord commends" (here κύριος would be applied to the exalted Jesus: Kramer, *Christ, Lord, Son of God,* sec. 43*a*, n. 570, and "about the Lord" corresponds to the use of the verbal root [ב לֹל, *hālal* *b*ᵉ] in v 17, ibid., 50*a*, n. 651).

The conclusion drives home Paul's chief thrust: only a Christian enterprise, which is both originated from God's plan, according to the divine κανών, and aims to promote his honor (of which the antithesis is self-praise) can stand ultimate scrutiny. This is a major affirmation in Paul's *apologia pro vita sua,* when he regards his *vita* as caught up in the ongoing mission of God, at Corinth and further afield. Similar sentiments are given in 1 Cor 15:10; Rom 15:17; Gal 2:8 (cf. Eph 3:7, 8).

Explanation

The apostle now takes the offensive, and opens his "defense" (paradoxically) by charging his enemies with a false set of values (v 12). At the same time, he makes it clear that he has not trespassed on the limits which God has set for his missionary service. He is, par excellence, the apostle to the Gentiles, a vocation spelled out to him at his conversion and call (according to Acts 9:15; 22:21) and accepted by the "pillar" apostles as part of the comity agreement at Jerusalem (Gal 2:9). Indeed, the mission to the Gentiles is his peculiar province which God himself apportioned him (v 13)—and Corinth falls in that category as a largely non-Jewish community.

This reference is clearly intended as a side-look at the Jewish Christian proselytizers who were molesting Gentile church members and endeavoring to impose the yoke of obedience and certain extraneous beliefs upon them (11:3, 4, 20). Paul replies that if any preacher is "out of bounds" at Corinth, it is not he himself, but the interlopers who had gone beyond the limit assigned to them and failed to respect the proper "base of operations" to which they were entitled (see 11:12).

Paul most carefully justifies his integrity here (v 14), insisting that when he first came to Corinth he did so with clear conscience and intended in no way to "poach" on the missionary territory of other Christians (vv 15, 16; cf. Rom. 15:20).

At Corinth he may justifiably claim to be the human founder of the church (1 Cor 3:6: "I planted"). What right have the rival preachers to encroach on his work (1 Cor 9:1; 2 Cor 3:2)? Their mandate does not operate at Corinth.

Yet the final arbiter in this matter of evangelistic "division of labor" and territorial comity is no human committee, nor does an agreement, made between Christians, mean much unless it is the Lord who directs. True—and herein is the relevance for modern missionary service—he expects his servants to honor their arrangements and not to act irresponsibly in defiance of agreements as to mission fields; but it is his work and whatever success is given comes from him to whom alone the credit and glory belong (vv 17, 18, quoting Jer 9:24).

Denney (309), as so often, applies the apostolic message in a timeless way:

> Two feelings are compounded all through this passage: an intense sympathy with the purpose of God that the Gospel should be preached to every creature—Paul's very soul melts into that; and an intense scorn for the spirit that sneaks and poaches on another's ground, and is more anxious that some men should be good sectarians than that all men should be good disciples.

C. The Emissaries Identified and Opposed (11:1–15)

Bibliography

Barrett, C. K. *Essays on Paul.* "Christianity at Corinth." 1–27. ———. ibid. "Paul's Opponents in 2 Corinthians." 60–86. ———. ibid. "ΨΕΥΔΑΠΟΣΤΟΛΟΙ (2 Cor 11.13)." 87–107. **Betz, H.-D.** *Der Apostel Paulus und die sokratische Tradition.* **Black, D. A.** *Paul, Apostle of Weakness.* **Ellis, E. E.** "Paul and His Opponents." In *Prophecy and Hermeneutic in Early Christianity,* 80–115. Grand Rapids: Eerdmans, 1978. **Fahy, T.** "St. Paul's 'Boasting' and 'Weakness.'" *ITQ* 31 (1964) 214–27. **Friedrich, G.** "Die Gegner des Paulus im 2 Korintherbrief." *Abraham unser Vater.* 181–221. **Georgi, D.** *Die Gegner des Paulus im 2. Korintherbrief.* **Goppelt, L.** *Apostolic and Post-Apostolic Times.* Tr. R. A. Guelich. New York: Harper/London: A. & C. Black, 1970. **Hainz, J.** *Ekklesia.* 157, 158. **Holsten, C.** "Zur Erklärung von 2 Kor 11, 4–6." *ZWT* 16 (1873) 1–56. **Horsley, G. H. R.,** ed. *New Documents Illustrating Early Christianity (1976).* North Ryde, NSW: Macquarie University, 1981. **Judge, E. A.** "Paul's Boasting in Relation to Contemporary Professional Practice." *ABR* 16 (1968) 37–50. ———. "Cultural Conformity and Innovation in Paul: Some Clues from Contemporary Documents" *TynB* 35 (1984) 3–24. **Käsemann, E.** *Die Legitimität des Apostels: eine Untersuchung zu II Korinther 10–13.* **Kee, Doyle.** "Who Were the 'Super-Apostles' of 2 Cor 10–13?" *RestQ* 23 (1980) 65–76. **Kleinknecht, K. T.** *Der leidende Gerechtfertigte.* **Marshall, P.** "Invective: Paul and his Enemies at Corinth." In *Perspectives on Language: Essays and Poems in Honor of Francis I. Andersen's Sixtieth Birthday.* Ed. E. W. Conrad and E. G. Newing. Winona Lake, IN: Eisenbrauns, 1987. **McClelland, S. E.** "'Super-Apostles, Servants of Christ, Servants of Satan,' A response" [to M. E. Thrall]. *JSNT* 14 (1982) 82–87. **Mozley, J. F.** "2 Cor 11:12." *ExpTim* 42 (1930–31) 212–14. **Munck, J.** *Paul and the Salvation of Mankind.* 1959. **Oostendorp, D. W.** *Another Jesus. A Gospel of Jewish Christian Superiority in II Corinthians.* Kampen: Kok, 1967. **Schlatter, A.** *Paulus, der Bote Jesu*[3], 1962. **Schütz, J. H.** *Paul and the Anatomy of Apostolic Authority.* **Theissen, G.** *The Social Setting of Pauline Christianity. Essays on Corinth.* ———. *Sociology of Early Palestinian Christianity.* Tr. J. Bowden. Philadelphia: Fortress Press, 1978. **Thrall, M. E.** "Super-Apostles, Servants of Christ and Servants of Satan." *JSNT* 6 (1980) 42–57. **Travis, S. H.** "Paul's Boasting in 2 Corinthians 10–12." *SE* VI (TU 112, 1973) 527–32. **Ward, R. B.** "The Opponents of Paul." *RestQ* 10 (1967) 185–95. **Zmijewski, J.** *Der Stil der paulinischen "Narrenrede."* Analyse der *Sprachgestaltung in 2 Kor 11, 1–12, 10 als Beitrag zur Methodik von Stiluntersuchungen neutestamentlicher Texte.* Köln-Bonn: Hanstein, BBB 52, 1978.

Translation

¹*I would* ᵃ *that you might put up with my little display of folly! Yes, please put up with me!* ᵇ ²*for I am jealous for you, with a jealousy God inspires [in me], because I have promised you in marriage to a single husband, even Christ, to present you to him an undefiled virgin.* ³*My fear, however, is that just as the snake led Eve astray by craftiness, so your minds should be corrupted from a sincere commitment* ᶜ *to Christ.* ⁴*For if the person who has come to you*
   proclaims a rival Jesus, whom we did not proclaim
   or if you welcome a different Spirit, which you did not welcome [in our message]
   or if [you accept] a different gospel, which you did not accept [as our Gospel]
   then, you put up with ᵈ *this person right well!*
⁵*For I counted myself to be in no way inferior to "the highest ranking apostles"!* ⁶*I may indeed be untrained in public speaking, but I am not [deficient] in knowledge [of the truth]. Rather, in every way we have made [God's truth] known to you as to all.*
⁷*Did I do wrong in humbling myself that you might be lifted up, because I proclaimed the Good News of God to you without levying a charge?* ⁸*Rather, I robbed other congregations, taking my expenses [from them] in fulfillment of my ministry to you* ⁹*and when I was with you and ran into need, I laid no [financial] burdens on anyone; for it was the brothers who arrived from Macedonia who made good my deficiency. In all ways I kept myself from being a burden to you, and I will continue to do so.* ¹⁰*As certain as God's truth is on my side, this boasting of mine will not be stopped in the districts of Achaia.* ¹¹*How so? Is it because I do not love you? God knows I do.*
¹²*The course I have taken I will keep to, that I may put an end to the opportunity of those men who are seeking such an opportunity to be regarded, in what they boast of, as just like us.* ¹³*On the contrary, these people are bogus apostles, workers of deceit, masquerading as Christ's apostles.* ¹⁴*Do not be surprised at that;* ᵉ *for Satan himself masquerades as a messenger of light.* ¹⁵*It is no great surprise, then, if his servants too masquerade as servants of righteousness. Their fate will be what their deeds deserve.*

Notes

ᵃReading ὄφελον (with no augment: BDF § 67.2) with P⁴⁶ ℵ B and other cursives. The reading ὤφελον seen in D³ F G K L Ψ is the form in classical Gr. but with εἴθε and a following infinitive: see BDF § 359.1 who takes the NT construction as used to express an unattained wish. Paul tends to use the ejaculation, more as a particle than as a verb, to convey irony: Gal 5:12; 1 Cor 4:8. Notice how ἀλλά modifies and corrects the unfulfilled wish. See *Note* b.

ᵇἀνέχεσθε is best taken as a kind of imperative (BDF § 448.6: "I will not only express the wish, but I forthwith entreat you"). The other option is to render the verb as indicative: "but you have already done so." Plummer, 293, thinks that with καὶ to emphasize what is now said, one gets more of a correction and as much emphasis if the indicative is understood. So Lietzmann,

144, who argues that ἀλλὰ καί must be adversative, reversing the previous statement, and so introducing a similar declarative clause. So too Bultmann, 201. But taking ἀλλὰ as copulative (Barrett, 271: "I wish you would . . . yes, do") makes the transition to what follows smoother (Robertson, *Grammar*, 1186).

ᶜThe textual issue turns on whether καὶ τῆς ἁγνότητος, "and (of) purity," is part of the original sentence after ἀπὸ τῆς ἁπλότητος, "from devotion" to Christ. The longer text is found in p⁴⁶ ℵ* B G syrʰ copˢᵃˑᵇᵒ goth eth; then those witnesses which omit the phrase (ℵᶜ Dᶜ H K P ψ lat syrᵖˑʰ arm) and those which have it—but exclude τῆς ἁπλότητος (Ambrose, Augustine with Lucifer—all Latin fathers) would be accounted for by the scribe's eye passing over words with identical endings (-οτητος in both instances: i.e., by homoeoteleuton). Yet D* itᵈ Epiphanius have the nouns in reverse sequence, so that cannot be the whole explanation. Lietzmann, 145, supposes that it was ἁγνὴν ("pure," v 2) that gave rise to the noun in v 3—a not unlikely idea. And Barrett, 270, has a point that the variable position of the reference to ἁγνότης suggests a later expansion of the text (on the principle *lectio brevior potior*). But Allo, 276, and Hughes, 376, defend the inclusion on ground of haplography rather than the omission as dittography (Windisch, 325). See *Textual Commentary*, 583, 584.

ᵈRead καλῶς ἀνέχεσθε (p⁴⁶ B D* 33 sa), "you bear with him quite beautifully," as an ironical statement (Plummer, 297). The variant ἀνείχεσθε (ℵ D³ and uncials, lat) adds the element of contingency, even though ἄν is missing: "if he proclaims . . . you *would* bear with him." But Paul is not in doubt about the way the Corinthians have given hospitality to the rival mission. Equally unlikely also is the view that wishes to take the sentence as interrogative, asking a simple question to do with a visitor on the scene. Schlatter, *Paulus*, 635, thinks the visitor was awaited from Jerusalem in the person of Peter who is expected as a judge (*Schiedsrichter*). Rightly Käsemann, *Die Legitimität*, 15, and Bultmann, 203, n. 16, insist that this identity is impossible, since the καλῶς construction with ἀνέχεσθε (1) refers to an actual, not hypothetical, case, and (2) corresponds to the tenor of v 19, which reveals a real problem, not an imaginary one, at Corinth. See Strachan, 18.

ᵉοὐ θαῦμα is read in ℵ B D* F G, with a variant οὐ θαυμαστόν in Dᵇˑᶜ E K. The latter is probably an attempt to turn a rare term into a well-known one, found often in LXX and not infrequently in NT.

Form/Structure/Setting

A major decision awaits the interpreter of 11:1–15. It is the simple choice of accepting this section as an interlude in which Paul turns aside from his chief theme of missionary service and the dispute of territoriality (in 10:12–18), only to revert to that topic in 11:16, with the common link that of "boasting" (καυχᾶσθαι in chap. 10 and 11:18–21 and following chaps.). The alternative is to see 10:13–18 as a digression, albeit related to the main theme. Then, at 11:1 the reader is confronted with the beginning of a new topic, heralded by an outburst of indignation (so Barrett, 271; Plummer, 292). Others see the two sections as vaguely related (Hughes, 372), but having no precise connection.

Our choice is to prefer the first option on the ground that Paul turns to meet a new threat hitherto not fully disclosed, namely, the presence and influence of rival mission preachers (in 11:4) whose activity is set before the Corinthians and whose effect on the congregation is then shown to be altogether baneful (in 11:13–15). True, "boasting" does occur in this pericope (11:10, 12), but the issue of apostolic authority and the question of *Missionsgebiet*, "missionary sphere of service," which was so prominent in 10:13–18, is not resumed until we get to 11:16 where the theme is continued with a fresh emphasis. The matter there is: Why have the Corinthians allowed the alien intruder to take control of them (11:20)? And, more particularly, why have they scorned *their* apostle, Paul himself, who has an impressive array of credentials to his account (11:21–33)? And is he not one who remained true to his set practice of refusing to receive money from the Corinthians (vv 8–11)? The center of the debate is, as Käsemann, *Die Legitimität,* 37 et passim, has definitively shown, that of apostolic legitimation and the crux of the matter turns on *Evidenzproblem* (Betz, *Der Apostel Paulus,* 132–37), i.e., what kind of proof (δοκιμή) validates the true servant of Christ and, more especially, where is the locus of Christian existence to be found? Is it in "boasting" because of success and accompanied with a lordly presence? Or is it to be seen in Paul's own strength-in-weakness? At the center of this section lies a sentence that sets the stage: in v 12 Paul makes the opponents' boasting in their gospel a pivotal issue. They maintained that they were acting out the terms of their ministry on the same terms as Paul's mission service. For Paul this is categorically denied, for reasons that go back to 10:13–18 and look ahead to the decisive refutation in 13:1–4. This—at its elemental level—is the nub of the discussion, and provides Paul with a chance (an "opportunity" [ἀφορμή] in 11:12) to state his τύπος ἀπολογητικός, "pattern of apologetic," as Windisch (8) calls it, citing Demetrius of Phalerum (*Typi epistolares,* 18). See too Betz's more nuanced designation of the chapters as "apology in letter-form" (ibid., 14).

This position regarding the several sections of chaps. 10–13 may be defended in various ways. But whatever decision is reached in regard to the present passage in 11:1–15, we will do well to heed Zmijewski's conclusions based on a comprehensive examination of the stylistic, rhetorical, and literary features of 11:1–12:10, which are the heart of the chapters (*Der Stil,* esp. 412–22, from which the following items are drawn). He sees the vv as containing an elaborately worded and artistically crafted *"Narrenrede,"* "discourse of fools," where irony, sarcasm, mock humility, word-play, diatribe, and rhetorical comparison (Gr. *synkrisis*) play a significant role. Yet he is not willing to abandon or play down the role of Paul's own personal contribution as autobiography (so Kleinknecht, *Der leidende Gerechtfertigte,* 264–66, who indeed calls Paul's interest in his biographical-evidential experiences the key to understanding him), and this interest is concentrated in the scope of his argument with its "list of trials" (*peristaseis*) in 11:22–33. In this instance Zmijewski is in agreement with the position found in Prümm, *Diakonia* 2:96, to the effect that, although Paul employs rhetorical forms, he shows no great interest in the literary type (*Genos*) as such, but only insofar as he can use it, and because he has been forced to deal with his opponents on their own ground; and he parts company with Betz's recourse to the form of the debate between the philosopher and the sophist as the overriding consideration in these two long chapters (ibid., 121, 122). Zmijewski (ibid., 424) points out stylistic peculiarities that can only be classed as semitic, e.g., *parallelismus membrorum,* or use of couplets, 12:2–47; a paratactic sequence with 11:8, 9, 32, 33 as examples; finite verbs with a participle in 11:5, 6; the argument *a minori ad maius,* which the OT writers and rabbis employed under the figure of "the light and the heavy" in 11:13, 14; the theological "divine passive" in 12:7*b,* i.e., "there was given me" by God; the placing of the verb at the head of the sentence in 12:1; the characteristic type of expression, such as "I escaped his hands" (11:33); the unusual Greek prepositional use of πρός with παρών, 11:9, "I was with you" and καυχᾶσθαι + ὑπέρ and ἐν in 12:5, 9 and εὐδοκῶ + ἐν in 12:10; the way of expressing "time when" in 12:2—all these features are cited as betraying a style indebted to an OT-rabbinic cast of mind. See J. H. Moulton-N. Turner, *Grammar* 4 (Edinburgh: T. & T. Clark, 1976) 86–99.

Betz, *Der Apostel Paulus,* of course, finds many contrasting parallels drawn from the Greek world and discovers one of his main supports in chap. 13 of our letter, especially 13:1–4, with which Zmijewski hardly deals. So a final decision must await our coverage of those latter vv.

For the present we may appeal to Zmijewski's main contention based on 10:11. (There are several subsidiary points which have intrinsic value, e.g., Paul's defense is christocentric: see 11:10, 23a; 12:9, 10; his pastoral motivations are paramount in all his relations with the Corinthians; and the central question is apostolic self-understanding, with its correlation of ἀσθένεια/ δύναμις, weakness/strength; ibid., 419–21.) We may find confirmation of seeing 10:13–18 as the central issue by following Zmijewski in pointing to 10:11 as setting the stage for all that follows (ibid., 432, 433). This v (10:11) takes us back to the earlier section which is chiefly preoccupied with missionary comity. But at Corinth there was a prior concern, which arose out of a contrast between Paul's person and his effective ministry (Windisch, 307). Continental scholars (e.g., Windisch, loc. cit.; Bultmann, 193; Schlatter, ibid., 622) have stressed how the antithesis of λόγος, "word," and ἔργον, "work," lies at the heart of Paul's Corinthian debate. In reply to the allegation that he was weak (i.e., timid and time-serving) and rhetorically ineffective, Paul retorts that, as he has shown strength in his letter at a distance (ἀπόντες), so when he does arrive at Corinth, he will manifest a similar forceful character (παρόντες τῷ ἔργῳ).

In this view, the sequence in 11:1–15 is designed to face two realities: (1) Paul's rivals, trading on their claim to be legitimate apostles at Corinth, have arrived in the city, and Paul gets wind of their activity (11:4); (2) he addresses the matter of what is to take place when he in turn will come to Corinth by denouncing these men in no uncertain terms (11:12–15), and blocking their appeal to the congregation. In the trial of strength between their claims and his ministry, he freely concedes *ad hominem* that he does not have their rhetorical skill (λόγος, linking with 10:11 where his forte is in letter-writing, not public utterance: see 1 Cor 2:1–5), but he builds his case for allegiance on what he has already revealed (φανερώσαντες, 11:6, linking with 4:2) to his people at Corinth, i.e., his Gospel and the ἀπόδειξις of the Spirit in his ministry "in every way" (linking with 6:4, ἐν παντὶ συνιστάντες ἑαυτοὺς ὡς θεοῦ διάκονοι; by contrast his enemies are Satan's διάκονοι, 11:15). The apostle's word (λόγος) and deed (ἔργον, i.e., his demeanor as a suffering apostle) thus go together and are "not to be separated" (Schlatter, ibid., 622, who adds that Paul "lives for his work which is the building up of the church"; therein lies his appeal to authority and his sense of "responsibility to and for the community" as Schütz, *Paul and the Anatomy of Apostolic Authority,* 182, describes it in terms of οἰκοδομή, citing 13:10). But that apostolic authority necessarily implies a concern to deal firmly with his direct antagonists and thereby to call back the Corinthians to a former allegiance, since he is Christ's servant (11:10), and committed to seek the well-being of his cause at Corinth. Bound up with that is Paul's own investment in Corinth as a key center of his mission strategy, so there is added poignancy in his christological invocation in 11:10, and in his eschatological *lex talionis* (11:15: their *telos* will match their deeds [ἔργα], linking with 10:11: so my deed [ἔργον] will be when I am present). Thus the circle of argumentation is closed at 11:15 as Paul pronounces a curse-formula on such ἔργα, which he has threatened to judge when he reaches Corinth and finds a pocket of opposition led by Satan's emissaries.

Within the larger frame of 11:1–15, vv 13–15 form a clearly demarcated unit, not only in content but also style (Zmijewski, *Der Stil*, 166, 167). The following features stand out: staccato expressions (vv 14a, 15a, 15b); noun-forms which predominate; parallelisms in sentence-structure; rhetorical figures such as *enumeratio*, in threes (v 13); words repeated, e.g., μετασχηματίζεσθαι (3x), διάκονοι (2x); contrasting pairs, e.g. "false apostles"—"apostles of Christ"; "Satan's servants"—"servants of righteousness," offset by synonyms: "servants" = "apostles of Christ"; a cyclic framing in v 15: οἱ διάκονοι—ὡς διάκονοι, ὧν—αὐτῶν, and epiphoric alliteration (v 13 with endings in -οι); more significant, perhaps, is the argumentation form: *propositio* (v 13); *ratio* (v 14); *conclusio* (v 15a) with a proleptic judgment-formula in v 15b. The entire subsection is artistically crafted in a circular way, with the opponents mentioned at the beginning and the conclusion; and the rabbinical argument *a fortiori* ("light"/"heavy") called into play (Bultmann, 211).

Other traits of style are shared by the surrounding vv and include: repetition (vv 9c, 12); a paraphrastic style (*Umschreibungsstil*) in v 7: ἁμαρτίαν ἐποίησα in place of ἡμάρτησα; and the insertingof words of powerful emotional content, e.g., συλᾶν (rob), ἀγαπᾶν (love), ἐκκόπτειν (cut off), φράσσειν (stop). See Zmijewski, ibid., 187.

Comment

1. ὄφελον ἀνείχεσθέ μου μικρόν τι ἀφροσύνης· ἀλλὰ καὶ ἀνέχεσθέ μου, "I would that you might put up with my little display of folly! Yes, please put up with me!" The form of this sentence, which in the view we have taken marks a slight digression from the previous theme of "boasting in mission" in 10:13–18 to which Paul will return in 11:16, is striking. The sentence joins two contrasting statements: an unrealizable wish (ὄφελον: a fixed form, functioning as a particle to introduce an unattainable wish, BDG, 599) and—by contrast (ἀλλά) but more a concession—a declaration that Paul's wish is to be granted, "yes, do what I cannot really ask." The middle term is the verb ἀνέχεσθαι, "to endure, bear with, put up with." Clearly something like the last-mentioned translation is required here (as in Mk 9:19, ἕως πότε ἀνέξομαι ὑμῶν;). Paul can hardly bring himself to ask for this indulgence, that the Corinthians will put up with his display of "folly" (ἀφροσύνη: "the decisive catchword for this sentence," and what is to come—see v 4—in the entire "Fool's Discourse" [*Narrenrede*]: so Zmijewski, *Der Stil*, 78). The first μου should be retained with the noun: "with this folly of mine" (Bultmann, 201; but most translators opt for "bear with me"). Paul will keep this thought before his readers (11:16,

17, 19, 21; 12:6, 11). ἄφρων/ἀφροσύνη, "fool/foolishness," is a technical expression in Jewish wisdom literature (especially in Prov and Eccl, as in Sir, Wisd Sol) in contrast to σοφός/σωφροσύνη, the wise/wisdom (so Windisch, 318). See the contrast in 1 Cor 1:18–2:6, on which cf. Barrett, "Christianity at Corinth," 6–14; E. E. Ellis, "Wisdom and Knowledge in 1 Cor," in *Prophecy and Hermeneutic in Early Christianity*, 45–62. The ironical reference in 11:19 with φρόνιμοι is not very different from Paul's use of σοφός in malam partem.

Paul's indulgence in "folly" is by his design, but he has been driven to it (so 12:11). To that extent Lietzmann, 144, is correct to find here a slogan, as if Paul had been accused of this practice, being a boastful person (10:1; cf. 5:13 where he faces the charge of being the opposite of σώφρων, a self-controlled individual). Yet Bultmann, 202, notes that the antithesis then would be μωρός (1 Cor 4:10) with the reproach of μωρία, "folly"—but that is in the eyes of the world, not in the eyes of a section of the church, we observe. For the figure of speech see BDF § 495.3.

2. ζηλῶ γὰρ ὑμᾶς θεοῦ ζήλῳ, ἡρμοσάμην γὰρ ὑμᾶς ἑνὶ ἀνδρὶ παρθένον ἁγνὴν παραστῆσαι τῷ Χριστῷ, "For I am jealous for you, with a jealousy God inspires [in me], because I have promised you in marriage to a single husband, even Christ, to present you to him an undefiled virgin." A Pauline pastoral aside, this sentence points to what underlies Paul's concern for this church as for all the churches (11:28); "for," γὰρ, gives the link. He is consumed with ζῆλος, "jealousy" or "zeal," a term drawn from the character of Yahweh as the sole husband of Israel (Hos 1–3; Ezek 16; Isa 50:1–2; 54:1–8; 62:5) who is spoken of, correspondingly, as his bride. The marriage image is persistent throughout both Testaments: see C. Chavasse, *The Bride of Christ* (London: Religious Book Club, 1930); J. P. Sampley, *"And the Two Shall Become One Flesh": A Study of the Traditions in Ephesians*, SNTSMS 16 (Cambridge: University Press, 1971), esp. 34–51 on the *hieros gamos* motif (but hardly a heavenly syzygy or union, as Windisch, 320–22, opines). R. A. Batey, *New Testament Nuptial Imagery* (Leiden: Brill, 1971) points out that the description of Christ as the bridegroom is often wrongly sentimentalized. One of its main emphases is the assertion of his lordship over the bride, the Church (ibid., 67, 68). See especially Eph 5:25–27, 31 f. and the bibliography in my article, *IDB* 1:209.

Paul's role in this partnership between Christ and his bride is one of φίλος τοῦ νυμφίου (John 3:29: Heb. šôš^ebîn, "groomsman," who acted as best man or escort; see *Comment*, p. 207). As such, he is greatly interested in siding with Christ's desire to have a pure bride, a *virgo intacta* (παρθένον ἁγνήν), and he expresses his feelings by a recourse to the OT imagery where Yahweh is said to be a "jealous God" (Exod 20:5), which is another side to his love. "All love involves jealousy, if its exclusive claim is set aside" (Goudge, 101); and Paul shares this attitude as a mark of his love for the Corinthians (see 6:14–7:4, a pledge to be renewed at 12:15: see Windisch, 319). If this is the ruling idea in Paul's verb ἡρμοσάμην, "I betrothed," (middle voice of ἁρμόζεσθαι: see BDF § 316.1; Moulton, *Grammar* 1:160, for Paul's personal interest), then it seems we should give extra weight to ἑνί with ἀνδρί, i.e., "one husband," as much as to "pure virgin." See Tasker, 145, who comments that the adding of "one" stresses that, "just as the marriage relationship is exclusive, so believers in Christ owe an exclusive loyalty to Him." So ἑνὶ ἀνδρί implies that the church is united to Christ and to no other alongside or in place of him (Bultmann, 202). To desert him is to forsake the true Pauline Gospel—as v 4 makes apparent—for "another Jesus," a rival spouse.

The presentation (the verb παραστῆσαι, "to offer, render," looks on to the Parousia, as in 4:14) of the churchly bride to her future husband is also part of Paul's task as an apostle, whether as a father-figure (1 Cor 4:15: see *Comment* on 6:12; 7:4), or more probably as an escort. But Paul's hopes are none too sanguine for the reason given in v 3. (The same verb, "to present," in a nuptial setting has a different point in Eph 5:27, with no eschatological dimension: H. Schlier, *Der Brief an die Epheser* [6] [Düsseldorf: Patmos Verlag, 1968] 252–80). The illustration of παρθένος in *P.Oxy.* 3177.2, 3 in reference to a woman and her mother throws some light on this v, though it is noted in Horsley, *New Docs* (1976) #25, " 'A Pure Bride' (2 Cor 11.2)," 71, 72, that "we have no analogy to a group of people being regarded collectively as a παρθένος" (virgin), which is not an OT ecclesiological title.

3. φοβοῦμαι δὲ μή πως, ὡς ὁ ὄφις ἐξηπάτησεν Εὔαν ἐν τῇ πανουρ-γίᾳ αὐτοῦ, φθαρῇ τὰ νοήματα ὑμῶν ἀπὸ τῆς ἁπλότητος [καὶ τῆς ἁγνότητος] τῆς εἰς τὸν Χριστόν, "My fear, however, is that just as the snake led Eve astray by craftiness, so your minds should be corrupted from a sincere commitment to Christ." The apprehension (φοβοῦμαι δὲ) expressly qualifies Paul's desire to lead the Corinthians to their full bridal dignity. The key verb is φθαρῆναι ἀπό, a construction evidently patterned on the similar πλανᾶσθαι ἀπό, "to go astray from" (Lietzmann, 145), with the preposition acting to express separa-tion instead of the more usual simple genitive (BDF § 211). The verb with ἀπό implies both a corrupting influence (i.e., leading to ruin) and a seduc-tion from what is right and pure. (See Zmijewski, *Der Stil*, 89, for the sense of καὶ ἀποστῇ [Heb 3:12] or μεταθῇ [Gal 1:6]). The situation is that alien powers have worked dangerously—in Paul's view—to turn the Corinthians' minds (νοήματα: as in 3:14; 4:4; and 10:5 seems germane, *pace* Barrett, 272) away from their true allegiance, expressed as ἁπλότης (see on 1:12, *si vera lectio*), "sincere devotion" or wholehearted commitment to Christ. If καὶ τῆς ἁγνότητος is read in addition as part of the original text (see *Notes*), the de-votion is also described as "pure," going back to v 3. ἁγνότης of a bride is a symbol of "pure doctrine" (Lietzmann, 145) and is a synonym for ἁπλότης (Zmijewski, *Der Stil*, 87).

The baleful effect, seen in the church's slide away from Paul's message, is traced to malign influence. Using the story of Gen 3, where human innocence is lost through "man's first disobedience," in turn abetted by Eve's deception (ἐξαπατᾶν here, used too in 1 Tim 2:14) and their succumbing to Satan's ad-vances, Paul is also drawing on an extra-canonical source. So Menzies, 77, 78, who couples vv 3 and 14 as showing Paul's acquaintance with Jewish *haggadah* or scripturally based "story." This is the rabbinical legend of the snake which sexually seduced Eve in the garden (*Yebam.* 103*b; Abod. Zar.* 22*b; Šabb.* 146*a*), but variants of the same account are found in the earlier Jewish apocalypses (*1 Enoch* 69:6; *2 Enoch* 31:6: "the devil entered paradise, and corrupted Eve. But Adam he did not contact." F. I. Andersen's tr.; *Apoc. Abr.* 23; and in the apocryphal *Life of Adam and Eve* and *Apoc. Mos.*). The theme is much developed in the second century apocryphal-heretical literature (*Prot. Jas.* 13; *Apocryphon of John* 23: the archon [Yaldabaoth] seduced her

[Eve]; and in the gnostic aetiology refuted by Irenaeus, Hippolytus [*Refut.* 5.26.22 f.], and Epiphanius *Haer.* 40.5.3. References are in Windisch, 323, 324). On the question of Eve's deception, see A. T. Hanson, "Eve's Transgression," *Studies in the Pastoral Epistles* (London: SPCK, 1968) 65–77; D. C. Verner, *The Household of God*, SBLDS 71 (Chico, CA: Scholars Press, 1983) 170; cf. *Ep. Diog.* 12:8.

Paul's primary source is, however, the canonical Genesis chap. 3 where at 3:13 (LXX) Eve remarks that "the serpent beguiled me and I did eat," which appears in our text with a slight recasting, and the simplex verb-form of LXX becomes ἐξηπάτησεν. There is also a parallel to ἐν τῇ πανουργίᾳ αὐτοῦ, "by his craftiness," in Gen 3:1 where the LXX φρονιμώτατος, "most clever," is given by Aquila and Symmachus as πανοῦργος (see Bauernfeind, *TDNT* 5:725, n. 17). This may be sufficient to account for Paul's use of the terms, though the identifying of Satan with the Edenic snake is not earlier than Wisd Sol 2:24, if it is made there (cf. *1 Clem* 3:4). Cf. Philo *Leg. All.* 3.59.

Betz, *Der Apostel* 104, 105, argues that πανοῦργος/πανουργία ("crafty"/"craftiness") goes back to the use of such terms in anti-sophistic polemic and in arguments against religious superstition (*Aberglaube*) by the philosophers. So it would be appropriate for Paul to retort—against his detractors who accused him of being a γόης or bogus apostle (see 12:16 for the reason)—that it is they who are insidious in their influence (cf. 2:17). Thereby he is preparing for the conclusion in 11:13–15: they are Satan's servants and false apostles. But it may be enough to see ἐν τῇ πανουργίᾳ αὐτοῦ as no more than a "targum-like addition to Gen 3, 13" (Windisch, 323), especially as ethical questions are involved, and Paul does fear that the Corinthian morals may have been corrupted (in 12:20, 21), in spite of Barrett's denial of this exact threat (274).

4. εἰ μὲν γὰρ ὁ ἐρχόμενος
    ἄλλον Ἰησοῦν κηρύσσει
    ὃν οὐκ ἐκηρύξαμεν,
    ἢ πνεῦμα ἕτερον λαμβάνετε
    ὃ οὐκ ἐλάβετε
    ἢ εὐαγγέλιον ἕτερον ὃ οὐκ ἐδέξασθε, κτλ.

"For if the person who has come to you proclaims a rival Jesus, whom we did not proclaim or if you welcome a different Spirit, which you did not welcome [in our message] or if [you accept] a different gospel, which you did not accept [as our Gospel] then, you put up with this person right well!" Arguably this is the most important, explicit—and discussed—v in the entire four chapter section (10–13). The reason is not far to seek, and Käsemann, *Die Legitimität*, 14, states the matter well: the v is "a key for the understanding of the opponents who appeared on the scene at Corinth and for the interpretation of ch. 10–13." He rightly dismisses the variant in textual evidence (see *Notes*) which supplies a reconstructed "reading" καλῶς ἀνείχεσθε (a suggested form of the verb, not documented: so Lietzmann, 145) or ἠνείχεσθε, which would be an imperfect tense to be explained as expressing an actual ("when another Christ is proclaimed, you have borne it well!") or a hypothetical clause ("if . . . would it be right for you to tolerate this?" See R. Reitzenstein, *Hellenistic Mystery-Religions*, tr. J. E. Steely [Pittsburgh: Pickwick Press, 1978]

465, who finally decides for a rendering, "would it then be well with you?" as though the Greek read καλῶς ἂν εἴχετε;). As Bultmann, 204, notes, if the element of doubt or contingency is introduced—as if the intruder was merely anticipated or the danger threatened in the distance—then it becomes difficult to connect v 4 with the foregoing, as γὰρ, "for," requires. And vv 19–21 make no sense since they *do* describe a very real and present danger, not one on the horizon or imagined. But we should pause to take note that with the explicit announcement of an alien presence at Corinth, this is a new situation to which Paul responds vehemently and by using some of the strongest language of condemnation found in his corpus (cf. nearest parallels in Gal 1:8; 2:11; 5:10; and Col 2:8). The reality of the new threat explains his earlier plea (vv 1–3: a call to put up with his "act of folly," *sc.* in boasting, to come later in the chapter), and accounts for this great fear of both the Corinthians' safety as a "pure bride" likely to be violated, and his own apostolic standing in the Aegean mission area. We touch here the nerve-ending of the debate. It centers on the men referred to in 10:12 who set up a comparison with Paul's missionary service and found him wanting, as in vv 5, 6. But this is a concession which he states only to deny by giving a different basis for criteria in the matter of legitimacy and apostolic ἐξουσία, "authority."

The designation ὁ ἐρχόμενος, lit., "he who comes" is telling: this group is evidently headed by a ringleader, since it appears that the rival mission had a spokesperson (Barrett, 275; hence the singular, as in 10:7 [τις], 10 [φησίν], 11 [ὁ τοιοῦτος], 11:20–21 [τις], which is not quite generic, as most writers on this text believe, including Plummer, 296; Allo, 279; and Zmijewski, *Der Stil*, 99, 100, 413, though the last-named does see the singular ὁ ἐρχόμενος as collective denoting the "head" of a group which had reached Corinth in a preaching mission, implied in κηρύσσει . . . ἐκηρύξαμεν). More to the point, perhaps, is the observation that (1) the party has come from outside, in contrast to 10:14, 15, and (2) it came on its own volition and was not sent as a true apostolic mission, in Paul's eyes. It had simply "come," unsent and without divine authorization; hence they were no true apostles (see Hughes, 377; Barrett, 275). (Maybe we should add "and without human authorization.") Rather, they were ψευδαπόστολοι (11:13)—here the group is clearly in view as one of several plural forms, as in 11:12 (τῶν θελόντων), 18 (πολλοί).

Granted that the visitors to Corinth have already reached the city in this v, we have to pose two different questions: (I) what kind of message did they bring? and (II) who may they have been in the light of (I) and the following v where the connection is not too clear (Windisch, *recht unklar*, 329)? But there is obviously some link with γὰρ to make the transition. And we cannot really keep the two questions of content and identity separate.

The lines of v 4 may be set down in a quasi-versified form, as Zmijewski (ibid., 92, 93) proposes, as three *cola,* with a rhythmical, rhetorical, and climactic appeal. The climax is reached with the ironical καλῶς ἀνέχεσθε, lit., "you put up with . . . right well!" presumably with a reference to ὁ ἐρχόμενος as the person(s) involved. The verb ἀνέχεσθαι belongs to a set-piece of what Prümm 1:595 and Zmijewski, ibid., 79, 418 have termed *Toleranzvokabeln,* "words of toleration," used ironically to pour scorn on the wayward hospitality—δέχεσθαι in 11:16 should be included—given by the Corinthians to these rival preachers and their message. The church has been open to these influences, and it has grown suspicious and hostile in regard to its true apostle. Hence Paul's plain speaking is directed to this exposé.

(I) As to *the content of the proclamation,* we may notice from the formal characteristics of the lines how Paul is encountering a threefold denial of his version of the kerygma. Yet these three items are all interlocked.

ἄλλος Ἰησοῦς, πνεῦμα ἕτερον, εὐαγγέλιον ἕτερον express teaching Paul treated as deviant; there is no vital distinction in meaning between ἄλλος and ἕτερος, as there is in Gal 1:6, 7. Moulton, *Grammar* 3:197, explains the change as stylistic. Both adjectives mean "different" in the bad sense of "alien," "rival." Nor is there a discernible difference between λαμβάνειν and δέχεσθαι, though in other contexts the latter denotes a voluntary act, not necessarily implied in the former verb (see 11:16). The issue is basically a christological one, as we shall see. So "Jesus" implies an understanding of the church's Lord at odds with Paul's, whether it was gnosticizing, docetic, ebionite (i.e., denying his divinity: so Héring, 79) or nationalistic (treating him as an earthly, Jewish messiah). We shall argue that it is the character of Jesus as setting the norm for Christian existence that is at stake. They preached a lordly figure, with themselves as his powerful and "charismatic" exponents (a trait denied in 4:5).

"Spirit" (πνεῦμα) is hardly a reference to the Holy Spirit as a person, since then we would have to suppose that they had a heterodox (and anachronistic) Trinitarian teaching. Héring, 79, appeals to the (later) *Gospel of the Hebrews* (Frag. 3, *New Testament Apocrypha* 1, ed. W. Schneemelcher, tr. R. McL. Wilson [London: Lutterworth Press, 1963] 164) where "my mother the Holy Spirit seized me by one of my hairs and carried me." But there is no trace of such bizarre pneumatology in 2 Corinthians. See, however, on 13:13. πνεῦμα will be the effects of Christian living seen in outward deportment: their attitude to living before the congregation betrays a spirit in contradiction of Paul's strength-as-weakness (ἀσθένεια) teaching and practice (Black, *Paul, Apostle of Weakness,* 132–38: idem, *"Paulus Infirmus:* the Pauline Concept of Weakness," *Grace Theological Journal* 5 [1984] 77–93). Finally, εὐαγγέλιον is really a misnomer in this context, since for Paul there is only one Gospel (Gal 1:6–9) and his opponents' message is more a *dysangelion,* i.e., bad news.

(II) As we now survey the multifaceted options to do with *who the intruders at Corinth were,* we may dismiss the idea that (1) it was a question of a Judaizing gospel as in Gal 1:6–9, since the terms λόγος and γνῶσις (found here) do not play a role in Paul's answer to the agitators in Galatia, and in 2 Corinthians there is a remarkable absence of key "Judaizing" terms such as circumcision, sabbath, law (Barrett, 30, to the contrary; but he overlooks the omission of νόμος, "law" in these chapters and indeed in the entire letter, a singular fact, as Bultmann, 204, indicates); and (2) Bultmann's view (205) that the Gospel brought to Corinth was one of "gnostic pneumatics" is equally unsatisfactory (so in Schmithals, *Gnosticism,* 124–35, who makes too much of finding here a set of "specific, dogmatic, christological teachings," e.g., a rejection of the human Jesus, based on 1 Cor 12:3, which Paul does not have in his polemical sights). We return, however, to Bultmann's ancillary proposals shortly.

There are several other options: (3) Oostendorp, *Another Jesus*, 83 et passim, maintains that these men were Jewish-Christians who stressed the supremacy of Israel and advocated the "Jewish-Christian superiority" of the original apostles. This view is closely associated with F. C. Baur's original hypothesis (in *Paul*, 274–77) that behind these emissaries were the figure of Peter and the influence of a Petrine party at Corinth. Barrett's position, which has the rival missionaries coming as "envoys of the Jerusalem church" (30–32, 276), does not require Peter's endorsement of their activities, assuming that it was the Twelve who are referred to in the "super-apostles" of v 5 (see Thrall, "Super-Apostles"). Most writers with few exceptions believe that, if vv 13–15 relate to the same persons, it becomes next to impossible to think of Paul as branding Peter or the Jerusalem leaders as messengers of Satan, especially at the moment when he is appealing to the Corinthians to support the collection for the saints in the Holy City (Kee, "Who Were the Super-Apostles?" 66).

M. E. Thrall, ibid., who sees the visitors as claiming Peter's name, has to regard Paul as momentarily forgetting the link with Peter and lashing out at these men (loc. cit., 50); or else she views Paul's condemnatory words on the "servants of Satan" as his retort in the spirit of Jesus' pronouncement on Peter as Satan's mouthpiece in Mark 8:33//Matt 16:23—a dubious expedient, made more difficult to accept by an appeal to Acts 3:1–10; 5:15, 16; 9:32–34, 36–43, where Peter is cast in the role of a *Wundermann*, a miracle-worker, which his followers at Corinth claimed to emulate. In her view, Paul's statement in 12:12 is consciously set to match the tradition in Acts 5:12. McClelland, "A Response," is correct to note that Paul asserts, not equality with, but superiority to the "super-apostles" (ibid., 84); however, his position which cuts the ties between the emissaries to Corinth and the church at Jerusalem is equally objectionable, since 11:22, 23 are linked, and there must be ample cause for Paul to assert his "Jewishness." On balance, we conclude that the intruders did have Jewish-Jerusalem connections, but the idea that Paul's severe judgment on them entailed a harsh verdict on Peter whom they claimed to represent seems unfounded.

Munck's objection (*Paul and the Salvation of Mankind*, 176–78) that the "apostles" in 11:5; 12:11 have no connection with Jerusalem or the Twelve can hardly be sustained, since (a) it ignores the need for Paul to assert his Jewishness in 11:22, 23; (b) it overlooks, in spite of his disclaimer (ibid., 178, n. 1) that Paul always speaks of the Jerusalem leaders as "the Twelve," never the "apostles," the data in Gal 1:17, and 1 Cor 15:5, 7 where the "apostles" must at least include the Twelve; and (c) it fails to account for the debate over territoriality in 10:16, resumed in 11:12.

So most proponents of this view believe that the mission may have asserted Peter's authority but did not come with his consent. The irony of Paul may be directed, not at the Jerusalem apostles themselves (whom Paul treated with some respect in Gal 2:2–9: see Barrett, "Paul and the 'Pillar' Apostles," *Studia Paulina*, FS de Zwaan, 1–19; but note οἱ δοκοῦντες/δοκοῦντες στῦλοι εἶναι "who *seemed* to be pillars," and 2:11 where Peter "stood condemned"), but rather against the followers of the Twelve who claimed (falsely) to be authorized by them (see Goppelt, *Apostolic . . . Times*, 100: "in order to justify their authority they emphasized their roots in Palestinian Judaism [xi.22 ff.], their contacts with the earliest apostles whom Paul then ironically called the 'superlative apostles' [xi.5; xii.11]. . . ." But they also, according to Goppelt, claimed to be gnostic emissaries by means of *pneuma* ["spirit"]; thus the triad "another Jesus," "a different Spirit," "a different Gospel" is understood in v 4).

(4) A sharper point on the implied Jewishness of the opponents is put by G. Theissen, *Social Setting*, 44–54, who wishes to see these men as itinerant preachers from Palestine who claimed to have their roots in the original company whom Jesus in his earthly ministry chose, called, and commissioned (ibid., 50). One strong point in this link is the way, according to Theissen, they put emphasis on their financial dependence on the community at Corinth, since they claimed to be the legitimate heirs of the Twelve who in the Mission Charge of the synoptic Gospels (Mark 6:7–13) were to be sustained by the people to whom they were sent. (See Theissen, *Sociology of Early Palestinian Christianity*, 8–14.) Paul, on the other hand, disavowed such an arrangement on grounds stated in 1 Cor 9:15–18, and for this reason he was held to be discredited as a genuine apostle (as well as lacking the charismatic signs that marked the first followers of Jesus: see Mark 6:7–13, as above). But this reconstruction does not explain the essentially christological basis of Paul's objection to these men, as Georgi, *Die Gegner*, 285, insists.

(5) Still another variation in this general designation of Jewish-Christian apostolic figures is offered by Käsemann, *Die Legitimität*, 14–30, for whom the "super-apostles" (in v 5) are the Twelve (ibid., 28), and the emissaries in v 4 have come on the scene believing that they enjoyed the sanction of the Jerusalem leaders; indeed they claimed that it was the Jerusalem "mother church" that had authorized them to bring the gentile congregation under their control. At the heart of this contention was their attachment to the historical Jesus, a privilege which Paul lacked (5:16). Käsemann introduces a new idea in his contribution, namely, that there are two sets of persons in view in vv 4–15; the *Überapostel*, the "super-apostles" who are the Jewish hierarchy, and the *Falschapostel*, ψευδαπόστολοι, "false apostles," in vv 13–15, as envoys of the mother church, which they claimed themselves to be. But Barrett, "Paul's Opponents," 70, is critical of this distinction and twofold identification, since Paul "does nothing to indicate that he is moving from one group to another"; and we are left to resolve the exegetical problem of how Paul's thought "jumps" (ibid., 24) across the transition from v 4 to v 5: preachers of a false message, he says, can hardly be the Twelve. Schütz, *Paul*, 169, n. 1, correctly observes the fundamental importance of this question for Käsemann, and notes that "[his] perfectly cogent question about how 11:4 and 11:5 can stand side by side" is not faced by his critics. We will return to this issue shortly (under sect. 7), and offer a reason.

(6) This diversification of opposition, divided into the categories of *Überapostel* and *Falschapostel* seems well-founded, but Käsemann's overall analysis has been faulted, notably by G. Friedrich, "Die Gegner," on the evidence that Paul raises no criticism of his enemies at Corinth on the score that they are nomistic in religion: Paul does not attack their teaching of "righteousness by works" (*Werkgerechtigkeit*); and, while other points registered by Friedrich,

for example, that Palestinian Jews made no appeal to miracles, visions, demonstrations of the Spirit, cannot really stand (cf. Theissen, *Sociology*), his main contention seems solid. We are therefore led to ask if these opponents were hellenistic Jews, tinged with gnostic flavor, an idea already conceived by Windisch, 328.

This is Friedrich's own view, but its chief exponent is Georgi, *Die Gegner*, with agreement from Bornkamm, *Paul*, 172; Rissi, *Studien*, 42–44; Collange, *Enigmes*, 18–20 et passim; and to an extent, Schütz, *Paul*, 177–86. At the center of this presentation is the postulating of a group of hellenistic Jewish missionaries who modeled their lifestyle and preaching on wandering religious teachers in antiquity, known by the generic term of "divine men" (θεῖοι ἄνδρες, Georgi, ibid., 205–18). The pattern was that of prophecy, miracle-working, and a powerful presence with letters to accredit them (Georgi, ibid., 241–46). The starting point is the discussion over self-recommendation and boasting, but it comes to a practical matter which underlies much of chaps. 10–12, i.e., Paul's refusal to accept maintenance at Corinth, a practice which these opponents found incredible since they claimed to be religious teachers who deserved their rewards (11:7–11; 12:13–18). Paul, on the other side, refused such honors, and is held in low esteem since he carried no marks (σημεῖα, "signs") to accredit his ministry. This is brought out in the threefold analysis of 11:4. These missionaries proclaim "another Jesus": in their estimate "Jesus" is the figure of charismatic power, the θεῖος ἀνήρ of the early miracle-stories, and essentially κατὰ σάρκα (5:16). This is the core of the opposition to Paul, since the litmus test is christological (Georgi, 285: "the distinction [between Paul and the enemies] is above all in Christology"). As they patterned their ministry on the Jesus-figure who resembled the Moses of Philonic Judaism (see *Comment* on 3:1–18), they claimed that they were the mouthpiece of divine revelation in the new age of eschatological fulfillment (13:3: here the test—δοκιμή—is the issue of who speaks the truly authentic divine "word"). On all counts where they contrast their ministry and behavior with Paul's, he cuts a sorry figure (see 12:11, οὐδέν εἰμι, "I am nothing"): he is ineffectual as a speaker, sickly in body and unable to cure his malady, timid and cowardly in failing to come to Corinth, and lacking in all the demonstrable signs of "power" (δύναμις/πνεῦμα: see Georgi, "Mission als pneumatische Demonstration," ibid., 210–18), which they claimed chiefly in professing an attachment to the pneumatic, non-crucified Jesus. So a "different πνεῦμα" betrays a "rival εὐαγγέλιον (gospel)," as Paul calls it.

Paul's response is to assert the validity of *his* Gospel as the true "power of God," expressed in the suffering Lord (κύριος, his favorite term) who came to his glory only along a road of humiliation and self-abnegation. Paul's ministry shares these qualities, since he does not proclaim himself except as a δοῦλος, "servant," of the church's Lord (4:5) and has a life of "strength-in-weakness" as the distinguishing mark of the true πνεῦμα and the inalienable εὐαγγέλιον. Georgi's argumentation, at least, illumines 11:4, and shows its coherence with the general tenor, not only of chaps. 10–13, but of Paul's consistent self-presentation throughout the epistle, especially in 2:17–4:15.

The chief criticism has been leveled at the assumption of a θεῖος ἀνήρ figure in Greco-Roman society, and in fact it has been queried whether such an identifiable "type" ever existed (see C. H. Holladay, *Theios Aner in Hellenistic-Judaism*, 237–41, who offers as a fundamental criticism of the use of the expression *theios aner* its intrinsic ambiguity and the imprecision of the equation *theios aner* = miracle-worker). Partly to offset (in advance) that charge of imprecision and to avoid undue recourse to problematic texts to do with Greek heroes or vague hellenistic figures like Apollonius of Tyana, Friedrich, ibid., 196–208, turns attention to some better attested examples, and points to Stephen and his associates in Acts 6, 7. The example of Stephen and his διακονία, "ministry," fills the role of a hellenistic Jewish-Christian leader, with ostensible charisma (Acts 6:9, 10; cf. Philip in 8:6) and exercising an effective and extended ministry (Acts 11:19, 20). He is credited with "signs and wonders" (Acts 6:8), with visions (Acts 7:55), and dramatic power in speech and reasoning (λόγος). At a more tenuous point Philip's being transported in an ecstasy (Acts 8:39) is cited as being matched by Paul's use of ἁρπάζειν, "to snatch," in 12:2; more convincing is the way both Stephen's speech and martyr's experience, in the narrative of Acts, pick up the theme of δόξα, "glory," which Paul is concerned to reinterpret in our letter (3:6–4:6) in such a way as to suggest that he is rebutting an exegesis, presumably Jewish-Christian, that extolled Moses' glory (Exod 34:29–35) and authority as a "divine man." For the opponents of Paul, Jesus was regarded as the second Moses, not the suffering servant of God (Friedrich, 191). The next step is to associate Stephen's Christology of a "righteous man" (Acts 7:52) with the θεῖος ἀνήρ model, and to predicate this teaching of the Jewish-Christian mission in 2 Cor 11:4. Friedrich (ibid., 212), concludes: it is understandable that such an independent mission would come to Corinth from Stephen's circle. He then proceeds to trace a line of development from Acts 6 through the Jewish Christianity of Matthew's Gospel and the rival preachers in Phil 1:15–18 to 2 Cor chapters 3, 10–13—a bold expedient indeed!

(7) Friedrich's hypothesis is probably too neatly and narrowly framed. Yet it contains some suggestive ideas which we may take over, as we attempt a summing up and aim to reach a tentative conclusion. The innovative idea of Käsemann that two sets of *dramatis personae* are on view in 11:4–15 commends itself, and Barrett's counterargument that Paul does not give a hint of making a distinction may be answered by an appeal to Paul's needful ambivalence. He clearly has to denounce the opposition since his credentials at Corinth are at risk. Hence the overt denunciation, with irony (11:4) and invective (11:13–15), is in order to achieve his purpose. But, on the other side, he shows deference to the Jerusalem leadership, not least because he is anxious to cement relations between the gentile mission churches and the mother community at Jerusalem. Hence he has devoted his energies to gathering the collection, with this end in view (see *Comment* on 9:12–15). Yet, inasmuch as the preachers have come claiming some authorization from the "pillar" apostles, or at least as representing Jewish Christianity (implied in 11:22), making themselves out to be "servants of Christ" (11:23: see Georgi, *Gegner*, 31–38, 254), Paul must put the "super-apostles" in their place in a slightly derogatory way, while respecting their status in terms of the Jerusalem concordat (Gal 2:6–9). Both allusions to οἱ ὑπερλίαν ἀπόστολοι (11:5; 12:11) answer the accusation that he is inferior to them, a charge he denies by the

simple statement that he has the requisite credentials to stand alongside them; indeed, he is "superior," as he magnifies his office as "apostle to the Gentiles" (Rom 11:23) and eschatological person at the turning-point of the ages (2 Cor 5:16–6:2). In 11:6 he has "knowledge," i.e., the authentic Gospel of 4:4–6, which conveys saving truth from God, and in 12:12 he has "signs of an apostle" which God has wrought through his gentile-oriented ministry (as in Rom 15:19–20). On both counts, he places his apostolate on a par with Jerusalem, and more, he claims a special dispensation for it (3:6–12). In so doing he cuts the ground from under the feet of the emissaries who were using his lack of "signs" as a weapon to attack him and so to brand his apostleship as spurious (so Käsemann).

But why is Paul's indignation so virulent in 11:13–15? The answer is given in Bultmann's exposition of 11:4. The alien "Jesus-Spirit-Gospel" triad adds up to a wrong-headed perception of the entire Christian kerygma as Paul understood it. The Christ they proclaimed is κατὰ σάρκα (5:16) which means that the power on display is visible and self-centered. The πνεῦμα is manifest in a spirit of ἐξουσία, which they construed as lordly power which in turn leads to a posture of καυχᾶσθαι, "boasting" (see Travis, "Paul's Boasting," 527–32). The "gospel" is branded as a false message since it contradicts Paul's message of the cross and of the Christ who "did not please himself" (Rom 15:3). They glory in outward appearance (5:12), because they have no place for the hiddenness of Christ's weak demeanor (10:1; 13:3, 4) and the life based on "faith" (5:7). The summary of v 4 provided by Fallon (94) makes these points clear: "another Jesus" for the opponents is the wonder-working Jesus, rather than Paul's crucified and risen Lord. The alien "spirit" is the spirit of power and ecstasy which these messengers claimed to possess and embody in their ministry, rather than the Spirit of Christ which Paul exemplified. The new "gospel" is the message of power and present glory, based on demonstrable tokens of the divine and evidences of authority in their lives as Christ's servants (v 13), rather than Paul's kerygma of the suffering Christ whose power is displayed incognito and in patient love (13:3, 4). Above all, the contrast is seen in the way the rival preachers overlooked, and Paul expounded, the truth that the "true apostle" not only is a proclaimer of the passion story; he also lives it out (Schlatter, *Paulus*, 553; Friedrich, ibid., 189).

This account of 11:4 leading to the judgmental tones of 11:13–15 is, in our view, eminently satisfying and coherent. It has the merit of viewing Paul's total response to Corinthian problems as consistent throughout the letter, and yet it gives recognition to a fresh outbreak of severe opposition which Paul sees to be deserving of condemnation because: (a) it attacks his apostolate, and that spells a falsifying of his Gospel; (b) it explains why Paul has to approach his self-defense obliquely in vv 4, 5 since he wants to retain links with the στῦλοι, "pillar"-leaders, and the mother church; and (c) it gives a rationale for his fierce tones in vv 13–15 since these men have adopted a wrongheaded Christology branded as satanic which, for Paul, leads inevitably to an unworthy lifestyle in the congregation (6:3–13; see 11:19, 20; 12:20, 21 for what this influence on the Corinthians led to). The ones he opposes are no better than "unbelievers" held in Satan's power (4:4) and from whom the Corinthians have already been warned to dissociate themselves (6:14–7:1). Paul has already issued a call to reconciliation (5:19), and he can see no future for his cause at Corinth if the false apostles are permitted to have their way. Hence the pericope closes with a peremptory note of warning (11:15).

5. λογίζομαι γὰρ μηδὲν ὑστερηκέναι τῶν ὑπερλίαν ἀποστόλων, "For I counted myself to be in no way inferior to 'the highest ranking apostles'!" The verb "I counted" (λογίζομαι: see 10:2) is something of a technical expression in this setting; it picks up the Corinthian acceptance of false estimates of Paul's mission, and his call to them to "consider" the facts of the case (10:7). Now it is the apostle's turn to make a reckoning in his own defense. He perhaps is repeating a watchword at Corinth (so Betz, ibid., 68); and he uses a form of the verb ὑστερηκέναι which may be classed as "present perfect" (BDF § 341), i.e., "I am not inferior." He gives his assessment of what was evidently an innuendo cast at him: that he is inferior to the "exalted apostles," mildly ironical in reference to the Jerusalem leaders (Héring, 79; Käsemann, Die Legitimität, 28: the Überapostel are to be equated with the Urapostel, and so most commentators [not, however, Windisch, Bultmann, 205: see BGD 841]; but Zmijewski [ibid., 116], has recently reopened the issue of this identification on the stylistic grounds of the way the singular ὁ ἐρχόμενος merges into the plural form τῶν ὑπερλίαν ἀποστόλων; so, he maintains, there is no distinction between the "visitor" [v 4] and the "supreme apostles"; but this cannot be so—unless we are ready to accept the equation of the apostolic figures in both v 5 and v 13, or to deny a reference to them in both places, so McClelland, "Response"). Paul's use of ὑπερλίαν, "exceedingly," "beyond measure," is exceptional, since the adverb is a NT hapax, and Paul does not pause to explain. We may presume that it is an ironical, and mildly derogatory, term. Cf. Zmijewski (ibid., 116, 117). Our rendering with quotation marks added tries to make this point.

The linking γὰρ has to be respected, for it marks the transition between v 4 and v 5, which is difficult to account for on any showing. See earlier, p. 338. Our interpretation seeks to connect the vv on the score that the intruders are appealing to the "super-apostles" in Jerusalem, whether rightly or (more probably) wrongly. And Paul has to assert at least his parity with the latter authorities and probably his elevated role as apostle to the Gentiles par excellence. The next v will explain in what respect he reserves this right.

6. εἰ δὲ καὶ ἰδιώτης τῷ λόγῳ, ἀλλ᾽ οὐ τῇ γνώσει, ἀλλ᾽ ἐν παντὶ φανερώσαντες ἐν πᾶσιν εἰς ὑμᾶς, "I may indeed be untrained in public speaking, but I am not [deficient] in knowledge [of the truth]. Rather, in every way we have made [God's truth] known to you as to all." Again, this is a pivotal and perplexing v; it is clearly autobiographical and self-revealing, even if there is no subject expressed or copulative (BDF § 128.2), yet it is equally polemical. The preceding v is, in our view, something of a parenthesis which has the apostolic authority of the Twelve in mind. Now, having claimed to be their equal partner and a special apostle in the sense of 1 Cor 15:8–11 (cf. Eph 3:2–10), Paul reverts to the menace at Corinth. His opponents there put him in the category of being ἰδιώτης, "untrained" in rhetorical forms (but was he talking tongue-in-cheek?—see Judge, "Paul's Boasting," who treats

the term as ironical and as a species of *asteismos* or *prospoiēsis*, affectation for effect [37]) as an amateur or layperson, not a professional public speaker (Judge, *TynB*, 12–14, 35). Apparently he accepts this designation, if in a concessive way (so with εἰ καὶ: BDF § 374; Zmijewski, ibid., 118) and maybe he is again ironical (Allo, 279). Then, the weight of the sentence lies in the ἀλλά (2x), "but," contrasts. Granting for the sake of argument that he is to be ranked as an unskilled person in speaking (τῷ λόγῳ; see BDF § 197 for the dative) by his detractors' standards, nevertheless (ἀλλ᾿) he does have the really important qualifications, i.e., γνῶσις, knowledge of God and his Gospel (1 Cor 1, 2: Barrett, "Christianity at Corinth," 6–14); and "nevertheless" (ἀλλ᾿) he has made this Gospel known in ways that count (ἐν παντί will then correspond exactly with 6:4) and to all who are the true objects of Paul's mission in the *Missionsgebiet* of 10:13–18. Once more the verb φανερώσαντες (which lacks a definite object, and forms a rhetorical figure of brachylogy or compressed speech: we must add "it," i.e., τὴν γνῶσιν from the previous clause which means the Gospel as God's truth) is chosen with care, since the issue of φανέρωσις, "manifestation," was much ventilated at Corinth (see on 4:2, in a context where πανουργία, "craftiness," suggests the opposite, namely, a secretive and deceitful dealing with the message).

If Paul's writing is a species of "clipped speech," there is no need to suspect a textual omission or corruption (Schlatter, *Paulus*, 642, cited in Bultmann, 206, who lists the multiplicity of variant readings, none compelling and all designed to clarify the meaning, to correct the majority witnesses, and to amplify, as Lietzmann, 147, does by supplying after φανερώσαντες, the words τὸ μυστήριον τῆς γνώσεως/τῆς πίστεως, "the mystery of the knowledge/of the faith"). But R. Reitzenstein, *Hellenistic Mystery-Religions*, 466, concludes that the end of v 6 makes an impossible transition to v 7. He wants to supply, after ἐν παντὶ, ἀμέμπτους ἡμᾶς: "we are blameless."

The interpretation offered above is only one of several possibilities: (1) Bultmann, 205, 206, sees in Paul's disavowal of λόγος a turning away from gnostic speculations, as in 1 Cor 2:4, in the interest of a true evangelical γνῶσις. (2) Käsemann, *Legitimität*, 9, reckons that the issue is that Paul is no glossolalic; he is lacking in ecstatic speech, and so is no genuine πνευματικός (but see 1 Cor 14:18). (3) Betz, ibid., 59, sees a contrast between the arguments of the sophists and the philosophers (Socrates is called ἰδιώτης ἄνθρωπος, "a plain man," in Plato, *Ion* 532D, whereas the sophists were famed for rhetorical skill; see Munck, *Paul and the Salvation*, 158, n. 2; Travis, "Paul's Boasting," 528–31), with Paul siding with the Cynic distinction between form (*Aussprache*, λόγος) and content (*Inhalt*, γνῶσις). But Barrett, 280, notes how γνῶσις may have a loose definition in this and other contexts in the Corinthian correspondence. (4) Hughes, 380–82 sees only a general contrast, based on Paul's adherence to "plain speaking" and his studied avoidance of human rhetoric that would adulterate the word of the Gospel. This is true, but it can hardly be the sole explanation of a text which has a set of semitechnical terms in it (ἰδιώτης, λόγος, γνῶσις).

7. ἢ ἁμαρτίαν ἐποίησα ἐμαυτὸν ταπεινῶν ἵνα ὑμεῖς ὑψωθῆτε, ὅτι δωρεὰν τὸ τοῦ θεοῦ εὐαγγέλιον εὐηγγελισάμην ὑμῖν; "Did I do wrong in humbling myself that you might be lifted up, because I proclaimed the Good News of God to

you without levying a charge?" Paul's irony continues. The introductory ἤ is probably meant to mark a question (Zmijewski, *Der Stil*, 122–26; BGD, 342; BDF § 440.1). The issue raised turns on Paul's refusal to accept monetary support for his ministry at Corinth (see 1 Cor 9:6–18). The question had been discussed earlier, but now it receives sharper focus by the implied allegation that, since he preached his message without charge, he was no true apostle. So Paul asks querulously: Did I do a wrong thing (lit., ἁμαρτίαν ἐποίησα, "commit sin") in making my policy not to accept payment for my preaching? "Paul's irony is here at its most bitter" (Barrett, 281), with the emphasis in the sentence falling on the juxtaposed words δωρεὰν τὸ τοῦ θεοῦ εὐαγγέλιον, "the Gospel of God" offered "for nothing" (Plummer, 303).

The position taken by the apostle has two features in its background. (1) The sophists justified taking money for their teaching on the ground that if teaching was given freely it was worth nothing—a counterargument raised against the condemnation of their practice by Socrates (Xenophon *Mem.* 1.6.1), Plato (*Gorg.* 520; *Apol.* 20), and Aristotle (*Eth. Nic.* 9.1.5–7), who objected to selling wisdom for money (see Plummer, 302). (2) But from another angle, Greek attitudes would make Paul's habit of supporting himself by his trade (1 Cor 4:12; 1 Thess 2:9; cf. 2 Thess 3:7–9; and the witness in Acts 18:3 [on which see R. F. Hock, *The Social Context of Paul's Ministry*, 59–65, who suggests that Paul's tentmaking activity meant a loss of social esteem], 20:34) difficult to justify. The typical Greek "upper class" sentiment, represented by Aristotle (*Pol.* 3.5), was to treat manual labor with disdain, and insist that no free citizen—certainly no philosopher—should get himself entangled in physical work, except under extreme pressure. Paul's opponents may well have reflected these two attitudes (so in v 12; Paul is answering attacks made on him in this paragraph; so Goudge, 103) when it came to their criticisms of Paul's ministry at Corinth where he was known to have refused maintenance and to have labored with his own hands.

The question is raised at this point as to why Paul took this position, especially as he acknowledged freely that he has the "rights" (ἐξουσίαι, a plural) to be supported, and also to "refrain from working for a living" (1 Cor 9:4–6)—concessions he traces back to some "word of the Lord" (9:14: Theissen, *Social Setting*, 40–44, who gives a special slant to this "privilege" by arguing that the charge leveled at Paul was that he had deliberately evaded the requirement of "charismatic poverty" and that his recourse to working for his living displayed a lack of trust in God's provision for missionaries). Paul insisted that his setting aside the "privilege" (not a duty) of maintenance and depending on the congregation was justified on OT grounds; but more pointedly, he stood by his freedom because only in this way would he be able to avoid placing an obstacle in the path of the Gospel (1 Cor 9:12; the wording is similar in 2 Cor 6:3; cf. 2:17; 1 Thess 2:5; the implication is that he does not wish to prevent people from becoming Christians) which comes via his ministry exercised *gratis*, i.e., grace-wise. In 1 Cor 9:17 he further argued that he ought to reinterpret and replace the notion of "apostolic obligation" by the sense of a privilege which he felt free to decline (to use the distinction of B. Gerhardsson, *Memory and Manuscript*, ASNU 22, tr. E. J. Sharpe [Copenhagen/Lund: Gleerup, 1961] 207)—but for a different reason again. Here he stands on its head the idea of receiving wages for services rendered and argues that to proclaim the Gospel freely is its own reward. He is the Gospel's δοῦλος, and a slave cannot expect to be paid for doing what he is told to do (see Holmberg, *Paul and Power*, 88–95, esp. 93).

The situation, however, is not as simple as it appears. Paul did consent to receive help from the Macedonians, as in v 9; and we are left to guess what prompted him to insist on a principle at Corinth, only to waive it in respect of other churches. Holmberg (ibid., 93, 94) is probably right to see Paul's policy as informed by a pragmatic, not doctrinaire, approach. The contingency of events at Corinth forced him to make an issue of apostolic freedom, whereas, if two conditions were met, Paul felt free to accept support, though Phil 4:10–20 is noteworthy for his detached attitude to the Philippians' repeated gifts (see Martin, *Philippians*, NCB, 160–69, commenting on his paradoxical *"danklose Dank,"* "thankless thanks," as Lohmeyer and others have called it). The two caveats are: (1) only when Paul had left a church he had founded did he accept money from it (Plummer, 205); and (2) only as there was a cordial relationship between the apostle and the church, expressed in κοινωνία, "fellowship" (cf. Nickle, *The Collection*, 105, 106, for this term as a synonym for money contributions: see earlier on 8:4; 9:13), did Paul consent to receive support, as with the Philippian church.

This analysis (drawn from Holmberg, ibid., 94, 95) not only answers Betz's negative assessment (*Der Apostel Paulus*, 104; "we cannot avoid the impression that, in 1 Cor 9, we do not learn the real reasons for Paul's conduct"; in a similar vein, Barrett, 281), but throws considerable light on our present v and what follows. The Corinthians, abetted by the rival missionaries, had objected that Paul's behavior was inconsistent: it betrayed a further example of vacillation and double-dealing (see on 1:17–20); it showed favoritism and a lack of love for them (v 11; 12:13, 15); and it made his raising of the Jerusalem collection a dubious enterprise, since it could be seen now as a roundabout and underhanded way of claiming status as an apostle (Georgi, *Die Gegner*, 241). More especially, Paul's entire attitude could be taken as a proof of his lack of apostolic standing, since he was now manifestly seen to be inferior to the "superlative apostles" who did use the Jesus-tradition of Matt 10:8–10//Luke 10:7 (Q [*Did.* 13:1, 2]; see D. L. Dungan, *The Sayings of Jesus in the Churches of Paul* [Oxford: Blackwell, 1971] 76–80) to claim support. Moreover, if Georgi's argument (ibid., 237, n. 6) is feasible, the inference the Corinthians apparently drew, as reflected in 12:13, is that Paul had not shared the fullness of the πνευματικά, "spiritual gifts," with them, and hence his establishment of the church in their city was defective. This was a further illustration of his false claim to be an apostle (Lietzmann, 158).

With such a background we may appreciate the heavy religious tones of this present v (7): words like ἁμαρτία ("sin"), ταπεινοῦν ("humble"), ὑψοῦν ("exalt") are theological (Fallon, 96), along with εὐαγγελίζεσθαι/εὐαγγέλιον ("preach, Gospel"). We may suggest that they are chosen as if to stress how strongly Paul felt that his cause at Corinth was at stake. They are both negative (ἁμαρτίαν ποιεῖν is a self-originated objection [*Selbsteinwurf*]; Windisch, 334; Zmijewski, ibid., 177) and positive (the redundant εὐαγγέλιον/εὐηγγελισάμην is best classed as a rhetorical *figura etymologica;* Zmijewski, 181). The ironical tone does nothing to lessen the seriousness of the situation. Paul came to Corinth not only as a servant figure (a trait they misunderstood: see 10:1) but with the Gospel of the humiliated and exalted Lord (see 8:9; 13:4; Phil 2:6–11; in Martin, *Carmen Christi* [2] [1983 ed.] xviii, xix, xxxv–xxxix. The reasons are given there for seeing the exaltation of Christ as the lifting up of the humble Jesus whose cross in v 8c sets the pattern for and reinterprets all notions of present authority and cosmic lordship). Now, on reflection, Paul is asking the readers to consider whether the initial evangelism and founding of the church "under the cross" (1 Cor 1:18–2:5) was a terrible mistake! He will raise the matter in a parallel way at 11:21; 12:13, where his ἀσθένεια, "weakness," is the issue, which in turn is joined to his proclamation of a weak Jesus (13:4). See Güttgemanns, *Der leidende Apostel und sein Herr*, 177, 178.

8. ἄλλας ἐκκλησίας ἐσύλησα λαβὼν ὀψώνιον πρὸς τὴν ὑμῶν διακονίαν, "Rather, I robbed other congregations, taking my expenses [from them] in fulfillment of my ministry to you." The contrast is marked by the use of some vivid and bold language, as Paul now answers his own rhetorical question. He admits that he did draw funds from other churches (notably at Philippi: Phil 2:25; 4:10–20). The strong term ἐσύλησα, "I robbed," is a verb used in classical Greek of stripping a dead soldier of his armor on the field of battle (see Hughes, 385). The military metaphor is continued with a reference to ὀψώνιον, "a soldier's pay for buying rations" (see Deissmann, *Bible Studies*, 266. Cf. Luke 3:14; 1 Cor 9:7. Dungan, *Sayings of Jesus*, 29, has proposed that the Philippian church gave Paul "financial support in sufficient amount so that it could be termed a salary," appealing to Phil 4:15–17; 2 Cor 11:8, 9). But R. F. Hock, (*The Social Context of Paul's Ministry* [Philadelphia: Fortress Press, 1980] 92), has challenged this deduction since (1) ὀψώνιον means simply "provisions" (cf. C. Caragounis, "ὀψώνιον: A Reconsideration of its Meaning," *NovT* 16 37–57); (2) Paul's other term is δόμα, "gift," Phil 4:17; and (3) in 2 Cor 12:14 Paul refers only to his "expenses" for a projected trip to Corinth, which must be borne by the Corinthians themselves.

Paul explains how he could be said to "plunder" other congregations (is he looking ahead to what he charges his accusers with: extorting money from the Corinthians, 11:19?). He took gifts from other Christians—by using his rights as apostle of Christ, 1 Thess 2:6: see Holmberg, ibid., 91—only to make good his ministry (διακονία) at Corinth, that is, to fulfill it in a way consonant with his proclamation of a crucified Lord and a Gospel of free grace (its δωρεάν-character), two aspects of the Pauline message that, we have suggested, became formulated in a sharper way at the close of his Aegean campaign (see *Introduction*, pp. lix–lxi).

9. καὶ παρὼν πρὸς ὑμᾶς, "and when I was with you," on the initial visit to Corinth (Acts 18:1–17). Perhaps the other churches of v 8 had aided Paul with travel funds and living costs to get him from Macedonia to Corinth (so Bultmann, 207). When Paul "fell into want" (ὑστερηθείς, aorist participle), as funds ran out or work was not possible (1 Cor 4:12; 1 Thess 2:9), then he was relieved of acute distress by the arrival of supplies (προσανεπλήρωσαν; the verb suggests "replenish besides," or to "add something in addition") brought by Christian brothers from Macedonia, probably Silas and Timothy

(Acts 18:5). Paul is at pains to explain this circumstance in order to make his chief point: οὐ κατενάρκησα οὐθενός, "I laid no [financial] burdens on any-one," lit., "I put pressure on no one." The simplex verb ναρκᾶν is used of numbing by applying pressure (Gen 32:25–33, LXX), and with the prefix κατα- means "to impose a burden" (see BGD, 414, 415 for Latin *gravare;* Vulgate has *onorosus fui* as equivalent to ἐβάρυνα). But there may be an insidious nuance, suggesting a charge that Paul "pressured" the Corinthians for his own financial ends (12:16, 17; Bultmann, 208). If so, he denies it in both places. Bruce, 238, suggests a parallel to καταναρκᾶν, "to be numb," in the colloquialism "to sting someone for so much" in the sense of overcharging, cheating. But "sting" has yet another colloquial meaning in American English.

Rather, ἐν παντὶ ἀβαρῆ ἐμαυτὸν ὑμῖν ἐτήρησα, "in all ways I kept myself from being a burden to you." An answer to an accusation found elsewhere (12:16; 1 Thess 2:9; cf. 2 Thess 3:8; 1 Tim 5:16) follows. The root βαρ- is paralleled in the papyri with the sense of "burden" as a way of imposing a financial charge (see J. G. Strelan, "Burden-Bearing and the Law of Christ: A Re-Examination of Galatians 6:2," *JBL* 94 [1975] 266–76).

10. ἔστιν ἀλήθεια Χριστοῦ ἐν ἐμοὶ ὅτι ἡ καύχησις αὕτη οὐ φραγήσεται εἰς ἐμὲ ἐν τοῖς κλίμασιν τῆς Ἀχαΐας, "As certain as God's truth is on my side, this boasting of mine will not be stopped in the districts of Achaia." The opening words are an oath-formula (Bultmann, *Schwurformel,* 208), as in Rom 9:1, and Χριστοῦ is subjective genitive, "Christ's truth," since it is Christ speaking through the apostle as in 13:3 (cf. 5:20 similarly, with a change of the divine name). Paul calls for some attestation that he is speaking the truth; but it is also ironical, since "boasting" (καύχησις) is the very practice he only resorts to under duress (11:21; 12:11; καύχησις is a decisive watchword in the entire "Fool's Speech" account where it plays a significant role: see 11:12, 16, 17, 18, 30; 12:1, 5, 9; Zmijewski, *Der Stil,* 139). Perhaps we should read here an indignant tone, in response to the imputation of the charge that he has dealt suspiciously and selfishly with the Corinthians by seeking to get the collection from them in his own interests. It is hardly likely that the subject of καύχησις is not Paul but the Achaean Christians, as suggested by Bachmann, 371, and Prümm, *Diakonia Pneumatos* 1:622. The sequence which flows into v 12 is against that view. There it is another's boasting that Paul confronts.

So he returns in his outburst to face those who "boast" of their mission in the area that was demarcated to him (10:13–18). This is referred to in the phrase ἐν τοῖς κλίμασιν τῆς Ἀχαΐας, in the districts (BGD, 436: κλίμα is a biblically rare term: so Windisch, 337, n. 1; Allo, 284; the entire province of southern Greece, called here τῆς Ἀχαΐας) of Achaia. He avers that his apostolic confidence in his mission to Achaia, rightly—he claims—belonging to his sphere of service, will not be curtailed. The last verb, φράσσειν, is either "to obstruct" or "to be obstructed," hence "to silence." With "boast-ing" it is presumably the second idea, but the thought may be compressed, as though the real issue was Paul's boasting *in this region,* where his authority had been challenged by the rival preachers on the scene at Corinth. Then, what he is affirming is his right to be in Achaia, and so "my boasting [*sc.* of my mission] shall not be restricted (*beschränkt* . . .) or cut off" (*unterbunden werden:* so Bultmann, 208, if the verb has a background in the picture of blocking a road, as in Hos 2:6; Lam 3:9; or damming a river as in Prov 25:16; Judith 16:3; the latter idea is supported by Plummer, 306). This is a plausible rendering.

11. διὰ τί; ὅτι οὐκ ἀγαπῶ ὑμᾶς; ὁ θεὸς οἶδεν, "How so? Is it because I do not love you? God knows I do." Paul's self-reflecting protestation of love mirrors both his pastoral concern (see 12:15) and his response to the implied innuendo that he did *not* love the Corinthians. Whether they had questioned his love for them in view of his practice regarding apostolic support, or the opponents in 11:4 had sowed this suspicion in their minds is not clear. Either way, it is a situation calling for redress. He retorts warmly but affectionately (a trait noted earlier in 6:11–13; 7:2, 3). Yet the sentences are complex and elliptical, and evidently set in a question-and-answer dialogue schema which has overtones of religious pathos and is reinforced by an "asseveration formula" (ὁ θεὸς οἶδεν, God knows!). See Zmijewski, ibid., 140–43. διὰ τί; (see BDF § 299): Why am I determined not to relinquish my (rightful) claims to Corinth as my field of mission work, my *Arbeitsraum*? It is not a sign of Paul's disfavor, or (more likely) of his preference for other churches (11:28), that he has not taken support from the Corinthians. The appeal to God clinches his response (as in 11:31; 12:2).

12. ὃ δὲ ποιῶ, καὶ ποιήσω, ἵνα ἐκκόψω τὴν ἀφορμὴν τῶν θελόντων ἀφορμήν, ἵνα ἐν ᾧ καυχῶνται εὑρεθῶσιν καθὼς καὶ ἡμεῖς. It is possible to take the opening clause leading to the first ἵνα in two ways: either "but what I am doing I will also continue to do, that . . ." (ἵνα), or, "what I am doing and will continue to do [is] in order that" (ἵνα). The latter is preferred by Allo, 284, on the score that the sense goes back to v 9 where Paul says that he will refrain from placing burdens on the Corinthians. Either way, the point is the same. Paul's financial practice has come in for criticism, and it is time to address those who evidently were responsible for mounting this attack on him and maligning him to the Corinthians. So the target is in the words τῶν θελόντων ἀφορμήν, "those men who are seeking such an opportunity." ἀφορμή is "occasion," "opportunity" (a neutral term which we select, but with the recall of its original sense of "base of operations for an expedition," BGD, 127), or even "pretext" (Héring, 79), and Paul's reaction to what they are seeking is in the verb ἐκκόψω: "that I may put an end to," lit., "cut off" (ἐκκόπτειν is a horticultural term for pruning in Rom 11:23, 24; Matt 3:10; 7:19; but also a medical word for "amputate": Stählin, *TDNT* 3:857–60). Drastic action is here envisaged, akin to what he threatened the Corinthians with earlier, if they remain obdurate and side with the opponents (see 10:6, 8). The emotional language is evident (Zmijewski, ibid., 153) and prepares for vv 13–15.

The second ἵνα-clause is dependent on τῶν θελόντων κτλ, and gives the substance of what constitutes their "opportunity" (Bultmann, 209): they desire, literally, to be "seen or regarded" (ἵνα . . . εὑρεθῶσιν: perhaps the element of surprise is contained in the verb, as in Gal 2:17; so Lightfoot) in that which is their boast (ἐν ᾧ καυχῶνται) as doing the same work as we do (καθὼς καὶ ἡμεῖς). A number of interpretations may be reviewed. (1) The underlying objection Paul has against them is their "pride" (καυχᾶσθαι) in laying claim to the same mission territory as he believes he has, i.e., at Corinth. So they are interlopers, who have entered upon a field of mission service where they do not belong. As long as Paul persists in his mission work based on a crucified Jesus and a Gospel freely offered (the δωρεάν-principle, -*Grundsatz:* so Bultmann, 209), they will not have room to maneuver in Corinth. He will effectively check their activity as poachers on his field of operation.

Other interpretations are: (2) They were standing on their assumed dignity as true apostolic missionaries, and they were a burden to the Corinthians. So Paul wants to ease his readers of just that burden (Plummer, 307, 308) by resisting the intruders. (3) They were guilty of jealousy (Bultmann: *ihr Motiv ist also Eifersucht* ["therefore their motive is jealousy"] 209), and sought to win the Corinthians—perhaps in the name of the Jerusalem mother church to whose jurisdiction, they asserted, the Corinthians rightly belonged (but this is not Bultmann's position)—or at least, to capture them to their side (see v 20). (4) What was at stake was apostolic support which they claimed was rightfully theirs (their καύχησις: so Kümmel, 210, 211, citing Windisch, 339, 340). So when Paul does not permit himself to be supported by the community, he robs his opponents of the occasion to boast of their apostolic office (*Apostelamt*). (5) Yet another interpretation (Fallon, 97) wishes to retain the second ἵνα-clause as dependent on the main verb ἐκκόψω. The translation follows: "in order to cut off the opportunity from those who would like an opportunity (and) in order that in what they boast they may be found even as we are," i.e., fools. The point is that they seek an opportunity to place Paul on the same level as themselves by using categories of validation for their ministry (commendations from other churches, impressive speech, miracle-powers, demonstrations of "spirit," the right of maintenance). But it is hard to see how Paul's action in not receiving aid would deny that course to them, which is what the joining of ἐκκόψω and the second ἵνα requires. But see Bruce, 238.

We opt for the view stated above under (1) on the main ground that, if the issue is the presence of men who purported to be true representatives, legitimately moving to Corinth as their base of operations and claiming to have a "gospel" which Paul treated as spurious (11:4), then it explains the transition to v 13, with its opening indictment: οἱ γὰρ τοιοῦτοι ψευδαπόστολοι: "for such people are bogus apostles," wrongly named ἀπόστολοι, since no one has *sent* them, and so they have no warrant to be in Corinth. And the very title they claim, namely, to be sent *by Christ,* is only an empty mockery, for they have arrived at Corinth with a perverse message and an accompanying lifestyle (see on 11:4, 20), which denies the Pauline Gospel and promotes sub-Christian morality (12:20, 21).

13. οἱ γὰρ τοιοῦτοι ψευδαπόστολοι, ἐργάται δόλιοι, μετασχηματιζόμενοι εἰς ἀποστόλους Χριστοῦ, "On the contrary, these people are bogus apostles, workers of deceit, masquerading as Christ's apostles." Here for the first time the intruding mission which has come as an expedition to Corinth (see previous v on ἀφορμή) is exposed—albeit from Paul's perspective. The antecedent to γὰρ is Paul's refusal to grant these people any legitimacy in what he claims as his mission-sphere, whatever "base of operations" they may lay a claim to. See Zmijewski, ibid., 151, connecting vv 12 and 13; on v 12 he writes: "in the chosen expressions (ἀφορμή, ἐκκόπτειν) the situation of conflict is clearly

reflected as the apostle's following 'invective' (13–15) against his opponents will reach its high point." So Paul must denounce them to the errant Corinthians who have been taken in, and he must do so in strong language.

οἱ τοιοῦτοι (see Rom 16:18) is more pointed than οὗτοι, the general demonstrative pronoun, with a "negative-warning accent" (Zmijewski, ibid. 155), and it clearly marks out the target of Paul's shafts. There are three designations, all fixed terms relating to the early Christian mission (Windisch, 342) but each given a pejorative connotation in Paul's hands. (1) ψευδαπόστολοι, a NT *hapax* (see Rengstorf, *TDNT* 1:446) and a composite term made up of ἀπόστολος, "apostle," *in bonam partem* as Christ's representative and delegate in several senses, listed by Barrett, *Signs of an Apostle*, 70–73, with the negative prefix ψευδο-, "false," to reverse the meaning, as in similar formations: 1 Cor 15:15: ψευδομάρτυρες; Gal 2:4; 2 Cor 11:26, ψευδάδελφοι. With these terms as examples, Wendland, 237, is probably correct to believe that ψευδαπόστολοι is Paul's own coinage. The term is intended ironically since, in this context, there is a *contradictio in adjecto*. The basis of Paul's argument requires the affirmation that he alone has been sent to Corinth; they have not, and so their "mission" (implied in ἀποστέλλειν, "to send") is a misnomer. We translate "bogus apostles" to pick up this idea, coupled with the following denunciation of them as "masquerading" (μετασχηματίζειν) as something they are not. So they are also "false" apostles, since they bring a εὐαγγέλιον ἕτερον (v 4). The two sides of the word are evident: subjectively, their conduct betrays them, or they act as if they were truly "like us" (v 12), and objectively—even if they do regard themselves as "servants of Christ" (11:23)—they are carriers of an alien message (against C. Kruse, *New Testament Foundations of Ministry* [London: Marshall, Morgan & Scott, 1983] 105, who sees the Corinthians themselves influencing the "false apostles"). See Bultmann, 210, who highlights the second element: they are *Lügenapostel*, so Zmijewski, 156; but not gnostics or Judaizers (*pace* Bultmann and Barrett, "ΨΕΥΔΑΠΟΣΤΟΛΟΙ [2 Cor. 11.13]," esp. 102, 103), since the point of distinction between them and Paul is Christology, not speculation, and not the Torah or circumcision or sabbath rites; all these latter items are conspicuous by their absence from 2 Corinthians. So Georgi, *Die Gegner*, 285, 249, who concludes his section, ibid., 39–49, by observing that the difference between Paul and his enemies lies in the issue of who has the ability and authority to engage in missionary activity in areas where there is conflict; so the debate turns on who has the valid "signs of an apostle" (12:12) in both message and manner of living, and in true credentials (see Ollrog, *Paulus und seine Mitarbeiter* [1979] 83, n. 111).

(2) ἐργάται δόλιοι, lit., "deceitful workers"; NEB, "crooked in all their practices," where the adjective picks up the thought of "craftiness," πανουργία, which has already been mentioned (v 3). Paul has warned his readers against succumbing to allurements which will lead to a false "gospel"; here it is better to render by a noun form: "workers of deceit" (cf. 2:17; 4:2: μηδὲ δολοῦντες τὸν λόγον τοῦ θεοῦ; Phil 3:2, though it is almost certain that the persons are not exactly identical, given the stress on "covenantal nomism" in the latter chap.). ἐργάται, however, is the more important term since it consistently stands for those engaged in Christian missionary activity (Matt 9:37//Luke

10:2: cf. Luke 10:7 = 1 Tim 5:18; 2 Tim 2:15; *Did.* 13:2). The men involved here took possession of a Christian standing as part of their "missionary apostolate" (*Sendungsapostolat*), claiming to be "working" as servants of Christ, as Christian preachers (Georgi, ibid., 50); it is this self-description that Paul denies to them by his negative δόλιοι. They are, in his eyes, arrogant in this pretentious claim (Zmijewski, ibid., 157). Later he will spell out the criterion for this evaluation in terms of their unethical behavior (11:20; perhaps also 12:20, 21), but here he turns back on them the very allegation they have introduced against him at Corinth (as a later v shows; 12:16, πανοῦργος δόλῳ, "being crafty . . . I captured you by deceit").

(3) A further reason for Paul's antipathy is that they have "masqueraded as Christ's apostles," using the verb μετασχηματίζειν, "to disguise" (Schneider, *TDNT* 7:957–59). At the heart of the verb is σχῆμα, "what is apparent" as an object's form or shape (Prümm, *Diakonia* 1:628, n. 3). According to outward appearances they set themselves forth as apostles *of Christ,* but in reality they are no better than emissaries of Christ's great enemy, Satan (see 2:11; 4:4; 6:15; an apparent dualism, comments Windisch, 341, but this is not certain). So Paul's designation with the verb serves to pour scorn on their claim to be "Christ's apostles" (clearly a self-chosen title in 11:23 where their διακονία is in view). And Paul will go on to explain how this masquerade can happen—and has happened.

14. καὶ οὐ θαῦμα· αὐτὸς γὰρ ὁ σατανᾶς μετασχηματίζεται εἰς ἄγγελον φωτός, "Do not be surprised at that; for Satan himself masquerades as a messenger of light." The transition-formula καὶ οὐ θαῦμα is exceptionally striking, full of irony and appeal. They adopt, he remarks, the role of their master, Satan, who [habitually] transforms himself—unless the present tense μετασχηματίζεται is simply a way to denote the present danger looming large at Corinth—into an angel of light. There is a warning note in καὶ οὐ θαῦμα, lit., "and no wonder," but it is not a sad remark by way of commentary (Barrett, 286) so much as a strident call to be alert; and its staccato tone matches the οὐ μέγα οὖν in v 15a (Zmijewski, ibid., 164).

The link between the opponents and the source of their mischief follows a maximlike form, ὁ δοῦλος ὡς ὁ κύριος αὐτοῦ, Matt 10:25 (Plummer, 309: "Like master, like man"). The middle term is the ability to clothe oneself in a form (σχῆμα) which is deceptive (reverting to δόλιοι in v 13; but the reference to the much earlier discussion in 3:18, proposed by Fallon, 97, seems "far-fetched," in both senses!). Where Paul derived the scenario of Satan's disguise is not certain. The story in Gen 3 holds no reference to Satan's becoming "an angel of light"; nor indeed to Satan at all. The nearest canonical parallel is Job 1:6–12 (Windisch, 342). The closest parallel is the pseudepigraphical *Life of Adam and Eve* 9:1 where Satan changed himself into the shining form of the angels and joined in a discussion with Eve. This story connects with 11:3 which relates Eve's deception by the snake, which is closely associated with the devil in Jewish, Christian, and gnostic texts (see above). Similarly in *Apoc. Moses* 17:1, Eve, in recalling this incident, describes Satan as appearing in the form of an angel: "and he sang hymns like the angels. Then I bent over the wall and saw him, [looking] like an angel." Yet nowhere is the precise expression ἄγγελος φωτός, or its equivalent found. Paul evidently is writing *ad hoc;* and there is much evidence that the idiom is not strange to him. Already in 4:6; 6:14–7:1, he has used the antithesis of light/darkness to denote a moral contrast (cf. Col 1:12, 13; Eph 5:11–14; 6:12); in rabbinic Judaism there is the tradition that prior to his fall Satan was a glorious angel (K. L. Schmidt, "Luzifer als gefallene Engelsmacht," *ThZ* 7 [1951] 261–79); ἄγγελος will be used to denote satanic force in 12:7; and the purveyors of erroneous teaching are likened to an "angel from heaven" (ἄγγελος ἐξ οὐρανοῦ) in Gal 1:8, an idea that Prümm, *Diakonia* 1:629, wants to press on the analogy that the rivals' claim to be "apostles" is seen in their role as (Satan's) "messengers" (an alternative meaning of ἄγγελος). From all the data it looks as though the ascription to Satan of the role as an "angel of light" is Paul's own work, still there is ample background material on which he could have drawn.

15. The rare expression οὐ μέγα οὖν εἰ, "it is not great surprise then if," lit., "it is therefore no great thing if." But μέγα looks back to θαῦμα in v 14, and in any case, the literal rendering is misleading. It *was* a great thing for deceivers to have reached Corinth and to have entered the church; Paul cannot be minimizing the danger nor dismissing it trivially.

The καὶ, "too," carries an adverbial force (= "likewise": BDF § 442.10), linking what v 14 has stated, that Satan masquerades as an angel of light, with the actions of the opponents who are now "likewise" dubbed οἱ διάκονοι αὐτοῦ, "his servants," and disguised as "servants of righteousness" (qualitative genitive). That their pretensions are vain on both counts is Paul's point. Once more we have to go on to v 23 to see the implication of Paul's denial. The deceivers lack the required credentials to be Christ's servants and apostles. Rather, their message and the behavior they display in the Corinthian congregation brand them as Satan's agents. Their claim is to be "agents of righteousness," not preachers of the law (νόμος is absent), but the claim is dismissed as their wearing the mask of Christ's true διάκονοι, as though they were what they claimed to be (Bultmann, 211: professing to serve the power of righteousness, so Ziesler, *The Meaning of Righteousness*, 161). Paul had earlier used the expression ἡ διακονία τῆς δικαιοσύνης, "the ministry of righteousness," for his own Gospel (3:9; 5:19–21; see too 6:7), and there are two ways to explain the phrase here: (1) Paul is basing an invented claim he puts into the opponents' mouths on the "title of the apostle" (Windisch, 343) which he asserts for himself, as in 3:9. (2) The adversaries themselves *did* lay claim to this self-designation, so it has to be understood positively (Georgi, ibid., 249; he makes it the equivalent of "apostle," following Plummer, 321, ibid., 30; thus what they assert in calling themselves διάκονοι δικαιοσύνης is that they are accredited apostles). Perhaps, in this second view, it is the moral character of the men that is asserted; then Paul is making a rejoinder. In spite of their claim to be upright, they are self-deceived; and Paul cannot accept this designation any more than he can the other titles (so Barrett, 287). Thrall, "Super-Apostles," 50–55, wants to take the titles at face value, and to see Paul's recognition of these claims as valid. But that assumption is virtually impossible to reconcile with Paul's invective in this pericope, as illustrated in Zmijewski's treatment (177, 188, 189) which shows how the manner and content of the writing are uniformly condemnatory.

Whatever else these persons were, they have put on a makebelieve appearance, which disastrously has enticed and corrupted the Corinthians (11:1–6) to the point where Paul evidently holds that only the severest warning will suffice (as in 12:20; 13:2, 5, 10). It is a surprising thing that in all this discussion Paul never once names his adversaries, nor designates them in any way other than by pejorative and descriptive phrases that carry their own condemnation. Marshall, "Invective: Paul and his Enemies," finds this feature significant as a rhetorical device. Not naming or offering a periphrasis of the enemy was done for several reasons: (1) the person(s) was (were) well known (perhaps too well known); (2) it made the person(s) available to caricature; (3) it would be used in comparison (*synkrisis*); and (4) it could lead to both an outright condemnation and an oblique allusion to cause them shame. He finds some of these features illustrated in 10:12, 18 (they commend themselves as "self-recommenders" filled with ὕβρις), in 11:4 (the visitor arrives on the scene, claiming support of the "superlative apostles" [11:5; 12:11]), and in 11:12. "This periphrastic device enabled Paul to denigrate anonymously the conduct of his enemies and to compare it unfavourably with his own exemplary behaviour as an apostle" (Marshall). He does not attack them directly . . . for to do so would have destroyed the "form" of his argument and to have lost his dignity (C. Forbes, cited in Marshall).

His last clause is therefore a sentence of judgment, based on their "works"—a common Jewish norm for the divine reckoning (Ps 62 [LXX 61] 13; Prov 24:12; *Apoc. Bar.* 11:9; *T. Abr.* 9:8; Acts 10:35; James 2:14–26; 3:13; 1 John 3:7, 12, 18). Their τέλος (Delling, *TDNT* 8:54–56), "end," in the sense of "destiny," "fate," will correspond to what they have done, specifically in introducing alien teaching (11:4) and seducing the congregation (11:3, 20). The final clause says no more than that God will judge them (Bultmann, 211). But the stylistic climax lends weight to this section. It closes, then, on the somber note of retribution (*lex talionis*) to be classified as a "statement of sacred law," of the order "destruction to the destroyer" (1 Cor 3:17; so E. Käsemann in his *New Testament Questions of Today*, tr. W. J. Montague [London: SCM Press, 1969] 66–81). The appeal to the divine court is found elsewhere in Paul (Rom 2:16; 3:8; 1 Cor 4:5; Phil 3:19: cf. Acts 17:31), but this is certainly the most forthright and categorical declaration that the rival preachers in the Pauline congregations have forfeited all right to the titles they profess, and in the end the reward they will receive is the penalty of the misdeeds they have enacted. They have done Satan's work; to Satan's fate they will go.

The "cosmic" setting of vv 13–15 is well brought out by Kleinknecht, *Der leidende Gerechtfertigte*, 292, 293, who shows how the vocabulary, idioms, and concepts in vv 13–15 are all chosen to demonstrate that Paul's engagement is with no familiar earthly power; but rather he shares in the conflict between God and his nonhuman adversary, Satan. Paul's role is as God's advocate and "fellow-warrior" (*Mitkämpfer*), a link going back to 10:3–6, but also picking up the imagery of 11:8, we may add. The next section will show the valid credentials he has which authorize him to engage in this conflict as "apostle of Christ."

Explanation

One of the difficulties we face as we read Paul's correspondence with the churches of his day is that of not knowing precisely the background to the turns of phrase he employs. It is true that we have a good picture of the overall scene at Corinth, but some smaller details remain—and perhaps must always remain—obscure to us. The present chapter, along with chap. 12, is a good illustration.

Obviously, at places Paul is ironical (vv 1, 8, 11). He finds it necessary, if distasteful, to explain why he is required to justify himself and put his actions in the clear. But it is needful because of the close link that he claims with the church (v 2), likened here to the bride of Christ.

Because he cares so much for Christ's people, he is most solicitous lest they should be led astray (v 3). How could this happen, we may inquire?

Some important vv sketch in the character of the men who are later severely reprimanded (vv 13–15). Three descriptions of their work are given in this section.

(1) Their most dangerous work was that of enticing the believers away from a singlehearted devotion to Christ, and in attempting this (cf. Mark 13:22) they were doing the devil's work for him, as the serpent did in Eden (vv 3, 14; both texts are based on Gen 3:4, 13, and Jewish apocalyptic demonology). If this seems a staggering thought, we may recall Mark 8:33; Matt 7:15–23; Gal 1:6–10; 1 John 4:1–6; Rev 2:20–24.

(2) These men—Paul's antagonists—are errorists, preaching a different gospel which centered in a different Jesus from the person of the Pauline message (v 4). It is true that Paul prefaces his statement with an "if," but "he is not likely to cherish real fears on the ground of imaginary suppositions" (Strachan, 18); so "if" (v 4) really means "as is the case." It is difficult to be sure what this warning is intended to refer to. Was it a purely human Jesus whom the false teachers presented, or a heretical picture altogether, like the later Gnostics, who turned him into a sort of demi-god? We cannot tell. But the total impression suggests a " 'divine man' Jesus" whose wonder-working power was claimed as a quality shared by these teachers.

(3) These men claimed the authority of the Jerusalem apostles, surnamed ironically "extra-special messengers" (Phillips). They bolstered their opposition to Paul by appealing (perhaps on their own initiative) to Peter, James and John against him. But Paul knows of no such rivalry or inferiority (vv 5, 6).

When we turn to vv 7–11, the "little foolishness" of v 1 is now explained. What agitated Paul's mind and caused him a certain reluctance was his self-justification of policy. He had refused to accept maintenance from the churches (v 7).

The implication of this is that he had been taken to task on this score, with the innuendo that he did not claim his (rightful) due because he knew in his heart that he had no apostolic standing and so professed no entitlement to it.

But Paul takes pains to go into the matter in some detail, although he has already made his position clear in 1 Cor 9. In effect, he is reiterating the same disinterested concern to offer his services freely (v 7: "without cost to you"). He does this, not because of any inferiority complex or unwillingness to receive financial help. Indeed, he had already received and gratefully acknowledged help from the Macedonian churches (v 9), notably the Philippians who had sent regularly a gift (Phil 4:15–19) to relieve his need.

The issue at Corinth—as at Thessalonica—turned on the construction which his enemies placed on his receiving money. Both at Corinth and in other places (1 Thess 2:9; cf. 2 Thess 3:8, 9) Paul intentionally refrained from exercising his prerogative—and not always for the same reason.

A further point emerges in v 11. Paul's refusal to accept sustenance at Corinth was being used in another way. His enemies were accusing him of being spurious and so honestly refusing the support; his friends were professing to be grieved that he took this line of action, which they interpreted as a sign that he had no regard for them and that they had fallen into disfavor. Hence the heart's cry, "God knows I do (love you)!"

Paul claimed two privileges as a servant of Christ: (1) the right of maintenance by the churches (1 Cor 9:3–14), and (2) the right to refuse this (1 Cor 9:12, 15; cf. Acts 18:3; 20:34). We should also note what he claims for others (Gal 6:6; see too 1 Tim 5:17, 18; 2 Tim 2:6). There is an important pastoral bearing of this on (a) lay ministry, and (b) full-time pastoral ministry. If a church calls a minister, does it not thereby pledge to that person freedom from financial strain?

Reverting to the dispute which had entailed this explanation of his attitude to maintenance, Paul hits out at the false teachers who were troublemakers at Corinth. If they simply attacked him and sought to discredit his work, that would have been one thing; far more serious was their advocacy of a false gospel, by which they placed themselves under the judgment of Galatians 1:6–9.

They professed to be able to draw upon apostolic authority for their credentials. Paul warmly retorts: " 'Apostles'? They are spurious apostles, false workmen—they are masquerading as 'apostles of Christ' " (v 13, Moffatt). For in so doing they are emulating their leader, Satan, who himself masquerades as a messenger of God.

The lesson is clear: appearances are deceptive. So we should not be too readily impressed by the superficial attractiveness of teachers who claim to be heaven-sent messengers. The test is more rigorous and vital: what do they teach, and does their character conform to the message they bring—and do both doctrine and manner of life square with God's revelation? We may recall Jesus' teaching here (Matt 7:15–22). And the Pastor's no less stringent criteria (2 Tim 3:10–17) are apropos. Note also the serious admonitions of John (1 John 4:1–5; 2 John 7–11) and the Didachist (*Did.* 11:7–12:5).

V 14 raises an interesting point. Gen 3 tells of the devil's use of the serpent who in turn enticed Eve by a specious promise and a piece of trickery (see 1 Tim 2:14), but no mention is made of the devil's transformation into an angel of light. Paul here is evidently drawing upon a Jewish tradition which related how Satan once took the form of "an angel" and joined the other angels in praising God. The bearing of this suggested background has obvious meaning when it comes to the issue of the sources of Paul's thought.

Paul again does not mince his words about those who practice a deceit which Satan has inspired. They are his agents at Corinth, and will share his fate (15; cf. Matt 25:41, 46).

D. Paul's "Fool's Story" (11:16—12:10)

Note: It is best to divide this lengthy section into smaller units, as follows:
1. Boasting: True and False (11:16–21a)
2. Paul's Trials (11:21b–33)
3. Paul's Ecstasy and Its Evaluation (12:1–10)

1. BOASTING: TRUE AND FALSE (11:16–21a)

Bibliography

Barrett, C. K. "ΨΕΥΔΑΠΟΣΤΟΛΟΙ (2 Cor 11.13)." In *Essays on Paul,* chap. 5. **Berger, K.** "Die impliziten Gegner: Zur Methode des Erschliessens von 'Gegner' in neutestamentlichen Texten." In *Kirche,* FS Günther Bornkamm, ed. D. Lührmann and G. Strecker, 373–400. Tübingen: Mohr, 1980. **Betz, H.-D.** *Der Apostel Paulus.* BHT 45. Tübingen: Mohr, 1972. **Bowersock, G. W.** *Greek Sophists in the Roman Empire.* Oxford: Clarendon Press, 1969. **Deissmann, G. A.** *St. Paul.* Tr. W. D. Wilson. London: Hodder & Stoughton, 1925. **Judge, E. A.** "Paul's Boasting in Relation to Contemporary Professional Practice." *ABR* 16 (1968) 37–50. ———. "The Early Christians as a Scholastic Community." *JRH* 1 (1960–61) 125–37. ———. *The Social Pattern of Christian Groups in the First Century.* London: Tyndale Press, 1960. ———. "St. Paul and Classical Society." *Jahrbuch für Antike und Christentum* 15 (1972) 29 ff. **Kleinknecht, K. T.** *Der leidende Gerechtfertigte.* **Lattey, C.** "λαμβάνειν in 2 Cor. xi.20." *JTS* 44 O.S. (1943) 148. **Malherbe, A. J.** *Social Aspects of Early Christianity.* Baton Rouge/London: Louisiana State University Press, 1977. ———, ed. *The Cynic Epistles.* Missoula: Scholars Press, 1977. **Marshall, P.** "Invective: Paul and His Enemies in Corinth." (Forthcoming). **Theissen, G.** *The Social Setting of Pauline Christianity.* **Walter, E.** "Die Kraft wird in der Schwachheit vollendet." *GuL* 28 (1955) 248–55. **Weiss, J.** "Beiträge zur paulinischen Rhetorik." In *Theologischen Studien B. Weiss,* 165–247. Göttingen: Vandenhoeck & Ruprecht, 1897. **Zmijewski, J.** *Der Stil der paulinischen "Narrenrede,"* 1978.

Translation

[16] *I say again, let no one take me for a fool. But even if you do, please accept me and let me play the fool's part: let me in turn have a little boast.* [17] *What I am speaking, it is not on the Lord's authority, but (as it were) in my foolishness and on the ground of my making a proud boast.* [18] *Since there are many who are boasting as "people of the world,"* [a] *I too will boast.* [19] *For you gladly put up with fools, since you are wise people yourselves!* [20] *Indeed, you put up with the one who enslaves you, the one who exploits you, the one who lays hands on you, the one who lords it over you, even when he deeply insults you!* [21a] *I say this to my shame: I admit that (as it were) "we were weak."* [b]

Notes

ᵃ κατὰ τὴν σάρκα is read by ℵ² B D¹ ψ TR, with the shortened κατὰ σάρκα in P⁴⁶ ℵ* D* G. The latter is probably superior as a corrector would supply the article (Windisch, 346, n. 3). Cf. Allo, 290; Prümm, *Diakonia* 1:631. The sense is not affected.

ᵇ ἠσθενήκαμεν (P⁴⁶ ℵ B). The smoother verb form ἠσθενήσαμεν (in D E G and uncials) is secondary. Cf. Allo, 290, 292 however.

Form/Structure/Setting

Two issues need to be stated and considered under this head: (I) the stylistic character of the section which begins at 11:16 (or strictly 11:1) and extends to chapter 12; and (II) the link between vv 16–21 and the preceding sections, notably 11:1–15; and reverting (we shall argue) more particularly to 10:13–18.

I. The form of this section of the letter has been the subject of some investigation as part of a wider interest in Paul's use of Greek rhetorical patterns and devices. The features we are concerned with are chiefly irony, invective, parody, diatribe, antithesis, paradox, lists of trials, and expostulation. Chaps. 10–13 contain several examples of these, but it is in 11:1–12:11 that Paul's writing takes on the cast of an extended appeal, best described as a "Fool's Speech" (*Narrenrede:* the limits of the passage are set by the catchword ἀφροσύνη, "foolishness," in 11:1 and 12:11 [ἄφρων], and so provides an example of *inclusio*). Zmijewski, *Der Stil,* has offered the latest and most detailed treatment, providing a useful overview of study, since J. Weiss's *Beiträge zur paulinischen Rhetorik* (1897).

The landmark contributions may be set down as these: (1) Weiss's own work, which noted the sentence structures in Paul's controversial letters, was a groundbreaking enterprise. He perceived that rhetorical forms could be more easily appreciated by the ear than the eye, since they were essentially a style of the spoken word (*Sprechstil*). Formal characteristics such as poetic couplets (*parallelismus membrorum*), stanzas (see Martin, *Carmen Christi*², 24), and cynic-stoic diatribe, or debating style, in Paul were first recognized by Weiss.

(2) E. Norden's equally pioneering works, notably *Die antike Kunstprosa* (Leipzig, 1913; Stuttgart: Teubner, 1974 ed.) and *Agnostos Theos. Untersuchungen zur Formengeschichte religiöser Rede* (Leipzig/Berlin: Teubner, 1913; 1956 reprint) explored the evidence in Paul's letters of indebtedness to the background of classical Greek forms, and the apostle was firmly set in the milieu of Greek antiquity as far as some features of his letter-writing habits were concerned.

(3) R. Bultmann's *Der Stil der paulinischen Predigt und die kynisch-stoische Diatribe* (FRLANT 13 [Göttingen: Vandenhoeck & Ruprecht, 1910]) was devoted to Paul's use of the argumentative feature of diatribe, especially with reference to Epictetus whose works were the study of A. Bonhöffer, *Epiktet und das Neue Testament* (Giessen: Töpelmann, 1911; 1964 reprint). In particular Bultmann noted that diatribe is a considerable feature of rhetorical antithesis (ibid., 109), but it was left to later investigators (notably N. Schneider [see later]) to develop the theological purpose served by this rhetorical *figura*.

(4) Paul's rhetoric as a theme of his letter was popularized by G. A. Deiss-mann, *Paulus: eine kultur- und religionsgeschichtliche Skizze* [2] (Tübingen: Mohr, 1925), and his Jewish-hellenistic background was brought out as a key to his thought, but at the expense of understanding his corporate relationships with the churches and his polemics.

. (5) Paul's role as a child of the Jewish-hellenistic synagogue has been more recently investigated in the work by H. Thyen, *Der Stil der jüdisch-hellenistischen Homilie* (FRLANT 65 [Göttingen: Vandenhoeck & Ruprecht, 1955]) where the use of LXX in the synagogue was shown to have influenced the apostle's way of composition and argument.

(6) W. Bujard's *Stilanalystische Untersuchungen zum Kolosserbrief* (SUNT 11 [Göttingen: Vandenhoeck & Ruprecht, 1973]) offered to explore a threefold step into Paul's spiritual and literary background: the likenesses and differ-ences seen when his career was influenced by (a) his ancestral home; (b) his synagogue training and experience; and (c) his life in Tarsus (ibid., 132). The author's hope was to secure a "unified perspective" based on his style, i.e., sentence formation, flow of thought, rhetorical engagement (ibid., 221).

(7) Five special features have been fruitfully considered in more recent times, and they are especially deserving of notice since they bear directly on the exegesis and understanding of 2 Cor 10–13.

(a) N. Schneider, *Die rhetorische Eigenart der paulinischen Antithese* (HUTh 11 [Tübingen: Mohr, 1970]) gave special attention to one important feature of Paul's style, "antithesis." He sought to show that, in contrast to ancient rhe-torical forms in the classical Greek writers, Paul's debt was more in the direc-tion of *koine* Greek and the Old Testament–late Jewish texts (ibid., 63), and has a strong theological interest (ibid., 65–67).

(b) H.-D. Betz's *Der Apostel Paulus und die sokratische Tradition* (1972) is a monograph devoted to the last four chapters of 2 Corinthians, which section he finds best designated "an apology in letter-form" (ibid., 14) sharing the literary features of "antisophist tendency" (14). The opponents of Paul are cast in the role of sophists, while Paul himself is portrayed as the philoso-pher in this debate (18). As far as the setting and interpretation of 2 Cor 10–13 are concerned, Betz makes three points central: (*i*) the entire "praise speech," where Paul is "boasting" is conformed to the rhetorical model of περιαυτολογία, known from Plutarch, *On Self-Praise Without Offending* (Gr. περὶ τοῦ ἑαυτὸν ἐπαινεῖν ἀνεπιφθόνως [75, 95]); (*ii*) the "catalogue of trials" (περιστάσεις, *peristaseis:* see on 6:4) (11:23–33) shares in the literary form of the cynic-stoic diatribe (98); (*iii*) the section 12:2–4 is a parody on a "journey to heaven" motif, portrayed in highly ironical tones (89), while 12:7*b*–10 is a parodied "aretalogy," an encomium of praise devoted to gods, heroes, and illustrious people in Greco-Roman society by extolling their virtues and powers. Paul uses the form of this *topos* only to offset it by the "signs of the apostle" in 12:12 (93: see *Comment* on 12:1–10), a verse which highlights his "endurance" and leads to his "weaknesses" (13:1–3). This is the "proof" (δοκιμή) or evidence he brings out to refute their appeal to their "signs" or credentials. He plays the part of the "wise fool" to answer the charge that he is a false apostle.

In hellenistic debate between the sophist and the philosopher (typified in Socrates), the latter is often caricatured as "a fool" because he was believed to have lost the measure ($\mu\acute{\epsilon}\tau\rho o\nu$) of himself and his world. This appears to be the charge against Paul who replies in the style of the philosopher responding to the sophist. He will not boast of himself; but if he does, it is to show up his opponents who claimed ecstatic experiences, including an "ascent to heaven" as part of their special equipment. Paul recalls that he too can "boast" of this experience, but he argues that even this paranormal event proves nothing regarding his credibility as an apostle, and in any case he refuses to divulge the mystic secrets he overheard (12:4). Only in his weakness will he glory; and that becomes the criterion of his apostolate. His adopting the language and thought-forms of his opponents serves only to undercut the value they gave to the sophists' role (12:1, regarding $\kappa\alpha\nu\chi\tilde{\alpha}\sigma\theta\alpha\iota$: "there is nothing to be gained by it").

(c) The strictly autobiographical dimension of Paul gets only a minor place in Betz's appeal to rhetorical patterns such as apology and parody. On the contrary, Zmijewski's *Der Stil* (1978) seeks to emphasize the part played by "boasting in weakness" (11:30; 12:9) in Paul's own life-experience. The key to his use of rhetorical forms is biography, since he is at pains always to point out that the *"Narrenrede"* is after all only one ingredient in a letter written by Paul to a specific congregation facing specific trials (ibid., 421). Hence the dialogue element must be coupled with the rhetorical parallels (ibid., 422).

(d) Zmijewski's chief contention (against Betz) is reinforced by the latest writer on the style of 2 Cor 10–13, K. T. Kleinknecht, *Der leidende Gerechtfertigte* (1984). He stresses the epistolary, autobiographical, and apologetic elements, but he also introduces a wider concern to establish a theological setting for those four chapters. This he finds in the role of the suffering apostle who sides with God in the struggle against his foes (ibid., 293). The *Denkrahmen* (frame of thought) of Paul is basically Jewish, and what moves him primarily is a desire to stress the notion of "glorying in weakness" as a way of understanding his own life and ministry; hence the biographical dimension is the key (ibid., 295, 296).

(e) E. A. Judge, with C. Forbes and P. Marshall, has set Paul's boasting on the background of his appeal to a sophisticated, rhetorically trained congregation at Corinth. Paul's use of set forms is no accident, since he is one of them (in spite of 10:10), and his adopting the role of a fool is explained as a tactic of "non-conformity" (Marshall's term). When he disavows rhetoric, he does so self-consciously, since he believes such display would be incongruent with his Gospel and his idea of apostleship. But he is at heart a hellenist who differs from his opponents and the Corinthians only on the single point that he is moderate in the claims he makes, while they (the opponents in 11:6; 12:11) are men of $\H{\upsilon}\beta\rho\iota\varsigma$, "pride" (but they accepted this character since for them it was a virtue; Paul's estimate is seen in the verb $\epsilon\pi\alpha\acute{\iota}\rho\epsilon\sigma\theta\alpha\iota$, "to assume superiority, to lord it over" another, in v 20; that is, it is condemned as Pauline *hybris:* Zmijewski, ibid., 212). The rivals of Paul are "hybrists"— but this is not a pejorative term so much as a tribute to the self-praise which

was native to Greek self-esteem. Did Paul know how to handle them? is the
question that Marshall poses. But his self-chosen delimiting of the response
to exclude Paul's theology is a weakness in an otherwise illuminating
study.

II. It is not unproblematical to suggest a transition to the section commencing at 11:16. Two possibilities are available. On the one hand, since the
link between 11:16 ("I repeat, let no one think me foolish," RSV) and 11:1
("Bear with me in a little foolishness") is clear, it looks at first glance as if
v 16 simply resumes the theme of "foolishness," after a digression in which
Paul has exposed the character and characteristics of his opponents. But the
two vv do not say the same thing (Plummer, 313: against Lietzmann, 149,
"the meaning is indeed the same"; Bultmann, 211; Zmijewski, Der Stil, 193).
In v 1 the call is, Bear with me in my folly; at v 16 the accent is rather,
Don't think me a fool. In v 1 Paul is tentative and proffers a request he
thinks will not be refused; in v 16 he is even less sure, and is apparently
certain that he is regarded as a fool in the eyes of the Corinthians. The
reason is probably to be sought in the unmasking of the enemy and his
influence at 11:4, 13–15. Paul has developed a much more serious attitude
as the chapter has unfolded. Perhaps the hook-words ἐδέξασθε–δέξασθε (vv
4, 16) give the explanation. They have "accepted" the alien teaching; the
best he can hope for is that they will "accept" him as a fool, ad absurdum.

The second possibility, on the other hand, is to treat 11:1–15 in toto as a
diversion from the chief theme begun in 10:13–18 where the topic was Paul's
mission to Corinth and the issue of boasting in the sphere of service. Now
after explaining the real nature of the threat in 11:4, 5, 13–15, Paul picks
up the earlier matter and develops it in terms of "boasting." His taking the
role of the fool is part of the general treatment of "commending oneself"
which goes back to 10:16–18; that passage closed on the scriptural note of
Paul's true boast—in the Lord who appointed and authorized him to the
service that brought him first to Corinth.

In our view, this linkage is to be preferred on the following grounds: (1)
The "vocabulary of toleration" (with δέχεσθαι and ἀνέχεσθαι [vv 1, 4, 19, 20])
shows that what is at stake is not a clash of personalities but the issue of
legitimacy of mission and the evidence of genuine apostolicity (see Käsemann,
Die Legitimität, 37–51), which will get Paul into the subsequent discussion of
his trials, weaknesses, and credentials. (2) The contrast of κατὰ κύριον and
κατὰ σάρκα (lit., "according to the Lord"/"according to [the] flesh") in vv
17, 18 lies at the heart of the short pericope. The reference to κύριος, "Lord,"
looks back to 10:17, where true boasting has to be "in the Lord" (ἐν κυρίῳ),
and only those whom the Lord recommends will be approved (δόκιμοι) in
10:18. The antithesis is to boast on the basis of σάρξ, "flesh," which is tied
to the rival claim in 10:15: they boast in their κανών. But we refuse to do
that since all such pride, says Paul, is determined by the self-life which has
come under the judgment-power of the cross (Gal 6:13, 14; Phil 3:3), just
as the trait that it inspires in others leads to their claim to be φρόνιμοι, "wise
people" (the phrase is used by Paul ad absurdum, whereas Paul is ἀσθενής "a
weak man," v 21a). Clearly, however, φρόνιμοι is "the subjective self-evaluation
of the Corinthians" (Prümm, Diakonia 1:634), which has come about, thanks

to the rival mission. (3) On the lexical evidence καυχᾶσθαι/καύχησις is the most frequent word group in vv 16–21*a* (4x), and while "foolishness" is an important subtheme, it gains its importance only since Paul has to face the wider issue of "boasting, true and false." On "self-praise" as a theme for reciprocal condemnation, see K. Berger, "Die impliziten Gegner," 385.

As to a suggested classification of vv 16–21*a*, Zmijewski (ibid., 217) has proposed the term "ironical concession," as Paul puts himself on the side of his opponents in challenging their authority as missioners in Corinth. Their presence is seen in πολλοί ("many," v 18), suggesting a considerable presence. The section is, however, no simple confrontation with rival preachers on the human level (κατὰ σάρκα: cf. 10:3); *rather it is a defense of true apostolicity,* a theme which has been begun earlier.

Paul sets out his position vis-à-vis the opponents in several ways: (a) they rule over the congregation (v 20), he is the Corinthians' sponsor as a bridegroom's agent (vv 2, 3); (b) where the Corinthians have been "fleeced," Paul has proclaimed a "free" Gospel (vv 7–11); (c) in place of enticing words which have ensnared the church members (v 18), Paul's message is the truth of Christ (v 10) and the only Gospel of God (vv 4, 7); (d) instead of self-praise, Paul has come with a lowly posture (v 7*a*); (e) far from inflicting injury on them, he loves them (v 11).

Yet it is clear that they were not easily convinced of Paul's motives. So he has to adopt a stance that is difficult to explain. He will take the fool's part. And this boasting as a fool is undertaken to appeal to their "shame," though in line with his posture he writes, "To *my* shame." He will come before them as a weak person (v 21), which is the charge levied at him (10:1), a charge he refutes (10:2). He moves over to the opponents' opinion of him in 10:10 (Bultmann, 214) with "a weak presence and feeble speech." His point is: let me grant those traits; which would you have, my feebleness, or the opponents' self-styled powerful presence and rhetorical persuasiveness? The verbal key to the discussion can easily be missed: it is ὡς, "as it were," in v 17 and ὡς ὅτι in v 21*a*, which is not a causal particle (= "since we are weak," so Bachmann, 377; Windisch, 348; Schlatter, *Paulus,* 651; Lietzmann, 148 [but not Kümmel, 211]), but rather explicative. The latter sense is supported by Bultmann, 214, who takes ὡς ὅτι as depending on λέγω and explaining the verb (a parallel is in 5:19). See too BDF § 396 who takes it as equivalent to ὅτι = "that"; but Héring, 83, makes it the same as ὡς "*as if* we were weak." On balance the ὡς more likely qualifies the force of the ὅτι, "intimat-[ing] that what is introduced by ὅτι is given as the thought of another, for the correctness of which the speaker does not vouch" (Plummer, 317; Allo, 290: ὅτι "indicates ordinarily the opinion of other people"). The other option is to make the particle comparative (see BGD, 589: "as I must concede when I compare my conduct with the violent treatment you have had from others" [v 20]; so NIV). But whether Paul's writing of ὡς ὅτι introduces an explanation, "I must confess to my shame . . . I have been weak," or a comparison, "I have been too weak to imitate the opponents," in both instances it is a mark of irony. Paul seems consciously to be reflecting on what they have rumored about him: he is weak. And he takes this assessment at face value as a "concession" (*Einräumung,* so Prümm, *Diakonia* 1:635), and acts out the fool's role.

Herein is the key to the entire "Foolish Discourse" of 11:1–12:10, as a "self-caricature," a grotesque parody of Paul as a servant of Christ (Zmijewski, ibid., 230).

Comment

16. πάλιν λέγω, "I say again," pointing back to 11:1. The modern equivalent is "I repeat," but we have retained "say" for λέγω to show the contrast with λαλῶ in v 17, "I am speaking," and the *inclusio* at v 21.

The key term is ἄφρων, "fool": not a dim-witted person or clown, a jester (as in "play the fool"), but in the technical sense of the person in hellenistic-Roman society who had lost the correct measure (μέτρον) of himself and the world around him (Fallon, 92). Like Socrates, the true philosopher was often seen as a fool, especially by the sophists (see G. W. Bowersock, *Greek Sophists*, for the development of the sophist movement in the second century A.D.; G. C. Field, "Sophists," *Oxford Classical Dictionary*[2], ed. N. G. L. Hammond and H. H. Scullard [Oxford: Clarendon Press, 1970], *s.v.*) because he was reckoned (δοκεῖν: on the construction see BDF § 397; the verb is ingressive here in v 16a) to have lost the true measure.

The concessive clause begins with εἰ δὲ μή γε, "but even if you do" (an elliptical construction, BDF § 439, 480.6, and meaning "otherwise"), i.e., receive me as a fool, which is how I present myself to you and how I expect you to receive a fool. The ἄν joined with καί as κἄν implies "at least," "though only" (BDF § 374; Bultmann, 211). δέξασθε is the verb of 11:4 for the reception already accorded the intruders' message. Paul is making capital out of the contrast by this catchword.

ἵνα κἀγὼ μικρόν τι καυχήσωμαι. His taking the fool's part is the way he centers attention on "boasting," the main item in his rejoinder. His attitude to boasting is negative, since it stands opposed to the OT *testimonium* in 10:18, and Bultmann notes (212) how καυχᾶσθαι is thought of as a species of ὕβρις in Greek philosophical opinion (cf. Plutarch, *De se ipsum citra invidiam laudando* [*Moralia* 539A ff.]; Betz, ibid., 75, 95). The Corinthian opponents, however, have taken the sophists' part in the debate, and forced Paul to play the game on their terms (12:11). But he is doing it self-consciously with tongue-in-cheek and as a concession. μικρόν, "a little," is the figure of speech, *litotes*, chosen to poke fun (by understatement) at the large claims the adversaries were making. After καυχᾶσθαι used transitively (BDF § 148.2) it signifies "a little [share in] boasting."

17. A parenthesis follows, introduced by ὃ λαλῶ, "What I am speaking." The verb, then repeated, points on to 13:3: the Corinthians were seeking "evidence" of Christ's speaking (λαλοῦντος Χριστοῦ) through Paul. He implies that it is not in his enforced καυχᾶσθαι that Christ's message is made known—only as a boasting in his weaknesses (11:30). So he is not speaking κατὰ κύριον, "on the Lord's authority," but ὡς ἐν ἀφροσύνῃ, "as it were, in [my] foolishness," an antithesis; so Schneider, *Die rhetorische Eigenart*, 50, 51, 62, for the formula "*non* x, *sed* y." And the antithesis functions rhetorically as a *correctio*, as Paul confronts the opposition (Schneider, ibid., 47–49).

His speaking "as (ὡς) a fool" rests on (ἐν) ταύτῃ τῇ ὑποστάσει τῆς καυχήσεως, "the ground (ὑπόστασις: a difficult term to find the English equivalent for, as in 9:4. See *Comment* there. The choice is between "confidence" or "plan"; we have followed Héring's appeal [82] to etymology, and he renders "supposition" or "ground") of my boasting." The last-named idea, implying that Paul is making a "hypothesis" by adopting the stance of a fool, is endorsed by ὡς, also implying a role which the speaker is playing "in the matter of this boasting" (Hughes, 398, n. 60; Bultmann, 212), is also possible, but less emphatic. Paul is showing why he is adopting a fool's part.

18. ἐπεὶ πολλοὶ καυχῶνται κατὰ σάρκα, κἀγὼ καυχήσομαι, "Since there are many who are boasting as 'people of the world,' I too will boast." Again, the ironical tone is unmistakable. (οἱ) πολλοί, the "many," suggests an opposition in some strength, as in 2:17. But it may be stylistic (cf. Phil 3:18), intended to maximize the seriousness of the danger *in Paul's eyes.* The object which is the opponents' proud claim is not mentioned: it is inferred from 10:16: ἐν ἀλλοτρίῳ κανόνι εἰς τὰ ἕτοιμα καυχήσασθαι, "to boast about what has already been done in another person's sphere [of service]."

More important is the adverbial phrase κατὰ σάρκα, lit., "according to the flesh." Σάρξ, "flesh," in this context has been shown by E. Schweizer *TDNT* 7:128, to be the decisive distinction, in moral terms, between humankind and God; and κατὰ σάρκα is the same as κατὰ ἄνθρωπον (1 Cor 3:3), particularly since the former term σάρξ speaks of what constitutes the race of sinful creatures. Σάρξ is human frailty which concurs in sin's appeal and powerful attack, leading men and women to live independently of God. In this context, the opponents' boasting as σαρκικοί, "people of the world" (1 Cor 3:1, 3; cf. Phil 3:3; Gal 5:13–26), refers to trust in outward display and demonstrations of spirit, their reliance on "sight" (εἶδος, 2 Cor 5:7), and their glorying in "the outward" (2 Cor 5:12), where Paul's point of reference is "in the Lord" (ἐν κυρίῳ, 11:17, 18) or κατὰ κύριον, "as a Christian" (Héring, 81) whose only hope is in Christ and his own weakness (13:1–3). So when Paul consents to boast, it will be in those qualities—his weaknesses—which most obviously demonstrate his own vulnerability and frailty (12:5).

19. ἡδέως γὰρ ἀνέχεσθε τῶν ἀφρόνων φρόνιμοι ὄντες, "For you gladly put up with fools, since you are wise people yourselves!" The adverb ἡδέως, lit., "sweetly, gladly," when used with ἀνέχεσθαι, "to put up with," only increases the degree of irony, as part of the "toleration" speech employed by the apostle. The verb runs parallel with δέξασθε in v 16, and both comment on the surprising hospitality given to the intruding missionaries. The Corinthians are adept at welcoming all and sundry—surely they can find room for Paul the fool! They are φρόνιμοι, "wise," not really, of course, but in the ironical strain. The designation is Paul's commentary on their pretensions. This is the natural way to understand Paul's stance. Bultmann, 213, maintains, on the contrary, that what is in view is not the Corinthians' tolerance of erroneous teachers but their patience with Paul when he speaks to them as a fool. This is possible, but that view concedes that they are φρόνιμοι. More likely, Paul uses φρόνιμοι in a derogatory manner, much the same as in 1 Cor 4:10.

A new proposal, ventilated by P. Richardson ("The Thunderbolt in Q and the Wise Man in Corinth," in *From Jesus to Paul,* FS F. W. Beare [Waterloo, Ont.: Laurier University Press, 1984] 91–111, deserves to be noticed here, though the author does not specifically relate his suggestion to 2 Cor 10–

13). The point made is that the debate at Corinth centers on Paul's position regarding wisdom and the distinctive emphasis found in the logia tradition (Q), notably in Matthew 11:25–27, which is associated by Richardson with Apollos and his party. The Corinthians' claim to be "wise" ($\phi\rho\acute{o}\nu\iota\mu\omega$) must be taken seriously—not sarcastically—and it marks the devotion they showed not only to a wisdom Christology but to the representatives of Apollos' mission to Corinth. Although the conclusion is not drawn, it would assist our understanding of 11:4, 13–15 if this argument is sound. Then, we could identify the reference to "another Jesus" and appreciate the dynamics of the polemic between Paul and the rival preachers: it centers in "wisdom," and the issue has to do with whose type of wisdom is kerygmatic, Paul's wisdom of the cross or Apollos' "wisdom of the wise," as Paul viewed it (1 Cor 1:19; 3:18, 19; 4:19). To complement Richardson's argument, we may see the relevance of the verb $\mu\epsilon\tau\alpha\sigma\chi\eta\mu\alpha\tau\acute{\iota}\zeta\epsilon\sigma\theta\alpha\iota$ in 11:13–15 in the light of 1 Cor 4:6 (ibid., 105), and also the use made of the same OT testimony, "Let the one who boasts boast in the Lord," in 1 Cor 1:30 and 2 Cor 10:18 against a similar background. But this reconstruction implies that $\phi\rho\acute{o}\nu\iota\mu\omega$ is used in a nonpejorative way, which is not probable, given the irony that pervades the whole section.

20. $\dot{\alpha}\nu\acute{\epsilon}\chi\epsilon\sigma\theta\epsilon$ $\gamma\grave{\alpha}\rho$ $\epsilon\grave{\iota}$ $\tau\iota\varsigma$ $\dot{\upsilon}\mu\hat{\alpha}\varsigma$ $\kappa\alpha\tau\alpha\delta\upsilon\lambda o\hat{\iota}$, $\epsilon\grave{\iota}$ $\tau\iota\varsigma$ $\kappa\alpha\tau\epsilon\sigma\theta\acute{\iota}\epsilon\iota$, $\epsilon\grave{\iota}$ $\tau\iota\varsigma$ $\lambda\alpha\mu\beta\acute{\alpha}\nu\epsilon\iota$, $\epsilon\grave{\iota}$ $\tau\iota\varsigma$ $\dot{\epsilon}\pi\alpha\acute{\iota}\rho\epsilon\tau\alpha\iota$, $\epsilon\grave{\iota}$ $\tau\iota\varsigma$ $\epsilon\grave{\iota}\varsigma$ $\pi\rho\acute{o}\sigma\omega\pi o\nu$ $\dot{\upsilon}\mu\hat{\alpha}\varsigma$ $\delta\acute{\epsilon}\rho\epsilon\iota$, "Indeed, you put up with the one who enslaves you, the one who exploits you, the one who lays hands on you, the one who lords it over you, even when he deeply insults you!" This is a most revealing sentence, providing new information about the outlook and behavior of the false apostles. The style has many impressive features, such as *enumeratio*, as five verbs are listed in succession, and in a climactic way, following the "law of increasing members" (Zmijewski, ibid., 207) with each verb adding extra weight to Paul's exposé. The emphasis of a string of verbs, with two *hapaxes*, found only here in the NT, is enhanced by the anaphorical repetition of [$\epsilon\grave{\iota}$] $\tau\iota\varsigma$ five times, "the one who," and epiphoric assonance (hence the sonorous -οι, -ει, -ει, -αι, -ει; see W. Bujard, *Stilanalystische Untersuchungen*, 184). Moreover, the intention is clear, though it is debated whether the verbs' meanings are to be construed literally (Allo, 290; Barrett, 291, partly undecided), or metaphorically (so Lietzmann, 211; Windisch, 347; Bultmann, 213), or rhetorically, i.e., as figures of speech in the debate (so Betz, ibid., 116, 117). Paul evidently is continuing in an ironical vein and professing to be "alienated" from his readers who have permitted themselves to be assaulted by his foes. The two key verbs are (1) $\lambda\alpha\mu\beta\acute{\alpha}\nu\epsilon\iota$, lit., "takes," but it may mean "lays hands on" perhaps with a sexual connotation of "violate, deflower," with a retrospective allusion to 11:2, 3, where the church is a virgin bride in danger of being seduced and raped (see Zmijewski, ibid., 212); and (2) $\dot{\epsilon}\pi\alpha\acute{\iota}\rho\epsilon\tau\alpha\iota$, possibly translated as "is lifted up," as in 10:5, but more likely in the moral sense of "is presumptuous, puts on airs, acts arrogantly," and so "lords it over" you. It is used of those who stand over against the Corinthians and their freedom in Christ. The notion of irresponsible, lordly control seems implied, and exposes the nature of the opposition in direct contrast to Paul's pastoral solicitude in 1:24, [$o\dot{\upsilon}$] $\kappa\upsilon\rho\iota\epsilon\acute{\upsilon}o\mu\epsilon\nu$ $\dot{\upsilon}\mu\hat{\omega}\nu$ $\tau\hat{\eta}\varsigma$ $\pi\acute{\iota}\sigma\tau\epsilon\omega\varsigma$, "we are not ruling over your faith."

The other verbs are just as telling. The Corinthians have been open-hearted to the arrivals in their city, and have welcomed them even if the latter intended to "enslave" (καταδουλοῦν). Galatians 2:4 has the identical verb, but hardly the same enemy is in view there. "Bondage to the law" (Plummer, 316; Hughes, 199; Tasker, 157) is scarcely in the setting of this passage where νόμος, "law," is absent altogether. καταδουλοῦν is rather the policy of those who set themselves up as masters, claiming the Corinthians as δοῦλοι, "slaves," whereas Paul is δοῦλος of Christ (4:5). See Windisch, 347; but Betz, ibid., 116, n. 535, 117, thinks Paul's estimate is more of a caricature.

κατεσθίειν, lit., "to eat up," with the prefix κατα as intensive (see MM *s.v.* for uses in the papyri). The opponents are thought to be swallowing up the congregation, not in a literal sense of harming them but as exploiting them for personal gain. See the idea in Mark 12:40 // Luke 20:47 where the same verb is used of devouring property, i.e., to appropriate illegally (BGD, 422). The intruders as greedy persons guilty of πλεονεξία is what is meant, a theme to be taken up in self-defense at 12:16–18. So the issue may be Paul's "right to maintenance" as an apostle, which he waived but the false apostles have traded on (Barrett, 291; Lietzmann, 149; Bultmann, 213); or else in reference to the collection, which, however, does not figure prominently in chaps. 10–13 (Betz, ibid., n. 6).

λαμβάνει, "takes," either has a neutral flavor, "to make captive" as in 12:16 or, as has been suggested (see above), there is a more aggressive meaning, "to violate," "to take advantage of" in a sexual way. "Lay hands on" is the meaning offered by Lattey and may be understood in either way, but note his appeal to LXX where λαμβάνειν renders לָקַח, *lāqaḥ*, "to seize" (Kümmel, 211).

ἐπαίρεται, "lords it over you," is even stronger in its association of the insolence and haughty dealing with the congregation that Paul attributes to the adversaries at Corinth. But notice the way this verb reappears in 12:7 as a denial of Paul's *hybris* (Betz, ibid., 95, 102).

εἰς πρόσωπον δέρειν, "to strike on the face." A physical assault is almost certainly implied in this verb, though it could be a vivid picture word for the insult that was like a blow. Philostratus, *Life of Apollonius* 7.23, has the phrase μόνον οὐκ ἐπὶ κόρρης παίει: it is almost as if the popular philosophers are given a blow about the ears when they are accused of groveling before wealthy men or conniving at their deeds. The charge is ὕβρις, it is alleged, since it is assumed that "all excess of wealth engenders insolence."

The verb denotes a calculated insult (akin to the scene in Luke 22:63) and shares the Jewish imagery of directing a blow to a person's face as a way of humiliating him (see Matt 5:39: "striking on the right cheek" is a peculiarly insulting assault, which meant a buffet with the back of the hand. Hence the Mishnah, *B. Qam.* 8.6, prescribes a specially heavy fine for such an action: see T. W. Manson, *The Sayings of Jesus* [London: SCM Press, 1945] 51). The link with 2 Cor 12:7, με κολαφίζῃ, "it may batter me" (cf. the verb in Matt 26:67—another passion-narrative term), is to be noted.

21a. κατὰ ἀτιμίαν λέγω, ὡς ὅτι ἡμεῖς ἠσθενήκαμεν, "I say this to my shame: I admit that (as it were) 'we were weak.'" This two-member sentence sums up and forms a conclusion to a set piece (vv 16–21a, λέγω comes at both ends). Once again Paul's "ironical concession" (*ironische Einräumung*) results in a stylized form, in which he abruptly concedes that, since his readers are self-evidently φρόνιμοι, his enacting the role of the fool is bound to seem a disgrace, unworthy of their consideration. "*My* shame" is the true reading (Plummer, 317).

Moreover, the ironical comparison between ἄφρων and φρόνιμος leads to an admission that, though Paul's enemies have shown a strong attitude, he has been weak by contrast. Paul's preface of ὡς ὅτι before the verb marks a stance he is adopting (see above, p. 361). Later (at 13:3, 4), Paul will give a fuller assessment in a non-ironical way. For the moment he is agreeing with the verdict at 10:10, and hiding his apostolic ἐξουσία in a guise of assumed ἀσθένεια to point up the contrast between himself and the Corinthian opponents who have so influenced the church.

Explanation

More irony peeps through at v 16. Possibly, as on previous occasions in his running debate with the opponents, the term "fool" was one which formed the substance of a charge brought against him. And when we remember that he includes the little term "too" (v 16, RSV), it seems that the pattern of boasting had already been set by the alien teachers themselves; why should not Paul then have his turn?

Verse 17 is rightly enclosed in parentheses; it is a qualification which the writer feels he must insert lest his readers should fail to catch the spirit in which he is writing. He is not "boasting" "after the Lord," which means here "as a Christian" (so NEB), but as a man who deliberately puts himself in the place of those whose pretensions he wants to expose; Paul is arguing *ad hominem,* to use the technical term.

The opponents have been conspicuously successful in the inroads they have made into the Corinthian assembly, and v 20 is a surprising statement of the way in which they have been accorded hospitality. The Corinthians have shown a singular lack of discernment, almost naïveté, in welcoming the false prophets with their grandiose claims and pretensions; will they (Paul is asking) extend the same attitude to him as he plays the role of a fool?

They have tolerated these men, allowing themselves to be ordered about, robbed of their money (cf. 2:17), and duped by these false teachers—even to the point of being insulted by them in a way which any Jew would regard as a most humiliating experience—a blow on the face. Paul, in this tremendously sarcastic passage, now simply asks for a hearing as he will present his case. "What a pity we are not like that—you seem to prefer bullies" is his final thrust (v 21).

2. PAUL'S TRIALS   (11:21b–33)

Bibliography

Betz, H.-D. *Der Apostel Paulus und die socratische Tradition.* **Bultmann, R.** *Der Stil der paulinischen Predigt und die kynisch-stoische Diatribe.* **Burchard, Ch.** *Der dreizehnte Zeuge.*

Traditions- und Kompositionsgeschichtliche Untersuchungen zu Lukas' Darstellung der Frühzeit des Paulus. FRLANT 105. Göttingen: Vandenhoeck & Ruprecht, 1979. **Casson, L.** *Travel in the Ancient World.* Toronto: Hakkert, 1974. **Collins, J. N.** "Georgi's envoys in 2 Cor. 11:23." *JBL* 93 (1974) 88–96. **de Vaux, R.** *Early History of Israel.* Tr. David Smith. Philadelphia: Westminster Press, 1978. **Fridrichsen, A.** "Zum Stil des paulinschen Peristasenkatalogs. 2 Cor. 11, 23ff." *SO* 7 (1928) 25–29. ———. "Peristasenkatalog und res gestae: Nachtrag zu 2 Cor. 11, 23ff." *SO* 8 (1929) 78–82. **Georgi, D.** *Die Gegner des Paulus im 2. Korinther,* 1964. **Horsley, G. H. R.,** ed. *New Documents Illustrating Early Christianity: A Review of Greek Inscriptions and Papyri Published in 1978.* North Ryde, NSW, Australia: Macquarie University, 1983. **Hort, F. J. A.** "A Note on κόφινος, σπυρίς, σαργάνη." *JTS* O.S. 10 (1909) 567–71. **Jervell, J.** *The Unknown Paul.* chap. 5: "The Signs of an Apostle." Tr. R. A. Harrisville. Minneapolis: Augsburg, 1984. **Jewett, R.** *A Chronology of Paul's Life.* Philadelphia: Fortress, 1979. **Judge, E. A.** "The Conflict of Educational Aims in NT Thought." *Journal of Christian Education* 9 (1966) 32–45. **Kleinknecht, K. T.** *Der leidende Gerechtfertigte.* 1984. **Marshall, P.** "Enmity and Other Social Conventions in Paul's Relations with the Corinthians." Diss., Macquarie University, 1980. Forthcoming in WUNT. **Ogg, G.** *The Chronology of the Life of Paul.* London: Epworth Press, 1968. (American Title: *Odyssey of Paul*) 16–23. **Osborne, R. E.** "Paul's Silent Years." *JBL* 84 (1965) 59–65. **Rauer, M.** *Die "Schwachen" in Korinth und Rom nach den Paulusbriefen.* BS 21:2–3. Freiburg: Herder, 1923. **Schürer, E.** *The History of the Jewish People in the Age of Jesus Christ.* Ed. G. Vermes and F. Millar. Edinburgh: T. & T. Clark, 1973. 1:340–53. **Starcky, J.** "The Nabateans: A Historical Sketch." *BA* 18 (1955) 84–106. **Steinmann, A.** *Aretas IV. König der Nabatäer. Eine historisch-exegetische Studie zu 2 Kor 11, 32f.* Freiburg: Herder, 1909. **Theissen, G.** *The Social Setting of Pauline Christianity,* 1982. **Thrall, M. E.** "Super-Apostles, Servants of Christ, and Servants of Satan." *JSNT* 6 (1980) 42–57. **Travis, S. H.** "Paul's Boasting in 2 Corinthians 10–12." *SE* 6 (1973) 527–32. **van Unnik, W. C.** "Tarsus or Jerusalem. The City of Paul's Youth." In *Sparsa Collecta,* pt. 1, 259–327. NovTSup 29. Leiden: Brill, 1973.

Translation

²¹ᵇ *Yet—speaking foolishly—whenever anyone presumes to make a claim, I too can do the same.* ²² *Do they claim to be Hebrews? So am I. Do they claim to be Israelites? So am I. Are they Abraham's descendants? So am I.* ²³ *Are they Christ's servants? I am more one than they—even if I am out of my senses in claiming this— with far more toils, in prison more often, in suffering beatings beyond number, at death's door frequently.* ²⁴ *Five times I took thirty-nine lashes from the Jews.* ²⁵ *Three times I was beaten with rods. Once I was stoned. Three times I was shipwrecked. A night and a day I have spent adrift on the open sea.* ²⁶ *During my frequent journeys I have been exposed to dangers from rivers, dangers from brigands, dangers from my own people, dangers from Gentiles, dangers in the town and in the country, dangers at sea, dangers at the hands of false brothers.* ²⁷ *I have lived my life in toil and hard work, through many a night without sleep, in hunger and thirst, often deprived of food, suffering from cold and destitution.* ²⁸ *And, aside from all the other things, there is the daily pressure* ᵃ *that concern for all the congregations brings me.* ²⁹ *Who is the weak person? Then, I am that person. Who is tripped up? Then, I am the one to feel indignation.*

³⁰ *If there has to be boasting, I will boast [only] of my weakness.* ³¹ *The God and Father of our Lord Jesus—he who is ever-blessed—knows that I do not lie.*

³²*At Damascus, the ethnarch under king Aretas was guarding the city of the Damascenes in order to capture* ᵇ *me,* ³³*and I had to be lowered in a basket through a window by the wall so that I could escape out of his clutches.*

Notes

ᵃTwo variations are found in this v. ἐπίστασις (so Nestle-Aland²⁶) is read by P⁴⁶ ℵ B D F G, while ἐπισύστατις, a cognate noun but suggesting a more violent reaction ("uprising, disturbance, insurrection," BGD, 301; cf. Num 16:40) is witnessed by K L M P. Also μοι (P⁴⁶ ℵ* B) is a stronger reading than μου (ℵ² D ψ TR lat Ambst), since ἐπί + dative is more normal (BDF § 202). The μου would indicate Paul's pressure on others, which is a less natural connection.

ᵇπιάσει με without auxiliary verb has apparently only a limited attestation (B D* lat syrᵖ copˢᵃ), whereas θέλων, "wishing," is added by ℵ D² ψ syrʰ bo TR, in the interests of a smoother text, and should be rejected.

Form/Structure/Setting

This section is dominated by the use of the *peristaseis*-list, i.e., a list of trials, endured by moral philosophers and teachers (cf. Epictetus *Diss.* I:11, 33; 18, 22; II:19, 24; Seneca *Epp.* 41.4; 82.14; see Bultmann, *Der Stil,* 19, 71–80, and in his Commentary on 2 Cor, 116, 117, 170–76, 230, 231, for comparisons between Paul and the cynic-stoic preacher). There are obvious differences as well; not least in that the popular moral philosopher suffered περιστάσεις as a totally human experience, where Paul saw a divine purpose running through all his life's hardships (cf. A. Bonhöffer, *Epiktet,* 301; Zmijewski, *Der Stil,* 322, noting how the christological formulation is seen at its clearest in 12:9, 10).

Another setting for such parallel lists is touched on by Fridrichsen, loc. citt., that with the paradox of "boasting" as a sign of evidence—but the evidence turns out to be that of "weakness"—we should think of "the inscriptions of oriental kings, the *res gestae* of Roman emperors, and [the exploits of gods and heroes recounted in] Greek novels" (so Kümmel, 211). See Bultmann, 217, who notes how, even with the formal similarities between the *res gestae* of hellenistic rulers and Roman emperors, still it remains true that the Paul in this list of 2 Cor 11 is far removed from the miracle-working Paul of the apocryphal Acts. See, however, J. Jervell, "The Signs of an Apostle," 90–95, for a different evaluation. Bultmann takes the witness of 12:12 to be exceptional, whereas Jervell finds Paul's miraculous activity in several other places (Rom 15:19; Gal 3:1–5; 1 Thess 1:5). See later, p. 436.

Paul's indebtedness to such forms of trial-lists is clear from 2 Cor 4:8–10; 6:4–10; 1 Cor 4:10–13; Rom 8:35–9. The commonest links in style and theme are (1) use of the preposition ἐν, "in," to denote the circumstances posing trials; (2) rhetorical questions (seen in 2 Cor 11:22–23a, 29); (3) the overcoming of hazards (11:32, 33), and above all (4) the christological component, giving this body of literature its Christian flavor.

The "Fool's Speech" here begins in earnest at 11:21b, to be continued into 12:11. The exordium is at v 23, while vv 24–27 give the litany of afflictions endured by Paul in his missionary service. Throughout he is "speaking as a fool," and consciously setting his service as a διάκονος Χριστοῦ, a "servant of Christ," in antithesis to the claims of the rival mission preachers. There is a special point to some of these features. The travel risks which are described in such detail in vv 25–27, 31–33, illustrate how Paul is standing on its head the conventional *topos* of self-praise (see Marshall, "Invective"; idem, "Enmity"). All travel on ancient trade routes by land or sea involved much risk-taking (cf. L. Casson, *Travel,* chaps. 9–11), and the usual way to acknowledge a safe return home from a trip was to make a thank-offering to the gods (Homer *Od.* 1.5.12–16. Horsley, *New Documents 1978,* gives examples from the papyri, #18). Paul turns the note of praise into one of celebrating his weakness, not his success; and he probably brings the list to an unexpected climax by a little story (*narratiuncula*) that could illustrate his (apparent) humiliation and cowardice (see *Comment* on 11:30–33).

To achieve his purpose Paul's narration is carefully and logically constructed. Already we have observed the introductory theme stated in 11:16–21*a*, in which v 21*b* is a "reflecting observation" (Zmijewski, 276, who writes *reflexive,* surely meaning *reflektierende;* cf. Kleinknecht, ibid., 286, n. 139).

The catalogue-list is then stated in vv 23–29, after setting the stage at v 22 in a fourfold way: are these opponents Hebrews, Israelites, Abraham's seed, servants of Christ? The mounting emphasis is to be seen in the terms used, moving from the general to the particular. There is even the possibility of an increase in syllabic quantities in the terms used, from three syllables in Ἑβραῖοι to six in διάκονοι Χριστοῦ as though to stress the writer's "impressionistic style" (Zmijewski, ibid., 254, n. 166; cf. Judge, "Paul's Boasting," 48–50).

A further "reflecting observation" comes at 11:30, 31, to be followed by a report on the Flight from Damascus as a narrative interlude (11:32, 33). At this point Paul is ready to introduce a second main section (12:1–10) on "Visions and Revelations." This skeletal analysis of vv 21–33 shows how Paul is both employing a rhetorical pattern of his day, and fitting in the autobiographical details with a double aim, which is to use a "Boasting Talk" (*Ruhmesrede*) (1) to show how he can be "bold" (τολμᾶν, 11:21*b,* in support of 10:2 which threatens drastic action at Corinth if he finds the church still unsubdued) and yet (2) to qualify that "boldness" in terms of his role as a suffering apostle whose "power" is perfected only in "weakness" (12:9, 10, linked with 11:21). All the literary devices, patterns and "tricks" are pressed into service to establish these two goals.

The chief items of interest in the field of style and form are:

(1) Climactic development, seen in the way the sentences increase in emphasis and insistence, e.g., κόποι—φυλακαί—πληγαί—θάνατοι (vv 22, 23, 28, 32, 33), with the stylistic variation of "once," "thrice" (2x), "five times," though not in order. These multiple-words are part of the "memorial chronicle" of the *res gestae* literature (Fridrichsen, "Peristasenkatalog," 81, 82). An "eightfoldness" (5 + 3) has been detected in the listing of the dangers of Paul (Zmijewski, ibid., 251). See the diagram later for vv 26, 27.

(2) Even more carefully structured is the sequence of ideas in which generalized statements are unpacked in the details that follow on directly. This feature is best seen in a schematic, as indicated by Kleinknecht's chart (288). Specially to be observed are the arrowed lines showing the climactic arrangement in the vertical markers:

Analysis of 11:21–29

21 Ἐν ᾧ δ᾽ ἄν τις τολμᾷ,   ἐν ἀφροσύνῃ λέγω;   τολμῶ | κἀγώ.

22 Ἑβραῖοί   εἰσιν;   κἀγώ.
    Ἰσραηλῖταί   εἰσιν;   κἀγώ.
    σπέρμα Ἀβραάμ εἰσιν;   κἀγώ.

23 διάκονοι Χριστοῦ   εἰσιν;   παραφρονῶν   λαλῶ,   ↓ὑπὲρ   ἐγώ.

            ἐν   κόποις*   περισσοτέρως,
            ἐν   φυλακαῖς*   περισσοτέρως,
            ἐν   πληγαῖς*   ὑπερβαλλόντως,↓

        ↓ ἐν   θανάτοις   πολλάκις ─────────
24   ὑπὸ | Ἰου | πεντάκις 40–1 | ἔλαβον,
25 | τρὶς | ἐρραβδίσθην,
                                          | ἅπαξ | ἐλιθάσθην,
                                          | τρὶς   ┌──── | ἐναυάγησα,
                                                    νυχθήμερον ἐν τῷ
                                                    βυθῷ πεποίηκα·

26   ὁδοιπορίαις   πολλάκις, ─────┐
                            | κινδύνοις   ποταμῶν,
                            | κινδύνοις   λῃστῶν,
                            | κινδύνοις ἐκ γένους,
                            | κινδύνοις ἐξ ἐθνῶν,
                            | κινδύνοις ἐν πόλει,
                            | κινδύνοις ἐν ἐρημίᾳ,
                            | κινδύνοις ἐν θαλάσσῃ,
                            | κινδύνοις ἐν ψευδαδέλφοις,

27 κόπῳ καὶ μόχθῳ   ἐν ἀγρυπνίαις*   πολλάκις,
   ἐν λιμῷ καὶ δίψει,   ἐν νηστείαις*   πολλάκις,
   ἐν ψύχει καὶ γυμνότητι·

28 χωρὶς τῶν παρεκτὸς ἡ ἐπίστασίς μοι καθ᾽ ἡμέραν,
   ἡ μέριμνα πασῶν τῶν ἐκκλησιῶν.

29 τίς ἀσθενεῖ   καὶ οὐκ   ἀσθενῶ;
    τίς σκανδαλίζεται καὶ οὐκ ἐγὼ πυροῦμαι;

Key to Symbols

↓   = line of development

┆   = formal equivalent in lines, with links in case-ending and word-play, word-usage, etc.

*   = also in 2 Cor 6:5, 6

(3) The biographical elements are an evident feature, with the *Aktionsart* of the aorist tenses of the verbs: ἔλαβον—ἐρραβδίσθην—ἐλιθάσθην—ἐναυάγησα. Some of these verbs are "complexive (constative)" aorists denoting repeated actions provided the repetition is summed up and has a terminus: τρὶς ἐρραβδίσθην in v 25 (BDF § 332.2). Other aorists are better classed as "narra-

tive" aorists, which give information of a biographical nature (Windisch, 324: the verbs yield "concrete biographical data, known only in part from the Acts of the Apostles," vv 25, 27, 31–33). Other verb tenses, e.g., the perfect πεποίηκα (v 25), stand alongside the aorists without apparent reason (BDF § 343.2). The verb-uses share an epic quality, or else have a "horror" element (e.g., v 25), or yield a dramatic emphasis, which is detected in the perfect in πεποίηκα by A. T. Robertson, *Grammar*, 896, 897, and in the question-and-answer dialogue with word-play in vv 22–23*a*, regarded as "close to a dramatic dialogue" (Windisch, 350). To this we may add the rhetorical questions of v 29, both of which have a histrionic effect when read out aloud.

(4) Repetition in the plural nouns is marked as a feature, e.g., κινδύνοι, "dangers," is eight times repeated, where the plural is natural. But θάνατοι, "deaths," is unnatural as a plural, and ὁδοιπορίαι, "journeys," is plural to account for all the dangers that are listed (Fridrichsen, "Zum Stil," 27). And "Damascus"—"Damascenes" results in an overweighted sentence (v 32).

(5) Nouns are grouped in twos by association, e.g., κόπῳ καὶ μόχθῳ—ἐν λιμῷ καὶ δίψει—ἐν ψύχει καὶ γυμνότητι, with the adverb πολλάκις linking the parts and providing a "functional power" (Fridrichsen, ibid., 27) to add to the gravity of Paul's recital. Parallelism in this arrangement is noted by Bujard, *Stilanalytische Untersuchungen*, 187. But the terms are also linked in an interesting way by Zmijewski (ibid., 263) who sees a schema of

(1) synonym
   "toil"   (paired with) . . .   "hard work"
(2) antonym
   "hunger"   (paired with) . . .   "thirst"
(3) metonym
   "naked" (i.e., "destitute")   (paired with). . .   "cold"

(6) Liturgical formulations (v 31, "the God and Father of the Lord Jesus") coupled with an oath formula (v 31: οὐ ψεύδομαι, a *litotes* = I am speaking the truth) give an added weightiness to the narrative, to stress how Paul is under pressure to declare his own interest, as part of a task to assert his own credibility as an apostle at Corinth.

(7) The continuing features of paradox, irony, and "rhetorical comparison" (*synkrisis:* for this term as a literary genre see Prümm, *Diakonia* 2:368, 369) are sustained into chap. 12, with a touch of humor added. In v 33 Paul closes the *cursus honorum* with a section (30–33) which has been variously assessed. Some have regarded the Flight from Damascus episode as a gloss added in dictation by Paul's scribe (Windisch, 364), or as an afterthought (Lietzmann, 151), or as a topic which had been exploited by his enemies who tried to show how he was a cowardly man (10:1, 10), or as a little story with no apparent reason for its inclusion here (Bultmann, 220). Much more likely is the attempt to find the rationale for the episode in Paul's rhetorical purpose, either as a climax of his "tale of woe and weakness," as though to prove the depth of degradation he was put to in his service of Christ; or because he wishes to stress "descent" over the wall as a foil to prepare for his "ascent" to the heavenly regions in 12:2–4 (Harris, 393). An interesting

sidelight is provided by Judge, "Conflict" (45), and Travis, "Boasting" (530), who see Paul's unceremonious exit down from the city wall in a humble fish-basket as a parodic counterpoint to the honor given to the Roman soldier who in storming an enemy city was the first over the wall. He was rewarded with the dignity of *corona muralis* (Livy 23.18), a crown to mark his bravery at the wall. Paul's claim is to be "let down" and so to escape; so he once more turns the contemporary practice on its head in his role as fool and a person of "weak presence" (10:1, 10). So 11:30. Whatever the precise reason for this recall of the Damascus interlude, it is a powerfully ironical and playful story, tinged with humor and exactly in place; and it is biographical as well as rhetorical as a parody in form.

Comment

21b. ἐν ᾧ δ' ἄν τις τολμᾷ, ἐν ἀφροσύνῃ λέγω, τολμῶ κἀγώ, "Yet—speaking foolishly—whenever anyone presumes to make a claim, I too can do the same." Obviously the parenthetic ἐν ἀθροσύνῃ λέγω as the second member of a three-part sentence is determinative. He will continue his role-playing as ἄφρων, and the *"Narrenrede,"* "Fool's Discourse," opens with Paul's entering into a dialogical comparison with his opponents. The issue turns on the idea expressed in τολμᾶν, "to be bold," whether as courageous or, more appropriately here, as insolent or arrogant. The conditional clause with ἐν ᾧ δι' ἄν marks the situation, since it is clear that Paul is accusing his rivals of just this attitude in the light of their conduct in v 20. Paul is drawn into the contest because of these traits displayed by the opponents; hence the repetitive τολμῶ, "I too am bold" based on the principle, what they are, I am also (so Windisch, 350). Yet the intermediate, "I am speaking foolishly," betrays the ironical stance the speaker is taking, an admission reinforced by v 23, παραφρονῶν λαλῶ, "I am speaking like a madman." The brief formulation here is well designed with the ἀφροσύνη-motif casting a shadow over the three words, each ending in -ω to produce an assonance: λέγω—τολμῶ—κἀγώ.

τολμᾶν has four meanings in the NT, as listed by Fitzer, *TDNT* 8:184, 185: "to dare" in a neutral way (Rom 5:7); to dare as a confession of courage; to dare = to pressure (Lietzmann, 149); to be insolent. Fitzer's view is to see a double-entendre in our v, as though Paul were paying courtesy to the ones addressed. But the polite way of praising them for courage (second sense) as dialogue partners (*Gesprächspartner*) shows only in an ironical and sarcastic way that the speaker is presumptuous (third sense). The real explanation, however, seems to be that τολμᾶν is the opponents' slogan word, used contemptuously of Paul (10:1, 2), and here he turns it back to them, but in an *ad hominem* way. Granted that they are bold in the claims they make as Christ's professed servants, Paul will set down his list of credentials—an act of boldness in both senses mentioned earlier. In that way he will try to show how *their* boldness is presumptuous (fourth sense). The issue is basically one of apostolic self-awareness (Fitzer, ibid.) on which Paul is being challenged and which he seeks to reassert—but in this circuitous, ironical way, by speaking κατὰ σάρκα, not κατὰ κύριον and forgetting (on purpose) the restriction and caution of 10:17, 18.

We have taken the view that Paul's reference in τις, "anyone," looks back to 11:13–15, the false apostles who in turn can be heard voicing their claims in vv 22, 23a. Barrett, 292, wishes to widen the scope, and he believes that Paul's thought here moves beyond his immediate rivals to center on the leaders at Jerusalem who stand behind them. So, in his interpretation, the fourfold designation in vv 22, 23a applies to the "pillar" apostles, but—in spite of a superficial parallel in 1 Corinthians 15:9–11, where the issue of rival preachers is not to the fore—it is less convincing to have Paul's mind turn from the immediate scene. The links with 10:13–18, in our understanding, are too strong to ignore, and we maintain that the four designated titles in the next vv make more sense if they refer to a Jewish mission which not only made large claims for itself but acted upon those claims in coming to Corinth to challenge Paul's authority, which would not be true of the Jerusalem στῦλοι.

22, 23a. Ἑβραῖοί εἰσιν; κἀγώ. Ἰσραηλῖταί εἰσιν; κἀγώ. σπέρμα Ἀβραάμ εἰσιν; κἀγώ. διάκονοι Χριστοῦ; κἀγώ, παραφρονῶν λαλῶ, ὑπὲρ ἐγώ, "Do they claim to be Hebrews? So am I. Do they claim to be Israelites? So am I. Are they Abraham's descendants? So am I. Are they Christ's servants? I am more one than they—even if I am out of my senses in claiming this." Four "titles of honor" are made central to the rhetorical questions, to each of which Paul provides a retort: κἀγώ = καὶ ἐγώ by crasis, lit., "and I am" three times, with the final question answered by ὑπὲρ ἐγώ, a phrase difficult to render. See below.

The literary form is to be classified as a "rhetorical asyndeton" (BDF § 494) demonstrating the "lively style of colloquial speech." The increasing force of the words used is to be seen, showing that "servants of Christ" is the most audacious of all the claims made and surpassed. Moreover, Paul's disclaimer, παραφρονῶν λαλῶ (from the verb παραφρονεῖν, "to conduct oneself in an irrational manner" [BGD, 623]), shows how Paul regarded the final claim to be paramount. The inference is that there is no higher office than to be Christ's διάκονος—but that title is one he is not willing to grant to his opponents. If this is so, they cannot be the same as the Twelve, but the term must refer to the emissaries who presumed to arrive at Corinth with the authority of the Jerusalem leaders.

To be sure, ὑπὲρ ἐγώ in part of Paul's reply is ambiguous, and it is not easy to decide between "I more," i.e., I am a better servant (cf. NIV, RSV), and "I have more credentials to show as a servant," where the list of trials shows how Paul has "more" (ὑπέρ). (There is a third possibility, however; see later.) But ὑπέρ is better taken as adverbial (BDF § 230) as if it were μᾶλλον (Phil 3:4; so Lietzmann, 151; Windisch, 353; Bultmann, 217; Héring, 83), and the first rendering is preferred. Throughout, the style is "plerophoric" (Bujard, *Stilanalytische Untersuchungen*, 162), i.e., it has a degree of fullness that seeks to overwhelm the readers with ringing tones (ibid., 184) and emphatic figures of speech. So the adverbs with ὑπέρ ("more") and περισσοτέρως ("more") and πολλάκις ("often"), all with a rhetorical comparison in view, play a vital role.

The four titles used to challenge the opponents are not to be taken as synonyms, therefore (as Lietzmann, 150, supposes), nor variations to be accounted for on rhetorical grounds. But Windisch (350) and Bultmann (215) are wise not to draw too fine a distinction between the various names by regarding them all as "titles of honor" or *Ehrenprädikate*. On the other hand, there is much to be said of Georgi's point (*Die Gegner*, 76–82) that διάκονοι Χριστοῦ is the all-determinative expression, which holds the clue to the others. The last-named title is then a Christian self-understanding by which they viewed their Jewish-Christian position as the true essence of the apostolic διακονία: "Hebrews" ('Εβραῖοι) represents the outer "shape" of their profession; "Israelites" ('Ισραηλῖται) is the inner character of that national identity; while σπέρμα 'Αβραάμ, "seed of Abraham," is an honorific title they lay claim to since it embodies the name of the father of all the faithful. διάκονοι Χριστοῦ places the capstone on their right to office as representing an important function they felt commissioned to exercise on the basis of the earlier designations. In all, therefore, the titles stand for a missionary awareness implied in their being sent (*ein missionarisches Sendungsbewusstsein*, Zmijewski's phrase, ibid., 241). And we have to assume that the "sending party" was claimed—and only claimed—to be Jerusalem (against Thrall, "Super-Apostles"); Paul grants them *e concesso* the titles he states, without necessarily endorsing them all in their case. Indeed, if 11:13–15 relates to the same body of missionaries, their assumption of the title διάκονοι Χριστοῦ is misplaced, since they are more rightly branded as ψευδαπόστολοι and ἀπόστολοι of Satan. This factor seems to make a conclusion regarding an earlier phrase stronger, namely, the ὑπέρ-adverb in "I am more" has an exclusive force. It is time to consider this usage with ὑπέρ more fully.

The option we observed above was to take ὑπέρ as either comparative or as marking a contrast. On either view, the sense would be "I am more a servant of Christ than the opponents (are)," tacitly according to them the title διάκονοι Χριστοῦ (so Lietzmann, 151; Allo, 294; Wendland, 241), or "my service is better than theirs (is)"; so I have more reason to claim the title (cf. Windisch, 353). But we may construe the force of the adverb as superlative or exclusive: I am a servant of Christ, and when they claim it they err, since it is a "mad claim" (*Wahnsinn*) in any case, and can only be made if the speaker is manifestly παραφρονεῖν λαλῶν, "speaking as a person out of his senses." Then, Paul proceeds, *if* I have to state my claim to be Christ's διάκονος, let me rehearse the evidence, which my rivals cannot produce. And, paradoxically, that leads him to provide evidence of his weakness, not his mighty works (v 30). So Paul on this basis does have a *Rechtanspruch*, a rightful claim.

'Εβραῖοι (here, Acts 6:1; Phil 3:5 in NT) has two meanings: (1) a pure-blooded Jew; (2) a speaker of Hebrew as a language. The latter was regarded as a valuable asset (cf. de Vaux, *Early History*, 209, 210). Also there is some suggestion that the term implied "born in Israel," at least as far as family connections went, and so not a hellenistic Jew (Windisch, 350; contra Georgi, ibid., 51–63; but see Kümmel's rejoinder [211] in favor of taking the "Hebrews" as Palestinian Jews who made their chief accusation against Paul the fact that he did not have a personal knowledge of the earthly Jesus [5:16]. The "double front" on which Paul had to fight them was [a] their Palestinian connection, and [b] their attachment to "spiritual gnosis"). See Gutbrod, *TDNT* 3:390; and van Unnik, "Tarsus or Jerusalem," on Paul's early days in Jerusalem, whatever his family history in Cilicia might have contributed to his formative years.

Ἰσραηλῖται (as in John 1:47; Rom 9:4; 11:1; cf. Gal 6:16) is a term of social and religious distinction (Barrett, 293). It denotes membership in the community of salvation-history and a share in God's purposes (Windisch, 350).

σπέρμα ᾿Αβραάμ is more complex, with a diverse background (see John 8:33, 37; Heb 2:16; Rom 9:7; 11:1; and especially Gal 3:16, where "Abraham's seed" is given a christological twist; it may have been a slogan introduced to the Galatians to offer them membership in the chosen [and mystical] community of heavenly salvation; R. Jewett, "The Agitators and the Galatian Congregation," *NTS* 17 [1970–71] 198–212, going back to H. J. Holtzmann, *Lehrbuch der hist.-krit. Einleitung in das NT* [Freiburg: 1886] 243 who makes σπέρμα ᾿Αβραάμ a Jewish-Christian motto, pointing to their origin as Jerusalem-oriented: so Jewett, 204; Georgi, ibid., 63–82, esp. 74–76).

If "Abraham" was a name being used in the propaganda of the Jewish-Christian mission, and "seed of Abraham" was their term which Paul takes up, it is likely that, on the basis of evidence in Philo, what made Abraham important was his role as the first believer and also as a "man of the Spirit" (*Pneumatiker;* Georgi, ibid., 78, 79, citing W. L. Knox, "Abraham and the Quest for God," *HTR* 28 [1935] 55–59). The missionaries claimed equally to be πνευματικοί and to be preachers with both a self-understanding and a mission-consciousness (Georgi, 82) based on the "model" (*Vorbild*) of Abraham. Zmijewski, ibid., 240, prefers to see the issue centered in the divine promises which the patriarch inherited (Rom 4:16, 18; 9:6–9; Gal 3:29: Jeremias, *TDNT* 1:8, 9). Paul is claiming this title, "seed of Abraham," for himself as a badge of honor to mark out his Christian self-identity over against his rivals. But the term σπέρμα ᾿Αβραάμ elsewhere suggests a wider currency in the early church. It was evidently the occasion of discussion with claims and counterclaims.

διάκονοι Χριστοῦ, "Christ's servants." Here Paul states the fundamental matter of the debate between himself and the antagonists at Corinth. He will deny this title to them only because for him it is *the* hallmark of his life and life's work. He is a missionary-servant, clothed with apostolic "right" which in turn has brought him to Corinth as his μέτρον τοῦ κανόνος (10:13), a privilege he cannot share with the rival preachers. Again, it is an open question whether they claimed this title as part of their functional legitimation in their *Missionsgebiet* as "men sent on a mission" (Käsemann, *Die Legitimität*, 36, 37). That supposition, if we accept it, would explain why (1) Paul used the term, which would par excellence include himself (and exclude them, in his reckoning), and (2) he does not use ἀπόστολοι Χριστοῦ Ἰησοῦ (see 1:1), a term he cannot write of others who, in his eyes, are ψευδαπόστολοι and ἀπόστολοι of Satan (11:13, 15).

Perhaps the ὑπέρ ἐγώ in his response, "I am more one than they," is meant to take a snide glance at the ὑπερλίαν ἀπόστολοι (11:5) whose authority was being invoked in the intruding mission, especially as these leaders will shortly reappear on the scene (12:11). The irony of Paul's words is self-evident, in any case, and with all the "tricks" of hyperbole, comparison and dramatic narration he will proceed to detail his life as θεοῦ διάκονος (6:4), "a servant of God."

23b. ἐν κόποις περισσοτέρως, ἐν φυλακαῖς περισσοτέρως, ἐν πληγαῖς ὑπερβαλλόντως, ἐν θανάτοις πολλάκις, "with far more toils, in prison more often, in suffering beatings beyond number, at death's door frequently." A series of terms each accompanied with ἐν forms a catalogue of missionary experience, each item also accompanied by an adverb. His first two comparisons shade off into an exaggerated emphasis with (lit.) *"countless* beatings . . . deaths *often."*

The substantives κόποι—φυλακαί—πληγαί—θάνατοι are in ascending order of danger, to be construed with ἐγενόμην, "I was," *ad sensum.* κόπος is a word for physical toil, but applied to Christian service as in 1 Cor 15:58; 1 Thess 1:3; 2:9; 3:5 as well as in our letter at 6:5; 10:15. See too Phil 2:16 for the verb (Martin, *Philippians,* NCB, 106). The prison experiences (in Acts 16:23–30; cf. 1 Cor 15:32; 2 Cor 1:8–10; Rom 16:3–7; see Martin, *Colossians and Philemon* NCB [1981] 26–32 for a consideration of the data, both NT and extra-biblical, in regard to Paul's imprisonments; *1 Clem.* 5:6 speaks of Paul's being in chains seven times) and the reference here parallel 6:5: ἐν φυλακαῖς. The adverb περισσοτέρως, "more often," may suggest comparison with other missionaries, i.e., I have been in captivity more often than they; but in view of the next phrase it may be rather a stylistic trait used for effect.

ἐν πληγαῖς ὑπερβαλλόντως, lit., "in beatings (cf. 6:5) very exceedingly," which is an obvious hyperbole if taken in the sense of "times without number" (an exaggeration found in the hellenistic *Perisistasenkatalog* with the profusion of trials enumerated for effect, so Fridrichsen, "Zum Stil," 26); but the adverb could be rendered "beyond measure," a reference to the degree of physical suffering Paul endured as a sign of courage (10:1, 10), a topic under question at Corinth. The only thing he could not afford to do in this debate was to overplay his sufferings without a basis in fact, and so lay himself open to the charge of protesting too much. Héring, 83, renders "beyond all reason," i.e., for no cause, *re incognita* (as in Acts 16:37), his case not having been tried in court.

ἐν θανάτοις πολλάκις, lit., "in deaths often," suggests a constant exposure to death and its threats (see 1:9, 10; 4:11; 1 Cor 15:32; Rom 8:36). "Mortal dangers" (Héring, 83) gives the exact sense (so Prümm, *Diakonia* 1:642). In a document which acknowledges divine deliverance from danger (σωθεὶς ἐγ μεγάλου κινδύνου) Stratoneikos also confesses to have been often "near death" (ἰσοθανάτους)—a parallel phrase to our text. See Horsley, *New Docs* (1983), 59.

24. The particular form of physical punishment Paul suffered is described in a Jewish idiom. ἔλαβον, "I took" (as my penalty, Str-B 3:527–30) the statutory thirty-nine lashes, prescribed in Mishnah, *Mak.* 3.10, on the basis of Deut 25:2, 3, which gave the maximum as forty. Jewish law safeguarded the human person by ensuring the number was not exceeded by a miscount. The punishment was a synagogue discipline, as a verdict of the *bet dîn,* "house of judgment," for several offenses (see the list in *Mak.* 3.1–9, including the trespass of entering into the Jerusalem Temple in an unclean state. Cf. Acts 21:28 which, however, is later chronologically than the writing of 2 Cor: Barrett,

296). The five occasions on which Paul claims to have been beaten perhaps belong to an early period of his mission service, in the so-called "silent years" (cf. Osborne, "Paul's Silent Years") where he (apparently) was banished as a member of the synagogue community (see Schürer, *History,* II.2.262). Meeks, *First Urban Christians,* 26, joins this verse to 1 Cor 9:20 to postulate a mission of Paul to the Jews with the result that he suffered the synagogue penalties levied on a false teacher of Israel. But Luedmann, *Paul, Apostle to the Gentiles,* 121, n. 91, rejects the inference. Both Acts and the rest of the Pauline letters are silent regarding a synagogue mission. However, Acts is incomplete in other respects regarding Paul's early Christian life (Hengel, *Acts and the History of Earliest Christianity,* 109). The form "forty less one" is rabbinic, yet Greek usage of the phrase is attested (BDF § 236.4).

25. τρὶς ἐρραβδίσθην, ἅπαξ ἐλιθάσθην, τρὶς ἐναυάγησα, νυχθήμερον ἐν τῷ βυθῷ πεποίηκα, "Three times I was beaten with rods. Once I was stoned. Three times I was shipwrecked. A night and a day I have spent adrift on the open sea." The penalty of being beaten with rods (ῥαβδίζειν) has a technical side, referring to a punishment (*virgis caedere* as a *verberatio*) inflicted by the Roman magistrate, as in Acts 16:22 (the lictors [ῥαβδοῦχοι, lit., "rod-bearers"] acted for the magistrates), though Windisch, 356, wants to interpret the Greek verb in its LXX background. In a strict sense Paul as a Roman citizen was exempt from this punishment (see T. Mommsen, "Die Rechtsverhältnisse des Apostels Paulus," *ZNW* 2 [1901] 90; A. N. Sherwin-White, *Roman Society and Roman Law in the New Testament* [Oxford: Clarendon, 1963] 48–98). But there were occasions when even the profession of being a Roman citizen went unheeded (Cicero *In Verrem* 5.62–66: the case of a Roman citizen beaten at Messina, in spite of his cry "I am a Roman *civis*").

Paul suffered this indignity three times, we are told; a fact which is sad evidence that Roman governors were not always meticulous in upholding the law, (Livy, 10.9), and a miscarrage Paul comments on as ὑβρισθέντες . . . ἐν Φιλίπποις, "outrageously treated at Philippi" (1 Thess 2:2). So it was not the fact that Paul chose not to exercise his civic privilege that brought on him the suffering, as Bultmann, 217, thinks. Florus who succeeded Albinus as procurator or Judea in A.D. 64/65 had soldiers of equestrian rank flogged, ignoring their rights as Romans (Josephus, *JW* 2.308). In Paul's case the beating was administered as a public warning, or because he was treated as a social pest.

The one instance of stoning (λιθάζειν) is recorded in connection with Paul's visit to Lystra (Acts 14:5, 19). This punishment was a Jewish procedure, usually as a capital sentence passed on apostates, blasphemers and adulterers (Deut 17:5; 22:22–24; Mishnah, *San.* 7.56–60). See Acts 5:26; 7:58; John 8:5; 10:31–33; 11:8; Heb 11:37. Paul's reference is naturally not to a death sentence, though the record in Acts speaks of him nearly dying (Acts 14:19).

The three incidents of shipwreck (ναυαγεῖν, a mariner's term) are quite unknown to us. The detailed episode of Acts 27 is, of course, subsequent to the time of this writing, though in the narrative of Paul's mission journeys he had already made several trips by sea (listed in Barrett, 298). Hair-raising experiences at sea were commonplace in hellenistic romances, a fact seized on by Conzelmann (*Die Apostelgeschichte* [HNT 7] Tübingen: Mohr, 1963) 146,

147, to account for the apparent verisimilitude of Luke's writing in Acts 27; but see the robust rejoinder of R. P. C. Hanson, "The Journey of Paul and the Journey of Nikias," *SE* 4, TU 102 (1968) 315–18. The one instance of the verb in a nonliteral sense in the NT is 1 Tim 1:19, a sense found in Philo *Mut. Nom.* 215; *de Somn.* 2.143.

Further adventures at sea exposed Paul to risk as he recalled "a period of a night and a day" (νυχθήμερον: BDF § 161.2) "spent on the open sea." The verb is πεποίηκα, in this context, "I have been," an unusual perfect, used for dramatic effect (see earlier, p. 371), or because the experience is vividly before the writer's eye. See further Moulton, *Grammar* 1:144. The entire phrase "to be on the deep" is reminiscent of OT imagery (Pss 68:3; 67:23, LXX) and suggests to Windisch, 357, "probably an oriental-didactic exaggeration," but there is no reason for this judgment. The Hebrew native horror of the ocean (*tᵉhôm*, תהום) which is associated with the forces of anarchy and primeval chaos: see G. von Rad, *Theology of the Old Testament*, trl. D. M. G. Stalker (London: Lutterworth Press, 1962) 1:150, 151, may well account for such a reference, ἐν τῷ βυθῷ πεποίηκα. Another such experience awaited him (Acts 27:44*a*).

26. ὁδοιπορίαις πολλάκις, κινδύνοις ποταμῶν, κινδύνοις λῃστῶν, κινδύνοις ἐκ γένους, κινδύνοις ἐξ ἐθνῶν, κινδύνοις ἐν πόλει, κινδύνοις ἐν ἐρημίᾳ κινδύνοις ἐν θαλάσσῃ, κινδύνοις ἐν ψευδαδέλφοις, "During my frequent journeys I have been exposed to dangers from rivers, dangers from brigands, dangers from my own people, dangers from Gentiles, dangers in the town and in the country, dangers at sea, dangers at the hands of false brothers." The "catalogue of trials" continues, with a generalizing rubric, ὁδοιπορίαις πολλάκις, "often in my travels," a phrase used of his mission service, which is then made the heading under which Paul recites the varied dangers he has encountered. The term κινδύνοις is eight times repeated, for effect; we must note that all the hazards came to him in direct consequence of his appointment to service as ἀπόστολος. Only as a "servant of Christ" did he endure these hardships, not as a private person or a tourist. The groups of dangers are (1) physical and (2) personal, taking them in reverse order.

(1) "Rivers" (ποταμοί) would be natural barriers to be crossed or forded, often difficult at flood-tide.

"Town" (πόλις): perhaps "city" suggests too grand a place. The word implies a place where people live, in contrast to the desert.

"Country" (ἐρημία): again, not quite our understanding of wilderness, but rather an uninhabited area or a region with only a sparse population. Both topographical settings would present different dangers to the lonely traveler.

"Sea" (θάλασσα) reverts to the earlier mention of Paul's exposure to danger in the shipwrecks he endured and while he was adrift at sea (v 25). The preposition ἐν, "in," suggests the location of these sources from which threats to him came.

(2) At the personal level, with a change of preposition to ἐκ, "from" (suggesting origin, BDF § 166), Paul met troubles arising from a series of individuals and personal groups:

λῃσταί ("brigands") roamed in bands to attack unwary, unprotected travelers; or maybe the allusion is to highwaymen, as Rengstorf thinks, *TDNT* 4:260.

γένος, "my own people," with the possessive adjective added *ad sensum* to mark the threats from his fellow Jews is next. This was a frequent and doleful feature of Paul's life according to Acts (9:23, 29; 13:8, 45; 14:2, 19; 17:5; 18:6, 12; 20:3, 19; 21:11, 27). Yet his love for his compatriots was unwearying (Rom 9:1–5; 11:1; cf. Rom 10:1).

In contrast, the threats (in Acts) from ἔθνη, "the Gentiles," were less severe and less frequent (Acts 16:20; 19:23), but it was still a constant risk he ran, just as he was called to be an apostle to the Gentiles (see Rom 15:16; cf. Eph 3:1, 6), the reason, it may be, that ἔθνη are specifically referred to here.

ψευδάδελφοι, "false brothers," as a term is a "new Christian formation" (Windisch, 358) and in particular a Pauline expression, patterned on ψευδ- + noun as in Gal 2:4; 2 Cor 11:13. In the series of the trial-list it stands as the climax, to attract to itself greater emphasis, and there is no logical reason why the previous member on the list (ἐν θαλάσσῃ) should suggest the next item, which is ψευδάδελφοι, as J. Weiss, "Beiträge," 186, noted long ago. Windisch, 358, suggests a misplacement of the last term, but this results in an anticlimactic ending with ἐν θαλάσσῃ in his schema. Others (Lietzmann, 151; Prümm, *Diakonia* 1:643; Wendland, 242) have sought to explain the work of false brothers as in some way connected with Paul's dangers at sea, or as Paul's putting together two comparable dangers ("sea"—the worst elemental threat; "false brothers"—the worst human danger. That would be the case, if we regarded the events of v 25, "shipwrecks," as the most life-threatening of all the hazards he met). Or else, Paul simply sought to bring his list up to date, by concluding with ψευδάδελφοι, because *they* were now his most urgent problem, and the Corinthians needed to know how he felt about his present encounter with the "false apostles" (Zmijewski, ibid., 259, against Bultmann, 218, who thinks Paul has all false brothers, wherever they are found, in mind. This is not very likely, nor is Barrett's view [299] very plausible that Paul included "false brothers" because he has mentioned Jews and Gentiles already, though he is right to note that they are professed Christians). In our view, the term ψευδάδελφοι is placed at the end of the list deliberately to bring the list to a powerful (if lamentable) conclusion, and to drive home to the Corinthian readers that their hospitality to such people (11:4, 19) is a source of great grief to him now. These men are no less than his rivals; and worse, they are Satan's agents (vv 13–15).

27. κόπῳ καὶ μόχθῳ . . . A
 ἐν ἀγρυπνίαις πολλάκις . . . B
 ἐν λιμῷ καὶ δίψει . . . A
 ἐν νηστείαις πολλάκις . . . B
 ἐν ψύχει καὶ γυμνότητι, . . . A

"I have lived my life in toil and hard work, through many a night without sleep, in hunger and thirst, often deprived of food, suffering from cold and destitution." This sentence, which carries the marks of a generalizing summary with its own unifying theme within the "catalogue of trials" (so Weiss, "Beiträge," 186; Fridrichsen, "Zum Stil," 26, 27; Windisch, 359; Allo, 297; Plummer, 327; Héring, 86) concentrates on what the apostle lacked in direct consequence of his missionary service (Wendland, 242). The phrases are put together to form a schema with the pattern A-B-A-B-A; or alternatively, two

pairs, κόπῳ καὶ μόχθῳ/ἐν λιμῷ καὶ δίψει, each followed by a phrase with ἐν
. . . πολλάκις, are joined, and a concluding coda to form a third line is all
the more effective by ending abruptly with ἐν ψύχει καὶ γυμνότητι. This three-
line strophe is carefully crafted (Weiss, "Beiträge," 186), with the last line
ending on the note of "rest." Repetitions and prolixities abound with the
use of synonyms or near equivalents (e.g., "toil"/"hard work," "cold"/
"nakedness" [Bujard, *Stilanalytische Untersuchungen*, 187]), and πολλάκις, "often," links the lines together. "Fullness" and "intensity" are conveyed through
the choice and placing of the words (Zmijewski, ibid., 261).

Paul's purpose is evidently to show the deprivations that characterized
his life as an apostle (cf. 1 Cor 4:9–13).

κόπος reverts to v 23; cf. 1 Cor 15:10, 58, and see 2 Cor 6:5; μόχθος,
"hard work," is a virtual synonym. He uses the pair together in 1 Thess
2:9; 2 Thess 3:8, "a coupling beloved by Paul" (Allo, 297, who seeks to
distinguish between a passive and an active nuance in the words in the order
in which they are used). Together the pair of words acts as a heading for
what follows.

ἀγρυπνία[ι], lit., "wakefulness," "inability to sleep," may imply three ideas:
nocturnal activity, e.g., travel or work at night (Sir 38:26–30; 2 Macc 2:26,
LXX, used of writing a book at night), or sleeplessness on account of worry
or fear (cf. Sir 34 [31]:2, LXX: Windisch, 359), or a voluntary vigil as an
exercise of the spiritual life (Müller-Bardorff, *TLZ* 81 [1956] 347–52, referred
to at 6:5, see *Comment*). It is difficult to be certain whether the sleepless
nights were voluntary or a necessity (Acts 16:25 may be cited for the latter).
The second choice seems more probable if Paul is insistent on proving the
cost of his service as an apostle.

Certainly the couplet ἐν λιμῷ καὶ δίψει speaks of enforced hardship. λιμός
is "hunger," with its partner διψός, "thirst," joined in Rom 8:35. The latter
noun is a NT *hapax* (Allo, 297), though the verb is found elsewhere. Paul's
suffering here may witness to his poverty; more likely it describes his rigorous
life of travel, not an involuntary fast (Plummer, 328).

νηστείαι, "fasts," poses the same question: voluntary, as a spiritual discipline, or going without food because of a hard life? Allo (298) and Barrett
(300) suggest the former, opposed by Windisch (359) who rejects Paul's asceticism here, attributing deprivation of food to part of Paul's necessitous life
or explained because of his frequent imprisonments. Prümm, *Diakonia* 1:643,
n. 5, leaves it open, as we must, though Zmijewski, ibid., 263, has a point
that, in the "catalogue of trials" patterns, such an experience fits more naturally as a trial of destiny and suffering, forced on the philosopher and endured
in the interests of a good cause. Cf. Betz, *Der Apostel Paulus*, 98.

The final pair touches a low rung in the scale of values. ψῦχος, "cold"
and γυμνότης, lit., "nakedness," go together as marks of extreme loss, including a loss of dignity and self-esteem. See 1 Cor 4:11; Rom 8:35, with the
undertone of "shame" that characterizes the nakedness of the afflicted and
disgraced persons in Scripture (Gen 2:25; 3:7, 10, 11; Ezek 16:8; Nah 3:5;
Mic 1:11; Rev 3:18). In the context of Paul's *cursus honorum*, it is paradoxical
that the last specific item should be a mention of what his mind could regard
only with distaste and horror (see on 5:3).

28. χωρὶς τῶν παρεκτὸς is a puzzling introduction; it is capable of several interpretations. It seems clear, in spite of the asyndeton and the awkward nominative to follow (ἡ ἐπίστασις), that Paul intended this rhetorical formula, understood with γινομένων, to move the list to a conclusion (Windisch, 360). The question is: Does he mean, "the remainder, which I have omitted as too incidental" (Denney, 340; Plummer, 329), or "besides those things which are external" (Barrett, 300, as though it read τὰ ἔξω or τὰ ἔξωθεν)? The former interpretation by supplying, with Chrysostom, an *ad sensum* τὰ παραλειφ-θέντα, "the matters I have left out or overlooked," seems better (so Windisch, 360; Prümm, ibid., 637, Tasker, 164). The reason lies in the meaning behind ἡ ἐπίστασις . . . [ἡ μέριμνα] which is ungrammatical as a "compound verbal substantive" (BDF § 202.2) governing the dative μοι, "pressure . . . on me," which is "concern" for all the churches. It must then be said that these pastoral matters were not "external" in the sense that they did not involve Paul in personal relations. The climax of the trials–list is yet another evidence of his apostolicity, and in order to hasten to the theme of pastoral solicitude, he seems quickly and with an anacoluthon to pass over other matters he might have referred to. So χωρὶς τῶν παρεκτὸς is an "interruption" (Zmijewski, ibid., 268), passing over what he might have mentioned in order to come to what he needs to say to the Corinthians. In the spirit of his language earlier (6:11–13; 7:2–4) he puts his finger on his "concern" (μέριμνα) for all his congregations, not least the people at Corinth.

ἐπίστασις, "attention" or "care" required of me, the burden of oversight which lies upon me (see BGD, 300), is a synonym with μέριμνα, a word of human emotion, whether expressed as "anxiety" or "concern" (the cognate verb is in Phil 2:20; 4:6; 1 Cor 7:32, 33, 34; 12:25; cf. 1 Pet 5:7); or else the construction with ἐπίστασις is explained by μέριμνα, a nominative in apposition. The first word (see *Notes* for textual variation) suggests from its etymology the force of events which press on a person (see Acts 24:12; so Bachmann, 380, who thereby accounts for the dative μοι). But that general sense may have two nuances: (1) pressure exerted by friends or associates; (2) pressure caused by troublesome things or circumstances (cf. 2 Macc 6:3, LXX; so Windisch, 360). If we look forward to v 29, τίς ἀσθενεῖ, κτλ., it seems evident that what is in view is Paul's pastoral concern, his "all-inclusive care for his entire work" as a servant of Christ and Christ's people (Wendland, 242). This perspective helps us to elucidate μέριμνα, which normally for Paul has a pejorative sense (Phil 4:6; 1 Cor 7:32–34) except in 1 Cor 12:25 and here, where "concern" is altruistic and unself-regarding.

The "concern," μέριμνα *in bonam partem*, weighed upon Paul's spirit as a daily responsibility (καθ᾽ ἡμέραν; cf. 4:16: ἡμέρᾳ καὶ ἡμέρᾳ) and was carried on behalf of "all the congregations," not simply the Corinthian church, but certainly including these house groups. This statement of Paul's pastoral regard stands at the high-point of the "list of trials," and it is at once "graphic, informative and communicative" of his service for the churches as their authentic messenger, founder and guide (Zmijewski, ibid., 270). At a deeper level still, he is their father-in-God (see *Comment* on 7:2–4; 12:14).

29. Two illustrations of what μέριμνα, "concern," meant in Paul's life as church leader are expressed in a set of parallel questions. Both have καὶ

occurring in the middle, and it is most likely that the word in both cases functions as καί-*consecutivum* (BDF § 442.2), i.e., it is to be rendered "and so, so," or conceivably—as in our translation—"then." The accent falls, not on the question itself, but on what comes as the second-member reply in the composite sentence, which is to be taken positively. "Who is weak?" Then, *I* most obviously am weak, emphasizing the self-evident nature of the response Paul makes for himself. Similarly, "Who is tripped up?" Then, *I* am the one to feel indignation.

The first of the two verbs is ἀσθενεῖν, "to be weak"—a key word in the Fool's Speech of the chapter (11:21*a*, 30; 12:5, 9, 10). The verb has a wide range of meanings: bodily weakness or sickness (Allo, 299, who translates as *malade*), or the religious sense of a sensitive conscience (Rom 14:1, 2; 15:1; 1 Cor 8:11, 12), or a trait of inability to lead within the congregation (so Rauer, *Die "Schwachen" in Korinth*, 67, on the basis of the data in 1 Cor 8:9; cf. 1 Cor 8:10, 11; 10:15, 31: see G. Theissen, *Social Setting*, chap. 3, "The Strong and the Weak in Corinth," 121–43).

If we take σκανδαλίζειν, "to fall by stumbling," to be in strict parallelism, it seems that the two meanings carry a religious connotation; the cross references in Rom 14:13 (πρόσκομμα . . . σκάνδαλον), 14:21 (προσκόπτει) and 1 Cor 8:13 (σκανδαλίσω) suggest that this is so. So Prümm, *Diakonia* 1:644; Windisch, 361; Bultmann, 219, all of whom support the figurative meaning of "weak." Then, Paul is saying that, where there is a person who lives under the liability of a weak faith or a troubled conscience, I too share that condition, in the spirit of 1 Cor 9:22, "to the weak I became weak." But this seems a new tack for Paul to pursue, quite unexpected in this context. Bultmann senses the difficulty when he comments that Paul's καὶ οὐκ ἀσθενῶ, "I too am weak," or "am I not weak?" does not signify accommodation to the stand-point of the "weak" but a shared concern.

We choose therefore to see a literal meaning in both instances, preparing for what is to follow in v 30, which "fixes the meaning of *weakness* in the sense adopted in verse 29" (Barrett, 302) and 12:5, 9, 10 where Paul's physical weaknesses that have been on display throughout the "list of trials" are clearly meant. But "weakness," as in 10:10, is not only physical; it is Paul's entire bearing as an unimpressive figure and an outwardly nonpowerful presence at Corinth. Both those ideas—physical weakness and a "non-charismatic *persona*"—interlock, however. They fit into Black's analysis of ἀσθένεια as (1) weakness as a sign of humanity in its earthiness and dependence on God and (2) weakness as a christological aspect of Paul's apostolic life, since his weakness is "in Christ," the one who "was crucified in weakness" (2 Cor 13:4). See *Paul, Apostle of Weakness*, 228–40.

σκανδαλίζεσθαι is taken to mean "to be enticed into evil or that which is false" (Bultmann, 219). But the two verbs are not synonyms, since weakness is a neutral condition, as part of Paul's human lot, whereas to be "scandalized" implies a fall into sin (Schlatter, *Paulus*, 656; Stählin, *TDNT* 7:356), for which a person is held accountable. The point is, therefore, somewhat different. In the second question, the idea is "if a believer is led astray (*sc.* as the Corinthians had been, exactly as in 11:2, 3), I am the one (as father and founder of the congregation) to 'burn' " (πυροῦσθαι, with love, as I seek to reclaim the errant Christian, or with indignation, at those who lead others astray in reference to 11:13–15; both meanings are possible, as the "blazing fire" of zeal [7:11] for God's work at Corinth may be in the spirit of Jer 20:9). Pastoral care of this kind is what Paul regards as the truest sign of being an apostle: "not one's performance of wonders but rather one's love for the community" (Fallon, 102, 103). Paul is weak along with those who are weak in the sense that they are without power to work wonders. He is angered when the Corinthians are led astray from the true Gospel, and consequently his work at Corinth is in jeopardy.

30–33. Already we have mentioned (p. 371) the sudden shift to a narrative episode, which is a problem to some commentators. There is, however, no real reason to question these vv as in place here since they form a powerful continuation and climax in the list of Paul's apostolic exploits and experiences. In the previous catalogue he has been adopting the posture of a "fool" and boasting without measure, in what French calls a *gasconnade*, speech of a braggart. As if to remind the readers that this is his style, he repeats the theme of his own "weakness" as a ground for καυχᾶσθαι, and takes up in a "crowning illustration" (Black, ibid., 145, from Barrett, 303) the charge which has been leveled at him (11:21).

εἰ καυχᾶσθαι δεῖ, τὰ τῆς ἀσθενείας μου καυχήσομαι, "If there has to be boasting, I will boast [only] of my weakness." This is a good example of the rhetorical form *inversio* in that the accusative object comes before the predicate καυχήσομαι and the τὰ is left without definite connection with τῆς ἀσθενείας μου. So the commentators see the link in different ways: what Paul boasts in are the evidences of his weakness (Windisch, 362), or the results of his weakness (Schlatter, *Paulus*, 657), or simply the things that made up his weak condition (Prümm, *Diakonia* 1:644; Barrett, 302).

The future tense of καυχήσομαι has the ring of a solemn vow, and takes the reader back to v 10 (Windisch, 362). This connection is to be preferred to seeing the present v as opening a new section (proposed by Hughes, 418). The v is more of a summary of what has gone before, as Paul is responding to his critics, perhaps even citing their own slogan καυχᾶσθαι δεῖ, "one must boast" (as Betz, ibid., 72–74, 90 suggests), in the light of 12:1, which is Paul's retort that such boasting does no good and certainly does not build up the congregation (12:19). Yet Paul's irony tempers his statement in v 30, and paradoxically he parades the very evidence his opponents would ridicule.

31. The "solemn oath formula" (Bultmann, 219) also goes back to v 10, thus indicating the connection. Paul invokes the name of God to certify that he is speaking the truth; this will be the issue posed at 13:3. The fulsome divine predications, ὁ θεὸς καὶ πατήρ, "the God and Father," τοῦ κυρίου Ἰησοῦ, "of [our] Lord Jesus," ὁ ὢν εὐλογητὸς εἰς τοὺς αἰῶνας, "he who is ever-blessed," contribute to the weightiness of Paul's vow, making the entire sentence artistically rich in construction by the addition of a Jewish eulogistic formula and a christological expansion: so "God is/be blessed" (εὐλογητός = בָּרוּךְ, *bārûk*: Beyer, *TDNT* 2:759–65; Str-B 3:64, 530) as in a prayer-speech (see *Comment* on 1:3); and Jesus is Lord (κύριος) as a confessional utterance in early Christianity (Rom 10:9; 1 Cor 12:3; Phil 2:11). Moreover, the supplement of καὶ πατήρ

τοῦ κυρίου both recalls 1:3 and will be found with expansion in later liturgical ascriptions: Eph 1:3; 1 Pet 1:3; Hippolytus, *Apostolic Tradition* Sec. 7, Cuming's ed. 12. The verbal ὁ ὤν, using the participle as a substantive has here an individualizing sense (so BDF § 413.1): "he who is"; cf. Rom 1:25; 9:5 (which has the same construction).

The claim οὐ ψεύδομαι, "I am not lying," is a *litotes* for what is more simply expressed "I am speaking the truth," as in 11:10. But the use of the ψευδ-verb must inevitably recall 11:13–15 where the *Lügenapostel*, "false apostles" (ψευδαπόστολοι; cf. v 26) are branded as servants of Satan. Paul here, in invoking the divine names to justify his truth-claims, is also asserting his true apostolic office. The oath is retrospective and looks back immediately to his "boasting-in-weakness" as the authentic validation of his ministry (so Hughes, 419, 420; contra Tasker, 167, who takes the divine witness to go back to what is said in vv 23–27; Calvin and Strachan, 28, refer the attestation to what is to come in vv 32, 33).

32, 33. As we noted, there are those (e.g., Goudge, 110) who see these vv as a gloss which has crept into the text. Windisch, 364, and Héring, 87, think of the episode as an added postscript, mentioned to Timothy in the course of dictation. But it is safer to assume that the vv do serve a purpose, if such a purpose can be discovered, since we must ask why an editor would have inserted the vv here (Barrett, 303). We have mentioned (p. 371) some possibilities. The most plausible are: (1) This experience left its indelible mark on his memory "like Paul's first apprenticeship" of active service—*haec persequutio erat quasi primum tirocinium Pauli* (Calvin)—at the very beginning of his missionary life (so Strachan, 28; Denney, 345; Wendland, 243, who dates the event within two years of Paul's conversion). (2) Since Paul's exit from Damascus may have been known to his enemies, it was being used as a sign of his cowardice. His first act as a Christian is said to have been a flight, so he is a weak person, a coward. He felt it incumbent to give his version of what happened, and since it could not be fitted easily into the "catalogue of trials" list, he placed it here as a postscript (see Menzies, 88, 9). (3) A parallel is sought by Fridrichsen, "Zum Stil," 29, in the "epic chronicle-style" of contemporary *Peristasenkatalog*, where the touch of humor blends with irony (Allo, 300, 301); (4) it is a simple illustration of his humiliation, as a proof of divine deliverance (with no overtone of disgrace) as in Acts 9:23–25 (Plummer, 333; cf. Lietzmann, 151). (5) The movement down from the city wall prepares—by contrast—the reader for the next pericope which has Paul lifted up to the heavenly regions (12:1–4). So the nexus is one of descent-ascent (Zmijewski, ibid., 289).

The last-named seems most likely, if we have to choose, with one additional factor not usually considered. The analogy of the Roman soldier's reward for scaling the besieged city walls, mentioned by Judge, "Conflict" (45), and Travis, "Paul's Boasting" (530), has been noted. Paul's turning this idea upside down leads him to pour ridicule on the entire notion of boasting (as he does explicitly in 12:11). But it has not been connected with the imagery of 10:4, 5, where Prov 21:22 is in Paul's mind, πόλεις ὀχυρὰς ἐπέβη σοφὸς καὶ καθεῖλεν τὸ ὀχύρωμα, ἐφ᾽ ᾧ ἐπεποίθεισαν οἱ ἀσεβεῖς, "A wise man scales the cities of the mighty and brings down the stronghold in which the godless trust," LXX. We submit that this OT v may still be in Paul's thought as he writes of the Flight from Damascus; he is deliberately setting off his life of weakness against the exploits of the "wise," whether the emissaries (as at 10:5) or the Corinthians themselves (as at 11:19) who exulted in their powerful presence and wonderful deeds. Paul, by contrast, cut a poor figure. They scaled the city walls of the mighty; he only managed to be let down in a fish-basket. They brought down the stronghold of the enemy; he had to rely on others to assist him to escape from his enemy, Aretas' guards. They were victorious; he suffered defeat. Yet that defeat was his glory, and he uses the story as the evidence that it was the Lord who brought him through, and in him he could boast (10:17, 18). The same is true when he knew experiences of the opposite character (12:1–4, 9*b*). In both humiliation (11:32, 33) and exaltation (12:1–4), Paul's attitude is unwavering: boasting achieves nothing, except when it is practiced within the limits of God's appointment (10:13) and relies on Christ's grace (12:9).

The ethnarch or city governor ruled Damascus under Aretas IV, a title borne by Nabataean vassal kings. This Aretas was reigning at Petra from 9 B.C. to A.D. 39/40 (Steinmann, *Aretas IV*). He was the father-in-law of Herod Antipas who divorced Aretas' daughter to marry Herodias (Mark 6:17, 18), who was his niece and sister-in-law. Aretas was angry with this action, and took his revenge several years later. In A.D. 36 with Vitellius, Roman legate of Syria, who was also determined to settle a score against Herod who had gained favor with the emperor Tiberius at Vitellius' expense (Josephus *Ant.* 18.104, 5), Aretas moved. He invaded Petra where he defeated Herod's army (*Ant.* 18.116). Tiberius took this defeat as an insult to Rome's ally, so Vitellius was ordered to launch a reprisal against Aretas. But Tiberius' death in A.D. 37 prevented its being carried out. Aretas does not seem to have had control of Damascus, since Vitellius' route suggests that he had no need to oust Aretas from such a strategic city, and the Roman legions stationed in Syria would have deterred any precipitate adventure to gain the city. The absence of Roman coins between A.D. 34 and 62 seems to be a happenstance, and most modern historians do not use this negative factor to prove that Aretas was in control of Damascus, until the early years of Caligula's reign. This emperor showed a friendly attitude to Aretas, and present opinion (reported in Jewett, *A Chronology*, 30–33; yet challenged by Luedemann, *Paul*, 31; cf. Burchard, *Zeuge*, 150–58) is that Aretas' control of Damascus is to be dated from A.D. 37. Since Aretas died in A.D. 39/40, Paul's flight may be dated within this two year span (cf. Hughes' note, 424–28; Ogg, *Chronology*, 22, 23 agrees).

Perhaps the safest conclusion is that Paul's exit must be located prior to Aretas' death. If Paul's visit to "Arabia" and Damascus in Gal 1:17 is the same event as the one referred to in our v (see Luedemann, ibid., 63), then Paul's danger followed some time later, and prompted his flight. But Paul's own chronology is silent as to when this occurred, hence the "three years later" of Gal 1:18 is presumably to be dated from his flight, itself variously to be dated A.D. 31, 34, or 37 (Luedemann, ibid., 262; Jewett, ibid., 99).

The ethnarch is identified as "probably . . . the leader of the semiautonomous Nabataean community in Damascus . . . (who) acted as their spokesman and representative in dealings with the civic and provincial authorities" (Bruce,

245; E. Schürer, "Der Ethnarch des Königs Aretas," *TSK* 72 [1899] 95–99, thinks of a local sheik). The Jewish elements in the population may have been organized under an ethnarch, as in Alexandria (Josephus *Ant.* 14.117, referring to Strabo). The question is sometimes asked whether hostility to Paul came from inside the city; or, were the city walls watched from outside πιάσαι με, "in order to capture me"? Jewett's argument (ibid., 30, 31) is conclusive against E. Haenchen, "The Book of Acts as Source Material for History of Early Christianity" in *Studies in Luke-Acts* (FS. P. Schubert, ed. L. E. Keck and J. L. Martyn, [London: SPCK, 1968] 268–69) and Bultmann, 219, that Aretas' men must have been within the city; "it would be absurd to drop over the wall into the hands of an encircling force that could not harm one within the city itself."

The details of the incident are rich in personal names: Damascus-Damascenes, (a "pleonastic occasion," amplifying the κίνδυνοι ἐν πόλει of v 26: Windisch, 366), ὁ ἐθνάρχης (on the article, BDF § 268.1, but here more likely used to fix the identity of the person concerned with Paul's danger), Aretas. All these names are intended to give historical credibility to what happened, and we may further suspect that the double allusion to Damascus carries the suggestion that it was in that city that Paul received both his call to new life and his commission to service, according to Acts 9:15–17; 22:15; 26:17, 18; the mission to the Gentiles is especially stressed in the last-named reference. See D. M. Stanley, "Paul's Conversion in Acts: Why the Three Accounts?" *CBQ* 15 (1953), 315–38.

The other terms used in the narrative, φρουρεῖν, "to guard" (cf. Phil 4:7; Gal 3:23 in a figurative way); πιάζειν, "to seize, lay hold of" (Acts 12:4; John 7:30 with a view to doing away with a person; so Acts 9:24, ὅπως αὐτὸν ἀνέλωσιν) add to the dramatic appeal, while σαργάνη (and not σπυρίς as in Acts 9:25, or κόφινος, Mark 6:43) is properly a "net to catch fish" (Prümm, 1:657) or perhaps a rope- or mat-basket used to conceal weapons under bran or wool (Hort, loc cit., 571). In any case it was an unceremonious way of leaving the city. The "shame" in the word-choice would be intensified if we followed the conclusion of Prümm, ibid.; Schlatter, *Paulus,* 657, n. 1, and Windisch, 365. They note the descriptions of Paul's being let down (χαλᾶν: a fishing term, Luke 5:4, 5; cf. Acts 27:17) "by a window" ("a little door": διὰ θυρίδος, cf. *Oxy.P.* I. 69.7: "stolen barley smuggled διὰ τῆς . . . θυρίδος") and διὰ τοῦ τείχους, lit., "through the wall" (not "over the wall"), since it was through an aperture in the wall that Paul escaped. And they conclude that the phrases are modeled on the escape of the spies from Rahab the prostitute's house (Jos 2:15–18). Further, in our suggestion given above, we may use the point that Paul never actually got "over the wall" (as in Acts 9:25) like the victorous and courageous Roman, but had to make do with being bundled through the window set in the wall, like some load of merchandise! Or even, if Hort's discussion (loc. cit., 571) is recalled, that Paul had to be smuggled out of the city. But the final word is one of deliverance (ἐκφεύγειν) from hostile hands (a Hebraic expression with ἐκ; cf. Luke 1:71; Moulton, *Grammar* 4:92) by the hand of God.

Barrett, 304, draws some contrast with Acts 9:23–25 which—if the incidents are the same, as seems very probable—tones down the humiliation suffered, but accentuates the threat to Paul's life. 2 Cor 11:27–33 as a whole stresses the apostle's extreme fortunes as a suffering person, but (in agreement with the *Tendenz* of Acts; on questionable attempts to harmonize the details in Acts and Paul here, see Burchard, *Zeuge,* 158, n. 100) he is also an exceptional leader, as 12:1–10 will show.

Explanation

Having taken up his assumed position of foolishly boasting, Paul goes on to give a record of his past life of service for Christ's sake and the Gospel's.

The true tests of apostleship, he avers, are not in loud claims and unsupported pretensions. The acid test is found in the appellant's record of suffering, service, and sympathy with others for their good. See Rom 15:15–19; cf. 2 Tim 2:10; 3:10–12.

Paul has a notable record of his trials, and in retelling them, he tells us many things that we would never otherwise have known.

He begins by claiming a pure descent as a true Jew (v 22). Then he proceeds to show that he is a true "minister of Christ" (v 23) by reciting a catalogue of privations and sufferings. Added to the physical strain of a life of hardship (vv 23–27) there was a mental and spiritual liability also to be carried: "my anxiety for all the churches" (v 28); and no church gave him more anxiety than Corinth! Finally, he adds the ever-pressing and exacting responsibility of the "care of souls," watching for the opportunity to help others in distress, entering sympathetically into their deep need, and sharing something of their travail (v 29).

As a postscript he rounds off with a personal account of the Damascus episode (cf. Acts 9:23–25). Why is this event, in itself, trivial in contrast with the hair-raising experiences and hazards of vv 23–27, put last? One possible solution is that Paul's objectors had fastened on this incident, distorted it, and turned it into an accusation of a cowardly escape from Damascus. Also possible is the view adopted by Calvin that Paul singles out this experience for mention because it left upon his mind an ineffaceable impression as the first trial after his conversion that he knew for the sake of his loyalty to Christ. This commentary has sought to find a deeper reason in the link between 10:4–5 and 11:32, 33, both united by military language and reflecting the soldier's courage and heroism. Paul, on the other hand, has to concede that he is not a person of such distinction. Unlike the proud vainglory of military prowess, his apostolic career opened on the note of humiliation and disgrace. But God was with him, and delivered him (1:8–10), even if the badges of honor he wore were his scars in service (Gal 6:17).

3. Paul's Ecstasy and Its Evaluation (12:1–10)

Bibliography

Barré, M. L. "Qumran and the Weakness of Paul." *CBQ* 42 (1980) 216–27. **Baumgarten, J.** *Paulus und die Apokalyptik.* WMZANT 44. Neukirchen-Vluyn: Neukirchener

Verlag, 1975. **Betz, H.-D.** "Eine Christus-Aretalogie bei Paulus (2 Cor 12, 7–10)." *ZTK* 66 (1969) 288–305. **Bieder, W.** "Paulus und seine Gegner in Korinth." *TLZ* 17 (1961) 319–33. **Binder, H.** "Die angebliche Krankheit des Paulus." *TZ* 32 (1976) 1–13. **Bowker, J. W.** " 'Merkabah' Visions and the Visions of Paul." *JJS* 16 (1971) 157–73. **Cambier, J.** "Le critère paulinien de l'apostolat en 2 Cor 12, 6s." *Bib* 43 (1962) 481–518. **Güttgemanns, E.** *Der leidende Apostel und sein Herr.* Göttingen: Vandenhoeck & Ruprecht, 1966. **Jervell, J.** "The Signs of an Apostle." In *The Unknown Paul.* **Jewett, R.** *Paul's Anthropological Terms.* Leiden: Brill, 1971. **Lincoln, A. T.** *Paradise Now and Not Yet.* SNTS 43. Cambridge: University Press, 1981. ———. "Paul the Visionary: the Setting and Significance of the Rapture to Paradise in 2 Corinthians 12:1–10." *NTS* 25 (1979) 204–20. **Marshall, P.** "A Metaphor of Social Shame: ΘΡΙΑΜ-ΒΕΥΕΙΝ in 2 Cor. 2:14." *NovT* 25 (1983) 302–17. **Mullins, T. Y.** "Paul's Thorn in the Flesh." *JBL* 76 (1957) 299–303. **Nisbet, P.** "The Thorn in the Flesh." *ExpTim* 80 (4, 1969) 126. **O'Collins, G. G.** "Power Made Perfect in Weakness: 2 Cor 12:9–10." *CBQ* 33 (4, 1971) 528–37. **Park, D. M.** "Paul's ΣΚΟΛΟΨ ΤΗ ΣΑΡΚΙ: Thorn or Stake?" *NovT* 22 (1980) 179–83. **Price, R. M.** "Punished in Paradise (An Exegetical Theory on 2 Corinthians 12:1–10)." *JSNT* 7 (1980) 33–40. **Rowland, C.** *The Open Heaven. A Study of Apocalyptic in Judaism and Early Christianity.* London: SPCK, 1982. 380–86. **Saake, H.** "Paulus als Ekstatiker. Pneumatologische Beobachtungen zu 2 Kor 12, 1–10." *Bib* 53 (1972) 404–10; also in *NovT* 15 (1973) 153–60. **Schmithals, W.** *Gnosticism in Corinth.* **Scholem, G.** *Jewish Gnosticism, Merkabah Mysticism and Talmudic Tradition.* New York: Jewish Theological Seminary of America, 1960. **Sevenster, J. N.** and **W. C. van Unnik,** eds. *Studia Paulina in honorem Johannis de Zwaan.* Haarlem: de Erven F. Bohn N. V., 1953. **Smith, N. G.** "The Thorn That Stayed. An Exposition of 2 Cor 12:7–9." *Int* 13 (1959) 409–16. **Spittler, R. P.** "The Limits of Ecstasy: An Exegesis of 2 Corinthians 12:1–10." In *Current Issues in Biblical and Patristic Interpretation,* in honor of Merrill C. Tenney, ed. G. F. Hawthorne, 259–66. Grand Rapids: Eerdmans, 1975. **Wilckens, U.** *Weisheit und Torheit.* BHT 26. Tübingen: J. C. B. Mohr, 1959. **Wood, J. E.** "Death at Work in Paul." *EvQ* 54 (1983) 151–55. **Zmijewski, J.** "Kontextbezug und Deutung von 2 Kor 12, 7a: Stilistische und Strukturale Erwägungen zur Lösung eines alten Problems." *BZ* n.s. 21 (1977) 265–77. ———. *Der Stil der paulinischen "Narrenrede."* BBB 52. Köln-Bonn: Hanstein, 1978.

Translation

[1]*I must go on boasting.* [a] *Though it is of no advantage,* [b] *I will come* [c] *to visions and revelations of the Lord.* [2]*I know a man in Christ who fourteen years ago— whether in the body or out of the body, I do not know, only God knows—was caught up to the third heaven.* [3]*And I know that this man—whether in the body or apart from* [d] *the body, I do not know, only God knows—* [4]*was caught up to paradise and he heard unspeakable words which a human being is not permitted to utter.* [5]*I will boast on behalf of this man, but I will not boast on my behalf, except in* [my][e] *weaknesses.* [6]*Even if I should choose to boast,* [f] *I would not be foolish, for I speak the truth. But I refrain* [from boasting] *so that no one will think more of me than what he sees in me* [g] *or hears from me,* [7]*even the extraordinary revelations. Therefore,* [h] *in order that I should not become conceited, I was given a thorn in the flesh, a messenger of Satan, in order to batter me, that I should not become conceited.* [i] [8]*Concerning this I pleaded with the Lord three times to take it away from me.* [9]*And he said to me, "My grace is sufficient for you, for* [my][j] *power is fulfilled* [k] *in weakness." Therefore I will most gladly boast in my weaknesses, in order that the power of Christ*

may rest upon me. [10] *For this reason I delight in weaknesses, in insults, in* [1] *anguish, in persecutions and* [m] *distress, for the sake of Christ; when I am weak, then I am powerful.*

Notes

[a] A few MSS ($\aleph^2$ H vg) have ϵi before $\kappa \alpha v \chi \hat\alpha \sigma \theta \alpha \iota$, though the addition is not likely to be original (Plummer, 339). Our text is supported by P^{46} $\aleph$ B D F G H* 0243 it syr cop (see 11:30). We also find $\delta\epsilon$ for $\delta\epsilon\hat\iota$ in $\aleph$ D* ψ bo. This may be a result of a copyist leaving off the *iota* (Hughes, 428, n. 97). Another variation is $\delta\acute\eta$ for $\delta\epsilon\hat\iota$. This is found in K Athan Chrys. This change may have resulted from the similarity in the sound of $\delta\epsilon\hat\iota$ and $\delta\acute\eta$. But Hughes (ibid.) is correct to admit that the reverse could also be true (see 1 Cor 6:20). Metzger (*Textual Commentary,* 584) believes we have the original in the text of Nestle-Aland[26]. His position is not accepted by all (see Hughes; and Windisch, 367, thinks that the text is corrupt).

[b] The text is supported by P^{46} $\aleph$ B F G 0243 cop. One variation is to have $\sigma v \mu \phi \acute\epsilon \rho \epsilon \iota$ (D*) instead of $\sigma v \mu \phi \acute\epsilon \rho o v$. Also we find $\sigma v \mu \phi \acute\epsilon \rho o v \ \mu o \iota$ (D^1 H ψ it vg).

[c] The use of $\mu \acute\epsilon v$ and $\delta \acute\epsilon$ is to be noted. (See *Comment.*) We find $\gamma \grave\alpha \rho$ in D ψ syr and $\delta \acute\epsilon \ \kappa \alpha \grave\iota$ in B.

[d] $\grave\epsilon \kappa \tau \acute o \varsigma$ is supported by $\aleph$ D^2 F G H ψ 0243. The text (with $\chi \omega \rho \grave\iota \varsigma$) is found only in P^{46} B D*, but it is felt that this is the earliest reading. Most likely $\grave\epsilon \kappa \tau \acute o \varsigma$ was introduced into v 4 as a result of the influence of v 2 (Metzger, ibid., 585).

[e] $\mu o v$ does not appear in the text (P^{46} B D* 0243). In some manuscripts ($\aleph$ D^2 F G ψ Ambst) $\mu o v$ is found after $\tau \alpha \hat\iota \varsigma \ \grave\alpha \sigma \theta \epsilon v \epsilon \acute\iota \alpha \iota \varsigma$. In spite of the text not having $\mu o v$, we have included "my" in brackets, *ad sensum.*

[f] We note that $\theta \acute\epsilon \lambda \omega$ is found in P^{46}.

[g] $\tau \iota$ (P^{46} $\aleph^2$ D* ψ 0243 vg Ambst) is included in the Nestle-Aland[26] text, but it is done so in brackets. The shorter reading ($\aleph$* B D^2 G cop^{sa,bo}) has strong witnesses. It is not too hard to see that $\tau \iota$ is both superfluous and awkwardly placed. This may be the main reason it was dropped (Metzger, ibid., 585).

[h] A question surrounds the first five words of 12:7 ($\kappa \alpha \grave\iota \ \tau \hat\eta \ \grave v \pi \epsilon \rho \beta o \lambda \hat\eta \ \tau \hat\omega v \ \grave\alpha \pi o \kappa \alpha \lambda \acute v \psi \epsilon \omega v$). The issue is whether these words should conclude the sentence begun in 12:6 or should begin a new sentence. Also, there is a question as to whether or not $\delta \iota \acute o$ should be included. This inferential conjunction is absent from P^{46} D ψ it vg syr cop^{sa}. But because of the strength of the Alexandrian witness ($\aleph$ A B G 33 81 1739) and the application of the rule *difficilior lectio potior,* it appears that $\delta \iota \acute o$ should be retained (see Metzger, ibid., and helpful note by Hughes, 448, n. 138). $\delta \iota \acute o$ normally begins a sentence. Thus, if $\delta \iota \acute o$ is retained, then 12:7a should be attached to 12:6. Barrett argues that 12:7a begins a new sentence (313, 314). Zmijewski uses structural analysis to show that 12:7a is part of 12:6 (see "Kontextbezug"; also see by same writer, *Der Stil,* 355–57; and 353, 354 for reasons for believing $\delta \iota \acute o$ is authentic). Metzger believes that some copyists mistakenly began a new sentence with 12:7a and this led to some witnesses omitting $\delta \iota \acute o$ (ibid.).

[i] Some MSS ($\aleph$* A D F G 33) omit the second $\grave\iota v \alpha \ \mu \grave\eta \ \grave v \pi \epsilon \rho \alpha \acute\iota \omega \mu \alpha \iota$ from 12:7. This may be due to some copyist evaluating such a clause as superfluous and unnecessary. It would make more sense to drop this clause from the original than to insert it later on. The clause is found in P^{46} B ψ 81 1739 syr cop goth arm and no doubt reflects Paul's desire to emphasize the reason for the thorn in the flesh.

[j] Later MSS ($\aleph^2$ A^2 D^2 ψ 0243 syr^{bo}), including the TR, read $\grave\eta \ \gamma \grave\alpha \rho \ \delta \acute v v \alpha \mu \iota \varsigma$. This appears as a later addition in order to help clarify the saying (Metzger, ibid., 585). Earlier witnesses (P^{46vid} $\aleph$* A* B D* F G it vg cop goth eth) omit the possessive pronoun $\mu o v$.

[k] $\tau \epsilon \lambda \epsilon i o \hat v \tau \alpha \iota$ is found in $\aleph^2$ D^2 E K L P. The stronger witness supports the text $\tau \epsilon \lambda \epsilon \hat\iota \tau \alpha \iota$ ($\aleph$* A B D* F G).

[l] $\kappa \alpha \grave\iota$ is found before $\grave\alpha v \acute\alpha \gamma \kappa \alpha \iota \varsigma$ in P^{46} $\aleph$*.

[m] The text is supported by P^{46} $\aleph$* B 104 326 1175 1838. Other variant readings are $\kappa \alpha \grave\iota \ \grave\epsilon v$ (0243 630 1739 1881) and $\grave\epsilon v$ ($\aleph^2$ A D G K P ψ 33 614 1241). The first variant reading is simply a result of conflating the text. The second variant reading, namely, the replacing of $\kappa \alpha \grave\iota$ with $\grave\epsilon v$, is more likely an attempt by copyists to continue the series with the preposition $\grave\epsilon v$ (Metzger, ibid., 586).

Form/Structure/Setting

The thrust of what Paul has to say in the present passage is that his strength comes through admission of his weakness. He learned this lesson and shares it with the Corinthians in 12:1–10 in a highly polemical setting. The overall picture of our passage is that Paul has taken up the posture of boasting (12:1*a;* Zmijewski, *Der Stil,* 325). As will be stated, he has been forced to do so by the Corinthians (12:11). Paul sees no value in such boasting (as his opponents evidently do), yet he goes on to relate the incident of his vision (12:1*b*–4). He exhibits concern not to draw attention to himself in this rehearsal by speaking in the third person. Paul knew "this man" who had a heavenly vision. The vision contained words that cannot be uttered by him or any mortal (12:4). In v 5, Paul begins to share with his readers that he is the "mystery" man of 12:2–4. Yet he refrains from using this fact as an opportunity to present his own apostolic person as something of great value. Rather, he turns toward his own weakness in continuity with 11:23–33. Instead of boasting in things that others cannot see, Paul urges his readers to look simply at what they know of him (12:6). (As will be seen, Paul offers demonstrable proofs of his apostleship, namely, his weakness and the fact that he was the one who founded the Corinthian church [Lincoln, *Paradise Now,* 76, 77]. The subject of "proof" [δοκιμή] will arise again in chap. 13). This leads into Paul's famous passage concerning the thorn in the flesh (12:7) and his prayer that it be removed (12:8). Having received an answer of no, Paul then proceeds to remark on the power of God coming through human weakness. In light of this experience (12:9), Paul boasts in his weaknesses, for in such weaknesses the power of Christ rests upon him. He then concludes our present passage by saying that he delights in weaknesses (12:10), for such is the time when he is strong, i.e., to do the work of an apostle (Phil 4:13).

This, in short, is a summary of 12:1–10. But we would be remiss if we failed to examine this passage with the intent to discover the literary style (see Zmijewski, *Der Stil,* 396–411). In 12:1–10, we have a mosaic of literary devices that yields an interesting picture. In this passage Paul is answering a criticism from his opponents, namely, that he boasts little, and even when he boasts, it is only of weakness. Paul's reply is to engage in an *ad hominem* argument. He will presently meet the opponents on their own level and then, in a masterful way, show that it is his ministry, not theirs, that is of God. (Our present passage brings to mind Paul's "opening of his heart" in 6:11–13 [see *Comment* on these verses]. In the earlier passage Paul's thoughts were not kept to himself, but rather he shared more than he intended. In our present passage, Paul again opens up his inner thoughts, this time sharing an experience that up till then was known only to him and God. In 10:13 he had backed away from boasting; now he is urged to it by serious threats to his apostolate at 11:4, 13–15.)

Paul follows 11:33—the lowering of him by his friends via the Damascus wall—with verses that seek to build up "a certain man." In apologetic form 12:1–6*a* appears as an aretalogy, i.e., a tribute of praise in honor of a great man as well as of a hellenistic deity. Paul seems to be building up this person only to point out that such a self-commendation is not the sign of a true apostle. Paul's picture here of a spectacular or even semidivine worker is reminiscent of the sophists (see *Comment* and Betz's argument; but note Zmijewski's [ibid., 379, n. 402; 411] reservations on the ground that the material is disparate). Paul seems to be attacking this way of promoting the Gospel, for 12:7–10 will lead the reader to see that expressing one's weakness is the only acceptable way to follow Christ in his service (see also 13:3–5; see Käsemann, *Die Legitimität,* 64: "this means that he wants to be understood only on the basis of his diakonia"). This final point is not confined only to the last part of 12:1–10. But in an opening irony, Paul introduces the thought in 12:1 that, while he must continue boasting, there is nothing to be gained by it (see J. L. Cheek, "Paul's Mysticism in the Light of Psychedelic Experience," *JAAR* 38 [1970], 381–89).

In 12:2–4 Paul reveals autobiographical information known before only to him and God. Fourteen years earlier (see *Comment* for discussion of the date of this vision) Paul was taken up into the third heaven, namely, paradise. The apostle relates twice that he is yet unsure as to whether this experience took place in the body or outside of it, i.e., with or without sensory perception. All the time he is describing this experience (though his description is vague and mysterious) he uses the third person. This may reflect Paul's Jewish background, or it may simpy suggest that he wants his readers to see that, though he experiences visions and revelations like his opponents, nevertheless the man about whom Paul speaks is not the one he desires to emulate. Windisch, 370, describes the pericope as *Bescheidenheitsstil,* a style that trades on the speaker's modesty, but this is to be questioned; see Zmijewski, ibid., 336. It is doubtful too that Paul is engaged in "the objectifying of the I" (Dunn, *Jesus and the Spirit* [Philadelphia: Westminster Press, 1975], 214, 215), nor is he employing the convention of the pseudonymity of the apocalyptic, in which an anonymous seer transfers his personal experience to a well-known figure (see Lincoln, *Paradise Now,* 75; contra J. Baumgarten, *Paulus und die Apokalyptik,* 143, 144). Paul neither is one who sells his teaching for profit nor baffles his hearers with mystical language simply for pride (like the sophists). Rather, in polemical fashion, 12:4 speaks of the things he knows as an apostle. He has heard inexpressible words. This paradoxical statement could not be verified by the Corinthians. The point is that Paul wants his readers to evaluate him on the basis of nothing except what they can see and hear of him (12:6) (i.e., the demonstrable evidence of his wretched experiences: see above). If Paul can convince them that this is the correct way, then, in turn, they should ask his opponents to provide similar tangible evidence. This is the challenge first posed in 11:21–23. And he trusts that his contest will lead the Corinthians to see that these opponents are indeed false in the sight of God.

In this section (vv 2–4) we note the parallel structures of Paul's two descriptions of his heavenly experience. The first description is found in v 2 and the second in vv 3, 4 (see Zmijewski, *Der Stil,* 335; Rowland, *The Open Heaven,* 381, for comment on the relation of the two vv).

	v 2		vv 3, 4
a)	οἶδα ἄνθρωπον ἐν Χριστῷ	a)	καὶ οἶδα τὸν τοιοῦτον ἄνθρωπον –
b)	πρὸ ἐτῶν δεκατεσσάρων –	b)	– – –
c)	εἴτε ἐν σώματι οὐκ οἶδα,	c)	εἴτε ἐν σώματι
d)	εἴτε ἐκτὸς τοῦ σώματος οὐκ οἶδα,	d)	εἴτε χωρὶς τοῦ σώματος οὐκ οἶδα,
e)	ὁ θεὸς οἶδεν –	e)	ὁ θεὸς οἶδεν –
f)	ἁρπαγέντα τὸν τοιοῦτον	f)	ὅτι ἡρπάγη
g)	ἕως τρίτου οὐρανοῦ	g)	εἰς τὸν παράδεισον
h)	– – –	h)	καὶ ἤκουσεν ἄρρητα ῥήματα, ἅ κτλ.

From this format, it appears that both descriptions are of the same event. V 3 begins with καὶ and some scholars (see *Comment*) think that this "and" introduces an additional vision. But it is doubtful that this is the case. More likely, vv 3, 4 reflect a repetition of the event described in v 2, and the second description is added to create a deeper impression (*Stilempfinden*, a semitic device like a *synthetic parallelism*). We see that Paul is speaking of only one event in vv 2–4 (see *Comment* for fuller discussion).

In 12:5 we have again Paul's use of irony (see 12:1). The man who had this vision can surely boast of greatness, but rather the correct way, according to Paul, is to boast of the nonspectacular, namely, weakness. In 12:5 Paul refers to himself as the man who had the vision. This "introduction" is seen in the somewhat parallel construction of v 5:

ὑπὲρ τοῦ τοιούτου καυχήσομαι,

ὑπὲρ δὲ ἐμαυτοῦ οὐ καυχήσομαι, εἰ μὴ ἐν ταῖς ἀσθενείαις

The last half of the second line points out that Paul has come in weakness (note adversative δέ; see Zmijewski, *Der Stil*, 347). The polemic which started in 12:4 continues in v 5, for Paul has now set himself off from his opponents. He continues this polemic in 12:6, though in a restrained manner. If Paul had boasted about his own accomplishments, he would be truthful, for he had many things of which to be proud. (No doubt Paul was suspicious of the veracity of his opponents' claims as in 11:21–23.) But instead of attacking his opponents in a more energetic manner, Paul begins a transition from the reasons for his being able to boast of himself to the reasons not to do so. The section of 12:7–10 becomes a discussion on weakness. Or, as Betz suggests, it is an "aretalogy of Christ" (see "Aretalogie"). In 12:7–10 Paul will explain that weakness is the way to power and this power comes from Christ, who was "crucified in weakness" (13:4). This has been called "the most celebrated paradox in the New Testament" by E. Fuchs (see Güttgemanns, *Der leidende Apostel*, 167, n. 110).

The idea of the thorn in the flesh has been the source of much discussion (see *Comment* for the various theories concerning the identity of the thorn). Paul is silent with respect to what this "thorn" was. Most likely, the Corinthians knew of what he was speaking. It has been noted that the account of the vision of Paul is placed between the experience of leaving Damascus hurriedly (11:32, 33) and mention of the thorn (Lincoln, *Paradise Now*, 84, 85). The vision is thus tempered and framed by the record of humiliating experiences. The thorn was given to prevent Paul from becoming conceited, literally "too uplifted" (see 11:20). In an indirect manner, Paul is still carrying on the polemic directed at his opponents. Had his opponents offered similar "guarantees" that they too would not be conceited? Or had they simply gloated all the more because of Paul's "thorn"? This becomes even more striking in that Paul was probably ridiculed for his thorn. If it was an illness or physical defect, then his enemies could ask why he could not heal himself (see Jervell on the "sick charismatic," "Der schwache Charismatiker," 196, 197: "Paul is . . . presented as the weak, sick charismatic"). But in a sense Paul is saying he has been healed, for the ailment is from God, and thus in God's power Paul is "made well."

A quick glance at v 7*b* reveals a chiastic, or criss-cross structure,

But to stop here with this observation overlooks the idea that between ἐδόθη and κολαφίζῃ we have another chiasmus (see Zmijewski, *Der Stil*, 366), namely

$$\begin{array}{l} \text{ἐδόθη μοι} \qquad\qquad\qquad \text{σκόλοψ τῇ σαρκί} \\ \text{ἄγγελος σατανᾶ} \qquad\qquad \text{με κολαφίζῃ} \end{array}$$

This second, or inner, chiasmus, highlights the point that the phrase "messenger of Satan" is in apposition to "thorn in the flesh" (Zmijewski, *Der Stil*, 365, n. 299; 366). There is much discussion as to whether the thorn in the flesh refers to an illness of Paul or an opponent of Paul. It is difficult to be certain about either (see *Comment* for discussion of both sides of the issue), but the important thing to remember is that God has given Paul something to keep him weak, in spite of his heavenly vision, and that his weakness (picking up 10:10) becomes the "criterion of ministry" (Jervell, ibid., 197; cf. Käsemann, *Die Legitimität*, 60–64).

From this account Paul, with God's power upon him, had turned weakness into victory. The personal nature of this transformation can be seen from the chiastic structure of 12:9, for the idea of grace and power is related to Paul's own person (O'Collins, "Power," 534; Plummer, 354; Zmijewski, ibid., 377).

$$\begin{array}{ll} \text{A ἀρκεῖ} & \text{C' ἡ γὰρ δύναμις} \\ \text{B σοι} & \text{B' ἐν ἀσθενείᾳ} \\ \text{C ἡ χάρις μου} & \text{A' τελεῖται} \end{array}$$

In a way Paul has experienced a cure, though not in the normal sense of the word. (Betz sees this v [12:9] as a healing oracle, "Aretalogie," 294–97, but Zmijewski's criticisms are well taken, ibid., 379. More apposite is the form of Jewish prayer-speech, e.g., Mark 14:32–36, Jesus in Gethsemane, Windisch, 389; cf. Plummer, 445; Allo, 312; Prümm, *Diakonia* 1:670.) Paul has received the power of Christ because he has accepted the answer of God, and proceeded to minister in spite of the thorn not being removed.

He brings our passage to a climax by using a slogan, a piece of paradox, to argue once more against his opponents. "When I am weak, then I am strong" refutes the position of his opponents. The apostle has shown that if one must boast, then it should only be in weakness, so as to provide an opportunity for God's strength to be manifest (10:17). This is easy to see in light of Paul's parallel constructions of vv 9b, 10. We cite Zmijewski (*Der Stil,* 388) who builds on Windisch (393).

9b: ἥδιστα οὖν . . . ἐν ταῖς ἀσθενείας . . . ἵνα ἐπισκηνώσῃ
                                          [. . . δύναμις τοῦ Χριστοῦ
10a: διὸ εὐδοκῶ . . . . . .   ἀσθενείαις, κτλ. . . . ὑπὲρ Χριστοῦ
10b: ὅταν γὰρ . . . . . .   ἀσθενῶ τότε δυνατός εἰμι

Paul's weaknesses—whether exhibited in his sufferings for the Gospel or centered in the thorn in the flesh—have been his criteria for true apostleship. He has entered into the fray, not in order to boast of his own achievement, but to boast of his weaknesses. By doing so he has offered the Corinthians an alternative to the opponents that harass him. The alternative is strength-based-on-weakness, a theme no doubt foreign to the opponents of Paul, but one that expressed the heart of his Gospel of a crucified Lord (Güttgemanns, ibid., 170: his weakness is the power of the crucified).

Comment

1. καυχᾶσθαι δεῖ, "I must go on boasting." Literally, the text runs "it is necessary to boast." The use of the impersonal verb δεῖ, "it is necessary," alerts the readers that the theme of boasting will remain in front of them. Paul has "boasted" throughout chaps. 10 (vv 8, 13, 15, 16, 17) and 11 (vv 10, 12, 16, 17, 18, 30), and he will continue this theme in our present chapter (vv 1, 5, 6, 9). Paul counterattacked his opponents in the previous chapter by presenting his list of accomplishments (Tasker, 169). He was a Jew of the highest quality (11:21, 22). Moreover, he had the credentials of a true apostle. He had suffered much for the cause of Christ (11:23–28). Yet, Paul was hesitant to boast about himself. Rather, Paul boasted in order to show the power of God. He had written earlier (10:17), "Let him who boasts boast in the Lord." Furthermore, in 11:30 Paul paves the way for similar boasting. He boasts in order to show his weakness. Denney sees Paul choosing to boast in things that men would judge as weak and shameful (343).

Paul was driven to boast (12:11). He has played the fool (γέγονα ἄφρων) for he has taken on the practice of boasting as the world does (κατὰ σάρκα, not κατὰ κύριον: see on 11:17; Windisch, 368). We note that in 12:1 Paul will continue this boasting, an idea suggested by the present tense. It is linked with 11:17 (Bultmann, 220). καυχᾶσθαι, "to boast," is a present infinitive, possibly Paul's way of showing that he will not cease to boast at this time (see 12:11). But there is a method to Paul's line of attack. He has to show that he is not inferior to the so-called "super-apostles" (11:5; 12:11). To do so, Paul boasts as do his opponents. But Paul's boasting will ultimately lead to God's glory, something his opponents do not set as their aim, in his estimation (10:12). It appears that Paul felt it imperative to boast in order both to gain the attention of the Corinthians and to overthrow the position of his opponents, though he had his doubts about its effectiveness.

Barrett views the sentence "I must go on boasting" as a Corinthian watchword (306). This is not an untenable position, for Paul has a habit of using slogans (see 1 Cor 6:12, 13; chap. 7 and, in our letter, on 5:18–21). If Paul was responding to the "mode of operation" of his opponents, it makes sense that he would use this watchword. The main thrust of the opening words of 12:1 is that Paul evidently considered boasting the best way to overcome the tide of opposition that was against him. He uses the opponents' term but "undercuts its value and hints at the genre of his language" by his addition in 12:1*b* (Fallon, 105).

οὐ συμφέρον μέν, "though it is of no advantage." We have already discussed the textual variations of this clause. There still remains the question of punctuation (see *Notes*). The KJV/AV puts a full stop after μέν. But this is not the best choice. Most likely, our present clause is a parenthesis between "I must go on boasting" and "I will go on to visions and revelations of the Lord" (Barrett, 306, 307; Zmijewski, *Der Stil*, 325, 326). This is seen in the construction of 12:1 by noting Paul's use of μέν and δέ. These particles bind together the second and the third clauses of our verse. Robertson calls the participle συμφέρον (from συμφέρειν) an accusative absolute (*Grammar*, 1130). But the syntax of this clause is not the major point for concern.

One question that surfaces is why the writer continues with such "foolish discourse" (as boasting: Héring, 89) if it is of no advantage. This would be a valid query if Paul is to be taken literally. Paul's normal usage of συμφέρειν usually describes the welfare of the Christian community, not of the individual (8:10; 1 Cor 6:12; 10:23; 12:7). Did Paul really feel that his boasting would build up the church? This is an issue put by Schlatter, *Paulus*, 658, who speaks of the "criterion of usefulness to the church" as a ruling factor in the discussion; it corresponds with οἰκοδομή in Paul's earlier writing to the Corinthians. (So Baumgarten, *Paulus*, 145, 146, who sets Paul's ecclesiology over against the rivals' "enthusiasm" and interest in personal ends.) In an indirect way, he does wish above all to build up the church (13:10), (but we will see that Paul apparently saw little value in dwelling on the visionary aspect of his life as an aid in edifying the church [Lincoln, *Paradise Now*, 72]). This is apparent if one refrains from interpreting these words with sterile literalness. Instead, the phrase "of no advantage" is most likely a polemical statement against his opponents, who have boasted to aid their own cause. Boasting of one's self is not a sign of apostleship. Paul sees boasting as useless unless in the final analysis it deflects glory away from man and directs it toward God. As we shall see, Paul's apostleship is marked by weakness, even in boasting. The "thorn in the flesh" is a means to lead to God's glory, not Paul's.

For Paul, boasting is of no advantage in and of itself. Filson is correct to note that Paul is attempting to show the Corinthians that they are wrong to see good in the boasting of the false apostles (405). If this last point is true, then the words "of no advantage"—if taken literally—do not reflect the total meaning of Paul. True, the apostle expresses his distaste for boasting by uttering these words. Nevertheless, he also senses that desperate situations call for desperate measures (Filson, ibid.). Possibly Paul has the same ambivalent emotions in his approach to boasting as he did when he wrote the painful, or severe, letter (2:4; 7:8). When Paul constructed the severe letter, he did so with much apprehension. Moreover, he was unsure of the outcome, for he might have been totally rejected by the Corinthians. Likewise, he cannot, with exactness, measure the outcome of his boasting. Yet, he feels it is a necessary evil. As Barrett writes, "It is not expedient to boast, but it might be even more inexpedient not to boast" (306). There may be a touch of irony in 12:1*b*, especially as at v 6 Paul will acknowledge that he is speaking only "as a fool."

ἐλεύσομαι δὲ εἰς ὀπτασίας καὶ ἀποκαλύψεις κυρίου, "I will come to visions and revelations of the Lord." If our assessment of 12:1*b* is correct, then Paul retains some embarrassment as he writes these words to the Corinthians. As a rule, Paul does not brag about his visions from the Lord. We must not let the several references in the Acts of the Apostles lead us to think otherwise about Paul (18:9, 10; 22:17–21; 23:11; 27:23, 24; of interest to the Corinthians may have been the vision at Corinth, in which Paul is strengthened by the Lord in a vision [ὅραμα; Acts 18:9] to stay in the city; yet it remains true that for Luke Paul is both a great miracle worker and a suffering figure who is by no means rescued through miracles: see Jervell, "The Signs of an Apostle," 85). Hughes is right in appreciating the event of 12:2–4 as possibly the "most intimate and sacred" of all Paul's religious experiences (428). Yet, Paul has been forced to share this event, and this sharing is accomplished through boasting (12:11).

To be more specific, Paul is using the *ad hominem* form of argumentation. He has already set down that the purpose of his boasting is to highlight his weaknesses (11:30). In 12:1 the apostle is reporting that boasting will help no one. Yet, Paul feels that he must take his opponents head-on if he is to convince the Corinthians that he remains the true apostle. In short, Paul shows that he too has revelations and visions. (The use of the plural ὀπτασίαι, "visions," and ἀποκαλύψεις, "revelations," suggests that Paul's original intention was to delineate several visionary experiences [Lincoln, *Paradise Now*, 72], but perhaps his reluctance to boast of such experiences led him to limit his "list" to only one.) He received "special" revelations. These revelations were understood by Paul as gifts from God (κυρίου is *gen. auctoris*). They were not given in order to authenticate his apostleship. Paul never uses his visions and revelations as signs to promote himself as "somebody special." (Bruce thinks that, in addition to confronting the position that the false apostles had visions and revelations, Paul may also be addressing the accusation that his ministry was based on an illusory vision, namely, the experience on the Damascus Road [246] in contrast perhaps to the "super-apostles.")

Paul's opponents could have leveled the charge against Paul that his lack of "visions" was proof that he was not a true apostle. But lack of frequent reference to visions and revelations is not grounds for concluding that Paul had little or no experience in this realm (Lincoln, "Paul the Visionary," 205). Rather, we have argued that Paul's reluctance to speak of visions stems from his desire to avoid drawing too much attention to himself. Paul proceeds with the account of his vision only with some embarrassment.

ἐλεύσομαι, "I will come," is the future of ἔρχεσθαι: εἰς, "to," helps to demonstrate the direction in which Paul's thinking is going. Though Paul is against boasting, nevertheless he comes to visions and revelations of the Lord. We may note that there is not a great difference between ὀπτασία, "vision," and ἀποκάλυψις "revelation." They are interchangeable terms (so Michaelis, *TDNT* 5:352, 353, who notes how at 12:7 Paul speaks only of ἀποκαλύψεις, "revelations"). The two words may be taken from the opponents' vocabulary (so Baumgarten, ibid., 137; perhaps they point to the "realized eschatology" of the gnosticizing opponents at Corinth; they may have claimed their experiences as the highest form of ecstasy, perhaps associated with glossolalia; so Schmithals, *Gnosticism*, 209–11). The latter word, ἀποκάλυψις, crops up frequently in his writings. Several times in eschatological contexts Paul employs this word (Rom 2:5; 8:19; 1 Cor 1:7; cf. 2 Thess 1:7, but in a way different from here; Bultmann, 220). Also, it is used in reference to his conversion (Gal 1:12), as well as to a special revelation that preceded a journey to Jerusalem (Gal 2:2). From this, it is apparent that "revelation" is of wider importance to Paul than "vision" (Denney, 346). But we should not press this too far (Barrett, 307). Plummer perhaps captures the flavor needed when addressing the subject of visions and revelations, for he remarks that not all visions reveal something and not all revelations require visions (338; see also Tasker, 170). But we should note that in 12:1 Paul appears to be saying that the vision of 12:2–4 is a source of revelation. (It is interesting to note, however, that 12:9 was probably a direct revelation, without the aid of a vision [Lincoln, *Paradise Now*, 72].)

This last point is seen from the construction in [εἰς] ὀπτασίας καὶ ἀποκαλύψεις κυρίου, "visions and revelations *of the Lord.*" Most scholars view this genitive as subjective, not objective (Barrett, 307; Plummer, 338; Bruce, 246; Tasker, 169, 170; Bultmann, 220; Lincoln, *Paradise Now*, 73; see also Zmijewski, *Der Stil*, 327, 328, "a genitive of origination," also see 330, 331; Georgi, *Die Gegner*, 298, n. 1, tries to see a distinction between Paul's use of κυρίου and the opponents' understanding; for him "the Lord" gave the revelations, whereas they took κυρίου as genitive of possession related to their transformation into Christ's image [?3:18] like a glorification). That is, more than likely Paul is speaking of visions and revelations given by the Lord rather than visions that see the Lord. But Lincoln is right to warn against too sharp of a distinction here ("Paul the Visionary," 205, 206). The author of the visions could also be the object of them (see also, Hughes, 428, n. 97; Dunn, *Jesus and the Spirit* [Philadelphia: Westminster Press, 1975], 414, n. 88, who argues that the genitive of 12:1 may have been deliberately ambiguous so that both thoughts are to be included).

It may be assumed that the opponents gloried in their transcendental experiences of "visions and revelations," though Windisch (368) is disposed to deny this ("it is nowhere *here* indicated that the opponents also can boast concerning such visions"). But Schmithals, *Gnosticism*, 209, is certainly correct to answer this denial, by pointing out that Paul's tack is not different from the one adopted in 11:22, 23; i.e., the comparison is "they—I too" or "they—I all the more." The difference, however, lies in the climax of the pericope, in v 9 where divine power in human weakness will be claimed as the "sole basis of the apostolic existence" (Baumgarten, ibid., 144), i.e., in a word from the Lord, not in a vision sent by the Lord. This is Paul's response; thereby he reduces the visionary experience to a revelation with a "word-of-God" character.

2. οἶδα ἄνθρωπον ἐν Χριστῷ πρὸ ἐτῶν δεκατεσσάρων, "I know a man in Christ who fourteen years ago." Immediately we are struck by Paul's use of the third person construction. It is accepted that Paul is referring to himself, but this has not prevented some helpful suggestions as to why Paul employed this use (see Zmijewski, *Der Stil,* 336). One idea is to see that Paul is reflecting the rabbinical use of "this man" for "I" (Str-B 3:531). Also, some see that Paul is distinguishing between two men within himself, namely, Paul the visionary and Paul the man (Wendland, 219). But Héring is right to counter that it was the man, not the visionary that was taken up (90). That is, the self did not necessarily leave the body (see Windisch, 369, 370). Another argument against this Philonic-hellenistic distinction (maintained by Reizenstein, *Hellenistic Mystery-Religions,* tr. J. E. Steely [Pittsburgh: Pickwick, 1978], 82, 83) is that Paul *remembers* the revelation, a point against the concept of two personalities. If Paul had a personality split into two, then it is unlikely he would remember the incident. An illuminating proposal has been given by Betz, who identifies the parallels between this parody of an ascension narrative (12:2–4; *Der Apostel Paulus,* 84–92) and Paul's line of reasoning in these verses. Paul is reacting, says Betz (ibid., 89), to opponents who are roughly congruent in style with the sophists of Socrates' time. We may recall that there was a reaction to the Socratic school that was centered in a group of teachers who took on the occupation of being a "wise person." These itinerant teachers taught for a fee. They were characterized as emphasizing material success, as well as using their influence for personal reasons.

Betz goes on to describe how the true philosopher used irony to vindicate himself. For the true philosopher, poverty and weakness authenticated the truth of his claim (ibid., 15–18, 20–38). Normally, this person would avoid boasting, but if forced to, would defend himself against false charges by boasting and by "playing the fool." In doing so, the philosopher would refrain from referring to himself directly and thus downplay his own accomplishment (ibid., 75–82). It is obvious that there are some similarities to Paul's situation. His opponents underline the material aspect of the ministry as well as use influence (in this case claimed from the Jerusalem hierarchy) as a weapon against the apostle. Likewise, Paul appears as one who "plays the fool" in order to show up his opponents as charlatans. But perhaps Betz has overstated his case, for it is doubtful that Paul was consciously following the Socratic line of thinking in this apology (Lincoln, "Paul the Visionary," 206). Barrett is probably right to notice an inner motivation for Paul's defense that is independent of tradition (307). And Kleinknecht, *Der leidende Gerechtfertigte,* 301–3, points to the biographical element in this *signum apostolicum* (see A. Henrichs's review of Betz in *JBL* 94 [1975] 312).

More likely, Paul's use of the third person is a means of reflecting his embarrassment (or reluctance) at boasting of what he has done or been a part of (see Furnish, 542–44). This makes sense in light of what is to follow. Paul will write in the *divinum passivum* in 12:7. What has happened has been done to Paul; he did nothing to obtain the vision (see Filson, 405). This can be seen from the phrase ἐν Χριστῷ, "in Christ." It is more than simply a reference to being "a Christian" (so Barrett, 308). It is Paul's way of showing that it was in Christ's power that the following visions and revelations took place (Plummer, 340). Nothing of Paul's ability is spoken of here. This is yet another example of how all Paul's actions point to Christ, since he is a person "(who lives) in Christ" (Allo, 304, on the ellipse). Tasker relates that experience to being "in Christ," which could be also interpreted to mean that any Christian can have this privilege of a vision, for there are no "favorites" in the economy of the church (170); but 11:12 denies that Paul's apostolate ranks on a par with that of his rivals.

πρὸ ἐτῶν δεκατεσσάρων, "who fourteen years ago." The vividness with which Paul remembers this event is evident in that he can remember the time when it took place. The time of fourteen years before the writing of this epistle (or at least before the writing of chaps. 10–13) places the period about A.D. 44 (Hughes, 430; Filson, 405; Denney, 347; Barrett suggests A.D. 40, 308; Lincoln, *Paradise Now*, 77, places it between A.D. 41 and 44; see R. E. Osborne, "St. Paul's Silent Years," *JBL* 84 [1965] 59–65). Whatever the date of Paul's experience, it was well before the founding of the Corinthian church. What remains a mystery is to what event specifically Paul is referring.

With the date of A.D. 44 in mind, it appears we can rule out every other visionary experience of Paul recorded in the NT. His conversion on the Damascus road, an experience that apparently Paul was more than willing to rehearse (at least from Acts 9:3–19; 22:6–10; 26:12–18), certainly took place long before A.D. 44. We can also dismiss the event of the trance Paul fell into described in Acts 22:17–21, for in this account the Lord in a vision came to Paul. We read nothing there of Paul being "caught up to the Lord" (Denney, 347, 348). Events that surely were later than A.D. 44 are the vision of the Macedonian man entreating Paul to come and help (Acts 16:9) and the vision he had in Corinth (Acts 18:9–10; Hughes, 430). The period of "fourteen years" found in Gal 2:1 is probably only coincidental and has nothing to do with 2 Cor 12:2 (see J. Knox, *Chapters in the Life of Paul* [New York: Abingdon-Cokesbury Press, 1950] 78, n. 3).

One suggestion for the occasion of the experience described in 12:2–4 is that it transpired while Paul was in Antioch (Hughes, 430, 431; Denney, 347). We read that Paul and Barnabas remained in Antioch a whole year (Acts 11:26). There is possibly a connection seen between the ecstatic experience (cf. 12:2–4) and the commissioning of Paul and Barnabas as missionaries (Acts 13:2, 3; so Allo, 304; Windisch, 369, 370). Perhaps in some small way, Paul related to the Christians at Antioch that he had received a vision at the hand of the Lord. Bruce only allows that we simply have a reference to an obscure period between the time when Paul was sent to Tarsus (Acts 9:30) and the meeting with Barnabas at Antioch (Acts 11:26; this can possibly be reconstructed from Galatians where Bruce places the visionary experience of Paul between Paul's departure for Syria-Cilicia [1:21] and his second post-conversion visit to Jerusalem [2:1], [Bruce, 246]; some strange proposals have been made to argue that Paul's spirit left his body at his stoning [Acts 14:19], or that he was one of the prophets mentioned in Acts 11:28, 29). All in all, we are better to recognize just how much conjecture is involved and agree with Denney that there is nothing that we know of the apostle with which we can identify his experience of 12:2–4 (347).

εἴτε ἐν σώματι οὐκ οἶδα, εἴτε ἐκτὸς τοῦ σώματος οὐκ οἶδα, ὁ θεὸς οἶδεν, "—whether in the body or out of the body, I do not know, only God knows." As Paul is relating the experience of "this man" (namely himself) he breaks his thought and inserts a parenthesis. It is as though Paul catches himself and wants to make a sudden (albeit too short) reference to the event of his vision. Barrett remarks in some detail that the words of this parenthesis are not without reason (308, 309). That is, there was a reason why Paul makes a statement concerning being "in" or "out of the body." On the one hand, Paul does not want to give an indication that he thinks the body is inherently evil. We saw this in our discussion of 5:1–10, where Paul sought to show that the whole person is involved in salvation, both body and spirit. In other words, Paul was probably well aware of the Corinthian-gnostic view that a religious experience was invalid unless it happened while one was out of the body (Philo wrote of Moses as having laid aside his body, *De Somn.* [1:36]). On the other hand, it could be that Paul was not intending to deny that one could have an "out of body" experience. Bultmann suggests that Paul's use of "body" (σῶμα) shows that the apostle left open the possibility of the soul's leaving the body for an encounter with the spiritual world (*Theology* 1:203). Elsewhere, Bultmann, in his commentary, 221, has a different idea to explain the expression: Paul is thought of as viewing his experience at a distance, as though he were simply an onlooker. Cf. Käsemann, ibid., 55: "to distance oneself from the event as reported." Such a "distancing" may also be seen in the contrast "I do not know . . . God knows" (Zmijewski, ibid., 337).

Paul may be relating his ignorance of his state at the time of this event (Denney, 347, 348). He simply is not sure whether he went to the "third heaven" in body or in spirit (this may suggest that Paul was alone at the time, for if others had been with him, they could have answered the question of whether or not his body remained in this world; see Plummer, 342). To say that ὁ θεὸς οἶδεν, "only God knows," may be an attempt by Paul to state his ignorance of the matter. Because he refrains from giving an opinion one way or the other his opponents cannot totally reject his boasting. By not eliminating the possibility that Paul could have remained in the body, he avoids undercutting the validity of his other visions. Moreover, it was not uncommon to boast of having come into bodily contact with the divine (Jewett, *Anthropological Terms,* 278). Also, by leaving the door open to an "out-of-the-body" experience, he affirms his teaching of 5:1–10 that there is existence for the soul apart from the body, and that this existence is "one of perceptive consciousness" (Hughes, 431). This latter point no doubt would have caught the attention of the opponents. To have an out-of-the-body experience would have satisfied some Corinthians (Jewett, ibid.). As we shall see, Paul never explains in detail this event. Thus, Paul may have carefully constructed the parenthesis of 12:2 (and 12:3) in order not to "prejudice" his account with either side (those wanting an "in-the-body" experience or those who seek an "out-of-the-body" one) by taking a stand on the issue (Jewett, ibid.). (See also Saake, esp. 405; also *NovT* 15 [1973] 154.) On the other side, Schmithals, *Gnosticism,* 211 (followed by Baumgarten, "Paulus," 143), sees great significance in the second phrase, ἐκτὸς τοῦ σώματος, suggesting that Paul considered it possible that he did not leave the body. Hence Paul is deliberately denying the central gnostic concern of dualism with its practice of a celestial journey apart from somatic encumbrance. There may be intended mockery here; in reply to his opponents' certain belief in the soul's heavenward ascent, Paul professes not to know.

Aside from the anthropological considerations of this parenthesis, there is a syntactical detail to note. The first use of σῶμα in this parenthesis is without the definite article, but the second has one. Plummer submits that ἐν σώματι is a colloquial expression, paralleling Paul's use of ἐν with οἴκῳ, "indoors, at home" (1 Cor 11:34; 14:35). For Plummer this anarthrous use of σῶμα is adverbial (343). Possibly the explanation is simply that ἐκτός is an example of an improper preposition. This is also seen in 12:3 where Paul replaces ἐκτός with χωρίς, "apart from." In both cases it appears we have improper prepositions, for "proper" prepositions do not always require the article (see Moule, *Idiom Book*, 83, 87, 114, 207).

ἁρπαγέντα τὸν τοιοῦτον ἕως τρίτου οὐρανοῦ, "was caught up to the third heaven." After the parenthesis, Paul completes his thought: "A certain man fourteen years before had been caught up to the third heaven." The use of ἁρπαγέντα (aorist passive participle of ἁρπάζειν [the same verb ἁρπάζειν is also found in v 4.]; such language reflects the idea of a "rapture of visions" [Lincoln, *Paradise Now*, 81]; see *Apoc. Mos.* 37:5; also the idea of "catch up" is found in Wisd Sol 4:11; Acts 8:39; Rev 12:5), "caught up," is limited in Pauline literature. It is only found in our present verse and in 1 Thess 4:17, when Paul speaks of living Christians being caught up with Christ in the air. In Paul's time it was not uncommon to hear of someone being "raptured" into heaven (see Lietzmann, 153; also Betz, *Lukian*, 38, 142, 169). Much of apocalyptic literature is the product of the seer being granted insight into truths that are in heaven (C. K. Barrett, "New Testament Eschatology," *SJT* 6 [1953] 138, 139). Barrett makes out a case for this when he cites several sources that parallel Paul's experience (309, 310). These sources are found in apocalyptic writings such as *1 Enoch* (39:3–4; 52:1), *2 Enoch* (7:1) and *3 Apoc. Bar.* (2:2). But we also come across mystical speculation in rabbinic literature. (Cf. Bowker, " 'Merkabah' Visions." In *Ḥag.* 14b there are four men who entered into paradise: Ben ʿAzzai, Ben Zoma, Acher, and R. Akiba. Of these four only R. Akiba returned unscathed: see Scholem, *Jewish Gnosticism*, 14–19; also see P. Schäfer, "New Testament and Hekhalot Literature: The Journey into Heaven in Paul and Merkavah Mysticism," *JJS* 35 [1984] 19–35; we shall see below that in 12:4 Paul describes his location as paradise, having changed the nomenclature from his earlier use of "third heaven.") Not surprisingly Barrett reports that hellenistic mysticism contains a similar phenomenon as found in Plato (see *Republic* 10:614–21; see too Philo *De Migr. Abr.* 34–35; *De Spec. Leg.* 3:1–2). Thus, Barrett is right when he concludes that Paul's rapture experience is not necessarily out of the ordinary. What is surprising is that Paul will soon depreciate the value of this experience (Barrett, 310).

What becomes a difficult question for scholars is one that centers on Paul's intended meaning behind his use of ἕως τρίτου οὐρανοῦ, "to the third heaven." A survey of extant literature does not really answer the question. The New

Testament is relatively silent concerning the number of heavens in Jewish cosmology. We find in Eph 1:10 the plural οὐρανοί, "heavens," but this does little to help us (Lincoln, "Paul the Visionary," 213). It has been noted that the plural "heavens," found in the New Testament, is probably the result of the Hebrew שָׁמַיִם, šāmayim, "heavens," which is dual in form. In Ps 63:33 the psalmist describes God as riding upon the "heaven of heavens." This verse has led Hughes (see 432–34), who builds upon Bengel, to hold that Paul's reference to the third heaven is in line with the threefold division in the Old Testament (cf. Neh 9:6; 1 Kings 8:27; 2 Chron 2:6; 6:18; Ps 148:4; also see C. R. Schoonhoven, *The Wrath of Heaven* [Grand Rapids: Eerdmans, 1966] 64). In this threefold division there is the atmospheric heaven, a stellar heaven (or firmament) and the limitless, or spiritual, heaven, where God is located (Lincoln, *Paradise Now*, 77, 78; Hughes, ibid.). If this evaluation is correct, then we could say that Paul ascended to the highest heaven. But this conclusion is not certain, for there were other conceptions of the number of heavens (Rowland, *The Open Heaven*, 381).

At the time of Paul and in Jewish antiquity, the idea of a sevenfold division of heaven was becoming popular. This concept can be found in *T. Levi* (3:1), *2 Enoch* (8–22) and *Asc. Isa.* (9). We also can locate the idea of seven heavens in rabbinic literature, such as the *Ḥag.* 11*b* (see *Pesiq. R.* 5; *Midr. Ps* 92; *Ab. R. Nat.* 37; *Pirqe R. El.* [154*b*]; see H. Traub *TDNT* 5:511–12). But three and seven are not the only numbers considered. The numbers *five* (see *3 Apoc. Bar.* 11:1, "And taking me from this, the angel led me to the fifth heaven") and *ten* (*2 Enoch* 20:3*b*, "and on the tenth heaven") are also suggested as identifying the levels of heavenly existence. With these differing accounts before them, some scholars have suggested that we simply cannot know the number of heavens in Paul's mind at the time of this writing (Bruce, 247; Filson, 405; see especially Barrett, 310, though he concedes that three seems a good possibility [Str-B, 3:531, 532]). Though certainty may remain beyond our grasp, it does appear probable that Paul had three heavens in mind.

The closing point of the preceding paragraph can be seen by Paul's use of ἕως, "up to." At first Plummer thinks that this "improper preposition" is not enough to prove that the third heaven is, in Paul's mind, the highest (343, 344). But Tasker is correct to conclude (and Plummer later comes to a similar conclusion) that it would seem illogical for Paul to write of such blessedness if he were not in the ultimate heaven (171). That is, Paul would be open to the criticism that his vision and revelation were inadequate if the Corinthians believed there to be seven heavens and Paul only "journeyed" to number three. This argument was observed long ago by Irenaeus (*Adv. Haer.* 2, 30, 7). Thus, logic dictates that ἕως, in all probability, was used by Paul to show that he—whether in the body or out of it—was raptured up to the highest heaven, namely, the third heaven. This conclusion is also supported in light of the use of ἕως, as found elsewhere in the New Testament. When used with the genitive, the preposition denotes "as far as" (Moule, *Idiom Book*, 85; BGD, 335). While one could argue that "as far as" does not say with certainty that Paul had reached the limit, our assumption appears to be the position with the least questions left unanswered. The use of ἕως in the New Testament (Acts 1:8; cf. *Ps. Sol.* 17:14) suggests that a limit had been reached. Also, in light of our preceding discussion, it seems that Paul needed to reach the zenith if he was to retain his credibility. Moreover, as we shall see in 12:4, the idea of "paradise" which is to be equated with the "third heaven" (Zmijewski, ibid., 339, but denied by Prümm, *Diakonia* 1:650) suggests even more that Paul had reached the upper level. From our viewpoint, we see Paul as probably thinking of a threefold division of heaven.

3. καὶ οἶδα τὸν τοιοῦτον ἄνθρωπον, "And I know that this man." This sentence begins a verse that parallels or repeats the event described in v 2. Plummer concludes that the opening καὶ strongly suggests that Paul is speaking of two separate events, one that took place in the third heaven and one in paradise, or at least two separate stages of the same event (344). Either hypothesis was popular with the patristic writers (Clem. Alex. *Strom.* 1:5; Irenaeus *Adv. Haer.* 2:55; Tert. *De praesc. haer.* 24) as well as with some modern commentators (Denney, 349; Plummer, 344; Filson, 406; Schlatter, *Paulus*, 662, 663). These positions take on strength if one considers paradise as distinguished from the third heaven, for then it is quite apparent that Paul's writing has been accurately perceived. But this has not been accepted by all. Some argue that paradise and the third heaven are equivalent (Hodge, 283; Windisch, 371, 372; Tasker, 171; Barrett, 310; Hughes, 435). Moreover, since there is only one date given (the fourteen years in 12:1) and only one description of the content (12:4, albeit Paul shares little with his readers), it appears that in 12:2 and 4 Paul is speaking of the same event (Lincoln, "Paul the Visionary," 211). Our present verse is a continuation of the subject of 12:2. See pp. 391, 392 and Zmijewski, ibid., 335, for a line-by-line comparison of v 2 with vv 3, 4, drawn from Windisch, 371.

The use of this connecting καὶ, if the last position is adopted, does not go unnoticed. It does suggest the idea of additional information, but not in terms of a second experience or stage. Rather, the καὶ suggests that Paul has added information concerning the third heaven. Namely, he clarifies somewhat his use of the term "third heaven" and describes it as paradise (see below). Hence, Paul resumes his retelling of a past experience (Hughes, 437).

εἴτε ἐν σώματι, κτλ. "—whether in the body or apart from the body, I do not know, only God knows." For the second time in a short span, Paul inserts a parenthesis into his letter. This second "change of direction," though not verbatim with the first parenthesis in 12:2b, is nevertheless congruent in thought (Barrett, 310). The only differences are that in 12:3 Paul uses the words οὐκ οἶδα, "I do not know," only once, and he uses χωρίς, "apart from," instead of ἐκτός. Neither change alters the meaning as described in 12:2. This would lead us to believe, in light of our earlier discussion, that Paul uses 12:3 to continue his description (begun in 12:2) of the visionary experience that transpired fourteen years before the writing of chaps. 10–13. We must not fail to see again Paul's use of the third person, as well as his admission of ignorance concerning the state he was in during this ecstatic experience, both evidently polemical devices to play down the opponents' claim to ecstatic experience as a validation of ministry. Paul, on the contrary, finds no edificatory value for the congregation in his experience.

4. ὅτι ἡρπάγη εἰς τὸν παράδεισον, "that was caught up to paradise." In this

verse Paul has changed the aorist participle ἁρπαγέντα (12:2) to the aorist passive indicative of ἁρπάζειν, namely, ἡρπάγη. But we must make note of how both uses of the verb, as well as διδόναι, "give" (found in 12:7 as ἐδόθη, "was given to me"), reflect passivity on Paul's part (the passive is also seen in 12:12, [κατειργάσθη]). We see that the agent of these passive verbs can be identified from their context as God. This use of the *passivum divinum* is important for understanding Paul's thought. His boasting cannot glorify himself, for God is the hidden agent behind these things. He took Paul up to the third heaven, namely paradise, as well as placed a thorn in his life. God also works through Paul (12:12). This fits well with our earlier discussion. Paul is God's apostle, for God has both proclaimed the message of reconciliation through the apostle (5:18–20), and ministered in service to the Corinthians through the same apostle. Now, however, he steps up the presentation because he is in a serious conflict with his opponents. So intense is this conflict that Paul shares an event in his life perhaps, up to this time, unknown except to the Lord and himself.

Paul states that he was caught up to παράδεισος, "paradise." This word is probably Persian in origin, meaning an enclosure or a nobleman's park. Both the Hebrew (פרדס, *pardēs;* cf. Eccl 2:5) and the Greek (παράδεισος) languages borrowed the word. Not all literature places the paradise in the third heaven. Sometimes we read that it is found in the seventh heaven (*Asc. Isa.* 9:7; Ḥag. 12*b*). More likely, though, Paul considers the third heaven and paradise the same. Just such an equation is found in 2 Enoch 8 and in *Apoc. Mos.* 37:5 (see also J. Jeremias, *TDNT* 5:765–73). An interesting note is that the LXX renders the earthly Garden of Eden (גן עדן, *gan ʿēdēn*) as παράδεισος (see Gen 2 and 3). The OT does not refer to the garden as the abode for the righteous after death or a final resting place for them. The development of the term is seen in apocalyptic literature (*T. Abr.* 20; *1 Enoch* 60:7–8; 61:12; 70:4; *2 Enoch* 9:1–42:3; *Apoc. Abr.* 21:6–7; see Windisch, 372, 373).

The word "paradise" occurs only three times in the New Testament. In addition to our present text, we find it in Jesus' statement to the penitent thief (Luke 23:43) and in Rev 2:7 ("To him who overcomes, I will give the right to eat from the tree of life, which is the paradise of God"). It appears certain that the paradise mentioned in Revelation and the paradise of our own text are one and the same. We might even link the paradise of Rev 2:7 with Rev 22:1–5, a description that reminds us of the paradise that was originally lost. The heavenly paradise of Rev 2:7 is located in the heavenly garden (Bruce, 247; cf. *T. Levi* 28:10; 4 Ezra 4:7–8; *3 Apoc. Bar.* 4:8; Ḥag. 15*b;* Gen. Rab. 65). The mention of paradise in Luke 23:43 offers us no location, but there is no doubt that it refers to the gathering of the righteous after death (Bruce; see Origen, *De Princ.* 2. 9, 6).

Hughes suggests that Paul's shift from "the third heaven" to "paradise" is for added information, that in this explication Paul discloses the nature of the third heaven (437). We are not privy to what Paul heard, as we shall see. Paul is granted the secrets of both the intermediate state and the glorious consummation (Lincoln, "Paul the Visionary," 214; but since he cannot reveal the content of the vision described in 12:2–4, this may be why Paul is so hesitant to expound the state of the believer after death [see 5:1–10]).

H. Bietenhard is too rigid when he concludes that Paul saw a vision of the world to come but not of the future (*Die himmlische Welt im Urchristentum und Spätjudentum* [Tübingen: Mohr, 1951] 167). We must not draw so sharp a distinction between the life hereafter and the future. Paul's understanding of eschatology will not permit it. (See Lincoln, *Paradise Now*, 84, who interprets 12:1–10 as a form of realized eschatology. But the drift of the passage is more antienthusiastic and opposed to a presently fulfilled eschatology; see Baumgarten, ibid., 146.) But we also must be cautious and concede that whatever teaching we have on these subjects (both the hereafter and the future), little has been related to us by Paul from the experience of 12:2–4. Whether because of being forbidden to speak by God concerning these things or because he was unable to translate heavenly thoughts into human language (see below), Paul shares no details with his readers. More pointedly the "inexpressible words" are a counterblast to gnosticizing secrets putatively revealed to the opponents.

καὶ ἤκουσεν ἄρρητα ῥήματα ἃ οὐκ ἐξὸν ἀνθρώπῳ λαλῆσαι, "and he heard unspeakable words which a human being is not permitted to utter." Unlike his gnostic and mystical counterparts, Paul says practically nothing about what he saw or heard while in paradise. Whether or not Paul created a play on words (Plummer thinks so, 345) is unclear, though we do notice paradoxical language. Paul heard words that are ἄρρητα (from ἄρ-ρητα, BDF § 11.1), "ineffable," "unspeakable" (KJV/AV), "inexpressible" (NIV). The use of ἄρρητα, with ἀ-*privatum*, so "unutterable" (see Barrett, 311), is similar to that use in the mystery religions (Héring, 91, n. 10; cf. Apuleius, *Metamorphoses* 11:23; Philo, *Legum Alleg.* 2:56; Euripides, *Bacch.* 472; Aristophanes, *Clouds*, 302; Herodotus 6:135; Lucian, *Menipp.* 2; see Windisch, 377, 378). Also, the notion of secret revelation (cf. *disciplina arcani*) is found in rabbinic literature (see J. Jeremias, *Jerusalem in the Time of Jesus*, tr. F. H. and C. H. Cave [London: SCM Press, 1969] 237–41; also see Spittler, "Limits," 263, 264). The idea of a sealed revelation (which is what Paul's revelation basically is) is found in the Old Testament (Isa 8:16; Dan 12:4; cf. 2 *Enoch* 17; Rev 14:3). Though Paul's experience was not "unusual," we go too far in thinking Paul is dependent on borrowed tradition in order to compose his thought of 12:2–4 (Barrett, 311).

A closer look at ἄρρητα ῥήματα reveals the meaning to be either words that are not able to be translated (Lincoln, "Paul the Visionary," 210) or those not able to be shared because of their sacredness (BGD 109), or simply "the language of the heavenly sphere" (Käsemann, ibid., 56, 57, which may be what Rom 8:26, 27 also refer to: see Käsemann, *Commentary on Romans*, tr. G. W. Bromiley [Grand Rapids: Eerdmans, 1980] 241, but this is unlikely [Martin, *The Worship of God*, 179], even if vv 2–4 in our chapter may be a reference to glossolalic speech as "celestial tongues" [1 Cor 13:1; 14:2, 14, 18: on these vv the present writer may refer to his *The Spirit and the Congregation*, esp. 66, 71]). It is not too hard to imagine that what Paul heard was ineffable. But the clause that follows ἃ οὐκ ἐξὸν ἀνθρώπῳ λαλῆσαι, "which a human being is not permitted to utter," places the emphasis on his being forbidden to relay what he heard (Lincoln, "Paul the Visionary," 216; *pace* Dunn, *Jesus and the Spirit*, 215, who argues for the ineffability of Paul's experience). Paul was not to tell anyone else what he heard. While οὐκ ἐξόν may mean "it is not possible," most likely it means "it is not lawful," for the usual idea behind ἔξεστι is "it is lawful" (Hughes, 439, n. 119).

But if our conclusion is true—that Paul is not permitted to share his adventure, except in general terms—then a needed question is, Of what value was Paul's experience? The sharing of this event would be quite valuable to the Corinthians in that they would be shown that indeed Paul can boast. Also they could see that his boasting, not that of his opponents, was grounded in God's strength. But moreover, and of utmost importance, this experience is invaluable to Paul in asserting his apostolic leadership at Corinth, and opposing a false eschatology of present glory, pneumatic ecstasy and a powerful presence in the influence of his rivals, whose ministry had so many tangible and sensory experiences to confirm it that it bypassed the weakness of the crucified Jesus and despised his suffering servant Paul (10:10; 13:1–4).

Tasker is correct in saying that "this particular revelation was for Paul alone" (172), as Paul's ministry was unique. Though we may come away somewhat frustrated and disappointed at the lack of information given here (as in 5:1–10), perhaps Calvin's dictum is right in that this experience was "to strengthen Paul by special means that he might not give way, but might persevere undaunted." This experience, though not communicable (as a result of its sacredness) must have had an untold influence on Paul. If this event transpired ca. A.D. 44, then it was an incalculable boost to him as he embarked on his ministry. We may never know the many times Paul received inner strength (inward renewal, 4:16–18) from his remembering this event. What is more, this "boast" did not end with him, but overflowed in blessing to the generation of his time (Hughes, 439).

5. ὑπὲρ τοῦ τοιούτου καυχήσομαι, "I will boast on behalf of this man." Paul continues his third person construction in a section (vv 5–7a) that looks like an insertion between vv 1–4 and 7b–9a, which are both "reports." He still refrains from signaling to his readers that he is the man who received this revelation. Some (Luther; Strachan, 29) have taken τοιούτου to be neuter, thus leaving us with the words "of an experience" instead of "on behalf of this man." But this view has not been generally accepted. For one thing, Paul has used τοιοῦτος as masculine in 12:2 and again in 12:3 to refer to a human being. For another, ὑπὲρ . . . ἐμαυτοῦ, found in 12:5b, provides balance and it is surely masculine as it refers to Paul. Moreover, if Paul was thinking of the experience of 12:2–4 (rather than the man) when he used τοιούτου, more likely than not he would have used the preposition ἐν (as he does with ἐν ταῖς ἀσθενείαις, 12:5b), for Paul's penchant is to use ὑπέρ, "on behalf of," with καυχᾶσθαι to signify a person (see 7:14; 9:2; cf. Hughes, 441, n. 120; Barrett, 311; Plummer, 345, 346; Bultmann, 224; see BDF § 196).

What Paul appears to be doing in 12:5 is preserving his desire to boast, but not in himself. The man mentioned in 12:5a of course is Paul. But by writing in this manner, he diverts any plaudits from himself, for in the second part of 12:5 he openly speaks of himself and does so only in terms of weakness. Paul is seeking to avoid the accusation that he has sought to enhance his person in the eyes of the Corinthians through self-commendation. The goal in 12:5 is to direct glory to God (Tasker, 172, 173).

It has been suggested that in 12:5 the apostle is distinguishing between two aspects of himself (as was discussed in 12:1). To be sure, on the surface it appears that way. But it is doubtful that he is discussing anthropology in our v. There does not appear to be a duality of personhood as much as a desire of Paul to direct attention to God (see Héring, 91). Käsemann's suggestion that Paul downplays his vision because it fails to build up the church (a similar idea of Paul's downplaying his gifts is found in 1 Cor 14:19 [the subject of tongues], *Legitimität,* 62–66; also see R. P. Martin, *The Spirit and the Congregation* [Grand Rapids: Eerdmans, 1984]) is closer to the truth than Lietzmann's contention (155) that the apostle distinguishes between "Paul the apocalyptist" and "Paul the man," but it still fails to capture the desire of Paul to stay out of the limelight. Barrett is correct to suggest that the apostolic sign of weakness was foremost on Paul's mind. If 12:5 is probably ironical and built on the antithesis καυχήσομαι/οὐ καυχήσομαι (Bujard, *Stilanalytische Untersuchungen,* 186) with a certain "distancing" between Paul the writer and his experience (see *Form/Structure/Setting*), Barrett's position is better (312). We shall see that the theme of weakness becomes an important one in 12:5*b*–10.

ὑπὲρ δὲ ἐμαυτοῦ οὐ καυχήσομαι εἰ μὴ ἐν ταῖς ἀσθενείαις, "but I will not boast on my own behalf, except in [my] weaknesses." For the first time since 12:1 Paul refers directly to himself. From 12:5*b* to 12:10 Paul is a visible figure in the discussion. And in 12:5*b* he presents the ground rules for the remainder of the passage. Apostolic weakness will be the topic of discussion. But this is not done in an attempt to gain pity; rather, it is to show that God works through this man. He is a legitimate apostle, and the Lord has appeared to him in a unique vision.

Earlier in this v we saw the use of ὑπὲρ with καυχᾶσθαι. In the second half of our present v the same construction appears, except in the negative (οὐ καυχήσομαι). Paul will not boast on his own behalf (note use of ἐμαυτοῦ, which is not ironical as Allo, 309, thinks), since this boasting could lead to his receiving a high place in the minds of the Corinthians for the wrong reasons. To ensure that this does not take place Paul adds "except in my weaknesses." Paul has put the idea of weakness before the Corinthians throughout this epistle. We saw this in 6:4–10 and more recently 11:23–28 (see Barré, "Qumran," 216–19). More specifically, in 11:30 Paul states that he will boast only to show his weakness. He illustrated the thought of 11:30 by relating the incident of being lowered down the Damascus wall (11:32, 33). In 12:7 Paul will again describe his weakness by speaking of the thorn in the flesh. Placed between the wall-incident and the thorn (both humbling experiences) is what may be called a highlight of Paul's life, namely, the ecstatic experience of fourteen years earlier (fourteen years, we may suppose, is a long time to remain silent about such a unique event as the experience of 12:2–4; such a silence may indicate that Paul considers any such experience as of little value for accrediting him in his apostleship [Lincoln, *Paradise Now,* 77]). It appears that Paul has left no room for the objection that he was no true apostle of God. At one extreme, Paul has placed before his critics the true sign of apostleship, namely, weakness. At the other extreme, Paul has been in the presence of the new world, with possibly an experience no one else could share. But Paul was still vulnerable to any detractor who did not accept his understanding of "vocation as weakness." This v therefore places side by side the two ideas of personal relationship to God and apostolic service in Paul's life (Kümmel, 212).

6. ἐὰν γὰρ θελήσω καυχήσασθαι, οὐκ ἔσομαι ἄφρων, ἀλήθειαν γὰρ ἐρῶ, "Even if I should choose to boast, I would not be foolish, for I speak the truth." The direction of our discussion of these words will point to the idea that Paul is writing in a polemical (though restrained) fashion. At the conclusion of 12:5, Paul has "introduced" himself into the present passage. (We know all along that the "other man" was Paul; but the Corinthians may not have been aware of that at the beginning of 12:1–10.) Our present v provides a transition (awkward with γάρ, which does not explain anything; Windisch, 381) for Paul's readers because 12:6–10 reads as though Paul has been talking explicitly about himself. Moreover, as was discussed above, the weakness of Paul now becomes an important theme of 12:6–10. Thus, 12:6 provides a shift for the Corinthians. Their attention is now focused on Paul and in turn on his weakness.

Paul keeps the idea of weakness before his readers, but he does so in an interesting way. He opens 12:6 with ἐὰν γὰρ θελήσω καυχήσασθαι, "even if I should choose to boast." The verb θέλειν, "to want," "to wish," is in the subjunctive mood. This is dictated by ἐάν (Plummer, 346, for grammatical usage). We note that there is little difference at times between the aorist subjunctive and the future indicative ("It is quite possible that the future indicative is just a variation of the aorist subjunctive," Robertson, *Grammar*, 924), but the idea of the subjunctive fits better into our context. Barrett notes that θέλειν carries with it an element of deliberate choice (312). Considering the *Sitz im Leben* of 2 Corinthians, we can see that a boast by Paul would have been both expected and probably appreciated by the Corinthians. But Paul has chosen another way to go; instead of boasting of himself, he boasts of God (10:17, 18).

Paul could choose to boast of himself, for he would have solid grounds on which to do so. Unlike his opponents, who probably boasted of visions they did not have (Barrett, ibid.), Paul has just related a vision which he has experienced. Paul's use of ἄφρων, "foolish" (see 11:16a), probably includes the idea of a person who is caught in making false claims. Paul avoids this problem because he speaks in truth (ἀλήθειαν . . . ἐρῶ: Zmijewski, ibid., 355), not only concerning the ecstatic experience of 12:2–4, but also about the other visions and revelations that he has been given and which he could relate if he were pressed to, but then he would be a "fool," or acting κατὰ σάρκα: so Bultmann, 225. Moreover, Paul's speaking in truth is a polemical stance against his opponents, as has been noted, for he did not consider his opponents as being truthful (see 13:8).

At first we might consider it a problem for Paul that he cannot offer "more proof" of his vision of 12:2–4. But this is just the point Paul will make. Neither can his opponents back up their claims in the sense of proving that they have experienced all the visions they may be reporting to the Corinthians. Paul will show that his visionary experience of 12:2–4 led to his being weak. Furthermore, Paul is saying that (as will be seen) his visions are not the criteria by which to judge him (Lincoln, *Paradise Now*, 74, 75). Rather, the way in which he has lived for God is the standard to use; or it is an appeal to the ministry that is performed according to the standard God has set (going back to 10:13–16). Paul's ministry is characterized by weakness and church planting. Even Paul's opponents cannot deny the veracity of the stripes he has suffered for the Gospel nor can they overlook that he was the one who founded the church at Corinth. They may evaluate Paul's sufferings incorrectly, but what he is should be evident to all. He is a weak servant of God, chosen by him to be an apostle, which is what he is to the Corinthians.

φείδομαι δέ, μή τις εἰς ἐμὲ λογίσηται ὑπὲρ ὃ βλέπει με ἢ ἀκούει [τι] ἐξ ἐμοῦ, "But I refrain [from boasting] so that no one will think more of me than what he sees in me or hears from me." Paul knows that some Corinthians will accept and believe his experience of 12:2–4. With this in mind, Paul expresses his wish that he not receive more credit than is due him (Héring, 92). If Paul is given too much praise for his vision, then the Gospel message would be clouded. This is the charge he brings against his opponents. Thus, Paul does not want to be regarded more highly than he should.

φείδομαι literally means "I spare" (see 1:23; 13:2; Rom 8:32; 11:21; 1 Cor 7:28; "I spare myself," Barrett, 312). If Héring is right that the idea of "not wishing to crush" those reading this message is behind our word, then possibly Paul also has his opponents directly in mind (92). This may explain the restraint that Paul exhibits in this polemic against his enemies. But when the verb is taken in the conative sense (Barrett's evaluation of the present tense, 312), it follows that Paul is refraining from leading the Corinthians down the wrong path. He could share more of his visionary experiences with the Corinthians, but he stops short of doing so (Bultmann, 225: "I could relate more experiences like that in vv 2–5; I truly have had them"). He takes this line of action so that people will not miss God's power in seeing his accomplishments and so that they will judge Paul by the acceptable criteria, i.e., not κατὰ σάρκα, but κατὰ κύριον (11:17, 18). The people of Corinth cannot evaluate his visions, for such experiences remain hidden from them. However, they can judge what they see in and hear in his case. The coupling of the verbs βλέπειν/ἀκούειν is to be taken as more than simple references to the everyday events in Paul's life. The verbs are to be understood as referring to his humility and (ἤ is copulative: BDF § 446.1) weakness and to his acceptance by God as a true and faithful apostle (Cambier, "Le critère paulinien," 498–505). Paul wished to be judged on more than simply the externals of his service (so Käsemann, *Legitimität*, 63, an idea going back to 5:12 [see *Comment* there]). His service is the means by which others may see that he is an ambassador for Christ; his weakness is a means by which the power of Christ is truly displayed, i.e., in line with 4:7 (see *Comment*).

The use of λογίσηται (aorist subjunctive from λογίζεσθαι) possibly carries with it the idea of commercial accounting (see Lietzmann, 155: Zmijewski, ibid., 359, citing Philem 18 to show it as a current metaphor; cf. BDF § 145.5). This would not be surprising in such a commerce-oriented city as Corinth; but it is evidently a slogan in this correspondence (11:5; see 10:2, 7, 11 to do with *Evidenzproblem*; Betz, ibid., 68, 74, 121, 134). Paul is emphatic in saying that one should not credit to his account any "wares" except those that are visible. His readers should turn from Paul's visions and reflect on the message he has preached and the sufferings he has endured. Paul invested himself greatly in the pathos of this v. Not only is he the subject of four verbs (θελήσω, ἔσομαι, ἐρῶ, φείδομαι), but we also see three uses of personal pronouns in 12:6b (ἐμέ, με, ἐμοῦ; also cf. ἐμαυτοῦ of 12:5). This should tell us that by the time the Corinthians read (or heard) the words in 12:7, they were prepared to link the "unknown man" of 12:2–5a with Paul. The double accusative in "more" and "me" is to the point (BDF § 157).

The apostle has exhibited much restraint at this point, for he could have directly attacked his opponents on the grounds that they misrepresented both himself and themselves. Rather, Paul leaves such a conclusion to be worked out in the mind of the Corinthians. He does this by indirectly showing that the true man of God will seek to avoid inordinate self-esteem based on visions and revelations. Perhaps the indefinite μή τις ("no one"; Paul is not excluding anyone) is Paul's way of showing hope that both the Corinthian church and his opponents will evaluate him on what is (to him at least) self-evident (Héring, 92).

7. καὶ τῇ ὑπερβολῇ τῶν ἀποκαλύψεων, "even the extraordinary revelations." The modern interpreter may wonder, after reading the Greek text of 12:7, if Paul set this text down the way he had intended (Barrett, 313). We have already examined the textual questions surrounding the v and have opted to view the above phrase as completing the sentence in v 6 (see *Notes* on 12:7). 12:6 had closed with Paul saying that he refrained from boasting about what was unseen. He wished the people to evaluate him on what was tangible, by something they could see, i.e., his trials. But we may wonder if Paul was convinced that, after telling them of his vision, his Corinthian readers would heed his concern (12:2–4; and we must remember that some may have known of Paul's other visions, especially the one in Corinth [Acts 18:9, 10]). There could possibly have been some who, with good intentions, would consider Paul to be an exceptional person because of his ecstatic experience. After all, Paul had his followers at Corinth ("I follow Paul"; 1 Cor 1:12). Moreover, he had won a majority back to him as recorded in 7:8–16. In spite of new and recurring problems, there were some who would take this new piece of information and place Paul high in their estimation. Paul's choice of ὑπερβολῇ, here a *dativus causae*, is somewhat ambiguous. The composite noun can mean either "excess" (ὑπέρ- of quantity) or "extraordinary" (ὑπέρ- of quality). Paul's use of the word in 2 Cor (4:17; 1:8; cf. also 4:7; Rom 7:13; Gal 1:13; 1 Cor 12:31) might tip the scales in favor of the qualitative aspect (so Zmijewski, "Kontextbezug," 272), but perhaps we should not draw too sharp a distinction here (see Héring, 92). The fact that ἀποκαλύψεις, "revelations," is plural has led Plummer, 347, to raise again the idea that 12:2–4 speaks of two separate revelations. But we have already judged this position to be doubtful (so Güttgemanns, *Der leidende Apostel*, 161, n. 55, who argues his case that v 7 moves "without a perceptible break" from the account in v 4, against several interpreters). Moreover, as has been stated before, the Corinthians were probably aware that Paul had some visions (but not nearly enough to satisfy the opponents). He had been accused of being out of his mind (5:13). But the significance of the vision in 12:2–4 is its dimension in terms of "revelation." In short, it probably fell as a bombshell on some, though ignored or scoffed

at by others. There was no way on Paul's part that he would become too proud or conceited over this incident (he will presently explain why to the Corinthians this is so). But there was always the possibility that some at Corinth would treat his mystical experience in a way that Paul himself would disown.

διὸ ἵνα μὴ ὑπεραίωμαι, ἐδόθη μοι σκόλοψ τῇ σαρκί, ἄγγελος σατανᾶ, ἵνα με κολαφίζῃ, ἵνα μὴ ὑπεραίρωμαι, "Therefore, in order that I should not become conceited, I was given a thorn in the flesh, a messenger of Satan, in order to batter me, that I should not become conceited." Discussion of this verse will not lead the exegete to certainty regarding the identity of Paul's "thorn in the flesh." As Hughes aptly writes, the thorn "is another one of those questions which, on the evidence available, must remain unanswered" (442). This is not to say that a study of past theories concerning the present topic will be of no benefit. Quite the contrary, for if we are to understand the basis for God's strength in Paul—namely, through weakness—then it is imperative that we consider the options and at least form general conclusions regarding Paul's situation. But this is to say that our present discussion offers no certain conclusion that has up to now eluded scholars.

διὸ ἵνα μὴ ὑπεραίρωμαι, "Therefore, in order that I should not become conceited." The use of διό, "therefore," alerts Paul's readers that some form of summary statement is to follow in this new sentence, a view to be argued for against other possibilities, e.g., that διό is an afterthought, a textual corruption, an unstressed anticipation of ἵνα, the next word; rather it introduces the "following connection" as an inferential conjunction (Zmijewski, *Der Stil*, 354; Bultmann, 226, both relying on E. Molland, "Διό" in *Serta Rudbergiana* [1931] 49, 50, which I have not been able to consult). Paul has presented the Corinthians with the information that he experienced a unique vision. In turn, he has related to them that, in spite of this event, he will not boast about it (though essentially he has already boasted and feels that he has joined [12:11] in the activity of his opponents, an activity which he devalues [12:1]). Thus, Paul now proceeds to give, in general terms, one reason why he is unable to boast: God has sought to keep Paul from becoming conceited. The ἵνα twice in one v, "in order that," alerts us to three purpose clauses in close symmetry. First, there was a reason for the giving of the thorn and that reason is that Paul should not become proud. Second, the satanic messenger came in order to batter him. Third, this encounter was (again) to prevent his conceit. The word for "exalting oneself" ("becoming conceited," ὑπεραίρομαι) is found only one other place in the NT (2 Thess 2:4), where Paul describes "the man of lawlessness" as exalting himself against God. If Paul felt inclined to exalt himself, i.e., to be independent of God as an act of ὕβρις, "pride," the thorn was sent to prevent that from happening. More important, if the Corinthians wanted to place Paul "on a pedestal," the thorn would prevent such action. That Paul was intent on showing that he was not free to put himself above others is seen in this construction (cf. Rom 12:3). The identical purpose clause ἵνα μὴ ὑπεραίρωμαι both begins and ends this verse. The emphasis is clear; Paul is weak and this is further demonstrated by the thorn in the flesh. (Surprisingly, the NIV fails to translate the second ἵνα μὴ ὑπεραίωμαι clause, and we may note how Schlatter, *Paulus*, 665, in recognizing a "medley of two kinds of composition," seeks to attach the clauses to two different parts of the sentence, going back to v 6 to connect the first ἵνα clause to the "abundance of revelations" as a kind of "intrusion.")

Paul confesses that he is not the agent responsible for this thorn. He reports that the thorn ἐδόθη μοι, "was given to me." It is doubtful that Satan is the giver, even if σκόλοψ τῇ σαρκί is the grammatical subject of ἐδόθη. If Paul had intended to convey such information, he most likely would have chosen a word other than διδόναι. This word was usually employed to denote that God's favor had been bestowed (cf. Gal 3:21; Eph 3:8; 5:19; 1 Tim 4:14). Plummer suggests that if Satan was the agent, ἐπιτίθημι, "lay upon" (Luke 10:30; 23:26; Acts 16:23), or βάλλω, "cast" (Rev 2:24), or ἐπιβάλλω, "put on" (1 Cor 7:35), would have been more appropriate (348). As mentioned earlier, we have an example of the *passivum divinum*. This "divine passive," speaking of God as the hidden agent behind events and experiences in human lives, fits well into Paul's thinking. He sees both the revelation and the thorn as from God. (Smith makes the point that Paul may not have viewed the thorn as a "gift." Moreover, he says that Paul refrains from saying the thorn was God's will ["The Thorn," 411]. Paul viewed the thorn as a bitter reality that drew him closer to God. But whether or not Paul saw this as a good thing in the beginning remains beyond our ability to answer.) Hence Zmijewski, ibid., 368, is correct when he writes that though "thorn" can be assumed to be the grammatical subject of "was given," in reality "the evidence points to God being the essential acting subject."

σκόλοψ τῇ σαρκί, ἄγγελος σατανᾶ, "a thorn in the flesh, a messenger of Satan." Much scholarship has been devoted to this phrase, yet undeniably mystery and uncertainty remain. And as will be seen, this attention is not limited to modern times only, but has marked exegetical and devotional study throughout church history.

σκόλοψ can be taken to mean "thorn" or "stake" (Schlatter [*Paulus,* 666] suggests that σκόλοψ could be equivalent to σταυρός, "cross"; cf. Origen *c. Celsum* 2.68). The more common rendering of "thorn" is well attested (see LXX [Num 33:55; Ezek 28:24; Hos 2:6], KJV/AV, RSV, NIV; note NEB has "a sharp physical pain," which is then interpreted in a footnote to be a "stake, *or* thorn, for the flesh"; see also BGD, 756; Delling, *TDNT* 7:411, 412). A case can be made for rendering "stake." Park argues that "stake" could have been a concept borrowed from the military ("Paul's ΣΚΟΛΟΨ," 180–82). Such stakes were used to slow an enemy's progress (as in the form of a fence or wall), or to torture and to execute an enemy (such as by impaling). The idea of "stake" looks plausible except that Park makes too much of the severity of Paul's problem (ibid., 182, 183). To say that "stake" implies the intensity of Paul's problem whereas thorn suggests he has a superficial affliction is not satisfactory. Furthermore, to portray the situation by suggesting that Paul was helplessly impaled on a stake (Hughes, 447) rather overlooks the power he felt was working in him. For these reasons we choose "thorn" as our rendering ("splinter," Bruce, 248; Plummer, 348). (For the moment, we postpone the discussion of the different possibilities that are attached to "thorn," in order to examine Paul's use of τῇ σαρκί.)

There is uncertainty in identifying Paul's use of σάρξ, in the expression "in the flesh." The question centers on whether to render this phrase "*in* the flesh" or *"for* the flesh." It is a question of whether to take τῇ σαρκί as locative dative or dative of disadvantage (Tasker, 174, *dativus incommodi*). (Allo's view [310] that the dative τῇ σαρκί is explanatory of μοι, "given to me, that is, to my flesh" [on the basis of Rom 7:18], is not likely. Rather the dative is explained as closely tied to the substantive [σκόλοψ; the usage as in 1 Cor 7:28] "by analogy" [BDF § 190.3].) If it is the former, then most likely Paul is speaking of a physical malady or ailment, for we should understand σάρξ in the neutral sense, namely, the physical body (Bruce, 248; Barrett, 315; Filson, 407; Schweizer, *TDNT* 7:125 for "flesh" as a synonym for man's corporeal existence; Bachmann, 392, n. 1: a metaphor for the most real physiological meaning of human life; so BGD, 743). (We have already discussed how Paul could use σάρξ in a nontheological manner; see *Comment* on 7:1.) The argument against taking the dative as locative is that, if Paul intended it this way, he would have included the preposition ἐν, "in" (Plummer, 348). On the contrary, it has been proposed that this is the dative of disadvantage (*"for* the flesh"). If this position is adopted, then σάρξ takes on the Pauline sense of man's lower nature (Tasker, 174). Opponents of this position argue that if Paul had wanted to convey this meaning of σάρξ he most likely would have contrasted it with some reference to the Spirit (Hughes, 448). On the basis of Hughes's thinking, we understand "flesh" to be of the nontheological category (see Jewett, *Anthropological Terms*, who interprets σάρξ as equal to σῶμα [158], but as belonging to the old eon [455]; cf. 5:17).

The exact meaning of thorn remains elusive. No one has yet given an interpretation that is generally accepted. There are historical surveys in Plummer, 348–51; Hughes, 443–46; Allo, 313–21; Güttgemanns, *Der leidende Apostel*, 162–64. The first interpretation was offered by Tertullian *de Pudicitia* 13.17, who took the thorn to mean Paul had a pain in the ear or head (also see Jerome and Pelagius). Chrysostom, *Hom.* 26, understands σατανᾶς, "Satan," in the general sense of adversary, and he concluded that Paul's thorn was his opponents. (Specifically, Chrysostom has Alexander the coppersmith in mind.) Recently this argument has been revived (Tasker, 176; Mullins, "Paul's Thorn"; Barré, "Qumran," 222–25, sees that there is a connection between 1QH 2:23–25 and 2 Cor 10–13, for in both contexts weakness is the result of persecution; Bieder, "Paulus," 319–33, argues that the opposition is that seen in 11:14 [332], heretical adversaries at Corinth who are Satan's emissaries; but can "messenger" be equated with διάκονοι? asks Güttgemanns, ibid., 164; see below). The support of this position is well worth noting.

There are four basic points that endorse the position that the thorn refers to Paul's opponents. First, the phrase ἄγγελος σατανᾶ, "messenger of Satan" (note σατανᾶ is a Doric genitive of σατανᾶς, which is of irregular declension), could refer to a person, for this is the normal use of ἄγγελος (it is not likely that as yet "angel" was a technical term). It appears that Paul does not use ἄγγελος except to refer to a person. Second, one must not forget that chaps. 10–13 describe Paul's fight against his adversaries. We see in 12:12 that Paul is in conflict with those who would question his apostleship. Moreover, in 11:13–15 Paul understands his conflict with his opponents as a conflict between God and Satan (see Kleinknecht, *Der leidende Gerechtfertigte*, 293). Paul sees himself as a representative of God and the false apostles as representing

Satan. In this conflict Paul views Satan as a (false) messenger of light (11:14). It follows that the use of messenger is in reference to a person, not an illness. If this is so, then the use of σκόλοψ in 12:7 should not be understood as referring to some physical malady.

A third point is seen in the clause ἵνα με κολαφίζῃ, "in order to batter me." The verb κολαφίζειν (see the uses in Mark 14:65; Matt 26:67; cf. 1 Cor 4:11) speaks of one who is beaten or battered about, especially by blows to the head (see K. L. Schmidt, *TDNT* 3:819–21; and idem, "Ἰησοῦς Χριστὸς κολαφιζόμενος und die 'colaphisation' der Juden," Mélanges offerts à Maurice Goguel, Bibliothèque Théologique [Paris: Delachaux & Niestlé, 1950]; *Aux sources de la tradition chrétienne*, FS M. Goguel). This has led some to conclude that the choice of σκόλοψ refers specifically to a person, thus pointing to Paul's opponents. A fourth item is that in the LXX we find thorn associated with opponents of Israel. The Canaanites, who are permitted to remain in Israel, are "thorns" (Num 33:55). In Ezekiel (23:24) the foes of Israel are described as "thorns." These four points show that a case can be made for considering Paul's thorn as the adversaries that dog him at Corinth (see also patristic support in Augustine, Theodoret, Theophylact).

However, there is much support for the view of the thorn as referring to something other than the opponents of Paul. The medieval thinkers (from Gregory the Great to Aquinas) understood the Vulgate rendering (however, a "misrendering," Hughes, 444; see 442–46 for a helpful excursus on the history of interpretation of the "thorn") of *stimulus carnis* to imply sexual temptation. The Reformers (such as Calvin and Luther) viewed Paul's thorn in the flesh as spiritual temptation. Few modern commentators adopt this view (but see J. J. Thierry, "Der Dorn im Fleische," *NovT* 5 [1962] 301–10). Rather, the majority opt for some form of physical ailment (see the full note in Windisch, 385–88, "Die Krankheit des Apostels Paulus," with bibliographical references). One common ailment suggested was a severe form of ophthalmia. This is inferred from the colorful language of Galatians. In 4:13 Paul speaks of a weakness of the flesh (σάρξ), and proceeds to acknowledge the willingness of the Galatians to pluck out their eyes and give them to him (4:15). Also, Paul is seen as closing the Galatian epistle by noting that the handwriting is his own, for this writing is in large letters (6:11). Also appeal is made to the (hypothetical) case of Acts 23:5 where Paul fails to recognize the high priest. This defective eyesight may stem from, as the theory goes, the scales that fell from Paul's eyes after his conversion experience (Acts 9:9, 18). This theory, though interesting, has received little support in recent times (though see Nisbet, "The Thorn").

Another ailment suggested is epilepsy (Lightfoot), possibly as a result of the experience Paul had at his conversion. That is, the fact that Paul fell down on the road to Damascus has been seen as evidence that Paul was epileptic, but this is doubtful (see Allo, 316).

One of the more attractive hypotheses is that of W. M. Ramsay (*St. Paul the Traveller and Roman Citizen*[18] [London: Hodder & Stoughton, 1935] 94–97; followed by Allo). Paul, it is said, suffered from a form of recurring malarial fever. It has been suggested that he contracted this disease (specifically Malta fever; so W. M. Alexander, "St. Paul's Infirmity," *ExpTim* 15 [1904] 469–

73; 545–48) in Pamphylia. For Ramsay, this theory covers all the symptoms Paul seems to exhibit. Accordingly, Paul was incapacitated by the attacks of this fever. If the fever seared the head, one can appreciate how Paul felt battered about.

Other forms of suffering have been suggested. The thorn, e.g., may have been the agony that Paul experienced at the Jewish rejection of the Gospel (Ph. H. Menoud, "L'écharde et l'ange satanique [2 Cor 12.7]," *Studia Paulina*, 169). We know this was a problem for Paul as recorded in Romans chaps. 9–11, especially 9:1–3. Menoud does make the point that Paul never mentions sickness in his tribulation-lists (Barré, "Qumran," 224, notes that 12:7 is framed by two such lists, namely, 11:21*b*–29 and 12:10*a*). Clavier ("La santé de l'apôtre Paul," *Studia Paulina*, 78, 79) believes that Paul suffered disorders to his nervous system as a result of the hardships he endured and the shock his psyche received from his visions and revelations. Yet, with all these physical ailments suggested, one wonders with Binder whether or not a person who was so often on the "battlefield" could have been so physically weak and still have withstood the rigors of Paul's life ("Die angebliche Krankheit").

But this is not to say that the supposition that Paul's suffering was physical cannot also be defended. It is worth noting that Satan is associated with physical illness in the biblical tradition. We see this in Job 2:5 where Satan is allowed (by God's permission) to inflict sickness. Also in Luke (13:16), Satan is credited as the one responsible for the woman being bent over for eighteen years. There is nothing to suggest that a "literal" messenger (ἄγγελος) was the agent for these respective illnesses. In addition, the term "angel of Satan" was not necessarily a common phrase (see Barrett, 315; Matt 25:41; Rev 12:7, 9; Str-B 1:136, 983–94). Contrary to those who see ἄγγελος as signifying a "person" (specifically, adversaries), Paul may have simply been attributing his ailment to satanic origin (possibly through demonic agency; Price, "Punished," 33–40, understands the thorn to be a demon), but always with the conviction that God was in control (Barrett, 316). Probably the most telling argument against the position that Paul was referring to human opponents as the thorn in the flesh (and by now it should be apparent that the possibilities offered concerning the thorn roughly fall into two categories, namely, human opponents and physical ailment) is found in 12:8. This verse relates that Paul prayed that God would remove the thorn. Would the apostle pray to be spared persecution? This is doubtful, since persecution was the fuel on which Paul seemed to thrive. The more he was persecuted the more he seemed determined to press the claims of his apostolate. Moreover, if this thorn was given to Paul near the time of his revelation of 12:2–4, then it is doubtful Paul was speaking of the opponents in 11:13–15 (against Bieder), for he had yet to confront them. Yet, we must honestly recognize (and so in recall of Binder's thesis) that a chronically ill Paul does not fit well with the picture of Paul found in the New Testament. Rather, Paul is one who must be seen as in robust health and with a strong constitution. On the other side, at Corinth where his apostolic role was under fire, any physical weakness would have seemed a liability, then Paul could not deny that the estimate of his person in 10:10; 11:21; 12:10, is valid, however much it was exploited by his traducers.

Something in the nature of defective speech has also been suggested as Paul's thorn (W. K. L. Clarke, *New Testament Problems* [London: SPCK, 1929] 136–40, followed in part by Barrett). This could account for his making a bad first impression at Corinth (1 Cor 2:1–5; 2 Cor 10:10). Moreover, it may supply the reason why he was impressive in his letters, but "deficient" in his speech (10:1, 9, 10, 11; 11:6). Such an ailment would not prove incapacitating nor drain one's strength, yet it would be humiliating, evoking ridicule and scorn (see Marshall, "A Metaphor of Social Shame," *NovT* 25 [1983] 315, 316, who identifies the thorn as a "socially debilitating disease or disfigurement which was made the subject of ridicule and invidious comparison," which discredited the value of the vision-audition experience. He argues that the upshot of the pericope is the idea: God defeated his apostle, in line with 2:14, as Marshall interprets the verb there). But again this is only a guess. We simply do not know the meaning behind "the thorn in the flesh." At best we can say with Bruce that the thorn attacked Paul some time after the ecstatic experience. From the present tense of κολαφίζειν it appears that this was a continual problem. It seems also likely that Paul suffered a kind of physical disorder, but even that is uncertain. In all probability, the Corinthians knew of what Paul spoke. We, however, are left on the outside listening to one side of a two-sided conversation. We will probably never know the truth (or, at least, never know for sure we have the truth).

But this examination of the possible meanings of thorn is worthwhile. From studying the possibilities we can see two important points and several consequences. First of all, the thorn was inherently evil. Nowhere does Paul infer that this thorn was good. It was used to buffet Paul and caused him great consternation and pain (so Zmijewski, ibid., 370, 371, who remarks that, while the image of a thorn is a plastic one, it does have the connotation of the *painful side* of Paul's sufferings). Second, and more important, the thorn served a good purpose as a gift from God. The importance of the passive verb ἐδόθη, "was given," can hardly be exaggerated. God is the unseen agent behind the bitter experience. The paradox is that behind the nonpersonal, passive word form of the verb lies "the veiled allusion to God as author" (Prümm, *Diakonia* 1:657). Some momentous consequences follow. First, this passive formulation with the divine concealed in a human trial places the experience on a theological plane, where the need for a theodicy is urgent. Paul will partly address this issue in vv 9, 10 by introducing the christological motif and a vindication of his service for Christ. Then, Paul's suffering is viewed within the context of divine grace which not only allowed the affliction but sustained the sufferer in it (Schlatter, *Paulus*, 668). The thorn humbled (and humiliated) Paul; he could never revel in his great vision for very long before he would be reminded of his thorn. But, third, this negative factor, as 12:9, 10 tell us, was an opportunity for God to demonstrate his power. Paul acknowledged God's power as he acknowledged his own weakness. Maybe Paul reflected many times that, if he had not received the vision, he would have not received the thorn. But this made little or no difference to him. Because of his weakness, he became a powerful instrument for God. Paul's own personal interest is shown in the *inclusio* and chiastic form:

8. ὑπὲρ τούτου τρὶς τὸν κύριον παρεκάλεσα ἵνα ἀποστῇ ἀπ᾽ ἐμοῦ, "Concerning this I pleaded with the Lord three times to take it away from me." In 12:8 Paul proceeds to some autobiographical material concerning his beseeching the Lord to remove this messenger of Satan. Grammatically speaking, ὑπὲρ τούτου refers to ἄγγελος σατανᾶ instead of σκόλοψ ἐν σαρκί. This is because ἀποστῇ (from ἀφιστάναι, "to take away," again passive) is used of persons, not things, throughout the NT (Hughes, 449, n. 139; cf. 1 Tim 4:1; 2 Tim 2:19; Heb 3:12; Luke 4:13). At first thought, we might be inclined to translate the οὗτος/τούτου as "he" (so Barrett, 316) instead of "this matter" or simply "it" (neuter; NIV; KJV/AV; RSV; NEB). This personification is tempting but undesirable. At best all we can say is that Paul considered the "messenger of Satan" in a quasi-personal sense (Zmijewski, Der Stil, 375; Hughes, 441, n. 120). We need to note that in 12:7 the phrase "messenger of Satan" appears in apposition to the words "thorn in the flesh"; thus the "it" of 12:8 (the object that Paul wished removed from his life) may mean either the thorn or the messenger, without affecting the meaning of the v (12:8; see Form/Structure/Setting). As stated earlier, it is quite probable that Paul did not have any special person in mind when he wrote 12:7. Any persecution from opponents, especially that resulted in suffering, would not have been an item Paul would have sought to evade. For Paul, his sufferings, in some way, reflected the sufferings of Jesus (Col 1:24). The οὗτος (see BDF § 290.3) most likely is a reference to Paul's thorn; the use of the "messenger of Satan" probably is Paul's way of saying that evil forces (though permitted by God) were a part of his life.

Paul reports: τρὶς τὸν κύριον παρεκάλεσα, "three times I pleaded with the Lord." In all probability, κύριος here is the personal object of a prayer directly to Christ (Bultmann, 227). This can be seen from 12:9, which speaks first of "my power" (which refers to Christ) and then "Christ's power." Héring takes this as the only occasion (to the point of its being true "undeniably," 93, n. 20) during which Paul prayed directly to Christ and not to God the Father. But see possible examples to the contrary (1 Thess 3:12–13; 1 Cor 1:2; 16:22; and also Filson, 409; R. J. Bauckham, "The Worship of Jesus in Apocalyptic Christianity," NTS 27 [1980–81] 322–41; P. F. Bradshaw, Daily Prayer in the Early Church [London: Alcuin Club/SPCK, 1981] 36; R. T. France, "The Worship of Jesus" in Christ the Lord, FS D. Guthrie, ed. H. H. Rowdon [Leicester: IVP, 1982] 17–36). Immediately, the reader is impressed by the number of times Paul sought (παρεκάλεσα: BDF § 392; but not "begged" [see Barrett, 316, and 8:6; 9:5 but see on 10:1, 2]) a subsequent cure (A. Deissmann, Light From the Ancient East, 153, 308, speaks of an interesting parallel with the prayer of M. Julius Apellas). The number three is a reminder of Jesus' temptations in the Garden of Gethsemane and the three times he petitioned the Father to remove the cup from him. Chrysostom and Calvin suggest that τρίς is symbolic, representing many times. But also the "three" could reflect the Jewish importance attached to this number when related to blessings (see Acts 10:16; John 21:17: also *Midr. Tehuma* 22.2). And three-fold prayers are well attested in Greco-Roman religion (Windisch, 389, 390; cf. Betz, "Aretalogie," 293). Whatever Paul's meaning, it remains a question as to whether these three occasions of prayer were the result of three separate attacks of his malady or all are located during the time shortly after the first attack. The latter makes sense in light of the point that Paul had had sufficient time to accept this affliction and had learned to live with it (Bruce, 249). This is seen in what follows especially if the aorist tense in παρεκάλεσα "suggests that the fact [of prayer] had passed, so that Paul no longer prayed for this object" (Allo, 312), while the next line has a notable change of tense. But maybe the "three times" prayer is a stereotyped expression for urgency in praying (so Güttgemanns, ibid., 166 n. 94).

9. καὶ εἴρηκέν μοι, "And he said to me." In oracular form (Betz, "Aretalogie," 294 ff., *"eine indikativische Heilsbestätigung,"* esp. 297) the answer to his prayer came. It was not what he desired; rather (we may suppose) it was what he needed. The attention of most readers is drawn to the answer that follows but we should not overlook the construction of these opening words. εἴρηκεν, "he said," is the perfect of λέγω (12:9 is a "fair example of the true Greek perfect," Moule, *Idiom Book,* 15, against other suggestions: that the perfect is the same as an aorist tense [Windisch, 390, n. 1: cf. 11:25], or that the classification is that of a "narrative perfect," BDF § 343.2). That the use of the perfect speaks of something that happened in the past is evident. This suggests a decision that is regarded as final by Paul (Bachmann, 401). But more than that, Paul's choice of the perfect tells us that he still hears the echo of this divine oracle (εἰρηκέναι is frequently used of divine utterances [Plummer, 354; Acts 13:34; Heb 1:13; 4:3, 4; 10:9; 13:5: these references are to OT citations]). The answer, coming after Paul's third petition, "was ever sounding in the apostle's ears" (Hodge, 286). When we examine the content of this answer, we shall see the reason. In all probability, what he had heard in the past remains a present source of power and comfort (Bruce, 249). While some could argue that the perfect can be understood in a punctiliar sense it is not likely in this case. We noted in 12:8 that παρεκάλεσα was in the aorist. Paul had pleaded with the Lord, but this was a thing of the past (Allo, 312, cited above). Paul's use of the perfect and the aorist together in 12:8, 9 appears as a conscious attempt on his part to tell the Corinthians that he had ceased to petition God to remove the thorn (aorist), while he still keeps the answer as an ever-present source of comfort (perfect). In 12:9*a*, though the answer was a thing of the past, it resounded with vibrancy and vitality in the present. The answer was final, but it also was advantageous for Paul for it was a means to strengthen him. In spite of his weakness, Paul would be strengthened. Though he had a thorn in the flesh, he still could carry on his work for God. This is indeed marked as "the veritable highpoint of the entire sentence sequence" (Zmijewski, *Der Stil,* 378), in the light of the next line.

ἀρκεῖ σοι ἡ χάρις μου, ἡ γὰρ δύναμις ἐν ἀσθενείᾳ τελεῖται, "My grace is sufficient for you, for [my] power is fulfilled in weakness." The words that follow—

"he said to me"—reveal the answer Paul received. Hughes has called this answer, "the summit of the epistle. . . . From this vantage-point the entire range of Paul's apostleship is seen in focus" (451). Though his petition for removal of the thorn was denied, Paul appears confident that, whenever the messenger of Satan "beats him about," he will have the strength to overcome. The words recorded here may have been a direct communication to Paul from Christ (O'Collins, "Power," 530; these may be the only words of the risen Christ that we find in Pauline literature, though we may question O'Collins's position in light of 1 Cor 11:23–26: but he is correct if the issue is one of discovering *oratio recta:* see D. E. Aune, *Prophecy in Early Christianity* [Grand Rapids: Eerdmans, 1983] 247, 248, 261, 269, 321).

Paul's use of χάρις, "grace," may or may not refer specifically to his situation of 12:1–10. χάρις has received wide use in our present epistle (1:2, 12; 4:15; 8:1, 2, 4, 6, 7, 9, 19; 9:8, 14). For Paul "grace" can speak of his special call to apostleship (1 Cor 15:10; cf. Rom 1:5; 12:3). The fundamental aspect of grace is God's love toward man shown in Christ (8:9). Through it a person can be assured that no suffering (Rom 8:38, 39) can overpower those who are in Christ (Barrett, 316). This grace is the way by which "any man becomes the sort of Christian that he is" (ibid.). No doubt Paul had in mind the thorn in the flesh when he related the wording of 12:9. But it is possible that he also had in mind the many sufferings that had accompanied his apostleship. We simply have to remember the tribulation-lists that dot the horizon of 2 Corinthians (6:4–10; 11:23–28; 12:10). Taking this one step farther, we may have a general principle for Christians concerning weakness (Bultmann, 228, 229: see below). That is, we see a law in 12:9 regarding Christian service (Käsemann, *Legitimität,* 39). O'Collins, however, disagrees ("Power," 534). This last discussion will come up again (see below) at the conclusion of our comment on 12:9. For now it is sufficient to note that the grace of God was exhibited in Paul's life though weakness ("This Divine gift is perpetually sufficient, good for his whole life," Plummer, 354).

ἀρκεῖν, "to be sufficient," carries with it the idea of "being enough" (see G. Kittel, *TDNT* 1:464–67); here the verb has a theological nuance, which makes it distinctive. The stoic parallels, e.g., Epictetus *Diss.* I.1, 7–13, IV.10, 14–16, are not really to the point, since the point of comparison is not inner freedom or adequacy but the possession of the Spirit or God's gift and an admission of human weakness to be reinforced by the divine strength; Bultmann, 228, makes this clear, drawing a contrast between Paul and the stoics. The contrast between Paul and Judaism is striking as well, since Deut 3:26 is no adequate parallel, as this is more a pious resignation to necessity than a positive accession of δύναμις, "strength." What we can say is that Paul is convinced that neither the thorn nor trials of any sort will cause him to cease in his service to God. The following clause restates the same theme.

The power (δύναμις) spoken of is the power of Christ. This is why the "my" is inserted in the translation (see also NIV; RSV; KJV/AV; Bruce, 249; but the "my" is absent from NEB and also from Barrett, 316, and is a secondary textual reading). At the conclusion of 12:9 Paul again speaks of the δύναμις τοῦ Χριστοῦ, "the power of Christ" (see Tasker, 179). It is right to take δύναμις and χάρις as synonyms (O'Collins, "Power," 522; Bultmann, 229). By understanding power to represent the power of Christ, Paul is close to personifying power in our present v (Héring, 93). See 1 Cor 1:24 where Christ is said to be the power of God. This personification suggests that Christ reaches fulfillment (τελεῖν) in Paul (Windisch, 391; Gal 2:20 as a *unio mystica*). But such an understanding of Paul is unusual, for he likes to speak of believers being ἐν Χριστῷ, "in Christ." In this phrase, Christ is treated as a personality in whom all Christians are incorporated (see C. F. D. Moule, *The Phenomenon of the New Testament*, SBT 2d ser. 1 [Naperville: Allenson, 1967] 21–42).

The power Paul experienced is fulfilled (τελεῖται: Delling, *TDNT* 8:58–61) in weakness (ἀσθένεια: here "the most outstanding example of Paul's usage of ἀσθένεια"; Black, *Paul*, 151). The concept behind "fulfillment" is that of bringing to completion (τελείωσις). Some translate it as bringing power to perfection. But "perfection" does not here speak of moral behavior, rather of God's power as it is made the main focus of Paul's work. This is the main thrust behind 12:1–10. But unlike Paul's opponents—in whom God's glory was not an aim—the apostle boasts of his weakness (in particular, his thorn). Barrett is certainly correct, if slightly anachronistic, when he writes, "Divine power is scarcely perceptible in the impressive activities of the ecclesiastical potentates with whom Paul has to contend" (317).

Some maintain that Paul's choice of τελεῖν is a deliberate rebuttal of the gnostics. The connection is made when τέλειος is considered synonymous with πνευματικός (see Schmithals, *Gnosticism*, 163, 164; also see E. Güttgemanns, *Der leidende Apostel*, 168; U. Wilckens, *Weisheit*, 218, n. 2). But the alternative proposal of Georgi that Paul's opponents were Jewish Christian missionaries cannot be ignored (see also O'Collins, "Power," 531; see Betz, "Aretalogie," 304, 305). If this position is true, then we can say, as does O'Collins, that the gnostics did not have a monopoly on the use of δύναμις and ἀσθένεια. Moreover, Paul was not consciously responding to the Gnostics in this emotional and intimate passage under study. What can be said is that the fulfillment of God's power comes not in heavenly visions and ecstatic demonstrations, but in earthly weakness (see Güttgemanns, ibid.). And to mark off Paul from his opponents, it is clear that, while both groups shared a revelatory experience, Paul—unlike his rivals—does not report a healing, to provide a proof of the validity of his apostleship (Fallon, 106).

The notion of weakness is an important idea in 12:9, 10. (The noun appears three times and the verb once.) O'Collins is right in pointing out that "Paul understands his weakness Christologically" ("Power," 532: so Güttgemanns, ibid., 169, 170, tellingly). What Paul has suffered has been done so for Christ. Furthermore, in the crucifixion, Paul can see Christ as weak (Wilckens, ibid., 48; cf. 13:4). He can also see God's power manifested (fulfilled) in the resurrection. Thus, in Christ's suffering, God's power was completed. That Paul is weak (and even weaker because of the thorn) is yet the "best possible hope for the display of divine power" (Barrett, 317).

ἥδιστα οὖν μᾶλλον καυχήσομαι ἐν ταῖς ἀσθενείαις μου, "Therefore I will most gladly boast in my weaknesses." Having received the assurance that his weaknesses will not hinder his work for God, Paul presents the ruling attitude that prevails in his life. Instead of asking God yet again to remove the thorn, Paul understood this liability as a means tending to God's glory. The οὖν, "therefore," tells Paul's readers that he has concluded something about his situation (BDF § 451.1). ἥδιστα, "all the more gladly," is the superlative of ἡδέως (thus a possible rendering is the elative "most gladly," Barrett, 317). Paul's prayer (12:8) was answered in the negative. In time, Paul has come to accept this answer as in his best interest. That καυχήσομαι is in the future tense should not lead us to think Paul has yet to boast in his afflictions. A quick glance at 4:7–18 affirms that Paul glories in God, not himself. But he had been driven (12:11) to boast by the exigencies of the new situation consequent on the arrival of "false apostles" in 11:4, 13–15. He has related his vision to the Corinthians. In turn, he says, as we have noticed, that this vision was not his "badge" of apostleship. Rather, his sufferings prove him a *bona fide* minister of God. Even more, Paul revels in his weaknesses, for in them God uses him as an instrument for truth and righteousness (6:4–10).

A question centers on Paul's use of μᾶλλον. It has the idea of "rather" behind it (BGD, 489). It is doubtful that it goes with ἥδιστα as μᾶλλον does not strengthen superlatives (Plummer; cf. BDF § 246). Paul will boast in his weaknesses rather than in something else (Robertson, *Grammar*, 664). Possibly the something else is "revelations and visions" (*pace* Plummer, 355).

ἵνα ἐπισκηνώσῃ ἐπ᾿ ἐμὲ ἡ δύναμις τοῦ Χριστοῦ, "in order that the power of Christ may rest upon me." The ἵνα introduces the reason (or purpose; we shall discuss the issue of whether weakness is a means to finding a power already within, or a means to receiving power from outside) that Christ's power rests on Paul. This conjunction governs the subjunctive mood, an example of which we find in ἐπισκηνώσῃ (from ἐπισκηνοῦν). We might note that the use of the verb in 12:10 is a *hapax legomenon*. Plummer (355) calls the idea behind ἐπισκηνοῦν a "bold metaphor." What we see is the Hebrew concept concerning the presence of God as it was found in the Jewish Tabernacle and first Temple. Many have noticed this point (Plummer, 355; Strachan, 33; Héring, 94; Tasker, 179; Hughes, 452; Barrett, 367; Schlatter, 669; Hodge, 287; Güttgemanns, ibid., 169; Bultmann, 230) and related it to the Hebrew term שְׁכִינָה, *šᵉkînāh*. This OT-Jewish term referred to the presence of God dwelling with the people (Exod 40:34). In the NT the root σκην- clearly suggests the Hebrew root for "abide," namely, שָׁכַן, *šākan*. It is said in John 1:14 that Christ was "dwelling among us" (literally, "pitching his tent"), and in Revelation (7:14; 12:12; 13:6; 21:3) that God will dwell with the saints (cf. also Ezek 37:27 and Zech 2:10, both in the LXX; see also Philo, *Quis div. haer.*, 23). In some sense then, the power of Christ alighted on Paul as a result of his accepting God's will not to remove the thorn (see chap. 5 where Paul also uses the tent imagery in his discussion). But in examining this point, we are led to ask another question: Did Paul see weakness as a means of revealing a power already present in him, or is weakness the door through which comes the power of Christ? Another way to phrase the question is to inquire whether the prefix ἐπι- in the verb ἐπισκηνοῦν is vertical (i.e., Christ's power descending *onto* Paul from above: so Windisch, 392; Lietzmann, 156), or horizontal (i.e., Christ's power expressing itself *through* Paul and his apostolic career, so Michaelis, *TDNT* 7:389; cf. Schlatter, *Paulus*, 669; Allo, 312).

Bultmann interprets 12:9 as referring to a revelatory function of weakness. For him, struggle is not approved by God as a means for living the Christian life. Rather, for Bultmann, God is only satisfied with total surrender, which signifies no more struggle. By doing this, the person will know and, only then will he truly know, that he is a sinner (see *Theology* 1:285, 349, 351 and in his commentary, 228–30). By discerning weakness, a person discovers the power within. For Bultmann, Paul's dictum (12:9) for power holds true for any Christian. Plummer concurs, for he writes that God's power becomes more evident in weakness, not more real (354). Betz views the weakness of Paul, not as the indwelling of the messenger of Satan but as an "epiphany" (*"eine Epiphanie"*) of the crucified Lord ("Aretalogie," 303).

An opposite point of view is taken by Käsemann. He understands weakness as an ontological reality (see *Legitimität*, 39: also see 13:3, 4). Windisch (391, 392) sees Paul's weakness as a precondition for the power of Christ to enter him. Strachan shows a similar understanding, but O'Collins may be right in spotting a Pelagian tendency in Strachan's thinking ("Power," 530).

O'Collins favors the position that weakness is ontological rather than revelatory ("Power," 537). However, he does allow for "something in the order of revelation." The ontological reality of the gift of power leads to an "epiphany" of this presence. Possibly O'Collins sums up best the role that weakness played in Paul's life. What we can see is that Paul has experienced a higher degree of communion with God because of suffering in general and the thorn in particular. We probably will never know the invaluable aid the experience of 12:1–10 played in strengthening Paul over the arduous years of his ministry.

O'Collins, however, parts company with Käsemann (who is followed by Schmithals, *Gnosticism,* 163; Windisch, ibid.; Wendland, 224, 225) concerning whether or not Paul's teaching of 12:9 is to be understood as a general rule for the Church as a whole. O'Collins (ibid.) maintains that in 12:1–10 Paul is speaking of himself—his vision (12:1), his thorn (12:7), his prayer 12:8—and thus we should follow Betz's contention ("Aretalogie," 297) that the oracle was directed at Paul and not the community. But we wonder if Paul would want to be understood like this. More likely he would not accept this exclusivist interpretation, for it would make him out as somebody special. This is an elitist idea that Paul fights against throughout his letter (1:24; 3:3, 18; 6:3; 7:3; 10:13; 11:21, and esp. 13:9). (Surprisingly, O'Collins admits that Christians have the right to apply Paul's words of 12:9 to their lives ["Power," 534]. But this, in effect, undercuts O'Collins's position.)

10. διὸ εὐδοκῶ ἐν ἀσθενείαις, ἐν ὕβρεσιν, ἐν ἀνάγκαις, ἐν διωγμοῖς καὶ στενοχωρίαις, ὑπὲρ Χριστοῦ, "For this reason, I delight in weaknesses, in insults, in anguish, in persecutions and distress for the sake of Christ." We observed the use of διό in 12:7. Possibly this is a connection between the thought there (*"therefore* in order that I not become conceited") and the summary he gives in this v. Paul has not fallen into conceit because of the thorn in the flesh God gave him; yet, Paul has overcome—in a spiritual sense—this thorn and its attendant weakness by accepting it and learning to live with it. He has overcome his handicap because the power of Christ rests upon him, exactly as in 4:7.

Because this power is now Paul's (in a secondary sense), he delights (εὐδοκεῖν) in what has happened to him. The rendering of εὐδοκῶ as "content" (RSV) or "well content" (NEB; Barrett, 317; also see Phillips, "I can even enjoy") misses the point of this verse. Paul is so aware ("conscious," is how Tasker, 179, puts it) of the power of Christ (i.e., the grace of Christ) that he delights in (a semitism with ב, *b^e*, BDF § 196, 206.2, and implying consent to, approval of, saying yes to [*ja sagen zu*, Bultmann, 230]) his afflictions and weaknesses (ἀσθένειαι, κτλ.: a mini "catalogue of crises"). ὕβρεις, "insults," a noun to be taken passively (G. Bertram, *TDNT* 8:305), is used by Paul only here (see Acts 27:10, 21), and has specific allusion to his Corinthian enemies who resisted him in mockery (11:19–21) and by opposing his Gospel. So Windisch, 393. The ASV translation of "injuries" for ἐν ὕβρεσιν is not commonly followed. For "in anguish" (ἐν ἀνάγκαις) see *Comment* on 6:4. Here it goes in close association with "insults," directed at his apostolic work.

διωγμοί translates as "persecutions" and suggests such persecutions as those resulting from religious reasons (BGD, 201; Rom 8:35; cf. 2 Thess 1:4; 2 Tim 3:11). We have στενοχωρίαι in 6:4, and cf. 4:8 for the verb.

The tribulation-list supplements and illustrates Paul's discussion on weakness. We note that the afflictions are endured ὑπὲρ Χριστοῦ "for the sake of (lit., "on behalf of") Christ." Such an idea repels the mistaken concept of suffering that has sometimes pervaded church history. Those who have experienced or encouraged self-afflicted wounds, endured martyrdom simply as a means of seeking to become righteous, and practiced asceticism solely as a means of securing God's favor are guilty of emphasizing merit, not faith (cf. Ignatius of Antioch). Human suffering in and of itself does not display divine power. Such bravado only produces rewards for the morbid fanatic or the foolish (Tasker, 179). Or, as Hughes proposes, "a joyless theology of insecurity" is the outcome of such endeavors. Rather, Paul exhibits a joyful walk with God undergirded by a firm security in God's grace. So deep-seated is Paul's delight that what he has endured does not compare to what is his in Christ.

ὅταν γὰρ ἀσθενῶ, τότε δυνατός εἰμι, "When I am weak, then I am powerful." This sentence is the gnomic climax of 12:1–10. Perhaps this is a parody (Betz), but no more than in a peripheral sense (Barrett, 317, 18; Zmijewski, *Der Stil*, 395, who treats the dictum as a paradoxical keyword which expresses the highpoint of the section). Paul has stated in succinct terms and a concise manner the essence of his apostolic ministry. The temporal particle ὅταν, "when," introduces the idea of the indefinite. (Possibly, if being weak referred to a specific time, then we would have had ὅτε. In one sense, Paul is weak because of the thorn. But in an added sense, Paul has brought his whole ministry [weaknesses, insults, anguish, persecutions, and distress] into the picture. Paul is not only concerned with the thorn when he writes 12:10*b;* he is concerned with his ministry [or any Christian's ministry in general].) Whenever God's servants humble themselves and acknowledge their weakness, then the power of Christ can flow through them. This is a justification of "My grace is sufficient for you" (Plummer). God has more than compensated for the fact that the thorn was not removed. In short, the response of 12:9*a* as a divine ἀπόκριμα is the "answer" in Paul's best interest. (We have translated δυνατός as "powerful," so that there is consistency in 12:9, 10 with respect to δύναμις, i.e., God's might in human frailty. This translation procedure is not usually followed.)

Explanation

The present passage provides one of the most enlightening treatments by Paul on the meaning of strength-in-weakness. Paul resisted the taunts of his opponents who insisted that they were better suited to represent the ministry of God in Corinth. The opponents came to this conclusion on the ground and evidence that they had demonstratable gifts that attracted attention to their own persons. Paul countered by insisting that his credentials were not spectacular visions (though he had visions to his credit); rather, he boasted of the power of Christ that rested upon and worked through him. And it was not as though Paul had no demonstrable gifts. He did have, namely, his weakness and his ministry to the Corinthians. Herein is the paradox. These were the reasons why Paul entered into a "debate" with his opponents. He wanted to show that boasting was of little value unless such boasting directed attention (and glory) to God. Because he was weak, Paul's ministry did just that. Thus, he has shown that boasting (in the common understanding of the word) was not of God. One should "boast" to glorify God, not oneself. But "boasting" now has assumed a different character, returning in thought to 10:17, 18.

Paul resisted the temptation of steering off the course set before him. He could have easily taken the detour of self-commendation in order to avoid the jibes and jabs of his opponents. He could have also taken such an alternate route in the hope of convincing the Corinthians (again) of his integrity and honest desire to better them. Paul remained faithful to the truth (13:8).

Paul recognized that his religious experiences (i.e., visions and revelations) were valid and helpful. He considered them a privilege and an honor. They were from God, and Paul never questioned the validity of them. Such times, especially that described in 12:2-4, were of much aid for Paul. It is highly unlikely that a recall of the vision (12:2-4) ever failed to strengthen Paul. But he never appealed to it to validate his apostolate. Instead, his appeal lies elsewhere, e.g., in 3:1-3; 13:1-4, 8, 9.

But Paul's greatest boast was the strength of Christ which resided in him. God had accepted Paul's weakness; and in a dialogic encounter Paul learned that such a thing—even a humiliating thorn in the flesh—can and does lead a person to God. By accepting God's will, Paul was able to grow as a minister of the Gospel, as well as a disciple of Christ. At firsthand, Paul understood the "weakness" Christ exhibited in going to the cross (13:4). Moreover, he saw the true power of God in the resurrection of the heavenly Lord who spoke to him. In 12:9, 10, Paul names a rule of life that overturns the world's understanding and yet provides a key to service in Christ. This rule is Paul's guide: "When I am weak, then I am powerful."

E. Paul's Apostolate Justified (12:11-18)

Bibliography

Barrett, C. K. "Paul's Opponents in 2 Corinthians." In *Essays on Paul*, chap. 4, 60–86. ———. "Titus." In *Essays on Paul*, chap. 7, 118–31. **Jervell, J.** "The Signs of an Apostle." Tr. R. A. Harrisville, in *The Unknown Paul.* ———. "Der schwache Charismatiker." In *Rechtfertigung.* FS E. Käsemann.

Translation

¹¹ *I have become a fool;* ^a *you compelled me to do it. For I ought to be commended by you; for in no way am I inferior to the "highest ranking apostles"—though I am nothing.* ¹² *The marks* ^b *of a [true]* ^c *apostle were displayed [by God]* ^d *among you in all persistence, [along with]* ^d *signs* ^e *and wonders and mighty works.* ¹³ *How were you inferior to the other churches, except that I, myself, was not a burden to you? Forgive me this wrong!* ¹⁴ *I am now ready to visit you a third time,* ^f *and I will not be a burden, because I seek you and not your possessions. For children ought not to save up for their parents, but parents for their children.* ¹⁵ *I will most gladly spend and be spent on your behalf. If* ^g *I love* ^h *you more, will you love me less?* ⁱ ¹⁶ *Though I was not a burden to you,* ^j *yet, crafty fellow that I am, I caught you by trickery.* ¹⁷ *Did I take advantage of you by any of the men I sent to you?* ¹⁸ *I urged Titus [to visit you]* ^k *and I sent the brother with him. Did Titus take advantage of you? Did we not walk in the same spirit and follow the same course?*

Notes

^a Some MSS (ψ 0243 syr) add καυχώμενος ("I have become a fool through boasting") but our text is well supported (P⁴⁶ ℵ A B D* F G K 33 81 1175 1736). As Tasker remarks, the "sentence is more vigorous without" the addition (179).

^b We follow the NEB and understand the first σημεῖον to be used differently from the second one of 12:12. Accordingly, we have rendered the second term as "signs," but the first as "marks" (contra BGD, 748; see *Comment*).

^c This is not in the text but is implied by the needed sense.

^d In light of our decision in *Note* b, we insert the words "by God," "along with," to show that the marks of an apostle effected by God were accompanied by signs and wonders and mighty works. See Rom 15:18, 19 for parallel. The Greek text, however, does not have the words in the brackets. See *Comment* for use of datives for the three nouns that follow.

^e The text is supported by P⁴⁶ ℵ B 0243 33 81 1175 1739. Also σημείοις (without τε; A D* Ambst) and ἐν σημείοις (ℵ² D²) are noted. See Plummer, 360.

^f K L P 614 629 945 1241 omit τοῦτο, but most likely the text is right (ℵ A B F G).

^g The TR has καί after εἰ (ℵ² D¹ K L P vg syr goth arm eth). Some MSS (D* it^{d,g,r} Ambst) omit εἰ altogether. But the text has the strongest support (P⁴⁶ ℵ* A B F G 33 cop).

^h A difficult decision is called for concerning the correct reading of "If I love you more, will you love me less?" First issue is the question of punctuation (see *Note* i), and second is the question of whether to include the verb ἀγαπῶ (ℵ* A 33 104*) or the participle ἀγαπῶν (P⁴⁶ ℵ² B D F G ψ 0243). The confusion over which verbal form to keep could be the result of either the adding or dropping of ν before η (ΑΓΑΠΩ[Ν]ΗΣΣΟΝ). The participial form is the more difficult because, unlike anywhere else, Paul demands that the reader supply the verb εἰμι. The greater external evidence has led scholars to include ἀγαπῶν, but internal considerations influenced them so as to show ν in brackets (ἀγαπῶ[ν], Metzger, *Textual Commentary*, 586, 587).

ⁱMany MSS (p⁴⁶ ℵᶜ B D ψ 0243 81 1739 1881 it vg goth Chrys) have v 15 ending in a period. Other MSS (ℵ* A 33 syr cop) have the ending of v 15 as a question mark. The context suggests the latter. See Tasker, 182.

ʲThe text is found in A B D² ψ 0243. Other variant readings are p⁴⁶ οὐκ ἐβάρησα (also in D*) and οὐ κατενάρκησα ὑμῶν (ℵ F G 81 104 1881).

ᵏThese words in brackets, though not found in the Greek text, are implied, as though ἵνα ἔρχηται πρὸς ὑμᾶς were understood (Windisch, 403).

Form/Structure/Setting

Paul ceases his boasting in 12:11–18 (Barrett, 319) and turns instead to the defense of his behavior. Once more, in 12:11–18, Paul is defending his motives for acting the way he did. The first subject to be discussed is Paul's boasting and apostleship. Paul had not wanted to boast but had been driven (ἠναγκάσατε, 12:11) to do so because the Corinthian church abdicated its responsibility to defend him (cf. 5:12). Let us review the setting. When Paul's opponents attacked him, apparently few, if any, of the church came to his defense. (The first time the Corinthian church failed to speak on Paul's behalf was the occasion when the offender confronted Paul [cf. 2:5–11; 7:12]. This occasion sparked off the writing of the "severe letter" [2:3, 4]. Apparently after the return of Titus to Paul in Macedonia [7:5–7] and the good report that he brought, the church was infiltrated by some that opposed Paul, probably the so-called "false apostles" [11:4, 13]. It appears that these opponents attacked Paul's apostolate. [Paul may have learned of the sudden change of events as he made his way toward Corinth from Macedonia.] The church followed the same course of action with regard to these opponents as it had done when the offender opposed Paul, namely, it did nothing at the time. The reaction of the church to the opponents is the impetus behind Paul's writing chaps. 10–13.) Hence, Paul played the fool (γέγονα ἄφρων, 12:11). 12:11a appears to complete an *inclusio* that started in 12:6 and closes the "ring-composition" begun at 11:1. The intervening vv form a separate literary unit, a "Fool's Talk," (*Narrenrede*). In 12:6 Paul speaks of boasting, but not as a fool in the general sense. In 12:11, he reminds the Corinthians that, if they think he is a fool, they must remember that they forced him to act like one. (By noticing this *inclusio*, we see that 12:1–10 and 12:11–18 are connected.) Paul had taken up and played the role of a fool in order to overcome his opponents. This role parallels the true philosopher who sought to prove that his weaknesses authenticated his claims. The philosopher, as a rule, avoided boasting. If forced to boast, he would play the part of the fool (by a use of irony, parody, and invective) in order to defend himself against false charges. See earlier, pp. 329, 359, 360. 12:6–11 contains the account of the thorn in the flesh as a counterpoint to his insistence in "boasting" (12:1). Paul has boasted, but only in his weakness since he saw the thorn as sent by God and a reality he had to come to terms with. Yet, if his boasting was taken as a "self-commending action," Paul reminds the Corinthians that such a course of action on his part would not have been necessary—had they defended him.

The Corinthians ought (ὤφειλον, 12:11) to have refuted Paul's opponents.

After all, had Paul not come to them as a loving father? Had he not been the one apostle with a commission (10:13–16) to found the church? Nevertheless, the apathetic Corinthians had once more opted to do nothing. Or worse, they sided with the intruders and gave them a welcome (11:4, 19). This reflects "consistency" on their part, for such action is reminiscent of the action they took during Paul's painful visit. And their instability made them easy prey. Even though Paul has been hurt again, he will not turn and leave his children. (Would his opponents have done likewise? That is, would they have been so loving and patient if they had received such treatment as Paul had?) In a sudden change, Paul brings in the "super-apostles" and insists that in no way is he inferior (ὑστέρησα, 12:11) to those leaders whose authority the rival mission evidently claimed to represent. (There is much uncertainty surrounding the identity of these ὑπερλίαν ἀπόστολοι in 12:11, cf. 11:5. Were they the Jerusalem apostles or the false apostles of 11:13? Or, were they the Jerusalem leaders whose name was being used, as we propose? See earlier, pp. 336–42. In any case, we note the sarcastic tone of Paul. See *Comment* on 11:5. It is the position of this commentary that the "super-apostles" and the "false apostles" [11:13] are two different groups. The former probably refers to Peter, James, and John. [Cf. also Gal 2:9, where we read of the "pillar–" στῦλοι– apostles.] The latter describes a group opposed to Paul, possibly a group of self-appointed emissaries, who sought to proselytize among the Corinthians; see Harris, 312–14; Barrett, 30–32; and for a recent treatment, D. A. Carson, *From Triumphalism to Maturity* [Grand Rapids: Baker, 1984] 16–29.) This sudden "insertion" of the term "super-apostles" is probably a side-glance at the "false apostles." The latter were claiming authority from the former (though it is doubtful the former gave the latter such authority). Paul is now centering on his apostleship and has left the subject of boasting. In polemical fashion, Paul retorts that he "is nothing." This is probably a borrowed phrase, most likely coming as a taunt from his opponents similar to 1 Cor 15:8 (ἐκτρῶμα, "one untimely born," or "little one," a term of reproach: Martin, *The Spirit and the Congregation*, 92, 93, 99, 100). The irony of calling himself "nothing" is noteworthy. Paul is "nothing" because he admits his weaknesses and confesses that everything he has is from God. But if Paul were pressed he would admit that to say he is nothing is equivalent to saying that in Christ's power he is everything and more. He is more than the opponents that slur him and not any less than the super-apostles. See the use of this "self-depreciation" motif in Eph 3:7, 8.

Paul continues his polemic in 12:12. He suggests that the marks of an apostle (not necessarily limited to "signs, wonders and mighty works") were performed (*sc.* by God through me: Rom 15:18, 19) among the Corinthians in great persistence (ἐν πάσῃ ὑπομονῇ). Paul has probably borrowed some words of the Corinthians and built his case upon them. More likely than not, he was accused of not having the marks or signs of a true apostle. This is evident in that the marks that Paul boasted of—weakness and suffering—were not considered by others as proof of apostleship. Paul is called (by implication) an "inferior" apostle. If Paul's "thorn in the flesh" was a physical ailment (see pp. 412–16), then the opponents could argue that Paul could not heal

himself (see Jervell, "Der schwache Charismatiker"). Also, we cannot rule
out that Paul's failure to do much for Epaphroditus (even though he did
recover) may have been another arrow shot at the apostle. See Phil 2:25–
28; we can well understand Paul's empathy for Epaphroditus, who like Paul,
may have been subject to suspicion as a sick Christian leader, incapacitated
by illness which rendered him out of commission. (The tradition in 2 Tim
4:20, "I left Trophimus as a sick person in Miletus" also confirms Paul's
inability to heal); see R. P. Martin, *Philippians*, NCB (Grand Rapids: Eerdmans,
1982) 122. Moreover, as will be seen, Paul did not accept money from the
Corinthians. The acceptance of money for ministry was considered by the
opponents as a "mark" of a true apostle (11:7–11). What Paul does (see
Comment) is to build a case that there are more important criteria to determine
whether or not a person is a true apostle. In fact, this is exactly what Paul
has done in chaps. 10, 11, and will return to in 13:4, 5. As the *Comment*
will show, Paul *can* perform the miraculous (see now Jervell, "The Signs of
an Apostle," esp. 90–94, who appeals to Rom 15:19; 1 Thess 1:5; 1 Cor
2:4; Gal 3:1–5; but in 2 Cor 12:12 he misses the point of the verb and the
inclusion of a set formula which is modified by ὑπομονή. In any case, Jervell
grants, "divine miraculous power is expressed in the weakness of the ailing
apostle" [94]). But more important, he can prove his apostleship by the suffering he has endured for Christ, the frailty of the messenger (4:7), and the
effectiveness of the message he brings (5:18–21).

After having defended his boasting and apostleship (12:11, 12), Paul turns
to a sore subject (the second topic of 12:11–18) between him and the Corinthians, namely, his refusal to receive maintenance from the church at Corinth
(12:13–16a). Apparently the Corinthian church felt slighted that he would
accept aid from other churches (11:9) but not from it. He had not been a
burden (οὐ κατενάρκησα). Again using irony, he argues that the Corinthian
church is not "inferior" because he refused its money. Perhaps Paul is not
being ironical when he writes "forgive me this wrong!" (χαρίσασθέ μοι τὴν
ἀδικίαν ταύτην). Such an idea is based on the assumption that Paul truly felt
he had offended the Corinthians, hence the church had the impression that
the apostle either doubted its willingness to help him or considered it cheap.
But Paul was aware that the opponents had fleeced the church (11:9, 20),
and he worked (probably at tentmaking) so as not to burden these people.
Moreover, he could not take the Corinthians' money, or they would assume
that he condoned this activity of the false apostles. Most likely, on balance,
the statement is ironical ("Forgive me this wrong" as in 11:7), one that does
not miss the mark in getting its point across.

Paul maintains in 12:14 that he will persevere in his policy of taking no
money from his children. Hodge (293) says of Paul that he is telling the
Corinthians "You must allow me a parent's privilege." We should not fail
to see that in 12:13, 14 Paul is still writing in polemical fashion. He is their
father and has never taken anything from the Corinthians that could have
caused a hardship to them. Paul simply quotes a natural rule of life (νόμος
φύσεως; Bultmann, 236, standing in tension with 1 Cor 9:14), and that
rule is that parents support their children, not vice versa. Paul is willing to

spend and be spent for his spiritual offspring (12:15). He hopes that his increased love will not be met with a decrease of love on the part of the Corinthians. This reference to loving the Corinthians may be Paul's response to a charge that he in fact does not love them (11:11; another charge mooted by his opponents). Paul concludes 12:13–16a with the statement that his future visit (number three) will not find a change in his attitude toward seeking financial help from the church at Corinth. What Paul has accomplished in 12:13–16a is to promote his sincerity toward the Corinthians in spite of appearances to the contrary. He is not out to make them feel inferior by taking assistance only from other churches. Rather (see *Comment*), he wants nothing but the best for the Corinthians (13:9). To take money from the Corinthians would not impoverish them. But it would condone the activity of misguided people (the opponents and their followers) who see the taking of money for preaching the Gospel as an authentic sign of an apostle. By refusing such procedures Paul continues his honest dealings with the Corinthians.

But 12:16b–18 presents us with a third area in which Paul has had to defend his behavior. Since the opponents could not deny that he refused direct aid from the Corinthian church (11:9), then it appears Paul was confronted with the charge of stealing the collection in spite of the safeguards of 8:20, 21 (see *Comment* there, and see Holmberg, *Paul and Power*, 92, for several other factors in the Corinthians' suspicious attitudes). Paul could refuse "over the table" payments—such as reimbursement for services rendered— because, his opponents argued, he was receiving money "under the table." He was covering up his real intention by the pretense of refusing the aid of the Corinthians. Paul reports his awareness that he is accused of taking advantage of the Corinthians (ἐπλεονέκτησα, 12:17, 18). In a stinging piece of irony Paul "admits" that his trickery (δόλος) has caught the Corinthians when he writes, "crafty fellow that I am" (12:16b). In a series of four questions, Paul then argues that the accusation that he is stealing from the Corinthians is ludicrous. The first two of these questions are constructed so as to expect a negative answer (17, μή; 18b, μήτι). Paul inquires of the Corinthians whether any of his emissaries, especially Titus, had ever cheated them (answering the implied charge that he acted in sly fashion to acquire money through agents: Georgi, *Die Gegner*, 241). Then in the other two questions (12:18c) we see that Paul desires affirmative answers (οὐ). The thrust of these final two questions is that, if the Corinthians compare Paul with Titus, then they will see that Paul walks in the same paths as does the trusted Titus. If they do not doubt Titus's sincerity, how can they doubt Paul's?

This passage, 12:11–18 as an apology for Paul's actions, basically ends Paul's polemic against his opponents in chaps. 10–13. Beginning in 12:19 and continuing for the remainder of the letter, he centers on his forthcoming visit to Corinth. His opponents, though never far from his mind, recede into the background of the present epistle. The remainder of 2 Corinthians describes Paul as one coming in the authority of the Lord, though 13:1–4 offer a classic statement on the nature of apostolic ministry, and 13:8–10 touch on the genius of his authority as concerned with οἰκοδομή, "upbuilding" (Strachan, 36).

Comment

11. γέγονα ἄφρων, "I have become a fool." At this point Paul's boasting comes to an end. What we have is the terminus of an *inclusio* begun at 11:1 (See *Form/Structure/Setting*). He has boasted often in chaps. 10–13 (10:8; 11:16–18; 12:5, 6), yet such action has been against his nature. No doubt Paul felt caught in a dilemma. If he did not boast, there was a good chance that the Corinthians would not give him the attention that he desired. If "boasting" was a "mark" of an apostle in the eyes of the Corinthians, then Paul had to boast. If Paul did boast, he was then joining in an activity which he detested, for it appears that such an activity was a full-time occupation of his opponents. In short, boasting was a "necessary evil" for Paul, called into play by the exigencies of the conditions at Corinth where he was encountering a struggle "with rhetorically trained opponents for the support of his rhetorically fastidious converts" (E. A. Judge, "Paul's Boasting," *ABR* 16 [1968] 48).

Paul has reluctantly boasted. We saw in 11:21–23 that he realizes he is being carried away by the boasting he is doing. (In 11:22 Paul defends his "Jewish" nature, thus suggesting that the opponents are Jewish.) When he commences to list his credentials, he catches himself and says "I am speaking as a fool" (11:21). A little later he inserts, "I must be out of my mind to talk like this" (11:23). Finally, in 11:30 Paul relates that his boasting points toward his weakness. Nevertheless, he continues his "bragging" by describing a certain revelation that he had fourteen years earlier (12:2–4). he concludes in 12:9, 10 that his weakness, including the thorn in the flesh, is a means for God's power to be manifested. Moreover, it is in such weakness that Paul believes he has found the locus of strength, i.e., it is the strength which comes from reliance on God in whom he boasts (10:17, 18).

In 12:11 Paul tries one more time to break away from his boasting, and this time he succeeds. He reflects his thought of 11:21 and 11:23 by stating he has made a fool of himself. He has been foolish (ἄφρων). He was bragging how he was a better Jew and a more devoted servant of Christ than his opponents. The use of the perfect (γέγονα, "have become") may suggest that Paul realizes his being foolish has been a fact for sometime. He has had to engage in this non-typical activity ("un-Christian," Barrett, 319) to remedy a critical situation. As we will see, though Paul recognizes that he has played the fool, he does not take responsibility for having to do so. The pastoral concerns (11:28) have driven him to an alien practice, albeit needful, as part of his argumentative strategy (see 1 Cor 9:22, 23).

ὑμεῖς με ἠναγκάσατε, "you compelled me to do it." Had it not been for the Corinthian behavior, Paul "would never have stooped to such folly" (Plummer, 358). We note that the pronoun ὑμεῖς, "you," stands immediately after the pause. This placement by Paul was not for stylistic reasons, but for emphasis (Filson, 410). It was the Corinthians who forced Paul to act the fool. ἠναγκάσατε (aorist of ἀναγκάζειν) suggests the idea of "compulsion," "necessity," or "constraint," an idea also found with ὤφειλον (imperfect, without ἄν, to denote necessity, obligation, duty; so BDF § 358.1). This power over someone else can be the result of either threats or persuasion. As is the case here, it suggests that Paul was compelled to boast because of the Corinthian behavior towards him. (It will be seen shortly that Paul considered this situation—when compared to the earlier one of the second visit—as critical. While Paul may have been humiliated earlier, he now fears that the message of Christ will be lost on the Corinthians, for they are following a teaching that is different from his own [11:4].) He has been forced to act foolishly, and he makes this point clear by including the personal pronoun, με, "me" as the object of ἠναγκάσατε.

ἐγὼ γὰρ ὤφειλον ὑφ᾽ ὑμῶν συνίστασθαι, "For I ought to be commended by you." With these words, Paul explains why he was compelled to boast by the Corinthians' behavior. He was their spiritual father (6:13; cf. 12:14). The Corinthians owed thanks and appreciation to him for their new life in the Gospel (1 Cor 4:15). All along they have owed a debt to Paul for his missionary work at Corinth (Filson, 410). Paul reminds them of this point. ὤφειλον, "ought," is the imperfect of ὀφείλειν, which means "to owe." The imperfect tense may suggest that Paul sees this "owing" as an ongoing activity, but see above for a more likely meaning. It can refer to financial debts (Matt 18:26, 30, 34; Luke 7:41; 16:5, 7; Philem 18), but more generally it speaks of obligation in the figurative sense (Rom 13:8; 15:1; 1 Cor 9:10; 11:7; 2 Cor 12:14; 2 Thess 1:3). Again, Paul's use of a pronoun is transparent. He places ἐγώ, "I," at the beginning of this clause. The boasting by Paul was the result of their failure "to commend" (συνίστασθαι is the present passive of συνιστάνειν, a key term in the letter, see 3:1, 2; 4:2; 5:12; 6:4; 10:12, 18) him to others, namely, his opponents. As the Corinthians were guilty before (chap. 7), they are guilty again of failing to defend their apostle against his adversaries (Tasker, 179).

To be sure, the commendation by the Corinthians of Paul was not the basis for his apostleship (1 Cor 4:3: "it is a very light matter for me to be assessed by you or by human opinion"). He opened both canonical Corinthian epistles with the idea that he was called by God to be an apostle. We saw in 2 Cor 5 that despite the lack of Corinthian support, Paul claimed to be a true apostle of God. He had withstood much suffering on behalf of the Gospel, as well as much pain because of the indifference of the Corinthians. Moreover, Paul still loved these people.

His apostleship was from God (Gal 1:1) and not liable to human judgment (1 Cor 4:3, 4). But Paul also viewed the Corinthians as the seal of his apostleship (1 Cor 9:2). Since the Corinthians had become Christians because of Paul, what other proof was needed to validate his work (3:2, 3)? Even so, as Barrett remarks, the Corinthians were still ashamed of "their cheap (xi.7–11; xii.13–18) and tongue-tied (x.1, 10; xi.6) apostle as they compared him with his domineering rivals (xi.20)" (319, 320).

It is ironic that Paul was accused of being fickle (1:15–23) by a group of people that exhibited fickleness almost at every turn. After Paul had left Corinth following his first visit, trouble erupted. Upon his painful visit, Paul was humiliated. Surprisingly (or not so, to some) the appearance of Titus with the "severe letter" in Corinth turned the Corinthians' affection back to Paul. However, shortly thereafter, the opponents of Paul (most likely the false apostles [11:13]) convinced the Corinthians to return to their estimate of him that had prevailed prior to Titus's visit. (This "pendulum effect" makes one wonder if Paul [or Titus] ever met these false apostles face to face. We almost get the idea that the latest arrival in Corinth [11:4] is the leader in charge. That is, it almost seems that the one in effective control of the Corinthian church was the person who visited the church most recently, whether it might be Paul or his opponents. This "rule," it was Paul's hope, would prove true on his third visit to Corinth. Hence it would appear that if and when Paul made his third visit [12:14; 13:7] he would win them over to his side yet again [see *Comment* on 13:10].)

From our earlier discussion it seems that the fault of the Corinthians was mostly their apathy and gullibility (see 11:19, 20). They never rejected Paul out of hand; rather they simply thought it better to do nothing in face of the attack on him (2:5–11). Likewise, the words of 12:11 suggest that the problem was the same as that behind 2:5–11. But now it took on a more sinister cast. The Corinthians should have commended Paul to his opponents, even more so now that he had been reconciled to them (7:2–16). Yet this failed to happen. And we have to postulate a dramatic and unprecedented turn of events following the arrival of a rival Christian mission at 11:4. Nor should it be disregarded that Paul's own missionary future may have given an added seriousness to this latest threat to his apostolic calling. If the intrusion of a missionary party, aiming to overthrow his credibility at Corinth, gained a firm foothold, the consequences for Paul would be serious, not only in view of his past investment at Corinth, but also regarding his future plans for westward adventures (Rom 15:18–29). His entire emphasis on "weakness-as-strength" (12:1–10; 13:1–4), based on the "shame" of the cross and the apostolate, gained fresh impetus at this crucial time in his life (see Introduction, pp. lviii–lix).

Therefore, this "relapse" on the part of the Corinthians was understood by Paul as a dangerous situation. We saw this earlier at 5:12 with its point that for the Corinthians to disregard Paul was, in his mind anyway, to disregard God (Bultmann, 149, cited on p. 230). But our present v underscores the thought that Paul sees this latest episode by the Corinthians as even more critical than the earlier one. These false apostles not only attack Paul, but preach a different Jesus and a different gospel (11:4). The silence of the Corinthians when they might have rallied on the behalf of Paul forced him to boast. This was not only to gain the attention of his readers, but was also an attempt to show the Corinthians the folly of their position and to lead them to free themselves from the evil influence of the opponents (Plummer, 358). No doubt Paul feared that the Corinthians were close to reverting to their pagan ways. The problem would be that their behavior (clearly delineated in vv 20, 21) would have the sanction of "Christian apostles." This may make it impossible for Paul, or any other true apostle, ever to make headway again at Corinth (*1 Clement* makes salutary reading, describing the state of the Corinthian church in A.D. 96—at least from the standpoint of a leader at Rome).

οὐδὲν γὰρ ὑστέρησα τῶν ὑπερλίαν ἀποστόλων, "for in no way am I inferior to the 'highest ranking apostles'." The apostle continues his discussion with the Corinthians concerning their failure to uphold him in the face of opposition. In an obvious piece of polemic, Paul blurts out that he is not inferior to the super-apostles. The opening word is οὐδέν, meaning "in no single thing" (Plummer, 358). We take note of its place in the emphatic position, signifying that in no single way is Paul inferior. Literally, ὑστερεῖν means "to come up short." In the earlier reference (11:5) to "super-apostles" the verb was in the perfect (ὑστερηκέναι), but in our present v we have the aorist tense (ὑστέρησα). The use of the latter may suggest that Paul is referring specifically (Bultmann, 233) to a previous stay in Corinth (Filson, 411; Plummer, 358; most likely it was his first visit, the one that lasted eighteen months, for his second visit was of short duration and of little effect). Barrett (cf. his "Paul's Opponents," 71) suggests that the aorist may point to a specific occasion when the Corinthians compared Paul to his rivals (320; but Betz, *Der Apostel Paulus*, 121, n. 572, thinks it simply looks back to the "Fool's Talk" section). If so, then the super-apostles must have been in Corinth at the same time and thus could be identified as the false apostles and not the Jerusalem apostles (11:13). But, as Barrett proceeds, if this aorist is constative, then Paul is speaking of his dealings with the Corinthians since the writing of chaps. 1–9, and he simply may be saying that he is equal to the super-apostles (those in Jerusalem) and thus not inferior. We saw earlier the question surrounding οἱ ὑπερλίαν ἀπόστολοι, the "highest ranking apostles." Were these apostles the leaders of Jerusalem or some other group? (See *Comment* on 11:5, 13.) Our conclusion is that Paul uses the term "super-apostles" to refer to the original apostles in Jerusalem, following Käsemann, *Legitimität*, 28, who equates *Überapostel* with *Urapostel*. It may seem odd that Paul would include a reference to these apostles of Jerusalem when it appears that 12:11–18 is directed toward the opponents (probably the false apostles, *Lügenapostel:* Friedrich, "Die Gegner," 192). Most likely though, Paul's use of the "super"-apostles is intended as an indirect polemic against the false apostles. If the false apostles (probably Jewish emissaries or "missionizers," at least in the sense of imposing Jewish-hellenistic ideas on the Corinthians, though not necessarily insisting on circumcision [since there is no reference to circumcision or the law as νόμος in 2 Cor], see Harris, 312, 313) claimed that they were patterned after the super-apostles, this would account for the reference. Then if Paul was at least equal to the super-apostles, how could he be an inferior apostle? Admittedly Paul brings in elements that at first seem out of place. But we must remember that Paul is dictating a letter replete with emotion and is not writing a treatise that demands flawless logic (see *Comment* on 11:5). Regardless of who the super-apostles are, it appears Paul is speaking in ironical fashion (see *Form/Structure/Setting;* Barrett, 320; Tasker, 179, 180) when he uses the term "super"-apostles with more than a hint of the Corinthian love of ὕβρις, "pride," as exemplified in his opponents (11:19, 20; see Marshall, "Invective: Paul and his Enemies at Corinth") who have "exceeded" the bounds of their mission (10:13–15; 11:12). This would explain the concentration on ὑπέρ- in this chapter. They have gone to excess in visiting Corinth.

εἰ καὶ οὐδέν εἰμι, "though I am nothing." Having said that he is not an inferior apostle, Paul does not want to appear to be overdoing it. The use of εἰ καὶ is probably concessive and the use of οὐδέν, "nothing," may reflect the language of his opponents (Tasker, 180). No doubt they considered him a nobody (cf. 6:9), and he is simply repeating the charge. We know that Paul could characterize himself in humble terms (10:1, 2; 1 Cor 15:8, 9; also see use of οὐδέν in Plato, *Phaedrus* 234; Epictetus, III.9.14; IV.8.25; see Betz, ibid., 122–27). But not to be overlooked is the possibility that the statement "though I am nothing" may be ironical (Bultmann, 233, who suggests too a statement of pathos in the light of 12:5–10). For Paul to say that he is nothing is not to admit to being worthless or useless. Quite the contrary, he is at least equal to these super-apostles, both in terms of faith and work (Filson, 411). He has argued throughout the epistle that his apostleship is second to none. Nevertheless, he acknowledges (again) that what he has is from God. Because the apostle refuses to brag (except when forced to), he is seen as nothing. Moreover, his points of weakness support the contentions of his opponents. In this sense, he is pleased to be considered as "nothing" (12:9, 10). He is nothing that Christ may be seen to be everything.

Some older commentators (e.g., Chrysostom) took εἰ καί as an introduction to 12:12 rather than a conclusion to 12:11. But this has found little support. Plummer maintains that to affix the εἰ καί to 12:12 ignores the μέν, as well as creates an awkward asyndeton for v 12 (358).

12. τὰ μὲν σημεῖα τοῦ ἀποστόλου κατειργάσθη ἐν ὑμῖν πάσῃ ὑπομονῇ, "The marks of a [true] apostle were displayed [by God] among you in all persistence." The main thrust of v 12 is that Paul has all the credentials in the contest of *Evidenz* (13:3: you want proof [δοκιμή]). What calls for discussion is whether the two uses of σημεῖον, "sign," refer to the same thing or whether they are different. We lean toward the latter interpretation (against NIV, but see RSV and NEB). The first use of σημεῖον (12:12a) is more general than the second (Denney, 361, 362). The second use refers to a "miraculous" action, but it is distinguished from the first in that the former is included in the latter (Hughes, 457). We agree with Hughes, who writes, "These 'signs of an apostle' [12:12a] which were witnessed by the Corinthians were accompanied by 'signs and wonders and mighty works' [12:12b]" (ibid.)

We have seen in chaps. 10–13 that Paul bases his apostleship on the call of God (1 Cor 1:1; 2 Cor 1:1). He has felt that this apostleship has been affirmed and confirmed in his life and ministry (3:1–3). Such thinking appears to be behind the first use of σημεῖον in our present v. When Paul speaks of "distinguishing marks," naturally he must be referring to something more than the miraculous (12:12b). He does not belittle this aspect of the apostleship, but if the idea of θεῖοι ἄνδρες, "divine men," or something like it, was present at Corinth, Paul would probably shy away from putting such proof forward as the only evidence of his apostleship. (Indeed Bultmann [234], quoting the verb κατειργάσθη, lit., "were done," says it "shows that Paul does not recognize himself as a θεῖος ἀνήρ.") Rather, we understand Paul to say that he, and not his adversaries, has the true signs, or marks, of apostleship. (In fact, Paul considered the miraculous as open to being counterfeited; see 2 Thess 2:9; cf. Käsemann, *Legitimität*, 52, who cites Mark 13:22 as well.) Hence, the first part of v 12 is speaking of the genuine proof of Paul's apostleship.

First and foremost in Paul's mind as a mark of a true apostle is that the result of his preaching is changed lives (Denney, 361). Only God can do that (1 Cor 3:5–9). Paul "founded" the church at Corinth; he came as an ambassador of reconciliation (5:18–21). The Corinthians were the seal of Paul's apostleship (1 Cor 9:2; 2 Cor 3:1–3). Paul's message had introduced the Corinthians to Christ, and this, in turn, led to changed lives. Could the false apostles say that their message had been as effective? In addition, another mark of Paul was his Christlike life (Hughes, 456). He had endured suffering on behalf of Christ (13:4). Moreover, Paul had shown both the offender and the church as a whole how God expects his people to live. Paul had forgiven the offender (arising from the painful visit, 2:5–11) and had welcomed the church back to his side with open arms (chap. 7). Not only that, but Paul had been honest with the Corinthians (an issue that comes up in vv 14–18). His motives were pure and his actions aboveboard. He exhibited a life of sincerity and holiness (1:12; 2:17; 3:4–6; 4:2; 5:11; 6:3–13; 7:2; 10:13–18; 11:6, 23–28). In summary of our present phrase, we see that Paul's ministry and life basically encompass the "signs of a true apostle." His preaching was instrumental in the formation of the Corinthian church; his life was one of purity and honesty. For Paul "the signs of an apostle were the insignia of the apostleship" (Hodge, 290).

The phrase "the signs (marks) of an apostle" was probably borrowed by Paul as a slogan (Bultmann, 233). Possibly this phrase was taken from the lips of his opponents, but more likely these words originated with the Corinthians themselves (Barrett, 321). With several different people approaching the Corinthians under the guise of apostleship and with these people all claiming that they were the true apostles, the proof, or sign, of apostleship was probably a concept often repeated. Most likely, the Corinthians sought some special signs in Paul, as they had seen in the "other" apostles (13:3, 5). That is, they were expecting proof of miraculous power in Paul. He has already provided such "evidence" in 12:1–10 (also see *Comment* on 12:12*b*). But Paul is insisting in 12:12*a* that such signs are not the primary criterion for deciding whether or not a person is an apostle. Instead, he is suggesting that the true signs of apostleship—his ministry and life—are the signs that matter the most (i.e., they aim to secure οἰκοδομή, "upbuilding," as in 1 Cor 14; Käsemann, ibid., 62). Paul was not about to say that he was the only one (in all the world) to exhibit signs of apostleship. He would never say, "I am the only true apostle." That Paul would not say this is seen in the use of the generic (Barrett, 320; Robertson, *Grammar,* 757) article τοῦ. Paul admitted (though sometimes sarcastically, Gal 2:9) that there were other true apostles (but we wonder if he felt that any of them suffered as much as he did; see 11:23 in the *argumentum ad insipientem*). Thus, he writes the "mark of a [true] apostle."

Paul writes that these marks κατειργάσθη, "were wrought" (aorist passive; i.e., "divine passive" used of God's action) among the Corinthians ἐν πάσῃ ὑπομονῇ, "in all persistence." His life and ministry were sustained by the power of God. Paul would not claim that he was responsible for surviving his hardships. The idea of "patience" or "endurance" (Barrett, 321) reflects the strain that had been upon Paul (6:4). Despite rejection, ridicule, and slander, Paul has remained true to the Corinthians. As any loving father would do, he has waited patiently for his children to return his love. Though the "spoilt children of the apostolic family" (Denney, 361) were wayward, Paul never fully abandoned them. Some interpreters see "patience" (Hughes, 457; Calvin: *primum signum nominat patientiam*) as a sign of apostleship. That is, patience is included as a service of apostleship rather than a description of how Paul performed his role before the church. But this position is not totally convincing. Héring (95) notes that patience is not necessarily to be included in the "signs" of an apostle, since suggesting such a description would be somewhat "pale" as a term used to summarize Paul's apostleship. Nevertheless, Héring is inadequate when he renders ὑπομονή as "perfect consistency." This definition fails to capture the depth of Paul's commitment, and ὑπομονή as "persistence" is to be given emphasis to qualify the list of credentials by providing a "horizon" (in the *peristaseis*-list of 11:23–33) in which these marvelous credentials have to be assessed (Bachmann, 405; Käsemann, ibid., 53).

σημείοις τε καὶ τέρασιν καὶ δυνάμεσιν, "[along with] signs and wonders and mighty works." We agree with the thought of the NEB that with a threefold description miracles "attended" ("accompanied," Barrett, 321) the true signs of the apostle (see above; see also *Notes* b, c, and d). The use of the three terms in the dative case suggests that this interpretation is correct (Barrett, ibid.). If Paul had sought to show that the "marks" of apostleship were "signs and wonders and mighty works" only, it would have made more sense for him to have employed the nominative case and constructed a predicate nominative ("the signs of apostleship are signs, wonders and mighty works"). But instead Paul seems to be suggesting the idea of "accompaniment" (see Moule, *Idiom Book*, 45). As we understand it, Paul stops short of saying that these credentials are the sole basis for anyone's apostleship. To say that "signs and wonders and mighty works" are the primary signs of apostleship goes against Paul's teaching of chaps. 11–13 (as well as chaps. 1–9). Earlier, Paul described his apostleship as true because he suffered much (4:7–15; 6:4–10). Also, his proclaiming of reconciliation has proved effective (5:18–21). Moreover, to "boast" of great miraculous power is to put one's own person forward in a way that Paul does not (4:5). Ample proof of this is seen in Paul's reluctance to share his revelations and visions (12:1–10). The conclusion is that Paul does not consider the miraculous as the main criterion by which to judge apostleship (*pace* Jervell, "Signs"). Rather, 12:12a suggests that there are other criteria by which any apostle should be evaluated. The thrust of this discussion is to show that, while Paul performed (or rather Christ worked through him) such miracles as "signs and wonders and mighty works" (Rom 15:19), he "boasted" more of the valid signs of the apostle (12:12a). This agrees with our earlier observations that Paul sought to set his apostleship off from the "false apostles." Miracles could be performed through trickery and deception (cf. Acts 8:13 and the LXX evidence, e.g., Exod 7:3, 11, 12; see also D. E. Aune, "Magic in Early Christianity," in *Aufstieg und Niedergang der römischen Welt*, 2/26.2, ed. H. Temporini and W. Haase [Berlin & New York: Walter de Gruyter, 1981] 1507–57). Paul summons the Corinthians to base their evaluation of him on the criteria of his ministry and life (note Isa 8:18 for "signs and portents," σημεῖα καὶ τέρατα in LXX, a phrase used of human beings, i.e., Isaiah's children). Yet, Paul does not deny that God's workers may have the ability to do the miraculous. Paul too can do such miracles (so 6:6, 7; so Bultmann, 234) and thus he includes the witness of 12:12*b*. In short, 12:12*b* says Paul equals anyone else in the ability to perform the miraculous. And 12:12*a* relates that he excels and surpasses the opponents that attack his apostleship, if in an *ad hominem* way.

The threefold expression σημεῖον καὶ τέρας καὶ δύναμις is not a common expression (Acts 2:22; Heb 2:4: other references have some words in the trio: Rom 15:19; 2 Thess 2:9). More often is found the pair, "signs and wonders," (Acts 2:43; 4:30; 5:12; 7:36; 14:3 [see also 8:3 for "signs and mighty works"]). "Signs and wonders" was probably a current phrase, possibly a hendiadys (Héring, 95). The second use of σημεῖον, "sign," in 12:12 is not the same as the first, we maintain. Whereas the former use spoke of "signs" in a general sense, the latter speaks in a more narrow way. The second use of "signs" constitutes one of the "signs of apostleship" (Hughes, 457). The basic meaning of "sign" is an event that increases spiritual understanding (Denney, 362; Filson, 411; note the Fourth Gospel's use of "signs" in R. T. Fortna, *The Gospel of Signs,* SNTSMS 11 [Cambridge: University Press, 1970]). τέρας, "wonder," carries with it the idea of astonishment or shock (Hughes, 457) or "awe" in the presence of the numinous. The term δύναμις, "mighty work," is an act in which the power of God is evident (Filson, 411). But there is some limitation to this revelatory power. See R. P. Martin, *Mark: Evangelist and Theologian* (Exeter: Paternoster/Grand Rapids: Zondervan, 1972) 170, for the judgment of K. Kertelge, *Die Wunder Jesu im Markusevangelium,* SANT 23 (1970), 125, that only under the rubric of εὐαγγέλιον, "Gospel," do the δύναμεις of Jesus receive their true significance. The same estimate would hold for Paul: in that section, *Mark,* 156–205, the present writer has tried to see a link between Mark and Paul's Gospel as the latter was (mis)understood at Corinth.

It could be argued that each term describes a different type of miracle. But Tasker is probably right when he argues that they are simply describing miracles from three different aspects (180, 181).

All these terms may describe healings (see Plummer, 360). We know that Paul was famous in the early church, according to Luke's Acts, for his healing miracles (Acts 13:11; 14:10; 15:12; 16:18; 19:11–12; 28:3–6, 8). He also himself remarks that he has seen miracles among many persons (Rom 15:19; cf. Gal 3:5). It is fair to conclude that Paul's use of "signs and wonders and mighty works" in 12:12*b* may refer to his healing miracles (Windisch, 379), but the evidence for Paul as a pneumatic leader is wider (see Holmberg, *Paul and Power,* 75–77). Essentially, the apostle is telling the Corinthians, perhaps with tongue-in-cheek, that he has done as much as his opponents. More obviously in the context of the four chapter letter, he is trying to show his readers that external signs are not enough. The "signs and wonders and mighty works" at best can be but a limited part of the criterion of apostleship. At their worst, they can deceive the people. From an analysis of the terms of 12:12*b* (see above) we deduce that Paul is attempting to convince the Corinthians that his works have pointed to God, while those of his opponents have not. Even in miracles Paul is quick to concede that God, not he, is the source of the "miracle-power."

But more than that, the works of Paul (in 12:12*b*) are the workings of, and not the proof for, his authentic apostleship. He is a true apostle because God called him. Paul is pleading with the Corinthians to dispense with the secondary criteria (signs, wonders, mighty works) and judge would-be apostles by the yardstick of the primary criterion, namely, the *signa apostolica* of the crucified Jesus (13:1–4). If the Corinthians would follow this standard, then Paul would be seen by them as not being inferior to the super-apostles or the false apostles. But until this is done, Paul may continue to seem second rate when compared with them. Yet his "servant role" is the pattern he has accepted, with a διακονία devoted to others (see Kleinknecht, *Der leidende Gerechtfertigte,* 303, who usefully makes it clear that all "signs" are subsumed under one *signum apostolicum,* namely, "service" in weakness and reliance on God).

13. τί γάρ ἐστιν ὃ ἡσσώθητε ὑπὲρ τὰς λοιπὰς ἐκκλησίας, "How were you inferior to the other churches." Having pleaded for the right to be considered a true apostle, Paul returns to a sore subject between him and the Corinthians. The question of why he had refused financial aid from Corinth surfaces again. In a way, he is continuing his discussion of 12:12 regarding the signs of apostleship (we note the γάρ, "for," which could be Paul's way of connecting the thought of the two vv, but see Liddell and Scott 1:338, who understand the γάρ as part of abrupt questions). Paul had been accused of not being a true apostle because he did not receive support from the Corinthians (11:7–11; cf. 1 Cor 9:4–18). Yet, in 12:11, 12, Paul had reiterated that he was not inferior to other apostles. He had received aid from other Christians (Phil 4:15–17; see Holmberg, *Paul and Power,* 89–93). Perhaps the Corinthians felt slighted that Paul did not let them help him (Tasker, 181), or more probably because they believed Paul had cheated them out of their full charismatic inheritance (v 13a). So Georgi, *Die Gegner,* 237, discussed earlier, p. 345. Moreover, possibly the Corinthian church felt inferior to other churches because of this stand of "independence," and waiver of apostolic rights of maintenance.

ἡσσώθητε (cf. Rom 11:12 and use of ἥττημα), taken with ὑπέρ, gives us the idea of "being inferior to" (Moule sees τί γάρ ἐστιν ὃ ἡσσώθητε as an example of "accusative of respect," *Idiom Book,* 131). In short, Paul is asking the Corinthians in what way they are inferior to other churches. Even though the other churches had been allowed to contribute to Paul's work, it appears that the Corinthians have not missed out on any blessings (Bruce, 250). On the contrary, since Paul was not a burden to them, they should take this abstinence as a mark that he was a true leader in not seeking to impose on them.

εἰ μὴ ὅτι αὐτὸς ἐγὼ οὐ κατενάρκησα ὑμῶν; "except that I myself was not a burden to you?" The only exception (εἰ μή) that Paul took with the Corinthians, as compared to the other churches, was that he did not receive financial support. But it must be apparent that he did this so as not to appear like his opponents (11:18, 19). It was permissible for apostles to accept money for the preaching of the Gospel (1 Cor 9:14), but the Corinthians apparently failed to realize that the person doing the preaching had the prerogative to accept or refuse aid (1 Cor 9:15; see earlier, p. 344). Paul chose to refuse because any acceptance might be misconstrued as a "sign of apostleship."

We may be sure that the signs of apostleship are here fresh in Paul's mind. He has already stated that he did not accept payment for his work among the Corinthians (11:9; 1 Cor 9). The use of the emphatic αὐτὸς ἐγώ, "I myself," may mean in comparison to other colleagues, but more likely is to be taken in regard to the false apostles (Plummer, 360; Héring, 96; Lietzmann, 158). Paul does not see the taking of money as an apostolic sign. κατενάρκησα (aorist of καταναρκᾶν) signals the idea of being a burden, possibly a financial one. This verb is found only with the genitive and only in 2 Corinthians (11:9; 12:13, 14). Paul had not become a burden to, or dead weight on, the Corinthians (Hughes, 387, and helpful note). He had not been a drain at all on their finances—unlike the interloping counterparts on the Corinthian scene. The remark is ironical.

χαρίσασθέ μοι τὴν ἀδικίαν ταύτην, "Forgive me this wrong!" In sustained irony, Paul asks for forgiveness. χαρίσασθε is the aorist imperative of χαρίζεσθαι. This is not primarily a theological word with Paul in this letter (Barrett, 323), but rather speaks of the forgiveness between two parties (2:7, 10). The ἀδικία, a word similar to ἁμαρτία in 11:7, rendered "wrong" (see 2:10; 7:12), is given in ironical fashion (though Paul may be serious and may have realized that he offended the Corinthians by seemingly rejecting their offer as too small). The irony in this verse has been evaluated as both affectionate (Hughes, 459) and bitter (Strachan, 34). Regardless of how one views Paul's emotion behind 12:13, it is doubtful that anyone escaped the sharp bite of his tongue and pen. Strachan is right to observe that the issue of Paul's refusal to accept payment for services rendered is one of the hardest and deepest disappointments of Paul's work with the Corinthians. That Paul thought of this often may be gathered from the amount of attention given to it. To compound his disappointment is the idea that by seeking to refrain from a dubious practice (with respect to his opponents) Paul is considered an inferior apostle.

14. ἰδοὺ τρίτον τοῦτο ἑτοίμως ἔχω ἐλθεῖν πρὸς ὑμᾶς, "I am now ready to visit you a third time." The subject of Paul's defense and his assuming the role of ἄφρων with a "fool's speech" has passed for the present. Having reiterated that he will not take maintenance (v 13), Paul informs the Corinthians that he is coming again to see them. He introduces this change of subject by the use of the interjection ἰδού, "behold" (Filson, 412; or better yet, "actually"). Paul himself is coming to visit the church.

A question surrounds the ambiguity of the Greek construction. The placement of ἑτοίμως ἔχω (cf. 10:6 for a possible Latinism), "am ready," between τρίτον τοῦτο (note τρίτον, "third," is emphatic [Plummer, 361]) and the infinitive ἐλθεῖν, "to come," is a problem (Moule, *Idiom Book*, 161). We are not sure, at least grammatically speaking, whether τρίτον τοῦτο is to be taken with ἑτοίμως ἔχω or with ἐλθεῖν (BDF § 154). If the former is true, then the meaning of our clause is, "For the third time I am preparing to visit you" (see R. A. Batey, "Paul's Interaction with the Corinthians," *JBL* 84 [1965] 139–46). In short, Paul is telling the Corinthians that he has prepared twice before to visit them, but such an event never happened. This leads to the conclusion that Paul is preparing for only his second visit. If we take the latter option, then we see Paul telling his readers that he is ready to visit them a third time. Most commentators prefer the latter interpretation as the one Paul intended (Allo, 326, 327). For one thing, as Allo remarks, Paul, in much clearer language, tells the Corinthians (in 13:1) that he is coming for a third visit. For another thing, such an interpretation lines up with our conclusion that Paul had made two earlier visits to Corinth. The first visit was the time at which Paul established the church (Acts 18); the second one was his intermediate or "painful" visit, chronicled for us (though quite briefly) in 2:1. Also see *Comment* on 13:2, because this v also suggests that Paul left Corinth after having given a warning of possible punishment for the church when he returns. It is doubtful if Paul's first visit would have ended on this unhappy note. Thus it appears that Paul took a second trip to Corinth, i.e., one that resulted in the "painful" visit. If Paul is planning his third visit, then we can rule out the notion that chaps. 10-13 are part of the "severe letter," for that letter was delivered in lieu of a visit, "painful" or otherwise (Bruce, 250; see Hughes, 459-62).

καὶ οὐ καταναρκήσω· οὐ γὰρ ζητῶ τὰ ὑμῶν ἀλλὰ ὑμᾶς, "and I will not be a burden, because I seek you and not your possessions." Paul has had to defend his policy of taking no remuneration from the Corinthians and, though he will again be in their midst, he does not plan to give up this policy. His return to Corinth is to reclaim the only prize he desires, namely, the Corinthians: "Not yours, but you" (Denney, 365).

Paul is coming to them in the same fashion as on his previous two visits. Paul will not be a burden to the Corinthians (καταναρκᾶν; see on previous v, and *Comment* on 11:9). He does not desire their possessions ("what is yours," τὰ ὑμῶν). He does not want to be a "sponge" (Plummer, 361) as the false apostles have been. 11:20 describes the false apostles as visitors who eat their hosts "out of house and home" (Barrett, 291). Moreover, Paul is seeking more importantly the Corinthians themselves. Paul is making a greater demand of the Corinthians than simply their property; he wants their hearts (Strachan, 35). As Plummer writes (361), "He [Paul] cares too much about them to care about their possessions." Rather, he asks of them much more than can be fulfilled by material means, an idea that is parallel with the Macedonian example in 8:5 (cf. Phil 4:17). He asks of the Corinthians to be restored to him, as was previously the case.

In yet another oblique glance at his opponents, Paul upholds his position that taking money is not to be construed as an apostolic sign. The Corinthians can keep their money: here he anticipates the accusation of money-grubbing in v 16. Paul will still come to them. But it is not as though he is coming as a defeated messenger. He is coming to set things straight (13:2). He hopes this forthcoming visit will not be a painful one. Possibly the Corinthians can straighten out their problems before he arrives (12:20, 21; 13:11). He has the authority of God—as his messenger—to bring the Gospel and its demands to the people (13:10). In addition, we should note that Paul is not seeking the Corinthians in order to make them *his* possession. On the contrary, his desire is that they should return to their espoused (but lately estranged) husband, namely, Christ (11:2). Paul desires neither the possessions of the Corinthians nor themselves solely for his personal satisfaction. Instead, he "seeks" (ζητεῖν, as in 13:3 of the Corinthians' desire to have Paul validate his apostolate; in 1 Cor 13:5 it is a corrective of their false ambition; see

Martin, *The Spirit and the Congregation,* 49, for the verb as a term in the moral life of early Christians) the Corinthians that they may return to Christ and his ways.

We opened the preceding paragraph by adverting to Paul's continued refusal to take money from the Corinthians: his denial was evidently written in polemical manner. Yet, this should not lead us to overlook the affection with which Paul wrote. Sometimes the severity that is found in chaps. 10–13 keeps us from seeing the tender heart Paul has for the Corinthians, so noteworthy in 6:11–13; 7:2–4. Hughes sees Paul's thought here as very tender (462). Allo (326) is right to point out that Paul exhibits similar compassion toward the Corinthians in our present passage as he did in chaps. 1–9. In no better way is this compassion seen than his recalling that he is the father and the Corinthians his children.

οὐ γὰρ ὀφείλει τὰ τέκνα τοῖς γονεῦσιν θησαυρίζειν ἀλλὰ οἱ γονεῖς τοῖς τέκνοις, "For children ought not to save up for their parents, but parents for their children." If only the Corinthians would remember that Paul is their spiritual father (1 Cor 4:15), then they would see that all he is doing is fulfilling a natural law, a νόμος φύσεως, as Chrysostom calls it, borrowing the term from Philo (see below) (Filson, 413). The parents, especially the father, are under obligation to provide support for the children. The use of ὀφείλειν was seen in 12:11. Paul is responsible to provide for the Corinthians.

In the light of the context, money is apparently a primary issue in Paul's discussion. The verb θησαυρίζειν carries with it more the idea of saving up than of simple help or support. This makes us wonder if the Corinthians had established a "super fund" for the other apostles. Also, its use could suggest a drive by the Corinthians to establish a special fund for Paul. After all, the Corinthians had demonstrated the ability to dig into their pockets, as evidenced by both the offering (chaps. 8–9) and the support given to the false apostles. In one sense, Paul is indirectly providing "financial" assistance to the Corinthians because they are not having to spend anything on him. In other words, since the Corinthians can keep their money that was earmarked for "apostolic preaching," in a sense Paul has "given" them money. But it is doubtful if Paul is speaking only of money when he talks of providing for his children. Paul will soon show that he has lifted the discussion to a higher level. Just as Paul asks from the Corinthians a greater gift than money, so he also offers a greater gift than money (12:15). He exercises the privilege of a father (Hughes, 463). This privilege is to give of himself, and to seek nothing in return but a loving response of the heart. This is a similar call to that of 6:11–13. In that passage Paul pleaded with the Corinthians to reopen their hearts to him. The apostle gives the most expensive love but is willing to bear the cost (Hughes, ibid.).

In 12:14*b*, as was the case in 7:12, the negation of one alternative does not completely rule out its validity. Rather, this construction οὐ [γὰρ] ὀφείλει, "ought not," suggests the superiority of the other alternative, but not exclusively so. That is, Paul is not saying that children should never help their parents, but instead he is laying down the accepted norm that parents usually help their children (Plummer, 362; Filson, 413). The obligation is squarely upon the shoulders of the parents, as Philo (*Vit. Mos.* 2.245) also observed:

νόμος φύσεως ἐστι κληρονομεῖσθαι γονεῖς ὑπὸ παίδων ἀλλὰ μὴ τούτους κληρονομεῖν, "it is a natural law that the sons are the inheritors of their fathers, not fathers of their sons." Windisch (399, 400) points out that this axiom is a general one, since parents not able to earn their own living must be cared for by their sons (and daughters). Bultmann, 236, sees here not a legal relationship (*Rechtsverhältnis*), but one of love (*Liebesverhältnis*), where the parent-child bond is all-important.

Yet we note that if Paul had followed his rule of 12:14b in strict adherence, then he would never have accepted help from other churches. This not to be the case, however, for the Macedonian Christians provided him with financial assistance. Possibly this "partiality" to one "child" over another was taken as another example of Paul's "inconsistency." We recall the charge of his "fickleness" earlier (1:15–23). Or, as was suggested above, some readers may have understood that Paul was unhappy with them or, worse yet, did not love them (11:11). Moreover, Paul was considered inferior as an apostle because he did not take money from the Corinthians for his preaching. But he is simply saying (in 12:14b) that the Corinthians are his children (Filson, 413, wonders if this use of "children" implies that a majority of the church supported Paul; but this is sentimental) in the faith and that he is more than glad (12:15) to labor on behalf of them with no monetary return (Filson, ibid.). We may ask, "Is it wrong for a father, in his good judgment, to treat his respective children [in Paul's case, different churches] in ways that are beneficial to them, even though each child may receive some different treatment?" If the father does so in love, then the answer to our question is no. Paul knew that the accepting of funds by the other apostles was seen by the Corinthians as an apostolic sign because it appealed to the dictum of the laborer being worthy of wages (1 Cor 9:14), evidently much in vogue in Judeo-Christianity (see earlier, pp. 344, 345, 348). Paul has argued that this deduction is incorrect (12:11–13) since the "privilege" *may* be honorably refused, and *must* be rejected if its acceptance is liable to misunderstanding and/or abuse. In order to help his children break out of this impasse, Paul refused such help. We also should note that Paul did not *demand* the gifts he received from the other churches (Plummer, 362). No matter what Paul did, he did not cease to be a father to the Corinthians (Calvin). Tasker points out that the proof of Paul's sincerity of motive for the Corinthians is seen in his refusal of any payment for services rendered (181, 182).

The drift of 12:14 is that Paul will not become a financial burden to the Corinthians. He will again refer to finances in 12:16. In fact, most of 12:14b–18 is concerned with this topic. But in 12:15 Paul insists that "spending" does not always entail money alone. He will show that he is willing to give everything of himself and asks for love, not money, in return. The verb θησαυρίζειν, "to save up," can have a nonmaterial sense (Matt 6:19, 20; Luke 12:21, 33).

15. ἐγὼ δὲ ἥδιστα δαπανήσω καὶ ἐκδαπανηθήσομαι ὑπὲρ τῶν ψυχῶν ὑμῶν, "I will most gladly spend and be spent on your behalf." Paul continues with his paternal affection. He will go beyond such expectations that are normally placed on parents. Sad to say, not every father would seek reconciliation with children who acted like the Corinthians. However, Paul goes beyond

natural responsibility (Filson, 413; this is to say that being a "natural" father does not make a man a true father). He is willing to extend himself to the uttermost limits of his capacity.

Despite the rejection Paul received from the Corinthians, he desired that they should know of his love for them. Paul's use of ἐγώ underscores his emphatic wish to set himself before the Corinthians as one who has great love for and devotion to them. He will "most gladly" (ἥδιστα: an elative form: BDF § 60.2: see 12:9) continue to offer his services to them. Paul gives two future tenses, δαπανήσω, "spend," and ἐκδαπανηθήσομαι, "be spent." The first suggests that Paul will spend his money, time, energy, and love for the church. The second future is in the passive voice. The verb with ἐκ has behind it the intent of "being utterly spent:" he is "sacrificing himself completely" (Bultmann, 236, who quotes Seneca, *Dial.* 1.5.4: *boni viri . . . impendunt, impenduntur et volentes quidem*, "good men . . . spend and are spent and that right willingly"). The use of ἐκ with δαπανᾶν also may carry with it the perfective force (see Robertson, *Grammar*, 596). A good example of how ἐκ transforms a verb into one of perfective force is seen also in 4:8. In that verse Paul is perplexed (ἀπορούμενοι), and then he adds that he is not perplexed leading to despair (ἐξαπορούμενοι). The point is that in 12:15 Paul will not withhold any resource he has, including himself. Bruce differentiates between δαπανᾶν and ἐκδαπανᾶν by connecting the former with Paul's resources and the latter with Paul himself (250). Whether or not we can make such a distinction is not clear. What is true here is that Paul will demonstrate his love to the Corinthians in such a way that no one could possibly deny that he cared for them deeply. Paul is speaking of more than just money in this v. He seeks to show his love for them in everything he does. Bruce (250, 251) is correct when he writes, "There is no limit to his [Paul's] love for them; it is sad that their love for him is so limited" (see also 6:11–13; 7:2–4). Paul is willing to expend himself ὑπὲρ τῶν ψυχῶν ὑμῶν, "on behalf of you." The idea of ψυχή being taken in the semitic sense of "you" is found in 1:23 (see also Barrett, 324).

Paul is ready to exhaust his energies in order to prove his love for the Corinthians. Even though 12:15 is in a context that primarily speaks to the issue of money, we may understand the v to speak of more than a money gift. Paul will spend himself—his energy, his health, if need be (Tasker, 182), his reputation, his affections—on the Corinthians. If anything, he will work all the harder at doing what he does best, namely, loving the Corinthians.

εἰ περισσοτέρως ὑμᾶς ἀγαπῶ[ν], ἧσσον ἀγαπῶμαι; "If I love you more, will you love me less?" See *Notes* for a discussion of textual concerns in this sentence. The clause under study appears as an answer to the charge of 11:11 ("because I do not love you?"; see Filson, 414). It is uncertain whether or not this sentence (in 12:15) is in the interrogative. Most understand it so (NIV; RSV; RV; NEB; Barrett, 324; Menzies, 97; contra Phillips; KJV/AV; Allo). Less critical is whether one should read the verb (ἀγαπῶ) or the participle (ἀγαπῶν). There is little difference between "If I love you more, will you love me less?" and "Loving you more, am I loved less?" The use of the ἀγαπῶ appears to be more Pauline (Barrett, 324). Also, the older MSS are to be read in such a way as to conclude that the present clause is not dependent on the first clause of 12:15a (see Tasker, 182). But by putting 12:15b in the form of a question, Paul can be seen making his point with not so blunt a condemnation as the KJV/AV suggests ("though the more abundantly I love you, the less I be loved"). By taking Paul's writing in the form of a question, we leave open the way for the Corinthians to change and to return Paul's love with a love of their own (Filson, 414). Possibly Paul is making an impassioned appeal to the Corinthians when he puts this question before them (Tasker, 182).

The term περισσοτέρως, "more," ("more abundantly," "more intensely"; see 7:13: the comparative adverb should be taken with ἧσσον: the *more* I love . . . the *less* should I be loved?) shows that v 15b continues the thought of v 15a. Paul has already told the Corinthians that when he comes a third time and renews the intensity of his love for them he will show to what extent he can be "spent" for them. Also, v 15b introduces a fear implicitly contained in v 15a. If Paul proceeds to expend both his resources and his energy to the point of exhaustion, then what happens if this new campaign is not well received by the Corinthians? What happens if Paul is loved less in spite of his effort? The answer is that Paul would most likely have been devastated, though he was willing to come to Corinth a third time to find out. Though Paul's question of v 15b leaves open the way for the Corinthians to rectify the situation, it also conveys a fear Paul has: "Will my increased affection result in less love from the Corinthians?" (ἧσσον from ἥσσων, "less"). Whether or not Paul's fear came to pass is not known for sure. See *Comment* on 13:10.

16. ἔστω δέ, ἐγὼ οὐ κατεβάρησα ὑμᾶς, "Though I was not a burden to you." The remaining verses of this section (16–18) speak of an even more serious charge against Paul. As will be seen in vv 17, 18, Paul repels the accusation that he swindled the Corinthians by pocketing the offering intended for the poor of Jerusalem. Even his severest critics could not deny that he had refrained from both asking and receiving help from the Corinthians; nevertheless they could conjure up another line of attack.

Paul's use of ἔστω δέ (lit., "so be it"; see Tasker, 182) suggests that he assumes that his readers concede him the point that he has not been a direct burden on anyone. The use of καταβαρεῖν in 12:16 reflects the idea of "weighing down." (This word is not that of 12:13, 14, as it is a *hapax legomenon* [but cf. 11:9, ἀβαρῆ]). Plummer notes that Paul never uses ἔστω this way anywhere else (363). But Robertson suggests that 12:15b is the subject of ἔστω (*Grammar*, 392). In effect, he is arguing that Paul intends to be understood as saying, "though I am loved the less, yet I have not been a burden to you." But the words that follow (17, 18) suggest otherwise. Paul is ready to take on the imputation that he has battened on the generosity of the congregation, even though this charge contradicts the earlier allegation that he is no apostle and does not love the Corinthians because he did *not* receive money at Corinth (11:11). Bultmann (237) thinks that the various charges emanated from different groups.

ἀλλὰ ὑπάρχων πανοῦργος δόλῳ ὑμᾶς ἔλαβον, "Yet, crafty fellow that I am, I caught you by trickery." No doubt Paul's opponents were embarrassed by his refusal to take money for his services. To be sure, the false apostles had argued (with a considerable degree of success) that maintenance was an apostolic sign. But even such a position was not enough. Possibly the opponents felt that they wanted to make sure that Paul would not be seen in a good light. Perhaps some Corinthians had begun to question why the false apostles had to be paid, or at least why they had to be paid so much (reflected in 11:20). So, to cover their tracks, they invented the story that the reason Paul refused money was obvious. It was not that his motives were high, but that the Corinthians were supporting him, though indirectly (Hughes, 464). The picture painted was this: Paul could appear independent of the Corinthians because he was taking their money in an underhanded way, namely, by using his associates to set aside some of the offering for himself. (Strachan [35, n. 1] wonders if possibly some of the money was set aside under the pretense of travel expenses. [This idea of bureaucratic expenses is of no little concern even in our present day.]). Hughes adroitly offers another possibility for a motive of the opponents in attacking Paul (465). Most likely they would have enjoyed the money set aside for the collection themselves. But since it was earmarked for Jerusalem, and thus, inaccessible to their hands, they did the next best (or worst) thing. They sought to destroy a reputation in order to vent their anger and frustration. They may have hoped that any future offerings would be curtailed in the light of Paul's "misbehavior." The result of the Corinthians' withdrawing from the Pauline "collection for the saints" would be more money for the false apostles.

It is unclear whether Paul is reacting directly to a charge of the Corinthians or of his opponents. The RSV includes the words "you say," an addition not found in the Greek. Perhaps Filson's suggestion is a better one. It is that we should supply the words "they say" (414). This would reflect the point that the charge of impropriety with respect to the collection was initially the work of the opponents. Most likely, the accusation originated with the opponents, but the Corinthians themselves kept such an innuendo alive.

ὑπάρχων is the participle of ὑπάρχειν, "to exist," "to be" (see 8:17; Gal 1:14; 2:14). Plummer views Paul's choice of ὑπάρχων as almost equivalent to φύσει ("the nature of"). In ironical tones, Paul writes that he deliberately outwitted the Corinthians. The participle is understood as causal in our verse (Moule, *Idiom Book*, 103). πανοῦργος, "crafty," "cunning," "unscrupulous," is an adjective that is not found elsewhere in the New Testament. Héring translates it as a man "capable of anything" on the ground that "crafty" weakens the import of what Paul is saying (96 n. 31). We note that πανοῦργος is found in the LXX (mainly wisdom literature: see Windisch, 403; but Betz, *Der Apostel Paulus*, 104–6, has an interesting consideration of the wider application of use in the philosopher-sophist debate; πανουργία is a slogan in the antisophist polemic, as it is linked with γοητεία, sorcery; the opposite of πανουρία is ἁπλότης, cf. 11:3). Paul's use of the noun πανουργία in 4:2 and 11:3 (cf. also Eph 4:14 and Luke 20:23) indicates that this term was much in the air at Corinth, as charge and countercharge. In the former verse Paul tells his readers that he remembers practices that involve deception. In the latter verse he is speaking of how the devil connived to lead Eve astray. (This has to be connected to his opponents in 11:4, 5.) Almost certainly

Paul's choice of πανοῦργος is polemic in intent. He rejects such behavior; his opponents are connected to the guilt of his adversary. We may also see some polemic in Paul's employment of ἔλαβον (second aorist of λαμβάνειν), a verb also used in 11:20. In both instances, it is a metaphor for hunting and fishing. In 11:20, Paul was blasting his opponents who sought and succeeded in "capturing" the Corinthians. In our present v Paul is seen to be "stalking" his prey, that he too may "win" the Corinthians. Regardless of Paul's polemic intent, we must not downplay his ironical streak; indeed the two features go hand in hand.

The instrument by which Paul "caught" the Corinthians was his "trickery" (δόλῳ, from δόλος, meaning "deceit" or "bait"; see Héring, 196; cf. 4:2 for use of the cognate verb). In the light of the hunting metaphor of ἔλαβον, it appears Paul is referring to the insinuation that the collection was offered as bait to entrap the Corinthians. Then, when entrusted with the catch, Paul pilfered the money box. Sad to say, the accusations included (apparently) Paul's associates, for what follow in rapid succession are four questions which imply that accusing fingers were also pointing at Paul's coworkers. Barrett is right to indicate that it is difficult to believe that chaps. 8 and 9 with their approval of these colleagues and Paul's insistence on probity, especially financial, were written after chaps. 10–13 (324). His point—with which we agree—is that there is no reference in the earlier chapters to any accusation against Paul. It is hardly the case that Paul would have left such a hurtful charge out of his discussion, if indeed chaps. 10–13 preceded 8 and 9.

17. μή τινα ὧν ἀπέσταλκα πρὸς ὑμᾶς, δι᾿ αὐτοῦ ἐπλεονέκτησα ὑμᾶς; "Did I take advantage of you by any of the men I sent you?" Paul begins his series of rhetorical questions by asking, in a general tone, if any of his emissaries had ever exploited the Corinthians. (It should be noted that there are four questions in the Greek text. The English translation runs more smoothly, however, by incorporating the last two questions of 12:18 into one question for translation.) Paul hopes for the answer no, as seen from μή. Paul's construction in 12:17 is not as smooth as the English may suggest. This anacoluthon may result from the influence of Semitisms. Moule argues that the use of "an indeclinable and genderless relative followed by a pronoun indicating its case and gender" is a construction that influenced NT writers (*Idiom Book*, 176). But we may question, with Hughes, why, if this is true, Paul did not use διά τινός instead of τινά, for δι᾿ αὐτοῦ takes up the thought of τινά. Hughes argues that what we have is an "accusative of respect" (465, n. 153). Paul may have put τινά here for emphasis. Or, as Barrett suggests (325), the anacoluthon may simply be the result of the emotion with which Paul writes these words. As Héring (96, n. 32) notes, this was not uncommon in Paul's time (see BDF § 466). It is easier if we regard ὧν as a compression for τούτων οὕς (Bultmann, 237).

Paul's thinking in our v may be a reflection of earlier transactions between the Corinthians and Paul's helpers. In 8:20, 21, Paul is explicit in wanting the offering to be collected in a manner that is above suspicion. The use of ἀπέσταλκα (the perfect of ἀποστέλλειν) suggests the "perfect of broken continuity" (Moulton, *Grammar* 1:144; Robertson, *Grammar*, 896; Bultmann, ibid., however, sees no reason for the tense, as in 11:25). This "iterative perfect" is Paul's way of asking his readers to recall any instance, even one, in which his coworkers "took advantage" of the Corinthians. The aorist ἐπλεονέκτησα (from πλεονεκτεῖν) carries with it the idea of cheating and defrauding as in 2:11; 7:2. In 2:11 it is used in connection with the possibility that Satan may outwit the church. In 7:2, Paul urges his readers to accept him as a person who is not out to take advantage of anyone. With this in mind, Paul's use of this verb in 12:17 probably reflects a polemical stance on his part. He is asking the Corinthians to examine the record and step forward with a specific complaint instead of hiding behind generalizations, none of which is easily proved or disproved (Barrett, 325). In the next verse we see that Paul narrows down the choice for the Corinthians by identifying the emissaries that he has sent to them.

18. παρεκάλεσα Τίτον καὶ συναπέστειλα τὸν ἀδελφόν, "I urged Titus [to visit you] and I sent the brother with him." The words in the bracket, though absent from the Greek text, are nevertheless implied (Barrett, 325; Windisch, 403). But our major concern here is to know what visit it is to which Paul is referring. Is it the one mentioned in 8:6a, or the one in 8:16–24?

At an earlier time Titus visited Corinth and started a collection (8:6). From what Paul tells us, Titus did not complete the collection at that time, and was urged to return to finish what he had started. It is unclear whether Titus started the collection at the same time that he delivered the "severe letter" or whether the visit mentioned in 8:6 was earlier. Although we cannot rule out the possibility that Titus commenced the collection project when the church repented at the reading of the "severe letter," this conclusion may be only our wishful thinking. For one thing, it appears that the collection began over a year before the writing of chap. 8 (8:10; Tasker, 113). If so, the collection would probably have started before the sending of the "severe letter." Also, if 8:6 is the visit of Titus with the "severe letter," then it seems that Paul would have highlighted the beginning of the collection when he congratulated the Corinthians for obeying Titus on the occasion of his visit bearing this letter (7:15) (though we can conjecture that the Corinthians obeyed Titus's plans to carry on with the collection, which was started earlier). Moreover, it may have been too presumptuous to initiate an offering immediately on the heels of the "severe letter." Thus, it seems safe to assume that the visit of Titus mentioned in 8:6 was earlier than his visit following Paul's "painful" visit.

With respect to the visit described in 8:16–24, it is not clear whether this one had taken place yet. Allo (329) assumes the aorists of 8:17 (ἐξῆλθεν) and 8:18 (συνεπέμψαμεν) are genuine, and that Titus had left Paul (before the writing of chap. 8) with the two brothers. But Allo is not convincing, for ἐξῆλθεν can be taken as an epistolary or anticipatory aorist (Hughes, 468; Tasker, 119). Thus, the visit planned in 8:16–24—the one on which Titus will be accompanied by two brothers (8:18, 22)—had not taken place at the writing of chap. 8, and probably had not taken place at the writing of chaps. 10–13. In other words, Titus was with Paul when he wrote both letters (chaps. 1–9 and 10–13). It would make sense for Paul to include in 12:17, 18, Titus's visit to the Corinthians with the two brothers, if indeed, this visit had taken place. But apparently it had not. Moreover, the mention of Titus in

12:18 speaks of his being accompanied (συναπέστειλα) by only one brother, τὸν ἀδελφόν. This seems to rule out the equation of 12:18 and 8:16–24 as speaking of the same visit, for the latter vv indicate that two brothers were to accompany Titus. Thus we are left with the conclusion that 8:6 and 12:18 speak about one and the same visit (unless, of course, Paul's reference in 12:18 is to a visit not mentioned in 2 Corinthians).

Paul urged Titus (παρεκάλεσα, aorist of παρακαλεῖν) and sent with (συναπέστειλα, aorist of συναποστέλλειν) him a brother (τὸν ἀδελφόν). We note that παρακαλεῖν is found in both 8:6 and 12:18 and may be grounds for connecting the two vv as describing the same visit. Also, it appears that the aorists of 12:18 are genuine (as they are in 8:6), and thus we see another link between 8:6 and 12:18. What must remain a mystery is, if 8:6 and 12:18 describe the same visit, why Paul did not mention the brother in 8:6. Possibly at the time of the writing of 8:6, Paul did not deem it important to mention the other brother (see also Bruce, 251; see also Barrett, "Titus," 127). This is possible in that Paul was not defending his action toward the offering when he composed chaps. 1–9, while he was having to defend it in chap. 12. Whatever the reason, it seems more logical to equate 8:6 and 12:18 (Hughes, 467–69). Moreover, the person of Titus is more important to Paul's argument. For one thing, Titus was a Gentile (no doubt an important item with the Corinthians). For another thing, Titus had the confidence of the Corinthians. He had started the collection in Corinth and had been the one to deliver the "severe letter." Whatever one's conclusion about 12:18a, Titus must be seen as playing a vital role in Paul's self-defense.

μήτι ἐπλεονέκτησεν ὑμᾶς Τίτος; "Did Titus take advantage of you?" Paul probably knows full well that the Corinthians are not about to doubt Titus's integrity. Here he asks them whether or not Titus defrauded them. Again Paul constructs the question so that an answer "no" is expected (see Moule, Idiom Book, 156). The use of μήτι instead of μή (12:17) may be an intensification by Paul. Also, the use of πλεονεκτεῖν in 12:18 as in 12:17 shows an effort to relate Paul to Titus. If Titus was above reproach, then it was "ludicrous" (Plummer, 365) to think Paul had cheated. To accuse Paul of dishonesty would be to do likewise to Titus. Paul is obviously hoping that his defense will work, though Bultmann (238) is right to observe, and then to respond to the charge, that there is an element of "circularity" (Zirkelbeweis) in the apostle's argument (so Windisch, 404: Paul appeals to Titus to prove his integrity, then defends Titus's integrity by linking it to his own).

οὐ τῷ αὐτῷ πνεύματι περιεπατήσαμεν; οὐ τοῖς αὐτοῖς ἴχνεσιν; "Did we not walk in the same spirit and follow the same cause?" Paul's final two questions (given as one in the English) make a shift in the argument. Instead of expecting a negative answer as in the first two questions (with the inclusion of μή and μήτι), Paul constructs both questions in such a manner as to expect an answer in the affirmative. (Both questions have οὐ.) περιπατεῖν, lit., "to walk," carries with it the ethical sense of "to live." Paul is saying that he "walks" in the same spirit as Titus. The "we" may simply refer to Paul or may include the joint thought of Paul and Titus. The understanding is little affected in either case, for Paul is simply arguing that both he and Titus have done nothing wrong (Barrett, 325).

τῷ αὐτῷ πνεύματι, "in the same spirit," presents a few problems. Tasker follows the RV with a capitalized "Spirit" (for πνεῦμα) and argues that Paul refers to the Holy Spirit (184). That is, "Paul and Titus were inspired and guided by the Holy Spirit." But more likely we are to take "in the same spirit" in parallel with "in the same steps." This leads us to see the nontheological use of πνεῦμα (Barrett, 326; Héring, 97; see 6:6, 7), as associating the two men as leaders. Literally, ἴχνος means "footprint" (see Rom 4:12). In both questions here we find the pronoun αὐτός in the attributive position, thus underlining Paul's theme of "oneness" with Titus.

With this verse Paul concludes his argument against those who would slight his integrity. As will be apparent, 12:19 takes a new turn in the Pauline train of thought. For the present, Paul has no more to say about his behavior and probity. If the Corinthians doubt Paul's pastoral integrity, then there is not much more that he can do or say. But evidently Paul does not give up hope, for he continues on the assumption that they will accept him (13:1–10).

Explanation

With the conclusion of 12:11–18 we see the ending of Paul's self-defense or *apologia* in 2 Corinthians. This epistle has centered primarily on the defense of his apostleship. Before offering the Corinthians final instructions and warnings in anticipation of his next visit, Paul reviews charges made against him. In general, apostolic integrity has been called into question. He has been attacked as an "inferior apostle" out to fleece the people of Corinth. Specifically, the charge is that he has failed to take remuneration for his services because he has used the guise of collecting an offering for the poor of Jerusalem. Paul is accused of setting aside money for his own purpose. To the contrary, he has argued vigorously that such insinuations border on the unbelievable. The Corinthians are not spared the biting sarcasm of Paul's tongue and pen.

Vv 11–13. Again Paul reminds his readers that all he is writing has a distinct purpose in view—and the mood he is adopting as much as the contents of the letter are both dictated by the immediate situation at Corinth. They have compelled him to play the part of a braggadocio, and to parade himself as though he were out of his mind with conceit and self-importance (v 11). He has bragged without restraint—and all to show that the accusations leveled at him by those who are undermining the Corinthian community are without substance.

These three vv (11–13) really give a résumé of his case against the opponents:

(i) "He is nobody," they say; very well, Paul replies, but he is not, on any showing, a bit inferior to the so-called "super-apostles" to whose authority his enemies were laying claim (v 11).

(ii) "He is a plain, ordinary man, ungifted and undistinguished"; but Paul has a ready answer: I have the signs to accredit me as an apostle—miracles, wonders and deeds of power; and even something more convincing still, the persistence to cope with fractious people (v 12)!

(iii) "He doesn't really care for you Corinthians; he has neglected the church"; and Paul can say that this insult is without foundation, and cannot be substantiated. Yet, ironically, only in one matter is it true: "I did not make myself a burden to you by taking your money (cf. 11:20). Please forgive me for failing to sponge on you!" (v 13).

Vv 14–18. Paul turns to consider future relations with the Corinthian church (14), holding out the promise of a third visit. This implies, as we saw earlier, an intermediate visit, referred to in 2:1. Now, as he contemplates the visit ahead, he makes it clear that what he wants is not money but the wholehearted acceptance by the church of his authority, a submission to Christ and a confidence in himself, with a clearing of the air of all suspicious and mutual recriminations.

But perhaps the Corinthians still believe that he has deceived them with clever tricks (v 16). This insinuation maintains that Paul was astute enough not to take any money directly from them; but he shared in the proceeds for the collection which they gave to his agents, notably Titus. The answer to this is a reminder of the facts which relate to the mission of Titus and the unnamed brother of v 18 (the same man as in 8:22? but this may be doubted). This latter person would be a man well known to the Corinthians and who would be able to testify to Titus's honesty—and incidentally to Paul's too. His presence would guarantee the integrity of the other Christians involved in the collection scheme (cf. 8:6).

F. Warnings and a Third Visit Promised (12:19–13:10)

Bibliography

Barrett, C. K. "Paul's Opponents in 2 Corinthians." In *Essays on Paul*, chap. 4, 233–54. **Betz, H.-D.** *Der Apostel Paulus und die socratische Tradition.* **Black, D. A.** *Paul, Apostle of Weakness.* 160–67. **Eckstein, H.-J.** *Der Begriff Syneidesis bei Paulus*, WUNT 2d ser. 10. Tübingen: Mohr, 1983. **Güttgemanns, E.** *Der leidende Apostel und sein Herr.* 142–54. **Johnston, G.** "2 Cor 13:8." *ExpTim* 5 (1893–94) 68, 69. **Kennedy, H. A. A.** "Weakness and Power." *ExpTim* 13 (1901–02) 349, 350. **Roetzel, C. J.** *Judgement in the Community: A Study of the Relationship Between Eschatology and Ecclesiology in Paul.* 1972. **Vielhauer, Ph.** *Oikodome* in his *Aufsätze zur Neuen Testament.* München: Chr. Kaiser Verlag, 1979 ed. **Vliet, H. van.** *No Single Testimony: A Study on the Adopting of the Law of Deut 19:15 par. into the New Testament.* Utrecht: Kemink & Zoon, 1958. **Wiles, G. P.** *Paul's Intercessory Prayers.* SNTSMS 24. Cambridge: University Press, 1974. **Wilckens, U.** *Weisheit und Torheit.* BHT 26. 1959.

Translation

[19] *Have you been thinking all along* [a] *that we are defending ourselves before* [b] *you?* [c] *We are speaking before God in Christ and all that we do, beloved, is for your edification.* [20] *For I fear that when I come I shall not find you as I wish and*

that I will not be found by you as you wish. [*For I fear*] *that there will be strife,* [d]
jealousy, [e] *outbursts of anger, selfish ambitions, slander, gossiping, conceit and disorder.*
[21] *I am afraid that when I come,* [f] *my God will again humble me before you and
that I will mourn* [g] *for many who have sinned earlier and have not repented of the
impurity, fornication, and licentiousness in which they indulged.*

[13:1] *This will be my third visit to you. "On the evidence of two or three witnesses,
every matter is established."* [2] *As I said during my second visit, I now* [h] *say while
absent: when I return I will not spare those who have sinned earlier or anyone else,* [i]
[3] *since you seek proof that Christ is speaking through me. He is not weak towards
you, rather he is powerful among you.* [4] *For in fact* [j] *he was crucified in* [k] *weakness,
yet he lives by the power of God. For indeed we are weak in him,* [l] *but we shall live
with him* [m] *by God's power when serving you.* [n] [5] *Examine yourselves to see if you
are in the faith; test yourselves. Or do you not know that Jesus Christ* [o] *is in you—
unless you fail the test?* [p] [6] *I hope that you will realize that we do not fail the test.*
[7] *We pray* [q] *to God that you might do nothing wrong, not that we would appear as
having passed the test, but rather that you might do right even if we appear to
have failed.* [8] *For we cannot do anything against the truth, but only for the truth.*
[9] *For we rejoice when we are weak, though you are strong. Our prayer is for your
restoration.* [10] *This is why I write these things while I am yet absent, so that when
I am present I might not have to act harshly in accordance with the authority which
the Lord has given to me, the authority for building you up, not tearing you down.*

Notes

[a] P[46] includes οὐ, which makes 12:19a a question expecting an affirmative answer. The variant
may have been influenced by 5:12, or it may be an assimilation to the preceding questions in
12:18, which begin with οὐ. If the latter is true, then it appears that the copyists of the earliest
documents understood 12:19a as a question (cf. Hughes, 469, n. 156). See also *Note c.* The
TR has the easier reading of πάλιν, which may be an assimilation to the πάλιν in 3:1 and 5:12.
But the text, πάλαι, is the more difficult rendering and, in light of its support (ℵ* A B F G 33
330 1175 1739 1881 lat), is retained.

[b] D ψ have κατενώπιον. The text, κανέναντι, has much greater support (P[46] ℵ A B F G 33 81
7775 1739 1881).

[c] Opinion is divided over whether to take 12:19a as a question (KJV/AV; RSV; NIV; Phillips)
or a statement (RV; ASV; NEB; TEV/GNB; *Diglot*). But Tasker is right (184) in that either choice
retains the correct meaning behind the sentence. See Bratcher, *Diglot* (1964); *Translator's Guide*
(1983), 139.

[d] The singular ἔρις is found in P[46] ℵ A 0243 33 1739 1881 (the text), whereas the plural
ἔρεις is found in B D F G ψ syr[h]. The plural is most likely the result of a copyist's desire to
align ἔρις with the other plurals in this verse. See *Note e.*

[e] The singular ζῆλος has support from P[46] A B D* F G 33 syr[p] bo[ms]. The plural ζῆλοι, found
in ℵ D[1] ψ 0143 syr[h], is an attempt to bring ζῆλος in line with the many other plurals of 12:20
(see *Note* d).

[f] ἐλθόντα με ταπεινώσῃ ὁ θεός μου πρὸς ὑμᾶς is found in ℵ ψ 0243. Also, there is the variant
reading ἐλθόντα με πρὸς ὑμᾶς ταπεινώσῃ με ὁ θεός μου (D[1] syr[p] Tert). The two readings may be
attempts to correct the difficult grammar of the text (see *Comment*). The text is supported by
P[46] ℵ* A B F G 33 81 1175. (See also Plummer, 360.)

[g] We find ταπεινώσει in P[46] D F G L P 1175, but this future indicative raises questions, especially
if μή does not go with ἐλθόντος (see *Comment*). It appears that an οὐ should replace the μή if
ταπεινώσει is to be included. Against Plummer (371), it does not appear that the text ταπεινώσῃ
is a correction.

[h] γράφω follows νῦν in D[1] vg[ms] syr[sa], but there appears no reason why, if γράφω was the
original, it should have been omitted (Metzger, *Textual Commentary*, 587). Furthermore, the text
has better support P[46] ℵ A B D* F G 0243 1175 1739 1881). See Hughes 476, n. 169.

[i] ὅτι is found before ἐπεὶ in F G Ambst, but this is probably only an attempt to emphasize the causal nature of the clause.

[j] Several MSS (א² A D¹ ψ lat syr Ambst) have καὶ γάρ εἰ which leaves us with "for if he was crucified. . . ." The text (without εἰ) is supported by P⁴⁶ א* B D* F G 0243 33 81 1739. Barrett (327) appears correct when he observes that the variant reading "lacks the vigour" of the text found in Nestle-Aland[26]. This "lack" is noticed because εἰ ("if") destroys the equal emphasis between weakness and power. For Barrett, such an inequality of importance is less than Pauline.

[k] The usual rendering of ἐξ (from ἐκ) is "from," "out of." But the context of our verse demands the idea of "by reason of." See BGD, 235.

[l,m] Assimilation is seen in many MSS (א A F G syrᵖ bo), for it appears the use of σὺν αὐτῷ in 13:4c resulted in the replacing of ἐν by σὺν at the conclusion of 13:4b. There also appears to have been an inverse assimilation, for the σὺν of 13:4c was replaced by ἐν in P⁴⁶ᵛⁱᵈ D* 33 (Metzger, *Textual Commentary*, 587, 588). But it appears that the text (B D ψ 0243 vg syrʰ sa) is to be preferred. The first variant reading does not appear to have as strong a support as our text. The second variant reading, if accepted, would weaken Paul's attempt to show that he is in union with Christ. The σὺν captures this thought better than ἐν (though we disagree with taking σὺν as an indication that Paul is talking of the future life in 13:4b [contra Barrett, 327, 337]).

[n] εἰς ὑμᾶς is omitted in B D². But it is doubtful if this phrase would have been inserted in such an awkward place. See Hughes, 479, n. 175.

[o] The words Ἰησοῦς Χριστός (found in B D ψ vgᵐˢ syr) are reversed in א A F G P 0243 1175 1739 1881 Ambst. See Plummer (376).

[p] There are different ways to interpret the punctuation of this verse. One way is to end this verse with a question mark (KJV/AV; RSV; NIV; NEB). Another way is to create a series of questions. Also, the whole verse can be understood as a statement (Phillips).

[q] εὐχόμεθα (P⁴⁶ א A B D* F G K P 33 81 1175 lat) is to be preferred to εὔχομαι (D² ψ 0243 vgᵐˢˢ syrᵖ saᵐˢ Ambst). See Plummer, 337.

Form/Structure/Setting

This passage is the last major section of the epistle. The subject differs from that of the preceding verses in that Paul ceases to "boast" and instead turns his attention to the forthcoming visit (12:20, 21; 13:1; cf. 12:14). He is concerned that the Corinthians repent before he reaches their city (see Acts 20:2).

Paul attempts to persuade the Corinthians that his boasting (12:1–18) was not for the purpose of outdoing his opponents. "His aim in self-defence is to build up a Church, not merely to refute slander" (Strachan, 36; see too Bultmann, 239: "the motive of his remark [in 12:19] is not one of self-defense, but rather the upbuilding or going forward of the congregation"). He begins this attempt by asking the Corinthians if they think he has been defending (ἀπολογοῦμαι) himself (12:19). He was led to ask this question in light of the previous vv which reflect his activity of boasting. Rather, Paul says, everything that has taken place has been for the edification (οἰκοδομή: a key word for Paul; see later) of the church. He is the builder of this church and is concerned that it should be a "living" church. The thrust of 12:19–21 (the first part of our passage) is Paul's exhortation to the Corinthians to repent, for he is aware that problems persist in the church. Paul's awareness of these problems is evidenced by his fear (φοβοῦμαι) that he may have to discipline the church when he arrives. He conveys the idea of such fear in 12:20a. In this verse, we notice a chiastic, or criss-cross, structure (Plummer, 368; Furnish, 561).

A   θέλω ──────────────── B   κἀγὼ εὑρεθῶ ὑμῖν οὐ

B¹   οὐχ εὕρω ὑμᾶς ────── A¹   θέλετε

What Paul is saying is that when he comes "he may not find the Corinthians" (B) as "he wishes" (A), namely repentant and willing to accept him as a true apostle. Likewise, "the Corinthians may not find him" (B¹; see *Comment*) as "they wish" (A¹), for he may be forced to come with a rod. That is, if the Corinthians do not correct the problems of their church, then Paul will have no choice but to correct the situation himself.

These problems are spelled out in 12:20*b* and 12:21*b*. The former contains a list of eight sins betraying a divided church. Plummer takes these eight vices as a series of four pairs (369). A case can be made out for linking ἔρις, "strife," and ζῆλος, "jealousy," for Paul used them as a pair in 1 Cor 3:3 (ζῆλος καὶ ἔρις; see also Rom 13:13). However, the second two, θυμός, "outburst of anger," and ἐριθεία, "selfish ambition," are found together again only in Rom 2:8, and even then there appears little attempt by Paul to show that in his thinking they are considered as paired with each other. (In Rom 2:8, θυμός, with the aid of a καί, is matched with ὀργή.) Also, none of the other four vices listed in 12:20*b*—καταλαλία, "slander"; "gossiping" (only in 12:20); φυσίωσις, "conceit" (only in 12:20); or ἀκαταστασία "disorder" (6:5; 1 Cor 14:33)—is ever paired with another elsewhere in the NT. All of this suggests that Plummer's thinking is too ingenious. Furthermore, if Paul had wanted to structure this list of 12:20*b* in terms of a series of pairs, most likely he would have constructed it with the aid of καί, as he did when he used pairs in 6:8, 9.

12:21*b* lists sins that reveal a church beset by sexual immorality. These sins are ἀκαθαρσία, "impurity"; πορνεία, "fornication"; and ἀσέλγεια, "licentiousness." The use of only one article (τῇ) for all three sins listed may indicate that Paul considered them as synonyms, but see Tasker (185, 186). We can find the same triad of sins listed in Gal 5:19, but in an order different from that found in 12:21 and without an article.

A comparison of these two lists (12:20*b* and 12:21*b*) leads us to conclude that they are dissimilar in nature. The former reflects sins of a church rent by division; the latter describes a church beset by sexual immorality. Is Paul speaking of the same situation, and if he is, does he have two separate groups of people in sight? The answer to the first part of the question is affirmative. On this point we agree with Barrett ("Paul's Opponents," 74, 75). It is doubtful Paul would juxtapose two separate situations when he is keeping his intended visit in the foreground of this discussion (12:20, 21; 13:1, 2). More than likely, 12:20*b* and 12:21*b* both describe the present situation at Corinth. But when answering the second part of our question, we part company with Barrett's affirmation and think more of distinguishing two sets of problems. Barrett's reasoning is as follows. It appears that Paul has divided those of Corinth into two groups. Specifically, Paul views as "new sinners" those who have accepted the teaching of the false apostles and thus have "fallen" into strife and its kindred sins. This group, according to Barrett, is spoken of in 12:20*b*. And Paul sees as "old sinners" those who have failed to repent of their libertine tendencies, namely their sexual immorality. This group is discussed in 12:21*b*. While we applaud Barrett's conclusion that 12:20, 21 speak of the present situation in Corinth, nevertheless, as will be maintained in 13:2 (*Form/Structure/Setting*) and later in the *Comment*, we suggest that Barrett's proposal that Paul has separated (in his mind) the Corinthians into the two groups described above is too neat. Our argument against Barrett will be explained below but, suffice it to say, it is doubtful that Paul is restricting his use of προαμαρτάνειν (both here and in 13:2) to refer to only those guilty of immorality. More likely, Paul is thinking of all those who have persisted in their sin, regardless of whether that sin is strife or immorality.

The second section of our passage falls at 13:1–4. These vv deal specifically with just how severe Paul may have to be with the Corinthians. The visit in mind will be Paul's third (τρίτον) to Corinth. (The first one led to the founding of the church; the second one was the "painful" or "interim" visit; see 2:1.) We note that the mention of his third visit in 13:1 links 13:1–4 to 12:19–21 in that Paul discussed his forthcoming visit twice in the latter passage. (Paul speaks of his coming in 12:20 [ἐλθών] and in 12:21 [ἐλθόντος, though this genitive absolute is a source of much discussion, see *Comment*].) Paul concludes 13:1 with a reference to Deut 19:15 ("On the evidence of two or three witnesses, every matter is established," these words of Paul approximate the verse in Deuteronomy [LXX], though they are nearer to the wording of Matt 18:16). This deuteronomic reference is used by the apostle to establish the validity of his disciplining (if needed) the Corinthians. (For a discussion of the possible meanings behind the "two or three witnesses," see *Comment* on 13:2.)

Another obvious link between 12:19–21 and 13:1–4 is found in 13:2. In that verse Paul uses the perfect participle προημαρτηκόσιν (see below and 12:21). In 13:2, Paul again warns the Corinthians that he will not spare (οὐ φείσομαι) anyone that persists in resisting his authority. Paul does not list specific sins in 13:2, as he did in 12:20 and 12:21. But the absence of such a detailed list does not lessen the import of what he has to say. As he said before (προείρηκα) during his second visit (ὡς παρὼν τὸ δεύτερον) and he now repeats while absent (ἀπών), he will spare no one (see 1:23).

A literal translation of 13:2 proves awkward to English readers. But this should not cause us to overlook the literary structure of 13:2*a*. An examination of the Greek text reveals that Paul has provided his readers with a series of three pairs of phrases linked by καὶ (Hughes, 476):

προείρηκα καὶ προλέγω
ὡς παρὼν τὸ δεύτερον καὶ ἀπὼν νῦν
τοῖς προημαρτηκόσιν καὶ τοῖς λοιποῖς πᾶσιν.

We notice that in this v Paul exhibits his penchant for stringing together words that begin with προ- (see 9:5; Gal 5:21; Rom 8:29; 1 Tim 1:18; 5:24; 2 Tim 3:4). One of these words, προημαρτηκόσιν (perfect participle), reminds us of 12:21*b*, which includes προημαρτηκότων (perfect participle; from προαμαρτάνειν, as is the previous verb). In 12:21*b* those "sinning beforehand" were pictured as those committing sexual immorality. Barrett reasons that the use of "sinning beforehand" in 12:21 implies that its use in 13:2 is the same. That is, προαμαρτάνειν, found in 13:2, is meant to single out those who have failed to repent of their libertine tendencies. While it is agreed that the perfect tense refers to the past, is it to be understood that in 13:2 Paul is thinking only of those who have committed fornication and kindred sins when he uses προημαρτηκόσιν? This writer thinks not. It makes more sense to understand Paul as thinking of *all* those who failed to repent, without regard to a specific type of sin. Otherwise it appears that he is not concerned with those who supported the false apostles (who, Barrett assures us, had visited Corinth since Paul's "painful visit," 7). Furthermore, to suggest that τοῖς λοιποῖς πᾶσιν, "to all the rest," refers specifically to those that have followed the false apostles is hard to reconcile with his teaching concerning these apostles. It is difficult because it makes Paul look as if he threw in this phrase as an afterthought. This hardly seems reasonable in light of the attention Paul has given to the false apostles in these chaps. (10–13). Instead, the phrase "all the rest" is meant to complement the phrase "those who sinned earlier." The latter phrase reflects the Corinthian offenders known to Paul. The former phrase includes anyone at Corinth that may be sinning, but of whom Paul is unaware (Tasker, 186).

13:3 continues the thought of Paul coming to deal harshly with the Corinthians. In ironic fashion, he assumes that the Corinthians will hear Christ speaking in him. The Corinthians want proof (δοκιμή) that Paul is a full-fledged apostle of Christ. The irony comes in that the proof Paul will give them is the opposite of what they are asking for (Plummer, 374; Wilckens, *Weisheit*, 218, who notes a rehearsal of the debate in 12:12 on "signs and wonders" as the sine qua non of a *Pneumatiker*, which Paul is not). The Corinthians want signs, wonders, and miracles (12:12). This is what they expect when they hear that Paul is going to offer them proof that Christ is in him. But the proof that they will receive is the wrath of Paul directed at them (Black, *Paul*, 162). His discipline (whether it be a tongue-lashing or an excommunication) will be his way of providing proof for the Corinthians. Yet the Christ whom Paul embodies is known by "weakness," and Paul paradoxically has no inherent power (v 4*b*); only the power conditioned by the suffering apostolate, which in turn is based on the cross. There God showed how his weakness is stronger than human strength (1 Cor 1:25*b*). So "power" and "weakness," which seem to be mutually contradictory and to exclude each other, are brought together in this way: "they are experienced *together*, being for Paul two aspects of the same reality" (Black, ibid., 163; see too Wilckens, *Weisheit*, 48: "ἐξ ἀσθενείας corresponds with ἐκ δυνάμεως"; Güttgemanns, ibid., 153, 154, utilizes the idea of "hidden power" revealed in the weakness of the crucified Jesus, which is the power of love; Bultmann, 245: "this is why the δύναμις of Christ will be effectual in Paul who is despised as ἀσθενής and actually lives in ἀσθένεια, namely, that with Christ himself ἀσθένεια and δύναμις are bound up together").

So, Paul is not bent on disciplining the Corinthians if they will repent, and it is his pastoral concern (11:28, 29) which speaks of the vulnerable love he has for these folk, revealing all the native weakness (12:10) that motivated him to deal with persistent love (12:15). This is the reasoning behind chaps. 10–13. The letter will precede Paul to Corinth. He hopes that it will take effect as did the "severe letter." The result of the latter was that reconciliation took place (alas, temporarily) between the apostle and the Corinthians. With this hope of Paul's in mind, we suggest that 13:3*b*, 4 is a transitional section, for in it he begins to describe his wish that the church will repent before he arrives. If this is so, then he will not have to discipline the church.

13:3*b* reflects a chiastic structure:

A   εἰς ὑμᾶς   B'   δυνατεῖ
B   οὐκ ἀσθενεῖ   A'   ἐν ὑμῖν

Christ has not been weak (B) toward the Corinthians (A); rather he is powerful (B') among them (A') (see Furnish, 570). The idea of weakness and power is continued in 13:4. This verse expresses thoughts that are written as a parallelism.

καὶ γὰρ ἐσταυρώθη ἐξ ἀσθενείας,
ἀλλὰ ζῇ ἐκ δυνάμεως θεοῦ,
καὶ γὰρ ἡμεῖς ἀσθενοῦμεν ἐν αὐτῷ,
ἀλλὰ ζήσομεν σὺν αὐτῷ ἐκ δυνάμεως θεοῦ εἰς ὑμᾶς

We notice that each sentence commences with καὶ γὰρ and that the second part of each sentence begins with an adversative ἀλλὰ. In the first sentence of 13:4, Paul remarks that Christ was crucified in weakness, but lives by the power of God. This thought is parallel to the second sentence of the v, in which Paul speaks of how he (notice the use of the first person plural for the first person singular; see M. Carrez, "Le 'nous' en 2 Cor.," *NTS* 26 [1979–80] 483: "to be weak and to live are based on the close fellowship with Christ, and it is this fellowship which unites Paul ['we'] and the Corinthians ['you'] in this life; in this way, Christ is presented as the one who gives the 'we' its meaning and its power, in a more personal and direct fashion than in 2 Cor 5.10") is weak in Christ, but will live in the power of God. From our discussion it is apparent that Paul has changed his topic from that of severe punishment to the optimistic attitude that the Corinthians will recognize that the lack of outward appearance of power is not to be equated with weakness. Why? Paul anticipates this question by showing that Christ is among the Corinthians (13:3*b*), yet even the risen Lord voluntarily followed a life of "weakness," for he chose the cross. The point for Paul is that he likewise has lived a life of weakness. If this is so, and if Christ is among the Corinthians, then Paul should be accepted for who he is because he is the one responsible for bringing the message of Christ to the Corinthians first (he was the "vehicle," as Bruce, 253, remarks). As 13:1–4 closes and 13:5–10 begins, we can see that punishing the church is not the main concern of Paul. Instead, by noting his themes of power and weakness, we (and, it may be, the Corinthians saw this) begin to understand that Paul wants the Corinthians to repent (13:10*a*), even if this means Paul will remain weak, a trait already visible in 4:7–10; 10:1; 11:21 (see *Comment*).

The third and final section of our passage is 13:5–10. This section is linked to the preceding one. We notice that the motifs of strength and weakness are dominant in the first ten verses of chap. 13. ἀσθενεῖν (13:3, 4, 9) and ἀσθένεια (13:4) provide the contrast to δυνατεῖν (13:3, 4, 8), δύναμις (13:4) and δυνατός (13:9; see Hughes, 483, n. 181). Also, the two sections (13:1–4 and 13:5–10) are similar in that the idea of "passing the test" (δοκιμή, 13:3; δοκιμάζειν; δόκιμος, 13:7) is found in both. We also note that the idea of "passing the test" is set against the idea of "not passing" in 13:5–7 (see ἀδόκιμος in 13:5, 6, 7; Hughes, 482, n. 178). 13:5–10 is Paul's exhortation to the Corinthians to "pass the test" (a key verb, δοκιμάζειν, with its cognates is used 17x in 1–2 Cor, and of these in 2 Cor 13:1–10 the frequency is 6x). And what is the test (δοκιμή)? It is that the Corinthians will realize that Christ is among them (because of Paul's apostolic presence as leader and letter-writer, 10:10), and that they must repent in order to acknowledge that presence. If they do so, and they repent, then Paul can come in a "non-severe" manner. His prayer (13:7, 9) is that they will repent and be restored (κατάρτισις). Paul's hope has two sides, namely that the Corinthians will pass the test, and also will avoid doing anything wrong, i.e., by resolving to turn from their pagan ways (12:20, 21).

13:5*b* is ironical (Barrett, 338; "mild irony," Hughes, 491). After exhorting the Corinthians to examine (ἑαυτοὺς πειράζετε, imperative) themselves to see "if they are in the faith" (ἐν τῇ πίστει); that is, to become aware of living in the new age (5:17), of being in Christ and having him in them; and after exhorting them to test (δοκιμάζετε, imperative) themselves, Paul moves to an ironical statement. This irony ("Do you not know that Jesus Christ is in you—unless you fail the test?") is for a distinct purpose. If the Corinthians examine themselves and find that indeed Christ is in them (which of course Paul knows is true and is confident that the Corinthians themselves will come to discover), then this should be sufficient proof that Paul is a true apostle, for he brought the Gospel first to Corinth. In 13:5*b* Paul appeals to the self-knowledge (ἐπιγινώσκετε) of the Corinthians. But even more, he invokes the reality of Christ in the congregation as a "critical power" (*als kritische Macht in der Gemeinde*, Bultmann, 248).

The idea of Paul's being a true apostle is continued in 13:6, where he offers the hope that the Corinthians will see that he has passed the test. (For Paul's possible different use of ἀδόκιμος, see *Comment.*) The two sides to Paul's hope (see above) are apparent in 13:7, where we find a balance of thought in the structure of the verse:

A μὴ ποιῆσαι ὑμᾶς κακὸν μηδέν
B ὑμεῖς τὸ καλὸν ποιῆτε.

Paul's prayer is that the Corinthians will avoid doing anything wrong (A) and instead do only what is right (B), even if this leads to Paul's appearing to have failed the test. He would like nothing more than for this to happen; then it would mean that the Corinthians had repented. If they repented, then Paul would appear to be "weak," for he would not only be "bold" in his letters, but face to face he would be "humble" (10:1; see Bultmann, 241).

It should be noted that Paul's use of the phrases "passing the test" (13:5) and "not passing the test" (13:5, 6, 7) make 13:5–7 a unit in itself. Also, it is apparent that Paul can oscillate between wanting to pass the test and seeming to fail it. The former speaks of his being accepted as an apostle; the latter refers to being judged as "weak," i.e., ineffectual, in another sense of ἀσθένης. Paul points out that everything is done according to the truth (ἀλήθεια; 13:8). If the Corinthians repent, then he will rejoice (χαίρειν) in his weakness (by weakness we mean not performing certain duties, such as the exercise of discipline or of his authority εἰς καθαίρεσιν, "to destroy"). But he has written all these things (13:10; that is, all of chaps. 10–13) so as to provide the Corinthians with one last opportunity to repent. Paul's goal is finally stated to edify the church. This may entail punishment, though Paul would prefer not to do so. But whether Paul comes as a "friend" or a "foe" (and he obviously left it up to the Corinthians to decide if this third visit would be a painful one in a manner reminiscent of 1 Cor 4:21), all is done in truth and for the edification of the church. Paul has the ἐξουσία, "authority," to edify the church, and this authority has come from God.

Comment

19. πάλαι δοκεῖτε ὅτι ὑμῖν ἀπολογούμεθα; "Have you been thinking all along that we are defending ourselves before you?" We have already discussed the textual problems that accompany this clause. See *Notes.* Also see further Moulton, *Grammar* 1:118. πάλαι, an adverb, designates a past time, possibly a period of long duration. The adverb, taken with the present of δοκεῖν, "to think," suggests the idea of "progressive" (Robertson, *Grammar,* 879) or "durative" (Moulton, *Grammar* 1:119) time, and this combination is equivalent to the English perfect tense. In a sense Paul is telling the Corinthians that he assumes that they have been thinking all along (BGD, 605) that he is defending himself before them. (Again we note Paul's use of the first person plural ἀπολογούμεθα [from ἀπολογοῦσθαι, "to defend oneself"], but most likely he is thinking only of himself in 12:19a. He may have Titus in mind, since he was mentioned by Paul in 12:18, but by now we are well aware of his use of "we" when he probably was only considering himself. Yet Carrez, "Le 'nous,' " 480, makes out a case for treating the "we" in 12:18, 19 [and so in this v] as "referring to actions that can be called *apostolic* in the larger sense of the word, even if in the strict sense only Paul is an apostle. . . . [The 'we' shows] that Paul and Silvanus and Timothy have ministerial solidarity with a common mission in their proclamation of the Gospel, their authority [but not their superiority] over the community, and it orients their exhortation" [his italics].)

Paul has been defending himself in the previous verses. He played the fool (11:21; 12:11) and presented himself as a leader worthy of the office of apostleship. Chaps. 10–13 have been another attempt by him to win the hearts of the Corinthians. But for Paul to make a defense (in the normal sense) for himself—a "self-regarding composition" (Barrett, 328) aimed at furthering his own interest, as well as commending his person before those sitting in judgment—would fall into his opponents' hands (Furnish, 566, 567).

These opponents would argue that Paul was writing out of self-interest and not out of an interest for his readers.

Possibly, all along Paul has been sitting in judgment on the Corinthians. Plummer considers this when he points out that the Corinthians should not misread their relationship to the apostle (367). In the past, Paul had come in weakness and, in turn, had suffered much humiliation. He was considered a "paper tiger," effective only at a distance (10:10). But as will unfold in our present section (12:19–13:10), Paul may come (and he is prepared to do so) with severe consequences for the Corinthians (10:2, 6, 11). This may be yet another "painful visit," for he is about to issue a warning that many may feel his wrath, if they continue in their errant ways. Yet, Paul acts only in love toward the Corinthians, and this letter's appeal (chaps. 10–13) gives one more opportunity for them to change. In essence, Paul has left the Corinthians to decide whether or not the third visit will be a painful one.

κατέναντι θεοῦ ἐν Χριστῷ λαλοῦμεν, "We are speaking before God in Christ." Paul continues the theme of "his working on the behalf of the Corinthians" (1:24). This was suggested in 12:15. According to 12:19*b*, we see that Paul is concerned for the Corinthians' welfare and not for his own gain. He is behaving as a "responsible theologian" (Barrett, 328). That Paul is not seeking his own good can be seen on two fronts. First, there is the evidence of 12:19*c*, which speaks of Paul's wanting to strengthen the Corinthians (see below). Then, the other front is seen in a "pair of guarantees" (Plummer, 368). Paul speaks "before God" and "in Christ." The idea of speaking "before God" (κατέναντι), a preposition meaning "in the sight of" (see 2:17; cf. 4:2), carries with it the possible idea of judgment. Everything that Paul does and says is under the scrutiny of the Lord (see 5:10). God expects Paul to be faithful to his call. In Paul's mind he has done nothing unworthy of this calling. To have been guilty of the accusations made against him by his opponents would have prevented Paul from inviting others, as well as God, to put his life and ministry under scrutiny. Moreover, Paul lives ἐν Χριστῷ. His being and existence are dependent upon this union. He has come in weakness, yet God has made him strong. It is noted that the phrase κατέναντι θεοῦ ἐν Χριστῷ λαλοῦμεν is also found in 2:17. In the latter verse Paul had just pointed out that he did not peddle the word of God; rather Paul preached it in sincerity before God in Christ. We also note that in the context of 2:17 Paul was arguing that there should be no need for him to commend himself again to the Corinthians (3:1; see also 1 Cor 4:3–5). A glance at the Pauline epistles reveals that Paul's conscience was always clear of wrongdoing (2 Cor 1:18, 23; 4:2; 5:11; 7:12; 11:11, 13; Rom 1:9; 9:1; Phil 1:8; 1 Thess 2:5, 19: see the recent monograph, H.-J. Eckstein, *Der Begriff Syneidesis*, esp. 224–32).

τὰ δὲ πάντα, ἀγαπητοί, ὑπὲρ τῆς ὑμῶν οἰκοδομῆς, "and all that we do, beloved, is for your edification." We saw in 12:19*b* that Paul was acting on behalf of the Corinthians. In our present text, he makes this even more explicit. All that is done is done for the building up (οἰκοδομή) of the Corinthians, corresponding in fact to the terms of his self-defense (Bultmann, 239).

τὰ πάντα, "all things," "everything," is taken by Plummer to mean only those things "spoken" by Paul (368). Plummer's reasoning is that, since there is no verb in 12:19*c*, then λαλεῖν of 12:19*b* is to be carried over to 12:19*c*. But we question if this line of interpretation is not too restrictive, especially in light of Paul's elaborate defense of his behavior in the matter of the offering (12:14–18). The point is that the Corinthians most likely would understand Paul to be describing his actions, as well as his words, when he speaks of τὰ πάντα. Not the least of these actions would be the "severe letter" because it seems likely that Paul was hoping that chaps. 10–13 would have a similar effect on the Corinthians, and that when he came a third time the reception would be a pleasant one.

Everything Paul did for the Corinthians was for their "edification" (Vielhauer, Oikodome, 72, 73, on building God's house as the apostle's missionary task). When combined with the genitive, ὑπέρ denotes the idea of "for the sake of." The metaphor of "building up" (οἰκοδομή) was a familiar one to the Corinthians (1 Cor 3:9; 8:1, 10; 10:23; 14:3, 4, 5, 12, 17, 26: see Martin, The Spirit and the Congregation, 62, 63; J. H. Schütz, Paul and the Anatomy of Apostolic Authority, 224, 225, 260, on 1 Cor 2:10–15). To build up or edify God's people was Paul's function as an apostle (Barrett, 328; idem, Signs of an Apostle). As 13:10 relates, Paul has received authority from the Lord to build up the church at Corinth. Though this edification may come in the form of harshness, such a ministry is not Paul's desire. Behind his sternness is love ("love is the criterion for determining what builds up"; so Schütz, ibid., 262). This is reflected in his use of ἀγαπητοί, "beloved" (Filson, 415; a term of endearment found here and in 7:1). As will be seen, Paul's prayer is that the Corinthians will heed his warning and correct their ways (13:7, 9). In fact, it appears that 12:19 reflects his themes of 12:1–18 (see Form/Structure/Setting). All that the apostle has done at Corinth has been to edify the Corinthian church, though it was not appreciated as such. Unlike his opponents, Paul has not been a burden on the church, nor a fair-weather friend to the Corinthians. On the contrary, he has sought to do nothing that would harm the Corinthians, an idea which is true though it cannot be deduced from 13:7, as Lietzmann, 161, supposes. If only the Corinthians would understand, then they could see that his "depreciation" of himself has not been due to a lack of, but rather a demonstration of, strength. His "tearing down" of himself was intended as a means to building up the church. Paul still hopes that such an action on his part will be successful. But he has some lingering doubts and fears.

20. φοβοῦμαι γὰρ μή πως ἐλθὼν οὐχ οἵους θέλω εὕρω ὑμᾶς, "For I fear that when I come, I shall not find you as I wish." Previously, Paul has dealt "passively" with the Corinthians. Instead of disciplining the offender during his "second visit," Paul retreated and allowed the church to do the correction (7:11; cf. 2:5–11). When Paul chided the church for its behavior during his "second visit," he did so through a letter, and even then he did not deliver it in person. Furthermore, Paul has been anything but aggressive when in Corinth (10:1). But this stance may change.

The thought of 12:20a is connected to that of 12:19c, as seen in the use of γάρ, "for" (Plummer, 368). Paul seeks to build up the Corinthians, but this building up must include a "cleansing" (cf. 6:14–7:1), and a renewed reconciliation which in turn requires a forsaking of pagan ways (vv 20, 21). His past attempts at building up the Corinthians, though effectual at times, proved only to be temporary successes. His attempts to correct the situation at Corinth with 1 Corinthians and with the "severe letter" were not lastingly effective. False teachers have intruded on to the scene (11:4) and have been accorded a welcome (11:19). So, the need for chaps. 10–13 reveals that the positive results of the "severe letter" have been reversed. The change in tone between chaps. 9 and 10 suggests that a new problem has arisen at Corinth. He will elucidate this problem in 12:20*b*. In 12:20*a* he lays the groundwork for the listing of the sins of 12:20*b*. In spite of his earlier efforts, Paul fears (φοβοῦμαι) that he will not find the Corinthians as he wishes. We note that μή πως follows verbs of apprehension (BGD, 519; BDF § 428.6; Moule, *Idiom Book*, 139). Paul is quite concerned that he will have to take decisive action against those of Corinth who persist in their sin. He will not shrink from such an unhappy task if it will help his children. We cannot but agree with Hughes (471, 472) who sees his paternal concern evident in this verse.

Yet, Paul is hopeful that such an unpleasant task will not be necessary. We note that εὕρω is in the subjunctive, not the indicative mood (from εὑρίσκειν). Perhaps this is Paul's way of saying that discipline is not necessarily a foregone conclusion (Bultmann, 239, cites 2:3 which speaks of Paul's *real* and enduring hopes). He seems to be allowing the Corinthians the opportunity to make right their wrongs. He wants the Corinthians to rid themselves of any undesirable qualities that would cause him not to be pleased with them at his coming. While Paul will exercise parental discipline if necessary, he also has the heart of a pastor and exudes pastoral wisdom (Hughes, 471) in that he permits the Corinthians time to rectify the situation. It is important to note that his concern for building up the Corinthians can be summed up in the options he provides for them. He will do whatever it takes to accomplish his goal. "He would prefer to effect the congregation's οἰκοδομή, not its καθαίρεσις (10.8; 13.10)" (Bultmann, 239). He is prepared to exercise swift and effective discipline on the Corinthians. Yet he hopes that the Corinthians will "build" themselves up by correcting their own situation as he returns to this call in 13:11 in a final plea for reconciliation (see Martin, *Reconciliation*, 90–93 for a review). We need to note this option of self-correction, for it is an underlying theme of 12:19–13:10. In short, Paul hopes for the best, yet is prepared for the worst.

κἀγὼ εὑρεθῶ ὑμῖν οἷον οὐ θέλετε, "and that I will not be found by you as you wish." The crasis κἀγὼ (καὶ ἐγὼ) places the "I" in the emphatic position of this clause. If Paul is fearful that he will not find the Corinthians as he wishes, he is just as honest in explaining to the Corinthians that they may not find him to be as they were accustomed (see *Form/Structure/Setting* for the chiastic structure of this verse). He lists the undesirable qualities of the Corinthians in 12:20*b*. He too will have undesirable qualities, most notably a "rod" (Barrett, 329). He will spare no one if such people fail to reform (13:2). Again we notice a subjunctive, namely, εὑρεθῶ (again from εὑρίσκεσθαι, though this time in the passive voice instead of the active). Thus, Paul leaves the door open for reform. In essence, he has given the Corinthians the opportunity to make this a pleasant visit for him if they so desire. The words of 1 Cor 4:21 (though speaking of a previous visit) capture the thought of 12:20*a* and *b*: "What do you prefer? Shall I come to you with a whip [rod], or in love and with a gentle spirit?" (NIV).

[φοβοῦμαι] μή πως ἔρις, ζῆλος, θυμοί, ἐριθεῖαι, καταλαλιαί, ψιθυρισμοί, φυσιὡσεις, ἀκαταστασίαι, "[For I fear] that there will be strife, jealousy, outbursts of anger, selfish ambitions, slander, gossiping, conceit, and disorder." The words "for I fear" are enclosed in brackets for they are not an actual part of the text, yet the English demands a verb (Barrett, 329). Moreover, Paul wants his readers to understand the first part of 12:20*b* in this manner. The μή πως calls for φοβοῦμαι in 12:20*b*, for there is no explicit verb in this clause. In 12:20*a* we saw that φοβοῦμαι anticipated μή πως, and it appears that Paul is doing the same in 12:20*b*.

What Paul fears he now specifically lists. In a previous comment on the sins listed in 12:20, we noticed that those sins in that v differ from the sexual impurity mentioned in 12:21. What Paul lists in 12:20*b* are sins that describe a divided church; what he lists in 12:21*b* are sins that reflect a moral condition beset by sexual impropriety. Whether Paul is consciously making these two lists dissimilar in order to isolate different components of the Corinthian scene is hard to determine. Barrett understands the sins of 12:20*b* to be the result of the work of the rival apostles ("Paul's Opponents," 75; see also *Form/Structure/Setting*). Since some Corinthians sided with Paul and some with his opponents the vices of 12:20*b* are a natural outgrowth of factions that support different leaders (see 1 Cor 1:10–17; 3:3). In line with this position, the sexual sins of 12:21 may reflect Paul's attack on those who have never changed their pagan ways (6:1) and remain untouched by his Gospel of reconciliation (5:20; 6:14). However, Paul may be simply including everybody at Corinth in his threat and not, as Barrett thinks, be dividing the church into different groups. Possibly he is simply expressing the thought that whether the readers were guilty of party faction or sexual impropriety or both, all refractoriness was liable to his wrath.

ἔρις, "strife," "discord," "contention." This word is found in vice-lists (see Rom 1:29; this may possibly reflect Paul's apprehension of the "heathen" tendencies of the Corinthians), sometimes with ζῆλος (Rom 13:13; see BGD, 309: S. Wibbing, *Die Tugend- und Lasterkataloge im Neuen Testament*. BZNW 25 [Berlin: Töpelmann, 1959] 96, 97). This pair of vices is also found in 1 Cor 3:3, which lies in the context of spiritual immaturity. Either consciously or unconsciously Paul is expressing the concern that the Corinthians (at least some of them) were almost back at the point at which he found them. "Strife" is an outgrowth of a worldly church (Phil 1:15; see Martin, *Philippians* [TNTC, 1959] 71–73, for ἔρις directed against Paul personally: see Bultmann, 239, 240, on the absence of the personal note in 2 Cor 12:20, but "if his apostolic authority falls, the moral life of the congregation also goes to pieces." The Corinthians need to take the responsibility for building themselves into an "acceptable" community for God). Thus again we see the building motif of Paul's ministry as in 1 Cor 3. For the apostle, God is the master builder (1 Cor 3:9), yet Paul remains a builder (1 Cor 3:10) in his own right. To be built by Paul is to be built by God: hence the claim of οἰκοδομή.

ζῆλος, "jealousy." Paul uses this word both in a good sense (2 Cor 7:7; 11:2) and a bad one (here and 1 Cor 3:3; see also Rom 13:13; Gal 5:20; *1 Clem* 5: on this see Martin, *Philippians*, 72, n. 1, against Cullmann, *Peter*² [tr. F. V. Filson; London: SCM Press, 1962] 105; see too James 3:14, 16 with ἐριθεία). The latter may reflect a sense of "rivalry" or "party-attachment"

(BGD, 337; see Héring, 97, n. 34). Apparently the Corinthians were capable of intense loyalty, but this loyalty shifted (from one leader to another) almost as though blown by the wind.

θυμός, "anger," "rage," "wrath." The plural of the text gives us the rendering "outbursts of anger" (see Büchsel *TDNT* 3:167, 168). It is not unusual to find that tempers are short when divisions are a part of the scene. The term is in the vice-list of Gal 5:20; Col 3:8; Eph 4:31.

ἐριθεία, "selfish ambition," has the Greek plural ἐριθεῖαι. Originally this word was used to describe one seeking political office for selfish reasons (Aristotle, *Polit.* 5, 3, 1302*b*; 1303*a*, 14). Such a description of a church cursed by strife and division suggests the quarrelsome spirit leading to intrigue and artifice, "machinations" (*Ränke*, so Bultmann, 240), and it tells us that Paul feared that his work was in jeopardy of collapsing unless drastic action was undertaken. The term is also found in vice-catalogues (Gal 5:20; cf. Phil 1:17; 2:3). (For the use of abstract expressions in the plural see BDF § 192.) See Büchsel, *TDNT* 2:660, 661.

καταλαλιά, "evil speech," "slander." The Greek plural (καταλαλιαί) is possibly used to show that there are several individual instances of this sin (BGD, 412). The noun is found again only in 1 Pet 2:11. The adjective κατάλαλος is used substantively in Rom 1:30. The verb καταλαλεῖν is found in James 4:11 where the most significant background is the setting among the priests in Jerusalem in the mid-60s: see Martin, "The Life-Setting of the Epistle of James in the Light of Jewish History," in W. S. LaSor FS, *Biblical and Near Eastern Studies*, ed. G. A. Tuttle (Grand Rapids: Eerdmans, 1978), 97–103, in reference to Josephus, *Ant* 20.180, who uses κακολογεῖν; 1 Pet 2:12; 3:16.

ψιθυρισμοί is from ψιθυρισμός and means "whisperer" or "tale-bearer," hence the idea of gossiping. Barrett views the use of the plural as an indication that gossiping was a prevalent offense at Corinth (329). This is the only verse in the NT in which the noun is found (outside the NT, the word still carries a pejorative sense, e.g., Ps 40:8; Sir 5:14; 21:28; *1 Clem* 30:3; 35:5: see Windisch, 409). The similar ψιθυριστής (first declension masculine) is found only once in the NT and that is in another vice-list (Rom 1:29). Again we see Paul's fear of pagan behavior in the Corinthians' immoral, antisocial conduct.

φυσιώσεις, "conceit." This Greek plural comes from φυσίωσις, which means "inflated," hence "conceited." The noun is a *hapax*. The verb φυσιοῦσθαι is found often in the canonical Corinthian correspondence (1 Cor 4:6, 18, 19; 5:2; 8:1; 13:4), thus suggesting that the sin of pride was ingrained in the church. This should hardly be a surprise in light of the fact that the church was the center of attention of both Paul and his correspondents. "The church of Christ was"—for them—"a stage on which they aspired to be conspicuous figures" (Denney, "The Superlative Way," in *The Way Everlasting* [London: Hodder & Stoughton, 1911], 152).

ἀκαταστασίαι, "disorders," is from a composite noun that suggests disturbance or social anarchy. We know that disturbances had been a part of Paul's ministry (6:5), but probably here it points to the idea of "self-seeking" and "small-minded" scheming (Barrett, 329). It appears that there is much unrest at Corinth (1 Cor 14:33: on this threat of a chaotic state in worship, see Martin, *The Spirit and the Congregation*, 82, 83). See too James 3:16.

It is an understatement to say that Paul was afraid of what he might find at Corinth upon his third visit. This list of sins reflects a church that was in turmoil. Little wonder that he was coming to correct the situation. If his appraisal was on target, then much of a remedial nature would have to take place. The use in our passage of words that are infrequent elsewhere in the NT presupposes that Paul thought the Corinthian situation exceptional. That is, there was not another church founded by Paul, as far as we know, that was so plagued by sin and division (but the case of the Philippian congregation needs to be considered: Martin, *Philippians,* NCB, 22, 23, 31–34). The similarity between 12:20*b* and the list of vices in the letter to the Romans (1:28–32; 13:13) shows how Paul considered the Corinthians' behavior as inconsistent with the Christian lifestyle (see 6:14–7:1). He now intends drastic measures as a possible means of making the situation right. What these measures might have been will be discussed below. The point is that the church at Corinth is as an unruly and wayward child, and discipline appears as the only remedy. However, as has been discussed and as needs to be kept in mind, Paul hopes that the Corinthians will come to their senses before he arrives. If this could happen, Paul would be satisfied (13:7).

21. μὴ πάλιν ἐλθόντος μου ταπεινώσῃ με ὁ θεός μου πρὸς ὑμᾶς, "I am afraid that when I come my God will humble me again before you." This verse, in some ways, continues Paul's concern of 12:20. But before deciding upon the degree of continuity between 12:20 and 12:21, there is a technical point before us. The grammar of 12:21 is somewhat confusing and needs examination before we are ready to judge the relationship between sins listed in 12:20*b* and in 12:21*b*.

Barrett remarks that the placement of πάλιν has left us with an "insoluble grammatical problem" (330). The problem centers on whether to take πάλιν with ἐλθόντος, "coming," or with ταπεινώσῃ, "humble." In other words, do we translate the first part of 12:21*a* as "when I come again, my God will humble me" (NIV; NEB; RSV; KJV/AV) or "when I come my God will humble me again" (Barrett, 330; Plummer, 369; Furnish, 562; Héring, 98; note that Phillips conveniently avoids the translation of πάλιν altogether). Each alternative is grammatically possible. Furthermore, it is difficult from the context to decide which of the two thoughts Paul had in mind.

By its position in the text, πάλιν can be taken with ἐλθόντος. Since πάλιν is next to this participle, the translation "coming again" is grammatically feasible. But one wonders with Barrett (330) if the phrase ἐλθόντος μου, "my coming," is only secondary to the thought of the main verb of the clause, namely, ταπεινώσῃ (aorist subjunctive of ταπεινοῦν, "to humiliate"). This can be seen in that ἐλθόντος μου is in the genitive absolute. It would seem more likely that Paul would have put the circumstantial participle in the accusative (ἐλθόντα) if he wanted to emphasize "his coming" in 12:21*a* (but see BDF § 423.2). The use of ἐλθόντα would be in agreement with με. Thus, the use of the genitive absolute (though strictly incorrect, Barrett, 330) suggests that Paul meant "his coming" to be a parenthetical statement in 12:21*a*. If so, then πάλιν would go with ταπεινώσῃ. The uncertainty surrounding the correct rendering of 12:21*a* is apparent, as seen in the different variants for this clause (see *Note* f; possibly these attempts at changing the reading are the result of endeavors to smooth out some of the grammar).

An examination of the context of 12:21a does not help to clear up the situation, though a logical argument can be made for taking πάλιν with ταπεινώσῃ instead of ἐλθόντος. Paul has just discussed what might happen during his next visit (12:14, 20); hence a return visit ("a coming again") is already in the mind of the Corinthians when he writes 12:21a. Thus, Paul would not be introducing a new theme by writing "when I come again." Yet, we agree with Bachmann (411, 412) that to emphasize "his coming again" in 12:21 appears superfluous. Why suggest that you are coming again (12:20) and then repeat the "again" in 12:21a? (Hughes argues that, if Paul wanted to emphasize the idea of his "coming again" in 12:21a, he would have prepared his reader by writing μὴ πάλιν ἐλθών in 12:20; [see 472, n. 166].) Plummer understands πάλιν to have been placed in the emphatic position. Thus, πάλιν, though adjacent to ἐλθόντος, should be taken with ταπεινώσῃ. As Plummer notes, Paul often uses ἔρχεσθαι without πάλιν when speaking of "coming back" (369). This is prevalent in the Corinthian correspondence (1 Cor 4:18, 19; 11:34; 14:6; 16:2, 5, 10, 11, 12; 2 Cor 1:15, 23; 2:3; 8:17; 12:20). If Plummer's thinking is correct, then it appears more likely that πάλιν goes with ταπεινώσῃ. From this, we have chosen to attach (with Bultmann, 240) πάλιν to ταπεινώσῃ, for we see this as the more logical approach. Admittedly, neither case for the place of πάλιν has overwhelming support. But we believe logic dictates that πάλιν be taken with ταπεινώσῃ. Thus, in summary of our discussion, the more likely solution is that Paul is fearing that he may be humbled again. We remember that he had a previous humiliation (the second visit, ἐν λύπῃ, see 2:1, 5; 7:2); and with the situation presently at Corinth he fears a recurrence of the earlier time.

Paul openly expressed his fear in 12:20 (φοβοῦμαι). Most likely he wants his readers to understand that he fears a second humiliation. The use of μὴ, understood as a conjunction, conveys the meaning of "lest." This idea for μὴ is not uncommon when the word follows verbs of fear (BGD, 517), though we would have to understand 12:21a elliptically. (Harris understands πάλιν to modify the entire clause. Thus 12:21a is rendered, "I fear lest again when I come my God should humiliate me in your presence," 401. He, however, seems to stand alone in this position.) What has to be asked is just exactly what is behind Paul's fear of a second humiliation? Is it to be different from his first humiliation? The answer to the second question is yes. Unlike the first time when Paul was probably humiliated by a specific offender, this time Paul will be humiliated by God. God is the subject of ταπεινώσῃ (aorist subjunctive) and Paul is the object (με). If Paul finds in the Corinthians the moral laxity he fears, he will be forced to mourn for his people and to take harsh actions. In this way Paul will be humiliated for he will feel that he failed in his mission (Furnish, 567; "their ruin is his defeat," Filson, 416; Lietzmann, 159: "the ταπείνωσις doubtless lies in the expression of sorrow over the failure of his work." Kümmel, 213, turns it around: Paul's "finding the Corinthians in an abject condition would be enough to humiliate him in the eyes of the Corinthians." Bultmann's view [241: but not following his textual expedient; see below] is best: Paul's fear is that he will have to employ strict methods. Then, the apostle's humiliation will consist in his having to use his ἐξουσία, which was given him [by God] for οἰκοδομή, for the purpose of its opposite, καθαίρεσις. Success or failure is hardly the issue;

the matter that causes pain is continuing resistance to "the truth" [i.e., Paul's own Gospel], as in 13:9, and that obstinacy seems to Paul to require the severest measure of discipline. Hence his fear that only a judicial sentence will suffice, an action that will show his stern face as part of the *opus alienum* of the Gospel). Thus the answer to our first question is that Paul's humiliation will lead him to purge the body of believers at Corinth. We remember that since Paul's second visit the only "sting" felt by the Corinthians was his drastic letter. Now, if his exhortation to repentance fails, they will feel his wrath.

The use of πρὸς ὑμᾶς, "before you," intensifies Paul's plea for a return by the Corinthians to the apostolic way. He wishes not to be humiliated again, especially before the Corinthians. Barrett suggests that Paul is concerned with being rejected by the Corinthians (330). Surely, Paul was concerned with this, and it would have been a devastating prospect. But in the light of our preceding discussion, it appears that the humilation that is in Paul's mind is not only rejection by the Corinthians, but more, his having to deal severely with the church. Whether rejected by the church or required to deal severely with it, Paul would be humiliated, for in either case this would mean that he still was not accepted as a true apostle of Christ. And, in a paradox, if he was to inflict discipline on refractory members at Corinth, then he would feel discredited, since his claim to apostleship served to upbuild, not pull down, the community. At this point his concept of authority differs markedly from that of his rivals. "By contrast with the authority claimed by the missionaries, Paul's authority in no way reflects credit upon himself; indeed, its proper and effective exercise can leave him discredited" (Ivor H. Jones, *The Contemporary Cross* [1973] 55). Failure to observe this paradox leads Bultmann (241) to think an οὐ ("not") has fallen out between μου and ταπεινώσῃ. This would leave us with Paul fearing that God would "not" humiliate him again. This is doubtful, and with Barrett we reject this argument (ibid., 331). Yet, in all this Paul holds out the possibility that he will not have to be humiliated in the presence of the Corinthians. The subjunctive mood of ταπεινώσῃ alerts us that Paul is not pessimistic that he will have to purge the Corinthians.

The Pauline expression of fear continues, "and that I will mourn for many who have sinned earlier and have not repented of the impurity, fornication, and licentiousness in which they indulged," with more insight into what specifically he is fearing. In 12:20 he related that there was much division and pettiness in the church. In our present v Paul is apprehensive that he will be humiliated before God. We saw how Paul's humiliation will be expressed in the actions he may have to take. He will have to discipline the Corinthians. But this is not a reason for Paul to boast. Rather, in his chastising of the Corinthians, Paul will be "mourning." πενθήσω (future of πενθεῖν), "I will mourn," shows us that Paul is still emotionally and pastorally invested in the church at Corinth. All the time he is contemplating having to punish the disobedient, he will be grieved. In contrast to the joy that the Corinthians earlier brought Paul (7:6), they will now become a source of grief. The objects of Paul's mourning are those who have sinned and not repented. (This is the only place in the NT that πενθεῖν is used as a transitive verb; see BDF

§ 148.2; also cf. Robertson, *Grammar*, 475; see 1 Esdr 1:30; 1 Macc 12:52; 13:26.) But this reaction of Paul is motivated by more than his usual displeasure at sin in general (e.g., 1 Cor 5:1–13). Paul has a stake in the condition of the readers. He is reacting specifically to the situation at Corinth in a manner akin to Phil 3:18 (also an emotional attitude to lapsing believers: Martin, *Philippians* [NCB] 143, 144, where the denial of the cross is shown in a consequent abandonment of the ethical demands of the Gospel, as here at Corinth; this is one more telltale piece of evidence of Paul's debate with Aegean churches at a crucial juncture in his life). While the sin of humanity in general distressed him (Rom 1:18–32), the setting at Corinth distresses him at a deeper level. Bruce sees an added dimension to Paul's heartache (252), for if he had to discipline many at Corinth, this would be an opportunity for the Jewish opposition to attack Paul's premise that circumcision is not needed by the Gentiles. Those that oppose Paul could argue that the indwelling of the Holy Spirit has not been enough and more is needed. The basis for their attack is that the Corinthians (Gentiles) are behaving as pagans. But this line of interpretation seems far-fetched since "circumcision" was not an issue in 2 Cor 10–13, and is not a word in the text.

Paul will be mourning over πολλοὺς τῶν προημαρτηκότων καὶ μὴ μετανοησάντων, "many who have sinned earlier and have not repented." Though both participles are in the genitive (which Bultmann, 241, finds *sinnlos*, "meaningless"), this does not imply that Paul is thinking in terms of the partitive, i.e., some who are sinning. Rather, the πολλοὺς suggests that all those sinning and unrepentant are the reason for Paul's grief. To interpret otherwise would suggest that there are some at Corinth who have sinned and not repented for whom Paul has no remorse. This is uncharacteristic of Paul (Barrett, 332).

The first genitive is the perfect active participle of προαμαρτάνειν, "to have sinned before" (BDG, 702; only here and in 13:2). Plummer interprets the perfect tense to indicate that some have persisted in sin (370). Also, the aorist participle of the second genitive (from μετανοεῖν) taken with ἔπραξαν (aorist of πράσσειν, "to practice," "to indulge in") suggests that those who have continued to sin failed to repent despite an earlier visit or letter by Paul (Hughes, 473). They had the opportunity to change, yet they did not take advantage of it. The combination of the perfect and the aorist is probably Paul's way of saying that the Corinthians had a specific opportunity to repent (the aorist underlies this failure; Plummer, 370) and did not do so (the perfect). Their sinning has persisted even at the writing of chapters 10–13.

A question surfaces as to what Paul may have meant in choosing the word προαμαρτάνειν. The prefix προ- suggests an earlier time. It is doubtful that the period in mind was before the conversion of the Corinthians (Plummer, 370). It is hardly conceivable that Paul would refer to sin committed before conversion as needing to be confessed. Windisch's earlier work, *Taufe und Sünde im ältesten Christentums bis auf Origenes* (1908), contains the remarkable theory that, in Paul's view, Christians who sin are not Christians at all, since for Paul all Christians are sinless. B. B. Warfield, *Perfectionism*, vol. 1 (New York: Oxford University Press, 1931), devotes an entire chapter to examining and refuting Windisch (239–301), and in particular his treatment of 12:21

(260–63). It is true *ipso facto* that conversion implies repentance of sin. More likely, Paul is referring to sin that has persisted since his second visit, or even the reading of the "severe letter." Paul was aware that some had not allowed God's grace to change their lives (6:1) and needed to heed the call, "Be reconciled to God" (5:20). He earlier remarked that there are some in the church who are not living as Christians (6:14–7:1). It is because of these that Paul fears he will have to mourn.

Paul lists specifically the types of sins that these unrepentant people have been guilty of and still are continuing to commit: ἀκαθαρσία, "impurity," especially sexual (cf. Rom 1:24; 6:19); πορνεία, "fornication" (a definite form of ἀκαθαρσία, Plummer [370]; cf. 1 Cor 5:1; 6:13, 18; 7:2; see B. Malina, "Does *porneia* mean Fornication? *NovT* 14 [1972] 10–17, and J. Jensen's rejoinder, "A Critique of Bruce Malina," *NovT* 20 [1978] 161–84); and ἀσέλγεια, "licentiousness," "excess," "revelry" (Rom 13:13). We find this same triplet in Gal 5:19, with the first two items in Col 3:5; Eph 5:3. The last-named is also in Eph 4:19; 1 Pet 4:3; Mark 7:22; cf. Jude 4; 2 Pet 2:2, 7, 18. The use of ἐπί with μετανοεῖν is common (Plummer, 370); ἐπί is used especially with verbs expressing emotion: BDF § 235.2. See Wisd Sol 12:19 and 1 Chron 21:15 (LXX). The use of a simple article with all three sins may suggest a unity and that all three words are synonyms (M. Zerwick, *Biblical Greek* [Rome: Biblical Institute Press, 1964] 184; see also BDF § 276). But Tasker is not convinced (185, 186). (See BDF § 294 for discussion of the attraction of ᾗ in place of ἥν.)

We now are prepared to address an issue introduced earlier. The sins just mentioned by Paul—dealing with sexual irregularity, a feature of life in ancient Corinth (see *Introduction*, pp. xxviii, xxix)—bear little similarity to the sins of v 20. Are we then to conclude that the list of 12:20 and that of 12:21 refer to separate situations? That is, does Paul refer to the influence of false apostles on the Corinthian church only when he lists the sins in 12:20, and then think of a separate situation (such as in 1 Cor 5 or 6) when he considers the sins of sexual impurity (12:21)? Barrett thinks not ("Paul's Opponents," 75, 76).

He argues that, although the theme of gnosticism has dropped out of 2 Corinthians, its effect (sexual immorality) has not disappeared from view. He argues that gnostic influence provided the inroads for sexual libertinism and that such behavior remained. The argument goes on to maintain that because of sexual immorality at Corinth Paul reacts to it in 12:21. In 12:20, Paul had displayed his awareness of the work of the false apostles. Moreover, new converts have accepted the teaching of those emissaries. The result of such an acceptance was division and jealousy. Thus, the two lists address the situation Paul may find upon his coming, though he (according to Barrett) has divided the sinners of Corinth into two separate groups. But we wonder if this is too neat a picture. We will see in 13:2 that Paul brings all the sinful together. Also, we note that in Rom 13:13 one can find ἀσέλγεια listed with ἔρις and ζῆλος. This suggests that for Paul, as for his Jewish teachers (e.g. in 'Aboṯ 5:9), sexual sins were not necessarily separate from sins such as strife and jealousy. Possibly he simply is pointing out that he is aware that those who persist in sins unbecoming of Christians are probably those who are responsible for the division in the church. In short, we take Barrett's cue one step further. We see these two lists as describing the present scene at Corinth, but also suppose that one group is guilty of both types of sins. To accept Paul and reject his message is to reject the Gospel and its moral demands (cf. the problem at Philippi). There is in Paul's mind no difference between those who tolerate immorality (Strachan [36] wonders if the delay of the Corinthians in dealing with the case of incest [1 Cor 5:1–6] may "have poisoned" the church) and those who accept the false apostles. Paul is not planning to punish two different "types" of sinners. Rather, he fears that he will simply have to punish the whole church.

13:1 τρίτον τοῦτο ἔρχομαι πρὸς ὑμᾶς, "This will be my third visit to you." Previously Paul had made two visits to Corinth. On the first one he founded the church; the second was the "painful visit." Since Paul had no intention of visiting the Corinthians when he wrote the "severe letter" (he sent Titus instead), it is highly unlikely that chaps. 10–13 are part or all of that letter. We note in 13:1a the use of a neuter adjective in place of a modified substantive. This was a common practice (see BDF § 154).

ἐπὶ στόματος δύο μαρτύρων καὶ τριῶν σταθήσεται πᾶν ῥῆμα, "on the evidence of two or three witnesses, every matter is established." This use of Deut 19:15 closely follows the text of the LXX, though Paul's verse is similar to Matt 18:16 (see R. H. Gundry, *The Use of the Old Testament in St. Matthew's Gospel*, NovTSup 18 [Leiden: Brill, 1967] 139, for textual peculiarities). The idea of needing multiple witnesses in order to prove a case is a point of Judaic thinking (see Vliet, *No Single Testimony*, 43–62, 96). Deut 19:15 was probably a "rule of living" for Paul (Vliet, 88). But there is disagreement as to the actual meaning that Paul intends here by its use.

Some interpreters think that Paul cites this verse from Deuteronomy so as to suggest that upon his third visit he will set up a formal investigation or judicial "proceeding" (*Verhandlung*) (Filson, 417; Tasker, 188; Hughes, 475; Allo, 335; Schlatter, *Paulus*, 675). In other words, Paul will hold court, and on the testimony of two or three witnesses, will convict and then punish the offenders. But this may not have been Paul's intention for including Deut 19:15, for much of what he would oppose was already a matter of record. The sins (12:20 and 21) were flagrant and out in the open (Lietzmann, 160: "clearly it is not a question of unmasking secret sinners, but of leading open sinners to repentance, for which witnesses cannot help"). There was little need to set up an "inquisition" (see Plummer, 372; Denney, 373), in order to discover the problem at Corinth.

Others hold that the visits themselves constituted the witnesses (Calvin, 169; Bachmann, 412; Plummer, 372; Bruce, 253; Strachan, 38; Windisch, 413). To take this position is to view the two previous visits plus the forthcoming one as the testimony sufficient to indict the offenders. This would have merit except it is hard to see that the first visit constituted a witness against the Corinthians (Furnish, 575), for on Paul's initial journey to Corinth he founded the church. It hardly makes sense that the original trip was meant as a warning to the Corinthians.

Another possible solution is to understand Paul's second visit and the letter which includes chaps. 10–13 and in particular the references in v 2 as making two witnesses against the Corinthians (Bultmann, 243). This is possible in light of 13:2*b* which may be an echo of Paul's warning at the time he departed after his second visit. But more likely is Barrett's (333) contention that Paul is simply letting the Corinthians know in a general way (not specifically connecting the cardinal numerals of Deut 19:15 with any ordinals) that they have had ample warning. (Héring wonders if Paul interpreted Deut 19:15 allegorically, 99, as he does in 1 Cor 9:9 in regard to Deut 25:4.) When Paul comes, no one can plead that opportunity was not available for repentance, or that warning was not given. In trying to match certain events one to one with the numbers "two" and "three" in Deut 19:15, we must not overlook the main reason for the inclusion of this OT verse. Paul is simply saying that when he arrives in Corinth he will (if needed) begin judgment. He will in fact begin immediately, for he has given more than ample warning of possible future actions on his part. Paul's use of Deut 19:15 was more a slipping into his rabbinic frame of mind than a recalling of specific incidents between himself and the church. His use of ῥῆμα probably reflects דָּבָר, *dābār*. (See Procksch, *TDNT* 4:92, 93.)

2. προείρηκα καὶ προλέγω, ὡς παρὼν τὸ δεύτερον καὶ ἀπὼν νῦν, "As I said during my second visit, I now say while absent." The structure of this verse has already been discussed (see *Form/Structure/Setting*). Paul reminds the Corinthians that there has been ample warning concerning his coming visit, namely his second visit and the utterances of chaps. 10–13. (Again we note that Bultmann's thesis is attractive with respect to Deut 19:15, but still it appears too neat. Would not Paul have held that any warnings by Titus— or any other fellow worker—were sufficient to get his point across to the Corinthians? Thus it appears, in a general way, that Paul believed that ever since his second visit, no matter in what manner the warning came, the Corinthians have no excuse for ignoring his word.) The second visit and the present letter (chaps. 10–13) are probably boundaries of the time period that Paul has in mind as he reflects on those who have disobeyed him. This period would have begun with his humiliation at his second visit and ended with the arrival of chaps. 10–13. In between these two events, possibly several exhortations urging acceptance of Paul were made. Most notable were the drastic letter and any additional *paraklesis* from Titus. In 12:21 and 13:2 Paul is mainly concentrating on what has happened since his second or interim visit.

He has not changed his thinking nor wavered from the threat he made as he left following his second visit. προείρηκα (perfect tense of προλέγειν) carries with it the idea of "telling beforehand" (BDG, 708). The use of προλέγειν can include the idea of a warning (Liddell and Scott 2:1488). We see that προείρηκα and προλέγω (present of προλέγειν) go with the adverbial clauses that follow. παρὼν (participle, present active, of παρεῖναι, "to be present") goes with προείρηκα; and ἀπὼν, "absent," is attached to προλέγω. In essence Paul is saying, "I warned you before at my second visit and I warn you now while I write these words" (Bultmann, 243). Plummer thinks that προείρηκα refers to the sins that happened before Paul's second visit and that προλέγω speaks of the period that covers the time after the same visit

(373). The period after the second visit includes the arrival at Corinth of the "severe" letter and will include the arrival of chaps. 10–13. These letters came in the absence of Paul. The apostle has left no loophole of escape for the Corinthians. Since his rejection by the church at the second visit (at a time when he gave a warning in person), he had been absent from the Corinthians. Yet, he had corresponded with them (notably through the "severe letter" and now in chaps. 10–13, but also chaps. 1–9). Despite accusations to the contrary (10:1–6, 9), Paul would punish anyone remaining in "sin" (i.e., rebellion against his Gospel) when he comes. But in the reading of chaps. 10–13, it is important to see that Paul is concerned with the present. If the Corinthians would repent, then he would feel vindicated. But until that comes about, he will remain inflexible over the sins of self-will (12:20) and self-indulgence (12:21), for the former are proof of the "carnality of religious contention" (Denney, 368), and the latter the destruction of personal purity. Just as he condemned such sins at his second visit, he still condemns them at this writing.

Paul hints at the prospect of his visit in the words, "when I return I will not spare those who have sinned earlier or anyone else." In these words, Paul joins together all the sinners at Corinth. He makes sure that no one can rightly assume that he will spare anyone unless such persons have repented of their sin. προαμαρτάνειν, "to sin beforehand," is found in 12:21. This suggests that Paul is making yet another warning to the many who heard his earlier warning at his second visit. The phrase τοῖς λοιποῖς πᾶσιν, "all the rest," or "anyone else," may refer specifically to the new converts who recently chose to go opposite to Paul's wishes (by following the rival preachers). It seems unlikely though that προαμαρτάνειν refers only to the sins of 12:21 and the "all the rest" only to the sins of 12:20, for if this were so, it would make Paul appear to include the sin of self-will as an afterthought. Rather, in 13:2 Paul does not necessarily differentiate between the sins of immorality and those of church division. Had not those who sinned by causing schism in the church sinned "beforehand"? Could not Paul's use of the phrase "all the rest" include all those who were guilty of both sexual immorality and strife, and yet, at the time of the writing of chaps. 10–13, were unknown to him? The answer to both questions is probably affirmative. In 13:2, Paul is addressing the present situation at Corinth in general and in broad terms. In this way no one was free to say that there was insufficient warning of impending "judgment." Also, none could claim an "excuse" on the premise that they had not been mentioned by Paul. He has covered the whole church constituency in 12:20 and 21; he does likewise in 13:2. For Paul, if some rejected his apostleship and so his message, they set themselves up as rejecters of the truth (13:8; see 4:2–4; 6:7). The sins of sexual impurity, as well as the sins of jealousy and divisiveness, are all a reflection of rejecting Paul and his message (as in the appendix of Rom 16:17, 18). In light of this, many in the church were subject to his vindicating, but not vindictive, wrath.

The remaining clause of 13:2 appears to be a rehearsal of Paul's words as he left Corinth following his second visit. The ὅτι probably fulfills the function of quotation marks (BDF § 470.2; Furnish, 570; Hughes, 476, n. 170). The recitative use of ὅτι would "help to refresh" the minds of the Corinthians. The use of ἐάν introduces the subjunctive, namely, ἔλθω, "when I return." The normal meaning of ἐάν is "if," but it can be taken as "when" (Tasker, 186, 187; Bruce, 253; Hughes, 476). It makes little sense to "threaten" someone if the person issuing the threat is doubtful of returning to make good on that threat. See John 16:7 and 1 John 3:2 where ἐάν is interpreted to mean "when" (see Tasker, ibid.). Phillips and NEB translate ἐάν in this way in 13:2. Moreover, see 1 Cor 16:10 where the RSV renders ἐάν as "when" ("when Timothy comes"). Our understanding of ὅτι as recitative suggests that ἐὰν ἔλθω εἰς τὸ πάλιν οὐ φείσομαι was a warning from Paul's lips verbatim, a warning delivered as he was leaving Corinth on his second visit. With this in mind we admit that such speech (ἐὰν ἔλθω) at the emotional departure of Paul following this humiliation may have included a "shade of uncertainty" (Hughes, ibid.). In light of Paul's appraisal of the Corinthian church as he himself departed Corinth, he may have been unsure that he would ever be able (or ever want) to return. But it seems a point of certainty that, as Paul wrote 13:2, the use of ἐάν does not include any suggestion of uncertainty. Otherwise, why spend the last several verses assuring the readers that he would spare no one who rejected his message if he, at the time of the writing of chaps. 10–13, was not positive he would return? We then take ἐάν to mean "when," for Paul is "definitely coming again and he is going to act" (Hughes, ibid.). (ἐάν, in this context, suggests a temporal use, an eventual condition; M. Zerwick, *Biblical Greek*, 320.)

The idea behind φείδεσθαι is that of sparing someone. Possibly this was a military term, suggesting sparing an enemy in battle, especially when the opportunity to kill the enemy presented itself and was not taken (see Liddell and Scott 2:1920). Paul has announced that when he comes, no one who deserves his wrath will escape. The perfect προημαρτηκόσιν suggests persistence in sin. Paul will not punish those who repent, but along the same lines, he will not spare those who persist in their sins. That is, Paul will not spare those who deserve punishment. We might ask what type of punishment he has in mind. One possibility is the punishment that was meted out to the offender who opposed Paul on his second visit. While we are unsure of what that punishment was, nevertheless it appears to have been effective (2:6–11; 7:9–12). Yet, we must remember that the majority of the Corinthians favored this action (2:6). The point is, will Paul have such backing at his third visit? Other possibilities for punishment are, or at least include, excommunication; but Barrett is probably correct in arguing that Paul would not necessarily be in a position to ask for excommunication at his third visit. He himself may end up being ejected and irrevocably disowned. Another possibility is the punishment of turning the opponents over to Satan. This was prescribed for the man guilty of incest (1 Cor 5:5); Hymenaeus and Alexander also were threatened with similar punishment, though in a different church setting (1 Tim 1:20). While such a course of action may seem extremely harsh (as well as somewhat vague, to our understanding), we must remember that his apostolic aim was that such persons be restored and that they be saved (1 Cor 5:5; see 13:9, 10). Though Paul could be severe, his goal was the good of the people (12:14). He was coming to punish those who sought to oppose Christ (note the use of εἰς suggests the idea of motion and rest— "a line ending at a point," Moule, *Idiom Book*, 68, 69).

3. ἐπεὶ δοκιμὴν ζητεῖτε τοῦ ἐν ἐμοὶ λαλοῦντες Χριστοῦ, "since you seek proof that Christ is speaking through me." ἐπεί, "since," is used by Paul in a causal sense (BDG, 284). The present clause is a continuation of the sentence that commenced in 13:2. In essence, Paul has conceded to the church the right to examine his work. In fact, he welcomed this opportunity. But the nub of the debate is that the criteria chosen by the Corinthians to evaluate his work are wrong (10:12; 11:12, 17; 12:11–18). They had been swayed by the opponents of Paul and thus used their supposed miraculous gifts and powerful speech as standards by which to decide that Paul was "inferior." But this conclusion drawn by the Corinthians was wrong, in Paul's estimation. Barrett is certainly correct when he writes, "The only test of the validity of any ministry is whether it conveys the word of Christ to his people" (335). In this light, had not Paul brought the word to the Corinthians (1 Cor 2:4), and thus been part of the reason for their conversion (1 Cor 4:15; 15:11; 2 Cor 3:1–3)? (That is, Paul is an agent for the reconciliation of the Corinthians to God, [5:18–21].) Paul has been the "stage" (Barrett, 335) or "vehicle" (Bruce, 253) for the coming of God's word in power. Though the messenger with the loudest and most impressive voice does not always constitute the one with authority, Paul seems to be saying with this causal clause (in ironical fashion) that he will make his voice to be heard in order to prove he is of Christ.

The Corinthians seek (ζητεῖτε) proof from Paul. δοκιμή, "proof," was used earlier in our present epistle (2:9; 8:2; 9:13). There Paul spoke of the Macedonian churches as having passed the test (8:2), as he had a former confidence in his Corinthian readers (2:9; 9:13). Here (13:3) Paul is ready to present the proof desired by the Corinthians (BDG, 202). From the instrumental use of ἐν, "in," (Furnish, 570), we see that the Corinthians were demanding proof that Paul was a true apostle of Christ. It is hardly an issue of Paul's "spirituality" (*Pneumatikertum*, Bultmann, 244) that is under consideration. Rather, it is the legitimacy of his apostolic office (Käsemann, *Die Legitimität*, 37–43, 47). In their eyes, and abetted by the rival mission preachers, the Corinthians viewed Paul as "weak" and "ineffectual" (10:1, 10); indeed, the deduction was evidently made that he was no true Christian (10:7: Käsemann, ibid., 11, 12). He must, then, be a charlatan, and a bogus apostle with no right to be at Corinth. Such evidences as would accredit him were external, tangible, charismatic "signs of inspiration" (Bultmann, ibid.; Schmithals, *Gnosticism*, 153–56; but cf. Betz, *Der Apostel Paulus*, 58), according to 12:12. The question of who is δόκιμος and who is ἀδόκιμος is the basic theological issue in 13:1–4 (Betz, ibid., 132–35).

Paul's rejoinder is to shift the evidence from the outward and demonstrable to the role of the prophet who (in 1 Cor 14:3) speaks (λαλεῖν) to the congregation's οἰκοδομή, as conveying the νοῦς Χριστοῦ, (1 Cor 2:16) and is possessed by the true spirit of God (1 Cor 7:40; cf. 1 Cor 14:37). Bultmann is exactly on target: the word of the accredited messenger of Christ—the sign that Christ is speaking in him—is not marked by its demonstrable form but by its meaningful content (*durch seinen sachlichen Gehalt*). It is not a performance to amaze people, but a word to address them, and so (Paul is sure) to have an effect in their lives (244).

The link with Moses (in the tradition of Exod-Num) as a "man of authority" who suffered criticism and disaffection is brought out by Hughes, 477, 478. To the extent that rebellion against Moses was taken to be tantamount to an affront to Yahweh, the analogy holds. And it is a fact that Paul has previously used the Exodus narratives in a typological sense (1 Cor 10:11: τυπικῶς). Paul remarked earlier that the Israelites of old had committed sexual immorality (1 Cor 10:8) and had tested (ἐπείρασαν) the Lord (1 Cor 10:9). These things about Israel had been recorded so that future generations would avoid similar sins (1 Cor 10:6 . . . . κακῶν; see 2 Cor 13:7, κακὸν). Could it be that Paul was thinking that the Corinthians, like old Israel, could repent and avoid punishment? (See 1 Cor 11:27–32; Martin, *Worship in the Early Church* [1974 ed.], 128; Roetzel, *Judgement,* 136–42.) Most likely the answer to that question is yes. Paul was reminding the Corinthians (with chaps. 10–13) that they had time to repent and must take advantage of this time (unlike the Israelites of Moses' day who failed to obey God). For Paul, 13:3a is the continuation of the thought in 13:2: "I will not spare since you desire to see Christ in me." Plummer is too pessimistic when he thinks that the Corinthians made it impossible for Paul to spare them (374). To be sure, if they do not correct their ways, such will be the result. But Paul's hope (see 13:7–10) is that he will be able to avoid punishing the Corinthians. This hope may come true, especially if chaps. 10–13 have a positive effect on the church as did the "severe letter."

ὃς εἰς ὑμᾶς οὐκ ἀσθενεῖ ἀλλὰ δυνατεῖ ἐν ὑμῖν, "He is not weak towards you, rather he is powerful among you." In this sentence Paul lays the groundwork for 13:4, from which 13:3b is understood. Christ has not been weak (ἀσθενής) towards the Corinthians ("towards you," εἰς ὑμᾶς; probably "you" means the whole church, Filson, 417) simply because Paul has chosen, up to this point, to come in gentleness. Rather, Christ has been powerful (δυνατός) among (ἐν ὑμῖν) this people. This is a surprising remark, prompting Bultmann, 244, to wonder if the text read ἐν ἡμῖν, "among us": cf. 10:4; 12:9, 10; or perhaps it is ironically framed: he is mightily in your midst, as you claim. If the latter, it indicates how a single revealing phrase can have two meanings. For the Corinthians, Christ was in their company as a wonder-worker, or in them as a pneumatic force; for Paul he was there to be their judge and criterion, exercising the prophetic role of ἐλέγχειν of 1 Cor 14:24, 25. We noticed the chiastic construction earlier (see *Form/Structure/Setting*). We might note that δυνατεῖν is found only in Paul in the NT (9:8; 13:3; Rom 14:4), and is always speaking of divine power. Paul has said that the Corinthians have failed to recognize the power of Christ just as they have failed to comprehend Paul's power. The church at Corinth equated great overt acts of apostleship with power. He is saying that just the opposite is true. This will come out in the discussion of 13:4. Simply put, Christ chose to take the form of a servant, not willing to punish those who opposed him. Yet this is a sign of power. Likewise, Paul has chosen the same path. As will be seen in 13:4, if the Corinthians accept that Christ's seemingly "weak" work was in fact accomplished by the power of God, then they must do the same with respect to Paul. After all, he was the one who brought them the message of Christ (4:7–15).

4. καὶ γὰρ ἐσταυρώθη ἐξ ἀσθενείας, ἀλλὰ ζῆ ἐκ δυνάμεως θεοῦ, "For, in fact, he was crucified in weakness, yet he lives by the power of God." See *Notes* for the several textual concerns of this verse. We noted earlier (see *Form/ Structure/Setting*) that 13:4a parallels 13:4b. In the former, Christ is depicted as having been crucified (ἐσταυρώθη, aorist) in weakness, "yet" (ἀλλά, adversative; see also BDF § 448.5) he is living (ζῆ, present) by (ἐκ; this marks the source, Plummer, 375) the power of God. Paul is determined to make his case, for he introduces 13:4a with καὶ γάρ, "for in fact." This use of these concessive conjunctions (see BDF § 457) is found at the beginning of both 13:4a and 13:4b.

Paul's christological understanding fits well into his argument of 13:4. Christ is both weak and strong. Barrett is right to point out that Christ's weakness, as exhibited in the crucifixion, is not the result of a lack of power (336; see Käsemann, *Die Legitimität*, 41). When Christ chose the cross, he did so because he was acting in God's power. Yet he assumed ἀσθένεια as a role. In taking God's will to be his own, Christ acted in power, despite the fact that the world would think otherwise (cf. Mark 15:30–32). His death on a cross was his own choice and not to be understood as submission to alien powers, such as satanic-demonic forces, as in gnostic ideology (see W. Grundmann, *TDNT* 2:316, 317). Always the weak Jesus remains the subject in dependence on God (against Windisch, 418), and the stress on his "weakness" is not simply a sign of true humanity (although it is that). Rather, Paul is polemicizing here against a *theologia gloriae*, "a theology of glory," that viewed Christ as a powerful figure *in his own right*. This is well brought out in W. Bieder, *ThZ* 17 (1961) 319, and is linked to Paul's dependence on God's κανών as opposed to his rivals' alleged independence (10:13–18; 11:12), loc. cit., 328. We may appeal to the christological hymn of Phil 2:5–11 (see R. P. Martin, *Carmen Christi*[2] [Grand Rapids, Michigan: Eerdmans, 1983], xxiii–xxxiii, 134–64, for a detailed examination of the manner in which Christ chose to come as a servant). We see the ideas of weakness (ἀσθένεια; Phil 2:7, 8) and of power (δύναμις; Phil 2:9; cf. also Rom 6:4; 8:11) side by side linked by the cross and the resurrection. The "hinge" comes at Phil 2:9, διὸ καί, "therefore, also" as transition point between ἀσθένεια and δύναμις. But the cross is not simply a past happening; it is caught up in his present, risen life where he remains as the crucified one, as the crucified Jesus is now the risen Lord (see Martin, *Carmen Christi*[2], xviii, xix, for this observation that makes the cross not a station on the way to his final glory, but the *esse* of that lordship, so that always his lordly power is conditioned by his continuing weakness, obedience, and humility). Christ is Lord of the Corinthians, but they must remember he chose the cross (1 Cor 1:18) as the means of reaching that exalted position. As follows in 13:4b, there is power-in-weakness, a model followed and exemplified by Paul. The "analogy" of Christ and Paul lies at the heart of this double sentence (Güttgemanns, *Der leidende Apostel*, 152–54).

καὶ γὰρ ἡμεῖς ἀσθενοῦμεν ἐν αὐτῷ, ἀλλὰ ζήσομεν σὺν αὐτῷ ἐκ δυνάμεως θεοῦ εἰς ὑμᾶς, "For indeed we are weak in him, but we shall live with him by God's power when serving you." Paul is trying to convince the Corinthians that his manner of dealing with them in the past has not been because he is an "inferior" apostle. Instead, he is asking them to consider that "weakness," not harshness and not overbearing superiority (11:19–21), is the correct stance of a true apostle of Christ. 13:4b parallels the thought of 13:4a. Christ came in weakness, yet God vindicated him with resurrection life (on Phil 2:9, see Martin, *Carmen Christi*[2], 229–35, where "reward" is ruled out by the verb χαρίζεσθαι, and any attempt to find a law *per aspera ad astra* [so Lohmeyer, *Kyrios Jesus*, 74], is equally to be questioned; the connection is rather one of "eschatological reversal" [*Umwertung*] applied to the godly righteous in Israel: see R. P. Martin, "Salvation and Discipleship in Luke's Gospel," in *Interpreting the Gospels*, ed. J. L. Mays [Philadelphia: Fortress Press, 1981] 214–30). Likewise, Paul came in "weakness" and thus he too will be vindicated like his Lord (see discussion below for the meaning behind Paul's use of the future tense of ζήσομεν). God regarded Christ's work as fully acceptable; Paul wishes that the Corinthians would see his work *mutatis mutandis* in the same light.

13:4 is a grand (and noble) attempt by Paul to convince the Corinthians of their wrongdoing. This attempt is grand, because the "model of Christ" (*Urbild:* a unique pattern) is presented as the one (*Vorbild:* an example to be followed) after which Paul patterned his ministry; it is noble, for Paul is paving the way for the Corinthians "to repent" before his coming. He is definitely coming to the Corinthians. When he arrives he will evaluate the situation there. If he finds that they have reconsidered his apostleship and come back to his teaching and if he finds they have repented of their wrongdoing, then he will remain "weak" (as he has done already, 11:21), for he will rejoice with them and will not have to punish anyone. They will reflect on the fact that Paul brought the message of reconciliation to them and that, because of him, Christ was among them, even in weakness, which is characteristic of his Gospel (1 Cor 1:17–2:5; see W. C. Robinson, Jr., "Word and Power [1 Corinthians 1:17–2:5]" in *Soli Deo Gloria*, FS W. C. Robinson, ed. J. M. Richards [Richmond, VA: John Knox, 1968] 68–82). If, however, they have changed neither their ways nor their attitude toward Paul, then he will come in "power." But unlike the past, when the Corinthians were merely spectators of Paul's battles (i.e., the possible skirmishes between Paul and his opponents), this third visit will find them receiving the brunt of Paul's rod. Yet in that stern face he will still be acting in weakness, i.e., sharing the humiliation of his crucified Lord (12:21; cf. 4:12, a dialectic his Corinthian detractors must have found difficult to comprehend, given their notions of "power" represented in forceful leadership and impressive ἀπόστολοι; see J. H. Schütz, *Paul*, 244–48). But, ironically, the new Paul will not be the type they want.

It appears that Paul and the Corinthians did not understand "power" in the same way. For them it was on display in an aggressive and a mighty personality. For the apostle, it is seen in weakness. What neither congregation nor opponents realize is that "in the meaningful necessities [12:10] of the apostle is mirrored the shape of the cross (*Kreuzgestalt*) of Jesus" (Käsemann, ibid., 42). Even if Paul must come and deal with the Corinthians harshly, he will still be acting out power in the form of weakness. The apostle hopes that he will appear "weak" in the sense that he will not have to act harshly with the Corinthians. Reasoning further, the apostle writes that God will vindicate his course of ministry by energizing him. Paul will live because of God's power. However, he is somewhat unclear as to when he sees this power being demonstrated for the Corinthians. In 13:4*b*, ζήσομεν is in the future tense. Does Paul mean that the Corinthians will not see this power until the next age, "the Kingdom come in power" (Barrett, 337)? Or is Paul speaking about the future in terms of when he gets to Corinth (Plummer, 375; Héring, 100, n. 3; Tasker, 188; Hughes, 479; Furnish, 571)? It is doubtful that Paul is speaking of the eschatological afterlife. There does not appear to be any reference to the future world in our passage of 12:19–13:10. Instead, Paul has centered on his coming visit, which leads us to see that he is speaking of living in power before the Corinthians during his third visit. The εἰς ὑμᾶς, "before you," is consistent with this position (Furnish, 571). Specifically, Paul will be living in the power of God when he gets to Corinth. But εἰς ὑμᾶς may mean no more than "to build you up"; see 12:15; Windisch, 419, gives parallels in 1:6; 4:12; see Betz, ibid., 99, 100, for Paul's ἀσθένεια as *Evidenz* in the debate at Corinth. This is then a link with 13:5 (Betz, 132–37, esp. 134). Ideally, the Corinthians will have repented before he arrives. This would confirm, at least in Paul's mind, that his ministry is definitely a ministry of "power," i.e., incognito and hidden under the aspect of the cross. If he is forced to punish some members, the hope is still that the church will accept him, and thus he can see validated his method of serving in "weakness." We must not forget that Paul is seeking to build up the church (13:10). A true demonstration of power is the ability to edify the people of God. Paul's end is to do just that, though his means may be painful for the Corinthians in the process.

5. ἑαυτοὺς πειράζετε εἰ ἐστὲ ἐν τῇ πίστει, "Examine yourselves to see if you are in the faith." 13:5 begins a new direction for Paul. In 12:19–13:3 he has elaborated on his coming visit. He has underlined the point that when he arrives, most likely he will act as "judge, jury, and executioner." That is, he will chasten those who refuse to follow the Gospel, a message presented to and lived out before the Corinthians by the preacher himself. But in 13:4 Paul appears to be taking a new tack. By appealing to the conscience of the church, Paul asks them to consider the paradigm of Christ. In essence, he is allowing the Corinthians the chance to correct the situation at Corinth themselves. This could be done either through self-confession by individual members or through the disciplining of offending members by the church or through both. The point is that Paul has begun in 13:4, and will continue throughout the remainder of chap. 13, to push for the Corinthians to reform themselves. No more will Paul threaten the Corinthians *ab extra;* now he will appeal to their hearts, in a style reverting to 6:11–13; 7:2–4.

ἑαυτοὺς πειράζετε, "examine yourselves." The ἑαυτοὺς is in the emphatic position (Windisch, 420). (The third person plural of the reflexive pronoun does duty for the first and second person plural; see Moule, *Idiom Book,* 120.) Paul wants to make sure that the Corinthians get his point. He exhorts the Corinthians to "examine" themselves, instead of subjecting him to scrutiny (Wiles, *Paul's Intercessory Prayers,* 243). Elsewhere Paul uses πειράζειν to mean "to tempt" (1 Cor 7:5; 10:3; Gal 6:1; 1 Thess 3:5). But it is doubtful Paul would "command" someone to perform an action that was essentially a temptation which might promote sin. Probably it is better to take πειράζειν (found only here in 2 Cor) as meaning "to discern what type of person someone is" (BDG, 640; the verb is to be understood in the "neutral" sense, see Plummer, 376). This fits into the theme of 13:5–10, for Paul is hoping that the Corinthians, upon self-examination of the conscience (Héring, 100), will see that Christ is "in," i.e., among, them. If the Corinthians discover this, then Paul will be seen as a true apostle and thus his message will be obeyed. If this message is accepted and followed, then when Paul arrives on his third visit, he will find the Corinthians as he desires.

Paul exhorts the Corinthians to examine themselves in order to determine "if" (εἰ) they are "in the faith" (ἐν τῇ πίστει). The phrase ἐν τῇ πίστει is found in 1 Cor 16:13 ("stand firm in the faith"). Furnish understands the phrase in our present verse to mean primarily obedience (577). πίστις can include the ideas of trust (a human attitude) and faithfulness (on the part of God; see Héring, 100, 101). Also, faith is understood to be genuine religion (BDG, 663) fides quae creditur (1:24: τῇ πίστει ἑστήκατε, with the article). The use of the phrase here suggests even more. Paul is speaking of a new situation and a new existence as Christian (5:17) (Héring, ibid.). In essence, this understanding encompasses all the meanings of "faith" suggested above, but with particular allusion to a correct appreciation of the Pauline Gospel versus the rival kerygma (11:4). ἐν τῇ πίστει can be understood as synonymous with Χριστὸς ἐν ὑμῖν, "Christ is among you." For Paul, "faith is the reality of the presence of Christ" (Wendland, 231; also see Héring, 100, n. 6, 101, n. 7). What Paul is doing is expressing the hope that the Corinthians will examine themselves to deal with the issue of whether or not they are walking in the way of Christ by following his apostle (1 Cor 11:1). Possibly Paul means for them to answer the question, "Do you really understand what it is to be a Christian?" (Furnish, 577). Instead of questioning Paul's work, the Corinthians should question their own attitudes, for their position before Christ is in danger (Filson, 420). In other words, Paul is directing the Corinthians to ask themselves, "Are we really Christians or have we lost that position?" Earlier (1 Cor 9:27; 2 Cor 6:1) Paul brought up the possibility that salvation, through careless living based on false hopes, could be lost (also see Gal 5:4). As a conscientious worker for God, Paul presents this message to the Corinthians in order for them to turn their judging eyes from the church leader to themselves, or, more to the point, to Christ in their midst as a "critical power" (Bultmann, as on p. 457).

ἑαυτοὺς δοκιμάζετε, "test yourselves." Again we notice the emphatic position of ἑαυτοὺς, and again see that the verb (in this case δοκιμάζειν) is in the imperative. δοκιμάζειν carries with it the idea of "proving in the expectation of approving" (Plummer, 376; see 8:22; 1 Cor 11:28; Rom 2:18; 14:22; Eph 5:10; 1 Thess 2:4). We anticipate the use of its cognate adjectives in 13:5–7 (cf. also 10:18). Paul has urged (note imperatives) the Corinthians to examine and to test themselves. His goal is that they should understand that Christ is "within" (ἐν) them (see use of irony in 13:5d below). Paul is concerned to have the Corinthians repent. If only the Corinthians realize that Christ is among them, then they will come to see that Paul has already ministered to them previously in accordance with God's will and can return (third visit) in a "weak" way. The highest hope of Paul is that the Corinthians should accept him as a true apostle and that then he need not punish them, in his ἐξουσία.

The litmus test of all Christian profession follows: "Or do you not know that Jesus Christ is in you—unless you fail the test?" Paul steps up his appeal to the Corinthians to prove to themselves that Christ is truly among them as they contend. The Corinthians are asked, "Have you no self-understanding or self-criticism?" (Bultmann, 247). The use of ἤ, "or," as an interrogative is not rare (1 Cor 6:16; Rom 6:3; 9:21). The prefix ἐπι- in ἐπιγινώσκειν conveys the idea of "complete" (Plummer, 376) or "thorough" (Hughes, 481, n. 177) knowledge. It is also used here to suggest the idea of being true members of Christ (BDG, 291). Paul is exhorting (even commanding; is this an attempt by Paul to see what influence he has over the Corinthians? will they obey his command?) the Corinthians to take their critical eyes and turn them upon themselves. It may be possible that the church will come to understand that indeed its members do walk in the faith. If so, then Paul has come to them in truth (13:8), and they are authentic proof of his apostolic credentials (2 Cor 3:1–3).

Paul concludes this v with a piece of irony (see *Form/Structure/Setting*). He adds "unless you fail the test." εἰ μήτι ("unless it were so," BDF § 376) includes the strengthened form of μή. The idea behind ἀδόκιμος (13:5, 6, 7) is "not passing the test" ("counterfeit," Bruce, 254). In spite of the closing words of 13:5, Paul (*contra* Filson, 420) is optimistic that the Corinthians will indeed pass the test. Tasker opines that Paul dismisses the idea that the Corinthians will fail (188). This is consistent with 13:7*a*, where Paul prays for a favorable outcome. Also, the Corinthians have responded favorably to Paul before. This was seen in their positive reactions to the "severe letter." Paul is more than willing to give the Corinthians the benefit of the doubt. It could be that his confidence in the Corinthians is a subtle polemic against his opponents. Would the opponents show as much patience toward the church if it threw its support behind Paul?

6. ἐλπίζω δὲ ὅτι γνώσεσθε ὅτι ἡμεῖς οὐκ ἐσμὲν ἀδόκιμοι, "I hope that you will realize that we do not fail the test." The first ὅτι introduces an objective clause ("I hope 'that' . . ."). Paul's hope is that the Corinthians will come to know that he passed the test. (Again we have Paul's oscillation between the first person singular and plural; see Plummer, 377; Carrez, "Le 'nous' en 2 Corinthiens," *NTS* 26 [1979–80] 474–86 remarks that "verse 6 is surprising . . . [with its sequence of] I-you-we. The attitude of 'you' Corinthians is such that it contests the recognition of Paul's apostolate. In that case, the community itself ceases to be apostolic. If Paul is *adokimos* [recognized as unfit], so is the community as well! Paul is not a minister who was intended to pass any sort of qualifying examination which would turn him into a candidate approved by the Corinthians. Verse 4 is quite clear on that point . . . to be weak and to live are based on close fellowship with Christ, and it is this fellowship which unites Paul ['we'] and the Corinthians ['you'] in this life. Thus Christ is presented as the person who gives meaning and force to the 'we' " [483].) There is probably no difference intended by Paul's choice

of γινώσκειν here and ἐπιγινώσκειν in 13:5 (compound verbs are often repeated in simplex form, Moulton, *Grammar*, 1:115). But γνώσεσθε is in the future, thus suggesting that the Corinthians are to test Paul again. They had done so on his first visit, for they accepted his message and the church was founded. Also, they had tested his work when they received the "severe letter." Again, they followed his advice. Now they are asked to evaluate him once more. He wishes them to see that he has not failed the test. The same word, ἀδόκι-μος, is found also in 13:5. But Héring notes a possible difference between the uses of the adjective in v 5 and v 6 with respect to the object of the testing. In 13:5, the consciences of the Corinthians were what Paul had in mind. But it is doubtful in 13:6 that he is asking the Corinthians to examine his conscience when he uses ἀδόκιμοι. More likely he is suggesting that his capabilities and credentials as an apostle should be scrutinized. That is, Paul is asking the Corinthians to test his apostleship (Héring, ibid.). In 13:6 he expresses the fear that the Corinthians will not accept his apostleship (Strachan, 39). This is not anything new to Paul, for much of 2 Corinthians has mirrored such fear. Paul's hope is that the Corinthians will realize that he is a true minister of God. If they do so, they will heed his warnings and respect his authority, which, in turn, will lead to repentance. If this happens, he will not have to be severe with them at his coming. Paul is not out to crush them, but rather to appeal to their consciences (Héring, 101). And in this appeal, Paul has built himself a strong case. He has described the work of Christ among the Corinthians as one of weakness, yet a work that is blessed by God (as in 1 Cor 9:1, 2: Wiles, *Paul's Intercessory Prayers*, 244, n. 3). Likewise, Paul has described his own ministry among the Corinthians as one done in weakness (1 Cor 2:3), yet with the same results. If the Corinthians examine themselves closely they will either find Christ absent from among themselves (a sure sign of disobedience), or they will discover that he is indeed among them. If the Corinthians arrive at the latter conclusion (and Paul hopes that they will), then they must accept Paul and reject the false emissaries. To do otherwise is to follow a different gospel (11:4). In short, to doubt Paul's apostleship should lead the Corinthians to doubt their Christian standing. Moreover, if the Corinthians accept Paul, that confirms their Christianity (Barrett, 338; Windisch, 420: "when it leads to self-examination . . . the congregation will find that its Christianity is genuine"). But Bultmann, 248, has some harsh words about this view. He remarks, "Rather the critical question is whether the Corinthians are conscious that Christ is living in the congregation as a critical power," with a play on *kritische*. Paul considers the Corinthians the seal of his apostleship; now they need again to remember this (see 1 Cor 9:1–3). "Their δοκιμή must demonstrate itself precisely in their recognition of Paul's δοκιμή," since he writes ὅτι ἡμεῖς οὐκ ἐσμὲν ἀδόκιμοι, not ἐστε ἀδόκιμοι. "The two recognitions coincide" (Bultmann, 248).

7. εὐχόμεθα δὲ πρὸς τὸν θεὸν μὴ ποιῆσαι ὑμᾶς κακὸν μηδέν, "We pray to God that you might do nothing wrong." Paul reports to the Corinthians that he (note the "we") is praying (present tense) for the Corinthians. The use of εὐχόμεθα πρός is not uncommon (LXX: Num 11:2; 21:7; 2 Kgs 10:2; see also Jub 22:27; 2 Macc 15:27). As he does in other epistles (Phil 1:9) Paul shares

the content of his prayer with his reader. He is praying to God that the Corinthians will refrain from doing wrong. Here Paul introduces (Furnish, 577) the other side to his hope that they may pass the test; and that other side is that they will not do any wrong ("no evil thing," Barrett, 339). ὑμᾶς, "you," is in the accusative and, grammatically speaking, can be taken as either the subject (so RSV) or the object of the aorist infinitive ποιῆσαι (from ποιεῖν). The latter, however, seems unlikely. If the Corinthians are the object, then the subject is understood to be either God (see Lietzmann, 160–62; but also see Kümmel, 214: "that God will cause no harm to you") or Paul himself (so NEB [1961 ed.] "[we pray] that we may not have to hurt you"). Either choice leaves us with an awkward thought, for what follows suggests that Paul wishes nothing but the best for the Corinthians. This is seen in the parallel thought of v 7c (ἵνα ὑμεῖς τὸ καλὸν ποιῆτε, "so that you might do right"; see *Form/Structure/Setting*). Also, Paul mentions in 13:9b that he is praying for their restoration (see Barrett, 339). The point is that to take ὑμᾶς as the object of ποιῆσαι is to place a thought out of line with Paul's thinking in 13:5–10. Most likely, ὑμᾶς is the subject of ποιῆσαι (Furnish, 572; Héring, 101; Bultmann, 249; Wiles, *Paul's Intercessory Prayers*, 244, n. 6, but not Lietzmann whom he lists). Paul's prayer is that they do nothing wrong. The "wrong" may have been a refusal to follow Paul's instructions to repent (12:20, 21). Also, the wrong may have been the action of rejecting Paul when he comes (Harris, 404). More simply, it is a negative way of stating the hope that they may not be ἀδόκιμοι.

οὐχ ἵνα ἡμεῖς δόκιμοι φανῶμεν, "not that we appear as having passed the test." After sharing the content of his prayer with the Corinthians, Paul gives his motive for such a prayer-report. He does this by first saying that his reasons for praying as he does are not selfish. If the Corinthians repent and reform, then Paul will be satisfied. But, as will be shown, if this reform takes place before his arrival, then apparently Paul will not *be seen* as (ὡς: the Corinthians' point of view) having passed the test. This is one way to assess the thinking behind the present words under study. But the ambiguity of the ἵνα clauses here and to follow makes it uncertain where the prayer-report closes. Either, with Plummer (377), the ἵνα clauses add explanations to the purpose of Paul's prayer that they do no wrong, or, as Wiles, ibid., 244, 245, n. 7, argues, the same clauses continue the content of his prayer: "and we do not pray that (οὐχ ἵνα) we may appear . . . but that (ἀλλ᾽ ἵνα) you may do what is right." On the latter construction, see BDF § 392.1, which is to be preferred. To be sure, Paul would very much like to be accepted as a true apostle. And, essentially, he will be accepted if the Corinthians repent. But in the eyes of his opponents, he will have failed the test of a "powerful and mighty" apostle, for when he comes he will not need to exercise authority in this manner. He will again be accused of being bold while away, but timid in person (10:1, 10). However, it is Paul's hope that the Corinthians repent before he arrives and so remove the necessity for him to establish his identity by a δοκιμή. This is the third consecutive verse in which Paul has referred to the idea of "passing a test." And in each instance, he has meant something different. The test in 13:5 appears to be an examination of the consciences of the Corinthians. In 13:6, Paul is asking the Corinthians "to test" his apostleship. In our present verse, Paul seems to be bringing another nuance out of the picture. In 13:7, he refers to the "standards" of his opponents. His opponents will be watching him closely to see if he comes as one carrying a potent rod. They will be judging him by whether or not he exerts his ἐξουσία, the central issue now ventilated. In other words, will he come in "outward power"? In summary, Paul is concerned that the tests imposed in 13:5 and 13:6, respectively, be passed. But he will be more than happy if he does *not* pass the test of 13:7. If he fails this one, that means he will not have to discipline the church, for its members will have repented. Though each separate use of "passing the test" has its own special characteristics, nevertheless there is a common denominator for all uses, namely, that the presence and power of Christ will be demonstrated in each instance. If the Corinthians examine their consciences and pass the test, they will see that Christ is among them "in power" (13:5). If the Corinthians see that Paul passes the test, they will see Christ's power-in-weakness in his apostleship (13:6). If the apostle does not "pass the test" of his opponents in that he does not have to discipline the Corinthians (13:7), then again the power and presence of Christ will be evident, for the Corinthians will have accepted Paul's work and apostleship (an apostleship sanctioned by God in power and in the presence of Christ). This common denominator is in itself a repetition of the thought of 13:4.

ἀλλ᾽ ἵνα ὑμεῖς τὸ καλὸν ποιῆτε, ἡμεῖς δὲ ὡς ἀδόκιμοι ὦμεν, "but rather that you might do right even if we appear to have failed." The words (ἀλλ᾽ . . . ποιῆτε) balance the thought expressed in 13:7a ("that you might do nothing wrong"). The ἵνα introduces the purpose (Plummer, 377) of Paul's prayer or its content (Wiles, 244, n. 7), as we saw. He is praying that they will do what is right (τὸ καλὸν). For the Corinthians to do right would be to accept Paul's message and repent of their sins, even if this meant Paul would look like he was doing wrong ("failed the test," again observing ὡς denoting the Corinthians' evaluative comment, and so not a true δοκιμή). Literally, ἀλλ᾽ . . . ὦμεν reads, "that you may do good while we may be rejected," (Filson, 420), sc. by you.

If the Corinthians respond favorably to Paul, he will be without proof of his ability to be "outwardly" strong (Hughes, 482). But this "absence of proof" will only be apparent to his enemies, for Paul's converts will note that the apostle is indeed powerful. The choice of the right way by the Corinthians is the main concern of Paul. He is more concerned with this action of the Corinthians than with his needing to discipline them. His concern for the salvation of the Corinthians is the important item for Paul (Héring, 101), as v 9b will clarify.

Such thinking on the part of Paul reminds the reader of 12:19, in which Paul remarks that all he does and says is for the edification (οἰκοδομή) of the church. Paul takes the rejection of the Gospel seriously. Thus the antithesis κακὸν/τὸ καλὸν may *seem* trite and platitudinous, but has to be viewed as part of Paul's *apologia pro vita et evangelio* (Prümm, *Diakonia* 1:724; Wiles, 245). This is illustrated in his agony over the rejection of the messiah by the Jews (Rom 9:2–4a; 10:1–3) and his equally intense feeling over false brothers (Rom 6:1–14; Phil 3:18, 19; cf. 2 Cor 11:13–15, 26). He is willing to do whatever is necessary to assist the Corinthians in living in accordance with his message, whether it be to chasten (though Paul wishes not to have to this, Tasker, 189) or to appear a failure.

Barrett takes Paul's willingness to be rejected as a sign that there is still the possibility the Corinthians may turn to do good and yet not accept Paul as apostle (but see *Comment,* v 9). In this, Barrett remarks, Paul "never appears more clearly as an apostle, an accredited representative of Jesus Christ, than he does here" (339; see also Denney, 380). It appears that Paul is prepared to take the sins of others upon himself and "to be counted a transgressor for their justification" (Barrett, ibid.). While this is a sobering thought, it may not be completely foreign to Paul's mind, for the idea of the apostolic suffering servant has arisen before in 2 Corinthians (see 6:1, 2).

8. οὐ γὰρ δυνάμεθά τι κατὰ τῆς ἀληθείας, ἀλλὰ ὑπὲρ τῆς ἀληθείας, "For we cannot do anything against the truth, but only for the truth." The thrust of this explanatory sentence (Wiles, ibid., 246) is that Paul can do nothing outside the realm of truth. It should not be hard to see that this thought expressed as a general maxim anticipates v 10. The γὰρ ("for") clause suggests that 13:8 continues the thought of the preceding verse (Tasker, 189; Barrett, 339; Hughes, 483). It follows that whatever action Paul takes—either coming in "weakness" or in "power"—is in line with "the truth." If things in Corinth are going well when Paul arrives, then his refusal to exercise authority is in line with the truth. Paul will not need to act harshly unless the truth is being opposed ("He must not allow authority to degenerate into authoritarianism," Hughes, 484). ἀλήθεια, "truth," in this verse, possibly means the Gospel (Denney, 381; Furnish, 573, 579; Filson, 421; Tasker, 189; cf. 4:2; 6:7; 11:10: cf. Gal 2:14). Bultmann understands "truth" to be Paul's teaching over against a different gospel (*TDNT* 1:244; cf. 11:4). Acting according to (ὑπέρ, "on behalf of") the truth is certainly Paul's duty, but for one so committed to the Gospel as Paul was it implies also acting out of practice (Johnston, "2 Cor 13:8," 68, 69). What Paul was doing in his weakness was reacting in his normal manner. His weak showing was in accordance with the truth just as his life was devoted to "the service of the overmastering ἀλήθεια" (Bultmann, 250). If Paul is forced to act harshly, this is not a sign of departing from the truth. Rather, it would be another side of the truth. While the idea is "obeying the truth," Quell has possibly gone too far when he considers that the idea of righteousness lies behind ἀλήθεια (*TDNT* 1:233: so Bultmann, 250), especially when we consider Paul's understanding of righteousness (Héring, 101, n. 9).

No doubt 13:8 is a polemic against Paul's opponents. Everything Paul has done has been in accordance with God's will as he understood it. He has always acted in truth. In essence, Paul has laid a foundation for his coming visit. Whatever he finds at Corinth and in whatever way he is led to act, it will be done for God's glory. Whether he rejoices at their repentance or attacks the church at large (possibly Paul saw a reformed church as a living church; Kennedy, "Weakness and Power," 350), Paul will (and always intends to) promote the will of God in his action. Thus, he is committed to serve "the truth," i.e., the Gospel entrusted to him, even in the dialectic of weakness-in-strength and acceptance-in-rejection, as well as death-in-life (see 4:12). To his mind, he will not violate this dictum during his third visit.

9. χαίρομεν γὰρ ὅταν ἡμεῖς ἀσθενῶμεν, ὑμεῖς δὲ δυνατοὶ ἦτε, "For we rejoice when we are weak, though you are strong." The γὰρ, "for," continues ("confirms," Plummer, 378) the thought of 13:8, or better v 7. We have previously discussed the use of ἀσθένεια and its cognates in our passage (see also 4:7–12; 11:21; 12:9). The two properties of Paul's teaching of strength-in-weakness are connected (Barrett, 340; see 13:4). Paul is "weak" (12:10) that the Corinthians might be "strong." This paradox was highlighted in 13:4 and touched on again in 13:7. Paul would be satisfied if he had to be "weak," as they said he was (10:10; 11:21, 30; 13:4), because the Corinthians had become "strong" as was their self-estimate (10:4; 11:19). So there is evidently an allusion in the dictum to the Corinthians' own slogan and catchword. Paul, however, is revising their understanding of what "weak" and "strong" consist in, as he views both terms in the light of the cross of Jesus (13:4; Güttgemanns, *Der leidende Apostel*, 153, 154).

τοῦτο καὶ εὐχόμεθα, τὴν ὑμῶν κατάρτισιν, "Our prayer is for your restoration." Paul adds to what he said in 13:7 about his prayers on behalf of the Corinthians. He prays now for their κατάρτισις, "restoration." This noun is a NT *hapax* and comes from καταρτίζειν (13:11; 1 Cor 1:10; Gal 6:1; 1 Thess 3:10; cf. Heb 13:21; 1 Pet 5:10; Mark 1:19; Matt 4:21). Also see the use of καταρτισμός (Eph 4:12). The RSV translates κατάρτισις here as "improvement," but this appears too weak a rendering (as does Lietzmann's *Besserung*, "betterment"). The word includes more than the idea of improvement (Héring, 102, n. 10), and is closer to the concept of "completion," "putting in proper condition," "restoring" (BDG 417, 418; see 13:11; cf. Gal 6:1). Originally, the idea was of setting dislocated bones (Liddell and Scott 1:910), hence the meaning of setting right what was wrong (Barrett, 340; Plummer, 378; Allo, 340). Though κατάρτισις suggests the attainment of religious and moral perfection (Filson, 421; but not "perfectionism," Hughes, 484), unity also cannot be far from Paul's mind (see 1 Cor 1:10). What Paul has in view is the restoration and repair of what has been broken. There were several relationships that had been fractured. For one, the relationship between Paul and the church was in need of repair. Something had happened after the time Titus left Corinth with a good report (7:2–16) that caused the church to become estranged from him. (Here the intrusion of a rival mission in 11:4, 13–15 probably explains the breakdown of good relations.) In chaps. 10–13 we find Paul attempting to mend a broken relationship. For another, the relationship between the Corinthians and God was likewise in need of attention. No doubt Paul saw that, if the Corinthians failed to accept him, then this relationship to God was at risk. (This point makes it difficult to accept Barrett's position that the Corinthians might repent and still fail to accept Paul, see above.) Also, fellowship among the members of the church itself was probably in disarray. If the Corinthians could rectify their relationship with God and his messenger, namely, Paul, then most likely unity and harmony would return to the church (13:11). It appears that disunity was prevalent in Corinth at this time; we can see this from the sins listed in 12:20, and *1 Clement* (A.D. 96) shows how the same factious spirit persisted.

Paul's prayer for the Corinthians was that they might do nothing wrong (13:7) and that they might be restored to God, to the apostle and to one another (13:9). His hope was that such events could take place before he arrived. Yet, he was prepared to punish those who remained obdurate if, when he arrived, he found that which he feared (12:20, 21). But even in this punishment, Paul was not out to make a name for himself (to "appear strong") by taking his cue from the opponents (11:19, 20). Rather, if forced to act severely with the Corinthians, he still hoped for the outcome of "restoration." In Paul's thinking, any discipline necessary was for the good of the church. He will elaborate on this point in 13:10. His goal was the edification (οἰκοδομή) of the church at Corinth. His hope was that this desired result would come about through the effort of writing chaps. 10–13. But, if need be, he will come "with a rod" (to use the imagery of 1 Cor 4:21).

10. διὰ τοῦτο ταῦτα ἀπὼν γράφω, "This is why I write these things while I am yet absent." διὰ τοῦτο, "this is why" ("for this case," Plummer, 378; cf. 14:1; 7:13; 1 Cor 4:17). In these opening words of 13:10, Paul reviews his purpose in what these four chapters (10–13) have been concerned to promote, namely, that there may be restoration and repentance. If these events take place while Paul is absent (ἀπὼν), then he will have no need to be severe with the Corinthians when he is present (παρὼν). The use of ἀπὼν and παρὼν together in 13:10 reminds us of 10:11; 13:2, where Paul speaks of his being present with and his being absent from the church. ἀπὼν is understood in both verses to relate to his absence while he is composing chaps. 10–13. As these chapters are read (either as a letter on its own, or simply as part of a larger letter) in his absence (cf. Polycarp, *Phil* 3:2), he warns the Corinthians, but more important, he offers the Corinthians a chance to return to his side. The use of παρὼν in 13:2 refers to a different visit from that mentioned in the παρὼν in 13:10. With respect to the former, Paul speaks of his painful (second visit); the latter use refers to the expected pleasant visit that is still yet to happen (the third visit; 13:1; 12:14). One might have expected the epistolary aorist (Moule, *Idiom Book*, 12, n. 1), but instead we find the present γράφω (Furnish, 574; see Robertson, *Grammar*, 845, 846). The ταῦτα, "these things," refers to everything in chaps. 10–13 (Furnish, 574; Filson, 422; Barrett, 340). Regardless of the chronology of chaps. 1–9 and 10–13 (see *Introduction*, pp. xxxviii–li), it is necessary to separate the two parts (Windisch, 425). That is, it is highly doubtful that chaps. 1–13 were composed as a single letter. More likely, they (1–9 and 10–13) were separate literary efforts of Paul. Paul has written the *apologia* of chaps. 10–13 in order to bring about results similar to those of the writing and reading of the "severe letter," but with increased intensity in response to a new situation in 11:4, 13–15, i.e., the presence and influence of alien teachers who promoted an anti-Pauline message.

ἵνα παρὼν μὴ ἀποτόμως χρήσωμαι, "so that when I am present I might not have to act harshly." Paul gives his purpose (seen in the ἵνα clause) for sending this letter to the Corinthians before he arrives. Paul hopes (and prays) that he will not (μὴ) have to "act," "proceed" (χρήσωμαι, subjunctive of χρῆσθαι), harshly (ἀποτόμως, adverb; see ἀποτομία, "severity," in Rom 11:22 [2x]). He wishes "restoration" and to enforce his final appeal he reverts to the possibility of his readers' remaining unmoved. So he returns to the warning notes struck in 12:19–13:4, or more pointedly in 10:8, 11.

κατὰ τὴν ἐξουσίαν ἣν ὁ κύριος ἔδωκέν μοι εἰς οἰκοδομὴν καὶ οὐκ εἰς καθαίρεσιν, "in accordance with the authority which the Lord gave me, the authority for building up, not tearing down." The words reflect Paul's opening thought of "the four chapter letter," for in 10:8 Paul reports to the Corinthians that he has received authority (ἐξουσία) from the Lord (ἔδωκεν is aorist) for building up (οἰκοδομή) and tearing down (καθαίρεσις). καθαίρεσις brings with it the idea of pulling down strongholds (10:4). Apparently, Paul is prepared to do battle with those who refuse to accept his instructions leading to repentance. But this is not his chosen goal. Rather, he wishes to fulfill his calling as apostle (1:1), namely building up of the Corinthians. In a paradoxical way, Paul assumes any "tearing down" on his part will, in the long run, contribute to the building up of the church. He will exercise power—either in mildness or in anger—and do whatever necessary to aid the church to reach its full maturity (v 9).

These words of 13:10 reiterate his topic introduced in 10:1, 2. He will not be "bold" unless forced to be so by the Corinthians. In these four chapters, he has presented his case and provided the evidence that is more than sufficient to convict (ἐλέγχειν, as a prophetic ministry: 1 Cor 14:24, 25; but see too Betz, *Der Apostel Paulus*, 77, on the role of ἐλέγχειν in rhetorical "comparison" [10:12]) any wrongdoers. Yet, his arguments have preceded his person in the form of a letter in the hope that those led astray by alien forces (11:1–3) will rectify the situation. Although we are left in the dark as to the outcome of this visit, we may hope that Harris is right in conjecturing that most likely the visit was not unpleasant (404, 405). There are several hints (though no direct evidence) that possibly Paul's third visit turned out to be somewhat positive. For one thing, if Paul visited Corinth during the time he was in Greece (a three-month period mentioned in Acts 20:2, 3) and if he wrote the Epistle to the Romans from Corinth (R. P. Martin, *New Testament Foundations 2* [Grand Rapids: Eerdmans, 1978], 190), then Rom 15:30, 31 may shed some light on our concern. In these vv, we see that Paul is apprehensive, but it is for the future, not necessarily the present. If our position is correct, then there appears to be no pastoral concern (11:28) for the situation in Corinth at the time of the writing to the Romans. If the Corinthian church was still the same as described in chaps. 10–13, then we could rightly expect Paul to ask for prayer for that situation. Moreover, we wonder if Paul would endeavor to compose an epistle if the environment was hostile to him—unless Romans has the shape of his "last will and testament." True, he wrote some of his epistles in the not-so-friendly environment of a prison. But in those instances he had no choice of being where he was when he composed. At least at Corinth he could have left if he was not wanted, assuming the seas were open to traffic after the close of the winter season.

Again we appeal to Romans (following Harris) when we note that Paul was laying plans for further evangelism (15:24, 28). Would he be so eager to press westward (i.e., towards Spain) if the Corinthian church was still in disarray? Moreover, it appears that the collection (2 Cor 8, 9) was completed among the Corinthians (Rom 15:26, 27). It is doubtful this would have transpired if the church had rejected Paul after reading chaps. 10–13. Yet there are no Corinthian delegates in the journey with the collection intended for Jerusalem, according to Acts 20:4, 5 (see earlier, pp. 285). (Harris also adds that the fact that 2 Cor was preserved argues in favor of a successful visit [the third].) But this leaves unanswered the question why the "severe letter" was not preserved if it also produced a desired effect. Admittedly, these facts do not shed a direct light on the outcome of Paul's third visit. Perhaps we are being too optimistic to suggest that Paul and the church at Corinth lived in renewed harmony. But at least we can say that there are some hints that all was not lost in the writing of chaps. 10–13. Possibly, the situation improved at Corinth. Harris's conjecture sheds no light on whether Paul had to use force on the Corinthians or whether he came to a people that had repented. It is not ruled out that Paul was finally accepted at Corinth. But we must note that if the situation at Corinth was pleasant for Paul, nevertheless the church eventually reverted to its old ways (see *1 Clement,* dated A.D. 96) and Paul's influence went generally into a decline.

Explanation

These verses (12:19–13:10) record Paul's warnings before he visits Corinth a third time. It appears that something happened after Titus left Corinth. Paul's co-worker had journeyed to the city with the "severe letter." We also know that the Corinthians repented after hearing the "severe letter"; thus, when Titus returned to Paul at Macedonia, he brought the apostle the good report that the Corinthians had realized their error and were in line with Paul's teaching (7:2–16). Because of this report, Paul penned chaps. 1–9 as a Letter of Thanksgiving. But either Titus misread the Corinthian situation or, more likely, some outsiders infiltrated the church (11:4, 13–15), for Paul apparently received word that, despite Titus's report, all was not well at Corinth. In chaps. 10–13 we see part, if not all, of the response Paul made to the Corinthian situation, now made worse by alien mission preachers.

Paul opens this response by warning that he will return to punish the Corinthians. He then describes why he (and his message) should not have been displaced in favor of the opponents who have influenced the Corinthians. So Paul engages in a "boasting" contest with his opponents, picking up the idea of 10:12. Our apostle argues passionately, and yet logically, that he is the one who is honest and loving towards the Corinthians. This theme of boasting is seen in the discussion of Paul's thorn, but it is here that Paul underlines his belief that he experiences the power of God in weakness. He continues his defense of his actions until 12:19, where he stops defending himself and concentrates on his coming visit to Corinth.

Paul threatens to come in a manner that will be displeasing to the Corinthians. Unlike his second visit, the third one will not find Paul backing away from opposition. His appointed task as apostle was to edify the church. Paul has received the authority to do so from God. This edification may not come except through Paul's disciplining the church and castigating such sub-Christian moods and practices as were known to him. He has learned that the church at Corinth is beset by features of division (12:20) and sexual immorality (12:21). But while Paul's words describing the possible punishment of the church are harsh (and we have no reason to doubt their sincerity), we will miss the true motivation behind Paul's writing of chaps. 10–13 if we fail to see that he wished to avoid stern action against the Corinthians. Instead,

Paul's goal is that chaps. 10–13 will lead the Corinthians to see that they are wrong, and in turn, will lead them to repent and accept Paul's ministry and message. If this change would occur, then the apostle would be satisfied.

The promise and prospect of a third impending visit (12:14) are renewed in 13:1. Paul has already issued a direct and strong warning, as an authoritative spokesperson of Christ (v 3), about the ethical laxity of the members who had sinned. He reiterates that warning (v 2) and tells them plainly that he will deal firmly with any repeated indiscipline and trifling with Christian moral standards. He is clearly an advocate of prescriptive ethics!

There is a veiled threat of some discipline (in vv 2, 3) which he will exercise, not in his own right or name, but simply and solely because he is the genuine messenger of Christ who seeks, as an overriding consideration, the highest welfare of the church (v 9).

Yet Paul's threat of a severe reprimand is tempered by some paradoxical thoughts (v 3*b*). He is weak in himself and seemingly powerless to remedy the menacing situation at Corinth; but clothed with an authority which derives from his status as Christ's apostle—almost his personal representative—Paul has the ability to cope firmly with this ugly problem and to bring to bear upon it in Christ's own power as head of his people. "The Church is subject to Christ" (Eph 5:24), and to the apostle who represents Christ to the congregation. Yet (if we recall 1:24) this authority is exercised in no dictatorial or authoritarian fashion, as though Paul were simply imposing his own personal whims and wishes on the church. It is an authority, exercised in the spirit of the Crucified (v 4), which will bring the Corinthians to see the folly of their ways. In other words, it is love that subdues—by turning disobedience and hostility into a glad acceptance of God's will and a willing alignment of selfish ends to his nobler purposes for human lives. It is the message of the cross applied to a difficult and delicate situation, created by a rebellious group at Corinth, sadly led astray (11:2, 3).

The key phrase is "crucified in weakness." We may consider Bonhoeffer's comment on this phrase: "God in human form—not, as in oriental religions, in animal form, monstrous, chaotic, remote, and terrifying, nor in the conceptual forms of the absolute, metaphysical, infinite, etc., nor yet in the Greek divine-human form of 'man in himself,' but 'the man for others' and therefore the Crucified, the man who lives out of the transcendent" (*Letters and Papers from Prison* [New York: Macmillan, 1972] 381, 382).

We are left in no doubt that Paul cherishes the church's highest good—their "restoration" (v 9), their "building up" (v 10), their stability as a Christian community with the Lord at the center (v 5). What are the ways to achieve these exemplary ends?

(i) Self-examination (v 5), which *may* be a painful process of self-analysis, deals ruthlessly with the present condition and does not refuse to face the unpleasant sight of past sins and failures. But this leads to:

(ii) Repentance, i.e., a confession of past evil ways as deserving of God's judgment and a turning from them (12:21) is needed. Paul has no room for cheap grace or any easy way back to favor. Penitence—and all that is involved in a forsaking of sinful practices and tempers—is an indispensable condition to restoration and renewed fellowship.

(iii) The apostle's prayers are also a force to be reckoned with (vv 7, 8), for he carried the burden of the church's good on his pastoral heart, and yearned to see them in right relationship with the Lord and himself.

(iv) Threatening, which Paul is not afraid to use (v 10), reminds his readers that he may have to deal severely with the offenders if they do not, in his absence, set matters right. And he will have no compunction in claiming the God-given authority which he has, as apostle to the Gentiles, to ensure the church's highest well-being.

(v) Optimism is a final factor, for Paul was irrepressibly hopeful for his churches. He has confidence that as the truth is mighty and it prevails (v 8), so, once the Corinthians perceive the truth of the appeal he makes, they will accept it and act upon it. Thus he expects that all will be put right in the end (v 9).

VIII. Conclusion (13:11-13)

Bibliography

Campbell, J. Y. "κοινωνία and Its Cognates in the New Testament." *JBL* 51 (1932) 352–80. **Champion, L. G.** *Benedictions and Doxologies in the Epistles of Paul.* Oxford: Published privately, 1934. **De Passe-Livet, J.** "L'existence chrétienne: participation à la vie trinitaire, 2 Cor 13, 11–13." *AsSeign* 31 (1973) 10–13. **Dobschütz, E. von.** "Zwei- und dreiliedrige Formeln. Ein Beitrag zur Vorgeschichte der Trinitätsformel." *JBL* 50 (1931) 117–47. **George, A. R.** *Communion with God in the New Testament.* London: Epworth Press, 1953. **Hainz, J.** *Koinonia: Kirche als Gemeinschaft bei Paulus.* BU 16. ———. *Ekklesia.* BU 9, 1972. Regensburg: Verlag F. Pustet, 1982. **Hermann, I.** *Kyrios und Pneuma.* Studien zur Christologie der paulinischen Hauptbriefe. SANT 2. München: Kösel-Verlag, 1961. 135–38. **McDermott, M.** "The Biblical Doctrine of κοινωνία." *BZ* n.f. 19 (1975) 64–77, 219–33. **Muellensiefern, R.** "Wie sind 2 Kor 13:13 die drei Teile des Segenswunsches inhaltlich auseinderzuhalten und miteinander zu verbinden?" *TSK* 72 (1899) 254–66. **Mullins, T. Y.** "Benediction as a New Testament Form." *AUSS* 15 (1977) 59–64. **Panikulam, G.** *Koinonia in the New Testament.* AnBib 85. Rome: Pontifical Biblical Institute, 1979. **Rigaux, B.** *The Letters of St. Paul.* Ed. and tr. S. Yonich. Chicago: Franciscan Herald Press, 1968. **Seesemann, H.** *Der Begriff KOINONIA im Neuen Testament.* BZNW 14. Giessen: Töpelmann, 1933. **Wainwright, A. W.** *The Trinity in the New Testament.* London: SPCK, 1962. 241, 242. **Wiles, G. P.** *Paul's Intercessory Prayers.* SNTSMS 24. 1974.

Translation

[11] *Finally, brothers, rejoice,* [a] *aim for restoration,* [b] *encourage one another,* [c] *be of the same mind,* [d] *live in peace. And the God of love and peace will be with you.* [12] *Greet* [e] *one another with a holy kiss.* [f,g] *All the saints send their greetings.* [13] *The grace of the Lord Jesus Christ* [h] *and the love of God and the fellowship* [i] *of the Holy Spirit be with you all.* [j,k]

Notes

[a] Although χαίρειν literally means "rejoice" (*gaudete*), there are several authorities that understand Paul's use in 13:11 as a common greeting: "farewell" (*valete*) (Plummer, 380; Denney, 384; Bultmann, 252; KJV/AV; RSV; NEB); "goodbye" (Barrett, 342; NIV). We, however, keep the meaning of rejoice and in doing so follow NASB; Furnish, 581; Hughes, 486; Moule, *Idiom Book*, 161; Phillips has "cheer up," which is less acceptable as too colloquial and so here meaningless. Filson believes that both options, "rejoice" or "farewell," are equally possible (422, 423). See BGD, 873, 874. For fuller treatment of this question, see *Comment.* Much depends on whether vv 11–13 are the close of the four-chapter letter (10–13) or of the redacted 2 Corinthian letter in toto, and inserted by the final editor. See later.

[b] The second person plural imperative ending -εσθε can be translated either as the middle or passive voice. The verb in question, καταρτίζεσθε (καταρτίζειν, "to restore"), is cognate with the noun κατάρτισις, "restoration," in 13:9, a point overlooked by Bultmann (252) who renders *bessert euch*, having treated Lietzmann's *Besserung* in v 9 as "somewhat weak." If the verb is translated in the passive voice, we render "be restored," *sc.* by God, as in 1 Thess 3:10 (Windisch,

426; Allo, 342; Furnish, 581, 582). If we choose the middle voice, our translation would be "aim for restoration" ("mend your ways," RSV; NEB; such a rendering is, however, regarded as too weak [Filson, 423]; "pull yourselves together" [Barrett, 342] is too colloquial; also the translations that give us "perfection" instead of "restoration" for καταρτίζειν do not help the understanding of this verse [RV; NIV; see Hughes, 486; Harris, 405]). As will be seen in the *Comment*, the most likely understanding in 13:11 is the middle voice for καταρτίζειν.

ᶜA decision is called for in regard to παρακαλεῖσθε as it was in respect to καταρτίζεσθε (note παρακαλεῖν is a contracted verb and we still have the second person plural imperative ending). Is παρακαλεῖσθε (from the verb that normally means "to exhort" or "to encourage" but with a wide range of meanings [see BGD, 617]) in the middle or passive voice? To translate it as the passive leaves us with "accept my appeal" (NIV; RSV; "take our appeal to heart," NEB; Hughes, 487; Furnish, 582; Plummer 380). But the middle voice, "Encourage one another," may be Paul's meaning (Phillips; Barrett, 342; Bultmann, 252, but his appeal to Windisch, 426, leads him to see encouragement as a "warning-call" [*Mahnung*] comparable with Heb 13:22). See *Comment* for more discussion.

ᵈφρονεῖτε (from φρονεῖν, "to think") is a contracted verb. The -ειτε can be taken either as a second person plural indicative or a second person plural imperative ending. But since φρονεῖτε comes in a series of imperatives there is little doubt that it should be taken as a paraenetic imperative as well.

ᵉἀσπάσασθε (from ἀσπάζεσθαι, "to greet") is an imperative, as are many of the verbs in 13:11. But in that v the imperatives are all in the present tense. Is there any significance in the use of the aorist (ἀσπάσασθε) in 13:12 after a string of present imperatives? Although the aorist does break a pattern, there may be no need to place too much emphasis on this change. (See Moule, *Idiom Book*, 8, 21; Moulton, *Grammar* 3:75; BDF § 320, 337.4.) See *Comment*.

ᶠThe text ἐν ἁγίῳ φιλήματι is supported by ℵ B D K, while some MSS (A F G L) have ἐν φιλήματι ἁγίῳ. The latter reading is probably an attempt to adapt 13:12 to other vv which also speak of the holy kiss (1 Cor 16:20; Rom 16:16; 1 Thess 5:26). See Plummer, 381.

ᵍSome versions and translations (TR, TEV/GNB) divide chapter 13 into only thirteen vv. In many other translations (KJV/AV; RV; ASV; RSV; NEB; NIV) chap. 13 had fourteen verses. The first appearance of chap. 13 with fourteen vv may have been the second edition (1572) of the Bishops' Bible (Furnish, 583). We follow Nestle-Aland²⁶ in verse numbering.

ʰΧριστοῦ is omitted in B ψ 1881.

ⁱThere is a question whether to translate κοινωνία as "fellowship" or as "participation." The question is whether to take τοῦ ἁγίου πνεύματος as a subjective genitive or an objective genitive. The former understanding lends itself to the idea of the "fellowship created and given by the Holy Spirit"; the latter suggests the idea of "participation in," or sharing in (as if κοινωνία = μετοχὴ καὶ μετάληψις) the Holy Spirit (see Hainz, *Koinonia*, 47–51). In the light of the two genitives (ἡ χάρις τοῦ κυρίου Ἰησοῦ Χριστοῦ and ἡ ἀγάπη τοῦ θεοῦ) preceding the present one which are subjective, we have opted to translate the present one as subjective also. But in doing so, we do not consider the alternatives as mutually exclusive (possibly both ideas are to be understood with Hainz, ibid. 54, who renders "fellowship through [mutual] sharing," *Gemeinschaft durch [gemeinsame] Teilhabe*). Moreover, our position that ἡ κοινωνία τοῦ ἁγίου πνεύματος is to be understood as a subjective genitive is by no means the only position that can be supported. See *Comment* for fuller discussion; Martin, "Communion," *IBD*, pt. 1, 307, 308.

ʲThe TR, following ℵᶜ k ψ itᵈ vg syr cop goth, adds ἀμήν. The text, which does not include ἀμήν, is supported by p⁴⁶ ℵ* A B F G 33 itᵍ vgᵐˢˢ armᵐˢˢ eth. See Metzger, *Textual Commentary*, 588. On Amen = אמן in Judeo-Christian liturgies, see R. Deichgräber, *Gotteshymnus und Christushymnus in der frühen Christenheit*, SUNT 5. Göttingen: Vandenhoeck & Ruprecht, 1967, 25–27.

ᵏAll of Paul's letters have a subscription added to the closing words of the apostle, and 2 Corinthians is no exception. The subscription to our present epistle is πρὸς Κορινθίους β̄ (see Metzger, ibid., for variant readings of the subscription). This simple reading follows the common pattern of other subscriptions to Pauline writings. The subscription functions as a title, an element that was not needed until the letters of Paul were collected into a corpus. (See Metzger, *The Text of the New Testament* [New York: Oxford University Press, 1968], 205, 206.) Of note is the subscription appended to our present epistle in the KJV/AV: "The second epistle to the Corinthians was written from Philippi, a city of Macedonia by Titus and Lucas." The KJV/AV is noted for such additions to the Pauline writings. The additions usually report the city where the letter was putatively written, as well as the name of the amanuensis or carrier of the epistle.

Form/Structure/Setting

These last verses constitute the closing words of our epistle. In general, these verses follow the normal pattern of the ending of Paul's letters. Such endings are devoted to greetings, doxologies and benedictions (see especially 1 Cor 16:19–24; Phil 4:21–23; see R. P. Martin, *New Testament Foundations 2* [Grand Rapids: Eerdmans, 1978] 246, 247; Champion, *Benedictions*, 20, 25–37; Rigaux, *Letters of St. Paul*, 131–33; W. Doty, *Letters in Primitive Christianity* [Philadelphia: Fortress, 1973] 39–43; Mullins, "Benediction," 59–64). It appears that Paul constructed and expected his letters to be read as part of the worship service (Martin, ibid.; it has been suggested that 1 Cor 16:20–24 not only functioned as a closing to the letter but also as a transition to the worship service itself, but see C. F. D. Moule, "A Reconsideration of the Context of Maranatha," *NTS* 6 [1959–60] 307–10, and M. Black, "The Maranatha Invocation and Jude 14, 15 [1 Enoch 1:9]," in *Christ and Spirit in the New Testament*, FS C. F. D. Moule, ed. B. Lindars and S. S. Smalley [Cambridge: University Press, 1973] 189–96).

It is thought by some (Strachan, 145) that originally 13:11–13 was the closing for 2 Cor 1–9 and when a redactor combined chaps. 1–9 with 10–13 into one letter (our canonical 2 Cor) he simply took the ending of 1–9 and placed it at the end of 10–13. In effect, the closing of 1–9 became the closing of 2 Corinthians. However, it can be argued, and quite logically, that 13:11–13 remains at its original place, namely, at the end of 10–13 (Plummer, 379, 380; Windisch, 426). It appears that the practice of Paul's time was for a redactor—when he combined two letters into one—to retain both the opening of the first letter and the closing of the second one. Only in compelling circumstances would a redactor do otherwise (Furnish, 585). Moreover, 13:11–13 is linked to the vv before it. In 13:9 we find the word meaning "to rejoice," χαίρειν. This is also found in 13:11. Also, in 13:9 Paul prayed for the restoration (κατάρτισις) of the Corinthians (to God and to Paul and to one other). In 13:11, καταρτίζειν, "to restore," is the verb that is cognate with κατάρτισις in 13:9. 13:11–13 would seem out of place if it followed 9:15 because Paul closes chap. 9 on such an optimistic note. The last few vv of chap. 9 speak of a church marked by unity; the last few verses of chap. 13 are an appeal to overcome disunity, for Paul exhorts the Corinthians to be of the same mind (φρονεῖτε). In addition, the end of 10–13 reflects in part the appeal found in the opening vv of these same chapters. In 10:8, 9, Paul begins by expressing the fear that he will have to deal harshly with the Corinthians (see also 12:19–13:10). By the end of chap. 13, he has toned down that threat, and has expressed the hope that the Corinthians will rectify the situation themselves. The point is that in the opening verses of chap. 10, as well as the closing verse of chap. 13, Paul is concerned to express his apprehension that the church situation needs correction. There is no hint of such trouble in chap. 9. In light of this discussion, it appears Strachan's position is too precarious to hold.

In these closing verses, Paul makes his final appeal to the Corinthians. This appeal is pointed but friendly (Filson, 422; Paul's appeal here is not as general as Harris [405] would have us believe). A brief outline of 13:11–

13 shows us that v 11 consists of succinct admonitions (Furnish, 585) to be followed by a greeting (12*a*, 12*b*) and the benediction (13). The apostle opens v 11 with the adverb λοιπόν, "finally," thus signaling that his composition is coming to a close. He still considers the church at Corinth to be dear to his heart. This is seen in the use of ἀδελφοί, "brothers," a term not otherwise used in chaps. 10–13, but it is at 1:8; 8:1. Paul then proceeds to exhort the Corinthians to Christian living by a series of imperatives. In 13:11*a* alone there are five imperatives, all in the present tense: χαίρετε, "rejoice" (or maybe χαίρετε is to be taken as a common greeting; see *Note* a and *Comment*); καταρτίζεσθε, "aim for restoration" (can be taken either as a middle or passive; see *Note* b and *Comment*); παρακαλεῖσθε, "encourage one another" (παρακαλεῖν can have numerous meanings; it can be taken as passive or middle in 13:11, see *Note* c and *Comment*); τὸ αὐτὸ φρονεῖτε, "be of the same mind"; εἰρηνεύετε, "live in peace." Although there are other endings to Paul's letters that contain some paraenesis (see Rom 16:17), we cannot help but notice the striking number of imperatives employed in 13:11*a*. This suggests that Paul is urgently (and passionately?) encouraging the Corinthians to remedy the situation in the church before he arrives. Such thinking by Paul is consistent with the main thrust of 13:5–10, in which he allows the Corinthians the opportunity to take care of their own problems. This tact of Paul does not eliminate or lessen his threat expressed in 10:6; 13:2; rather he says, "my threat will not be carried out if (and only if) you heed my warning." The very fact that Paul plans to send chaps. 10–13 to Corinth before his third visit is proof that he hopes it will not be necessary to punish the church. If the letter takes effect as did the "severe letter," then Paul's visit (the third one) will be a joyful one; there will be no need for him to discipline the church. As he concludes chaps. 10–13, he makes one last emotional appeal (13:11*a*) to the Corinthians. This appeal is brief, but nevertheless it is to the point.

The series of imperatives is connected to the following clause by the simple copulative. The clause is marked by the future of εἰμι, namely, ἔσται. The term "God of love" (ὁ θεὸς τῆς ἀγάπης) is not found elsewhere in the NT (or, in fact, anywhere in the OT, whether the LXX or Hebrew Bible), though the idea is found in other places (cf. Rom 5:8). The term "peace of God" occurs often (Rom 15:33; 16:20; 1 Cor 14:33; Phil 4:9; 1 Thess 5:23; 2 Thess 3:16; cf. also Heb 13:20). The latter term appears to be a common Pauline concluding formula (Barrett, 343). The inclusion of "God of love" with "God of peace" (1 Thess 3:11) may not be all that significant (Furnish, 586). There is one other variant in Rom 15:5. But what is important is the promise of v 11*b*, which is more effectively tied to the preceding admonitions by καί. The whole of v 11 parallels Paul's structure of Phil 4:8, 9*a*, and 4:9*b*:

admonition	$\longrightarrow$	promise
2 Cor 13:11*a*	$\longrightarrow$	13:11*b*
Phil 4:8, 9*a*	$\longrightarrow$	9*b*

Phil 4:8, 9*a* is a command to think on things that are pure and good, as well as a command to practice what Paul does and says and teaches. In 4:9*b*

(linked to Phil 4:8, 9*a* by a καὶ) is the promise that the God of peace will be with the Philippians.

A closer look reveals that these two passages have more in common. Both passages begin with λοιπόν (τὸ λοιπόν in Phil 4:8) though the use of this adverb in Phil may not signal the end of the letter (but see Martin, *Philippians* [NCB] 16–22, 157). Also, the call for the people to have the same mind (τὸ αὐτὸ φρονεῖν) is given by Paul in both contexts (see Phil 2:2, 5; 4:2; in the Philippian church the call was given specifically to Euodia and Syntyche). The admonitions (see above) in both letters are followed by the promise "the God of peace will be with you." The point of this discussion is that more than once (in the Aegean period of his correspondence) Paul has used the phrase "the peace of God be with you" to cement his admonitions (possibly, in Philippians, the peace of God in 4:9*b* completes an *inclusio* started in 4:7; see Martin, *Philippians* [NCB] 160). No doubt the connection between the two passages is more than a coincidence. After all, when Paul wrote to the Corinthians the churches of Macedonia were on his mind (chaps. 8 and 9); and in both sets of correspondence his relations with the congregations were a prime factor.

The promise of Paul (13:11*b*) may be an adaptation of a peace blessing, an example of which is found in Philippians, as well as other Pauline letters (see also Rom 15:33; 16:20; 1 Thess 5:23; cf. also 1 Cor 14:33; see Bultmann, 252). The use of the future ἔσται may suggest a conditional statement, "If you follow my appeal, then God will be with you" (see Barrett, 342; also cf. 6:17). But more likely Paul is saying, "Do what I urge you to do and in the process God will be with you," or he is expressing a surrogate for a peace-prayer (see Wiles, *Paul's Intercessory Prayers*, 36, 107) rather than making a declaration (Moule, *Worship in the New Testament* [London: Lutterworth Press, 1961] 78, 79) (see *Comment*). The latter slant is easier to understand if we take "peace" and "love" to be gifts of God, given by him to the Corinthians. However, if "love" and "peace" are understood as characteristics of God, then we may interpret 13:11*b* in the conditional sense (Tasker, 191; see Harris, 405). But Barrett may be correct in concluding that Paul could mean that "love" and "peace" are both characteristics and gifts of God.

After v 11, Paul turns to the subject of greetings. He implores the Corinthians to greet one another with a holy kiss. The aorist imperative ἀσπάσασθε stands out among the series of present imperatives of 13:11 (see *Note e* and *Comment*). The exhortation to give other Christians a holy kiss is common in Paul's letters (1 Cor 16:20; Rom 16:16; 1 Thess 5:26; see also 1 Peter 5:14; in every case ἀσπάσασθε is used). The fraternal kiss was not necessarily unique as a Christian practice, though its use in the synagogue liturgy is not attested (Windisch, 427). Nevertheless it did signify for the church fellowship and union based on reconciliation—a Jewish motif. The use of ἅγιος, "holy," may be an explicit attempt to show this (Plummer, 382). Though there is still uncertainty surrounding the exact meaning of the holy kiss in the church setting (see *Comment*), it would be possible to imagine that Paul was hoping that the kiss would represent mutual forgiveness and reconciliation among the church members in Corinth. Paul had urged other churches to greet one another with a kiss, but probably at no other time had he been so concerned that a church follow his advice as he was when he composed 13:12.

Verse 12*b* continues the greetings section of 13:11–13 with the reference to "all (πάντες) the saints (οἱ ἅγιοι)" who send their greetings. (Just who these persons are remains an uncertainty [see *Comment*].) Such a greeting can be found in Romans 16:6 and in a reverse way in Phil 4:22. Sometimes Paul sends the greetings of brothers (ἀδελφοί; see Phil 4:22; 1 Cor 16:20; see also Titus 3:15). The important thing to note is Paul's call for unity, as a theme running through the entire letter. He called for it in 13:11, and the exhortation in 13:12 was to offer a sign (holy kiss) that reflected unity. In 13:12*b* Paul reminds the Corinthians that they must become unified with an even greater number of Christians, namely, the other churches. The use of this part-verse is Paul's way of saying unity can be a way of life for God's people.

Paul closes with 13:13, the apostolic benediction, "a verse of capital importance" (Allo, 343). This particular benediction has been called the "most elaborate" in all of the Pauline writings (Filson, 424). Normally, Paul closes his letters with "May the grace of our Lord Jesus Christ be with you" (Rom 16:20*b*; 1 Cor 16:23; Gal 6:18; Phil 4:16; 1 Thess 5:28; 2 Thess 3:18; Philem 25; see also Col 4:18*b*; 1 Tim 6:21*b*; 2 Tim 4:22*b*; Titus 3:15*b*). Such a pattern for Paul may help to explain why grace appears first in 13:13; but see below. But in our present v we have the mention of Christ, God and the Holy Spirit together, and in that order. In other places Paul has included the three persons in his various discussions (see 1 Cor 12:4–6; see Martin, *The Spirit and the Congregation,* 10, 11; Hainz, *Ekklesia,* 325–27; also cf. Gal 4:4–6; Rom 8:5–11; Eph 4:4–6). But in no other place does Paul combine the three names in such a singular way, with χάρις, ἀγάπη, and κοινωνία associated in a remarkable fashion. We especially note in the last-named where πνεῦμα is linked with κοινωνία in a manner not quite identical with Phil 2:1 (Hainz, ibid. 327; idem, *Koinonia,* 55–61, against Hermann, *Kyrios und Pneuma,* 140–43).

The work of the three persons of the Trinity is given in separate clauses which may be parallel:

A   ἡ χάρις τοῦ κυρίου Ἰησοῦ Χριστοῦ
         καὶ
B   ἡ ἀγάπη τοῦ θεοῦ
         καὶ
C   ἡ κοινωνία τοῦ ἁγίου πνεύματος

The conclusion that these clauses are parallel holds up if we accept all three as subjective genitives. It is generally agreed that the first two clauses are subjective genitives (though Plummer, 384, suggests that the second may be objective). But there is still a question of how to interpret the third clause (see *Note* i). The exegesis of τοῦ ἁγίου πνεύματος as a subjective genitive leads to the understanding that Paul is speaking about the fellowship created and given by the Holy Spirit to be enjoyed among believers. Many hold to this position (Plummer, 383; Bruce, 255; Tasker, 191; Hughes, 488; Harris, 406; Schlatter, *Paulus, der Bote Jesu,* 62; Wendland, 234). But not all are convinced of this view (Barrett, 344; Hauck, *TDNT* 3:807; Furnish, 584; Windisch, 428; Lietzmann, 162; Bultmann, 253). This genitive could be interpreted as objective, and our third clause in this case would mean the participation in, or fellowship with, the Holy Spirit as a person (see *Comment*). Moreover, the third clause may not be parallel to the first two, if it is taken to be the only clause in Paul's mind connected with the statement μετὰ πάντων ὑμῶν, "with you all." But if we understand that Paul is speaking about all three "virtues"—grace, love and fellowship—as being with all the Corinthians (note Paul is concerned not to leave anyone out of his benediction), then all three clauses are more likely to be parallel. Maybe the answer lies in viewing Paul as meaning in the third clause *both* the fellowship created by the Holy Spirit *and* the fellowship with the Holy Spirit (Denney, 388; Hainz, *Koinonia*, 61). This will be taken up later (see *Comment*).

Setting aside the grammatical analysis, we must address another issue raised by this benediction. That issue has to do with the Trinitarian flavor of 13:13. When Paul put 13:13 together as a formula, he was not consciously echoing a developed doctrine of the Trinity (Barrett, 345). Moreover, it is doubtful that this formula (or any similar to it) circulated among other churches, for we do not find it in later epistles (Plummer, 382, 383). Jeremias thinks it was a baptismal form (cf. Matt 28:19; *Jerusalem zur Zeit Jesu* [Göttingen: Vandenhoeck & Ruprecht, 1958], II, 109), but more likely it was a spontaneous (Hughes, 488) confession of Paul's faith "in the historical and eschatological saving act of God" (Kümmel, 214). Even if thrice repeated baptism in the triune name became standard from the time of *Didache* 7 onward (see the texts in Martin, *The Worship of God*, 93, 94; the main references are Justin, *1 Apol*, 46; cf. 6:2; 65:3; 67:2, 13; Irenaeus, *Epideixis* 7; and Hippolytus, *Apostolic Tradition*, sec. 21 Cuming's text, 19), for Paul the primary focus was a confession of Christ. God had revealed his love through the death of his Son on the cross. The people of Corinth understood the love of God through the grace of Christ (2 Cor 8:9). Mention of Christ comes first in the benediction because the historical revelation of God's love was in Christ, and this revelation certified God's love for his people. In addition, these people were brought into the new life in the Spirit (Strachan, 145; Denney, 358). This thinking may explain why we see an "economic order" (i.e., the relationships of the persons of the Trinity to the world of humankind). Normally, the creeds have the sequence: Father, Son and Holy Spirit. But this is not Paul's understanding. It would be for the church of later times to hammer out the details of the doctrine of the Trinity (a term coined by Tertullian as *trinitas: de Pudicitia* 21; see also von Dobschütz, "Zwei- und dreiliedrige Formeln," esp. 141 ff.; J. N. D. Kelly, *Early Christian Doctrines* [London: A & C. Black, 1958] 109–37; idem, *Early Christian Creeds*[2] [London: Longmans, 1960], chaps. 1–3 for developments).

But this is not to deny (as Kümmel [214] does) that what we have is the "starting-point" (Barrett, 345) for the development of the credal statement of a Trinitarian confession (see 1 Peter 1:2). It was inevitable (Barrett, ibid.) that the church should seek to develop a doctrine that expressed (as best it could) its understanding of God (Filson, 425). Paul never confounded the distinction between God and Jesus Christ (see Phil 2:11; though 2 Cor 3:17

poses a problem of the relationship between the exalted Lord and the Spirit: see *Comment* there; and Hermann, ibid. 69–122; Hainz, *Koinonia*, 58–61). Maybe this caution is seen in the balanced clauses of 13:13. True, Paul was not writing in an attempt to defend the concepts of *una substantia et tres personae* (three persons and one substance); in this sense Paul was still a long way from the Trinitarian doctrines of the Church councils (Héring, 104). Paul's purpose is not to stress the individual hypostases of the Godhead; rather his emphasis is on the grace, love, and fellowship/participation that is available to the Corinthians (Barrett, 345). Paul's purpose in chaps. 10–13 has been to promote reconciliation within the church. God reconciled the Corinthians to himself through the work of Christ (5:18–21) and has given the Spirit (1:22; 5:5) as a sign of the new age begun but not yet realized. Since the Spirit in the letter has been claimed as *both* the mark of a "realized eschatology" which looked to ecstatic experience (which swallowed up the not yet in forceful speech and action [J. D. G. Dunn, *Jesus and the Spirit*, 330]) as validating apostolic ministry (3:1–6; 5:1–10; 11:4), *and* (in Paul's rejoinder) the evidence of unfulfilled hopes (5:5–7) that await the Parousia and a power that reinforced the not yet, it may be that the closing is also polemical. In particular, attention may be directed to 11:4 where the Corinthian readers have, under alien influences, accepted a "different spirit" (πνεῦμα ἕτερον) from the Spirit Paul knew, i.e., the Spirit of the crucified Jesus as seen in his ministry, now attacked (12:18).

The inclusion of the κοινωνία of this holy Spirit in his final wish-prayer (Wiles, *Paul's Intercessory Prayers*, 115, on the appeal to Christian experience, which now assumes a combative role, given the *Tendenz* of the four-chapter letter, 10–13, in our view) is to reinforce the plea that the Corinthians should return to his side by adhering to the truth (13:8) in their experience of God's grace in Christ by the Spirit, i.e., the truth that constitutes the church in being (Hainz, *Koinonia*, 61). Since God has acted (indicative), the Corinthians should live (imperative) as God's people. The God of love and peace offers himself through his Spirit in order to aid his people to live as they should. Paul's concern in 13:13 is to function as a pastor, not as a systematic theologian. Yet theology is here called into service to resist a false emphasis on the Spirit as claimed by the emissaries. We can say that at least we have the Trinitarian formula in "embryonic" form in this benediction (Harris, 406; Hainz, *Koinonia*, 47); and the close of the letter finds Paul reiterating his chief concern, to invoke divine resources to match his readers' needs in the face of threats and fears (11:2, 3; 12:21; 13:10).

Comment

11. λοιπόν, ἀδελφοί, "finally, brothers." Paul closes this letter with an appeal for unity. This appeal is given by one who is deeply concerned with the welfare of the church (see pp. 492, 493 for discussion of whether 13:11–13 was originally the conclusion of chaps. 1–9 or 10–13). λοιπόν, "finally," alerts the reader that Paul is bringing his correspondence to a close. The use of λοιπόν (instead of τὸ λοιπόν) is more colloquial (Plummer, 380). It is obvious that the adverb means "finally" in our present case. But care must be exercised

in exegeting this adverb, for it overlaps with the function of a particle (Moule, *Idiom Book,* 160, 161; see also Thrall, *Greek Particles,* 25–30). We see another use of τὸ λοιπόν in Phil 3:1, "Finally, my brothers, rejoice (χαίρετε) in the Lord." This may help our understanding of χαίρειν in 13:11 (see below).

ἀδελφοί, "brothers." This term of confidence suggests that Paul does not yet consider the situation at Corinth irreversible. The title to describe the Corinthians is "warm in tone" and says that Paul still considers the Corinthians as Christian believers (Filson, 422). He has used this term before with respect to the Corinthians (1:8; 8:1; but not in the four-chapter letter; in 1 Cor alone the term occurs twenty times). "Brothers" encompasses the whole congregation (Furnish, 581; 112, 113). The term "brother" was a common one among early Christians (Matt 23:8; cf. 12:50; see Deissmann, *Bible Studies* 87, 88, 142), and included the women of the congregation as well (Barrett, *1 Corinthians,* 31; cf. Gal 3:28; Col 3:2). The idea of "all" the congregation being included in Paul's appeal is also seen here (πάντες, v 12). ἀδελφοί is often found with παρακαλεῖν (Rom 16:17; 1 Cor 16:15; 1 Thess 4:10; 5:14) and this is true of our present verse.

χαίρετε, "rejoice." After affectionately addressing the church as "brothers," Paul launches into a "succession of staccato injunctions" (Hughes, 486). In a series of five imperatives Paul makes a final appeal for unity and harmony in the church at Corinth. If this appeal is effective, Paul will not have to discipline the church (13:10). χαίρειν, "to rejoice," has been understood to mean (in our present v) "farewell" (BGD, 874; NIV;KJV/AV; RSV; NEB; Plummer, 350; Denney, 384; "good-bye," Barrett, 342; as though the verb meant the same as ἔρρωσο, ἔρρωσθε or ἐρρῶσθαί σε/ὑμᾶς εὔχομαι). Verses cited in support of this position are Acts 15:23 [the opening of a letter from Claudius Lysias to Felix]; 23:26 [the opening of the letter from the Jerusalem council to the Gentile believers]; James 1:1; but all of these uses are at the beginning, not the ending of a letter (as in the case in 13:11). Phil 4:4 is also thought to support the position that χαίρειν is meant by Paul to be understood as "farewell," but it is not clear how this Philippian verse supports that position. Most likely, χαίρετε should be taken as "rejoice" (Hughes, 486; Furnish, 581; NASB; Moule, *Idiom Book,* 161). This is consistent with Paul's use of χαίρειν in 13:9, where he speaks of "rejoicing" at his being weak while the Corinthians are strong. Such an idea comports well with 13:11. Paul's hope is that the Corinthians will rejoice in spite of the bad report that has come to him and in spite of the threats he has made to the Corinthians (13:2). If the Corinthians obey Paul's advice (and take advantage of the opportunity to heed his warnings before he arrives at Corinth), then there is reason to hope. They can rejoice in that God loves them and Paul as apostle loves them (even if they questioned this: so 12:15). "Rejoice" is not too strong a translation for χαίρετε in this context, as Denney asserts (384), and neither is it incongruous in light of the threat of Paul to spare no one (οὐ φείσομαι), which is the point of 13:5–10. The Corinthians may rejoice in that they can remedy the situation if they choose to do so. There is no need for Paul to include χαίρειν to mean farewell, for he has already suggested the idea of good-bye by his use of λοιπόν.

καταρτίζεσθε, "aim at restoration." The issue of how to interpret this imperative—either middle ("mend your ways," RSV; NEB; "pull yourselves togeth-er," Barrett; 342; "set yourselves right," Héring, 102; NIV) or passive ("be restored"; see Windisch, 426; Allo, 342; Furnish, 581, 582)—has already been touched on (see *Note* b). The verb καταρτίζειν (see BGD, 417, 418) is cognate with the noun κατάρτισις, "restoration," in 13:9. In that v Paul was praying for the recovery of the Corinthians, presumably from erroneous ways to which they had succumbed (11:2, 3). Furnish (581, 582) interprets Paul as seeing the Corinthians as more or less passive with respect to the command to be reconciled. But we think that probably Paul is requiring some action on behalf of the Corinthians to rectify the situation, based on the middle voice which suggests action that is needed. To take the verb in the passive voice conveys the idea that Paul is lessening the burden on the Corinthians to act. This seems unlikely in light of his desire that the Corinthians should act before he arrives.

παρακαλεῖσθε, "encourage one another." Again we could translate παρακαλεῖν either as middle, "encourage one another" (Barrett, 342; Bruce, 254, 55), or passive, "accept my appeal" (NIV; RSV; NEB; Hughes, 487; Furnish, 582; Plummer, 380). Since Paul is hoping that the Corinthians will again live in harmony, we take the verb to be construed as the middle voice. Paul is seeking to encourage the Corinthians who in turn will engage in a mutual ministry of encouragement (Barrett, 342). The result of this encouragement is that they will be "comforted" ("comfort" is one of the many meanings for παρακαλεῖν; see BGD, 617 and *Comment* on 1:3–5). Tasker takes the idea of comfort found in 1:3–7 to be in the present v as well (191). If the Corinthians are seeking harmony with Paul and his teaching, what better way to achieve this than by encouraging and exhorting one another, perhaps also in the sense of mutual "reproof" for the disaffection caused by opposition to Paul (cf. 1 Thess 4:18; 5:11). See Bjerkelund, *PARAKALÔ*, 134, 137.

τὸ αὐτὸ φρονεῖτε, "be of the same mind." Paul continues his admonitions for the church to return to harmonious attitudes and living. The thought of "being of one mind" is also found in Romans (12:16; 15:5) and Philippians (2:2; 4:2). The use of "be of the same mind" in 13:11 signals that division is still a reality at Corinth (Filson, 423; see 1 Cor 1:10). Paul desires that God grant the Corinthians (Rom 15:5) something not attainable by human endeavor. He is not asking for each Corinthian to give up his or her individual-ity (Paul desires "Christian unity, not artificial uniformity," Hughes, 487). Rather, the apostle seeks unity for the Corinthians on a deeper level, one which is based on agreement of the mind which, in turn, leads to agreement in the truth (Hughes, ibid.; Tasker, 191). The verb φρονεῖν is an important verb in Paul's pastoral theology, especially when he faces congregations racked by dissension and disunity. See on Phil 2:2, 5; the verb "is both a summons to adopt an attitude and an exhortation to carry that attitude into practice" (Martin, *Philippians*, NCB, 90).

εἰρηνεύετε, "live in peace." The idea of being of the same mind leads on to Paul's plea that the Corinthians should live in peace. Peace is the natural result of being of one mind (Plummer, 380). Not to be of one mind is to invite sectionalism (Tasker, 191) and strife into the body of Christ (12:20). To live in peace is to experience God (see 13:11*b*). Paul will return to the idea of peace when he speaks of greeting other Christians with the holy kiss (13:12). See Rom 12:18 and 1 Thess 5:13 for other paraenetic calls, exhorting the readers to live in peace. Cf. Mark 9:50.

This appeal of Paul is presented by the use of present imperatives. This verb mood suggests continual or protracted action (Moule, *Idiom Book*, 20, 21, though, as we shall see in 13:12, this is not a rule without exceptions). Paul was saying that Christians must constantly strive for church harmony (cf. Eph 4:3).

καὶ ὁ θεὸς τῆς ἀγάπης καὶ εἰρήνης ἔσται μεθ' ὑμῶν, "And the God of love and peace will be with you." The copulative καὶ connects the exhortation of Paul (13:11a) to a promise of blessing (see Furnish, 586; 13:11b). We discussed earlier (see *Form/Structure/Setting*) how 13:11 is parallel to Phil 4:8, 9 both in thought and structure. In essence, Paul is telling the Corinthians that divine blessing awaits their right and responsive action. Possibly the blessing in 13:11b is an adaptation of a peace blessing, something not uncommon to Paul's thinking (Bultmann, 252; Rom 15:33; 16:20; 1 Thess 5:23; Phil 4:9; cf. 1 Cor 14:33; 2 Thess 3:16). Often Paul wrote to those who were experiencing difficulties themselves and prayed for their peace (G. F. Hawthorne, *Philippians*, WBC 43 [1983] 190). And in wishing people "peace," Paul was wishing for them the highest blessing of God (Martin, *Philippians* [TNTC 11] 173). Also, to think of God as the God of peace would likely be an uplifting and revitalizing experience for Paul himself, since his life at this juncture was characterized by so much hardship and disruption (Hawthorne, ibid.).

The thought of God as sending, or himself being, peace was an important one for Paul (see also C. Bigaré, "La paix de Dieu dans le Christ Jésus: Prière et mettre en pratique, Ph 4, 6–9," *AsSeign* 58 [1974] 11–15). The last imperative in the series (13:11a) exhorts the Corinthians to live in peace. This was made possible by the action of the Holy Spirit, who offered one of his fruit as peace (Gal 5:22). The idea of "the God of peace" being with the readers became a "prayer of benediction" for Paul (Hawthorne, ibid.). It is based on Jewish liturgical and paraenetic ascriptions (e.g., *T. Dan* 5:2: ὁ θεὸς τῆς εἰρήνης), but in the majority of NT references εἰρήνη is given "its comprehensive meaning of eschatological salvation. God is named by this title as the one through whom eschatological salvation comes" (R. Deichgräber, *Gotteshymnus und Christushymnus*, 94, 95).

Into the Pauline phrase "the God of peace" Paul inserted the words "the God of love." This latter phrase is not found anywhere in the NT, though the idea is there (Rom 5:8; 1 John 4:16). Furnish does not attach much significance to this insertion, but we suggest that Paul's use of "the God of love" is in anticipation of his benediction, which includes the words "the love of God" (13:13). After all, the Corinthian church was not noted for its love (hence the sad rebuke of 1 Cor 8:1). Instead of love, Paul had found jealousy and strife. Paul's hope and prayer is that the Corinthians will emulate "the God of love." The word for love is the well known term ἀγάπη, a term described in 1 Cor 13 as meaning the action that seeks the highest good of another (see Barclay, *New Testament Words* [Philadelphia: Westminster Press,

1974] 21, 22). Such action was sorely needed at Corinth, and Paul was hoping that the presence of "the God of love and peace" would be an incentive to encourage the Corinthians.

The conclusion to 13:11, ἔσται μεθ᾽ ὑμῶν, "will be with you," invites us to examine the basis for the promise of 13:11*b*. The use of the future ἔσται suggests the idea of possible conditionality (Harris, 405). Is Paul saying, if you follow my directions of 13:11*a*, then (and only then) the God of love and peace (these are characteristics of God) will be with you? This is the element of condition as implying more a wish than a declaration (see Wiles, *Paul's Intercessory Prayers*, 33, 34, drawing on W. C. van Unnik, "Dominus Vobiscum," in *New Testament Essays* in memoriam T. W. Manson, ed. A. J. B. Higgins [Manchester: University Press, 1959] 270–305), but that more is intended than a simple wish, i.e., expressing "a strong confidence of fulfillment" has been argued by B. van Elderen ("The Verb in the Epistolary Invocation," *CTJ* 2 [1967] 46–48). Or, is the apostle saying that in the process of fulfilling his demands of 13:11, God will provide the resources (gifts), namely, love and peace, to accomplish this task? Tasker leans toward the idea of condition (191), but we believe Barrett is closer to the truth when he suggests that both ideas (characteristics and gifts) are meant by Paul (343). This reflects Paul's use of the phrase "the God of peace" elsewhere. In Rom 15:33 there is no hint of condition, while in Phil 4:9 we again see ἔσται. Perhaps Hughes catches the sense of 13:11*b* when he remarks that it is God alone who supplies the grace to achieve the demands of 13:11*c*, but this "achievement" is not accidental, for each church member must make a conscious daily effort to practice love and peace. This ensures the presence of God, for the "promise [13:11*b*] cannot prevail where there is jealousy and strife" (488).

12. ἀσπάσασθε ἀλλήλους ἐν ἁγίῳ φιλήματι, "Greet one another with a holy kiss." Paul now turns to the theme of greeting, but in doing so he does not leave behind the theme of peace and harmony discussed in 13:11. To salute one with a holy kiss continues (Strachan, 145) the themes of 13:11. The kiss was a common Oriental form of salutation. Apparently there were different forms of this gesture meant for different occasions, such as the kissing of a ruler or the kissing of loved ones (Stählin, *TDNT* 9:119–24). The church took over this practice of kissing and invested it with "special and sacred meaning" (Harris, 405). From NT letters it appears that the practice of giving a kiss in the church was common (Rom 16:16; 1 Cor 16:20; 1 Thess 5:26; 1 Pet 5:14). Moreover, this form of greeting was probably a part of the liturgy (Stählin, ibid., 142–46; Justin, *1 Apology* 65:2; Windisch, 427: it played a role in the bishop's consecration in Hippolytus' rite in *Apostolic Tradition* Sec. 4 [Cuming's text, 10]), possibly preceding the celebration of the eucharist (cf. 1 Cor 16; 20*b*, 22) or the rite of baptism (Hippolytus, *Apostolic Tradition*, Sec. 21: Cuming's text, 21). The fact that the kiss was exchanged when the Christians met for worship (Tasker, 191) may explain the adjective ἅγιος, "holy," for this kiss was shared among the saints (ἅγιοι; see Filson, 423; Plummer, 382; it is uncertain whether the holy kiss was shared between men and women; see Athenagoras, *Legatio pro Christianis* 32, [MPG 6 col. 964], which speaks of someone possibly losing eternal life if one gives the

holy kiss with an ulterior [sexual] motive; Héring, 103). It is suggested that Paul implied that the Corinthians were to give one another (ἀλλήλους) the kiss that he would have given, if he were present (Barrett, *1 Corinthians*, 396).

Most likely, the kiss was already practiced in the Corinthian church. But Paul wanted it to be more than a meaningless gesture or worse, as Jerome (*Ep.* 82.3) was later to rebuke the person who harbored bitter thoughts at the eucharist and "when his hand is held out [to receive the communion elements], turn[ed] away his face, and in the midst of the sacred feast prof-fer[ed] the kiss of Judas." He wanted it to be an actual sign that represented an inward charity for all (Tasker, 191). The kiss was to symbolize family life and to show that each member of the Corinthian church considered every other member as a part of one family (Denney, 384). In addition, Paul hoped that the kiss would be a sign of forgiveness and reconciliation. As we shall see shortly, the exhortation to give a holy kiss was not unique to the Corinthian church.

The aorist imperative ἀσπάσασθε, "greet," is common to all the other occasions when Paul exhorts his readers to greet one another with a holy kiss (Rom 16:16; 1 Cor 16:10; 1 Thess 5:26; see too 1 Pet 5:14). What is of note for our present v is that the aorist imperative comes after the series of present imperatives in 13:11a. Strictly speaking, the aorist imperative commands something to be done once-for-all (but see Moule, *Idiom Book*, 20, 21; see also Moulton, *Grammar* 3:75). But it is doubtful Paul is simply saying that the Corinthians are to kiss each other only once. His use of the aorist imperative here simply reflects his normal exhortation to greet others with a holy kiss. The Corinthians would naturally assume that each time they came together to worship that they were to exchange the holy kiss. There may be some connection between the giving of the "kiss of peace" and the "liturgical" blessing of 13:13 (Lietzmann 162: idem, *Mass and Lord's Supper*. Tr. D. H. G. Reeve [Leiden: Brill, 1979] 186), but Barrett questions if the connection is as strong as it is sometimes made out to be (343).

In the history of the liturgy, "the kiss of peace" (together with the words of salutation *pax vobiscum*) played a significant, if varied, role. Justin's order of service, set in Rome in the mid-second century, placed the kiss prior to the presentation of bread and cup to the president of the eucharist, and after the common prayers were said by all. Roman and some other western usage retained this significance, namely, that the kiss of peace after praying is the "seal of prayer" (*signaculum orationis*, Tertullian, *de Orat.* 18, since no prayer is complete without it, except that on Good Friday the kiss was omitted). See Innocent's letter to Decentius (in A.D. 416) defending the place of the gesture at the close of the Canon, as marking the assent of the people to all that was done and giving their seal to it (*Ep. ad Decent.* 1). Tertullian makes much of the kiss as signifying joyous reconciliation in the spirit of Matt 6:16–18, against those in Carthage who withheld the rite after fasting.

In the Gallican and Mozarabic rites, as in the eastern liturgy, the kiss is situated before the Preface and so placed in connection with the Offertory (cf. Irenaeus *Adv. Haer.* 4.18.1). Support for this placement drew on Matt 5:23, 24 (cf. *Did.* 14.2), while the link of the kiss of peace with the Communion emphasized the leading idea of the sacrament of unity.

But not all the data are clear-cut, as J. H. Srawley (*The Early History of the Liturgy*[2] [Cambridge: University Press, 1947], passim), R. D. Richardson (in Lietzmann, *Mass and Lord's Supper*, 528–46), and G. Wainwright (*Doxology: The Praise of God in Worship, Doctrine, and Life* [New York: Oxford Univ. Press, 1980], 31, 32) make evident.

12. ἀσπάζονται ὑμᾶς οἱ ἅγιοι πάντες, "All the saints send their greetings." (See *Note* g for the differences in the v numbering of chap. 13.) Paul remarks that the Corinthians are part of a larger body, namely the universal church (1 Cor 12:28, and Martin, *The Spirit and the Congregation,* 31). Paul's habit of having those with him when he was writing his letters send greetings to his readers is well documented (Rom 16:3–23; 1 Cor 16:19, 20; Phil 4:21; Col 4:10–15; Titus 3:15; Philem 23; cf. 2 Tim 4:19–21). The identity of the saints in 13:12, 13 remains uncertain. They could be the Philippians or the Thessalonians or the Bereans. More likely, they are the Christians of Macedonia (Bruce, 255). But the most one can say is that the "saints" were those Christians in Paul's company when he wrote chaps. 10–13. In 1 Cor 16:20 Paul spoke of the "brothers" (instead of "the saints") greeting the Corinthians. It is doubtful that there is any difference between "brothers" and "saints" (Barrett, 343: on the latter term see *Comment* on 1:1, and note E. E. Ellis' theory that the designation οἱ ἀδελφοί [with the article] refers to "a relatively limited group of workers, some of whom have the Christian mission and/or ministry as their primary occupation," in "Paul and his Co-workers" in *Prophecy and Hermeneutic in Early Christianity* [Grand Rapids: Eerdmans, 1978] 15), but his equating of "brothers" and "fellow-workers" is by no means proved. Rather, in v 11, the term means "the church as a whole." So W.-H. Ollrog, *Paulus und seine Mitarbeiter,* WMANT 50 (1979) 78. The important thing to remember here is that Paul is calling for unity. Just as the holy kiss was an "epistolary greeting" (Harris, 405) that signified unity, so was the greeting from other "saints." The Pauline Christians throughout the churches were united in Christ, and firm in their devotion to Paul, at least by inference. πάντες, "all," is placed at the end of the sentence. This may be Paul's way of emphasizing (Plummer, 381) that the Corinthians—in spite of their previous behavior—are still considered by him to belong to the body of Christ. Thus, other Christians are one with them and will continue to be so (Hughes, 488). Unity remains in Paul's mind in vv 12, 13 and is suggested by his sending the greetings of others, despite the possibility that those who sent their greetings were personally unknown to the Corinthians (Tasker, 191).

13. ἡ χάρις τοῦ κυρίου Ἰησοῦ Χριστοῦ καὶ ἡ ἀγάπη τοῦ θεοῦ καὶ ἡ κοινωνία τοῦ ἁγίου πνεύματος μετὰ πάντων ὑμῶν, "The grace of the Lord Jesus Christ and the love of God and the fellowship of the Holy Spirit be with you all." The question of the Trinitarian flavor of 13:13 was discussed earlier (*Form/Structure/Setting*). Concerning the benediction of 13:13 Furnish writes: "No other Pauline letter concludes with a benediction so theologically imposing as the one" here (587). This verse appears as the construction of three parallel clauses.

ἡ χάρις τοῦ κυρίου Ἰησοῦ Χριστοῦ, "the grace of the Lord Jesus Christ." This phrase is usually found at the end of Paul's letters (Rom 16:20*b;* 1 Cor 16:23; Gal 6:18; Phil 4:23; 1 Thess 5:28; Philem 25; cf. 2 Cor 1:2; see Héring,

103). This common usage may explain why he placed it first among the three clauses. But since "grace" (χάρις, used christologically here and in 8:9; 12:9) is understood as both action and gift (Barrett, *1 Corinthians*, 398), Paul may be placing "the grace of the Lord Jesus Christ" at the opening of the v because it was through the cross (an observable event) that people came to understand the love of God and were thus led to life-in-the-Spirit (cf. Eph 2:18: on this v see Martin, *The Worship of God*, 92, citing J. D. Crichton, "To the Father through the Son in the Holy Spirit, is the underlying pattern of the history of revelation. So is it too of the liturgy" ["A Theology of Worship," in *The Study of Liturgy*, ed. C. Jones, G. Wainwright and E. Yarnold (London: SPCK, 1978) 19]). Thus it is logical that an early statement describing the work of Christ came first as conveying the knowledge of Christian salvation (only later did the Father's election take precedence: 1 Pet 1:2; Eph 1:3–14: 1 Tim 2:5). Undoubtedly the genitive (τοῦ κυρίου Ἰησοῦ Χριστοῦ) is subjective, for Paul is not speaking about the grace given to Christ by the believer, but rather the grace from Christ to and for his people.

καὶ ἡ ἀγάπη τοῦ θεοῦ, "and the love of God." The first clause is connected to the second one in 13:13 by the simple copulative "and." The phrase "love of God" is found also in Romans (5:8; 8:39). The love of God is closely related to the love of Christ (Rom 8:35, 37; cf. 2 Cor 5:14; Gal 2:20; see also Rom 8:39: "the love of God that is in Christ Jesus our Lord" [NIV]). The love of God is never seen more clearly than in the sending of his Son that God might reconcile the world to himself (5:18–21). Through Christ we receive God's saving grace (Rom 5:1, 2; Gal 1:15, 16; 2:12; 2 Cor 8:9; we also receive the love of the Spirit, Rom 15:30; see Filson, 425). Most likely this second clause of 13:13 is a subjective genitive, for it is not the Christian's love for God that is being highlighted (Tasker, 101; Furnish, 583; but see Plummer, 384).

καὶ ἡ κοινωνία τοῦ ἁγίου πνεύματος μετὰ πάντων ὑμῶν, "and the fellowship of the Holy Spirit be with you all." But while there is little debate as to whether the previous clauses of 13:13 contain a subjective genitive or not, with regard to our present clause there is much disagreement (see *Note* i). Both sides (taking the genitive as subjective versus objective [fellowship in *or* with the Spirit]) can make a strong case. If the genitive is taken as subjective, or genitive of origin (Hainz, *Koinonia* 50), or author (Prümm, *Diakonia* 1:730), then we understand Paul to be speaking of the fellowship created and given by the Holy Spirit to be enjoyed between members of the church. This follows logically in light of the two preceding clauses which are indubitably subjective genitives. It is not difficult to see that here Paul is concerned with the fellowship which the Spirit promotes among believers. The thrust of 13:11–13 has been to emphasize peace and harmony within the church at Corinth (Plummer, 383, 384; Bruce, 255; Tasker, 191, 192; Harris, 406; Schlatter, *Paulus*, 682; Wendland, 234; Schweizer, *TDNT* 6:434, who finally thinks the choice is immaterial). But it can also be said that Paul meant our present clause to be understood as an objective genitive, thus giving us a paraphrase that speaks of participation in the Holy Spirit, namely communion with him as a person (Barrett, 344; Hauck *TDNT* 3:807; Moule, *Idiom Book*, 41; Furnish, 584; Windisch, 428; Lietzmann, 214; see H. Seesemann, *Der Begriff KOINONIA* [62–

73] i.e., *Geistesgemeinschaft,* which Hainz, *Koinonia,* 48, comments drily, is more an illustration than an explanation of the Pauline phrase; Seesemann's term *innige Anteilnahme am* [73], "intimate participation in," is better, on his understanding; it is similar to 1 Cor 1:9). This latter position is based on other uses of κοινωνία in which "participation in" is the understanding (see 1 Cor 10:16 and Phil 3:10; also cf. Rom 15:27; Phil 2:1; Philem 6; see 2 Cor 1:7; 6:14; 8:4, 23; 9:13; see A. R. George, *Communion with God in the New Testament,* 175–77). Also, it is argued that "participation in the Holy Spirit" goes better with the phrase μετὰ πάντων ὑμῶν, "be with you all" than does "the fellowship given by the Holy Spirit" (Barrett, 344). But such a position is not convincing (see also B. Reicke, *Diakonie, Festfreude und Zelos* [Uppsala: Lundequistska bokhandeln, 1951]; J. Y. Campbell, "Κοινωνία and Its Cognates in the New Testament," *JBL* 51 [1932] 378, 379).

A third possible option is to take the phrase as understood in both ways, namely as a subjective and objective genitive (Filson, 425). As Denney explains it, there is not much difference between the idea of "the fellowship of the Holy Spirit" and the idea of "fellowship with one another" (386). We would not expect Paul to overlook the "communion" of believers with the Holy Spirit. Yet we may find it hard to understand why he would create three clauses (possibly parallel in structure, see pp. 495, 496), of which the first two clauses are subjective genitive, and then suddenly change to an objective genitive (but such "lack of concinnity" [*Inkonzinnität;* Hermann, *Kyrios und Pneuma,* 136] is not without parallel—see Phil 2:1, where Lohmeyer's structural analysis seems soundly based [on this see Martin, *Philippians,* TNTC, 46–50]; in any case Phil 2:1 is not precisely parallel with 2 Cor 13:13. W. Kramer, *Christ, Lord, Son of God,* SBT 50, tr. B. Hardy [London: SCM, 1966] 20*b,* believes the first two clauses are a pre-Pauline formulaic creation, engendered by Paul's own addition of the κοινωνία of the Spirit. By this addition he has destroyed the congruence of the binitarian credo by supplying the thought that the "Holy Spirit" is not the dispenser but is himself the gift of salvation. Given that *Sitz im Leben* of v 13, it is more likely that the third member clause stresses the church's creation by the Spirit, i.e., the genitive is subjective). More likely than not, the Corinthians understood Paul as speaking of the fellowship created by the Holy Spirit, since this idea would be more immediately relevant in context. But no matter what choice of interpretations of the genitive we make, in either case the function of the Spirit is to conjoin the work of Christ and God's love (see Rom 8:9). To take the genitive as objective is to hold that the grace of Christ and the love of God are present by the participation in the Holy Spirit (who realizes and effectuates the "grace" and "love" as "a divine work on earth": so Hermann, *Kyrios und Pneuma,* 136, 137). To take the genitive as subjective is to conclude that the fellowship with the Spirit is not primarily the sharing in the Spirit, but the sharing in the communion he creates among believers (Héring, 103), a sharing characterized by grace and love. But it is clearly possible to combine both syntactical points, and think of Paul as remarking on "the fellowship of the church through the common share in the Holy Spirit" (see Hainz, *Koinonia,* 61).

The idea of God's blessings being "with you all" is common to Paul's letter-closings (see Rom 16:20*b;* 1 Cor 16:23; 1 Thess 5:28). Sometimes he wishes the blessings of God to be with a person's spirit (Gal 6:18; Phil 4:23; Philem 25; cf. 1 Cor 12:18). An item of note is that usually Paul closed his letters with a hope of a blessing (*Segenswunsch*) rather than a promise (*Segensver-heissung,* in Deichgräber's terminology, ibid. 95). But except for here and in 2 Thess 3:18, he did not include the word πάντες, "all." Normally, he would say, "the grace of Christ be with you." But in 13:13 he writes "with you all." The πάντων, "all," is his way of emphasizing that he is speaking to everyone in the church (Plummer, 384). Paul has sought to show that no one is to be excluded from his appeal. He asks that all in the church heed his exhortation, and he hopes that all will reap the benefit of obedience. He opened 13:11 with the term "brothers," which also signifies he is speaking to all church members. He closes the passage (13:11–13), and the epistle as well, with the word "all," again including all readers in the scope of his paraenesis.

Explanation

Two final sections round off Paul's appeal and contain his "adieu"; perhaps we should also add, in view of 12:14 and 13:1, 2, 10, the note of "au revoir."

Vv 11–13 assure the Corinthian believers of his continuing interest, and call for harmony within a divided congregation. The divine blessing is promised (11*b*) to a fellowship whose reconciliation Paul fervently anticipates; the outward token of this is expressed in the practice of the "holy kiss." Associated with early Christian worship as a mark of true family life (Rom 16:16; 1 Cor 16:20; 1 Thess 5:26; 1 Pet 5:14), this practice persisted into the later liturgical life of the Church, and the references to it at the close of the NT epistles give extra support to the belief that these epistles were intended to be read out in public worship services (clearly in 1 Thess 5:27; Col 4:16; and probably Rev 1:3), and the reading was to be followed by the Lord's Supper. Then, the practice of the kiss would be an act of mutual affection and confidence, implying a putting away of all disagreements between the church members, in anticipation of a fresh realization of unity as they shared in a common loaf and cup (so Matt 5:23, 24; 1 Cor 10:16, 17). But Acts 20:37 reminds us that this practice was also simply a current demonstration of fraternal greeting.

The closing verse is the familiar apostolic benediction and a clear statement of NT Trinitarianism which is "economic," i.e., the relationships of the persons are described in connection with the world of men and women. Hence the order is that of Christian experience, and "the grace of the Lord Jesus Christ" stands first. For it is by him, incarnate, crucified and triumphant, that we come to know the Father's love (John 1:14–18; Rom 5:8–11; Heb 9:14) and to rejoice in the fellowship of the divine Spirit. The last phrase may mean either that fellowship which he promotes between believers (Eph 4:3) or the Christian's fellowship with him as a Person (John 14:17). A third view is preferable, namely, that the Holy Spirit's work is to create a true "fellowship of believers" to share in that work, which in turn is a sign of the new age (1:22; 5:5).

Ivor H. Jones, *The Contemporary Cross*, 57, 58, sums up the point of Paul's closing appeal, in the light of vv 5–10:

> We ought not to underestimate what Paul is asking of the Corinthians. He is asking them to make the kind of decision we find so difficult—for or against public lotteries, for or against comprehensive education, decisions which are complicated by prevailing trends and attitudes. He is asking them to make the sort of decision the ancient Israelites had to make when they witnessed the battle between Hananiah and Jeremiah, to decide between two prophets both acting in character and one of whom must be disastrously wrong if only they could see which it was and what a wrong decision might mean. That was the kind of decision which Paul was asking of them. Like those who listened to Jeremiah, those who listened to Paul in Corinth had to take up a challenge to realistic responsibility for one another.
>
> Like those who watched Jeremiah, those who had watched Paul had little to go on except that this man took his suffering for God seriously and responsibly, and had no doubt that this was what faith was about. But there was a further element in the total context in which their decision had to be made. Paul was addressing the community to whom it could be said by way of conclusion: "the grace of the Lord Jesus Christ, and the love of God, and fellowship in the Holy Spirit, be with you all" (13:13).

Index of Ancient Authors

Old Testament Apocrypha and Pseudepigrapha; and Other Jewish Writings

Other Christian Literature

Index of Modern Authors

(Excluding commentators referred to in the text)

Index of Principal Topics

Index of Biblical Texts

A. The Old Testament

B. The New Testament